BIOLOGICAL SCIENCE **1**

Organisms, Energy and Environment

D.J. TAYLOR B.Sc., Ph.D., C.Biol., F.I.Biol.
Director of Continuing Education
Strode's Sixth Form College, Egham

N.P.O. GREEN B.Sc., C.Biol., M.I.Biol.
Headmaster
St George's College, Buenos Aires, Argentina

G.W. STOUT B.Sc., M.A., M.Ed., C.Biol., F.I.Biol.
Formerly Headmaster
International School of Bophuthatswana, Mafikeng/Mmabatho,
Republic of Bophuthatswana, Southern Africa

Editor
R. SOPER B.Sc., C.Biol., F.I.Biol.
Formerly Vice-Principal and Head of Science
Collyers Sixth Form College, Horsham

CAMBRIDGE
UNIVERSITY PRESS

574

APG

PUBLISHED BY THE PRESS SYNDICATE OF THE UNIVERSITY OF CAMBRIDGE
The Pitt Building, Trumpington Street, Cambridge CB2 1RP, United Kingdom

CAMBRIDGE UNIVERSITY PRESS
The Edinburgh Building, Cambridge CB2 2RU, United Kingdom
40 West 20th Street, New York, NY 10011-4211, USA
10 Stamford Road, Oakleigh, Melbourne 3166, Australia

First published 1984
Ninth printing 1987
Second edition 1990
Fourth printing 1995
Third edition 1997

Printed in the United Kingdom at the University Press, Cambridge

Typeset in Times 10/12 pt

A catalogue record for this book is available from the British Library

ISBN 0 521 56721 1 paperback

Contents

Preface to the first edition

The fundamental aim underlying the writing of *Biological Science* was the desire to emphasise the unifying scientific nature of biological systems despite the amazing diversity in structure and function seen at all levels of biological organisation.

Books 1 and 2 comprise a complete text for the A-level student, following all syllabuses in Biological Sciences and incorporating all the topic areas recommended by the GCE Interboard Working Party on the A-level common core in Biology (published 1983). The text will also be relevant to all first-year University and Further Education College students studying the Biological Sciences.

Each chapter is designed to provide comprehensive, up-to-date information on all topics in Biological Sciences, and the accuracy and relevance of this information has been checked by leading authorities in the appropriate fields and by practising teachers and examiners. The text includes:
- clearly written factual material,
- a carefully selected series of thoroughly pretested practical investigations relevant to the A-level course,
- a variety of types of question designed to stimulate an enquiring approach and answers to them.

Whilst it is recognised that the study of Biological Science follows no set pattern, the content of books 1 and 2 has been arranged so that each book contains material approximating to each year of a two-year course.

The appendices, which provide information and techniques vital to the study of Biological Science at this level, recognise that many students do not study Chemistry and Physics to the same level. Mathematical, physical and chemical concepts related to Biological Sciences are emphasised throughout the text, as appropriate.

Preface to the third edition

Since its publication in 1984, *Biological Science* has become established as one of the most comprehensive and authoritative A level Biology texts. It has remained one of our aims in writing the third edition to maintain its reputation as an up-to-date and comprehensive resource for current A level syllabuses.

In recent years there have been significant changes in content and format of syllabuses, with modular courses becoming important alternatives to 'linear' courses, and a new agreed subject core for Biology being established by SCAA in 1993, which has subsequently been revised in 1997. A typical modern syllabus is now composed of a core containing the agreed basis of the subject, with options that develop depth and range of experience in more specialist areas. Typically these options also emphasise the social, ethical and applied aspects of the subject, and emphasise the growing importance of biological sciences in the modern world.

The revision for the third edition has been far more comprehensive than that carried out for the second edition, with many substantial as well as more subtle changes to the text, diagrams, photographs and tables. Much new material has been written, and material which is no longer relevant has been removed. In addition, some of the material in the appendices has been removed and placed in the relevant chapters.

In recognition of the importance and popularity of certain topics, particularly in option areas, three completely new chapters have been added. These provide comprehensive coverage of Microbiology and biotechnology (chapter 12), Human health and disease (chapter 15) and Applied genetics (chapter 25). In addition, there is far more extensive coverage of human nutrition in chapter 10 and human reproduction in chapter 21 in line with present syllabuses. Where relevant, the ethical and social implications of these topics are also discussed. A wider range of topical issues is also included in the Ecology chapter (chapter 10).

In line with the changing emphasis of syllabuses, Variety of life has been condensed from three chapters into one (chapter 2), with examples relevant to current syllabuses being chosen. The chapter includes a new introductory discussion on classification and use of keys. Other chapters have been updated where necessary. Physiological topics throughout the book have, in particular, been modified in the light of new knowledge as well as to match syllabus requirements. The text also takes into account the trend towards a greater focus on higher plants and humans.

In addition to the changes described, a major effort has been made to make the text suitable for a wider range of students. Consideration has been given to reducing unnecessary complexity, especially in the use of language. Particular care has been taken with the introduction to each topic. Some sections have been reorganised, subheadings added, and greater use made of numbered lists and bulleted points. It is hoped that these changes will improve the readability whilst retaining the vigour and depth of the text.

Revision of this edition of the book has largely been carried out by Dennis Taylor during a sabbatical from Strode's College. As in the second edition, the ecology chapters (10 and 11) have been revised by Rosalind Taylor of Kingston University. The new chapter on Health and disease was mostly written by Roland Soper. Academic referees have checked new text with the aim of making it as factually correct as possible. Nevertheless, in an undertaking this large, errors and inaccuracies are difficult to avoid completely, and the authors are always grateful for notification of any that are spotted.

Acknowledgements

The authors and publisher would like to acknowledge the many friends, colleagues, students and advisers who have helped in the production of *Biological Science*.

In particular, we wish to thank:
Dr R. Batt, Dr I. Benton, Dr Claudia Berek, Professor R.J. Berry, Dr A.C. Blake, Dr John C. Bowman, Dr John Brookfield, Mr R. Brown, Dr Stuart Brown, Dr Fred Burke, Mr Richard Carter, Dr Norman R. Cohen, Dr I. Côte, Dr K.J.R. Edwards, Mr Malcolm Emery, Mr Nick Fagents, Dr James T. Fitzsimons, Dr John Gay, Dr Brij L. Gupta, Vivienne Hambleton, Dr David E. Hanke, Dr R.N. Hardy, Reverend J.R. Hargreaves, Dr S.A. Henderson, Mr Michael J. Hook, Mr Colin S. Hutchinson, Illustra Design Ltd, Dr Alick Jones, Mrs Sue Kearsey, Dr Simon P. Maddrell FRS, Professor Aubrey Manning, Dr Chris L. Mason, Mrs Ruth Miller, Dr David C. Moore, A.G. Morgan, Dr Rodney Mulvey, Dr David Secher, Dr John M. Squire, Professor James F. Sutcliffe, Stephen Tomkins, Dr Eric R. Turner, Dr Paul Wheater, Dr Brian E.J. Wheeler, Dr Michael Wheeler.

The authors are particularly indebted to Mrs Adrienne Oxley, who patiently and skilfully organised the pretesting of all the practical exercises. Her perseverance has produced exercises that teachers, pupils and laboratory technicians can depend upon.

However, the authors accept full responsibility for the final content of these books.

Finally, the authors wish to express their thanks to their wives and families for the constant support and encouragement shown throughout the preparation and publication of these books.

We also wish to thank the following for permission to use their illustrations, tables and questions.
Figures: 2.2*a*, 2.37*c*, 2.38*b*, 2.40*a*, 2.40*b*, 2.46, 2.66*b*, 2.66*e*, 8.3 Heather Angel/Biofotos; 2.2*b* Stephen Krasemann/NHPA; 2.2*c* Gerard Lacz/NHPA; 2.6*b*, 5.3, 5.8 Andrew Syred 1995/Microscopix; 2.6*c*, 2.6*d*, 2.7, 2.17*b*, 2.18*b*, 2.25*a*, 2.25*c*, 2.26*a*, 2.27*b*, 2.32*b*, 2.37*d*, 2.48*e*, 2.48*f*, 2.48*g*, 2.66*c*, 2.66*d*, 5.1*b*, 5.13, 5.25, 5.28, 5.30, 5.31, 5.35, 6.3*e*, 6.3*f*, 6.4*a*, 6.4*b*, 6.5*d*, 6.6*e*, 6.7*b*, 6.9*c*, 6.9*d*, 6.10*b*, 6.12*b*, 6.12*c*, 6.12*e*, 6.13*b*, 6.13*d*, 6.15*b*, 6.16*c*, 6.16*d*, 6.22, 6.25, 6.29, 7.3, 7.4*a*, 7.4*b*, 7.6, 8.10*b*, 8.17, 8.19, 8.21*b*, 8.21*e*, 8.21*f*, 9.11*a*, 9.20*a*, 9.20*b*, 9.22*a*, 9.23, 9.33*a*, 9.33*b*, Biophoto Associates; 2.9 Professor Stanley Cohen/Science Photo Library (SPL); 2.12 Dr L. Caro/SPL; 2.18*c* Jurgen Dielenscheider/Holt Sudios International; 2.19*b* B. Heggeler/Biozentrum, University of Basel/SPL; 2.24 NIBSC/SPL; 2.27*a* Andrew Syred 1993/Microscopix; 2.37*b* Roy Edwards; 2.53 R. Umesh Chandron, TDR, WHO/SPL; 2.62*b*, 2.62*c* Shell International Petroleum Co.; 2.62*d* Stephen Dalton/NHPA; 3.1*b*, 3.1*c*, 3.11, 3.17*b* Andrew Lambert; 3.34*b*, 3.34*e* Sir John Kendrew; 3.34*d* Dr Arthur Lesk/SPL; 3.41 Dr J.M. Squire; 3.45 Professor M.H.F. Wilkins, Biophysics Department, King's College, London; 4.4*d* Clive Freeman, The Royal Institution/SPL; 5.5*a*, 5.5*b* A.M. Page, Royal Holloway College, London; 5.6 R. Maisonneuve, Publiphoto Diffusion/SPL; 5.12 Dr Glenn Decker, School of Medicine, John Hopkins University; 5.24 Don Fawcett/SPL; 5.29, 6.14*b*, 6.17*b*, 6.17*c*, 6.18*c*, 6.19*b* 6.20, 6.21, 6.23, 6.24, 6.26*a*, 6.31*a*, 8.16*b*, 8.21*a*,

9.12*e* Dr Paul Wheater; 5.33 Dr Klaus Weber; 6.3*d* Rothamsted Experimental Station; 6.5*c*, 6.6*d*, 6.12*f*, 7.12, 11.2, 11.3, 11.10 Centre for Cell and Tissue Research, York; 6.14*c*, 6.15*c* Life Science Images; 6.18*d* Mr P. Crosby, Department of Biology, University of York; 7.2 Andrew Mounter/Planet Earth Pictures; 7.8, 7.21*b*, 7.23 Dr A.D. Greenwood; 7.21*a* C.C. Black (1971) *Plant Physiology*, **47**, 15–23, with permission of the publisher; 8.1*a* R.L. Mathews/Planet Earth Pictures; 8.1*b* Nick Greaves/Planet Earth Pictures; 8.6*a* Kim Taylor/Bruce Coleman Ltd; 8.6*c*, 8.6*d* Dr Brad Amos/SPL; 8.7*b* Claude Nuridsany & Marie Perennou/SPL; 8.8 Alan Weaving/Ardea; 8.13*a* Charles Day; 8.13*b* King's College School of Medicine and Dentistry, London; 8.15*a*, 8.15*b*, 8.15*c*, 8.15*d* Dr C.A. Saxton, Unilever Research; 8.16*a* Dr L.M. Beidler/SPL; 8.18*b* Mehav Kulyk/SPL; 8.28, 9.35 National Medical Slide Bank; 8.30*a*, 8.30*b* Peter Menzel/SPL; 9.11*b*, 9.12*g* Dr Brij L. Gupta, Department of Zoology, Cambridge; 9.12*f* Bill Longcore/SPL; 9.13 E.F. van Bruggen, State University of Groningen; 9.20*c* Prof. P. Motta, Department of Anatomy, University La Sapienza, Rome/SPL; 9.22*b*, B. Siegwart, P. Gehr, J. Gil & E.R. Wiebel (1971) *Respir. Physiol.*, **13**, 141–59; 9.25 G.M.Hughes (1973) *The Vertebrate Lung*, Oxford Biology Readers, no.59; 9.35 National Medical Slide Bank; 10.16 Dr Martyn Waller; 10.20 Mark Mattock/Planet Earth Pictures; 10.27 Herbert Giradet/Panos Pictures; 10.30 Nick Garbutt/Planet Earth Pictures; 10.37 W. J. Allen/Chilworth Media Associates; 11.1, 11.13 Graham Page, Kingston University; 11.6 John Edward Leigh; 11.7 Nigel Luckhurst; 12.2 Simon Fraser/SPL; 12.4, 12.14*b* Hank Morgan/SPL; 12.5 National Dairy Council; 12.11*a*, 12.27 Andrew Syred/SPL; 12.11*b* National Institute for Research in Dairying, Reading; 12.12 Robert Longuehaye, NIBSC/SPL; 12.14*a*, 12.15 James Holmes/Celltech Ltd/SPL; 12.18 CEPHAS/Stuart Boreham; 12.19 Ricardo Arias, Latin Stock/SPL; 12.21 John Birdsall; 12.22 E. A. Rathbun & N. J. Brewin, John Innes Centre, Norwich; 12.23 Prof. David Hall/SPL; 12.24 David Hall/Panos Pictures; 12.25 Steve McCutcheon/FLPA; 12.26 Gist-Brocades; 12.31 Hattie Young/SPL.
Tables: 3.1 with permission of Plenum Publishing Corporation, copyright Plenum Publishing Corporation; 8.8, 8.9, 8.10 reproduced by permission of the Controller of Her Majesty's Stationery Office; 10.1 copyright © 1971 by W.B. Saunders Company, reprinted by permission of Holt, Rinehart & Winston, CBS Publishing; 11.5, 11.6 by permission of Griffin & George.
Questions: 10.14, 10.16 Open University Foundation Course (S100) Unit 20, copyright © 1971, Open University Press.
Cover: Mark Mattock/Planet Earth Pictures.

Chapter One

Introduction to the subject

Biology (*bios*, life; *logos*, knowledge) is a science devoted to the study of living organisms. Science has progressed by breaking down complex subjects of study into their component parts so that today there are numerous branches of biology, some of which are shown in fig 1.1. This principle is often called the 'reductionist' principle and, carried to its logical conclusions, it has focused attention on the most elementary forms of matter in living and non-living systems. This approach to study seeks fundamental understanding by looking at parts rather than the whole. An opposing approach, based on the 'vitalist' principle, considers that 'life' is something special and unique, and maintains that life cannot be explained solely in terms of the laws of physics and chemistry, having properties which are special to the system as a whole. The aim of biology must ultimately be to explain the living world in terms of scientific principles, although appreciating that organisms behave in ways which often seem beyond the capabilities of their component parts. Certainly the consciousness of living organisms cannot be described in terms of physics and chemistry even though the neurophysiologist can describe the working of the single neurone in physicochemical terms. Consciousness may be the collective working of millions of neurones and their electrochemical states, but as yet we have no real concept of the chemical nature of thought and ideas. Nor do we understand completely how living organisms originated and evolved. There have been many attempts to answer this questions from theological to biological and chapters 23–27 attempt to put the different viewpoints, but with the emphasis on the possible biological explanations.

Thus we are reduced to the position that we cannot define precisely what life is nor whence it came. All that we can do is to describe the observable phenomena that distinguish living matter from non-living matter. These are as follows.

Nutrition

All living organisms need food, which is used as a source of energy, and materials for the processes of life, such as growth. Only two sources of energy are used by living organisms, namely light and chemical energy. Those organisms specialised for using light energy carry out photosynthesis and contain pigments, including chlorophyll, which absorb light. They include plants, algae

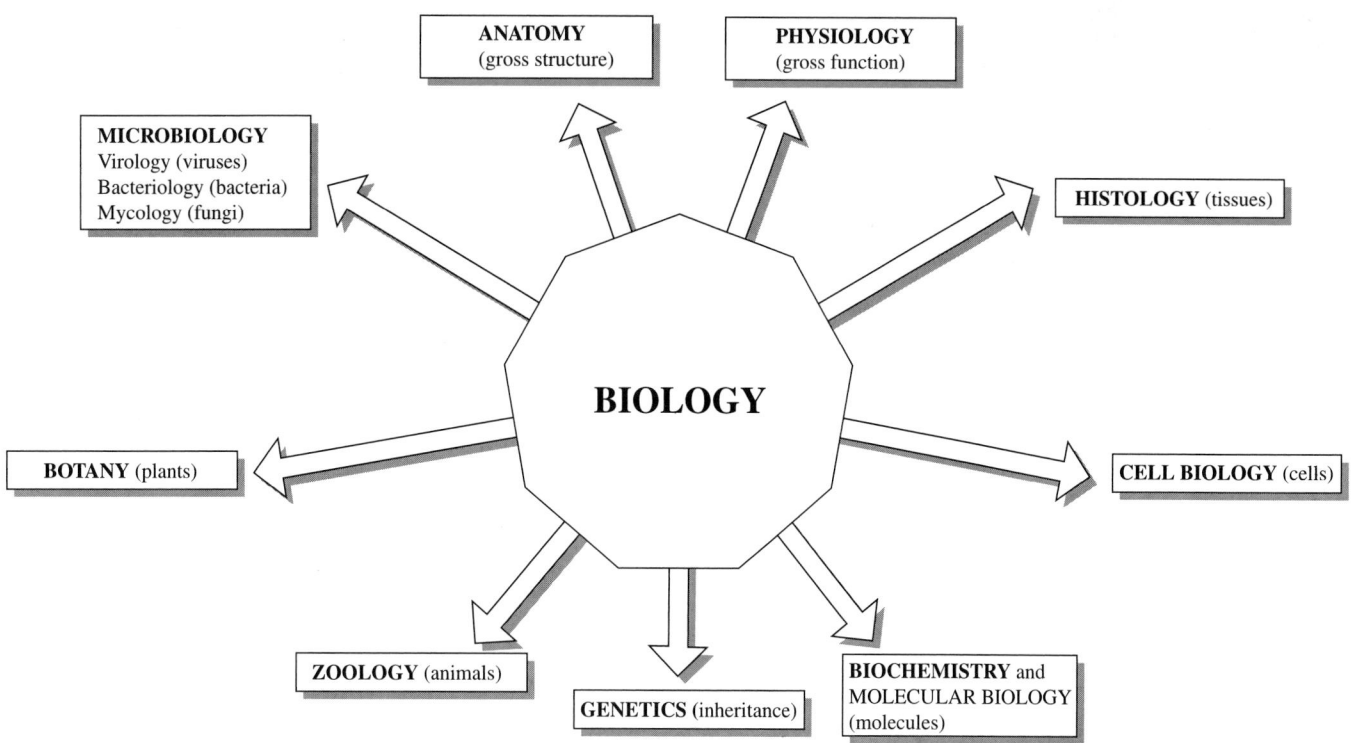

and some simple organisms including bacteria. These organisms which use chemical energy must obtain it from other living organisms. They include animals and fungi. Different methods of nutrition are responsible for some of the most fundamental differences between organisms.

Respiration

All life processes require energy and much of the food obtained by nutrition is used as a source of this energy. The energy is released during the breakdown of certain energy-rich compounds in the process of respiration. The energy released is stored in molecules of adenosine triphosphate (ATP). This compound had been found to occur in all living cells and is sometimes referred to as the 'universal energy carrier'.

Irritability

Living organisms have the ability to respond to changes in both the internal and external environments and thus ensure that they maximise their chances of survival. For example, the blood vessels in the skin of a mammal dilate (increase in diameter) in response to a rise in body temperature, and the consequent heat loss brings about a return to the optimum temperature of the body. A green plant on a window sill in a room grows towards light coming through the window, thus ensuring maximum exposure to light for photosynthesis.

Movement

Some living organisms, such as animals and some bacteria, have the ability to move from place to place, that is they locomote. This is necessary in order for them to obtain their food, unlike other organisms, such as plants, which can manufacture their own food from raw materials obtained in one place. Nevertheless, some movement of whole body structures can occur in plants, as when a leaf grows towards the Sun or a flower closes at night.

Excretion

Excretion is the removal from the body of waste products of metabolism. For example, the process of aerobic respiration produces a waste product, carbon dioxide, which can be harmful in excess and must be eliminated. Animals take in an excess of protein during nutrition and, since this material cannot be stored, it must be broken down and excreted. Animal excretion is, therefore, largely nitrogenous excretion.

Reproduction

The life span of organisms is limited, but they all have the ability to perpetuate 'life', thereby ensuring the survival of the species. The resulting offspring have the same general characteristics as the parents, whether such individuals are produced by asexual or sexual reproduction. The 'reductionist' search for the explanation of this inheritance has revealed the existence of molecules, known as nucleic acids (deoxyribonucleic acid, DNA, and ribonucleic acid, RNA), which contain the coded information passed between organisms from one generation to the next.

Growth

Non-living objects, such as a crystal or a stalagmite, grow by the addition of new material to their outside surface. Living organisms, however, grow from within, using food that they obtain from nutrition. The molecules are formed into new living material.

These seven characteristics can be observed to a greater or lesser extent in all living organisms. They are the *observable* outcome of the all-important property of living material, namely the extraction, conversion and use of energy from the environment. In addition, living material is able to maintain and even increase its own energy content. In contrast to this, dead organic matter tends to disintegrate as a result of the chemical and physical forces of the environment. In order to maintain themselves and prevent this disintegration, organisms have an inbuilt *self-regulating* system to ensure that there is no net energy loss. This control is referred to as homeostasis and operates at all levels of biological organisation, from the molecular level to the community level.

The characteristics of life outlined above are dealt with in detail in this book. Many of the chapters extend the explanations in terms of physical and chemical concepts, for it is in these fields that the major research and additions to our knowledge have come in recent years. The study of cell structure, DNA and genetics, protein synthesis, enzymes, hormones, the immune response, and many other aspects of the structure and function of living organisms, all provide some explanation of what is happening within the cells and bodies of organisms.

In the appendixes, in Book 2, you will find some basic information required by a biologist, including biochemistry, scientific method, the experimental approach, a glossary of terms and so on. The appendices are designed to supply information to those students which may be lacking in one or more of these areas. With this knowledge the student should strive to develop powers of critical observation and description which are part of the thinking processes underlying scientific enquiry.

Chapter Two

Variety of life

2.1 Classification

2.1.1 Why classify?

If you have ever watched a child playing with coloured sweets or sorting out stamps, football cards or other collectable items, you may have witnessed one of our most basic instincts in operation, the desire to sort out things into groups. This is an act of classification. **Classification** is grouping things together on the basis of features they have in common. The science of classification is called **taxonomy**. Why do we classify? Some biologists suggest that one reason *why* we classify things is because it has survival advantage. If our senses are besieged by an overwhelming number of different stimuli, we can begin to cope and make sense of things by classifying them. Our first classifications may go wrong; for example some small children may call anything with four legs a dog. But gradually we develop a system that enables us to cope with the complexity of the world.

Something like one-and-a-half million different kinds of living organisms have been discovered on this planet, and it has been estimated that there may be 10–100 million kinds. Not surprisingly therefore, there are records of our attempts to classify these organisms as far back as we can trace. The classifications differ according to the uses to which they are put. The ancient Chinese, for example, organised the animal kingdom into a number of groups, some of which may seem odd to us today, such as fabulous ones, stray dogs, those that have broken a flower vase and those that resemble flies at a distance. More obvious classifications might be into poisonous and edible plants or flying and non-flying animals. As we shall see, modern systems of classification often emphasise our ideas of evolutionary relationships between organism.

As we learn more about living organisms, our classifications are modified, but it is important to realise that there is no single perfect classification. They are all designed for our own convenience.

2.1.2 Taxonomy

The science of taxonomy has two branches, the naming of organisms, or **nomenclature**, and the placing of organisms into groups, or **systematics**. The latter is done on the basis of their similarities and differences.

Biological nomenclature is based on the **binomial system** pioneered by the work of the Swedish naturalist Carl Linnaeus (1707–78). In this system each organism has two Latin names: a **generic** name beginning with a capital letter and a **specific** name beginning with a lower case letter. For example, humans are named *Homo sapiens*; the genus is *Homo* and the species is *sapiens*. Italics are used to indicate Latin names. Alternatively, the words can be underlined, e.g. Homo sapiens. You should try to remember to do this when you use the Latin name of an organism. The genus may be abbreviated to one letter, e.g. *H. sapiens*. The Latin name is internationally agreed and avoids the confusion of local variations in common names. For example, in Britain, the plant *Caltha palustris* has at least 90 common names, including marsh marigold, kingcup, golden cup, brave celandine, grandfather's button and butter-flower. The puma, *Felis concolor*, has more than 20 common names. Additional confusion with English names comes when a single common name refers to more than one species. For example, there are more than 100 different plant species known as raspberries.

2.1.3 The taxonomic hierarchy

Linnaeus eventually extended the binomial system to include more groups than just genus and species. These he arranged in a hierarchy with the largest group, the **kingdom**, at the top of the hierarchy. The groups he proposed are still used today and, in descending order of size, are:

kingdom*
phylum – introduced by Haeckel late nineteenth century
class*
order*
family – introduced in Linnaeus' lifetime
genus*
species*

* introduced by Linnaeus

An actual example from the classification of the animal kingdom is shown in fig 2.1. You can see that each group, or taxon, may contain a number of groups (taxa) lower in the hierarchy. For example, the subphylum Vertebrata contains six classes and the genus *Homo* three species, two of which are extinct. Each group possesses features unique to that group. These are described as diagnostic features.

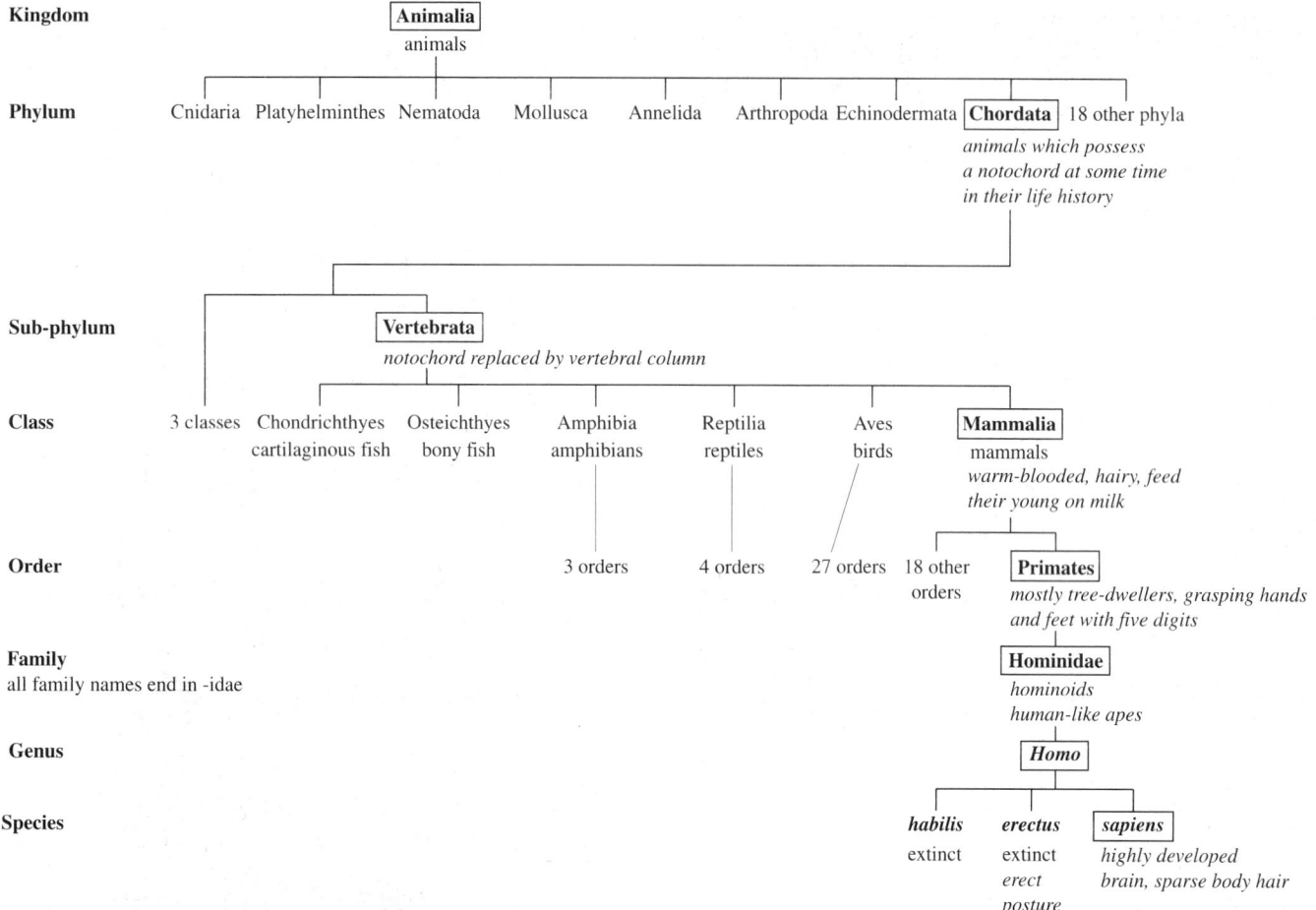

| Kingdom | | | | | | | | | **Animalia** | | |
| | | | | | | | | | animals | | |

| Phylum | Cnidaria | Platyhelminthes | Nematoda | Mollusca | Annelida | Arthropoda | Echinodermata | **Chordata** | 18 other phyla |

animals which possess a notochord at some time in their life history

| Sub-phylum | | **Vertebrata** |
notochord replaced by vertebral column

| Class | 3 classes | Chondrichthyes cartilaginous fish | Osteichthyes bony fish | Amphibia amphibians | Reptilia reptiles | Aves birds | **Mammalia** mammals |

warm-blooded, hairy, feed their young on milk

| Order | | | | 3 orders | 4 orders | 27 orders | 18 other orders | **Primates** |

mostly tree-dwellers, grasping hands and feet with five digits

Family
all family names end in -idae

Hominidae
hominoids human-like apes

Genus

Homo

| Species | | *habilis* | *erectus* | *sapiens* |
| | | extinct | extinct erect posture | *highly developed brain, sparse body hair* |

Fig 2.1 *Example of a hierarchy of taxonomic groups. Not all the groups of animals are shown. Note the use of Latin names, although most groups also have common English names.*

For example, only mammals (order Mammalia) possess hair, so hair is a diagnostic feature of mammals. Mammals, however, share with birds, reptiles, amphibians and fish all the diagnostic features of the preceding group in the hierarchy, namely the vertebrates.

Groups may be further subdivided into subgroups, such as subphylum Vertebrata (fig 2.1) or put together into supergroups, such as superclass, if it is convenient to do so. The hierarchies are constructed for our convenience, and they are frequently changed or modified.

2.1.4 Species

The term species has a more precise definition than the other levels in the hierarchy. It can be defined as a **group of closely related organisms which are capable of interbreeding to produce fertile offspring**. Occasionally two organisms which are genetically closely related can interbreed to produce *infertile* offspring. A cross (hybrid) between a donkey and a horse, for example, produces a mule, which is infertile. By definition, therefore, a donkey and a horse should be described as different species.

Mules show some of the advantages of both types of parent (**hybrid vigour**).

There are exceptions to the rule about fertile offspring. For example lions and tigers are considered as different species. If a male tiger mates with a female lion they can have fertile offspring (*tiglons*) although the offspring of female tigers and male lions (*ligers*) are *not* fertile. Normally tigers are forest dwellers and lions are plains dwellers, so they are ecologically isolated. Breeding has only been observed in captivity.

Each species possesses its own distinct structural, behavioural and ecological characteristics (fig 2.2) (see also chapter 27). As we progress up the taxonomic hierarchy, the number of similarities between the members of each group decreases. For example, members of the same genus have more characteristics in common than members of the same family or order.

As we have seen, a precise definition of a species is not really possible. This is not surprising because species can change (evolve) over time. According to the theory of natural selection this process takes place by survival of the fittest, in other words those best adapted to the environment. If the environment changes, then individuals which are better adapted will be selected, and over many generations the species will gradually change. If different populations of the same species become isolated from each

Fig 2.2 (a) Canis familiaris, *the domesticated dog. All breeds of dog are capable of interbreeding and are therefore placed in the same species.*
(b) Canis latrans, *the coyote, a common carnivore and scavenger of North America.*
(c) Canis lupus, *the grey wolf, distributed widely in the northern hemisphere where its range overlaps with the other two species. Coyotes and wolves have been known to mate successfully with dogs, producing fertile offspring.*
This illustrates the difficulty of deciding what exactly constitutes a species. It is often even more difficult to be precise with larger groups such as genus and order. All canines are placed in the order Carnivora.

other, for example by ecological or physical barriers such as oceans or mountain ranges, then the different populations may evolve in different ways until they cease to be capable of interbreeding. They become different species.

In some cases there are not necessarily sharp genetic boundaries between one species and another. For example, the herring gull and the lesser black-backed gull are described as different species because they show physical and behavioural differences and do not normally interbreed. However, they occasionally nest in the same place and a few mixed breeding pairs do occur (chapter 27).

2.1.5 Artificial and natural classification

There are two types of classification, artificial and natural. An **artificial classification** is based on one or a few easily observed characteristics, and is usually designed for a practical purpose with an emphasis on convenience and simplicity. The ancient Chinese system already mentioned is

an artificial classification. Linnaeus included all worm-like organisms in a single group, the Vermes. This included a wide range of animals, from simple nematode worms and earthworms to snakes. This was an artificial classification because it did not take account of important natural relationships, such as the fact that snakes have backbones and earthworms do not. Snakes have more in common with other vertebrates than with worms. An example of an artificial classification of fish could be to group them as freshwater fish, brackish-water fish and marine fish on the basis of their environment. This would be convenient for the purpose of investigating their mechanisms of osmoregulation. Similarly, all microscopic organisms are known as microorganisms (section 2.2), a convenient group for the purposes of study but not a natural group.

A **natural classification** tries to use natural relationships between organisms. It considers more evidence than artificial classifications, including internal as well as external features. Similarities of embryology, morphology, anatomy, physiology, biochemistry, cell structure and behaviour are all relevant. Most classifications in use today are natural and phylogenetic. A **phylogenetic classification** is one based on evolutionary relationships. In such a system organisms belonging to the same groups are believed to have a common ancestor. The phylogeny (evolutionary history) of a group can be shown by means of a 'family tree', as in fig 2.3.

Another way to classify organisms is to use a **phenetic classification**. This is an attempt to avoid the problem of establishing evolutionary relationships, which can be very difficult and very controversial, especially if there is little or no fossil evidence. The word 'phenetic' comes from the Greek *phainomenon*, 'that which is seen'. This classification is based solely on observable characteristics (phenetic similarity) and all characters used are considered of equal importance. All features of an organism can be considered, the more the better, and they do not necessarily have to be of evolutionary significance. Masses of data are collected and the degrees of similarities between different organisms are calculated, usually by computer because the calculations are extremely complex. The use of computers in taxonomy is known as **numerical taxonomy**. Phenetic classifications often resemble phylogenetic classifications, but they are not constructed with this in view.

2.1.6 Specimen identification and keys

A **key** is a convenient method of enabling a biologist to identify an organism. It involves listing the observable characteristics of the organism and matching them with those features which are diagnostic of a particular group. Most of the characteristics used in identification are based on easily observable features such as shape, colour and numbers of appendages, segments and so on. Hence identification is *artificial* and *phenetic* since it relies purely on the appearance (phenotype) of the organism. Despite this, most diagnostic keys enable organisms to be identified into a group which is part of a natural phylogenetic hierarchical classification system.

There are various types of diagnostic keys, but the simplest is called a **dichotomous key**. This is made up of pairs of statements called **leads**, numbered 1, 2, 3 and so on, where each lead deals with a particular observable characteristic. The paired statements of each lead should be *contrasting* and *mutually exclusive* and, by considering these in order, a large group of organisms may be broken down into progressively smaller groups until the unknown organism is identified.

The characteristics used in keys should be readily observable morphological features, and may be **qualitative**, such as shape of abdomen and colour, or **quantitative**, such as number of hairs and length of stem. Either may be used, but the characteristic must be constant for that species and not subject to variation as a result of environmental influences. In this respect size and colour are often bad examples to use since both can be influenced by the

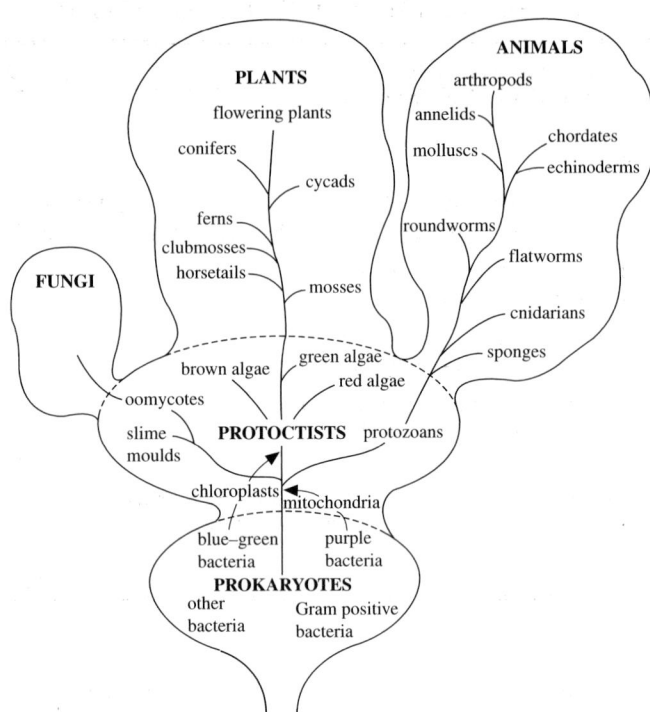

Fig 2.3 *An evolutionary tree of life, including the five kingdoms of Margulis and Schwartz (section 2.2). The lengths of the lines are not related to time.*

environment, the season, the age or state of the organism at the time of identification. Characteristics chosen should, if possible, exist in two or more states. For example, the characteristic 'stem shape' may exist in one of the two states, 'round' or 'square'.

After each statement there is a number referring to the next lead to be considered, if the statement matches the specimen. For example in the simple key to the cultivated members of the plant family Leguminosae (which includes peas and beans) shown in table 2.1, if the specimen has been keyed as far as lead 5 and it possesses branches without thorns or spines, the next lead to consider is lead 7, and so on.

2.2 Five kingdoms

Until relatively recently it was generally agreed that all organisms should be placed in just two kingdoms, the animal and plant kingdoms. The basic difference between animals and plants was that animals fed on organic material (are **heterotrophic**) whereas plants synthesised their own organic requirements from inorganic compounds (are **autotrophic**). More precisely, a heterotrophic organism is one which has an organic source of carbon, and an autotrophic organism is one which has an inorganic source of carbon, namely carbon dioxide. Animals typically search for their food and so show locomotion. For this they require a nervous system for coordination in the more complex animals, whereas plants are stationary and do not show locomotion or possess a nervous system.

Table 2.1 Extract of key to cultivated Leguminosae.

1	Woody trees and shrubs	2
	Herbaceous and annual plants	15
2	Climbing	3
	Non-climbing	4
3	Flowers bright red	Lobster claw
	Flowers mauve, sometimes white, forming sprays	Wisteria
4	Flowers all or partly yellow	5
	Flowers not yellow	8
5	Branches with thorns and spines	6
	Branches without thorns and spines	7
6	Leaves absent, plant spiny all over	Gorse
	Leaves present on young shoots, spines on older branches	Needlewhin
7	Young stem square, leaves small with three leaflets	Broom
	Stems not square, leaves longer than 2.5 cm	9
8	etc.	

However, this classification ignored the fact that all cellular organisms seem to fall into two natural groups, now known as prokaryotes and eukaryotes. These two groups are fundamentally different. The terms *prokaryote* and *eukaryote* refer to differences in the location of the DNA (the genetic material). In **prokaryotes** the DNA is not enclosed by nuclear membranes and lies free in the cytoplasm. The cells therefore lack true nuclei (*pro*, before; *karyon*, nucleus). The cells of **eukaryotes**, however, do contain true nuclei (*eu*, true). Eukaryotes evolved from prokaryotes.

Classifying all organisms as animals or plants presented other difficulties. For example, fungi are heterotrophic but non-motile, so should they be classified as animals or plants? Such problems have been solved by accepting that there should be more than two kingdoms. In 1982, Margulis and Schwartz proposed a system which used five kingdoms, the Prokaryotae and four eukaryote kingdoms (fig 2.4). This system has been widely accepted and is currently recommended by the Institute of Biology. The eukaryotes

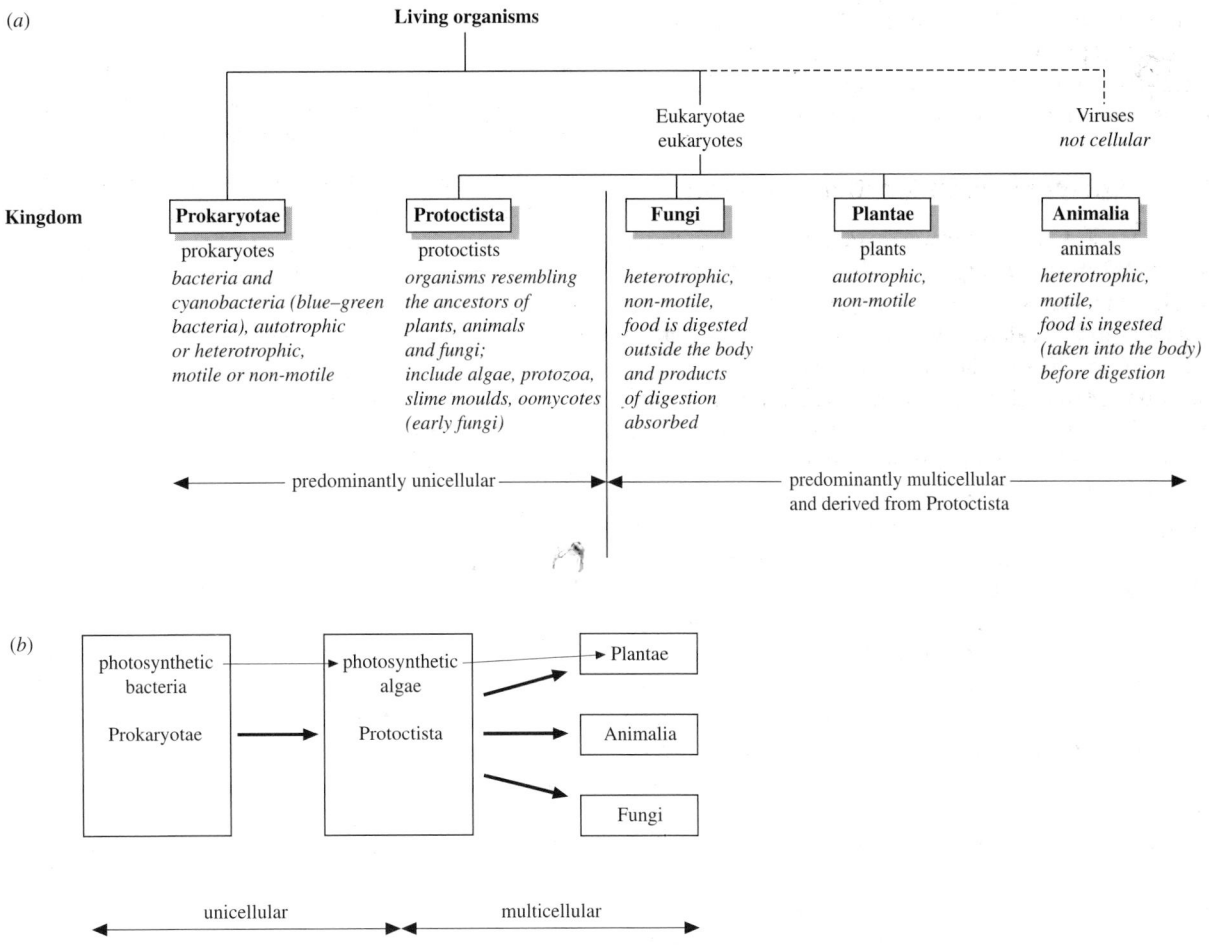

Fig 2.4 (a) *The five kingdom classification of living organisms, according to Margulis and Schwartz. Some of the chief characteristics of the kingdoms are shown. Viruses do not fit neatly into any classification of living organisms because they have a very simple, non-cellular structure and cannot exist independently of other organisms.*
(b) *Evolutionary relationships between the five kingdoms. The diagram shows the trend towards multicellular organisms, the first appearing among the protoctists.*

can be regarded as belonging to a superkingdom, the Eukaryotae. The most controversial group is the protoctists because it is probably an unnatural group. This is discussed later in section 2.6.

One group of 'organisms' that does not fit neatly into any classification scheme is the viruses. Viruses are extremely small particles consisting only of a piece of genetic material (DNA or RNA) in a protective coat of protein. They do not have a cellular structure, unlike all other organisms, and can only reproduce by invading living cells. Their origins are discussed in section 2.4 and they are shown as an extra group in fig 2.4a.

Although it is not a natural grouping, the smallest organisms are often collectively known as **microorganisms** or **microbes**. These include the bacteria (prokaryotes), viruses, fungi and protoctists. The grouping is a useful one for practical reasons because the techniques used in their study are often similar. For example, a microscope is needed to see them and sterile (aseptic) techniques are

needed for culturing them. The study of microorganisms is a branch of biology known as **microbiology**. Microorganisms have become increasingly important in the areas of biochemistry, genetics, agriculture and medicine, and are the basis of an important section of industry known as **biotechnology**. They will be discussed in chapter 12. Microorganisms, such as bacteria and fungi, are also important ecologically as decomposers (section 10.3.2).

2.3 Prokaryotes

The kingdom Prokaryotae is made up of organisms commonly known as bacteria. They are the most ancient group of organisms, having appeared about 3500 million years ago, and are the smallest organisms with a cellular structure. Their characteristics are summarised in table 2.2. They are mainly single cells, although the blue-green bacteria (Cyanobacteria) may form single rows of cells

Table 2.2 Major differences between prokaryotes and eukaryotes.

Feature	Prokaryote	Eukaryote
Organisms	Bacteria	Protoctists, fungi, plants and animals
Cell size	Average diameter 0.5–10 μm	10–100 μm diameter common; commonly 1000–10 000 times volume of prokaryotic cells
Form	Mainly unicellular	Mainly multicellular (except Protoctista, many of which are unicellular)
Evolutionary origin	3.5 thousand million years ago	1.2 thousand million years ago, evolved from prokaryotes
Cell division	Mostly binary fission, no spindle	Mitosis, meiosis, or both; spindle formed
Genetic material	DNA is circular and lies free in the cytoplasm (no true nucleus) DNA is naked (not associated with proteins or RNA to form chromosomes)	DNA is linear and contained in a nucleus. DNA is associated with proteins and RNA to form chromosomes
Protein synthesis	70S ribosomes (smaller) No endoplasmic reticulum present (Many other details of protein synthesis differ, including susceptibility to antibiotics, e.g. prokaryotes inhibited by streptomycin)	80S ribosomes (larger) Ribosomes may be attached to endoplasmic reticulum
Organelles	Few organelles None are surrounded by an envelope (two membranes) Internal membranes scarce; if present usually associated with respiration or photosynthesis	Many organelles Envelope-bound organelles present, e.g. nucleus, mitochondria, chloroplasts Great diversity of organelles bounded by single membranes, e.g. Golgi apparatus, lysosomes, vacuoles, microbodies, endoplasmic reticulum
Cell walls	Rigid and contain polysaccharides with amino acids; murein is main strengthening compound	Cell walls of green plants and fungi rigid and contain polysaccharides; cellulose is main strengthening compound of plant walls, chitin of fungal walls (none in animal cells)
Flagella	Simple, lacking microtubules; extracellular (not enclosed by cell surface membrane) 20 nm diameter	Complex, with '9+2' arrangement of microtubules; intracellular (surrounded by cell surface membrane) 200 nm diameter
Respiration	Mesosomes in bacteria, except cytoplasmic membranes in blue-green bacteria	Mitochondria for aerobic respiration
Photosynthesis	No chloroplasts; takes place on membranes which show no stacking	Chloroplasts containing membranes which are usually stacked into lamellae or grana
Nitrogen fixation	Some have the ability	None have the ability

called filaments. Some bacteria stick together in characteristic patterns, forming chains or clusters like bunches of grapes (fig 2.10), but the cells are totally independent of each other. Individual bacterial cells can only be seen with the aid of a microscope, which is why they are known as microorganisms. The study of bacteria is called **bacteriology** and is an important branch of microbiology.

Bacteria range in length from about 0.1 to 10 µm. Their average diameter is about 1 µm, enough room for 200 average-sized globular protein molecules (of 5 nm diameter) to fit across the cell. Such a molecule in solution can diffuse about 60 µm per second; thus no special transport mechanisms are needed for these organisms.

Bacteria occupy many environments, such as soil, dust, water, air, in and on animals and plants. Some are found in hot springs where temperatures may reach 78 °C or higher. Others can survive very low temperatures and periods of freezing in ice. Some have been found in deep cracks in the ocean floor, at very high pressures and temperatures of 360 °C. They form the starting point of unique food chains in these areas of the ocean.

Numbers of bacteria are enormous; one gram of fertile soil is estimated to contain 2.5 thousand million; 1 cm^3 of fresh milk may contain more than 3000 million. Together with fungi their activities are vital to all other organisms because they cause the decay of organic material and the subsequent recycling of nutrients. In addition, they are of increasing importance to humans, not only because some cause disease, but because their very diverse biochemistry can be used in many biotechnological processes. Their importance is discussed further in chapter 12.

2.3.1 Structure

Fig 2.5 shows the structure of a generalised bacterium, a typical prokaryotic cell. Figs 2.6a–d show a common rod-shaped bacterium, *Escherichia coli*, which lives in the gut of humans and other vertebrates. It is normally completely harmless. Its presence in water can be used as a very useful indicator of contamination by faeces. *E. coli* has been studied more than any other bacterium and is one of the few organisms whose entire genetic code has been determined. Note how little structure is visible in the cell of *E. coli* compared with a eukaryotic cell (figs 5.5 and 5.6). Fig 2.7 shows another rod-shaped bacterium which, unlike *E. coli*, possesses flagella.

Cell wall

The bacterial cell wall is strong and rigid due to the presence of **murein**, a molecule that consists of parallel

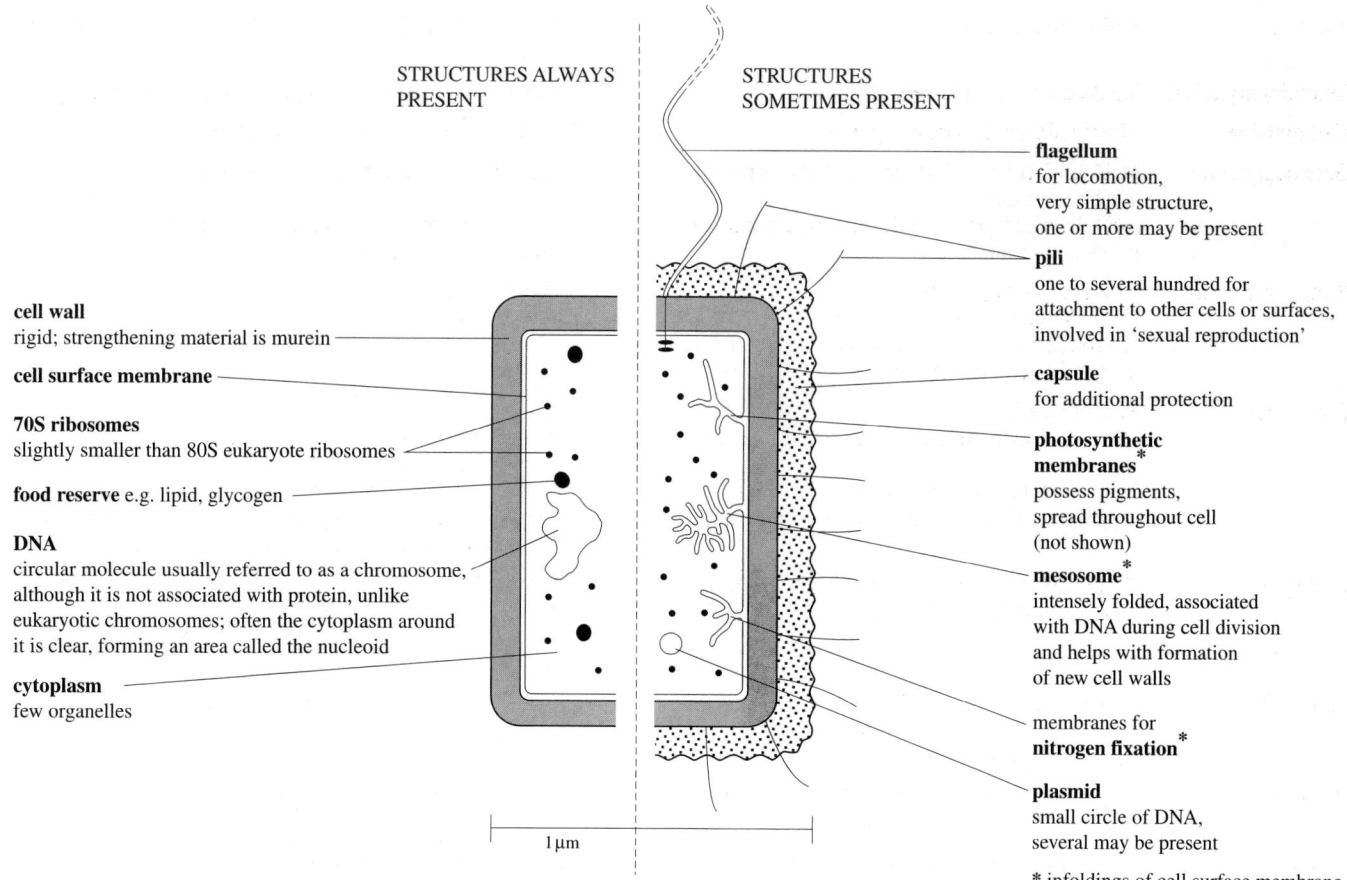

STRUCTURES ALWAYS PRESENT

STRUCTURES SOMETIMES PRESENT

cell wall
rigid; strengthening material is murein

cell surface membrane

70S ribosomes
slightly smaller than 80S eukaryote ribosomes

food reserve e.g. lipid, glycogen

DNA
circular molecule usually referred to as a chromosome, although it is not associated with protein, unlike eukaryotic chromosomes; often the cytoplasm around it is clear, forming an area called the nucleoid

cytoplasm
few organelles

1 µm

flagellum
for locomotion, very simple structure, one or more may be present

pili
one to several hundred for attachment to other cells or surfaces, involved in 'sexual reproduction'

capsule
for additional protection

photosynthetic membranes[*]
possess pigments, spread throughout cell (not shown)

mesosome[*]
intensely folded, associated with DNA during cell division and helps with formation of new cell walls

membranes for **nitrogen fixation**[*]

plasmid
small circle of DNA, several may be present

[*] infoldings of cell surface membrane

Fig 2.5 *Structure of a generalised rod-shaped bacterium (a typical prokaryote cell). The cell contains little structure compared with a eukaryotic cell.*

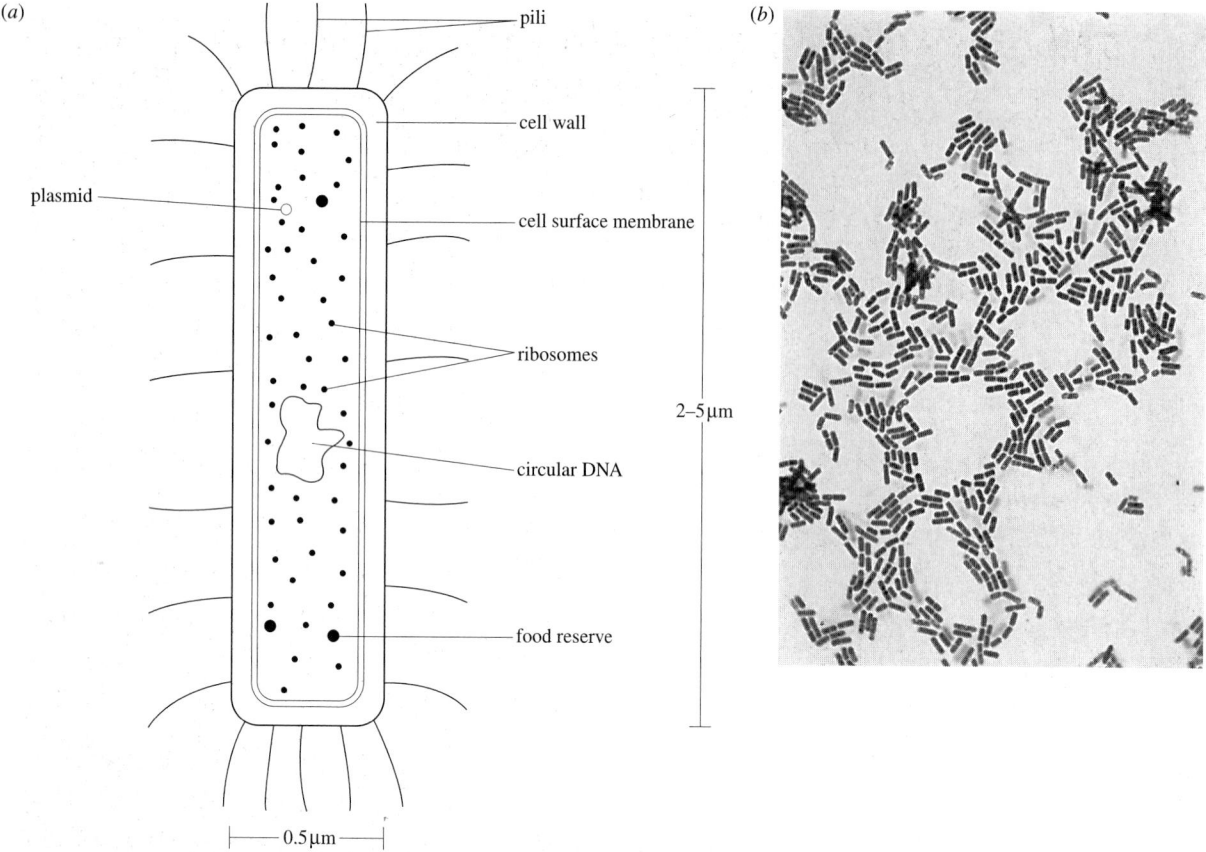

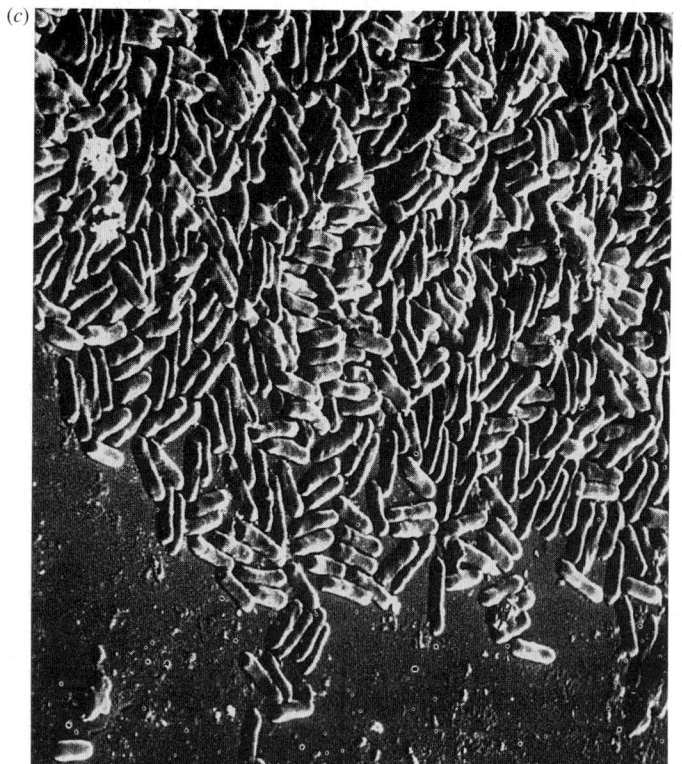

Fig 2.6 (a) *Structure of* Escherichia coli *(*E. coli*), a rod-shaped bacterium found in the gut of vertebrates.* (b) *Stained cells as they appear under a high-power light microscope (×1000).* (c) *Scanning electron micrograph of a colony of* E. coli. (d) *Transmission electron micrograph of a section of a dividing cell of* E. coli *(×50 000). This type of division is known as binary fission. The light areas contain DNA. The region containing the DNA is often referred to as the nucleoid.*

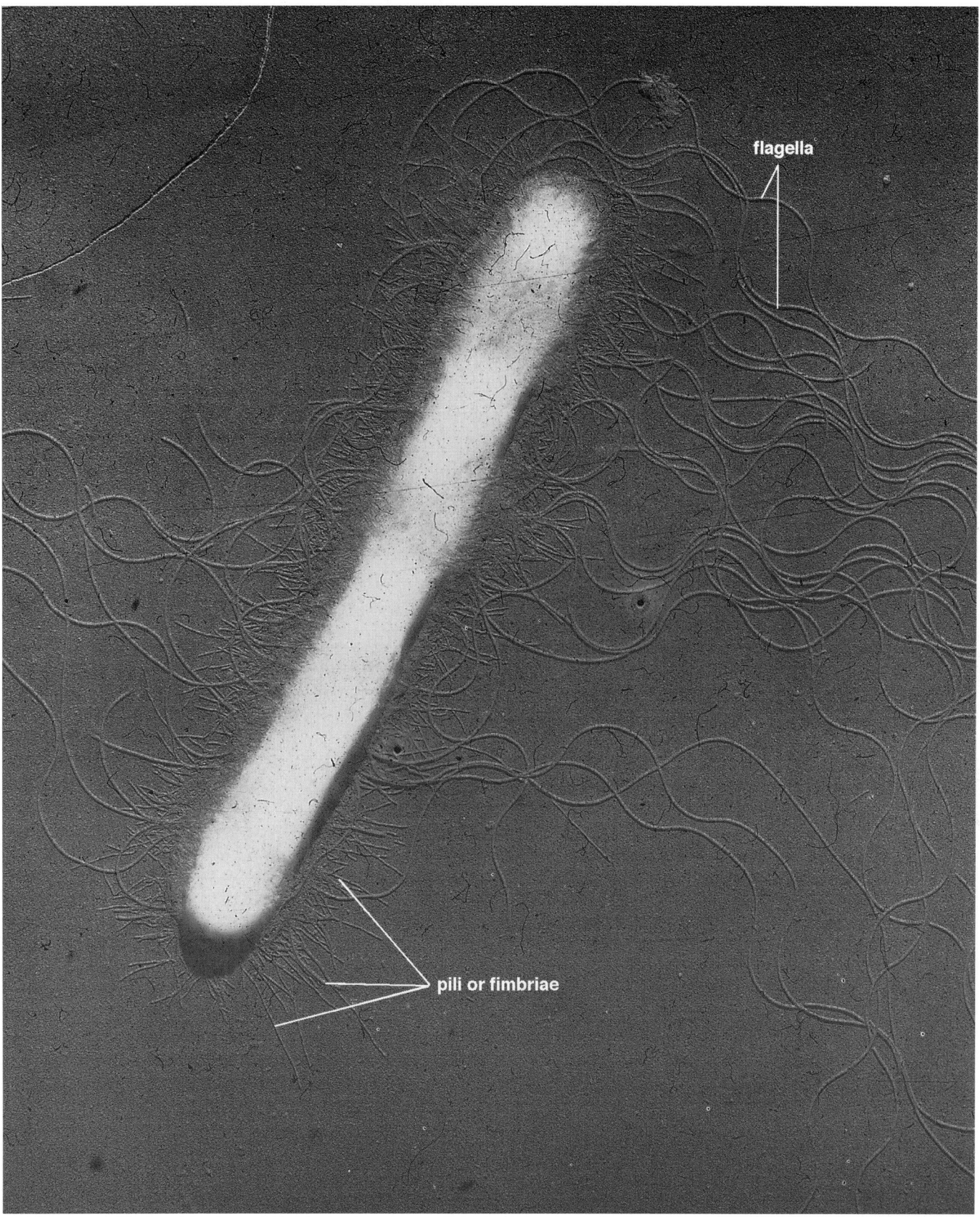

Fig 2.7 *Transmission electron micrograph of a rod-shaped bacterium to show shape, wall, pili and long wavy flagella (× 28 000). The specimen was sprayed with a heavy metal which is opaque to electrons. Sheltered areas remain uncoated, forming an electron-transparent shadow. The photograph is published as a negative to make the shadows black. The technique is known as shadowing and is useful for showing the surface structure of small objects.*

polysaccharide chains cross-linked at regular intervals by short chains of amino acids. Each cell is thus surrounded by a net-like sac which is really one huge molecule. The wall prevents the cell from bursting when it absorbs water (as a result of osmosis). Tiny pores allow the passage of water, ions and small molecules.

In 1884 a Danish biologist, Christian Gram, developed a stain which revealed that bacteria can be divided into two natural groups. We now know that this is due to differences in their wall structure. Some bacteria stain with Gram's stain and are called **Gram positive**, others do not and are called **Gram negative**. A practical exercise involving Gram staining is described in section 12.9.2.

In Gram positive bacteria, such as *Staphylococcus*, *Bacillus* and *Lactobacillus*, the murein net is filled with other components, mainly polysaccharides and proteins, to form a relatively thick wall. The walls of Gram negative bacteria, such as *Salmonella*, *E. coli* and *Azotobacter*, are thinner but more complex (fig 2.8). Their murein layer is coated on the outside with a smooth, thin, membrane-like layer of lipids and polysaccharides. This protects them from **lysozyme**, an antibacterial enzyme found in tears, saliva and other body fluids and egg white. Lysozyme digests the polysaccharide backbone of murein. The wall is thus punctured and lysis (osmotic swelling and bursting) of the cell can occur. The same outer layer also gives resistance to penicillin, which attacks Gram positive bacteria by interfering with the cross-linking in the murein of growing cells so making the walls weaker and more likely to burst when water enters by osmosis.

Cell surface membrane, mesosomes and photosynthetic membranes

Like all cells, the living material of bacterial cells is surrounded by a partially permeable membrane. The structure and functions of the cell surface membrane are similar to those in eukaryotic cells (section 5.9). It is also the site of some respiratory enzymes. In addition, in some bacteria it forms mesosomes and/or photosynthetic membranes.

Mesosomes are infoldings of the cell surface membrane (fig 2.5). They appear to be associated with DNA during cell division, organising the separation of the two daughter molecules of DNA after replication and helping in the formation of new cross-walls between the daughter cells.

Among photosynthetic bacteria, sac-like, tubular or sheet-like infoldings of the cell surface membrane contain the photosynthetic pigments, always including bacteriochlorophyll. Similar membranes are associated with nitrogen fixation.

Genetic material (bacterial 'chromosome')

Bacterial DNA is a single circular molecule of about 5 million base pairs and of length 1 mm (much longer than the cell). The total DNA (the genome), and hence the amount of information it contains, is much less than that of a eukaryotic cell: typically it contains several thousand genes, about 500 times fewer than a human cell. (See also table 2.2 and fig 2.5.)

Ribosomes

Ribosomes are the sites of protein synthesis (see table 2.2 and fig 2.5).

Capsules

Capsules are slimy or gummy secretions of certain bacteria which show up clearly after negative staining (when the background, rather than the specimen, is stained). In some cases these secretions unite bacteria into colonies. They also enable bacteria to stick to surfaces such as teeth, mud and rocks, and offer useful additional protection to the bacteria. For example capsulate strains of pneumococci grow in their human hosts causing pneumonia, whereas non-capsulate strains are easily attacked and destroyed by phagocytes, and are therefore harmless.

Spores

Some bacteria, mainly of the genera *Clostridium* and *Bacillus*, form endospores (spores produced inside cells). They are thick-walled, long-lived and extremely resistant, particularly to heat, drought and short-wave radiations. Their position in the cell is variable and is of importance in recognition and classification (see fig 2.10).

Flagella (singular flagellum)

Many bacteria are motile due to the presence of one or more flagella. The flagellum is a simple hollow cylinder of identical protein molecules. It is rigid and wave-shaped (fig 2.7). It propels the cell along by rotating at the base, providing a corkscrew-like motion rather than a beat. Examples of bacteria with flagella are *Rhizobium* (one flagellum) and *Azotobacter* (many flagella), both of which are involved in the nitrogen cycle.

Motile bacteria can move in response to certain stimuli, that is show tactic movements. For example, aerobic bacteria will swim towards oxygen (positive aerotaxis) and motile photosynthetic bacteria will swim towards light (positive phototaxis).

Flagella are most easily seen with the electron microscope using the technique of metal shadowing (fig 2.7).

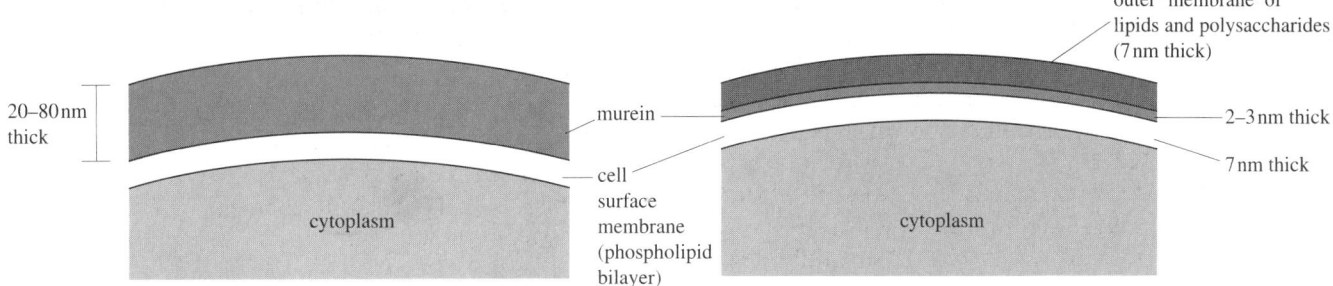

20–80 nm thick

murein

cell surface membrane (phospholipid bilayer)

cytoplasm

outer 'membrane' of lipids and polysaccharides (7 nm thick)

2–3 nm thick

7 nm thick

cytoplasm

Fig 2.8 *Cell wall structure in Gram positive (left) and Gram negative (right) bacteria. The Gram stain is easily washed out of the thin murein layer of Gram negative bacteria during the decolourising procedure of Gram staining.*

Pili (singular pilus)

Projecting from the walls of some Gram negative bacteria are numerous fine protein rods called **pili** or **fimbriae** (fig 2.7). They are shorter and thinner than flagella and are concerned with attachment to specific cells or surfaces. Various types occur, but of particular interest is the **F pilus**. This is involved in sexual reproduction (section 2.3.3).

Plasmids

In addition to the single circular DNA molecule found in all bacteria, some species also contain one or more plasmids (fig 2.9). A plasmid is a small, self-replicating circle of extra DNA. It possesses only a few genes, which generally give extra survival advantage. Some confer resistance to antibiotics. For example, some staphylococci contain a plasmid which includes a gene for the enzyme penicillinase. This breaks down penicillin, thus making the bacteria resistant to penicillin. The spread of such genes by conjugation (see reproduction) has important implications in medicine. Other plasmid genes are known which:

- confer resistance to disinfectants
- cause disease
- are responsible for the fermentation of milk to cheese by lactic acid bacteria
- confer ability to use complex chemicals as food, such as hydrocarbons, with potential applications in clearing oil spills and producing protein from petroleum.

2.3.2 Cell shape

Bacterial shape is an important aid to classification. The four main shapes found are illustrated in fig 2.10. Examples of both useful and harmful bacteria are given.

2.3.3 Reproduction

Growth of individuals and asexual reproduction

Bacteria have a large surface area to volume ratio and can therefore gain food sufficiently rapidly from their environment by diffusion and active transport mechanisms. Therefore, providing conditions are suitable, they can grow very rapidly. Important environmental factors affecting

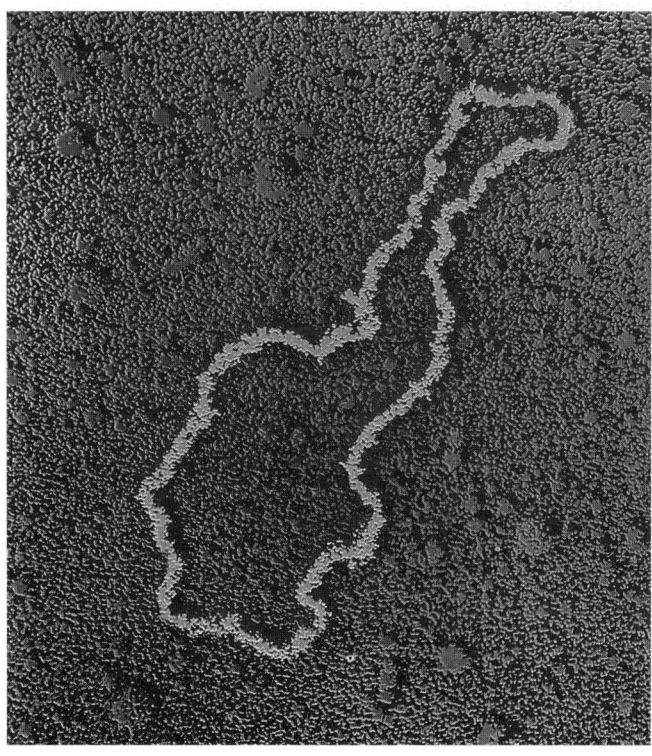

Fig 2.9 *Transmission electron micrograph of a plasmid of bacterial DNA.*

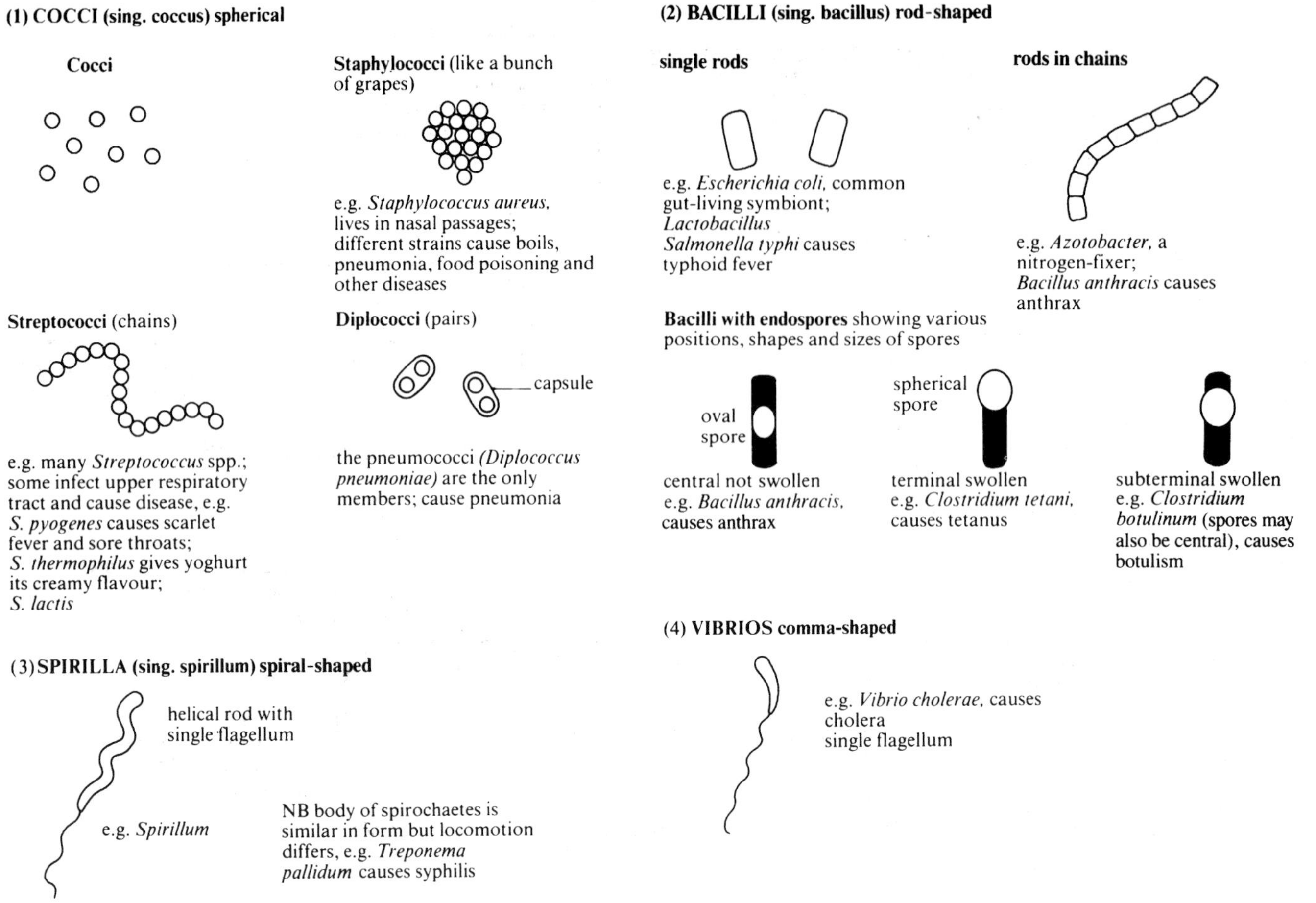

(1) COCCI (sing. coccus) spherical

Cocci

Staphylococci (like a bunch of grapes)

e.g. *Staphylococcus aureus,* lives in nasal passages; different strains cause boils, pneumonia, food poisoning and other diseases

Streptococci (chains)

e.g. many *Streptococcus* spp.; some infect upper respiratory tract and cause disease, e.g. *S. pyogenes* causes scarlet fever and sore throats; *S. thermophilus* gives yoghurt its creamy flavour; *S. lactis*

Diplococci (pairs)

capsule

the pneumococci *(Diplococcus pneumoniae)* are the only members; cause pneumonia

(3) SPIRILLA (sing. spirillum) spiral-shaped

helical rod with single flagellum

e.g. *Spirillum*

NB body of spirochaetes is similar in form but locomotion differs, e.g. *Treponema pallidum* causes syphilis

(2) BACILLI (sing. bacillus) rod-shaped

single rods

e.g. *Escherichia coli,* common gut-living symbiont; *Lactobacillus Salmonella typhi* causes typhoid fever

rods in chains

e.g. *Azotobacter,* a nitrogen-fixer; *Bacillus anthracis* causes anthrax

Bacilli with endospores showing various positions, shapes and sizes of spores

oval spore

central not swollen e.g. *Bacillus anthracis,* causes anthrax

spherical spore

terminal swollen e.g. *Clostridium tetani,* causes tetanus

subterminal swollen e.g. *Clostridium botulinum* (spores may also be central), causes botulism

(4) VIBRIOS comma-shaped

e.g. *Vibrio cholerae,* causes cholera single flagellum

Fig 2.10 *Forms of bacteria, illustrated by some common useful and harmful types.*

growth are temperature, nutrient availability, pH and ionic concentrations. Oxygen must also be present for obligate aerobes and absent for obligate anaerobes.

On reaching a certain size, dictated by the nucleus to cytoplasm ratio, bacteria reproduce asexually by binary fission, that is by division into two identical daughter cells (fig 2.11). Cell division is preceded by replication of the DNA and while this is being copied it may be held in position by a mesosome (figs 2.5 and 2.6c). The mesosome may also be attached to the new cross-walls that are laid down between the daughter cells, and plays some role in the synthesis of cell wall material. In the fastest growing bacteria such divisions may occur as often as every 20 minutes.

Sexual reproduction

In 1946 it was discovered that bacteria can take part in a primitive form of sexual reproduction. Gametes are not involved, but the essential feature of sexual reproduction, namely the exchange of genetic material, does take place and is called **genetic recombination**. The process was discovered using *E. coli* as follows. Normally *E. coli* can make all of its own amino acids, given a supply of glucose and mineral salts. Random mutations were induced by exposure to radiation and two particular mutants selected.

One could not make biotin (a vitamin) or the amino acid methionine. Another could not make the amino acids threonine and leucine. About 10^8 cells of each mutant were mixed and cultured on media lacking all four growth factors. Theoretically, none of the cells should have grown, but a few hundred colonies developed, each from one original bacterium, and these were shown to possess genes for making all four growth factors. Exchange of genetic information had therefore occurred, but no chemical responsible could be isolated. Eventually it was shown with the electron microscope that direct cell-to-cell contact, that is **conjugation**, can occur in *E. coli* (fig 2.12).

Conjugation therefore involves transfer of DNA between cells in direct contact. One cell acts as the donor ('male') and the other as the recipient ('female'). The ability to serve as a donor is determined by genes in a special type of plasmid called the sex factor, or **F factor** (F for fertility). This codes for the protein of a special type of pilus, the **F pilus** or sex pilus. This enables cells to come into contact. The pilus is hollow and it is believed that the DNA passes through the pilus from the donor (F^+) to the recipient (F^-). The process is described in fig 2.13.

Note that the donor retains the F factor and the recipient also becomes F^+. The process is slow, so the F^- cell can

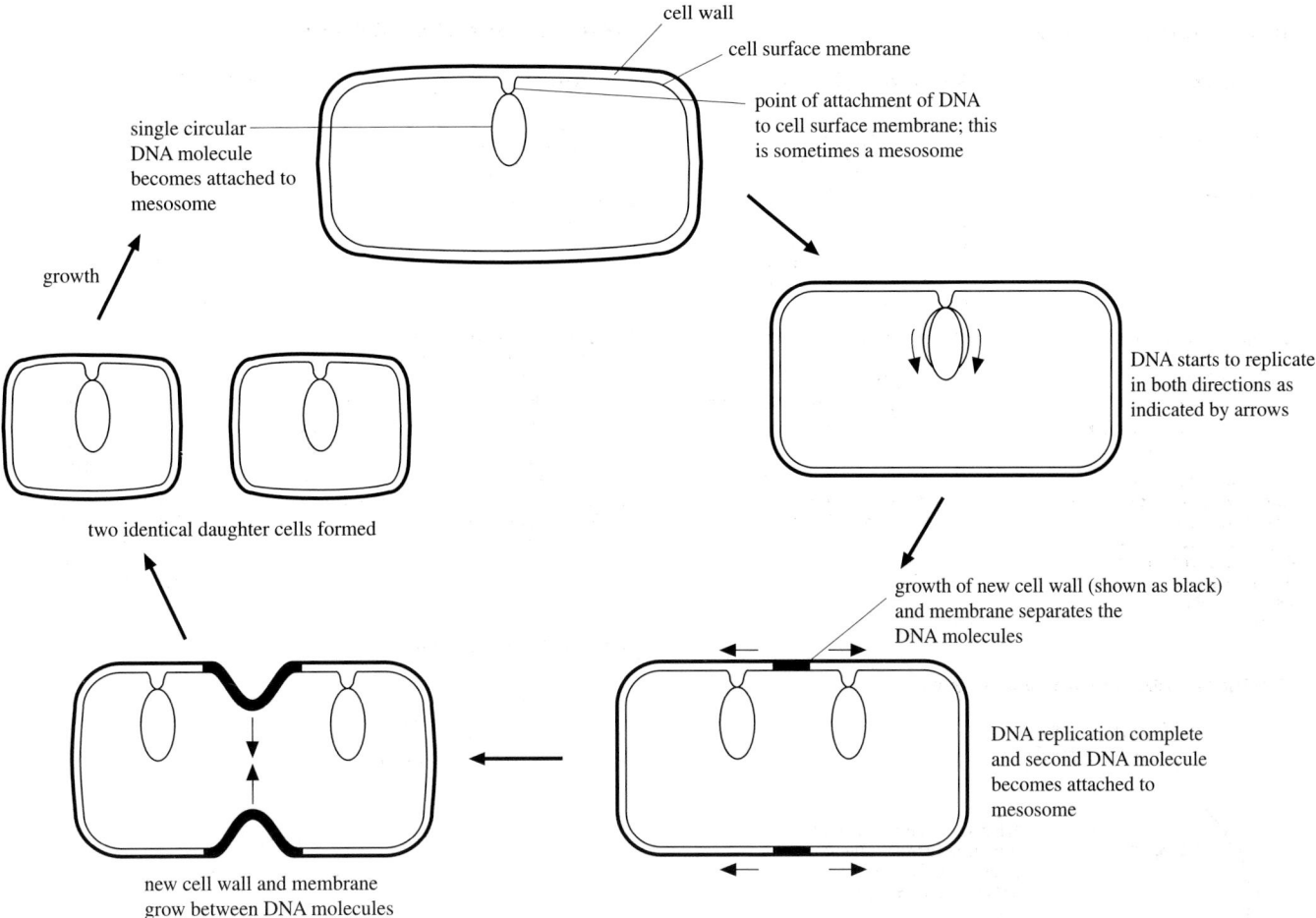

cell wall

cell surface membrane

point of attachment of DNA
to cell surface membrane; this
is sometimes a mesosome

single circular
DNA molecule
becomes attached to
mesosome

growth

two identical daughter cells formed

DNA starts to replicate
in both directions as
indicated by arrows

growth of new cell wall (shown as black)
and membrane separates the
DNA molecules

DNA replication complete
and second DNA molecule
becomes attached to
mesosome

new cell wall and membrane
grow between DNA molecules

Fig 2.11 *Binary fission in a bacterium, e.g.* E. coli.

replicate by binary fission one or several times before the process is complete, thus maintaining F⁻ cells in the population.

The F factor is particularly important because in a few cases, about 1 in 100 000, it becomes integrated with the rest of the DNA in the host cell. In such cases, the process of conjugation involves transfer of not only the F factor, but also the rest of the DNA. This takes about 90 min and separation may occur before exchange is complete. Such strains consistently donate all or large portions of their DNA and are called **Hfr strain**s (H = high, f = frequency, r = recombination), because the donor DNA can recombine with the recipient DNA.

2.3.4 Nutrition

Nutrition is the process of acquiring energy and materials. Living organisms can be grouped on the basis of their source of energy or source of carbon, the latter being the most fundamental material required for growth. Only two forms of energy can be used by living organisms to synthesise their organic requirements, namely light and chemical energy. Those that use light are known as **phototrophs** and those that use chemical energy are called **chemotrophs**. Phototrophs carry out photosynthesis.

As already noted, organisms can also be described as autotrophic or heterotrophic, depending on whether their source of carbon is inorganic (carbon dioxide) or organic respectively. Thus four nutritional categories can occur, as shown in table 2.3. There are examples of bacteria in all four categories. The largest group is the chemo-heterotrophic bacteria.

Chemoheterotrophic bacteria

These bacteria obtain energy from chemicals in their food. They use an enormous range of chemicals. There are three main groups, namely saprotrophs, mutualists and parasites.

A **saprotroph** is an organism that obtains its food from dead and decaying matter. The saprotroph secretes enzymes onto the organic matter to digest it. Thus digestion is outside of the organism. Soluble products of digestion are absorbed and assimilated within the body of the saprotroph.

Saprotrophic bacteria and fungi constitute the **decomposers** and are essential in bringing about decay and recycling of nutrients. They produce humus from animal and plant remains, but also cause decay of materials useful to humans, especially food. Their importance in the biosphere is stressed in chapter 10.

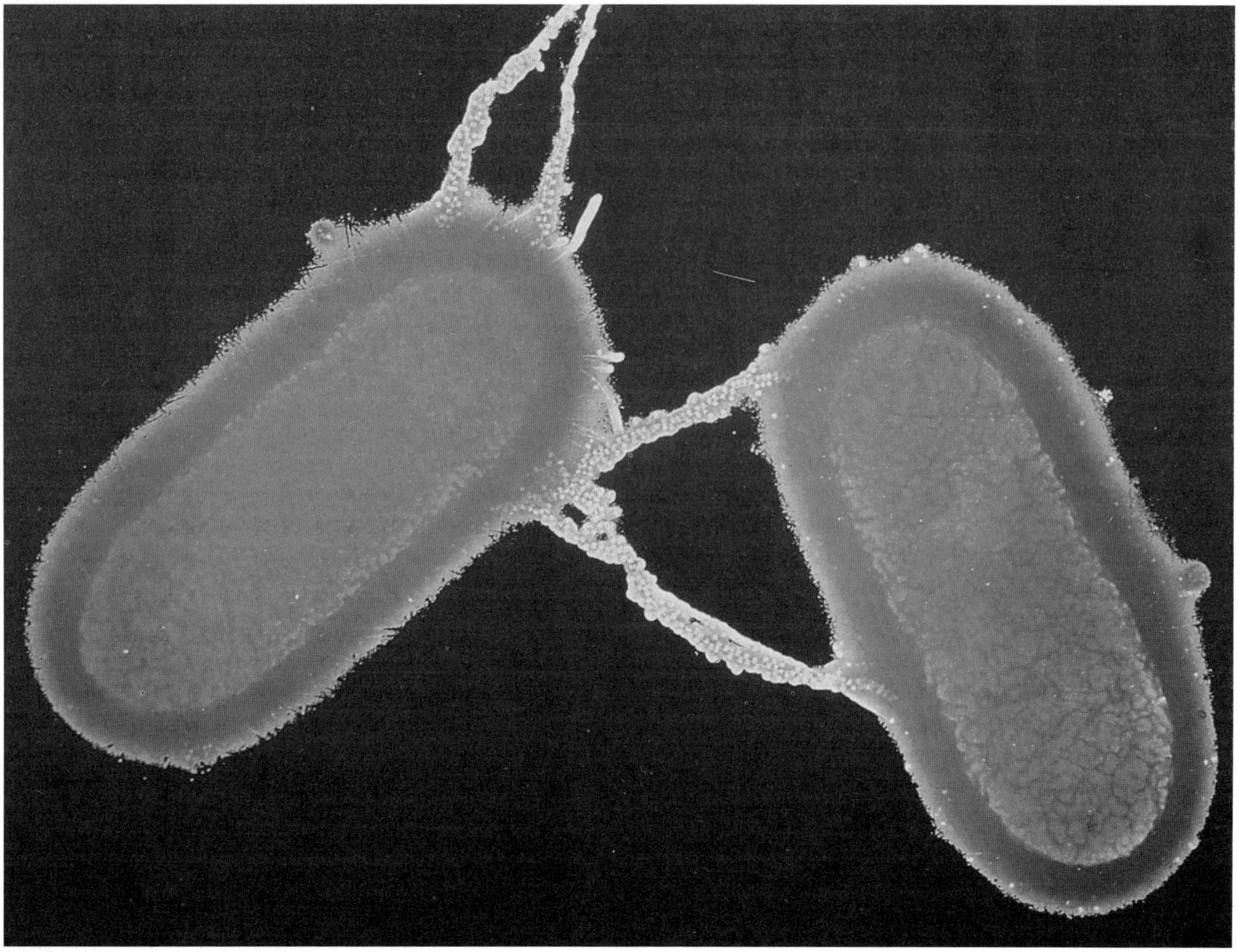

Fig 2.12 *Conjugating bacteria, one 'male' (left) with two 'females' (× 19 475). The second 'female' cell is beyond the top of the photograph.*

Mutualism (or symbiosis) is the name given to any form of close relationship between two living organisms in which both partners benefit. Examples of bacterial mutualists are *Rhizobium*, a nitrogen-fixer living in the root nodules of legumes such as pea and clover, and *Escherichia coli*, which inhabits the gut of humans and probably contributes vitamins of the B and K groups.

A **parasite** is an organism that lives in or on another organism, the **host**, from which it obtains its food and, usually, shelter. The host is usually of a different species and suffers harm from the parasite. Parasites which cause disease are called **pathogens**. Some examples are given in fig 2.10 and in chapter 15. Some parasites can only survive and grow in living cells and are called **obligate parasites**. Others can infect a host, bring about its death and then live saprotrophically on the remains; these are called **facultative parasites**. It is a characteristic of parasites that they are very exacting in their nutritional requirements, needing 'accessory growth factors' that they cannot manufacture for themselves but can only find in other living cells.

Photoautotrophic bacteria

Cyanobacteria, or blue-green bacteria, are examples of photoautotrophic bacteria. Algae and plants are also photoautotrophic. They all carry out photosynthesis and use carbon dioxide as a source of carbon (table 2.3). The process of photosynthesis first evolved in bacteria, possibly in blue-green bacteria. As we shall see later, the

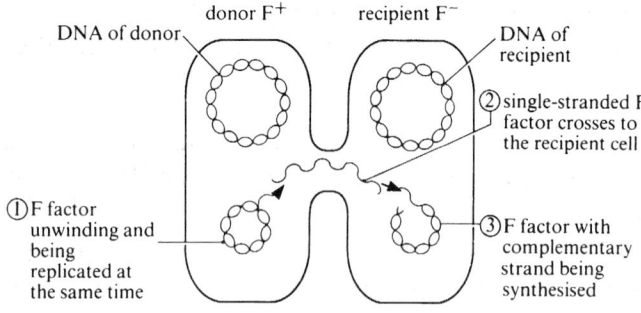

Fig 2.13 *Conjugation between two bacterial cells. 1, 2 and 3 represent successive stages in transfer of the F factor.*

Table 2.3 The four nutritional categories of living organisms, according to sources of energy and carbon. Examples are given of bacteria in each category. Plants are photoautotrophic. Fungi and animals are chemoheterotrophic.

		CARBON SOURCE	
		autotrophic source of carbon is inorganic (carbon dioxide)	**heterotrophic** source of carbon is organic
ENERGY SOURCE	**phototrophic** (photosynthetic) light energy used	**photoautotrophic** e.g. blue-green bacteria	**photoheterotrophic** e.g. purple non-sulphur bacteria
	chemotrophic (chemosynthetic) chemical energy used	**chemoautotrophic** e.g. *Nitrosomonas* and *Nitrobacter*, nitrifying bacteria involved in the nitrogen cycle	**chemoheterotrophic** most bacteria – all the saprotrophs, parasites and mutualists (symbionts)

chloroplasts of algae and plants are thought to be descendants of what were once free-living photosynthetic bacteria that invaded heterotrophic cells (section 2.6.1).

Blue-green bacteria are common in surface layers of both fresh water and sea water and are also found as gelatinous mat-like growths on shaded soil, rocks, mud, wood and some living organisms. Most blue-green bacteria are single cells but some are linked to form filaments sheathed in mucus, e.g. *Anabaena* and *Spirulina*. They differ from most bacteria, and resemble algae and plants, in producing oxygen from water during photosynthesis. Fig 2.14 shows the structure of *Anabaena*, a typical blue-green bacterium. Photosynthetic membranes characteristically run throughout the cytoplasm and it is here that the photosynthetic pigments are located. The pigments include chlorophyll *a*, again resembling algae and plants, as well as a characteristic blue-green pigment called phycocyanin. The cells of blue-green bacteria tend to be larger than those of other bacteria. The fact that blue-green bacteria produce oxygen in photosynthesis, have photosynthetic membranes running through the cell and contain chlorophyll *a*, indicate that they may be evolutionary links between the rest of the bacteria and eukaryotes.

Some blue-green bacteria, such as *Anabaena*, have the ability to **fix** nitrogen, that is to convert nitrogen gas from the air to ammonia which can then be used in synthesis of amino acids, proteins and other nitrogen-containing organic compounds. This is done in special cells called **heterocysts** which develop when there is a nitrogen shortage. These cells export the nitrogen compounds to neighbouring cells in exchange for other nutrients such as carbohydrate.

Chemoautotrophic bacteria

These are more commonly known as **chemosynthetic** bacteria. They use carbon dioxide as a source of carbon but obtain their energy from chemical reactions. The energy is obtained by oxidising inorganic materials such as ammonia and nitrite. Some are important members of the nitrogen cycle, carrying out a process called **nitrification.** This takes place in two stages. Firstly ammonia is oxidised to nitrite with a release of energy. This is carried out, for example, by *Nitrosomonas*. Secondly nitrite is oxidised to nitrate with the release of more energy. This is done, for example, by *Nitrobacter.*

(1) $$NH_4^+ \xrightarrow{\text{oxygen}} NO_2^- + \text{energy}$$

(2) $$NO_2^- \xrightarrow{\text{oxygen}} NO_3^- + \text{energy}$$

The importance of nitrification is discussed with the nitrogen cycle in section 10.4.1.

2.3.5 Population growth in bacteria

> **2.1** Consider the situation where a single bacterium is placed in a nutrient medium under optimal growth conditions. Assuming it, and its descendants, divide every 20 min, copy table 2.4 and complete it.
>
> Using the data from your table, draw graphs of number of bacteria (graph A) and $\log_{10}$ number of bacteria (graph B) on the vertical axes against time (horizontal axis). What do you notice about the shapes of the graphs?

The kind of growth shown in table 2.4 is known as **logarithmic**, **exponential** or **geometric**. The numbers form an **exponential series**. This can be explained by reference to line C in table 2.4 where the number of bacteria is expressed as a power of 2. The power can be called the logarithm or exponent of 2. The logarithms or exponents form a linearly increasing series 0, 1, 2, 3, etc., corresponding with the number of generations.

Returning to table 2.4, the numbers in line A could be converted to logarithms to the base 2 as follows:

A *Number of bacteria*	1	2	4	8	16	32	64	128	256	512	1024
D *Log₂ number of bacteria*		0	1	2	3	4	5	6	7	8	9	10

Compare line C with line D. However, it is conventional to use logarithms to the base 10, as in line B. Thus 1 is 10^0, 2 is $10^{0.3}$, 4 is $10^{0.6}$, etc.

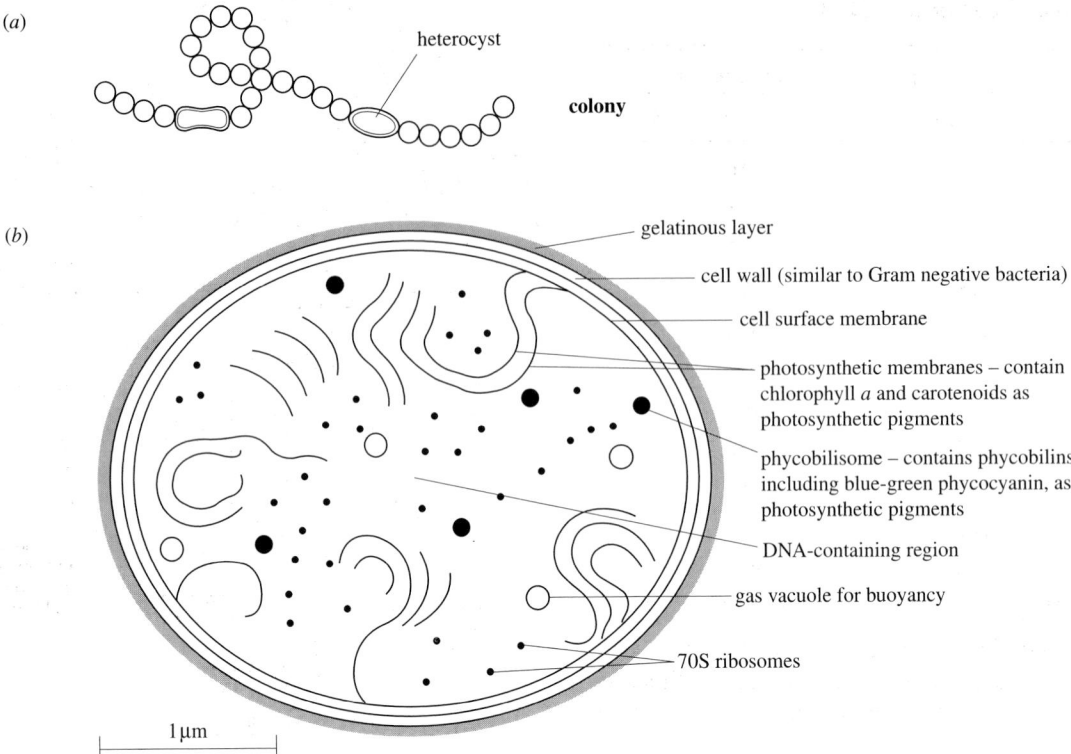

(a)

heterocyst

colony

(b)

gelatinous layer

cell wall (similar to Gram negative bacteria)

cell surface membrane

photosynthetic membranes – contain chlorophyll *a* and carotenoids as photosynthetic pigments

phycobilisome – contains phycobilins, including blue-green phycocyanin, as photosynthetic pigments

DNA-containing region

gas vacuole for buoyancy

70S ribosomes

1 μm

Fig 2.14 *Structure of a blue-green bacterium,* Anabaena. *Cells may occur singly* (b), *or in colonies* (a).

Table 2.4 Growth of a model population of bacteria.

Time (in units of 20 min)	0	1	2	3	4	5	6	7	8	9	10
A Number of bacteria											
B Log_{10} number of bacteria (to one decimal place)											
C Number of bacteria expressed as power of 2											

The curve in graph A is known as a **logarithmic** or **exponential curve**. Such growth curves can be converted to straight lines by plotting the logarithms of growth against time. Under ideal conditions, then, bacterial growth is theoretically exponential. This mathematical model of bacterial growth can be compared with the growth of a real population. Fig 2.15 shows such growth. The growth curve shows four distinct phases.

- During the **lag phase** the bacteria are adapting to their new environment and growth has not yet achieved its maximum rate. The bacteria may, for example, be synthesising new enzymes to digest the particular spectrum of nutrients available in the new medium.
- The **log phase** is the phase when growth is proceeding at its maximum rate, closely approaching a logarithmic increase in numbers when the growth curve would be a straight line.

- Eventually growth of the colony begins to slow down and it starts to enter the **stationary phase** where growth rate is zero, and there is much greater competition for resources. Rate of production of new cells is slower and may cease altogether. Any increase in the number of cells is offset by the death of other cells, so that the number of living cells remains constant. This phase is a result of several factors, including exhaustion of essential nutrients, accumulation of toxic waste products of metabolism and possibly, if the bacteria are aerobic, depletion of oxygen.

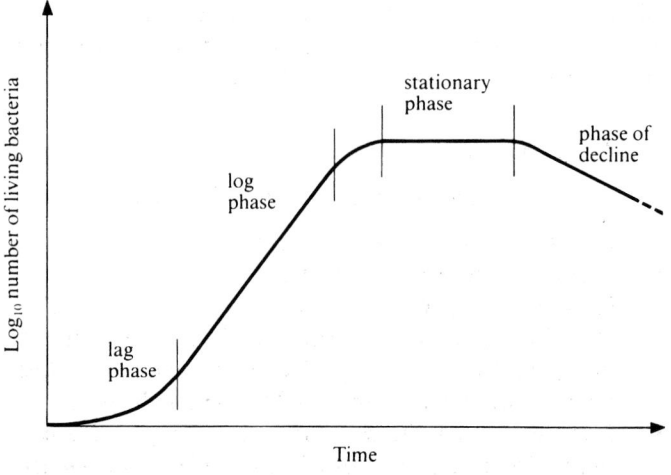

Fig 2.15 *Typical growth curve of a bacterial population.*

Table 2.5 Culture of bacteria at 30 °C.

Time/h	Number of cells in millions	
	living	living and dead
0	9	10
1	10	11
2	11	12
5	18	20
10	400	450
12	550	620
15	550	700
20	550	850
30	550	950
35	225	950
45	30	950

- During the final phase, the **phase of decline**, the death rate increases and cells stop multiplying. Methods of counting bacteria are described in the practical work in chapter 12.

2.4 Viruses

2.4.1 Discovery

In 1852, the Russian botanist D. I. Ivanovsky prepared an infectious extract from tobacco plants that were suffering from mosaic disease. When the extract was passed through a filter able to prevent the passage of bacteria, the filtered fluid was still infectious. In 1898 the Dutchman Beijerink coined the name 'virus' (Latin for poison) to describe the infectious nature of certain filtered plant fluids. Although progress was made in isolating highly purified samples of viruses and in identifying them chemically as nucleoproteins (nucleic acids combined with proteins), the particles still proved elusive and mysterious because they were too small to be seen with the light microscope. As a result, they were among the first biological structures to be studied when the electron microscope was developed in the 1930s.

2.4.2 Characteristics

Viruses have the following characteristics.

- They are the smallest living organisms.
- They do not have a cellular structure.
- They can only reproduce by invading living cells. Therefore they are all parasitic. They are **obligate endoparasites**, meaning that they can only live parasitically inside other cells. Most cause disease.
- They have a simple structure, consisting of a small piece of nucleic acid, either DNA or RNA, surrounded by a protein or lipoprotein coat.

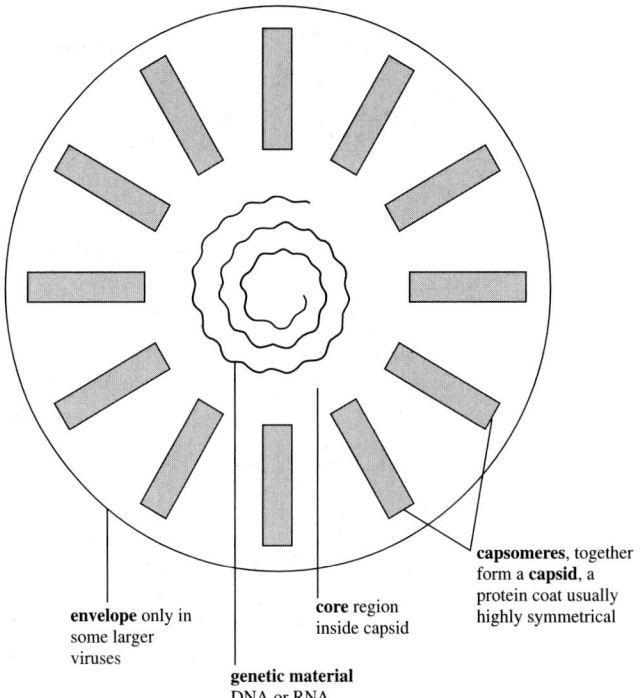

capsomeres, together form a **capsid**, a protein coat usually highly symmetrical

core region inside capsid

envelope only in some larger viruses

genetic material DNA or RNA

Fig 2.16 *A generalised virus.*

- They are on the boundary between what we regard as living and non-living.
- Each type of virus will recognise and infect only certain types of cell. In other words, viruses are highly specific to their hosts.

These characteristics will now be examined in more detail.

Size

Viruses are the smallest living organisms, ranging in size from about 20–300 nm; on average they are about 50 times smaller than bacteria. They cannot be seen with the light microscope and they pass through filters which retain bacteria.

Origin

The question is often posed, 'Are viruses living?'. If, to be defined as living, a structure must possess genetic material (DNA or RNA), and be capable of reproducing itself, then the answer must be that viruses are living. If to be living demands a cellular structure then the answer is that they are not. It should also be noted that viruses are not capable of reproducing outside the host cell.

We can understand viruses much better if we understand their evolutionary origins. It is suspected, though not proven, that viruses are pieces of genetic material that have 'escaped' from prokaryote and eukaryote cells and have the potential to replicate themselves when they get back into a cell environment. A virus survives in a purely inert state outside cells, but has the set of instructions (genetic code) necessary to re-enter a particular type of cell and instruct it to make many identical copies of itself. It is therefore reasonable to suppose that viruses must have evolved after cells evolved.

Structure

Viruses have a very simple structure consisting of the following:

- **core** – the genetic material, either DNA or RNA. The DNA or RNA may be single-stranded or double-stranded.
- **capsid** – a protective coat of protein surrounding the core.
- **nucleocapsid** – the combined structure formed by the core and capsid.
- **envelope** – a few viruses, such as the HIV and influenza viruses, have an additional lipoprotein layer around the capsid derived from the cell surface membrane of the host cell.
- **capsomeres** – capsids are often built up of identical repeating subunits called capsomeres.

The overall form of the capsid is highly symmetrical and the virus can be crystallised, enabling information about its structure to be obtained by X-ray crystallography as well as electron microscopy. Once the subunits of a virus have been made by the host, they can self-assemble into a virus. Fig 2.16 shows a simplified, generalised structure of a virus.

Certain types of symmetry are common among capsids, notably polyhedral and helical symmetry. A polyhedron is a many-sided figure. The most common polyhedral form in viruses is the icosahedron, which has 20 triangular faces with 12 corners and 30 edges. Fig 2.17*a* shows a regular icosahedron, and fig 2.17*b* the herpes virus, which has 162 capsomeres arranged into an icosahedron.

Helical symmetry is well illustrated by the tobacco mosaic virus (TMV), an RNA virus (fig 2.18*a* and *b*). Here the capsid is made up of 2130 identical protein capsomeres. TMV was the first virus to be isolated in a pure state. It causes a mottled yellowing of tobacco leaves called leaf mosaic (fig 2.18*c*). The virus can spread extremely rapidly, either mechanically if infected plants, or plant parts, come into contact with healthy plants, or even as airborne particles such as the smoke of cigarettes made from contaminated leaves.

Viruses that attack bacteria form a group called **bacteriophages**, or simply phages. Some of these have a distinct icosahedral head, with a tail showing helical symmetry (fig 2.19). Fig 2.20 shows simplified diagrams of some viruses and their relative sizes, and summarises their structures.

2.4.3 Life cycle of a bacteriophage

The life cycle of typical bacteriophage is shown in fig 2.21. *E. coli* is a typical host and can be attacked by at least seven strains of phage, known as T1 to T7. A T-even phage (for instance T2) is illustrated in figs 2.19*a* and *b* and 2.22.

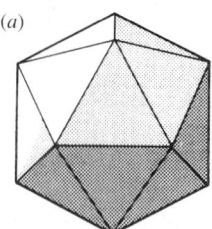

(a)

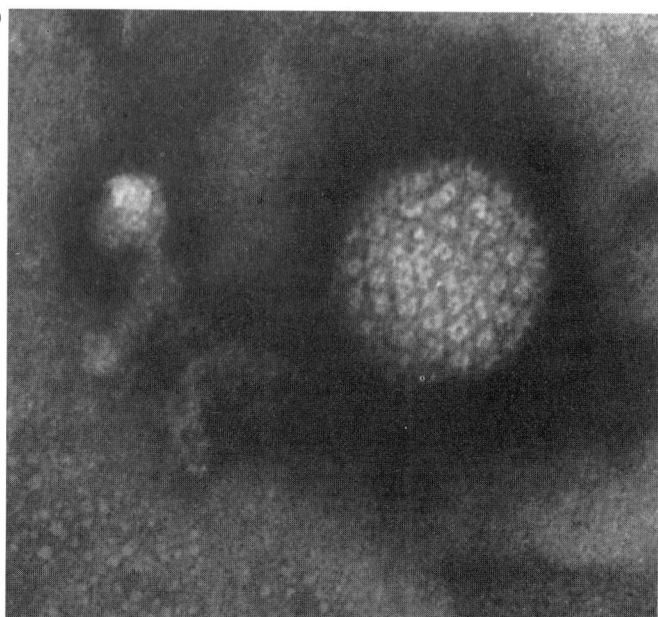

(b)

Fig 2.17 *(a) Solid model of an icosahedron. (b) Electron micrograph of a negatively stained herpes simplex virus. Negative staining stains the background, not the specimen. Note how the detailed structure of the virus is revealed. Individual capsomeres are just visible where the stain has penetrated between them.*

The life cycle is the same in principle for all phages. Some complete the life cycle without a break. Such life cycles are called **lytic** cycles. However, some phages, such as lamda phage, insert their DNA into the host DNA and remain dormant for many generations. Each time the host cell divides the phage DNA is copied with the host cell DNA. This dormant stage of the phage is called the **prophage**. Eventually it is activated again and completes its life cycle, causing death of the host cell in the usual way. Such phages are described as **lysogenic**.

2.4.4 Viruses as agents of disease

Viruses can also infect eukaryotic cells and, as in prokaryotic cells, each has its own specific host. For example, TMV will attack only tobacco plants. Between them, viruses cause a wide range of diseases among plants, animals and fungi. Diseases of humans caused by viruses include measles, German measles (rubella), chickenpox, influenza, herpes and AIDS.

Viruses cause many different diseases in almost every other kind of organism.

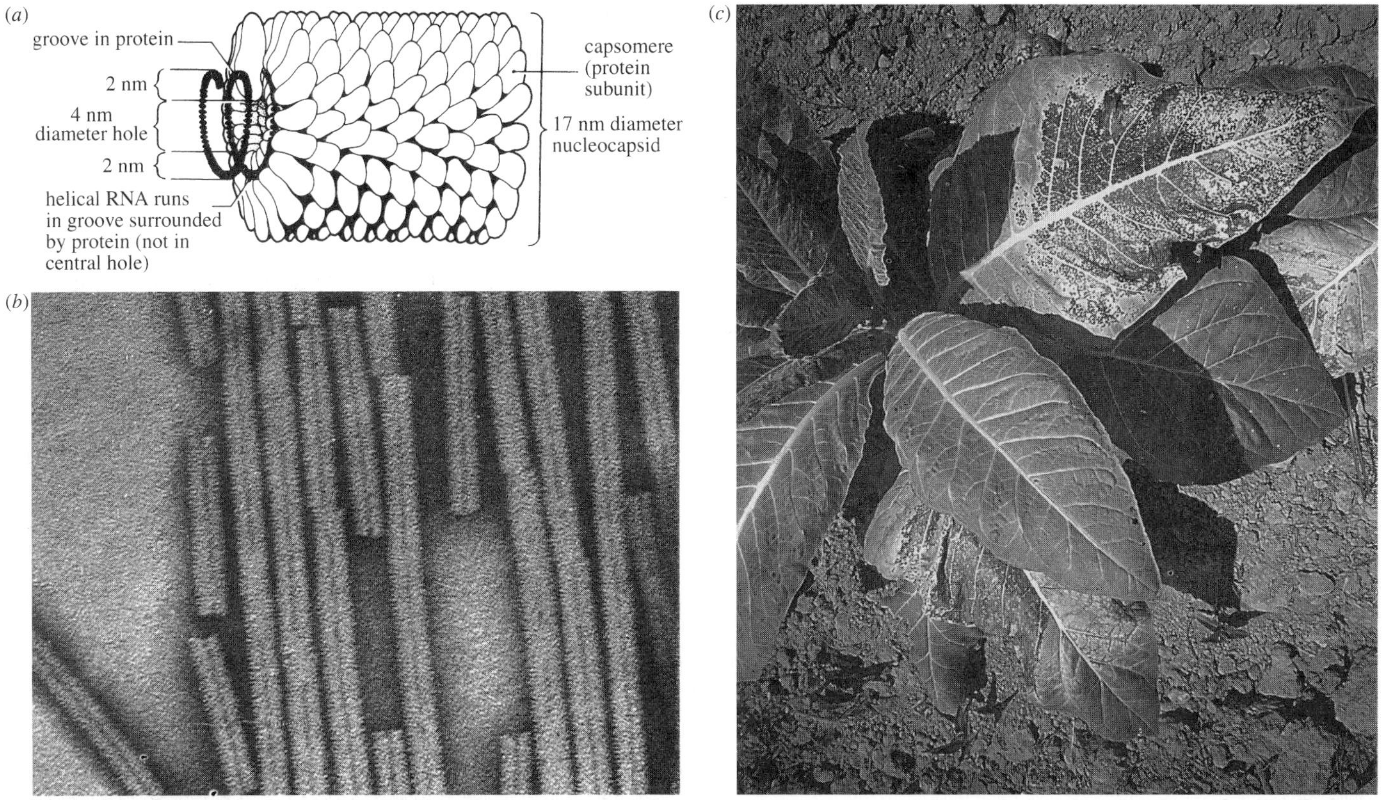

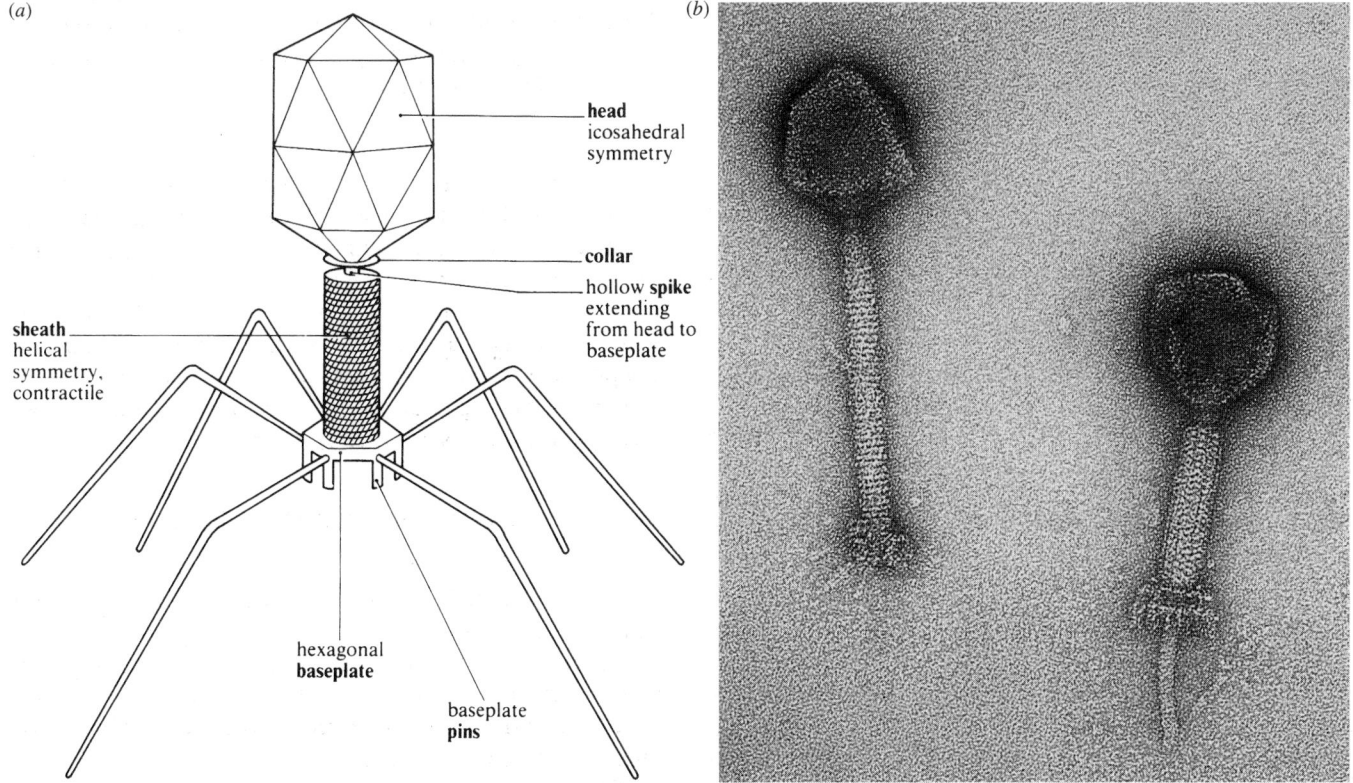

Fig 2.18 (a) *Structure of tobacco mosaic virus (TMV) showing helical symmetry of the capsid. Only part of the rod-shaped virus is shown. The drawing is based on X-ray diffraction, biochemical and electron microscope data.*
(b) *Electron micrograph of a negatively stained tobacco mosaic virus (× 800 000). The capsid (coat) is made of 2130 identical protein capsomeres. (c) Tobacco plant infected with TMV. Note the characteristic mosaic pattern on the leaves where tissue is dying.*

(a)

groove in protein

2 nm

4 nm diameter hole

2 nm

helical RNA runs in groove surrounded by protein (not in central hole)

capsomere (protein subunit)

17 nm diameter nucleocapsid

(b)

(c)

(a)

head icosahedral symmetry

collar

hollow **spike** extending from head to baseplate

sheath helical symmetry, contractile

hexagonal **baseplate**

baseplate **pins**

(b)

Fig 2.19 (a) *Structure of a T2 bacteriophage.* (b) *Electron micrograph of negatively stained bacteriophages.*

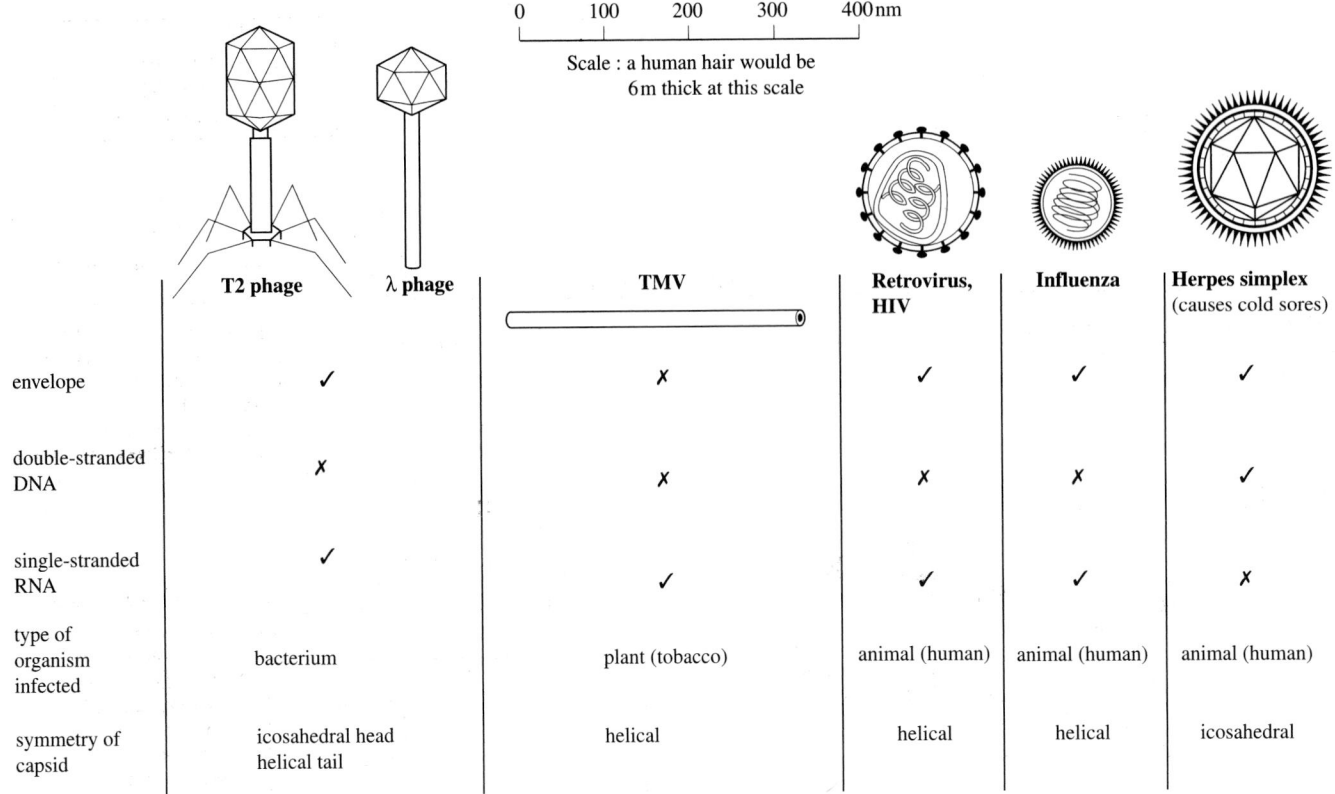

	T2 phage	λ phage	TMV	Retrovirus, HIV	Influenza	Herpes simplex (causes cold sores)
envelope	✓		✗	✓	✓	✓
double-stranded DNA	✗		✗	✗	✗	✓
single-stranded RNA	✓		✓	✓	✓	✗
type of organism infected	bacterium		plant (tobacco)	animal (human)	animal (human)	animal (human)
symmetry of capsid	icosahedral head helical tail		helical	helical	helical	icosahedral

Fig 2.20 *Some simplified diagrams of viruses showing different sizes and symmetry. The T2 phage is shown with its tail fibres released prior to infection; the λ (lambda) phage does not have tail fibres.*

2.4.5 Structure and life cycle of a retrovirus, HIV

AIDS (acquired immunodeficiency syndrome) is of particular interest because it is a relatively new disease, the first cases being reported in the United States in 1981. The virus which causes it is **HIV**, or **human immunodeficiency virus**. This is also of interest because it belongs to a group of RNA viruses known as **retroviruses**. This name comes from the fact that these viruses can convert their RNA back into a DNA copy using an enzyme known as reverse transcriptase. Normally a section of DNA (a gene) is copied to make RNA, a process called **transcription**. Making DNA from RNA is therefore reverse transcription, and the enzyme controlling it is called **reverse transcriptase**. The enzyme has proved extremely useful in genetic engineering (chapter 25).

Fig 2.21 shows the structure of the HIV virus and fig 2.23 summarises its life cycle (see also fig 2.24). It infects and destroys certain white blood cells called T helper lymphocytes, thus crippling the immune system. The disease is discussed in chapter 15.

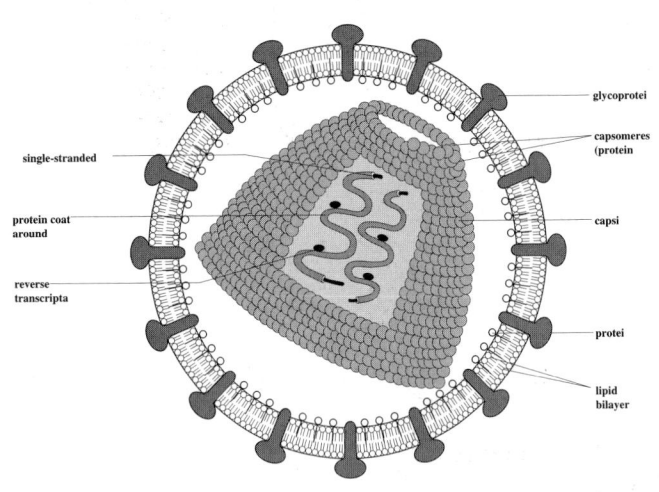

glycoprotei

capsomeres (protein

single-stranded

capsi

protein coat around

reverse transcripta

protei

lipid bilayer

Fig 2.21 *Structure of the HIV virus, an example of a retrovirus. The cone-shaped capsid is made of a helical spiral of capsomeres. It is cut open to reveal the two copies of the RNA genetic code. Reverse transcriptase is an enzyme which converts single-stranded RNA into double-stranded DNA copies. The capsid is enclosed in a protein shell which is anchored in a lipid bilayer, or envelope, obtained from the cell surface membrane of the previous host cell. This envelope contains viral glycoproteins which bind specifically to helper T-cell receptors, enabling the virus to enter its host.*

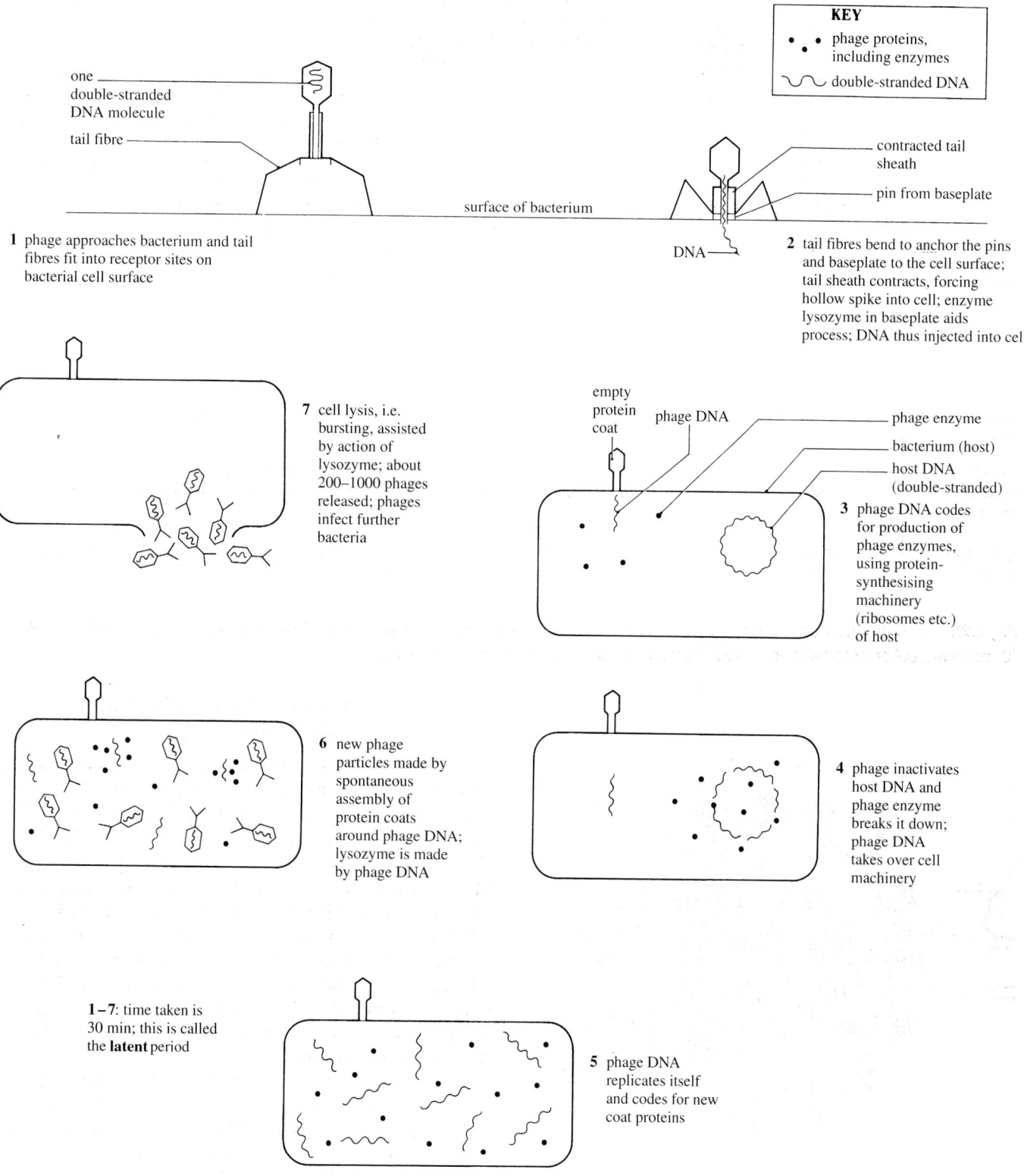

Fig 2.22 *Life cycle of a bacteriophage.*

KEY

• • • phage proteins, including enzymes

〜 double-stranded DNA

one double-stranded DNA molecule

tail fibre

surface of bacterium

contracted tail sheath

pin from baseplate

DNA

1 phage approaches bacterium and tail fibres fit into receptor sites on bacterial cell surface

2 tail fibres bend to anchor the pins and baseplate to the cell surface; tail sheath contracts, forcing hollow spike into cell; enzyme lysozyme in baseplate aids process; DNA thus injected into cell

7 cell lysis, i.e. bursting, assisted by action of lysozyme; about 200–1000 phages released; phages infect further bacteria

empty protein coat

phage DNA

phage enzyme

bacterium (host)

host DNA (double-stranded)

3 phage DNA codes for production of phage enzymes, using protein-synthesising machinery (ribosomes etc.) of host

6 new phage particles made by spontaneous assembly of protein coats around phage DNA; lysozyme is made by phage DNA

4 phage inactivates host DNA and phage enzyme breaks it down; phage DNA takes over cell machinery

1–7: time taken is 30 min; this is called the **latent** period

5 phage DNA replicates itself and codes for new coat proteins

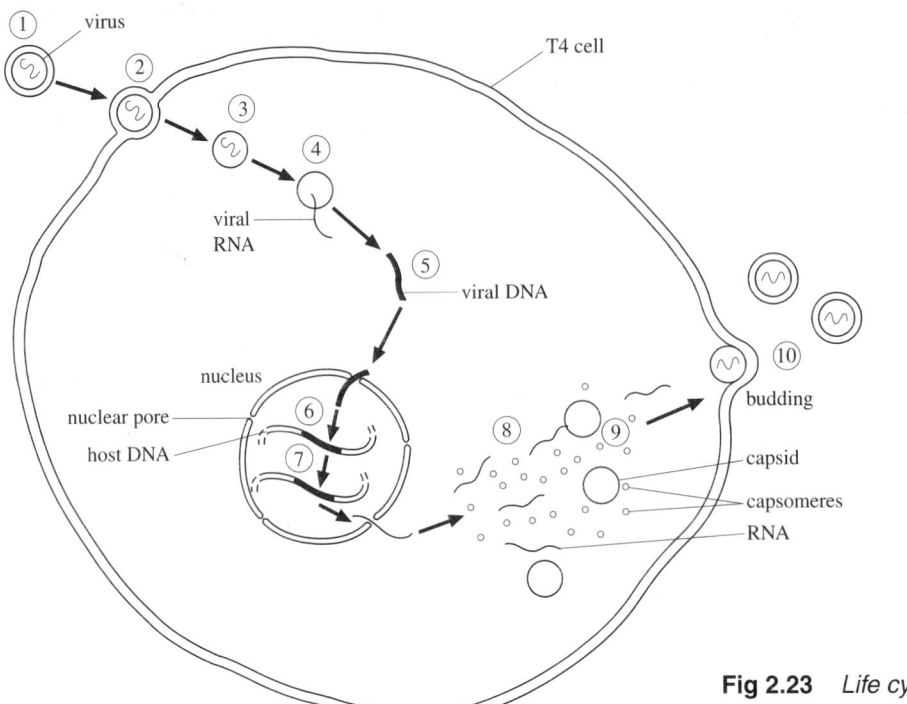

Fig 2.23 *Life cycle of the HIV virus.*

① Virus approaches a T4 lymphocyte cell.

② Virus glycoprotein attaches to a specific receptor protein in the cell surface membrane.

③ Virus enters the cell by endocytosis.

④ The viral RNA is released into the cytoplasm of the host cell, together with the enzyme reverse transcriptase.

⑤ A double-stranded DNA copy of the single-stranded virus RNA is made using reverse transcriptase.

⑥ The DNA copy enters the nucleus and inserts itself into the host DNA. Whenever the cell divides, it also makes a copy of the viral DNA, increasing the number of infected cells.

⑦ After a period of inactivity known as the **latency period**, which lasts on average 5 years, the virus becomes active again. The stimulus for converting a latent virus into an active virus is poorly understood.

⑧ New RNA is produced (transcription) and viral proteins are made using the host's protein synthesising machinery.

⑨ New viral particles assemble.

⑩ Virus particles bud off from the cell surface membrane of the host by exocytosis.

⑪ The cell eventually dies as a result of the infection.

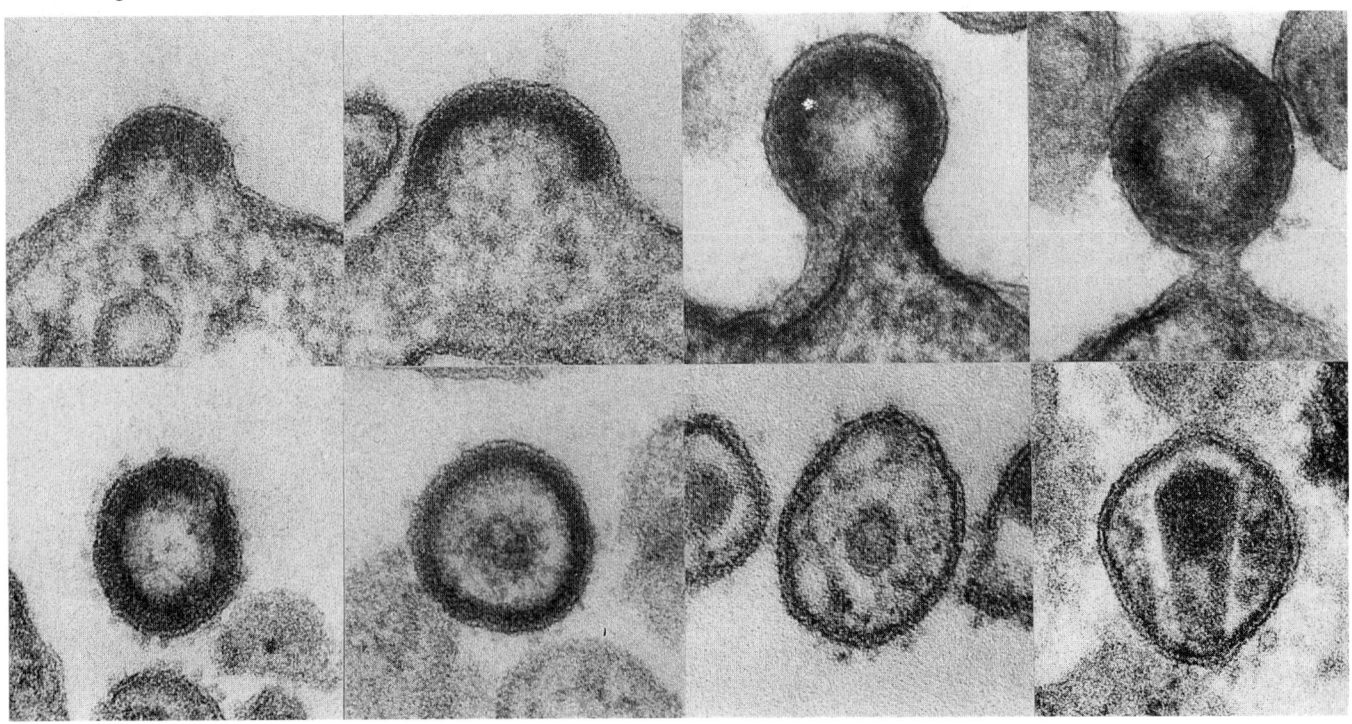

Fig 2.24 *HIV emerging from infected cell.*

2.5 Kingdom Fungi

The fungi are a large and successful group of organisms of about 80 000 named species. They range in size from the unicellular yeasts to the large toadstools, puffballs and stinkhorns, and occupy a very wide range of habitats, both aquatic and terrestrial. They are also of major importance for the essential role that they play in the biosphere, and for the way in which they have been exploited by humans for economic and medical purposes.

Fungi include the numerous moulds which grow on damp organic matter (such as bread, leather, decaying vegetation and dead fish), the unicellular yeasts which are abundant on the sugary surfaces of ripe fruits and many parasites of plants. The latter cause some economically important diseases of crops, such as mildews, smuts and rusts. A few fungi are parasites of animals, but these are less significant in this respect than bacteria.

The study of fungi is called mycology (*mykes*, mushroom). It forms a branch of microbiology because many of the handling techniques used, such as sterilising and culturing procedures, are the same as those used with bacteria (see chapter 12).

2.5.1 Classification and characteristics of Fungi

As discussed in section 2.2, fungi are eukaryotes that lack chlorophyll, and are therefore heterotrophic, like animals. However, they have rigid cell walls and are non-motile, like plants. In the past, they were regarded as plants, but modern classifications, such as that shown in fig 2.4, place them in a separate kingdom. Their classification and characteristics are summarised in table 2.6. The two largest and most advanced groups are the Ascomycota and the Basidiomycota. Structure and nutrition of fungi are discussed in more detail below.

> **2.2** Using those features of the kingdom Fungi given in table 2.6, prepare a table of differences between fungi and typical plant cells.

Table 2.6 Classification and characteristics of fungi.

Kingdom Fungi

General characteristics
Heterotrophic nutrition because they lack chlorophyll and are therefore non-photosynthetic. They can be parasites, saprotrophs or mutualists. Nutrition is absorptive; digestion takes place outside the body and nutrients are absorbed directly. Digestion does not take place inside the body, unlike animals.
Rigid cell walls containing chitin as the fibrillar material. Chitin is a nitrogen-containing polysaccharide, very similar in structure to cellulose. Like cellulose it has high tensile strength. It therefore gives shape to the hyphae and prevents osmotic bursting of cells.
Body is usually a mycelium, a network of fine tubular filaments called hyphae. These may be septate (have cross-walls), e.g. *Penicillium*, or aseptate (no cross-walls), e.g. *Mucor*.
If carbohydrate is stored, it is usually as glycogen, not starch
Reproduce by means of spores
Non-motile

Phylum Zygomycota	*Phylum Ascomycota*	*Phylum Basidiomycota*
Asexual reproduction by conidia or sporangia containing spores	Asexual reproduction by conidia. No sporangia	Asexual reproduction by formation of spores. Not common
Non-septate hyphae and large well-developed branching mycelium	Septate hyphae	Septate hyphae
e.g. *Rhizopus stolonifer*, common bread mould, a saprotroph *Mucor*, common moulds, saprotroph	e.g. *Penicillium* and *Aspergillus*, saprotrophic moulds *Saccharomyces* (yeast), unicellular saprotrophs *Erysiphe*, obligate parasites causing powdery mildews, e.g. of barley	e.g. *Agaricus campestris*, field mushroom, saprotroph

2.5.2　Structure

The body structure of the fungi is unique. It consists of a mass of fine, tubular branching threads called **hyphae** (singular hypha), the whole mass being called a **mycelium**. Each hypha has a thin rigid wall whose chief component is chitin, a nitrogen-containing polysaccharide which is also found as a structural component in the exoskeletons of arthropods (section 2.8.6). The hyphae are not divided into true cells. Instead, the protoplasm is either continuous or interrupted at intervals by cross-walls called **septa** which divide the hyphae into compartments similar to cells. Unlike normal cell walls their formation is not a consequence of nuclear division, and a pore normally remains at their centre allowing protoplasm to flow between compartments. Each compartment may contain one, two or more nuclei, which are distributed at more or less regular intervals along the hyphae. Hyphae having cross-walls are called **septate**, as in *Penicillium* (fig 2.25). Hyphae lacking cross-walls are called **non-septate (aseptate)** as in *Mucor* (fig 2.26).

Within the cytoplasm the usual eukaryote organelles are found, such as mitochondria, Golgi apparatus, endoplasmic reticulum, ribosomes and vacuoles. In the older parts, vacuoles are large and cytoplasm is confined to a thin peripheral layer. Sometimes hyphae aggregate to form more solid structures such as the spore-producing bodies of the mushrooms. The yeasts are unusual in being unicellular fungi and therefore lack the typical hypha structure, e.g. *Saccharomyces* (fig 2.27).

Penicillium, *Mucor* and *Rhizopus* are known as moulds. They are widespread saprotrophs, that is they feed on dead organic matter. They are convenient fungi to study because they are easy to grow in culture and show the typical hyphal growth of fungi.

Penicillium species form blue, green and sometimes yellow moulds, common, for example, on bread and decaying fruit. The mycelium forms a circular colony of small diameter with septate hyphae and the spores give colour to the colony (fig 2.25a). *Penicillium* reproduces asexually by means of spores called **conidia**. These are found at the tips of special hyphae called **conidiophores** (fig 2.25b and c). They are not enclosed in a sporangium, but are naked and free to be dispersed as soon as they mature. The structure of the hyphae is shown in fig 2.25d. The economic importance of *Penicillium* is discussed in section 12.11.1.

Mucor is a genus which includes a number of well-known moulds. It is common in soil and may also be found growing on bread. It forms more or less circular colonies when grown on agar. Its hyphae are aseptate and profusely branching (fig 2.26b). It produces spores in spherical **sporangia** borne on very long stalks known as **sporangiophores** (fig 2.26a and b). These are numerous in the more mature parts of the mycelium and resemble a collection of pins; hence *Mucor* is often referred to as pin mould. Sporangia are clearly visible using the low power of a microscope. Mucor grows rapidly and can cover a petri dish in 3 days at 20 °C. Internally, its hyphae have the same typical eukaryotic structure as *Penicillium* (fig 2.25d) except that the hyphae of *Mucor* lack cross-walls. *Rhizopus* is very similar to *Mucor*. Some hyphae, called *stolons*, are arch-shaped and produce tufts of short, root-like hyphae at their tips. Two or more sporangiophores grow from the same point, unlike *Mucor* where sporangiophores occur singly.

> **2.3**　What is the purpose of the sporangiophores?

Yeasts are unicellular, saprotrophic fungi. They occur widely in nature and are particularly common on the sugary surfaces of ripe fruits. The bloom on grapes, for example, is due to yeast. The fermentation (anaerobic respiration) of the sugars by yeast produces alcohol, a fact made use of by humans for thousands of years and which forms the basis of the wine and brewing industries. Under appropriate conditions yeast cells multiply rapidly by budding, a form of asexual reproduction (fig 2.27a). Yeast cells show the usual eukaryotic features (fig 2.27b and c).

2.5.3　Nutrition

Fungi are heterotrophic, that is they require an organic source of carbon. In addition, they require a source of nitrogen, usually organic such as amino acids; inorganic ions such as K^+ and Mg^{2+}; trace elements such as Fe, Zn and Cu; and organic growth factors such as vitamins. The exact range of nutrients required, and hence substrates on which they are found, is variable. The nutrition of fungi can be described as absorptive because they absorb nutrients directly from outside their bodies. This is in contrast to animals, which normally ingest food and then digest it within their bodies before absorption takes place. With fungi, digestion, if necessary, is performed by the fungus secreting enzymes out of its body on to its food.

Fungi obtain their nutrients as saprotrophs, parasites or mutualists. In this respect they are like most bacteria.

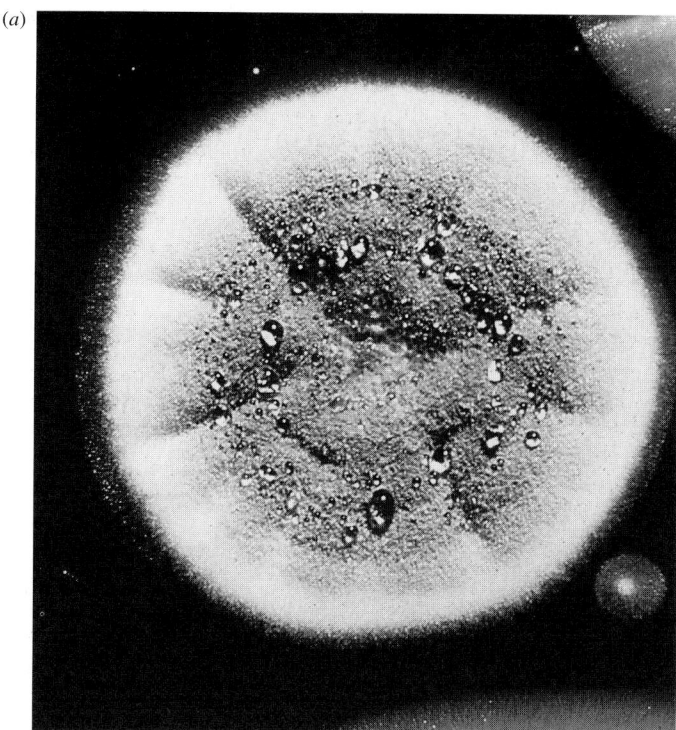

(a)

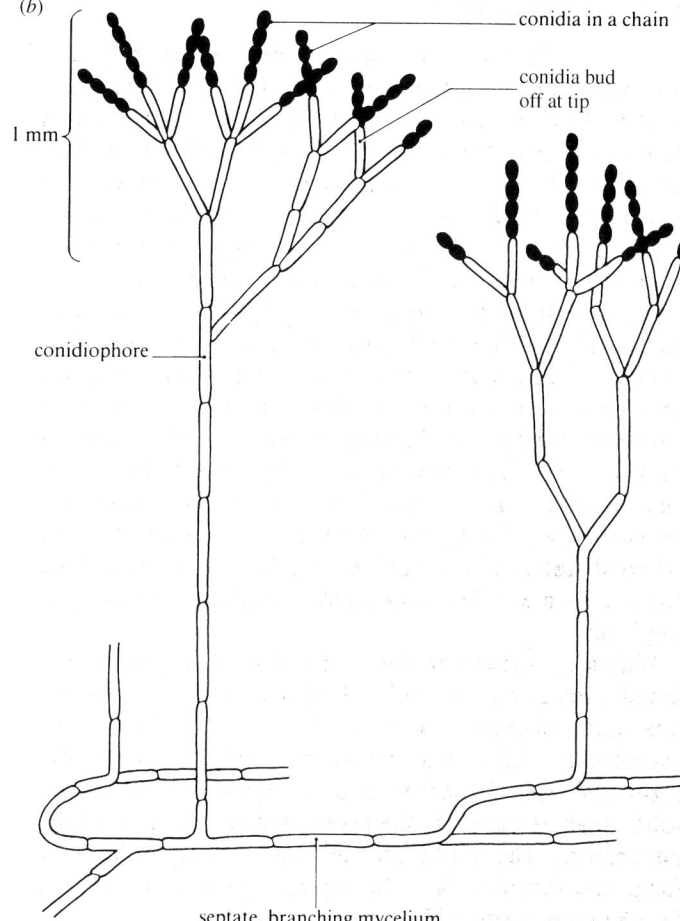

(b)

conidia in a chain

conidia bud
off at tip

1 mm

conidiophore

septate, branching mycelium

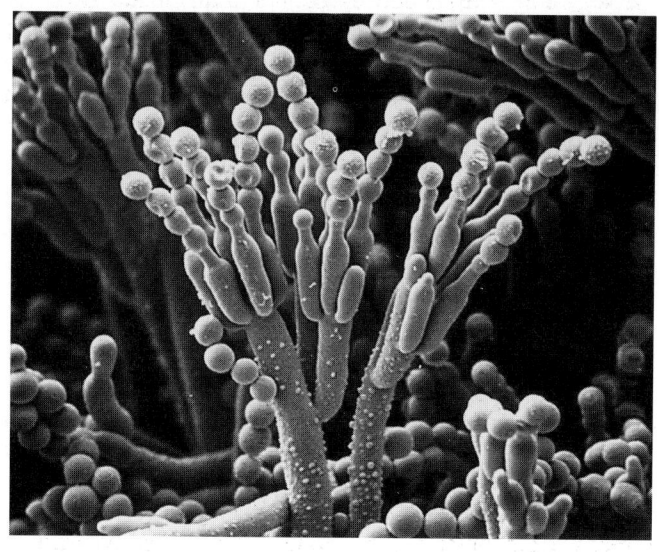

(c)

Fig 2.25 (a) Penicillium *growing on nutrient agar in a petri dish. It typically produces a relatively small circular mycelium. The young outer edge of the mycelium appears white, whereas the mature central portion appears darker where coloured spores have been produced.*
(b) Penicillium *showing asexual reproduction. It has a characteristic brush-like arrangement of conidia.*
(c) *Scanning electron micrograph of conidiophore and conidia (spores) of* Penicillium. *(d) LS hypha showing fine structure visible with electron microscope.*

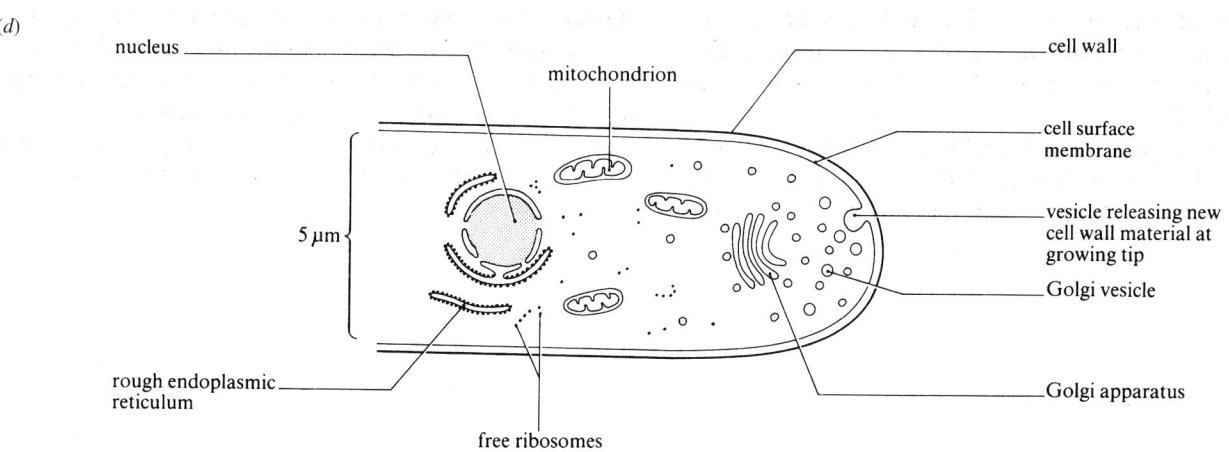

(d)

nucleus

mitochondrion

cell wall

cell surface
membrane

vesicle releasing new
cell wall material at
growing tip

Golgi vesicle

5 μm

Golgi apparatus

rough endoplasmic
reticulum

free ribosomes

27

Saprotrophs

Saprotrophic organisms feed on dead organic material. Fungal saprotrophs produce a variety of digestive enzymes. If they secrete the three main classes of digestive enzymes, namely carbohydrases (digest carbohydrates) such as amylases (digest starch), lipases (digest lipids) and proteases (digest proteins), they can utilise a wide range of substrates. For example the *Penicillium* species form green and blue moulds on substrates such as soil, damp leather, bread and decaying fruit.

The hyphae of saprotrophic fungi are usually chemotropic, that is they grow towards certain substrates in response to chemicals diffusing from these substrates.

Fungal saprotrophs usually produce large numbers of light, resistant spores. This allows efficient dispersal to other food sources. Examples are *Mucor, Rhizopus* and *Penicillium*.

Saprotrophic fungi and bacteria together form the decomposers which are essential in the recycling of nutrients. Especially important are the few that secrete the enzymes cellulase and lignase, which break down cellulose and lignin respectively. Cellulose and lignin (a complex chemical found particularly in wood) are important structural components of plant cell walls, and the rotting of wood and other plant remains is achieved partly by decomposers secreting cellulase and lignase.

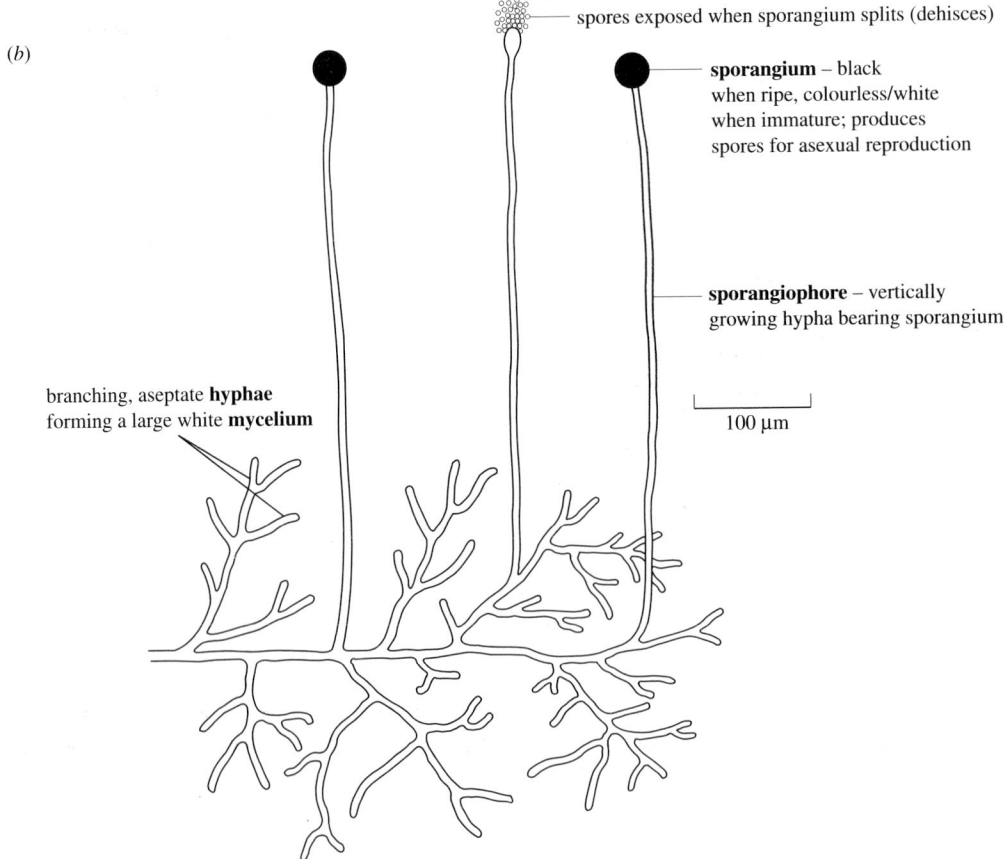

spores exposed when sporangium splits (dehisces)

sporangium – black when ripe, colourless/white when immature; produces spores for asexual reproduction

sporangiophore – vertically growing hypha bearing sporangium

100 μm

branching, aseptate **hyphae** forming a large white **mycelium**

Fig 2.26 (a) *A scanning electron micrograph of part of the mycelium of* Mucor hiemalis *showing sporangia (× 85).*
(b) *Mycelium of* Mucor *as seen with low power of a light microscope.*

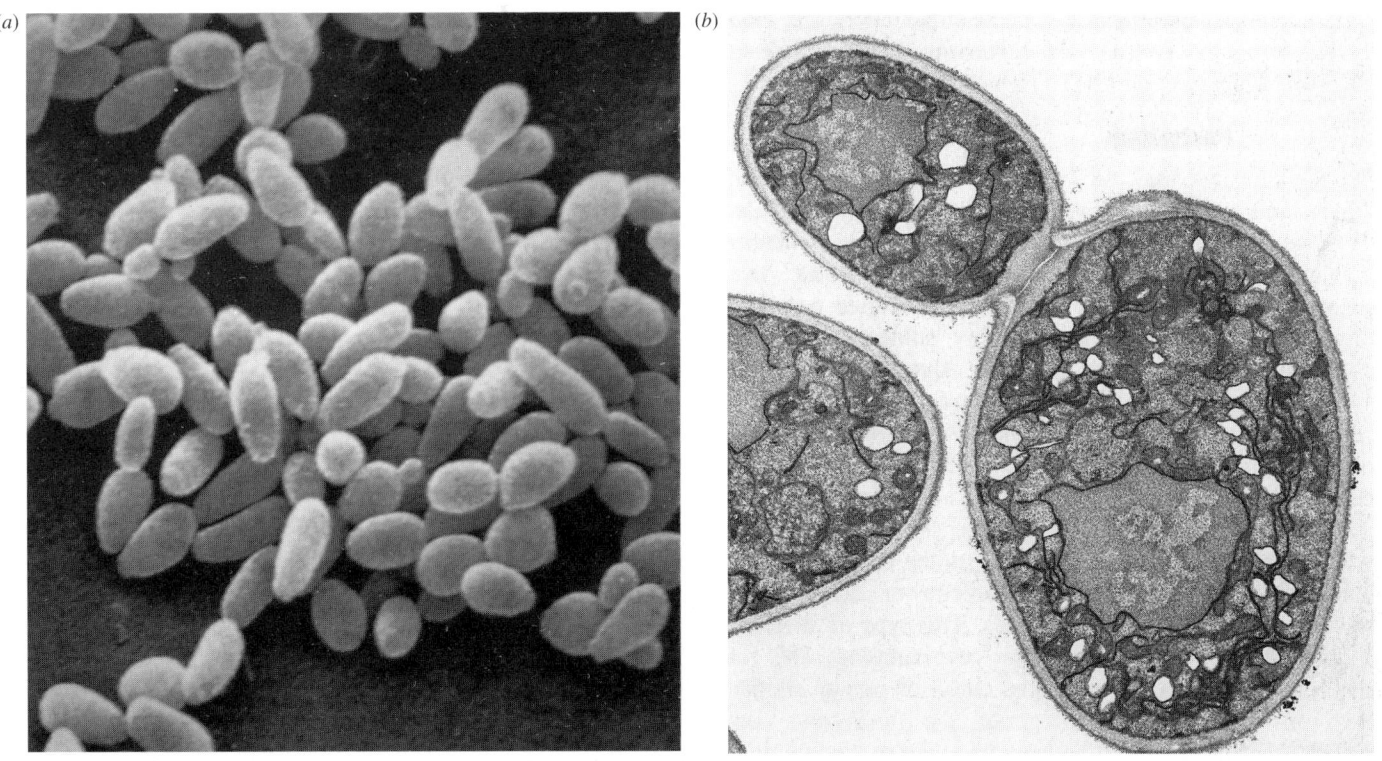

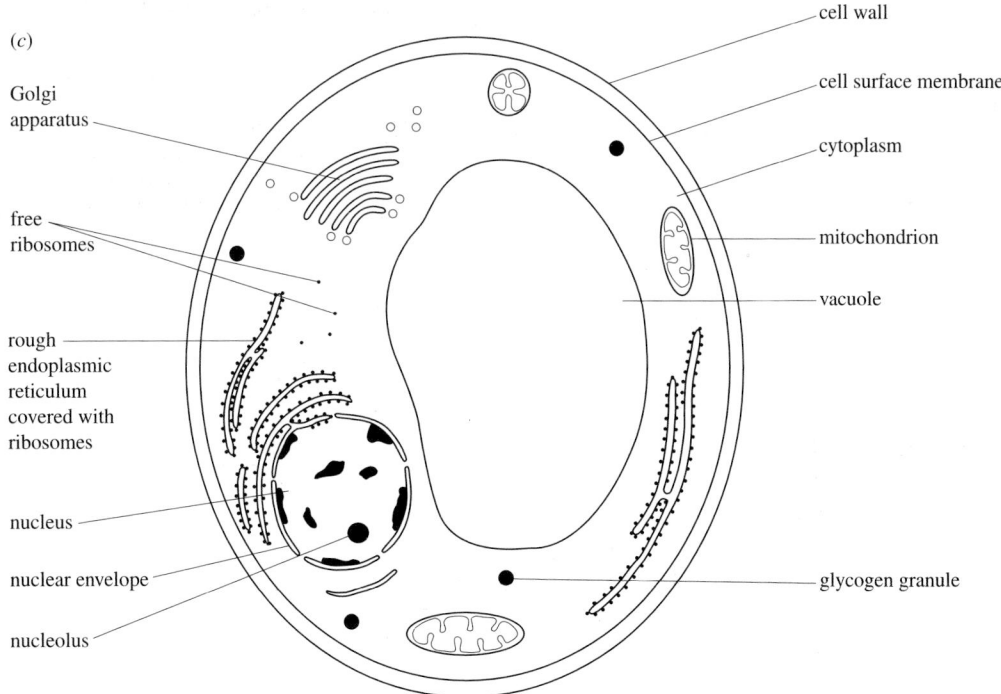

Fig 2.27 *Structure of yeast (*Saccharomyces*). (a) Budding cells as seen with a light microscope (× 4000). (b) Yeast cell seen with a transmission electron microscope (× 10 000). (c) Diagram of fine structure visible with an electron microscope.*

Some fungal saprotrophs are of economic importance, such as *Saccharomyces* (yeast) used in brewing and breadmaking and *Penicillium* (section 12.11.1) which is used in medicine.

Parasites

Fungal parasites may be facultative or obligate (section 2.3.4), and more commonly attack plants than animals. Obligate parasites do not normally kill their hosts, whereas facultative parasites frequently do and then live saprotrophically off the dead remains. Obligate parasites include the powdery mildews, downy mildews, rusts and smuts, which attack cereals and many other crops.

Once inside the plant, hyphae normally grow between cells. Facultative parasites commonly produce enzymes called pectinases which digest the middle lamellae between cells and cause 'soft rot' of the tissue, reducing it to a mush. Subsequently they may invade cells and kill them with the aid of cellulase which digests the cell walls. Cell constituents may be absorbed directly or digested by secretion of further fungal enzymes. This type of attack is shown by *Pythium* (the cause of 'damping off' of seedlings) and *Phytophthora* (the cause of potato blight), both of which belong to a group, the Oomycota, now regarded as ancestral to fungi and classified in the kingdom Protoctista (see section 2.6.2).

An example of a facultative parasite which infects humans is the yeast *Candida albicans*. This is a normal and usually harmless part of the surface or gut microflora of about 5% of the adult human population. However, particularly if the balance of natural microorganisms living on or in the body is disturbed by the use of antibiotics or prolonged use of steroid drugs (which have the side-effect of suppressing the body's immune system), the yeast may grow out of control and become pathogenic, that is cause disease. It causes a condition known as **thrush** (**candidiasis** or candidosis). Damp conditions are needed and it can infect the mouth (oral thrush) and vagina. The latter is associated with increased vaginal discharge and there may be itching or soreness on passing urine. It is very common, but not serious and can be controlled with antifungal drugs.

Mutualism (symbiosis)

Two important types of mutualistic union are made by fungi, namely lichens and mycorrhizas. Lichens are associations between fungi and green algae or blue-green bacteria. Lichens are commonly encrusted on exposed rocks and trunks of trees; they also hang from trees in wet forests. It is believed that the alga contributes organic food from photosynthesis, while the fungus is protected from high light intensity and is able to absorb water and mineral salts. The fungus can also conserve water, enabling some lichens to grow in dry conditions where no plants exist.

A mycorrhiza is an association between a fungus and a plant root. The fungus absorbs mineral salts and water which pass to the plant, and in return receives organic products of photosynthesis. Mycorrhizas are considered in more detail in section 7.10.2.

2.6 Kingdom Protoctista

(Greek *protos*, very first; *ktistos*, to establish)

2.6.1 Classification and characteristics of protoctists

In section 2.2 it was noted that in the five kingdom classification of Margulis and Schwartz (fig 2.4), the Protoctista is probably the most controversial group because it is the least natural. It is really a collection of all the eukaryotic organisms that do not fit neatly into the other three eukaryote kingdoms. Many are unicellular.

The Protoctista contains eukaryotes that are generally regarded as identical or similar to the ancestors of modern plants, animals and fungi (fig 2.28). It includes organisms which resemble early plants (algae), early animals (protozoa) and early fungi (Oomycota). It also includes a group known as the slime moulds which produce spores like fungi but can creep slowly over surfaces and are therefore motile like animals. The earliest eukaryotes were probably unicellular organisms which moved by beating flagella.

The group is fascinating to those interested in evolution because these organisms are the link between prokaryotes and the more modern eukaryotes like plants and animals. For example, during the 1960s it was discovered that mitochondria, the 'powerhouses' of cells that provide energy in aerobic respiration, contained their own DNA and ribosomes which resemble those of prokaryotes. There is now good evidence, based on an examination of the base sequences in the mitochondrial DNA, that mitochondria were formerly aerobic bacteria (prokaryotes) that invaded an ancestral eukaryote cell and 'learned' to live symbiotically within it. Now all eukaryotic cells contain mitochondria, and the mitochondria can no longer live independently.

Like mitochondria, chloroplasts, the chlorophyll-containing organelles responsible for photosynthesis, also contain their own prokaryotic DNA and ribosomes. These seem to have evolved from photosynthetic bacteria which invaded heterotrophic animal-like cells, turning them into algae which are autotrophic. It is also likely that red algae may have evolved in this way from blue-green bacteria and that green algae evolved from green bacteria known as prochlorophytes.

The theory that mitochondria and chloroplasts are the descendants of symbiotic bacteria is known as the **endosymbiont theory**. An endosymbiont is an organism that lives symbiotically *inside* (endo-) another organism.

2.6.2 Phylum Oomycota

Oomycotes are close relations of the fungi and have a similar structure, but are now regarded as a more ancient group. Their cell walls contain cellulose, not chitin, as the strengthening material. Their hyphae are aseptate. In

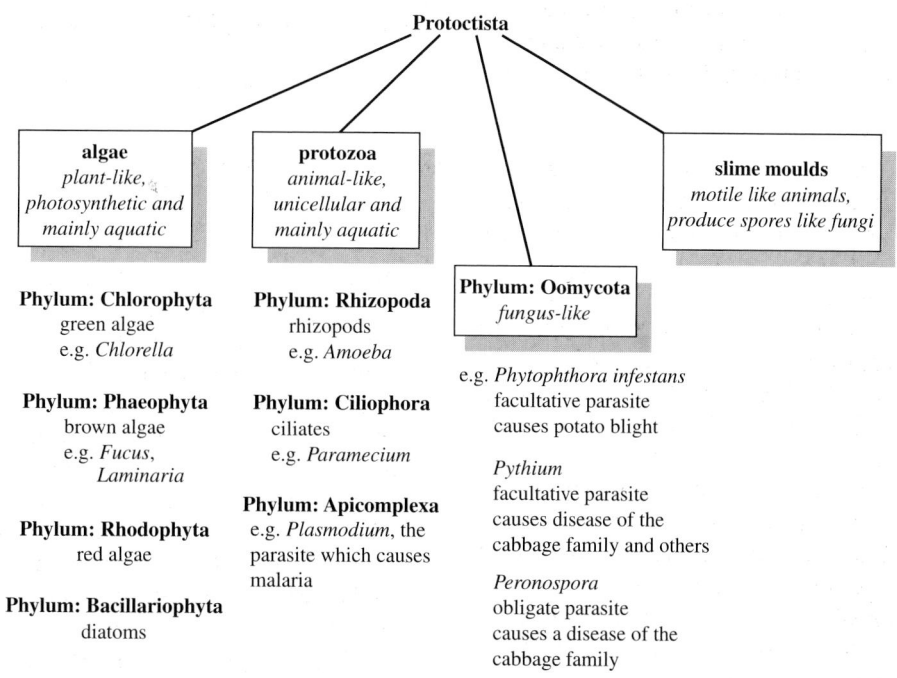

Fig 2.28 *The main groups of Protoctista and some examples of the phyla and genera they contain. Not all groups or phyla are shown.*

this phylum are a number of pathogenic organisms, including the downy mildews. One of these, *Phytophthora infestans*, will be studied as an example of a parasite which is generally described as obligate. *Peronospora*, an obligate parasite, will also be mentioned for comparison. Finally, *Pythium* will be examined as a typical example of a facultative parasite. An obligate parasite is one which can only survive and grow in living cells whereas facultative parasites typically bring about the deaths of their hosts before living saprotrophically on the remains.

Phytophthora infestans

Phytophthora infestans is a pathogen of economic importance because it parasitises potato crops, causing a potentially devastating disease known as potato blight. It does not grow independently of its host and in this respect resembles obligate parasites. It is similar in its structure and mode of attack to another member of the Oomycota, *Peronospora*, which is a common, but less serious, disease of wallflower, cabbage and other members of the plant family Cruciferae.

The *Phytophthora* mycelium overwinters in potato tubers and grows up to the leaves in spring. Blight is usually first noticed in the leaves in August.

A mycelium of branched, aseptate hyphae spreads through the intercellular spaces of the leaves, giving off branched **haustoria** which push into the mesophyll cells and absorb nutrients from them (fig 2.29). Haustoria are typical of obligate parasites. They are specialised penetration and absorption devices. Each is a modified hyphal outgrowth with a large surface area which pushes into cells without breaking their cell surface membranes

and without killing them. In warm, humid conditions the mycelium produces long, slender structures called **sporangiophores** which emerge from the lower surface of the leaf through stomata or wounds. These branch and give rise to **sporangia** (fig 2.29). In warm conditions sporangia may behave as spores, being blown or splashed by raindrops on to other plants, where further infection takes place. A hypha emerges from the sporangium and penetrates the plant through a stoma, lenticel or wound. In cool conditions, the sporangium contents may divide to form swimming spores (a primitive feature) which, when released, swim in surface films of moisture. They may encyst until conditions are suitable once more for hyphal growth, then produce new infections.

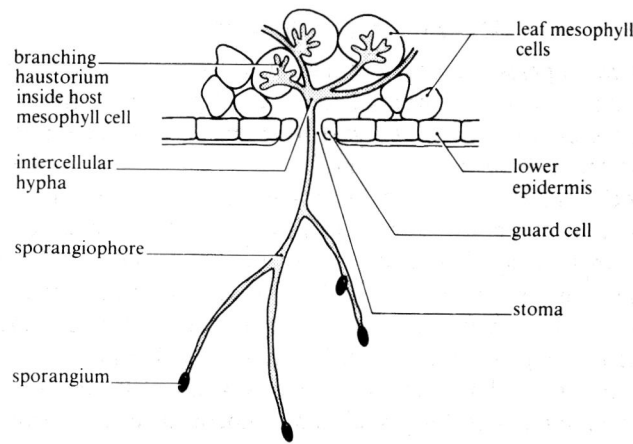

Fig 2.29 Phytophthora infestans *growing in a diseased potato leaf, with sporangiophores emerging from the underside of the leaf.*

31

Diseased plants show individual leaflets with small, brown, dead, 'blighted' areas. Inspection of the lower surface of an infected leaflet reveals a fringe of white sporangiophores around the dead area. In warm, humid conditions, the dead area spreads rapidly through the whole leaf and into the stem. Some sporangia may fall to the ground and infect potato tubers. Here infection spreads very rapidly, causing a form of dry rot in which the tissues are discoloured a rusty brown in an irregular manner from the skin to the centre of the tuber.

First the base and then the rest of the plant becomes a putrid mass as the dead areas become secondarily infected with decomposing bacteria (saprotrophs). *Phytophthora* thus kills the whole plant, unlike its close relative *Peronospora* which is an obligate parasite. In this respect, *Phytophthora* is not a typical obligate parasite and it is sometimes described as facultative, though the distinction is perhaps not worth stressing here.

The organism normally overwinters as a dormant mycelium within lightly infected potato tubers. Except where the potato is native (Mexico, Central and South America) it is thought that the organism rarely reproduces sexually, unlike *Peronospora*, but under laboratory conditions it can be induced to do so. Like *Peronospora*, it produces a resistant resting spore. It is the result of fusion between an antheridium (male) and an oogonium (female), and a thick-walled spore is produced. This can remain dormant in the soil over winter and cause infection in the following year.

In the past, *Phytophthora* epidemics have had serious consequences. The disease is thought to have been accidentally introduced into Europe from America in the late 1830s and caused a series of epidemics that totally destroyed the potato crop in Ireland in 1845 and in subsequent years. Widespread famine resulted and many starved to death, victims as much of complex economic and political influences as of the disease. Many Irish families emigrated to North America as a result.

The disease is also of interest because in 1845 Berkeley provided the first clear demonstration that microorganisms cause disease by showing that the organism associated with potato blight caused the disease, rather than being a by-product of decay.

Knowledge of the life cycle of potato blight has since led to methods of controlling the disease. These are summarised below.

- Care must be taken to ensure that no infected tubers are planted.
- New plantings must not be made in soil known to have carried the disease a year previously, since the organism can survive up to one year in the soil. Crop rotation may therefore help.
- All diseased parts of infected plants should be destroyed before lifting tubers, for example by burning or spraying with a corrosive solution such as sulphuric acid. This is because tubers can be infected from decaying haulms (stems) and aerial parts.

- Since the organism can overwinter in unlifted tubers, care must be taken to ensure that all tubers are lifted in an infected field.
- The organism can be attacked with copper-containing fungicides, such as Bordeaux mixture. Spraying must be carried out at the correct time to prevent an attack, since infected plants cannot be saved. It is usual to spray at fortnightly intervals, from the time that the plants are a few centimetres high until they are well matured. Tubers intended as seed potatoes can be sterilised externally by immersion in a dilute mercury(II) chloride solution.
- Accurate monitoring of meteorological conditions, coupled with an early warning system for farmers, can help to decide when spraying should be carried out.
- Breeding for resistance to the blight has been carried out for some years. The wild potato, *Solanum demissum*, is known to show high resistance and has been used in breeding experiments. One great obstruction to producing the required immunity lies in the fact that the organism exists in many strains and no potato has been found to be resistant to all of them. New strains of the organism may appear as new strains of potato are introduced. This is a familiar problem in plant pathology and emphasises the need for conservation of the wild ancestors of our modern crop plants as sources of genes for disease resistance.

Pythium

Unlike *Phytophthora, Pythium* is a relatively unspecialised parasite, attacking a great variety of plants and causing a soft rot. It causes 'damping off' in seedlings. It needs damp conditions since it produces swimming spores during asexual reproduction. It can grow on the living plant or on its dead remains, so is a facultative parasite. It can also live saprotrophically in wet soil. It produces extracellular enzymes which help it attack and kill its host rapidly. The first enzymes produced are pectinases which diffuse ahead of the growing fungus and digest the pectin in the middle lamellae which hold the cells together. As a result the plant tissue dissolves into a mush (soft rot). The plant collapses. Later other enzymes are produced which digest the contents of the plant cells, but it does not produce haustoria, unlike *Phytophthora*. Products of digestion are absorbed by the hyphae which grow between the cells.

Damping-off of seedlings is due to destruction of the first shoot as it appears above the soil. Watery spots first appear on the stem at soil level. As these darken, the stem collapses. It can be a serious problem in horticulture, forestry and agriculture. Members of the cabbage family (crucifers) are particularly susceptible, especially when the seedlings are grown in crowded conditions.

2.6.3 Algae

The algae form a large group of protoctistans of great biological importance and significance to humans. No single characteristic is diagnostic. They are best thought of as photosynthetic eukaryotes that evolved in, and have remained in, water. A few algae have escaped to live successfully on land, but unlike plants, which evolved on land, these are insignificant in number compared with those in the oceans and fresh water. The bodies of algae lack true stems, roots and leaves. Such a relatively undifferentiated body is called a **thallus**.

The algae fall naturally into distinct groups, chiefly on the basis of their photosynthetic pigments. These groups are given the status of phyla in modern classifications. Only four of the phyla are shown in fig 2.28. Characteristics of the algae and of two of the main phyla are shown in table 2.7. Two examples of algae, namely *Chlorella* (phylum Chlorophyta) and *Fucus* (phylum Phaeophyta) are examined in more detail below.

2.6.4 Phylum Chlorophyta (green algae)

Chlorella

Chlorella is a unicellular, non-motile green alga. Its structure is shown in fig 2.30. Its habitat is freshwater ponds and ditches. It is easily cultured and has been used as an experimental organism in research on photosynthesis (section 7.6) as well as being investigated as an alternative source of food (single cell protein, section 12.12.3).

2.6.5 Phylum Phaeophyta (brown algae)

Fucus

Fucus is a relatively large and complex brown alga. Its body is a thallus which is differentiated into a stipe, holdfast and fronds (note these are not true stem, roots and leaves). It is a marine alga, common on rocky shores off the British coast. It is well adapted to the relatively harsh conditions of the shore, where it is alternately exposed and covered by the tides.

There are three common species and these are often found at three different levels, or zones, on the shore, a phenomenon called **zonation** (section 10.6.4). They are principally zoned according to their ability to withstand exposure to air. Their chief recognition features and positions on the shore are noted below.

F. spiralis (flat wrack) – towards high tide mark. If suspended, the thallus adopts a slight spiral twist.

F. serratus (common, serrated or saw wrack) – middle zone. Edge of the thallus is serrated.

F. vesiculosus (bladder wrack) – towards low tide mark. Possesses air bladders for buoyancy. The external features of *F. vesiculosus* are shown in fig 2.31.

Adaptations to environment. Before discussing the adaptations of *Fucus* to its environment, some mention must be made of the nature of this environment, which is relatively hostile. Being intertidal, the different species are subjected to varying degrees of exposure to air when the tide recedes. Therefore they must be protected against drying out. Temperatures may change rapidly, as when a cold sea advances into a hot rock pool. Salinity is

Table 2.7 Classification and characteristics of two of the main groups of algae.

Algae

General characteristics
Almost all are specialised for an aquatic existence
Great range of size and form, including unicellular, filamentous, colonial and thalloid forms. A thallus is a body which is not differentiated into true roots, stems and leaves and lacks a true vascular system (xylem and phloem). It is often flat
Photosynthetic, eukaryotic

Phylum Chlorophyta ('green algae')	*Phylum Phaeophyta* ('brown algae')
Dominant photosynthetic pigment is chlorophyll; therefore green in appearance. Chlorophylls *a* and *b* present (as in plants)	* Dominant photosynthetic pigment is brown and called fucoxanthin. Chlorophylls *a* and *c* present
Store carbohydrate as starch (insoluble)	* Store carbohydrate as soluble laminarin and mannitol. Also store fat
Mostly freshwater	Nearly all marine (three freshwater genera only)
Large range of types, e.g. unicellular, filamentous, colonial, thalloid	Filamentous or thalloid, often large
e.g. *Chlorella*, a unicellular, non-motile alga *Chlamydomonas,* a unicellular, motile alga *Spirogyra,* a filamentous alga *Ulva,* a thalloid, marine alga	e.g. *Fucus*, a thalloid, marine alga *Laminaria,* large thalloid, marine alga; one of the kelps

* a diagnostic feature.

another factor to which the organism has adapted, and this may increase in an evaporating rock pool, or decrease during rain. The surge and tug of the tide, and the pounding of waves, are additional factors which demand mechanical strength if they are to be withstood. Large waves can pick up stones and cause great damage as they crash down.

Morphological adaptations (overall structure). The thallus is firmly anchored by a holdfast (fig 2.31). This forms an intimate association with its substrate, usually rock, and is extremely difficult to dislodge. In fact, the rock often breaks before the holdfast.

The thallus shows dichotomous branching (branching into two at each branch point). This minimises resistance to the flow of water which can pass between the branches. The thallus is also tough but non-rigid and its midrib is strong and flexible.

F. vesiculosus possesses air bladders for buoyancy, thus holding its fronds up near the surface for maximum interception of light for photosynthesis.

Chloroplasts are mainly located in the surface layers for maximum exposure to light for photosynthesis.

Physiological adaptations. The dominant photosynthetic pigment is the brown pigment **fucoxanthin**. This is an adaptation for photosynthesising under water because fucoxanthin strongly absorbs blue light, which penetrates water much further than longer wavelengths such as red light.

The thallus secretes large quantities of mucilage which fills spaces within the body and exudes on to its surface. This helps to prevent desiccation by retaining water.

The solute potential of the cells is higher (less negative) than that of sea water, so water is not lost by osmosis.

Reproductive adaptations. Release of gametes is synchronised with the tides. At low tide the thallus dries and squeezes the sex organs, which are protected by mucilage, out of the conceptacles. As the tide advances, the walls of the sex organs dissolve and release the gametes.

The male gametes are motile and chemotactic, attracted by a chemical secretion of the female gametes.

The zygote develops immediately after fertilisation, minimising the risk of being swept out to sea.

2.6.6   Protozoa

Like the algae, the protozoans form a large group of protoctistans. They are unicellular, animal-like cells with heterotrophic nutrition. There are over 50 000 known species and they are found in all environments where water is present. Most are free-living and there are various methods of locomotion. Some, however, are parasites, including one (*Plasmodium*) which causes the disease which is estimated to have killed more humans than any other, namely malaria. It is still one of the world's worst killers.

A free-living protozoan, *Paramecium*, is chosen for study in this section as being typical of this level of organisation. *Plasmodium* is studied in Book 2 in chapter 15 on disease.

2.6.7   Phylum Ciliophora (ciliates)

Ciliates are a type of protozoan (fig 2.28). They have the following characteristics:

* unicellular, heterotrophic;
* possession of **cilia**, fine hairs which beat and cause movement of water, either for locomotion or feeding;
* a definite shape due to the presence of a thin, flexible outer region of cytoplasm, called the **pellicle**, which is covered by the cell surface membrane;
* a complex cell structure with a macronucleus and a micronucleus.

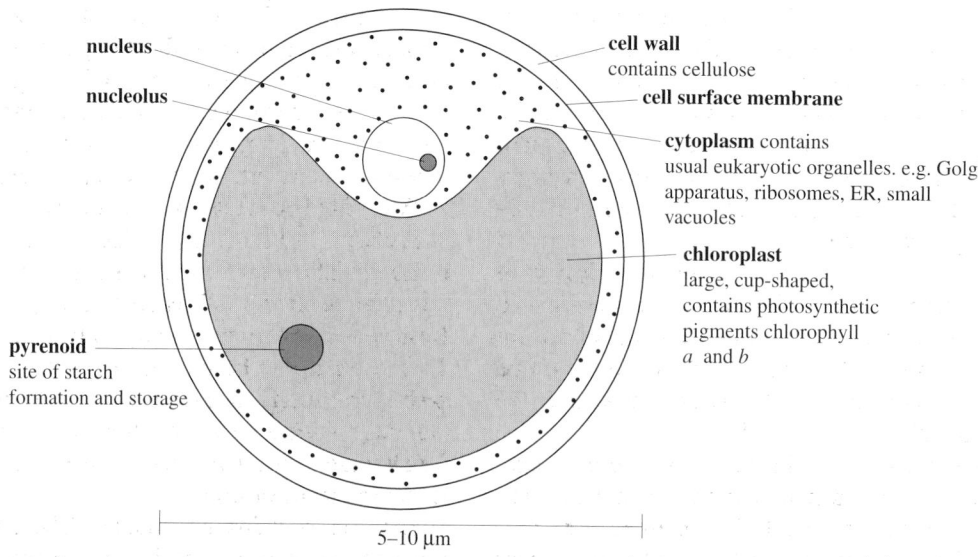

Fig 2.30 *Structure of* Chlorella, *a green alga.*

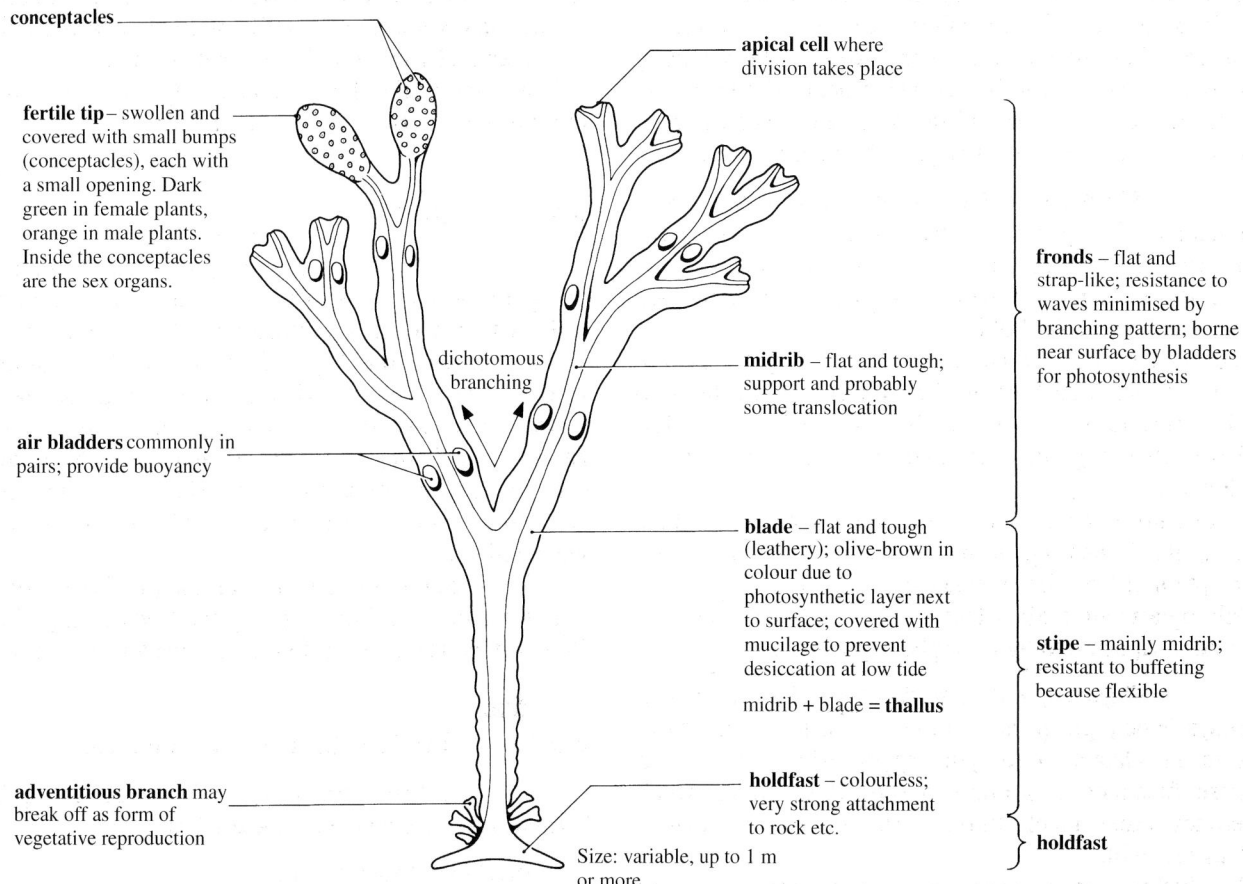

conceptacles

fertile tip – swollen and covered with small bumps (conceptacles), each with a small opening. Dark green in female plants, orange in male plants. Inside the conceptacles are the sex organs.

air bladders commonly in pairs; provide buoyancy

dichotomous branching

adventitious branch may break off as form of vegetative reproduction

Size: variable, up to 1 m or more

apical cell where division takes place

fronds – flat and strap-like; resistance to waves minimised by branching pattern; borne near surface by bladders for photosynthesis

midrib – flat and tough; support and probably some translocation

blade – flat and tough (leathery); olive-brown in colour due to photosynthetic layer next to surface; covered with mucilage to prevent desiccation at low tide

midrib + blade = **thallus**

stipe – mainly midrib; resistant to buffeting because flexible

holdfast – colourless; very strong attachment to rock etc.

holdfast

Fig 2.31 *External features of* Fucus vesiculosus, *with notes on structure, particularly adaptations to environment.*

A common example of a ciliate is *Paramecium*. It lives in stagnant water, or slow-flowing fresh water that contains decaying organic matter. Fig 2.32 shows the complex cell structure typical of the ciliates. The complexity of the cell is explained by the fact that it has to perform all the functions of a whole organism, such as feeding, osmoregulation and locomotion. The body shape is characteristic, being blunt at the front (anterior) end and tapered at the back (posterior). Cilia occur in pairs. They run in rows diagonally across the body, causing the body to rotate as they beat and move the cell forward. Between the cilia are holes leading into chambers called **trichocysts**. From these chambers, sharply tipped fine threads can be discharged which are probably used for anchorage during feeding.

Beneath the pellicle is a layer of **ectoplasm**, a clear, firm cytoplasm in the form of a gel. **Basal bodies** (identical to centrioles) are found here. They are the structures from which cilia are formed. There is also a network of fine fibres running between the basal bodies which may be involved in coordinating the beat of the cilia.

The bulk of the cytoplasm is in the form of **endoplasm**, which exists in a more liquid state than the ectoplasm. Here most of the organelles are found. The **oral groove** is a shallow groove found on the ventral (lower) surface near the front of the organism. It tapers back into a narrow tube-like **gullet** at the end of which the endoplasm is exposed to form a 'mouth' or **cytostome**. Both the oral groove and gullet are lined with cilia which beat and cause a current of water to flow towards the cytostome, carrying food particles such as bacteria in suspension. The food particles are ingested into a food vacuole formed by the endoplasm (endocytosis). The vacuoles follow a distinct pathway through the endoplasm, finishing at the **cytoproct** or anal pore, where undigested material is egested (exocytosis). During their movement through the cytoplasm, lysosomes add digestive enzymes to the vacuoles and products of digestion are absorbed into the surrounding cytoplasm.

Two fixed **contractile vacuoles** are present in the endoplasm (fig 2.32). They are responsible for osmoregulation, that is the maintenance of a constant water potential inside the cell (chapter 20). As a result of living in fresh water, water constantly enters the cell by osmosis. This water has to be pumped out by an energy-consuming active transport mechanism to prevent the cell from bursting. Around each contractile vacuole a number of canals radiate outwards and collect water before emptying it into the main vacuole.

The cell contains two nuclei. The larger, bean-shaped **macronucleus** is polyploid (has more than two sets of chromosomes). It controls metabolic activities apart from

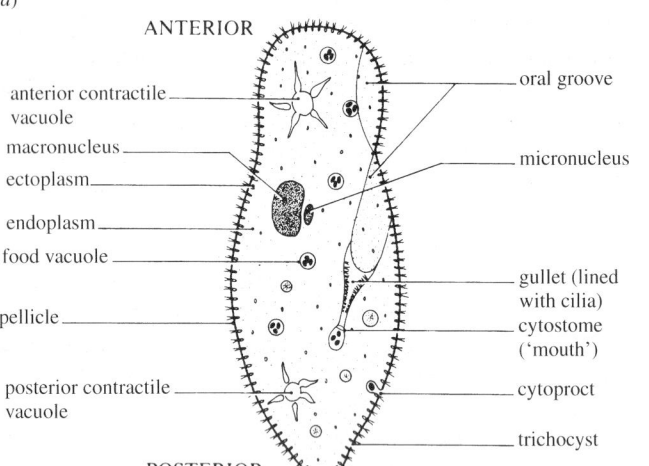

(a)

ANTERIOR

anterior contractile vacuole

macronucleus

ectoplasm

endoplasm

food vacuole

pellicle

posterior contractile vacuole

POSTERIOR

oral groove

micronucleus

gullet (lined with cilia)

cytostome ('mouth')

cytoproct

trichocyst

cilia

(b)

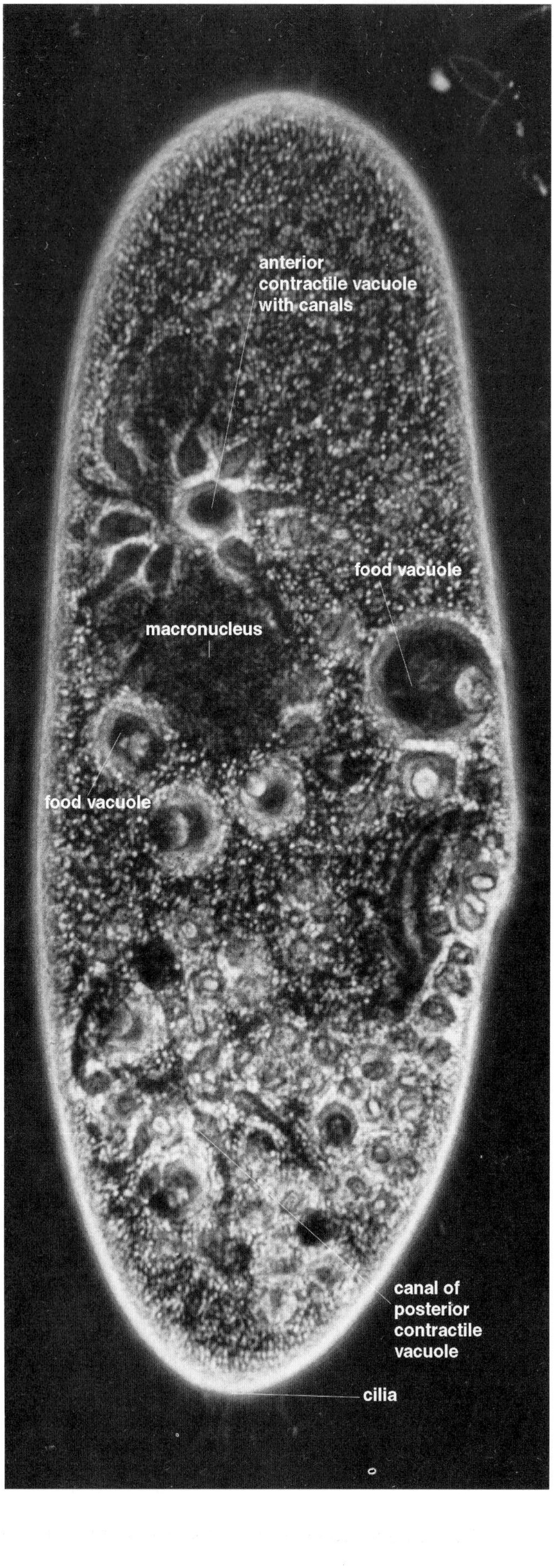

anterior contractile vacuole with canals

food vacuole

macronucleus

food vacuole

canal of posterior contractile vacuole

cilia

Fig 2.32 (a) Paramecium caudatum – *structures visible under the light microscope.* (b) Paramecium caudatum *as seen with a light microscope (x 832).*

reproduction. The **micronucleus** is diploid. It controls reproduction and the formation of new macronuclei during nuclear division.

Paramecium can reproduce both asexually (by transverse binary fission) and sexually (by conjugation).

2.6.8   Phylum Apicomplexa

This group of protozoans also possesses a pellicle, giving the cell a definite shape. Most, however, possess no special structures for locomotion and have limited movement. Their most distinguishing characteristic is the production of spores during asexual and sexual reproduction. An example is the parasite *Plasmodium* which causes malaria in humans and is discussed in chapter 15.

2.7   Kingdom Plantae

Although life probably began on this planet about 3.5 thousand million years ago, it was not until about 420 million years ago that the first organisms colonised the land. These were the earliest plants. Plants are autotrophic eukaryotes which have become adapted for life on land. The only other autotrophic eukaryotes are algae, which are specialised for life in water. Remember, **autotrophic** means that the organism has an inorganic source of carbon, that is carbon dioxide. Nutrition involves acquiring energy as well as carbon (see section 2.3.4) and plants are photoautotrophic, meaning that their source of energy is light. Their method of nutrition is more commonly referred to as **photosynthesis**.

The story of plant evolution is mainly of gradually improving adaptation to life on land. It is this story which will be one of the main themes in our study of plants. The classification of those plants which we shall consider in this book is shown in fig 2.33, together with a summary of some of the main trends in plant evolution which relate to adaptation to life on land and which will also be studied in this section.

2.7.1 Phylum Bryophyta (liverworts and mosses)

Bryophytes are the simplest land plants. They are thought to have evolved from green algae. The phylum contains two main classes, the Hepaticae, or liverworts, and the Musci, or mosses. Neither group is particularly well adapted for life on land and they are mainly confined to damp, shady places. The classification and characteristics of the bryophytes are summarised in table 2.8.

Bryophytes are small simple plants, with strengthening and conducting tissues absent or poorly developed. There is no true vascular tissue (xylem or phloem). They lack true roots, being anchored by thin filaments called **rhizoids** which grow from the stem. Water and mineral salts can be absorbed by the whole surface of the plant, including the rhizoids, so that the latter are mainly for anchorage, unlike true roots. (*True* roots also possess vascular tissue, as do *true* stems and leaves.) The plant surface lacks a cuticle, or

has only a delicate one, and so there is no barrier against loss (or entry) of water. Nevertheless, most bryophytes have adapted to survive periods of dryness using mechanisms that are not fully understood. For example, it has been shown that the well-known xerophytic moss *Grimmia pulvinata* can survive total dryness for longer than a year at 20 °C. Recovery is rapid as soon as water becomes available.

Alternation of generations

In common with all plants and some advanced algae, such as *Laminaria*, bryophytes show alternation of generations. Two types of organism, a haploid gametophyte generation and a diploid sporophyte generation, alternate in the life cycle, summarised in fig 2.34. The haploid generation is called the **gametophyte** (*gameto*, gamete; *phyton*, plant) because it undergoes sexual reproduction to produce gametes. Production of gametes involves mitosis, so the gametes are also **haploid**. The gametes fuse to form a **diploid** zygote which grows into the next generation, the diploid sporophyte generation. It is called the **sporophyte** because it undergoes asexual reproduction to produce spores. Production of spores involves meiosis, so that there is a return to the haploid condition. The haploid spores give rise to the gametophyte generation. One of the two generations is always more

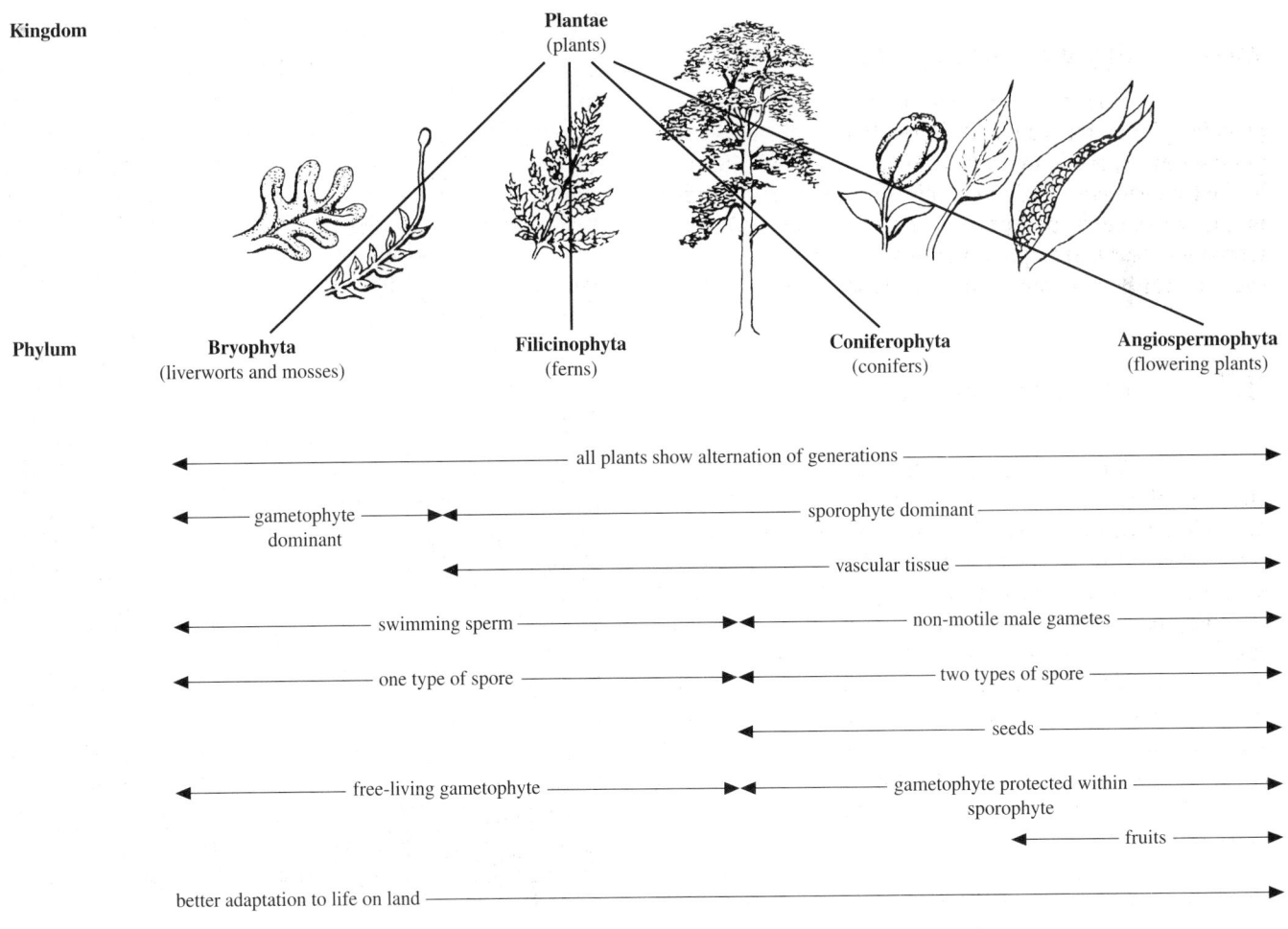

Fig 2.33 *Classification of plants and some of the main trends in plant evolution.*

Table 2.8 Classification and characteristics of the phylum Bryophyta (bryophytes).

Phylum Bryophyta

General characteristics
Alternation of generations in which the gametophyte generation is dominant
No vascular tissue, that is no xylem or phloem
Body is a thallus, or differentiated into simple 'leaves' and 'stems'
No true roots, stems or leaves: the gametophyte is anchored by filamentous rhizoids
Sporophyte is attached to, and is dependent upon, the gametophyte for its nutrition
Spores are produced by the sporophyte in a spore capsule on the end of a slender stalk above the gametophyte
Live mainly in damp, shady places

Class Hepaticae (liverworts)	*Class Musci* (mosses)
Gametophyte is a flattened structure that varies from being a thallus (rare) to 'leafy' with a stem (majority), with intermediate lobed types	Gametophyte 'leafy' with a stem
'Leaves' (of leafy types) in three ranks along the stem	'Leaves' spirally arranged
Rhizoids unicellular	Rhizoids multicellular
Capsule of sporophyte splits into four valves for spore dispersal: elaters aid dispersal	Capsule of sporophyte has an elaborate mechanism of spore dispersal, dependent on dry conditions and involving teeth or pores
e.g. *Pellia*, a thallose liverwort *Marchantia*, a thallose liverwort, with antheridia and archegonia on stalked structures above the thallus *Lophocolea*, a leafy liverwort, common on rotting wood	e.g. *Funaria* *Mnium*, a common woodland moss similar in appearance to *Funaria* *Sphagnum*, bog moss: forms peat in wet acid habitats (bogs)

conspicuous and occupies a greater proportion of the life cycle; this is said to be the **dominant** generation. In the bryophytes, the gametophyte generation is dominant. In all other plants the sporophyte generation is dominant. It is customary to place the dominant generation in the top half of the life cycle diagram.

Fig 2.34 should be studied carefully because it summarises the life cycle of all plants, including the flowering plants, which are the most advanced. One point that must be remembered is that gamete production involves mitosis, not meiosis as in animals; meiosis occurs in the production of spores.

Class Hepaticae – liverworts

Characteristics of the Hepaticae are summarised in table 2.8. They are more simple in structure than mosses and, on the whole, more confined to damp and shady habitats. They are found on the banks of streams, on damp rocks and in wet vegetation. Most liverworts show regular lobes, or definite 'stems' with small, simple 'leaves'. The simplest of all though are the thalloid liverworts where the body is a flat thallus with no stem or leaves.

An example is *Pellia*, a liverwort that is common throughout Britain. The plant is a dull green with flat branches about 1 cm wide. Its external features are shown in fig 2.35.

Class Musci – mosses

Characteristics of the Musci are summarised in table 2.8. They have a more differentiated structure than liverworts

but, like liverworts, are small and found mainly in damp habitats. They often form dense cushions.

Funaria is a common moss of fields, open woodland and disturbed ground, being one of the early colonisers of such ground. It is especially associated with freshly burned areas, for example after heath fires. It is also a common weed in greenhouses and gardens. Its external features are illustrated in fig 2.36.

As with liverworts, water is essential for fertilisation. When the surface of the plant is wet, mature antheridia absorb water and burst, releasing the male gametes (sperm) onto the surface. The sperm each have two flagella. They swim towards the archegonia, each of which contains one female gamete or ovum. Fertilisation, that is fusion of the sperm nucleus with the ovum nucleus, takes place in the archegonium. The product is a diploid zygote which grows out of the archegonium to become a new sporophyte.

2.7.2 Phylum Filicinophyta (ferns)

Characteristics of the Filicinophyta are summarised in table 2.9. They are usually restricted to damp shady habitats. Few ferns are capable of growing in full sunlight, although bracken (*Pteridium*) is a common exception. Ferns are common in tropical rain forests, where temperature, light and humidity are favourable.

Ferns are vascular plants, meaning that they contain vascular tissue. **Vascular tissue** is made up of xylem and phloem. These tissues are concerned with translocation (transport) of water and nutrients round the plant body.

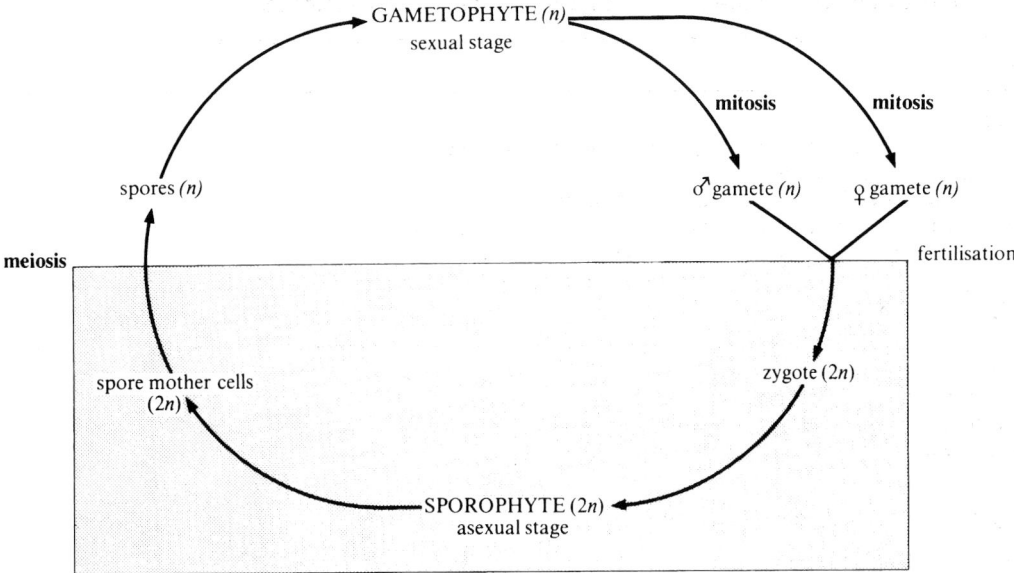

Fig 2.34 *Generalised life cycle of a plant showing alternation of generations. Note the haploid stages (n) and diploid stages (2n). The gametophyte is always haploid and always produces gametes by mitosis. The sporophyte is always diploid and always produces spores by meiosis.*

Xylem carries mainly water and mineral salts, whereas **phloem** carries mainly organic solutes in solution such as sugars. Vascular tissue is a major evolutionary advance compared with the simple conducting cells of some bryophytes and algae. It is found only in the sporophyte generation, and is one reason why the sporophyte generation becomes conspicuous in all vascular plants.

Vascular tissue has two important properties. First, it forms a **transport system**, conducting food and water around the multicellular body, thus allowing the development of large, complex bodies. Secondly, these bodies can be **supported** because xylem, apart from being a conducting tissue, contains lignified cells of great strength and rigidity. Another lignified tissue, sclerenchyma, also develops in vascular plants and supplements the mechanical role of xylem (section 6.2.1).

The sporophyte generation possesses true roots, stems and leaves. Roots penetrate the soil with the result that water and dissolved nutrients can be obtained more easily. Xylem conducts it to other parts of the plant.

Once plant bodies could achieve support above the ground, there must have been competition for light, so there would be a tendency for taller forms to evolve. Ferns and tree-ferns were the dominant vegetation for about 70 million years, from the Devonian to the Permian eras. After this conifers and, later, flowering plants largely replaced them (see the geological time scale in the appendix in Book 2).

Despite these advances in adapting to a land environment, which are associated with the sporophyte generation, in ferns there remains a major problem with the gametophyte. This is even smaller and more susceptible to desiccation (drying) than the bryophyte gametophyte. It is called a **prothallus**, and produces sperm which must swim to reach the female gametes, as is the case in bryophytes.

Table 2.9 Characteristics of the phylum Filicinophyta (ferns).

Phylum Filicinophyta (ferns)

General characteristics
Alternation of generations in which the sporophyte is dominant
Gametophyte is reduced to a small, simple prothallus
Vascular tissue present (xylem and phloem) in sporophyte: sporophyte therefore has true roots, stems and leaves
Leaves relatively large and called fronds
Spores produced in sporangia which are usually in clusters called sori

e.g. *Dryopteris filix-mas* (male fern)
Pteridium (bracken)

The male fern (Dryopteris filix-mas)

Dryopteris filix-mas is probably the most common British fern and is found in damp woods, hedgerows and other shady places throughout the country. The fronds (leaves) of the sporophyte may reach a metre or more in height and grow from a thick horizontal stem, or **rhizome**. This bears **adventitious roots**. Branches from the main stem may eventually break away and give rise to separate plants, a form of vegetative reproduction. The bases of the fronds are covered with dry brown scales called **ramenta** that protect the young leaves from frost or drought. The young leaves show a characteristic tightly rolled structure. The ramenta gradually become smaller and less dense up the main axis of the frond. This axis is called the **rachis**, and the leaflets either side are called the pinnae. The small rounded subdivisions of the pinnae are called **pinnules**. The external features of the sporophyte of *Dryopteris filix-mas* are

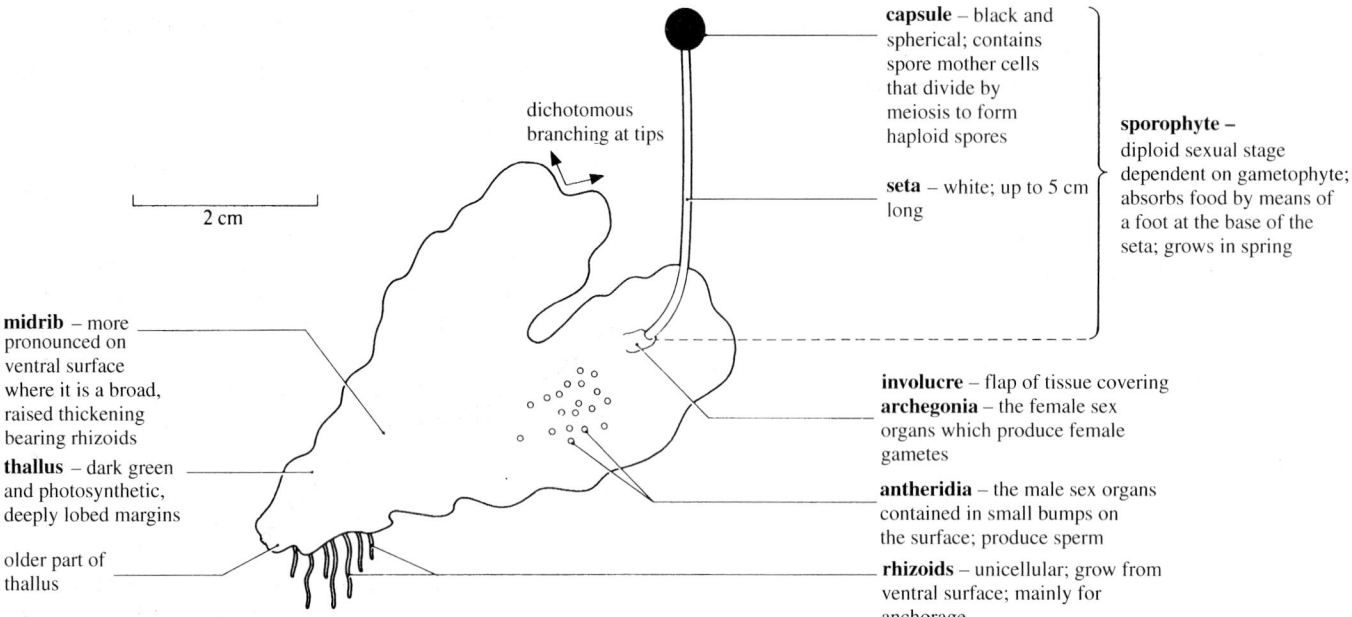

Fig 2.35 *External features of* Pellia, *a liverwort. The gametophyte is shown with the dependent sporophyte generation attached.*

Labels in Fig 2.35:

capsule – black and spherical; contains spore mother cells that divide by meiosis to form haploid spores

seta – white; up to 5 cm long

sporophyte – diploid sexual stage dependent on gametophyte; absorbs food by means of a foot at the base of the seta; grows in spring

dichotomous branching at tips

2 cm

midrib – more pronounced on ventral surface where it is a broad, raised thickening bearing rhizoids

thallus – dark green and photosynthetic, deeply lobed margins

older part of thallus

involucre – flap of tissue covering

archegonia – the female sex organs which produce female gametes

antheridia – the male sex organs contained in small bumps on the surface; produce sperm

rhizoids – unicellular; grow from ventral surface; mainly for anchorage

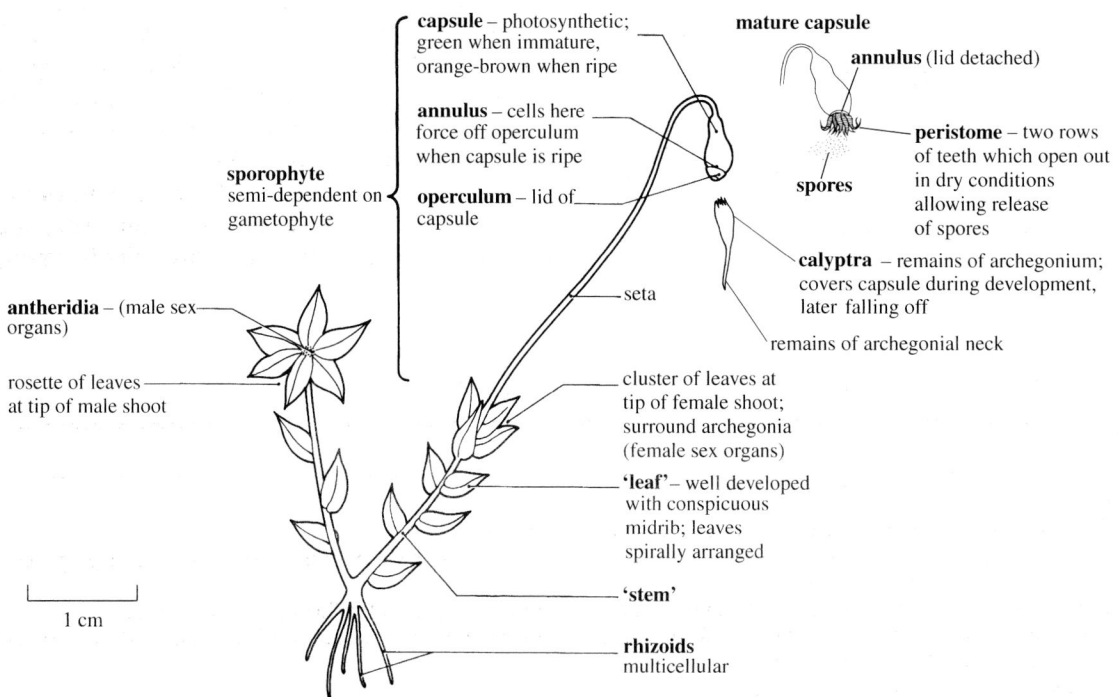

Fig 2.36 *External features of* Funaria, *a moss. The gametophyte is shown with the semi-dependent sporophyte generation attached.*

Labels in Fig 2.36:

capsule – photosynthetic; green when immature, orange-brown when ripe

mature capsule

annulus (lid detached)

annulus – cells here force off operculum when capsule is ripe

operculum – lid of capsule

sporophyte semi-dependent on gametophyte

peristome – two rows of teeth which open out in dry conditions allowing release of spores

spores

calyptra – remains of archegonium; covers capsule during development, later falling off

remains of archegonial neck

antheridia – (male sex organs)

rosette of leaves at tip of male shoot

seta

cluster of leaves at tip of female shoot; surround archegonia (female sex organs)

'leaf' – well developed with conspicuous midrib; leaves spirally arranged

'stem'

rhizoids multicellular

1 cm

shown in fig 2.37. The gametophyte is shown in fig 2.38.

Spores are produced during late summer in structures called **sporangia**. Sporangia develop in clusters called **sori** on the undersides of pinnules (fig 2.37*c*, *d* and *e*). Each sorus has a protective covering called an **indusium**. Inside each sporangium diploid spore mother cells divide by meiosis to produce haploid spores. When mature, the indusium shrivels and drops off, and the exposed sporangium walls begin to dry out. Eventually the wall ruptures and spores are catapulted from the sporangium (fig 2.37*e*).

The spores germinate to form the gametophyte generation. The gametophyte is a thin heart-shaped plate of cells about 1 cm in diameter (fig 2.38). It is green and photosynthetic and is anchored by unicellular rhizoids to the soil. This delicate prothallus lacks a cuticle and is prone to drying out, so can only survive in damp conditions.

The gametophyte (prothallus) produces simple antheridia and archegonia on its lower surface. These sex organs protect the gametes within them. Gametes are produced by mitosis of gamete mother cells, the antheridia producing sperm and each archegonium an ovum, as in the bryophytes. Each sperm has flagella. When ripe, and conditions are wet, each antheridium releases its sperm, which swim through a film of water towards the archegonia. The product of fertilisation is a diploid zygote. Note that fertilisation is still dependent on water as in the bryophytes.

The zygote grows into the sporophyte generation. The young embryo absorbs nutrients from the gametophyte until its own roots and leaves can take over the role of nutrition (fig 2.38b). The gametophyte soon withers and dies.

2.7.3 Seed-bearing plants

The most successful group of plants have seeds. They probably have their origin among extinct seed-producing members of the ferns and their close relatives. Classification and characteristics of the seed-bearing plants are summarised in table 2.10.

Table 2.10 shows the two main groups of seed-bearing plants, the **conifers** and **angiosperms**. The latter are commonly known as the **flowering plants**. In conifers, ovules (later seeds) are located on the surfaces of specialised scale leaves called ovuliferous scales. These are arranged in cones. In angiosperms, ovules, and therefore seeds, are enclosed, giving more protection.

2.7.4 Phylum Coniferophyta (conifers)

Characteristics of the Coniferophyta are summarised in table 2.10.

Conifers are a successful group of plants of worldwide distribution, accounting for about one-third of the world's forests. They are trees or shrubs, mostly evergreen, with needle-like leaves. Most of the species are found at higher altitudes and further north than any other trees. Conifers are commercially important as 'softwoods', being used not only for timber but for resins, turpentine and wood pulp. They include pines, larches (which are deciduous), firs, spruces and cedars. A typical conifer is *Pinus sylvestris*, the Scots pine.

Pinus sylvestris is found throughout central and northern Europe, Russia and North America. It is native to Scotland, though it has been introduced elsewhere in Britain. It is planted for timber and ornament, being a stately, attractive tree up to 36 m in height with a characteristic pink to orange-brown flaking bark. It grows most commonly on sandy or poor mountain soils and consequently the root system is often shallow and spreading. Its external features are illustrated in fig 2.39.

Each year a whorl of lateral buds around the stem grows out into a whorl of branches. The roughly conical appearance of *Pinus* and other conifers is due to the transition from whorls of shorter (younger) branches at the tops to longer (older) branches lower down. The latter usually die and drop off as the tree grows, leaving the mature trees bare for some distance up their trunks (fig 2.39).

The main branches and trunk continue growth from year to year by the activity of an apical bud. They are said to show **unlimited growth**. They have spirally arranged scale

Table 2.10 Classification and characteristics of the seed-bearing plants.

Seed-bearing plants

General characteristics
Sporophyte is the dominant generation; gametophyte generation is severely reduced
Sporophyte produces two types of spores (in other words, it is **heterosporous**). The two types are microspores and megaspores; microspore = pollen grain, megaspore = embryo sac
The embryo sac (megaspore) remains completely enclosed in the ovule (megasporangium); a fertilised ovule is a seed*
Water is not needed for sexual reproduction because male gametes do not swim (except in a few primitive members); they are conveyed to the ovum by a pollen tube to effect fertilisation*
Complex vascular tissues in roots, stems and leaves

Phylum Coniferophyta (conifers)	*Phylum Angiospermophyta* (flowering plants)
Usually produce cones on which sporangia, spores and seeds develop	Produce flowers in which sporangia, spores and seeds develop*
Seeds are not enclosed in an ovary. They lie on the surface of specialised leaves called ovuliferous scales in structures called cones*	Seeds are enclosed in an ovary*
No fruit because no ovary	After fertilisation, the ovary develops into a fruit*
	Classes Dicotyledoneae and Monocotyledoneae (see table 2.11)

*diagnostic feature.

(a)

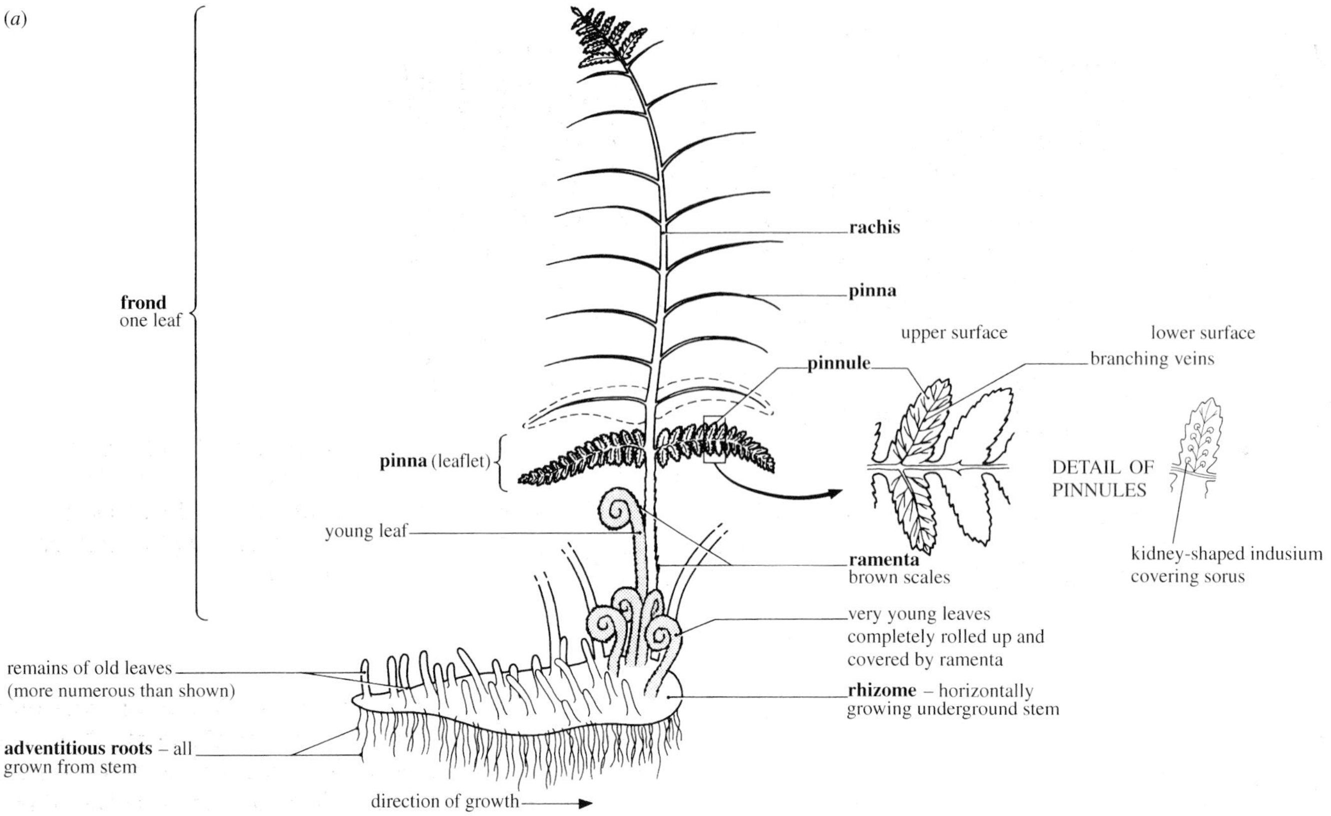

frond
one leaf

rachis

pinna

upper surface   lower surface
                       branching veins

pinnule

pinna (leaflet)

DETAIL OF
PINNULES

young leaf

ramenta
brown scales

kidney-shaped indusium
covering sorus

remains of old leaves
(more numerous than shown)

very young leaves
completely rolled up and
covered by ramenta

rhizome – horizontally
growing underground stem

adventitious roots – all
grown from stem

direction of growth

(b)

(c)

Fig 2.37 *External features of the sporophyte generation of Dryopteris filix-mas, the male fern. (a) Diagram with details of one pair of pinnae; others have the same structure. (b) The fronds. (c) Underside of frond showing sori (some covered with indusium). (d) and (e) opposite.*

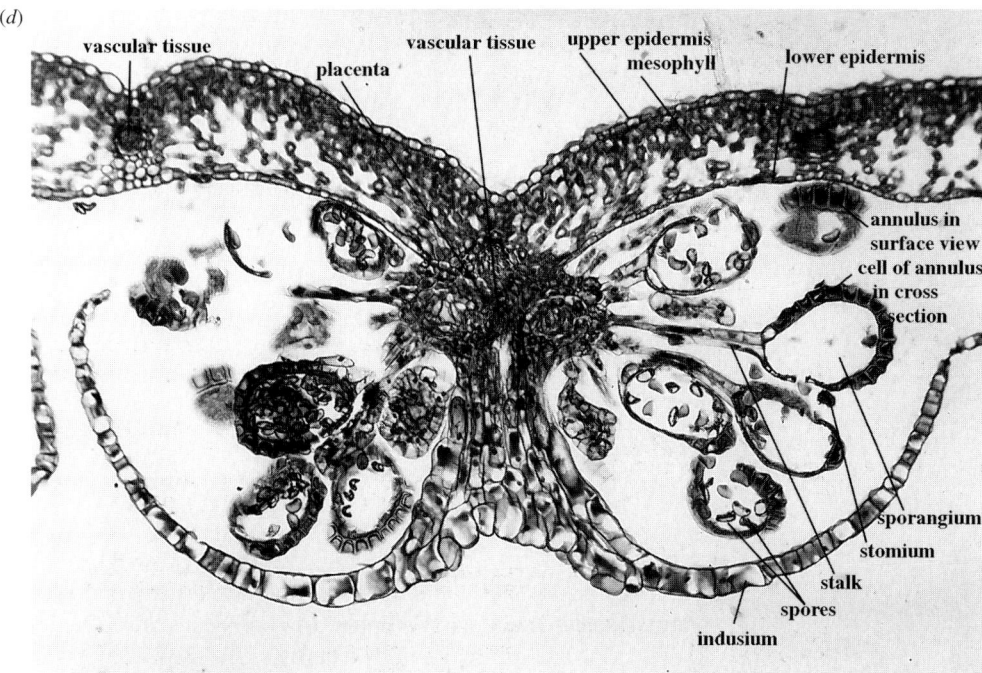

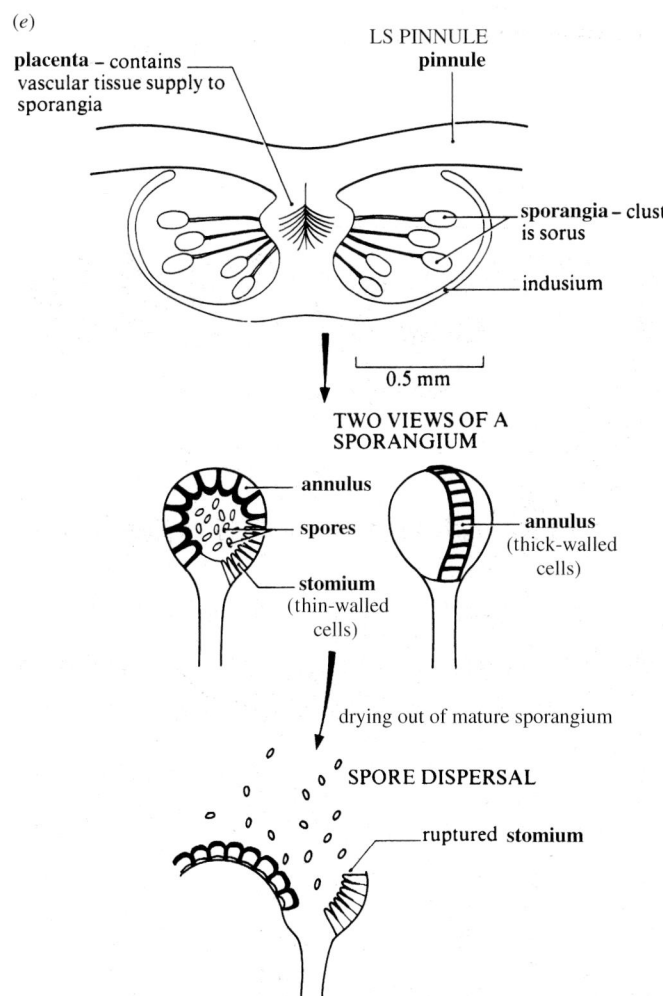

(d)

vascular tissue   vascular tissue   upper epidermis
placenta   mesophyll   lower epidermis

annulus in
surface view
cell of annulus
in cross
section

sporangium
stomium
stalk
spores
indusium

Fig 2.37 (cont.)   (d) *LS of a sorus as seen with a light microscope.* (e) *LS of sorus, details of sporangium and spore dispersal.*

(e)

placenta – contains
vascular tissue supply to
sporangia

LS PINNULE
pinnule

sporangia – cluster
is sorus

indusium

0.5 mm

TWO VIEWS OF A
SPORANGIUM

annulus
spores
stomium
(thin-walled
cells)

annulus
(thick-walled
cells)

drying out of mature sporangium

SPORE DISPERSAL

ruptured **stomium**

leaves, in the axils of which are buds that develop into very short branches (2–3 mm) called **dwarf shoots**. These are shoots of **limited growth** and at their tips grow two leaves. Once the shoot has grown, the scale leaf at its base drops off leaving a scar. The leaves are needle-like, reducing the surface area available for the loss of water. They are also covered with a thick, waxy cuticle and have sunken stomata, further adaptations for conserving water. These xeromorphic features ensure that the tree does not lose too much water from its evergreen leaves during cold seasons, when water may be frozen or difficult to absorb from the soil. After two to three years the dwarf shoots and leaves drop off together, leaving a further scar.

The tree is the sporophyte generation. In spring, male and female cones are produced on the same tree. The male cones are about 0.5 cm in diameter, rounded and found in clusters behind the apical buds at the bases of new shoots. They develop in the axils of scale leaves in the place of dwarf shoots. Female cones arise in the axils of scale leaves at the tips of new strong shoots, at some distance from the male cones and in a more scattered arrangement. Since they take three years to complete growth and development, they are of various sizes, ranging from about 0.5–6 cm on a given tree. They are green when young, becoming brown or reddish-brown in their second year. Both male and female cones consist of spirally arranged, closely packed sporophylls (modified leaves) around a central axis (fig 2.39).

Each sporophyll of a male cone has two **microsporangia** or **pollen sacs** on its lower surface. Inside each pollen sac, meiosis takes place to form haploid **pollen grains** or **microspores**. These contain the male gametes. Each grain has two large air sacs to aid in wind dispersal. During May the cones become yellow in appearance as they release clouds of pollen. At the end of the summer they wither and drop off.

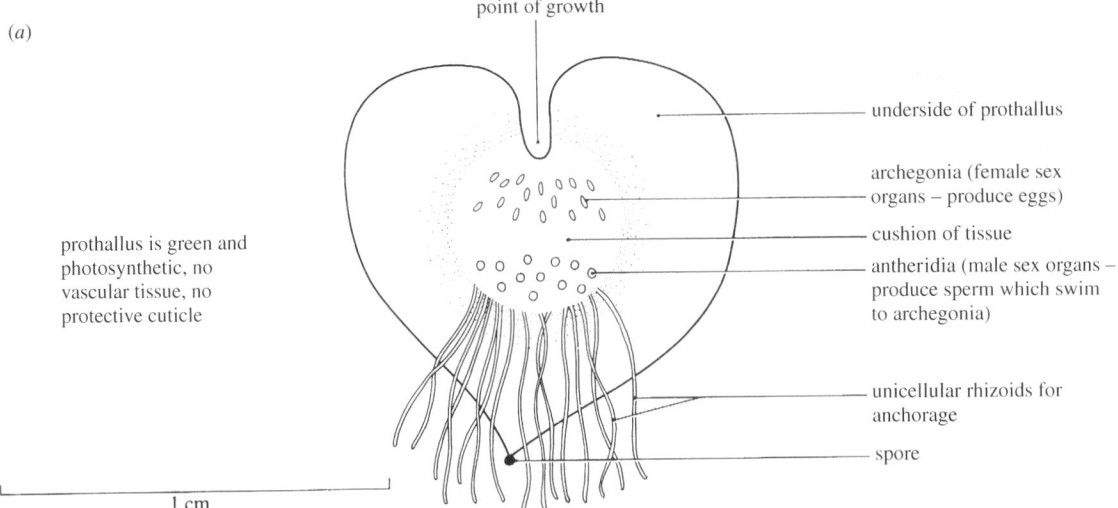

(a)

point of growth

underside of prothallus

archegonia (female sex organs – produce eggs)

cushion of tissue

antheridia (male sex organs – produce sperm which swim to archegonia)

prothallus is green and photosynthetic, no vascular tissue, no protective cuticle

unicellular rhizoids for anchorage

spore

1 cm

1 mm

first sporophyte leaf

sporophyte stem

gametophyte prothallus

apical notch of prothallus

Fig 2.38 *External features of the gametophyte generation of* Dryopteris, *known as the prothallus. (a) The prothallus is green and photosynthetic. It has no vascular tissue and no protective cuticle. (b) Prothallus with the first frond of the next sporophyte generation growing from it. At first the sporophyte is dependent on the gametophyte for water and minerals but it soon becomes an independent plant and the gametophyte dies.*

Each sporophyll of a female cone consists of a lower bract scale and a larger upper **ovuliferous scale**. On its upper surface are two ovules side by side, inside which the female gametes are produced. Pollination takes place during the first year of the cone's development, but fertilisation does not take place until the pollen tubes grow during the following spring. The fertilised ovules become winged seeds. They continue to mature during the second year and are dispersed during the third year. By this time the cone is relatively large and woody and the scales bend outwards to expose the seeds prior to wind dispersal.

2.7.5 Phylum Angiospermophyta (flowering plants)

Characteristics of the Angiospermophyta are summarised in table 2.10.

Angiosperms are better adapted to life on land than any other plants. After their appearance during the Cretaceous period, 135 million years ago, they rapidly took over from conifers as the dominant land vegetation on a world scale, and spread as different habitats were successfully exploited. Some angiosperms even returned to fresh water, and a few to salt water.

One of the most characteristic features of angiosperms, apart from the enclosed seeds already mentioned, is the presence of **flowers** instead of cones. This has enabled many of them to utilise insects, and occasionally birds or even bats, as agents of pollination. In order to attract these animals, flowers are usually brightly coloured, scented and offer pollen or nectar as food. In some cases the flowers have become indispensable to the insects. The result is that, in some cases, the evolution of insects and flowering plants has become closely linked and there are many highly specialised, mutually dependent, relationships. The flower generally becomes adapted to maximise the chances of pollen transfer by the insect and the process is therefore more reliable than wind pollination. Insect-pollinated plants need not, therefore, produce as much pollen as wind-

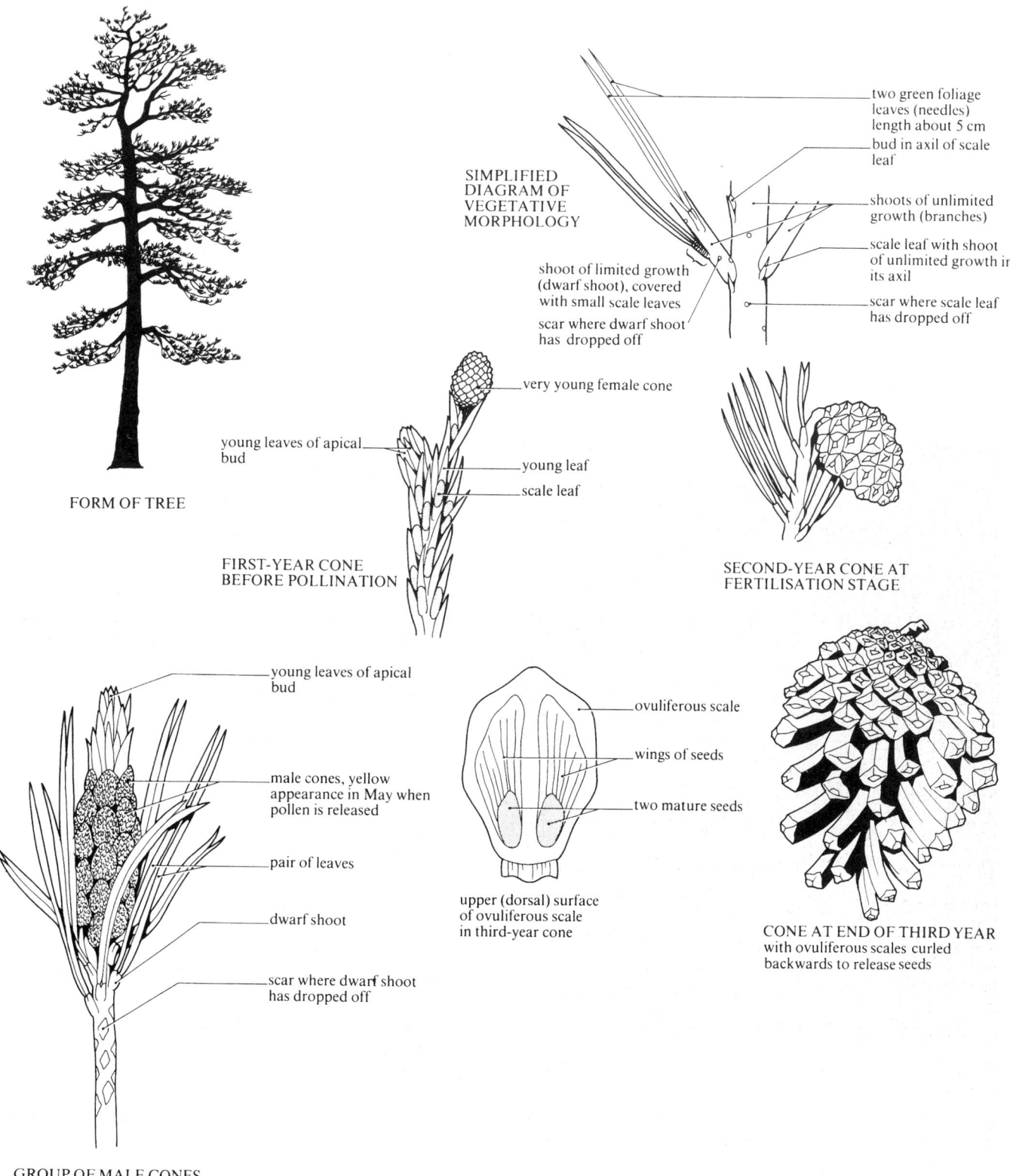

FORM OF TREE

SIMPLIFIED DIAGRAM OF VEGETATIVE MORPHOLOGY

two green foliage leaves (needles) length about 5 cm

bud in axil of scale leaf

shoots of unlimited growth (branches)

scale leaf with shoot of unlimited growth in its axil

scar where scale leaf has dropped off

shoot of limited growth (dwarf shoot), covered with small scale leaves

scar where dwarf shoot has dropped off

very young female cone

young leaves of apical bud

young leaf

scale leaf

FIRST-YEAR CONE BEFORE POLLINATION

SECOND-YEAR CONE AT FERTILISATION STAGE

young leaves of apical bud

male cones, yellow appearance in May when pollen is released

pair of leaves

dwarf shoot

scar where dwarf shoot has dropped off

GROUP OF MALE CONES

ovuliferous scale

wings of seeds

two mature seeds

upper (dorsal) surface of ovuliferous scale in third-year cone

CONE AT END OF THIRD YEAR with ovuliferous scales curled backwards to release seeds

Fig 2.39 *External features of the sporophyte generation of* Pinus sylvestris, *the Scots pine.*

pollinated plants. Nevertheless, many flowers are specialised for wind pollination.

Dicotyledons and monocotyledons

The angiosperms are divided into two major groups that are given the status of classes. The most commonly used names for the two groups are the monocotyledons and dicotyledons, usually abbreviated to **monocots** and **dicots**. A summary of the ways in which they differ is given in table 2.11 (see also fig 2.40). The modern view is that monocots probably evolved from dicots.

Angiosperms may be **herbaceous** (non-woody) or **woody**. Woody plants become shrubs or trees. They grow large amounts of secondary xylem (wood) that offers support, as well as being a conducting tissue, and is produced as a result of the activity of the vascular **cambium**. This is a layer of cells found between the xylem and phloem in stems and roots. These cells retain the ability to divide. The new xylem produced is called **secondary xylem** or wood.

Herbaceous plants, or herbs, rely on turgidity and smaller quantities of mechanical tissues such as collenchyma, sclerenchyma and xylem for support, and they are consequently smaller plants. They either lack a vascular cambium or, if present, it shows restricted activity. Many herbaceous plants are **annuals**, completing their life cycles from germination to seed production in one year. Some produce organs of perennation such as bulbs, corms and tubers by means of which they overwinter or survive periods of adverse conditions such as drought (chapter 21). They may then be **biennial**, in which case they produce their seeds and die in their second year, or **perennial**, in which case they survive from year to year. Shrubs and trees are perennial, and may be **evergreen**, producing and shedding leaves all year round so that leaves are always present, or **deciduous**, shedding leaves in seasons of cold or drought.

The structure of representative angiosperms is described in figs 2.41–44 to illustrate their diversity.

2.7.6 Adaptations of plants to life on land

Having examined the distinguishing features of the four main groups of plants, namely bryophytes, ferns, conifers and flowering plants, we are now in a position to understand more clearly the evolutionary progress that plants have made on adapting to life on land.

The problem

Probably the greatest single problem to overcome in making the transition from water to land is that of drying out, or **desiccation**. Any plant not protected in some way, for example by a waxy cuticle, would tend to dry out and die very rapidly. Even if this difficulty is overcome, there remain other problems, notably that of successfully achieving sexual reproduction. In the first plants this involved a male gamete which had to swim in water to reach the female gamete.

The first plants to colonise the land are generally thought to have evolved from the green algae, a few advanced members of which evolved reproductive organs, namely archegonia (female) and antheridia (male), that enclosed and thus protected the gametes within. This, and certain other factors that helped to prevent desiccation, enabled some of them to invade the land.

Table 2.11 Major differences between dicotyledons and monocotyledons.

	Class Dicotyledoneae	Class Monocotyledoneae
Examples	Pea, rose, buttercup, dandelion	Grasses, iris, orchids, lilies
Leaf morphology	Net-like pattern of veins (reticulate venation) Lamina (blade) and petiole (leaf stalk) Dorsal and ventral surfaces differ	Veins are parallel (parallel venation) Typically long and thin (grass-like) (fig 2.40) Identical dorsal and ventral surfaces
Stem anatomy	Ring of vascular bundles Vascular cambium usually present, giving to rise to secondary growth	Vascular bundles scattered Vascular cambium usually absent, so no secondary growth (exceptions occur, e.g. palms)
Root morphology	Primary root (first root from seed) persists as a tap root that develops lateral roots (secondary roots)	Adventitious roots from the base of the stem take over from the primary root, giving rise to a fibrous root system
Root anatomy	Few groups of xylem (2–8) (see chapter 13) Vascular cambium often present, giving rise to secondary growth	Many groups of xylem (commonly up to 30) Vascular cambium usually absent, so no secondary growth
Seed morphology	Embryo has two cotyledons (seed leaves)	Embryo has one cotyledon
Flowers	Parts mainly in fours and fives Usually distinct petals and sepals Often insect pollinated	Parts usually in threes No distinct petals and sepals. These structures are combined to form 'perianth segments' Often wind pollinated

One of the main evolutionary trends in plants is their gradually increasing independence from water.

The main problems associated with the transition from an aquatic to a terrestrial environment are summarised below.

- **Desiccation.** Air is a drying medium and water is essential for life for many reasons (section 3.1.2). Means of obtaining water and conserving it are required.
- **Reproduction.** Delicate sex cells must be protected and motile male gametes (sperm) require water if they are to reach the female gametes.
- **Support.** Air, unlike water, offers no support to the plant body.
- **Nutrition.** Plants require light and carbon dioxide for photosynthesis, so at least part of the body must be above ground. Minerals and water, however, are at ground level or below ground, and to make efficient use of these, part of the plant must grow below ground in darkness.
- **Gaseous exchange.** For photosynthesis and respiration, carbon dioxide and oxygen must be exchanged with the atmosphere rather than a surrounding solution.
- **Environmental variables.** Water, particularly large bodies of water like lakes and oceans, provides a very constant environment. A terrestrial environment, however, is much more subject to changes in important factors such as temperature, light intensity, ionic concentration and pH.

Liverworts and mosses

Mosses are well adapted to a terrestrial environment in their mode of spore dispersal, which depends on the drying out of the capsule and the dispersal of small, light spores by wind. However, they still show a great reliance on water for the following reasons.

- They are still dependent on water for reproduction because sperms must swim to the archegonia. They are adapted to release their sperms when water is available since only then do the antheridia burst. They are partly adapted to land because the gametes develop in protective structures, the antheridia and archegonia.
- There are no special supportive structures, so the plants are restricted in upward growth.
- They are dependent on availability of water and mineral salts close to or at the surface of the soil, because they have no roots to penetrate the substrate. However, rhizoids are present for anchorage, an adaptation to a solid substratum.

> **2.4** Liverworts and mosses have sometimes been described as the amphibians of the plant world. Briefly explain why this should be.

Fig 2.40 *Structure of* (a) *a monocotyledonous leaf and* (b) *a dicotyledonous leaf.*

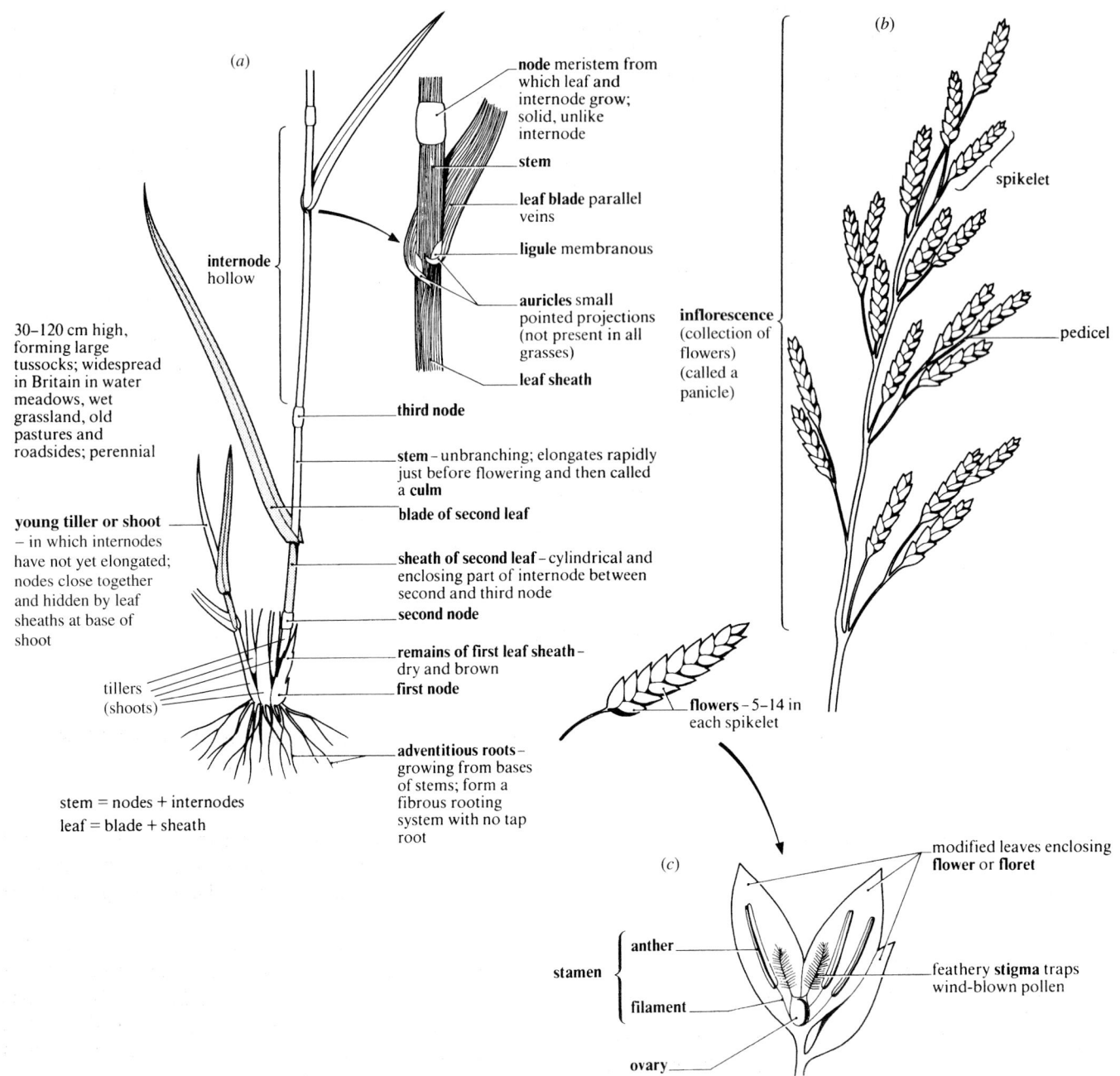

Fig 2.41 *Vegetative and floral morphology of the grass meadow fescue (Festuca pratensis), an herbaceous monocotyledon. The second leaves are shaded. Leaves are typically in two rows, alternating on opposite sides of the stem.*
(a) Vegetative morphology. (b) Floral morphology – the inflorescence. (c) Detail of one open flower or floret: two small petal-like structures (lodicules) which enclose the ovary have been omitted.

Ferns

2.5 How are ferns better adapted to life on land than liverworts or mosses?

2.6 In what main respects are mosses, liverworts and ferns poorly adapted to life on land?

Seed-bearing plants – conifers and flowering plants

One of the main problems for plants living on land is the vulnerability of the gametophyte generation. For example, in ferns the gametophyte is a delicate prothallus and it produces male gametes, or sperm, dependent on water for swimming. In seed plants, however, the gametophyte generation is protected and very much reduced.

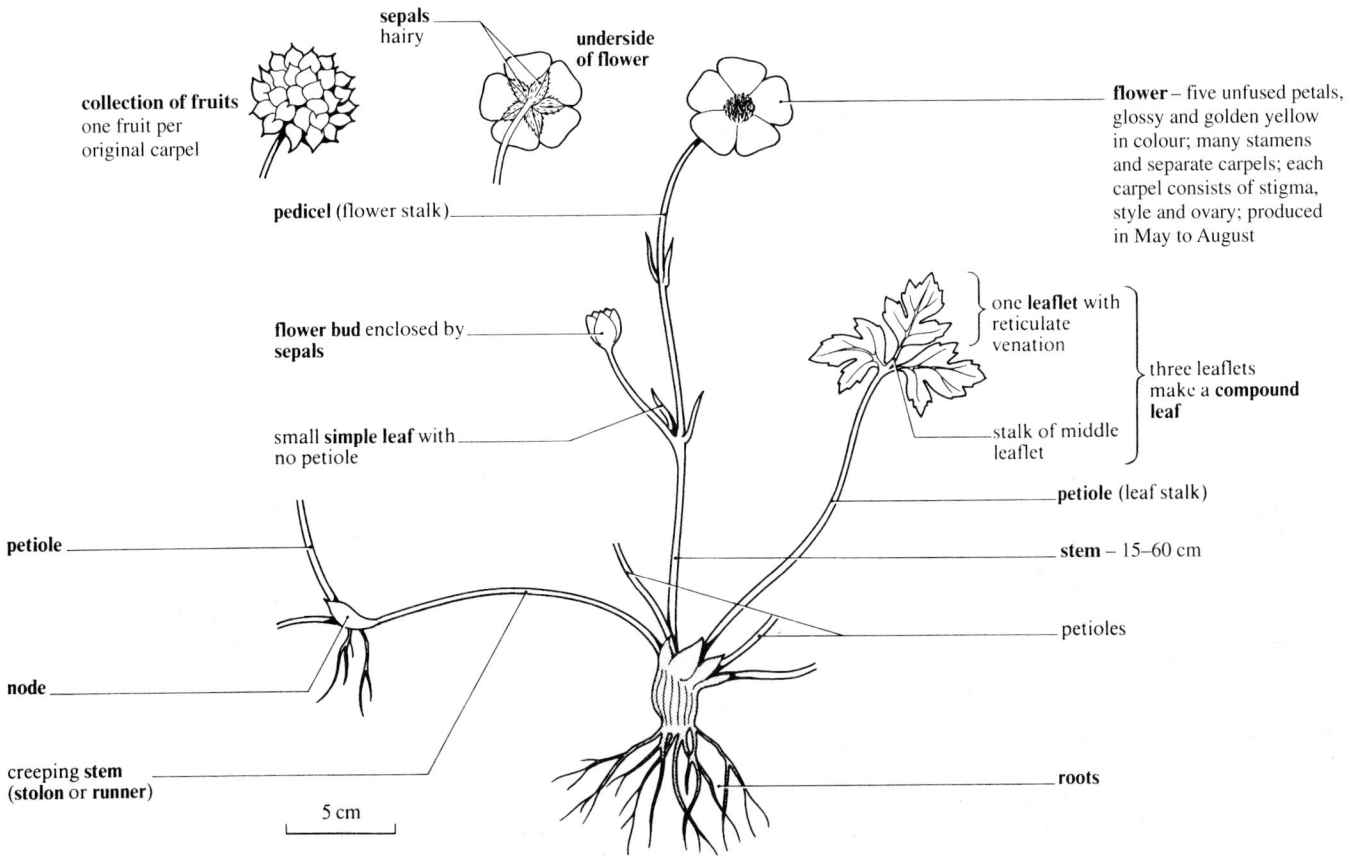

Fig 2.42 *Vegetative and floral morphology of the creeping buttercup (*Ranunculus repens*), an herbaceous dicotyledon. It is a common perennial plant throughout Britain, found in wet fields, woods, gardens and on waste ground.*

Three important advances have been made by seed plants, first the development of two types of spore (heterospory), secondly the development of non-swimming gametes and thirdly the development of seeds.

Heterospory and non-swimming male gametes. An important evolutionary advance was made when certain ferns and their close relatives developed two types of spore. This is known as **heterospory**, and the plants are described as heterosporous. *All* seed-bearing plants are heterosporous. They produce large spores called **megaspores** in one type of sporangium (megasporangium) and small spores called **microspores** in another type of sporangium (microsporangium). When spores grow they form gametophytes (fig 2.34). Megaspores produce female gametophytes and microspores produce male gametophytes. In seed-bearing plants the gametophytes produced by megaspores and microspores are very small and never released from the spores. Thus the gametophytes are protected from desiccation, an evolutionary advance. However, sperms from the male gametophyte still have to travel to the female gametophyte. This is made easier by dispersal of the microspores. Being very small they can be produced in large numbers and blown away from the parent sporophyte by wind. By chance they can be brought into closer proximity to the megaspores, which in seed plants stay attached to the parent sporophyte (fig 2.45). This is the basis of **pollination** in seed plants, where microspores are in fact the pollen grains. Inside the pollen grains male gametes form.

In seed plants another evolutionary advance has occurred. The male gametes no longer have to swim to the female gametes because seed plants have evolved pollen tubes. These grow from the pollen grains to the female gametes and deliver the male gametes. There are no longer any swimming sperm, just male nuclei.

Thus for the first time, plants evolved a mechanism for fertilisation which was not dependent on water. This is one of the main reasons why seed plants are so much more successful than other plants at exploiting dry land. Pollination was originally achieved by wind, a fairly haphazard process involving large wastage of pollen. However, early in the evolution of seed plants flying insects appeared (in the Carboniferous era about 300 million years ago) bringing the possibility of more efficient pollination by insects. The flowering plants have exploited this method to a high degree, although conifers are still wind-pollinated.

Seeds. In the early heterosporous plants, megaspores were released from the parent sporophyte like the microspores. However, in the seed plants megaspores are retained on the parent plant within the megasporangium.

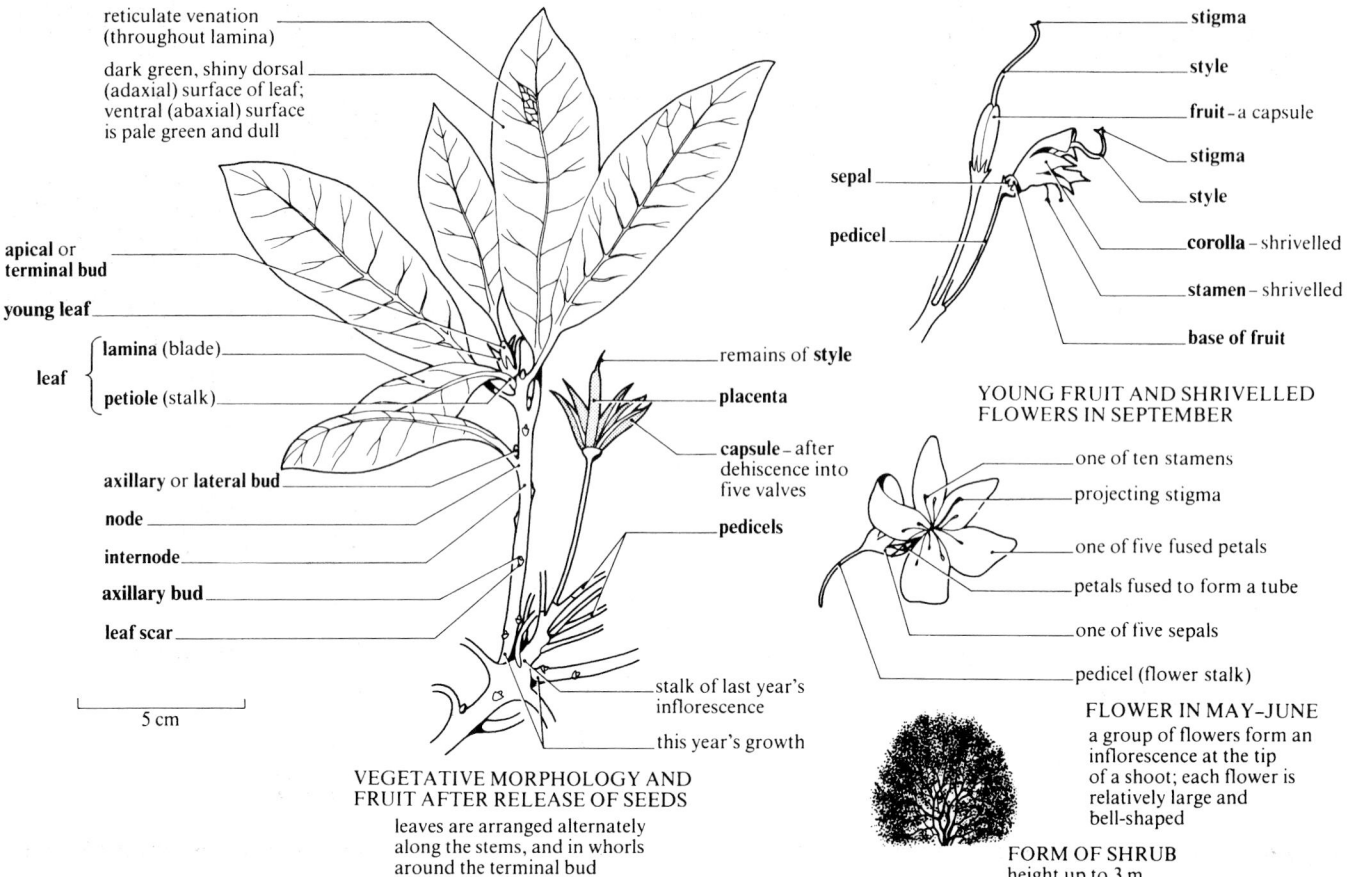

Fig 2.43 *Vegetative and floral morphology of the wild rhododendron,* R. ponticum, *an evergreen dicotyledonous shrub. It is commonly planted in woods and gardens. Originally introduced, it has become naturalised, favouring acid soils (sandy or peaty) on heaths and in woods.*

This is known as an **ovule** in seed plants (fig 2.45). The ovule contains the female gamete. Once this is fertilised the ovule is known as the **seed**. Thus a seed is a fertilised ovule. The ovule/seed brings the following advantages.

- The female gametophyte is protected by the ovule. It is totally dependent upon the parent sporophyte and is not susceptible to desiccation as would be a free-living gametophyte.
- After fertilisation it develops a food store, supplied by the parent sporophyte plant to which it is still attached. The food will be used by the developing zygote (the next sporophyte generation) at germination.
- The seed is specialised to resist adverse conditions and can remain dormant until conditions are suitable for germination.
- The seed may be modified to facilitate dispersal from the parent gametophyte.

The seed is a complex structure because it contains cells from three generations, a parent sporophyte, a female gametophyte and the embryo of the next sporophyte generation. All the essentials for life are supplied by the parent sporophyte and it is not until the seed is mature,

containing a food store and an embryo sporophyte, that it is dispersed from the parent sporophyte.

> **2.7** The chances of survival and development of wind-blown pollen grains (microspores) are much less than those of spores of *Dryopteris*. Why?
>
> **2.8** Suggest reasons for the fact that megaspores are large and microspores are small.

2.7.7 Summary of adaptations of seed-bearing plants to life on land

The major advantages that seed plants have over other plants are as follows.

- The gametophyte generation is very reduced. It is always protected inside a sporophyte, which is well adapted for life on land, and is totally dependent on the sporophyte. In other plants the gametophyte is susceptible to drying out.
- Fertilisation is not dependent on water. The male gametes are non-motile and carried within pollen

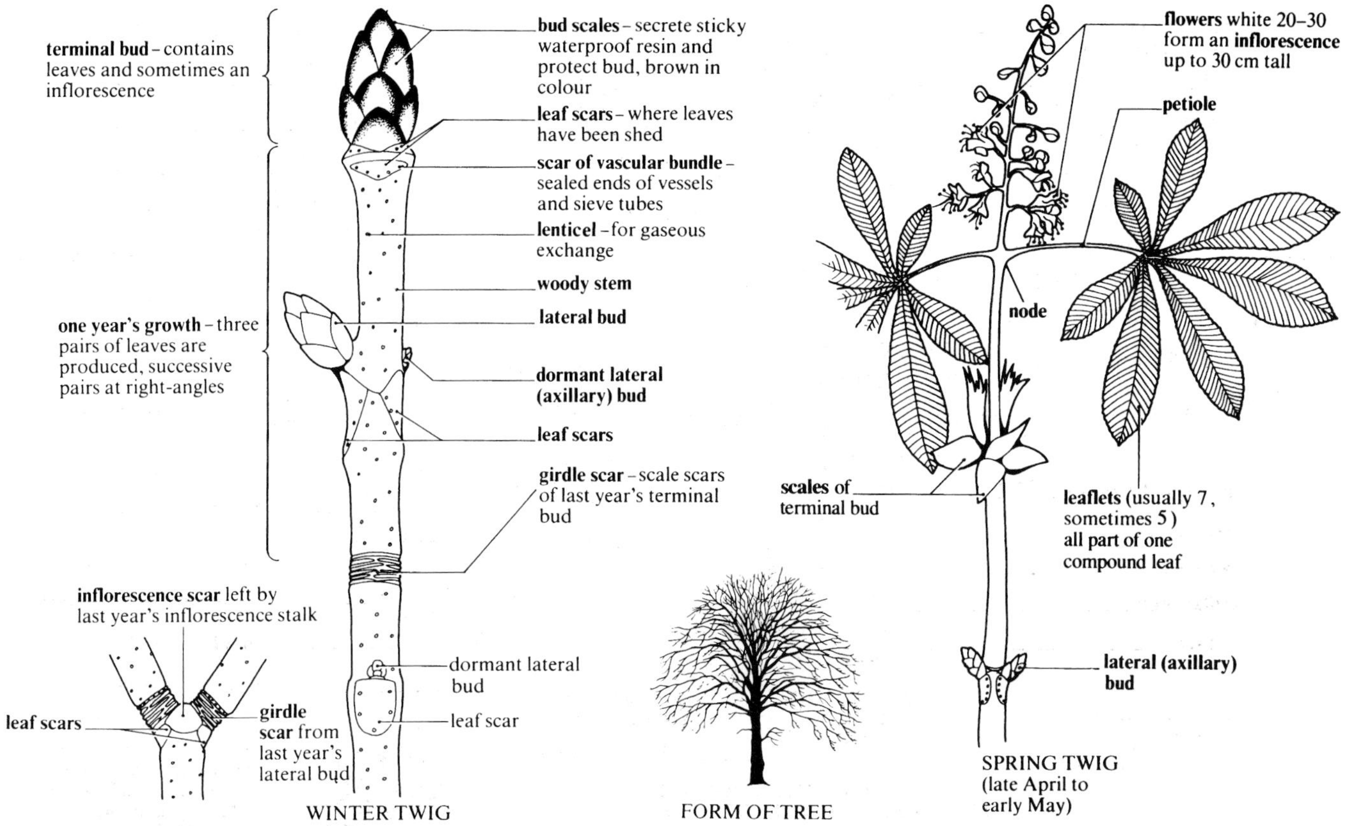

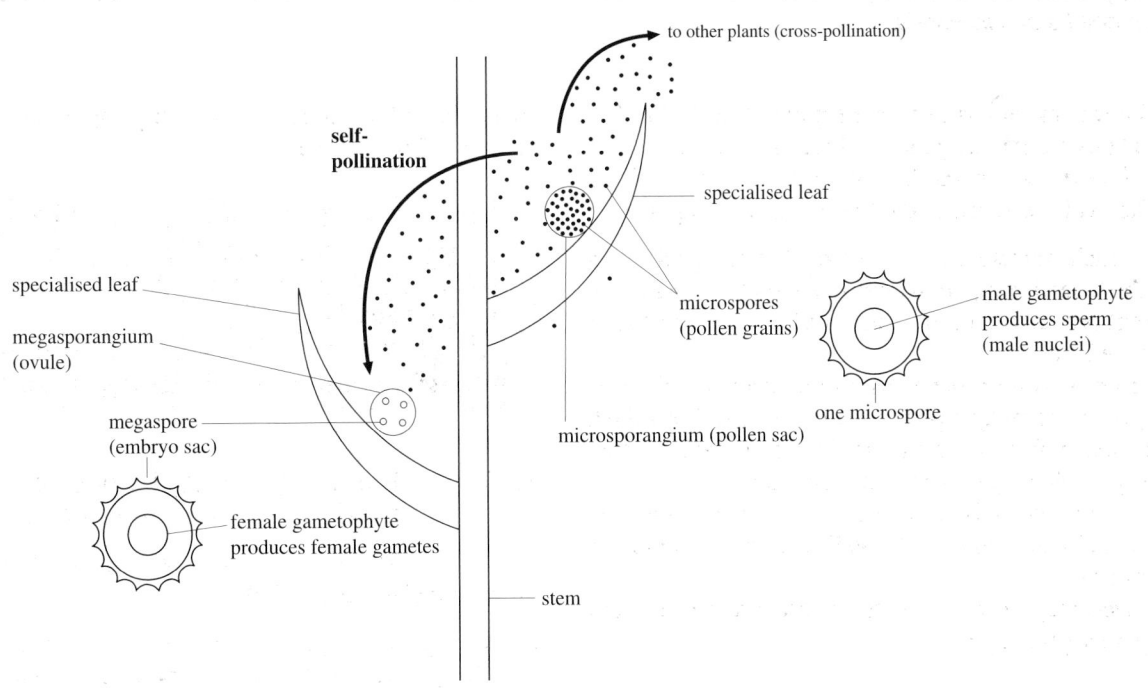

Fig 2.44 *Vegetative and floral morphology of the horse chestnut* (Aesculus hippocastanum)*, a deciduous dicotyledonous tree. The tree may reach 30 m or more in height.*

WINTER TWIG

terminal bud – contains leaves and sometimes an inflorescence

bud scales – secrete sticky waterproof resin and protect bud, brown in colour

leaf scars – where leaves have been shed

scar of vascular bundle – sealed ends of vessels and sieve tubes

lenticel – for gaseous exchange

woody stem

lateral bud

one year's growth – three pairs of leaves are produced, successive pairs at right-angles

dormant lateral (axillary) bud

leaf scars

girdle scar – scale scars of last year's terminal bud

inflorescence scar left by last year's inflorescence stalk

leaf scars

girdle scar from last year's lateral bud

dormant lateral bud

leaf scar

FORM OF TREE

SPRING TWIG (late April to early May)

flowers white 20–30 form an **inflorescence** up to 30 cm tall

petiole

node

scales of terminal bud

leaflets (usually 7, sometimes 5) all part of one compound leaf

lateral (axillary) bud

Fig 2.45 *Diagram illustrating the principles of heterospory and pollination.*

to other plants (cross-pollination)

self-pollination

specialised leaf

microspores (pollen grains)

male gametophyte produces sperm (male nuclei)

one microspore

specialised leaf

megasporangium (ovule)

megaspore (embryo sac)

microsporangium (pollen sac)

female gametophyte produces female gametes

stem

grains dispersed by wind or insects. Final transfer of the male gametes to the female gametes after pollination is by means of pollen tubes.

- The fertilised ovule (seed) is retained for some time on the parent sporophyte from which it obtains protection and food before dispersal.
- Many seed plants show secondary growth with production of large amounts of wood. This provides support. Such plants become trees or shrubs and are able to compete effectively for light and other resources.

Some of the important evolutionary trends are summarised in fig 2.33. Seed plants have other features which are not unique to them as a group but which are also adaptations to life on land.

- True roots enable water in the soil to be reached.
- The plant is protected from desiccation by an epidermis with a waterproof cuticle (or by cork after secondary growth has taken place).
- The epidermis of aerial parts, particularly leaves, has many small holes, called **stomata**, which allow gaseous exchange between plant and atmosphere.
- Plants can show specialised adaptations to hot dry environments (chapters 19 and 20).

2.8   Kingdom Animalia (animals)

2.8.1   Evolutionary trends

Animals make up one of the four eukaryote kingdoms, as shown in fig 2.4. They are all multicellular, since the animal-like unicellular organisms are placed in the Protoctista. They differ from plants in being heterotrophic rather than autotrophic. They differ from fungi, which are also multicellular, heterotrophic eukaryotes, in the way they obtain their food. Fungi can be described as absorptive and animals ingestive. Fungi digest food outside their bodies and absorb the products, whereas animal nutrition typically involves **ingestion** (taking in of food) followed by digestion inside the body. Any undigested food is **egested** (got rid of outside the body). A number of feeding habits have developed, including carnivorous, herbivorous, omnivorous and parasitic modes of life. Whereas fungi grow on their food, animals often have to seek it. If they do, this requires locomotion, the ability of the animal to move from one place to another, and this in turn requires a nervous system with sense organs and effectors. Locomotion of larger animals requires muscles and a skeleton, which is also needed for support.

In studying animals, we shall be looking at the evolutionary trends which have led to more and more complex levels of organisation within their bodies. One group of animals, the sponges (fig 2.46), do not form true tissues (table 2.12), but in all other animals tissues are formed. A **tissue** is a group of cells, often similar in structure and origin, operating together to perform a

Fig 2.46   *Breadcrumb sponge* (Halichondria panicea).

specialised function. Many different tissues can be formed, each performing a different function. This is called **differentiation** or **division of labour**. The same principle operates at the subcellular level, with different cell organelles showing specialisation for different functions.

Division of labour generally increases efficiency. Higher levels of organisation than the tissue occur. A number of tissues working together form an **organ**, such as the stomach, and a group of organs working together forms a **system**, such as the digestive system. The various systems together make the organism.

Just as the activity of cells is coordinated within a tissue, so organs and systems must be coordinated. This is achieved by hormones and a nervous system. As we shall see, the evolutionary development of more complex tissues, organs and systems was also accompanied by basic changes in body plan and, eventually, the need for transport systems within the body, particularly a blood system. Blood is a liquid tissue which is circulated by contractile vessels or a heart.

Table 2.12 Characteristics of the phylum Porifera (sponges).

Phylum Porifera

Characteristic features
Some cell differentiation, but no tissue organisation
Body has two layers of cells
Adults do not show locomotion
All marine
Body frequently lacks symmetry
Single body cavity
Numerous pores in body wall
Usually a skeleton of calcareous or silica-rich spicules, or horny fibres
No differentiated nervous system
Asexual reproduction by budding
All are hermaphrodite
Great regenerative power
'Dead-end' phylum – it has not given rise to any other group of organisms

Representatives of the main animal phyla will now be studied to examine some of the more important of these developments.

2.8.2 Phylum Cnidaria (cnidarians)

Classification and characteristics of the Cnidaria (the C is not pronounced), are summarised in table 2.13. The cnidarians include jellyfish, sea anemones and corals.

Diploblastic

The body plan is relatively simple, consisting of two layers of cells, an outer **ectoderm** and an inner **endoderm** as shown in fig 2.47. This is known as the diploblastic level of organisation. The ectodermal cells face outwards into the environment and the endodermal cells face inwards into the **enteron**, a cavity with a single opening to the environment, the 'mouth'. Feeding is by means of tentacles arranged around the mouth. Both ingestion (taking in food) and egestion (getting rid of undigested food) take place through this opening. There is some specialisation of cells, so it can be argued that the tissue level of organisation has been achieved. For example, batteries of stinging cells known as **nematoblasts** occur in the ectoderm of the tentacles. These can discharge threads of three types which can penetrate, cling to or kill the prey. The ectoderm also contains sensory cells, which connect with nerve cells, forming a communication network through the mesogloea. Cells containing contractile, muscle-like fibrils allow movement of the body and tentacles, and locomotion in jellyfish. In the endoderm are cells specialised for various aspects of digestion and absorption.

Radial symmetry

Cnidarians are radially symmetrical, meaning that they can be cut in half across any diameter and the two halves will be identical (like a cake). Radial symmetry tends to be associated with organisms which do not show locomotion (see also echinoderms, section 2.8.8). Most animals show bilateral symmetry (associated with locomotion) which not only gives a more compact and streamlined shape but allows greater specialisation of body parts.

Polyps, medusae and polymorphism

Two basic body types occur in the cnidarians, the polyp and the medusa (see fig 2.47). The **polyp** is cylindrical and **sessile**. A sessile organism is one that remains attached to a surface such as a rock throughout its life and shows little or no locomotion. The **medusa** is umbrella-shaped and free-swimming or floating. The two types sometimes alternate in the life cycle, in which case the medusa can act as a dispersal stage (see *Obelia* below). In this situation polyps reproduce asexually by budding off medusae, and the medusae reproduce sexually to produce larvae which develop into polyps. Individual polyps within colonies can also vary in form. For example, they may be specialised for feeding or for asexual reproduction (see *Obelia* below). The situation in which individuals of a species exist in two or more different forms is known as **polymorphism**.

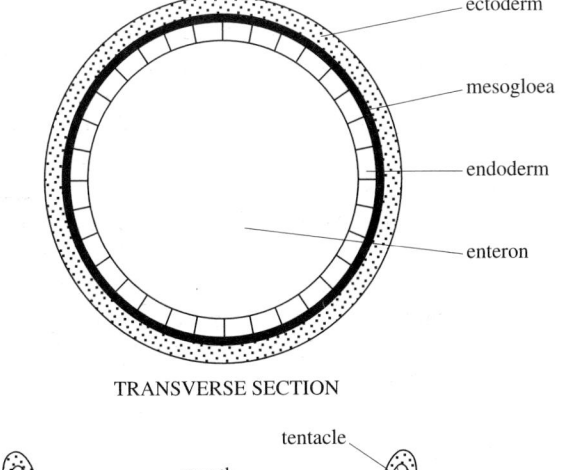

TRANSVERSE SECTION

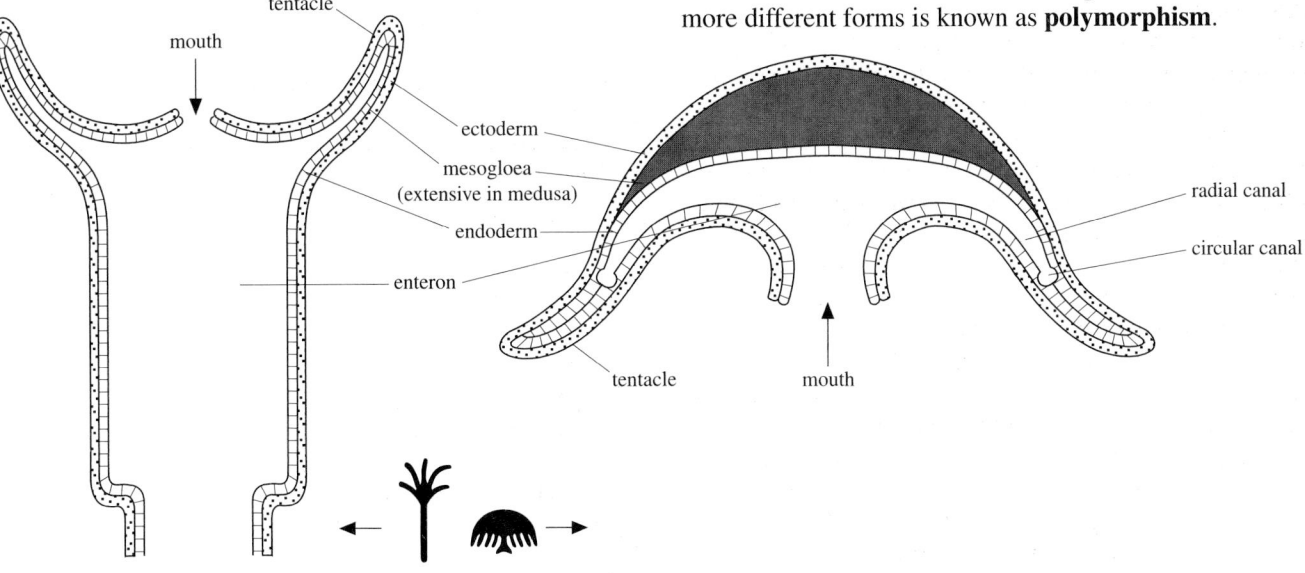

polyp

medusa

Fig 2.47 *Body plan of cnidarians.*

Table 2.13 Classification and characteristics of the phylum Cnidaria (cnidarians).

Phylum Cnidaria

Characteristic features
Diploblastic animals: body wall composed of two layers of cells, an outer **ectoderm** and an inner **endoderm**; these layers are separated by a structureless, gelatinous layer of **mesogloea** which may contain cells that have migrated from other layers*
Tissue level of organisation achieved
Radial symmetry
Body is basically sac-shaped with a single opening, the 'mouth', for ingestion and egestion. The single cavity within the sac is called the **enteron** and is where digestion takes place
Two structural types, **polyps** and **medusae**. Polyps are sessile (stay in one place) and may be solitary, e.g. *Hydra,* or colonial, e.g. *Obelia.* Medusae are free-swimming and solitary*
Polymorphism exhibited, that is individuals have specialised shapes with different functions – a form of division of labour

Class Hydrozoa (hydroids*)*	*Class Scyphozoa* (jellyfish*)*	*Class Anthozoa* (corals and sea anemones*)*
Polyp dominant in life cycle	Small polyp sometimes present as a larval stage	Polyp only – more complex than those of the Hydrozoa
Medusa simple	Large highly organised medusa dominant in life cycle	No medusa
Polyps solitary or colonial		Polyps solitary (anemones, some corals) or colonial (most corals)
Nematoblasts (stinging cells)	Nematoblasts	Nematoblasts
e.g. *Hydra* (no medusa phase) *Obelia*	e.g. *Aurelia* (jellyfish)	e.g. *Actinia* (beadlet anemone) *Madrepora* (coral)

* diagnostic features.

Size

Cnidarians are still relatively small animals. The few large jellyfish consist mainly of mesogloea which is not made of living cells. With only two layers of cells, nutrients can diffuse rapidly from the feeding cells in the endoderm to the ectoderm. In addition, all cells are in direct contact with the water of the environment, so gaseous exchange can take place very efficiently by diffusion. The organism has a large surface area to volume ratio.

Fig 2.48 shows a variety of cnidarians. *Obelia, Aurelia* and *Actinia* are all marine species (live in the sea). *Obelia* is a good example of polymorphism, with colonial polyps alternating with a small jellyfish stage in the life cycle. It is common in shallow waters attached to rocks, shells, the fronds of large seaweeds or piers. *Actinia* is very common around the shores of Britain, particularly in sheltered places such as cracks in rocks and rock pools.

2.8.3 Phylum Platyhelminthes (flatworms)

Classification and characteristics of the Platyhelminthes are summarised in table 2.14.

The triploblastic condition

This is the condition in which a third layer, called the **mesoderm** develops in the embryo. This separates the ectoderm from the endoderm (fig 2.55a). The presence of mesoderm in the body is significant for several reasons.

- It allows triploblastic organisms to increase in size and this results in considerable separation of the alimentary canal from the body wall.
- It has been used to form a variety of organs, which may combine together and contribute towards an organ system level of organisation. Examples of such systems include the central nervous system and digestive, excretory and reproductive systems.
- It enables the improvement of the muscular activity of triploblastic organisms. This is necessary as their increased size renders the ciliary or flagellar mode of locomotion inadequate.

This increase in size, however, poses problems of transport of materials between the endodermal and ectodermal layers. In some animals the mesoderm completely fills the space between the endoderm and ectoderm (the **acoelomate condition**, fig 2.55a), in which case the transport problems are overcome by a flattening of the body, so maintaining a large surface area in relation to volume. Thus diffusion of materials between environment

Fig 2.48 *A variety of cnidarians.* (a) Hydra *– a freshwater, solitary cnidarian.* (b) Obelia *– a marine, colonial cnidarian with two types of polyp and a medusoid form.* (c) Aurelia *– a jellyfish.* (d) Actinia *– a sea anemone.* (e) Aurelia *medusa.* (f) Obelia *colony.* (g) Hydra. (e)–(g) overleaf.

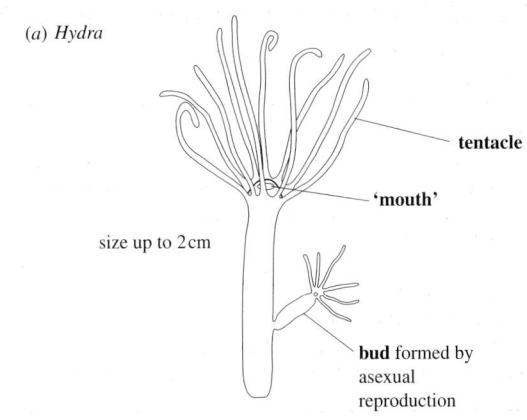

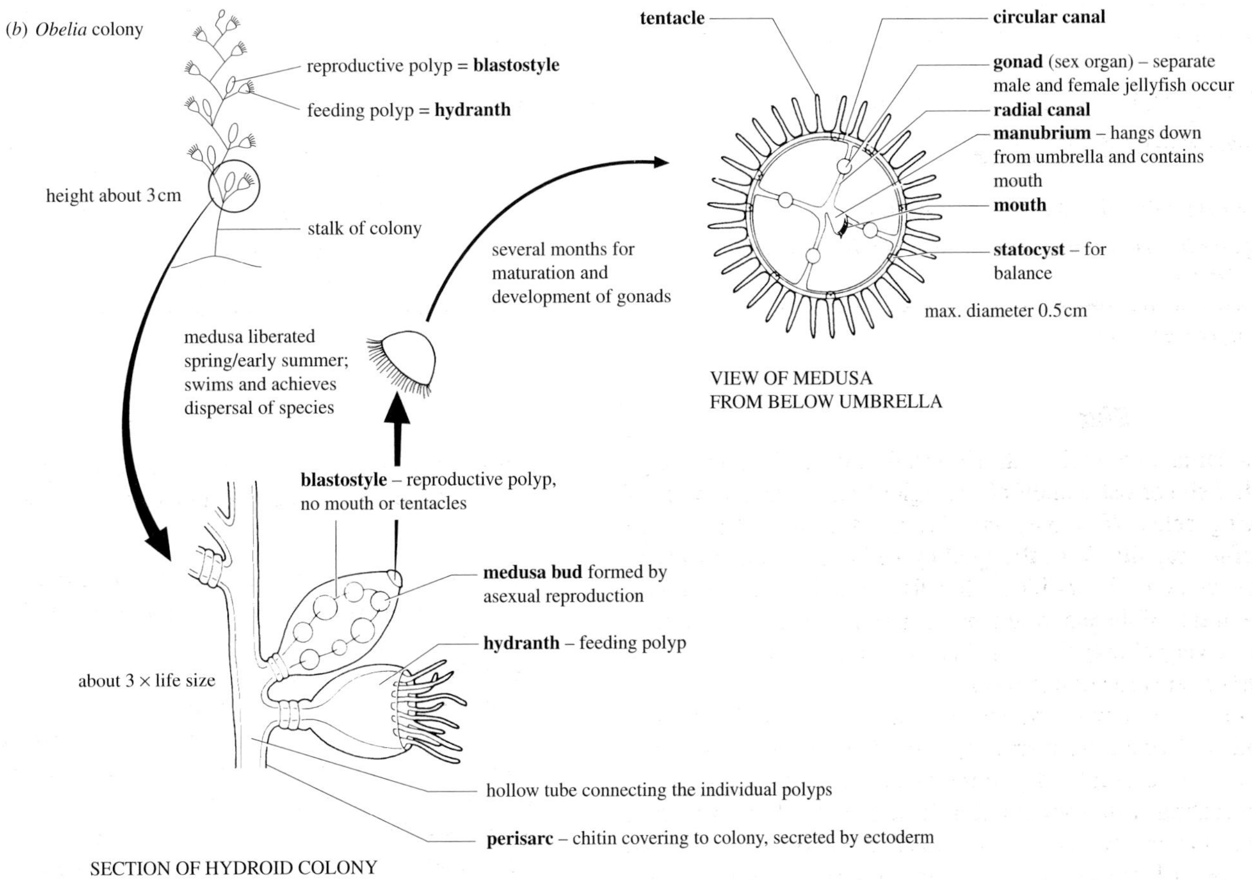

(a) *Hydra*

tentacle

'mouth'

size up to 2 cm

bud formed by asexual reproduction

(b) *Obelia* colony

reproductive polyp = **blastostyle**

feeding polyp = **hydranth**

height about 3 cm

stalk of colony

several months for maturation and development of gonads

medusa liberated spring/early summer; swims and achieves dispersal of species

blastostyle – reproductive polyp, no mouth or tentacles

medusa bud formed by asexual reproduction

hydranth – feeding polyp

about 3 × life size

hollow tube connecting the individual polyps

perisarc – chitin covering to colony, secreted by ectoderm

SECTION OF HYDROID COLONY

tentacle

circular canal

gonad (sex organ) – separate male and female jellyfish occur

radial canal

manubrium – hangs down from umbrella and contains mouth

mouth

statocyst – for balance

max. diameter 0.5 cm

VIEW OF MEDUSA
FROM BELOW UMBRELLA

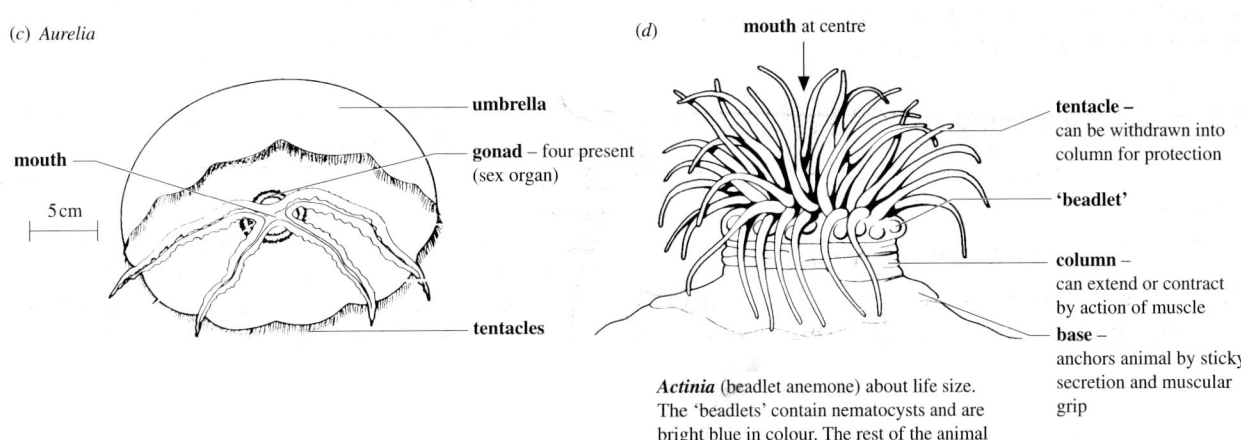

(c) *Aurelia*

mouth

5 cm

umbrella

gonad – four present (sex organ)

tentacles

(d)

mouth at centre

tentacle – can be withdrawn into column for protection

'**beadlet**'

column – can extend or contract by action of muscle

base – anchors animal by sticky secretion and muscular grip

Actinia (beadlet anemone) about life size. The 'beadlets' contain nematocysts and are bright blue in colour. The rest of the animal is a dark red or olive green colour.

55

(e)

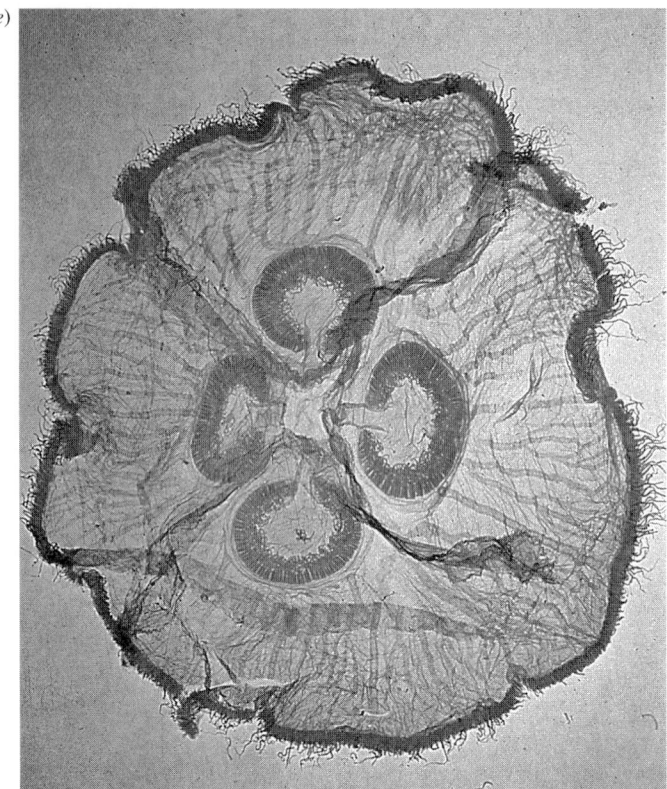

(f)

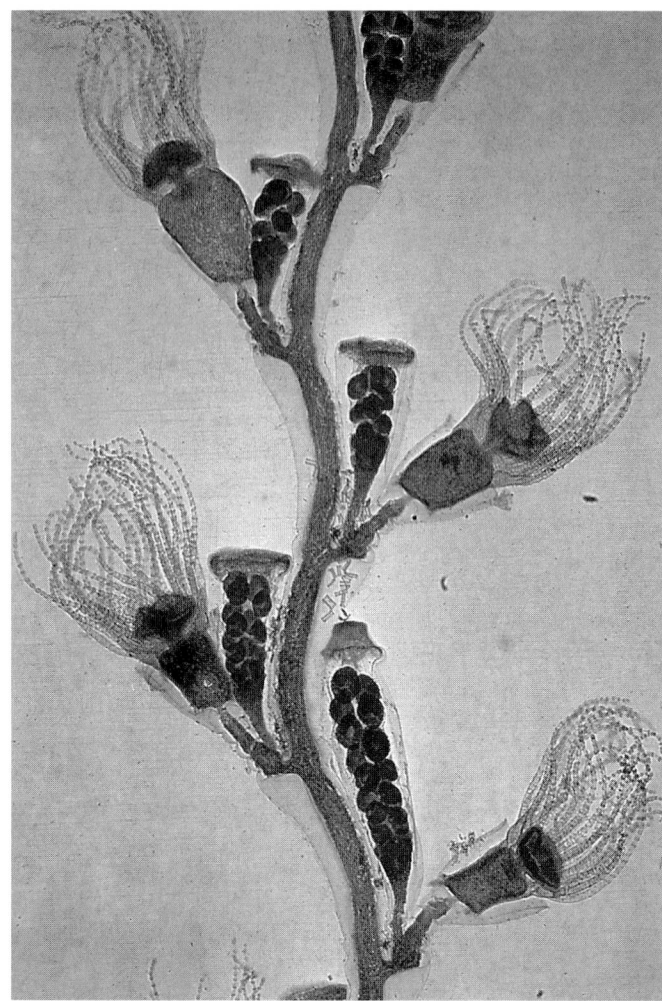

Fig 2.48 (cont.)

(g)

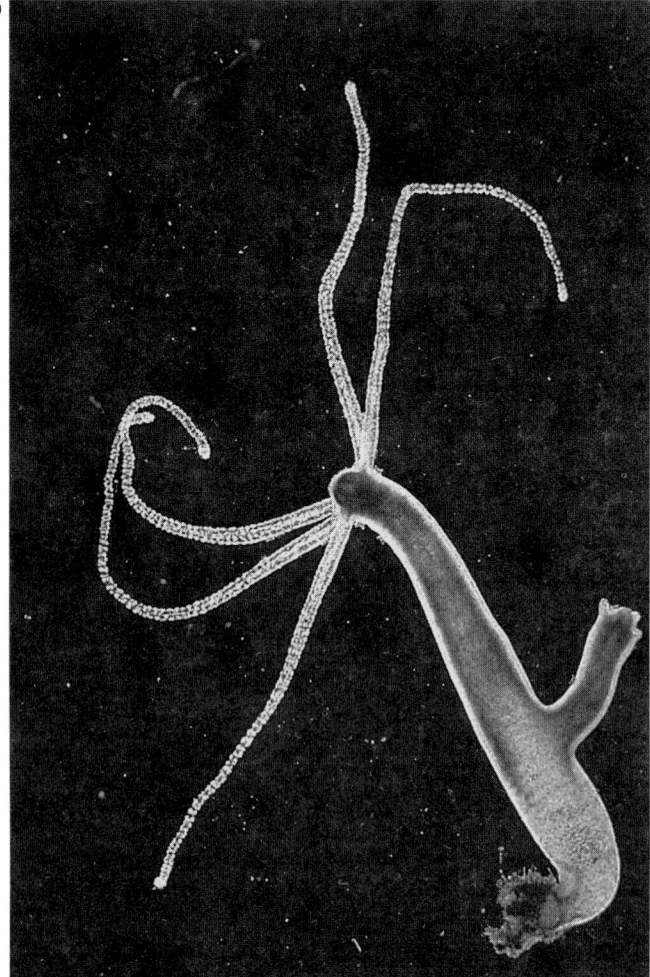

and tissues is rapid enough to satisfy metabolic requirements. In other animals a space (the **coelom**) develops within the mesoderm (the **coelomate condition**) and transport systems are developed which carry materials from one part of the body to another.

The platyhelminths are constructed on the triploblastic body plan and are the earliest animals to have developed organs and organ systems from the mesoderm. They are acoelomate and therefore have flat bodies – hence their common name of flatworms. Much of the mesoderm remains undifferentiated and forms a packing tissue, the **mesenchyme**, which supports and protects the organs of the body.

The phylum is divided into three classes; two of these are completely parasitic, whereas the other class, the most typical, contains free-living forms. The platyhelminths possess a clearly differentiated 'head' situated **anteriorly** (at the front), and a distinct **posterior** (back) end. There are clearly defined **dorsal** (upper) and **ventral** (lower) surfaces. Many structures (such as eyes) are symmetrically arranged on the right- and left-hand sides of the body. Such organisation, where the right side is approximately the mirror image of the left and where there is a distinct anterior end, is called **bilateral symmetry**.

Table 2.14 Classification and characteristics of the phylum Platyhelminthes (flatworms).

Phylum Platyhelminthes

Characteristic features
Triploblastic
Bilateral symmetry
Unsegmented (like nematode worms, unlike annelid worms)
Acoelomate
Flattened shape
Mouth but no anus

Class Turbellaria (turbellarians)	*Class Trematoda* (flukes)	*Class Cestoda* (tapeworms)
Free living; aquatic	Endoparasitic (live inside host) or ectoparasitic (live on outer surface of host)	Endoparasitic (live inside host)
Delicate, soft body	Leaf-like shape	Elongated body divided into proglottides which are able to break off
Suckers rarely present	Usually ventral sucker in addition to sucker on 'head' for attachment to host	Suckers and hooks on 'head' (scolex) for attachment to host
Outer suface covered with cilia for locomotion; cuticle absent	Thick cuticle with spines (protection); no cilia in adult (locomotion not needed because not parasitic)	Thick cuticle (protection); no cilia in adult
Enteron present	Enteron present	No enteron (no digestion required – absorbs predigested food from host)
Sense organs in adult	Sense organs only in free-living larval stages	Sense organs only in free-living larval stages
e.g. *Planaria*	e.g. *Fasciola* (liver fluke) *Schistosoma* (blood fluke) – cause of schistosomiasis (bilharzia) in many tropical countries	e.g. *Taenia* (tapeworm)

No transport system has developed, because in the basic body structure all parts are in close proximity to food and oxygen supplies. All platyhelminths are thin and flat, providing a large surface area to volume ratio for gaseous exchange. Many forms possess a much-branched gut, which ramifies throughout the body to facilitate absorption of food materials. In addition, excretory material is collected from all parts by a branched system of excretory tubes.

Class Turbellaria

Planaria is a free-living, carnivorous flatworm found in freshwater streams and ponds. It remains under stones during the day, emerging only at night to feed. It is black in colour and can measure up to 15 mm in length. It has an elongated, extremely flattened body, with a relatively broad anterior 'head' possessing a pair of eyes in the dorsal surface, and a posterior end that is clearly tapered. *Planaria* is bilaterally symmetrical, a body design associated with an active mode of life (fig 2.49).

There is a single gut opening, the mouth, which is located on its ventral surface towards the posterior end of the body. *Planaria* feeds on small worms, crustacea and on the dead bodies of larger organisms.

Class Trematoda

Fasciola hepatica, the liver fluke (fig 2.50), belongs to the class Trematoda, which is one of the major groups of

parasites in the animal kingdom. It is **endoparasitic**, meaning it lives inside its host. It lives in the bile ducts of sheep, its most important, or **primary**, **host**. Other primary hosts are cattle and, occasionally, humans.

Many differences exist between *Fasciola* and the free-living *Planaria*. These differences can be attributed to the adaptations that *Fasciola* has evolved in order to survive as an endoparasite. Associated with its parasitic mode of life is a complex life history, involving three larval stages (the miracidium, redia and cercaria), which provide opportunities for increasing its numbers during the life cycle. The large numbers of offspring produced in this way help to offset the high mortality rate that inevitably occurs during infection of new hosts. For a part of its life history *Fasciola* infests a **secondary host**, the freshwater snail (*Limnea*), in which some of its larval stages are able to live and multiply.

Each stage in the life history of *Fasciola* shows structural, physiological and reproductive adaptations suited to its mode of life. Some of these are listed below and shown in fig 2.50. The life cycle is summarised in fig 2.51.

Adult fluke. The body is thin and flat and attaches to the lining of the bile duct. The body wall protects the fluke against the host's enzymes. The gland cells situated here also secrete material which protects the parasite against the host's antitoxins.

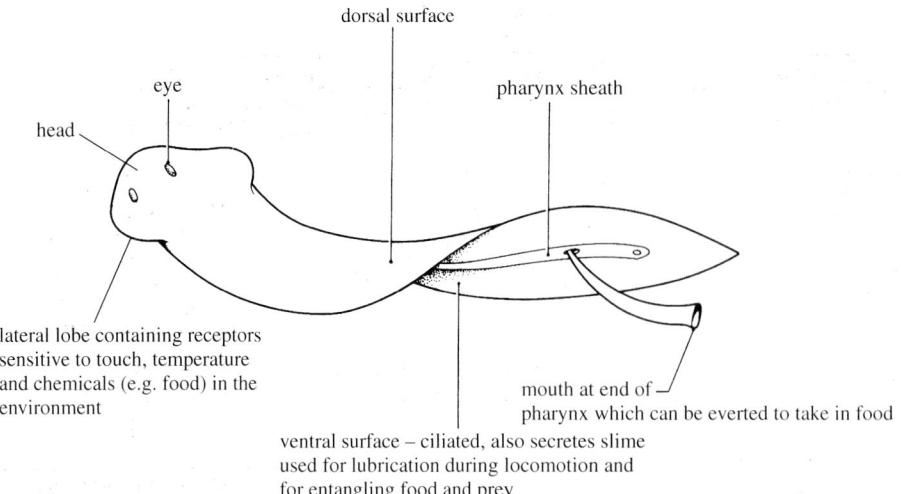

Fig 2.49 Planaria *showing external features.*

A **hermaphrodite** (male and female sex organs in the same organism) reproductive system ensures that self-fertilisation or cross-fertilisation can occur. The fluke can survive anaerobically if there is a shortage of oxygen.

Miracidium. This is the first of the larval stages of *Fasciola* (fig 2.51). Its main function is to find the secondary host, for which it needs sense organs and the ability to move. It also produces more larvae (sporocysts – see below). It has a ciliated epidermis which allows it to swim in water or in moisture on vegetation.

The miracidium is attracted to its secondary host, the freshwater snail, by chemotaxis (locomotion in a particular direction in response to a chemical stimulus). It attaches at its anterior end to the snail's foot, and a gland secretes protein-digesting enzymes onto the surface of the snail to help in the penetration of the host's tissues. Penetration is further helped by muscle cells which help the larva to wriggle through the tissues of the host. In this way it migrates to the digestive glands. There are special germ cells present inside the miracidium which give rise to the next larval forms.

Sporocyst. The function of this stage is to increase numbers to compensate for wastage of larvae that do not find hosts. It is an immobile, closed sac containing germ cells, which multiply to form many rediae, the next larval stage.

Redia. This is a multiplication and feeding stage. It has a muscular pharynx to suck in fluids and tissues from its host. Muscle cells aid locomotion of the larva. Germ cells multiply into more rediae, or into cercariae. There is a pore for the escape of the new rediae or the cercariae.

Cercaria. This bears many features in common with the adult fluke, which include oral and ventral suckers for anchorage to suitable substrates such as grass. There is also a tail to assist in locomotion through

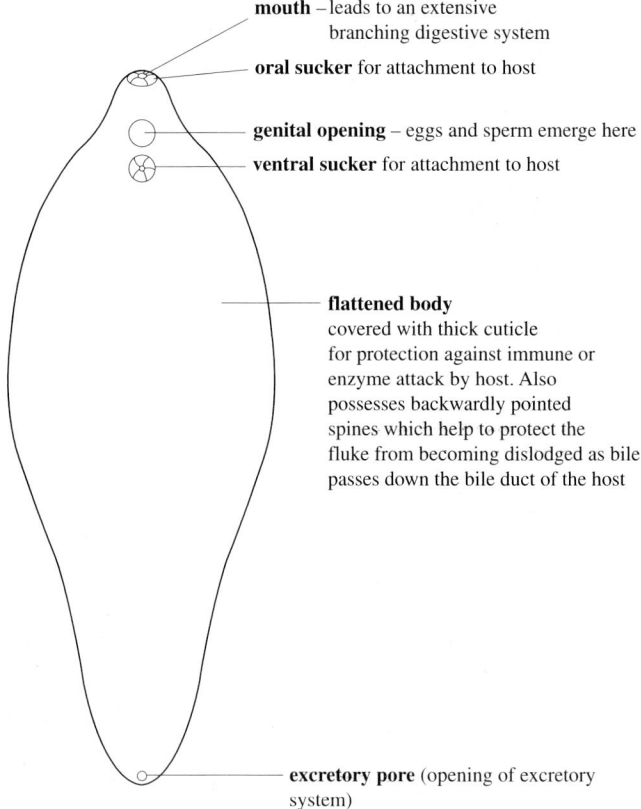

Fig 2.50 *External features of* Fasciola hepatica, *the liver fluke. The fluke lives in the bile duct of the host.*

water or moisture on vegetation. Glands are present which secrete a cyst wall (fig 2.51). The encysted cercaria undergoes no further development until it is swallowed by a sheep. It has considerable powers of resistance to low temperatures, but is susceptible to desiccation.

Limnea is an amphibious snail inhabiting ponds, muddy tracks and damp vegetation. It is able to withstand adverse conditions. Therefore the sporocyst and redia stages of

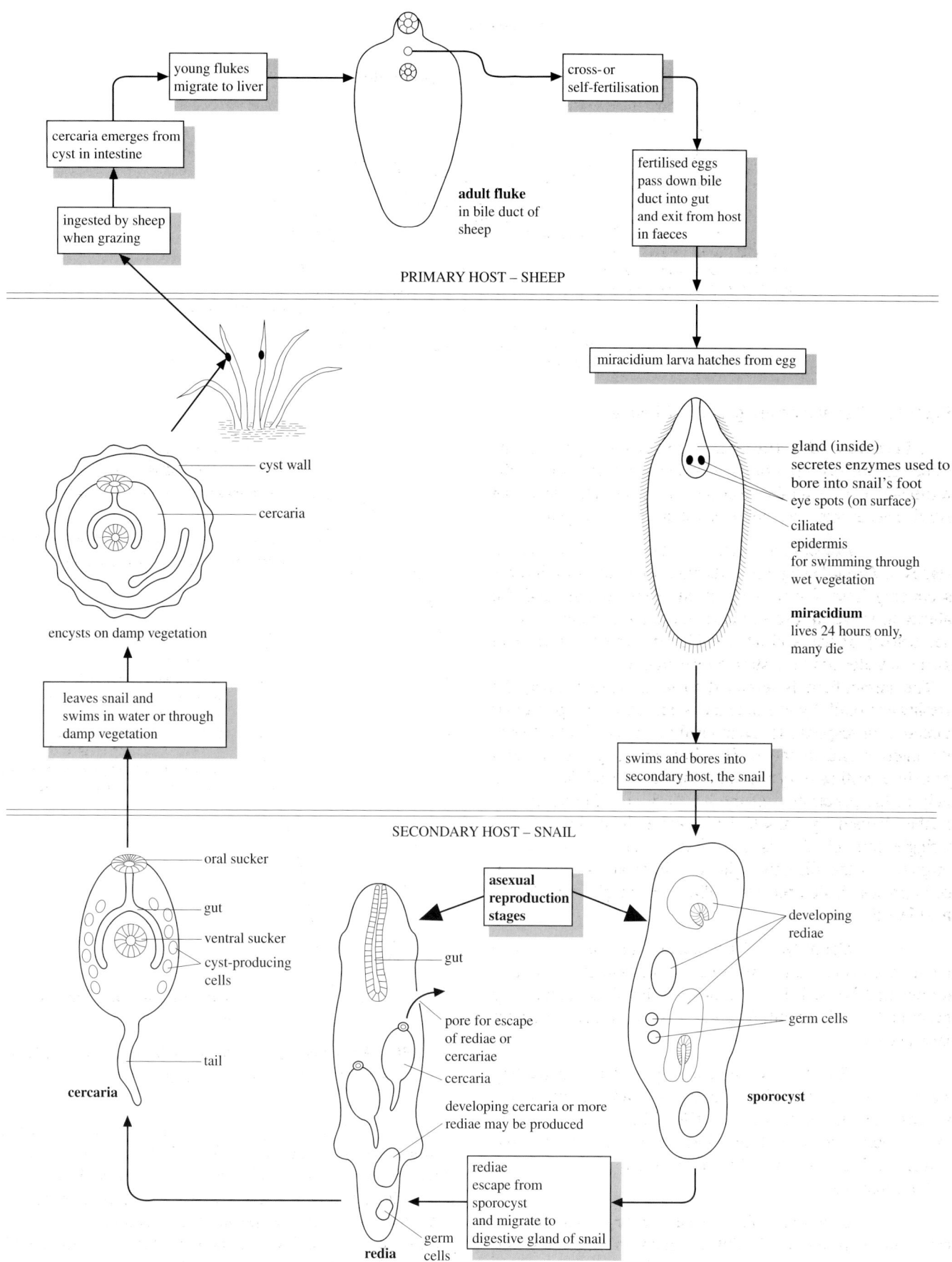

Fig 2.51 *Life cycle of* Fasciola hepatica, *the liver fluke.*

Fasciola's life history, which develop within the snail, are themselves directly protected from such unfavourable conditions. Indeed, in conditions of low temperature, rediae produce daughter rediae instead of cercariae. The rediae remain within the snail and can overwinter within the host, only producing cercariae when warmer weather returns in the spring. *Limnea* is also a very rapid breeder. It has been estimated that one snail may produce up to 160 000 offspring in 12 weeks. If all of these offspring contain developmental stages of *Fasciola,* then the chances of cercariae escaping from the snails and entering new, uninfected primary hosts will be considerably increased. The amphibious mode of life of *Limnea* ensures that when the cercariae escape there is water available in which to disperse.

The release of young adult flukes from the encysted cercaria takes place in the gut of the sheep or cow. The process is initiated in the stomach by high carbon dioxide levels and a temperature of around 39 °C. Under these conditions the parasite releases protein-digesting enzymes which digest a hole in the cyst wall. Emergence of young flukes is triggered off by the presence of bile in the digestive juices of the small intestine.

The young flukes burrow through the intestinal wall and migrate to the liver. For a time they feed on liver tissue, but about six weeks after infection they become permanently attached in the bile ducts.

Fasciola can have several effects on its primary host. A heavy infection can cause death. Liver metabolism of the host is interfered with when the young flukes migrate through it. Cells are destroyed and bile ducts may be blocked; large-scale erosion of the liver (liver rot) will cause dropsy. Little, or absence of, bile in the gut can affect digestion, and the excretory wastes of *Fasciola* can have a toxic effect on the host.

The following measures can be taken against *Fasciola.* Drainage of the pasture land and introduction of snail-eating geese and ducks to the pastures (a method of biological control) will help to remove the secondary host *Limnea.* The filling in of ponds and use of elevated drinking troughs will also help to achieve this. Use of lime on the land will help to prevent the hatching of the eggs of the parasite, as they will not hatch in water with a pH of more than 7.5. For sheep which are already infected, the administration of carbon tetrachloride kills flukes in the liver.

2.8.4 Phylum Nematoda (nematodes or roundworms)

The nematodes are simple worms, with slender cylindrical bodies tapering at each end. Like platyhelminths they are triploblastic with no blood system. They are neither acoelomate nor coelomate (section 2.8.5), but have a simple internal body structure which we need not consider here. Although extremely common in water, soil (as many as 100 000 million per hectare), and a wide range of other habitats, these worms are mostly microscopic or too small to be seen easily. New species are constantly being discovered; one appears to be unique to German beer mats. The roundworms, flukes and tapeworms form the three largest groups of animal parasites. Their characteristics are summarised in table 2.15. An example is *Ascaris* (fig 2.52). One species, *Ascaris lumbricoides,* is a common parasite of the intestine of humans and pigs. It is a creamy white colour and relatively large, about the size of an earthworm (up to 20 cm long). Heavy infections can cause obstructions in the gut. The eggs, which pass out in the faeces, are very resistant and can survive for years. The male is smaller than the female and is more curved at its posterior end. Another well-known nematode parasite is *Wuchereria bancroftii,* which infects the human lymphatic system and causes elephantiasis (fig 2.53). The legs can

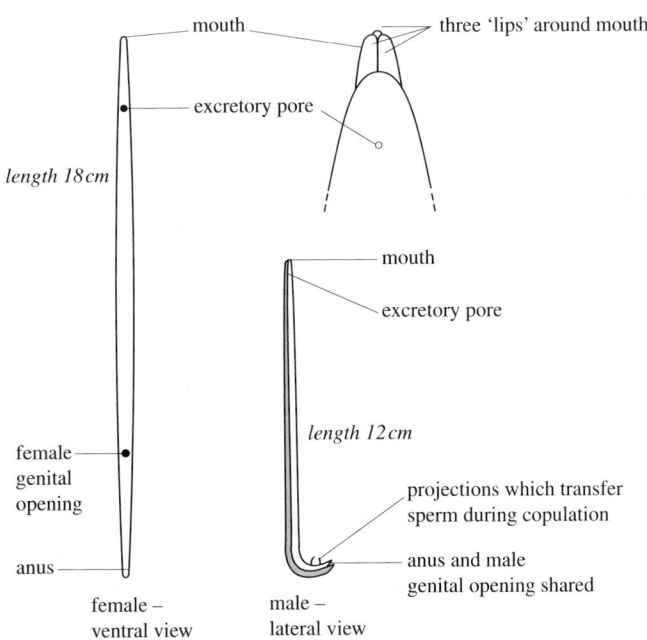

Fig 2.52 Ascaris lumbricoides, *a common gut parasite of humans and pigs.*

Table 2.15 Characteristics of the phylum Nematoda (nematodes or roundworms).

Phylum Nematoda

Characteristic features
Triploblastic
Bilateral symmetry
Elongated, round 'worms' with pointed ends*
Unsegmented (like flatworms, but unlike annelid worms)
Alimentary canal with mouth and anus
Sexes separate
Some free living, many important plant and animal parasites
Anterior end shows a degree of cephalisation (development of a head)

* diagnostic feature.

swell enormously, resembling those of an elephant. Nematodes can also attack plants, including a wide variety of crops.

2.8.5 Phylum Annelida (annelids or segmented worms)

Classification and characteristics of the annelids are summarised in table 2.16. A variety of annelids is illustrated in fig 2.54. *Nereis* and *Lumbricus* are described in more detail later. Annelids are coelomates.

The coelomate body plan

It has been seen in the platyhelminths that the mesoderm completely fills the space between the ectodermal and endodermal layers and forms a solid middle layer. Such a condition, without a coelom, is said to be **acoelomate** (fig 2.55*a*).

In the annelids and later animal groups, an extensive internal space or body cavity is developed, called a **coelom**. This arises as a split in the mesoderm during development of the embryo. The cavity formed is filled with coelomic fluid, and splits the mesoderm into two layers, the **somatic mesoderm** to the outside and the **splanchnic mesoderm** to the inside (fig 2.55*b*). The somatic mesoderm is attached to the ectoderm and these together form the body wall. The splanchnic mesoderm is attached to the endoderm to form the muscular wall of the gut. The coelom thus separates the body wall from the gut wall.

The majority of the mesoderm which lines the coelom develops into muscle; that of the body wall aids locomotion of the whole animal, whilst that of the gut causes peristalsis of food. Transport of materials between the gut wall and the body wall (and vice versa) is achieved by a well-developed blood vascular system. Note that the gut cavity is in the endoderm. The lining of the coelom is called the **peritoneum**. Portions of the peritoneum which connect the gut wall to the body wall across the coelom are called **mesenteries**. Any organs, such as reproductive or excretory organs, which project into the coelom are bounded by peritoneum (fig 2.55*b*).

Biological significance of the coelom

- Because the coelom separates the gut from the body wall, muscular movements of the body wall, associated with locomotion, can be separated from muscular movements of the gut wall, which move food through the gut (peristalsis) and help to churn the food. Greater powers of locomotion result, and different parts of the gut can become differentiated for different functions, for example a stomach for churning food. This allows a greater variety of diets.

- The coelom also provides a cavity in which organs can grow, develop and function independently of other organs.

- Increasing size and complexity are possible. These bring about additional problems of transport and

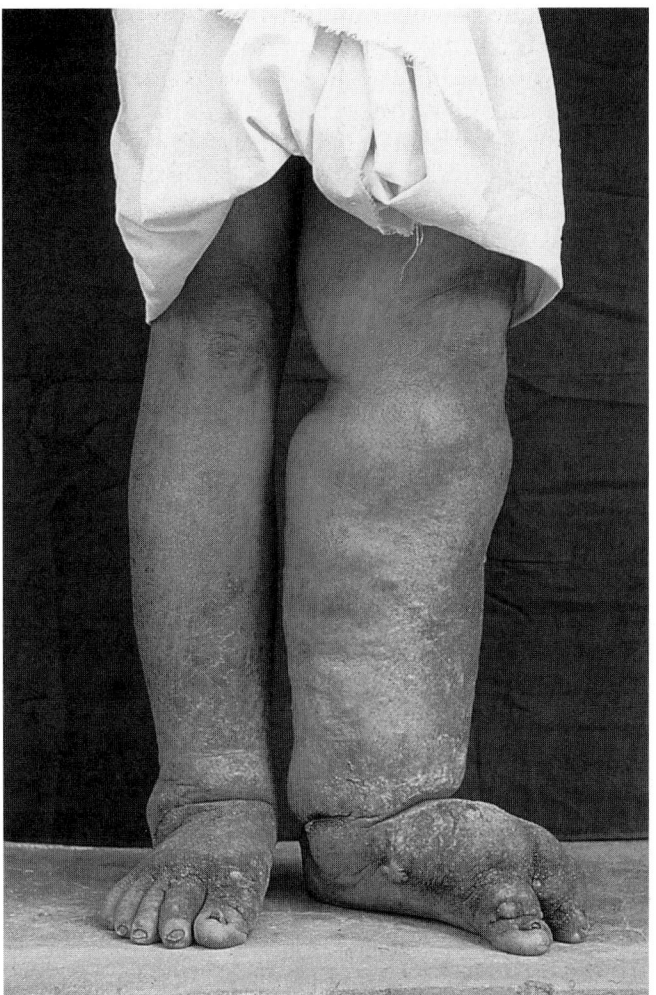

Fig 2.53 *Person suffering from elephantiasis.*

coordination. For example, food is digested in the gut, but the cells of the body wall are separated from the gut by the coelom. Similarly, the gut is some distance from the body surface where gaseous exchange takes place. As body size increases the problems get greater, as already noted at the beginning of section 2.8.3, and some kind of transport system becomes necessary. All coelomates possess a blood vascular system. A **vascular system** is a system of tubes. **Blood** is a liquid tissue which is circulated round the body by the pumping action of muscle in the walls of contractile vessels or a heart. These contain valves to maintain a one-way flow.

Greater complexity also requires more complex coordination and therefore a more elaborate nervous system. **Cephalisation** (development of a head) is part of this trend. (See also size and surface area:volume ratio below.)

- The coelom performs an additional specialised function in annelids. Here it acts as a **hydrostatic skeleton**, in other words a fluid skeleton. Skeletons serve three main functions, namely support, protection and locomotion. Being a liquid, coelomic fluid is incompressible.

Table 2.16 Classification of the phylum Annelida (annelids or segmented worms).

Phylum Annelida

Characteristic features
Triploblastic, coelomate
Bilateral symmetry
Metameric segmentation
Prostomium, a lip-like extension of the first segment situated above the mouth
Definite cuticle (outer covering)
Chaetae, hair-like structures made of chitin and arranged segmentally (except leeches)*

Class Polychaeta (polychaetes or bristleworms)	*Class Oligochaeta* (oligochaetes or earthworms)	*Class Hirudinea* (leeches)
Marine	Inhabit fresh water or damp earth	Ectoparasites with anterior and posterior suckers
Distinct head	No distinct head	No distinct head
Chaetae numerous on lateral extensions of the body called parapodia*	Few chaetae – in pairs or single, no parapodia*	Small fixed number of segments, no chaetae or parapodia*
No clitellum	Clitellum or 'saddle' which secretes a cocoon in which the eggs are deposited	No clitellum
e.g. *Arenicola* (lugworm) *Nereis* (ragworm)	e.g. *Lumbricus* (earthworm)	e.g. *Hirudo* (leech)

*diagnostic features.

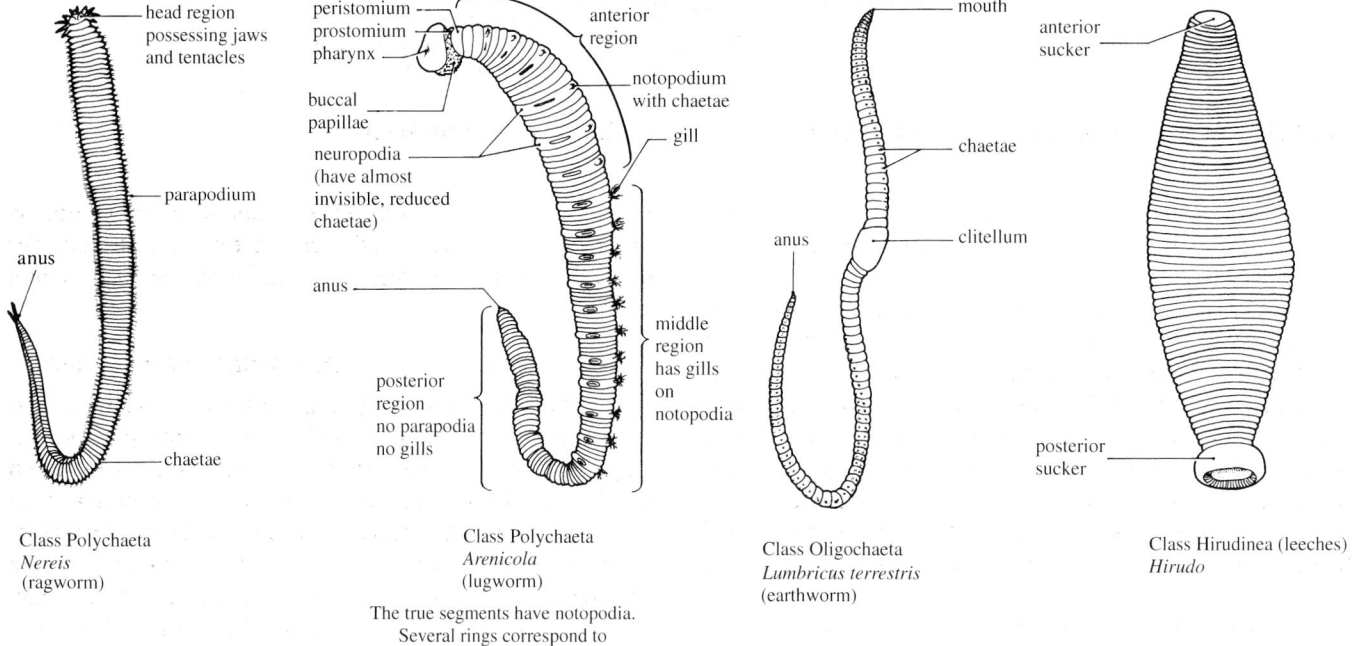

Fig 2.54 *A variety of annelids.*

Contraction of muscles can therefore change the shape of the worm but not its volume. During locomotion parts of the body alternately become longer and thinner, then shorter and fatter as different sets of muscles exert pressure on the coelomic fluid. Protection is provided by the ability of fluid to dissipate external forces rapidly and equally in all directions.

• Coelomic fluid may help to circulate food, waste materials and respiratory gases, although this function is mainly carried out by the blood vascular system.

Metameric segmentation

Another evolutionary advance which took place amongst the coelomates was **metameric segmentation**. This is the division of the body transversely into a number of similar parts or segments. Thus a series of similar segments occurs

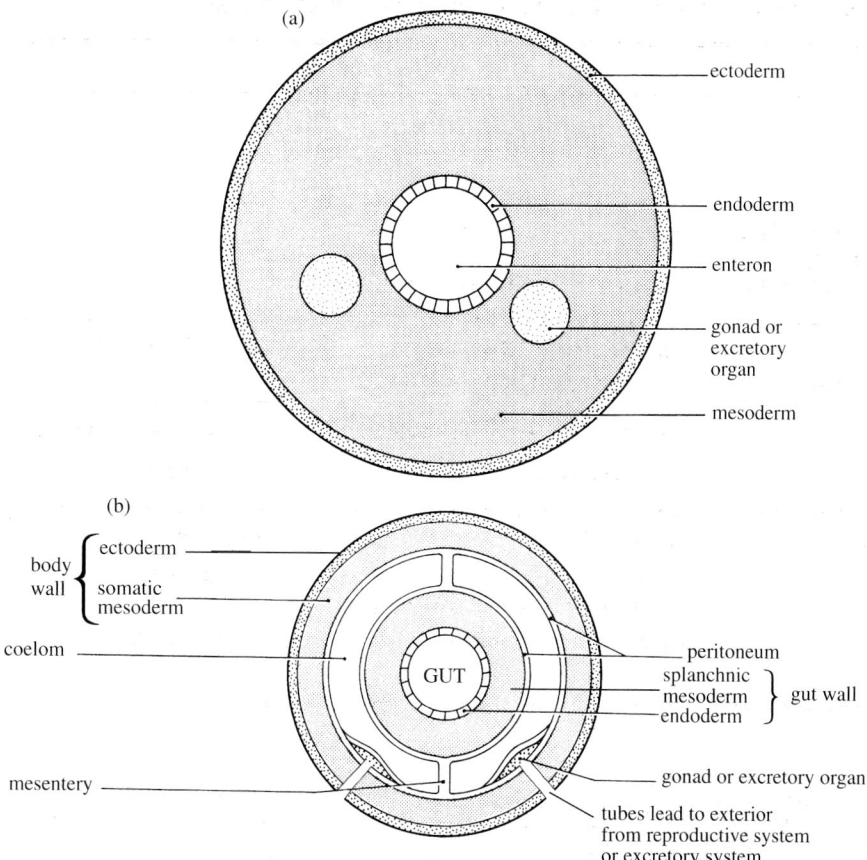

Fig 2.55 (a) *Transverse section of a generalised acoelomate.* (b) *TS generalised coelomate.*

along the length of the body. It originates in the mesoderm but usually affects both mesodermal and ectodermal regions of the body.

Metameric segmentation is most clearly seen in annelids, where the subdivisions may appear externally as constrictions of the body surface. Internally the segments are separated from each other by layers (septa) extending across the coelom. Each segment contains its own blocks of muscle, blood vessels, nerve cells and, in some groups, reproductive organs. However, the segments are not totally independent even in the annelids. The nervous system and blood system, in particular, must also run the length of the body.

Once segmentation and a basic plan for each segment was established, it was possible for evolutionary changes to take place within individual or small groups of segments, and for greater specialisation and division of labour of parts of the body to take place. This occurs in a number of ways. Different functions may be carried out in different segments; fusion of segments can occur, as happens in cephalisation where several segments fuse to form a head; or even loss of some segments, as shown by arthropods. Arthropods have fewer segments and, as we shall see in section 2.8.6, external segmentation is often less obvious, as in the cephalothorax of crustaceans. Internally, however, segmentation in arthropods is almost as clear as in annelids.

In the chordates (section 2.8.9) external segmentation is lost, but certain systems still show clear segmentation, for example the muscle blocks in embryos, and the spinal nerves.

Size and surface area:volume ratio

Organisms with a relatively large surface area:volume ratio can rely on diffusion to satisfy their transport needs. Oxygen, nutrients and waste products such as carbon dioxide can diffuse sufficiently rapidly for the organism to survive without a special transport system. Diffusion, however, is only effective over very short distances. As size of a regular figure increases, volume increases faster than surface area so the surface area:volume ratio decreases. This can be shown most easily with a cube, as in fig 2.56, but the same principle applies to spheres, cells and whole living organisms. If the living organism is flattened as volume increases, its surface area can remain high, as occurs in platyhelminths where diffusion is still adequate to satisfy transport needs. However, coelomate animals cannot escape the need for specialised gaseous exchange and transport systems.

Class Polychaeta

Arenicola, the lugworm, lives in burrows in sand or soft mud in the intertidal zone or below low tide (fig 2.54).

Nereis, the ragworm, is a cylindrical bristleworm (fig 2.57). It lives in estuaries under stones, or in mud or muddy sand burrows.

The segmented nature of the body of *Nereis* is clearly visible externally. All segments, apart from those most anterior and posterior, are very similar to each other. On either side of each segment is a projection, called the **parapodium**. It consists of an upper **notopodium** and a lower **neuropodium** (fig 2.57). From each of these structures two hair-like tufts of **chaetae** emerge. Two additional outgrowths of the parapodia are noticeable: a dorsal and a ventral cirrus. A **cirrus** (plural cirri) is a hair-like structure (from the Latin *cirrus*, curl of hair). The parapodia have a good blood supply and function as the animal's gaseous exchange surface. *Nereis* crawls by using its parapodia like paddles. It can also swim by means of its parapodia and lateral flexing of the body brought about by muscles in the body wall. The body is surrounded by a thin cuticle. The alimentary canal runs from mouth to anus. Prey is swallowed when the pharynx is retracted.

Nereis possesses a clearly differentiated head (fig 2.57); this clear cephalisation is typical of polychaete worms, but unlike the other annelids. The head consists of an anterior **prostomium**, the first segment, and posterior **peristomium**, the second segment. On the prostomium is a pair of sensory tentacles (dorsal in position) and two pairs of eyes, whilst a pair of fleshy 'palps' extend from its ventrolateral regions. These are sensitive to touch. The mouth is situated between the two headparts, and on the peristomium are four pairs of long, flexible hairs or cirri. These are also sensitive to touch and have chemoreceptors which are sensitive to various chemicals, giving the animal the equivalent of a sense of taste and smell.

Class Oligochaeta

Lumbricus, an earthworm, is an elongated, cylindrical organism, approximately 12–18 cm in length (fig 2.58). The anterior end of the body is tapered, whilst the posterior end is dorsoventrally flattened. Despite being a terrestrial animal, it has not fully overcome all the problems associated with life on land. In order to protect itself from desiccation it lives underground in burrows in damp soil, and emerges only at night to feed and reproduce.

The differences in body form exhibited by *Lumbricus* as compared with *Nereis* are the result of its adaptation to a subterranean life. The body is streamlined with no projecting structures which might impede its passage through the soil. The prostomium is a small, rounded structure without sensory appendages, overlying the mouth. Each segment, except the first and last, possesses four pairs of chaetae, two positioned ventrally and two ventrolaterally. The chaetae protrude from sacs located in the body wall and can be extended or withdrawn by the action of specialised muscles. They are used during locomotion for gripping the soil and for gripping the sides of the burrow if attacked by a predator. Longer chaetae are present on segments 10–15, 26 and 32–37, and are used during copulation. Another reproductive structure, the **clitellum**, is situated on segments 32–37. Here the epidermis is dorsally and laterally swollen with gland cells that form a very noticeable saddle. The clitellum helps in the processes of copulation and cocoon formation.

There is a mouth and anus at opposite ends of the body. *Lumbricus* feeds on detritus (fragments of decomposing organic material) by swallowing soil. The majority of the soil passes straight through the worm, much of it eventually being deposited as 'worm casts' on the surface of the ground.

Secretions of coelomic fluid via dorsal pores, and mucus from mucous glands in the epidermis (skin), keep the worm's thin cuticle moist. This helps prevent desiccation, improves gaseous exchange and also acts as a lubricant for movement through the soil. It is here that gaseous exchange occurs by diffusion, a process that is helped by the presence of networks of looped blood capillaries in the epidermal layer.

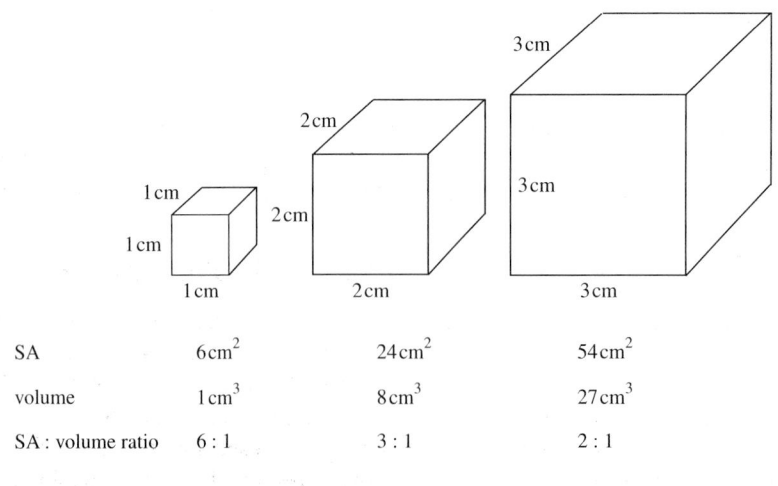

SA	6 cm^2	24 cm^2	54 cm^2
volume	1 cm^3	8 cm^3	27 cm^3
SA : volume ratio	6 : 1	3 : 1	2 : 1

SA = surface area

Fig 2.56 *Effect of increasing size on surface area:volume ratio.*

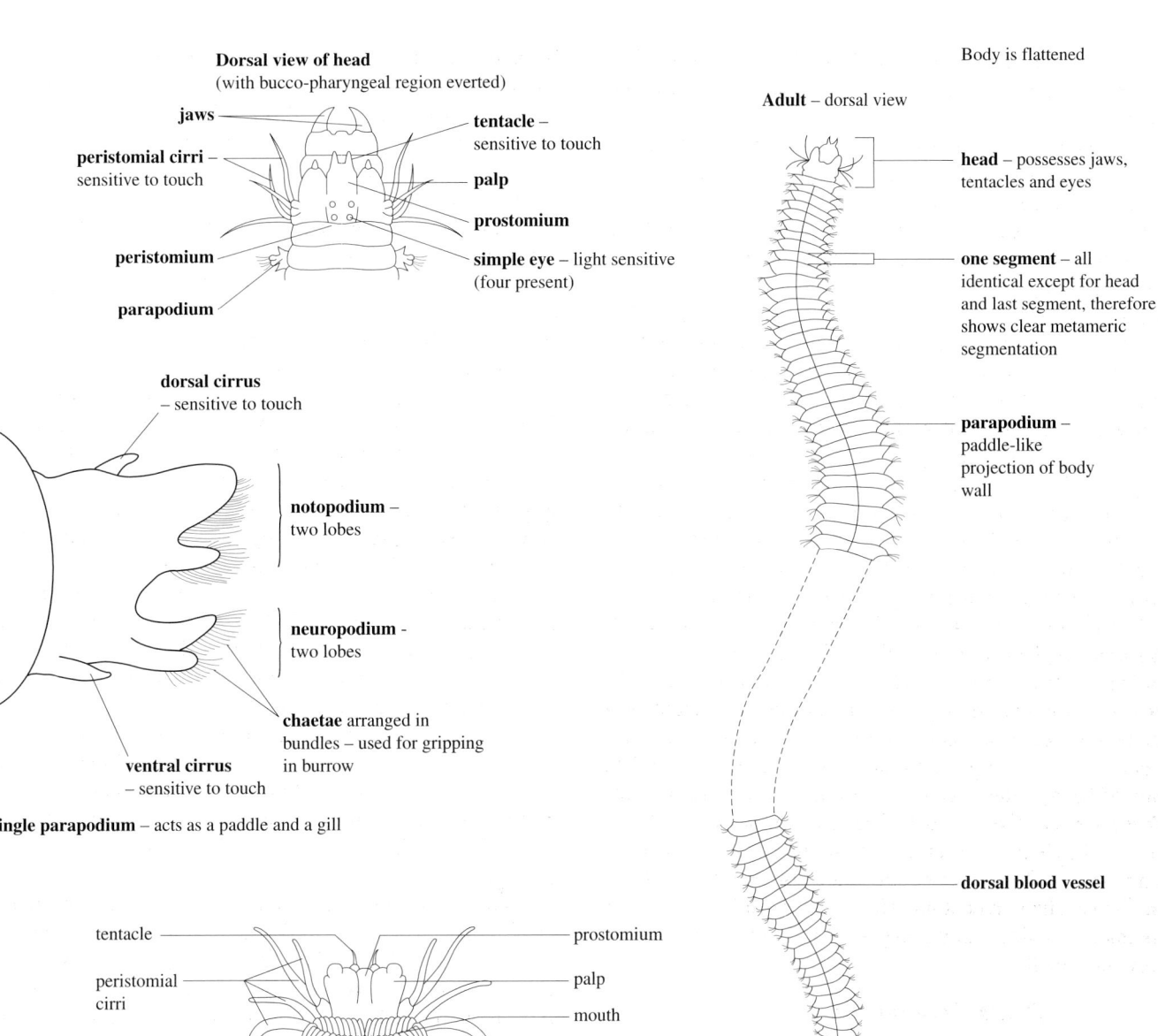

Fig 2.57 Nereis, *the ragworm.*

There is a pair of excretory and osmoregulatory tubes, called nephridia, in every segment except the first three and the last one. They open on to the surface of the worm via pores.

The reproductive system and behaviour of earthworms is very complex. This is due to their terrestrial mode of life and the necessity to avoid desiccation of gametes and fertilised eggs. *Lumbricus* is hermaphrodite (has male and female sex organs). Contact between worms is infrequent, but when it does occur, because they are hermaphrodite, any two worms of the same species are able to copulate. The worms exchange sperm and both are fertilised.

The sex organs are grouped at the anterior end of each worm. The external features associated with reproduction are shown in fig 2.58. Mating and subsequent laying of fertilised eggs in cocoons is a complicated process during which the worms line up facing in opposite directions.

2.8.6   Phylum Arthropoda (arthropods)

Classification and characteristics of the arthropods are summarised in table 2.17. The phylum Arthropoda contains more species than any other phylum. More than three-quarters of all known species are arthropods, insects alone accounting for more than half the known species. They have exploited every type of habitat on land and in water.

The basic body plan of the arthropods has been

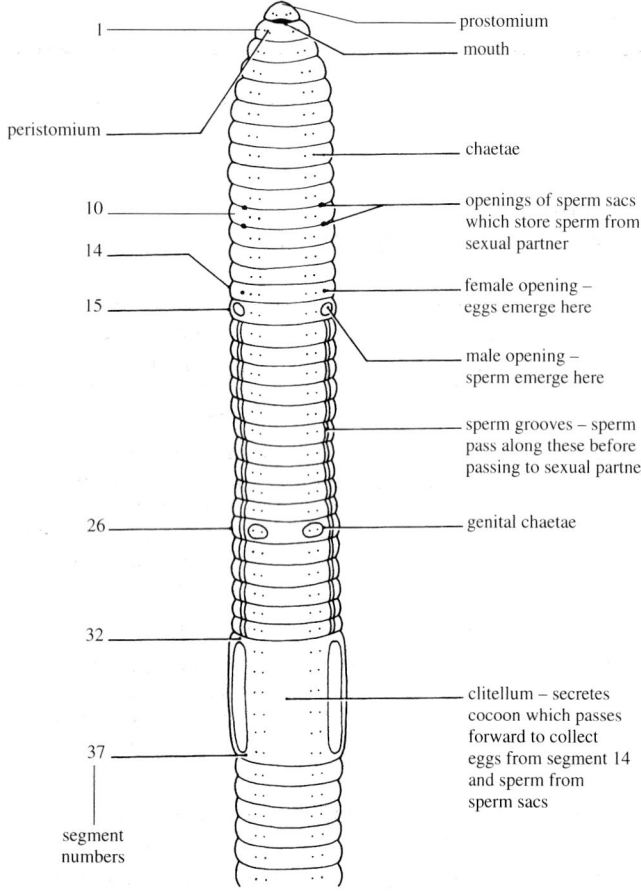

Labels on figure:
- prostomium
- mouth
- peristomium
- chaetae
- openings of sperm sacs which store sperm from sexual partner
- female opening – eggs emerge here
- male opening – sperm emerge here
- sperm grooves – sperm pass along these before passing to sexual partner
- genital chaetae
- clitellum – secretes cocoon which passes forward to collect eggs from segment 14 and sperm from sperm sacs
- segment numbers (1, 10, 14, 15, 26, 32, 37)

Fig 2.58 *Ventral view of anterior region of* Lumbricus terrestris.

extremely successful, and by a process known as **adaptive radiation** different forms have evolved to fill many different ecological niches from a single successful ancestral type (chapter 26). Insects, for example, have undergone adaptive radiation into types suitable for flying, burrowing, living an aquatic life, parasitism, etc.

The arthropod body design can be regarded as based on the segmented body plan of annelids. It shows clearly how metameric segmentation can be exploited. Ancestral arthropods possessed a series of similar simple appendages along the length of their bodies. These probably served a variety of purposes such as gaseous exchange, food gathering, locomotion and detection of stimuli. In the modern arthropods different segments have tended to become more specialised than in the annelids, so that more elaborate and specialised appendages appear as a result, with greater division of labour in the body. Segmentation is still visible externally but there tend to be fewer segments than in the annelids.

The other major characteristics of the arthropods are discussed below, and these, together with the advanced segmentation noted above, help to explain their success.

Exoskeleton or cuticle. This is secreted by the epidermis. It contains chitin, a nitrogen-containing polysaccharide which strongly resembles cellulose, the strengthening material of plant cell walls. Chitin has high tensile strength (it is difficult to break by pulling from both ends). The properties of the exoskeleton can be altered by combining chitin with other chemicals. For example, addition of mineral salts, particularly calcium salts, can make it harder, as in crustaceans. Protein can have the same effect. A range of hardness, flexibility and stiffness is therefore possible. Flexibility is important at joints. Advantages of the exoskeleton include:

- support, particularly on land;
- it provides an anchor for the muscles internally, particularly those involved in locomotion, including flight;
- protection from physical damage;
- addition of a layer of wax from special glands in the epidermis helps prevent desiccation on land;
- insect flight and the jumping ability of fleas and grasshoppers depends on the presence of a remarkably elastic protein in the exoskeleton;
- it has a low density, which is important for flying animals;
- flexible joints are possible between segments;
- it can be modified to form hard jaws for biting, piercing, sucking (fig 2.61*b*) or grinding;
- it can be transparent in places allowing, for example, entry of light into eyes and camouflage in water.

There are two disadvantages associated with the presence of an exoskeleton.

- Final body size is limited because, as already noted in the previous section, as body size increases the surface area:volume ratio decreases. The extent of the exoskeleton depends on the surface area whereas mass depends on the volume. An arthropod the size of an elephant would either not be able to support its own weight, or the exoskeleton would have to be so massive it would not be able to move. (The other important restriction on size of insects is their breathing mechanism which works mainly by diffusion through tubes called tracheae. The largest living insects are stick insects, of about 30 cm in length, and the larger beetles, such as the hercules beetle which weighs up to 100 g, the size of a mouse.)
- It restricts growth, so periodic moulting (ecdysis) is required if the animal is to grow. However, the arthropod is very vulnerable to attack by predators at this period, and generally seeks the protection of shelter before undergoing the process.

Table 2.17 Classification of the phylum Arthropoda (arthropods).

Phylum Arthropoda

Characteristic features
Triploblastic, coelomate
Metameric segmentation, bilateral symmetry
Exoskeleton* of chitin and sometimes calcareous matter; may be rigid, stiff or flexible
Each segment typically bears a pair of jointed appendages used for locomotion or feeding or sensory purposes*
Coelom much reduced, main body cavity a haemocoel

Superclass Crustacea (crustaceans)**	*Class Insecta* (insects)	*Class Chilopoda* (centipedes)	*Class Diplopoda* (millipedes)	*Class Arachnida* (arachnids)
Mainly aquatic	Mainly terrestrial	Mainly terrestrial	Terrestrial	Terrestrial
Cephalothorax (head and thorax not distinctly separate)	Well-defined head, thorax abdomen	Clearly defined head Other body segments all similar	Clearly defined head Other body segments all similar	Cephalothorax (head and thorax not distinctly separate); thorax separated from abdomen by a narrow waist-like constriction
Two pars of antennae	One pair of antennae	One pair of antennae	One pair of antennae	No antennae
At least three pairs of mouthparts	Usually three pairs of mouthparts	One pair of mouthparts (jaws)	One pair of mouthparts (jaws)	No true mouthparts but one pair of appendages used in capturing prey and one pair of sensory palps
Pair of compound eyes raised on stalks	Pair of compound eyes and simple eyes	Eyes simple, compound or absent	Eyes simple, compound or absent	Simple eyes only (no compound eyes)
Appendages often modified for swimming, as mainly aquatic; number of legs variable, sometimes 10	Three pairs of legs on thorax, one pair per segment. Usually one or two pairs of wings on thorax (on second and/or third segments)	Numerous legs, all identical, one pair per segment	Numerous legs, all identical, two pairs per segment	Four pairs of walking legs (segments 4–7)
Larval form occurs	Life cycle commonly involves metamorphosis either 'complete' or 'incomplete', with a larval stage	No larval form	No larval form	No larval form
Typical gaseous exchange by gills – outgrowths of the body wall or limbs	No gills in adult Gaseous exchange by tracheae (tubes inside body	Gaseous exchange by tracheae	Gaseous exchange by tracheae	Gaseous exchange by 'lung' books or 'gill' books or tracheae
e.g. *Daphnia* (water-flea) *Astacus* (crayfish) Also barnacles, prawns, crabs, lobsters, woodlice	e.g. *Periplaneta* (cockroach) *Apis* (bee) *Pieris* (white butterfly) Also bugs, beetles, fleas, wasps, flies, dragonflies, termites, grasshoppers, earwigs	Mainly carnivorous e.g. *Lithobius* (centipede)	Mainly herbivorous e.g. *Iulus* (millipede)	e.g. *Scorpio* (scorpion) *Epeira* (web-spinning spider) Also mites, ticks

* diagnostic features.
** This superclass contains many classes.

Jointed appendages. The word 'arthropod' means, literally, 'jointed foot'. Jointed appendages are one of the most obvious characteristics of arthropods. They are used for a wide variety of functions such as feeding, locomotion and sensory purposes (fig 2.59).

Haemocoel. In arthropods and molluscs, the coelom is almost completely obliterated during development by another cavity called the **haemocoel** (fig 2.60). It develops from the cavities of the blood vascular system and is therefore filled with blood. The blood is

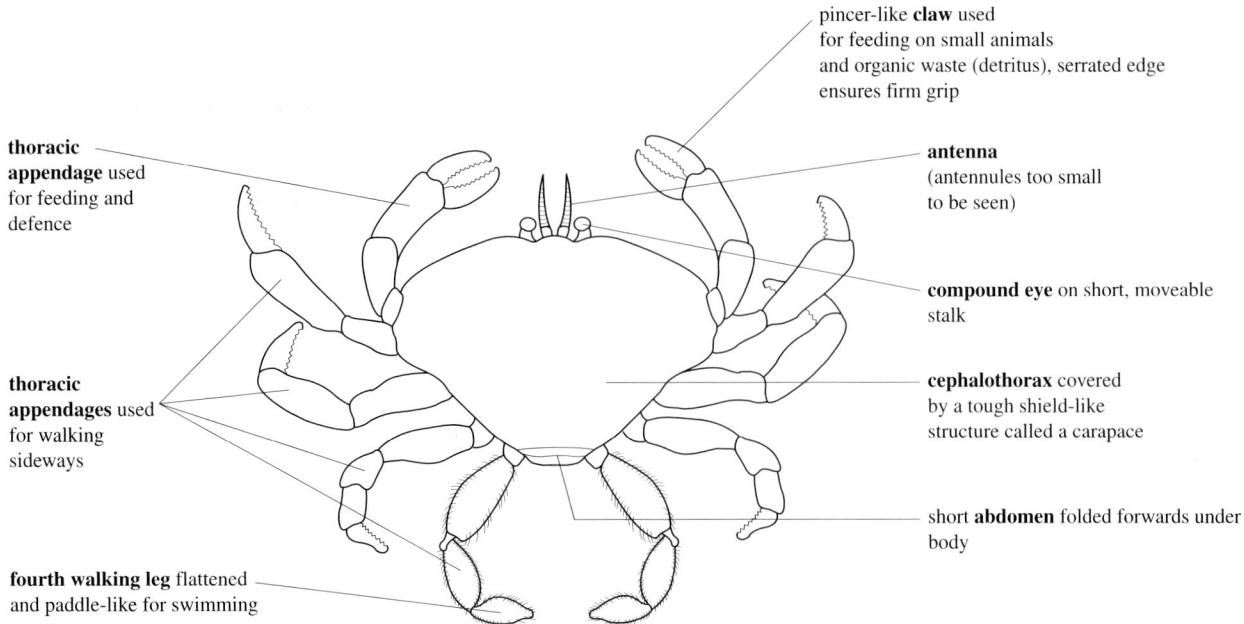

thoracic **appendage** used for feeding and defence

pincer-like **claw** used for feeding on small animals and organic waste (detritus), serrated edge ensures firm grip

antenna (antennules too small to be seen)

compound eye on short, moveable stalk

thoracic **appendages** used for walking sideways

cephalothorax covered by a tough shield-like structure called a carapace

short **abdomen** folded forwards under body

fourth walking leg flattened and paddle-like for swimming

Fig 2.59 *A crustacean* Carcinus maenas, *the shore crab. Dorsal view. Common on rocky shores and beaches. Separate sexes occur. The head is fused to the thorax to form a cephalothorax. The first three pairs of thoracic appendages, called maxillipeds, are involved in feeding but are not visible from the dorsal surface. Note that the appendages are jointed.*

generally circulated in the haemocoel, and through several attached blood vessels. The major organs are bathed in blood. The coelom still exists but is small and confined to the cavities of excretory organs and the reproductive ducts. The high blood volume to body volume in arthropods enables them to maintain a high metabolic rate, allowing them to be very active animals. The danger of blood loss from injury, though, is high.

Specialisation of body parts. The division of labour, which is much more pronounced in arthropods than annelids, has contributed to the development of distinct regions of the body, namely the **head** and, in many cases, a **thorax** and **abdomen**. The head possesses sensory receptors, such as eyes and antennae, as well as feeding appendages. In bilaterally symmetrical animals the front end (the head) is the first part to come into contact with new environments. Thus the front end becomes specialised. The brain is much larger than in annelids and cephalisation much more pronounced.

Flight. Insects have developed flight which greatly increases opportunities for finding food and escaping predators (fig 2.61a).

Insect life histories

Life histories of insects are very variable and often highly complex. In many, a process called **metamorphosis** (*meta*, change; *morphe*, form) occurs. This is a change of form or structure of the animal during the course of its life cycle.

In the more primitive insect groups the larval stages often resemble the adult (**imago**) during development. Each successive larval form (called a **nymph** or **instar**) usually looks more and more like the adult. This form of development is termed **hemimetabolous** or **incomplete metamorphosis**. The nymph possesses adaptive features which enable it to live in a different habitat and eat different food from that of the adult. This avoids competition for food between juvenile and adult. The locust shows this type of life cycle.

In groups which evolved later, the larval stages are quite distinct from the adult. The final larval moult produces a pupa, inside which metamorphosis produces the adult

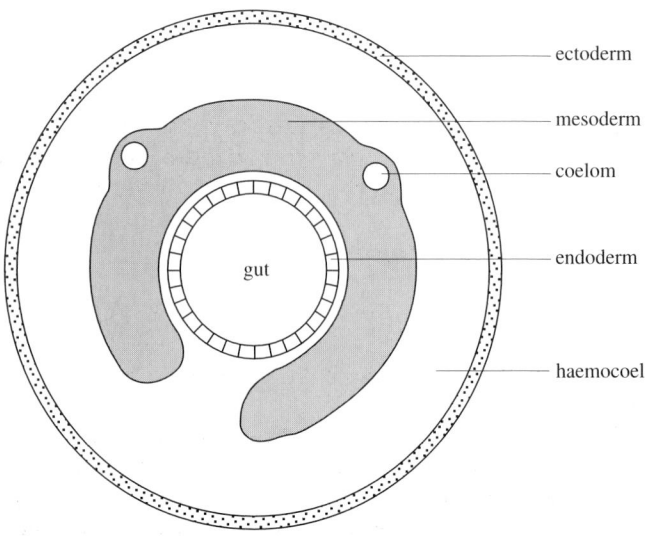

ectoderm

mesoderm

coelom

gut

endoderm

haemocoel

Fig 2.60 *The haemocoel condition (compare fig 2.55).*

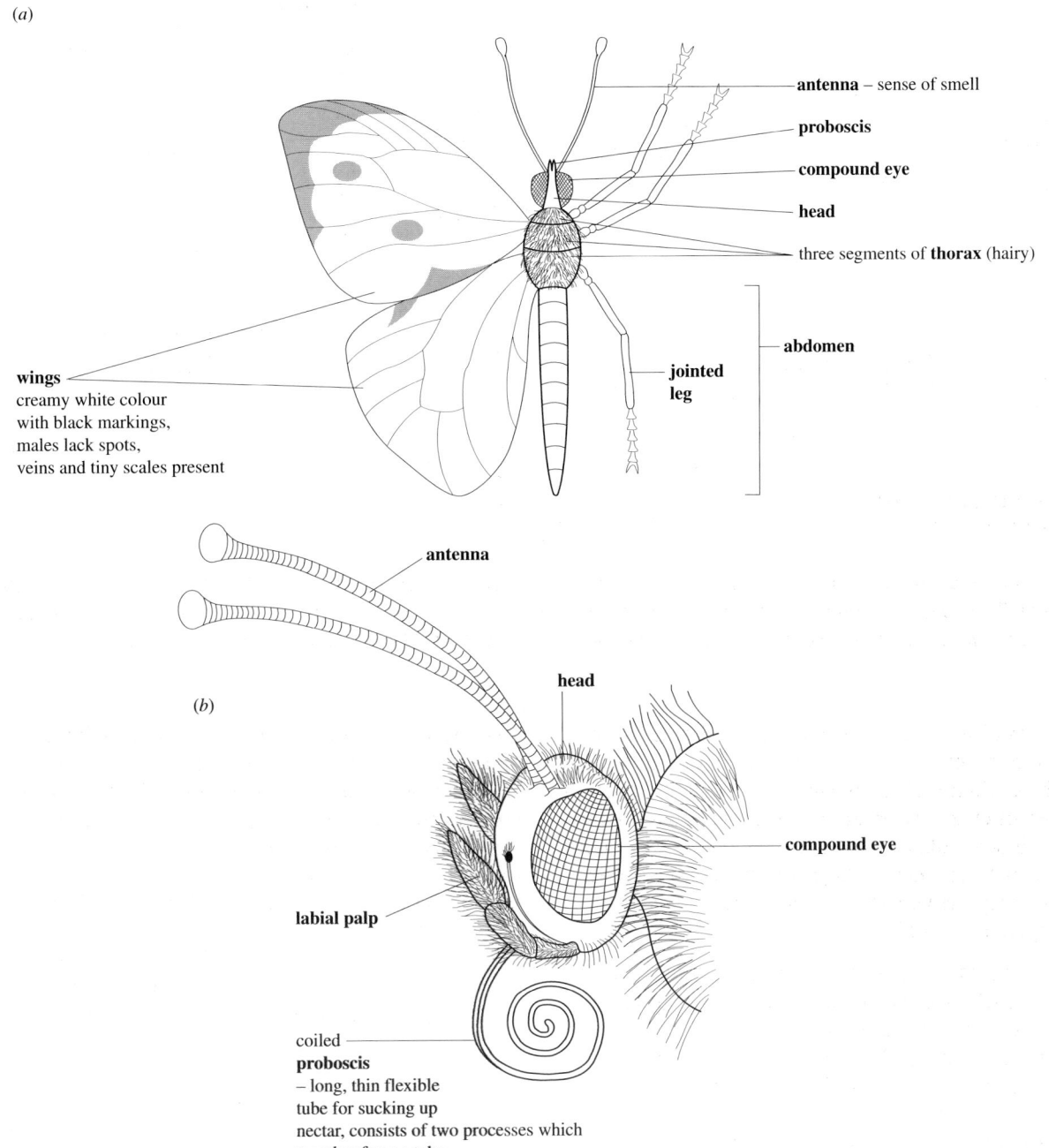

(a)

antenna – sense of smell

proboscis

compound eye

head

three segments of **thorax** (hairy)

abdomen

wings
creamy white colour
with black markings,
males lack spots,
veins and tiny scales present

jointed
leg

antenna

head

(b)

compound eye

labial palp

coiled
proboscis
– long, thin flexible
tube for sucking up
nectar, consists of two processes which
together form a tube

Fig 2.61   (a) *An insect,* Pieris brassicae, *the large (cabbage) white butterfly. Dorsal view, with wings shown on one side and legs the other. Wings are attached to the second and third thoracic segments, legs to all three thoracic segments. Pairs of spiracles, holes leading to the tracheae (respiratory tubes) are present on the first thoracic segment and the first eight abdominal segments.*
(b) *Detail of head of* Pieris.

tissues, using components from the degenerating larval tissues. This is called **holometabolous** or **complete metamorphosis**. An example of this type of life cycle is shown in fig 2.62.

Metamorphosis enables the juvenile and adult forms to live in different habitats and exploit different sources of food, that is to occupy different ecological niches. This reduces competition between juveniles and adults. For instance, dragonfly nymphs prey upon aquatic insects and exchange gases via gills whereas the adults attack terrestrial insects, live in air and exchange gases via tracheae. Also, lepidopteran (butterfly and moth) larvae generally feed on foliage and possess chewing mouthparts, whereas the adults drink nectar and have sucking mouthparts.

Once wings have fully developed, moulting is no longer possible. This restricts growth, so metamorphosis therefore allows the immature stages to provide the feeding and growing stages of the insect's life cycle.

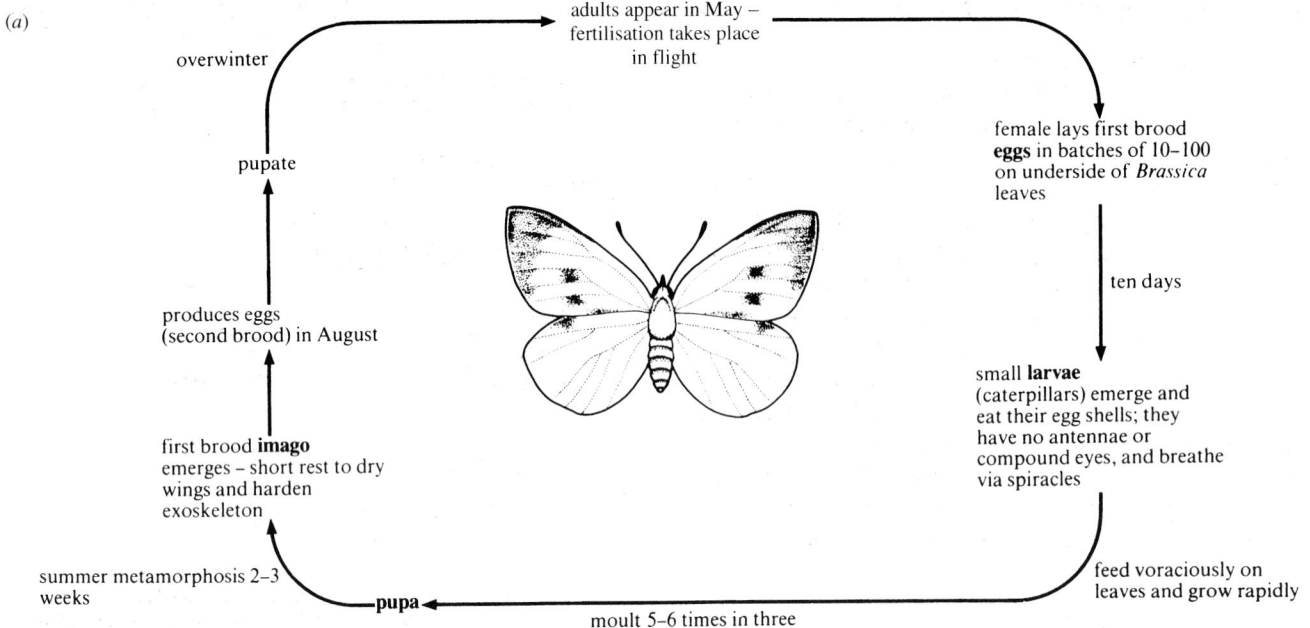

(a)

overwinter

pupate

adults appear in May – fertilisation takes place in flight

female lays first brood **eggs** in batches of 10–100 on underside of *Brassica* leaves

ten days

produces eggs (second brood) in August

first brood **imago** emerges – short rest to dry wings and harden exoskeleton

small **larvae** (caterpillars) emerge and eat their egg shells; they have no antennae or compound eyes, and breathe via spiracles

summer metamorphosis 2–3 weeks

pupa

moult 5–6 times in three weeks

feed voraciously on leaves and grow rapidly

NB pupation may last for only a few weeks in summer; if insect overwinters, then the pupa is the state maintained

(b)

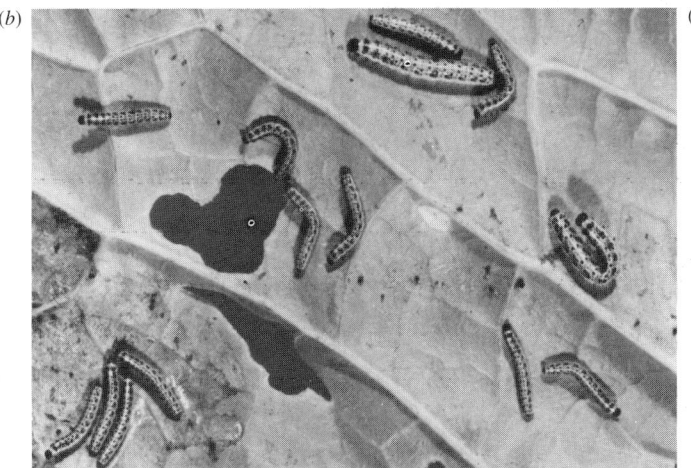

(c)

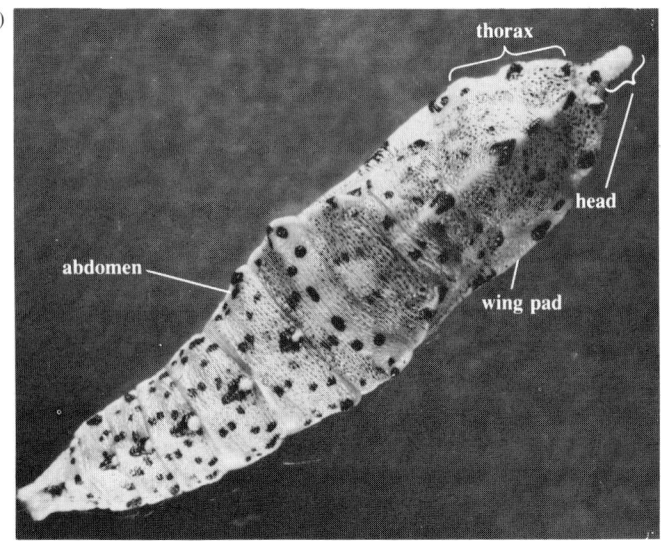

thorax

head

wing pad

abdomen

(d)

Fig 2.62 *Life cycle of cabbage white butterfly* (Pieris brassicae), *a member of the insect order Lepidoptera (butterflies and moths); (a) diagram of life cycle, an example of complete metamorphosis, (b) larvae (caterpillars), (c) pupa (chrysalis), (d) female imago (adult feeding from a buddleia bush).*

2.8.7 Phylum Mollusca (molluscs)

Classification characteristics of the Mollusca are summarised in table 2.18 (only three of the six classes are shown). The phylum consists of a diverse group of organisms which include slow-moving snails and slugs, relatively sedentary bivalves, such as clams, and highly active cephalopods (fig 2.63). With over 80 000 living species and 35 000 fossil species, the phylum is second only in size to the Arthropoda. One of the molluscs, the giant squid, is the largest non-vertebrate animal, weighing several tonnes and measuring 16 m in length.

The formation of a protective shell, and use of gills or lungs for gaseous exchange, has enabled molluscs to colonise aquatic and terrestrial environments and thus occupy a wide range of ecological niches. However, a shell can be handicap to locomotion, and some of the more active molluscs show a reduction or loss of the shell.

Fig 2.63 *A variety of molluscs.*

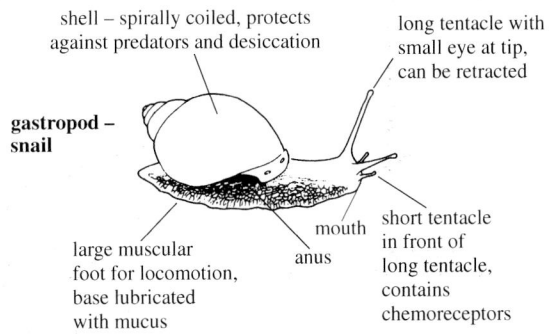

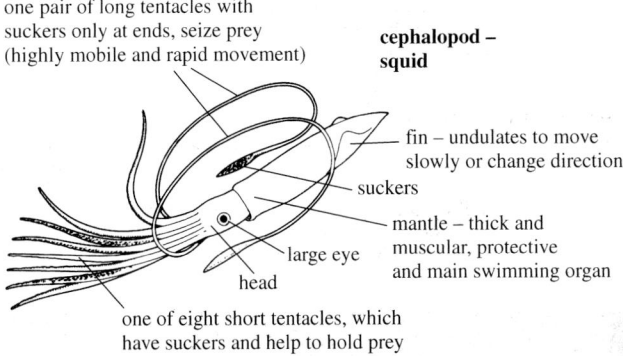

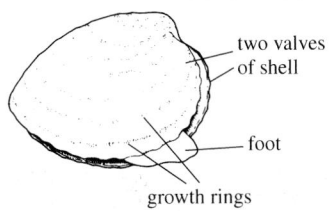

Table 2.18 Classification and characteristics of the phylum Mollusca (molluscs).

Phylum Mollusca

Characteristic features	
Unsegmented, triploblastic coelomates	foot and dorsal visceral hump*
Usually bilaterally symmetrical	Over the hump the skin (mantle) secretes a calcareous shell
Body soft and fleshy and divided into a head, ventral muscular	Main body cavity is a haemocoel
	No limbs

Class Gastropoda (gastropods)	*Class Pelycopoda* (bivalves)	*Class Cephalopoda* (cephalopods)
Terrestrial, marine and freshwater	Aquatic	Aquatic. Largest and most complex molluscs
Asymmetrical	Bilateral symmetry	Bilateral symmetry
Shell of one piece, usually coiled due to rotation of hump during growth	Shell consists of two hinged halves called valves (hence the term 'bivalve'. Body enclosed by the valves and laterally compressed)	Shell often reduced and internal or wholly absent
Large flat foot used in locomotion	Foot reduced in size and often used for burrowing in sand or mud	Adapted for fast swimming. Foot modified to form part of head and tentacles
Head, eyes and sensory tentacles	Head greatly reduced in size, tentacles absent	Head highly developed with tentacles with suckers, and well-developed eyes
Radula, a rasping tongue-like structure used in feeding	Filter feeder	Radula and horny beak
Anus is anterior	Anus is posterior	Anus is posterior
e.g. *Helix aspersa* (land snail) *Patella* (limpet) *Buccinum* (whelk) *Limax* (slug)	e.g. *Mytilus edulis* (marine mussel) *Ostrea* (oyster)	e.g. *Sepia officinalis* (cuttlefish) *Loligo* (squid) *Octopus vulgaris* (octopus)

* diagnostic features.

2.8.8 Phylum Echinodermata (echinoderms)

There are over 6000 known species of echinoderms. The word 'echinoderm' means 'spiny skin'; most have hard spiny or wart-like outgrowths. They are all marine, and are largely bottom-dwellers inhabiting shorelines and shallow seas. The adult forms show pentamerous symmetry (a form of radial symmetry) although the group is believed to have evolved from bilateral ancestors. Classification and characteristics of echinoderms are shown in table 2.19 and examples of echinoderms are shown in fig 2.64.

Table 2.19 Classification and characteristics of the phylum Echinodermata (echinoderms).

Phylum Echinodermata

Characteristic features
Triploblastic, coelomate
All marine
Adult shows five-way (pentamerous) radial symmetry*
Tube feet for locomotion*
Calcareous exoskeleton
No head. Mouth generally on lower (oral) surface of body, anus on upper (aboral) surface

Class Stelleroidea (starfish)	*Class Echinoidea* (sea urchins)
Star-shaped, flattened	Globular
Arms not sharply separate from disc	Does not possess arms
Few calcareous plates in body wall; movable spines	Numerous calcareous plates in body wall, attached to each other to form a rigid structure; relatively long movable spines
e.g. *Asterias*	e.g. *Echinocardium*

* diagnostic feature.

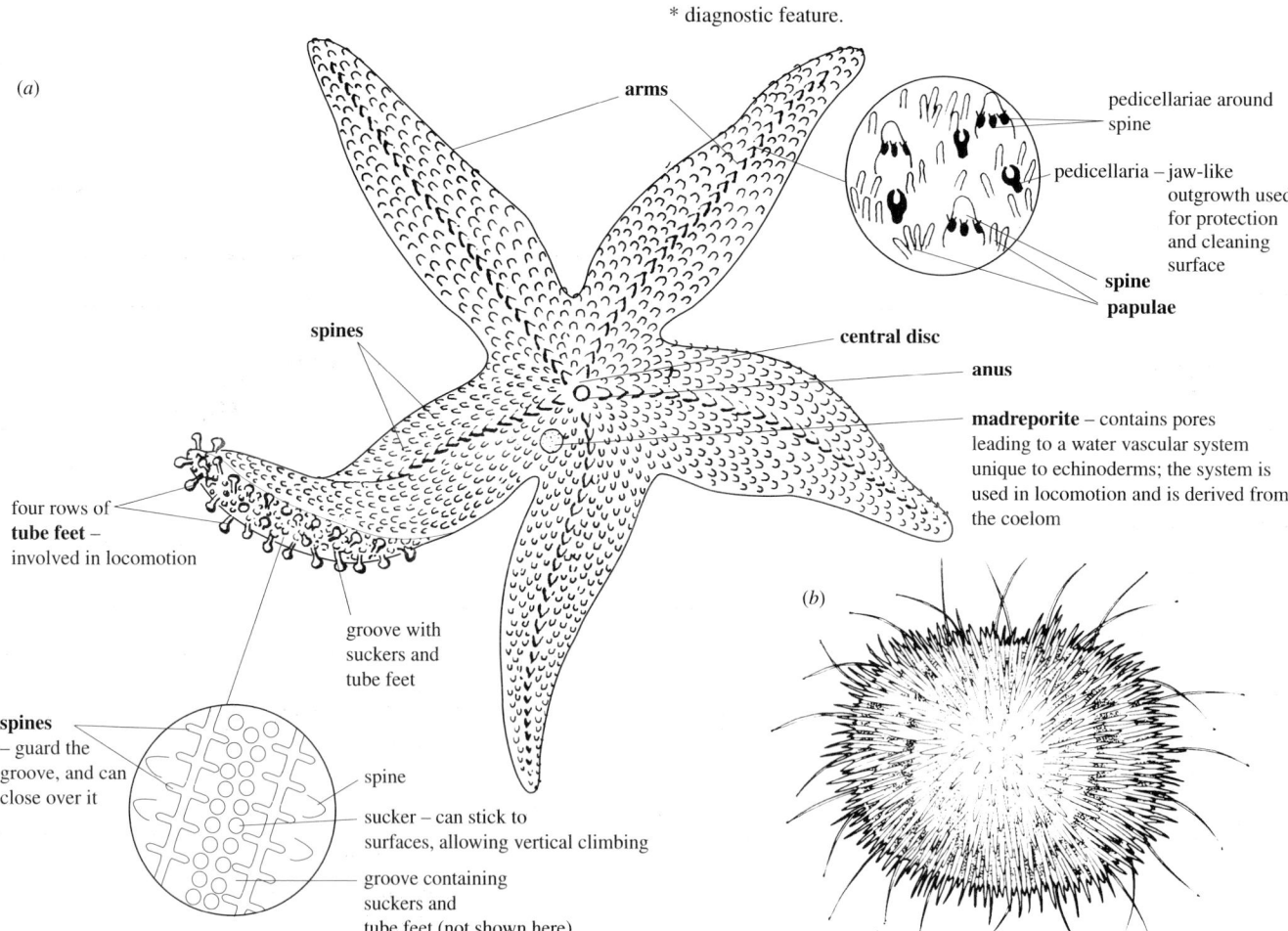

(a) arms
pedicellariae around spine
pedicellaria – jaw-like outgrowth used for protection and cleaning surface
spine
papulae

spines
central disc
anus
madreporite – contains pores leading to a water vascular system unique to echinoderms; the system is used in locomotion and is derived from the coelom

four rows of **tube feet** – involved in locomotion

groove with suckers and tube feet

(b)

spines – guard the groove, and can close over it
spine
sucker – can stick to surfaces, allowing vertical climbing
groove containing suckers and tube feet (not shown here)

Fig 2.64 (a) Asterias, *the common starfish. One arm is turned to show the lower side. Circles contain magnified views. The mouth is in the centre of the lower surface, known as the oral surface. The top side is known as the aboral surface.* (b) Echinocardium – *sea urchin.*

Phylum Chordata (chordates)

Classification and characteristics of the Chordata are summarised in table 2.20. The chief distinguishing feature of the chordates is the presence of a dorsal, longitudinally running rod, the **notochord**. It lies between the dorsal nerve tube and the gut (fig 2.65). It increases internal support and locomotory power and probably evolved originally in the swimming larval forms of chordate ancestors. It still exists in something like its original form in the few remaining groups of non-vertebrate chordates, but in most chordates it is mainly replaced during embryonic development by the bony vertebrae of the **vertebral column**, or **backbone**. Animals possessing a vertebral column are known as **vertebrates**; all other animals are **non-vertebrates**. We shall only consider the vertebrate chordates here. They are such an important natural group that they are given the status of a subphylum (Vertebrata).

The basic body plan of chordates is shown in figs 2.65a and b. Representative examples of vertebrates are shown in fig 2.66.

Table 2.21 provides a summary of the key features of evolutionary significance in the different animal phyla.

Table 2.20 Classification and characteristics of the phylum Chordata (chordates).

Phylum Chordata

Characteristic features
Notochord present at some stage in the life history. This is a flexible rod of tightly packed, vacuolated cells held together with a firm sheath*
Triploblastic coelomate
Bilateral symmetry
Pharyngeal (visceral) clefts present (slits in the pharynx)*
Dorsal, hollow nerve cord*
Segmental muscle blocks (myotomes) on either side of the body
Post-anal tail (tail starts posterior to anus)*
Limbs formed from more than one body segment*

Subphylum Vertebrata (vertebrates)

Characteristic features
Notochord replaced in adult by a vertebral column (backbone), a series of vertebrae made either of bone or cartilage*
Well-developed central nervous system including brain.* Skull protects the brain
Internal skeleton
Pharyngeal clefts (gill slits), few in number
Two pairs of fins or limbs.* These are attached to the rest of the skeleton by girdles, pectoral and pelvic*

Table 2.20 (cont.)

Class Chondrichthyes (cartilaginous fish)	Class Osteichthyes (bony fish)	Class Amphibia (amphibians)	Class Reptilia (reptiles)	Class Aves (birds)	Class Mammalia (mammals)
Skin with placoid (tooth-like) scales	Skin with cycloid scales (thin, round and made of bone)	Soft moist skin can be used for gaseous exchange to supplement lungs. No scales	Dry scaly skin with horny scales	Skin bears feathers, legs have scales	Skin bears hair with two types of glands, sebaceous and sweat
Cartilaginous skeleton	Bony skeleton	Bony	Bony	Bony	Bony
Paired, fleshy pectoral and pelvic fins Asymmetric tail fin helps prevent sinking (no air bladder or swim bladder for buoyancy)	Paired pectoral and pelvic fins supported by bony rays, giving greater manoeuvrability. Symmetrical tail fin	Two pairs pentadactyl limbs	Two pairs pentadactyl limbs usually present	Two pairs pentadactyl limbs, front pair form wings	Two pairs pentadactyl limbs
Visceral clefts present as separate gill openings; five pairs	Visceral clefts present as separate gill openings, but covered by a bony flap (operculum), four pairs	Visceral clefts present in aquatic larva (tadpole) only, lungs in adult, which is usually terrestrial Metamorphosis from larva to adult in life cycle	Visceral clefts never develop gills	Visceral clefts never develop gills	Visceral clefts never develop gills
No external ear	No external ear	No external ear	No external ear	No external ear	External ear (in addition to middle and inner ear)
Eggs produced, internal fertilisation	Eggs produced, external fertilisaton	Eggs produced, external fertilisation. Adults must return to water for reproduction	Fertilised yolky eggs laid on land or eggs retained until hatching. Eggs have a leathery skin. Internal fertilisation	As reptiles but eggs in calcareous shells, internal fertilisation.	Only two genera lay eggs, the spiny anteater and the duck-billed platypus. Embryo develops in mother. Mother has mammary glands which produce milk for the newborn. Internal fertilisation
			Teeth lost and beak developed		Different types of teeth for different functions
					Muscular diaphragm between thorax and abdomen
Poikilothermic ('cold-blooded')	Poikilothermic	Poikilothermic	Poikilothermic	Homeothermic ('warm-blooded')	Homeothermic
e.g. *Scyliorhinus* (dogfish) Also sharks, skates and rays	e.g. *Clupea* (herring)	e.g. *Rana* (frog) *Bufo* (toad) Also newts and salamanders	e.g. *Natrix* (grass snake) *Crocodylus* (crocodile) Also lizards, alligators, turtles, tortoises. Dinosaurs were reptiles	e.g. *Columba* (pigeon) *Aquila* (eagle)	e.g. *Homo* (human) *Canis* (dog)

*diagnostic features.

74

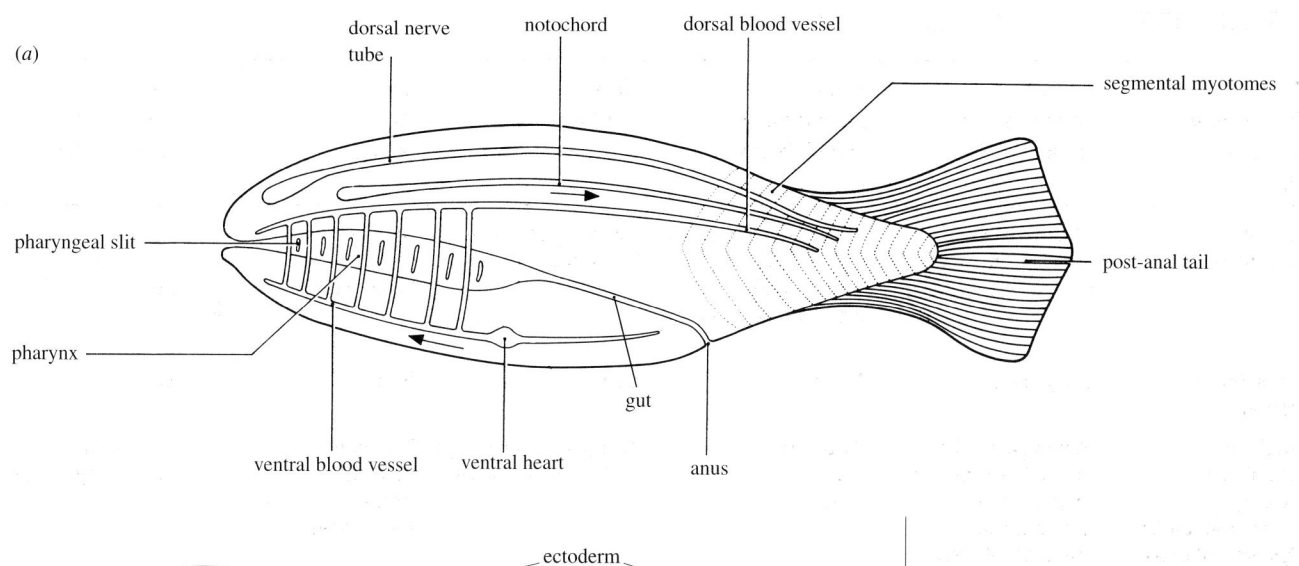

(a)

dorsal nerve tube

notochord

dorsal blood vessel

segmental myotomes

pharyngeal slit

post-anal tail

pharynx

gut

ventral blood vessel

ventral heart

anus

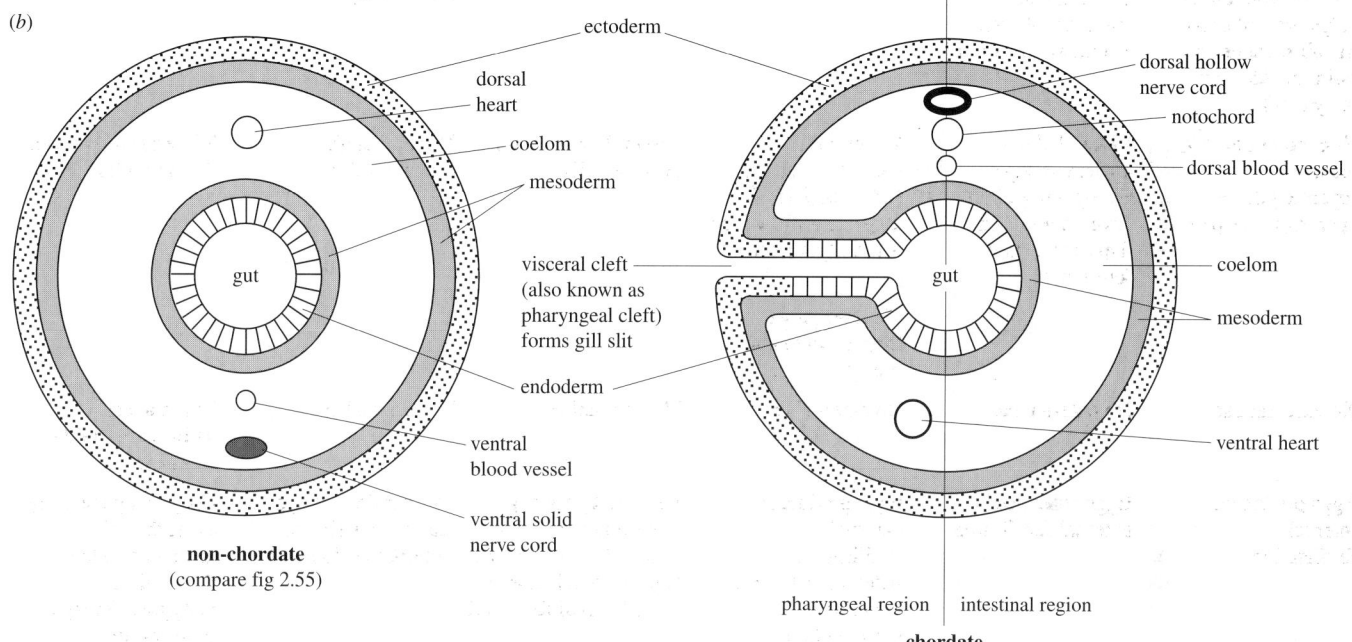

(b)

ectoderm

dorsal heart

coelom

mesoderm

gut

dorsal hollow nerve cord

notochord

dorsal blood vessel

coelom

mesoderm

visceral cleft (also known as pharyngeal cleft) forms gill slit

endoderm

gut

ventral blood vessel

ventral solid nerve cord

ventral heart

non-chordate
(compare fig 2.55)

pharyngeal region | intestinal region

chordate

Fig 2.65 (a) *Diagram showing basic chordate body plan.*
(b) *Transverse sections of a non-chordate coelomate and a chordate for comparison.*

Table 2.21 Summary of some key features of evolutionary significance in animal phyla.

Phylum	Radial symmetry	Diploblastic	Bilateral symmetry	Triploblastic	Acoelomate	Coelomate	Haemocoel	Metameric segmentation
Cnidaria	●	●	✕	✕	–	–	–	–
Platyhelminthes	✕	✕	●	●	●	✕	✕	✕
Nematoda	✕	✕	●	●	body cavity develops differently		✕	✕
Annelida	✕	✕	●	●	✕	●	✕	●
Arthropoda	✕	✕	●	●	✕	●	●	●
Mollusca	✕	✕	●	●	✕	●	●	✕
Echinodermata	●	✕	✕	●	✕	●	✕	✕
Chordata	✕	✕	●	●	✕	●	✕	●

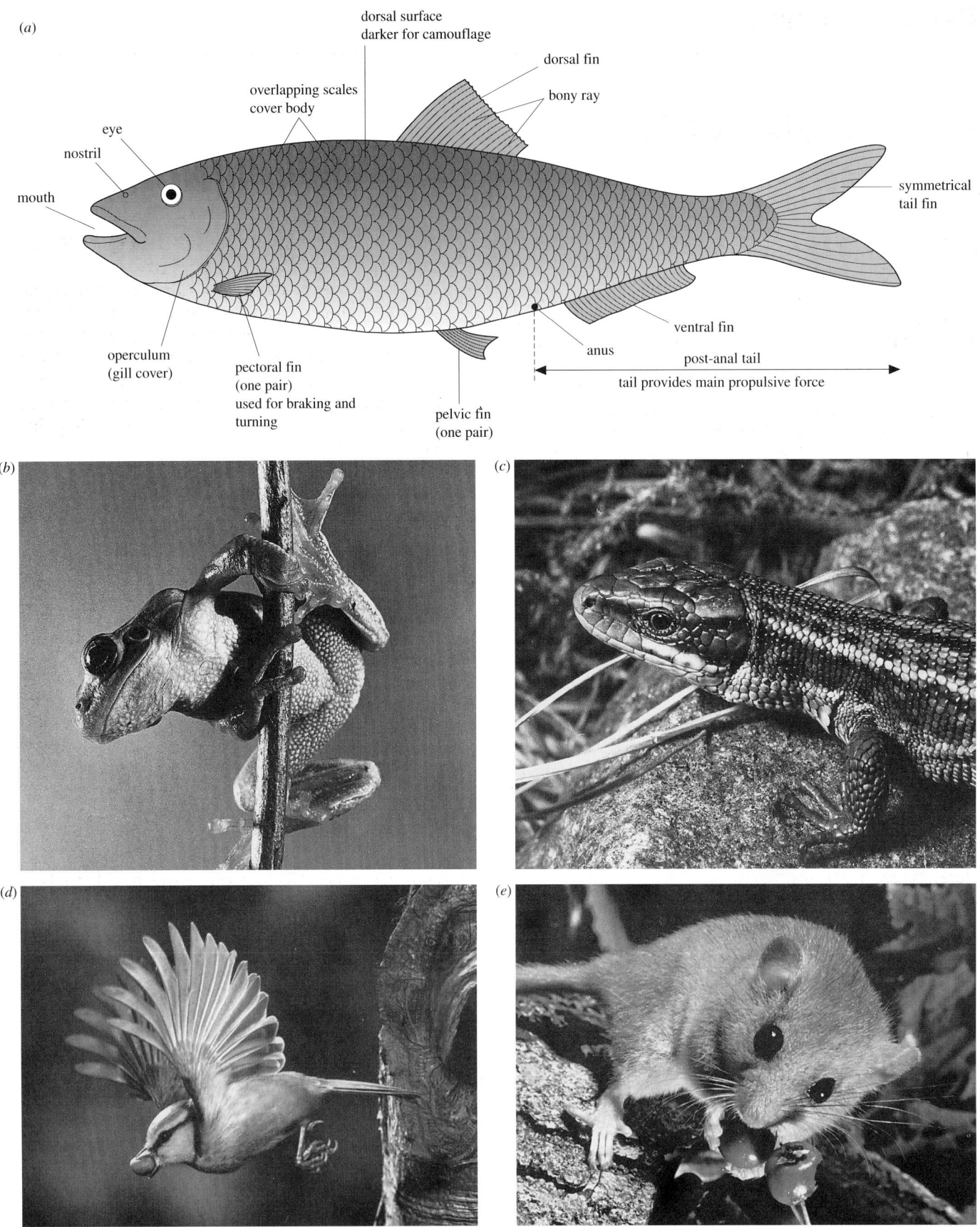

Fig 2.66 (a) Clupea harengus, *the herring, a bony fish. The paired pectoral and pelvic fins control pitch (swimming up or down). The single dorsal and ventral fins control roll (leaning to sides) and yaw (turning).* (b) *European tree frog (*Hyla arborea*).* (c) *Lizard.* (d) *Blue tit (*Parus caeruleus*).* (e) *Dormouse (*Muscardinus avellinarius*).*

Chapter Three

Chemicals of life

3.1 Introduction to biochemistry

Biochemistry is the study of the chemicals of living organisms. It has been closely associated with the great expansion in biological knowledge that has taken place during the twentieth century. Its importance lies in the fundamental understanding it gives us of the way in which biological systems work. This finds application in fields like agriculture, with development of pesticides, herbicides and so on; medicine, including the whole pharmaceutical industry; fermentation industries with their vast range of useful products, including baked products; and food and nutrition, including dietetics, food production and preservation. Many of the exciting new developments in biology, like genetic engineering, biotechnology, 'designer' proteins and molecular approaches to genetic disease, are underpinned by an understanding of biochemistry.

Biochemistry is also one of the great unifying themes in biology. At this level, what is often striking about living organisms is not so much their differences as their similarities.

3.1.1 Elements found in living organisms

The Earth's crust contains approximately 100 chemical elements and yet only 16 of these are essential for life. These 16 are listed in table 3.1. The four most common elements in living organisms are, in order, hydrogen, carbon, oxygen and nitrogen. These account for more than 99% of the mass and numbers of atoms found in all living organisms. The four most common elements in the Earth's crust, however, are oxygen, silicon, aluminium, and sodium. The biological importance of hydrogen, oxygen, nitrogen and carbon is largely due to their having valencies of 1, 2, 3 and 4 respectively and their ability to form more stable covalent bonds than any other elements with these valencies. The appendix contains a summary of some basic chemistry, including covalent bonding (appendix, Book 2) which you might find useful to revise before reading this chapter.

The importance of carbon

It is sometimes said that life on our planet is based on carbon. Carbon is an element that is found in all organic molecules. The term organic, meaning living, was used originally because it was thought that only living things could make organic compounds. This myth was dispelled in 1828 when the German chemist Wöhler synthesised the organic molecule urea from inorganic starting materials. This made scientists realise that there was no 'magic' or special life force needed to make the biochemicals of life, and today we have even reached the point where we could in theory synthesise DNA, the genetic material, from inorganic starting materials, and hence 'create' life.

But why is carbon so important? Carbon forms strong covalent bonds, in other words it shares electrons, with other elements. It forms four such bonds, that is it has a valency of four. A simple example is methane, whose **molecular formula** is CH_4 and whose structural formula is shown in fig 3.1. (See also appendix 1, Book 2.) Box 3.1 should be consulted for help with writing formulae.

Table 3.1 The elements found in living organisms.

Chief elements of organic molecules	Ions	Trace elements	
H hydrogen	Na^+ sodium	Mn manganese	B boron
C carbon	Mg^{2+} magnesium	Fe iron	Al aluminium
N nitrogen	Cl^- chlorine	Co cobalt	Si silicon
O oxygen	K^+ potassium	Cu copper	V vanadium
P phosphorus	Ca^{2+} calcium	Zn zinc	Mo molybdenum
S sulphur			I iodine

Elements in each column are arranged in order of atomic mass, not abundance. Those in the first three columns are found in all organisms.
(Based on A. L. Lehninger, *Biochemistry*, Worth. N.Y. 1970).

(a)

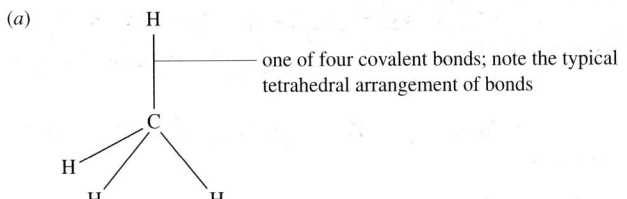

one of four covalent bonds; note the typical tetrahedral arrangement of bonds

(b)

(c)

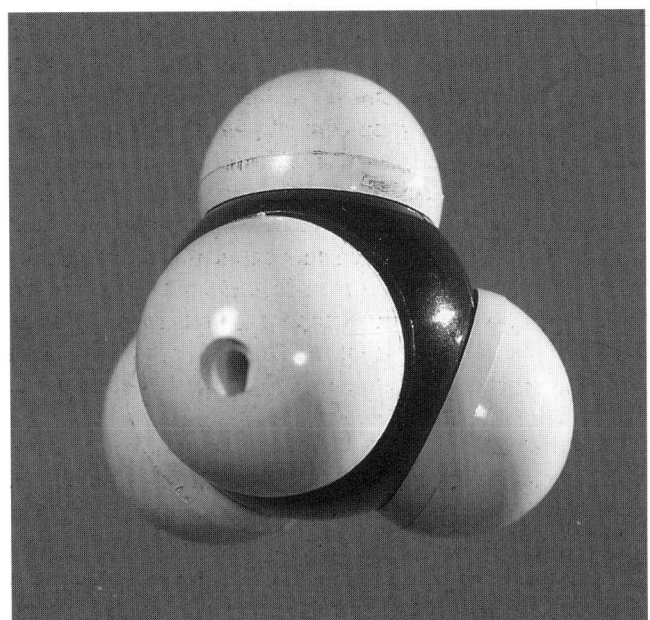

Fig 3.1 *Structure of methane, a simple organic molecule. (a) Structural formula. Carbon typically forms four covalent bonds when combining with other elements or with other carbon atoms. (b) and (c) show two ways of representing molecules as models. (b) A ball-and-stick model shows the arrangement of bonds clearly. In this case the tetrahedral arrangement of C bonds is shown. (c) A space-filling model gives a more realistic appearance, showing how close the atoms really are.*

Box 3.1 Writing formulae

Structural formulae are commonly simplified so that emphasis can be placed on the more important chemical groups. A simple example is ethanoic acid, shown in fig 3.2. The simplified version of the structural formula omits the carbon atoms and any hydrogen atoms joined directly to carbon atoms. We know the valency of carbon is 4, so it is possible to deduce the location of missing carbon atoms. The molecular formula can be represented as $CH_3.COOH$. This could also be written as $C_2H_4O_2$ but the former version is much more useful because it gives information about the relative positions of groups present. These, in turn, determine the properties of the molecules.

structural formula

can be written as

Fig 3.2 *Two ways of representing the structural formula of ethanoic acid, CH_3COOH.*

3.1 From what you have read, what is the difference between molecular and structural formulae?

The explanation for the importance of carbon lies in the way carbon atoms can join to each other, forming either chains or rings as shown in fig 3.3. These chains and rings are the skeletons of organic molecules and hence of life itself. They are very stable because the covalent bonds linking the carbon atoms together are strong. Atoms or particular groups of atoms of other elements (referred to simply as **groups**) can be attached at various positions to

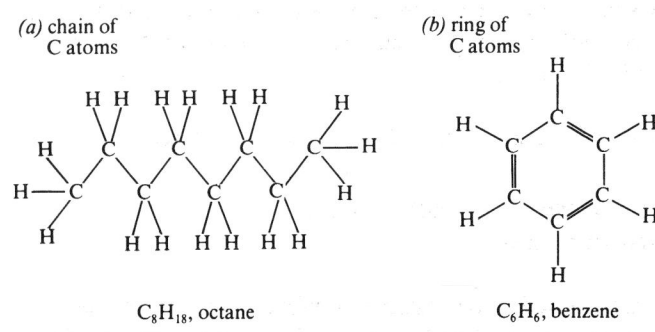

(a) chain of C atoms

C_8H_{18}, octane

(b) ring of C atoms

C_6H_6, benzene

Fig 3.3 *Examples of chain and ring structures formed by C–C bonds.*

Table 3.2 Some common chemical groups found in organic molecules.

Aldehyde group $-C\begin{smallmatrix}H\\\\O\end{smallmatrix}$ or –CHO

Keto group $\begin{smallmatrix}-C-\\|\\C=O\\|\\-C-\end{smallmatrix}$

Hydroxyl group –OH

Carboxyl group –COOH or $-C\begin{smallmatrix}O\\\\O-H\end{smallmatrix}$

Carbonyl group >C=O   (this group is part of the aldehyde, keto-
and carboxyl groups)

Amino group $-N\begin{smallmatrix}H\\\\H\end{smallmatrix}$

Sulphydryl group –S–H

Phosphate group $-O-\overset{\underset{\displaystyle O}{|}}{\underset{\displaystyle O}{\overset{\displaystyle O}{P}}}-O-H$

the carbon skeleton. Some common groups are shown in table 3.2. Each group has its own particular properties. For example, the carboxyl group, –COOH, is responsible for the acidic nature of fatty acids and amino acids.

Notice the use of shorthand methods to show chemical formulae in table 3.2.

Thus the group $C\begin{smallmatrix}H\\\\O\end{smallmatrix}$ is written as –CHO.

> **3.2** Fig 3.3 shows structural formulae of octane and benzene. Draw simplified versions of the structural formulae of (a) octane and (b) benzene, using the convention described in fig 3.2 in box 3.1.

Multiple bonds.   Note also in table 3.2 and in fig 3.3 that carbon can form double bonds with itself, C=C. In fact, carbon, oxygen and nitrogen can all form strong multiple bonds:

double bonds: >C=C<   >C=O   >C=N–

triple bonds: –C≡C– –C≡N
(rare in nature)

Compounds containing double (=) or triple (≡) carbon–carbon bonds are called **unsaturated**. In a **saturated** carbon compound, all carbon–carbon bonds are single.

> **3.3** Draw the structural formula for the unsaturated organic compound ethene, C_2H_4.

Summary.   The important chemical properties of carbon are:

- it is a relatively small atom with a low mass,
- it has the ability to form four strong, stable covalent bonds,
- it has the ability to form carbon–carbon bonds, thus building up large carbon skeletons with ring and/or chain structures,
- it has the ability to form multiple covalent bonds with other carbon atoms, oxygen and nitrogen.

This unique combination of features is responsible for the enormous variety of organic molecules. Variation occurs in three major ways:

- **size**, determined by the number of carbon atoms in the skeleton,
- **chemistry**, determined by the elements and chemical groups attached to the carbon atoms, and how saturated the carbon skeleton is,
- **shape**, determined by geometry, that is angles of the bonds.

3.1.2   Biological molecules

Living organisms are made of a limited number of types of atom, shown in table 3.1, which combine to form molecules, the building blocks of life. These molecules vary enormously in size from simple molecules such as carbon dioxide and water to macromolecules (giant molecules) such as proteins. The smaller molecules are soluble, easily transported and frequently enter into the general chemical activity of cells known as metabolism. Larger molecules tend to be used for storage or for structural purposes, and some can be described as 'informational' molecules, concerned with carrying genetic information (DNA and RNA) and the expression of that information (proteins).

Of the smaller molecules, water is the most abundant, typically making up between 60–95% of the fresh mass of an organism. Certain simple organic molecules are also found in all living organisms; these are shown in fig 3.4 and act as building blocks for the larger molecules. They are the kinds of molecules which biologists speculate could have been made in the 'primeval soup' of chemicals which is thought to have existed in the early history of the planet, before life itself appeared (chapter 26). These simple organic molecules are made in turn from even simpler, inorganic molecules, notably carbon dioxide, nitrogen and water.

Importance of water

Without water, life could not exist on this planet. It is important for two reasons. Firstly it is a vital chemical

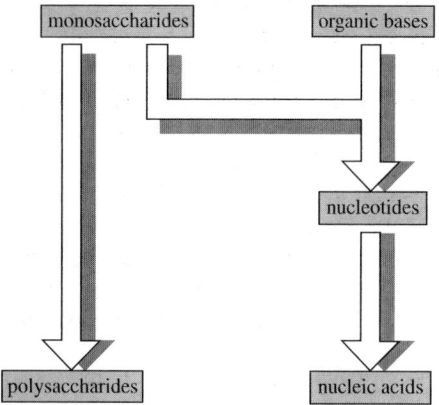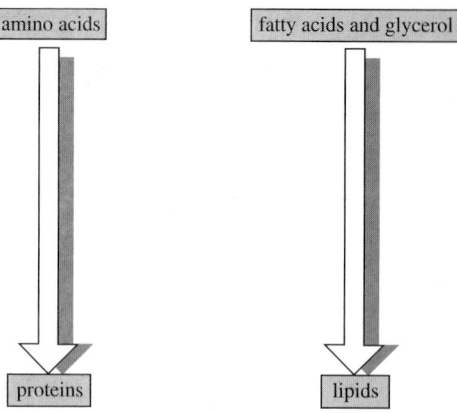

Fig 3.4 *The building blocks of life.*

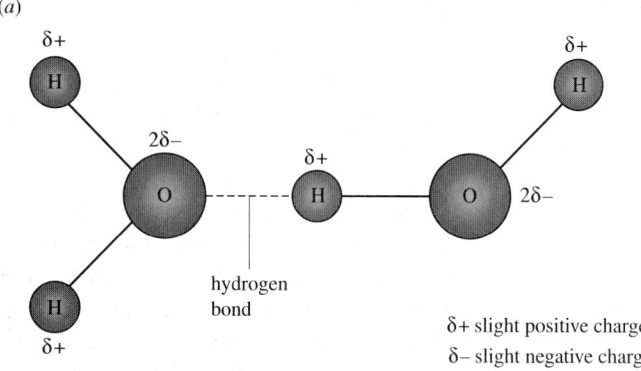

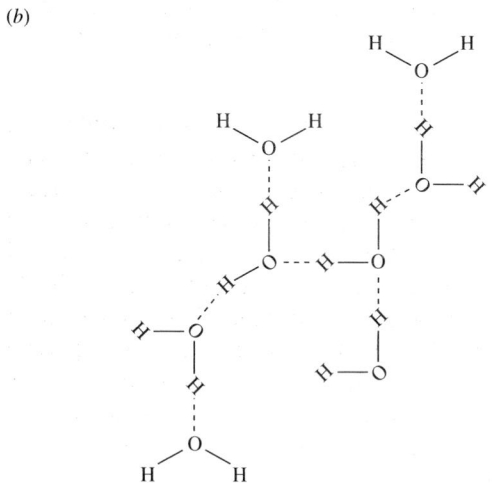

Fig 3.5 *Hydrogen bonding between water molecules.*
(a) *Two water molecules attracted to each other by hydrogen bonding.* (b) *Network of hydrogen-bonded water molecules held together by hydrogen bonding. Such networks are constantly forming and breaking in liquid water.*

constituent of living cells, and secondly it provides an environment for those organisms that live in water. It is worthwhile, then, looking at some of its chemical and physical properties.

These properties are rather unusual and due mostly to its small size, its polarity and to hydrogen-bonding between its molecules. Polarity is an uneven charge distribution within a molecule. In water, one part, or pole, of the molecule is slightly positive and the other slightly negative. This is known as a **dipole**. It occurs because the oxygen atom has greater electron-attracting power than the hydrogen atoms. As a result the oxygen atom tends to attract the single electrons of the hydrogen atoms. Electrons are negatively charged, so giving the oxygen atom a slightly negative charge relative to the hydrogen atom.

Water molecules therefore have a weak attraction for each other, with opposite charges coming together and causing them to behave as if they were 'sticky', like magnets (fig 3.5a). These attractions are not as strong as normal ionic or covalent bonds and are called **hydrogen bonds**. They are constantly being formed, broken and re-formed in water (fig 3.5b). Although individually weak, their collective effect is responsible for many of the unusual physical properties of water. With these features in mind, some of the biologically significant properties of water can be examined.

Biological significance of water

Solvent properties. Water is an excellent solvent for polar substances. These include ionic substances like salts, which contain charged particles (ions), and some non-ionic substances like sugars that contain polar groups (slightly charged) such as the slightly negative hydroxyl group (–OH). On contact with water, the ions and the polar groups are surrounded by water molecules which separate (dissociate) the ions or molecules from each other. This is what happens when a substance dissolves in water (fig 3.6).

Once a substance is in solution its molecules or ions can move about freely, thus making it more chemically reactive than if it were solid. Thus the majority of the cell's

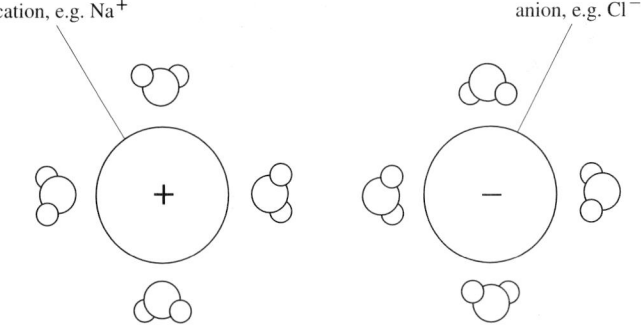

cation, e.g. Na⁺

anion, e.g. Cl⁻

oxygen (slight negative charge) faces the ion

hydrogen (slight positive charge) faces the ion

Fig 3.6 *Distribution of water molecules around ions in a solution. Note that the more negatively charged oxygen atom of water faces inwards to the cation but outwards from the anion. Water molecules have the effect of separating the ions because they collectively have a stronger attraction for the ions than the ions have for each other. If the ions were not separated they would form a solid crystal, for example sodium chloride crystals (common salt). Water has the effect of dissolving the salt.*

chemical reactions take place in aqueous solutions. By contrast, non-polar molecules, such as lipids, are repelled by water and usually group together in its presence, that is non-polar molecules are **hydrophobic** (water-hating). Such hydrophobic interactions are important in the formation of membranes and help to determine the three-dimensional structure of many protein molecules, nucleic acids and other cell structures.

Water's solvent properties also mean that it acts as a transport medium, as in the blood, lymphatic and excretory systems, the alimentary canal and in xylem and phloem.

High heat capacity. The heat capacity of water is the amount of heat required to raise the temperature of 1 kg of water by 1 °C. Water has a high heat capacity. This means that a large increase in heat energy results in a relatively small rise in temperature. This is because much of the energy is used in breaking the hydrogen bonds (overcoming the 'stickiness') which restrict the movement of the molecules.

Temperature changes within water are minimised as a result of its high heat capacity. Biochemical processes therefore operate over a smaller temperature range, proceeding at more constant rates and are less likely to be inhibited by extremes of temperature. Water also provides a very constant external environment for many cells and organisms.

High heat of vaporisation. Latent heat of vaporisation is a measure of the heat energy required to vaporise a liquid, that is to overcome the attractive forces between its molecules so that they can escape as a gas. A relatively large amount of energy is needed to vaporise

water (make it evaporate or boil away into gas). This is due to the hydrogen bonding. As a result, water has an unusually high boiling point for such a small molecule.

The energy transferred to water molecules to allow them to vaporise results in a loss of energy from their surroundings, that is cooling takes place. This is made use of in the sweating and panting of mammals, the opening of the mouth of some reptiles, such as crocodiles, in sunshine, and may be important in cooling transpiring leaves. The high heat of vaporisation means that a large amount of heat can be lost with minimal loss of water from the body.

High heat of fusion. Latent heat of fusion is a measure of the heat energy required to melt a solid, in this case ice. With its high heat capacity, water requires relatively large amounts of heat energy to thaw it. Conversely, liquid water must lose a relatively large amount of heat energy to freeze. Contents of cells and their environments are therefore less likely to freeze. Ice crystals are particularly damaging if they develop inside cells.

Density and freezing properties. The density of water decreases below 4 °C and ice therefore tends to float. It is the only substance whose solid form is less dense than its liquid form.

Since ice floats, it forms at the surface first and the bottom last. If ponds froze from the bottom upwards, freshwater life could not exist in temperate or arctic climates. Ice insulates the water below it, thus increasing the chances of survival of organisms in the water. This is important in cold climates and cold seasons, and must have been particularly so in the past, such as during Ice Ages. Also, the ice thaws more rapidly by being at the surface. The fact that water below 4 °C tends to rise also helps to maintain circulation in large bodies of water. This may result in nutrient cycling and colonisation of water to greater depths.

High surface tension and cohesion. Cohesion is the force whereby individual molecules stick together. At the surface of a liquid, a force called surface tension exists between the molecules as a result of cohesive forces between the molecules. These cause the surface of the liquid to occupy the least possible surface area (ideally a sphere). Water has a higher surface tension than any other liquid. The high cohesion of water molecules is important in cells and in translocation of water through xylem in plants (chapter 13). At a less fundamental level, many small organisms rely on surface tension to settle on water or to skate over its surface.

Water as a reagent. Water is biologically significant as an essential metabolite, that is it participates in the chemical reactions of metabolism. In particular, it is used as a source of hydrogen in photosynthesis (section 7.6) and is used in hydrolysis reactions.

Some of the biologically important functions of water are summarised in table 3.3.

Table 3.3 Some biologically important functions of water.

All organisms

Structure – high water content of cells (70–95% typical)

Solvent and medium for diffusion

Reagent in hydrolysis

Support for aquatic organisms

Fertilisation by swimming gametes

Dispersal of seeds, gametes and larval stages of aquatic organisms, and seeds of some terrestrial species e.g. coconut

Plants

Osmosis and *turgidity* (important in many ways, such as growth (cell enlargement), support, guard cell mechanism)

Reagent in photosynthesis

Transpiration

Translocation of inorganic ions and organic compounds

Germination of seeds – swelling and breaking open of the testa and further development

Animals

Transport in blood vascular system, lymphatic system, excretory system

Osmoregulation

Cooling by evaporation, such as sweating, panting

Lubrication, as in joints

Support – hydrostatic skeleton of e.g. annelid worms

Protection, for example lachrymal fluid (tears), mucus

Migration in ocean currents

3.1.3 Macromolecules

Simpler organic molecules often associate to form larger molecules. A **macromolecule** is a giant molecule made from many repeating units. Molecules built like this are known as **polymers**. The individual units are known as **monomers**. The units are joined by a chemical process known as **condensation**, which means removal of water. They can be broken down again by the opposite process, **hydrolysis**, or addition of water. There are three important types of macromolecule in biology, namely **polysaccharides**, **proteins** and **nucleic acids** and their constituent monomers are **monosaccharides**, **amino acids** and **nucleotides** respectively.

Macromolecules account for over 90% of the dry mass of cells. Polysaccharides tend to be used for food storage or structural purposes, whereas nucleic acids and proteins can be regarded as 'informational' molecules. This means that the *sequence* of subunits is important in proteins and

nucleic acids and is much more variable than in polysaccharides, where only one or two different subunits are normally used. The reasons for this will become clear later. In the rest of this chapter, we shall be studying the three classes of macromolecules and their subunits in detail. Lipids, which are generally much smaller molecules, will also be studied since they are made from simple organic molecules (fig 3.4).

3.2 Carbohydrates

Carbohydrates are substances which contain the elements carbon, hydrogen and oxygen and have the general formula $C_x(H_2O)_y$, where x and y are variable numbers; their name (hydrate of carbon) is derived from the fact that hydrogen and oxygen are present in the same proportions as in water, namely two hydrogen atoms to one oxygen atom. In addition, they have the following properties:

- all are aldehydes or ketones,
- all contain several hydroxyl groups.

Their chemistry is determined by these groups. For example, aldehydes are very easily oxidised and hence are powerful reducing agents. The structures of these groups are shown in table 3.2.

Carbohydrates are divided into three main classes, monosaccharides, disaccharides and polysaccharides, as shown in fig 3.7.

3.2.1 Monosaccharides

Monosaccharides are single sugar units. Their general formula is $(CH_2O)_n$ and some of their properties are shown in fig 3.7. They are classified according to the number of carbon atoms as trioses (3C), tetroses (4C), pentoses (5C), hexoses (6C) and heptoses (7C). Of these, pentoses and hexoses are the most common.

> **3.4** What would be the molecular formula of pentoses and hexoses?

The chief functions of the common monosaccharides are summarised in table 3.4. It will be seen from table 3.4 that monosaccharides are important as energy sources and as building blocks for the synthesis of larger molecules.

Aldoses and ketoses

In monosaccharides, all the carbon atoms except one have a hydroxyl group attached. The remaining carbon atom is either part of an aldehyde group, in which case the

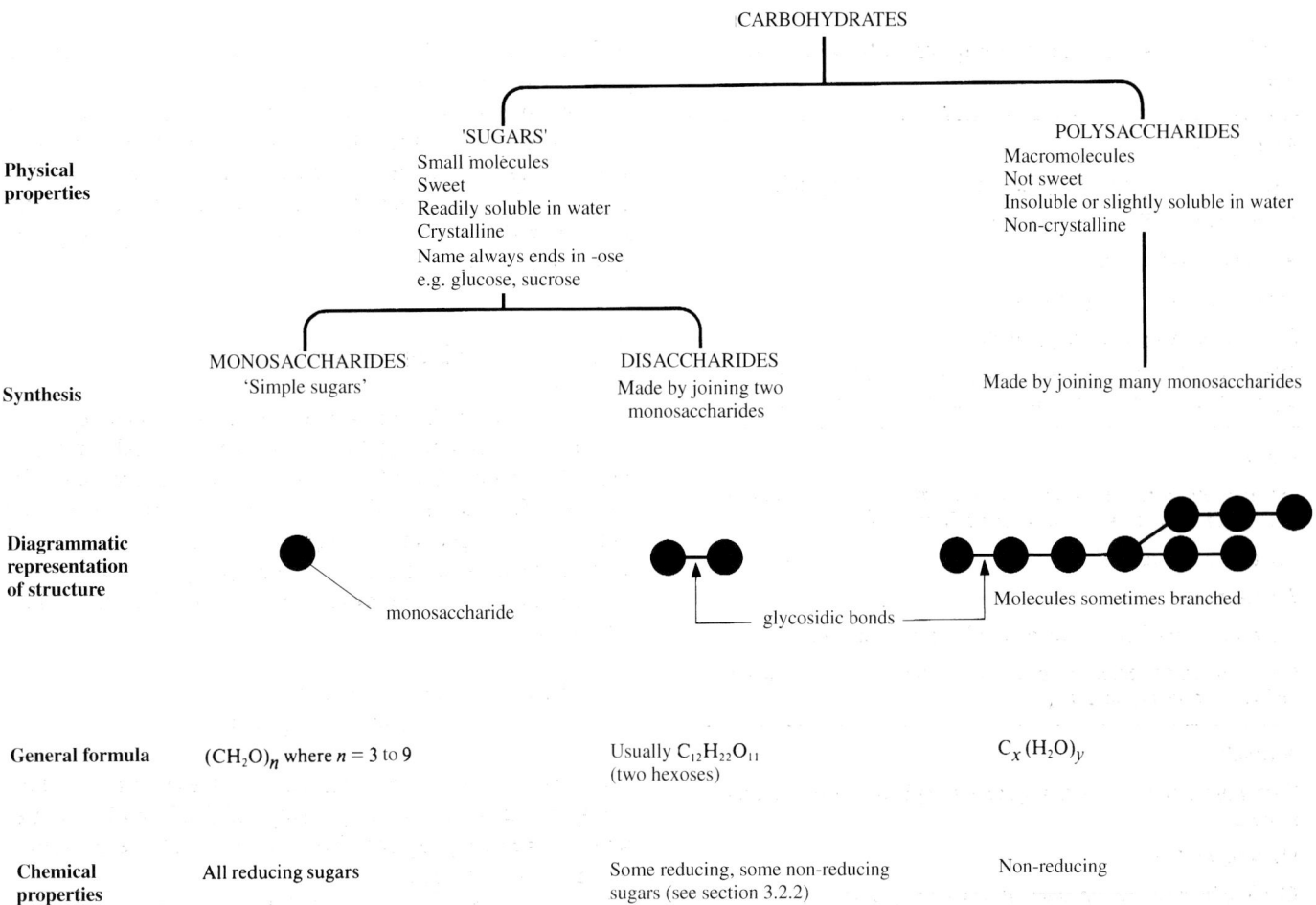

	'SUGARS' Small molecules Sweet Readily soluble in water Crystalline Name always ends in -ose e.g. glucose, sucrose		POLYSACCHARIDES Macromolecules Not sweet Insoluble or slightly soluble in water Non-crystalline
Physical properties			
Synthesis	MONOSACCHARIDES 'Simple sugars'	DISACCHARIDES Made by joining two monosaccharides	Made by joining many monosaccharides
Diagrammatic representation of structure	monosaccharide	glycosidic bonds	Molecules sometimes branched
General formula	$(CH_2O)_n$ where $n = 3$ to 9	Usually $C_{12}H_{22}O_{11}$ (two hexoses)	$C_x(H_2O)_y$
Chemical properties	All reducing sugars	Some reducing, some non-reducing sugars (see section 3.2.2)	Non-reducing

Fig 3.7 *Classification of carbohydrates. Note that monosaccharides and disaccharides are both referred to as sugars. They share certain properties, such as sweetness of taste.*

Table 3.4 Chief functions of monosaccharides.

Trioses $C_3H_6O_3$ e.g. glyceraldehyde, dihydroxyacetone
Intermediates in respiration (see glycolysis), photosynthesis (see dark reactions) and other branches of carbohydrate metabolism

Pentoses $C_5H_{10}O_5$ e.g. ribose, deoxyribose, ribulose

- Synthesis of nucleic acids; ribose is a constituent of RNA, deoxyribose of DNA

- Synthesis of some coenzymes, e.g. ribose is used in the synthesis of NAD and NADP

- Synthesis of ATP requires ribose

- Ribulose bisphosphate is the CO_2 acceptor in photosynthesis and is made from the 5C sugar ribulose

Hexoses $C_6H_{12}O_6$ e.g. glucose, fructose, galactose

- Source of energy when oxidised in respiration; glucose is the most common respiratory substrate and the most common monosaccharide

- Synthesis of disaccharides; two monosaccharide units can link together to form a disaccharide

- Synthesis of polysaccharides; glucose is particularly important in this role

monosaccharide is called an **aldose** or **aldo sugar**, or is part of a keto group, when it is called a **ketose** or **keto sugar**. Thus all monosaccharides are aldoses or ketoses. The two simplest monosaccharides are the trioses glyceraldehyde and dihydroxyacetone. Glyceraldehyde has an aldehyde group and dihydroxyacetone has a keto group (fig 3.8). In general, aldoses, such as ribose and glucose, are more common than ketoses, such as ribulose and fructose.

> **3.5** If you have little experience of chemistry, it might be useful to answer the following with reference to fig 3.8.
> (a) What is the valency of each element?
> (b) What is the total number of each type of atom? Does it conform with the molecular formula?
> (c) How many hydroxyl groups does each molecule contain? Could this have been predicted knowing they were trioses?

A suitable monosaccharide to study in more detail is glucose, the most common monosaccharide. It is a hexose, and therefore has the formula $C_6H_{12}O_6$. Its structure is shown in fig 3.9.

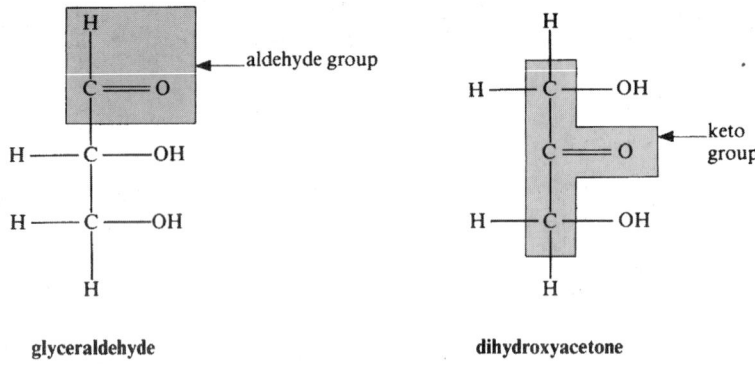

Fig 3.8 *Structures of glyceraldehyde and dihydroxyacetone. Note carefully the positions of the aldehyde and keto groups. Aldehyde groups are always at the end of the chain of C atoms.*

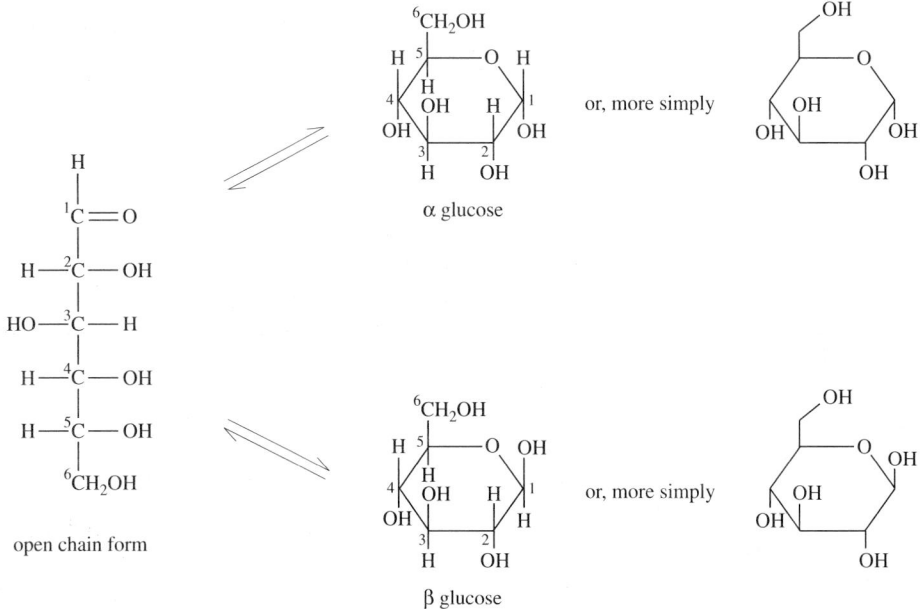

Fig 3.9 *Structure of the open chain and α and β ring forms of glucose. The three forms exist in equilibrium in aqueous solution, with 0.02% open chain, 36% α glucose and 64% β glucose.*

Open chain and ring forms

Fig 3.9 shows glucose as having either an 'open chain' or ring structure. The open chain form can be straight, but because of the bond angles between carbon atoms it is possible for sugars with five and six carbon atoms to bend and form stable ring structures. In hexoses like glucose, the first carbon atom combines with the oxygen atom on carbon atom number five to give a six-membered ring, as shown in fig 3.9. Note that oxygen is part of the ring and that one carbon atom, carbon atom number 6, sticks up out of the ring. In pentoses, the first carbon atom joins with the oxygen atom on the fourth carbon atom to give a five-membered ring, as shown in fig 3.10.

The ring structures of pentoses and hexoses are the usual forms, with only a small proportion of the molecules existing in the open chain form at any one time. The ring structure is the form used to make disaccharides and polysaccharides.

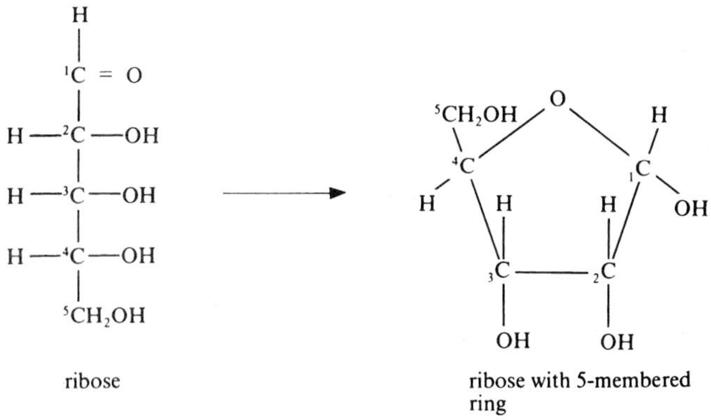

Fig 3.10 *Open chain and ring forms of ribose.*

Alpha (α) and beta (β) isomers

Fig 3.9 shows that glucose can exist in two possible ring forms, known as the **alpha (α)** and **beta (β) forms**. The

Fig 3.11 *Space-filling models of α and β glucose.*

hydroxyl group on carbon atom 1 can project below the ring (α glucose) or above the ring (β glucose). Molecules like this which have the same chemical formula but with different structures are said to be isomers of each other. Fig 3.11 shows space-filling models of the two isomers. At any given moment in a glucose solution, some of the molecules will be in the open chain form and some in the ring form. This is more stable and therefore more common. A glucose molecule can switch spontaneously from the open chain form to either of the two ring forms and back again. Overall an equilibrium is reached where the proportions of the different forms remain constant (fig 3.9).

As stated above, only the ring form can be used to make disaccharides and polysaccharides. Despite the relatively small difference in structure between α and β glucose, there are important consequences. Later we shall see that α glucose is used to make the polysaccharide starch and β glucose the polysaccharide cellulose, molecules which have very different properties.

3.2.2 Disaccharides

Fig 3.7 summarises some of the properties of disaccharides. They are formed when two monosaccharides, usually hexoses, combine by means of a chemical reaction known as a **condensation**. This means removal of water, and is shown in fig 3.12:

$$C_6H_{12}O_6 + C_6H_{12}O_6 \underset{\text{hydrolysis}}{\overset{\text{condensation}}{\rightleftharpoons}} C_{12}H_{22}O_{11} + H_2O$$

The bond formed between two monosaccharides as a result of condensation is called a **glycosidic bond** and it normally forms between carbon atoms 1 and 4 of neighbouring units (a 1,4 bond or 1,4 linkage). The process can be repeated many times to build up the giant molecules of polysaccharides (fig 3.12). The monosaccharide units are called residues once they have been linked. Thus a maltose molecule contains two glucose residues.

The most common disaccharides are maltose, lactose and sucrose:

maltose = glucose + glucose
lactose = glucose + galactose
sucrose = glucose + fructose

Maltose occurs mainly as a breakdown product during digestion of starch by enzymes called amylases. This commonly occurs in animals and in germinating seeds. The latter is made use of in brewing beer when barley grain is used as the source of starch. Germination of the barley is stimulated and this results in the conversion of the starch to maltose, a process known as malting. The maltose is then fermented by yeast to alcohol. This involves conversion of maltose to glucose by the action of the enzyme maltase, a process which also occurs in animals during digestion.

Lactose, or milk sugar, is found exclusively in milk and is an important energy source for young mammals. It can only be digested slowly, so gives a slow steady release of energy.

Sucrose, or cane sugar, is the most abundant disaccharide in nature. It is most commonly found in plants, where it is transported in large quantities through phloem tissue. It makes a good transport sugar because it is very soluble, and can therefore be moved efficiently in high concentrations. It is also relatively unreactive chemically. This means it tends not to enter into general metabolism on its way from one place to another. It is sometimes stored for the same reasons. It is obtained commercially from sugar cane and sugar beet and is the 'sugar' we normally buy in shops.

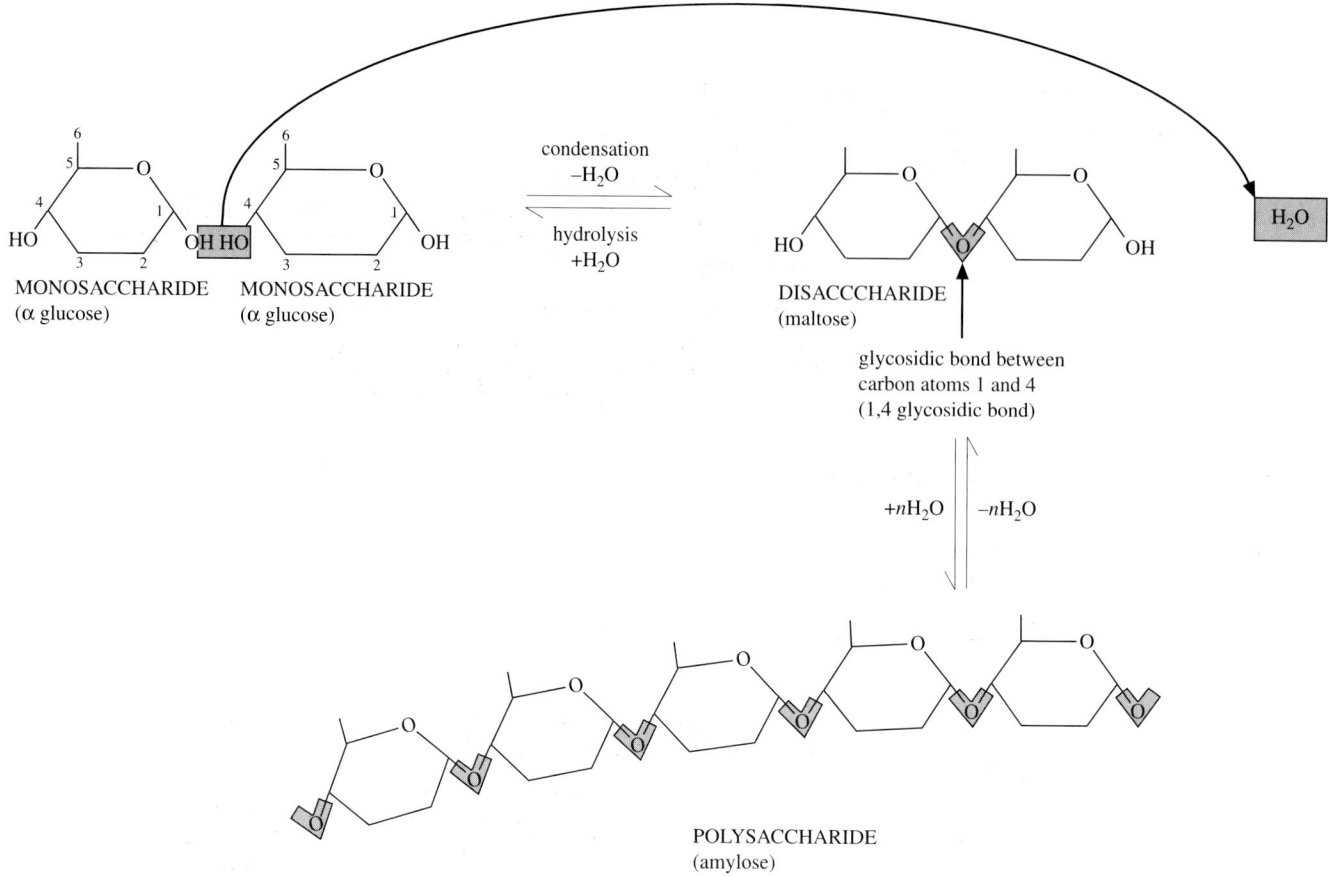

Fig 3.12 *Formation of a disaccharide and a polysaccharide from monosaccharides. In the example illustrated, α glucose is used to make maltose, then starch.*

Reducing sugars

All monosaccharides and some disaccharides, including maltose and lactose, are reducing sugars, meaning that they can carry out a type of chemical reaction known as **reduction**. Sucrose is the only common non-reducing sugar. Two common tests for reducing sugars, Benedict's test and Fehling's test (section 3.7) make use of the ability of these sugars to reduce copper from a valency of 2 to a valency of 1. Both tests involve use of an alkaline solution of copper(II) sulphate ($CuSO_4$) which is reduced to insoluble copper(I) oxide (Cu_2O).

Ionic equation: $Cu^{2+} + e^- \longrightarrow Cu^+$
blue solution   brick-red precipitate

3.2.3   Polysaccharides

Fig 3.7 summarises some of the properties of polysaccharides. They function chiefly as food and energy stores (for example starch and glycogen) and as structural materials (for example cellulose). They are convenient storage molecules for several reasons: their large size makes them more or less insoluble in water, so they exert no osmotic or chemical influence in the cell; they fold into

compact shapes (see below) and they are easily converted to sugars by hydrolysis when required.

As we have already seen, polysaccharides are polymers of monosaccharides.

Starch

Starch is a polymer of α glucose (fig 3.12). It is a major fuel store in plants, but is absent from animals where the equivalent is glycogen (see below). It can easily be converted back to glucose for use in respiration. In germinating seeds the glucose may also be used to make cellulose and other materials needed for growth.

Starch has two components, **amylose** and **amylopectin**. Amylose has a straight chain structure consisting of several thousand glucose residues joined by 1,4 bonds as shown in fig 3.12. These bonds cause the chain to coil helically into a more compact shape. Amylopectin is also compact as it has many branches, formed by 1,6 glycosidic bonds (fig 3.13). It has up to twice as many glucose residues as amylose. A suspension of amylose in water gives a blue-black colour with iodine–potassium iodide solution, whereas a suspension of amylopectin gives a red-violet colour. This forms the basis of the test for starch (section 3.7).

Starch molecules accumulate to form starch grains. These are visible in many plant cells, notably in the

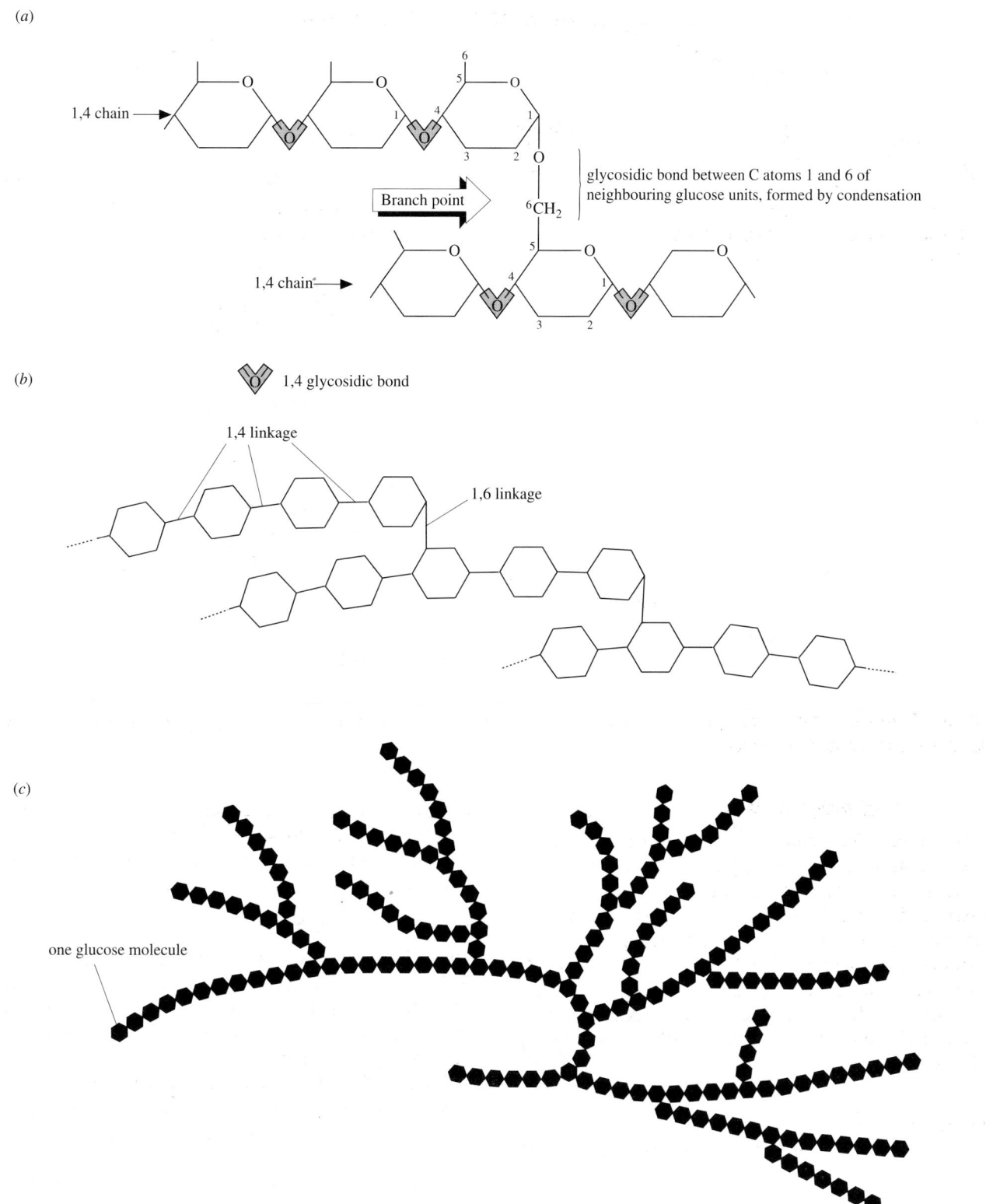

(a)

1,4 chain →

glycosidic bond between C atoms 1 and 6 of neighbouring glucose units, formed by condensation

Branch point

1,4 chain →

(b)

1,4 glycosidic bond

1,4 linkage

1,6 linkage

(c)

one glucose molecule

Fig 3.13 *Structure of amylopectin and glycogen at three levels of 'magnification'. (a) formation of one branch, (b) several branches, (c) highly branched structure of whole molecule. The 1,6 linkages cause branching and the 1,4 linkages cause the chains to turn and coil.*

chloroplasts of leaves (fig 7.6), in storage organs such as the potato tuber, and in seeds of cereals and legumes. The grains appear to be made of layers of starch and are usually of a characteristic size and shape for a given plant species.

Glycogen

Glycogen is the animal equivalent of starch, being a storage polysaccharide made from α glucose; many fungi also store it. In vertebrates, glycogen is stored chiefly in the liver and muscles, both centres of high metabolic activity, where it provides a useful energy reserve. Its conversion back to glucose is controlled by hormones, particularly insulin, as

described in chapter 9. It is very similar in structure to amylopectin (fig 3.13), but shows more branching. It forms tiny granules inside cells which are usually associated with smooth endoplasmic reticulum (fig 5.12).

Cellulose

Cellulose is a polymer of β glucose. Unlike starch and glycogen it has a structural role. When two molecules of β glucose line up, the –OH group on carbon atom 1 can only line up alongside the –OH group on carbon atom 4 if one of the molecules is rotated at 180° to the other (fig 3.14). This is because the –OH group on carbon atom 1 projects below

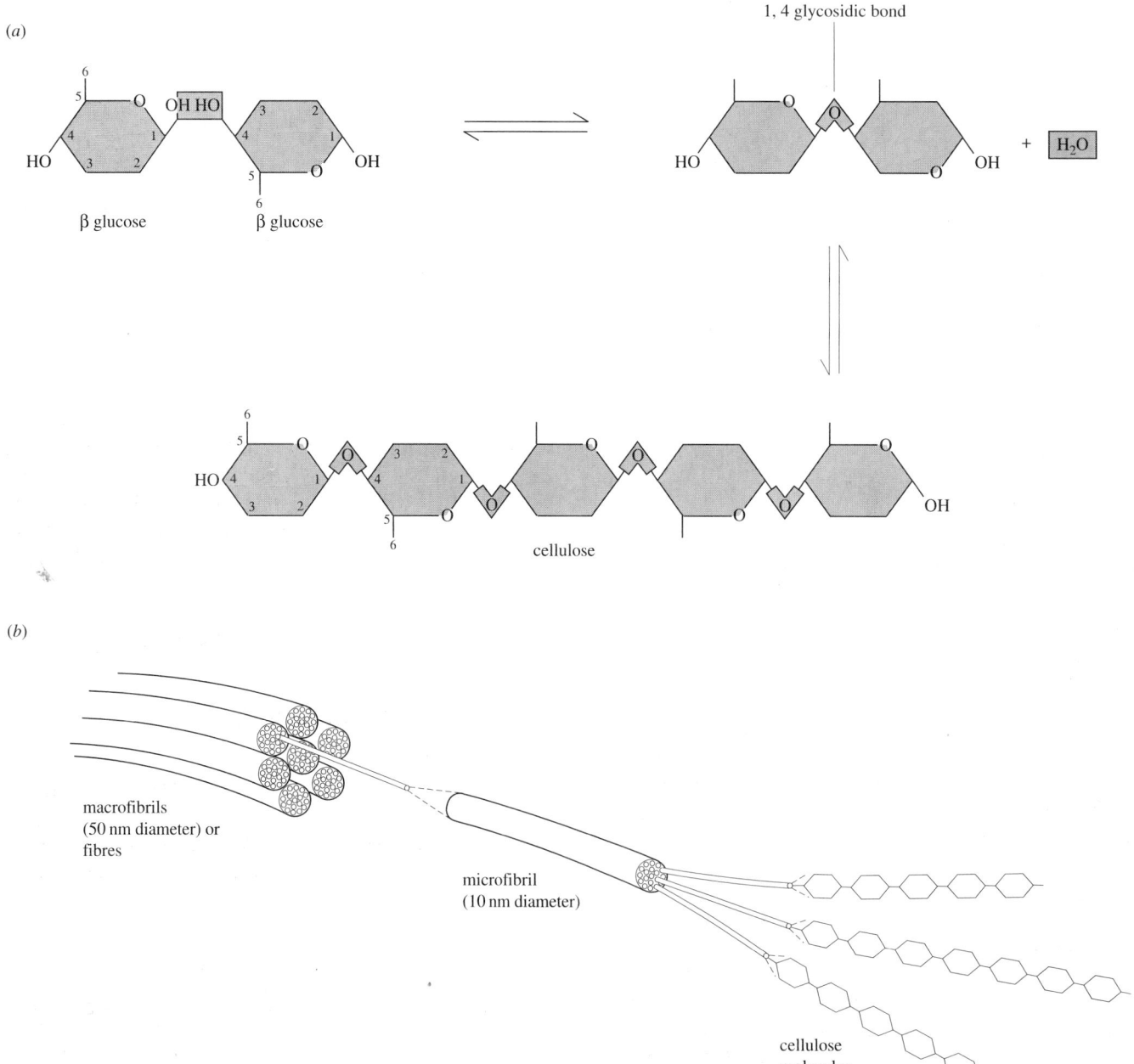

Fig 3.14 *Structure of cellulose. (a) Formation of cellulose from β glucose. Note that the β glucose molecules are rotated at 180° to each other so that OH groups on carbon atoms 1 and 4 can come alongside each other during condensation and formation of glycosidic bonds. (b) Packing of cellulose molecules into microfibrils and macrofibrils (fibres).*

the ring and the –OH group on carbon atom 4 projects above the ring. This rotation of successive residues is the underlying reason why cellulose has a different structure to starch.

About 50% of the carbon found in plants is in cellulose and it is the most abundant organic molecule on Earth. It is virtually confined to plants, although it is found in some nonvertebrate animals and ancestral fungi. Its abundance is due to its being a structural component of all plant cell walls, making up about 20–40% of the wall on average. The structure of the molecule reveals its suitability for this role. It consists of long chains of glucose residues with about 10 000 residues per chain (fig 3.14a). The β 1,4 linkages make the chains straight in contrast to starch where α 1,4 linkages cause the chains to be curved. Hydroxyl groups (–OH) project outwards from each chain in all directions and form hydrogen bonds with neighbouring chains. This cross-linking binds the chains rigidly together. The chains associate in groups of about 60 to 70 to form microfibrils, which are arranged in larger bundles to form macrofibrils (fig 3.14b). These have tremendous tensile strength (some idea of this strength can be obtained by trying to break a piece of cotton by pulling on both ends – cotton is almost pure cellulose). In cell walls the macrofibrils are arranged in several layers, in a glue-like matrix made of other polysaccharides as described in section 5.10.10 and shown in fig 5.35. This gives added strength.

Plant cells are therefore wrapped in several layers of cellulose. This prevents the cells from bursting when water enters by osmosis and also helps to determine the shapes of cells, since the direction in which they expand depends on the way the layers are arranged. As a cell inflates with water, pressure develops inside it and the cell becomes turgid. Turgid cells help support plants which lack wood. Despite their combined strength, the layers are fully permeable to water and solutes, an important property in the functioning of plant cells.

Apart from being a structural compound, cellulose is an important food source for some animals, bacteria and fungi. The enzyme cellulase, which catalyses the digestion of cellulose to glucose, is relatively rare in nature and most animals, including humans, cannot utilise cellulose despite its being an abundant and potentially valuable source of glucose. Ruminant mammals like the cow, however, have bacteria living symbiotically in their guts which digest cellulose. The abundance of cellulose and its relatively slow rate of breakdown in nature have ecological implications because it means that substantial quantities of carbon are 'locked up' in this substance, and carbon is one of the chief materials required by living organisms. Commercially, cellulose is extremely important. It is used, for example to make cotton goods and is a constituent of paper and Sellotape.

3.2.4 Compounds closely related to polysaccharides

Chitin

Chitin is closely related to cellulose in structure and function, being a structural polysaccharide (fig 3.15). It occurs in some fungi, where its fibrous nature contributes to cell wall structure, and in some animal groups, particularly the arthropods where it forms an essential part of the exoskeleton. Structurally it is identical to cellulose except that the hydroxyl (–OH) group at carbon atom 2 is replaced by $-NH.CO.CH_3$. It forms bundles of long parallel chains like cellulose.

Murein

Murein is a polysaccharide which acts as the strengthening material of bacterial cell walls (section 2.31). It is similar in structure to chitin, containing nitrogen like chitin.

> **3.6** What structural features of carbohydrates account for the fact that a wide variety of polysaccharides exists?

3.3 Lipids

Lipids are sometimes classified loosely as those water-insoluble organic substances which can be extracted from cells by organic solvents such as ether, chloroform and benzene. They cannot be defined precisely because their chemistry is so variable, but we can say that true lipids are formed by condensation reactions between fatty acids and an alcohol.

> **3.7** What is a condensation reaction?

3.3.1 Constituents of lipids

Fatty acids

Fatty acids contain the acidic group –COOH (the carboxyl group) and are so named because some of the larger molecules in the series occur in fats. They have the general formula R.COOH where R is hydrogen or a group such as

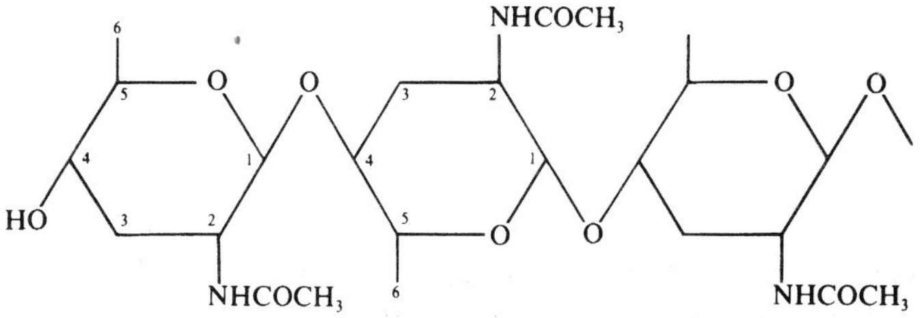

Fig 3.15 *Structure of chitin.*

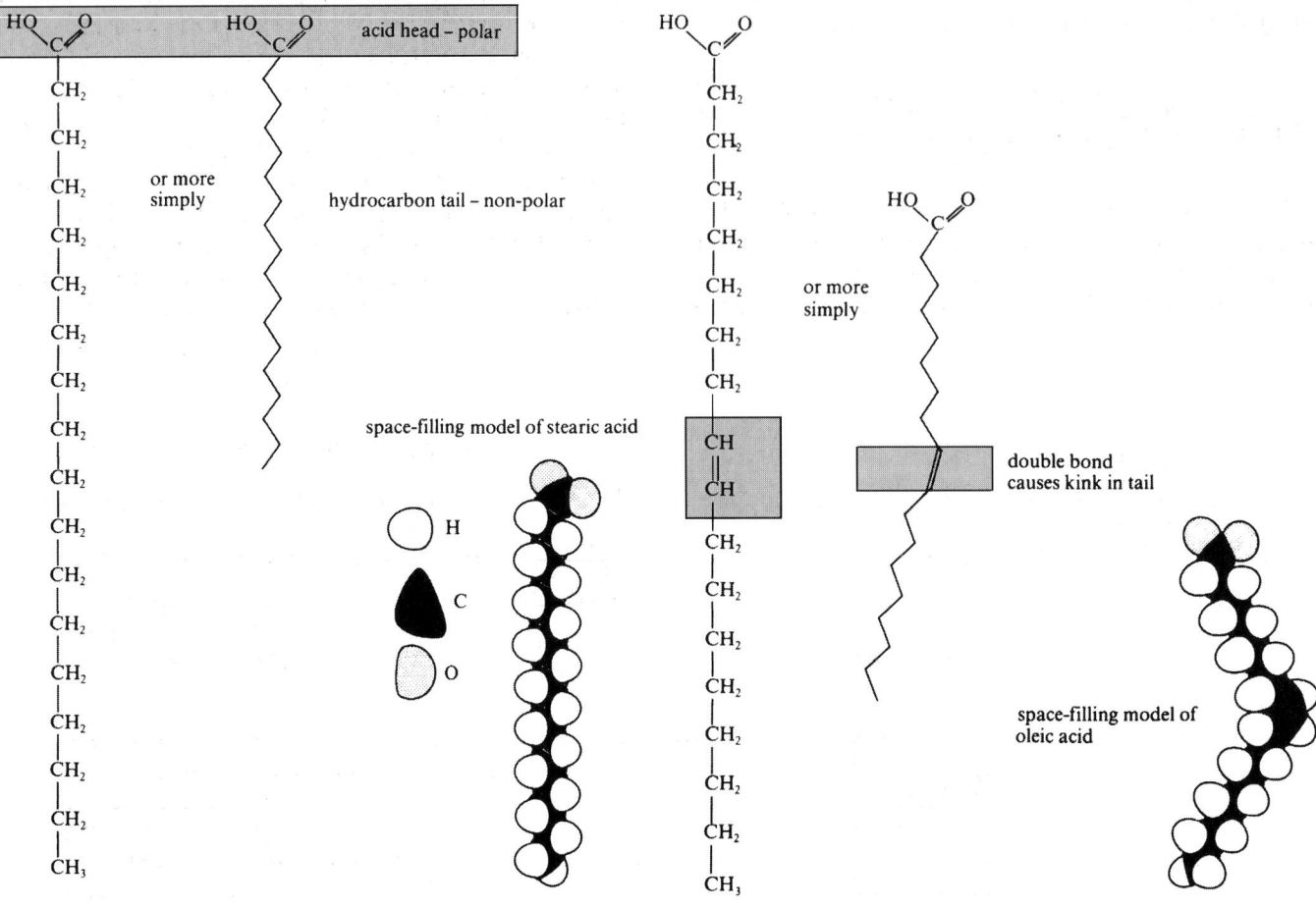

stearic acid, $C_{17}H_{35}COOH$, a saturated fatty acid; in palmitic acid, $C_{15}H_{31}COOH$, the tail is two carbon atoms shorter

acid head – polar

or more simply

hydrocarbon tail – non-polar

space-filling model of stearic acid

H
C
O

oleic acid, $C_{17}H_{33}COOH$, an unsaturated fatty acid

or more simply

double bond causes kink in tail

space-filling model of oleic acid

Fig 3.16 *Some examples of common fatty acids.*

–CH$_3$, –C$_2$H$_5$, and so on, increasing by –CH$_2$ for each subsequent member of the series. There are usually many carbon atoms in the fatty acids used to make lipids. Most naturally occurring fatty acids have an even number of carbon atoms between 14 and 22 (most commonly 16 or 18). The most common fatty acids are shown in fig 3.16. Note the characteristically long chain of carbon and hydrogen atoms forming a **hydrocarbon tail**. Many of the properties of lipids are determined by these tails, including their insolubility in water. The tails are said to be **hydrophobic**, meaning water-hating (*hydro*, water; *phobos*, fear).

Fatty acids sometimes contain one or more double bonds (C=C), such as oleic acid (fig 3.16). In this case they are said to be **unsaturated**, as are lipids containing them. Fatty acids and lipids lacking double bonds are said to be **saturated**. Unsaturated fatty acids melt at much lower temperatures than saturated fatty acids. Oleic acid, for example, is the chief constituent of olive oil and is liquid at normal temperatures (melting point 13.4 °C), whereas palmitic and stearic acids (melting points 63.1 °C and 69.6 °C respectively) are solid at normal body temperatures.

3.8 Cells of poikilothermic ('cold-blooded') animals usually have a higher proportion of unsaturated fatty acids than homoiothermic ('warm-blooded') animals. Can you account for this?

Alcohols

Most lipids are **triglycerides**. These are made from the alcohol glycerol (fig 3.17).

3.3.2 Formation of a lipid

Glycerol has three hydroxyl (–OH) groups, all of which can condense with a fatty acid. Usually all three undergo condensation reactions as shown in fig 3.17, and the lipid formed is therefore called a **triglyceride**.

3.3.3 Properties and functions of triglycerides

Triglycerides are the commonest lipids in nature and are further classified as fats or oils, according to whether they are solid (fats) or liquid (oils) at 20 °C. The higher the proportion of unsaturated fatty acids, the more likely they are to be liquid at a given temperature.

3.9 Tristearin and triolein are both lipids. Which is more likely to be an oil?

Triglycerides are non-polar. In other words, there is no uneven distribution of charge within the molecule. This means that they do not form hydrogen bonds with water molecules and therefore do not dissolve in water – they are hydrophobic. They are less dense than water and therefore float. Their tails vary in length according to the particular fatty acids used. Tristearin is an example of a lipid. It is made from three stearic acid molecules (fig 3.16), so its *tails* are 17 carbon atoms long. A space-filling model of tristearin is shown in fig 3.17.

A major function of lipids is to act as energy stores. They have a higher calorific value than carbohydrates, that is a given mass of lipid will yield more energy on oxidation than an equal mass of carbohydrate. This is because lipids have a higher proportion of hydrogen and an almost insignificant proportion of oxygen compared with carbohydrates.

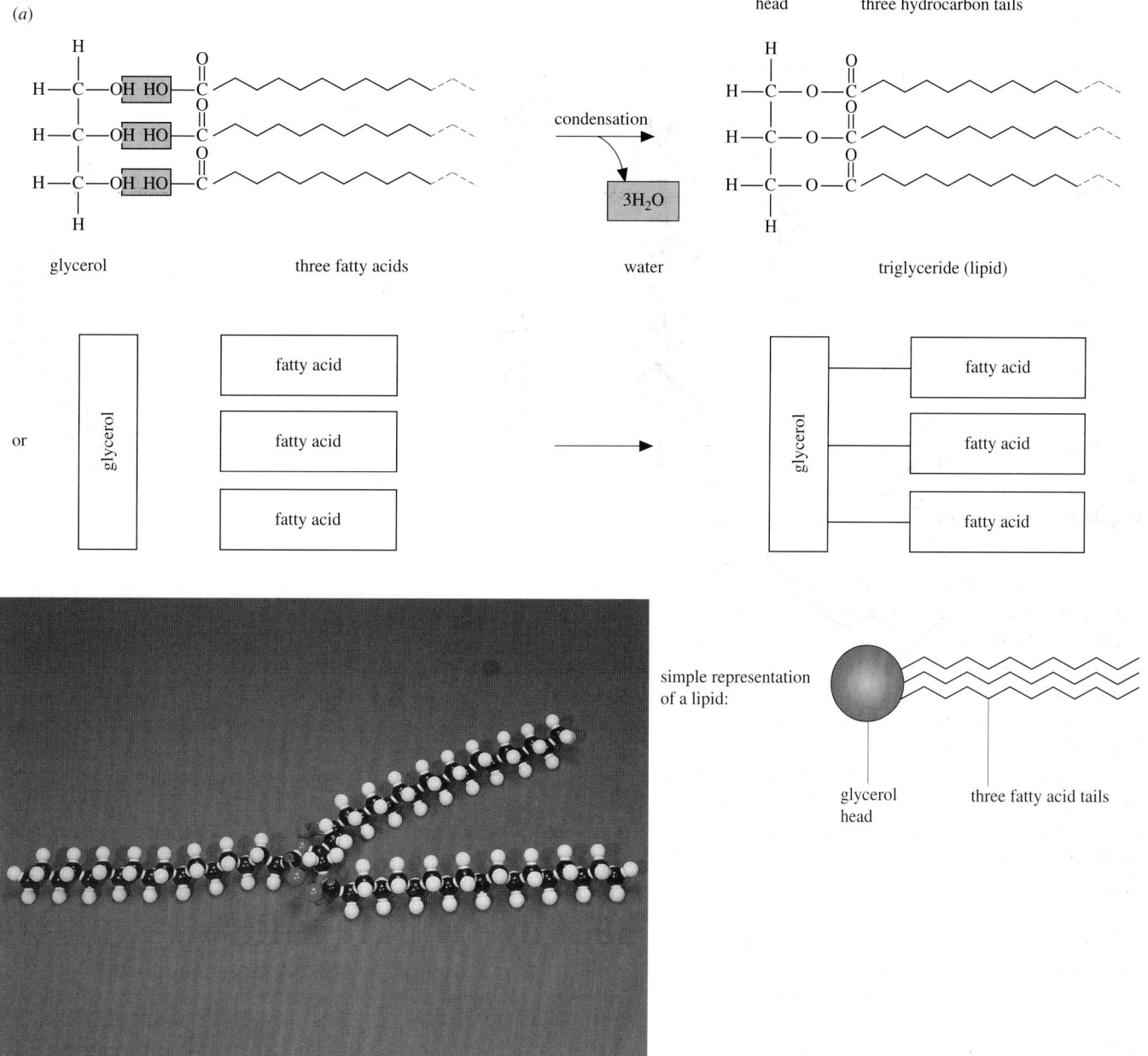

Fig 3.17 (a) *Formation of a triglyceride from glycerol and three fatty acids by three condensation reactions.*
(b) *A space-filling model of tristearin, an example of a triglyceride.*

Animals store extra fat when hibernating, and fat is also found below the dermis of the skin of vertebrates where it serves as an insulator. Here it is extensive in mammals living in cold climates, particularly in the form of blubber in aquatic mammals such as whales, where it also contributes to buoyancy. Plants usually store oils rather than fats. Seeds, fruits and chloroplasts are often rich in oils and some seeds are commercial sources of oils, for example the coconut, castor bean, soyabean and sunflower seed. When fats are oxidised, water is a product. This metabolic water can be very useful to some desert animals, such as the kangaroo rat, which stores fat for this purpose (chapter 20).

> **3.10** A camel stores fat in the hump primarily as a water source rather than as an energy source.
> (*a*) By what metabolic process would water be made available from fat?
> (*b*) Carbohydrates could also be used as a water source in the same process. What advantage does fat have over carbohydrate?

3.3.4 Phospholipids

Phospholipids are lipids containing a **phosphate group**. The commonest type is formed when one of the three –OH groups of glycerol combines with phosphoric acid instead of a fatty acid (fig 3.18). The other two –OH groups combine with fatty acids as in the formation of a triglyceride.

The molecule consists of a phosphate head, which is shaded in fig 3.18, with two hydrocarbon tails from the two fatty acids. The phosphate head carries an electrical charge and is therefore soluble in water; in other words it is **hydrophilic**, or water-loving. The tails, however, are still insoluble in water. Thus one end of the molecule is soluble and the other is not. This is important in the formation of membranes (section 5.9).

3.3.5 Glycolipids

Glycolipids are associations of lipids with carbohydrates. The carbohydrate forms a polar head to the molecule, and glycolipids, like phospholipids, are found in membranes.

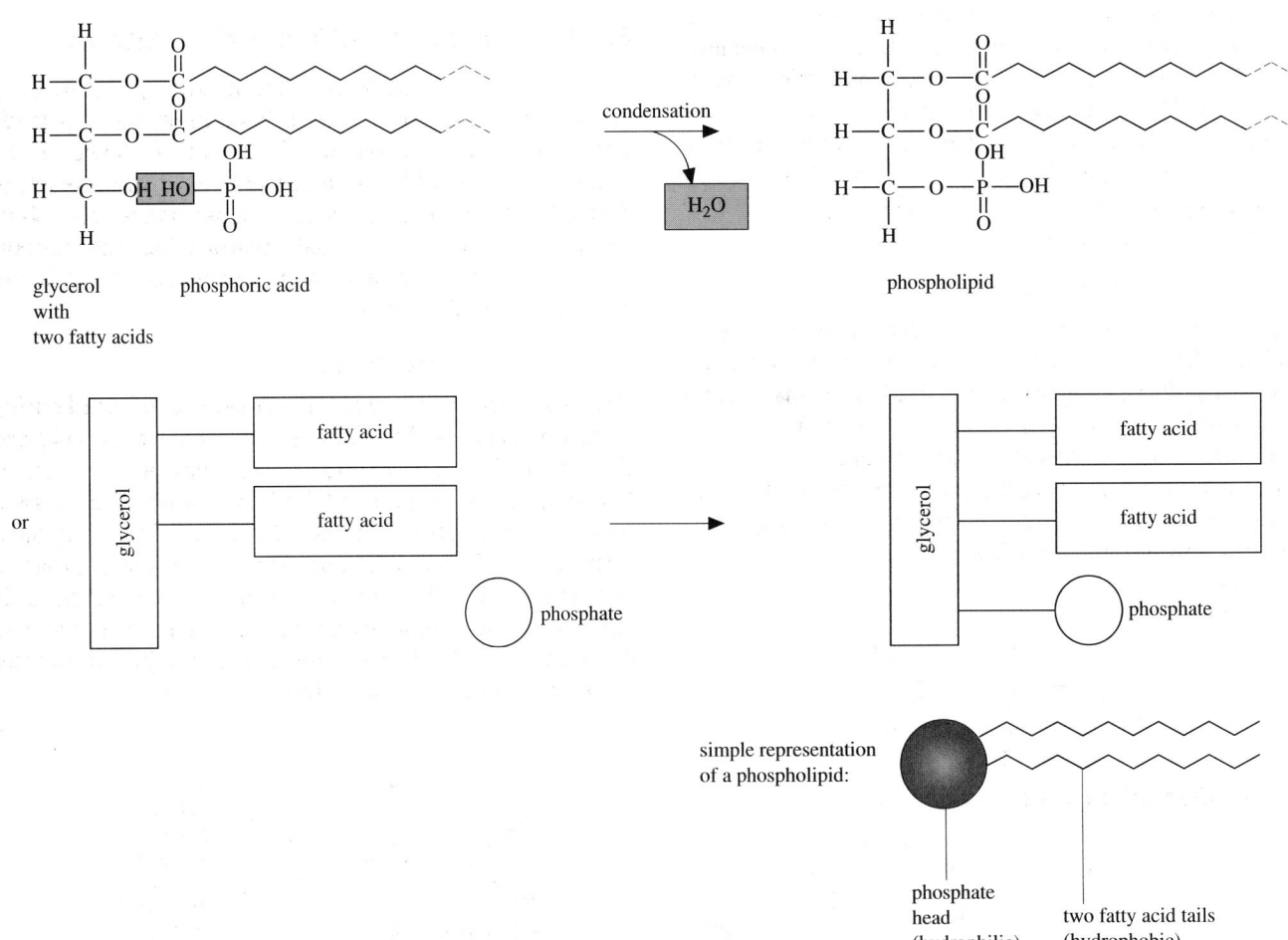

Fig 3.18 *Formation of a phospholipid. The structure can be shown simply as a head with two tails. The phosphate head is strongly polarised and is therefore water soluble (hydrophilic), unlike the non-polar tails (hydrophobic). This is a biologically important property in membranes.*

3.4 Amino acids

Amino acids are the basic units from which proteins are made. Over 170 amino acids are currently known to occur in cells and tissues. Of these, only 20 are commonly found in proteins. These are listed in table 3.5.

Plants are able to make all the amino acids they require from simpler substances. However, animals are unable to synthesise all that they need, and therefore must obtain some 'ready-made' amino acids directly from their diet. These are termed **essential** amino acids. Animals can make the other amino acids they require from these. Note that the essential amino acids are only described as 'essential' because they cannot be synthesised; the non-essential amino acids are just as necessary to make proteins.

3.4.1 Structure and range of amino acids

The general formula of an amino acid is shown in fig 3.19. There is a central carbon atom, known as the α carbon atom, to which is always attached an acidic carboxyl group, **–COOH**, a basic amino group, **–NH₂** and a **hydrogen** atom. The fourth position is the only variable part of the molecule. The group here is known as the **R group**. This group gives each amino acid its uniqueness. Table 3.5 shows the names, three-letter abbreviations and R groups of the 20 commonly occurring amino acids.

The simplest amino acid, and therefore the easiest one to learn as an example, is **glycine**, where R is simply hydrogen (fig 3.20*a*). When R is –CH₃, the amino acid **alanine** is formed (fig 3.20*b*).

Rare amino acids

A small number of rare amino acids occur in the proteins of organisms. They are made from some of the common amino acids. For example, hydroxyproline is made from proline, and is found in the protein collagen; hydroxylysine is made from lysine, and is also found in collagen.

There is no DNA code for the rare amino acids, and they are made from their parent amino acids *after* they have been incorporated into a protein.

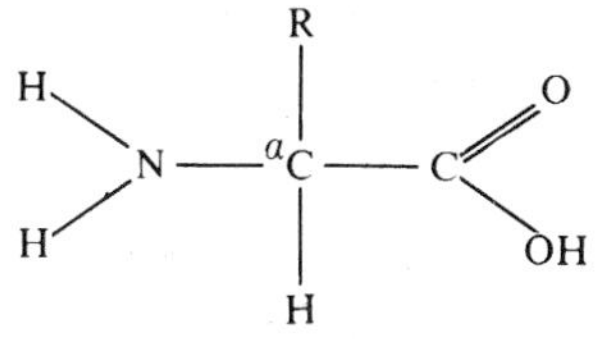

Non-protein amino acids

Over 150 of these are known to occur, either free or in a combined form in cells, but never in proteins. For example, GABA (γ aminobutyric acid) is virtually unique to the nervous system. It is an inhibitory neurotransmitter, important in the brain.

3.4.2 Amino acids are amphoteric

Molecules like amino acids which contain both an acid and a basic part are described as **amphoteric**. They exist mainly as ions and can carry both a positive charge on the basic part and a negative charge on the acid part. Such ions are described as dipolar and are called zwitterions (fig 3.21). This explains the fact that amino acids and proteins can be made to move in an electrical field, as when they are separated by electrophoresis (appendix 1, Book 2). The charge on the amino acid can be affected by changes in its environment. For example, making a solution more acid would increase the concentration of hydrogen ions, and hence positive charges, and these would tend to cancel out the negative charges on the amino acid.

3.4.3 Bonds used in protein structure

Amino acids combine to form proteins. They are joined together by a type of bond known as a **peptide bond**. Once these bonds have been formed, however, the protein typically folds into a particular shape as a result of four other types of bond, namely ionic bonds, disulphide bonds, hydrogen bonds, and hydrophobic interactions. Studying these bonds helps us to understand the structure and behaviour of proteins.

Peptide bond

This is formed when a water molecule is eliminated during a reaction between the amino group of one amino acid and the carboxyl group of another. Elimination of water is known as **condensation** and the bond formed is a covalent bond called a **peptide bond** (fig 3.22). The compound formed is a **dipeptide**. It possesses a free amino group at one end, and a free carboxyl group at the other. This enables further combination between the dipeptide and other amino acids. If many amino acids are joined together in this way, a **polypeptide** is formed (fig 3.23).

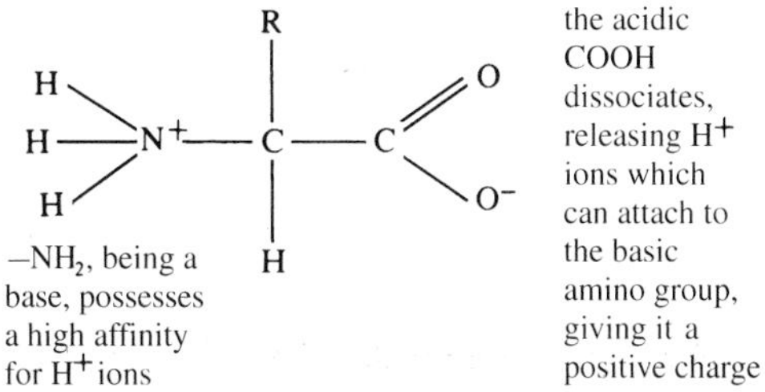

Fig 3.19 *General formula of an amino acid.*

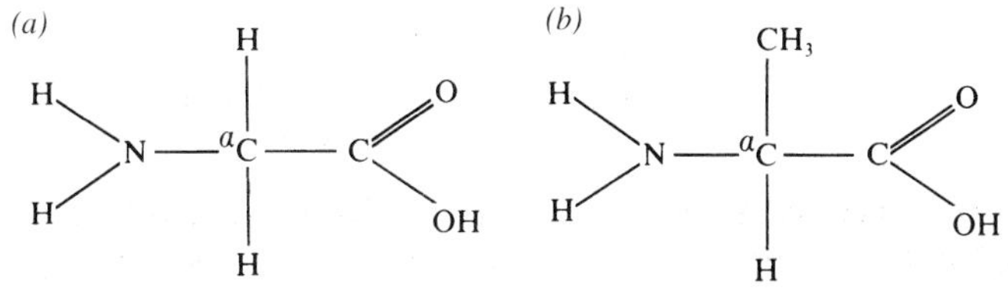

Fig 3.20 *(a) Glycine. (b) Alanine.*

–NH₂, being a base, possesses a high affinity for H⁺ ions

the acidic COOH dissociates, releasing H⁺ ions which can attach to the basic amino group, giving it a positive charge

Fig 3.21 *Neutral zwitterion form of an amino acid.*

Table 3.5 The 20 common amino acids found in proteins. Only the R groups are shown. The box represents the constant part of the molecule, shown fully only in alanine. The amino acids are arranged into four categories. All are neutral except for the acidic and basic ones. The two acidic one have an extra COOH group. The three basic ones contain extra nitrogen. Two amino acids contain sulphur, an extra element. Those labelled essential are essential in the diet of humans. Three amino acids are described as aromatic, having rings of carbon atoms.

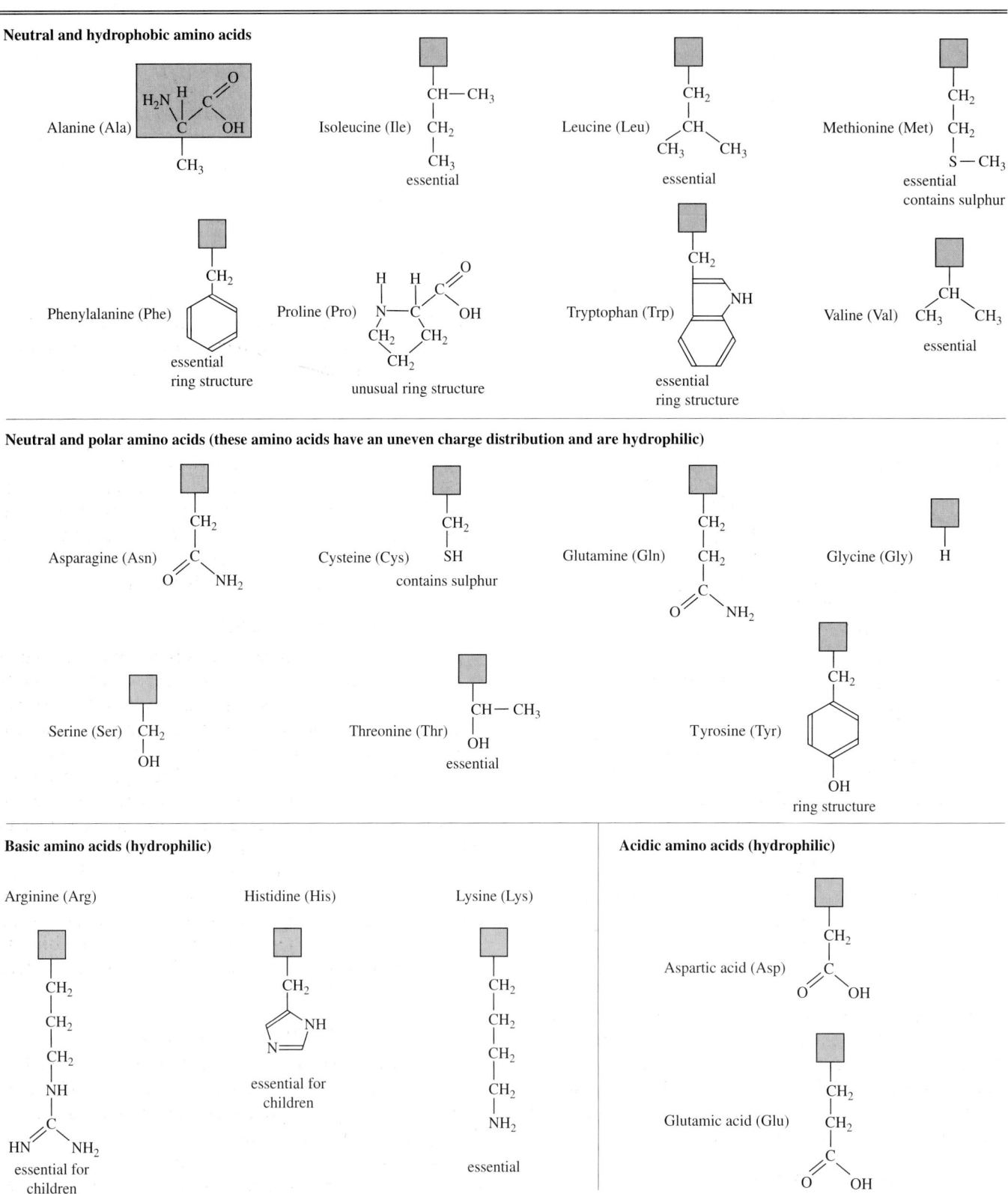

Neutral and hydrophobic amino acids

Neutral and polar amino acids (these amino acids have an uneven charge distribution and are hydrophilic)

Basic amino acids (hydrophilic)

Acidic amino acids (hydrophilic)

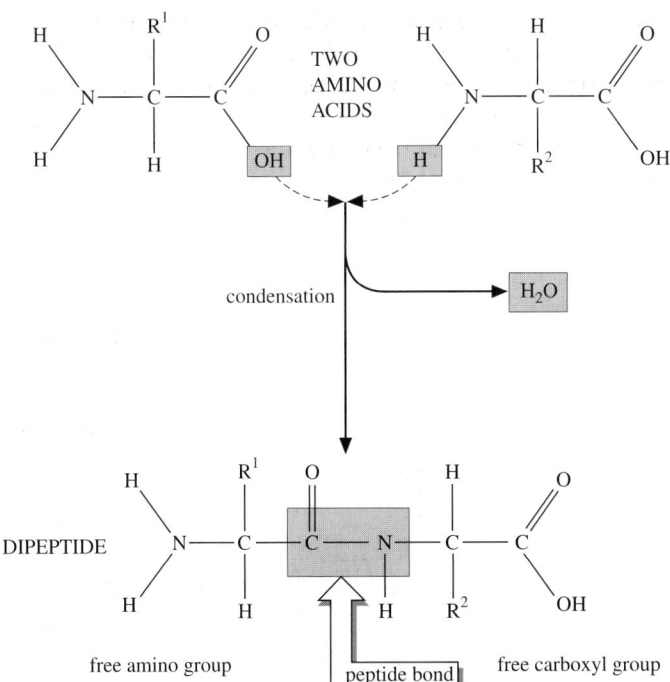

Fig 3.22 *Formation of a dipeptide by a condensation reaction between two amino acids. Condensation is removal of water.*

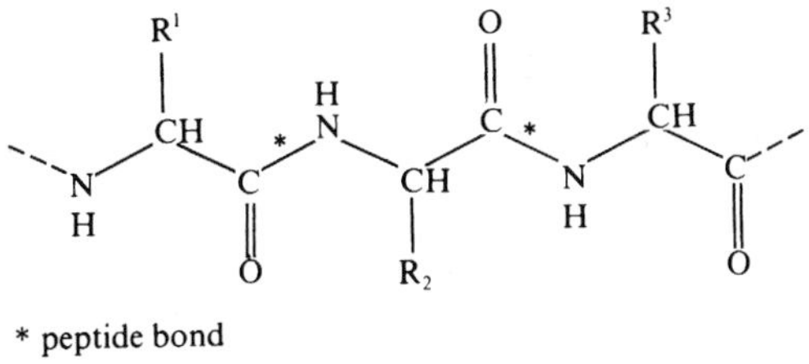

* peptide bond

Fig 3.23 *Part of a polypeptide showing the joining of three amino acids.*

> **3.11** Write down the structural formula of the tripeptide formed by alanine, glycine and serine joined together in that order.

Ionic bond

Acidic and basic R groups exist in an ionised (charged) state at certain pHs. Acidic R groups are negatively charged and basic R groups are positively charged. They can therefore be attracted to each other, forming ionic bonds (fig 3.24). In an aqueous environment this bond is much weaker than a covalent bond and can be broken by changing the pH of the medium. This helps to explain the disruptive effect that changes in pH can have on protein structure (section 3.5.4). For example, adding acid to milk makes it curdle because the ionic bonds in casein (milk protein) are broken and the protein ceases to be soluble.

Disulphide bond

The amino acid cysteine contains a sulphydryl group, –SH, in its R group. If two molecules of cysteine line up

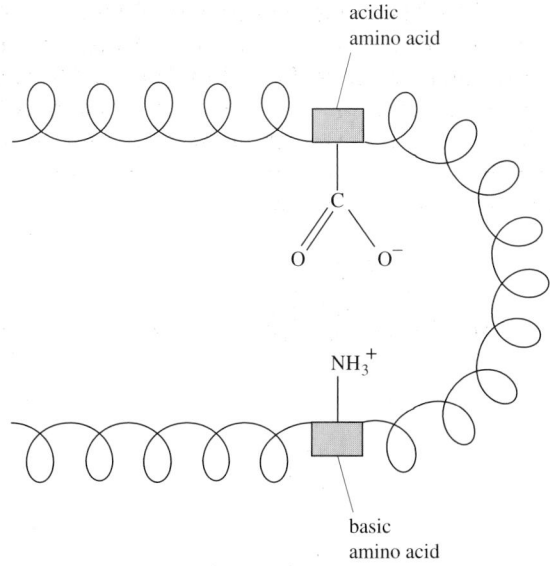

Fig 3.24 *Ionic bond formation. The polypeptide chain of the protein is represented by a coiled spring. The relevant amino acids are shown as boxes with side groups (R groups) attached.*

alongside each other, neighbouring sulphydryl groups can be oxidised and form a disulphide bond (fig 3.25). Disulphide bonds may be formed between different chains of amino acids (see insulin, fig 3.28) or between different parts of the same chain (fig 3.29). In the latter case the disulphide bonds make the molecule fold into a particular shape. They are strong and not easily broken.

Hydrogen bond

Hydrogen bonds have already been discussed in the section on water (section 3.1.2). When hydrogen is part of an OH or NH group it becomes slightly positively charged (electropositive). This is because the electrons that are shared, and which are negatively charged, are attracted more towards the O or N atoms. The hydrogen may then be attracted towards a neighbouring electronegative oxygen or nitrogen atom, such as the O of a C=O group or the N of an NH group (fig 3.26). C=O and NH groups occur along the length of polypeptide chains, as shown in fig 3.23, and they can interact to produce regular shapes such as the α helix discussed later. The hydrogen bond is weak, but as its occurrence is frequent, the total effect makes a considerable contribution towards molecular stability, as in the structure of the α helix (fig 3.30) and silk.

Hydrophobic interactions

Some R groups are non-polar and therefore hydrophobic, such as those on the amino acids tyrosine and valine (table 3.5). If a polypeptide chain contains a number of these groups and is in an aqueous environment, the chain will tend to fold so that the maximum number of hydrophobic groups come into close contact and exclude water (fig 3.27). This is how many globular proteins fold up. The hydrophobic groups tend to point inwards towards

95

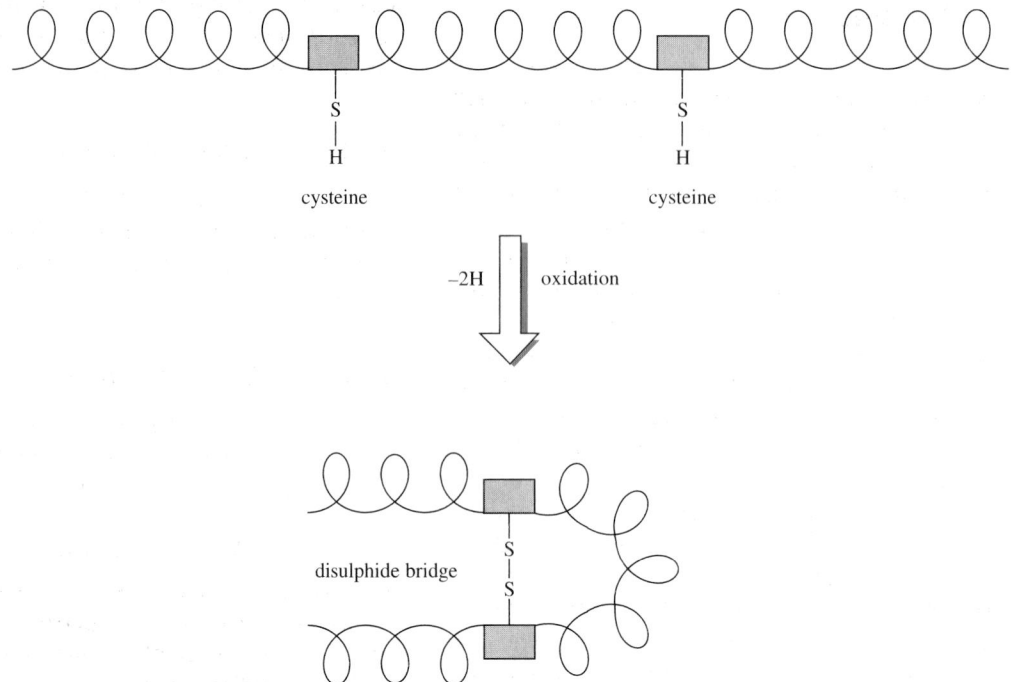

Fig 3.25 *Formation of a disulphide bond between the sulphydryl groups of two cysteines.*

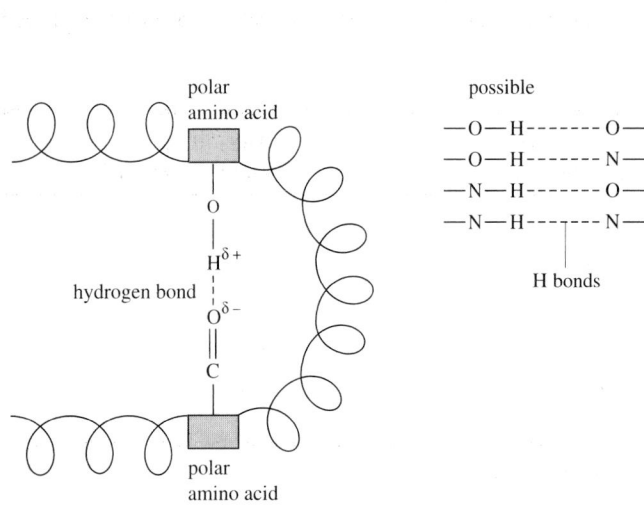

Fig 3.26 *Formation of a hydrogen bond. Hydrogen bonds may form between R groups of polar amino acids or between the C=O and N–H groups either side of peptide bonds (for example, see α helix and β sheet in next section).*

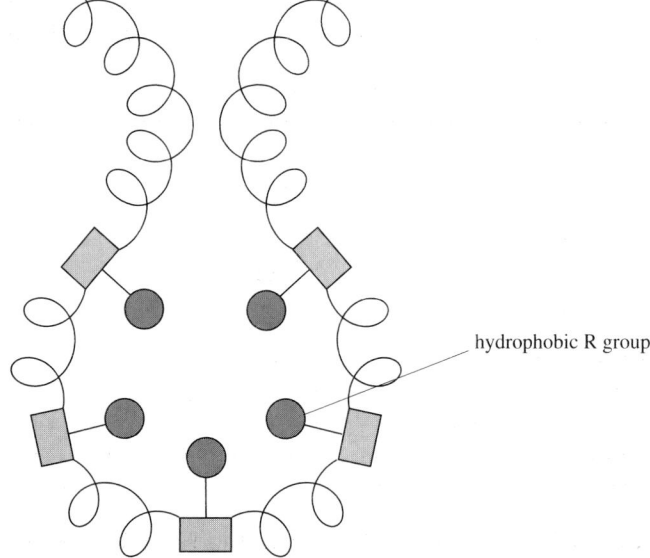

Fig 3.27 *Hydrophobic interactions between hydrophobic R groups. These create a hydrophobic region within the molecule which excludes water.*

the centre of the roughly spherical molecule while the hydrophilic groups face outwards into the aqueous environment, making the protein soluble. In the same way membrane proteins can have hydrophobic regions inside the membrane alongside the hydrophobic tails of the phospholipids, while the hydrophilic regions face outwards alongside the hydrophilic phosphate heads of the phospholipids (fig 5.15).

3.5 Proteins

Proteins are made from amino acids and therefore always contain the elements carbon, hydrogen, oxygen and nitrogen, and in some cases sulphur. Some proteins form complexes with other molecules containing phosphorus, iron, zinc and copper. Proteins are macromolecules of high M_r (relative formula mass or molecular mass), typically between several thousands and several millions, consisting of chains of amino acids. They are polymers and amino acids are the monomers. There are 20 different amino acids which are commonly found in naturally occurring proteins. The potential variety of proteins is unlimited because the sequence of amino acids in each protein is specific for that protein (chapter 23) and is genetically controlled by the DNA of the cell in which it is made. Proteins are the most abundant organic molecules to be found in cells and form over 50% of their total dry mass. They are an essential component of the diet of animals and may be converted to both fat and carbohydrate by the cells. Their diversity enables them to display a great range of structural and metabolic activities within the organism.

3.5.1 Size of protein molecules

Simple peptides containing two, three or four amino acid residues are called di-, tri- and tetrapeptides respectively. Polypeptides are chains of many amino acid residues (up to several thousand – table 3.6). A protein may possess one or more polypeptide chains.

3.5.2 Classification of proteins

Because of the complexity of protein molecules and their diversity of function, it is very difficult to classify them in a single, well-defined fashion. Three alternative methods are given in tables 3.7, 3.8 and 3.9.

3.5.3 Structure of proteins

Each protein possesses a characteristic three-dimensional shape, its **conformation**. There are four separate levels of structure and organisation as follows.

Primary structure

The **primary structure** is the sequence of amino acids in a polypeptide chain. The first person to work out the complete amino acid sequence of a protein was Fred Sanger, working at the Cavendish laboratory in Cambridge, where Watson and Crick also determined the structure of DNA. He worked with the hormone insulin, the smallest protein he could find. It took ten years and the results were published in 1953 (fig 3.28). Max Perutz, another great molecular biologist of the Cavendish, recalls 'it caused a sensation, because it proved

Table 3.6 Sizes of some proteins.

Protein	M_r (molecular mass)	Number of amino acids	Number of polypeptide chains
Ribonuclease	12 640	124	1
Lysozyme	13 930	129	1
Myoglobin	16 890	153	1
Haemoglobin	64 500	574	4
TMV (tobacco mosaic virus)	about 400 000 000	about 336 500	2130

The largest protein complexes are found in viruses where M_rs of over 400 000 000 are commonly found.

Table 3.7 Classification of proteins according to structure.

Type	Nature	Function
Fibrous	Secondary structure most important (little or no tertiary structure) Insoluble in water Physically tough Long parallel polypeptide chains cross-linked at intervals forming long fibres or sheets	Perform structural functions in cells and organisms e.g. **collagen** (tendons, bone, connective tissue), **myosin** (in muscle), **silk** (spiders' webs), **keratin** (hair, horn, nails, feathers)
Globular	Tertiary structure most important Polypeptide chains tightly folded to form spherical shape Easily soluble	Form enzymes, antibodies and some hormones, e.g. **insulin** Other important roles
Intermediate	Fibrous but soluble	e.g. **fibrinogen** – forms insoluble fibrin when blood clots

Table 3.8 Classification of proteins according to composition.

Proteins

Simple	Conjugated
Only amino acids form their structure (see tables 3.7 and 3.9)	Complex compounds consisting of globular proteins and tightly-bound non-protein material; the non-protein material is called a **prosthetic** group

Conjugated proteins

Name	Prosthetic group	Location
Phosphoprotein	Phosphoric acid	Casein of milk Vitellin of egg yolk
Glycoprotein	Carbohydrate	Membrane structure Mucin (component of saliva)
Nucleoprotein	Nucleic acid	Component of viruses Chromosomes Ribosome structure
Chromoprotein	Pigment	Haemoglobin – haem (iron-containing pigment) Phytochrome (plant pigment) Cytochrome (respiratory pigment)
Lipoprotein	Lipid	Membrane structure Lipid transported in blood as lipoprotein
Flavoprotein	FAD (flavine adenine dinucleotide, see section 9.3.5)	Important in electron transport chain in respiration
Metal proteins	Metal	E.g. nitrate reductase, the enzyme in plants which converts nitrate to nitrite

Table 3.9 Protein classification according to function. Proteins are also important in membranes where they function as enzymes, receptor sites and transport sites.

Type	Examples	Occurrence/function
Structural	Collagen Keratin Elastin Viral coat proteins	Component of connective tissue, bone, tendons, cartilage Skin, feathers, nails, hair, horn Elastic connective tissue (ligaments) 'Wraps up' nucleic acid of virus
Enzymes	Trypsin Ribulose bisphosphate carboxylase Glutamine synthetase	Catalyses hydrolysis of protein Catalyses carboxylation (addition of CO_2) of ribulose bisphosphate in photosynthesis Catalyses synthesis of the amino acid glutamine from glutamic acid + ammonia
Hormones	Insulin Gucagon ACTH	Help to regulate glucose metabolism Stimulates growth and activity of the adrenal cortex
Respiratory pigment	Haemoglobin Myoglobin	Transports O_2 in vertebrate blood Stores O_2 in muscles
Transport	Serum albumin	Transport of fatty acids and lipids in blood
Protective	Antibodies Fibrinogen Thrombin	Form complexes with foreign proteins Forms fibrin in blood clotting Involved in blood clotting mechanism
Contractile	Myosin Actin	Moving filaments in myofibrils of muscle Stationary filaments in myofibrils of muscle
Storage	Ovalbumin Casein	Egg white protein Milk protein
Toxins	Snake venom Diphtheria toxin	Enzymes Toxin made by diphtheria bacteria

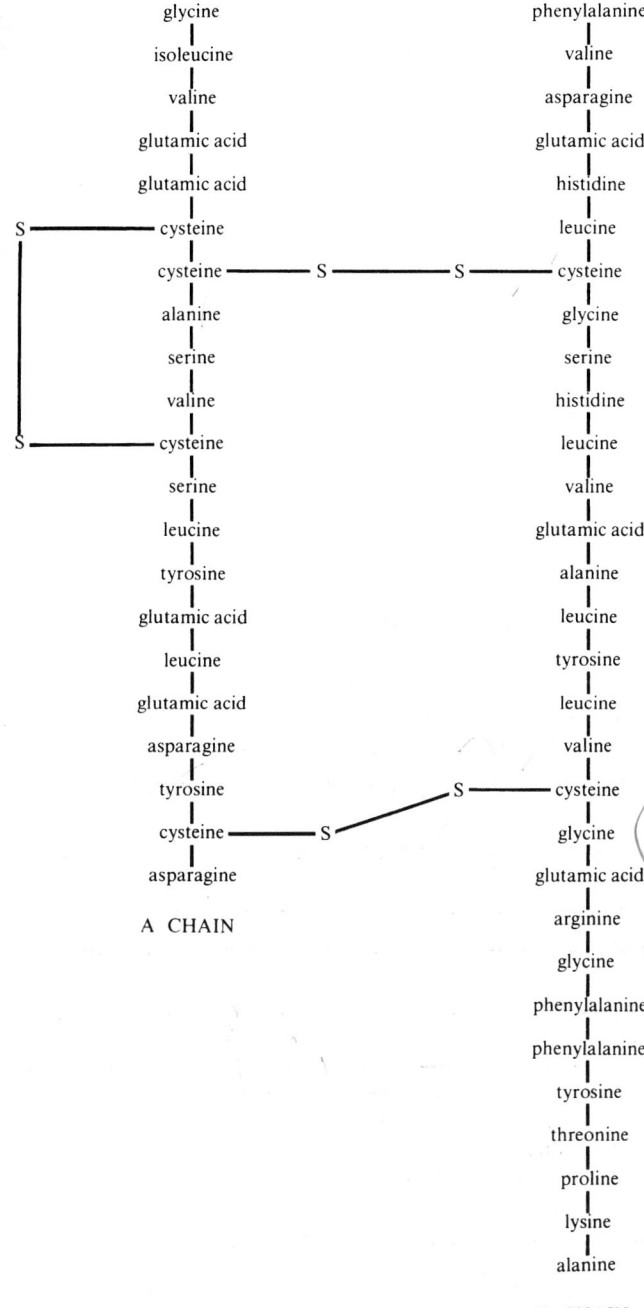

A CHAIN

B CHAIN

Fig 3.28 *Primary structure (sequence of amino acids) of insulin. The molecule consists of two polypeptide chains held together by two disulphide bridges.*

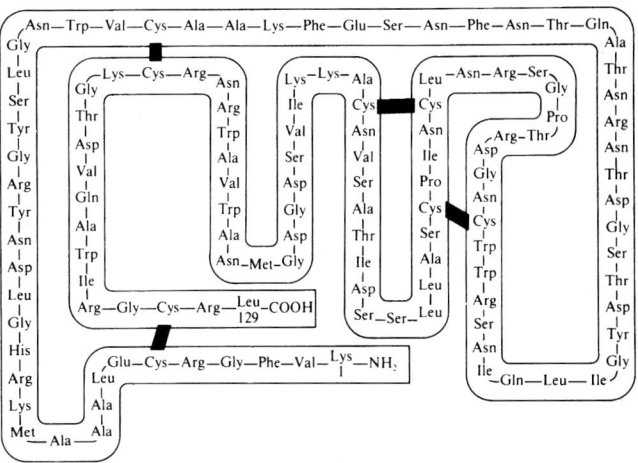

Fig 3.29 *The primary structure of lysozyme. Lysozyme is an enzyme that is found in many tissues and secretions of the human body, in plants, and in the whites of eggs. Its function is to catalyse the breakdown of the cell walls of bacteria. The molecule consists of a single polypeptide chain of 129 amino acid residues. There are four intrachain disulphide bridges.*

There are thousands of different proteins in the human body, all composed of different arrangements of the 20 fundamental amino acids. The sequence of amino acids of a protein dictates its biological function. In turn, this sequence is strictly controlled by the sequence of bases in DNA (chapter 23). Substitution of just a single amino acid can cause a major alteration in a protein's function, as in the condition of sickle cell anaemia (chapter 24). Analysis of amino acid sequences of similar proteins from different species is of interest, because it offers evidence about the possible evolutionary relationships between different species. This is dealt with in chapter 26.

3.12 (*a*) Let the letters A and B represent two different amino acids. Write down the sequences of all the possible tripeptides that could be made with just these two amino acids.
(*b*) From your answer to (*a*), what is the formula for calculating the number of different tripeptides that can be formed from two different amino acids?
(*c*) How many polypeptides, 100 amino acids in length, could be formed from two different amino acids?
(*d*) How many polypeptides, 100 amino acids in length (a modest length for a protein), could be made using all 20 common amino acids?
(*e*) How many peptides/polypeptides could be made (any length) from all 20 common amino acids?

Secondary structure

In addition to the primary structure there is a specific **secondary structure**. The most common secondary

for the first time that protein has a specific arrangement of amino acids along its chain.' Sanger was awarded the Nobel prize for his work in 1958 (and has since won a second for work on nucleic acids). Insulin is a protein of 51 amino acids. It is made of two polypeptide chains held together by disulphide bridges.

Today, much of the amino acid sequencing is accomplished by machine and well over one hundred thousand protein primary structures are known. Another example, lysozyme is shown in fig 3.29. Table 3.6 shows the number of amino acids in some proteins.

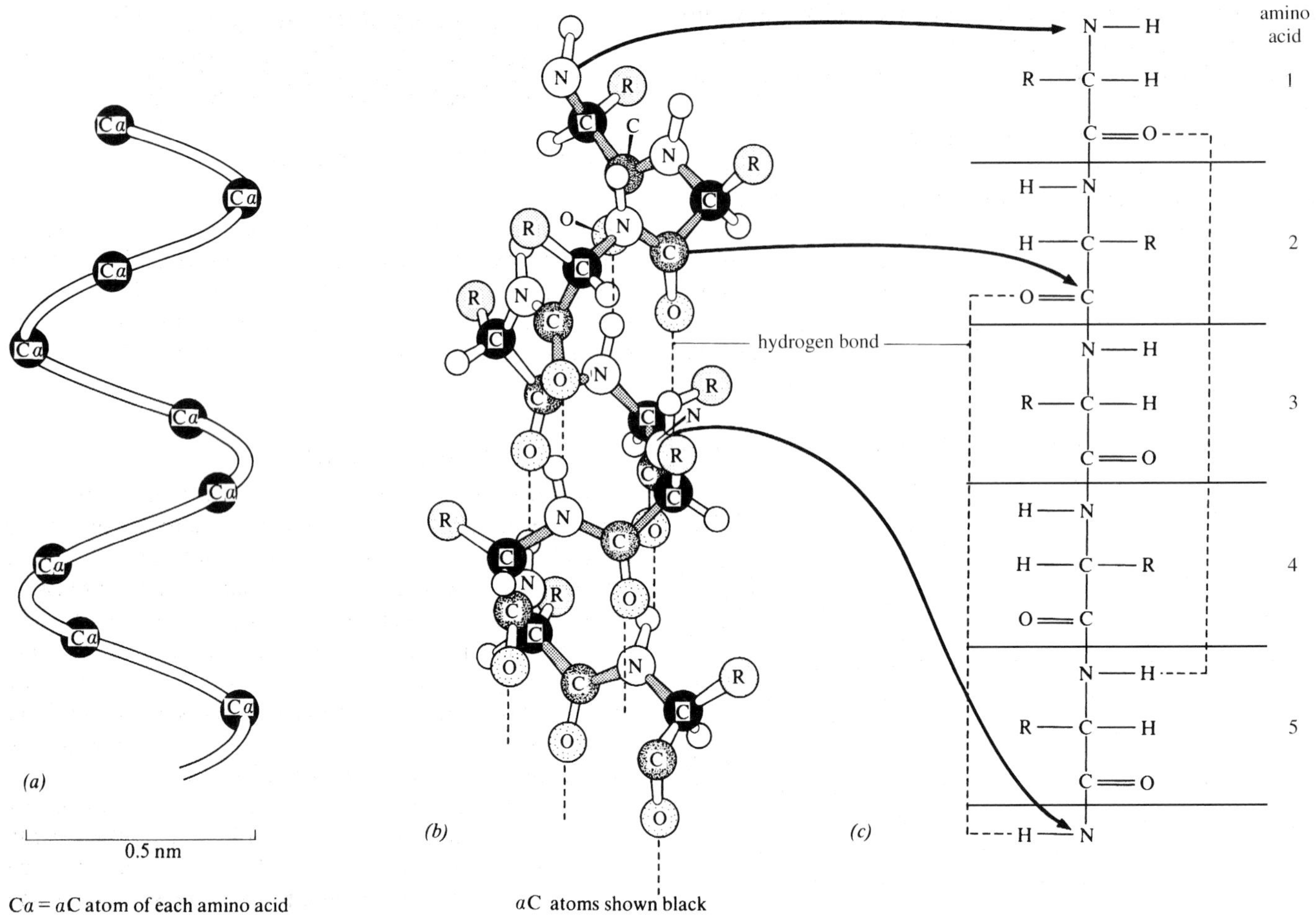

(a)

0.5 nm

Ca = aC atom of each amino acid

(b)

aC atoms shown black

— hydrogen bond —

(c)

amino acid

R — C — H   1

H — N

H — C — R   2

O = C

N — H

R — C — H   3

C = O

H — N

H — C — R   4

O = C

N — H

R — C — H   5

C = O

H — N

(d)

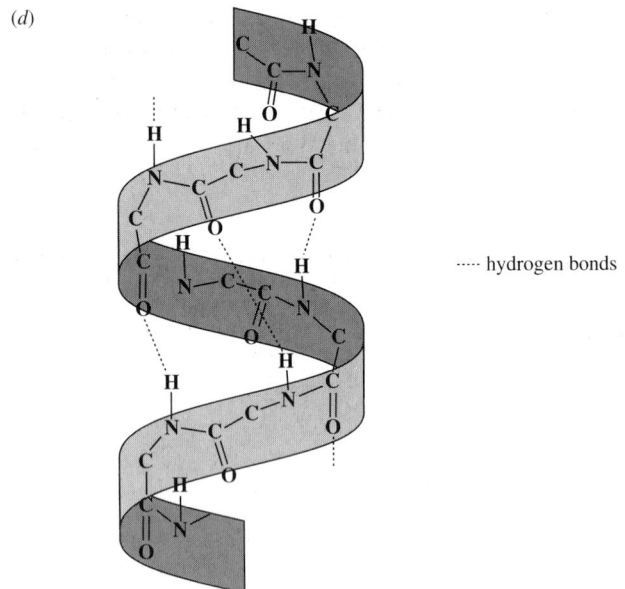

····· hydrogen bonds

Fig 3.30 *Structure of the α helix. (a) Only the α C atoms are shown. A line joining them describes an α helix. (b) The entire α helix. (c) Part of the α helix straightened out. Hydrogen bonds hold the helix in place. (d) α helix shown as a ribbon.*

structure is an extended spiral spring, the α helix, whose structure is maintained by many hydrogen bonds which are formed between neighbouring CO and NH groups. The H atom of the NH group of one amino acid is bonded to the O atom of the CO group four amino acids away (fig 3.30). Thus amino acid 1 would be bonded to amino acid 5, number 2 to number 6, and so on. X-ray diffraction data indicate that the α helix makes one complete turn for every 3.6 amino acids.

A protein which is entirely α-helical, and hence fibrous, is **keratin**. It is the structural protein of hair, wool, nails, claws, beaks, feathers and horn, as well as being found in vertebrate skin. Its hardness and stretchability vary with the degree of cross-linking by disulphide bridges between neighbouring chains.

Theoretically, all CO and NH groups can participate in hydrogen bonding as described, so the α helix is a very stable, and hence a common, structure. α-helical regions are rigid and rod-like. Most proteins are globular molecules in which there are also regions of β sheet (see below) and irregular structure. The fact that they are not entirely α-helical is due mainly to interference with hydrogen bonding by certain R groups, the occurrence of disulphide bridges between different parts of the same chain and the inability of the amino acid proline to make hydrogen bonds.

Another type of secondary structure is the β-**pleated sheet**. The protein that makes silk, namely **fibroin**, is entirely in this form. It is the protein used by silkworms when spinning their cocoon threads. It is made up of a number of adjacent chains which are more extended than the α helices. They are arranged in a parallel fashion, either running in the same direction or in opposite directions as in fig 3.31. They are joined together by hydrogen bonds formed between the C=O and NH groups of one chain and the NH and C=O groups of adjacent chains. Again, all NH and C=O groups are involved in hydrogen bonding, so the structure is very stable and rigid. The whole structure is known as a β-**pleated sheet**. The β sheet of silk has a high tensile strength (cannot be stretched), but the arrangement of the polypeptides makes the silk very supple. In globular proteins a single polypeptide chain commonly folds back on itself several times to form regions of β-pleated sheet.

Yet another arrangement is seen in the fibrous protein collagen, another structural protein like keratin and silk, and one that possesses great tensile strength. Here three polypeptide chains are wound around each other like the strands of a rope to form a **triple helix**. There are about 1000 amino acid residues in each chain, and the complete triple-helix compound is called **tropocollagen**. Each chain is itself in the form of a loose helix (not an α helix) (fig 3.32). The three strands or chains are held together by hydrogen bonds. Many triple helices can lie parallel to form fibrils. They are joined by covalent bonds between neighbouring chains. Fibrils in turn unite to form fibres. The large-scale structure of collagen is therefore built up in

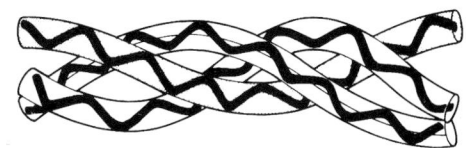

Fig 3.32 *Collagen triple-helix structure.*

stages, as with cellulose. The fact that the protein is extremely resistant to stretching is an essential part of its functioning, for example in tendons, bone, skin, teeth and connective tissue. Proteins which exist entirely in the form of helical coils, such as keratin and collagen, are exceptional.

Tertiary structure

Usually the polypeptide chain bends and folds extensively, forming a precise, compact 'globular' shape. This is the protein's tertiary structure and it is maintained by the interaction of the four types of bond already discussed, namely ionic, hydrogen and disulphide bonds as well as hydrophobic interactions (fig 3.33). The latter are quantitatively the most important and occur when the protein folds so as to shield hydrophobic side groups from the aqueous surroundings, at the same time exposing hydrophilic side chains, as described above.

The tertiary structure of a protein can be determined by X-ray crystallography. By early 1959, and after many years' work, John Kendrew and Max Perutz had built the first atomic model of myoglobin showing secondary and tertiary structures using this technique (fig 3.34). They received the Nobel prize for their work in 1962:

primary structure — single polypeptide chain of 153 amino acids, the sequence was elucidated in the early 1960s;
secondary structure — about 75% of the chain is α-helical (8 helical sections);

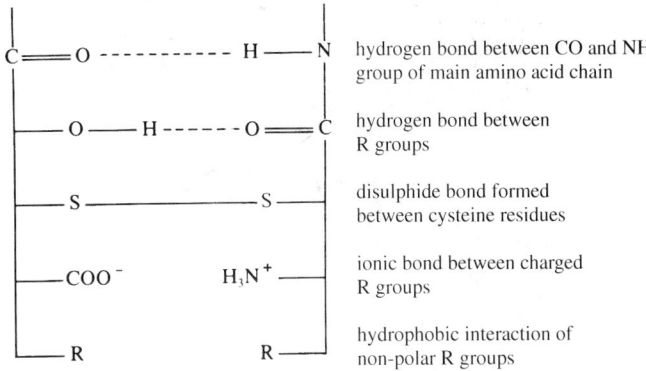

Fig 3.33 *Summary of types of bond stabilising secondary and tertiary structures of proteins. Hydrophobic interactions (associations of non-polar molecules or parts of molecules) to exclude water molecules in the aqueous environment of the cell are particularly important in maintaining structure, as in membranes.*

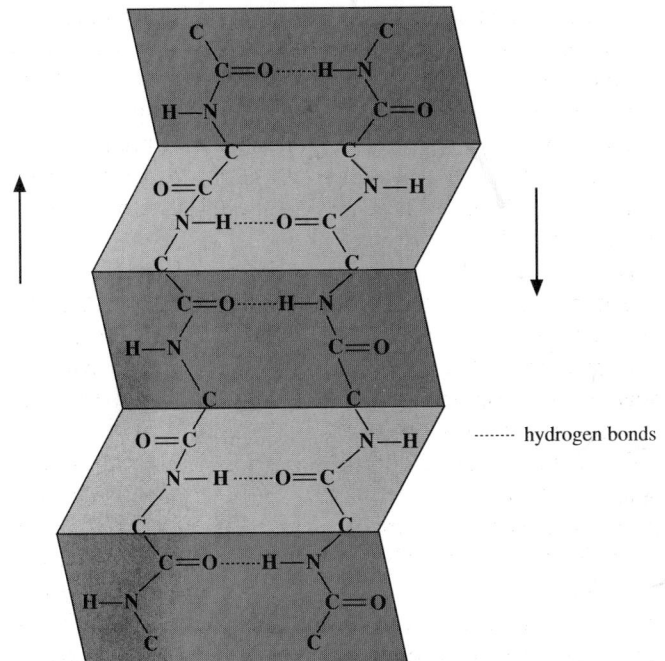

········ hydrogen bonds

Fig 3.31 *β-pleated sheet. The chains are held parallel to each other by the hydrogen bonds that form between the NH and CO groups. The side groups (R) are not shown but would project above and below the plane of the sheet.*

(a)

H₂N— Val — Leu — Ser — Glu — Gly — Glu — Trp — Gln — Leu — Val — Leu — His — Val — Tyr — Ala — Lys — Val —

Glu — Ala — Asp — Val — Ala — Gly — His — Gly — Gln — Asp — Ile — Leu — Ile — Arg — Leu — Phe — Lys —

Ser — His — Pro — Glu — Thr — Leu — Glu — Lys — Phe — Asp — Arg — Phe — Lys — His — Leu — Lys — Thr —

Glu — Ala — Glu — Met — Lys — Ala — Ser — Glu — Asp — Leu — Lys — Gly — His — His — Glu — Ala — Glu —

Leu — Thr — Ala — Leu — Gly — Ala — Ile — Leu — Lys — Lys — Gly — His — His — Glu — Ala — Glu —

Leu — Lys — Pro — Leu — Ala — Gln — Ser — His — Ala — Thr — Lys — His — Lys — Ile — Pro — Ile — Lys —

Tyr — Leu — Glu — Phe — Ile — Ser — Glu — Ala — Ile — Ile — His — Val — Leu — His — Ser — Arg — His —

Pro — Gly — Asn — Phe — Gly — Ala — Asp — Ala — Gln — Gly — Ala — Met — Asn — Lys — Ala — Leu — Glu —

Leu — Phe — Arg — Lys — Asp — Ile — Ala — Ala — Lys — Tyr — Lys — Glu — Leu — Gly — Tyr — Gln — Gly — COOH

(b)

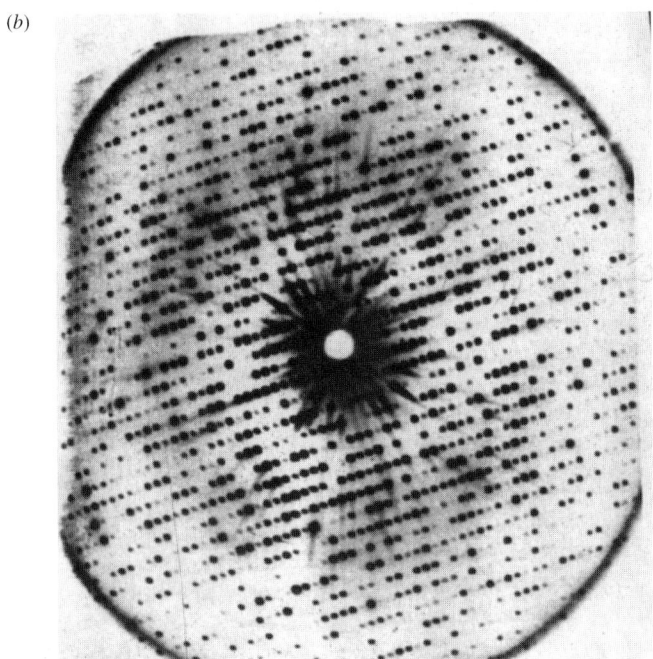

(c)

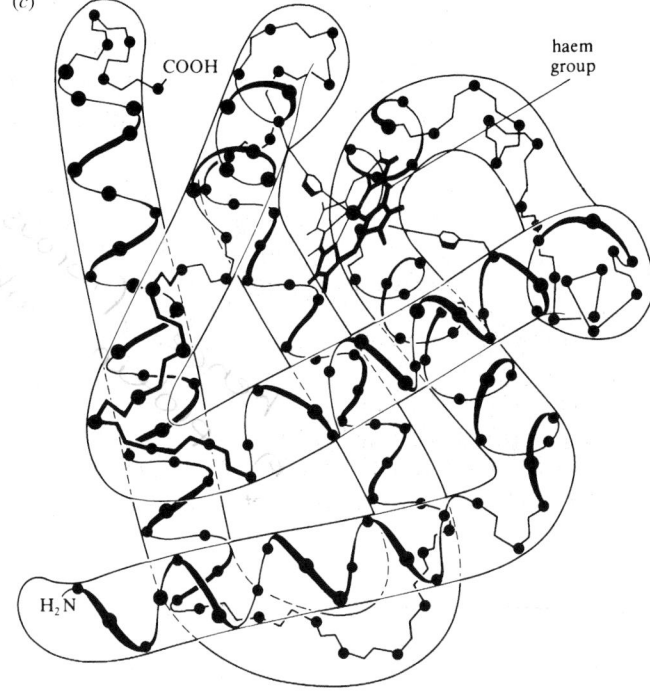

COOH

haem
group

H₂N

Fig 3.34 (a) *Primary structure of myoglobin.* (b) *X-ray diffraction pattern of myoglobin (sperm whale). The regular array of spots is a result of scattered (diffracted) beams of X-rays striking the photographic film after passing through pure crystals of myoglobin. The photograph is a two-dimensional section through a three-dimensional array of spots. The pattern and intensity of the spots are used to determine the arrangement of atoms in the molecule. From J. C. Kendrew,* Scientific American, *December 1961.* (c) *Conformation of myoglobin deduced from high resolution X-ray data. There are eight sections of α helix surrounding a haem group which forms a flat disc.* (d) *Another way of representing the three-dimensional structure of proteins is to show α helices as cylinders, as in this computer-generated diagram of myoglobin. Note the eight α-helical regions. The haem group is shown in the form of a space-filling model held in place by two amino acids (small white balls).*

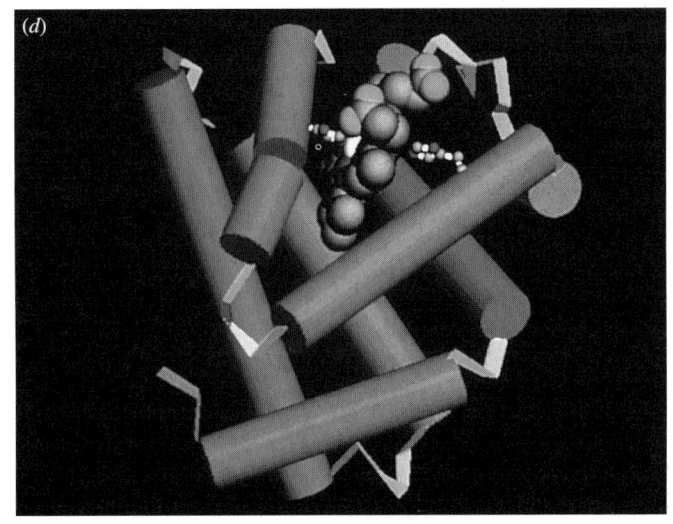

(d)

(e)

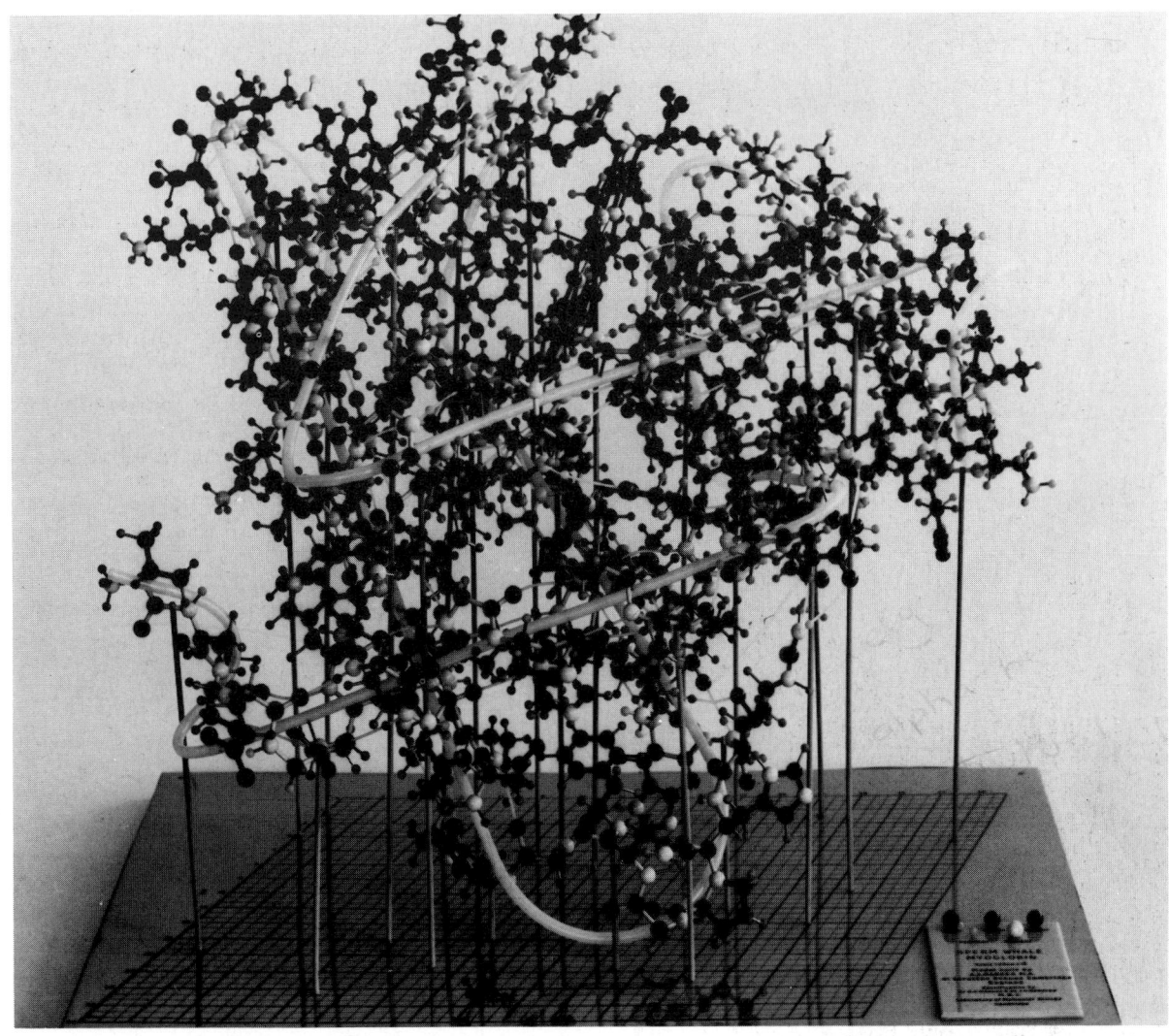

Fig 3.34 (cont.)   (e) *Ball-and-stick model of myoglobin.*

tertiary structure   –   non-uniform folding of the α-helical chain into a compact shape;

prosthetic group   –   haem group (contains iron).

Myoglobin is formed in muscle where its function is to store oxygen. Oxygen combines with the haem group as in haemoglobin. The haem group gives muscle its red appearance. Further information about the functions of myoglobin can be found in chapter 14. The elucidation of tertiary structure ·is still very time-consuming. Use of computers and other techniques to predict tertiary structure, based on knowledge of primary and secondary structures, is a fast-growing area of molecular biology. From this follows the possibility of designing proteins with particular shapes for particular functions, with important applications in industry and medicine.

Fig 3.34 shows several ways of representing the three-dimensional structure of a protein. Figure 3.35 shows a further method. The precise shapes formed are essential for the functioning of those proteins with tertiary structure. This is well illustrated by enzymes, as shown in section 4.1.2.

Quaternary structure

Many highly complex proteins consist of more than one polypeptide chain. The separate chains are held together by hydrophobic interactions and hydrogen and ionic bonds. Their precise arrangement is known as the **quaternary structure**. Haemoglobin shows such a structure. It is the red oxygen-carrying pigment found in the red blood cells of vertebrates. It consists of four separate polypeptide chains of two types, namely two α chains and two β chains. These resemble myoglobin in structure. The two α chains each contain 141 amino acids, while the two β chains each contain 146 amino acids. The complete structure of haemoglobin was worked out by Kendrew and Perutz and is illustrated in fig 3.36.

As is typical of globular proteins, its hydrophobic side chains point inwards to the centre of the molecule, and its hydrophilic side chains face outwards, making it soluble in water. A mutation which causes one of the hydrophilic amino acids to be replaced by a hydrophobic amino acid, thereby reducing its solubility, is responsible for the disease sickle cell anaemia (chapter 24).

Fig 3.35 *Tertiary structure of lysozyme. The arrows represent a region of β sheet. α helices are shown as regular coils. The rest of the molecule is represented as a ribbon and the four disulphide bridges as black zig-zags (compare fig 3.29).*

Fig 3.36 *Structure of haemoglobin. The molecule consists of four chains: two α chains and two β chains. Each chain carries a haem to which one molecule of oxygen binds. The assembly of a protein from separate polypeptide chains is an example of quaternary structure.*

The protein coats of some viruses, such as the tobacco mosaic virus, are composed of many polypeptide chains arranged in a highly ordered fashion (fig 2.14).

3.5.4 Denaturation and renaturation of proteins

Denaturation is the loss of the specific three-dimensional shape of a protein molecule. The change may be temporary or permanent, but the amino acid sequence of the protein remains unaffected. If denaturation occurs, the molecule unfolds and can no longer perform its normal biological function. A number of agents may cause denaturation as follows.

Heat or radiation. e.g. infra-red or ultra-violet light. Kinetic energy is supplied to the protein causing its atoms to vibrate violently, so disrupting the weak hydrogen and ionic bonds. Coagulation of the protein then occurs.

Strong acids and alkalis and high concentrations of salts. Ionic bonds are disrupted and the protein is coagulated. Breakage of peptide bonds may occur if the protein is allowed to remain mixed with the reagent for a long period of time.

Heavy metals. The positively charged ions of heavy metals (cations) form strong bonds with the negatively charged carboxyl groups on the R groups of proteins and often disrupt ionic bonds. They also reduce the protein's electrical polarity (its overall charge) and thus increase its insolubility. This causes the protein to precipitate out of solution.

Organic solvents and detergents. These reagents disrupt hydrophobic interactions and form bonds with hydrophobic (non-polar) groups. This in turn causes the disruption of hydrogen bonding. When alcohol is used as a disinfectant it functions to denature the protein of any bacteria present.

Renaturation

Sometimes a protein will spontaneously refold into its original structure after denaturation, providing conditions are suitable. This is called **renaturation**, and is good evidence that tertiary structure can be determined purely by primary structure and that biological structures can spontaneously assemble according to a few general principles.

3.6 DNA and RNA, the nucleic acids

Nucleic acids, like proteins, are essential for life. They form the genetic material of all living organisms, including the simplest virus. The term 'nucleic acid' comes from the fact that they are found mainly in the nucleus. Stains for nucleic acids show up nuclei very clearly under the light microscope.

Discovery of the structure of DNA (deoxyribonucleic acid), one of the two types of nucleic acid, represents one of the outstanding milestones in biology because it finally solved the problem of how living organisms store the information needed to control their activities and pass this information on to subsequent generations. Fig 3.4 shows that nucleic acids are made up of units called **nucleotides**. These are arranged to form extremely long molecules known as **polynucleotides**. Thus, to understand their structure, it is necessary first to study the structure of the nucleotide.

3.6.1 Structure of nucleotides

A nucleotide has three components, a 5-carbon sugar, a nitrogenous base and phosphoric acid.

Sugar. The sugar has five carbon atoms; therefore it is a pentose. There are two types of nucleic acids, depending on the pentose they contain. Those containing ribose are called ribonucleic acids or RNA and those containing deoxyribose (ribose with an oyxgen atom removed from carbon atom 2) are called deoxyribonucleic acids or DNA (fig 3.37).

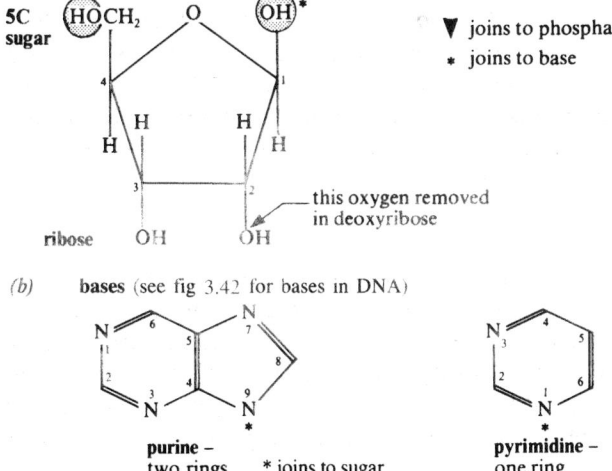

Fig 3.37 (a) *Ribose, deoxyribose,* (b) *bases and* (c) *phosphoric acid, the components of nucleotides.*

Bases. Each nucleic acid contains four different bases, two derived from purine and two from pyrimidine. The nitrogen in the rings gives the molecules their basic nature. The two purines are adenine (A) and guanine (G). The two pyrimidines are thymine (T) and cytosine (C) in DNA, with uracil (U) in place of thymine in RNA. Thymine is chemically very similar to uracil (it is 5-methyl uracil, that is uracil with a methyl group, $-CH_3$, on carbon atom 5). Purines have two rings and pyrimidines have one ring in their structure.

Note that the bases are commonly represented by their initial letters A, G, T, U and C.

Phosphoric acid (fig 3.37). This gives nucleic acids their acid character.

Fig 3.38 shows how the sugar, base and phosphoric acid combine to form a nucleotide. The combination of a sugar with a base occurs with the elimination of water and therefore is a condensation reaction. A nucleotide is formed by further condensation with phosphoric acid.

Different nucleotides are formed according to the sugars and bases used.

Nucleotides are not only used as building blocks for nucleic acids, but they form several important coenzymes, including adenosine triphosphate (ATP), cyclic AMP, coenzyme A, nicotinamide adenine dinucleotide (NAD) and its phosphate NADP, and flavine adenine dinucleotide (FAD) (section 4.5.3).

3.6.2 Formation of dinucleotides and polynucleotides

Two nucleotides join to form a **dinucleotide** by condensation between the phosphate group of one with the sugar of the other, as shown in fig 3.39. The process is repeated up to several million times to make a polynucleotide. An unbranched sugar–phosphate backbone is thus formed, as shown in fig 3.40.

3.6.3 Structure of DNA

Like proteins, polynucleotides can be regarded as having a primary structure, which is the sequence of nucleotides, and a three-dimensional structure. Interest in the structure of DNA intensified when it was realised in the early part of this century that it might be the genetic material. Evidence for this is presented in chapter 23.

By the early 1950s the Nobel prize-winning chemist Linus Pauling of the USA had worked out the α-helical structure which is common to many fibrous proteins, and was applying himself to the problem of the structure of DNA, which evidence suggested was also a fibrous molecule. At the same time Maurice Wilkins and Rosalind Franklin of King's College, London were tackling the same problem using the technique of X-ray crystallography. This involved the difficult and time-consuming process of preparing pure fibres of the salt of DNA through which

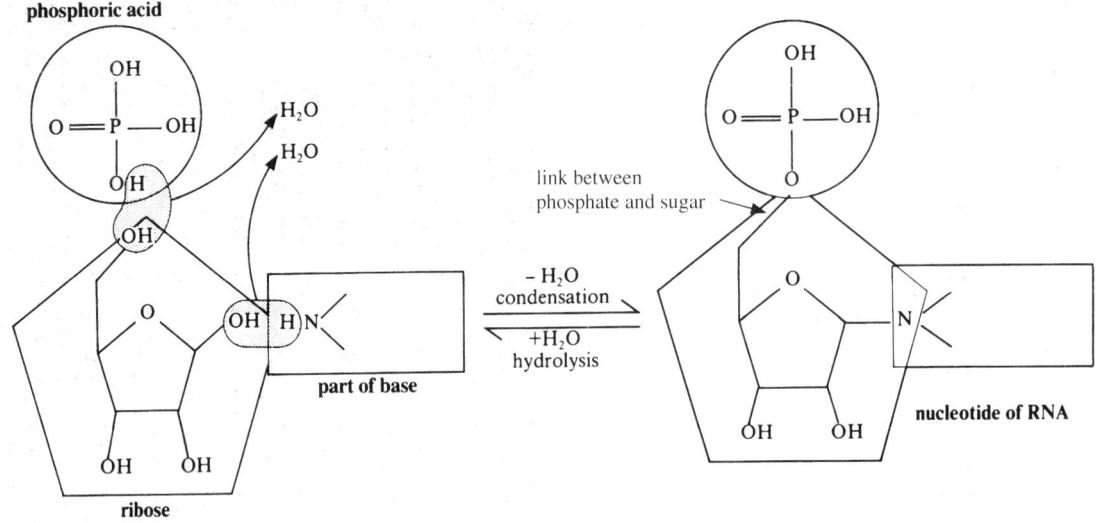

phosphoric acid
OH
O=P—OH
O H
OH
H_2O
H_2O
OH
H N
part of base
OH
OH
ribose
- H_2O
condensation
+H_2O
hydrolysis
link between
phosphate and sugar
OH
O=P—OH
O
O
N
OH
OH
nucleotide of RNA
diagrammatically:
phosphate
sugar (pentose)
base
+ $2H_2O$
nucleotide

Fig 3.38 *Formation of a nucleotide.*

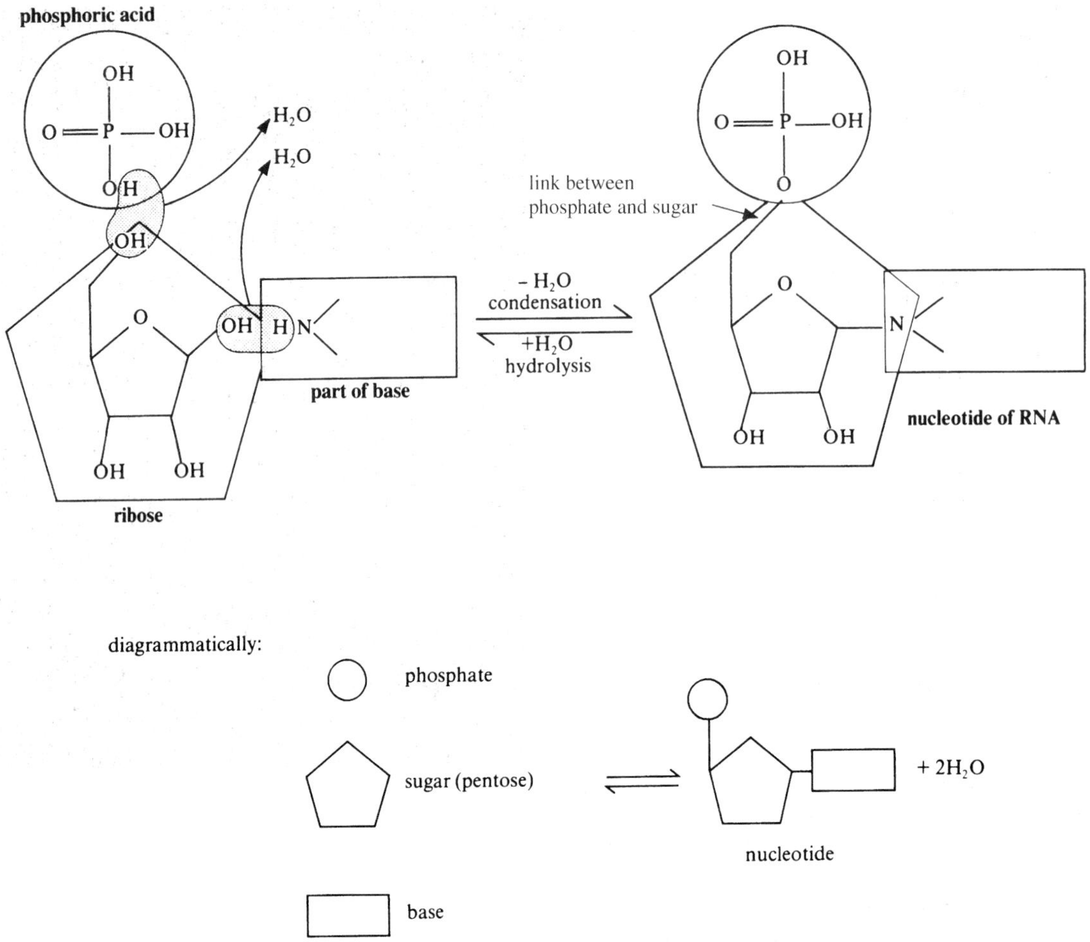

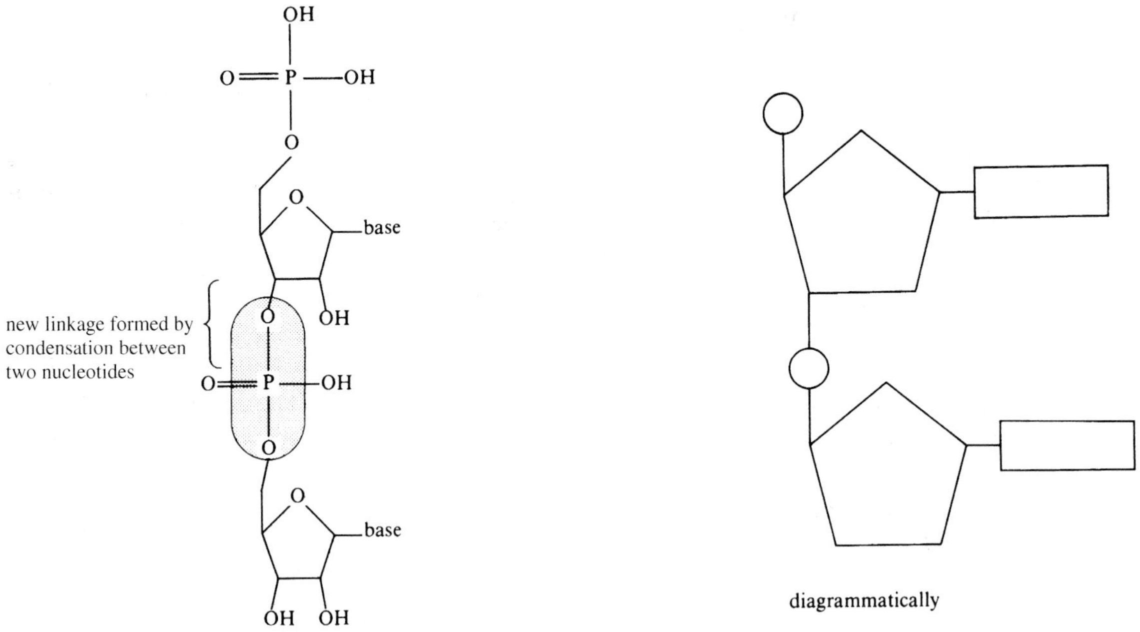

OH
O=P—OH
O
O
base
new linkage formed by
condensation between
two nucleotides
O
OH
O=P—OH
O
O
base
OH OH
diagrammatically

Fig 3.39 *Structure of a dinucleotide.*

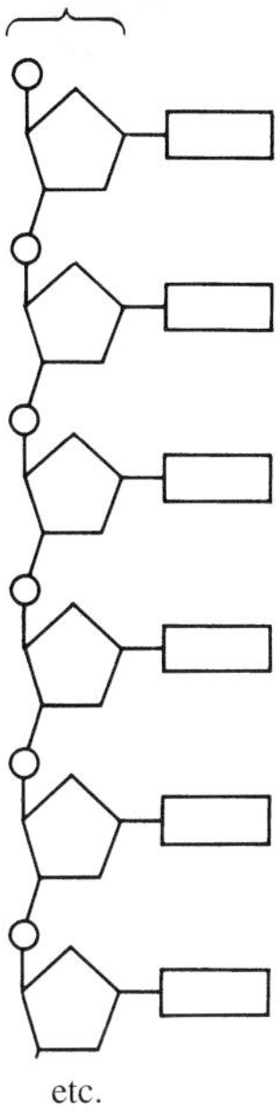

sugar–phosphate backbone

up to 5 million nucleotides, forming a polynucleotide (nucleic acid)

etc.

Fig 3.40 *Formation of a polynucleotide.*

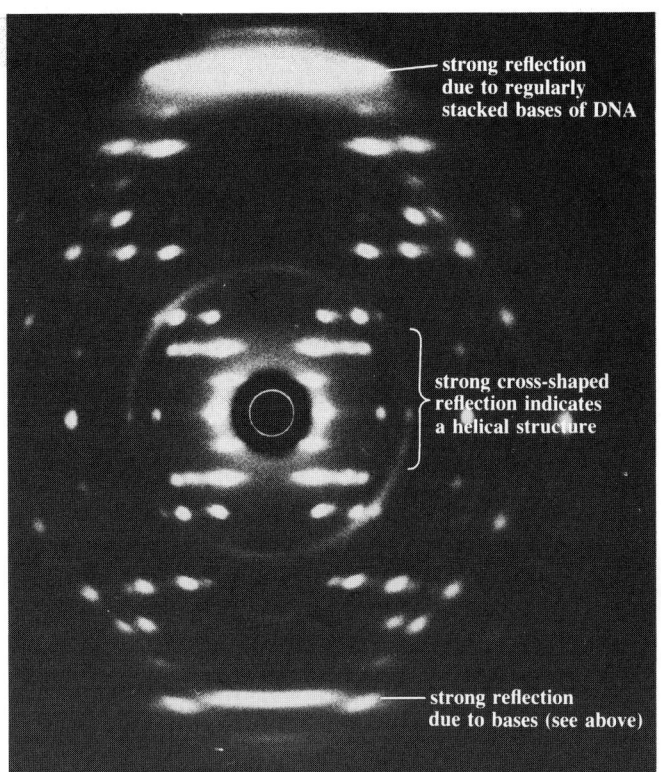

strong reflection due to regularly stacked bases of DNA

strong cross-shaped reflection indicates a helical structure

strong reflection due to bases (see above)

X-rays could be passed in order to obtain complex X-ray diffraction patterns (fig 3.41). These reveal the gross structure of the molecule but are not as detailed as those from pure crystals of proteins.

Meanwhile, James Watson and Francis Crick of the Cavendish Laboratory in Cambridge had chosen what was to prove the successful approach. Using all the chemical and physical information they could gather, they began building scale models of polynucleotides in the hope that a convincing structure would emerge. Watson's book *The Double Helix* provides a fascinating insight into their work.

Two lines of evidence proved crucial. Firstly, they were in regular communication with Wilkins and had access to the X-ray diffraction data, against which they were able to test their models. These data strongly suggested a helical structure (fig 3.41) with regularity at a spacing of 0.34 nm along its axis. Secondly, they realised the significance of some evidence published by Erwin Chargaff in 1951 concerning the ratio of the different bases found in DNA. Although important, the significance of this had been overlooked. Table 3.10 shows some of Chargaff's data, and supporting data obtained since.

3.13 Examine the table. What does it reveal about the ratios of the different bases?

Watson and Crick had been exploring the idea that there may be two helical chains of polynucleotides in DNA, held together by pairing of bases between neighbouring chains. The bases would be held together by hydrogen bonds.

Fig 3.41 *X-ray diffraction photograph of a fibre of DNA. This is the kind of pattern from which the double helical structure was originally deduced (photograph by courtesy of Dr J. M. Squire).*

Table 3.10 Relative amounts of bases in DNA from various organisms.

Source of DNA	Adenine	Guanine	Thymine	Cytosine
Human	30.9	19.9	29.4	19.8
Sheep	29.3	21.4	28.3	21.0
Hen	28.8	20.5	29.2	21.5
Turtle	29.7	22.0	27.9	21.3
Salmon	29.7	20.8	29.1	20.4
Sea urchin	32.8	17.7	32.1	17.3
Locust	29.3	20.5	29.3	20.7
Wheat	27.3	22.7	27.1	22.8
Yeast	31.3	18.7	32.9	17.1
Escherichia coli (a bacterium)	24.7	26.0	23.6	25.7
φX174 bacteriophage (a virus)	24.6	24.1	32.7	18.5

Amounts are in molar proportions on a percentage basis.

Fig 3.42 shows how the base pairs are joined by hydrogen bonds. Adenine pairs with thymine, and guanine with cytosine; the adenine–thymine pair has two hydrogen bonds. Watson tried pairing the bases in this way, and recalls 'my morale skyrocketed, for I suspected that we now had the answer to the riddle of why the number of purine residues exactly equalled the number of pyrimidine residues'.* He noticed the neat way in which the bases fit and that the overall size and shape of the base pairs was identical, both being three rings wide (fig 3.42). Hydrogen bonding between other combinations of bases, while possible, is much weaker. The way was finally open to building the now commonly accepted model of DNA, whose structure is summarised in figs 3.43–45.

Features of the DNA molecule

Watson and Crick showed that DNA consists of two polynucleotide chains. Each chain forms a right-handed helical spiral and the two chains coil around each other to form a double helix (fig 3.43). The chains run in opposite directions, that is are **antiparallel**. Each chain has a sugar–phosphate backbone with bases which project at right-angles and hydrogen bond with the bases of the opposite chain across the double helix (fig 3.44). The sugar–phosphate backbones are clearly seen in a space-filling model of DNA (fig 3.45). The width between the two backbones is constant and equal to the width of a base pair, that is the width of a purine plus a pyrimidine. Two purines

* From *The Double Helix*, James D. Watson, Weidenfeld & Nicolson, 1968.

would be too large, and two pyrimidines too small, to span the gap between the two chains. Along the axis of the molecule the base pairs are 0.34 nm apart, accounting for the regularity indicated by X-ray diffraction. A complete turn of the double helix comprises 3.4 nm, or ten base pairs. There is no restriction on the sequence of bases in one chain, but because of the rules of base pairing, the sequence in one chain determines that in the other. The two chains are thus said to be **complementary**.

Watson and Crick published their model in 1953 in the journal *Nature* and, together with Maurice Wilkins, were awarded the Nobel Prize for their work in 1962, the same year that Kendrew and Perutz received Nobel prizes for their work on the three-dimensional structure of proteins, also based on X-ray crystallography. Rosalind Franklin died of cancer before the prizes were awarded and Nobel prizes are not awarded posthumously.

To act as genetic material, the structure had to be capable of carrying coded information and of accurate replication. Its suitability for this was not overlooked by Watson and Crick who, with masterly understatement near the end of their paper said 'It has not escaped our notice that the specific pairing we have postulated immediately suggests a possible copying mechanism for the genetic material.' *In a second paper that year they discussed the genetic implications of the structure, and these are dealt with in chapter 23. This discovery, in which structure was shown to be so clearly related to function even at the molecular level, gave great impetus to the science of molecular biology.

3.6.4   Structure of RNA

RNA is normally single stranded, unlike DNA. Certain forms of RNA do assume complex structures, notably transfer RNA (tRNA) and ribosomal RNA (rRNA). Another form is messenger RNA (mRNA). These are involved in protein synthesis and are discussed in chapter 23.

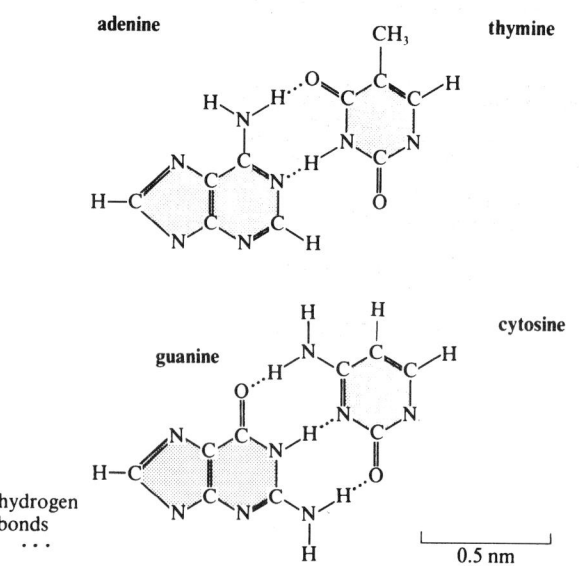

Fig 3.42 *Adenine–thymine and guanine–cytosine base pairs.*

* Watson, J. D. & Crick, F.H.C. (1953) *Nature* 171, 737.

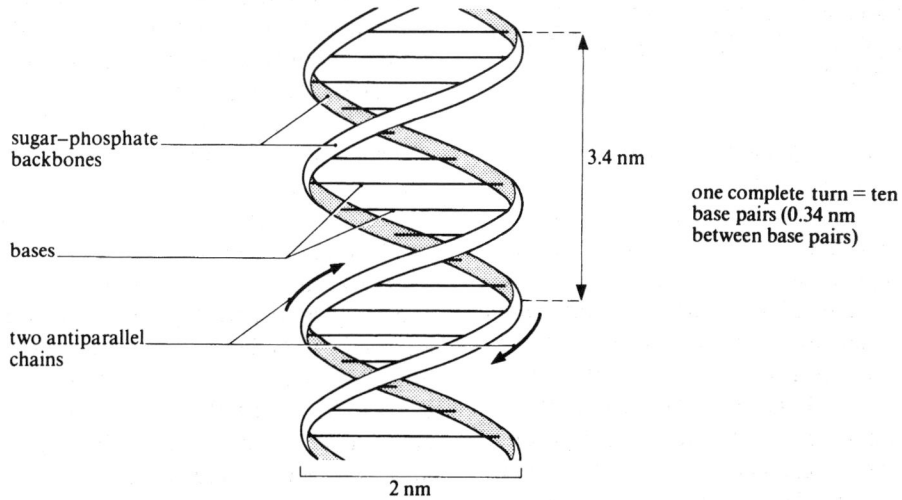

Fig 3.43 *Diagrammatic structure of DNA.*

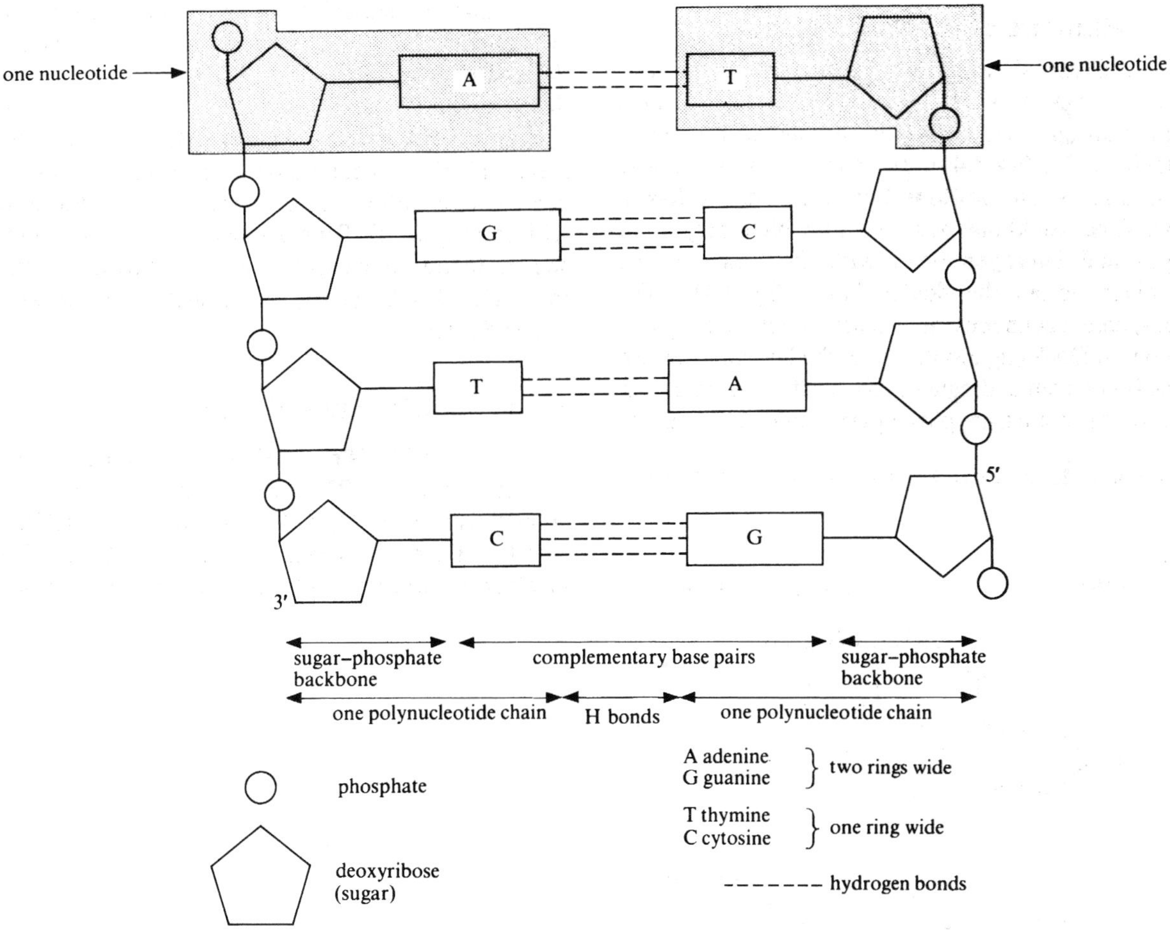

sugar–phosphate backbones

bases

two antiparallel chains

3.4 nm

one complete turn = ten base pairs (0.34 nm between base pairs)

2 nm

one nucleotide →

← one nucleotide

A ----- T

G ===== C

T ===== A

C ===== G

5'

3'

sugar–phosphate backbone

complementary base pairs

sugar–phosphate backbone

one polynucleotide chain

H bonds

one polynucleotide chain

○ phosphate

⬠ deoxyribose (sugar)

A adenine
G guanine } two rings wide

T thymine
C cytosine } one ring wide

- - - - - - hydrogen bonds

Fig 3.44 *DNA – diagrammatic structure of straightened chains.*

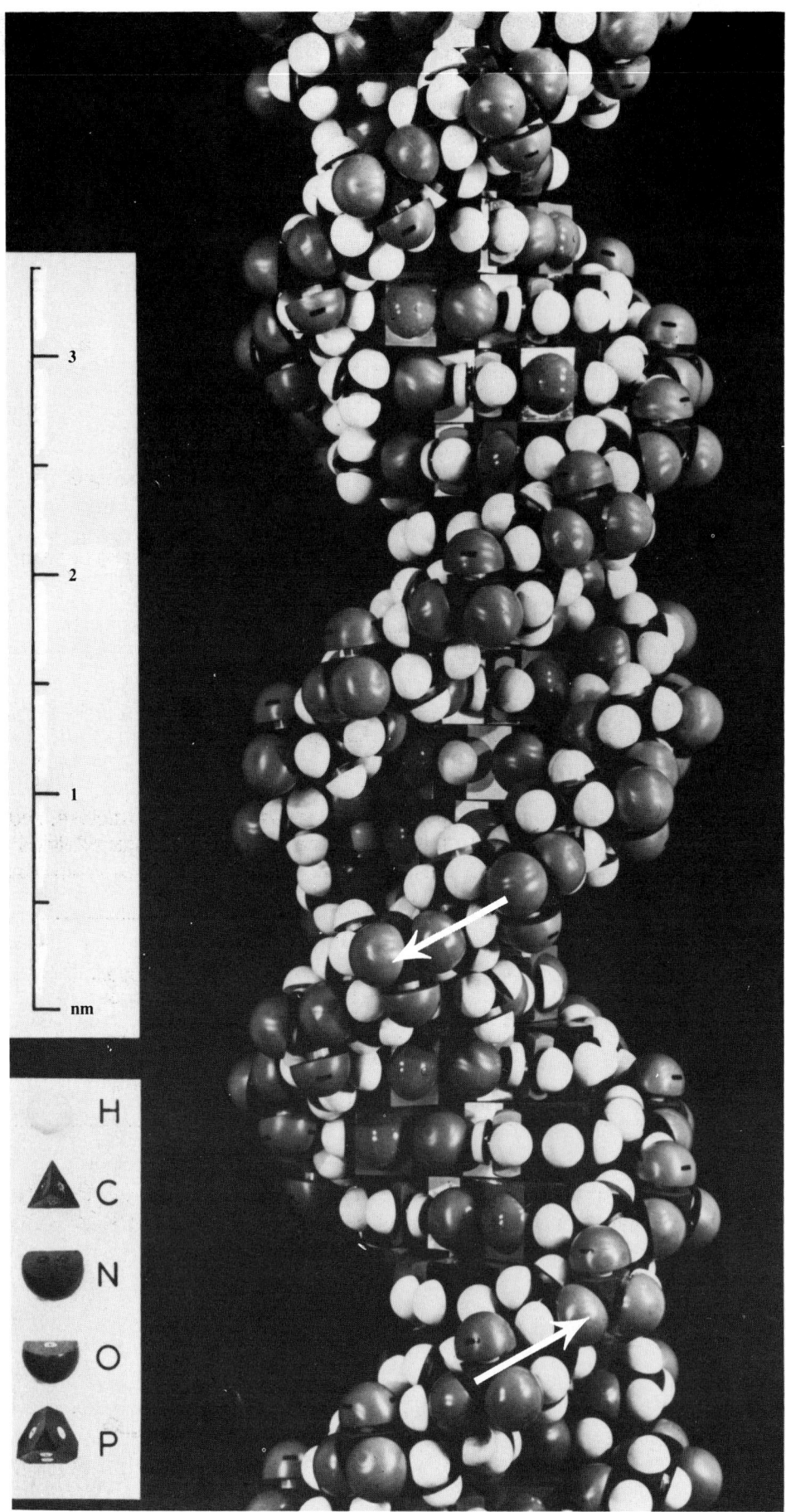

Fig 3.45 *Space-filling model of DNA. Arrows indicate the directions of the two antiparallel sugar–phosphate backbones.*

3.7 Identification of biochemicals

In this section are described some simple tests which can be carried out to identify some of the common biochemicals. More elaborate techniques exist for identifying and separating biochemicals. Of particular importance are chromatography and electrophoresis and these are described in the appendix in Book 2.

It is recommended that you first familiarise yourself with the following tests by using pure samples of the chemicals being tested. Once the techniques have been mastered and familiarity with the colour changes obtained, extracts from various tissues can be studied.

Experiment 3.1: Identification of biochemicals in pure form

NB Any heating that has to be done in the following tests should be carried out in a water bath at the boiling point of water. Direct heating of test-tubes should not take place.

Materials

pH paper
test-tubes
test-tube rack
Bunsen burner
teat pipettes
spatula
1 cm^3 syringe
iodine/potassium iodide solution
Benedict's reagent
dilute sulphuric acid
sodium hydrogencarbonate
Sudan III
Millon's reagent
5% potassium hydroxide solution
1% copper sulphate solution
DCPIP (dichlorophenolindophenol) solution
1% starch solution (cornflour is a recommended source)
1% glucose solution
1% sucrose solution (Analar sucrose must be used to avoid contamination with a reducing sugar)
olive oil or corn oil
absolute ethanol
egg albumen
1% lactose solution
1% fructose solution

Carbohydrates

Reducing sugars. The reducing sugars include all monosaccharides, such as glucose and fructose, and some disaccharides, such as maltose. The only common *non*-reducing sugar is sucrose. Use 0.1–1% sugar solutions.

Test	Observation	Basis of test
Benedict's test		
Add 2 cm^3 of a solution of the reducing sugar to a test-tube. Add an equal volume of Benedict's solution. Shake and bring gently to the boil.	The initial blue colouration of the mixture turns green, then yellowish and may finally form a brick-red precipitate.	Benedict's solution contains copper sulphate. Reducing sugars reduce soluble blue copper sulphate, containing copper(II) ions (Cu^{2+}) to insoluble red-brown copper oxide containing copper(I). The latter is seen as a precipitate.

Additional information

The test is **semi-quantitative**, that is a rough estimation of the amount of reducing sugar present will be possible. The final precipitate will appear green to yellow to orange to red-brown with increasing amounts of reducing sugar. (The initial yellow colour blends with the blue of the copper sulphate solution to give the green colouration.)

Test	Observation	Basis of test
Fehling's test Add 2 cm^3 of a solution of the reducing sugar to a test-tube. Add 1 cm^3 of Fehling's solution A and 1 cm^3 of Fehling's solution B. Shake and bring to the boil.	The initial blue colouration of the mixture turns green to yellow and finally a brick-red precipitate is formed.	As Benedict's test.

Additional information
Not as convenient as Benedict's test because Fehling's solutions A and B have to be kept separate until the test. Also it is not as sensitive.

Non-reducing sugars. The most common non-reducing sugar is sucrose, a disaccharide. If reducing sugars have been shown to be absent (negative result in above test) a brick-red precipitate in the test below indicates the presence of a non-reducing sugar. If reducing sugars have been shown to be present, a heavier precipitate will be observed in the following test than with the reducing test if non-reducing sugar is also present.

Test	Observation	Basis of test
Add 2 cm^3 of sucrose solution to a test-tube. Add 1 cm^3 dilute hydrochloric acid. Boil for one minute. Carefully neutralise with sodium hydrogencarbonate (check with pH paper) – care is required because effervescence occurs. Carry out Benedict's test.	As Benedict's test.	A disaccharide can be hydrolysed to its monosaccharide constituents by boiling with dilute hydrochloric acid. Sucrose is hydrolysed to glucose and fructose, both of which are reducing sugars and give the reducing sugar result with the Benedict's test.

Starch. This is only slightly soluble in water, in which it forms a colloidal suspension. It can be tested in suspension or as a solid.

Test	Observation	Basis of test
Iodine/potassium iodide test Add 2 cm^3 1% starch solution to a test-tube. Add a few drops of I$_2$/KI solution. Alternatively add the latter to the solid form of starch.	A blue-black colouration.	A polyiodide complex is formed with starch.

Cellulose and lignin. See appendix A2 (staining) in Book 2.

Lipids

Lipids include oils (such as corn oil and olive oil), fats and waxes.

Test	Observation	Basis of test
Sudan III Sudan III is a red dye. Add 2 cm^3 oil to 2 cm^3 of water in a test-tube. Add a few drops of Sudan III and shake	A red-stained oil layer separates on the surface of the water, which remains uncoloured.	Fat globules are stained red and are less dense than water.
Emulsion test Add 2 cm^3 fat or oil to a test-tube containing 2 cm^3 of absolute ethanol. Dissolve the lipid by shaking vigorously. Add an equal volume of cold water.	A cloudy white suspension	Lipids are immiscible with water. Adding water to a solution of the lipid in alcohol results in an emulsion of tiny lipid droplets in the water which reflect light and give a white, opalescent appearance.
Grease spot test Rub a drop of the sample into a piece of paper. Allow time for any water to evaporate. Gentle warming will speed up the process.	A permanent transparent spot on the paper.	

Proteins

A suitable protein for these tests is egg albumen.

Test	Observation	Basis of test
Millon's test Add 2 cm^3 protein solution or suspension to a test-tube. Add 1 cm^3 Millon's reagent and boil. NB Millon's reagent is poisonous: take care!	A white precipitate forms which coagulates on heating and turns red or salmon pink.	Millon's reagent contains mercury acidified with nitric acid, giving mercury(II) nitrate and nitrite. The amino acid tyrosine contains a phenol group which reacts to give a red mercury(II) complex. This is a reaction given by all phenolics and is not specific for proteins. Protein usually coagulates on boiling, thus appearing solid. The only common protein lacking tyrosine likely to be used is gelatin.
Biuret test Add 2 cm^3 protein solution to a test-tube. Add an equal volume of 5% potassium hydroxide solution and mix. Add two drops of 1% copper sulphate solution and mix. No heating is required.	A mauve or purple colour develops slowly.	A test for peptide bonds. In the presence of dilute copper sulphate in alkaline solution, nitrogen atoms in the peptide chain form a purple complex with copper(II) ions (Cu^{2+}). Biuret is a compound derived from urea which also contains the $-CONH-$ group and gives a positive result.

Vitamin C (ascorbic acid)

This test can be conducted on a quantitative basis if required, in which case the volumes given below must be measured accurately. A suitable source of vitamin C is a 50/50 mix of fresh orange or lemon juice with distilled water. Vitamin C tablets may also be purchased.

Test	Observation	Basis of test
Using 0.1% ascorbic acid solution as a standard. Add 1 cm³ of DCPIP solution to a test-tube. Fill a 1 cm³ syringe with 0.1% ascorbic acid. Add the acid to the DCPIP drop by drop, stirring gently with the syringe needle. Do not shake.* Add until the blue colour of the dye just disappears. Note the volume of ascorbic acid solution used.	Blue colour of dye disappears to leave a colourless solution.	DCPIP is a blue dye which is reduced to a colourless compound by ascorbic acid, a strong reducing agent.

* Shaking the solution would result in oxidation of the ascorbic acid by oxygen in the air. The effects of shaking and of boiling could be investigated.

DNA

See Feulgen's stain (appendix table A2.2 in Book 2).

3.15 How could you determine the concentration of ascorbic acid in an unknown sample?

3.16 You are provided with three sugar solutions. One contains glucose, one a mixture of glucose and sucrose, and one sucrose.
(a) How could you identify each solution?
(b) Supposing that the apparatus were available, and time permitted, briefly discuss any further experiments you could perform to confirm your results.

3.17 How would you make 100 cm³ of a 10% glucose solution?

3.18 Starting with stock solutions of 10% glucose and 2% sucrose how would you make 100 cm³ of a mixture of final concentration 1% sucrose and 1% glucose?

Experiment 3.2: Identification of biochemicals in tissues

A biochemist is often faced with the problem of wanting to identify chemicals (qualitative analysis) or to measure their amounts (quantitative analysis) in living tissue. Sometimes the chemical can be tested for directly, but often some kind of extraction and purification process must first be embarked upon.

A convenient exercise is to take a range of common foods and plant material and to test for the range of biochemicals listed in experiment 3.1. An extraction procedure is designed where possible to give a clear, colourless solution for testing, and you should note the rationale behind the procedures so that you could design your own if necessary.

Materials

As for experiment 3.1 up to DCPIP solution
pestle and mortar
microscope
slides and cover-slips
razor blade
watch glass
Schultz's solution
phloroglucinol + conc. hydrochloric acid
potato tuber
apple
cotton wool
woody stem
seeds/nuts
soaked peas
beans

Microscopic examination of thin sections of tissue

Suitable for: Visible storage products, particularly starch grains, such as potato tuber.

As above with appropriate staining or other chemical testing

Suitable for: Reducing sugars – Mount in a few drops of Benedict's reagent, heat gently to boiling; add water if necessary to prevent drying.
Starch – Mount section in dilute iodine/potassium iodide solution.
Protein – Mount in a few drops of Millon's reagent, heat gently to boiling; add water if necessary to prevent drying.
Oil and fat – Stain material, such as seed, with Sudan III and wash with water and/or 70% ethanol. Then section and mount.
Cellulose, lignin, etc. – see appendix A2.4.2 for staining.

Testing a clear, aqueous solution

Decolourise tissue if necessary: Pigments may interfere with colour tests but can usually be removed with an organic solvent such as 80% ethanol or 80% propanone.

Care must be taken to avoid naked flames. However, remember these solvents may also remove lipids and soluble sugars. *Suitable for:* Removing chlorophyll from leaves.

Homogenise (grind) material: Sugars and proteins – Small pieces of solid material can be ground with a small quantity of water using a pestle and mortar or a food mixer. The ground material should be squeezed through several layers of pre-moistened fine muslin or nylon and/or filtered or centrifuged to remove solid material. This may be unnecessary if a fairly colourless, fine suspension is obtained. The clear solution can be tested as usual, with further dilution if necessary. The solid residue may also be tested if appropriate.

Lipids – Grind material, transfer to a test-tube and boil. Lipids will escape as oil droplets. Perform the Sudan III test. Alternatively take thin shavings of nuts or other foods, including coloured foods, and do the emulsion test.

Suitable for:

fruit, such as apple, orange	(vitamin C, sugars)
nuts	(oils)
castor oil seed	(oil)
pea seed	(protein)
pine kernels	(protein and oil)
potato	(starch, vitamin C)
egg	(protein)

Subdivision of the above materials, such as into seeds, flesh, skin and juice, may be possible.

Chapter Four

Enzymes

Enzymes can be defined as biological catalysts. A **catalyst** is a substance which speeds up a chemical reaction but remains unchanged itself at the end. Enzymes are *biological* catalysts because they are protein molecules made by living cells. A typical human cell contains several thousand enzymes. They are used to catalyse a vast number of chemical reactions at temperatures suitable for living organisms, that is between approximately 5 and 40 °C. High temperatures would be needed, as well as marked changes in other conditions, if the same speeds of reaction were to be achieved outside the organism. These would be lethal to a living cell. Enzymes are vitally important because in their absence reactions in the cell would be too slow to sustain life.

The chemical (or chemicals) which an enzyme works on is called its **substrate**. An enzyme combines with its substrate to form a short-lived enzyme/substrate complex. This proximity of the enzyme with the substrate in the complex greatly increases the chances of a reaction occurring. Once a reaction has occurred, the complex breaks up into **products** and enzyme. The enzyme remains unchanged at the end of the reaction and is free to interact again with more substrate.

substrate + enzyme $\rightleftharpoons$ enzyme/substrate complex $\rightleftharpoons$ enzyme/ product complex $\rightleftharpoons$ enzyme + product(s)

or $\qquad$ E + S $\rightleftharpoons$ ES $\rightleftharpoons$ EP $\rightleftharpoons$ E + P

Anabolism and catabolism

The sum total of all the chemical reactions going on in cells is known as **metabolism**. Metabolism can be divided into two types, namely anabolism and catabolism. These two types of activity often take place in different parts of the cell. **Catabolic reactions** involve the breakdown of molecules and usually release energy. They often involve oxidation or hydrolysis. **Anabolic reactions** involve the synthesis of molecules and usually require energy. They often involve condensation. All these reactions are catalysed by enzymes. An example of an enzyme involved in anabolism is glutamine synthetase, which catalyses the synthesis of the amino acid glutamine from glutamic acid and ammonia:

$$\text{glutamic acid + ammonia + ATP} \xrightarrow[\text{synthetase}]{\text{glutamine}} \text{glutamine + water + ADP + P}_i$$

(ATP is adenosine triphosphate, ADP is adenosine diphosphate and P_i is inorganic phosphate.) An example of an enzyme involved in catabolism is amylase:

$$\text{starch + water} \xrightarrow{\text{amylase}} \text{maltose}$$

Metabolic pathways

Commonly, a number of enzymes are used in sequence to convert one substance into one or several products via a series of intermediate compounds. The chain of reactions is referred to as a **metabolic pathway**. Many such pathways are going on at the same time in the cell. The reactions proceed in a controlled manner due to the specific nature of enzymes. A single enzyme generally will catalyse only a single reaction. Thus enzymes serve to control the chemical reactions that occur within cells and ensure that they proceed at an efficient rate.

4.1 Properties of enzymes

Enzymes possess the following major properties.

- All are globular proteins.
- Being proteins, they are coded for by DNA.
- They are catalysts (see above).
- Their presence does not alter the nature or properties of the end product(s) of the reaction.
- They are very efficient. In other words, a very small amount of catalyst brings about the change of a large amount of substrate. For example, one molecule of the enzyme catalase can catalyse the decomposition of about 600 thousand molecules per second of hydrogen peroxide to water and oxygen at body temperature. The efficiency of catalase compared with an inorganic catalyst such as manganese dioxide can easily be demonstrated by adding them separately to hydrogen peroxide and observing the rate of oxygen evolution. A good source of catalase is liver. An average enzyme undergoes about 1000 reactions per second. Without a catalyst at all, reaction rates would be millions of times slower.
- They are highly specific, that is an enzyme will generally catalyse only a single reaction. Catalase, for example, will only catalyse the decomposition of hydrogen peroxide.

- The catalysed reaction is reversible.
- Their activity is affected by pH, temperature, substrate concentration and enzyme concentration. These factors are considered in section 4.3.
- Enzymes lower the activation energy of the reactions they catalyse (see section 4.1.1).
- Enzymes possess active sites where the reaction takes place. These sites have specific shapes (see section 4.1.2).

4.1.1 Activation energy

Consider a mixture of petrol and oxygen maintained at room temperature. Although a reaction between the two substances is thermodynamically possible, it does not occur unless energy is applied to it, such as a simple spark. The same is true of a match. The chemicals in the match head are capable of reacting with an overall release of energy. However, a little energy must be put in to get the reaction started (heat energy generated by friction on the matchbox). This energy is called the **activation energy**. It is the energy required to make the substances react. Enzymes, by functioning as catalysts, serve to reduce the activation energy required for a chemical reaction to take place (fig 4.1). They speed up the overall rate without altering, to any great extent, the temperature at which it occurs.

4.1.2 Mechanism of enzyme action

Enzymes are very specific and it was suggested by Fischer in 1890 that this was because the enzyme had a particular shape into which the substrate or substrates fit exactly. This is often referred to as the 'lock and key' hypothesis, where the substrate is imagined being like a **key** whose shape is complementary to the enzyme or **lock**. This is shown diagrammatically in fig 4.2. The site where the substrate binds in the enzyme is known as the **active site** and it is this which has the specific shape.

Most enzymes are far larger molecules than the substrates they act on and the active site is usually only a very small portion of the enzyme, between 3 and 12 amino acids. The remaining amino acids, which make up the bulk of the

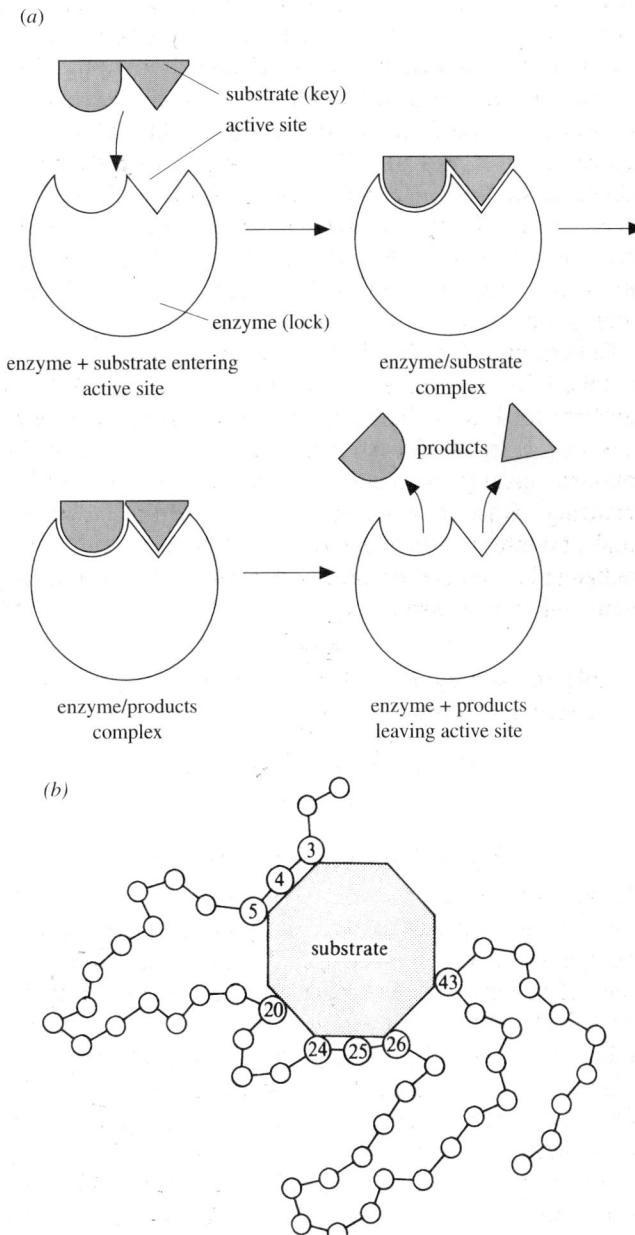

(a)

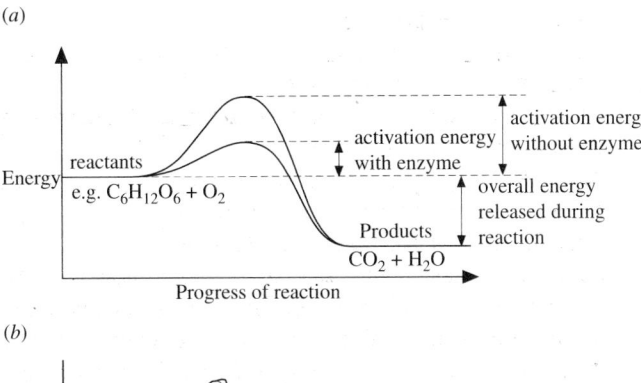

(b)

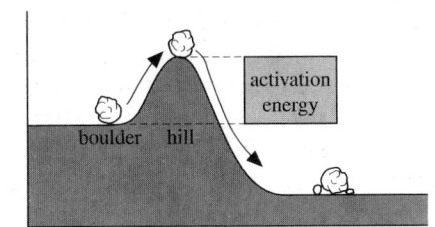

Fig 4.1 *Activation energy. (a) Activation energy for an enzyme-catalysed and an uncatalysed reaction. (b) An analogous situation where rolling a boulder down a hill will result in release of more energy than is used to start it rolling.*

Fig 4.2 *(a) Fischer's 'lock and key' hypothesis of enzyme action. (b) A more realistic diagrammatic representation of an enzyme–substrate complex. The positions of the amino acids of the active site are numbered according to their position in the primary structure of the enzyme.*

enzyme, function to maintain the correct globular shape of the molecule which, as will be explained below, is important if the active site is to function at the maximum rate.

Once formed, the products no longer fit into the active site and escape into the surrounding medium, leaving the **active site** free to receive further substrate molecules.

In 1959 Koshland suggested a modification to the 'lock and key' model known as the **'induced fit' hypothesis**. Working from evidence that suggested that some enzymes and their active sites were physically rather more flexible structures than previously described, he proposed that the active site could be modified as the substrate interacts with the enzyme. The amino acids which make up the active site are moulded into a precise shape which enables the enzyme to perform its catalytic function most effectively (fig 4.3). A suitable analogy would be that of a hand changing the shape of a glove as the glove is put on. Further refinements to the hypothesis have been made as details of individual reactions became known. In some cases, for example, the substrate molecule changes shape slightly as it enters the active site before binding.

Fig 4.4 shows how techniques such as X-ray crystallography and computer-assisted modelling have enabled us to visualise enzymes combining with their substrates. The example shown is lysozyme.

Fig 4.3 *Diagrams to show Koshland's induced fit hypothesis. (a) Simple diagram illustrating the principle. (b) More realistic diagram (From J. C. Marsden & C. F. Stoneman (1977)* Enzymes and equilibria, *Heinemann Educational Books).*

4.2   The rate of enzyme reactions

The rate of an enzyme reaction is measured by the amount of substrate changed, or amount of product formed, during a period of time.

The rate is determined by measuring the slope of the tangent to the curve in the initial stage of the reaction (shown as (*a*) in fig 4.5). The steeper the slope, the greater is the rate. If activity is measured over a period of time, the rate of reaction usually falls, most commonly as a result of a fall in substrate concentration (see next section).

4.3   Factors affecting the rate of enzyme reactions

When investigating the effect of a given factor on the rate of an enzyme-controlled reaction, all other factors should be kept **constant** and at **optimum levels** wherever possible. Initial rates only should be measured, as explained above.

(*a*)

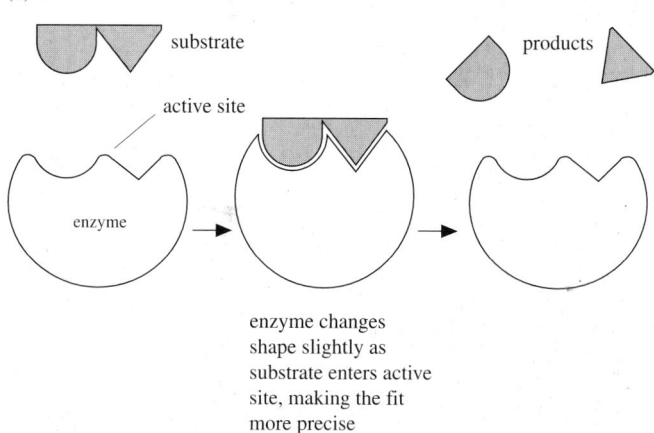

enzyme changes shape slightly as substrate enters active site, making the fit more precise

(*b*)

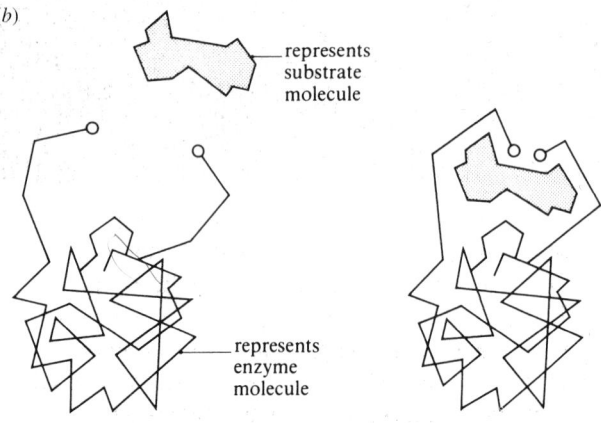

when the substrate combines with the enzyme it induces change of shape so that the active groups of the enzyme are brought together

larger and smaller compounds are unsuitable for reacting with the enzyme

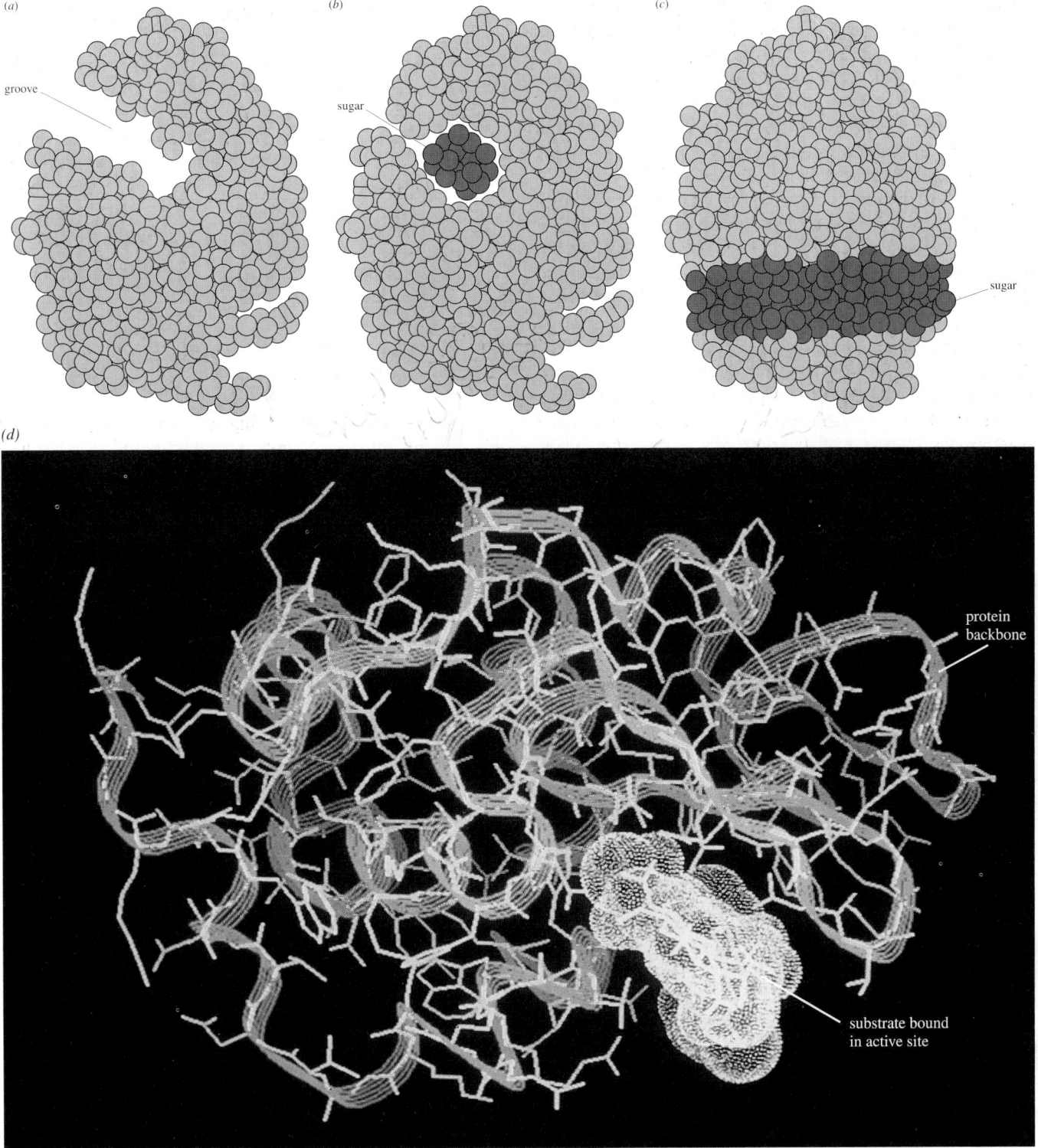

Fig 4.4 *How the enzyme lysozyme works. These computer-generated models show the tertiary structure of lysozyme before and after binding its substrate. (a) Side view of the groove-shaped active site which runs across the molecule. (b) Side view of active site with substrate molecule in place. Note the slight change in shape of the enzyme which has resulted from substrate binding. This is an example of 'induced fit', first proposed by Koshland in 1959. The substrate is a short chain of sugars which slides neatly into the groove and is split by the enzyme. These sugar chains are found in bacterial cell walls and their breakdown by the enzyme results in bacterial death – the cell explodes as a result of osmosis because the cell wall loses its rigidity. Lysozyme is a common enzyme found in human tears, saliva and mucus as a protective enzyme. (c) Front view of active site with substrate molecule in place. (d) Computer-generated model of lysozyme showing the substrate bound in the active site.*

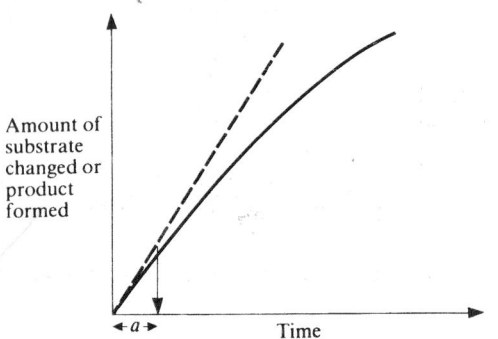

Fig 4.5 *The rate of an enzyme-controlled reaction.*

4.3.1   Enzyme concentration

Provided that the substrate concentration is maintained at a high level, and other conditions such as pH and temperature are kept constant, the rate of reaction is proportional to the enzyme concentration (fig 4.6). Normally reactions are catalysed by enzyme concentrations which are much lower than substrate concentrations. Thus as the enzyme concentration is increased, so will be the rate of the enzyme reaction.

4.3.2   Substrate concentration

For a given enzyme concentration, the rate of an enzyme reaction increases with increasing substrate concentration (fig 4.7). The theoretical maximum rate (V_{max}) is never quite obtained, but there comes a point when any further increase in substrate concentration produces no significant change in reaction rate. This is because at high substrate concentrations the active sites of the enzyme molecules at any given moment are virtually saturated with substrate. Thus any extra substrate has to wait until the enzyme/substrate complex has released the products before it may itself enter the active site of the enzyme.

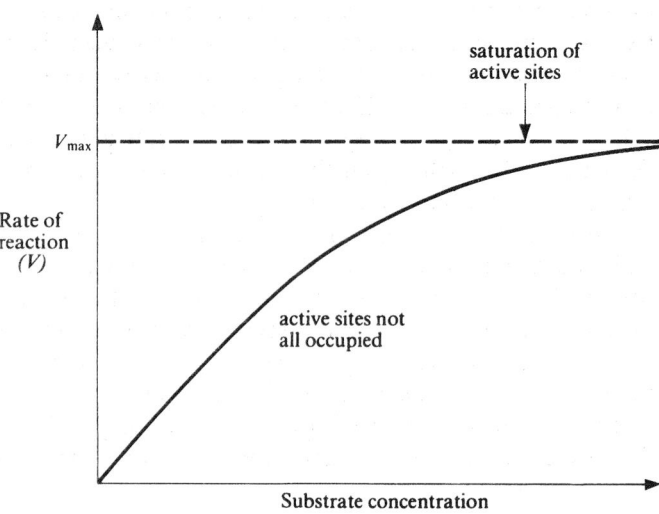

Fig 4.7 *Effect of substrate concentration on the rate of an enzyme-controlled reaction.*

4.3.3   Temperature

Heating increases molecular motion. Thus the molecules of the substrate and enzyme move more quickly and chances of their bumping into each other are increased. As a result there is a greater probability of a reaction occurring. The temperature that promotes maximum activity is referred to as the optimum temperature. If the temperature is increased above this level, then a decrease in the rate of the reaction occurs despite the increasing frequency of collisions. This is because the secondary and tertiary structures of the enzyme have been disrupted, and the enzyme is said to be denatured (fig 4.8). In effect, the enzyme unfolds and the precise structure of the active site is gradually lost. The bonds which are most sensitive to temperature change are hydrogen bonds and hydrophobic interactions.

Most mammalian enzymes have a temperature optimum of about 37–40 °C, but enzymes with higher optima exist. For

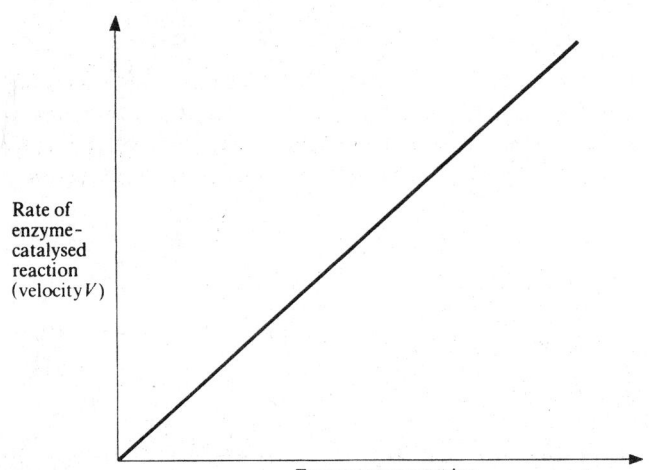

Fig 4.6 *Relationship between enzyme concentration and the rate of an enzyme-controlled reaction.*

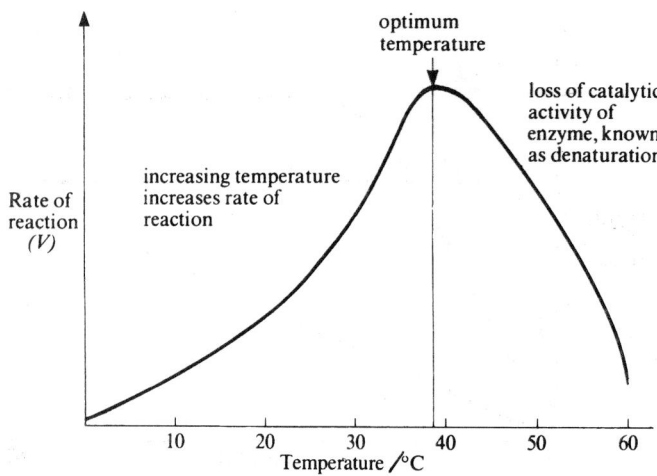

Fig 4.8 *Effect of temperature on the rate of an enzyme-controlled reaction.*

example, the enzymes of bacteria living in hot springs may have an optimum temperature of $70\,°C$ or higher. Such enzymes have been used in biological washing powders for high temperature washes. If temperature is reduced to near or below freezing point, enzymes are **inactivated**, not denatured. They will regain their catalytic influence when higher temperatures are restored.

Today techniques of quick-freezing food are in widespread use as a means of preserving food for long periods. This not only prevents growth and multiplication of microorganisms, but also deactivates their digestive enzymes thus making it impossible for them to decompose food. The natural enzymes in the food itself are also inactivated. However, once frozen, it is necessary to keep the food at subzero temperatures until it is to be prepared for consumption.

> **4.1** Study fig 4.9 carefully and comment on the shapes of the curves given for the enzyme reaction at different temperatures.

Temperature coefficient, Q_{10}

The effect of temperature on the rate of a reaction can be expressed as the temperature coefficient, Q_{10}.

Q_{10} = rate of reaction at $(x + 10)\,°C$/rate of reaction at $x\,°C$

Over a range of $0–40\,°C$, Q_{10} for an enzyme-controlled reaction is 2. In other words, the rate of an enzyme-controlled reaction is doubled for every rise of $10\,°C$.

4.3.4 pH

Under conditions of constant temperature, every enzyme functions most efficiently over a particular pH range. Often this is a narrow range. The optimum pH is that at which the maximum rate of reaction occurs (fig 4.10 and table 4.1). When the pH is altered above or below this value, the rate of enzyme activity diminishes. As pH

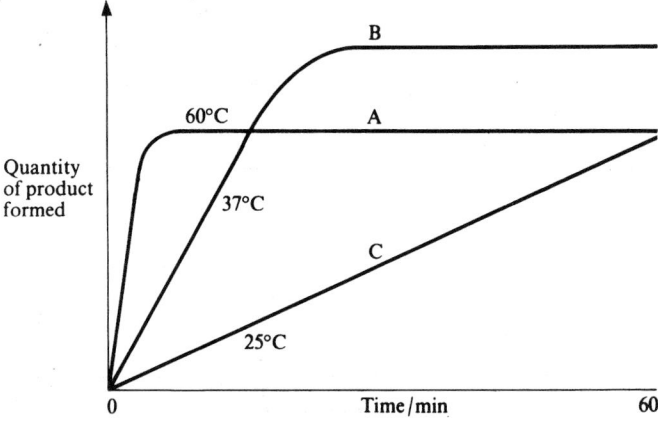

Fig 4.9 Time course of an enzyme reaction at various temperatures.

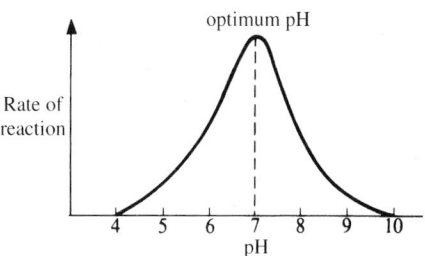

Fig 4.10 Effect of pH on the rate of an enzyme-controlled reaction.

Table 4.1 Optimum pH values for some enzymes.

Enzyme	Optimum pH
Pepsin*	2.00
Sucrase	4.50
Enterokinase	5.50
Salivary amylase	4.80
Catalase	7.60
Chymotrypsin	7.00–8.00
Pancreatic lipase	9.00
Arginase	9.70

* found in stomach with hydrochloric acid.

decreases, acidity increases and the concentration of H^+ ions increases. This increases the number of positive charges in the medium. Changes in pH alter the ionic charge of the acidic and basic groups and therefore disrupt the ionic bonding that helps to maintain the specific shape of the enzyme (section 3.5.3). Thus the pH change leads to an alteration of enzyme shape, including its active site. If extremes of pH are encountered by an enzyme, then it will be denatured.

> **4.2** (a) In fig 4.11, what is the optimum pH for the activity of enzyme B?
> (b) Give an example of an enzyme which could be represented by (i) activity curve A, (ii) activity curve B.
> (c) Why does the enzyme activity of C decrease at pH values between 8 and 9?
> (d) Why is pH control important in cells?
> (e) $1\,cm^3$ of a catalase solution was added to hydrogen peroxide solution at different pH values and the time taken to collect $10\,cm^3$ of oxygen was measured. The results are given below.
>
> | pH of solution | Time to collect gas/min |
> |---|---|
> | 4.00 | 20.00 |
> | 5.00 | 12.50 |
> | 6.00 | 10.00 |
> | 7.00 | 13.60 |
> | 8.00 | 17.40 |
>
> Draw a graph of these results and comment on them.

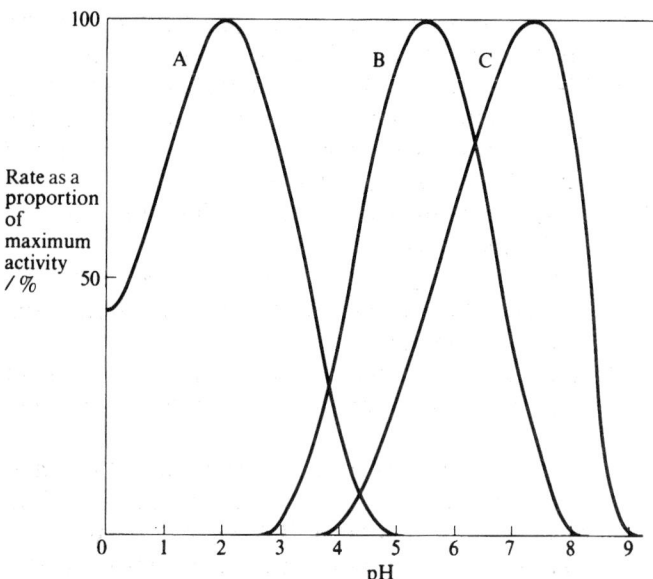

Fig 4.11 *The effect of pH on the activity of three enzymes, A, B and C.*

4.3.5 Practical work

Experiment 4.1: To determine the effect of enzyme concentration on the hydrolysis of sucrose by sucrase (invertase)

Materials

2% sucrose solution
1%, 0.75%, 0.5% sucrase (invertase) solutions
Benedict's reagent
12 test-tubes and rack
water baths at 38 °C and 100 °C
glass rods
stopclock
distilled water
labels
Bunsen burner

Method

(1) Add $2 \, cm^3$ of clear blue Benedict's reagent to $2 \, cm^3$ of clear colourless 1% sucrase solution. Heat the mixture in the water bath maintained at 100 °C for 5 min (Benedict's test).

(2) Repeat (1) using $2 \, cm^3$ of clear colourless 2% sucrose solution and then $2 \, cm^3$ of distilled water.

(3) Boil $5 \, cm^3$ 1% sucrase solution.

(4) Take 8 clean, dry test-tubes, label 1–8, and add $1 \, cm^3$ Benedict's reagent to each.

(5) Add $5 \, cm^3$ of 2% sucrose solution to a test-tube labelled S and place in the water bath maintained at 38 °C throughout the experiment.

(6) Add $5 \, cm^3$ of 1% sucrase solution to a test-tube labelled E and place in the water bath at 38 °C.

(7) Leave both test-tubes and contents in the water bath for 5 min to allow them to equilibrate with their surroundings.

(8) Add the enzyme solution to the sucrose solution, invert the test-tube to thoroughly mix the two solutions.

(9) Immediately start the stopclock and replace the tube containing the reaction mixture in the water bath.

(10) Throughout the experiment agitate the mixture continuously to ensure thorough mixing.

(11) After 30 s of incubation remove $1 \, cm^3$ of mixture and place in test-tube 1.

(12) Repeat this procedure every 30 s placing the samples in tubes 2–8 in turn.

(13) Heat tubes 1–8 in the water bath at 100 °C for 5 min. Note the time when the first positive reducing sugar test is obtained indicated by a brick-red precipitate.

(14) Repeat the experiment using the boiled enzyme from (3).

(15) Repeat the entire sequence/experiment twice using the 0.75% and 0.5% sucrase solutions.

(16) Record your observations and comment on your results.

Experiment 4.2: To investigate the distribution of catalase in a soaked pea, and to determine the effect of different temperatures on its activity

Catalase is an enzyme which catalyses the decomposition of hydrogen peroxide, liberating oxygen gas as shown by effervescence:

$$2H_2O_2 \xrightarrow{\text{catalase}} 2H_2O + O_2$$

Hydrogen peroxide is a toxic by-product of metabolism in certain plant and animal cells, and is efficiently removed by catalase, which is one of the fastest acting enzymes known.

Materials

a supply of soaked peas
hydrogen peroxide solution
test-tubes and rack
water baths at 40 °C, 60 °C, 70 °C, 80 °C and 100 °C
clock
thermometer
scalpels, scissors and forceps
test-tube holder
glass rod
white tile

Method

(1) Test for the presence of catalase by crushing a soaked pea and adding a few drops of hydrogen peroxide solution.

(2) Remove the seed coats from three soaked peas and test separately for catalase activity in both the seed coats and the cotyledons.

(3) Place two test-tubes containing distilled water in a water bath at 40 °C.

(4) Boil three whole peas in a test-tube and then place the boiled peas in one of the tubes in the water bath.

(5) Place three whole unboiled peas in the other test-tube in the water bath.

(6) Allow enough time for the peas to reach the temperature of the water bath (at least 10 min).

(7) Test each pea for catalase activity.

(8) Repeat the experiment at 50, 60, 70, 80 and 100 °C.

(9) Record your observations and comment on your results.

Experiment 4.3: To investigate the effect of different pH values on enzyme activity

Materials

Benedict's reagent
buffer solutions at pH 3, 5, 7, 9, 11
1% starch solution
water bath at 38 °C
Bunsen burner
asbestos mat
test-tube holder, test-tubes and rack
5 cm³ graduated pipettes
thermometer
stopclock
distilled water
stock solution of salivary amylase (such as contained in saliva)

Method

(1) Rinse out the mouth with 5 cm³ of distilled water and spit this out.

(2) Swill 10 cm³ of distilled water round the mouth for 1 min and then collect this liquid.

(3) Make up the volume of salivary amylase to 40 cm³ with distilled water.

(4) Test the salivary amylase, starch and buffer solutions for the presence of reducing sugar using Benedict's reagent.

(5) Label a test-tube pH 3 and add 2 cm³ of starch solution.

(6) Add 2 cm³ of buffer solution pH 3 to the same test-tube and mix the two solutions thoroughly.

(7) Boil at least 4 cm³ of enzyme solution and place 4 cm³ in a labelled test-tube.

(8) Add 4 cm³ of unboiled enzyme solution to another labelled test-tube and place all three test-tubes in the water bath and allow the solutions to reach 38 °C (approximately 1 min).

(9) Place a small quantity of Benedict's reagent in each of 11 test-tubes and label them 1–11.
The following three stages must be carried out very quickly.

(10) When the solutions in the water bath have equilibrated, add the buffered starch solution to the unboiled enzyme solution.

(11) Mix the two solutions thoroughly by inverting the test-tube and replace the tube in the water bath.

(12) Start the stopclock and immediately remove a small quantity of reaction mixture (approximately the same volume as the Benedict's reagent) and place it in the test-tube labelled 1.

(13) Throughout the experiment the mixture must be shaken vigorously.

(14) After one minute of incubation remove a second, approximately equal, volume of the mixture and place it in test-tube 2.

(15) Repeat the removal of similar-sized samples of mixture at minute intervals for a further 9 min and place in test-tubes 3–11.

(16) Perform Benedict's tests on test-tubes 1–11 and note the time of incubation at which a positive result (a brick-red precipitate) is first achieved.

(17) Repeat the experiment using the boiled enzyme solution from (7).

(18) Repeat the entire experiment using each of the other buffer solutions.

(19) Plot a graph of time taken for hydrolysis to occur against pH and comment on your results.

4.4   Enzyme inhibition

A variety of small molecules exists which can reduce the rate of an enzyme-controlled reaction. They are called enzyme inhibitors. It is important to realise that inhibition is a normal part of the regulation of enzyme activity within cells. Many drugs and poisons also act as enzyme inhibitors. Inhibition may be competitive or non-competitive. Non-competitive inhibition may be reversible or non-reversible.

4.4.1   Competitive inhibition

This occurs when a compound has a structure which is sufficiently similar to that of the normal substrate to be able to fit into the active site. Normally it does not take part in a reaction but while it remains there it prevents the true substrate from entering the active site. The genuine substrate and the inhibitor therefore **compete** for a position in the active site, and this form of inhibition is called **competitive inhibition**. A characteristic feature of competitive inhibition is that if the substrate concentration is increased, the rate of reaction increases.

> **4.3** Why should the rate of reaction increase under these conditions?

A diagram illustrating the principle of competitive inhibition, and an example, is shown in fig 4.12.

The knowledge of competitive inhibition helps us to understand the effect of a group of antibiotics known as

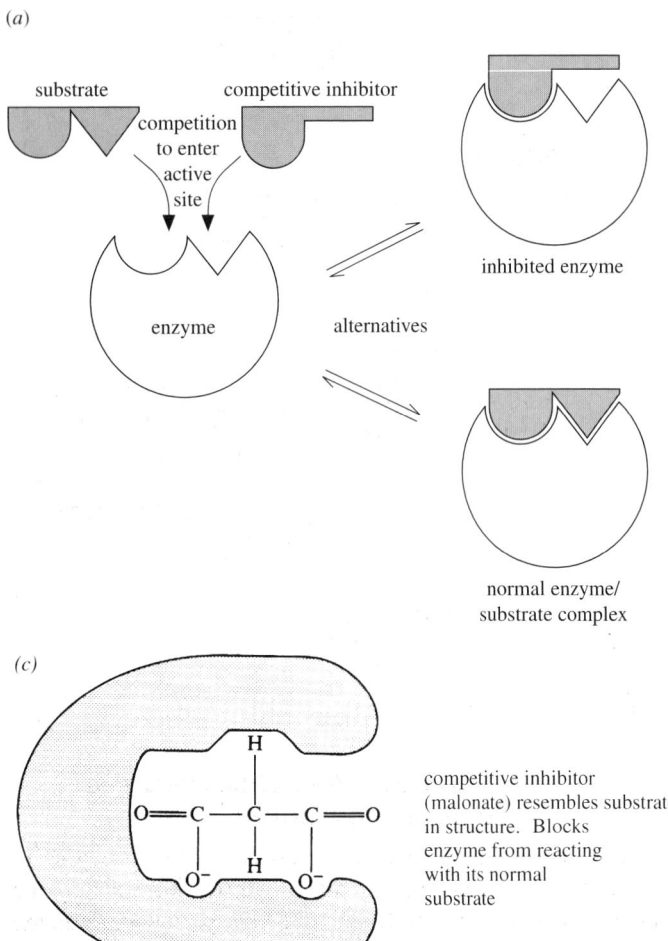

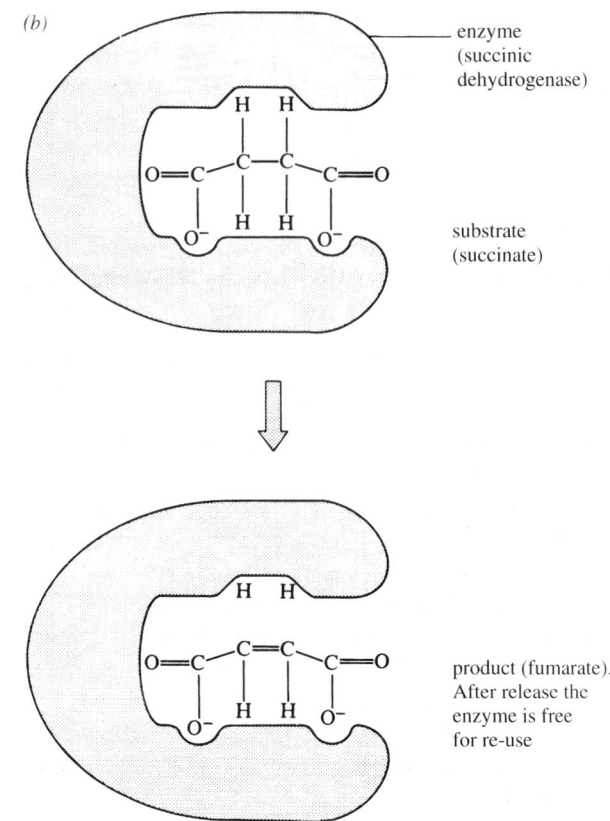

(a)

competitive inhibitor

competition to enter active site

substrate

enzyme

alternatives

inhibited enzyme

normal enzyme/substrate complex

(c)

competitive inhibitor (malonate) resembles substrate in structure. Blocks enzyme from reacting with its normal substrate

(b)

enzyme (succinic dehydrogenase)

substrate (succinate)

product (fumarate). After release the enzyme is free for re-use

Fig 4.12 *Competitive inhibition. (a) Principle illustrated by a simple diagram. (b) Action of the enzyme succinic dehydrogenase on succinate. (c) Competitive inhibition of the enzyme by malonate.*

sulphonamides. Antibiotics destroy infectious microorganisms without damaging host tissues. Sulphonamides were the first antibiotics to be used and were developed during the 1930s. During the Second World War they were used extensively to prevent the spread of microbial infection in wounds. They are similar in structure to PAB (para-aminobenzoate), a substance essential for the growth of many pathogenic (disease-causing) bacteria. The bacteria require PAB for the production of folic acid, an important enzyme cofactor. Sulphonamides act by inhibiting an enzyme needed for the synthesis of folic acid from PAB.

Animal cells are insensitive to sulphonamides even though they require folic acid for some reactions. This is because they use pre-formed folic acid and do not possess the necessary metabolic pathway for making it.

4.4.2   Non-competitive reversible inhibition

This type of inhibitor has no structural similarity to the substrate and combines with the enzyme at a point other than its active site. It does not affect the ability of the substrate to bind with the enzyme, but it makes it impossible for catalysis to take place. The rate of reaction decreases with increasing inhibitor concentration. When inhibitor saturation is reached, the rate of the reaction will be almost nil. It is a characteristic of this type of inhibition that an increase in substrate concentration does not affect the rate of reaction, unlike with competitive inhibition.

4.4.3   Non-competitive irreversible inhibition

Some chemicals cause irreversible inhibition of enzymes. Two examples will be given.

Very small concentrations of chemical reagents such as the heavy metal ions mercury (Hg^{2+}), silver (Ag^+) and arsenic (As^+), or certain iodine-containing compounds completely inhibit some enzymes. They combine permanently with sulphydryl (–SH) groups (fig 4.13). These may be in the active site or elsewhere. Either way, the change in structure of the enzyme makes it ineffective as a catalyst. The change may cause the protein of the enzyme molecule to precipitate.

Another example of irreversible inhibition is provided by the nerve gas DFP (diisopropylfluorophosphate) designed for use in warfare. It combines with the amino acid serine at the active site of the enzyme acetylcholinesterase. This enzyme deactivates the neurotransmitter substance

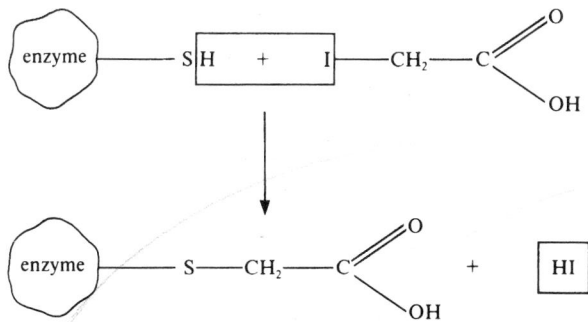

Fig 4.13 *Irreversible inhibition of an enzyme by iodoacetic acid. The iodine reacts with sulphydryl groups.*

acetylcholine. Neurotransmitters are needed to continue the passage of nerve impulses from one nerve cell to another across a synaptic gap (chapter 17). When the impulse has been transmitted, acetylcholinesterase functions to deactivate acetylcholine almost immediately by breaking it down. If acetylcholinesterase is inhibited, acetylcholine accumulates and nerve impulses cannot be stopped, causing prolonged muscle contraction. Paralysis occurs and death may result since the respiratory muscles are among those affected. Some insecticides currently in use, including those known as organophosphates (such as parathion), have a similar effect on insects, and can also cause harm to the nervous and muscular systems of humans who are overexposed to them.

> **4.4** Suggest why it is that substrate concentration has no effect on non-competitive inhibition.

4.4.4 Allosteric enzymes

One of the commonest ways of regulating metabolic pathways in cells is by means of allosteric enzymes. These are enzymes which are 'designed' to change shape (*allo*, different; *steric*, shape). They are regulated by compounds which act as non-competitive inhibitors. These compounds bind to the enzyme at specific sites well away from the active site. They modify enzyme activity by causing a reversible change in the structure of the enzyme's active site. This in turn affects the ability of the substrate to bind to the enzyme (unlike non-competitive reversible inhibition (section 4.4.2)). Compounds of this nature are called **allosteric inhibitors**. Allosteric inhibition is shown in fig 4.14.

An example of this is provided by one of the reactions of glycolysis, the series of reactions that forms the first part of cell respiration. The purpose of cell respiration is to produce ATP. When ATP is at a high concentration, it inhibits one of the enzymes of glycolysis allosterically. However, when cell metabolism increases and more ATP is used up, the overall concentration of ATP decreases and the pathway once again comes into operation because the inhibitor, ATP, has been removed. This is also an example of end-product inhibition.

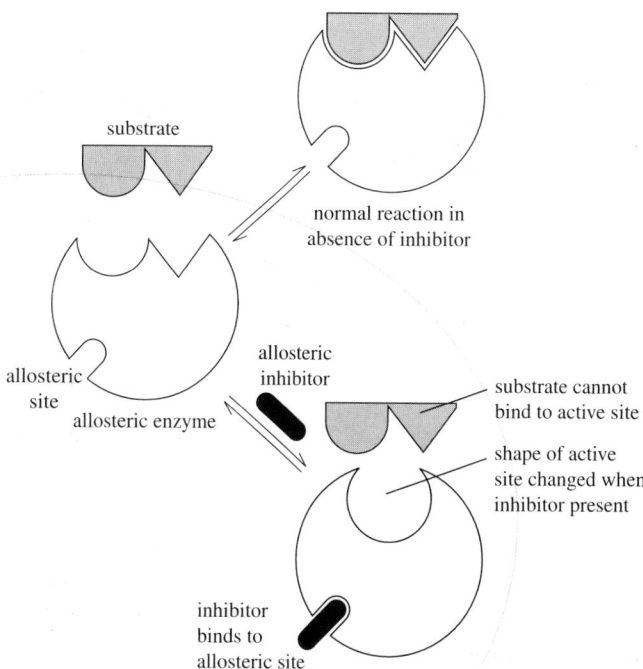

Fig 4.14 *Allosteric inhibition.*

End-product inhibition (negative feedback inhibition)

When the end product of a metabolic pathway begins to accumulate, it may act as an allosteric inhibitor of the enzyme controlling the first step of the pathway. Thus the product starts to switch off its own production as it builds up. The process is self-regulatory. As the product is used up, its production is switched back on again. This is called end-product inhibition and is an example of a **negative feedback** mechanism (fig 4.15) (see also chapter 19).

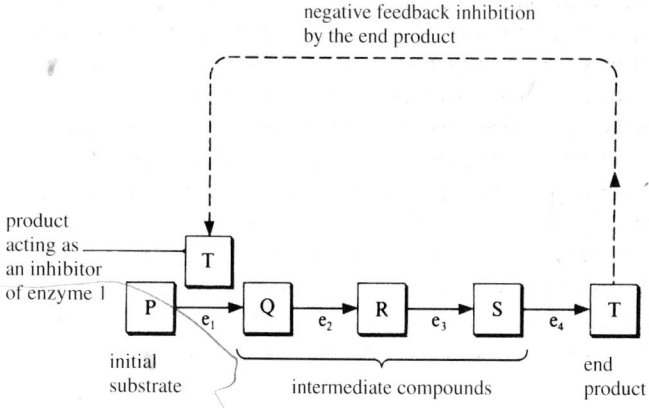

Fig. 4.15 *End-product inhibition. e_1–e_4 are different enzymes of a metabolic pathway.*

4.5 Enzyme cofactors

Many enzymes require non-protein components called cofactors for their efficient activity. They were discovered as substances that had to be present for enzyme activity, even though, unlike enzymes, they were stable at relatively high temperatures. Cofactors may vary from simple inorganic ions to complex organic molecules, and may either remain unchanged at the end of a reaction or be regenerated by a later process. There are three recognised types of cofactor: inorganic ions, prosthetic groups and coenzymes, which will be examined in the following sections.

4.5.1 Inorganic ions (enzyme activators)

These are thought to mould either the enzyme or the substrate into a shape that allows an enzyme/substrate complex to be formed, hence increasing the chances of a reaction occurring between them and therefore increasing the rate of reaction catalysed by that particular enzyme. For example, salivary amylase activity is increased in the presence of chloride ions.

4.5.2 Prosthetic groups (for example FAD, haem)

If the cofactor is tightly bound to the enzyme on a permanent basis it is known as a **prosthetic group** (from the Greek *prosthesis*, meaning 'addition'). Prosthetic groups are organic molecules. They assist the catalytic function of their enzymes, as in flavine adenine dinucleotide (FAD). This contains riboflavin (vitamin B_2), the function of which is to accept hydrogen (fig 4.16). FAD is concerned with cell oxidation pathways and is part of the respiratory chain in respiration (chapter 9).

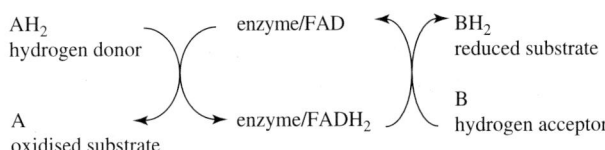

Net effect: 2H transferred from A to B. One enzyme acts as a link between A and B. Both AH_2 and B fit into the active site and FAD passes H_2 from one to the other.

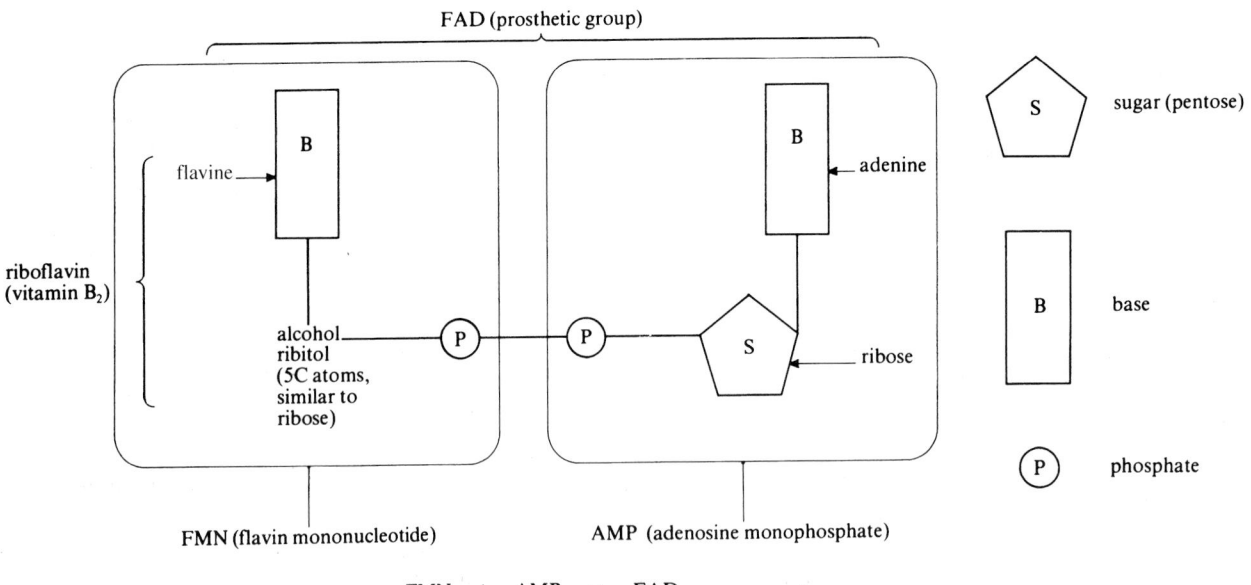

Fig 4.16 *Structure of FAD (flavine adenine dinucleotide), a prosthetic group. FAD is a dinucleotide, formed by the joining of two nucleotides. Nucleotides consist of a sugar, base and phosphate. The two nucleotides in this case are FMN and AMP. Note that riboflavin (vitamin B_2) is part of the structure of one of the nucleotides (FMN), explaining the need for this vitamin in the diet.*

Haem

Haem is an iron-containing prosthetic group. It has the shape of a flat ring (a '**porphyrin ring**' as is found in chlorophyll) with an iron atom at its centre. It has a number of biologically important functions.

Electron carrier. Haem is the prosthetic group of cytochromes (see respiratory chain, chapter 9), where it acts as an electron carrier. In accepting electrons the iron is reduced to Fe(II); in handing on electrons it is oxidised to Fe(III). In other words it takes part in oxidation/reduction reactions by reversible changes in the valency of the iron.

Oxygen carrier. Haemoglobin and myoglobin are oxygen-carrying proteins that contain haem groups. Here the iron remains in the reduced, Fe(II) form (see chapter 14).

Other enzymes. Haem is found in catalases and peroxidases, which catalyse the decomposition of hydrogen peroxide into water and oxygen. It is also found in a number of other enzymes.

4.5.3 Coenzymes (for example NAD, NADP, coenzyme A, ATP)

Like prosthetic groups, coenzymes are organic molecules which act as cofactors, but unlike prosthetic groups they do not remain attached to the enzyme between reactions. All coenzymes are derived from vitamins.

NAD (nicotinamide adenine dinucleotide) (fig 4.17)

This is derived from the vitamin nicotinic acid (niacin) and can exist in both a reduced and an oxidised form. In the oxidised state it functions as a hydrogen acceptor.

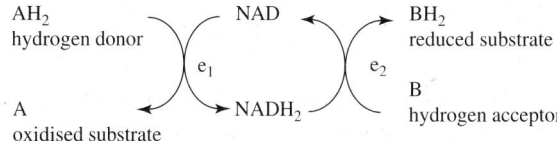

where e_1 and e_2 are two different dehydrogenase enzymes.

Net effect: 2H transferred from A to B. Here the coenzyme acts as a link between two different enzyme systems e_1 and e_2.

4.6 Summarise the characteristic properties of enzymes.

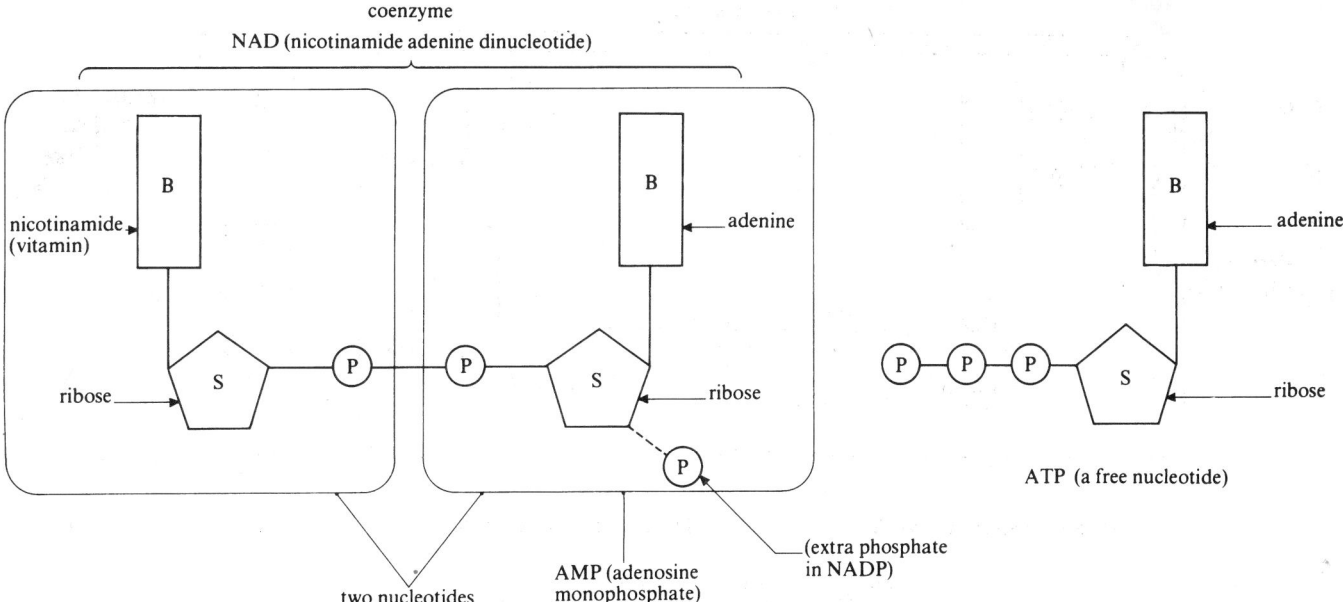

Fig 4.17 *Structure of the coenzyme NAD (nicotinamide adenine dinucleotide) and NADP (NAD with an extra phosphate). NAD and NADP are dinucleotides (see fig 4.16). Note that nicotinamide, also known as niacin, is a vitamin and is part of the structure of one of the nucleotides. AMP is closely related to ATP, the latter having two more phosphate groups. ATP is the energy carrier in cells and is made during cell respiration.*

Chapter Five

Cells

5.1 The cell concept

One of the most important concepts in biology is that **the basic unit of structure and function in living organisms is the cell**. This is known as the **cell theory** and was proposed jointly by two scientists, namely Schleiden, a Belgian botanist, in 1838 and Schwann, a German zoologist, in 1839. The discovery was due to the fact that during the nineteenth century there were dramatic improvements in the quality of lenses for use in microscopy and this in turn led to great interest in the structure of living organisms. Other important discoveries were made during the century, as shown in table 5.1. An essential part of the cell theory is the idea, first proposed in 1855, that **new cells only come from pre-existing cells**.

5.1.1 Why cells?

A cell can be thought of as a bag of chemicals which is capable of surviving and replicating itself. Inside the bag, the chemicals differ in various ways from those outside the bag. Without a barrier between the bag and the

Table 5.1 Some historically important events in cell biology.

1590	Jansen invented the **compound microscope**, which combines two lenses for greater magnification.
1665	Robert Hooke, using an improved compound microscope, examined cork and used the term 'cell' to describe its basic units. He thought the cells were empty and the walls were the living material.
1650–1700	Antony van Leeuwenhoeck, using a good quality simple lens (mag. × 200), observed nuclei and unicellular organisms, including bacteria. In 1676, bacteria were described for the first time as 'animalcules'.
1700–1800	Further descriptions and drawings published, mainly of plant tissues, although the microscope was generally used as a toy.
1827	Dolland dramatically improved the quality of lenses. This was followed by a rapid spread of interest in microscopy.
1831–3*	Robert Brown described the nucleus as a characteristic spherical body in plant cells.
1838–9*	Schleiden (a botanist) and Schwann (a zoologist) produced the 'cell theory' which unified the ideas of the time by stating that **the basic unit of structure and function in living organisms is the cell**.
1840*	Purkyne gave the name **protoplasm** to the contents of cells, realising that the latter were the living material, not the cell walls. Later the term **cytoplasm** was introduced (cytoplasm + nucleus = protoplasm).
1855*	Virchow showed that **all cells arise from pre-existing cells by cell division**.
1866	Haeckel established that the nucleus was responsible for storing and transmitting hereditary characters.
1866–88	Cell division studied in detail and chromosomes described.
1880–3	Chloroplasts discovered.
1890	Mitochondria discovered.
1898	Golgi apparatus discovered.
1887–1990	Improvements in microscopes, fixatives, stains and sectioning. Cytology[†] started to become experimental. Cytogenetics[‡], with its emphasis on the functioning of the nucleus in heredity, became a branch of cytology.
1900	Mendel's work, forgotten since 1865, was rediscovered giving an impetus to cytogenetics. Light microscopy had almost reached the theoretical limits of resolution, thus slowing down the rate of progress.
1930s	Electron microscope developed, enabling much improved resolution.
1946 to present	Electron microscope became widely used in biology, revealing much more detailed structure in cells. This 'fine' structure is called **ultrastructure**.

* significant events in the development of the cell concept.   † cytology – the study of cells, especially by microscopy.

‡ cytogenetics – the linking of cytology with genetics, mainly relating structure and behaviour of chromosomes during cell division to results from breeding experiments.

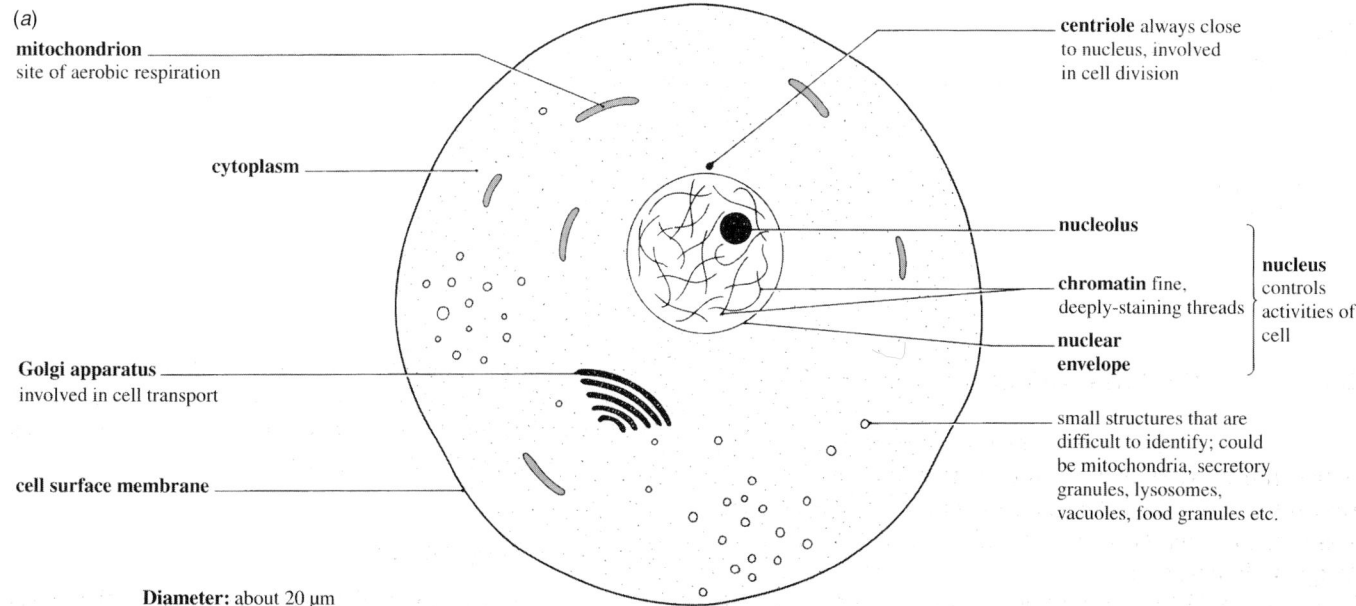

(a)

mitochondrion
site of aerobic respiration

cytoplasm

Golgi apparatus
involved in cell transport

cell surface membrane

Diameter: about 20 μm

centriole always close
to nucleus, involved
in cell division

nucleolus

chromatin fine,
deeply-staining threads

**nuclear
envelope**

nucleus
controls
activities of
cell

small structures that are
difficult to identify; could
be mitochondria, secretory
granules, lysosomes,
vacuoles, food granules etc.

environment the chemicals would mix freely by diffusion and the differences could not be maintained. Life could not exist. The barrier is a very thin membrane. This acts rather like a border control between two countries, controlling the traffic of molecules into and out of the cell. *All* living cells are surrounded by a membrane. It is known as a **cell surface membrane** to distinguish it from any membranes that occur inside the cell. The way in which it controls exchange between the cell and its environment is discussed in section 5.9.8.

5.2   Cells as seen with the light microscope

By the end of the nineteenth century most of the structures visible with a light microscope had been discovered. (A light microscope is one which uses light as a source of radiation.) The cell could be described as a small unit of living protoplasm, always surrounded by a cell surface membrane and sometimes, as in the case of plants, by a non-living wall. The most conspicuous structure in the cell is the **nucleus**, which contains a deeply staining material known as **chromatin** (meaning coloured material). This is the loosely coiled form of chromosomes. Chromosomes appear as thread-like structures just before nuclear division. They contain **DNA**, the genetic material. DNA controls the cell's activities and can replicate itself so that new cells can form.

Figs 5.1a and 5.2a show the structure of generalised animal and plant cells as seen with a light microscope. (A generalised cell is one which shows *all* the typical features found in a cell.) The only structures shown which had not been discovered by the end of the nineteenth century are lysosomes. Examples of particular types of cell are shown in figs 5.1b and 5.2b – see also fig 6.16, epithelial cells from the small intestine, and fig 6.2, plant parenchyma cell.

(b)

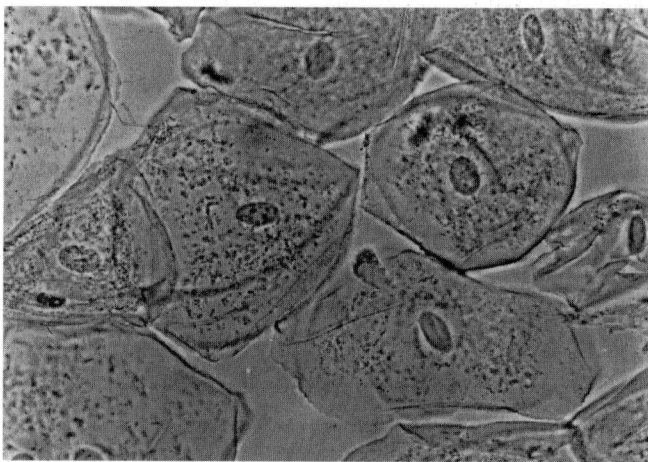

Fig 5.1 (a) *Generalised animal cell as seen with a light microscope.* (b) *Cells from the lining of the human cheek showing typical characteristics of an animal cell. Each cell contains a central nucleus surrounded by cytoplasm containing many organelles such as mitochondria (x400).*

The living material between the nucleus and the cell surface membrane is known as **cytoplasm**. This contains a variety of organelles. An **organelle** is a **distinct part of a cell which has a particular structure and function**. The organelles are described later (figs 5.12 and 5.13, and section 5.10). The only organelle found in animal cells which is absent from plant cells is the centriole. Basically, plant cells are very similar to animal cells but have more structures. The chief differences are the presence in plant cells of:

• a relatively rigid **cell wall** outside the cell surface membrane; pores containing fine threads known as **plasmodesmata** link the cytoplasm of neighbouring cells through the cell walls;

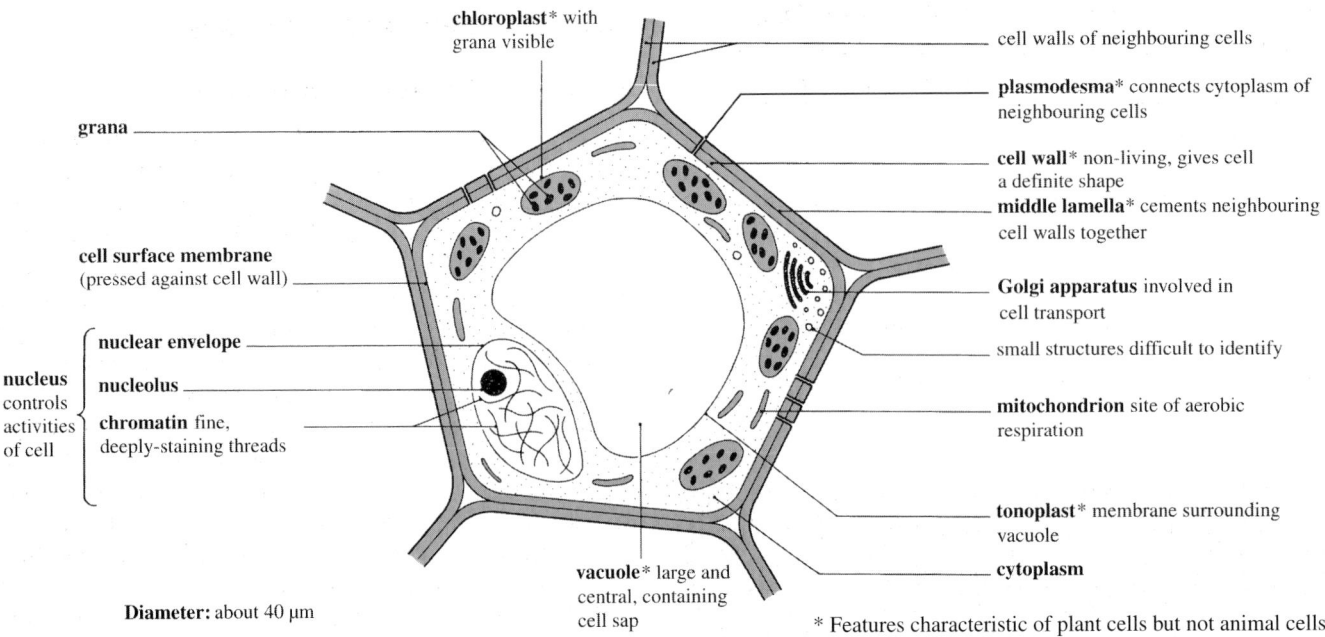

chloroplast* with grana visible

grana

cell surface membrane
(pressed against cell wall)

nuclear envelope

nucleus controls activities of cell

nucleolus

chromatin fine, deeply-staining threads

cell walls of neighbouring cells

plasmodesma* connects cytoplasm of neighbouring cells

cell wall* non-living, gives cell a definite shape

middle lamella* cements neighbouring cell walls together

Golgi apparatus involved in cell transport

small structures difficult to identify

mitochondrion site of aerobic respiration

tonoplast* membrane surrounding vacuole

cytoplasm

vacuole* large and central, containing cell sap

Diameter: about 40 μm

* Features characteristic of plant cells but not animal cells.

Fig 5.2 *Generalised plant cell as seen with a light microscope.*

- **chloroplasts** in photosynthetic plant cells;
- a **large central vacuole**: animal cells may have small vacuoles such as phagocytic vacuoles (figs 5.22 and 5.31).

Use of the light microscope is described at the end of this chapter (section 5.11).

5.3   Prokaryotes and eukaryotes

As described in chapter 2, there are two fundamentally different types of cell, the prokaryote cell and the eukaryote cell. In prokaryotes the DNA lies free in the cytoplasm in a region known as the **nucleoid**. There is no true nucleus. In eukaryotes the DNA is found inside a nucleus, a structure which is surrounded by two membranes, the **nuclear envelope**. The DNA is also associated with protein to form **chromosomes**. The differences between prokaryote and eukaryote cells are summarised in chapter 2 (table 2.2 and section 2.3).

5.4   Compartments and division of labour

Eukaryotic cells are far larger and more complex than prokaryotic cells. They contain many organelles. The eukaryotic cell has often been compared to a factory where, although different machines and people have different jobs, all are working together with one purpose. Efficiency is improved by '**division of labour**', the sharing out of jobs. In the cell each organelle has its own role, involving its own specialised structure and chemistry. The mitochondrion, for example, is the powerhouse of cells,

providing energy in the form of ATP from the specialised reactions of respiration. It has a particular structure which enables it to do this efficiently. The cell as a whole is, in effect, divided up into compartments. This **compartmentation** is often achieved by membranes. Most organelles are surrounded by membranes so that, just as the cell surface membrane controls exchange between the cell and its environment, each membrane-bound organelle can have its own particular unique set of chemicals and chemical reactions. The electron microscope reveals even more structural organisation than the light microscope, as we shall see in section 5.8.

5.5   Units of measurement

Before proceeding further, it is useful to remind yourself of just how small cells are, and of the units of measurement which we have to use in describing them. Table 5.2 summarises the most useful units of measurement. Fig 5.3 shows bacteria on the surface of the sharp end of a pin, which measures about 100 μm in diameter. (The symbol μm is a micrometre.) Between 50 and 100 μm is about the lowest limit of what is visible unaided with the human eye. A very fine human hair is about 30 μm in diameter. Eukaryotic cells vary greatly in size (the largest algal cell is 50 mm in diameter!) but the average animal cell is about 20 μm in diameter compared with about 40 μm for an average plant cell. The average mitochondrion and bacterium are about 1 μm in diameter (a convenient reference size to try to remember). The smallest cell organelles, ribosomes, are about 20 nm in diameter; a DNA molecule is 2 nm in diameter and the smallest atom, a hydrogen atom, is 0.04 nm in diameter.

130

Table 5.2 Units of measurement used in cell biology.

Unit	Symbol	Fraction of a metre	Also
millimetre	mm	one thousandth, 10^{-3} m	
micrometre	μm*	one millionth, 10^{-6} m	one thousandth of a millimetre
nanometre	nm	one thousand millionth, 10^{-9} m	one thousandth of a micrometre

* μ is the Greek letter mu.
The metre, symbol m, is the internationally agreed basic unit of length.

Fig 5.3 *Scanning electron micrograph of bacterial cells on the point of a pin.*

5.6 Electron microscopy

5.6.1 Electron microscopes

By the early 1900s progress on understanding cell structure was limited by the fact that no matter how good the quality of a light microscope, its maximum magnification is limited to about ×1500. This is due to the nature of light itself. Light is a form of electromagnetic radiation, as shown in fig 5.4. One of the properties of light is that it can behave like a series of waves. Wavelengths between about 400 nm (violet) and about 700 nm (red) cause a response in the human eye. However, there is a continuous spectrum of radiation of different wavelengths known as the **electromagnetic spectrum**, of which visible light is only a small part (fig 5.4). All the waves travel at the speed of light, but the shorter the wavelength, the greater the energy that the waves carry. It is not possible to view objects smaller than half the wavelength of the radiation used by the viewer. This is because the object has to be large enough to interfere with the passage of the waves. The smallest object we can view using visible light is therefore about 200 nm in diameter, half the size of the wavelength of violet light. Remembering the dimensions we noted in the previous section, it becomes clear why structures like mitochondria (1 μm, or 1000 nm) are only just visible as granules inside cells. Some organelles, such as ribosomes, are completely invisible using a light microscope. If we want to know more about the detailed structure of mitochondria, ribosomes and the other cell components, then light microscopes are inadequate.

With these limitations in mind, scientists deliberately set out to invent a different kind of microscope, one which used radiation of a much shorter wavelength. At one stage, an X-ray microscope was built, but the best choice turned out to be the electron microscope. Here the radiation used

Fig 5.4 *The electromagnetic spectrum. Visible light makes up only a small part of the spectrum. (Waves are not drawn to scale.)*

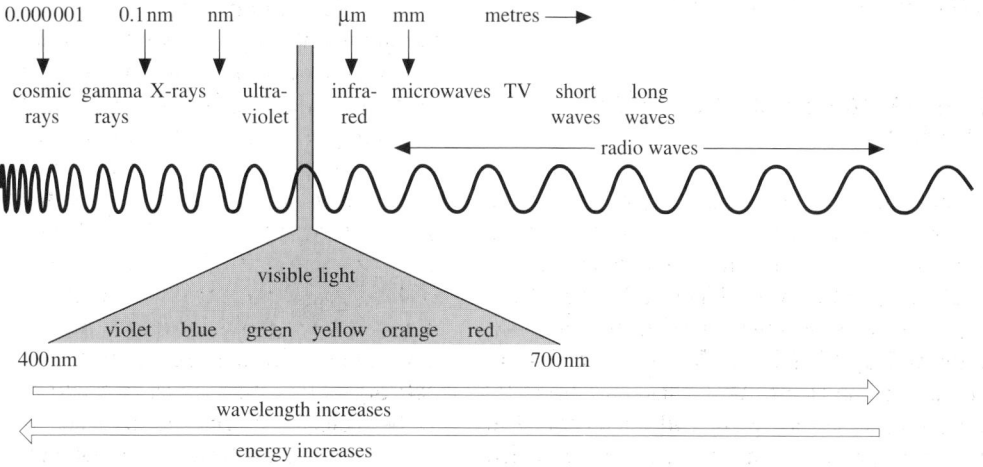

is electrons. Electrons are negatively charged particles which can be found in orbit around the nuclei of atoms. Under certain circumstances they can behave as waves. They have two great advantages over light. Firstly, they have extremely short wavelengths, about the same as X-rays (fig 5.4). Secondly, because they are negatively charged, a beam of electrons can easily be focused through a specimen using electromagnets. This involves bending the beam of electrons just as glass lenses are used to bend light.

With the electron microscope, magnifications up to ×250 000 are commonly obtained with biological material. With some materials even higher magnifications are possible, and even individual atoms have now been seen.

5.6.2 Resolution and magnification

The ability to distinguish between two separate objects is known as **resolution**. If two separate objects cannot be resolved, they will be seen as one object. Resolution is not the same as **magnification**. If you take a photograph and keep on magnifying it (enlarging it), you will not eventually be able to see atoms. Magnification can be increased, *but* the resolution of the photograph stays the same. We enlarge photographs in order to see them more clearly, but if we go too far the picture breaks up into separate blurred dots. Another way of explaining the difference between resolution and magnification is to study a picture of a cell taken with a light microscope and an electron microscope at the same magnification (fig 5.5). Note the difference in clarity between the two pictures in fig 5.5. The resolution is much greater in the electron microscope. The shorter wavelengths of electrons are said to have greater resolving power than those of light.

The resolution of an electron microscope is about 0.5 nm in practice, compared with 200 nm for the light microscope. This does not mean that electron microscopes are better. They are used for different jobs. Light microscopes are still important for getting an overall view of cells or tissues, and preparation of material for them is much quicker and easier. They can also be used to view living material, which is not possible with an electron microscope.

5.6.3 Principles and limitations of electron microscopes

Development of electron microscopes started in the 1930s and they came into regular use in the 1950s.

Fig 5.6 shows a modern transmission electron microscope and fig 5.7 the pathway of the electron beam. A transmission electron microscope (TEM) is one in which the electron beam is transmitted *through* the specimen before viewing, and was the first type to be developed.

The electron microscope is like an upside-down light microscope. The radiation enters at the top and the specimen is viewed at the bottom. The principle is the same as in a light microscope in that a beam of radiation is focused by condenser lenses through the specimen, and then the image

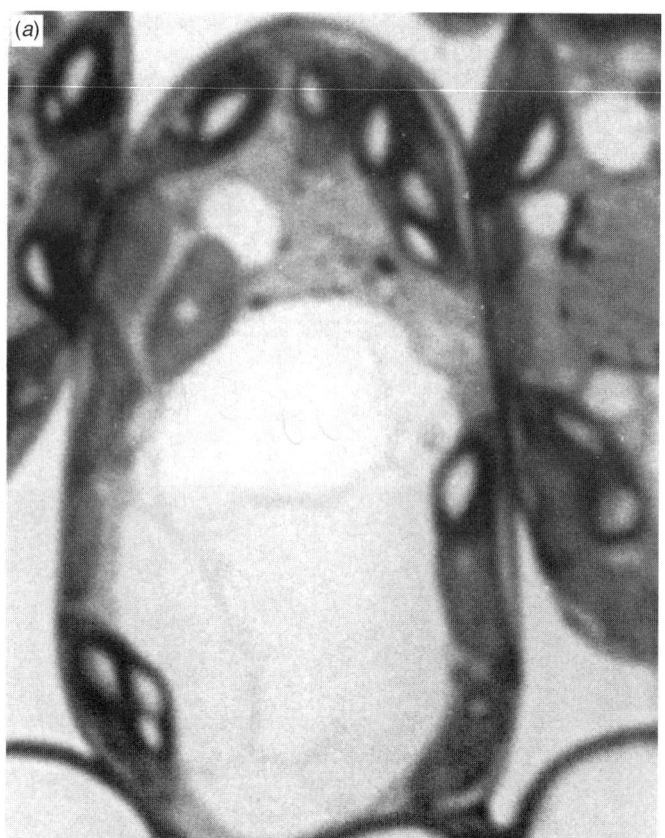

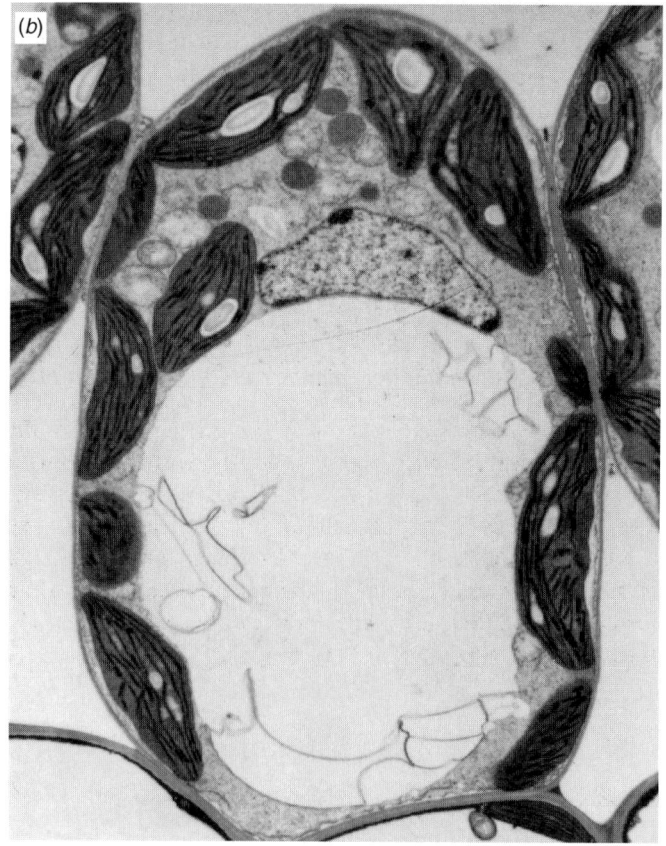

Fig 5.5 *Photographs of the same plant cells seen* (a) *with a light microscope, and* (b) *with an electron microscope, both shown at a magnification of about x2500.*

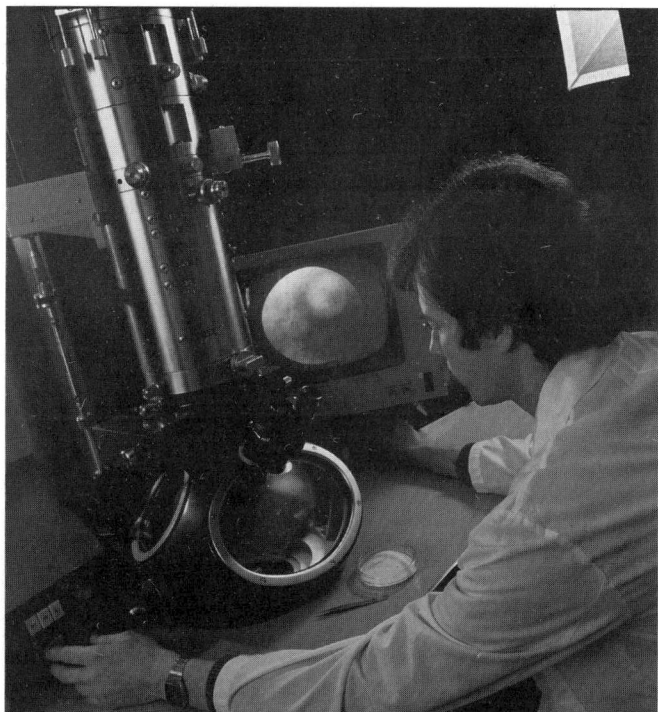

Fig 5.6 *A modern transmission electron microscope.*

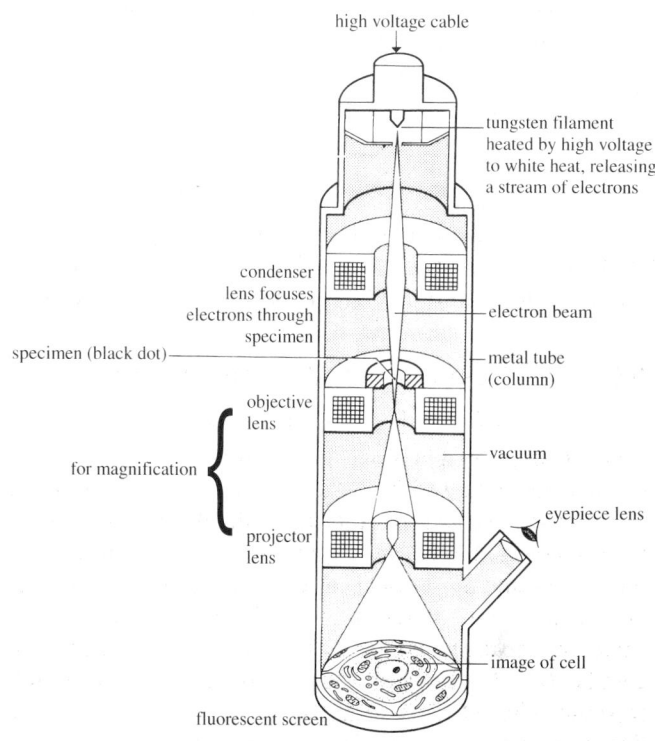

Fig 5.7 *Pathway of the electron beam in the transmission electron microscope.*

is magnified by further lenses. Table 5.3 summarises some of the similarities and differences. A high voltage, such as 50 000 V, is passed through a tungsten filament, like the filament of a light bulb, at the top of the column. The white hot filament releases a stream of electrons, kicked out of their orbits by the high voltage. Electromagnets focus the beam. The inside of the column has to be kept under a high vacuum, otherwise the electrons would collide with air molecules and be scattered. Only very thin sections (slices) of material or very small particles can be observed, because electrons are easily absorbed by larger objects. Those parts of the specimen which are more dense absorb electrons and appear blacker in the final picture. Density differences can be made greater by using stains which contain heavy metals such as lead and uranium.

Electrons cannot be seen with the human eye, so the image is made visible by shining the electrons on to a fluorescent screen. This gives a black-and-white picture. The screen can be lifted out of the way to enable the electrons to pass on to a photographic film so that a permanent record can be obtained of any interesting features. A photograph taken with an electron microscope is called an **electron micrograph**.

Advantage:

- high resolution (0.5 nm in practice).

Disadvantages:

- the specimen must be dead because it is viewed in a vacuum;
- it is difficult to be sure that the specimen resembles a living cell in all its details because preservation and

Table 5.3 Comparison of light and electron microscopes.

	Transmission electron microscope	*Light microscope*
Radiation source	electrons	light
Wavelength	about 0.005 nm	400–700 nm
Max. resolution in practice	0.5 nm	200 nm
Max. useful magnification	×250 000 (on screen)	×1500
Lenses	electromagnets	glass
Specimen	nonliving, dehydrated, relatively small or thin	living or nonliving
	supported on a small copper grid in a vacuum	usually supported on a glass slide
Common stains	contain heavy metals to reflect electrons	coloured dyes
Image	black and white	usually coloured

staining may change or damage the structure;

- expensive to buy and run;
- preparation of material is time-consuming and requires expert training;
- the specimen gradually deteriorates in the electron beam. Photographs must therefore be taken if further study is required.

5.6.4 Scanning electron microscope

Another kind of electron microscope is the scanning electron microscope (SEM) in which the electron beam is scanned to and fro across the specimen and electrons that are reflected from the surface are collected. They are used to form a TV-like image on a cathode ray tube.

Advantages:

- surfaces of structures are shown;
- great depth of field, meaning that a large part of the specimen is in focus at the same time. This gives a very striking three-dimensional effect (fig 5.8);
- much larger samples can be examined than with a TEM.

Disadvantage:

- resolution (5–20 nm) is not as great as with a TEM (0.5 nm).

5.7 Cell fractionation

Microscopy makes a very valuable contribution to our understanding of cells. However, other techniques are also needed if the functions of organelles are to be studied. A common approach to studying function is to isolate a particular cell organelle from other cell components and try to make it perform its normal functions in a test tube. A common procedure is to grind up (homogenise) cells in a suitable medium (with correct pH, ionic composition and temperature). This can be done with

a homogeniser (food mixer). The mixture is then centrifuged. The faster the rotation of the centrifuge, the smaller the particles which will be sedimented. Fig 5.9 illustrates the principle. A series of increasing speeds can be used. After each speed, the supernatant (the liquid above the pellet) can be drawn off and recentrifuged. A series of pellets containing cell organelles of smaller and smaller size can therefore be obtained. This is known as **differential centrifugation**. The high speeds require a special centrifuge known as an **ultracentrifuge**.

5.8 Ultrastructure of animal and plant cells

The fine structure of the cell as seen with the electron microscope is known as **ultrastructure**. Figs 5.10 and 5.11 show diagrams of generalised animal and plant cells as seen with the electron microscope and figs 5.12 and 5.13 show actual electron micrographs (pictures taken with an electron microscope), together with summaries of the structures and functions of the different parts seen.

> **5.1** With reference to figs 5.1, 5.2, 5.10 and 5.11, what additional structures are revealed by the electron microscope compared with the light microscope?
>
> **5.2** With reference to figs 5.1, 5.2, 5.10 and 5.11, what structures are found (*a*) in plant cells but not in animal cells, and (*b*) in animal cells but not in plant cells?

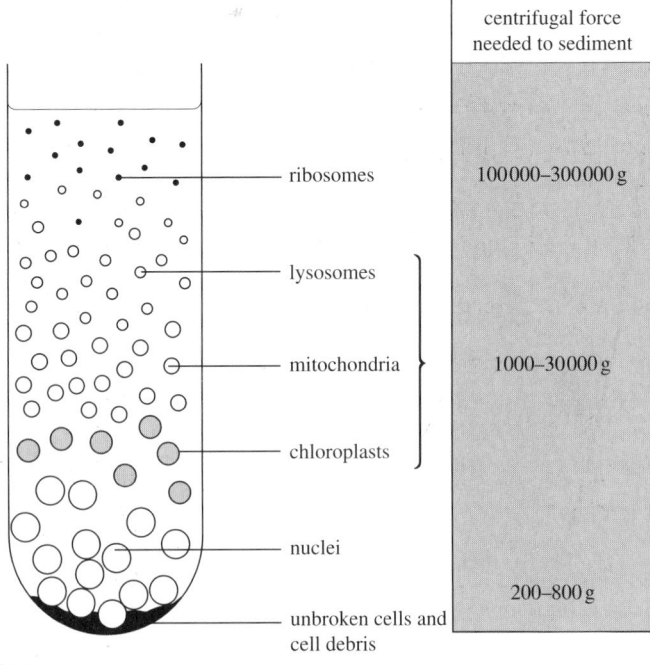

Fig 5.9 *Fractionation of cell components by centrifugation. Centrifugal forces are measured in g (number of times gravity).*

Fig 5.8 *Scanning EM of front view of a spider.*

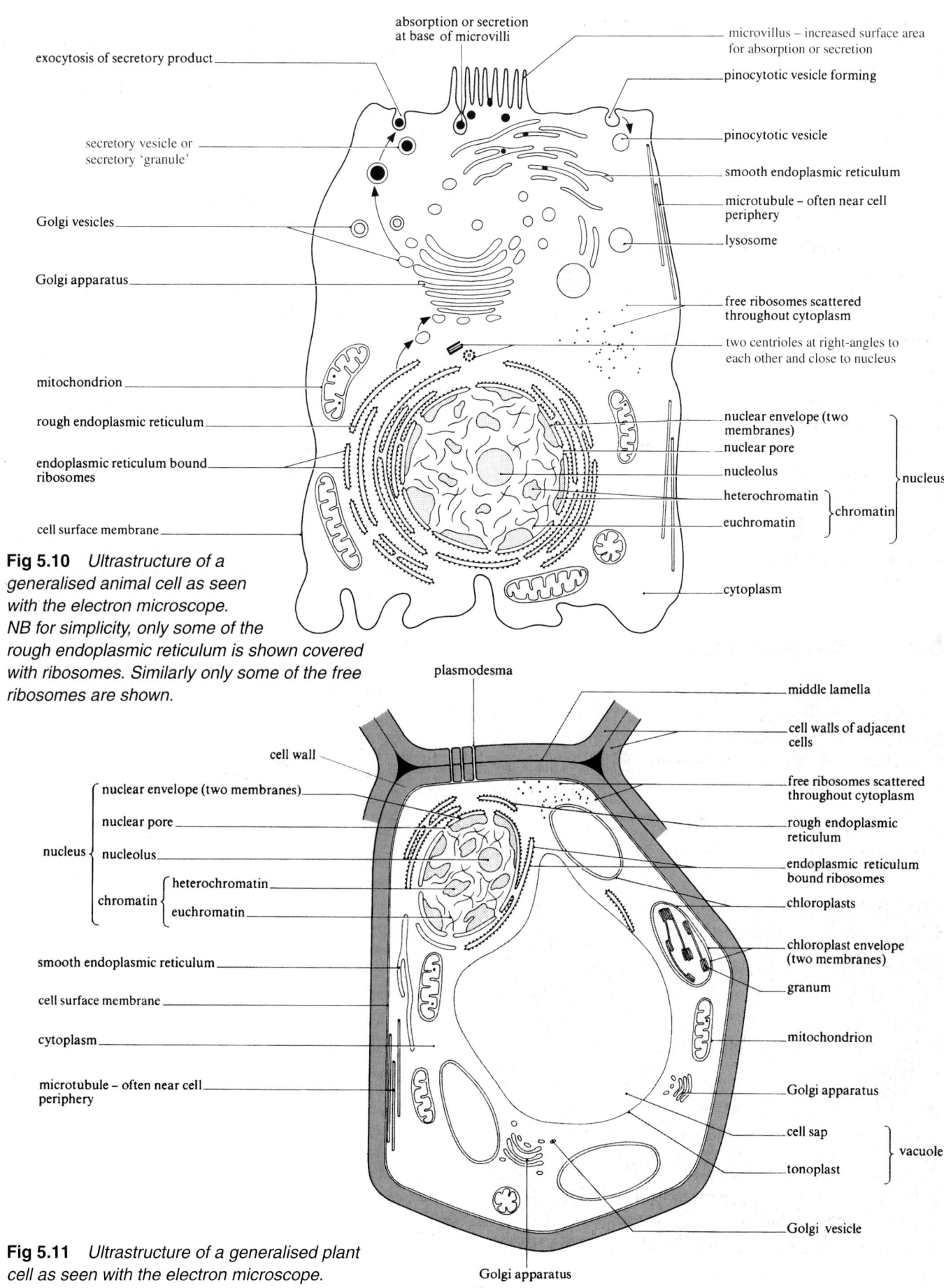

absorption or secretion at base of microvilli

microvillus – increased surface area for absorption or secretion

exocytosis of secretory product

pinocytotic vesicle forming

pinocytotic vesicle

secretory vesicle or secretory 'granule'

smooth endoplasmic reticulum

microtubule – often near cell periphery

Golgi vesicles

lysosome

Golgi apparatus

free ribosomes scattered throughout cytoplasm

two centrioles at right-angles to each other and close to nucleus

mitochondrion

nuclear envelope (two membranes)

rough endoplasmic reticulum

nuclear pore

endoplasmic reticulum bound ribosomes

nucleolus

nucleus

heterochromatin

chromatin

cell surface membrane

euchromatin

Fig 5.10 *Ultrastructure of a generalised animal cell as seen with the electron microscope. NB for simplicity, only some of the rough endoplasmic reticulum is shown covered with ribosomes. Similarly only some of the free ribosomes are shown.*

cytoplasm

plasmodesma

middle lamella

cell wall

cell walls of adjacent cells

nuclear envelope (two membranes)

free ribosomes scattered throughout cytoplasm

nuclear pore

rough endoplasmic reticulum

nucleus

nucleolus

endoplasmic reticulum bound ribosomes

chromatin

heterochromatin

chloroplasts

euchromatin

chloroplast envelope (two membranes)

smooth endoplasmic reticulum

granum

cell surface membrane

mitochondrion

cytoplasm

Golgi apparatus

microtubule – often near cell periphery

cell sap

vacuole

tonoplast

Golgi vesicle

Fig 5.11 *Ultrastructure of a generalised plant cell as seen with the electron microscope.*

Golgi apparatus

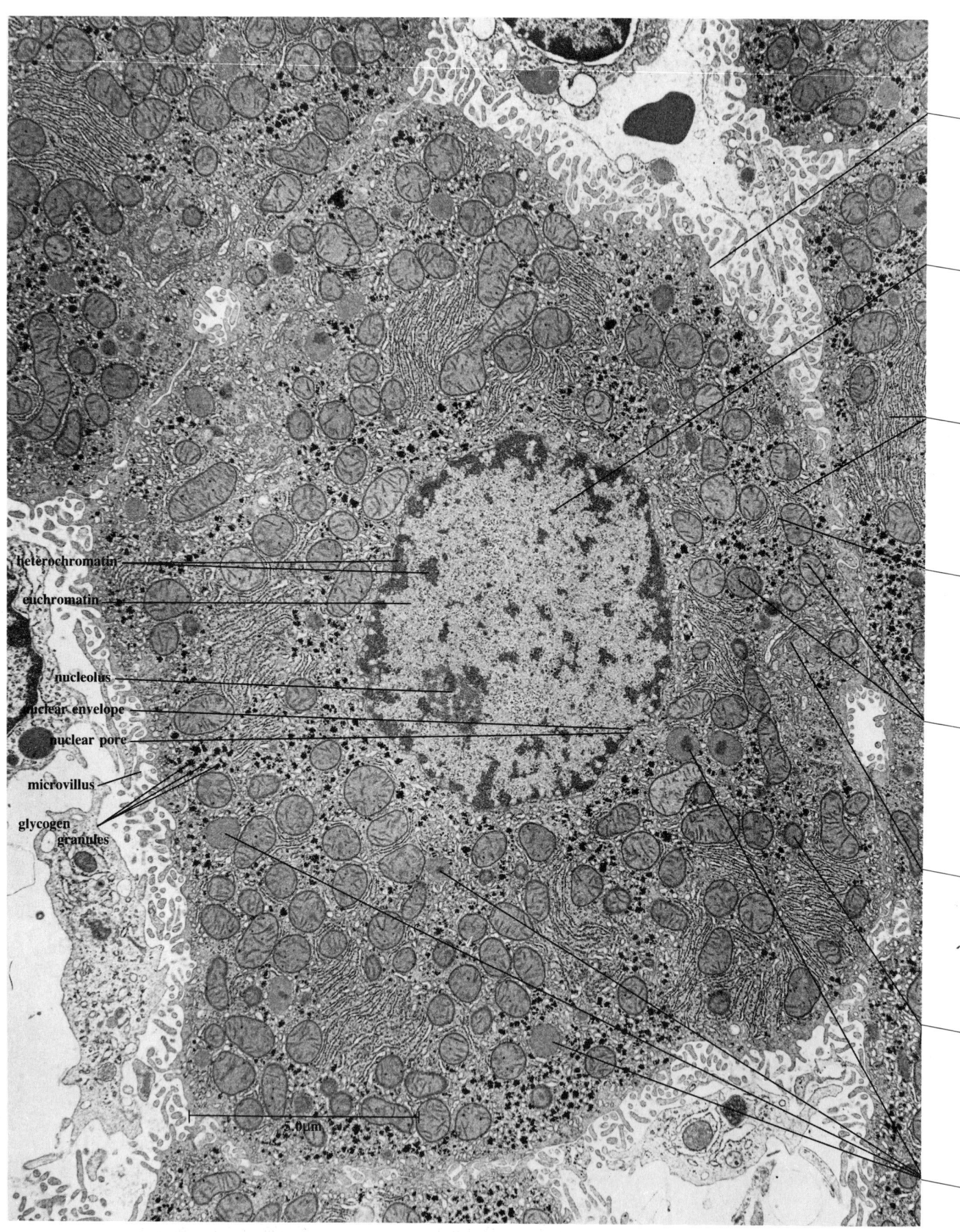

heterochromatin

euchromatin

nucleolus

nuclear envelope

nuclear pore

microvillus

glycogen
granules

1.0μm

Fig 5.12 *Electron micrograph of a thin section of a representative animal cell, a rat liver cell (x9600).*

Diagram	Structure	Functions
Cell surface membrane	'Trilaminar' appearance (3 layers), a pale layer sandwiched between 2 dark layers	A partially permeable barrier controlling exchange between the cell and its environment
Nucleus nuclear envelope (two membranes) nuclear pore heterochromatin euchromatin nucleolus chromatin	Largest cell organelle, enclosed by an **envelope** of two membranes that is perforated by **nuclear pores**. It contains **chromatin** which is the extended form taken by chromosomes during interphase. It also contains a **nucleolus**.	Chromosomes contain DNA, the molecule of inheritance. DNA is organised into genes which control all the activities of the cell. Nuclear division is the basis of cell replication, and hence reproduction. The nucleolus manufactures ribosomes.
Endoplasmic reticulum (ER) ribosomes — cisterna	A system of flattened, membrane-bounded sacs called **cisternae**, forming tubes and sheets. It is continuous with the outer membrane of the nuclear envelope.	If ribosomes are found on its surface it is called **rough ER**, and transports proteins made by the ribosomes through the cisternae. **Smooth ER** (no ribosomes) is a site of lipid and steroid synthesis.
Ribosomes large subunit small subunit	Very small organelles consisting of a large and a small subunit. They are made of roughly equal parts of protein and RNA. Slightly smaller ribosomes are found in mitochondria (and chloroplasts in plants).	Protein synthesis. They are either bound to the ER or lie free in the cytoplasm. They may form **polysomes** (polyribosomes), collections of ribosomes strung along messenger RNA.
Mitochondria (sing. mitochondrion) phosphate granule ribosome matrix crista envelope (two membranes) circular DNA	Surrounded by an envelope of two membranes, the inner being folded to form **cristae**. Contains a **matrix** with a few ribosomes, a circular DNA molecule and phosphate granules.	In aerobic respiration cristae are the sites of oxidative phosphorylation and electron transport, and the matrix is the site of Krebs cycle enzymes.
Golgi apparatus Golgi vesicles Golgi body	A stack of flattened, membrane-bounded sacs, called **cisternae**, continuously being formed at one end of the stack and budded off as vesicles at the other.	Internal **processing** and **transport** system. Processing of many cell materials takes place in the cisternae, e.g. proteins from the ER. Golgi vesicles transport the materials to other parts of the cell or to the cell surface membrane for secretion. **Makes lysosomes.**
Lysosomes	A simple spherical sac bounded by a single membrane and containing digestive (hydrolytic) enzymes. No internal structure visible.	Many functions, all concerned with breakdown of structures or molecules. For example, get rid of old organelles, digest bacteria taken in by phagocytosis.
Microbodies	A roughly spherical organelle bounded by a single membrane. Its contents appear finely granular except for occasional striking crystalloid or filamentous deposits.	All contain catalase, an enzyme that breaks down hydrogen peroxide. All are associated with oxidation reactions. In plants, are the site of the glyoxylate cycle.

137

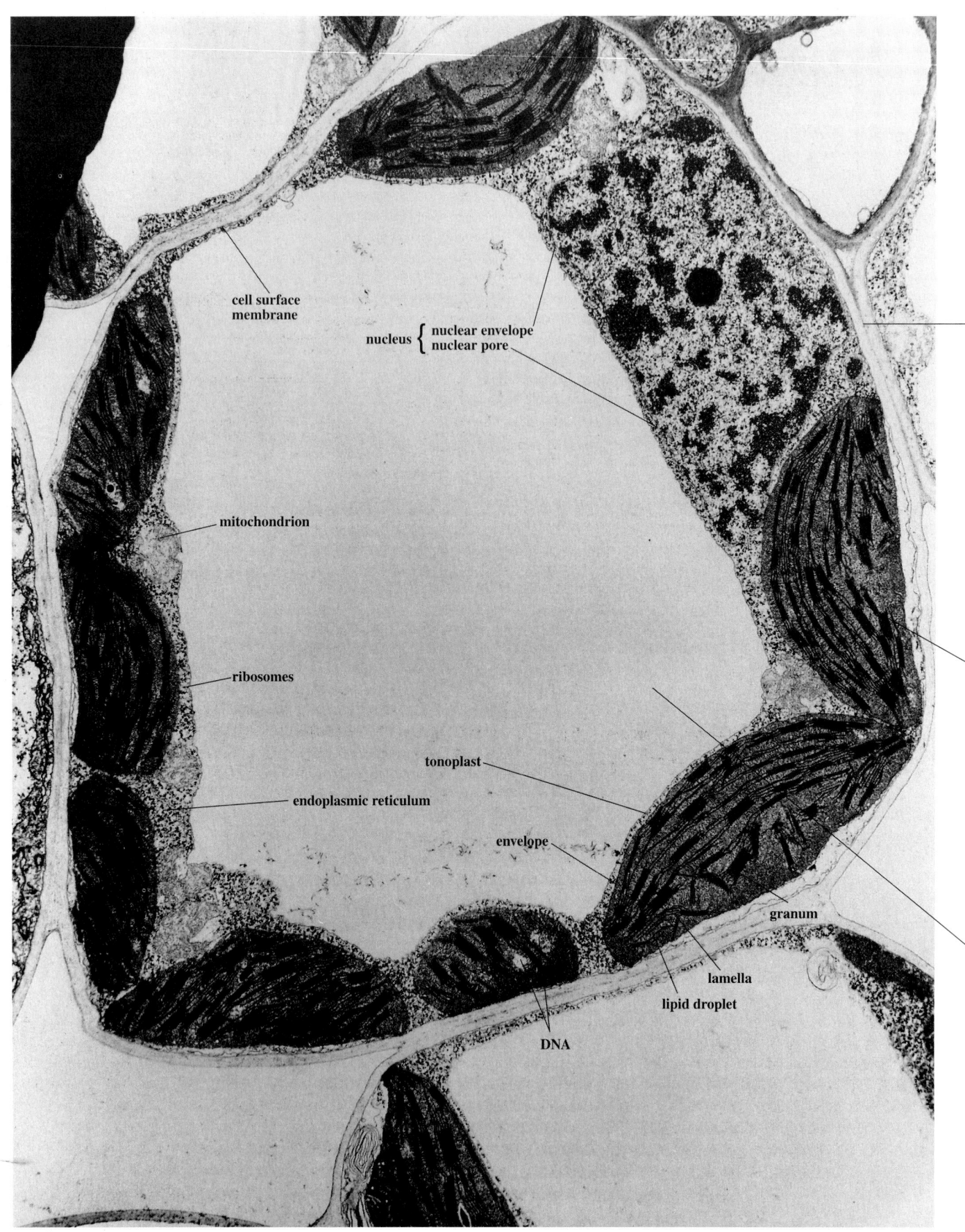

cell surface membrane

nucleus { **nuclear envelope** **nuclear pore**

mitochondrion

ribosomes

tonoplast

endoplasmic reticulum

envelope

granum

lamella

lipid droplet

DNA

Fig 5.13 *Electron micrograph of a thin section of a representative plant cell, a leaf mesophyll cell (x15 000).*

	Diagram	Structure	Functions
Cell wall, middle lamella, plasmodesmata (sing. **plasmodesma**)	cell wall; intercellular air space; cell surface membrane	A rigid cell wall surrounding the cell, consisting of cellulose microfibrils running through a matrix of other complex polysaccharides. May be secondarily thickened in some cells.	Provides mechanical support and protection. It allows a pressure potential to be developed which aids in support. It prevents osmotic bursting of the cell. It is a pathway for movement of water and mineral salts. Various modifications, such as lignification, for specialised functions.
	middle lamella	Thin layer of pectic substances (calcium and magnesium pectates).	Cements neighbouring cells together.
	plasmodesma	A fine cytoplasmic thread linking the cytoplasm of two neighbouring cells through a fine pore in the cell walls. The pore is lined with the cell surface membrane and has a central tubular core, often associated at each end with ER.	Enables a continuous system of cytoplasm, the **symplast**, to be formed between neighbouring cells for transport of substances between cells.
	Detail of plasmodesma — ER; tubular core		
Chloroplast	photosynthetic membranes with chlorophyll; lamella; granum; stroma; envelope (two membranes); circular DNA; lipid droplet; ribosomes; starch grain	Large plastid containing chlorophyll and carrying out **photosynthesis**. It is surrounded by an envelope of two membranes and contains a gel-like **stroma** through which runs a system of membranes that are stacked in places to form **grana**. It may store starch. The stroma also contains ribosomes, a circular DNA molecule and lipid droplets.	It is the organelle in which photosynthesis takes place, producing sugars from carbon dioxide and water using light energy trapped by chlorophyll. Light energy is converted to chemical energy
Large central vacuole	(Smaller vacuoles may occur in plant and animal cells such as food vacuoles, contractile vacuoles.)	A sac bounded by a single membrane called the **tonoplast**. It contains **cell sap**, a concentrated solution of various substances, such as mineral salts, sugars, pigments, organic acids and enzymes. Typically large in mature cells.	Storage of various substances including waste products. It makes an important contribution to the osmotic properties of the cell. Sometimes it functions as a lysosome.

cell wall

chloroplast

large central vacuole

5.9　Cell membranes

Cell membranes are important for a number of reasons. They separate the contents of cells from their external environments, controlling exchange of materials such as nutrients and waste products between the two. They also enable separate compartments to be formed *inside* cells in which specialised metabolic processes such as photosynthesis and aerobic respiration can take place. Chemical reactions, such as the light reactions of photosynthesis in chloroplasts, sometimes take place on the surface of the membranes themselves. Membranes also act as receptor sites for recognising hormones, neuro-transmitters and other chemicals, either from the external environment or from other parts of the organism. An understanding of their properties is essential to an understanding of cell function.

5.9.1　Membranes are partially permeable

It has been known since the turn of the century that cell membranes do not behave simply like semi-permeable membranes that allow only the passage of water and other small molecules such as gases. Instead they are better described as **partially permeable**, since other substances such as glucose, amino acids, fatty acids, glycerol and ions can diffuse slowly through them. They also exert a measure of active control over which substances they allow through.

5.9.2　Membranes contain proteins and lipids

Early work showed that organic solvents, such as alcohol, ether and chloroform, penetrate membranes even more rapidly than water. This suggested that membranes have non-polar portions and contain lipids. This was later confirmed by chemical analysis which showed that membranes are made almost entirely of proteins and lipids. The proteins are discussed later. The most common lipids are phospholipids.

5.9.3　Phospholipids

The structure of phospholipids is described in chapter 3 (fig 3.18). Each phospholipid molecule consists of a polar* head containing phosphate, and two non-polar hydrocarbon tails from the fatty acids used to make the molecule. **Polar** means there is an uneven distribution of charge within the molecule, making it soluble in water. The phospholipid molecule is unusual because the head is hydrophilic (water-loving) and the tails are hydrophobic (water-hating).

If a thin layer of phospholipid molecules is spread over the surface of water, they arrange themselves into a single layer, as shown in fig 5.14. The non-polar hydrophobic tails project out of the water, whilst the polar hydrophilic heads lie in the surface of the water.

If the phospholipid is present in large enough amounts to more than cover the surface of the water, or if it is shaken up with the water, particles known as **micelles** are formed, in which hydrophobic tails project inwards away from the water as shown in fig 5.15. Figs 5.15*b* and 5.15*c* show an arrangement known as a **bilayer** in which two layers of phospholipid molecules occur. It is now known that phospholipid bilayers like this are the basic structure of cell membranes.

5.9.4　Proteins

A technique known as freeze fracturing has helped us to understand how proteins fit into the phospholipid bilayer. In this technique cells are rapidly frozen and then fractured with a sharp metal blade. The technique allows membranes to be split and the surfaces inside to be examined. Freeze fracturing reveals the presence of particles, mainly proteins, which penetrate into, and often right through, the phospholipid bilayer. In general, the more metabolically active the membrane, the

*Remember that polar groups or molecules possess an uneven distribution of charge and have an affinity for water (hydrophilic); non-polar groups or molecules do not mix with water (hydrophobic) (section 3.1.2).

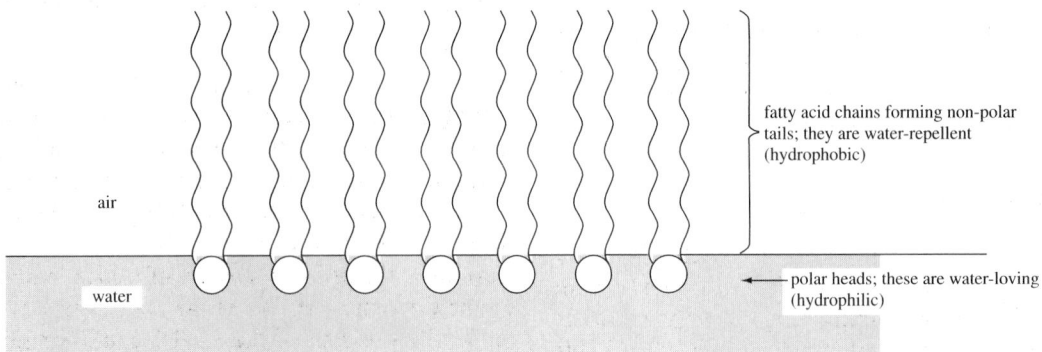

Fig 5.14　*Single layer of phospholipid molecules on the surface of water.*

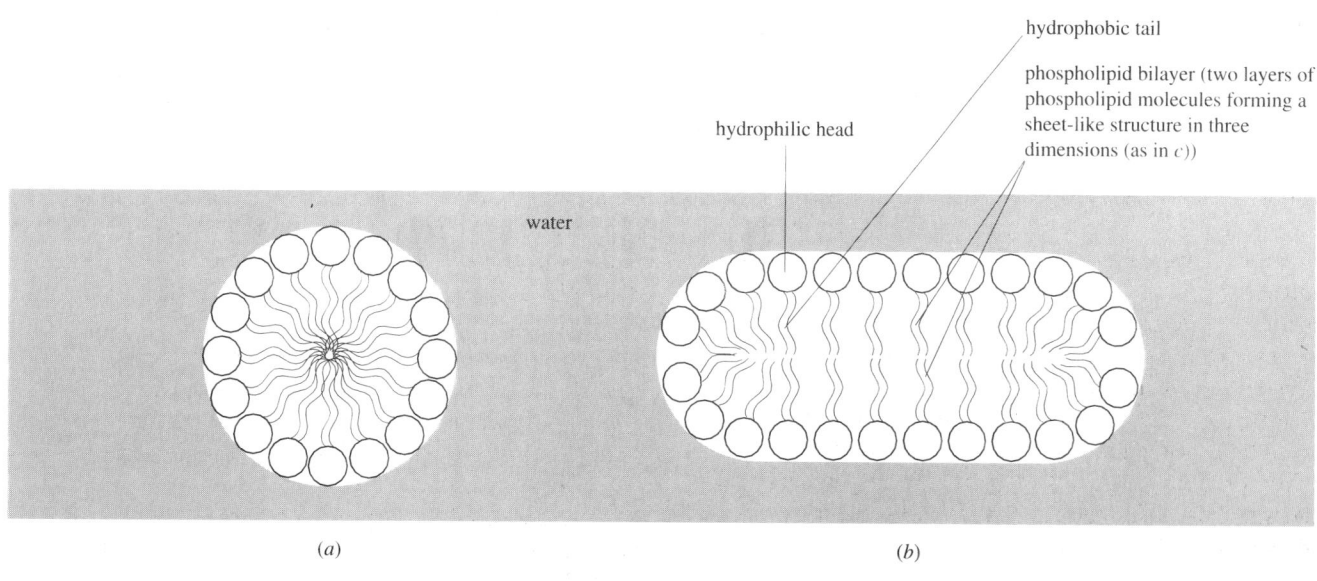

hydrophobic tail

phospholipid bilayer (two layers of phospholipid molecules forming a sheet-like structure in three dimensions (as in *c*))

hydrophilic head

water

(a)

(b)

(c)

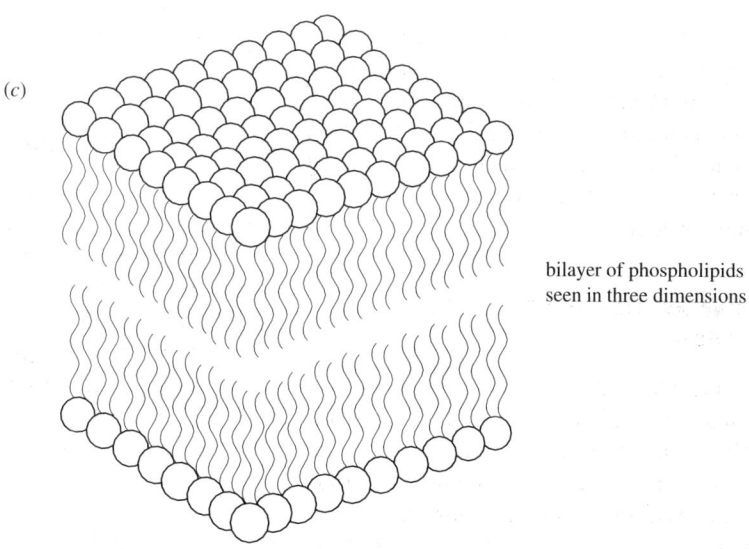

bilayer of phospholipids seen in three dimensions

Fig 5.15 *Sections through* (a) *a spherical micelle and* (b) *two layers (a bilayer) of phospholipids.* (c) *Sheet-like bilayer seen in three dimensions.*

more protein particles that are found; chloroplast membranes (75% protein) have many particles (fig 7.12), whereas the metabolically inert myelin sheath (18% protein) has none. The inner and outer sides of membranes also differ in their particle distribution.

5.9.5　Glycolipids and cholesterol

Membranes also contain glycolipids and cholesterol. Glycolipids are lipids combined with carbohydrate. Like phospholipids, they have polar heads and non-polar tails. Cholesterol is closely related to lipids and is slightly polar at one end.

5.9.6　The fluid mosaic model of membrane structure

In 1972, Singer and Nicolson put forward the **'fluid mosaic' model** of membrane structure in which protein molecules float about in a fluid phospholipid bilayer. The scattered protein molecules resemble a mosaic but, since the phospholipid bilayer is fluid, the proteins form a fluid mosaic pattern. The thin sheet-like structure surrounds the cell like the skin of a soap bubble, swirling in much the same way. It has the consistency of olive oil. An artist's impression of the model and a simplified diagram are shown in fig 5.16.

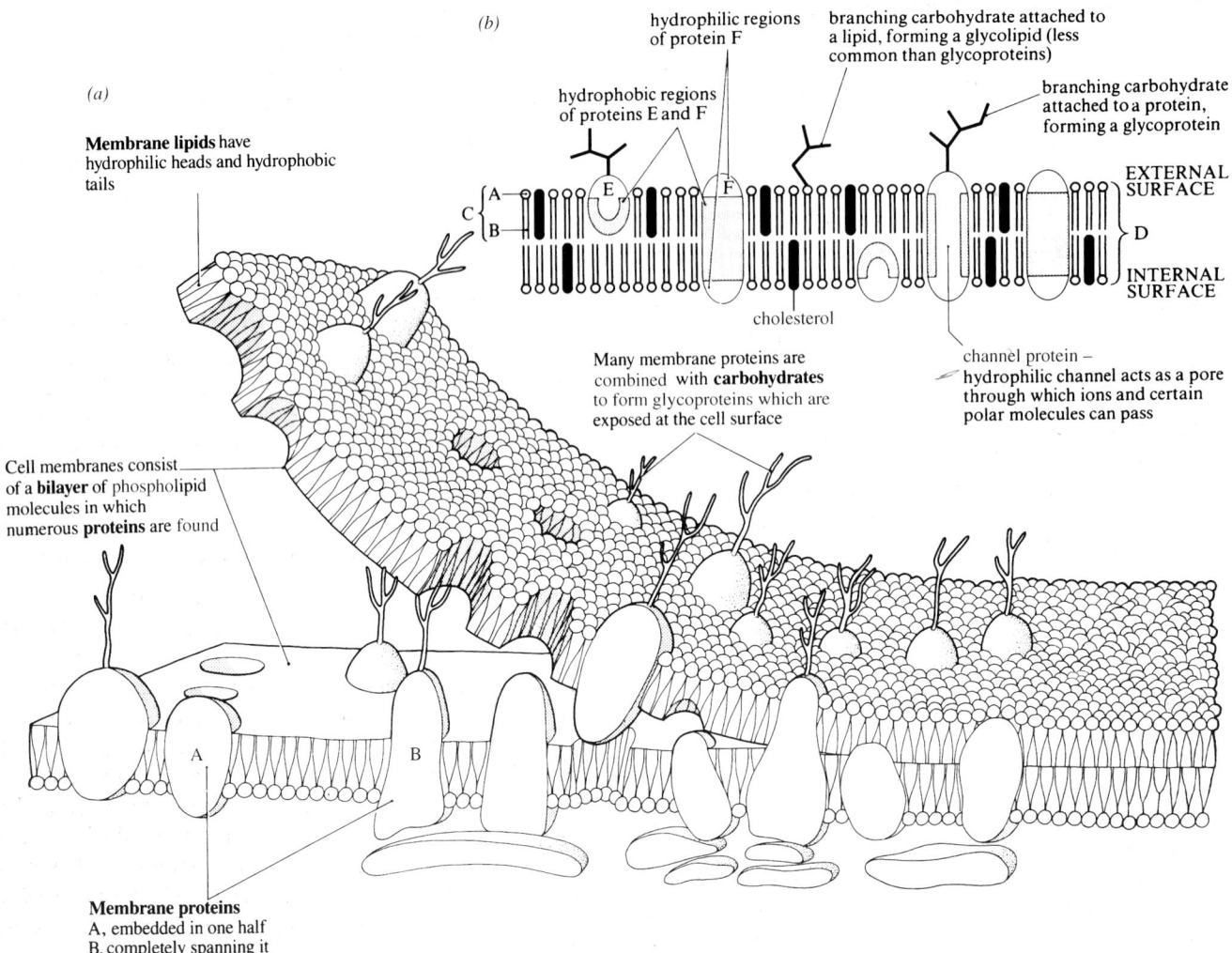

Fig 5.16 (a) *Artist's impression of the fluid mosaic model of membrane structure.* (b) *Simplified diagram of fluid mosaic model. Note glycoproteins and glycolipids are found only on the external surface.*

5.3 What are the structures represented by the labels A, B, C and D in fig 5.16*b*?

The membrane has the following features.

- It is about 7 nm thick.
- The basic structure is a phospholipid bilayer.
- The hydrophilic phosphate heads of the phospholipids face outwards into the aqueous environment inside and outside the cell.
- The hydrocarbon tails face inwards and create a hydrophobic interior.
- The phospholipids are fluid and move about rapidly by diffusion in their own layers.
- Some of the fatty acid tails are saturated and some are unsaturated (see chapter 3, fig 3.17). Unsaturated tails are bent and fit together more loosely. Therefore the more unsaturated the tails are, the more fluid the membrane is.
- Most protein molecules float about in the phospholipid bilayer forming a fluid mosaic pattern.

- The proteins stay in the membrane because they have regions of hydrophobic amino acids which interact with the fatty acid tails to exclude water. The rest of the protein is hydrophilic and faces into the cell or out into the external environment, both of which are aqueous.
- Some proteins penetrate only part of the way into the membrane while others penetrate all the way through.
- Some proteins and lipids have short branching carbohydrate chains like antennae, forming glycoproteins and glycolipids respectively.
- Membranes also contain cholesterol. Like unsaturated fatty acids, cholesterol disturbs the close packing of phospholipids and keeps them more fluid. This can be important for organisms living at low temperatures when membranes can solidify. Cholesterol also increases flexibility and stability of membranes. Without it, membranes break up.
- The two sides of a membrane can differ in composition and function.

142

5.9.7 Functions of membranes

The phospholipid bilayer provides the basic structure of membranes. It also restricts entry and exit of polar molecules and ions. The other molecules have a variety of functions.

- **Channel proteins and carrier proteins** – these are involved in the selective transport of polar molecules and ions across the membrane (see facilitated diffusion and active transport in section 5.9.8).
- **Enzymes** – proteins sometimes act as enzymes, for example the microvilli on epithelial cells lining some parts of the gut contain digestive enzymes in their cell surface membranes.
- **Receptor molecules** – proteins have very specific shapes as discussed in chapters 3 and 4. This makes them ideal as receptor molecules for chemical signalling between cells. For example, hormones are chemical messengers which circulate in the blood but only bind to specific target cells which have the correct receptor sites. Neurotransmitters, the chemicals which enable nerve impulses to pass from one nerve cell to the next, also fit into specific receptor proteins in nerve cells.
- **Antigens** – these act as cell identity markers or 'name tags'. They are glycoproteins, that is proteins with branching carbohydrate side chains like 'antennae'. There is an enormous number of possible shapes to these side chains, so each type of cell can have its own specific markers. This enables cells to recognise other cells, and to behave in an organised way, for example during development of tissues and organs in multicellular organisms. It also means that foreign antigens can be recognised and attacked by the immune system.
- **Glycolipids** also have branching carbohydrate side chains and are involved in cell–cell recognition. They may act as receptor sites for chemical signals. With glycoproteins they are also involved in sticking the correct cells together in tissues.
- **Energy transfer** – in photosynthesis and respiration proteins take part in the energy transfer systems that exist in the membranes of chloroplasts and mitochondria respectively.
- **Cholesterol** acts like a plug, reducing even further the escape or entry of polar molecules through the membrane.

5.9.8 Transport across the cell surface membrane

Cell membranes are only about 7 nm wide but they present barriers to the movement of ions and molecules, particularly polar (water-soluble) molecules such as glucose and amino acids that are repelled by the non-polar, hydrophobic lipids of membranes. This prevents the aqueous contents of the cell from escaping. However, transport across membranes must still occur for a number of reasons, for example:

- to obtain nutrients;
- to excrete waste substances;
- to secrete useful substances;
- to generate the ionic gradients essential for nervous and muscular activity;
- to maintain a suitable pH and ionic concentration within the cell for enzyme activity.

In the following account, movement across the cell surface membrane will be discussed, although similar movements occur across the membranes of cell organelles within cells. There are four basic mechanisms, namely **diffusion, osmosis, active transport** and **bulk transport (endocytosis** or **exocytosis)**. The first two processes are passive, that is they do not require the expenditure of energy by the cell; the latter two are active, energy-consuming processes.

Diffusion and facilitated diffusion

Diffusion is the movement of molecules or ions from a region of their high concentration to a region of their low concentration down a diffusion gradient. The process is passive, that is it does not require energy and happens spontaneously. For example, if a bottle of perfume were opened in a closed room, the perfume would eventually spread by diffusion until an equilibrium was reached where the perfume was evenly spread throughout the room. This occurs by the random motion of molecules which is due to their kinetic energy (energy of movement). Each type of molecule moves down its own diffusion gradient independently of other molecules. For example, oxygen diffuses from the lungs into the blood while at the same time carbon dioxide diffuses in the opposite direction.

Three factors in particular affect the rate of diffusion.

(1) The steepness of the diffusion gradient, or difference in concentration between point A and point B: the steeper the gradient, the faster the rate of diffusion. It is an advantage for cells to maintain steep diffusion gradients if rapid transport is required. This can be achieved in the lungs, for example, by speeding up the flow of blood through the lungs or by breathing faster.

(2) The greater the surface area of a membrane through which diffusion is taking place, the greater the rate of diffusion. The larger the cell, assuming it is roughly spherical, the smaller its surface area in relation to its volume. This places a limit on cell size. For example, a very large aerobic cell could not obtain oxygen fast enough to satisfy its needs if it relied on diffusion alone. Microvilli increase the surface area of animal cells for absorption purposes.

(3) Rate of diffusion decreases rapidly with distance (it falls in proportion to the square of the distance). Diffusion is therefore only effective over very short distances. This is another factor which limits cell size. Cells rely on diffusion for internal transport of

molecules so most are no larger than 50 μm in diameter, with no part of the cell more than 25 μm from the cell surface. An amino acid molecule, for example, can travel a few micrometres in several seconds but would take several days to diffuse a few centimetres. It is also essential that membranes are thin so that molecules or ions can cross them rapidly.

The factors affecting the rate at which molecules cross cell membranes by diffusion are summarised in Fick's law. This states that the rate is proportional to:

$$\frac{\text{surface area of membrane} \quad \times \quad \text{difference in concentration across the membrane}}{\text{thickness of membrane}}$$

We can now consider which molecules cross membranes by diffusion. The respiratory gases oxygen and carbon dioxide diffuse rapidly through membranes. Water molecules, although very polar, are small enough to pass between the hydrophobic phospholipid molecules without interference. However, ions and larger polar molecules such as amino acids, sugars, fatty acids and glycerol are repelled by the hydrophobic region of the membrane and diffuse across extremely slowly. Other mechanisms are required for these substances.

Some ions and polar molecules can diffuse through special transport proteins called **channel proteins** and **carrier proteins**. These contain water-filled hydrophilic channels or pores whose shape is specific for a particular ion or molecule. Alternatively several proteins combine, forming a channel between them. Diffusion can occur through the channel in either direction. Since diffusion would not be possible without the protein or proteins, the process is known as **facilitated diffusion**. Transport proteins which allow the passage of ions are called ion channels. Ion channels are usually 'gated', which means they can exist in open or closed states. Gated ion channels are important in the conduction of nerve impulses.

Channel proteins have a *fixed* shape (fig 5.16*b*). It has been shown that the disease cystic fibrosis is caused by a fault in a protein which acts as a chloride ion channel. **Carrier proteins** undergo rapid *changes* in shape, up to 100 cycles per second. They exist in two forms, known as the 'ping' and 'pong' states. Fig 5.17 shows how they work. The binding site faces outwards in one state and into the cell in the other state. The higher the concentration of the solute molecule or ion, the greater its chance of binding. If, as in the case of glucose in the example shown in fig 5.17, there is a higher concentration outside the cell, there will be a net movement of the solute into the cell. Glucose can enter red blood cells in this way. The movement has all the characteristics of diffusion although it is facilitated by the protein. Another example is the movement of chloride and hydrogencarbonate ions into and out of blood cells during the 'chloride shift'. This is one way in which cells achieve partial and selective permeability.

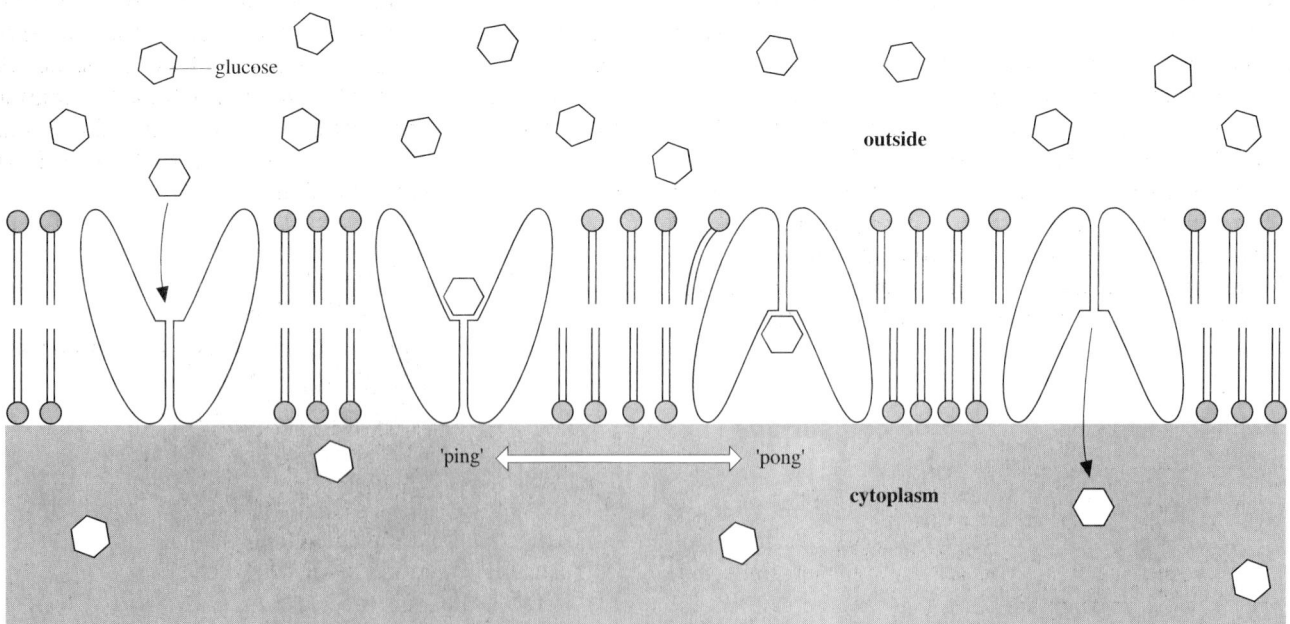

Fig 5.17 *Facilitated diffusion through a carrier protein. The protein alternates rapidly between two different shapes, 'ping' and 'pong'. A higher concentration of glucose (hexagons) is shown outside the cell resulting in a net movement of glucose into the cell down a diffusion gradient.*

144

Osmosis

Osmosis is the passage of water molecules from a region of their high concentration to a region of their low concentration through a partially permeable membrane. It is best regarded as a form of diffusion in which only water molecules move. Consider the situation in fig 5.18. The solute molecules are too large to pass through the pores in the membrane, so equilibrium can only be achieved by the movement of water molecules. Solution A has the higher concentration of *water*, so there will be a net movement of water from A to B by osmosis. At equilibrium there will be no further net movement of water. The tendency of water molecules to move from one place to another is measured as the **water potential**, represented by the symbol Ψ (Greek letter psi). Water *always* moves from a region of higher water potential to one of lower water potential. Solute molecules reduce Ψ (in effect, they dilute the water!). The extent by which they lower Ψ is known as the **solute potential**, given the symbol Ψ_s. The effects of different solutions on red blood cells are shown in fig 5.19. Osmosis in plant cells is considered in chapter 13.

> **5.4** In fig 5.18, which solution has (*a*) the higher concentration of water molecules, (*b*) the higher concentration of solute molecules, (*c*) the higher water potential, (*d*) the more negative solute potential?
>
> (*e*) Which of the following two values of water potential is the higher, −2000 kPa or −1000 kPa?

Active transport

Active transport is the **energy-consuming transport** of molecules or ions across a membrane **against** a concentration gradient. Energy is required because the substance must be moved **against** its natural tendency to diffuse in the opposite direction. Movement is usually in one direction only, unlike diffusion which is reversible. The energy is supplied in the form of a molecule known as ATP, which is an energy carrier made in respiration. Without respiration, active transport is therefore impossible.

The major ions inside cells and in their environments are sodium ions (Na^+), potassium ions (K^+) and chloride (Cl^-)

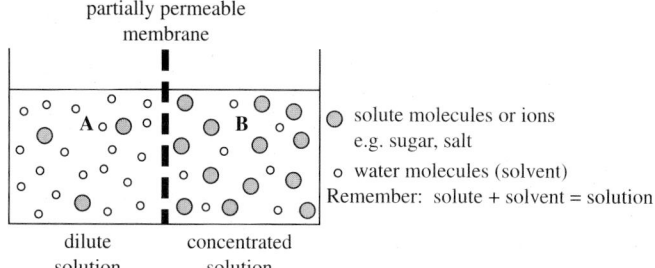

Fig 5.18 *Two solutions separated by a partially permeable membrane.*

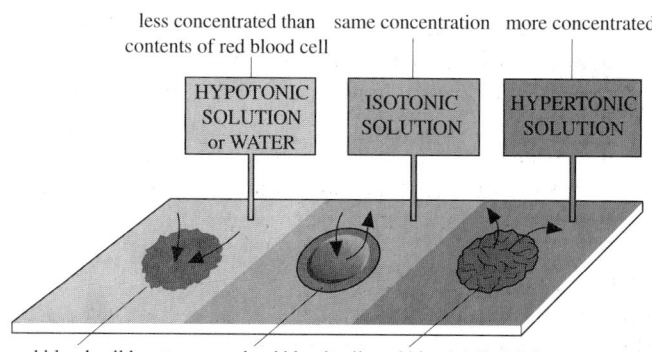

arrows represent net movement of water by osmosis

Fig 5.19 *Effects of different solutions on red blood cells. In a hypotonic solution, the solution has a higher water potential than the contents of the red cell. Water therefore enters by osmosis and the cell bursts, dispersing the cell contents. A hypertonic solution has a lower water potential than the cell contents, so water leaves the cell by osmosis and the cell shrinks. In an isotonic solution, water potential of the cell equals that of the external solution and no net movement of water occurs. The cell remains normal. Blood plasma must be kept isotonic to red blood cells and other body cells.*

ions. Look at fig 5.20 which shows that the concentrations of these ions are very different inside and outside a human red blood cell. For example, like most cells, there is a much higher potassium content inside than outside, and a higher concentration of potassium inside than sodium.

If respiration of the red blood cells is inhibited, for example with cyanide, the ionic composition of the cells gradually changes until it comes into equilibrium with the plasma. This suggests that the ions can diffuse passively through the cell surface membrane of the cells, but that normally respiration supplies the energy for active transport to maintain the concentrations shown in fig 5.20. In other words, sodium is actively pumped out of the cell and potassium is actively pumped in.

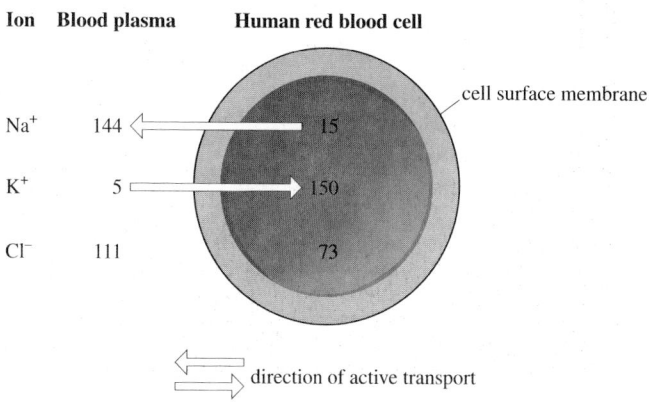

Fig 5.20 *Concentrations of Na^+, K^+ and Cl^- ions in red blood cells and their environment (measured as mM).*

Active transport is achieved by **carrier proteins** situated in the cell surface membrane. Unlike the situation described for facilitated diffusion, the carrier proteins involved in active transport need a supply of energy to keep changing shape. The energy is provided by ATP from respiration.

In recent years it has been shown that the cell surface membranes of most cells have **sodium pumps** that actively pump sodium ions out of the cell. In animal cells, the sodium pump is coupled with a potassium pump which actively moves potassium ions from outside to inside the cell. The combined pump is called the **sodium–potassium pump** (Na^+–K^+ pump). Since this pump is a common feature of almost all animal cells and has a number of important functions, it provides a good example of active transport. Its importance is revealed by the fact that more than a third of the ATP consumed by a resting animal is used to pump sodium and potassium.

The pump is a carrier protein which spans the membrane from one side to the other (fig 5.21). On the inside it accepts sodium and ATP, while on the outside it accepts potassium. The transfer of sodium and potassium across the membrane is brought about by changes in the shape of the protein. Note that for every $2K^+$ taken into the cell, $3Na^+$ are removed. Thus a potential difference is built up across the membrane, with the inside of the cell being negative. This tends to restrict the entry of negatively charged ions (anions) such as chloride. This explains why the chloride concentration inside red blood cells is less than outside (fig 5.20) despite the fact that chloride can diffuse in and out by facilitated diffusion. Similarly, positively charged ions (cations) tend to be attracted into cells. Thus both concentration and charge are important in deciding the direction in which ions cross membranes.

The pump is essential in controlling the osmotic balance of animal cells (osmoregulation). If the pump is inhibited, the cell swells and bursts because a build-up of sodium ions results in excess water entering the cells by osmosis. This explains why bacteria, fungi and plants, which have cell walls, do not need the pump. The pump is also important in maintaining electrical activity in nerve and muscle cells and in driving active transport of some other substances such as sugars and amino acids. Also, high concentrations of potassium are needed inside cells for protein synthesis, glycolysis, photosynthesis and other vital processes.

5.5 Explain the following observations.

(*a*) When K^+ ions are removed from the medium surrounding red blood cells, entry of sodium into the cells and exit of potassium increase dramatically.

(*b*) If ATP is introduced into cells, the exit of Na^+ is stimulated.

Active transport is important in many other situations. It is particularly associated with epithelial cells, as in the gut lining and kidney tubules (nephrons), because these are active in secretion and absorption.

Active transport in the intestine. When the products of digestion are absorbed in the small intestine they must pass through the epithelial cells lining the gut wall. After that, glucose, amino acids and salts pass through the cells of the blood capillary walls, into the blood and then travel to the liver. Soon after feeding, relatively high concentrations of digested foods are found in the gut and absorption is partly a result of diffusion. However, this is very slow and must be supplemented by active transport. Such active transport is coupled to a sodium–potassium pump as shown in fig 5.22.

As sodium is pumped out by the sodium–potassium pump, so it tends to diffuse back in. Situated in the

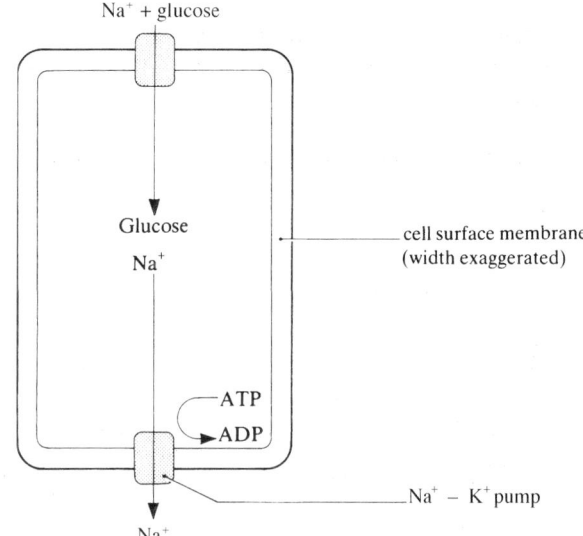

Fig 5.22 *Active transport of glucose through the cell surface membrane of an intestinal cell or kidney cell. (Based on Fig 36-12, L. Stryer (1981) Biochemistry, 2nd ed., Freeman.)*

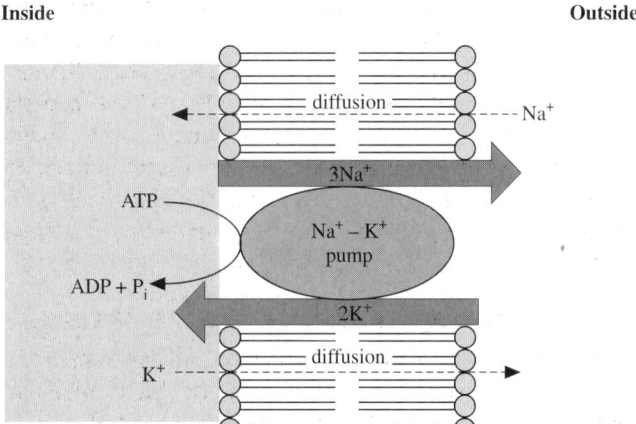

Fig 5.21 *Sodium–potassium pump.*

membrane is a carrier protein which requires both sodium and glucose to function. These are transported together by **facilitated diffusion** into the cell. A similar sodium–amino-acid carrier protein operates in the active transport of amino acids into cells, the active part of the process being the pumping back of sodium ions.

Active transport in nerve cells and muscle cells. In nerve cells and muscle cells a sodium–potassium pump is responsible for the development of a potential difference, called the **resting potential**, across the cell surface membrane (see conduction of nerve impulses, chapter 17, and muscle contraction, chapter 18).

In muscle cells another important carrier protein is the calcium pump. Muscle cells contain a specialised form of endoplasmic reticulum called sarcoplasmic reticulum. Calcium is pumped into it from the surrounding cytoplasm by the calcium pump. Muscle contraction is triggered by the sudden release of the calcium ions in response to a nerve impulse.

Active transport in the kidney. Active transport of glucose and sodium occurs from the proximal convoluted tubules of the kidney and the kidney cortex actively transports sodium. These processes are described more fully in chapter 20.

Active transport in plants. An example of active transport in plants is the active loading of sugar into phloem ready for transport round the plant (chapter 13). This is particularly important in leaves.

Endocytosis and exocytosis

Endocytosis and exocytosis are active processes involving the bulk transport of materials through membranes, either into cells (endocytosis) or out of cells (exocytosis) (fig 5.23).

Endocytosis occurs by an infolding or extension of the cell surface membrane to form a vesicle* or vacuole*. It is of two types.

*Vacuole – fluid-filled, membrane-bound sac; vesicle – small vacuole.

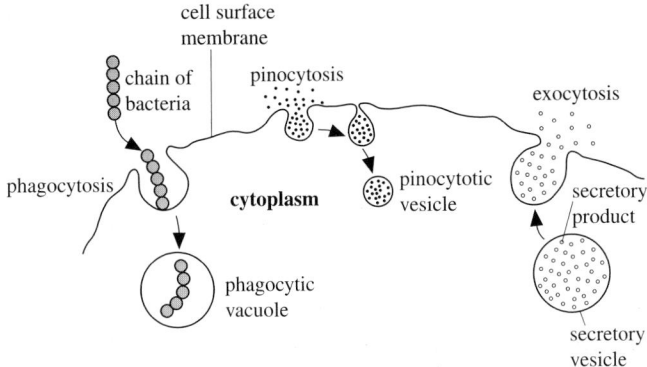

Fig 5.23 *Endocytosis and exocytosis.*

- **Phagocytosis** ('cell eating') – material taken up is in solid form. Cells specialising in the process are called **phagocytes** and are said to be **phagocytic**. For example, some white blood cells take up bacteria by phagocytosis. The sac formed during uptake is called a **phagocytic vacuole**.
- **Pinocytosis** ('cell drinking') – material taken up is in liquid form. Vesicles formed are often extremely small, in which case the process is known as **micropinocytosis** and the vesicles as **micropinocytotic vesicles**. Pinocytosis is used by the human egg cell to take up nutrients from the surrounding follicle cells. In the thyroid gland, the hormone thyroxine is stored as thyroglobulin in hollow structures called follicles. When required, thyroglobulin is taken up by pinocytosis by the follicle cells and then converted to thyroxine for release into the blood. Pinocytosis is very common in both animal and plant cells (fig 5.10).

Exocytosis is the reverse process of endocytosis. Waste materials may be removed from cells, such as solid, undigested remains from phagocytic vacuoles, or useful materials may be secreted. Secretion of enzymes from the pancreas is achieved in this way (fig 5.29). Plant cells use exocytosis to export the materials needed to form cell walls (fig 5.30).

5.10   Structures found in cells

5.10.1   The nucleus

Nuclei are found in all eukaryotic cells, the only common exceptions being mature phloem sieve tube elements and mature red blood cells of mammals. In some protozoa, such as *Paramecium*, two nuclei exist, a micronucleus and a meganucleus. Normally, however, cells contain only one nucleus. Nuclei are conspicuous because they are the largest cell organelles, and they were the first to be described by light microscopists. They are typically about $10\,\mu m$ in diameter.

The nucleus is vitally important because it controls the cell's activities. This is because it contains the genetic (hereditary) information in the form of DNA. The DNA can also replicate itself which can be followed by nuclear division, thus ensuring that the daughter nuclei also contain DNA. Nuclear division precedes cell division, producing two daughter nuclei with exactly the same DNA content as the parent nucleus. The nucleus is surrounded by a nuclear envelope and contains chromatin and one or more nucleoli.

Nuclear envelope and nuclear pores

What looks like a single membrane around the nucleus in the light microscope is actually a **nuclear envelope** composed of two membranes. The outer membrane is continuous with the endoplasmic reticulum (ER) as shown in figs 5.10, 5.11 and 5.24, and like the ER it may be

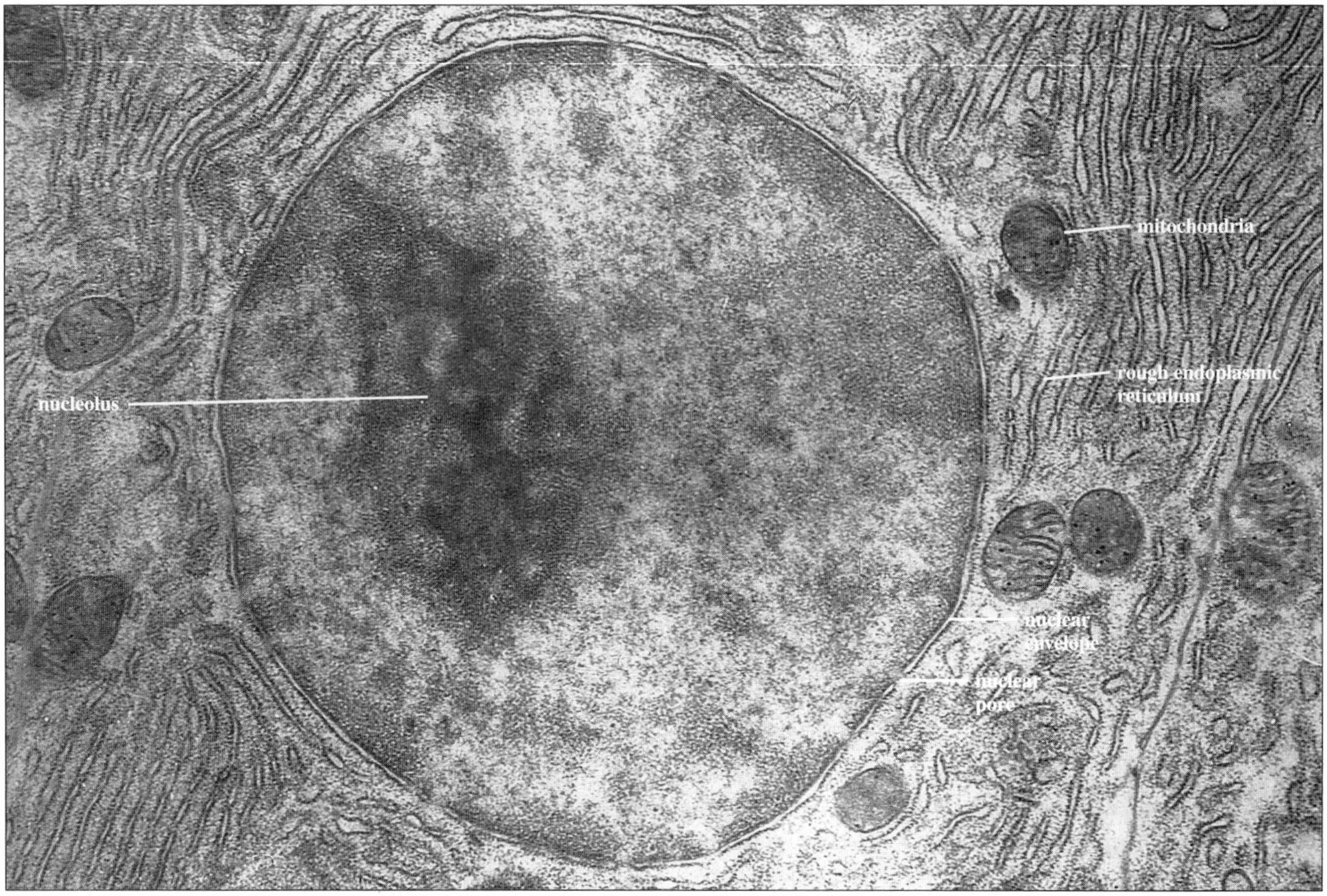

Fig 5.24 *Transmission EM of a nucleus. Note, in reality, the endoplasmic reticulum is continuous with the nuclear envelope.*

covered with ribosomes carrying out protein synthesis. The nuclear envelope is perforated by nuclear pores (fig 5.24) and these are particularly well revealed by freeze etching (fig 5.25). Nuclear pores allow exchange of substances between the nucleus and the cytoplasm. For example, the messenger RNA (mRNA) and newly made ribosomes can leave, and molecules needed for the manufacture of ribosomes and DNA (proteins and nucleotides) and the regulation of DNA (e.g. some hormones) can enter. The pore has a definite structure formed by fusion of the outer and inner membranes of the envelope. This controls the passage of molecules through the pore.

Chromatin

Chromatin is composed mainly of coils of DNA bound to basic proteins called **histones**. The DNA is so long (in humans there is an average of about one metre's length in each nucleus!) that it has to be packaged in an organised manner or it would get tangled like an unravelled ball of string. DNA is wound around the histones which form bead-like structures called nucleosomes, and these in turn are regularly packed in the chromatin.

The term chromatin means 'coloured material' and refers to the fact that this material is easily stained for viewing with the microscope. During nuclear division chromatin

Fig 5.25 *Electron micrograph of freeze-etched nucleus showing nuclear pores (x 30 000). In this technique, instantly frozen cells are split open with a metal blade. They fracture along planes of weakness, often through membranes. Removal of the ice leaves an etched surface.*

stains more intensely and becomes more conspicuous because it condenses into more tightly coiled threads called **chromosomes**. During interphase (the period between nuclear divisions) some of it becomes looser and more scattered. However, some remains tightly coiled and continues to stain intensely. This is called **heterochromatin** and is seen as characteristic dark patches, usually occurring near the nuclear envelope (figs 5.10–13 and fig 5.24). The remaining, loosely coiled chromatin is called **euchromatin**. This is thought to contain the DNA which is genetically active during interphase.

Nucleolus

The **nucleolus** appears as a rounded, darkly stained structure inside the nucleus (figs 5.12 and 5.24). Its function is to make ribosomes. One or more nucleoli may be present. It stains intensely because of the large amounts of DNA and RNA it contains. RNA is a molecule similar to DNA which is copied from DNA. The densely staining core of the nucleolus is made up of the DNA from one or several chromosomes. This contains many copies of the genes that code for the RNA needed to make ribosomes (ribosomal RNA or rRNA). During nuclear division nucleoli seem to disappear, but this is because the DNA disperses. They reassemble after nuclear division.

Around the central core of the nucleolus is a less dense region where ribosomal RNA is beginning to be folded and combined with proteins to make ribosomes. The partly assembled ribosomes move out through the nuclear pores into the cytoplasm, where assembly is completed.

5.10.2 Cytoplasm

The living contents of eukaryotic cells are divided into nucleus and cytoplasm, the two together forming the protoplasm. Cytoplasm is an aqueous (water-containing) substance containing a variety of cell organelles and other structures such as insoluble waste or storage products.

The soluble part of the cytoplasm forms the 'background material' or **'ground substance'** between the cell organelles. It contains a skeleton of very fine fibres (section 5.10.7) but otherwise appears transparent and structureless in the electron microscope. It is about 90% water and forms a solution which contains all the fundamental biochemicals of life. Some of these are ions and small molecules in true solution, such as salts, sugars, amino acids, fatty acids, nucleotides, vitamins and dissolved gases. Others are large molecules such as proteins which form colloidal solutions. A **colloidal solution** is one in which the solute molecules are relatively large (see appendix 1 in Book 2). It may be a sol (runny) or a gel (jelly-like); often the outer regions of cytoplasm are more gel-like.

Apart from acting as a store of vital chemicals, the ground substance is the site of certain metabolic pathways, an important example being glycolysis.

When *living* cytoplasm is examined, great activity is usually seen as cell organelles such as mitochondria move about.

5.10.3 Endoplasmic reticulum (ER)

One of the most important discoveries to be made when the electron microscope was introduced was the occurrence of a system of membranes running through the cytoplasm of all eukaryotic cells. This network, or reticulum, of membranes was named the **endoplasmic reticulum** (ER) and, although it is often extensive, it cannot be seen with a light microscope. The membranes are often covered with small particles called **ribosomes**.

In sections, the ER typically appears as pairs of parallel lines (membranes) running through the cytoplasm, as shown in fig 5.24. Occasionally though, a section will glance through the surface of these membranes and show that, in three dimensions, the ER is usually sheet-like rather than tubular. A possible three-dimensional structure is shown in fig 5.26. The ER consists of flattened, membrane-bound sacs called **cisternae**. These may be covered with ribosomes, forming **rough ER**, or ribosomes may be absent, forming **smooth ER**, which is usually more tubular.

Rough ER is concerned with the **transport of proteins** which are made by ribosomes on its surface. Details of protein synthesis are given in chapter 23. The growing protein, which consists of a chain of amino acids, is bound to the ribosome until its synthesis is complete. A receptor in the membrane of the ER provides a channel through which the protein can pass into the ER once it has been made.

The protein is now transported through the cisternae, usually being extensively modified en route. For example, it may be converted into a glycoprotein. The protein commonly travels to the Golgi apparatus from where it can be secreted from the cell or passed on to other organelles in the same cell. The enzymes in lysosomes have followed this route (see also fig 5.29).

One of the chief functions of smooth ER is **lipid synthesis**. For example, in the epithelium of the intestine the smooth ER makes lipids from fatty acids and glycerol absorbed from the gut, and passes them on to the Golgi apparatus for export. Smooth ER also makes **steroids**, which are a type of lipid. Some steroids are hormones, such as the corticosteroids made in the adrenal cortex and the sex hormones such as testosterone and oestrogen. In muscle cells a specialised form of smooth ER, called **sarcoplasmic reticulum**, is present.

5.10.4 Ribosomes

Ribosomes are tiny organelles, about 20 nm in diameter, that are found in large numbers throughout the cytoplasm of living cells, both prokaryotic and eukaryotic. A typical bacterial cell contains about 10 000 ribosomes, while eukaryotic cells possess many more times this number. They are the sites of protein synthesis.

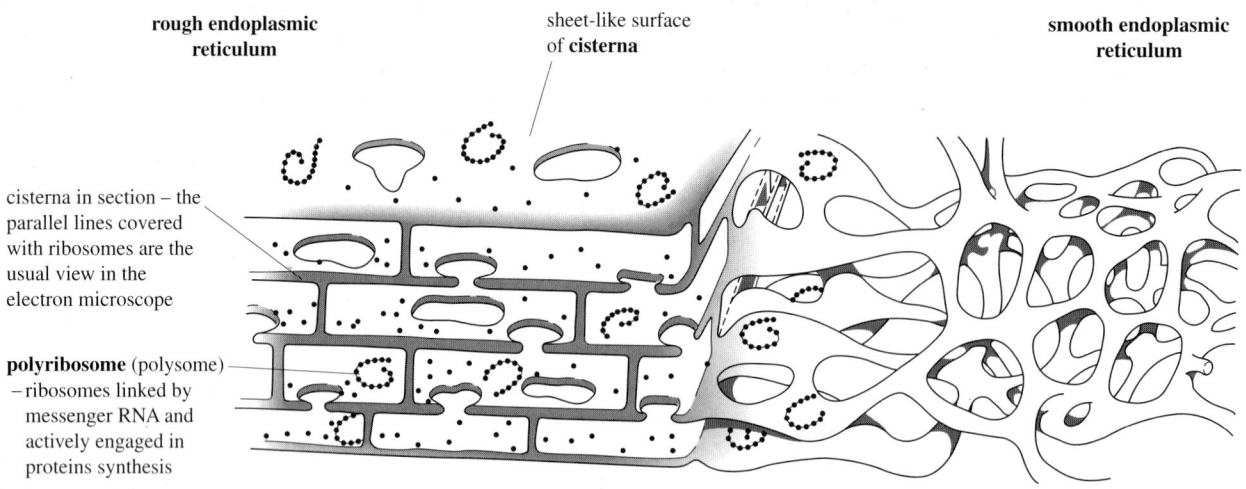

rough endoplasmic reticulum

sheet-like surface of **cisterna**

smooth endoplasmic reticulum

cisterna in section – the parallel lines covered with ribosomes are the usual view in the electron microscope

polyribosome (polysome) – ribosomes linked by messenger RNA and actively engaged in proteins synthesis

Fig 5.26   *Three-dimensional model of endoplasmic reticulum.*

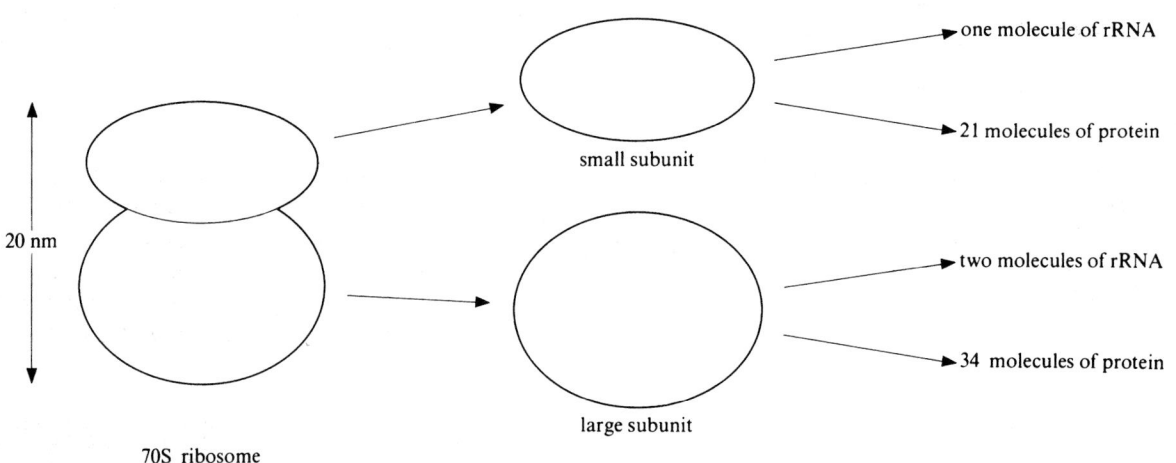

20 nm

small subunit

one molecule of rRNA

21 molecules of protein

large subunit

two molecules of rRNA

34 molecules of protein

70S ribosome

Fig 5.27   *Structure of a 70S ribosome. (The subunits of 80S ribosomes possess more proteins and the large subunit possesses three rRNA molecules.)*

Each ribosome consists of two subunits, one large and one small as shown in fig 5.27. Being so small they are the last organelles to be sedimented in a centrifuge, requiring a force of 100 000 times gravity for 1–2 h (fig 5.9). Sedimentation has revealed two basic types of ribosome, called 70S* and 80S ribosomes. The 70S ribosomes are found in prokaryotes and the slightly larger 80S ribosomes occur in the cytoplasm of eukaryotes. Chloroplasts and mitochondria contain 70S ribosomes, revealing their prokaryotic origins (section 7.4.1).

Ribosomes are made of roughly equal amounts of RNA and protein. The RNA is termed **ribosomal RNA (rRNA)** and is made in the nucleoli. The distribution of rRNA molecules and protein molecules is given in fig 5.27. Together these molecules form a complex three-dimensional structure.

During protein synthesis at ribosomes, amino acids are joined together one by one to form polypeptide chains. The process is described in detail in chapter 23. The ribosome acts as a binding site where the molecules involved can be precisely positioned relative to each other. These molecules include messenger RNA (mRNA), which carries the genetic instructions from the nucleus, transfer RNA (tRNA), which brings the required amino acids to the ribosome, and the growing polypeptide chain. In addition there are chain initiation, elongation and termination factors. The process is so complex that it could not occur efficiently, if at all, without the ribosome.

Two populations of ribosomes can be seen in eukaryotic cells, namely free and ER-bound ribosomes (figs 5.24 and 5.26). All of the ribosomes have an identical structure but some are bound to the ER by the proteins that they are making. Such proteins are usually secreted. An example of a protein made by free ribosomes is haemoglobin in young red blood cells.

During protein synthesis, the ribosome moves along the thread-like mRNA molecule. Rather than one ribosome at a

*S = Svedberg unit. This is related to the rate of sedimentation in a centrifuge; the greater the S number, the greater the rate of sedimentation.

time passing along the RNA, the process is carried out more efficiently by a number of ribosomes moving along the mRNA at the same time, like beads on a string. The resulting chains of ribosomes are called **polyribosomes** or **polysomes**. They form characteristic whorled patterns on the ER as shown in fig 5.26.

5.10.5 Golgi apparatus

The Golgi apparatus was discovered by Camillo Golgi in 1898, using special staining techniques. However, its structure was only revealed by electron microscopy. It is found in virtually all eukaryotic cells and consists of a stack of flattened, membrane-bound sacs called **cisternae**, together with a system of associated

vesicles (small sacs) called **Golgi vesicles**. It is difficult to build up a three-dimensional picture of the Golgi apparatus from thin sections, but it is believed that a complex system of interconnected tubules is formed around the central stack, as shown in fig 5.28.

At one end of the stack new cisternae are constantly being formed by vesicles from the smooth ER. This 'outer' or 'forming' face is convex, whilst the other end is the concave 'inner' or 'maturing' face where the cisternae break up into vesicles again. The whole stack consists of a number of cisternae moving from the outer face to the inner face.

The function of the Golgi apparatus is to transport and chemically modify the materials contained within it. It is particularly important in secretory cells, a good example being provided by the pancreas. Here specialised cells secrete the digestive enzymes of the pancreatic juice into the pancreatic duct, along which they pass to the duodenum. Fig 5.29a is an electron micrograph of such cells, and fig 5.29b is a diagram showing the secretion pathway.

(a)

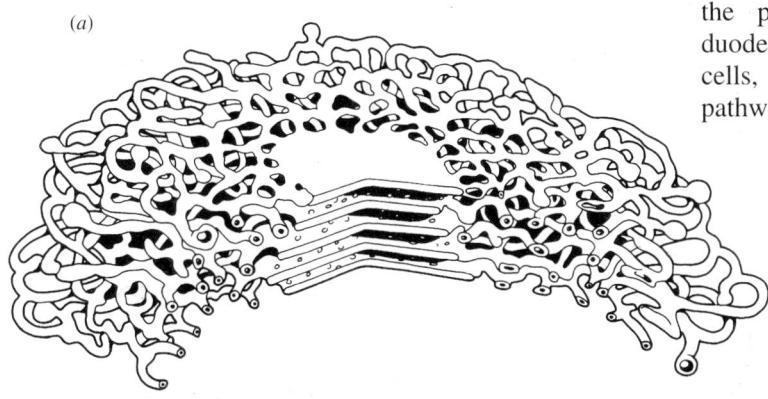

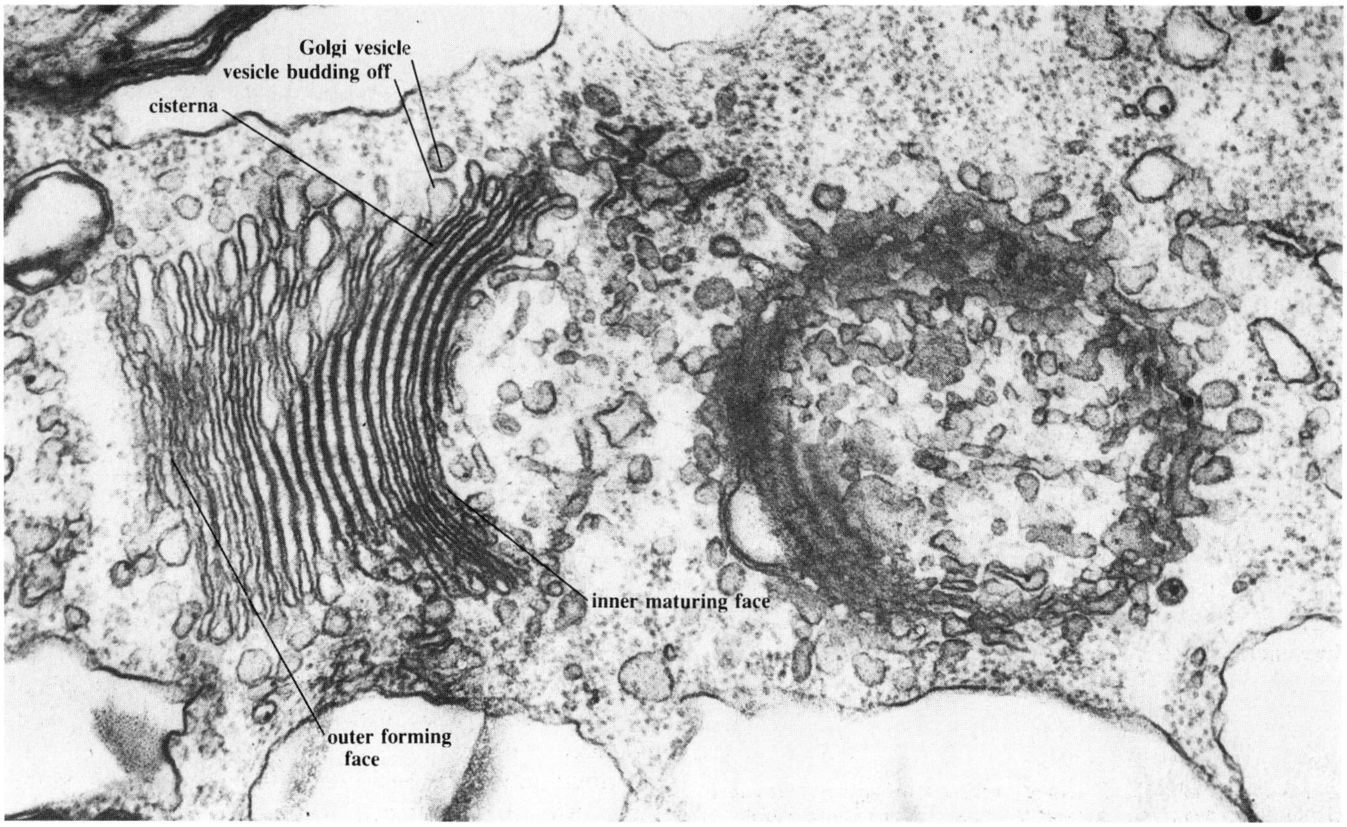

Fig 5.28   (a) *The three-dimensional structure of the Golgi apparatus. (b) Transmission electron micrograph showing two Golgi apparatuses. The left-hand one shows a vertical section. The right-hand one shows the topmost cisterna viewed from above (x50 000).*

(b)

Golgi vesicle
vesicle budding off
cisterna

inner maturing face

outer forming face

151

(a)

G
S
S
G
S
lumen of pancreatic duct
M
G
N
M
RER
M

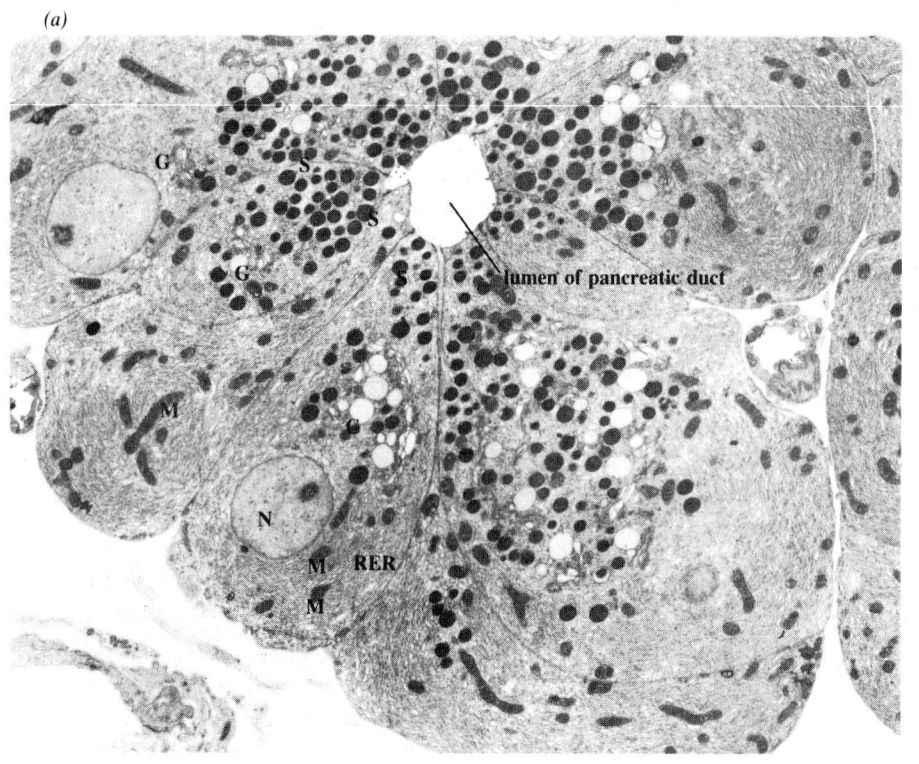

Fig 5.29 (a) *Electron micrograph of a group of enzyme-secreting pancreatic cells (x10 400). N, nucleus; M, mitochondrion; G, Golgi apparatus; S, secretory granules; RER, rough endoplasmic reticulum. (below)* (b) *Diagram of the synthesis and secretion of a protein (an enzyme).*

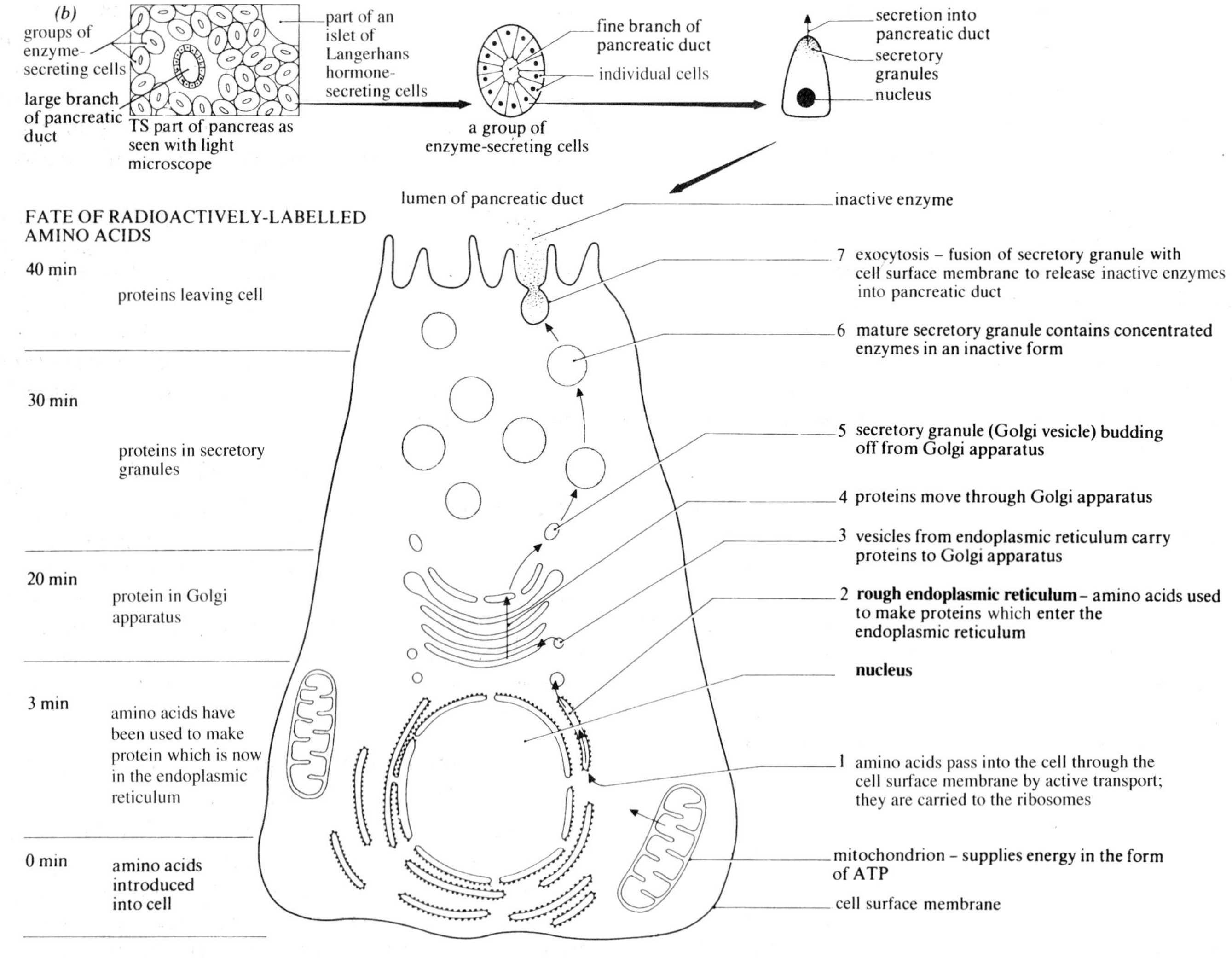

(b)
groups of enzyme-secreting cells
large branch of pancreatic duct
part of an islet of Langerhans hormone-secreting cells
TS part of pancreas as seen with light microscope
fine branch of pancreatic duct
individual cells
a group of enzyme-secreting cells
secretion into pancreatic duct
secretory granules
nucleus
FATE OF RADIOACTIVELY-LABELLED AMINO ACIDS
40 min
proteins leaving cell
30 min
proteins in secretory granules
20 min
protein in Golgi apparatus
3 min
amino acids have been used to make protein which is now in the endoplasmic reticulum
0 min
amino acids introduced into cell
lumen of pancreatic duct
inactive enzyme
7 exocytosis – fusion of secretory granule with cell surface membrane to release inactive enzymes into pancreatic duct
6 mature secretory granule contains concentrated enzymes in an inactive form
5 secretory granule (Golgi vesicle) budding off from Golgi apparatus
4 proteins move through Golgi apparatus
3 vesicles from endoplasmic reticulum carry proteins to Golgi apparatus
2 rough endoplasmic reticulum – amino acids used to make proteins which enter the endoplasmic reticulum
nucleus
1 amino acids pass into the cell through the cell surface membrane by active transport; they are carried to the ribosomes
mitochondrion – supplies energy in the form of ATP
cell surface membrane

Details of the pathway have been confirmed by using radioactively labelled amino acids. These get used by the cell to make protein. Because they are radioactive they can be traced as they pass through different cell organelles. This is done by homogenising samples of tissue at different times after supplying the amino acids, separating the cell organelles by centrifugation (fig 5.9) and finding which organelles contain the highest proportion of the radioactivity. After concentration in the Golgi apparatus, the protein is carried in Golgi vesicles to the cell surface membrane. The final stage in the pathway is secretion of the inactive enzyme by reverse pinocytosis. The digestive enzymes secreted by the pancreas are synthesised in an inactive form so that they do not attack and destroy the cells that make them. An example is trypsinogen which is converted to active trypsin in the duodenum.

In general, proteins received by the Golgi apparatus from the ER have had short carbohydrate chains added to make them glycoproteins (like the membrane proteins shown in fig 5.16). These carbohydrate 'antennae' can be remodelled in the Golgi apparatus, possibly to become markers that direct the proteins to their correct destinations. However, the exact details of how the Golgi apparatus sorts and directs molecules are unknown.

The Golgi apparatus is also sometimes involved in the secretion of carbohydrates, an example being provided by the synthesis of new cell walls by plants. Fig 5.30 shows the intense activity which goes on at the 'cell plate', the region between two newly formed daughter nuclei where the new cell wall is laid down after nuclear division.

Golgi vesicles are steered into position at the cell plate by microtubules (section 5.10.7). The membranes of the vesicles become the new cell surface membranes of the daughter cells, while their contents contribute to the middle lamella and new cell walls. Cellulose is added separately and involves microtubules, not the Golgi apparatus.

Secretion of enzymes by pancreatic cells and the formation of new plant cell walls are good examples of division of labour, where many cell organelles combine to perform one function.

The goblet cells of the respiratory pathway and gut secrete a glycoprotein called mucin which forms mucus in solution. Mucin is released by the Golgi apparatus. The Golgi apparatus in the leaf glands of some insectivorous plants such as sundews secretes a sticky slime and enzymes which trap and digest insects. The slime, wax, gum and mucilage secretions of many cells are released by the Golgi apparatus.

A second important function of the Golgi apparatus, in addition to secretion, is the **formation of lysosomes** which is described below.

5.10.6 Lysosomes

Lysosomes are found in most eukaryotic cells. They are surrounded by a single membrane and are simple sacs that contain digestive enzymes, such as proteases, nucleases and lipases which break down proteins, nucleic acids and lipids respectively. Such enzymes carry out hydrolysis reactions (adding water) and work best in an acid environment. The contents of the lysosome are therefore acidic. The enzymes have to be kept apart from the rest of the cell or they would destroy it. In animal cells, lysosomes are usually spherical and 0.2–0.5 µm in diameter (fig 5.31).

In plant cells the large central vacuoles may act as lysosomes, although bodies similar to the lysosomes of animal cells are sometimes seen in the cytoplasm.

The enzymes contained within lysosomes are synthesised on rough ER and transported to the Golgi apparatus. Golgi vesicles containing the processed enzymes later bud off to form the lysosomes. Lysosomes have a number of functions, summarised below and in fig 5.32.

Digestion of material taken in by endocytosis (route 1, fig 5.32)

The process of endocytosis is explained in section 5.9.8. Lysosomes may fuse with the vesicles or vacuoles formed by endocytosis, releasing their enzymes into the vacuole and digesting the material inside. This material might be taken in for food, as in the food vacuoles of some protozoans, or for defensive purposes, as in the case of phagocytic vacuoles formed by white blood cells when engulfing bacteria (fig 5.23). The products of digestion are absorbed and assimilated by the cytoplasm of the cell leaving undigested remains. The vacuole usually migrates to the cell surface membrane and releases its contents (exocytosis).

An interesting example of the role of lysosomes occurs in the thyroid gland. In section 5.9.8 the uptake of thyroglobulin by pinocytosis was described. The pinocytic vesicles so formed fuse with lysosomes, and the thyroglobulin is hydrolysed by lysosomal enzymes to produce the active hormone thyroxine. The lysosome then fuses with the cell surface membrane, thus secreting the hormone into the blood.

Autophagy (route 2, fig 5.32)

Autophagy is the process by which unwanted structures within the cell are engulfed and digested within lysosomes. They are first enclosed by a single membrane, usually derived from smooth ER, and this structure then fuses with a lysosome to form an '**autophagic vacuole**', in which the unwanted material is digested. This is part of the normal turnover of cytoplasmic organelles, old ones being replaced by new ones.

Release of enzymes outside the cell (exocytosis) (route 3, fig 5.32)

Sometimes the enzymes of lysosomes are released from the cell. This occurs during the replacement of cartilage by bone during development. Similarly, bone may be broken down during the remodelling of bone that can occur in response to injury, new stresses and so on. Sperm contain a

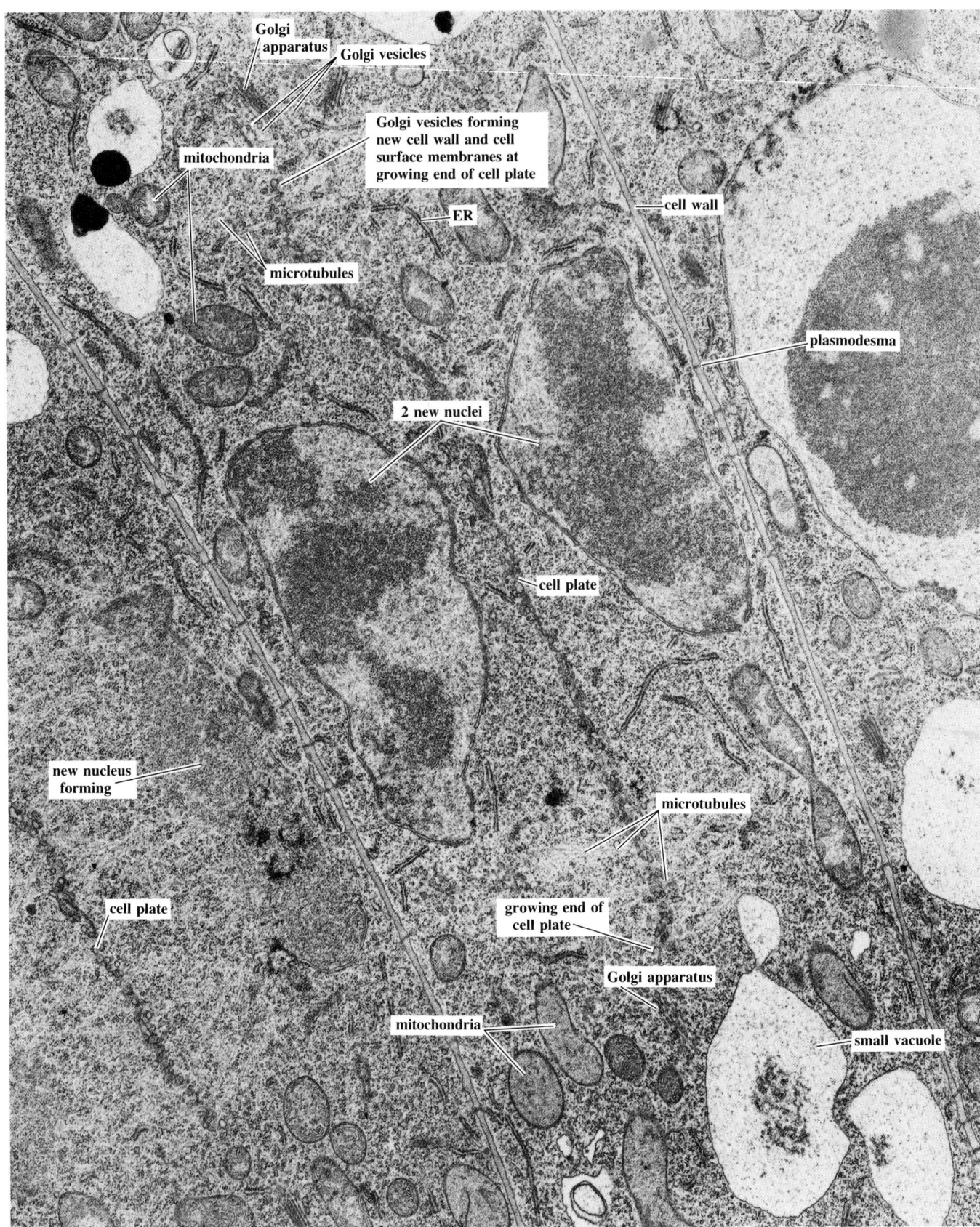

Fig 5.30 *Electron micrograph of a dividing plant cell. The dividing cell runs diagonally across the picture. Each of the two new cells is forming a cell wall from the centre of the cell outwards to the edge. The growing wall is known as the cell plate because it looks like a plate in three dimensions. Note the close association of Golgi apparatus and microtubules with the growing end of the cell plate (x15 000).*

154

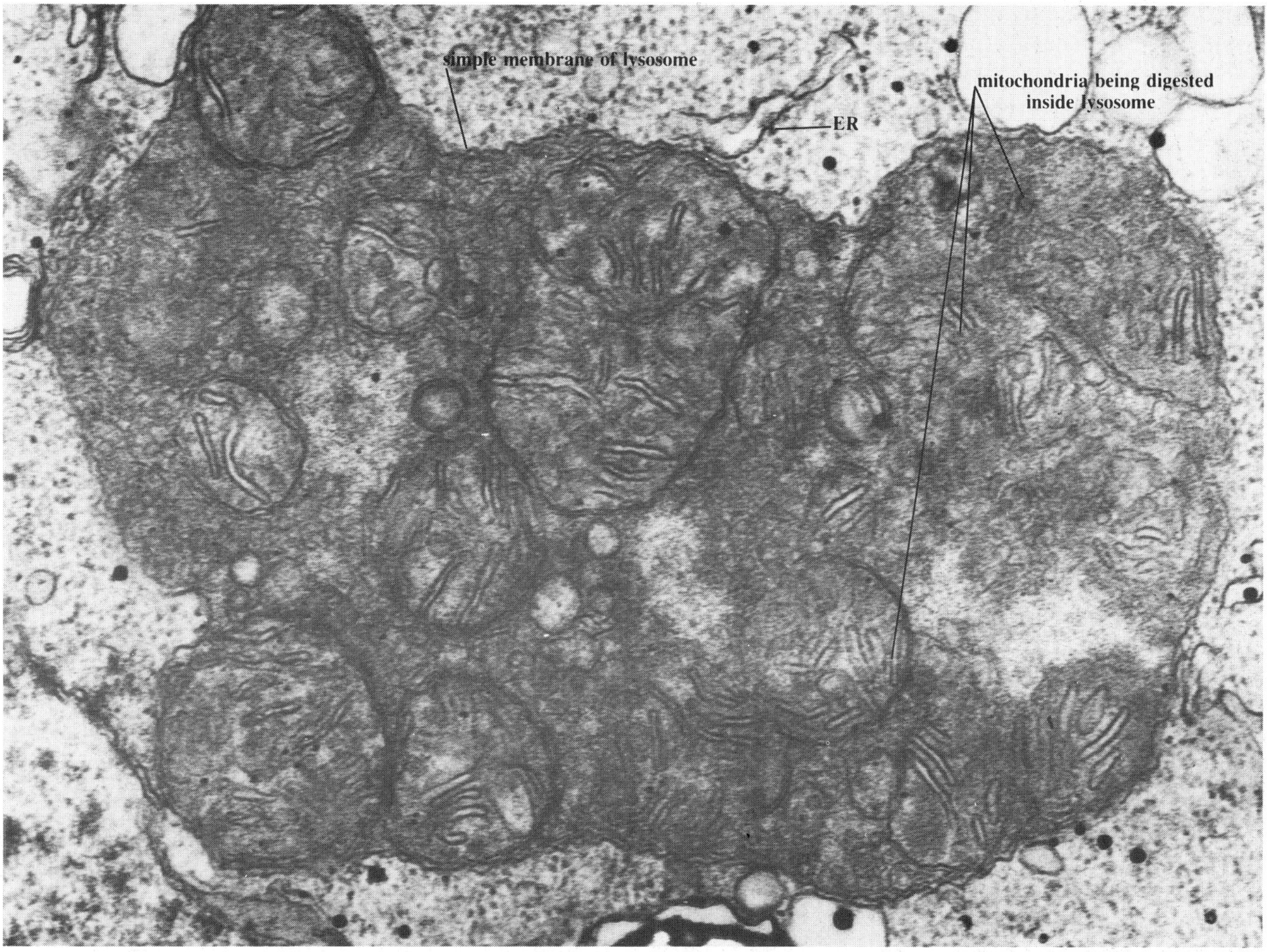

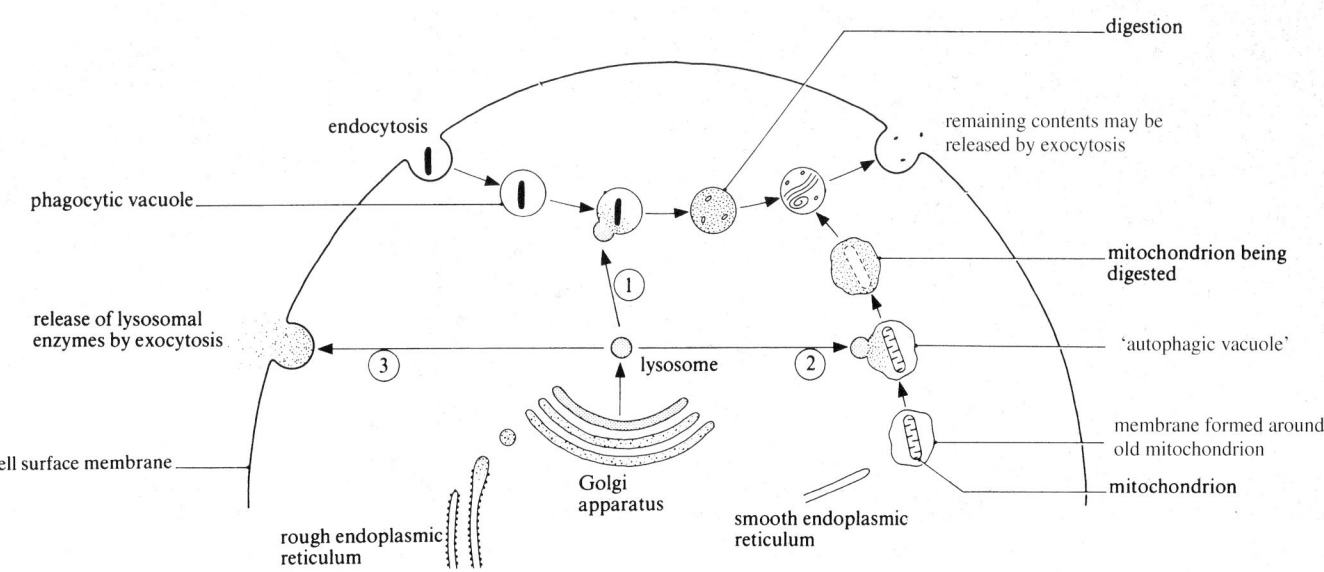

Fig 5.31 *Electron micrograph of a lysosome which has engulfed some old mitochondria and is digesting them (x90 750).*

Labels on Fig 5.31: simple membrane of lysosome; ER; mitochondria being digested inside lysosome

Labels on Fig 5.32: digestion; endocytosis; remaining contents may be released by exocytosis; phagocytic vacuole; mitochondrion being digested; release of lysosomal enzymes by exocytosis; 'autophagic vacuole'; lysosome; membrane formed around old mitochondrion; cell surface membrane; mitochondrion; Golgi apparatus; rough endoplasmic reticulum; smooth endoplasmic reticulum

Fig 5.32 *Three possible uses of a lysosome. The numbers 1, 2 and 3 refer to the order in which these pathways are discussed in the text.*

special lysosome called the **acrosome**. This releases its enzymes outside the cell to digest a path through the layers of cells surrounding the egg just before fertilisation.

Autolysis

Autolysis is the **self-digestion** of a cell by releasing the contents of lysosomes within the cell. In such circumstances lysosomes have sometimes been aptly named 'suicide bags'. Autolysis is a normal event in some differentiation processes and may occur throughout a tissue, as when a tadpole tail is reabsorbed during metamorphosis. Another example occurs in the uterus. During pregnancy the uterus grows much larger to accommodate the growing baby. After birth, it gradually returns to its normal size by self-digestion (autophagy) of many of the cells. Autolysis also occurs in muscles which are not exercised! It also occurs after cells die and is one reason why food deteriorates unless refrigerated. Sometimes it occurs as a result of certain lysosomal diseases.

5.10.7   Microtubules

Using electron microscopy, structure has been revealed in the apparently structureless 'background' or ground substance of the cytoplasm. Networks of fibrous protein structures have been shown to exist in all eukaryotic cells. These are known collectively as the **cytoskeleton**. The fibres are of at least three types: **microtubules**, **microfilaments** and **intermediate filaments**. Together,

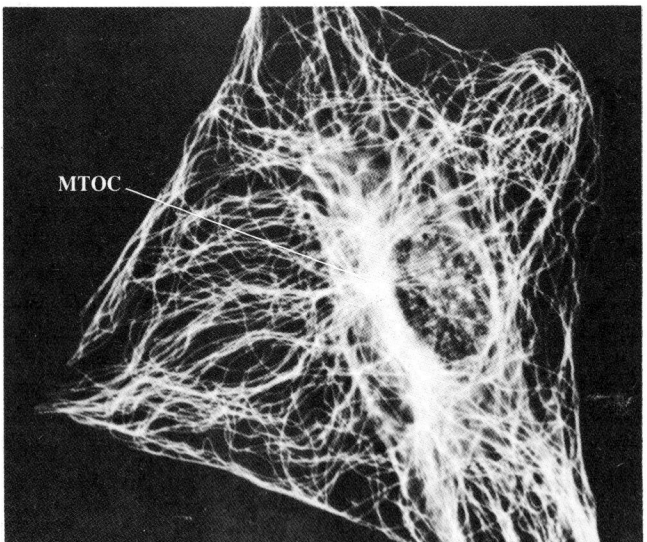

Fig 5.33 *Distribution of microtubules in a cell. The microtubules radiate from the microtubule-organising centre (MTOC) lying just outside the nucleus. The MTOC contains the centriole at its centre. The microtubules are made visible by attachment of a fluorescent antibody which binds specifically to the microtubule protein. The cell is a fibroblast, a cell which is commonly found in connective tissue and makes collagen.*

they are concerned with movement, the ability of cells to maintain their shapes, and with various other activities such as endocytosis and exocytosis. Only microtubules will be considered here.

Nearly all eukaryotic cells contain microtubules (fig 5.33). They are very fine, unbranched, hollow tubes. They have an external diameter of about 24 nm and walls about 5 nm thick made up of helically arranged subunits of a protein called tubulin, as shown in fig 5.34. Their typical appearance in electron micrographs is shown in fig 5.30. Growth of microtubules occurs at one end by addition of tubulin subunits. It apparently requires a template to start and certain very small ring-like structures that have been isolated from cells, and which consist of tubulin subunits, appear to serve this function. In intact cells, centrioles also serve this function and are therefore sometimes known as microtubule-organising centres, or MTOCs. Centrioles contain short microtubules.

Microtubules are involved in a number of cell processes, some of which are described below.

Centrioles and nuclear division

Centrioles are small hollow cylinders (about 0.3–0.5 μm long and about 0.2 μm in diameter) that occur in pairs in most animal cells. Each contains nine triplets of microtubules. At the beginning of nuclear division the centrioles replicate themselves and the two pairs migrate to opposite poles of the spindle, the structure on which the chromosomes line up. The spindle itself is made of microtubules ('spindle fibres') using centrioles as MTOCs. The microtubules control separation of chromatids or chromosomes by a sliding motion as described in chapter 23. Cells of higher plants lack centrioles, although they do produce spindles during nuclear division. The cells are thought to contain smaller MTOCs that are not easily visible even with the electron microscope.

Basal bodies, cilia and flagella

Cilia and flagella are organelles that have identical structures, although flagella are longer. They are outgrowths from cells which can beat either in one direction (cilia) or like a wave (flagella). The organelle can

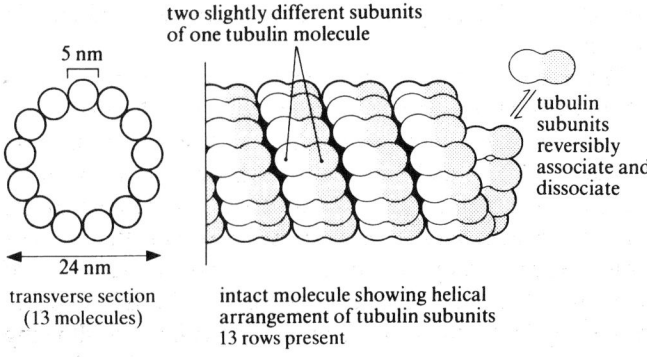

two slightly different subunits of one tubulin molecule

5 nm

24 nm

transverse section
(13 molecules)

tubulin subunits reversibly associate and dissociate

intact molecule showing helical arrangement of tubulin subunits
13 rows present

Fig 5.34 *Arrangement of tubulin subunits in a microtubule.*

be used for locomotion of single cells or to move fluids over the surfaces of cells, as cilia do when they move mucus through the respiratory tract. At the base of every cilium and flagellum is a **basal body**. Basal bodies are identical in structure to centrioles and are probably made by replication of centrioles. Like centrioles, they also seem to act as MTOCs because cilia and flagella contain a characteristic '9 + 2' arrangement of microtubules (chapter 18).

In cilia and flagella, microtubules undergo sliding motions which are responsible for the beating movements. Further details are given in chapter 18. Note that bacterial flagella are simpler than eukaryotic flagella and do not have basal bodies.

Intracellular transport

Microtubules are involved in the movements of other cell organelles such as Golgi vesicles, an example being the guiding of Golgi vesicles to the cell plate shown in fig 5.30. There is a constant traffic in cells of Golgi vesicles, of vesicles from the ER to the Golgi apparatus, lysosomes, mitochondria and other organelles. Such movements stop if the microtubule system is disrupted.

Cytoskeleton

Microtubules also have a structural role in cells, their long, fairly rigid, tube-like structure acting like a skeleton in forming part of the 'cytoskeleton'. They help to determine and maintain the shapes of cells during development, often being found in a zone just beneath the cell surface membrane (figs 5.10 and 5.11). Animal cells in which microtubules are disrupted change to a spherical shape. In plant cells the alignment of microtubules exactly corresponds with the alignment of cellulose fibres during formation of the cell wall, thus helping to determine cell shape.

5.10.8   Microvilli

Microvilli are finger-like extensions of the cell surface membrane of some animal cells (figs 5.10 and 5.12). They increase the surface area by as much as 25 times and are particularly numerous on cells specialised for absorption, such as epithelial cells in the intestine and kidney nephrons. The increase in surface area also improves the efficiency of digestion in the gut because certain digestive enzymes are attached to their surface (see section 8.3.8).

The microvilli can just be seen with a light microscope as a fringe across the top of the cell called a **brush border**.

Each microvillus contains bundles of actin and myosin filaments. Actin and myosin are the proteins found in muscle which cause muscle contraction. At the base of the microvillus actin and other filaments join up with filaments from neighbouring microvilli to form a network of filaments. The system as a whole allows the microvilli to remain upright and retain their shape, while still allowing their movement through the interactions of actin and myosin (similar to muscle contraction).

5.10.9   Mitochondria

Mitochondria are found in all aerobic eukaryotic cells and their structure and function are briefly summarised in fig 5.12. Their chief function is aerobic respiration and they are described in detail in section 9.3.

5.10.10   Cell walls

Plant cells, like those of prokaryotes and fungi, are surrounded by a relatively rigid wall which is secreted by the living cell (the protoplast) within. Plant cell walls differ in chemical composition from those of the prokaryotes and the fungi (table 2.2). The wall laid down during cell division of plants is called the **primary wall**. This may later be thickened to become a **secondary wall**. Formation of the primary wall is described in this section and an early stage of wall formation is shown in fig 5.30.

Structure of the cell wall

The primary wall consists of cellulose fibrils running through a **matrix** of other polysaccharides. Cellulose is a polysaccharide whose chemical structure is described in section 3.2.3. It has a high tensile strength which approaches that of steel. The matrix consists of polysaccharides which are usually divided for convenience into **pectins** and **hemicelluloses**. **Pectins** are acidic and have a relatively high solubility. The **middle lamella** that holds neighbouring cell walls together is composed of sticky, gel-like magnesium and calcium salts (pectates) of pectins.

Hemicelluloses are a mixed group of alkali-soluble polysaccharides. Like cellulose they form chain-like molecules, but the chains are less organised, shorter and more branched.

Cell walls are hydrated and 60–70% of their mass is usually water. Water can move freely through free space in the cell wall.

In some cells, such as leaf mesophyll cells, the primary wall remains the only wall. In most, however, extra layers of cellulose are laid down on the inside surface of the primary wall (the outside surface of the cell surface membrane), thus building up a secondary wall. Within each layer of the secondary wall the cellulose fibres are usually orientated at the same angle, but the fibres of different layers are orientated at different angles, forming a strong cross-ply structure. This is shown in fig 5.35.

Some cells, such as xylem vessel elements and sclerenchyma, undergo extensive **lignification** whereby lignin, a complex polymer (not a polysaccharide), is deposited in all the cellulose layers. In some cells, such as protoxylem, the lignification is only partial. In others it is complete, apart from 'pits' where groups of plasmodesmata were originally present in the primary wall (section 6.1.3 and fig 6.8). Lignin cements and anchors cellulose fibres together. It acts as a very hard and rigid matrix, giving the cell wall extra tensile and particularly compressional strength which prevents buckling. It is the main supporting material of trees. It also protects cells from physical and chemical damage. Together with cellulose, which remains in the wall, it is responsible for the unique characteristics of wood as a construction material.

Box 5A Composite materials

Mechanically strong materials, like cell walls, in which more than one component is present are known as **composite materials** and they are generally stronger than any of their components in isolation. Fibre–matrix systems are used widely in engineering and a study of their properties is an important branch of both modern engineering and biology. The matrix transfers stress to the fibres, which have a high tensile strength. The matrix also improves resistance to compression and shear. An example of a composite material traditionally used in engineering is reinforced concrete in which a concrete matrix is reinforced in various ways, such as by steel rods. More modern and lighter structural materials are fibreglass and carbon fibre in which a plastic matrix is reinforced with glass or carbon fibres. Other biological composites include wood, bone, cartilage and arthropod exoskeletons, which are rigid, and connective tissue and skin, which are flexible.

Fig 5.35 *Electron micrograph of layers from the wall of the green seaweed* Chaetomorpha melagonium *showing cellulose microfibrils about 20 nm wide; the contrast is due to shadowing with a platinum/gold alloy.*

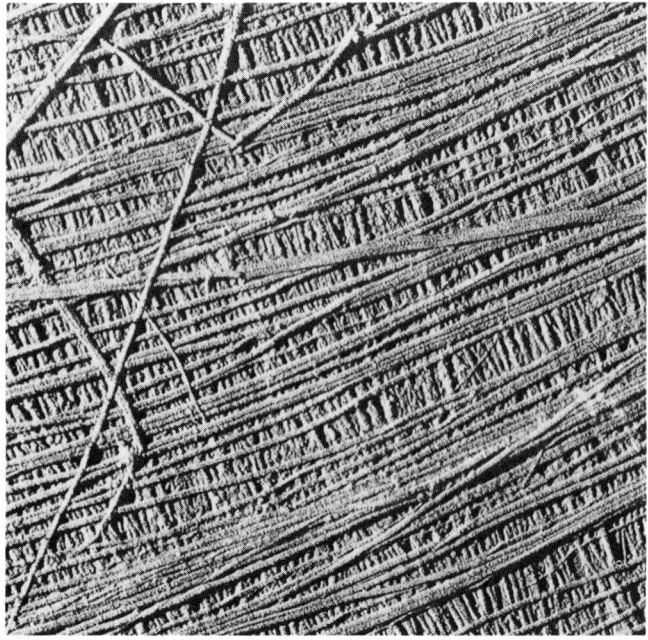

Functions of the cell wall

The main functions of plant cell walls are summarised below.

(1) Mechanical strength and skeletal support is provided for individual cells and for the plant as a whole. Extensive lignification increases strength in some walls (small amounts are present in most walls) and is particularly important in trees and shrubs.

(2) Cell walls are fairly rigid and resistant to expansion and therefore allow development of turgidity when water enters the cell by osmosis. This contributes to the support of all plants and is the main source of support in herbaceous plants and organs, such as leaves, which do not undergo secondary growth. The cell wall also prevents the cell from bursting when exposed to a dilute solution.

(3) Orientation of cellulose microfibrils limits and helps to control cell growth and shape because the cell's ability to stretch is determined by their arrangement. If, for example, cellulose microfibrils form hoops in a transverse direction around the cell, the cell will stretch, as it fills with water by osmosis, in a longitudinal direction.

(4) The system of interconnected cell walls (the **apoplast**) is a major pathway of movement for water and dissolved mineral salts (chapter 13). The walls are held together by middle lamellae. The cell walls also possess minute pores through which structures called **plasmodesmata** can pass, forming living connections between cells and allowing all the protoplasts to be linked in a system called the **symplast** (chapter 13).

(5) Cell walls develop a coating of waxy cutin, the cuticle, on exposed epidermal surfaces reducing water loss and risk of infection. Cork cell walls undergo impregnation with suberin which serves a similar function after secondary growth.

(6) The walls of xylem vessels and sieve tubes are adapted for long-distance translocation of materials through the cells, as explained in chapters 6 and 13.

(7) The cell walls of root endodermal cells are impregnated with suberin that forms a barrier to water movement (chapter 13).

(8) Some cell walls are modified as food reserves, as in storage of hemicelluloses in some seeds.

(9) The cell walls of transfer cells develop an increased surface area and the consequent increase in surface area of the cell surface membrane increases the efficiency of transfer by active transport (chapter 13).

5.10.11 Plasmodesmata

Plasmodesmata (singular *plasmodesma*) are living connections between neighbouring plant cells which run through very fine pores in the walls (fig 5.13). The cell surface membranes of neighbouring cells are continuous and line the pores. Running through the centre of each pore is smooth endoplasmic reticulum. Communication and coordination between plant cells is therefore made easier since molecules and ions do not have to cross a cell surface membrane. Movement is, however, regulated. Viruses can take advantage of these pores and can spread through plasmodesmata.

Sieve plate pores of phloem sieve tubes are formed from plasmodesmata (chapter 6).

5.10.12 Vacuoles

A vacuole is a fluid-filled sac bounded by a single membrane. Animal cells contain relatively small vacuoles, such as phagocytic vacuoles, food vacuoles, autophagic vacuoles and contractile vacuoles. However, plant cells, notably mature parenchyma cells, have a large central vacuole surrounded by a membrane called the **tonoplast** (fig 5.11). The fluid they contain is called **cell sap**. It is a concentrated solution of mineral salts, sugars, organic acids, oxygen, carbon dioxide, pigments and some waste and 'secondary' products of metabolism. The functions of vacuoles are summarised below.

(1) Water generally enters the concentrated cell sap by osmosis through the partially permeable tonoplast. As a result a pressure builds up within the cell and the cytoplasm is pushed against the cell wall. Osmotic uptake of water is important in cell expansion during cell growth, as well as in the normal water relations of plants.

(2) The vacuole sometimes contains pigments in solution. These include **anthocyanins**, which are red, blue and purple, and other related compounds which are shades of yellow and ivory. They are largely responsible for the colours in flowers (for example in roses, violets and *Dahlia*), fruits, buds and leaves. In the latter case they contribute to autumn shades, together with the photosynthetic pigments of chloroplasts. They are important in attracting insects, birds and other animals for pollination and seed dispersal.

(3) Plant vacuoles sometimes contain hydrolytic enzymes and act as lysosomes. After cell death the tonoplast, like all membranes, loses its partial permeability and the enzymes escape causing autolysis.

(4) Waste products and certain secondary products of plant metabolism may accumulate in vacuoles. For example, crystals of waste calcium oxalate are sometimes observed. Secondary products like alkaloids and tannins may offer protection from consumption by herbivores. Latex, a milky liquid, may accumulate in vacuoles, as in dandelion stems. The latex of the rubber tree contains the chemicals needed for rubber synthesis, and the latex of the opium poppy contains alkaloids such as morphine from which heroin is obtained.

(5) Some of the dissolved substances act as food reserves, which can be utilised by the cytoplasm when necessary, for example sucrose and mineral salts.

5.10.13 Chloroplasts

Chloroplasts contain chlorophyll and carotenoid pigments and carry out photosynthesis. They are found mainly in leaves and are described in section 7.4.1.

5.11 Use of the hand lens and microscope

5.11.1 The hand lens

This is a convex lens mounted in a frame. The frame may be small (pocket lens), or much larger for aiding dissection (tripod lens). The hand lens should be held close to the eye and the object brought towards the lens until an enlarged image can be seen. If a drawing is to be made, then the magnification of the drawing in relation to the size of the object must be calculated.

$$\text{drawing magnification} = \frac{\text{linear dimension of the drawing}}{\text{linear dimension of the object}}$$

For example: $\dfrac{6\ \text{cm wide drawing}}{2\ \text{cm wide object}} = \text{magnification} \times 3$

5.11.2 The light microscope

The **compound microscope** uses the magnifying powers of two convex lenses to produce a magnified image of a very small object.

Magnification

The magnification of the object is the multiple of eyepiece and objective lens magnifications (table 5.4).

Table 5.4 Magnification of the microscope.

Objective lens	Eyepiece lens	Magnification of the object
×10	×6	×60
×40	×6	×240
×10	×10	×100
×40	×10	×400

Parts of the microscope

Examine a microscope and identify the parts shown in fig 5.36. The microscope is an expensive instrument and should be handled carefully, paying attention to the following.

- Keep the instrument in a box (or under a cover) when not in use in order to maintain it in a dust-free state.
- Lift the microscope by its supporting arm only. Also support it from below with one hand. Place it on a bench gently to avoid unnecessary jarring.
- The lenses must be kept clean by wiping with a lens tissue (see below).

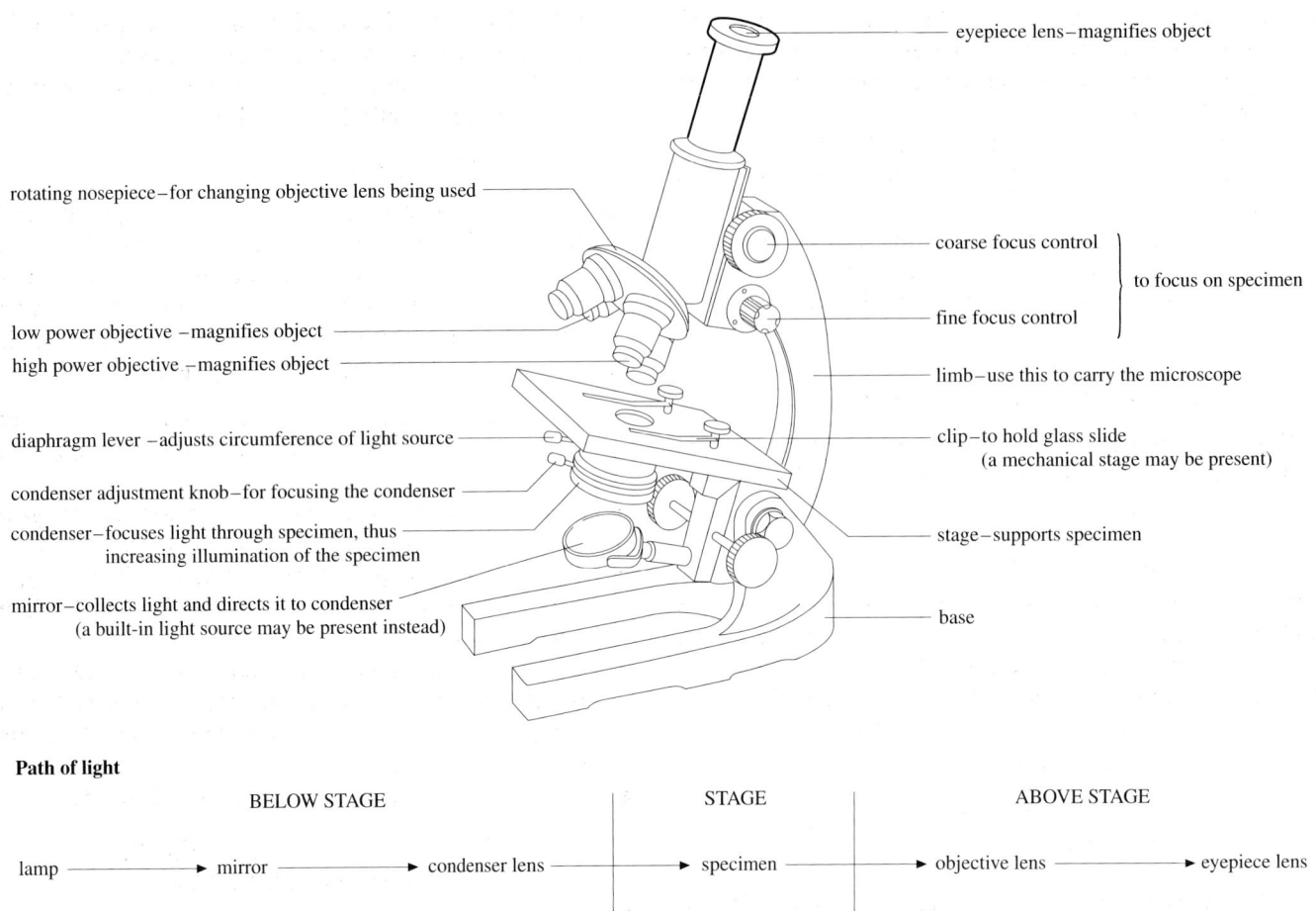

Labels on diagram:

eyepiece lens – magnifies object

rotating nosepiece – for changing objective lens being used

coarse focus control ⎫
fine focus control ⎭ to focus on specimen

low power objective – magnifies object

high power objective – magnifies object

limb – use this to carry the microscope

diaphragm lever – adjusts circumference of light source

clip – to hold glass slide (a mechanical stage may be present)

condenser adjustment knob – for focusing the condenser

condenser – focuses light through specimen, thus increasing illumination of the specimen

stage – supports specimen

mirror – collects light and directs it to condenser (a built-in light source may be present instead)

base

Path of light

BELOW STAGE	STAGE	ABOVE STAGE
lamp → mirror → condenser lens	→ specimen →	objective lens → eyepiece lens

Fig 5.36 *A compound light microscope.*

Cleaning lenses and slides

Dirt (dust, grit, grease etc.) is a common problem, and lenses and slides need regular cleaning. They can be cleaned before use, but if, during use, dirt is a problem, try to isolate the cause. For example, look down the eyepiece lens and try moving the slide or rotating the eyepiece lens to see if the dirt moves in either case. If it does not, the problem could be a dirty objective lens, mirror or lamp surface of condenser lens.

Remove conspicuous dust or grit by blowing, and then sweeping gently with a brush or piece of lens tissue. Huff on the slide or lens to dampen the surface, then polish clean and dry with a lens tissue. (This is specially prepared tissue with all traces of wood fibre removed, which could cause scratching of the lenses. Do not use ordinary tissue. Nappy liners are suitable.)

If necessary, the eyepiece lens can be removed for cleaning and the objective lenses can be unscrewed. Replace them immediately after cleaning to prevent dust from entering the microscope.

Remember:

- handle prepared slides at the ends or edges – do not place fingers on cover-slips.
- never touch lenses with your fingers.

- keep the stage clean.
- keep microscopes and slides covered when not in use.

Adjustment of the microscope for low power work

- Place the microscope on the bench and sit behind it in a comfortable position. Arrange other equipment around it. The object on the stage must be illuminated and this can be done with light from a built-in light source, from a window or a bench lamp. Light from the latter two sources shines on the understage mirror so that the curved surface reflects it up through the hole in the stage. The flat mirror is used to shine light through a sub-stage condenser, if there is one fitted. Light should be evenly spread across the field of view.

- Using the coarse adjustment screw, rack up the tube and turn the nosepiece until the lowest power objective (usually ×10 or 16 mm) *clicks* into line with the microscope tube. The magnifying power of the lens is usually inscribed on its barrel.

- Place the slide to be examined on the microscope stage so that the specimen is over the middle of the hole in the stage, and light can be seen passing through it.

- Viewing the stage and the slide *from the side*, rack down the low power objective using the coarse focus adjustment until the low power objective is about 5 mm from the slide.
- Looking through the microscope, slowly rack up by means of the coarse adjustment until the object is in focus.
- The microscope must **always** be focused **upwards, never downwards.** It is very easy to pass through the plane of focus when looking through the microscope and focusing downwards, and as a result damage the slide.
- Keep both eyes open and use each eye in turn.

Common problems are focusing on dust or dirt on surface of the cover-slip, and having the objective lens too far from the slide.

Moving the specimen

Note the direction in which the specimen moves when the slide is moved to the *left*, to the *right*, *away* and *towards* you. This knowledge will help you locate the specimen or follow a moving one. If a calibrated mechanical stage is present, this can be used as a reference to locate part of the specimen on future occasions.

Adjustment of the microscope for high power work

- High power work needs artificial light for sufficient illumination. Use a bench lamp or microscope lamp with an opal bulb. If a filament bulb is used, it will be necessary to place a sheet of paper between the bulb and the microscope. Swing the mirror so that the flat surface is uppermost and the light is thrown up into the microscope.
- To focus the condenser, leave the slide on the stage. Rack up the sub-stage condenser (fig 5.36) until within 5 mm of the stage. Look down the microscope and rack up the coarse adjustment until the object comes into focus. Now adjust the focus of the condenser until the image of the lamp is just superimposed on the slide. Put the condenser just out of focus so that the lamp image disappears. The lighting should now be at its optimum. Incorporated with the condenser is the **diaphragm.** This adjusts the opening through which light passes and the aperture should be as wide as possible. The definition will then be at its best.
- Turn the nosepiece until the high power objective lens ($\times 40$ or 4 mm) clicks into place. If focus has already been achieved under lower power, the nosepiece should automatically bring the high power lens into approximate focus. Adjust carefully using the fine adjustment and always focusing upwards.
- If the focus is still not correct after moving the higher power objective lens then use the following procedure. Look at the stage from the side, lower the tube until the objective lens is almost touching the slide. Watch the

reflection of the objective lens in the slide and then aim to make the lens and its image almost meet.
- Look into the microscope and rack up slowly using the fine adjustment until the object is in focus.

Oil immersion

For higher magnification than normal high power work ($\times 400$) an oil immersion lens can be used. The light-gathering properties of the lens are greatly increased by placing a fluid between the objective lens and the cover-slip. The fluid must have the same refractive index as the lens itself, so the fluid used is generally cedarwood oil.

- Place the slide on the stage and focus as normal for high power work. Replace the objective lens with an oil immersion lens.
- Place a drop of cedarwood oil on top of the glass cover-slip over the top of the object to be examined.
- Focus the object again under low power, then swing in the oil immersion objective lens so that the tip is in contact with the oil.
- Look down the microscope and very carefully adjust the lens using the fine adjustment. Remember that at the plane of focus the lens is only 1 mm from the cover-slip of the slide.
- After use, clean the oil from the lens with soft tissue.

Measurement of size with the microscope (micrometry)

It is obviously important to be able to make accurate measurements of the real sizes of structures seen with the microscope. Measurement of microscopic objects is called **micrometry.** This can be done using specially designed scales, or micrometers. One scale is placed in the eyepiece lens (the **eyepiece micrometer** or **eyepiece graticule**) and one on the stage (the **stage micrometer**) (fig 5.37). The micrometers have equally spaced divisions. The size of these is not relevant for the eyepiece graticule, but is a known value for the stage micrometer.

Be careful not to get fingerprints on the micrometers. Handle the eyepiece micrometer by the edges only, so that it does not get scratched.

Before using the eyepiece micrometer to measure a particular structure, you will have to find out the real width of each unit on the scale at each magnification. In other words you will have to calibrate the micrometer. This can be done by replacing the specimen with the stage micrometer, and using this to measure the eyepiece units at each magnification.

- Unscrew the top lens of the eyepiece. Check that the eyepiece micrometer is the correct way up, and insert it in the eyepiece. It will lie flat on a ledge inside the eyepiece. Replace the top lens.
- Place the stage micrometer on the stage. Arrange it so that light is passing through the scale (the location of the scale should be clear if viewed carefully with the eye).

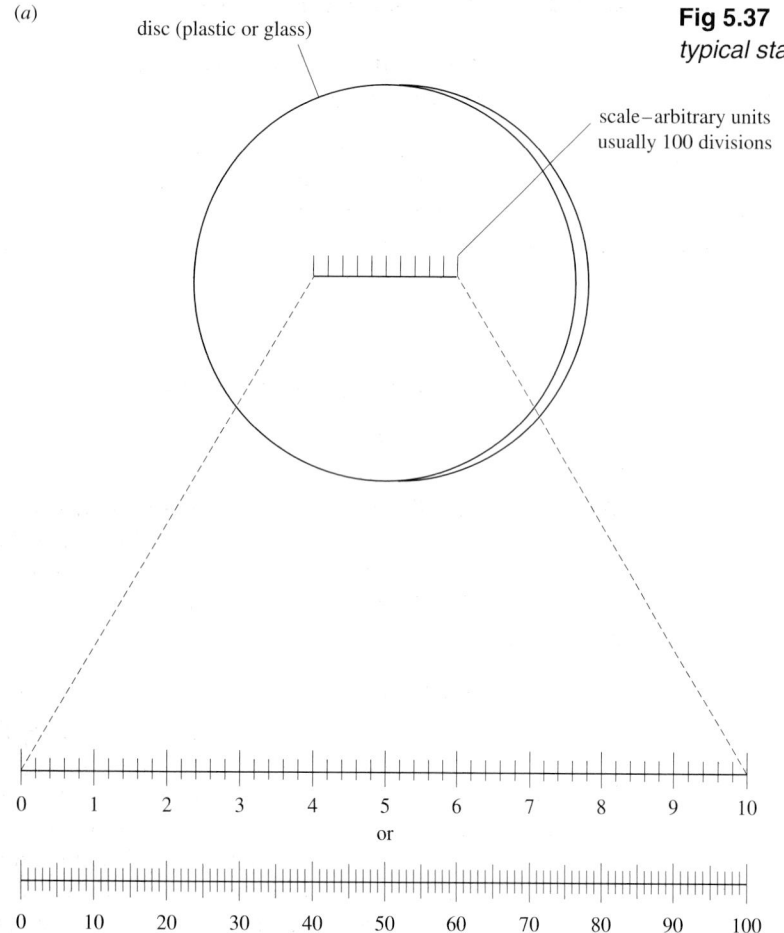

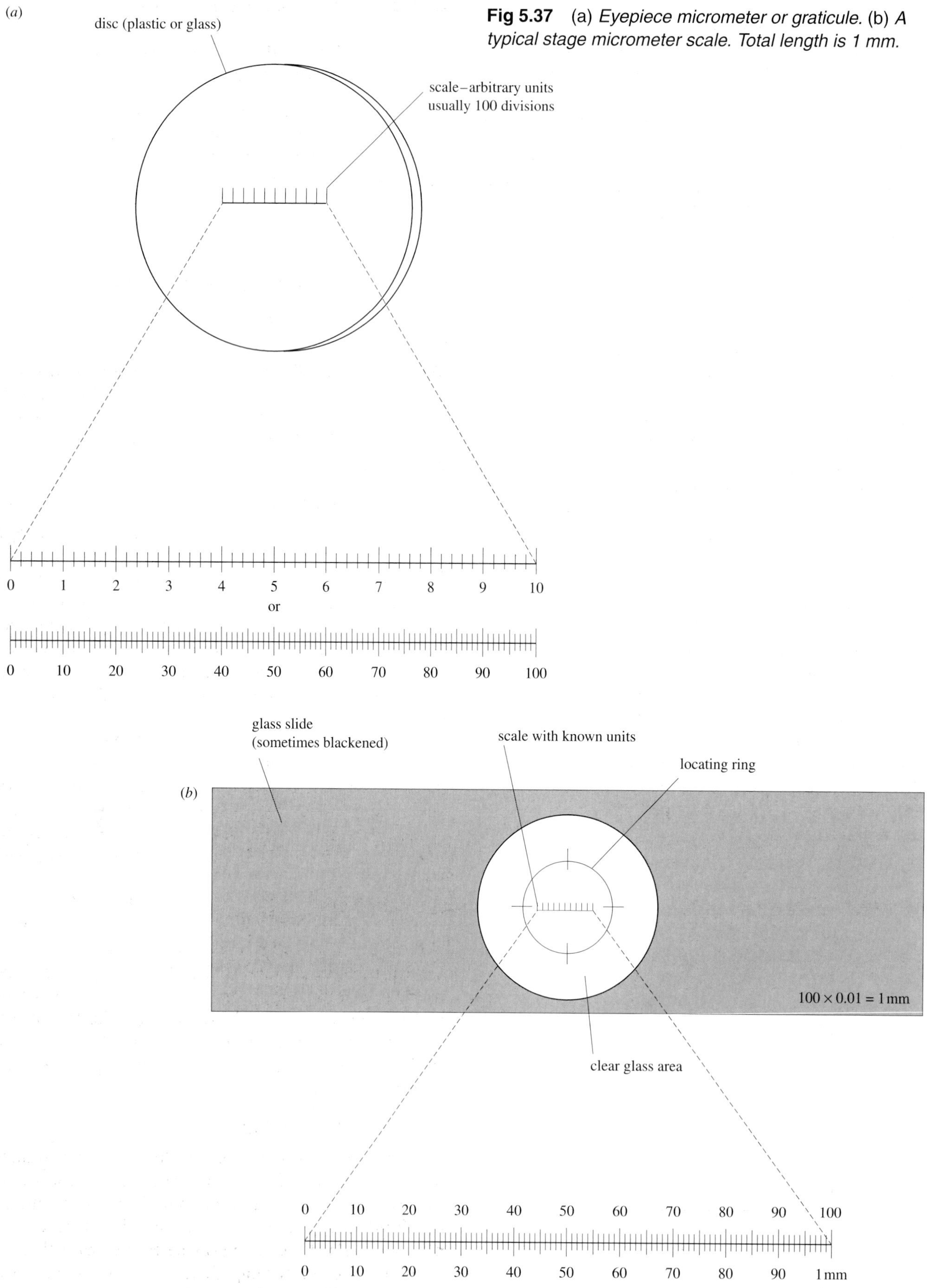

disc (plastic or glass)

scale–arbitrary units
usually 100 divisions

Fig 5.37 (a) *Eyepiece micrometer or graticule.* (b) *A typical stage micrometer scale. Total length is 1 mm.*

0   1   2   3   4   5   6   7   8   9   10

or

0   10   20   30   40   50   60   70   80   90   100

glass slide
(sometimes blackened)

scale with known units

locating ring

(b)

$100 \times 0.01 = 1\,mm$

clear glass area

0   10   20   30   40   50   60   70   80   90   100

0   10   20   30   40   50   60   70   80   90   1 mm

- Click the low power objective into position and focus on the stage micrometer scale.
- Rotate the eyepiece lens to line up the eyepiece scale parallel with the stage micrometer scale, and adjust the position of the stage micrometer so that the two scales are lined up next to each other and one can be read off against the other.
- Find out, as accurately as you can, how many stage micrometer divisions correspond to a known number of eyepiece units. (Choose as many units as possible for greatest accuracy.)
- The real width of the stage micrometer divisions will be 0.1 mm or 0.01 mm, which will be written on the slide. Using this information you can calculate the width of one eyepiece unit for this objective lens.
- Repeat the procedure for the other objective lenses that you intend to use for measuring (and any further eyepiece lenses, if necessary). Each eyepiece micrometer needs to be calibrated only once for a particular set of lenses and microscope.
- When the stage micrometer is replaced with a specimen, any part of the specimen can be measured in eyepiece units. Always rotate the eyepiece lens to line up the scale alongside the part to be measured.

It is easier to convert eyepiece units to real measurements if a graph is used. The vertical axis should represent eyepiece units, e.g. 100, and the horizontal axis should represent the actual distance in millimetres (see fig 5.38). Plot the actual length of 1 and 100 eyepiece units for each magnification, joining the two points with a straight line. Plot one graph for each magnification between the same axes, using appropriate scales for the horizontal axis. You can now read off the value in millimetres of any given number of eyepiece units for any magnification. It is useful to keep the graph with the microscope.

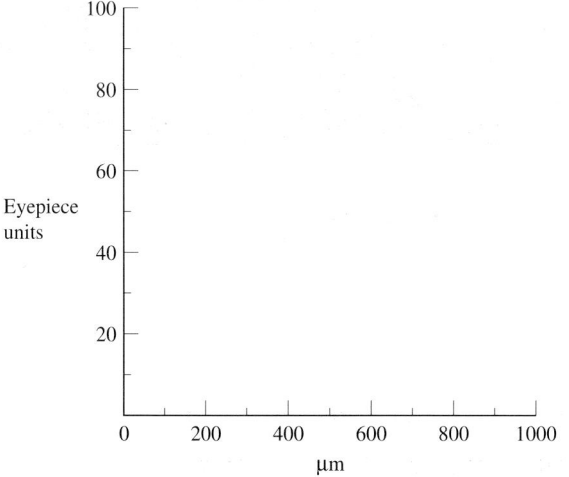

Fig 5.38 *Graph for converting eyepiece units to µm.*

5.12 Microscope techniques

5.12.1 Preparation of material for the microscope

Biological specimens may be examined in a living or preserved form. In the latter case material can be sectioned for closer examination and treated with a wide variety of stains to reveal and identify different structures. Preparations of freshly killed material may be temporary or permanent.

5.12.2 Permanent preparations

Fixation

This is the preservation of material in a life-like condition. Tissues must be killed rapidly and this is best achieved with small pieces of living material. The chemical used is called a **fixative**. By this method the original shape and structure are maintained and the tissue hardens so that thin sections can be cut.

Dehydration

Dehydration, or removal of water, is done to prepare the material for infiltration with an embedding medium or mounting medium (see below) with which water will not mix. Also bacterial decay would eventually occur if water were present. For preservation of fine detail, dehydration should be gradual and carried out by a series of increasingly concentrated ethanol/water or propanone (acetone)/water mixtures, finishing in 'absolute' (pure) ethanol or propanone.

Clearing

Alcohol does not mix with some of the common embedding and mounting media. Where this is the case, it is replaced with a medium (**clearing agent**) which does mix, such as xylol. This also makes the material transparent.

Embedding

Very thin sections can be cut if the material is embedded in a supporting medium. For light microscopy, embedding involves impregnating the material with molten wax which is then allowed to set. A harder material (plastic or resin) must be used for electron microscopy because thinner sections are required, and so more rigid support is needed during cutting.

Sectioning

Most pieces of material are too thick to allow sufficient light to pass through for microscopic investigation. It is usually necessary to cut very thin slices of the material (**sections**) and this may be done with a razor or a microtome. Hand-sectioning can be carried out with a razor which must be of shaving sharpness. For ordinary work, sections should be 8–12 µm thick. The tissue must be held firmly between two pieces of elder pith. The razor is wetted with some of the liquid in which the tissue is stored and the cut is made through pith and tissue, keeping the razor horizontal and drawing it towards the body with a long oblique sliding movement. Cut several sections fairly rapidly. Be content with the thinnest sections showing representative portions of the tissue.

Embedded tissues can be sectioned with a **microtome.** For light microscopy, sections a few micrometres thick can be cut from wax-embedded tissues using a steel knife. The **ultramicrotome** is used for cutting extremely thin sections (20–100 nm) for electron microscopy, and has a diamond or glass knife.

The need for embedding can be avoided in light microscopy by using a **freezing microtome** which keeps the specimen frozen, and therefore rigid, during cutting.

Staining

Most biological structures are transparent, so that some means of obtaining contrast between different structures must be employed. The most common method is staining. Some of the stains used in light microscopy are shown in table 5.5.

Certain stains when used in low concentrations are non-toxic to living tissue and can therefore be used on living material. These are called **vital stains**, for example methylene blue and neutral red.

To stain wax-embedded sections, the wax is dissolved away and the material partially rehydrated before staining.

Mounting

For light microscopy, the final stained sections are 'mounted' on a glass slide in a resinous medium which will exclude air and protect them indefinitely, such as Canada balsam or euparol. The mounted specimen is covered with a glass cover-slip.

The sequence of events described above is typical for preparations of thin sections for permanent preparations. However, two common variations in the order of events are:

(*a*) if hand-cut sections of fresh material are used, sectioning precedes fixation;

(*b*) staining may follow fixation and be carried out at the appropriate stage of the dehydration sequence, for example a stain dissolved in 50% ethanol would be used after dehydration in 50% ethanol.

The above procedures are similar in principle for both light and electron microscopy, although details differ as outlined in table 5.6.

Table 5.5 Common stains for plant and animal tissues.

Stain	Final colour	Suitable for:
Permanent stains		
aniline blue (cotton blue) in lactophenol	blue	fungal hyphae and spores
borax carmine	pink	nuclei; particularly for whole mounts (large pieces) of animal material, e.g. *Obelia* colony
eosin	pink	cytoplasm (see haematoxylin)
	red	cellulose
Feulgen's stain	red/purple	DNA; particularly useful for showing chromosomes during cell division
haematoxylin	blue	nuclei; mainly used for sections of animal tissue with eosin as counterstain* for cytoplasm; also for smears
Leishman's stain	red-pink	blood cells
	blue	white blood cell nuclei
light green or fast green	green	cytoplasm and cellulose (see safranin)
methylene blue	blue	nuclei (0.125% methylene blue in 0.75% NaCl solution suitable as a vital stain)
safranin	red	nuclei; lignin and suberin of plants; mainly used for sections of plant tissue with light green as counterstain* for cytoplasm
Temporary stains		
aniline hydrochloride or aniline sulphate	yellow	lignin
iodine solution	blue-black	starch
phloroglucinol + conc. HCl	red	lignin
Schultz's solution (chlor-zinc-iodine)	yellow	lignin, cutin, suberin, protein
	blue	starch
	blue or violet	cellulose

*counterstain: two stains may be used (double staining) in which case the second is called the counterstain.

5.12.3 Temporary preparations

Temporary preparations of material for light microscopy can be made rapidly, unlike permanent preparations. They are suitable for quick preliminary investigations. The stages involved are fixation, staining and mounting. Sectioning may precede fixation, or macerated material, such as macerated wood, may be used. Fresh material may be hand-sectioned with a razor directly into 70% alcohol as a fixative. For staining and mounting, a

Table 5.6 Differences in preparation of material for light and electron microscopes.

Treatment	For light microscopes	For electron microscopes
Fixation	As for electron microscopy, or for example 99 parts ethanol: 1 part glacial ethanoic acid ('alcohol/acetic'), or 70% ethanol (but this causes shrinkage and damage to delicate structures)	Glutaraldehyde or mixture of glutaraldehyde and osmic acid (OsO_4) is often used. OsO_4 also stains lipids, and hence membranes, black. Smaller pieces of material fixed for more rapid and better preservation of fine structure
Dehydration	Ethanol or propanone series	Ethanol or propanone series
Embedding	Wax	Resin (e.g. araldite, epon) or plastic
Sectioning	Metal knife	Only diamond or glass knives are sharp enough to cut the ultrathin sections required
	Microtome used	Ultramicrotome used
	Sections are few micrometres thick	Sections 20–100 nm thick
Staining	Coloured dyes (reflect visible light)	Heavy metals, e.g. compounds of osmium, uranium, lead (reflect electrons)

number of temporary stains may be used; some suitable for plant materials are shown in table 5.5. In each case the material should be placed on a clean glass slide (wiped clean with alcohol) and a few drops of stain added. In the case of phloroglucinol, one drop of concentrated hydrochloric acid is also added. The specimen is then covered with a thin glass cover-slip to exclude air and dust, and to protect high power microscope objectives (fig 5.39). If the specimens begin to dry out, or if it is known that prolonged examination (longer than 10 min) is required, specimens should be mounted in glycerine after staining.

5.13 Recording by biological drawing

Purpose

- To provide a record of work for future reference.
- To encourage you to study more fully and accurately the specimen that you are investigating.
- To aid memory of what you see by actively recording.

Principles

- Drawing paper of suitable quality must be used. It must be capable of standing some rubbing out of incorrect pencil lines.

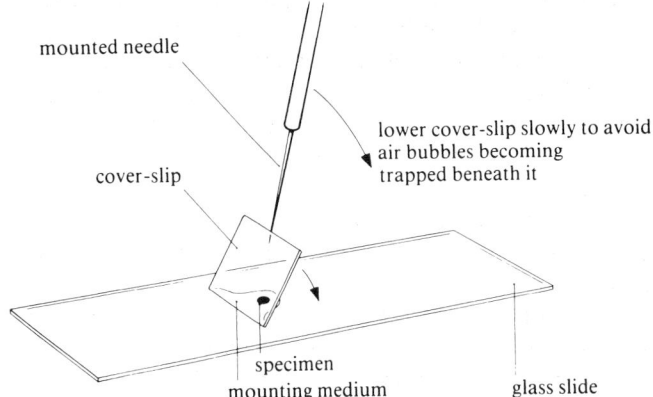

Fig 5.39 *Mounting a specimen and lowering a cover-slip on a glass slide.*

- Pencils should be sharp and of HB quality. No coloured pencils should be used.
- Drawing must be:
  (a) large enough – the greater the number of parts the larger the drawing. The drawing should normally occupy more than half the space available.
  (b) accurate – relative proportions of the various parts of the specimen should be observed and drawn carefully. If the subject has several similar parts, draw a small portion accurately.
  (c) drawn with lines sharp and clear – each line should be considered and then drawn without removing the pencil from the paper. Shading and colour should be avoided.
  (d) labelled – these should be as complete as possible with label lines that do not cross; space labels around the figure. Notes on observations can be added to the labels, such as intensity or colour of staining, shrinkage of tissue, unusual or typical features.
- Make two drawings if necessary:
  (a) a simple drawing of the main features, and
  (b) details of small parts only. For example, a lower power plan of a plant section should outline the different tissues but not include the individual cells. High power detail of the cells in a representative portion of the plan can then be drawn separately.
- Draw what you see and not what you think you should see, and certainly not a textbook copy.
- Every drawing should have a title, magnification, viewpoint of the specimen (such as TS, LS and so on) and explanatory notes. These should be placed in a standard position, such as the top right-hand corner of the page. A scale line should also be drawn where possible.
- Label lines should finish exactly at the structure named. They should be drawn with a ruler and should not cross each other. Labels should be arranged neatly around the drawing (lined up vertically where possible). All relevant structures should be labelled.

Experiment 5.1: Staining starch in plant tissues

A dilute solution of iodine in potassium iodide solution (I_2/KI) can be used to stain starch a deep blue-black colour. Starch is a carbohydrate which is commonly stored in the form of small grains in plant cells. Such grains can be seen clearly if the cut surface of a potato tuber is rubbed across a microscope slide and stained with I_2/KI solution. In addition to staining starch, I_2/KI solution stains lignified tissue (such as xylem and sclerenchyma) deep yellow, and unlignified tissue pale yellow. Nuclei stain more deeply yellow than the cytoplasm.

Materials

microscope and light source
eyepiece micrometer and stage micrometer
clean microscope slide and cover-slip
small brush for transferring sections
lens tissue
plain paper
mounted needle
teat pipette (if stain is not in a dropper bottle)
filter paper
iodine in potassium iodide solution
5% glycerol solution in dropper bottle
section of plant organ, e.g. stem of white deadnettle (*Lamium album*)

I_2/KI solution

Approx. 1 g iodine, 2 g potassium iodide, dissolved in 300 cm³ water. Concentration may be increased by using less water. Observe standard safety precautions when handling iodine.

Thin, fresh sections may be cut in the conventional way using a razor and supporting the stem between two pieces of pith. They should be cut into 70% alcohol.

Procedure

(1) Using a small brush, transfer a section of the plant organ to be studied to the centre of a microscope slide.

(2) Add two drops of I_2/KI solution, and one drop of 5% glycerol to slow down the rate of evaporation and stop the specimen drying out too quickly.

(3) Add a cover-slip as shown in fig 5.39.

(4) Examine the specimen carefully with a microscope. Note particularly the distribution of the darkly stained starch grains. Note also that any air bubbles will appear to have a thick black outline and are apparently empty. Ignore air bubbles.

(5) Draw a low power plan of your section of white deadnettle. Remember, the aim is to outline accurately the area occupied by each tissue. The following notes will also help.
  - White deadnettle has a special supporting tissue called **collenchyma** in each corner of its stem.
  - The vascular bundles are variable in size. Extra xylem and phloem *may* grow in between the vascular bundles, eventually making a continuous circle of vascular tissue.

(6) Label your low power plan and indicate the linear magnification of your drawing.

(7) State on the map which tissues contain starch. There is one layer of cells which is particularly abundant in starch grains. This is called the **starch sheath**. Draw this on your map and label it. Below your drawing, describe the *distribution* of starch grains within these cells.

(8) A biologist put forward the hypothesis that the average size of parenchyma cells in the cortex of the white deadnettle stem is greater near the centre of the stem than near the outside.

  Make appropriate measurements with the eyepiece graticule in the innermost and outermost regions of the cortex to test this hypothesis. Describe in detail the method you used.

  Record your results (measured in eyepiece units) in an appropriate manner and show your calculations.

  Convert your measurements to micrometres by calibrating your eyepiece micrometer.

  Do your measurements support the hypothesis?

Chapter Six

Histology

Histology is the study of tissues. All multicellular organisms possess groups of cells of similar structure and function assembled together to form tissues. A **tissue** can be defined as a group of physically linked cells and associated intercellular substances that is specialised for a particular function or functions. The cells of a tissue generally share a similar origin in the embryo. Tissues improve the efficiency with which the body functions by allowing division of labour, that is sharing of tasks, with each tissue being specialised for a particular job.

Higher levels of organisation than the tissue occur, particularly in animals. A number of tissues working together as a functional unit is called an **organ**, for example the stomach or the heart. In animals, organs form parts of even larger functional units known as **systems**, for example the digestive system (pancreas, liver, stomach, duodenum and so on) and the vascular system (heart and blood vessels).

The cells of a tissue may be all of one type, for example parenchyma, collenchyma and cork in plants and squamous epithelium in animals. Alternatively, the tissues may contain a mixture of different cell types, as in xylem and phloem in plants and some connective tissues in animals.

The study of tissue structure and function relies heavily on light microscopy and the associated techniques of preserving, staining and sectioning material. These techniques are described in sections 5.11 and 5.12.

In this chapter histology is studied at the level of detail which can be seen with the light microscope. In some cases, though, reference is made to structure as revealed by the electron microscope in order to provide greater clarification. In relating structure to function in tissues it is important to bear in mind the three-dimensional structures of the cells and their relationship to one another. This kind of information is usually 'pieced together' by examining material in thin section, most commonly in transverse section (TS) and longitudinal section (LS). Neither type of section alone can give all the information required, but a combination of the two can often reveal the necessary information. Some cells, such as xylem vessels and tracheids in plants, can easily be examined whole by macerating the tissues. This involves the breakdown of soft

---

* The structure of some plant tissue is dealt with elsewhere in this book. More detailed structure of phloem is given in chapter 13 where its structure is related to its function in translocation. Development of plant tissues from meristematic cells is discussed in chapter 22, together with secondary growth and the structure of wood (secondary xylem) and cork.

tissues leaving behind the harder, lignified xylem vessels, tracheids and fibres.*

Plant tissues can be divided into two groups:

- one type of cell   – parenchyma   section 6.1.1
       – collenchyma   section 6.1.2
       – sclerenchyma   section 6.1.3
- more than one type of cell
       – xylem   section 6.2.1
       – phloem   section 6.2.2

Animal tissues are divided into four groups:

- epithelial   section 6.3
- connective, including areolar tissue, fibrous tissue, adipose tissue, cartilage, bone   section 6.4
- muscle   section 6.5
- nervous tissue   section 6.6

Table 6.1 shows the characteristic features, functions and distribution of plant tissues. Fig 6.1 will help you to visualise the parts of the plant referred to when different tissues are being discussed.

6.1   Simple plant tissues – tissues consisting of one type of cell

6.1.1   Parenchyma

Structure

The structure of parenchyma is shown in fig 6.2. The cells may be roughly spherical or elongated.

Functions and distribution

- The cells are unspecialised and act as **packing tissue** between more specialised tissues, as in the central pith of stems and outer cortex of stems and roots (fig 6.1). They form a large part of the bulk of the young plant.
- The osmotic properties of parenchyma cells are important because, when turgid, they become tightly packed and provide **support** for the organs in which they are found. This is particular important in the stems of herbaceous plants where they form the main means of support. During periods of water shortage the cells of such plants lose water and this results in the plants wilting.

Table 6.1 Characteristic features, functions and distribution of plant tissues.*

Tissue	Main functions	Living or dead	Wall material	Cell shape	Distribution
Parenchyma	Packing tissue. Support in herbaceous plants. Metabolically active. Intercellular air spaces allow gaseous exchange. Food storage. Transport of materials through cells or cell walls.	Living	Cellulose, pectins and hemicelluloses	Roughly spherical to elongated	Cortex, pith, medullary rays in wood and packing tissue in xylem and phloem
Modified parenchyma					
(a) epidermis	Protection from desiccation and infection. Hairs and glands may have additional functions.	Living	Cellulose, pectins and hemicelluloses, and covering of cutin	Elongated and flattened	Single layer of cells covering entire primary plant body
(b) mesophyll	Photosynthesis (contains chloroplasts). Storage of starch.	Living	Cellulose, pectins and hemicelluloses	Roughly spherical, irregular (spongy) or column-shaped (palisade) depending on location	Between the upper and lower epidermis of leaves
(c) endodermis	Selective barrier to movement of water and mineral salts (between cortex and xylem) in roots. Starch sheath with possible role in gravity response in stems.	Living	Cellulose, pectins and hemicelluloses, and deposits of suberin	As epidermis	Around vascular tissue (innermost layer of cortex)
(d) pericycle	In roots it retains meristematic activity producing lateral roots and contributing to secondary growth if this occurs.	Living	Cellulose, pectins and hemicelluloses	As parenchyma	In roots between central vascular tissue and endodermis

NB The pericycle in the stem is made of sclerenchyma and has a different origin.

Tissue	Main functions	Living or dead	Wall material	Cell shape	Distribution
Collenchyma	Support (a mechanical function)	Living	Cellulose, pectins and hemicelluloses	Elongated and polygonal with tapering ends	Outer regions of cortex, e.g. angles of stems, midrib of leaves
Sclerenchyma					
(a) fibres	Support (purely mechanical)	Dead	Mainly lignin. Cellulose, pectins and hemicelluloses also present	Elongated and polygonal with tapering interlocking ends	Outer regions of cortex, pericycle of stems, xylem and phloem
(b) sclereids	Support or mechanical protection	Dead	As fibres	Roughly spherical or irregular	Cortex, pith, phloem, shells and stones of fruits, seed coats

Xylem	Mixture of living and dead cells. Xylem also contains fibres and parenchyma which are as previously described.				
tracheids and vessels	Translocation of water and mineral salts. Support.	Dead	Mainly lignin. Cellulose, pectins and hemicelluloses also present.	Elongated and tubular	Vascular system

Phloem	Mixture of living and dead cells. Phloem also contains fibres and sclereids which are as previously described.				
(a) sieve tubes	Translocation of organic solutes (food)	Living	Cellulose, pectins and hemicelluloses	Elongated and tubular	Vascular system
(b) companion cells	Work in association with sieve tubes	Living	Cellulose, pectins and hemicelluloses	Elongated and narrow	Vascular system

* Tissues associated with secondary growth, such as wood and cork, are described in chapter 22.

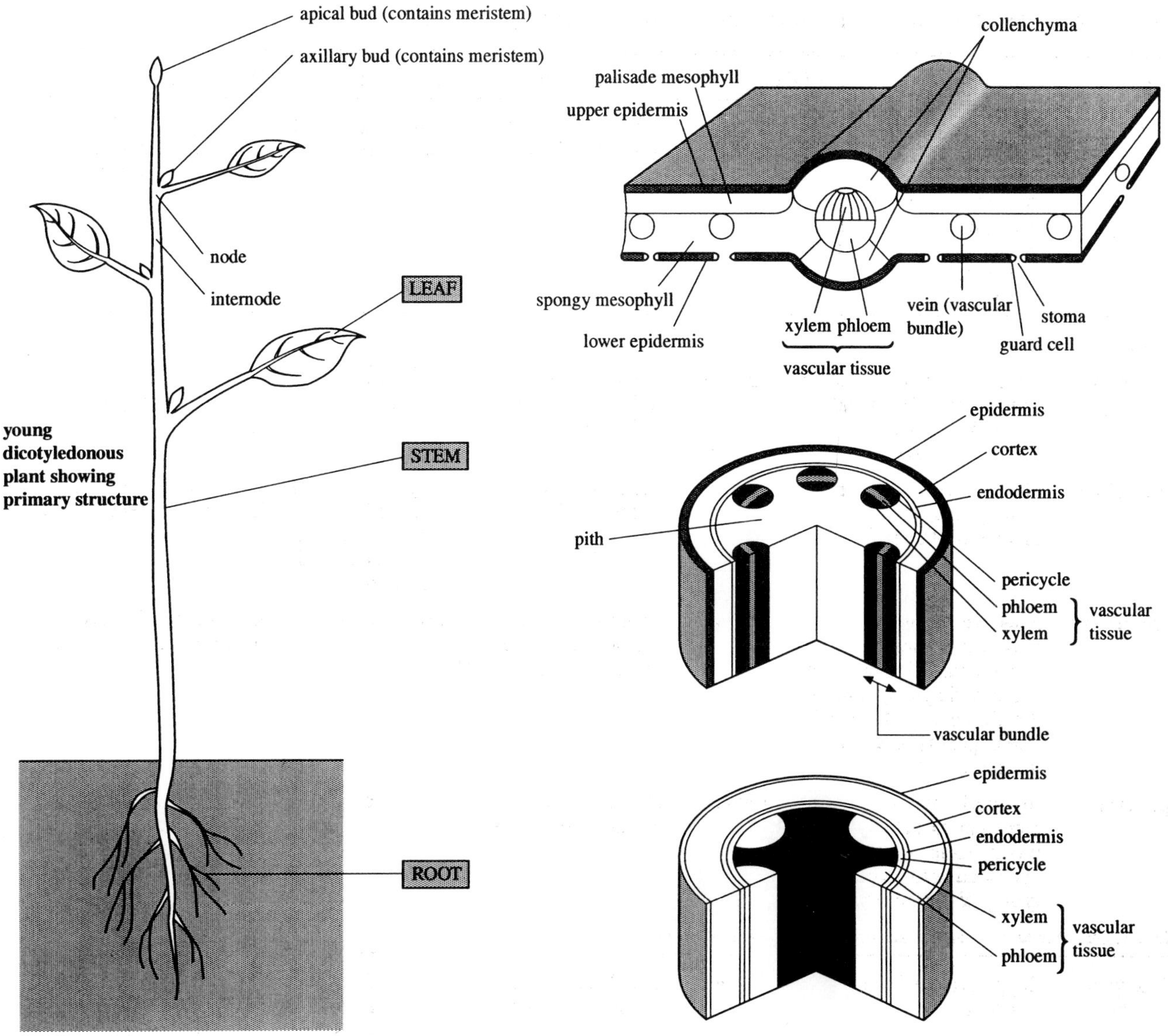

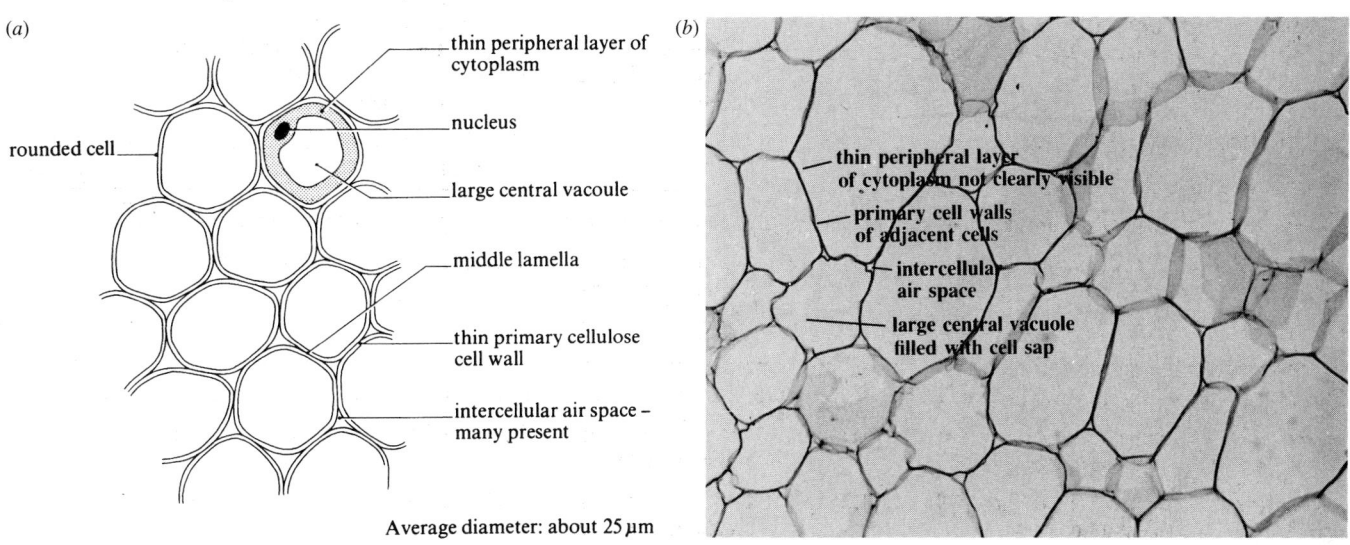

Fig 6.1 *Young dicotyledonous plant showing main features of primary structure of leaf, stem and root. The regions named are referred to during discussions of plant tissues.*

Fig 6.2 *Structure of parenchyma cells. (a) TS, cells are usually roughly spherical, though may be elongated.*
(b) TS Helianthus stem pith. Pith is the packing and supporting tissue found in the centre of the stems of dicotyledons.

- Although structurally unspecialised, the cells are **metabolically active** and are the sites of many of the vital activities of the plant body.
- A system of air spaces runs from the external environment where they open as stomata (pores in the leaf) or lenticels (special slits in woody stems). These air spaces run between the cells, thus allowing gaseous exchange to take place between living cells and the external environment. Oxygen for respiration and carbon dioxide for photosynthesis can thus diffuse through the spaces. This occurs readily in the spongy mesophyll layer of the leaf.
- Parenchyma cells are often sites of food storage, most notably in storage organs, such as potato tubers where the parenchyma cortex stores starch. Rare examples occur of parenchyma cells storing food in thickened cell walls, for example the hemicelluloses of date seed endosperm.
- The walls of parenchyma cells are important pathways of water and mineral salt transport through the plant (part of the 'apoplast pathway' described in chapter 13). Substances may also move through plasmodesmata between neighbouring cells.
- Parenchyma cells may become modified and more specialised in certain parts of the plant. Some examples of tissues that can be regarded as modified parenchyma are discussed below.

Epidermis. This is the layer, one cell thick, that covers the whole of the primary plant body (fig 6.1). Its basic function is to protect the plant from desiccation and infection. During secondary growth it may be ruptured and replaced by a cork layer as described in chapter 22. The structure of typical epidermal cells is shown in fig 6.3.

The epidermal cells secrete a waxy substance called **cutin** which forms a layer of variable thickness called the **cuticle** within and on the outer surface of the cell walls. This helps to reduce water loss by evaporation from the plant surface as well as helping to prevent the entry of pathogens (disease-causing organisms).

If the surfaces of leaves are examined in a light microscope it can be seen that the epidermal cells of dicotyledonous leaves are irregularly arranged and often have wavy margins (fig 6.3*b*) while those of monocotyledons tend to be more regular and rectangular in shape (fig 6.3*c*). At intervals, specialised epidermal cells called **guard cells** occur in pairs side by side, with a pore between them called a **stoma** (fig 6.1 and figs 6.3*b* and *c*). Guard cells have a distinctive shape and are the only epidermal cells that contain chloroplasts, the rest being colourless. The size of the stoma is adjusted by the turgidity of the guard cells as described in chapter 13. The stomata allow gaseous exchange to occur during photosynthesis and for respiration and are most numerous in the leaf epidermis, though they are also found in the stem. Water vapour also escapes through the stomata, and this is part of the process called transpiration.

Sometimes epidermal cells grow hair-like extensions which may be unicellular or multicellular and serve a wide variety of functions. In roots, unicellular hairs grow from a region just behind the root tip and increase the surface area for absorption of water and mineral salts. In climbing plants, such as goosegrass (*Galium aparine*), hooked hairs often occur and function to prevent the stems from slipping from their supports.

More often epidermal hairs are an additional protective feature. They may assist the cuticle in reducing water loss by trapping a layer of moist air next to the plant, as well as reflecting radiation. Some hairs are water absorbing, notably on xerophytic plants (plants adapted for dry conditions). Others may have a mechanical protective function as with short, stiff bristles. The hairs of the stinging nettle (*Urtica dioica*) are hard with a bulbous tip and, as they knock against an animal's body, their fragile tip breaks off and the jagged end pierces the skin. The cell contents at their bases enter the wound, acting as an irritant poison. Hairs may form barriers around the nectaries of flowers preventing access to crawling insects and helping to promote cross-pollination by larger flying insects.

Glandular cells are also a common feature of the epidermis and these may be hair-like. They may secrete a sticky substance that traps and kills insects, either for protection or, if the secretion contains enzymes, for digestion and subsequent absorption of food. Such plants may be regarded as carnivorous (fig 6.3*d*). Glandular hairs are sometimes responsible for the scents given off by plants, such as on the leaves of lavender (*Lavendula*).

Mesophyll (see also figs 7.3 and 7.4). This is the packing tissue found between the two epidermal layers of leaves (fig 6.1) and consists of parenchyma modified to carry out photosynthesis. Photosynthetic parenchyma is sometimes called **chlorenchyma**. The cytoplasm of such cells contains numerous chloroplasts where the reactions of photosynthesis occur. In dicotyledons there are two distinct layers of mesophyll: an upper layer consisting of column-shaped cells forming the **palisade mesophyll**, and a lower layer of more irregularly shaped cells, containing fewer chloroplasts, called **spongy mesophyll**. Most photosynthesis is carried out in the palisade mesophyll, while larger intercellular air spaces between spongy mesophyll cells allow efficient gaseous exchange.

Endodermis. This is the layer of cells surrounding the vascular tissue of plants and can be regarded as the innermost layer of the cortex (fig 6.1). The cortex is usually made of parenchyma, but the endodermis may be modified in various ways, both physiologically and structurally. It is more conspicuous in roots, where it is one cell thick, than in stems because in roots each cell develops a **Casparian strip**, a band of **suberin** (a fatty substance) that runs round the cell (fig 6.4). At a later stage further thickenings of the wall may take place. The

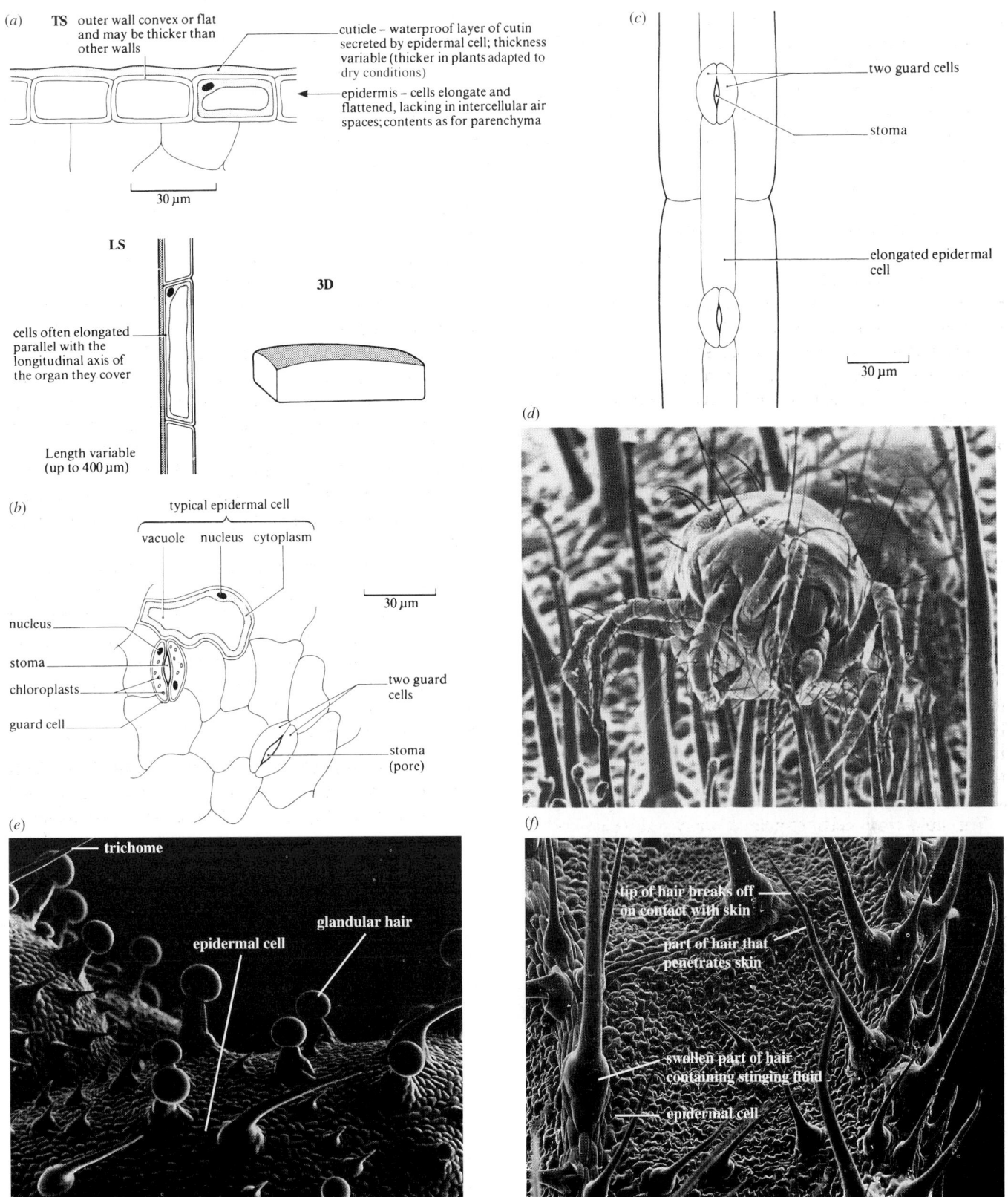

Fig 6.3 *Structure of epidermal cells. (a) Epidermal cells seen in TS, LS and three-dimensions. (b) Surface view of dicotyledon leaf epidermis. (c) Surface view of monocotyledon leaf epidermis. (d) Spider mite trapped and killed by the hair glands of a potato leaf. An enzyme capable of digesting animal matter has been found in one type of glandular hair in the potato, so the potato could be regarded as a carnivorous plant. Many other plants not normally thought of as carnivorous may have similar abilities. (e) Young leaf of* Cannabis sativa *with glandular hairs and trichomes.*
(f) Leaf surface of Urtica dioica *(stinging nettle).*

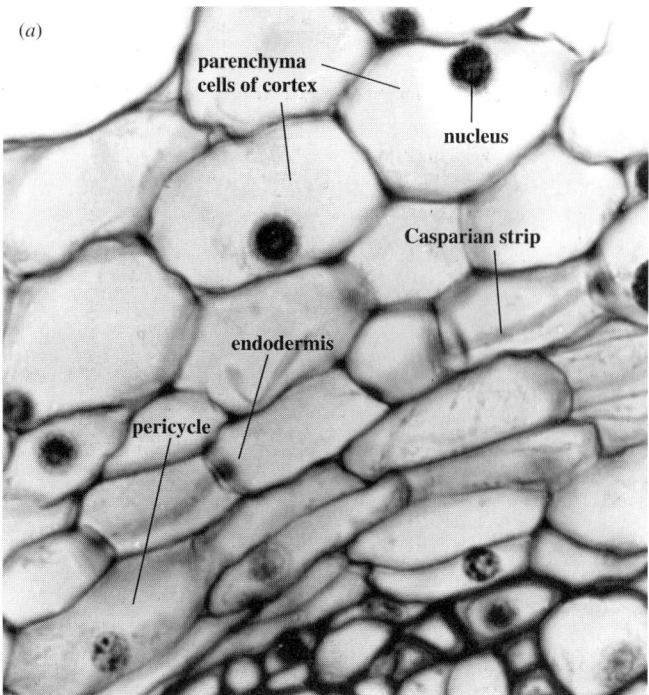

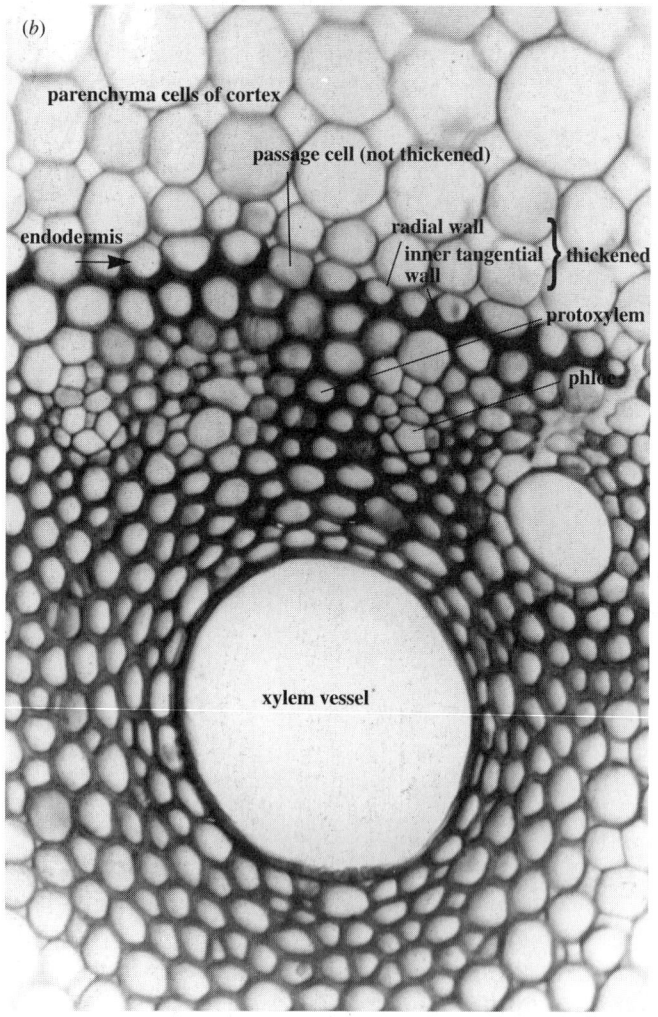

Fig 6.4 *Structure of root endodermis.* (a) *TS young endodermis with Casparian strip.* (b) *TS old dicotyledonous root showing endodermis.*

structure and function of root endodermis are discussed in chapter 13.

In the stems of dicotyledons the vascular bundles form a ring and the endodermis is the layer, one to several cells thick, immediately outside of this ring (fig 6.1). In this situation the endodermis often appears no different from the rest of the cortex, but may store starch grains and form a **starch sheath** which becomes visible when stained with iodine solution. These starch grains may sediment inside the cells in response to gravity, making the endodermis important in the geotropic response in the same way as root cap cells (chapter 16).

Pericycle. Roots possess a layer of parenchyma, one to several cells thick, called the **pericycle**, between the central vascular tissue and the endodermis (fig 6.1). It retains its capacity for cell division and produces lateral roots. It also contributes to secondary growth if this occurs. In stems there is usually no equivalent layer.

Companion cells. These are specialised parenchyma cells found adjacent to sieve tubes and are vital for the functioning of the latter. They are very active metabolically and have a denser cytoplasm with smaller vacuoles than normal parenchyma cells. Their origin, structure and function are described later in this chapter (section 6.2.2).

6.1.2 Collenchyma

Collenchyma consists, like parenchyma, of living cells but is modified to give **support** and **mechanical strength**.

Structure

The structure of collenchyma is shown in fig 6.5. It shows many of the features of parenchyma but is characterised by the deposition of extra cellulose at the corners of the cells. The deposition occurs after the formation of the primary cell wall. The cells also elongate parallel to the longitudinal axis of the organ in which they are found.

Function and distribution

Collenchyma is a **mechanical** tissue, providing support for those organs in which it is found. It is particularly important in young plants, herbaceous plants and in organs such as leaves where secondary growth does not occur. In these situations it is an important strengthening tissue supplementing the effects of turgid parenchyma. It is the first of the strengthening tissues to develop in the primary plant body and, because it is living, can grow and stretch without imposing limitations on the growth of other cells around it.

In stems and petioles its value in support is increased by its location towards the periphery of the organ. It is often found just below the epidermis in the outer region of the

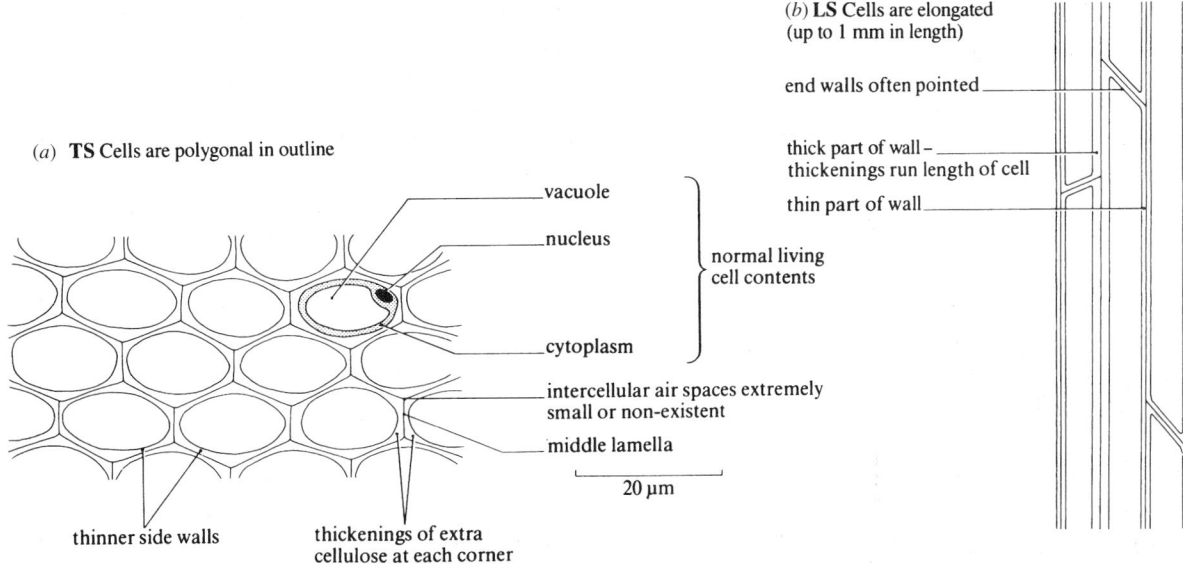

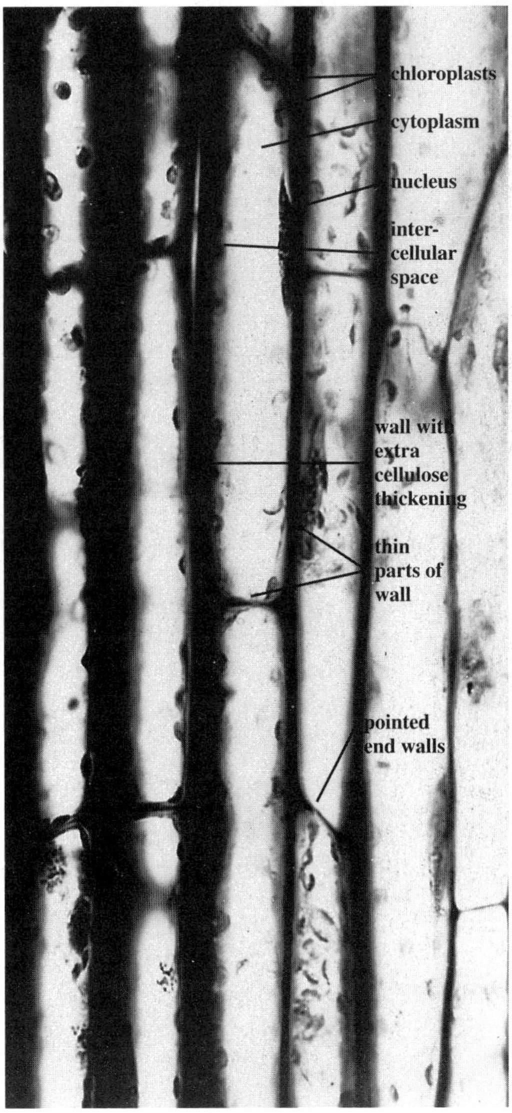

(a) **TS** Cells are polygonal in outline

vacuole

nucleus

}
normal living
cell contents

cytoplasm

intercellular air spaces extremely
small or non-existent

middle lamella

20 μm

thinner side walls

thickenings of extra
cellulose at each corner

(b) **LS** Cells are elongated
(up to 1 mm in length)

end walls often pointed

thick part of wall –
thickenings run length of cell

thin part of wall

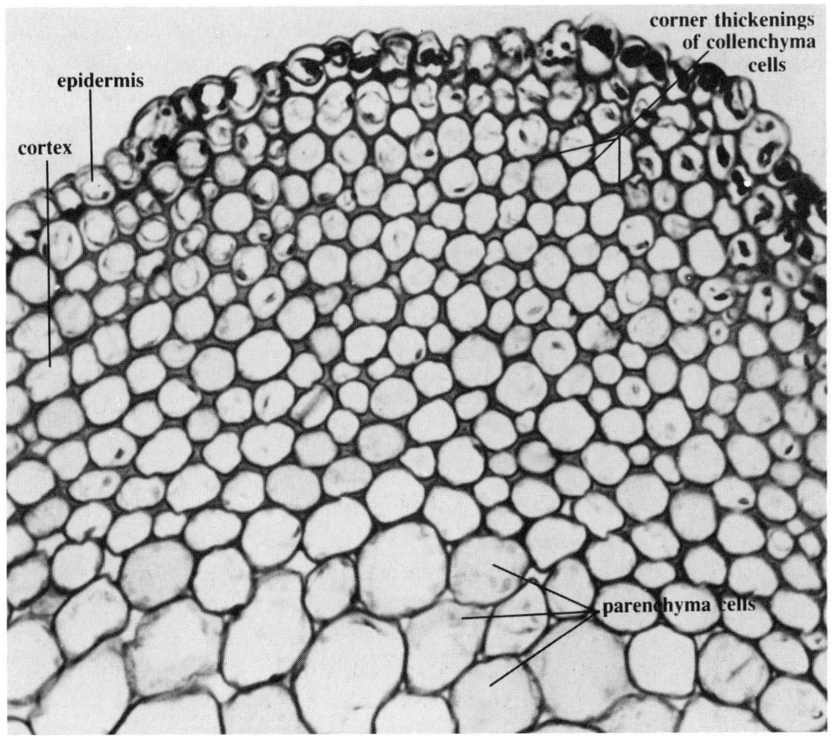

(c)

epidermis

cortex

corner thickenings
of collenchyma
cells

parenchyma cells

(d)

chloroplasts

cytoplasm

nucleus

inter-
cellular
space

wall with
extra
cellulose
thickening

thin
parts of
wall

pointed
end walls

Fig 6.5 *Structure of collenchyma cells. (a) TS, cells are
polygonal in outline. (b) LS, cells are elongated (up to 1 mm
in length). (c) TS collenchyma from* Helianthus *stem. (d) LS
collenchyma from* Helianthus *stem.*

cortex and gradually merges into parenchyma towards the inside, thus forming a hollow cylinder in three dimensions. Alternatively, strengthening ridges may be formed, as along the fleshy petioles of celery (*Apium graveolus*) and the angular stems of plants such as dead-nettle (*Lamium*). In dicotyledonous leaves it appears as solid masses running the length of the midrib, providing support for the vascular bundles (fig 6.1).

6.1.3 Sclerenchyma

The sole function of **sclerenchyma** is to assist in providing support and mechanical strength for the plant. Its distribution within the plant is related to the stresses to which different organs are subjected. Unlike collenchyma, the mature cells are dead and incapable of elongation so they do not mature until elongation of the living cells around them is complete.

Structure

There are two types of sclerenchyma cell, namely **fibres**, which are elongated cells, and **sclereids** or **stone cells**, which are usually roughly spherical, although both may vary considerably in size and shape. Their structures are shown in figs 6.6 and 6.7 respectively. In both cases the primary cell wall is heavily thickened with deposits of **lignin**, a hard substance with great tensile and compressional strength. A high tensile strength means that it does not break easily on stretching, and a high compressional strength means that it does not buckle easily.

Deposition of lignin takes place in and on the primary cellulose cell wall and, as the walls thicken, the living contents of the cells are lost with the result that the mature cells are dead. In both fibres and sclereids structures called **simple pits** appear in the walls as they thicken. These represent areas where lignin is not deposited on the primary wall owing to the presence of groups of **plasmodesmata** (strands of cytoplasm that connect neighbouring cells through minute pores in the adjacent cell walls). Each group of plasmodesmata forms one pit. The pits are described as simple because they are tubes of constant width. Their development is best explained diagrammatically as shown in fig 6.8.

Function and distribution of fibres

Individual sclerenchyma fibres are strong owing to their lignified walls. Collectively their strength is enhanced by their arrangement into strands or sheets of tissue that extend for considerable distances in a longitudinal direction. In addition, the ends of the cells interlock with one another, increasing their combined strength.

Fibres are found in the pericycle of stems, forming a solid rod of tissue 'capping' the vascular bundles of dicotyledons (see fig 6.1). They often form a layer in the cortex below the epidermis of stems or roots, in the same way as collenchyma, producing a hollow cylinder that contains the rest of the cortex and vascular tissues. Fibres

also occur in both xylem and phloem, either individually or in groups, as described in section 6.2.

Function and distribution of sclereids

Sclereids are generally scattered singly or in groups almost anywhere in the plant body, but are most common in the cortex, pith, phloem and in fruits and seeds.

Depending on numbers and position, they confer firmness or rigidity on those structures in which they are found. In the flesh of pear fruits they occur in small groups and are responsible for the 'grittiness' of these fruits when eaten. In some cases they form very resilient, solid layers, as in the shells of nuts and the stones (endocarp) of stone fruits. In seeds they commonly toughen the testa (seed coat).

6.2 Plant tissues consisting of more than one type of cell

There are two types of conducting tissue in plants, namely **xylem** and **phloem**, both of which contain more than one type of cell (fig 6.1). Together they constitute the **vascular tissue** whose function in translocation is described in chapter 13. Xylem conducts mainly water and mineral salts from the roots up to other parts of the plant, while phloem conducts mainly organic food from the leaves both up and down the plant. Both tissues may be increased in amount as a result of secondary growth as described in chapter 22. Secondary xylem may become extensive, when it is known as **wood**.

6.2.1 Xylem

Xylem has two major functions, the conduction of water and mineral salts, and support. Thus it has both a physiological and a structural role in the plant. It consists of four cell types, namely tracheids, vessel elements, parenchyma and fibres. These are illustrated in transverse and longitudinal section in fig 6.9.

Tracheids

Tracheids are single cells that are elongated and lignified. They have tapering end walls that overlap with adjacent tracheids in the same way as sclerenchyma fibres. Thus they have mechanical strength and give support to the plant. They are dead with empty lumens when mature. Tracheids represent the original, primitive water-conducting cells of vascular plants and are the only cells found in the xylem of the more ancestral vascular plants. They have given rise, in other plants, to xylem fibres and vessels which are described later. Despite their ancestral nature, they obviously function efficiently because conifers, most of which are trees, rely exclusively on tracheids to conduct water from the roots to the aerial parts. Water can pass through the empty lumens without being obstructed by living contents. It passes from tracheid to tracheid through the pits via the 'pit

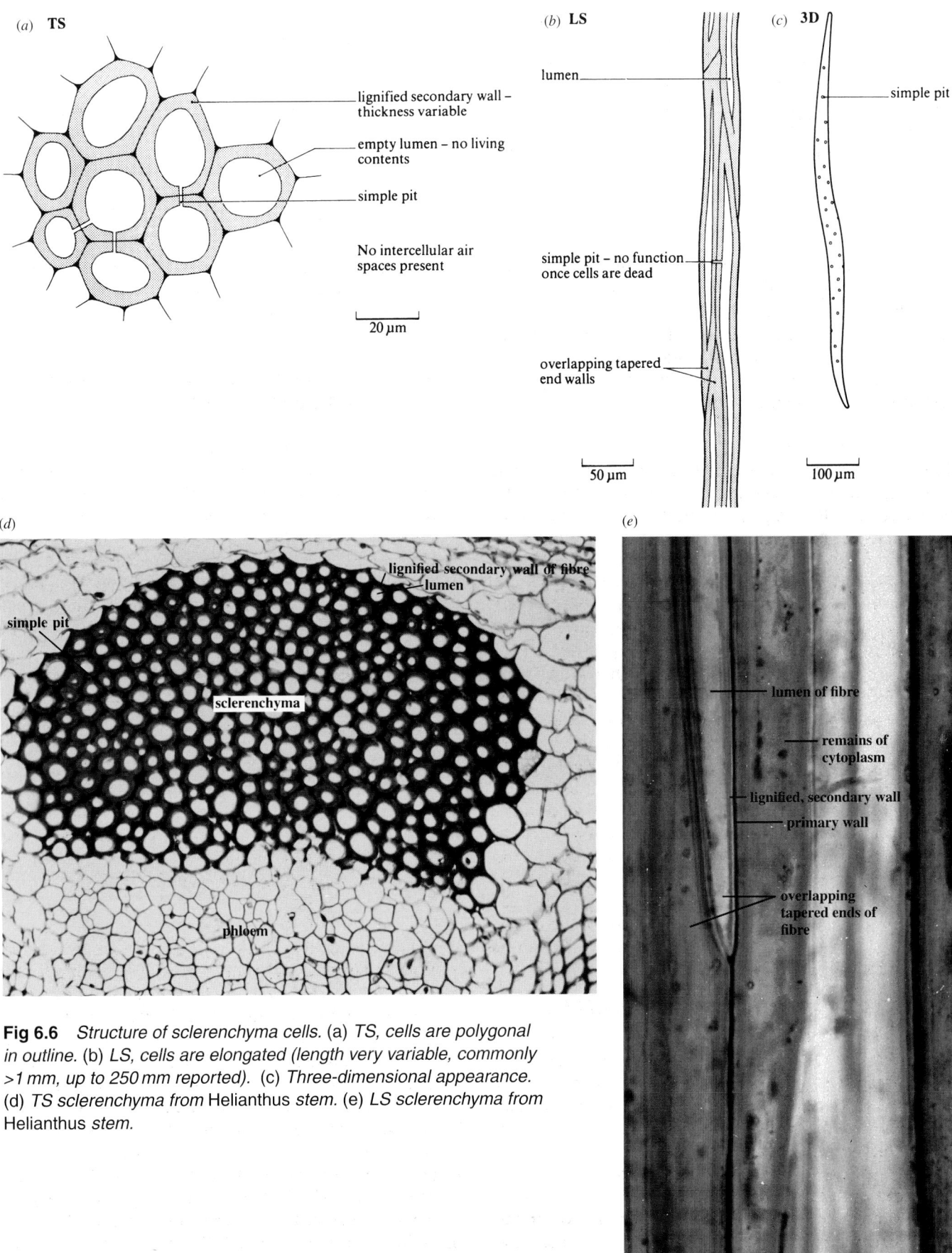

(a) **TS**

lignified secondary wall – thickness variable

empty lumen – no living contents

simple pit

No intercellular air spaces present

20 µm

(b) **LS**

lumen

simple pit – no function once cells are dead

overlapping tapered end walls

50 µm

(c) **3D**

simple pit

100 µm

(d)

lignified secondary wall of fibre
lumen

simple pit

sclerenchyma

phloem

(e)

lumen of fibre

remains of cytoplasm

lignified, secondary wall

primary wall

overlapping tapered ends of fibre

Fig 6.6 *Structure of sclerenchyma cells. (a) TS, cells are polygonal in outline. (b) LS, cells are elongated (length very variable, commonly >1 mm, up to 250 mm reported). (c) Three-dimensional appearance. (d) TS sclerenchyma from* Helianthus *stem. (e) LS sclerenchyma from* Helianthus *stem.*

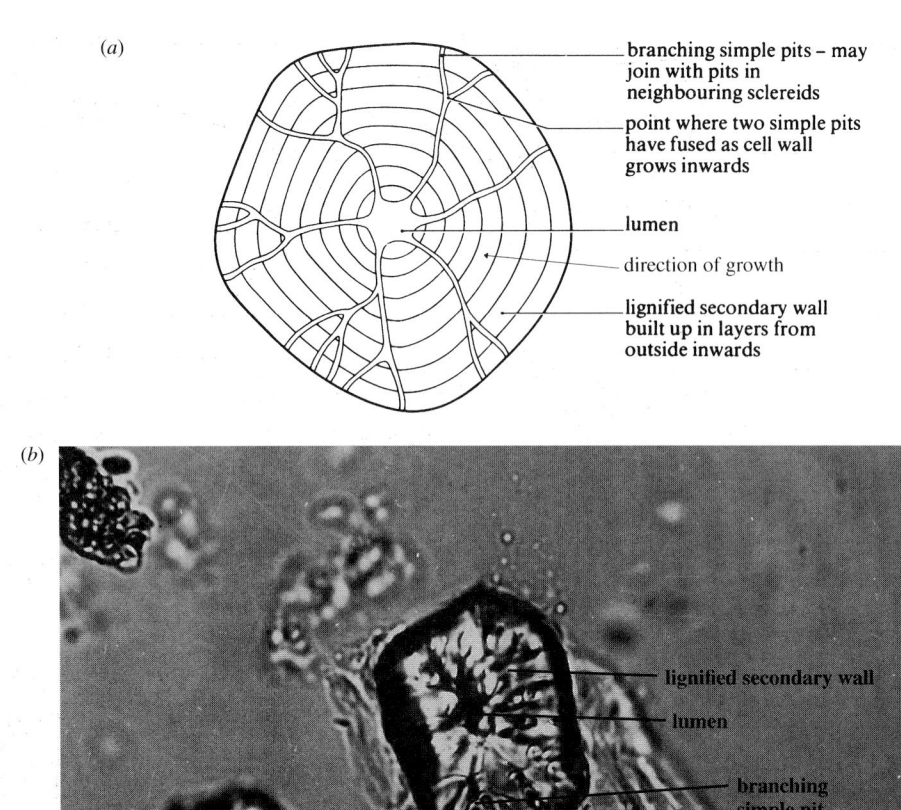

(a)

branching simple pits – may
join with pits in
neighbouring sclereids

point where two simple pits
have fused as cell wall
grows inwards

lumen

direction of growth

lignified secondary wall
built up in layers from
outside inwards

(b)

lignified secondary wall

lumen

branching
simple pit

primary
wall

Fig 6.7 *Structure of sclerenchyma sclereids.* (a) *TS or LS, cells are isodiametric.* (b) *Entire sclereid from macerated flesh of pear fruit (×400).*

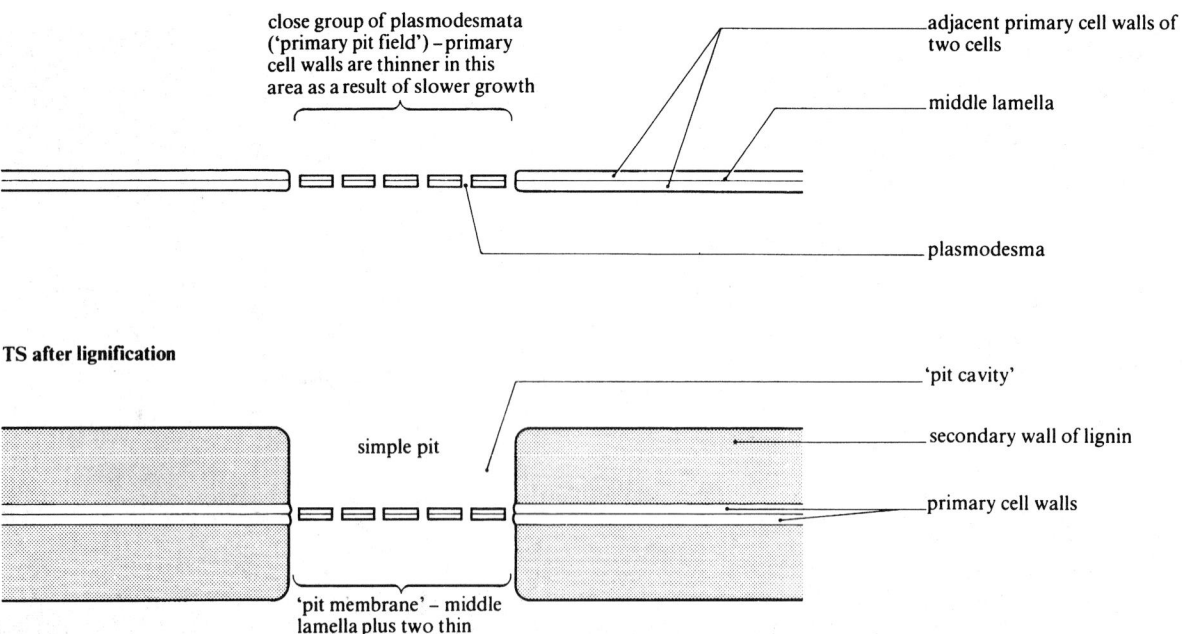

close group of plasmodesmata
('primary pit field') – primary
cell walls are thinner in this
area as a result of slower growth

adjacent primary cell walls of
two cells

middle lamella

plasmodesma

TS after lignification

'pit cavity'

simple pit

secondary wall of lignin

primary cell walls

'pit membrane' – middle
lamella plus two thin
primary walls

Fig 6.8 *Development of simple pits in sclerenchyma fibres and sclereids.*

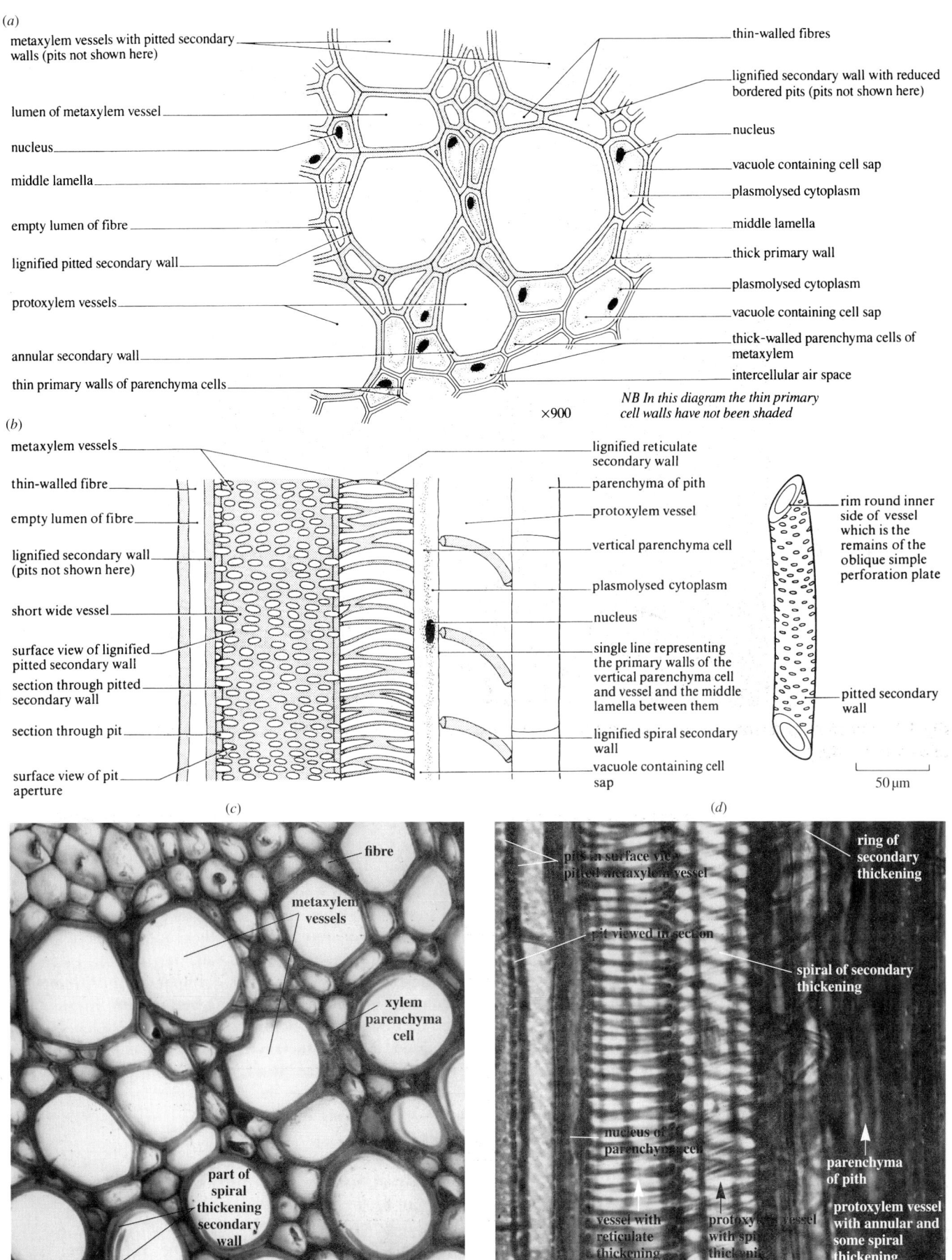

Fig 6.9 *Structure of primary xylem.* (a) *TS.* (b) *LS.* (c) *TS primary xylem from* Helianthus *stem.* (d) *LS primary xylem from* Helianthus *stem.*

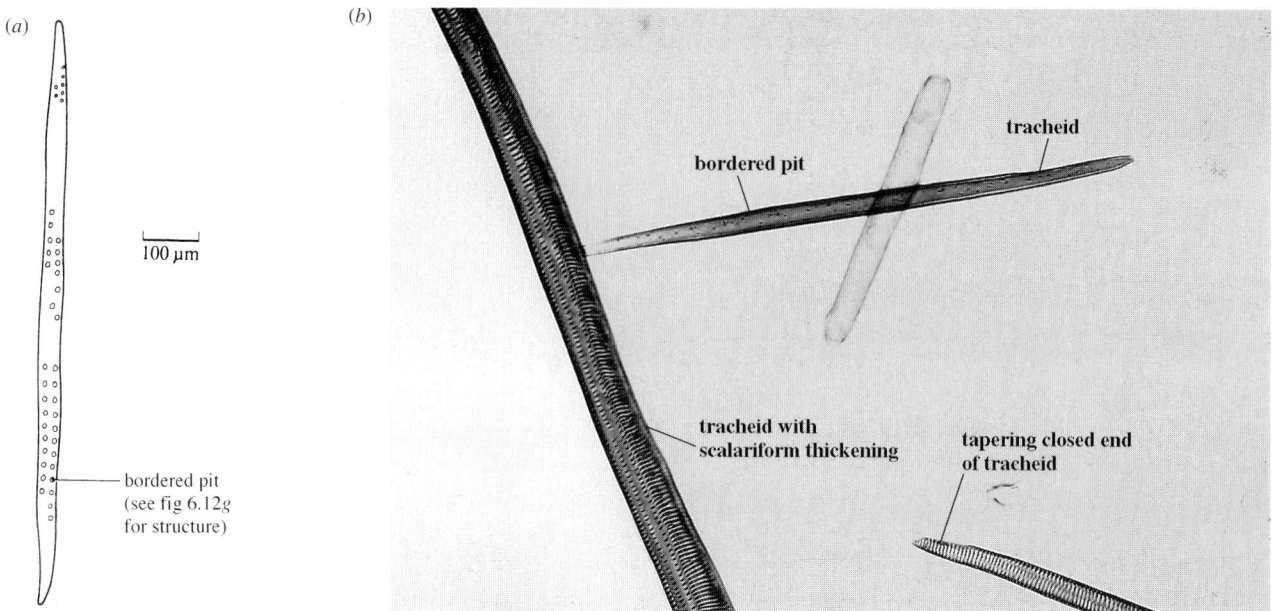

(a)

(b)

100 µm

bordered pit
(see fig 6.12g
for structure)

bordered pit

tracheid

tracheid with
scalariform thickening

tapering closed end
of tracheid

Fig 6.10 *Structure of tracheids. (a) Tracheid with bordered pits (tracheids may also have annular, spiral, scalariform and reticulate thickening, like vessels, see fig 6.12g). (b) Tracheids from macerated wood of* Pinus *(×120).*

membranes', formed as described in fig 6.8, or through unlignified portions of the cell walls. The pattern of lignification of the walls resembles that of vessels which are described below. Fig 6.10 illustrates the structure of tracheids. Flowering plants (angiosperms) have relatively fewer tracheids than vessels, and vessels are thought to be more effective transporting structures, possibly necessary owing to the larger leaves and higher transpiration rates of this group.

Vessels

Vessels are the characteristic conducting units of angiosperm xylem. They are very long, tubular structures formed by the fusion of several cells end to end in a row. Each of the cells forming a xylem vessel is equivalent to a tracheid and is called a **vessel element**. However, vessel elements are shorter and wider than tracheids. The first xylem to appear in the growing plant is called **primary xylem** and develops in the root and shoot apices. Differentiated xylem vessel elements appear in rows at the edges of the procambial strands. A vessel is formed when the neighbouring vessel elements of a given row fuse as a result of their end walls breaking down. A series of rims is left around the inner side of the vessel marking the remains of the end walls. The fusion of elements is shown in fig 6.11.

Protoxylem and metaxylem

The first vessels form the **protoxylem**, located in the part of the apex, just behind the apical meristem, where elongation of surrounding cells is still occurring. Mature protoxylem vessels can be stretched as surrounding cells elongate because lignin is not deposited over the entire cellulose

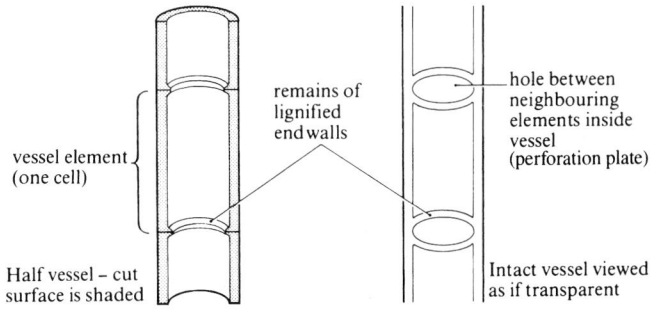

vessel element
(one cell)

remains of
lignified
end walls

hole between
neighbouring
elements inside
vessel
(perforation plate)

Half vessel – cut
surface is shaded

Intact vessel viewed
as if transparent

Fig 6.11 *Fusion of vessel elements to form a vessel.*

wall, but only in rings or in spirals as shown in fig 6.12. These act as reinforcement for the tubes during elongation of the stem or root. As growth proceeds, more xylem vessels develop and these undergo more extensive lignification, completing their development in the mature regions of the organ and forming **metaxylem**. Meanwhile, the earliest protoxylem vessels have stretched and collapsed. Mature metaxylem vessels cannot stretch or grow because they are dead, rigid, fully lignified tubes. If they developed before the living cells around them had finished elongating they would impose severe restraints on elongation.

Metaxylem vessels show three basic patterns of lignification, namely scalariform, reticulate and pitted, as shown in fig 6.12.

The long, empty tubes of xylem provide an ideal system for translocating large quantities of water over long distances with minimal obstruction to flow. As with tracheids, water can pass from vessel to vessel through pits

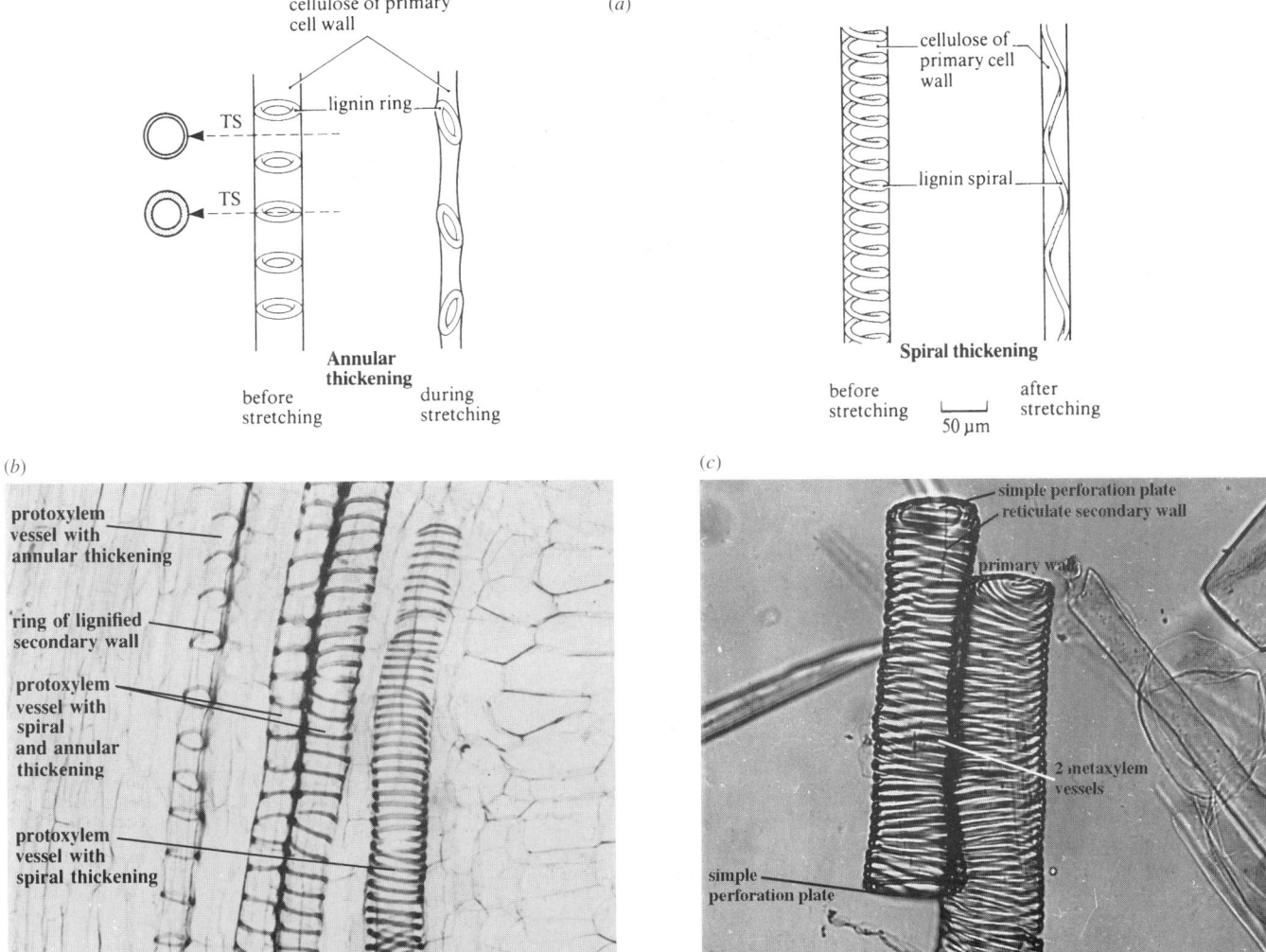

Fig 6.12 *Structure of protoxylem and metaxylem vessels. (a) Protoxylem vessels. (b) Micrograph of annular and spiral protoxylem vessels. (c) Micrograph of metaxylem reticulate vessels from macerated wood.*

or through unlignified portions of the cell wall. The walls also have high tensile strength, being lignified, which is another important feature because it prevents tubes collapsing when conducting water under tension (section 14.4).

The second main function of xylem, namely support, is also fulfilled by the collection of lignified tubes. In the primary plant body the distribution of xylem in the roots is central, helping to withstand the tugging strains of the aerial parts as they bend or lean over. In the stems the vascular bundles are arranged either peripherally in a ring, as in dicotyledons, or scattered, as in monocotyledons, so that in both cases separate rods of xylem run through the stem and provide some support. The supporting function becomes much more important if secondary growth takes place. During this process extensive growth of secondary xylem occurs which supports the large structure of trees and shrubs, taking over from collenchyma and sclerenchyma as the chief mechanical tissue. The nature

and extent of the thickness is modified to some extent by the stresses received by the growing plant, so that reinforcement growth can occur and give maximum support.

Xylem parenchyma

Xylem parenchyma occurs in both primary and secondary xylem but it is more extensive and assumes greater importance in the latter. It has thin cellulose cell walls and living contents, as is typical of parenchyma.

Two systems of parenchyma exist in secondary xylem, derived from meristematic cells called ray initials and fusiform initials, as described in chapter 21. The ray parenchyma is the more extensive. It forms radial sheets of tissue called **medullary rays** which maintain a living link through the wood between the pith and cortex. Its functions include food storage, deposition of tannins, crystals and so on, radial transport of food and water, and gaseous exchange through the intercellular spaces.

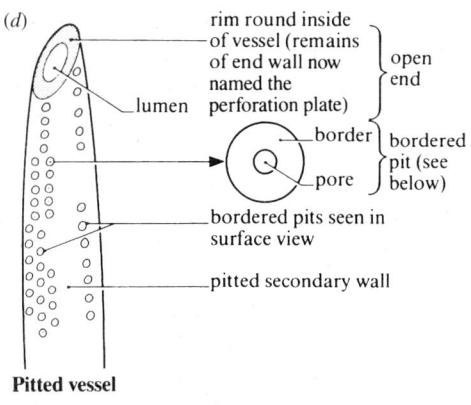

(d)

rim round inside
of vessel (remains
of end wall now
named the
perforation plate)
} open end

lumen

border } bordered pit (see below)

pore

bordered pits seen in
surface view

pitted secondary wall

Pitted vessel

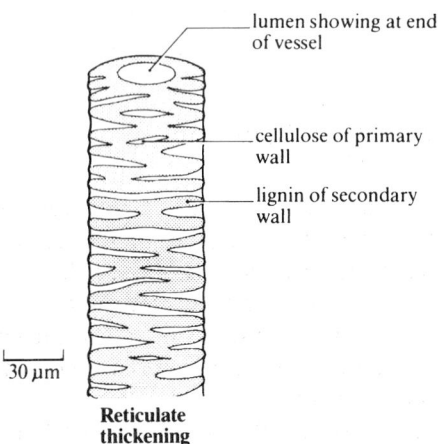

lumen showing at end
of vessel

cellulose of primary
wall

lignin of secondary
wall

30 µm

**Reticulate
thickening**

Size is very variable; the longest are several
metres in length, though commonly several
centimetres long.

Scalariform thickening is similar to reticulate but with fewer
interconnections between the bars of thickening. It is less
commonly seen. It usually grades into reticulate thickening by
progressive lignification

Fig 6.12 *(cont). (d) Pitted and reticulate metaxylem
vessels. (e) Micrograph of metaxylem pitted vessel from
macerated wood. (f) Scanning electron micrograph of
metaxylem vessels (×18 000). Appearance of these
vessels in TS will vary according to which part of the
vessel is sectioned as indicated in the diagram of
extreme left vessel in part (a). (g) TS bordered pit to
show structure.*

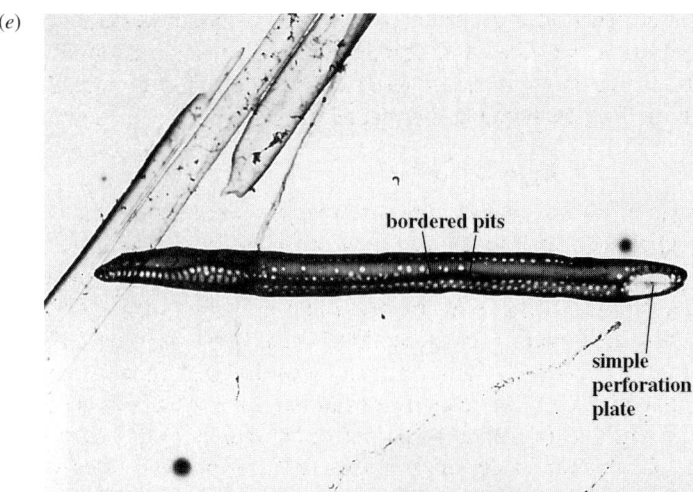

(e)

bordered pits

simple
perforation
plate

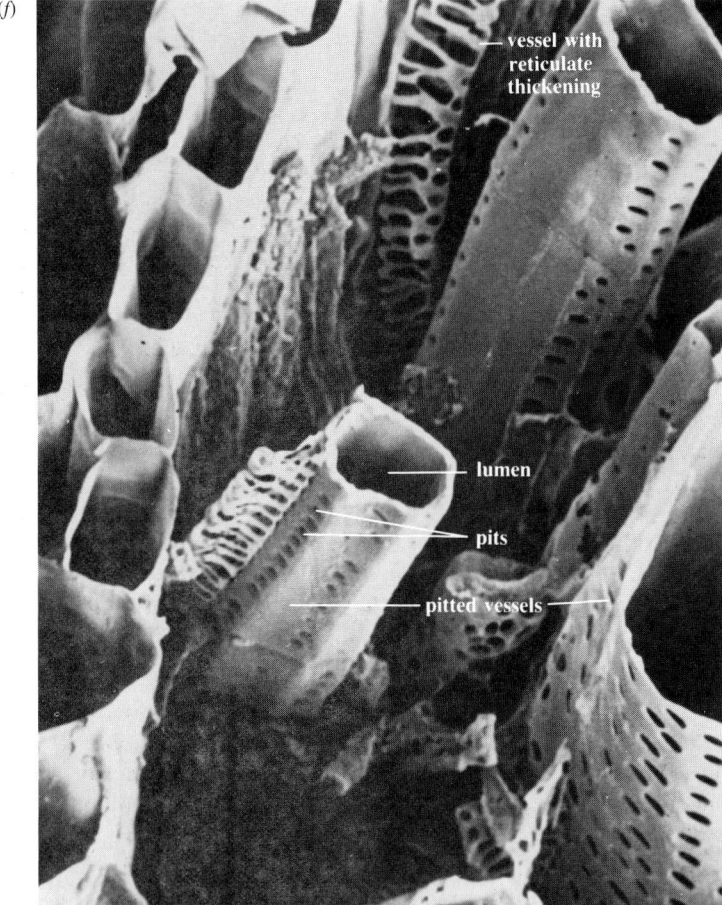

(f)

vessel with
reticulate
thickening

lumen

pits

pitted vessels

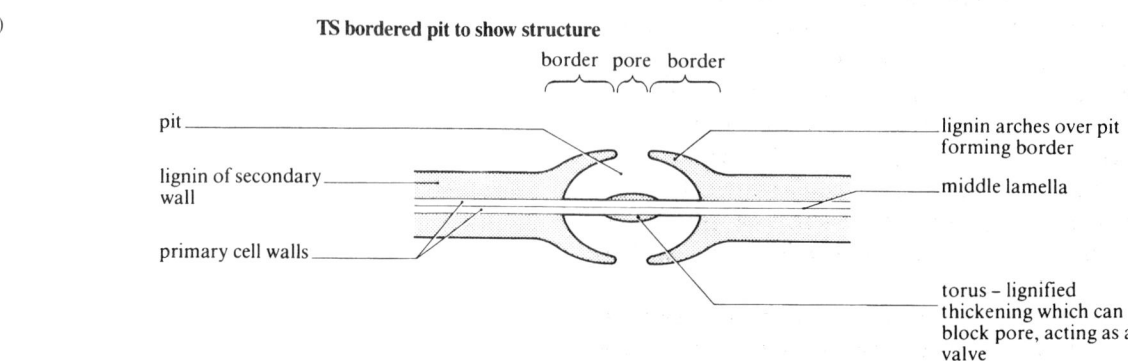

(g)

TS bordered pit to show structure

border pore border

pit

lignin of secondary
wall

primary cell walls

lignin arches over pit
forming border

middle lamella

torus – lignified
thickening which can
block pore, acting as a
valve

Fusiform initials normally give rise to xylem vessels or phloem sieve tubes and companion cells, but occasionally they give rise to parenchyma cells. These form vertical rows of parenchyma in the secondary xylem.

Xylem fibres

Xylem fibres, like xylem vessels, are thought to have originated from tracheids. They are shorter and narrower than tracheids and have much thicker walls, but they have pits similar to those in tracheids and are often difficult to distinguish from them in section because intermediate cell types occur. Xylem fibres closely resemble the sclerenchyma fibres already described, having overlapping end walls. Since they do not conduct water they can have much thicker walls and narrower lumens than xylem vessels and are therefore stronger and confer additional mechanical strength to the xylem.

6.2.2 Phloem

Phloem resembles xylem in possessing tubular structures modified for translocation. However, the tubes are composed of living cells with cytoplasm and have no mechanical function. There are five cell types in the phloem, namely sieve tube elements, companion cells, parenchyma, fibres and sclereids.

Sieve tubes and companion cells

Sieve tubes are the long tube-like structures that translocate solutions of organic solutes like sucrose throughout the plant. They are formed by the end-to-end fusion of cells called **sieve tube elements** or **sieve elements**. Rows of these cells can be seen developing from the procambial strands of apical meristems where primary phloem develops, together with primary xylem, in vascular bundles.

The first phloem formed is called **protophloem** and, like protoxylem, it is produced in the zone of elongation of the growing root or stem. As the tissues around it grow and elongate, it becomes stretched and much of it eventually collapses and becomes non-functional. Meanwhile, however, more phloem continues to be produced and the phloem that matures after elongation has ceased is called **metaphloem**.

Sieve tube elements have a very distinctive structure. Their walls are made of cellulose and pectic substances, like parenchyma cells, but their nuclei degenerate and are lost as they mature and the cytoplasm becomes confined to a thin layer around the periphery of the cell. Although they lack nuclei, the sieve elements remain living but are dependent on the adjacent companion cells which develop from the same original meristematic cell. The two cells together form a functional unit, the companion cell having dense, very active cytoplasm. The detailed structure of the cells is revealed by the electron microscope and is described in chapter 13.

A conspicuous and characteristic feature of sieve tubes that is visible in the light microscope is the **sieve plate**.

This is derived from the two adjoining end walls of neighbouring sieve elements. Originally plasmodesmata run through the walls but the canals enlarge to form pores, making the walls look like a sieve and allowing a flow of solution from one element to the next. Thus sieve tubes are spanned at intervals by sieve plates that mark successive sieve elements. The structure of sieve tubes, companion cells and phloem parenchyma as seen with the electron microscope is shown in fig 6.13.

Secondary phloem, which develops from the vascular cambium like secondary xylem, appears similar in structure to primary phloem except that it is crossed by bands of lignified fibres and medullary rays of parenchyma (chapter 22). It is much less extensive than secondary xylem and is constantly being replaced as described in chapter 22.

Phloem parenchyma, fibres and sclereids

Phloem parenchyma and fibres are found in dicotyledons but not in monocotyledons. Phloem parenchyma has the same structure as parenchyma elsewhere, though the cells are generally elongated. In secondary phloem, parenchyma occurs in medullary rays and vertical strands as already described for xylem parenchyma. Phloem parenchyma and xylem parenchyma have the same functions.

Phloem fibres are exactly similar to the sclerenchyma fibres already described. They occur occasionally in the primary phloem, but more frequently in the secondary phloem of dicotyledons. In secondary phloem they form vertically running bands of cells. Since the secondary phloem is subject to stretching as growth continues, the sclerenchyma probably helps to resist this pressure.

Sclereids occur frequently in phloem, especially in older phloem.

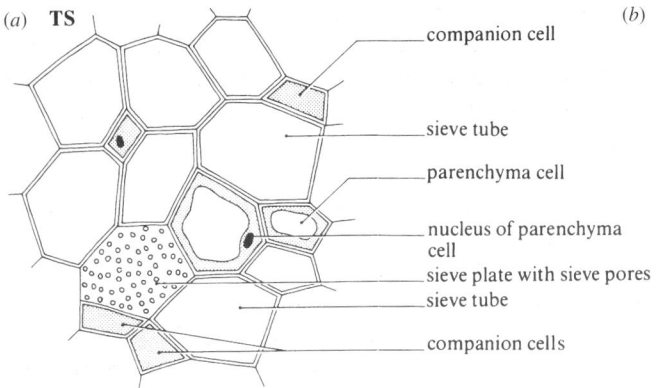

(a) **TS**

companion cell

sieve tube

parenchyma cell

nucleus of parenchyma cell

sieve plate with sieve pores

sieve tube

companion cells

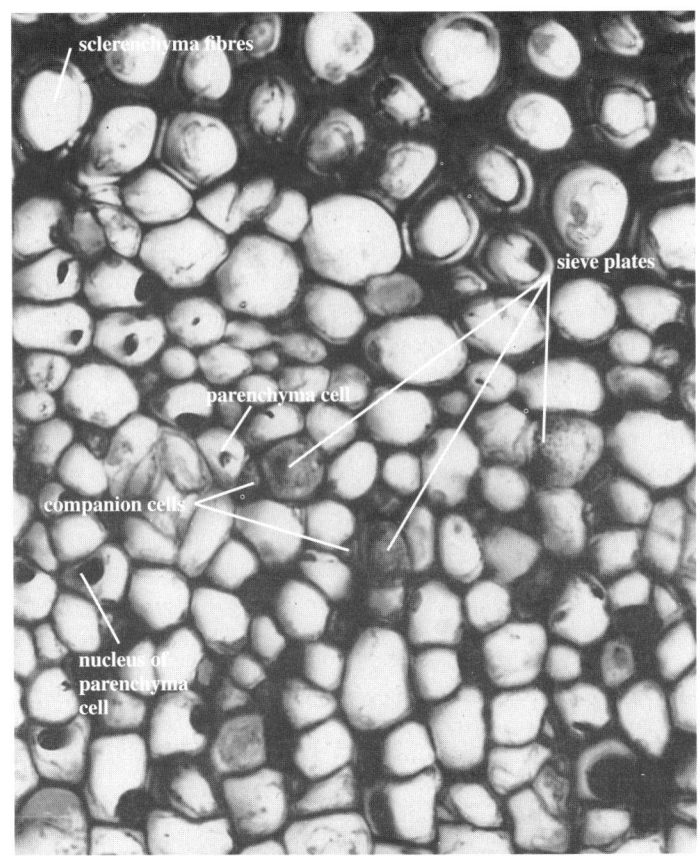

(b)

sclerenchyma fibres

sieve plates

parenchyma cell

companion cells

nucleus of parenchyma cell

Fig 6.13 *Structure of phloem.* (a) *Diagram of TS.* (b) *Micrograph of TS of primary phloem of* Helianthus *stem* (×450). (c) *Diagram of LS.* (d) *Micrograph of LS of primary phloem of* Cucurbita *stem* (×432).

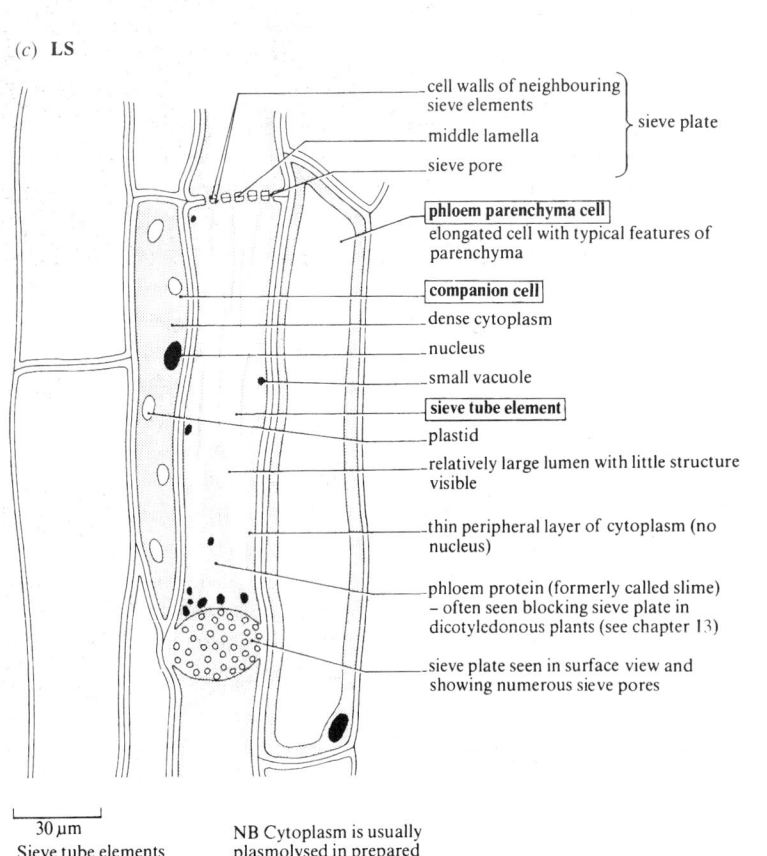

(c) **LS**

cell walls of neighbouring sieve elements

middle lamella } sieve plate

sieve pore

phloem parenchyma cell
elongated cell with typical features of parenchyma

companion cell

dense cytoplasm

nucleus

small vacuole

sieve tube element

plastid

relatively large lumen with little structure visible

thin peripheral layer of cytoplasm (no nucleus)

phloem protein (formerly called slime) – often seen blocking sieve plate in dicotyledonous plants (see chapter 13)

sieve plate seen in surface view and showing numerous sieve pores

30 μm

Sieve tube elements usually longer than shown

NB Cytoplasm is usually plasmolysed in prepared material

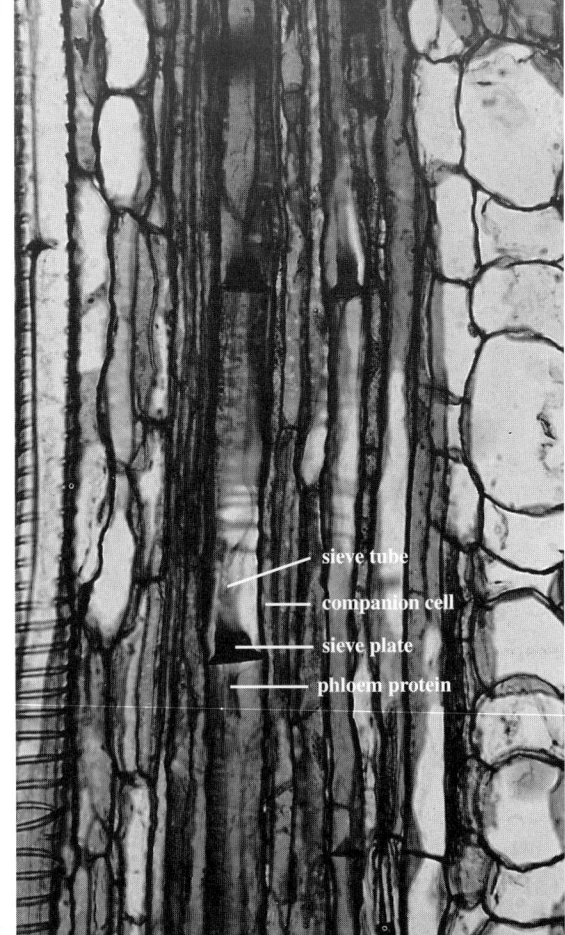

(d)

sieve tube

companion cell

sieve plate

phloem protein

6.3 Animal epithelial tissue

Epithelial tissue is arranged in single or multilayered sheets and covers the internal and external **surfaces** of the body of an organism.

Epithelial cells are held together by small amounts of a carbohydrate-based cementing substance and by special junctions between cells. The bottom layer of cells rests on a **basement membrane** composed of a network of fibres, which include collagen, in a matrix. (The term membrane here should not be confused with the cell membranes discussed in chapter 5 – the term simply means a thin layer.) It is not a barrier to diffusion. As epithelial cells are not supplied with blood vessels, they rely on diffusion of oxygen and nutrients from lymph vessels which run through nearby intercellular spaces. Nerve endings may occur in the epithelium.

Epithelial tissue functions to protect underlying structures from injury through abrasion or pressure, and from infection. Stress is combated by the tissue becoming thickened and keratinised, and where cells are worn off due to constant friction the epithelium shows a very rapid rate of cell division so that lost cells are quickly replaced. The free surface of the epithelium often has a specialised structure and may be absorptive, secretory or excretory in function, or bear sensory cells and nerve endings specialised for reception of stimuli.

Epithelial tissues are classified according to the number of cell layers and the shape of the individual cells, as shown in table 6.2. In many areas of the body the different cell types intermix and the epithelia cannot be classified into distinct types.

6.3.1 Simple epithelia

Squamous epithelium

The cells are thin and flattened. They are so thin that the nucleus causes a bulge (fig 6.14). The edges of squamous

Table 6.2 Classification of epithelial tissues.

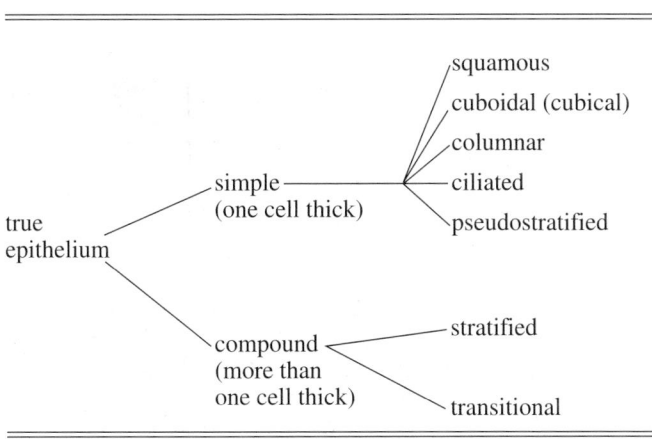

(c)

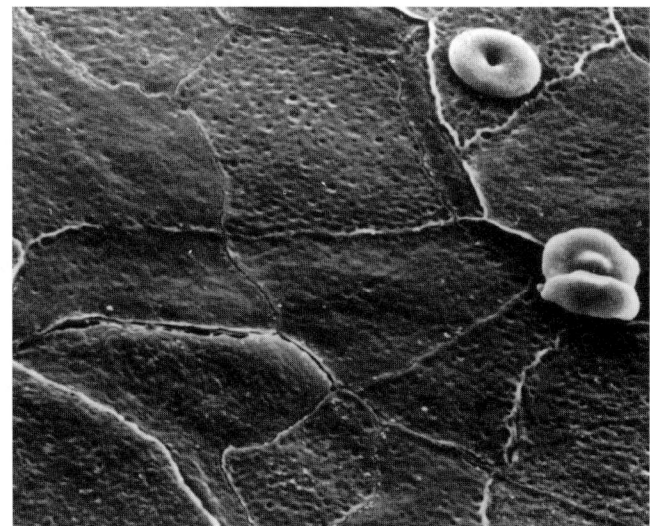

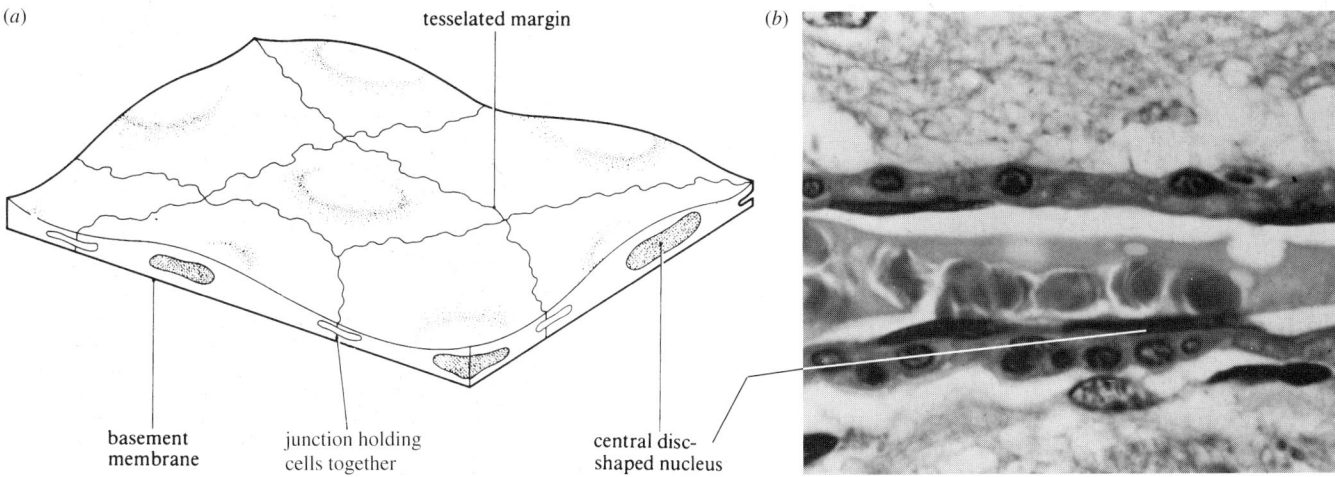

(a)

tesselated margin

basement membrane

junction holding cells together

central disc-shaped nucleus

(b)

Fig 6.14 *Simple squamous epithelium: (a) diagram; (b) photomicrograph (small blood vessel); (c) electron micrograph.*

cells are irregular as can be seen clearly in surface view. There are special junctions between neighbouring cells which help to bind them firmly together. Squamous epithelium occurs in areas such as the renal capsules of the kidney, the alveoli of the lungs and the blood capillary walls, where its thinness permits diffusion of materials through it. In blood vessels it is referred to as the **endothelium** (*endo*, inside). It also provides smooth linings to hollow structures such as blood vessels and the chambers of the heart, where it allows the relatively friction-free passage of fluids through them.

Cuboidal epithelium

This is the least specialised of all epithelia. The cells are roughly cube-shaped and possess a central spherical nucleus (fig 6.15). When viewed from the surface the cells are either pentagonal or hexagonal in outline. They form the lining of many ducts, such as the salivary and pancreatic ducts, and line the proximal and distal convoluted tubules and collecting ducts of the kidney where they are non-secretory. Cuboidal epithelium in other parts of the body is secretory and is found in many glands such as the salivary, sweat and thyroid glands.

Columnar epithelium

These cells are tall and quite narrow, thus providing more cytoplasm per unit area of epithelium (fig 6.16). Each cell possesses a nucleus situated at its basal end. Goblet cells, which secrete mucus, are often interspersed among the epithelial cells and the epithelium may be secretory and/or absorptive in function. There is frequently a conspicuous striated border or brush border of **microvilli** at the free surface end of each cell. This increases the surface area of the cell for absorption and secretion. Columnar epithelium lines the stomach, where mucus secreted by goblet cells protects the stomach lining from the acidic contents of the stomach and from digestion by enzymes. It also lines the intestine where mucus again protects it from self-digestion and at the same time lubricates the passage of food. In the small intestine digested food is absorbed through the epithelium into the bloodstream. Columnar epithelium lines and protects many kidney ducts, and is a component of the thyroid gland.

Ciliated epithelium

Cells of this tissue are usually columnar in shape but bear numerous cilia at their free surfaces (fig 6.17). They are always associated with mucus-secreting goblet cells, producing fluids in which the cilia set up currents. Ciliated epithelium lines the insides of the oviducts, ventricles of the brain, the spinal canal and the respiratory passages (trachea, bronchi and bronchioles), where it serves to move materials from one location to another. In the respiratory tract, for example, cilia waft mucus up to the throat for swallowing. The mucus traps bacteria, dust and other small particles, preventing it from reaching the lungs.

(a)

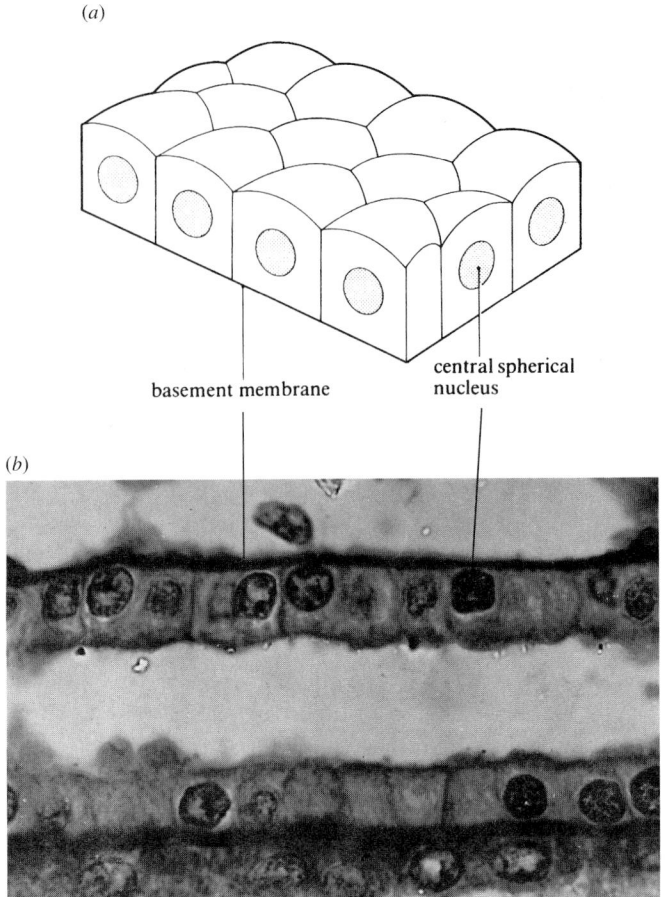

basement membrane   central spherical nucleus

(b)

(c)

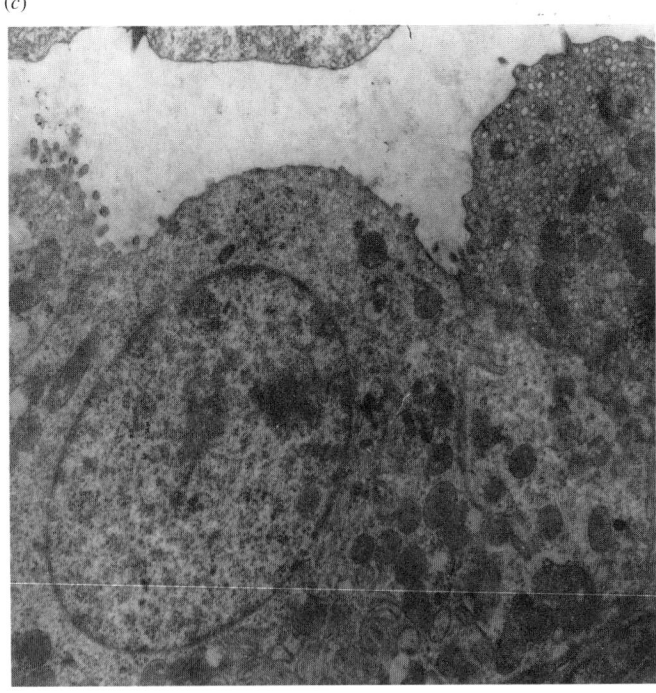

Fig 6.15 *Cuboidal epithelium: (a) diagram;*
(b) photomicrograph (kidney); (c) electron micrograph.

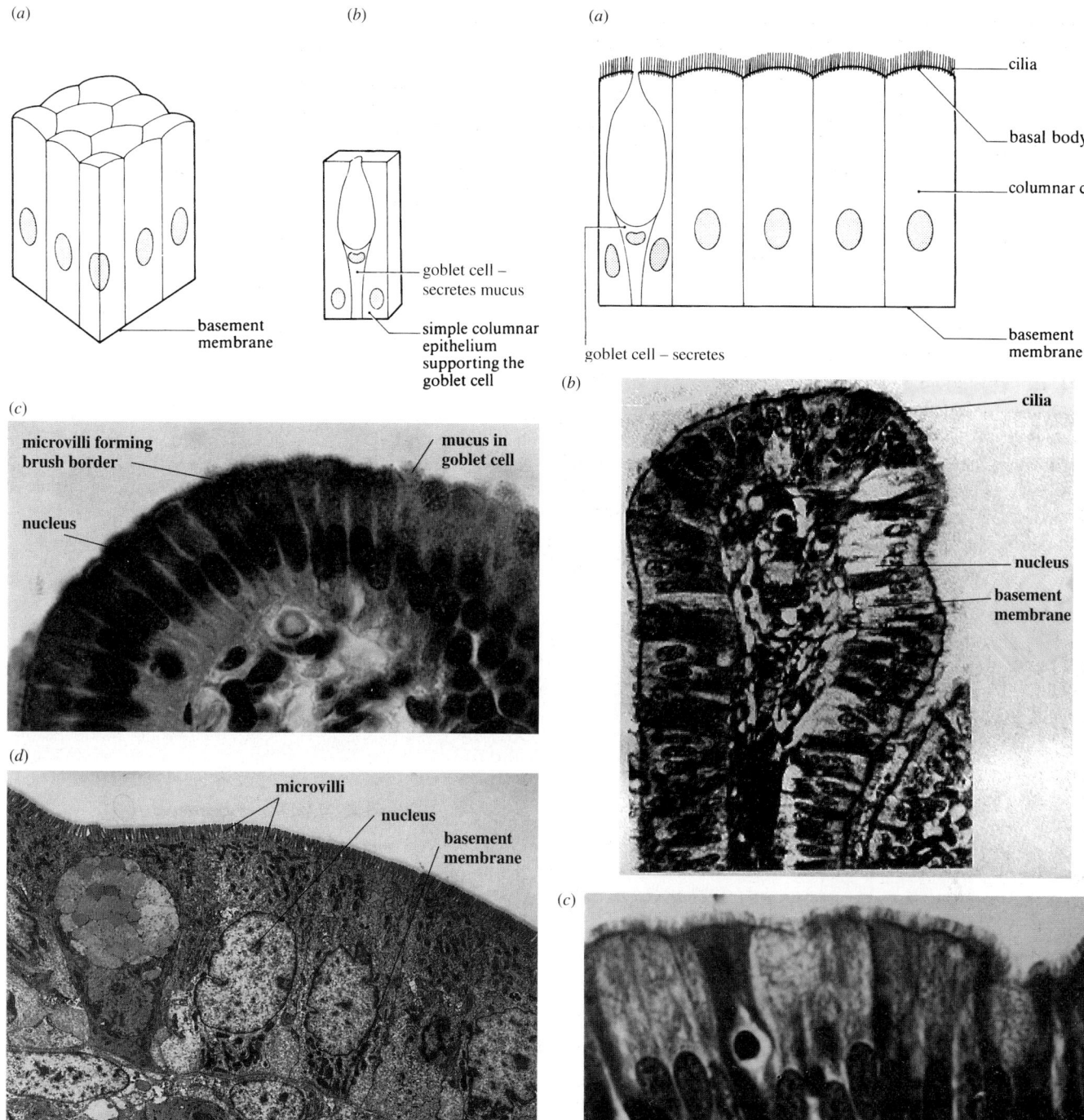

(a)

basement
membrane

(b)

goblet cell –
secretes mucus

simple columnar
epithelium
supporting the
goblet cell

(c)

microvilli forming
brush border

mucus in
goblet cell

nucleus

(d)

microvilli

nucleus

basement
membrane

Fig 6.16 (a) *Columnar epithelium; (b) showing goblet cell;
(c) photomicrograph (ileum); (d) electron micrograph
(ileum).*

(a)

cilia

basal body

columnar cell

basement
membrane

goblet cell – secretes

(b)

cilia

nucleus

basement
membrane

(c)

nucleus

Fig 6.17 *Ciliated columnar epithelium: (a) diagram;
(b) photomicrograph (oviduct); (c) photomicrograph
(trachea).*

185

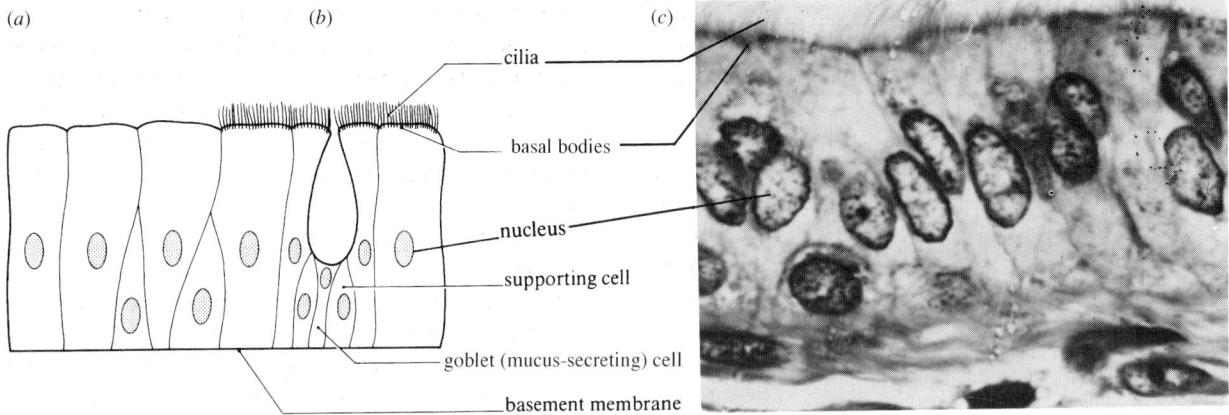

cilia

basal bodies

nucleus

supporting cell

goblet (mucus-secreting) cell

basement membrane

Fig 6.18 *Pseudostratified epithelium:* (a) *columnar;* (b) *ciliated;* (c) *photomicrograph of respiratory, ciliated epithelium;* (d) *scanning electron micrograph of cilia.*

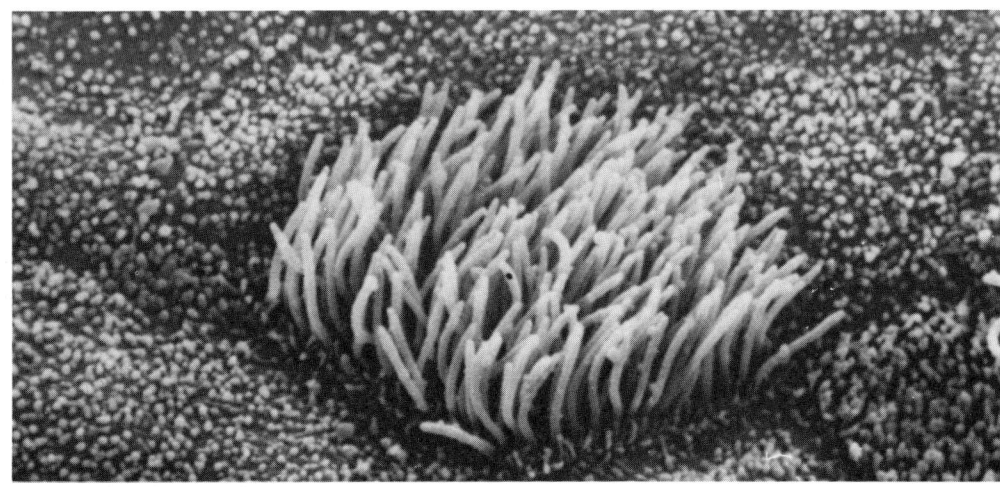

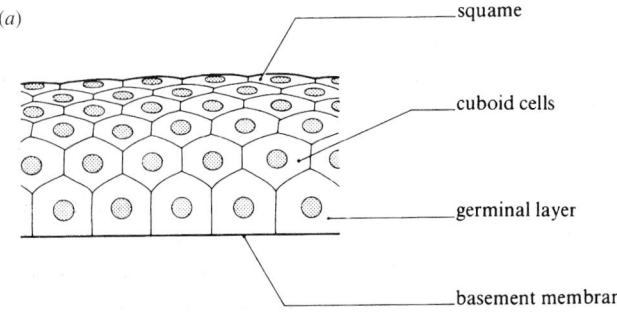

squame

cuboid cells

germinal layer

basement membrane

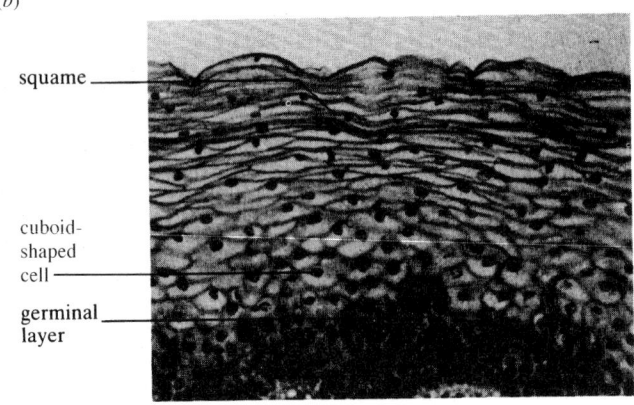

squame

cuboid-shaped cell

germinal layer

Fig 6.19 *Stratified squamous epithelium:* (a) *diagram;* (b) *photomicrograph (vagina).*

Pseudostratified epithelium

When viewed in section the nuclei of this type of epithelium appear to be at several different levels because not all the cells reach the free surface (fig 6.18). Nevertheless the epithelium is still only one layer of cells thick with each cell attached to the basement membrane. This epithelium is found lining the urinary tract and the respiratory passages (trachea, bronchi and bronchioles, where it is ciliated and columnar).

6.3.2   Compound epithelia

Stratified epithelium

This tissue is made up of a number of layers of cells. It is therefore thicker than simple epithelium and forms a relatively tough, impervious barrier. The cells are formed by mitotic divisions of a germinal layer which rests on the basement membrane (fig 6.19). The first-formed cells are cuboid in shape, but as they are pushed outwards towards the free surface of the tissue they become flattened. In this condition the cells are called **squames**. They may remain uncornified, as in the oesophagus, where the epithelium protects the underlying tissues against mechanical damage by friction with food just swallowed. In other areas of the body the squames may be transformed into a dead horny layer of **keratin** which eventually flakes away. In this condition the epithelium is said to be **cornified**, and is found in particular abundance on external skin surfaces, lining the buccal cavity (mouth) and the vagina, where it affords protection against abrasion.

According to the shape of the cells which make up the stratified epithelium, it may be termed stratified squamous (located in parts of the oesophagus), stratified cuboidal (in the sweat gland ducts), stratified columnar (in the mammary gland ducts), and stratified transitional (in the bladder).

Transitional epithelium

This is often regarded as a modified type of stratified epithelium. It consists of 3–4 layers of cells all of similar size and shape except at the free surface where they are more flattened (fig 6.20). The surface cells do not slough off, and all cells are able to modify their shape when placed under differing conditions. This property is important in locations where structures are subjected to considerable stretching, such as the bladder, ureter and the pelvic region of the kidney. The thickness of the tissue also prevents urine escaping into the surrounding tissues.

6.3.3   Glandular epithelia

Amongst the epithelial cells there may be individual glandular cells, such as the **goblet cells**, or aggregates of glandular cells forming a **multicellular gland**. An epithelium containing many goblet cells is called a mucous membrane.

6.4   Animal connective tissue

Connective tissue is the major **supporting tissue** of the body. It includes the skeletal tissues, bone and cartilage, and in addition it binds other tissues together. Connective tissue also forms sheaths like bags around the organs of the body, separating them so that they do not interfere with each other's activities, as well as surrounding and protecting blood vessels and nerves where they enter or leave organs. Connective tissue is a composite material made up of a variety of cells. It contains several types of **fibre** which are non-living products of the cells, and a fluid or semi-fluid background material or **matrix** between the cells.

The cells are usually widely separated from each other. An extensive blood supply runs through the tissue in some parts of the body, as in the dermis of the skin, but this is primarily concerned with supplying other structures, such as epithelium, with oxygen and nutrients rather than the connective tissue itself. Connective tissue may be subdivided into a number of types as indicated in table 6.3.

This tissue fulfils many functions other than packing and binding other structures together, such as providing protection against wounding or bacterial invasion (areolar tissue), insulation of the body against heat loss (adipose tissue), providing a supportive framework for the body (cartilage and bone) and producing blood cells.

6.4.1   Areolar, fibrous connective and adipose tissues

Areolar tissue is shown in fig 6.21, fibrous connective tissue in figs 6.22 and 6.23, and adipose tissue in fig 6.24.

6.4.2   Skeletal tissues

Cartilage

Cartilage is a connective tissue consisting of cells embedded in a matrix of **chondrin**. The matrix is deposited by cells called **chondroblasts** and possesses many fine fibrils mostly made up of collagen. Eventually the chondroblasts become enclosed in spaces called **lacunae**. In this condition they are termed **chondrocytes**. The margin of a piece of cartilage is enclosed by a dense layer of cells and fibrils called the **perichondrium**. From here new chondroblasts are produced, which are constantly added to the internal matrix of the cartilage.

Cartilage is a hard but flexible tissue. It is highly adapted to resist any strains that are placed upon it. The matrix is compressible and elastic and is able to absorb mechanical shocks, such as frequently occur between the surfaces of bones where they meet. The collagen fibrils resist any tension which may be imposed on the tissue.

Three types of cartilage are recognisable. For each type the organic components of the matrix are quite distinct.

Hyaline cartilage (fig 6.25). 'Hyaline' means glassy or shiny. The matrix is a semi-transparent material through which fine collagen fibrils run. The chondrocytes near the periphery are flattened in shape, whereas those situated internally are angular. Each chondrocyte is contained in a space called a **lacuna**, and

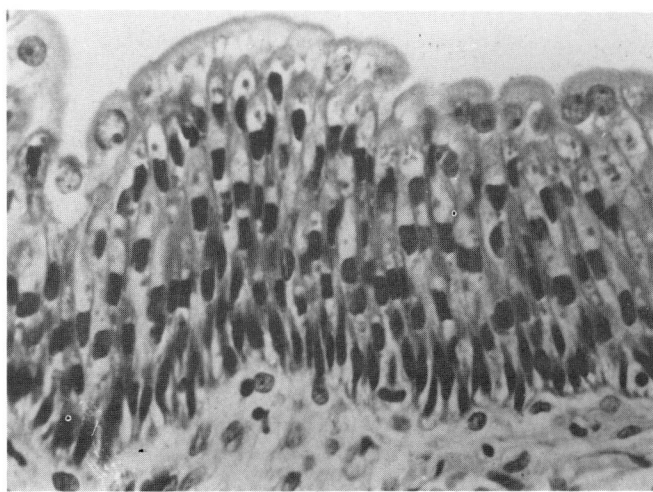

Fig 6.20 *Transitional epithelium (bladder).*

Table 6.3 Types of connective tissue

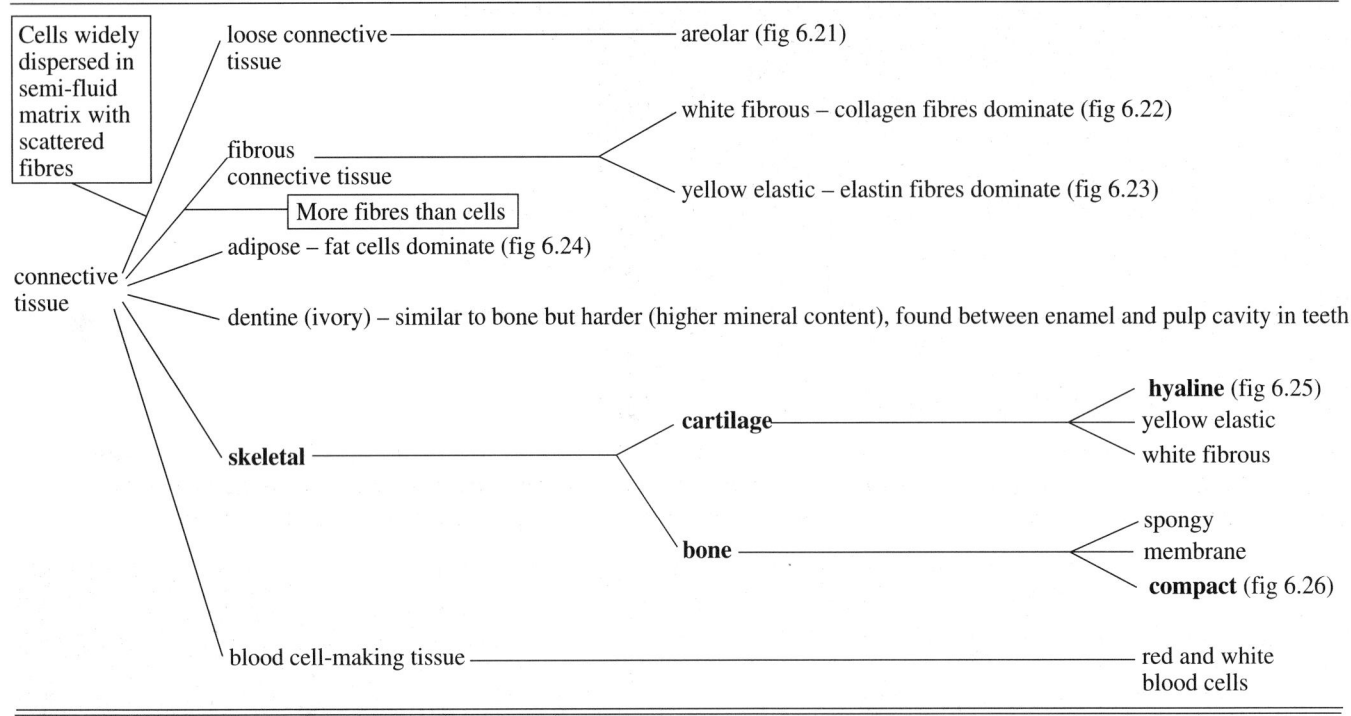

	loose connective tissue	areolar (fig 6.21)
Cells widely dispersed in semi-fluid matrix with scattered fibres	fibrous connective tissue *More fibres than cells*	white fibrous – collagen fibres dominate (fig 6.22)
		yellow elastic – elastin fibres dominate (fig 6.23)

connective tissue

adipose – fat cells dominate (fig 6.24)

dentine (ivory) – similar to bone but harder (higher mineral content), found between enamel and pulp cavity in teeth

skeletal — **cartilage** — **hyaline** (fig 6.25) / yellow elastic / white fibrous

bone — spongy / membrane / **compact** (fig 6.26)

blood cell-making tissue — red and white blood cells

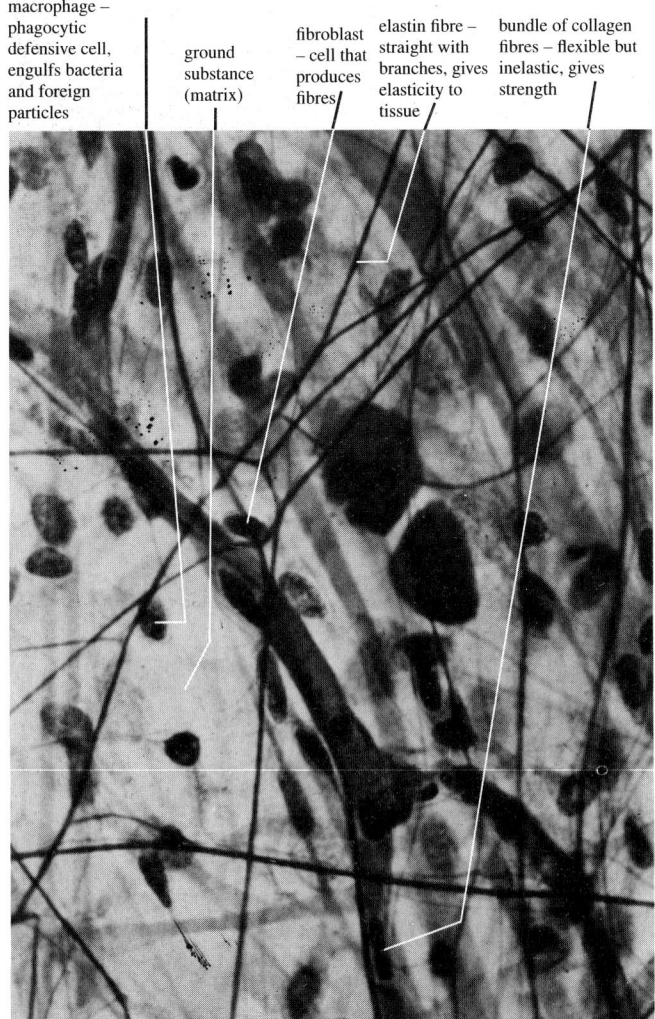

macrophage – phagocytic defensive cell, engulfs bacteria and foreign particles

ground substance (matrix)

fibroblast – cell that produces fibres

elastin fibre – straight with branches, gives elasticity to tissue

bundle of collagen fibres – flexible but inelastic, gives strength

Fig 6.21 *Loose areolar tissue. Cells are widely dispersed. Other cells not shown include fat cells (see adipose tissue), cells involved in response to injury (mast cells), and antibody-producing cells (plasma cells). Areolar tissue is found around all the organs of the body. The fibres are scattered randomly through the matrix.*

each lacuna may enclose one, two, four or eight chondrocytes.

Unlike bone, no processes extend from the lacunae into the matrix, neither are there blood vessels in this area. All exchange of materials between the chondrocytes and the matrix occurs by diffusion.

Hyaline cartilage is an elastic, compressible tissue located at the ends of bones and in the nose. C-shaped rings of hyaline cartilage keep open the air passages of the respiratory system (trachea, bronchi and larger bronchioles). It also forms the skeleton of cartilaginous fish such as sharks, and forms the embryonic skeleton in bony vertebrates.

Yellow elastic cartilage. The matrix is semi-opaque and contains a network of yellow elastic fibres. They confer greater elasticity and flexibility than is found in hyaline cartilage, and permit the tissue to recover its shape quickly after distortion. Examples of its occurrence are in the external ear and the epiglottis.

White fibrous cartilage. This contains large numbers of bundles of densely packed white collagen fibres embedded in the matrix. This provides greater tensile strength than hyaline cartilage, as well as a small degree of

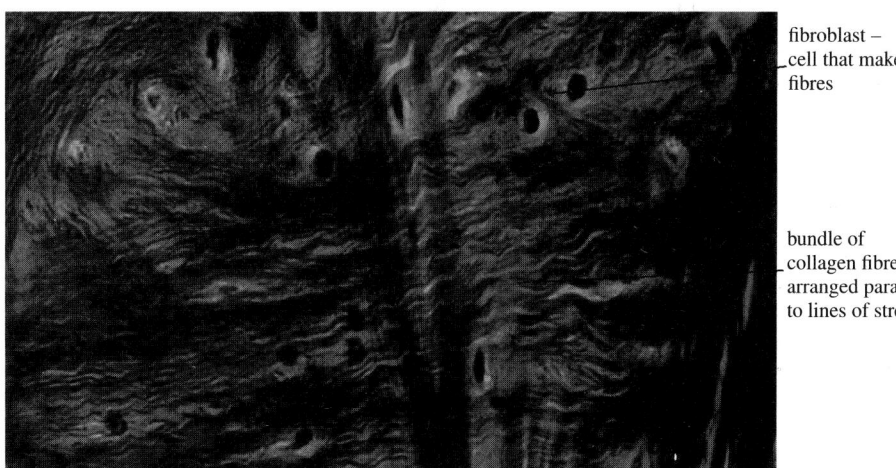

fibroblast – cell that makes the fibres

bundle of collagen fibres arranged parallel to lines of stress

Fig 6.22 *White fibrous tissue. This is composed mainly of parallel bundles of collagen fibres. It is strong and flexible but inelastic. Tendons are almost pure white fibres. They transmit the pull of muscle to bone. The tissue is also found in ligaments, the outer surface of the eye (sclerotic coat and cornea), and other places where strength is required.*

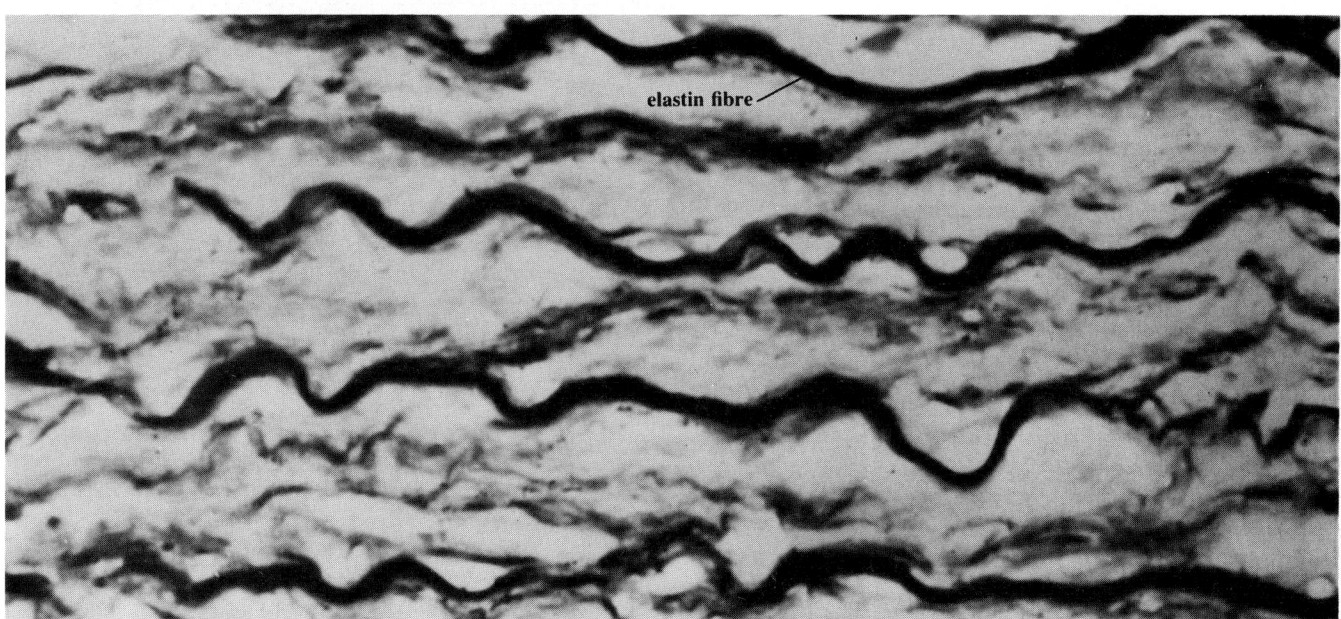

elastin fibre

Fig 6.23 *Yellow elastic tissue contains a network of elastin fibres. Elastin is an elastic protein. This tissue is common in elastic structures such as walls of arteries and alveoli of lungs. Also in ligaments.*

flexibility. White fibrous cartilage is located as discs between adjacent vertebrae (intervertebral discs) where it provides a cushioning effect. It is also found in the symphysis pubis (the region between the two pubic bones of the pelvis) and the ligamentous capsules surrounding joints.

Bone

Bone is the most abundant of all animal skeletal materials, and provides **support**, **protection** and some **metabolic functions**. The cells are embedded in a firm, calcified matrix. About 30% of the matrix is composed of organic material, consisting chiefly of collagen fibres and glycoproteins, whilst 70% is inorganic bone salts. The chief inorganic constituent of bone is needle-like crystals of hydroxyapatite, $Ca_{10}(PO_4)_6(OH)_2$, a form of calcium phosphate. Sodium, magnesium, potassium, chloride, fluoride, hydrogencarbonate and citrate ions are also present in variable amounts.

Bone cells, called **osteoblasts**, are contained in lacunae (spaces) which are present throughout the matrix. They lay down the inorganic components of bone. Fine canals containing cytoplasm connect the lacunae to each other and blood vessels passing through them provide the means by which osteoblasts exchange materials.

The structure of bone is specially designed to withstand the compression strains falling upon it and to resist tension.

Bone resorption and reconstruction processes enable a particular bone to adapt its structure to meet any change in the mechanical requirements of the animal during its

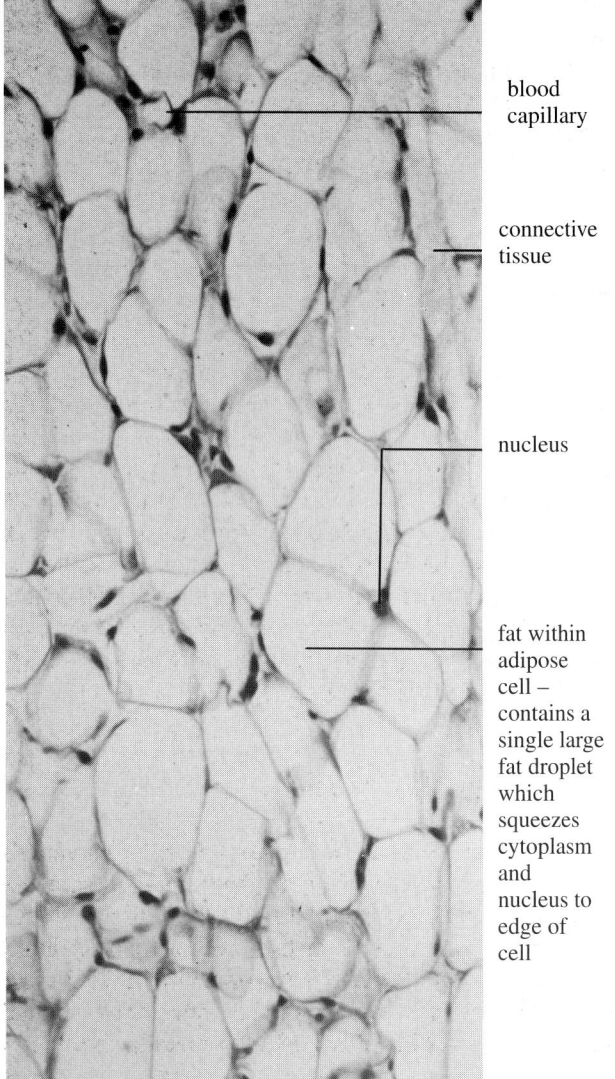

blood capillary

connective tissue

nucleus

fat within adipose cell – contains a single large fat droplet which squeezes cytoplasm and nucleus to edge of cell

Fig 6.24 *Adipose tissue. This tissue is common in the dermis of the skin and around the kidneys and heart. It acts as an energy store, a shock absorber and can insulate against heat loss.*

fibroblast – makes fibres

lacuna (space)

chondrocyte – cell that makes the matrix

collagen fibres

hyaline matrix

Fig 6.25 *Hyaline cartilage.*

development. Calcium and phosphate may be released into the blood as needed, under the control of two hormones, **parathormone** and **calcitonin** (chapter 17).

Compact or dense bone (fig 6.26). Compact bone is used in the growth of long bones (limb bones) and forms the long shaft of the bone between the two swollen ends. A transverse section of compact bone shows it to consist of numerous cylinders, each surrounding a central **Haversian canal**. One such cylinder plus its canal is termed a **Haversian system** or **osteon**. Each cylinder is itself made up of a set of concentric layers called **lamellae** which are cylindrical, an arrangement which increases strength.

Between the lamellae are numerous lacunae (spaces) containing living bone cells called **osteoblasts**. Each cell is capable of bone deposition. As osteoblasts mature they become less active and contain reduced quantities of cell organelles. They are then known as **osteocytes**. If structural changes in the bone are required they are activated and quickly regain the structure of osteoblasts.

Radiating from each lacuna are many fine channels called **canaliculi** containing cytoplasm which may link up with the central Haversian canal, with other lacunae or pass from one lamella to another.

An artery and a vein run through each Haversian canal, and capillaries branch from here and pass via the canaliculi to the lacunae of that particular Haversian system. They allow the passage of nutrients, respiratory gases and metabolic waste towards and away from the cells. A Haversian canal also contains a lymph vessel and nerve fibres. Transverse Haversian canals communicate with the marrow cavity in the centre of the whole bone and also interconnect with the longitudinal Haversian canals. These contain larger blood vessels and are not encircled by concentric lamellae.

The matrix of compact bone is composed of collagen, manufactured by the osteoblasts, and hydroxyapatite together with quantities of magnesium, sodium, carbonates and nitrates. The combination of organic with inorganic material produces a structure of great strength. The lamellae are laid down in a manner that is suited to the

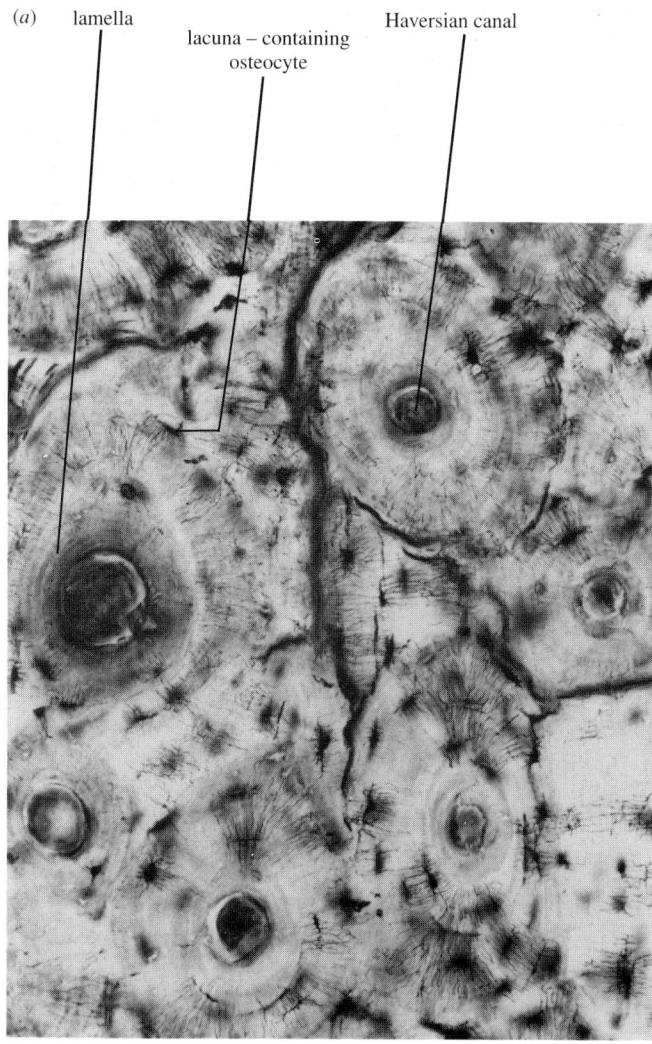

(a) lamella   lacuna – containing osteocyte   Haversian canal

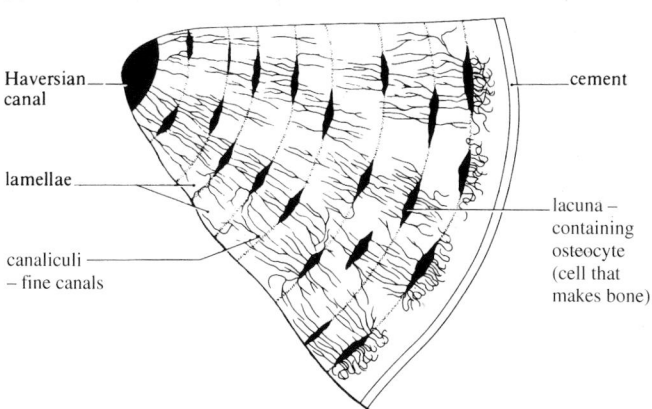

(b)

Haversian canal

lamellae

canaliculi – fine canals

cement

lacuna – containing osteocyte (cell that makes bone)

Fig 6.26 (a) *Part of a transverse section of a long bone.* (b) *TS Haversian system. The system forms a cylinder in three dimensions. The presence of large numbers of lamellae (layers) within each cylinder provides the bone with great strength despite its light weight.*

forces acting upon the bone, and the load that has to carried.

Covering the bone is a layer of dense connective tissue called the **periosteum**. Bundles of collagen fibres from the periosteum pierce the bone, providing an intimate connection between the underlying bone and periosteum and acting as a firm base for tendon insertions. The inner region of the periosteum has blood vessels and forms a layer which contains cells that can develop into osteoblasts.

Spongy bone. Spongy bone consists of a meshwork of thin, interconnecting bony struts called **trabeculae**. Its matrix contains less inorganic material (60–65%) than compact bone. The organic material is primarily composed of collagen fibres. The spaces between the trabeculae are filled with soft marrow tissue.

The trabeculae are orientated in the direction in which the bone is stressed. This enables the bone to withstand tension and compression forces effectively whilst at the same time keeping the weight of the bone to a minimum.

Spongy bone occurs in the embryo, growing organisms, and the swollen ends of long bones.

6.5   Muscle tissue

Muscle tissue makes up 40% of a mammal's body weight. It consists of highly specialised contractile cells or fibres held together by connective tissue. Three types of muscle are present in the body, namely **striated** (voluntary or skeletal), **smooth** (unstriated or involuntary) and **cardiac** (heart) muscle. Further details of striated muscle can be found in chapter 18 and of cardiac muscle in chapter 14.

6.6   Nervous tissue

Nervous tissue contains densely packed nerve cells called **neurones** (or **neurons**), which are specialised for conduction of nerve impulses. Among other cells present are receptor cells and Schwann cells (see below). Nervous tissue is frequently enclosed by connective tissue which contains blood vessels.

6.6.1   Neurones

These are the functional units of the nervous system. Neurones are capable of transmitting electrical impulses, and this provides the means of communication between **receptors**, the cells or organs which receive stimuli, and **effectors**, the tissues or organs which react to stimuli, such as muscles or glands (fig 6.27). Neurones which conduct impulses towards the central nervous system (the brain and spinal cord) are called **sensory neurones**, whilst **motor neurones** conduct impulses away from the central nervous system. **Interneurones** frequently connect

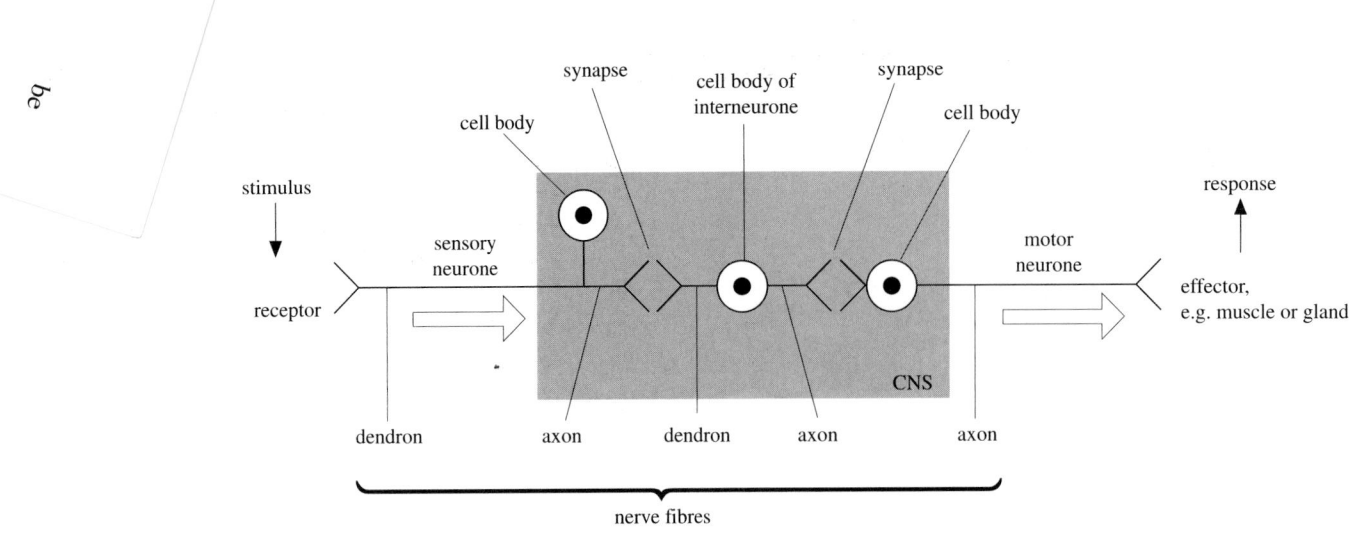

nerve
impulse

CNS   central nervous system (brain and spinal cord)(all cell bodies here)

Fig 6.27 *Simplified diagram of a nervous pathway. Alternative names of the neurones are:*
sensory neurone, *afferent neurone;*
motor neurone, *efferent neurone, effector neurone;*
interneurone, *intermediate neurone, association neurone, internuncial neurone, relay neurone.*
Use only one name for each!

sensory neurones with motor neurones. The structure of these neurones, and their alternative names, is shown in fig 6.28.

Each neurone possesses a **cell body** (fig 6.28), which contains a nucleus, most of the cell's other organelles and a variable number of **nerve fibres** extending from it. **Nissl's granules**, which are groups of ribosomes and rough ER associated with protein synthesis, and Golgi apparatus are present in the cell body (fig 6.29).

Nerve fibres which conduct impulses towards the cell body are called **dendrons** (fig 6.27). They are small, relatively wide, and break up into fine terminal branches called **dendrites** (*dendro*, tree). Nerve fibres which conduct impulses away from the cell body are termed **axons**, they are thinner than dendrites and may be several metres long.

The end of an axon breaks up into many fine branches with swollen endings called **synaptic knobs**. These do not join directly to the next nerve cell in the pathway. Instead, there is a tiny gap across which a chemical called a **neurotransmitter** must pass in order to stimulate the next nerve cell (or effector). The neurotransmitter is released from the synaptic knob in response to a nerve impulse travelling along the axon. The sites of these gaps are called **synapses** (fig 6.27).

Some nerve fibres are completely surrounded and insulated by a fatty **myelin sheath**. This is formed by another type of cell called a **Schwann cell**. The cell surface membrane of the Schwann cell becomes extended and wraps itself like a roll of carpet round and round the nerve fibre (fig 6.30). This extension forms the myelin sheath and is mainly lipid, lacking the protein normally found in membranes. The cytoplasm remains in a region called the **neurilemma** around the myelin sheath. Being lipid, the myelin sheath prevents movement of Na^+ and K^+ ions in and out of the nerve fibre. This movement is needed to conduct nerve impulses, so if the sheath were continuous, nerve impulses could not be transmitted. However, it is interrupted at regular intervals of about 1 mm by **nodes of Ranvier** (fig 6.28). The nodes occur between the Schwann cells, and one Schwann cell nucleus is visible in the sheath between each successive pair of nodes.

Nerve fibres with a myelin sheath are described as **myelinated**, for example spinal nerves. Some nerve fibres are non-myelinated. These lack nodes of Ranvier and are only partially surrounded by Schwann cells. Certain diseases involve destruction of myelin sheaths, notably multiple sclerosis and Tay–Sachs disease.

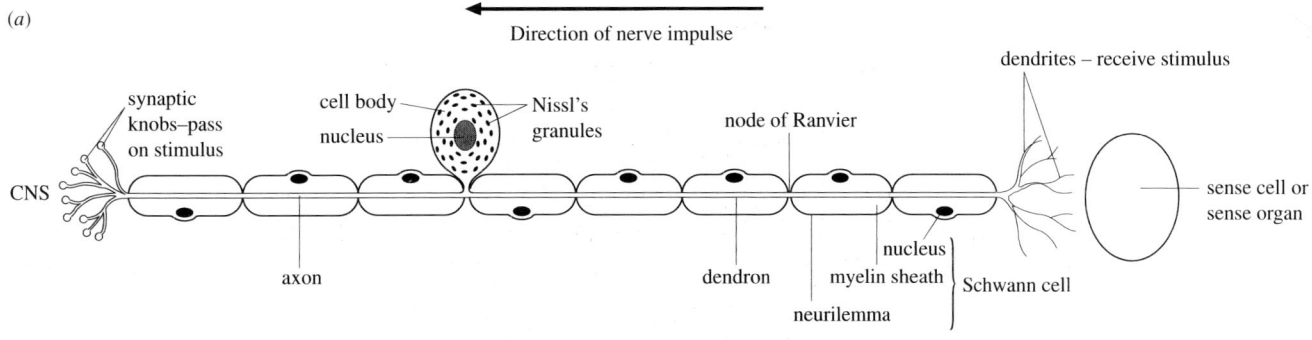

(a)

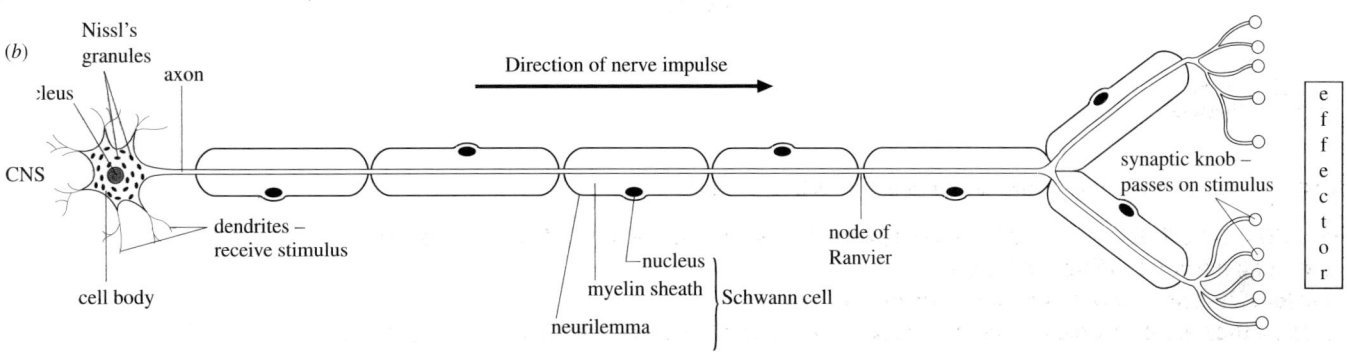

(b)

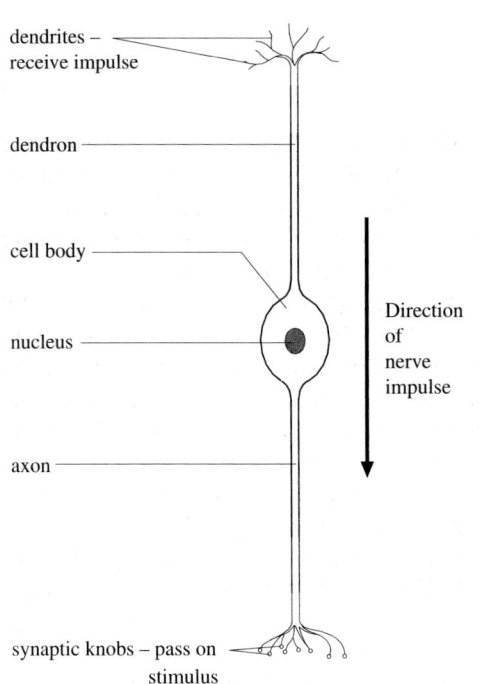

(c)

Fig 6.28 *Diagrams of* (a) *sensory neurone,* (b) *motor neurone,* (c) *interneurone.*

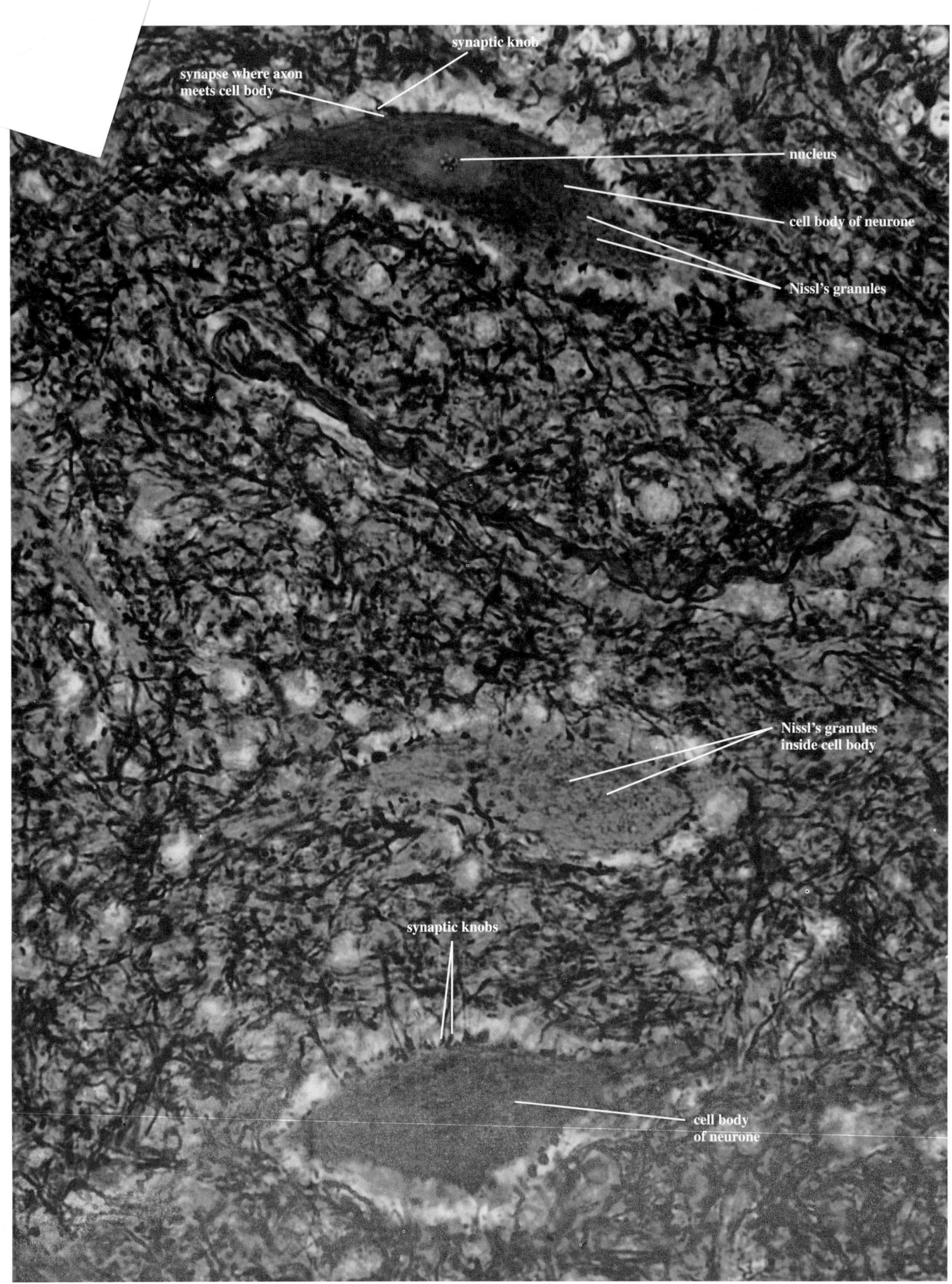

Fig 6.29 *Cell bodies of neurones with synapses and Nissl's granules.*

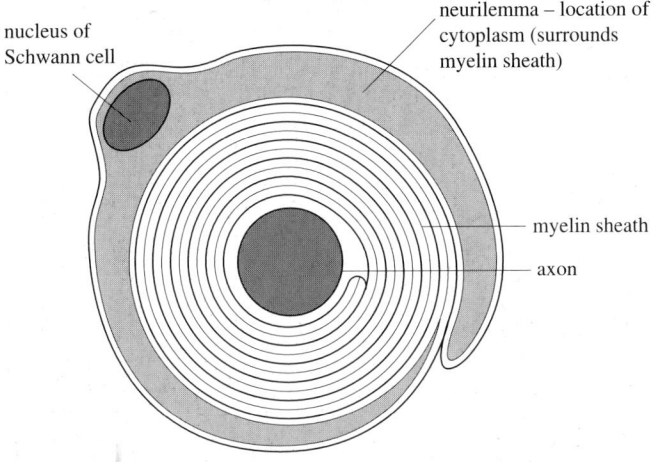

nucleus of Schwann cell

neurilemma – location of cytoplasm (surrounds myelin sheath)

myelin sheath

axon

Fig 6.30 *TS myelinated nerve fibre.*

6.6.2 Nerves

These consist of bundles of nerve fibres in a connective tissue sheath called the **epineurium**. Inward extensions of the epineurium, called the **perineurium**, divide the fibres into smaller bundles, whilst each fibre is itself surrounded by connective tissue called the **endoneurium** (fig 6.31). Nerves are classified according to the direction in which they convey nerve impulses. Sensory or afferent nerves, such as the optic and auditory nerves, convey impulses *to* the central nervous system, whilst efferent or motor nerves conduct impulses *away from* the central nervous system. Mixed nerves convey impulses in both directions (for example all spinal nerves).

The conduction of nervous impulses is discussed in chapter 17.

(*a*)

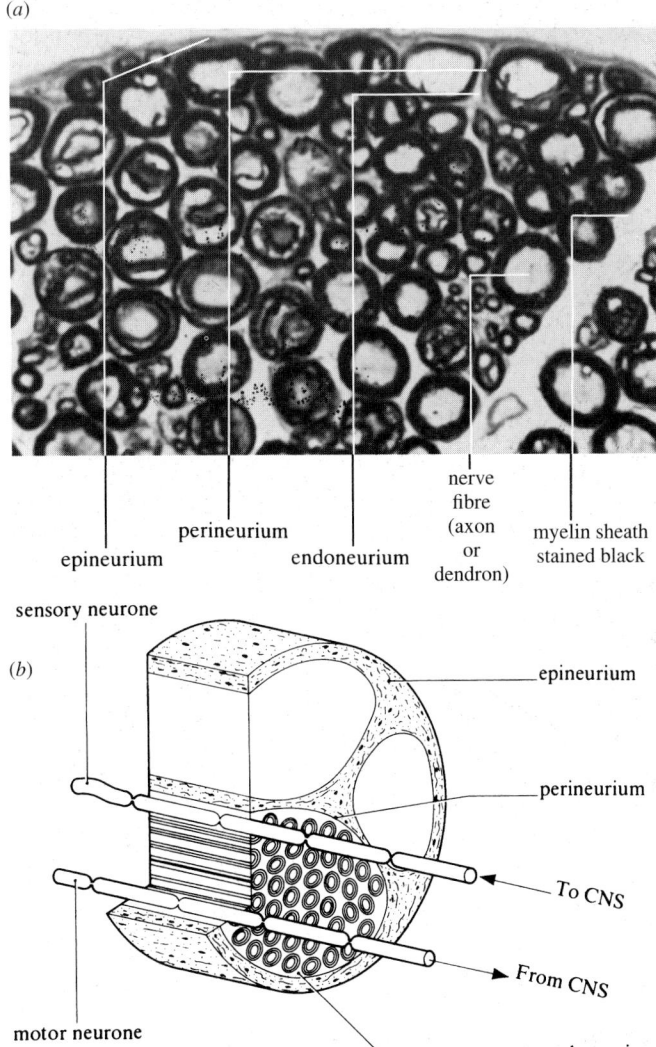

epineurium

perineurium

endoneurium

nerve fibre (axon or dendron)

myelin sheath stained black

sensory neurone

(*b*)

epineurium

perineurium

To CNS

From CNS

motor neurone

endoneurium

Fig 6.31 (a) *TS myelinated nerve,* (b) *diagram of a section of myelinated nerve.*

Chapter Seven

Autotrophic nutrition

Nutrition is the process of *acquiring* energy and materials. This is the theme of chapters 7 and 8. In chapter 9 **respiration** is considered, the process in which organisms *release* energy from the energy-rich compounds acquired by nutrition.

7.1 Why do living organisms need energy?

Energy may be defined as the **capacity to do work**. All living organisms may be regarded as working machines which require a continuous supply of energy in order to keep working, and so to stay alive. Energy can neither be created nor destroyed (**the law of conservation of energy**). It may occur in various forms, such as light, chemical, heat, electrical, mechanical and sound, and energy can be transferred from one form to another. A simple example would be striking a match, where, in the matchhead, chemical energy is transferred to heat, light and sound energy.

Some common examples of the use of energy in living organisms are:

- synthesis of substances for growth and repair, for example protein synthesis;
- active transport of substances into and out of cells against diffusion gradients, for example the sodium–potassium pump (section 5.9.8);
- phagocytosis, pinocytosis, and exocytosis (section 5.9.8);
- electrical transmission of nerve impulses;
- mechanical contraction of muscles and beating of cilia and flagella;
- heat energy released from respiration used to maintain a constant body temperature in birds and mammals;
- bioluminescence, that is the production of light by living organisms such as fireflies, glow-worms and some deep sea animals;
- electrical discharge, as in the electric eel.

The role of ATP as the energy carrier in cells is described in section 9.2.

7.2 Grouping organisms according to their energy and carbon sources

As stated above, nutrition involves acquiring both **energy** and **materials**. Carbon is the most fundamental material required by living organisms (section 3.1). Living organisms can be grouped on the basis of their source of **energy** or source of **carbon**.

Energy source

Despite energy existing in several forms, only two are suitable as energy sources for living organisms, namely **light energy** and **chemical energy**. Organisms using light energy are described as **photosynthetic** or **phototrophic** (*photos*, light; *trophos*, nourishment), while those using chemical energy are described as **chemotrophic**. Phototrophs contain pigments, including some form of chlorophyll, which absorb light energy and convert it to chemical energy.

Carbon source

Organisms which have an inorganic source of carbon, namely carbon dioxide, are described as **autotrophic** (*autos*, self) and those having an organic source of carbon are described as **heterotrophic** (*heteros*, other). Unlike heterotrophs, autotrophs synthesise their own organic requirements from simple inorganic materials.

These categories have already been discussed in section 2.3.4 and are summarised in table 2.3. An important principle that emerges is that chemotrophic organisms are totally dependent on photosynthetic organisms for their energy, and heterotrophic organisms are totally dependent on autotrophic organisms for their carbon.

By far the largest groups are the **photosynthetic organisms**, which include all green plants and algae, and the **chemoheterotrophic organisms**, which include all animals and fungi.

> **7.1** Define photoautotrophic and chemoheterotrophic.

Fig 7.1 illustrates further the relationship between the two main nutritional categories. It also gives a brief overview of how energy flows and carbon is cycled through living organisms and the environment, themes which are important in ecology (chapter 10).

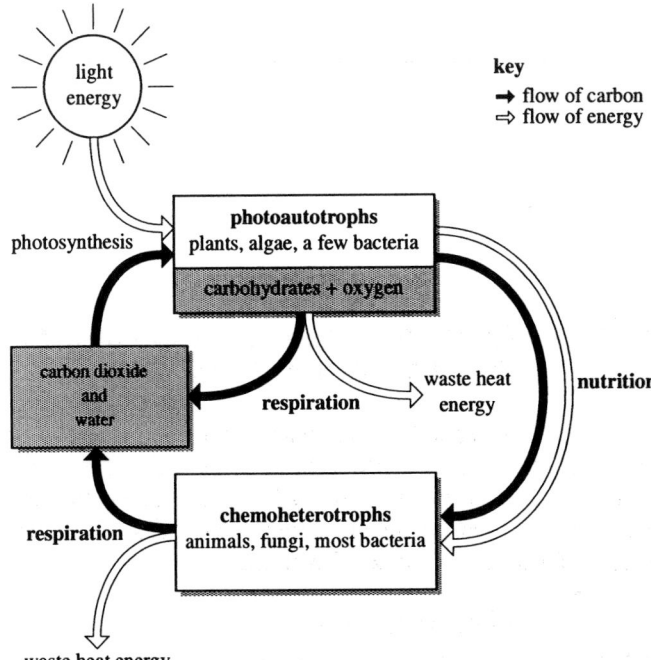

Fig 7.1 *Flow of energy (open arrows) and cycling of carbon (black arrows) through photoautotrophs and chemoheterotrophs, and balance between photosynthesis and respiration. Light energy is converted to chemical energy in photosynthesis and used, together with carbon dioxide and water, in the synthesis of organic materials from inorganic materials. Organic materials are the energy and carbon source for chemoheterotrophs. Energy and carbon dioxide are released again in the process of respiration (carried out by all living organisms). Every energy conversion is accompanied by some loss of energy as heat, which is waste energy.*

7.3   Importance of photosynthesis

Almost all life on Earth depends on photosynthesis, either directly or, as in the case of animals, indirectly. Photosynthesis makes both carbon and energy available to living organisms and produces the oxygen in the atmosphere which is vital for all aerobic forms of life. Humans also depend on photosynthesis for the energy-containing fossil fuels which have developed over millions of years.

Of the total amount of solar radiation intercepted by our planet, about half reaches its surface after absorption, reflection and scattering in the atmosphere. Of this, only about 50% is of the right wavelength to stimulate photosynthesis and, although estimates vary, it is likely that only about 0.2% of this is used in actual plant production (about 0.5% of the energy actually reaching plants). From this small fraction of the available energy virtually all life is sustained. About 40% of all photosynthesis is carried out by tiny algae, known as phytoplankton, which live in the oceans.

7.4   The structure of the leaf

In flowering plants the major photosynthetic organ is the leaf. As with all living organs, structure and function are closely linked. From the equation for photosynthesis

$$CO_2 + H_2O \xrightarrow[\text{chlorophyll}]{\text{sunlight}} (CH_2O)_n + O_2$$

carbon dioxide, water, carbohydrate, oxygen

it can be deduced that first the leaf requires a source of carbon dioxide and water, secondly it must contain chlorophyll and be adapted to receive sunlight, thirdly oxygen will escape as a waste product and finally the useful product, carbohydrate, will have to be exported to other parts of the plant or stored. In its structure the leaf is highly adapted to satisfy these requirements. Fig 7.2 shows the external structure of a leaf. Fig 7.3 shows a labelled photomicrograph of a leaf section which will help you in interpreting sections of dicotyledonous leaves. Fig 7.4 shows high power detail of a single palisade mesophyll cell. Fig 7.5 is a simplified drawing of a vertical section through a dicotyledonous leaf. (Advice on drawing from a light microscope is given in section 5.13.) The epidermises of different leaf types are shown in fig 6.3 and details of stomatal structure and function are dealt with in chapter 14.

The structure and function of different tissues in a dicotyledonous leaf are summarised in table 7.1.

> **7.2**   Make a list of the ways in which the structure of the leaf contributes to its successful functioning.

A final point to note is the arrangement of the leaves for minimal overlapping. Such leaf mosaics are particularly noticeable in some plants, such as ivy.

7.4.1   Chloroplasts

In eukaryotes, photosynthesis takes place in organelles called chloroplasts. They are found in the cytoplasm in numbers varying from one (as in the unicellular alga *Chlorella*) to about 100 (palisade mesophyll cells). They are about 3–10 μm (average 5 μm) in diameter, and so are visible with a light microscope (figs 7.3 and 7.4). Chloroplasts are surrounded by two membranes, which form the **chloroplast envelope**. They always contain **chlorophyll** and **other photosynthetic pigments** located on a system of membranes. The membranes run through a ground substance, or **stroma**. Their detailed structure is revealed by electron microscopy. Figs. 5.11 and 7.4 show the typical appearance of chloroplasts in a leaf mesophyll cell as seen at low power in

Fig 7.2 *External structure of a dicotyledonous leaf.*

Table 7.1 Relationship between structure and function in a dicotyledonous leaf.

Tissue	Structure	Function
Upper and lower epidermis	One cell thick. Flattened cells lacking chloroplasts. External walls covered with a cuticle of cutin (waxy substance). Contains stomata (pores) which are normally confined to, or more numerous in, the lower epidermis. Each stoma is surrounded by a pair of guard cells.	Protective. Cutin is waterproof and protects from desiccation and infection. Stomata are sites of gaseous exchange with the environment. Their size is regulated by guard cells, special epidermal cells containing chloroplasts.
Palisade mesophyll	Column-shaped ('palisade') cells with numerous chloroplasts in a thin layer of cytoplasm.	Main photosynthetic tissue. Chloroplasts may move towards light.
Spongy mesophyll	Irregularly shaped cells fitting together loosely to leave large air spaces.	Photosynthetic, but fewer chloroplasts than palisade cells. Gaseous exchange can occur through the large air spaces via stomata. Stores starch.
Vascular tissue	Extensive finely branching network through the leaf.	Conducts water and mineral salts to the leaf in xylem. Removes products of photosynthesis (mainly sucrose) in phloem. Provides a supporting skeleton to the lamina, aided, by collenchyma of the midrib, turgidity of the mesophyll cells, and sometimes sclerenchyma.

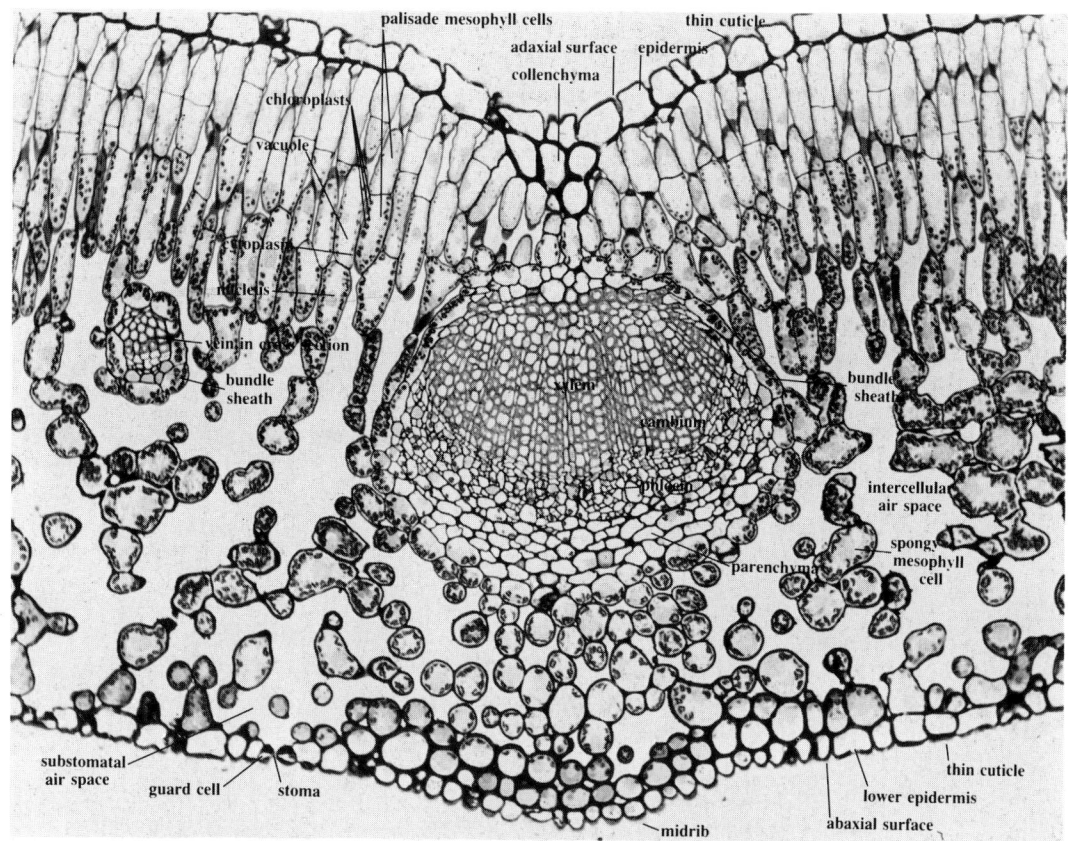

Fig 7.3 *TS lamina and midrib of a privet leaf (*Ligustrum*), a typical dicotyledon.*

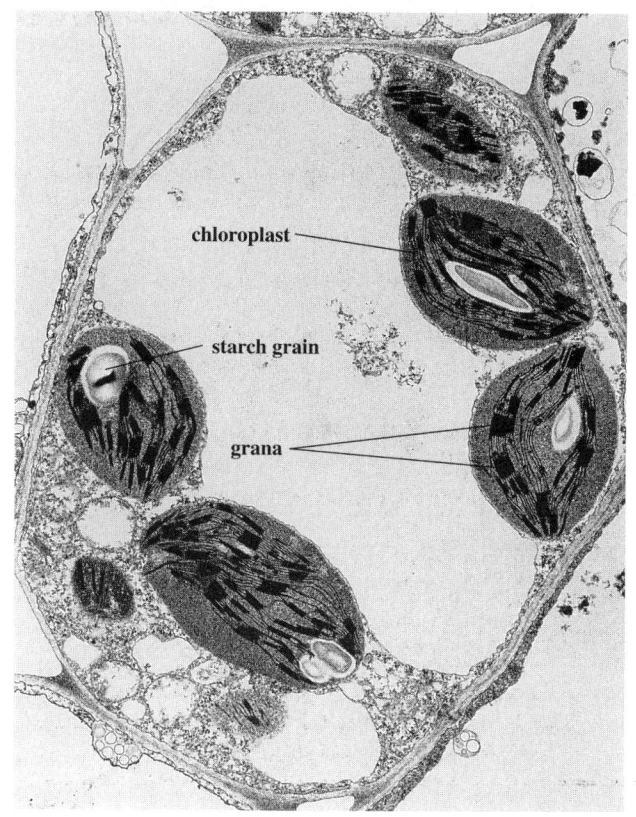

Fig 7.4 *Electron micrograph of a palisade mesophyll cell (x3000).*

the electron microscope. Figs 7.6 and 7.8 show electron micrographs and fig 7.7 a diagram of a chloroplast, illustrating the membrane system. The membrane system is the site of the **light-dependent reactions** in photosynthesis (section 7.6.2). The membranes are covered with chlorophyll and other pigments, enzymes and electron carriers. The system consists of many flattened, fluid-filled sacs called **thylakoids** which form stacks called **grana** at intervals, with lamellae (layers) between the grana. Each granum resembles a pile of coins and the lamellae are often sheet-like (fig 7.8). Grana are just visible under the light microscope as grains.

The stroma is the site of the **light-independent reactions** of photosynthesis (section 7.6.3). The structure is gel-like, containing soluble enzymes, particularly those of the Calvin cycle, and other chemicals such as sugars and organic acids. Excess carbohydrate from photosynthesis is sometimes seen stored as grains of starch. Spherical lipid droplets are often associated with the membranes. They become larger as membranes break down during ageing, presumably accumulating lipids from the membranes.

Protein-synthesising machinery and the endosymbiont theory

An interesting feature of chloroplasts, apart from photosynthesis, is their protein-synthesising machinery. During the 1960s it was shown that both chloroplasts and mitochondria contain DNA and ribosomes. This led to the

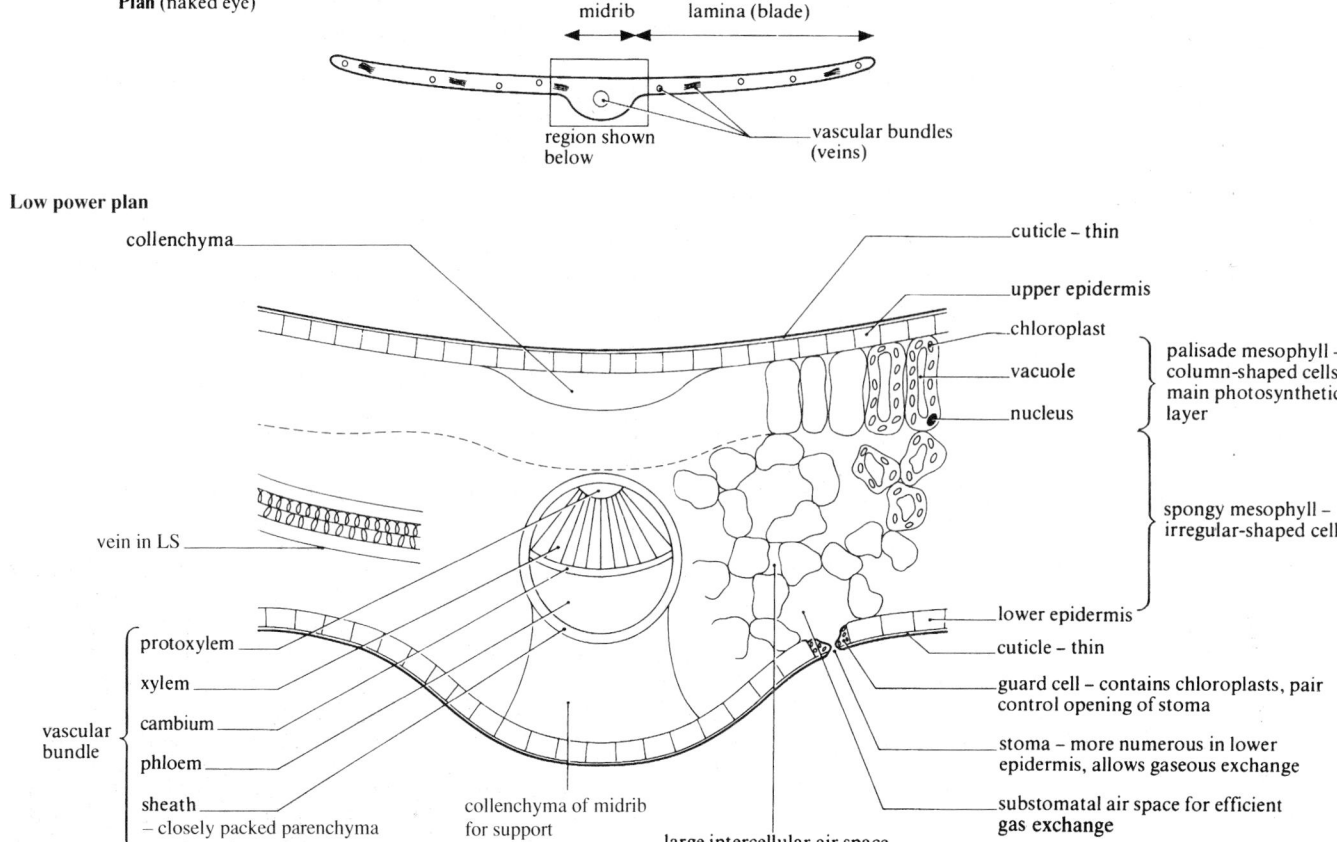

Plan (naked eye)

midrib — lamina (blade)

region shown below

vascular bundles (veins)

Low power plan

collenchyma

cuticle – thin

upper epidermis

chloroplast

vacuole

nucleus

palisade mesophyll – column-shaped cells, main photosynthetic layer

spongy mesophyll – irregular-shaped cells

vein in LS

protoxylem

xylem

cambium

phloem

sheath – closely packed parenchyma or sclerenchyma for support

vascular bundle

collenchyma of midrib for support

large intercellular air space

lower epidermis

cuticle – thin

guard cell – contains chloroplasts, pair control opening of stoma

stoma – more numerous in lower epidermis, allows gaseous exchange

substomatal air space for efficient **gas exchange**

Fig 7.5 *Diagrammatic transverse section of a typical dicotyledon leaf.*

suggestion that they might represent prokaryotic organisms which invaded eukaryotic cells at an early stage in the history of life. Thus the organelles represent an extreme form of symbiosis, a theory known as the **endosymbiont theory**. Some of the evidence for this is presented in table 7.2.

Photosynthetic bacteria (prokaryotes) do not contain chloroplasts. Instead their photosynthetic pigments are located in membranes distributed throughout the cytoplasm. Thus the whole cell is similar to one chloroplast, and is approximately the same size. It is now believed that

chloroplasts are the descendants of photosynthetic bacteria (see section 2.6.1).

It has been shown that, while chloroplasts and mitochondria do code for and make some of their own proteins, some of their genes have moved to the nucleus of the cell and so the task is now shared with nuclear DNA. This explains why they can no longer live independently.

Table 7.2 Comparison of prokaryotes, chloroplasts and mitochondria with eukaryotes.

	Prokaryotes, chloroplasts and mitochondria	*Eukaryotes*
DNA	Circular Not contained in chromosomes Not contained in nucleus	Linear Contained in chromosomes Contained in a nucleus
Ribosomes	Smaller (70S)	Larger (80S)
Sensitivity to antibiotics	Protein synthesis inhibited by chloramphenicol, not cycloheximide	Protein synthesis inhibited by cycloheximide, not chloramphenicol
Average diameter	Prokaryote cell: 0.5–10 μm Chloroplast: 1–10 μm Mitochondrion: 1 μm	Eukaryote cell: 10–100 μm

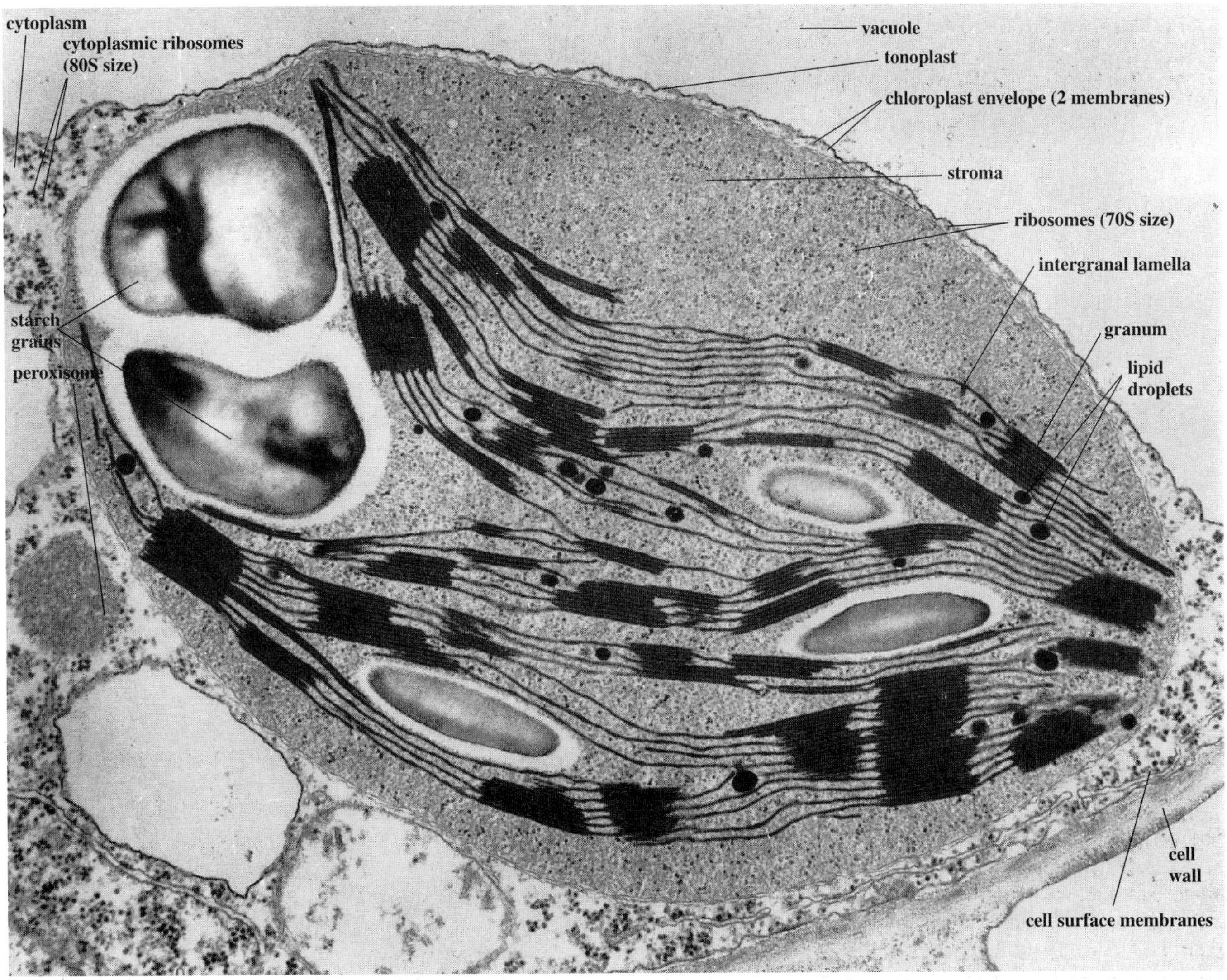

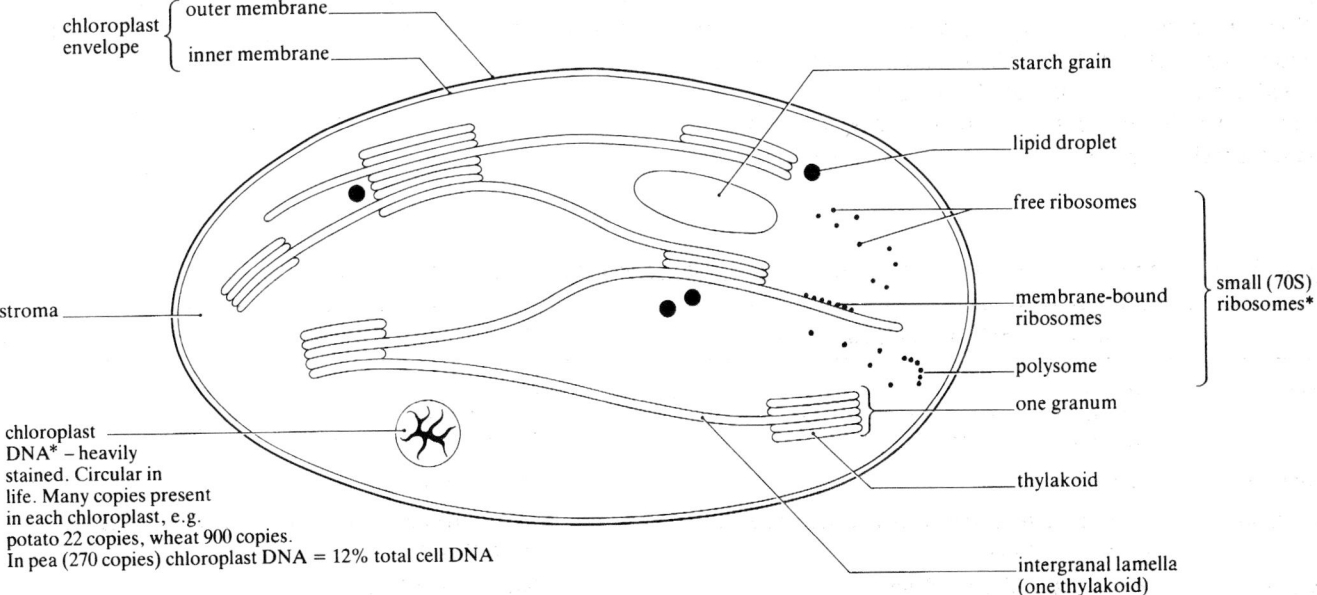

Fig 7.6 *Electron micrograph of a chloroplast (×15 800).*

cytoplasm

cytoplasmic ribosomes (80S size)

vacuole

tonoplast

chloroplast envelope (2 membranes)

stroma

ribosomes (70S size)

intergranal lamella

starch grains

peroxisome

granum

lipid droplets

cell wall

cell surface membranes

chloroplast envelope

outer membrane

inner membrane

starch grain

lipid droplet

free ribosomes

membrane-bound ribosomes

small (70S) ribosomes*

stroma

polysome

one granum

chloroplast DNA* – heavily stained. Circular in life. Many copies present in each chloroplast, e.g. potato 22 copies, wheat 900 copies. In pea (270 copies) chloroplast DNA = 12% total cell DNA

thylakoid

intergranal lamella (one thylakoid)

Fig 7.7 *Chloroplast structure. The membrane system has been reduced in extent to make the diagram simpler (*prokaryote-like protein synthesising machinery).*

201

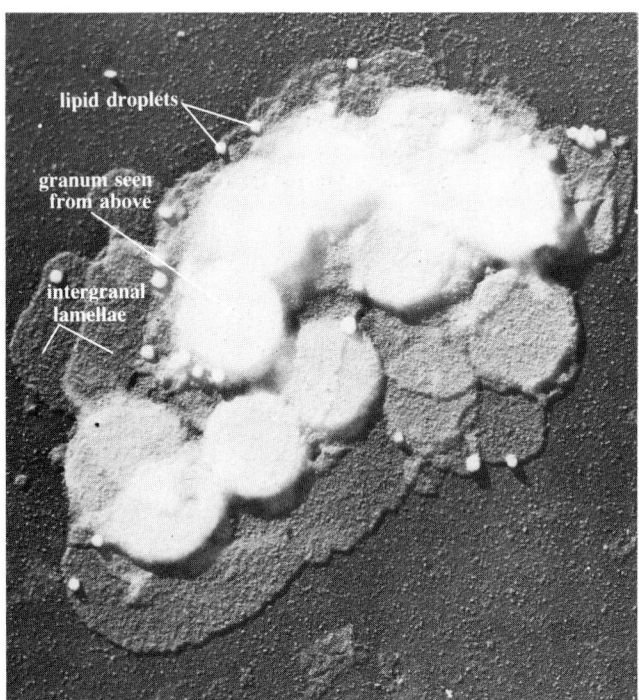

Fig 7.8 *Scanning electron micrograph of a 'stripped' chloroplast (a chloroplast whose outer envelope has been removed) looking down from above on the lamellae and grana which can be seen in three dimensions. Note that the lamellae are sheet-like and interconnect the grana. The preparation is a shadowed replica.*

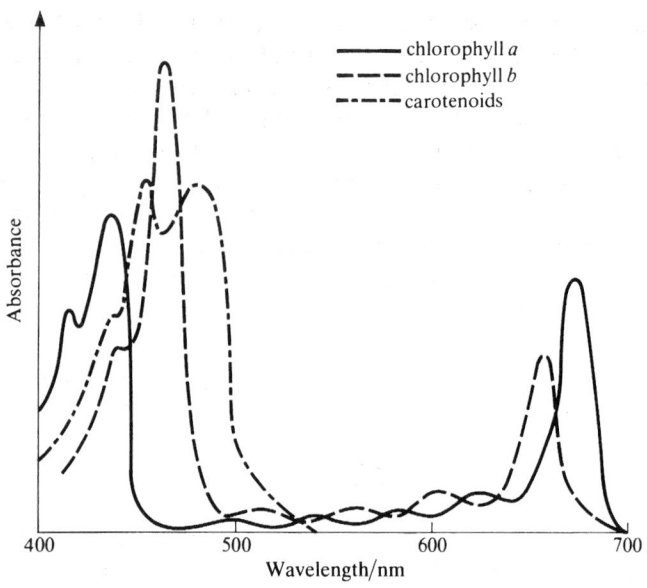

Fig 7.9 *Absorption spectra of chlorophylls a and b, and carotenoids. An absorption spectrum shows the amounts of light absorbed by a pigment at different wavelengths.*

7.5 Photosynthetic pigments

The photosynthetic pigments of higher plants fall into two classes, the **chlorophylls** and **carotenoids**. The role of the pigments is to absorb light energy, thereby converting it to chemical energy. They are located on the chloroplast membranes (thylakoids) and the chloroplasts are usually arranged within the cells so that the membranes are at right-angles to the light source for maximum absorption.

7.5.1 Chlorophylls

Chlorophylls absorb mainly red and blue-violet light, reflecting green light and therefore giving plants their characteristic green colour, unless masked by other pigments. Fig 7.9 shows the absorption spectra of chlorophylls *a* and *b* compared with carotenoids.

The chlorophyll molecule (fig 7.10) has a flat, light-absorbing head end which contains a magnesium atom at its centre. This explains the need for magnesium by plants and the fact that magnesium deficiency reduces chlorophyll production and causes yellowing. The chlorophyll molecule also has a long hydrocarbon tail which is hydrophobic (water-hating). The interior of membranes is also hydrophobic (section 5.9.6), so the tails project into the

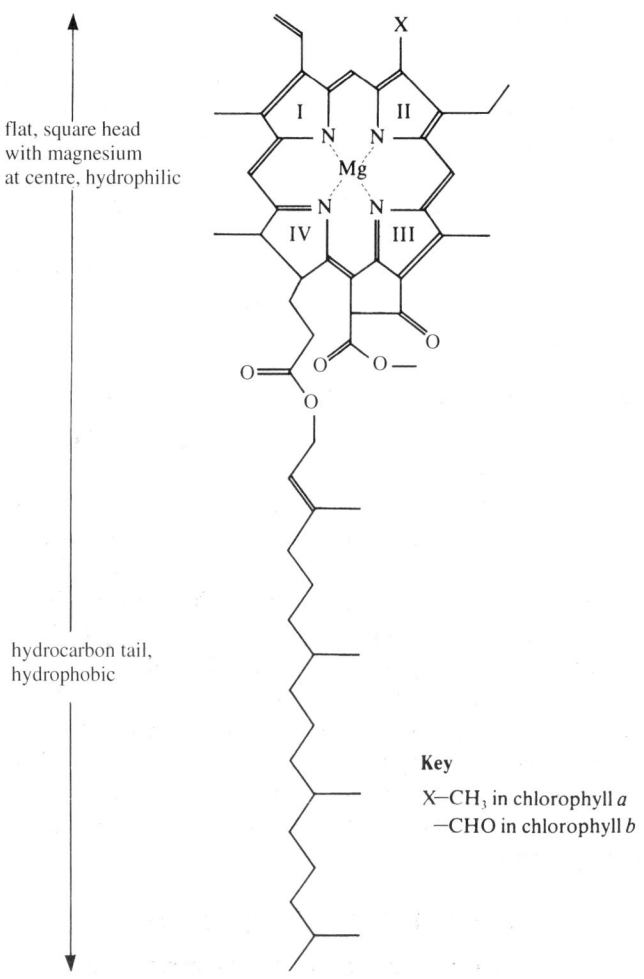

Fig 7.10 *Structure of chlorophyll.*

thylakoid membranes and act like anchors. The heads are hydrophilic and lie flat on the membrane surfaces like solar panels. Different chlorophylls have different side-chains on the head and this modifies their absorption spectra, increasing the range of wavelengths of light absorbed.

Chlorophyll *a* is the most abundant photosynthetic pigment. It exists in several forms, depending on its arrangement in the membrane. Each form differs slightly in its red absorption peak; for example, the peak may be at 670 nm, 680 nm, 690 nm or 700 nm.

7.3 How does the absorption spectrum of chlorophyll *a* differ from that of chlorophyll *b*?

7.5.2 Carotenoids

Carotenoids are yellow, orange, red or brown pigments that absorb strongly in the blue-violet range. They are called **accessory pigments** because they pass the light energy they absorb on to chlorophyll. Carotenoids have three absorption peaks in the blue-violet range of the spectrum (fig 7.9) and, apart from acting as accessory pigments, they may also protect chlorophylls from excess light and from oxidation by oxygen produced in photosynthesis. They are usually masked by the green chlorophylls but can be seen in leaves before leaf-fall because chlorophylls break down first. They are also found in some flowers and fruits where the bright colours attract insects, birds and other animals for pollination or dispersal; for example the red skin of the tomato is due to a carotene.

Carotenoids are of two types, carotenes and xanthophylls. The most widespread and important carotene is β-carotene, which is familiar as the orange pigment of carrots. Vertebrates are able to break the molecule into two during digestion to form two molecules of vitamin A.

7.5.3 Absorption and action spectra

When investigating a process such as photosynthesis that is activated by light, it is important to establish the action spectrum for the process and to use this to try to identify the pigments involved. An **action spectrum** is a graph showing the effectiveness of different wavelengths of light in stimulating the process being investigated. An **absorption spectrum** is a graph of the relative amounts of light absorbed at different wavelengths by a pigment. An action spectrum for photosynthesis is shown in fig 7.11, together with an absorption spectrum for the combined photosynthetic pigments. Note the close similarity, which indicates that the pigments, chlorophylls in particular, are those responsible for absorption of light in photosynthesis.

7.5.4 Excitation of chlorophyll by light

When a molecule of chlorophyll or other photosynthetic pigment absorbs light it is said to become **excited**. The energy from the light is used to boost

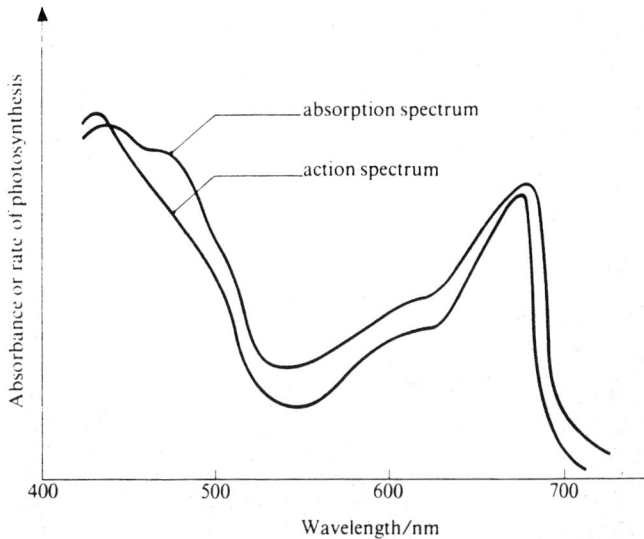

Fig 7.11 *Action spectrum for photosynthesis compared with absorption spectrum of photosynthetic pigments.*

electrons to a higher energy level. The energy of the light is now 'trapped' in the chlorophyll and has been transferred to chemical energy. This excited state is unstable and the molecule will tend to return to its unexcited state. For example, if a solution of chlorophyll has light shone through it and is then observed in darkness, it can be seen to fluoresce. This is because the extra energy of excitation is converted to light of a longer wavelength (less energy) and some waste heat energy. The excited electrons return to their original lower energy state. In the living plant the energy that is released can be passed to another chlorophyll molecule, as explained later. Alternatively, the excited electron itself may pass from the chlorophyll molecule to another molecule called an **electron acceptor**. As electrons have a negative charge, this will leave a positively charged 'hole' in the chlorophyll molecule.

$$\text{chlorophyll} \xrightarrow{\text{light energy}} \text{chlorophyll}^+ + e^-$$
$$\text{(reduced form)} \qquad \text{(oxidised form)} \qquad \text{electron}$$

Loss of electrons is known as **oxidation** and gaining electrons is **reduction**. Chlorophyll is therefore oxidised and the electron acceptor reduced. Chlorophyll replaces its electrons by removing low energy electrons from another molecule described as an **electron donor**.

The first stages in the process of photosynthesis involve both the movement of energy and of excited electrons between molecules within photosystems, as described below.

7.5.5 Photosystems

The chlorophyll and accessory pigment molecules are located in two types of photosystem, known as **photosystems I** and **II** (**PSI** and **PSII**). These photosystems are visible as particles in the thylakoid membranes, as shown in fig 7.12. Each contains an **antenna complex**, or **light-harvesting complex**, of pigment molecules.

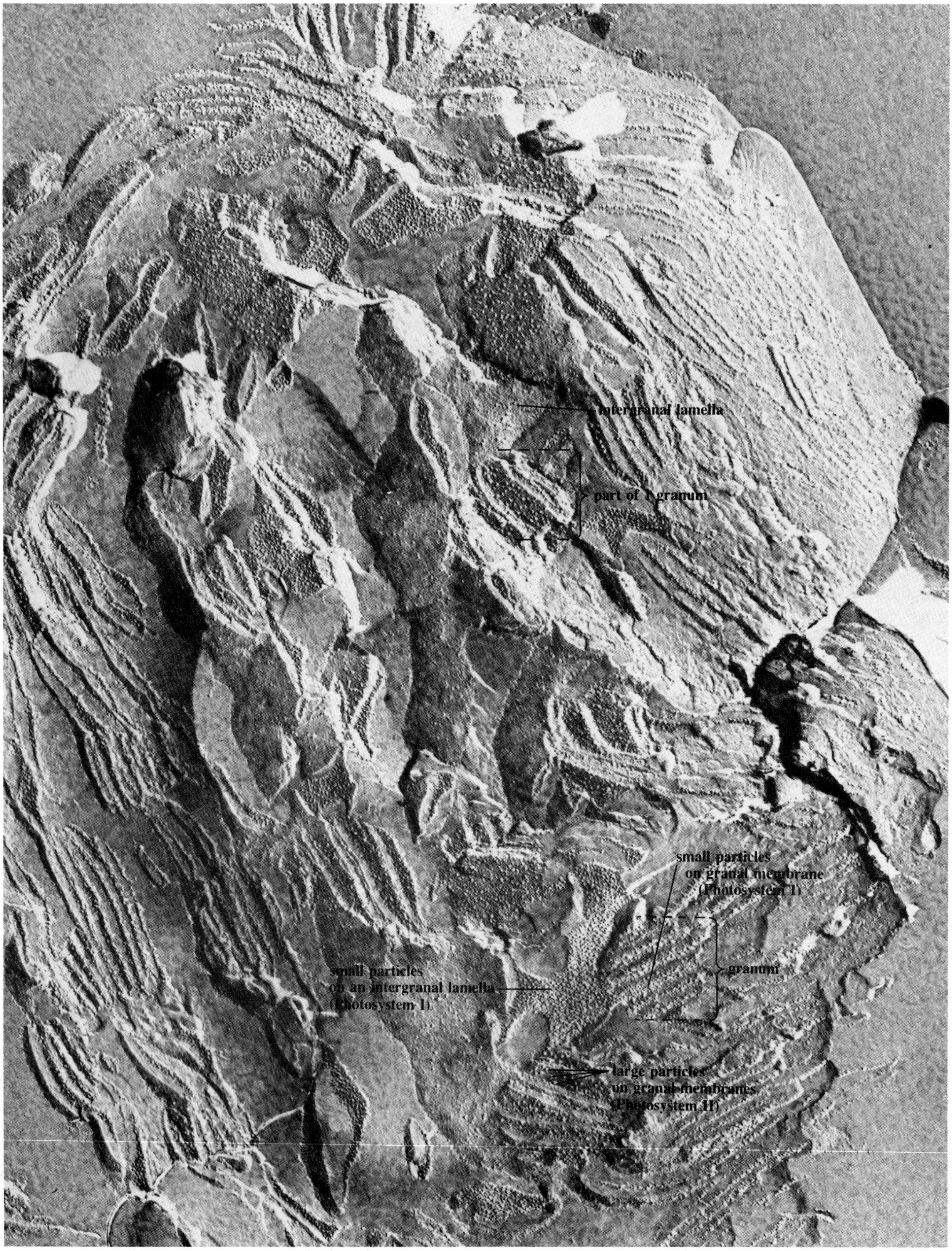
intergranal lamella
part of 1 granum
small particles
on granal membrane
(Photosystem 1)
granum
small particles
on an intergranal lamella
(Photosystem 1)
large particles
on granal membranes
(Photosystem II)

Fig 7.12 *Freeze-fractured isolated thylakoids of a chloroplast. The surfaces of fractured membranes are visible. Note the particles on the membranes. These are the photosystems. PSI particles are smaller than PSII particles.*

The light-harvesting complex contains 200–300 pigment molecules and collects light energy as shown in fig 7.13. Different pigments collect light of different wavelengths, making the process more efficient. All the energy is transferred from molecule to molecule, and finally to a specialised form of chlorophyll *a* known as P700 in PSI and P680 in PSII. P stands for pigment; their absorption peaks are at wavelengths of 700 nm and 680 nm respectively (both red light).

The chlorophylls P700 and P680 become 'excited' by the energy they absorb and release high energy electrons as described above. The fate of these electrons will be examined in section 7.6.2. We can now look at the overall process of photosynthesis.

7.6 Biochemistry of photosynthesis

A commonly used equation for photosynthesis is

$$6CO_2 + 6H_2O \xrightarrow[\text{chlorophyll}]{\text{light energy}} C_6H_{12}O_6 + 6O_2$$
$$\text{carbon} \qquad \text{water} \qquad\qquad \text{sugar} \qquad \text{oxygen}$$
$$\text{dioxide} \qquad\qquad\qquad\qquad \text{e.g. glucose}$$

This is useful for showing the formation of one molecule of sugar, but it should be realised that it is an overall summary of events. A better summary is

$$CO_2 + H_2O \xrightarrow[\text{chlorophyll}]{\text{light energy}} [CH_2O] + O_2$$

CH_2O does not exist as such, but represents a carbohydrate.

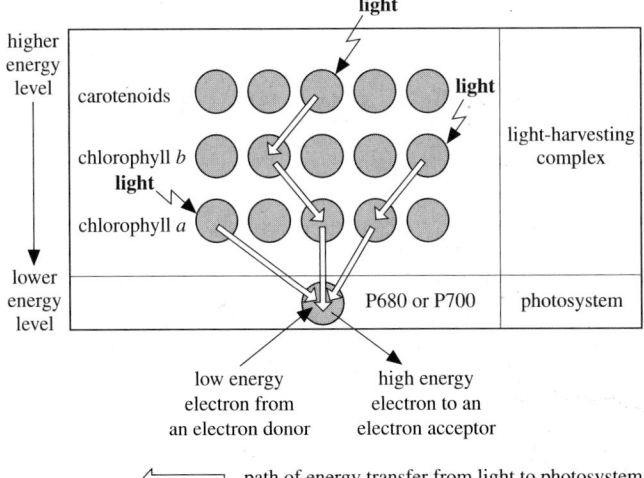

Fig 7.13 *Diagrammatic representation of a photosystem. Light may be absorbed by any of the pigment molecules in the light harvesting complex. The photosystem is located in the thylakoids. The two types of photosystem are visible as two different sized particles in fig 7.12.*

7.6.1 Source of oxygen

Looking at the equation above, a key question is whether the oxygen produced comes from carbon dioxide or water. The most obvious answer would seem to be carbon dioxide, so that the remaining carbon would be added to water to make carbohydrate. With the use of isotopes (appendix 1 in Book 2) in biology during the 1940s it became possible to answer the question directly.

The common isotope of oxygen has a mass number of 16 and is therefore represented as ^{16}O (8 protons, 8 neutrons). A rare isotope has a mass number of 18 (^{18}O). This is stable, but its greater mass can be detected with a mass spectrometer, an important analytical instrument which distinguishes between different atoms and molecules according to their masses. In 1941 an experiment was carried out which produced results summarised in the following equation

$$CO_2 + H_2^{18}O \longrightarrow [CH_2O] + {}^{18}O_2$$

The source of oxygen was thus shown to be water. The equation shows two atoms of oxygen coming from one molecule of water. So the balanced equation should be

$$CO_2 + 2H_2O \xrightarrow[\text{chlorophyll}]{\text{light energy}} [CH_2O] + O_2 + H_2O$$

This is the most accurate summary of photosynthesis and provides the extra information that water is produced, as well as used, in photosynthesis. This experiment provided a profound insight into the nature of photosynthesis because it showed that it takes place in two stages, the first of which involves acquiring hydrogen by splitting water into hydrogen and oxygen. This requires energy which must be provided by light (hence the process used to be called **photolysis**: *photos*, light; *lysis*, splitting). Oxygen is released as a waste product. In the second stage, hydrogen combines with carbon dioxide to produce carbohydrate. Addition of hydrogen is an example of a type of chemical reaction called **reduction** (appendix 1).

The fact that photosynthesis is a two-stage process was first established in the 1920s and 1930s. In the first stage the reactions require light and this stage was therefore called the **light reaction**. The second stage did not require light, and was called the **dark reaction**, although it takes place in light! These reactions are now more accurately referred to as the **light-dependent** and **light-independent** reactions. It is now known that the **light-dependent reactions take place on the chloroplast membranes** and the **light-independent reactions in the chloroplast stroma**.

Having established that photosynthesis proceeds by light-dependent reactions followed by light-independent reactions, it remained in the 1950s to discover the nature of these reactions.

7.6.2　Light-dependent reactions

We have seen that what the plant is doing in photosynthesis is making sugar using carbon dioxide and hydrogen (from water). This requires energy. The energy and the hydrogen are supplied by the light-dependent reactions which make ATP (adenosine triphosphate), an energy carrier, and reduced NADP.

ATP is the energy carrier of cells. Its structure is described in section 9.2.1 and its significance is summarised at the end of section 9.2.2. NADP (nicotinamide adenine dinucleotide phosphate) is a type of molecule known as a **hydrogen carrier**. It works in the same way as NAD. The structure of NAD and NADP is described in fig 4.17, and their roles as hydrogen carriers are described in section 4.2.3. It will help you if you read these references first.

ATP is made when energy is used to bond another phosphate to ADP, a process called **phosphorylation** (section 9.5.4). In photosynthesis the energy is supplied by light and the process is therefore called **photophosphorylation**. Reduced NADP is made from NADP in a process called **reduction**. The hydrogen comes from water. This also requires energy which is provided by light. The role of ATP and reduced NADP is simply to carry the energy and hydrogen into the light-independent reactions which follow.

We have seen already in section 7.5.5 that when light shines on photosystems I and II, high energy electrons are released by the chlorophyll molecules in the photosystems. It is the energy from these electrons that is used in the making of ATP and reduced NADP. The mechanism is shown in fig 7.14. The diagram contains a lot of information so should be studied carefully. Note that the vertical axis represents the energy level of the electrons.

The process depends on a flow of electrons from P680 and P700. Light provides the energy that causes this flow. Remember the equation

$$\text{chlorophyll} \xrightarrow{\text{light energy}} \text{chlorophyll}^+ + e^-$$
$$\text{(reduced form)} \qquad \text{(oxidised form)} \qquad \text{electron}$$

First, an electron from P680 or P700 is boosted to a higher energy level, that is it acquires excitation energy. Instead of falling back into the photosystem and losing its energy it is captured by an electron acceptor (X or Y in fig 7.14). This represents the important conversion of light energy to chemical energy. The electron acceptor is thus reduced and a positively charged (oxidised) chlorophyll molecule is left in the photosystem. The electron then travels downhill, in energy terms, from one electron acceptor to another in a series of oxidation–reduction (redox) reactions. The energy lost during this electron flow is 'coupled' to the formation of ATP. The pathway followed by the electron can be **cyclic**, returning to where it began, or **non-cyclic**, ending at NADP. When electrons are added to NADP it is changed to reduced NADP.

Non-cyclic photophosphorylation

Excited electrons from P680 (PSII) and P700 (PSI) reduce electron acceptors X and Y respectively, so that P680 and P700 become positively charged (oxidised). The electron donor which provides the replacement electrons for P680 is water. Water is split, releasing electrons which enter P680. Hydrogen ions and oxygen are also released. Oxygen escapes as a waste product (fig 7.14a).

Electrons flow from X along a chain of electron carriers, losing a little energy each time they move from one carrier to the next. Eventually they fill the positive holes left in P700. The energy from this flow is coupled to ATP production. Electrons also pass downhill in energy terms from Y to NADP along a chain of electron carriers and combine with hydrogen ions from water to form reduced NADP.

Cyclic photophosphorylation

In cyclic photophosphorylation, electrons from Y are recycled back to P700 via another chain of electron carriers. As the electrons pass down the chain their excitation energy is coupled to ATP production just as in non-cyclic photophosphorylation.

Table 7.3 shows the differences between cyclic and non-cyclic photophosphorylation.

The overall equation for non-cyclic photophosphorylation is

$$\text{H}_2\text{O} + \text{NADP}^+ + 2\text{ADP} + 2\text{P}_i \xrightarrow[\text{chlorophyll}]{\text{light energy}} \frac{1}{2}\text{O}_2 + \text{NADPH} + \text{H}^+ + 2\text{ATP}$$

Extra ATP can be made via cyclic photophosphorylation. The efficiency of energy conversion in the light-dependent reactions is high and estimated at about 39%.

Table 7.3　Comparison of cyclic and non-cyclic photophosphorylation.

	Non-cyclic	Cyclic
Pathway of electrons	Non-cyclic	Cyclic
First electron donor (source of electrons)	Water	Photosystem I (P700)
Last electron acceptor (destination of electrons)	NADP	Photosystem I (P700)
Products	Useful: ATP, reduced NADP Waste: O₂	Useful: ATP only
Photosystems involved	I and II	I only

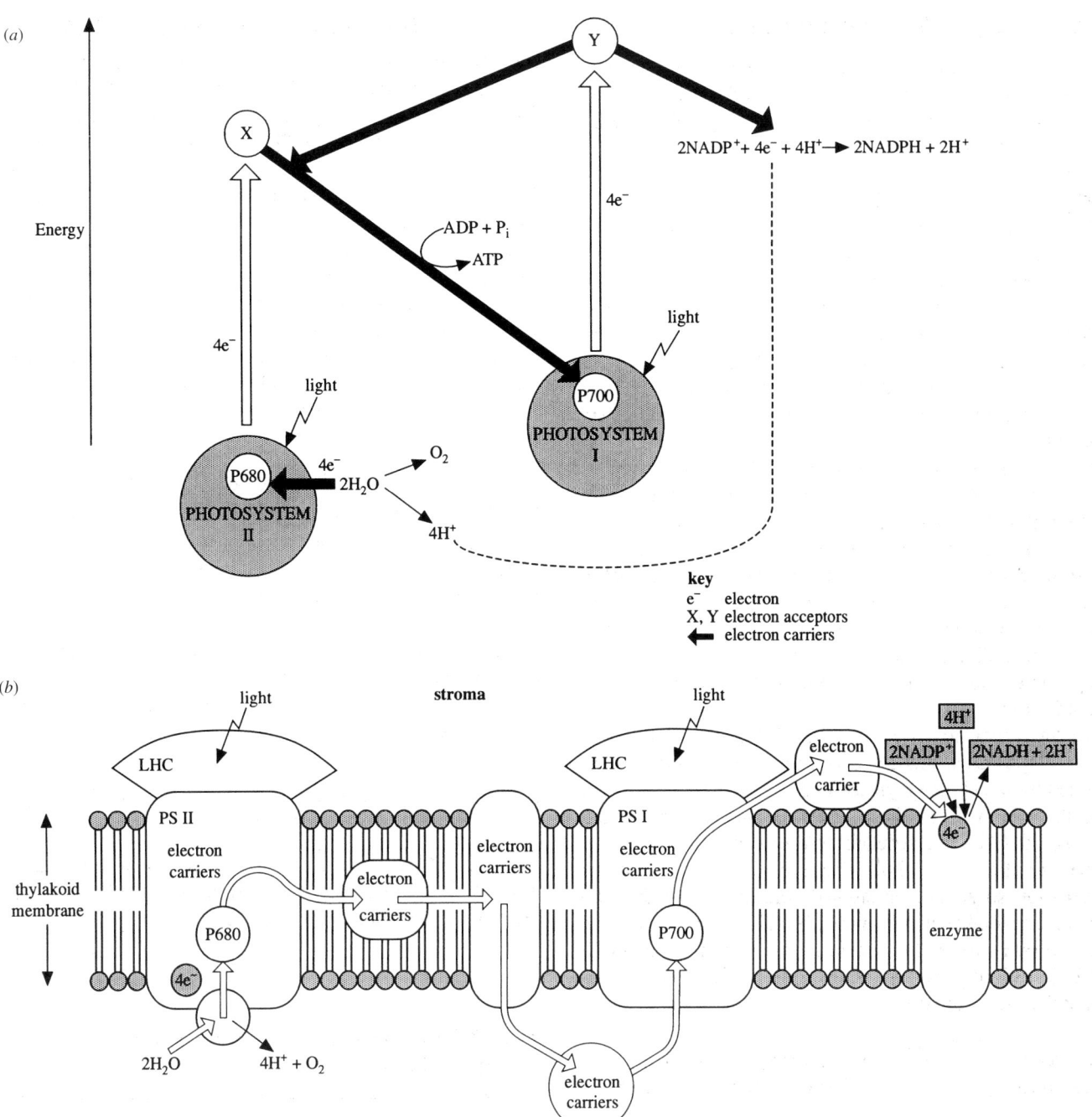

Fig 7.14 (a) *Electron flow in cyclic and non-cyclic photophosphorylation. Broad arrows represent the flow of electrons. As the electrons pass along the carriers they lose energy (see the vertical scale). The fall of electrons from a higher to a lower energy level can be used to drive the manufacture of ATP. Movement of four electrons is shown because two molecules of water are needed to release one molecule of oxygen, at the same time releasing four electrons. (b) The relationship between the electron flow and electron carriers in the cell surface membrane.*

7.6.3   Light-independent reactions

The light-independent (or dark) reactions, which take place in the stroma of the chloroplast, do not require light and use the energy (ATP) and reducing power (reduced NADP) produced by the light-dependent reactions to reduce carbon dioxide. The reactions are controlled by enzymes and their sequence was determined by Calvin, Benson and Bassham of the USA during the period 1946–53, work for which Calvin was awarded the Nobel prize in 1961.

Calvin's experiments

Calvin's work was based on use of the radioactive isotope of carbon, ^{14}C (half-life 5570 years, see appendix 1) which only became available in 1945. He also used paper chromatography, which was a relatively new but neglected technique. Cultures of the unicellular green alga *Chlorella* were grown in the now famous 'lollipop' apparatus (fig 7.15). The *Chlorella* culture was exposed to $^{14}CO_2$ for varying lengths of time, rapidly killed by dropping into hot methanol, and the soluble products of photosynthesis extracted, concentrated and separated by **two-dimensional paper chromatography** (fig 7.16 and appendix 1). The aim was to follow the route taken by the labelled carbon through intermediate compounds into the final product of photosynthesis. Compounds were located on the chromatograms by **autoradiography**. This technique uses photographic film sensitive to radiation from ^{14}C. The film is placed over the chromatograms. It becomes darkened where it covers radioactive compounds (fig 7.16). After only one minute of exposure to $^{14}CO_2$ many sugars and organic acids, including amino acids, had been made. However, using 5 s exposures or less, Calvin was able to identify the first product of photosynthesis as a 3C acid (an acid containing three carbon atoms), **glycerate phosphate** (GP). He went on to discover the sequence of compounds through which the fixed carbon passed and the various stages involved are summarised below. They have since become known as the **Calvin cycle** .

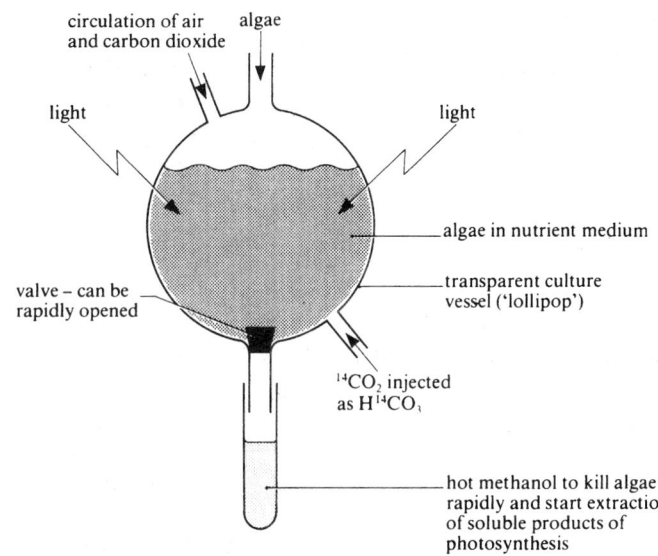

Fig 7.15 *Diagram illustrating the principle of Calvin's 'lollipop' apparatus. This comprises a thin, transparent vessel in which unicellular algae are cultured. Carbon dioxide containing radioactive carbon is bubbled through the algal suspension in experiments to determine the path taken by carbon in photosynthesis.*

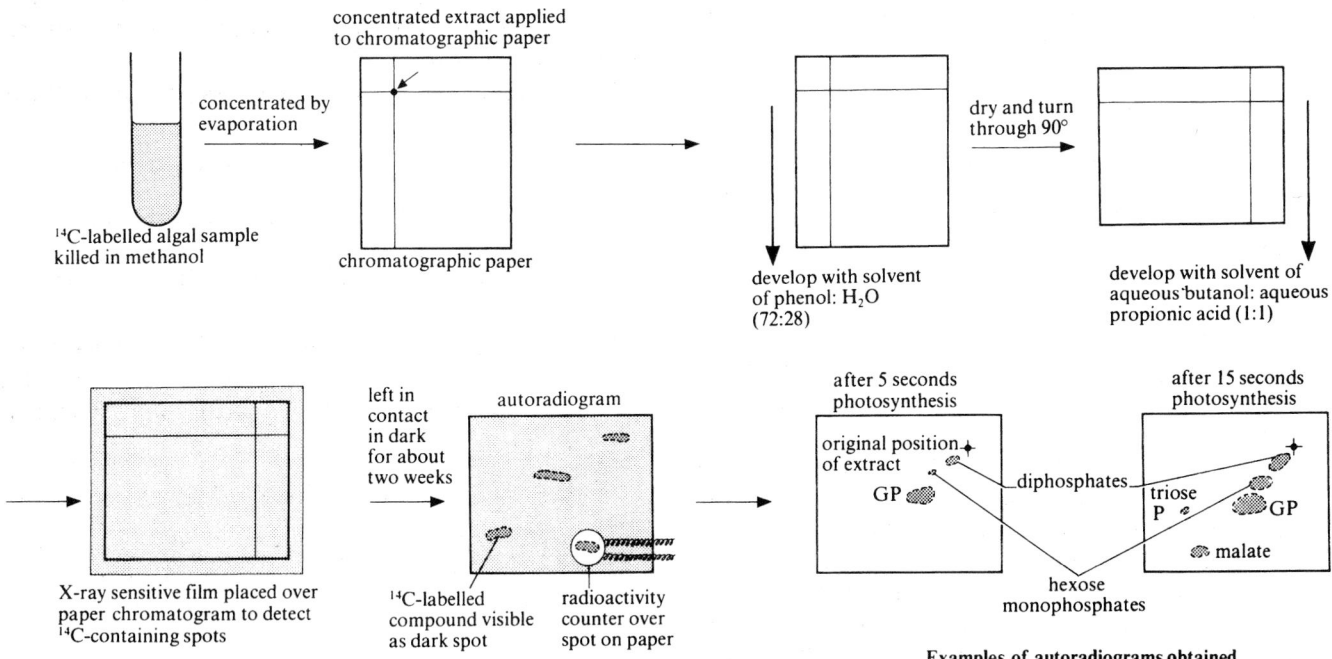

Fig 7.16 *Detection of the products of photosynthesis in algae after brief periods of illumination in the presence of radioactive carbon dioxide, $^{14}CO_2$. Paper chromatography is used to separate the products. Their positions on the paper enable them to be identified. The positions are found by exposing the paper to photographic film. Radiation from the radioactive products blackens the film.*

Stages in carbon pathway

Acceptance of carbon dioxide (carbon dioxide fixation).

$$RuBP + CO_2 + H_2O \xrightarrow{\text{RuBP carboxylase}} 2GP$$

(ribulose bisphosphate) 5C sugar — (glycerate phosphate) 3C acid

first product of photosynthesis

The carbon dioxide acceptor is a 5C sugar (a pentose), **ribulose bisphosphate** RuBP (ribulose with two phosphate groups). Addition of carbon dioxide to a compound is called **carboxylation**; the enzyme involved is a **carboxylase**. The 6C product is unstable and breaks down immediately to two molecules of **glycerate phosphate** (**GP**). This is the first product of photosynthesis. The enzyme ribulose bisphosphate carboxylase is present in large amounts in the chloroplast stroma, and is in fact the world's most common protein.

Reduction phase.

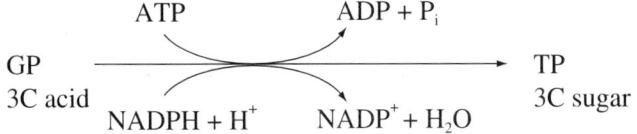

GP 3C acid — TP 3C sugar

$$\text{ATP} \qquad \text{ADP} + P_i$$
$$\text{NADPH} + H^+ \qquad \text{NADP}^+ + H_2O$$

GP is glycerate phosphate, a 3C **acid**. It contains the acidic carboxyl group (—COOH). TP is triose phosphate (glyceraldehyde phosphate), a 3C **sugar**. It contains an aldehyde group (—CHO).

The reducing power of reduced NADP and energy of ATP are used to remove oxygen from GP (reduction). The reaction takes place in two stages, the first using some of the ATP produced in the light-dependent reactions and the second using all the reduced NADP produced in these reactions. The overall effect is to reduce a carboxylic acid group (—COOH) to an aldehyde group (—CHO). The product is a 3C sugar phosphate (a triose phosphate), that is a sugar with a phosphate group attached. This contains more chemical energy than GP, and is the first carbohydrate made in photosynthesis.

Regeneration of the carbon dioxide acceptor, RuBP. Some of the triose phosphate (TP) has to be used to regenerate the ribulose bisphosphate consumed in the first reaction. This process involves a complex cycle, containing 3, 4, 5, 6 and 7C sugar phosphates. It is here that the

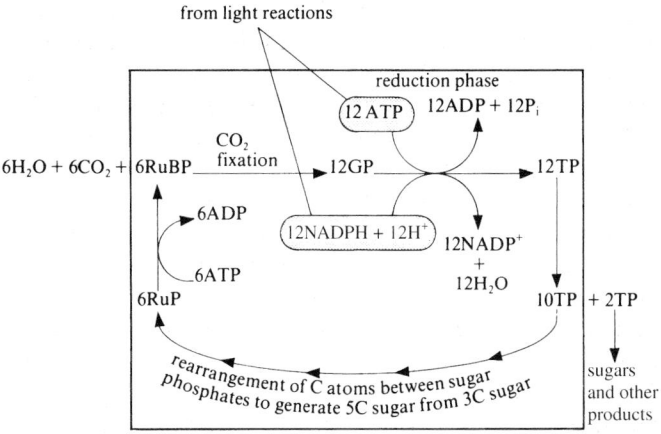

Fig 7.17 *Summary of the light-independent reactions of photosynthesis (Calvin cycle). RuBP, ribulose bisphosphate; RuP, ribulose phosphate; GP, glycerate-3-phosphate; TP, triose phosphate. Note that 10 × TP are used to make 6 × RuP, the 5C sugar ribulose phosphate. TP contains 3 carbon atoms. Therefore 10 × TP contains 30 carbon atoms. 6 × RuP also contains 30 carbon atoms (6 × 5C).*

remaining ATP is used. Fig 7.17 provides a summary of the light-independent reactions. In it the Calvin cycle is represented as a 'black box' into which carbon dioxide and water are fed and TP emerges. The diagram shows that the remaining ATP is used to convert ribulose phosphate (RuP) to ribulose bisphosphate (RuBP), but details of the complex series of reactions are not shown.

The overall equation for the light-independent reactions is

$$6H_2O + 6CO_2 \xrightarrow{\substack{18ATP \quad 18ADP + 18P_i \\ \\ 12NADPH + 12H^+ \quad 12NADP^+ + 12H_2O}} 2TP$$

The important point to note is that six molecules of carbon dioxide have been used to make two molecules of a 3C sugar, triose phosphate. The equation can be simplified by dividing by six

$$H_2O + CO_2 \xrightarrow{\substack{3ATP \quad 3ADP + 3P_i \\ \\ 2NADPH + 2H^+ \quad 2NADP^+ + 2H_2O}} [CH_2O] + 2H_2O$$

7.6.4 Summary of photosynthesis

Sugar is made during photosynthesis from carbon dioxide and water. The energy for the reaction comes from light and is stored within sugar which is an energy-rich molecule. It is important to realise that the energy in the sugar is the same energy that was in the form of light. Photosynthesis has transferred the energy from light to chemical energy in the sugar. The transfer of light energy into chemical energy is achieved by chlorophyll working in association with other molecules in the membranes of chloroplasts. The whole process involves two stages known as the light-dependent reactions and the light-independent reactions. In the light-dependent reactions electrons pass from one electron to another along chains of electron carriers, dropping in energy level with each move. The energy released is used to make ATP and the electrons reduce NADP. Water is split into hydrogen and oxygen and the oxygen is lost as a waste product. In the light-independent reactions the hydrogen (attached to NADP) and the ATP are used to reduce carbon dioxide to a 3C sugar. The overall equation is

$$CO_2 + H_2O \xrightarrow[\text{chlorophyll}]{\text{light energy}} [CH_2O] + O_2$$

Further summary notes are given in table 7.4.

7.7 Metabolism of glycerate phosphate and triose phosphate

Although triose phosphate is the end-product of the Calvin cycle, it does not accumulate in large quantities since it is immediately converted to other products. The most familiar of these are glucose, sucrose and starch, but fats, fatty acids and amino acids are also made rapidly. Strictly speaking, photosynthesis can be regarded as complete once triose phosphate is made, because subsequent reactions can also occur in non-photosynthetic organisms like animals and fungi. However, it is important to show here how glycerate phosphate and triose phosphate can be used in the synthesis of all the basic food requirements of plants. Fig 7.18 summarises some of the main pathways involved and shows what a central position the reactions of glycolysis and the Krebs cycle have in metabolism. These two pathways are discussed in chapter 9. Both glycerate phosphate and triose phosphate are intermediates in glycolysis.

Synthesis of carbohydrates

Carbohydrates are synthesised in a process which is, in effect, a reversal of glycolysis. The two most common carbohydrate products are sucrose and starch. Sucrose is the form in which carbohydrate is exported from the leaf in the phloem (chapter 13). Starch is a storage product and is the most easily detected product of photosynthesis.

Table 7.4 Summary of photosynthesis.

	Light-dependent reactions	Light-independent reactions
Location in chloroplasts	Thylakoids	Stroma
Reactions	Require light. Light energy causes the flow of electrons from electron 'donors' to electron 'acceptors', along a non-cyclic or a cyclic pathway. Two photosystems, I and II, are involved. These contain chlorophylls which emit electrons when they absorb light energy. Water acts as an electron donor to the non-cyclic pathway. Electron flow results in production of ATP (photophosphorylation) and reduced NADP.	Do not require light. Carbon dioxide is fixed when it is accepted by a 5C compound ribulose bisphosphate (RuBP), to form two molecules of a 3C compound glycerate phosphate (GP), the first product of photosynthesis. A series of reactions occurs called the Calvin cycle in which the carbon dioxide acceptor RuBP is regenerated and GP is reduced to a sugar. (See also fig 7.17.)
Overall equation	$2H_2O + 2NADP^+ \xrightarrow[\text{chlorophyll}]{\text{light}} O_2 + 2NADPH + 2H^+$ also $ADP + P_i \longrightarrow ATP$ (variable amount)	$CO_2 + H_2O \xrightarrow{\quad\quad} [CH_2O]$ with $3ATP \rightarrow 3ADP + 3P_i$ and $2NADPH + 2H^+ \rightarrow 2NADP^+ + 2H_2O$
Results	Light energy is converted to chemical energy in ATP and reduced NADP. Water is split into hydrogen and oxygen. Hydrogen is carried to reduced NADP and oxygen is a waste product.	Carbon dioxide is reduced to carbon compounds such as carbohydrates, using the chemical energy in ATP and hydrogen in reduced NADP.
Summary (omitting ATP and NADP)	light energy + chlorophyll; $2H_2O$; O_2; $4H^+ + 4e^-$	$[CH_2O] + 2H_2O$ sugar; $CO_2 + H_2O$; H_2O — sugar, containing energy from light, is made from carbon dioxide and water

210

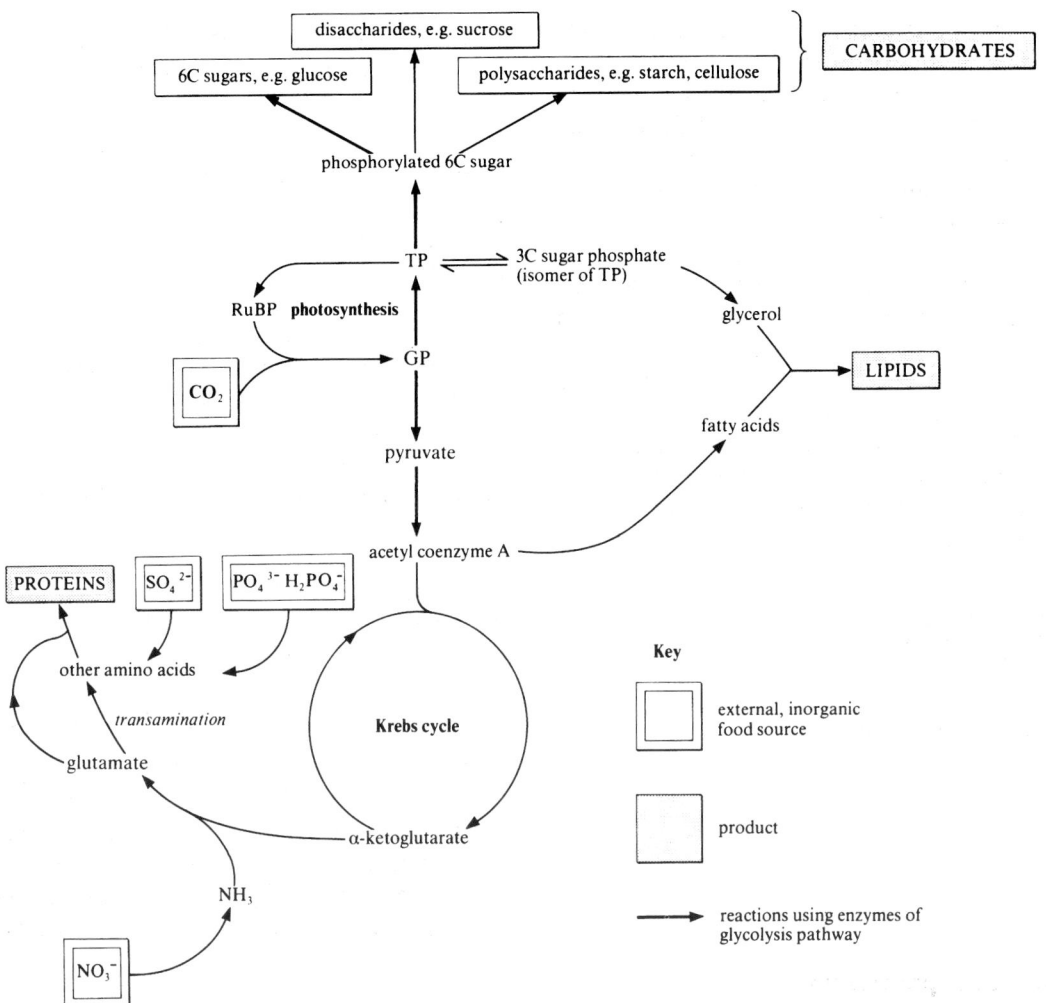

Fig 7.18 *Metabolism of GP and TP showing the relationship between photosynthesis and synthesis of food in plants. Main pathways only are shown. Some intermediate steps are omitted.*

Synthesis of lipids

Lipids are made from glycerol and fatty acids (section 3.3). **Glycerol** is made from triose phosphate. To make fatty acids, glycerate phosphate enters the glycolysis pathway and is converted to an acetyl group which is added to coenzyme A to form acetyl coenzyme A. The acetyl groups are converted to **fatty acids** in both cytoplasm and chloroplasts (not in mitochondria, where *breakdown* of fatty acids occurs).

Synthesis of proteins

Glycerate phosphate and triose phosphate contain the elements carbon, hydrogen and oxygen. Nitrogen and sulphur are also needed if amino acids and hence proteins are to be made. Plants obtain these elements from the soil, or surrounding water if aquatic. Nitrogen is taken up as nitrates or ammonia, and sulphur is taken up as sulphates.

Glycerate phosphate is first converted to one of the acids of the Krebs cycle via acetylcoenzyme A (fig 7.18). Synthesis of the amino acid is summarised below.

(1)
$$NO_3^- \xrightarrow[\text{nitrate reductase}]{\text{reduction}} NO_2^- \xrightarrow[\text{nitrite reductase}]{\text{reduction}} NH_3$$
nitrate   nitrite
from roots

(2) NH_3 + Krebs cycle acid $\longrightarrow$ amino acid
ammonia

For example,

$$NH_3 + \alpha\text{-ketoglutarate} + \frac{\text{reduced}}{\text{NADP}} \xrightarrow{\text{transaminase}} \text{glutamate} + \text{NADP}$$

Reaction (2) is the major route of entry of ammonia into amino acids. By a process called **transamination** other amino acids can be made by transferring the amino group ($—NH_2$) from one acid to another. For example,

glutamate + oxaloacetate $\xrightarrow{\text{transaminase}}$ α-ketoglutarate + aspartate
(amino   (a Krebs cycle   (a Krebs cycle   (amino acid)
acid)   acid)   acid)

Other synthetic pathways for amino acids also occur. Some amino acids are made in the chloroplasts. About one-third of the carbon fixed and about two-thirds of the nitrogen taken up by plants are commonly used directly to make amino acids.

7.8 Factors affecting photosynthesis

The rate of photosynthesis is an important factor in crop production since it affects yields. An understanding of those factors affecting the rate is therefore likely to lead to an improvement in crop management.

> **7.8** From the equation of photosynthesis what factors are likely to affect its rate?

7.8.1 Limiting factors

The rate of a biochemical process which, like photosynthesis, involves a series of reactions, will theoretically be limited by the slowest reaction in the series. For example, in photosynthesis the light-independent reactions are dependent on the light-dependent reactions for reduced NADP and ATP. At low light intensities the rate at which these are produced is too slow to allow the light-independent reactions to proceed at maximum rate, so light is a limiting factor. **The principle of limiting factors** can be stated thus:

when a chemical process is affected by more than one factor, its rate is limited by that factor which is nearest its minimum value: it is that factor which directly affects a process if its quantity is changed.

The principle was first established by Blackman in 1905. Since then it has been shown that different factors, such as carbon dioxide concentration and light intensity, interact and can be limiting at the same time, although one is often the major factor. Consider one of these factors, light intensity, by studying fig 7.19 and trying to answer the following questions.

> **7.9** In fig. 7.19
> (a) what is the limiting factor in region A?
> (b) what is represented by the curve at B and C?
> (c) what does point D represent on the curve?
> (d) what does point E represent on the curve?

Fig 7.20 shows the results from four experiments in which the same experiment is repeated at different temperatures and carbon dioxide concentrations.

> **7.10** In fig 7.20 what do the points X, Y and Z represent on the three curves?

In fig 7.20, experiments 1–4 show that once light intensity is no longer limiting, both temperature and carbon dioxide concentration can become limiting. Enzyme-controlled reactions like the light-independent reactions of photosynthesis are sensitive to temperature; thus an increase in temperature from 15 °C to 25 °C results in an

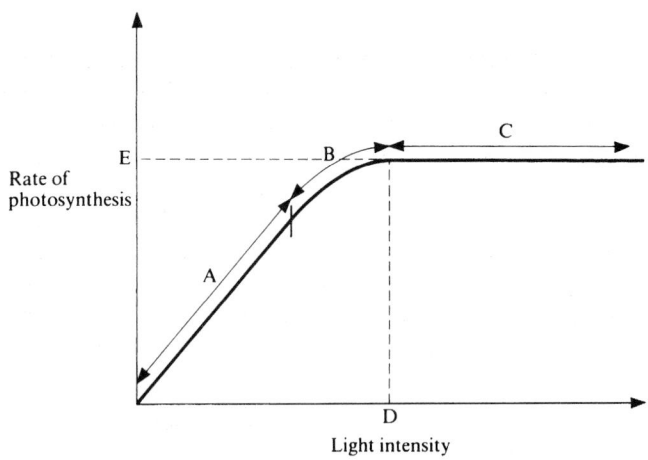

Fig 7.19 *Effect of light intensity on rate of photosynthesis.*

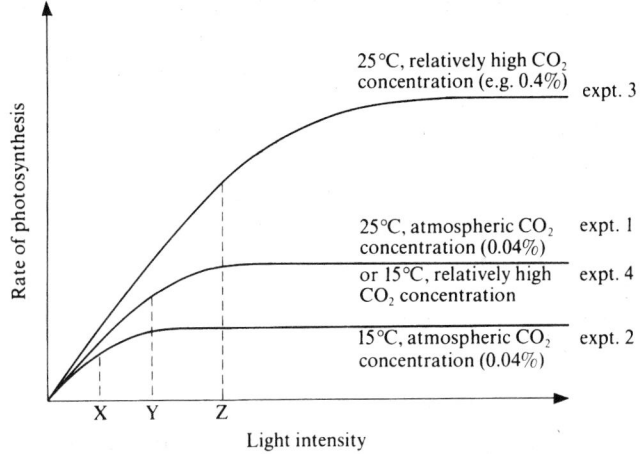

Fig 7.20 *Effect of various factors on rate of photosynthesis.*

increased rate of photosynthesis (compare experiments 2 and 1, or 4 and 3) providing light is not a limiting factor. Carbon dioxide concentration can also be a limiting factor in the light-independent reactions (compare experiments 2 and 4, or 1 and 3). In experiment 2, for example, temperature *and* carbon dioxide concentration are limiting, and an increase in either results in increased photosynthetic rate.

7.8.2 Reaction rate graphs

The chief external factors affecting rate of photosynthesis are light intensity, carbon dioxide concentration and temperature. Graphs representing their effects all have the form of fig 7.19, with external factors plotted on the horizontal axis. All show an initial linear increase in photosynthetic rate where the factor being investigated is limiting, followed by a decrease in the rate of increase and stabilising of rate as another factor, or factors, becomes limiting.

In the following it is assumed that factors other than the one under discussion are optimal.

Light intensity

In low light intensities the rate of photosynthesis increases linearly with increasing light intensity (fig 7.19). Gradually the rate of increase falls off as the other factors become limiting. Illumination on a clear summer's day is about 100 000 lux (10 000 ft candles), whereas light saturation for photosynthesis is reached at about 10 000 lux. Therefore, except for shaded plants, light is not normally a major limiting factor. Very high light intensities may bleach chlorophyll and slow down photosynthesis, but plants normally exposed to such conditions are usually protected by devices such as thick cuticles and hairy leaves.

Carbon dioxide concentration

Carbon dioxide is needed in the light-independent reactions where it is used to make sugar. Under normal conditions, carbon dioxide is the major limiting factor in photosynthesis. Its concentration in the atmosphere varies between 0.03% and 0.04%, but increases in photosynthetic rate can be achieved by increasing this percentage (see experiment 3, fig 7.20). The short-term optimum is about 0.5%, but this can be damaging over long periods; then the optimum is about 0.1%. This has led to some greenhouse crops, such as tomatoes, being grown in carbon dioxide-enriched atmospheres. At the moment there is much interest in a group of plants which are capable of removing the available carbon dioxide from the atmosphere more efficiently, hence achieving greater yields. These 'C$_4$' plants are discussed in section 7.9.

Temperature

The light-independent reactions and, to a certain extent, the light-dependent reactions are enzyme-controlled and therefore temperature-sensitive. For temperate plants the optimum temperature is usually about 25 °C. The rate of reaction doubles for every 10 °C rise up to about 35 °C, although other factors mean that the plant grows better at 25 °C.

> **7.11** Why should the rate decrease at higher temperatures?

Chlorophyll concentration

Chlorophyll concentration is not normally a limiting factor, but reduction in chlorophyll levels can be induced by several factors, including disease (such as mildews, rusts and virus diseases), mineral deficiency (section 7.10.1) and normal ageing processes (**senescence**). If the leaf becomes yellow it is said to be **chlorotic**, the yellowing process being called **chlorosis**. Chlorotic spots are thus often a symptom of disease or mineral deficiency. Iron, magnesium and nitrogen are required during chlorophyll synthesis (the latter two elements being part of its structure) and are therefore particularly important minerals. Potassium is also important. Lack of light can also cause chlorosis since light is needed for the final stage of chlorophyll synthesis.

Specific inhibitors

An obvious way of killing a plant is to inhibit photosynthesis, and various herbicides have been introduced to do this. A notable example is DCMU (dichlorophenyl dimethyl urea) which short-circuits non-cyclic electron flow in chloroplasts and thus inhibits the light-dependent reactions. DCMU has been useful in research on the light-dependent reactions.

Two other factors which are important when growing crops and which have more general effects on plant growth and photosynthesis are water supply and pollution.

Water

Water is a raw material in photosynthesis, but so many cell processes are affected by lack of water that it is impossible to measure the direct effect of water on photosynthesis. Nevertheless, by studying the yields (amounts of organic matter synthesised) of water-deficient plants, it can be shown that periods of temporary wilting can lead to severe yield losses. Even slight water deficiency, with no visible effects, might significantly reduce crop yields. The reasons are complex and not fully understood. One obvious factor is that plants usually close their stomata in response to wilting and this would prevent access of carbon dioxide for photosynthesis. Abscisic acid, a growth inhibitor, has also been shown to accumulate in water-deficient leaves of some species.

Pollution

Low levels of certain gases of industrial origin, notably ozone and sulphur dioxide, are very damaging to the leaves of some plants, although the exact reasons are still being investigated. It is estimated, for example, that cereal crop losses as high as 15% may occur in badly polluted areas, particularly during dry summers. Lichens are very sensitive to sulphur dioxide. Soot can block stomata and reduce the transparency of the leaf epidermis.

> **7.12** Suggest some habitats or natural circumstances in which (*a*) light intensity, and (*b*) temperature might be limiting factors in photosynthesis.

7.9 C$_4$ photosynthesis

In 1965 it was shown that the first products of photosynthesis in sugarcane, a tropical plant, appeared to be acids containing four carbon atoms (malic, oxaloacetic and aspartic) rather than the 3C acid GP of most temperate plants. Many plants, mostly tropical and subtropical and some of great economic importance, have since been identified in which the same is true and these are called **C$_4$ plants**. Examples are maize, sorghum, sugarcane and millet. Plants in which the 3C acid GP is the first product of photosynthesis are called **C₃ plants**. It is the biochemistry of these plants which has been described so far.

In 1966, two Australian workers, Hatch and Slack showed that C₄ plants were far more efficient at taking up carbon dioxide than C₃ plants: they could remove carbon dioxide from an experimental atmosphere down to 0.1 parts per million (ppm) compared with the 50–100 ppm of temperate plants. Hatch and Slack discovered a new carbon pathway in C₄ plants which is now called the **Hatch–Slack pathway**. The process in a typical C₄ plant, maize, will be described.

C₄ plants possess a characteristic leaf anatomy in which two rings of cells are found around each of the vascular bundles. The inner ring, or **bundle sheath cells**, contains chloroplasts which differ in form from those in the **mesophyll cells** in the outer ring. The chloroplasts in the plants are therefore described as **dimorphic** (two forms). Figs 7.21 *a* and *b* illustrate this so-called **'Kranz' anatomy** (Kranz means crown or halo, referring to the two distinct rings of cells). The biochemical pathway that takes place in these cells is summarised below and in fig 7.22.

7.9.1 Hatch–Slack pathway

The Hatch–Slack pathway is a pathway for transporting carbon dioxide and hydrogen from mesophyll cells to bundle sheath cells. Once in the bundle sheath cells, the carbon dioxide is released again and normal C₃ photosynthesis occurs (fig 7.22).

Acceptance of carbon dioxide (carbon dioxide fixation) in mesophyll cells

Carbon dioxide is fixed in the **cytoplasm** of the mesophyll cells as shown below:

$$\text{PEP} + \text{CO}_2 \xrightarrow{\text{PEP carboxylase}} \text{oxaloacetate}$$
$$\text{(phosphoenolpyruvate)} \qquad\qquad 4\text{C}$$
$$3\text{C}$$

The carbon-dioxide-acceptor is phosphoenolpyruvate (PEP) instead of the RuBP of C₃ plants, and the enzyme is PEP carboxylase instead of RuBP carboxylase. PEP carboxylase is much more efficient than the enzyme of C₃ plants for two reasons. Firstly, it has a much higher affinity for carbon dioxide, and secondly it is not competitively inhibited by oxygen. Oxaloacetate is converted to malate, a 4C acid.

Malate shunt

Malate is shunted through plasmodesmata in the cell walls to the chloroplasts of the bundle sheath cells, where it is converted to pyruvate, a 3C acid, by having carbon dioxide and hydrogen removed. The hydrogen is used to reduce NADP (fig 7.22). Note that in the mesophyll cells carbon dioxide and hydrogen are added and that in the bundle

(a)

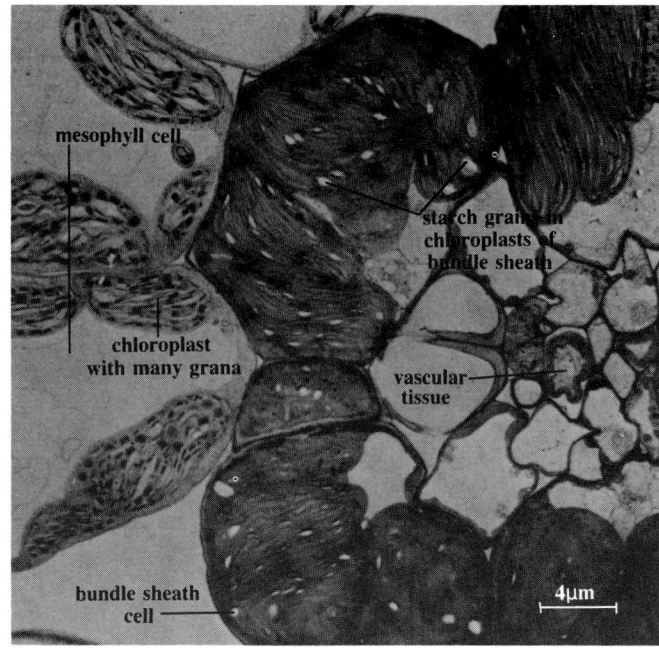

(b)

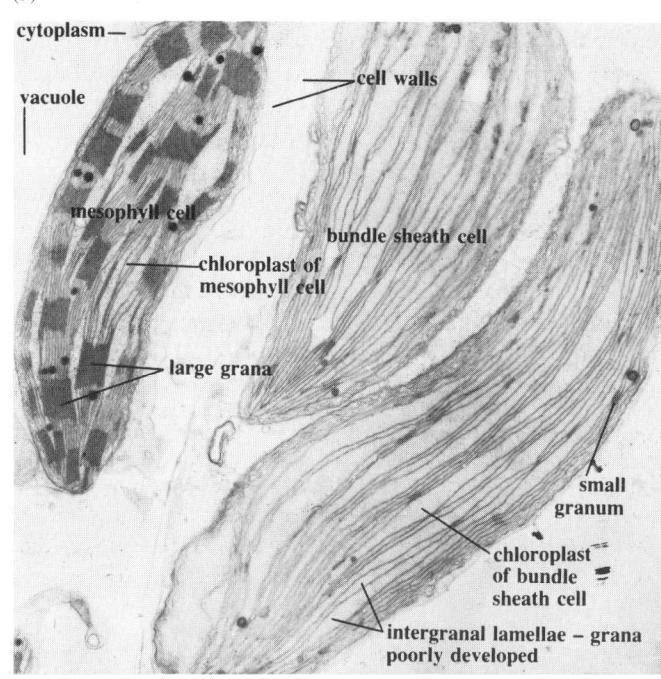

Fig 7.21 *'Kranz' anatomy, characteristic of C₄ plants. (a) Section of a leaf of crabgrass to show the difference between bundle sheath chloroplasts and mesophyll chloroplasts. Grana in the bundle sheath chloroplasts are only rudimentary, whereas they are prominent in chloroplasts of the mesophyll. Starch grains are present in both. (Magnification ×4000). (b) Electron micrograph of maize leaf showing two types of chloroplasts found in bundle sheath cells and mesophyll cells (×9900).*

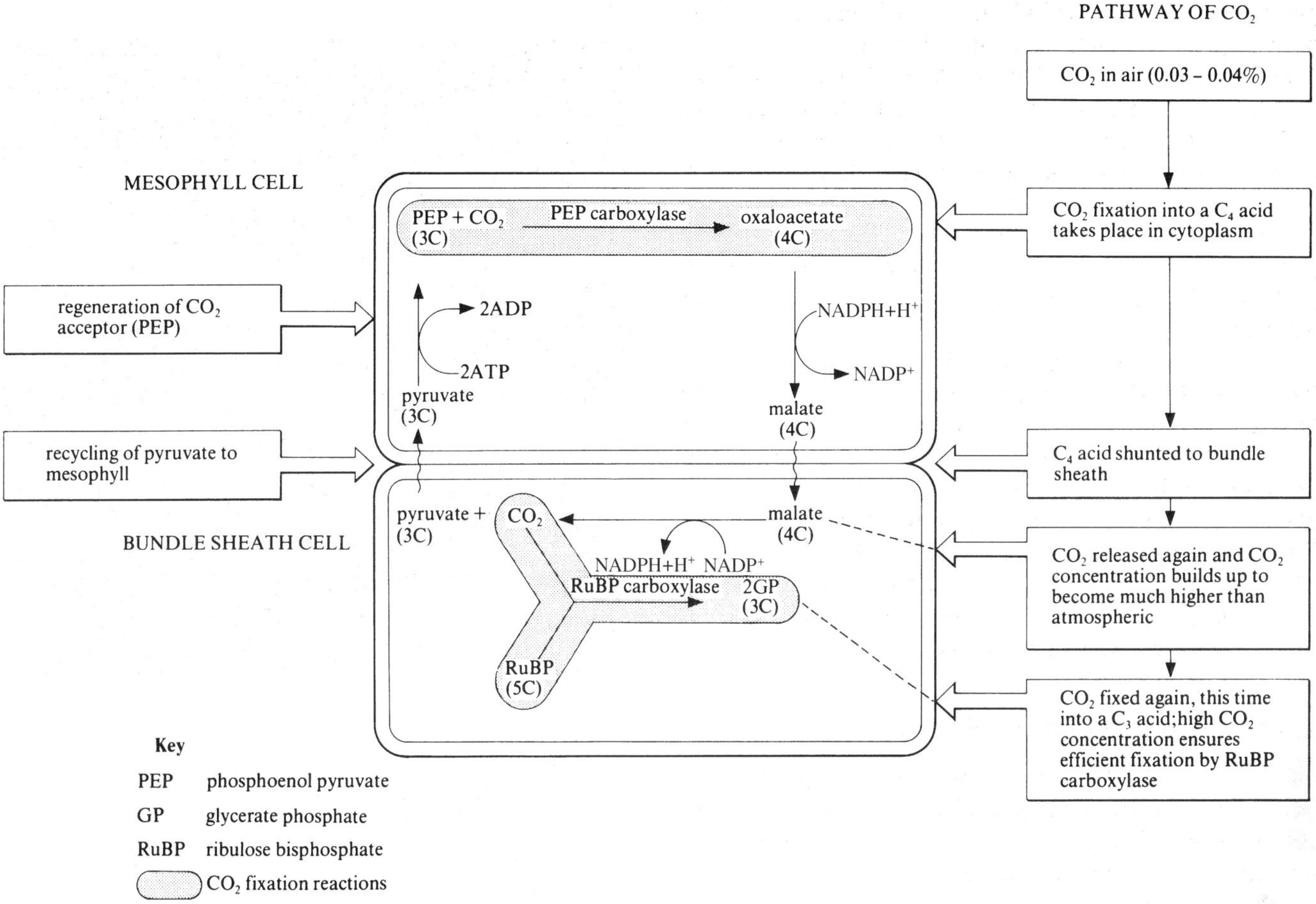

Fig 7.22 *Simplified outline of C$_4$ pathway coupled with C$_3$ fixation of carbon dioxide. Transport of carbon dioxide from air to bundle sheath is shown, together with final fixation of carbon dioxide into the C$_3$ acid GP.*

sheath cells they are removed again. The overall effect of this is to move carbon dioxide and hydrogen from the mesophyll cells to the bundle sheath cells.

Regeneration of the carbon dioxide acceptor

Pyruvate is returned to the mesophyll cells and is used to regenerate PEP by the addition of phosphate from ATP. This requires the energy from two high energy phosphate bonds.

7.9.2 Net result of C$_4$ pathway

The net result of the C$_4$ pathway is the use of two high energy phosphate bonds from ATP to transport carbon dioxide and hydrogen from the mesophyll cells to the chloroplasts of the bundle sheath cells. Since the transport requires energy from ATP, it can be regarded as a pumping mechanism.

7.9.3 Refixation of carbon dioxide in the bundle sheath cells

Carbon dioxide and reduced NADP are produced, as well as pyruvate, in the bundle sheath

chloroplasts (see malate shunt above). The carbon dioxide is then refixed by RuBP carboxylase in the C$_3$ pathway, and the reduced NADP used to reduce GP to sugar (section 7.6.3).

Since every carbon dioxide molecule has had to be fixed twice, the energy requirement for C$_4$ photosynthesis is roughly double that for C$_3$ photosynthesis. At first sight then, the transport of carbon dioxide and hydrogen by the C$_4$ pathway seems pointless. However, fixation using PEP carboxylase in the mesophyll is so efficient that a high concentration of carbon dioxide accumulates in the bundle sheath. This means that the RuBP carboxylase works at an advantage compared with the same enzyme in C$_3$ plants, where carbon dioxide is at atmospheric concentration. There are two reasons for this: firstly, like any enzyme it works much more efficiently at high substrate concentrations; secondly, oxygen is competitively excluded from the enzyme by carbon dioxide.

The main advantage of C$_4$ photosynthesis, therefore, is that it improves the efficiency of carbon dioxide fixation. It is an addition rather than an alternative to the C$_3$ pathway. As a result, C$_4$ plants are photosynthetically more efficient because the rate of carbon dioxide fixation is normally the limiting factor in photosynthesis. C$_4$ plants consume more energy by using the C$_4$ pathway, but energy is not normally the limiting factor in photosynthesis, and C$_4$ plants grow in regions of high light intensity as well as having modified chloroplasts for making more efficient use of available energy (see below).

7.9.4 Mesophyll and bundle sheath chloroplasts

Mesophyll chloroplasts are highly specialised for the light-dependent reactions of photosynthesis and bundle sheath chloroplasts are specialised for the light-independent reactions of C_3 photosynthesis. Table 7.5 summarises the important differences between mesophyll and bundle sheath chloroplasts, some of which are visible in fig 7.21.

7.13 Which type of chloroplast is specialised for light-dependent reactions and which for light-independent reactions?

7.14 Why is it an advantage that bundle sheath chloroplasts lack grana?

7.15 The malate shunt is, in effect, a carbon dioxide and hydrogen pump. What is the advantage of this?

7.16 What would be the effect of lowering oxygen concentrations on (a) C_3 photosynthesis, (b) C_4 photosynthesis? Explain your answers.

7.9.5 Significance of the C_4 pathway

The C_4 pathway is thought to be more recently evolved than the C_3 pathway, and involves a superior carbon-dioxide-fixing mechanism. Thus C_4 plants increase in dry mass more rapidly than C_3 plants and are more efficient crop plants in certain parts of the world (see below).

C_4 plants have evolved chiefly in the drier regions of the subtropics and tropics, for which they are adapted in two major ways. First, their maximum rate of carbon dioxide

Table 7.5 Differences between mesophyll and bundle sheath chloroplasts in C_4 plants.

Mesophyll chloroplasts	Bundle sheath chloroplasts
Large grana	No grana (or very few and small)
Therefore light-dependent reactions favoured, so plenty of ATP, reduced NADP and O_2 generated.	Therefore light-dependent reactions occur at very low rate, so little reduced NADP, ATP or O_2 generated
Virtually no RuBP carboxylase so no CO_2 fixation (CO_2 fixation occurs in cytoplasm by PEP carboxylase)	High concentration of RuBP carboxylase so CO_2 fixation occurs as in C_3 plants but more efficiently
Little starch	Abundant starch grains

fixation is greater; therefore the higher light intensities and temperatures of the tropics are more efficiently exploited. Light saturation takes place at much higher light intensities than with C_3 plants. In other words, the rate of photosynthesis carries on rising with increasing light intensity to a much higher level than with C_3 plants. Secondly, C_4 plants are more tolerant of dry conditions. Plants usually reduce their stomatal apertures in order to reduce water loss by transpiration, and this also reduces the area for carbon dioxide entry. Carbon dioxide is fixed so rapidly in C_4 plants that a steep carbon dioxide diffusion gradient can still be maintained between external and internal atmospheres, thus allowing faster growth than in C_3 plants. C_4 plants lose only about half the water that C_3 plants lose for each molecule of carbon dioxide fixed. The optimum temperature for growth of C_4 plants is also higher than it is for C_3 plants.

However, in cooler, moister, temperate regions with fewer hours of high light intensity, the extra energy (about 15% more) required by C_4 plants to fix carbon dioxide is more likely to be a limiting factor and C_3 plants may even have a competitive advantage in such situations. In temperate regions, C_3 crops, such as wheat, potato, tobacco, sugar beet and soya bean, grow more efficiently than C_4 crops, such as maize, sugar cane, sorghum and millet. A summary of the differences between C_3 and C_4 plants is given in table 7.6.

7.10 Mineral nutrition of plants and animals

Autotrophic nutrition involves not only the synthesis of carbohydrates from carbon dioxide and water, but also the subsequent use of minerals like nitrates, sulphates and phosphates to make other organic substances that are needed, such as proteins and nucleic acids. Heterotrophic organisms like animals also require certain minerals to supplement their organic food. In many cases the same nutrients are required and for the same reasons, so it is convenient to consider the whole area of mineral nutrition as a bridge between autotrophic nutrition (chapter 7) and heterotrophic nutrition (chapter 8).

A nutritional element essential for the successful growth and reproduction of an organism is called an **essential element**. The major essential elements for life are carbon, hydrogen, oxygen, nitrogen, sulphur, phosphorus, potassium, sodium, magnesium, calcium and chlorine. In addition, certain elements, the **trace elements**, are essential in trace amounts (a few parts per million). Of these, all organisms require manganese, iron, cobalt, copper and zinc; some also require combinations of molybdenum, vanadium, chromium and other heavy metals, as well as boron, silicon, fluorine and iodine (see table 3.1). All except carbon, hydrogen and oxygen are taken up as minerals from soil or water by green plants. The mechanism of uptake is discussed in chapter 13.

Table 7.6 Comparison of C_3 and C_4 plants.

	C_3 plants	C_4 plants	
Representative species	Most crop plants, e.g. cereals, tobacco, beans	Maize, sugarcane	
Light intensity for maximum rate of photosynthesis	10 000–30 000 foot candles	Not saturated at 10^5 lux	
Effect of temperature rise from 25 °C to 35 °C	No change in rate or lower rate	50% greater at 35°C	
Point at which no more CO_2 can be taken up	40–60 ppm CO_2	Around zero ppm CO_2	
Water loss per g dry mass produced	450–950	250–350	
Carbon dioxide fixation	Occurs once	Occurs twice, first in mesophyll cells, then in bundle sheath cells	
		Mesophyll cells	**Bundle sheath cells**
Carbon dioxide acceptor	RuBP, a 5C compound	PEP, a 3C compound	RuBP
Carbon dioxide-fixing enzyme	RuBP carboxylase, which is inefficient	PEP carboxylase which is very efficient	RuBP carboxylase, working efficiently because carbon dioxide concentration is high
First product of photosynthesis	A C_3 acid, GP	A C_4 acid, e.g. oxaloacetate	
Leaf anatomy	Only one type of chloroplast	'Kranz' anatomy, i.e. two types of cell, each with its own type of chloroplast	
Efficiency	Less efficient photosynthesis than C_4 plants. Yields usually much lower.	More efficient photosynthesis than C_3 plants but use more energy. Yields usually much higher.	

For heterotrophic organisms (animals and fungi) the trace elements (inorganic) are sometimes grouped with vitamins (organic) as **micronutrients**, since both are required in trace amounts and have similar fundamental roles in cell metabolism, often as enzyme cofactors. Vitamins are considered in chapter 8. Autotrophic organisms synthesise their own vitamins. The other essential elements are called **macronutrients**. Deficiency of any of the nutrients mentioned can lead to **deficiency diseases**.

Some examples of the functions of the major minerals are given in table 7.7. A study of the table will reveal that mineral elements are taken up by plants as separate ions, either anions (negatively charged) or cations (positively charged). This is also true of trace elements, though their ions are not shown in the table.

Animals do not obtain all their essential elements in the form of minerals. Much of their nitrogen, for example, is ingested in the form of proteins.

A balance of trace elements is essential for soil fertility. Extreme cases are known of plants thriving in areas of high metal contamination, such as on spoilage tips from mines or over natural mineral deposits, and such plants can prove toxic to grazing animals. On the other hand, they can be useful to humans if they help to cover former unsightly areas.

7.10.1 Mineral element deficiencies

It is not always easy, or possible, to isolate the effects of individual minerals. In plants, for example, chlorosis (lack of chlorophyll) can be caused by lack of magnesium or iron, both having different roles in chlorophyll synthesis (tables 7.7 and 7.8). A common deficiency disease of sheep and cattle called scour, which causes diarrhoea, is due to copper deficiency induced by high levels of molybdenum in the pastures. Different effects may occur in different organisms; lack of manganese, for example, causes grey speck in oats, marsh spot in beans and poor flavour in oats.

The close interaction and varied effects of mineral elements are due to their fundamental effects on cell metabolism. However, it is possible by various means, such as experimentally manipulating mineral uptake, to show that specific sets of symptoms are associated with deficiencies of certain elements. Such knowledge is of importance in both medicine and agriculture because deficiency diseases are common worldwide, both in humans and in their crops and animals.

Table 7.7 Some mineral elements that are essential macronutrients and examples of their uses in living organisms.

MACRONUTRIENTS			Common deficiency diseases or symptoms		Common food source for humans
Element and symbol	*Taken up by plants as*	*General importance*	*Plants*	*Humans*	
Nitrogen, N	Nitrate, NO_3^- Ammonium, NH_4^+	Synthesis of proteins, nucleic acids and many other organic compounds, e.g. coenzymes and chlorophyll.	Stunted growth and strong chlorosis, particularly of older leaves	Kwashiorkor due to lack of protein	Protein, e.g. lean meat, fish and milk.
Phosphorus, P	Phosphate, PO_4^{3-} Orthophosphate, $H_2PO_4^-$	Synthesis of nucleic acids, ATP and some proteins. Also, phosphate is a constituent of bone and enamel. Phospholipids in membranes.	Stunted growth, particularly of roots		Milk is rich in phosphorus
Potassium, K	K^+	Mainly associated with membrane function, e.g. conduction of nervous impulses, maintaining electrical potentials across membranes, Na^+/K^+ pump in active transport across membranes, anion/cation and osmotic balance. Cofactor in photosynthesis and respiration (glycolysis). Common in cell sap of plant vacuoles.	Yellow and brown leaf margins and premature death	Rarely deficient	Vegetables, e.g. brussels sprouts (= buds), and meat
Sulphur, S	Sulphate, SO_4^{2-}	Synthesis of proteins (e.g. keratin) and many other organic compounds, e.g. coenzyme A.	Chlorosis, e.g. 'tea-yellow' of tea		Protein, e.g. lean meat, fish and milk
Sodium, Na	Na^+	Similar to potassium, but usually present in lower concentrations. Often exchanged for potassium.		Muscular cramps	Table salt (sodium chloride) and bacon
Chlorine, Cl	Chloride, Cl^-	Similar to Na^+ and K^+, e.g. anion/cation and osmotic balance. Involved in 'chloride shift' during carbon dioxide transport in blood. Constituent of hydrochloric acid in gastric juice.		Muscular cramps	Table salt and bacon
Magnesium, Mg	Mg^{2+}	Part of structure of chlorophyll. Bone and tooth structure. Cofactor for many enzymes, e.g. ATPase.	Chlorosis		Vegetables and most other foods
Calcium, Ca	Ca^{2+}	Formation of middle lamella (calcium pectate) between plant cell walls and normal cell wall development. Constituent of bone, enamel and shells. Activates ATPase during muscular contraction. Blood clotting.	Stunted growth	Poor skeletal growth, possibly leading to rickets	Milk, hard water

Table 7.8 Some essential trace mineral elements and examples of their uses in living organisms.

TRACE ELEMENTS – all cations except boron, fluorine and iodine			Common deficiency diseases or symptoms		Common food source for humans
Element and symbol	Substance containing	Examples of functions	Plants	Humans	
Manganese, Mn	Phosphatases (transfer PO_4 groups)	Bone development (a 'growth factor')	Leaf-flecking, e.g. 'grey-speck' in oats	Poor bone development	Vegetables and most other foods
	Decarboxylases } Dehydrogenases }	Oxidation of fatty acids, respiration, photosynthesis			
Iron, Fe	Haem group in: haemoglobin and myoglobin }	Oxygen carriers		Anaemia	Liver and red meat, some vegetables, e.g. spinach
	Cytochromes	Electron carriers, e.g. respiration, photosynthesis			
	Catalase and } peroxidases }	Break down H_2O_2			
	Intermediate in chlorophyll synthesis	Chlorophyll synthesis	Strong chlorosis, particularly in young leaves		
Cobalt, Co	Vitamin B_{12}	Red blood cell development		Pernicious anaemia	Liver and red meat (as vitamin B_{12}).
Copper, Cu	Cytochrome oxidase	Last electron carrier in respiratory chain – oxygen converted to water	Dieback of shoots		Most foods
	Plastocyanin	Electron carrier in photosynthesis			
	Tyrosinase	Melanin production		Albinism	
Zinc, Zn	Alcohol dehydrogenase	Anaerobic respiration in plants (alcohol fermentation)	'Mottle leaf' of *Citrus*		
	Carbonic anhydrase	Carbon dioxide transport in vertebrate blood	Malformed leaves, e.g. 'sickle leaf' of cocoa		Most foods
	Carboxypeptidase	Hydrolysis of peptide bonds in protein digestion			
Molybdenum, Mo	Nitrate reductase	Reduction of nitrate to nitrite during amino acid synthesis in plants	Slight retardation of growth; 'scald' disease of beans		Most foods
	Nitrogenase	Nitrogen fixation (prokaryotes)			
Boron, B	—	Plants only. Normal cell division in meristems. Mobilisation of nutrients?	Abnormal growth and death of shoot tips, 'heart-rot' of beet; 'stem-crack' of celery	Not needed	
Fluorine, F	Associated with calcium as calcium fluoride in animals	Component of tooth enamel and bone		Dental decay more rapid	Milk, drinking water in some areas
Iodine, I	Thyroxine (Probably not required by plants)	Hormone controlling basal metabolic rate		Goitre; cretinism in children	Seafoods, salt

Experiments on plants were done in the late nineteenth and early twentieth century, particularly by German botanists, using the now classic water culture or sand culture techniques. In these experiments, plants are grown in prepared culture solutions of known composition. Many economically important plant deficiency diseases are now catalogued with the aid of colour photography, enabling rapid diagnosis.

7.10.2 Special methods for obtaining essential elements

Insectivorous plants

Insectivorous or carnivorous plants are green plants which are specially adapted for trapping and digesting small animals, particularly insects. In this way they supplement their normal autotrophic nutrition (photosynthesis) with a form of heterotrophic nutrition. Such plants typically live in nitrogen-poor habitats, and use the animals principally as a source of nitrogen. Having lured the insect with colour, scent or sweet secretions, the plant traps it in some way and then secretes enzymes and carries out extracellular digestion. The products, notably amino acids are absorbed and assimilated.

Some of the plants are interesting for the elaborate nature of their trap mechanisms, notably the Venus fly trap (*Dionaea muscipula*), pitcher plants (*Nepenthes*) and sundews (*Drosera*). *Drosera* is one of the few British examples, most being tropical or subtropical. It is found on the wetter heaths and moors which are typically acid, mineral-deficient habitats. The details of the various trap mechanisms are outside the scope of this book.

Mycorrhizas

A mycorrhiza is a mutualistic (symbiotic) association between a fungus and a plant root. It is likely that the great majority of land plants enter into this kind of relationship with soil fungi. They are of great significance because they are probably the major route of entry of mineral nutrients into roots. The fungus receives organic nutrients, mainly carbohydrates and vitamins, from the plant and in return absorbs mineral salts (particularly phosphate, ammonium, potassium and nitrate) and water, which can pass to the plant root. Generally only young roots are infected. Root hair production either ceases or is greatly reduced on infection. A network of hyphae spreads through the surrounding soil, covering a much larger surface area than the root could, even with root hairs. It has been suggested that plants of the same species, or even different species may often be interconnected with mycorrhizas, a concept which could radically alter our view of natural ecosystems.

Two groups of mycorrhizas occur, the ectotrophic and endotrophic mycorrhizas. **Ectotrophic mycorrhizas** form a sheath around the root and penetrate the air spaces between the cells in the cortex, but do not enter cells. An extensive intercellular net is formed. They are found mainly in forest trees such as conifers, beech, oak and many others, and involve fungi of the mushroom group. Their 'fruiting bodies' (mushrooms) are commonly seen near the trees.

Endotrophic mycorrhizas occur in virtually all other plants. Like ectotrophic mycorrhizas, they also form an intercellular network and extend into the soil, but they appear to penetrate cells (although in fact they do not break through the cell surface membranes of the root cells).

As we learn more about mycorrhizas, it is likely that the knowledge will be applied with advantage to agriculture, forestry and land reclamation.

Root nodules

Nitrogen fixation in root nodules of leguminous plants is discussed in chapter 13. The bacteria which inhabit the nodules stimulate growth and division of the root parenchyma cells resulting in the swelling or nodule.

7.11 Experimental work

Experiment 7.1: Investigating the Hill reaction

The Hill reaction

In 1939 Robert Hill, working in Cambridge, discovered that isolated chloroplasts were capable of releasing oxygen in the presence of an oxidising agent (electron acceptor). This has since been called the Hill reaction. A number of chemicals substitute for the naturally occurring electron acceptor NADP, one of which is the blue dye DCPIP (2,6 dichlorophenolindophenol) that turns colourless when reduced:

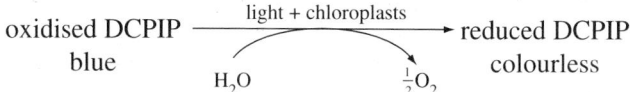

$$\text{oxidised DCPIP} \xrightarrow[\text{H}_2\text{O} \quad \frac{1}{2}\text{O}_2]{\text{light + chloroplasts}} \text{reduced DCPIP}$$

oxidised DCPIP — blue   reduced DCPIP — colourless

Isolation of chloroplasts

Materials

spinach, lettuce or cabbage leaves
scissors
cold pestle and mortar (or blender or food mixer)
muslin or nylon
filter funnel
centrifuge and centrifuge tubes
ice–water–salt bath
glass rod

Solutions (see notes)

0.05 M; phosphate buffer solution, pH 7.0

isolation medium
DCPIP solution (reaction medium)

Method

Chloroplasts can be isolated by grinding spinach, lettuce or cabbage leaves in a cold medium of suitable osmotic and ionic strength and pH, such as 0.4 M sucrose, 0.01 M KCl and 0.05 M phosphate buffer, pH 7.0. Solutions and apparatus must be kept cold during the isolation procedure if biochemical activity is to be preserved. The operation should also be performed as rapidly as possible, so study the method carefully and assemble the apparatus first.

Sufficient chloroplasts can be isolated using this method to supply several groups of students, if it is not practicable for all groups to prepare their own.

(1) Cut three small spinach, lettuce or cabbage leaves into small pieces with scissors, avoiding midribs and petioles. Place in a cold mortar or blender containing 20 cm³ of cold isolation medium (scale up quantities for blender if necessary).

(2) Grind vigorously and rapidly (or blend for about 10 s).

(3) Place four layers of muslin or nylon in a funnel and wet with cold isolation medium.

(4) Filter the homogenate through the funnel and collect in pre-cooled centrifuge tubes supported in an ice–water–salt bath. Gather the edges of the muslin and wring thoroughly into the tubes.

(5) Ensure that each centrifuge tube contains about the same volume of filtrate.

(6) If your bench centrifuge has a fixed speed, spin the filtrate for 2–5 min (a small pellet is required, but the time taken should be minimal).

   If a bench centrifuge with variable speed is available, spin the filtrate at 100–200 times gravity for 1–2 min. Respin the supernatant (the liquid above the sediment) at 1000–2000 times gravity for up to 5 min (sufficient time to get a small chloroplast pellet).

(7) Pour away the supernatant. Resuspend the pellet of one centrifuge tube in about 2 cm³ of isolation medium using a glass rod. Transfer the suspension from this tube to the second centrifuge tube and resuspend the pellet in that tube. (Alternatively, if more than one student group is to be supplied, use 2 cm³ in each tube and use one tube per group.)

(8) Store this chloroplast suspension in an ice–water–salt bath and use as soon as possible.

The Hill reaction

The chloroplast suspension can now be used to study the Hill reaction. The DCPIP solution should be used at room temperature.

Prepare the following tubes:

(1) 0.5 cm³ chloroplast suspension + 5 cm³ DCPIP solution. Leave in a bright light.

(2) 0.5 cm³ isolation medium + 5 cm³ DCPIP solution. Leave in a bright light.

(3) 0.5 cm³ chloroplast suspension + 5 cm³ DCPIP solution. Place immediately in darkness.

(4) It is useful to add 0.5 cm³ chloroplast suspension to 5 cm³ distilled water as a colour standard, showing what the final colour will be if the DCPIP is reduced.

Record your observations after 15–20 min.

If a colorimeter is available, the progress of the reaction can be followed by measuring the decrease in absorbance of the dye as it changes from the blue oxidised to the colourless reduced state. Prepare the mixtures given above for tubes (2) to (4) in colorimeter sample tubes. Insert a red (or yellow) filter and set the colorimeter at zero absorbance using tube (4) as a blank. Then set up tube (1) and immediately take a reading from this tube and return it to the light. Take further readings at 30 s intervals. Plot the rate of the reaction graphically. Once reduction is complete, take a reading from tube (3). Tube (2) can be checked for reduction of dye by first setting the colorimeter at zero with a blank of isolation medium. Ideally the time for complete reduction is about 10 min.

Notes

Prepare the solutions as follows.

0.05 M phosphate buffer solution, pH 7.0

$Na_2HPO_4.12H_2O$	4.48 g	(0.025 M)
KH_2PO_4	1.70 g	(0.025 M)

Make up to 500 cm³ with distilled water and store in a refrigerator at 0–4 °C.

Isolation medium

sucrose	34.23 g	(0.4 M)
KCl	0.19 g	(0.01 M)

Dissolve in phosphate buffer solution at room temperature and make up to 250 cm³ with the buffer solution. Store in a refrigerator at 0–4 °C.

DCPIP solution (reaction medium)

DCPIP	0.007–0.01 g	(10^{-4} M approx.)
KCl	0.93 g	(0.05 M)

Dissolve in phosphate buffer solution at room temperature and make up to 250 cm³. Store in a refrigerator at 0–4 °C. Use at room temperature.

(NB Potassium chloride is a cofactor for the Hill reaction.)

7.17 What change, if any, did you observe in tube (1)?

7.18 What was the purpose of tubes (2) and (3)?

7.19 What other organelles apart from chloroplasts might you expect in the chloroplast suspension?

7.20 What evidence have you that these were not involved in the reduction of the dye?

7.21 Why was the isolation medium kept cold?

7.22 Why was the isolation medium buffered?

7.23 What was (*a*) the electron donor, and (*b*) the electron acceptor, in the Hill reaction?

7.24 During the Hill reaction, DCPIP acts between X and PSI as shown in (fig 7.14*a*) and oxygen is evolved. Does the Hill reaction involve cyclic or non-cyclic photophosphorylation, or both? Give your reasons.

7.25 Fig 7.23 shows the appearance of the chloroplasts after being used in the experiment. The photograph demonstrates the consequences of transferring chloroplasts from the hypertonic isolation medium containing sucrose to the hypotonic reaction medium.

(*a*) How do the chloroplasts in fig 7.23 differ in appearance from normal chloroplasts?

(*b*) Can you explain why transferring the chloroplasts to a medium lacking sucrose should bring about this change?

(*c*) Why was this change desirable before carrying out the Hill reaction?

7.26 What significance do you think the discovery of the Hill reaction might have had on the understanding of the photosynthetic process?

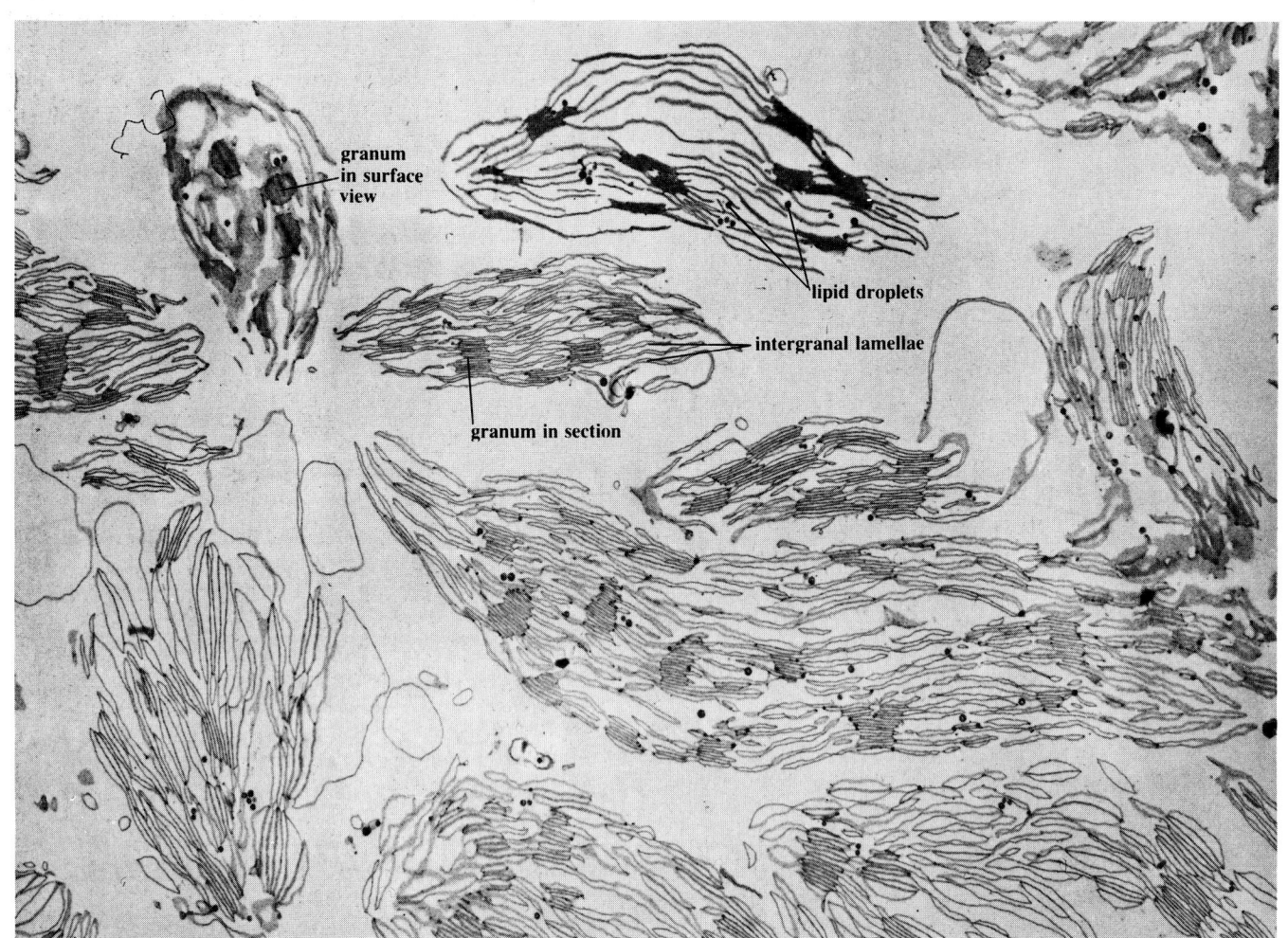

Fig 7.23 *Electron micrograph of chloroplasts after isolation in a dilute medium (×13 485). Envelopes and stroma are lost.*

Experiments: To investigate conditions required for, and products of, photosynthesis

As an indication that photosynthesis has occurred some production of the process can be identified. The first product is glycerate phosphate which is rapidly converted to a number of compounds, including sugars and then starch. The latter can be tested for very easily and can be taken as an indication that photosynthesis has occurred, providing that the precaution is taken of starting the experiment with a destarched leaf or plant.

Destarching a plant

A plant can be destarched by leaving it in the dark for 24–48 h. It is advisable to check that destarching is complete before attempting the following experiment.

> **7.27** Why does this result in destarching?

Experiment 7.2: To test a leaf for starch

Materials

leaf to be tested	hot water bath
test tube	90% ethanol
forceps	iodine/potassium iodide solution
white tile	

Method

Starch can be detected using iodine/potassium iodide solution (I_2/KI) but the leaf must first be decolourised because the green colour of the chlorophyll masks the colour change. This is achieved by placing the leaf in a test-tube of boiling 90% ethanol in a water bath for as long as necessary (naked flames must be avoided because ethanol is highly inflammable).

The decolourised leaf is rinsed in hot water to remove any ethanol and soften the tissues, spread on a white tile, and iodine solution poured on its surface. The red-brown solution stains any starch-containing parts of the leaf blue-black.

Experiment 7.3: To investigate the need for carbon dioxide

Materials

destarched leafy plant such as potted geranium (*Pelargonium*)	cotton wool
	starch test materials
	250 cm^3 conical flask
	clamp and clamp stand
light source such as a bench lamp	lime water
	20% potassium hydroxide solution

Method

Fig 7.24 illustrates a suitable procedure for investigating the need for carbon dioxide. The plant should be left for several hours in the light before testing the relevant leaves for starch.

> **7.28** Describe the conditions to which you would subject the control leaf.

A more satisfactory experiment showing the use of carbon dioxide is one involving the uptake of $^{14}CO_2$ (radioactively labelled carbon dioxide) into sugars and other compounds.

7.11.1 Measuring rates of photosynthesis

> **7.29** From the equation for photosynthesis, what changes in the substances taken up and produced might be used to measure the rate of photosynthesis?

In section 7.8 certain external factors (such as light intensity, carbon dioxide concentration and temperature) were shown to affect the rate of photosynthesis. When a particular factor is being investigated, it is essential that other factors are kept constant and, if possible, at optimum levels so that no other factor is limiting.

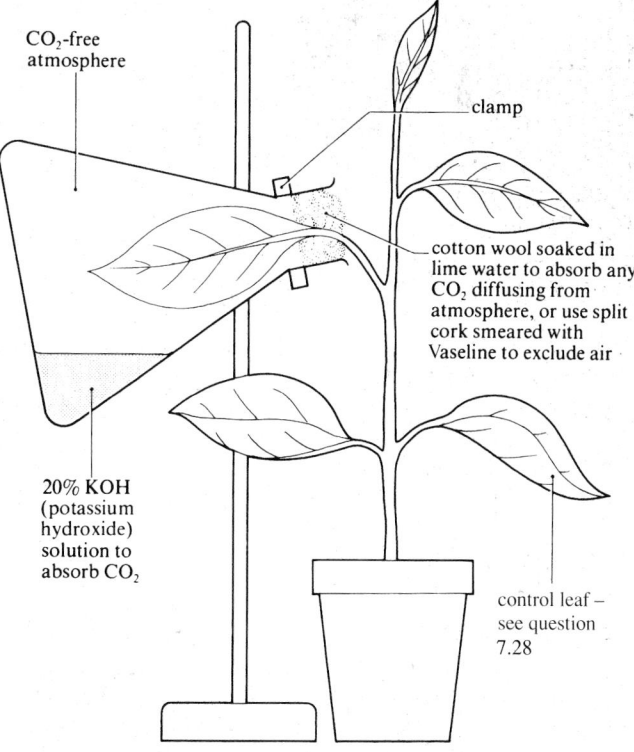

CO$_2$-free atmosphere

clamp

cotton wool soaked in lime water to absorb any CO$_2$ diffusing from atmosphere, or use split cork smeared with Vaseline to exclude air

20% KOH (potassium hydroxide) solution to absorb CO$_2$

control leaf – see question 7.28

Fig 7.24 *Investigating the need for carbon dioxide in photosynthesis.*

The rate of oxygen evolution

Measuring the rate of oxygen evolution from a water plant is the simplest way to measure the rate of photosynthesis.

Experiment 7.4: To investigate the effect of light intensity on the rate of photosynthesis

Materials

apparatus for collecting gas as shown in fig 7.25	metre rule
	stopclock
test-tube	light source such as bench lamp
400 cm³ beaker	
thermometer	Canadian pondweed (*Elodea*), previously well illuminated for several hours
mercury vapour lamp or projector lamp	
sodium hydrogen-carbonate	detergent (washing-up liquid)

Method

It is advisable to use *Elodea* that has been well illuminated and is known to be photosynthesising actively. The addition of 2–10 g of sodium hydrogencarbonate to each dm³ of pond water may stimulate photosynthesis if there are no obvious signs of bubbles being produced (this increases carbon dioxide availability). The water could also be aerated for an hour before the experiment.

(1) Cut the stem of a bubbling piece of *Elodea* to about 5 cm long with a sharp scalpel and place it, cut surface upwards, in a test-tube containing the same water that it has been kept in.

(2) Stand the test-tube in a beaker of water at room temperature. Record the temperature of the water, which acts as a heat shield, and check it at intervals throughout the experiment. It should remain constant and the water be renewed if necessary.

(3) Fill the apparatus with tap water, ensuring that no air bubbles are trapped in it and push the plunger well in to the end of the syringe (fig 7.25).

(4) Darken the laboratory. Place a bright light source 5 cm from the plant.

(5) Allow the plant to adjust to the light intensity (equilibrate) for 2–3 min. Ensure that the rate of bubbling is adequate (such as more than 10 bubbles per minute). A trace of detergent is sometimes sufficient to lower the surface tension to allow freer escape of bubbles.

(6) Position the *Elodea* so that its bubbles are collected in the capillary tube of the apparatus. Start timing.

(7) Collect a suitable volume of gas in a known period (for example 5–10 min). Measure the length of the bubble by drawing it slowly along the capillary tube by means of a syringe. The bubble can thus be positioned along the scale.

(8) Draw the bubble into the plastic tube connector where it will not interfere with subsequent measurements and repeat the procedure at increasing distances between the light source and *Elodea*, such as 10, 15, 20, 30, 40 and 80 cm. In each case allow time for the plant to equilibrate. The following three measurements are required under each condition: (*a*) the distance between plant and light source, (*b*) the time taken to collect the gas, and (*c*) the length of the gas bubbles collected (this measurement is directly proportional to volume and is used as a measurement of volume).

Results

The intensity of light falling on a given object is inversely proportional to the square of the distance from the source. In other words, doubling the distance between the weed and the lamp does not halve the light intensity received by the weed, but quarters it.

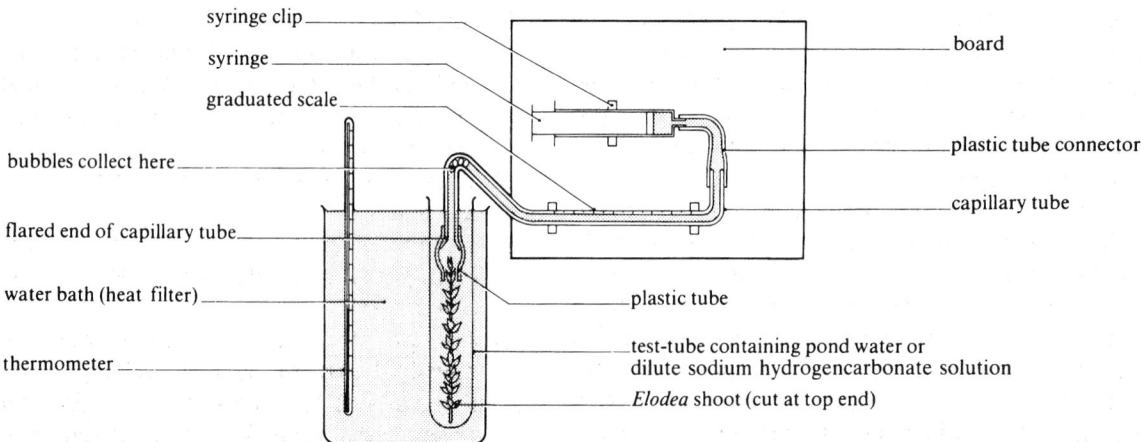

Fig 7.25 *Apparatus for measuring the rate of oxygen evolution by a water plant during photosynthesis.*

$$LI \propto 1/d^2$$

where LI is the light intensity and d is the distance between object and light source. Plot a graph with rate of photosynthesis on the vertical axis (as length of gas bubble per unit time) and LI on the horizontal axis (as $1/d^2$ or, more conveniently, $1000/d^2$).

> **7.30** (*a*) State the relationship between gas production and light intensity demonstrated by your results.
>
> (*b*) Why was the laboratory darkened and the temperature kept constant?
>
> **7.31** What are the main sources of inaccuracy in this experiment?
>
> **7.32** If the gas is collected and analysed it is found *not* to be pure oxygen. Can you account for this?
>
> **7.33** Why is it advisable to aerate the water before beginning the experiment?

If a simpler, quicker, though slightly less accurate method is required, the rate of oxygen evolution can be determined by counting the number of bubbles evolved from the cut end of a stem of *Elodea* in a given time period. This can be just as satisfactory, but errors may occur through variations in bubble size. This problem is less likely to arise if a trace of detergent is added to lower the surface tension (see (5) above). The *Elodea* can be anchored to the bottom of the tube with plasticine if necessary.

7.12 Compensation points

Photosynthesis results in uptake of carbon dioxide and evolution of oxygen. At the same time respiration uses oxygen and produces carbon dioxide. If light intensity is gradually increased from zero, the rate of photosynthesis gradually increases accordingly (fig 7.20). There will come a point, therefore, when photosynthesis and respiration exactly balance each other, with no net exchange of oxygen and carbon dioxide. This is called the **compensation point**, or more precisely the **light compensation point**, that is the light intensity at which net gaseous exchange is zero.

Since carbon dioxide concentration affects the rate of photosynthesis there also exists a **carbon dioxide compensation point**. This is the carbon dioxide concentration at which net gaseous exchange is zero for a given light intensity. The higher the carbon dioxide concentration, up to about 0.1% (1000 ppm, parts per million), the faster the rate of photosynthesis. For most temperate plants the carbon dioxide compensation point, beyond which photosynthesis exceeds respiration, is

50–100 ppm, assuming light is not a limiting factor. Atmospheric carbon dioxide concentrations are normally in the range 300–400 ppm, and therefore under normal circumstances of light and atmospheric conditions this point is always exceeded.

Experiment 7.5: To investigate gaseous exchange in leaves

Materials

four test-tubes thoroughly cleaned and fitted with rubber bungs	unbleached cotton wool no. 12 cork borer water bath with test-tube clamps
forceps	bench lamp
test-tube rack	freshly picked leaves
2 cm³ syringe	hydrogencarbonate
aluminium foil	indicator

The hydrogencarbonate indicator (bicarbonate indicator) solution should be freshly equilibrated with the atmosphere by bubbling fresh air through it until cherry red. Hydrogencarbonate indicator is supplied as a concentrated solution and must be diluted by a factor of ten for experimental use. To equilibrate with atmospheric carbon dioxide, air from *outside* the laboratory should be pumped through the solution. A suitable method is to place the solution in a clear glass wash-bottle to which a tube is attached whose free end is hung from a window. A filter pump is then used to bubble air through the solution until there is no further colour change. The colour of the indicator at this stage is a deep red but will appear orange-red in the test-tubes. Time must be allowed for this procedure before the start of the experiment (100 cm³ of indicator will need to be aerated for at least 20 min).

Method

(1) Label four test-tubes A, B, C and D.
(2) Rinse the four tubes and 2 cm³ syringe with a little of the indicator solution.
(3) Add 2 cm³ of the indicator solution to each tube by means of the syringe. Avoid putting fingers over the ends of the tubes since the acid in sweat will affect the indicator. Also avoid breathing over the open ends of the tubes.
(4) Cover the outside of the tubes A and C with aluminium foil.
(5) Set up the tubes as shown in fig 7.26, using two leaf discs per tube cut from a fresh leaf with a number 12 cork borer.
(6) Arrange the tubes in such a way that they are equally illuminated by a bench lamp.
(7) Place a heat filter in the form of a glass tank of water between the tubes and the light source to prevent a rise in temperature during the experiment.

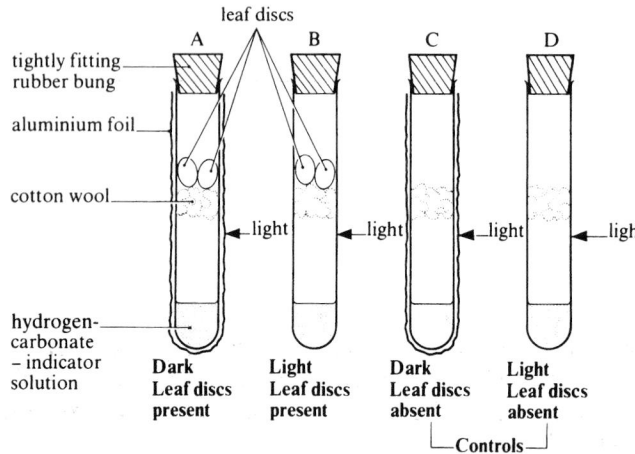

leaf discs

A   B   C   D

tightly fitting rubber bung

aluminium foil

cotton wool

light←→light←→light←→light

hydrogen-carbonate – indicator solution

Dark Leaf discs present   **Light Leaf discs present**   **Dark Leaf discs absent**   **Light Leaf discs absent**

Controls

Fig 7.26 *Experiment to investigate gas exchange in leaf discs.*

Alternatively, the tubes can be clamped in a water bath.

(8) Note the colour of the indicator in each tube.

(9) At intervals shake the tubes gently and leave for at least 2 h, preferably overnight. Record the final colour of the indicator in each tube as seen against a white background.

Results

Results can be interpreted using the following guide to colour changes.

yellow   orange   red   purple

←— net carbon dioxide production —| |— net carbon dioxide uptake —→

←————————— increasing acidity —————————→

←————————— increasing alkalinity ————————→

If conditions become more acidic, this can be assumed to be the result of carbon dioxide being produced and dissolving in the indicator solution. If conditions become less acidic, this indicates a lowering of carbon dioxide concentration.

Modifications of this experiment

(1) **Comparing rates of photosynthesis**. By using leaf discs as described, rather than whole leaves, comparative studies may be carried out using different light intensities, or, for example, old and young leaves on the same plant, yellow and green areas of variegated leaves, leaves of different species (such as a C_3 and a C_4 plant – see C_4 photosynthesis). To compare the rates of photosynthesis, colours of the indicator solutions can be compared during or at the end of the experiment as appropriate. If light intensity is investigated, a mercury vapour lamp should be used. An interesting comparison can be made between shade-loving plants, such as enchanter's nightshade (*Circaea lutetiana*), and other species to determine whether the former are capable of photosynthesising at lower light intensities (that is they have lower light compensation points).

(2) **Using water plants instead of leaf discs**. Water plants such as *Elodea* may be used, providing they are washed well in distilled water to remove traces of dirt and pond water in order to minimise any contribution from microorganisms. The plants should be placed directly in sufficient indicator solution to cover them. The solution has little effect on the plants during the course of the experiment.

Chapter Eight

Heterotrophic nutrition

As noted at the beginning of chapter 7, nutrition is the process of acquiring energy and materials for cell metabolism, including the maintenance and repair of cells, and growth. **Heterotrophic organisms**, or heterotrophs, are organisms that feed on an **organic source of carbon** (fig 8.1). It would be useful, if you have not already done so, to read sections 7.1 and 7.2 at this stage.

The survival of heterotrophs is dependent either directly or indirectly on the activities of autotrophs. All animals and fungi and the majority of bacteria are heterotrophic (table 2.3). The great majority obtain their energy from their food and these will be studied in this chapter. A few

Fig 8.1 (a) *Zebra eating grass. The grass contains energy obtained from sunlight, and carbon obtained from carbon dioxide, during the process of photosynthesis (autotrophic nutrition). The zebra obtains its energy and carbon from the grass (heterotrophic nutrition).*
(b) *Lion eating zebra. The lion is a carnivore, the zebra a herbivore.*

bacteria, however, are able to use light energy to synthesise their organic requirements from other organic raw materials. These are called **photoheterotrophs** (table 2.3).

The way in which heterotrophs obtain their food varies considerably. However, the way in which it is processed into a usable form within the body is very similar in most of them. It involves the following processes:

- **digestion** – reducing large complex food molecules into simpler soluble ones;
- **absorption** – taking the soluble molecules from the region of digestion into the tissues of the organism;
- **assimilation** – using the absorbed nutrients for a particular purpose.

For convenience, the main forms of heterotrophic nutrition may be classified as **holozoic**, **saprotrophic** (or saprophytic), **mutualistic** and **parasitic**, although some overlap between groups may occur. These will be studied in section 8.1.

8.1   Forms of heterotrophic nutrition

8.1.1   Holozoic nutrition

The term **holozoic** is applied mainly to free-living animals which have a specialised digestive tract, the **alimentary canal**. Most animals are holozoic.

The characteristic processes involved in holozoic nutrition are as follows.

- **Ingestion** is the taking in of food.
- **Digestion** is the breakdown of large organic molecules into smaller, simpler soluble molecules. Often two types of digestion occur. **Mechanical digestion** involves mechanical breakdown of the food, for example by teeth. **Chemical digestion** involves the activity of enzymes. The type of chemical process these enzymes catalyse during digestion is **hydrolysis**. Digestion may be either **extracellular** (outside the cell) or **intracellular** (inside the cell).
- **Absorption** is the uptake of the soluble molecules from the digestive region, across a membrane and into the body tissue proper. The food may pass directly into cells or first pass into the bloodstream to be transported to other regions of the body.

- **Assimilation** is using the absorbed molecules to provide either energy or materials to be incorporated into the body.
- **Egestion** is the elimination from the body of undigested waste food materials.

Animals which feed on plants are called **herbivores**, those that feed on other animals are **carnivores**, and those that eat a mixed diet of animal and vegetable matter are termed **omnivores**. Some animals take in food in the form of relatively small particles (microphagous feeders), for example earthworms and filter feeders like mussels. Some ingest food in liquid form (fluid feeders) such as aphids, butterflies and mosquitoes. Some take in food in the form of relatively large pieces (macrophagous feeders), for example *Hydra* and sea anemones, which use tentacles to catch their prey, and large carnivores such as sharks.

8.1.2 Saprotrophic nutrition (*sapros*, rotten; *trophos*, feeder)

Organisms which feed on dead or decaying organic matter are called **saprotrophs**. Other terms sometimes used which mean the same thing are saprophytes (saprophytic nutrition) and saprobionts (saprobiotic nutrition). Many fungi and bacteria are saprotrophs, for example the fungi *Mucor*, *Rhizopus* and yeast. Saprotrophs secrete enzymes onto their food where it is digested. The soluble end-products of this extracellular digestion are then absorbed and assimilated by the saprotroph. Saprotrophs feed on the dead organic remains of plants and animals and contribute to the removal of such remains by decomposing it. Many of the simple substances formed are not used by the saprotrophs themselves but are absorbed by plants. In this way the activity of saprotrophs provides important links in nutrient cycles by making possible the return of vital chemical elements from the dead bodies of organisms to living ones.

The saprotrophic nutrition of Mucor and Rhizopus

Mucor and *Rhizopus* are common fungi known as pin moulds. They are often found growing on bread, although they can also live in soil. The structure of *Mucor* is described in section 2.7.2. *Rhizopus* has a very similar structure and is even more common. Both are easy to culture in a laboratory. Their hyphae penetrate the food on which they grow and secrete hydrolysing enzymes from their tips. This results in extracellular digestion as shown in fig 8.2. Carbohydrase and protease enzymes carry out the extracellular digestion of starch to glucose and protein to amino acids respectively. The thin, much-branched nature of the mycelium of *Mucor* and *Rhizopus* ensures that there is a large surface area for absorption. Glucose is used during respiration to provide energy for the organism's metabolic activities whilst glucose and amino acids are used for growth and repair. Excess glucose is converted to

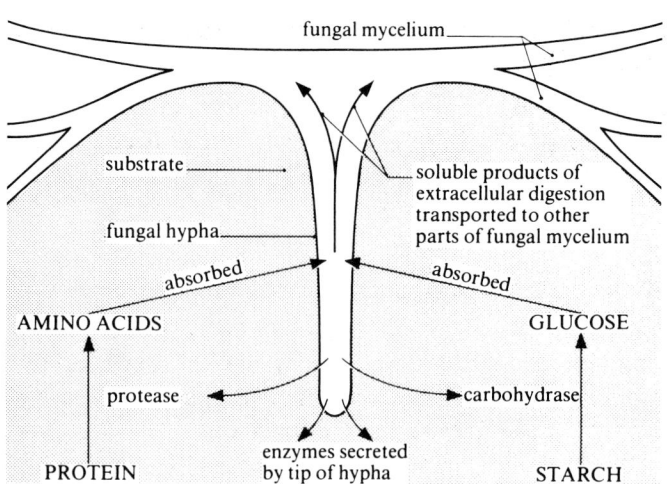

Fig 8.2 *Extracellular digestion and absorption in* Mucor *and* Rhizopus.

glycogen and fat, and excess amino acids to protein granules for storage in the cytoplasm.

8.1 Briefly describe the ways in which *Mucor* and *Rhizopus* are important to humans.

8.1.3 Symbiosis: mutualism, parasitism and commensalism

The term **symbiosis** means literally 'living together' (*syn*, with; *bios*, life). It was introduced by the German scientist de Bary in 1879 who described it as 'the living together of dissimilarly named organisms'; in other words, it is an association between two or more organisms of different species. Since de Bary's time the term symbiosis has been restricted by many biologists to meaning a close relationship between two or more organisms of different species **in which all partners benefit**.

Since the 1970s symbiosis has become more important as a topic in biology. For example, we now know that the great majority of plants obtain their minerals with the assistance of fungi, and that much nitrogen fixation is carried out by symbiotic bacteria; knowledge of rumen fermentation, involving symbiotic organisms, is of importance in increasing cattle productivity. At the same time biologists have become increasingly aware that the exact degree of closeness, benefit or harm in a relationship is very variable. Most modern biologists therefore prefer to use something like de Bary's original definition of symbiosis, a move approved by the Society for Experimental Biology in 1975*.

The following definitions will therefore be used in this book. Emphasis is placed on whether the relationship is beneficial or not to both partners.

Symbiosis – the living together in close association of two or more organisms of different species. Many associations involve three or more partners. Nutrition is commonly involved. Three common types of symbiotic relationship are:

- **mutualism** – in which both partners benefit;
- **parasitism** – in which one partner benefits and causes harm to the other;
- **commensalism** – in which one partner benefits but the other receives no harm or benefit.

Mutualism

Mutualism is a close association between two living organisms of different species which is beneficial to both partners. For example, the sea anemone *Calliactis* attaches itself to a shell used by a hermit crab (fig 8.3). The anemone obtains nourishment from the scraps of food left by the crab, and is transported from place to place when the crab moves. The crab is camouflaged by the anemone and may also be protected by the stinging cells in its tentacles. It seems that the anemone is unable to survive unless attached to the crab's shell, and, if the anemone is removed, the crab will seek another anemone and actually place it on its shell.

Herbivorous ruminants contain a vast number of cellulose-digesting bacteria and ciliates (see section 8.6.2). These can only survive in the anaerobic conditions found in a ruminant's alimentary canal. Here the bacteria and ciliates feed on the cellulose contained in the host's diet, converting it into simple compounds which the ruminant is then able to further digest, absorb and assimilate itself.

An important example of mutualism is the formation of root nodules by *Rhizobium*, a bacterium. This is described in section 7.10.2. Other examples are mycorrhizas (section 7.10.2) and endosymbiosis (section 8.1.3).

Fig 8.3 *Sea anemones attached to a whelk shell inhabited by a hermit crab.*

* References: SEB symposia XXIX, *Symbiosis*, CUP (1975) D.H. Jennings & D.L. Lee (eds,); G.H. Harper, (1985) 'Teaching symbiosis' *J. Biol. Ed.* 19 (3), 219–23; D.C. Smith & A.E. Douglas (1987) *The Biology of Symbiosis*, Arnold.

Parasitism (para, beside; sitos, food)

Parasitism is a close association between two living organisms of different species which is beneficial to one (the **parasite**) and harmful to the other (the **host**). The parasite obtains food from the host and, generally, shelter. A successful parasite is able to live with the host without causing it any great harm. The degree of benefit or harm may be difficult to establish.

Parasites which live on the outer surface of a host are termed **ectoparasites** (for example ticks, fleas and leeches). Such organisms do not always live a fully parasitic existence. Those that live within a host are **endoparasites**, such as *Plasmodium* (a protozoan that causes malaria (chapter 15), the tapeworm *Taenia*, and the liver fluke *Fasciola*. If the organism has to live parasitically at all times, it is said to be an **obligate** parasite, for example the fungus-like organism *Phytophthora* which causes potato blight (section 2.8.2). Facultative parasites are fungi that can feed either parasitically or saprotrophically, for example *Candida*, which causes thrush in humans (section 2.7.3) and *Pythium*, a fungus-like organism which causes 'damping-off' of seedlings (section 2.8.2). Sometimes facultative parasites kill their hosts and then live saprotrophically on the dead remains, as does *Pythium*.

Parasites are highly specialised, possessing numerous adaptations, many of which are associated with their host and its mode of life. This is particularly well illustrated by the tapeworm (*Taenia*) which is specialised for life in the gut, and the liver fluke (*Fasciola*) which lives in the bile duct. The life cycle of the liver fluke is described in section 2.10.3 and fig 2.5.1.

Like the liver fluke, *Taenia* belongs to the group of animals known as flatworms. It shows many adaptations to its mode of life compared with a free-living flatworm such as *Planaria* (section 2.10.3). Some of these adaptations are shown in fig 8.4 and some relating to feeding are discussed below.

Unlike free-living flatworms, the tapeworm has no gut or feeding structures of its own since it can absorb pre-digested food through its cuticle. (The large surface area to volume ratio of flatworms means that no special internal transport system, such as a blood system, is necessary as materials can diffuse rapidly to all parts of the body.) Tapeworms need no special sense organs like eyes since they live in a dark, constant environment and do not need to move around to obtain food. No special locomotory organs are present (free-living flatworms have simple eyes and show a gliding motion caused by cilia). The nervous system of tapeworms is therefore relatively poorly developed compared with free-living flatworms. The tapeworm can also withstand the low oxygen levels of the gut and respire anaerobically.

Table 8.1 shows some of the structural, physiological and reproductive modifications used by various parasites. Microorganisms which cause disease may be regarded as parasites (section 8.1.3).

Fig 8.4 *Structure of an adult tapeworm (Taenia).*

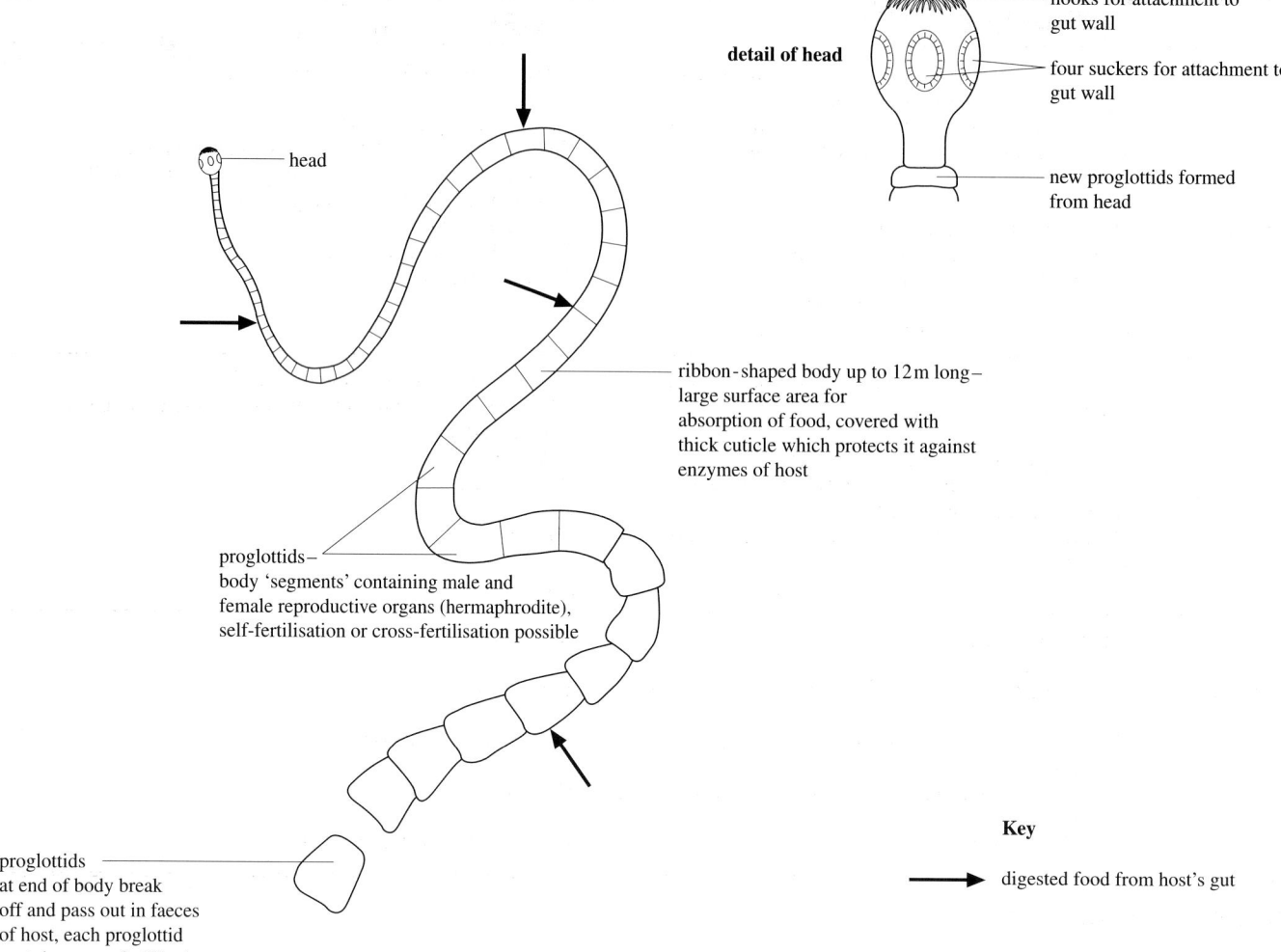

detail of head

hooks for attachment to gut wall

four suckers for attachment to gut wall

new proglottids formed from head

head

ribbon-shaped body up to 12 m long – large surface area for absorption of food, covered with thick cuticle which protects it against enzymes of host

proglottids – body 'segments' containing male and female reproductive organs (hermaphrodite), self-fertilisation or cross-fertilisation possible

proglottids at end of body break off and pass out in faeces of host, each proglottid contains many fertilised eggs

Key

→ digested food from host's gut

8.2 List the structural, physiological and reproductive features that make *Fasciola* (liver fluke) a successful parasite.

Commensalism (com-, *together; mensa, table*)

Commensalism is a close association between two living organisms of different species which is beneficial to one (the commensal) and does not affect the other (the host). Commensalism means literally 'eating at the same table' and is used to describe symbiotic relationships which do not fit conveniently into the mutualism and parasitism categories. For example, the colonial hydrozoan *Hydractinia* attaches itself to whelk shells inhabited by hermit crabs. It obtains nourishment from the scraps of food left by the crab after it has eaten. In this particular case the crab is totally unaffected by the association. An orchid or lichen (the commensal) growing on a tree (the host) would be another example.

8.2 Feeding mechanisms in a range of animals

8.2.1 Filter feeding

Filter feeders strain small particles of organic matter from water. Many molluscs feed in this way. An example is *Mytilus edulis*, the common mussel, which is found attached to rocks and stones in shallow coastal waters (fig 8.5). It belongs to a group of molluscs known as bivalves. These have a shell with two halves, or valves, which are hinged together. Inside the shell are two large gills, one on each side. The gills are covered with fine beating hairs called **cilia**. The movement of the cilia causes a current of water to enter the animal via one tube (the **inhalant siphon**) and leave via another tube (the **exhalant siphon**) (fig 8.5). The water which enters contains the food of the mussels, such as microscopic protozoa and algae. Numerous secretory cells scattered among the cilia produce streams of sticky mucus which trap the food particles. The trapped food is then swept by special bands of cilia towards the mouth which is located near the front end of the 'gill'. Ciliated structures surround the mouth and sort out the food

Table 8.1 Some structural, physiological and reproductive specialisations of parasites.

	Type of modification	Examples
Structural	Absence or degeneration of feeding and locomotory organs – characteristic of gut parasites.	*Fasciola* (liver fluke), *Taenia* (tapeworm)
	Highly specialised mouthparts as in fluid feeders.	*Pulex* (flea), *Aphis* (aphid)
	Development of haustoria in some parasitic green plants.	*Cuscuta* (dodder) (a flowering plant belonging to the family Convolvulaceae which does not possess chlorophyll and parasitises a variety of green plants)
	Boring devices to enter host.	nematode worms
	Attachment organs such as hooks or suckers.	*Taenia*, *Hirudo* (leech), *Fasciola*
	Outer covering resistant to attack by enzymes.	*Taenia*, *Fasciola*
	Reduction of sense organs associated with the constancy of the parasite's environment.	*Taenia*
Physiological	Enzyme production to digest host tissue external to parasite.	fungi, *Plasmodium* (a protozoan which infects mammals and birds, and in the case of humans causes malaria)
	Anticoagulant production in blood feeders.	*Pulex*, *Hirudo*
	Chemosensitivity in order to reach the optimum location in the host's body.	*Plasmodium*
	Production of digestive enzymes to aid penetration into host.	*Cuscuta*
	Ability to respire adequately in anaerobic conditions.	gut parasites
Reproductive	Hermaphrodite condition allowing self-fertilisation, if necessary.	*Taenia*, *Fasciola*
	Enormous numbers of reproductive bodies, i.e. eggs, cysts and spores.	*Taenia*, *Fasciola*
	Resistance of reproductive bodies when external to the host.	*Phytophthora* (potato blight)
	Employment of specialised reproductive phases in the life cycle.	*Fasciola*
	Use of secondary hosts as vectors.	*Taenia*, *Fasciola*, *Plasmodium*

Fig 8.5 *Filter feeding in the mussel (*Mytilus edulis*).*

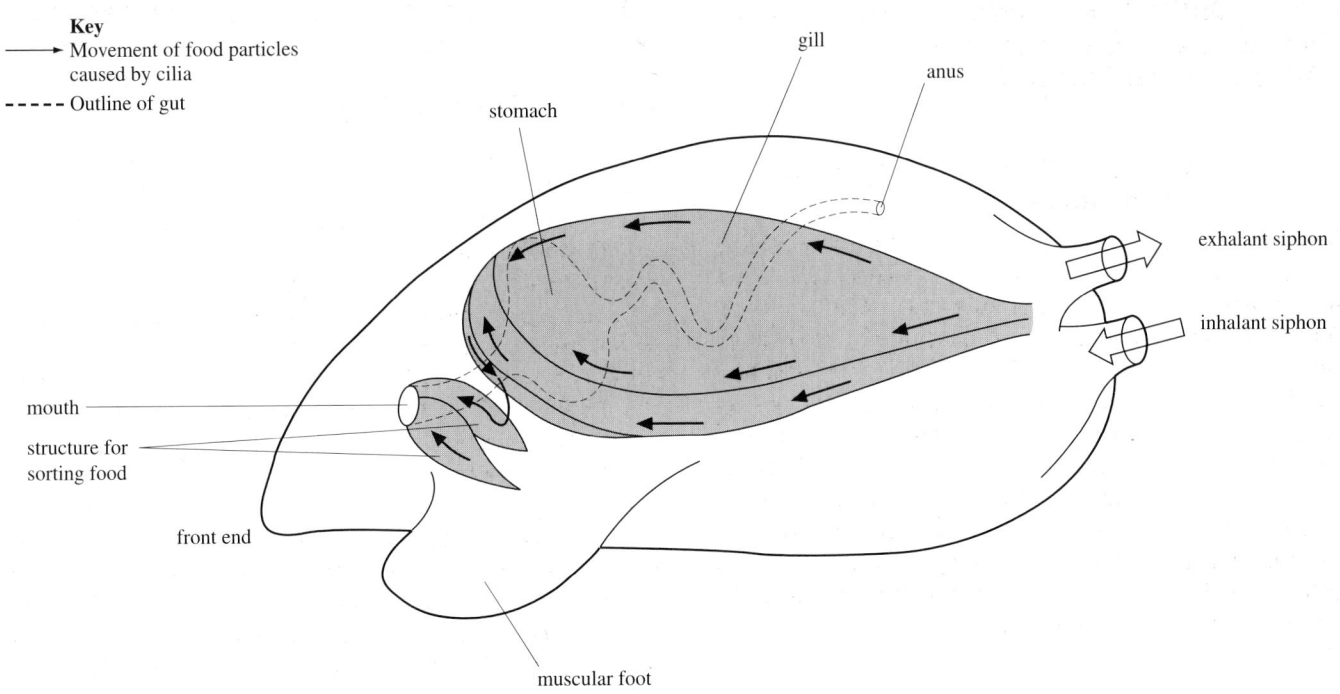

Key

→ Movement of food particles caused by cilia

----- Outline of gut

gill

anus

stomach

exhalant siphon

inhalant siphon

mouth

structure for sorting food

front end

muscular foot

particles to some extent before they enter the mouth. The alimentary canal of the mussel consists of a stomach and short intestine which ends at the anus near the exhalant siphon.

8.2.2 Feeding with tentacles

The phylum Cnidaria contains animals which have a simple structure (section 2.10.2). Cnidarians include jellyfish, sea anemones and the freshwater *Hydra*. They are all carnivores and possess tentacles for capturing food. The tentacles surround the mouth as shown in figs 2.47 and 2.48. There is no true gut, only a simple sac called an **enteron**, with one opening, the mouth. Food is placed in the mouth (**ingestion**) and any undigested remains eventually leave through the mouth (**egestion**).

Along the outside surface of the tentacles are batteries of stinging cells called **nematoblasts**. These cells have projecting hair-like triggers which, when stimulated, release their contents explosively (fig. 8.6). Usually, they have to be stimulated in two ways at the same time, for example by touch and exposure to appropriate chemicals ('scent'). Many types of nematoblasts exist. Some have barbs which penetrate the prey in the initial explosive discharge. Others have minor hooks that cling to the prey, and long hollow threads that release poison (the sting of a jellyfish) which can paralyse and even kill the prey. Sometimes the threads are sticky and loop round the prey, entangling it. The animal then grasps the prey with its tentacles, which pass it to the mouth for ingestion. The mouth opens widely and the prey enters the internal cavity (enteron) for the first, extracellular phase of digestion. Once the food has been reduced to small fragments, these are engulfed by phagocytosis into cells lining the enteron and digestion is finished intracellularly. Examples of the prey of *Hydra* include the water flea (*Daphnia*) and *Cyclops*, both common, small crustaceans found in fresh water.

8.2.3 Detritus feeding

Detritus is fresh or decaying organic matter. It is commonly found at the soil surface. An organism which is specialised for feeding on detritus is called a **detritivore**. An example of a detritivore is the earthworm. Detritivores often represent the first stage in recycling dead materials and therefore play an important role in ecosystems. The earthworm (fig 2.58) consumes fragments of detritus, especially vegetation, either at the soil surface, or after the food has been pulled into its burrow by its mouth. Pieces of food are torn off, moistened by alkaline secretions of the pharynx and swallowed. Earthworms can also feed on organic material contained in the soil which they swallow during burrowing activity.

The alimentary canal is straight and runs from mouth to anus. It is specialised at various points along its length for digestion and absorption of the ingested food. Any undigested material is egested from the anus as 'worm casts'.

Charles Darwin was the first person to point out how valuable earthworms are in maintaining soil structure and fertility. Fertile soil may contain over two million earthworms per hectare. By grinding soil as it passes through their guts, and depositing it at the surface as worm casts, earthworms break it down into fine particles, improving its texture and keeping it turning over (an estimated 50 tonnes per hectare per year). Nitrogenous waste included in the worm casts also adds nutrients which can be used by plants. Excess calcium is also got rid of as calcium salts and these reduce soil acidity, generally improving conditions for plant growth. The burrows of the worms help to aerate the soil, improving drainage and allowing more oxygen to reach plant roots. By pulling down surface detritus into their burrows they increase the overall rate of decomposition and increase productivity of an ecosystem.

8.2.4 Biting and chewing mouthparts

Many insects are herbivorous and have mouthparts for biting and chewing vegetation. Many are pests because they attack crops. The locust is an important example. The mouthparts of the locust are complex (fig 8.7). To understand the arrangement of the mouthparts it helps to know a little about the construction of the insect body as a whole. The body is made up of a series of segments (section 2.10.6). Each segment can bear a pair of jointed appendages. These can be modified in the head region for feeding. The locust uses appendages on segments 4, 5 and 6 of the head. These surround the mouth which is located on the lower surface of the head. Fig 8.7 shows that, in succession, there is an upper lip (**labrum**), a pair of jaws (**mandibles**), a pair of **maxillae** and a lower lip (**labium**). The jaws are on segment 4, the maxillae on segment 5 and the lower lip (a fused pair of appendages) on segment 6.

When feeding, a leaf is gripped between the upper and lower lips. The jaws work from side to side to cut, shred and crush small pieces from the leaf, with some help from the maxillae. The lower lip, containing saliva, again with help from the maxillae, then pushes the moistened food into the mouth where it is swallowed. Sensory processes called **palps** allow the locust to feel, smell and taste the food.

Locusts are a serious pest in warm parts of the world such as Africa, India, Pakistan, the Middle East and South America. Locust plagues in ancient Egypt are reported in the Bible. Outbreaks occur at irregular intervals and last for a few seasons. Populations build up from low density to high density in key 'outbreak centres' as food becomes limited and it becomes essential for a large proportion of the population to migrate to a new habitat. At this stage the locusts collect and migrate together as winged adults in vast swarms which can contain as many as 10 000 million locusts. These swarms are capable of eating more than 100 000 tonnes of food per day (fig 8.8). They can completely strip large areas of vegetation, devastating crops and causing famine. International cooperation means that

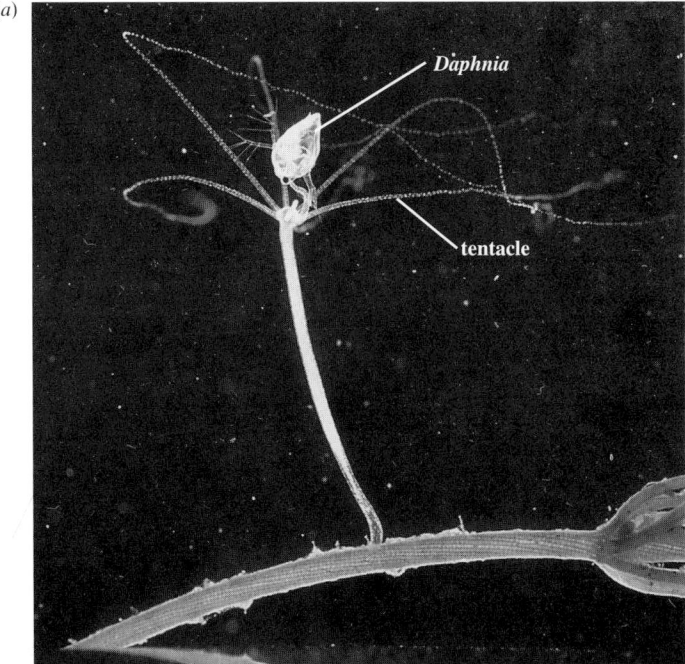

(a)

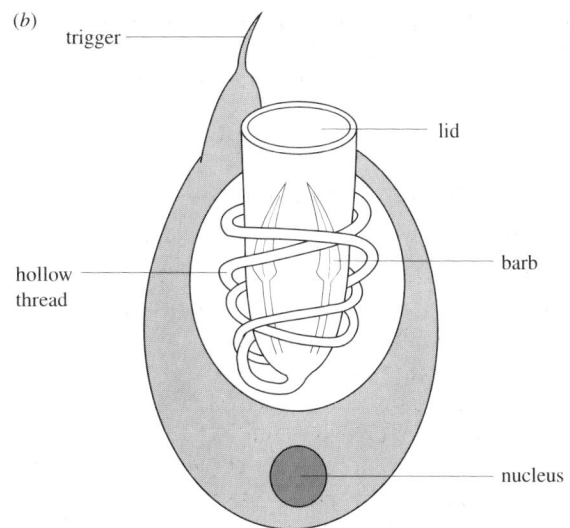

(b)

trigger

lid

hollow
thread

barb

nucleus

before discharge

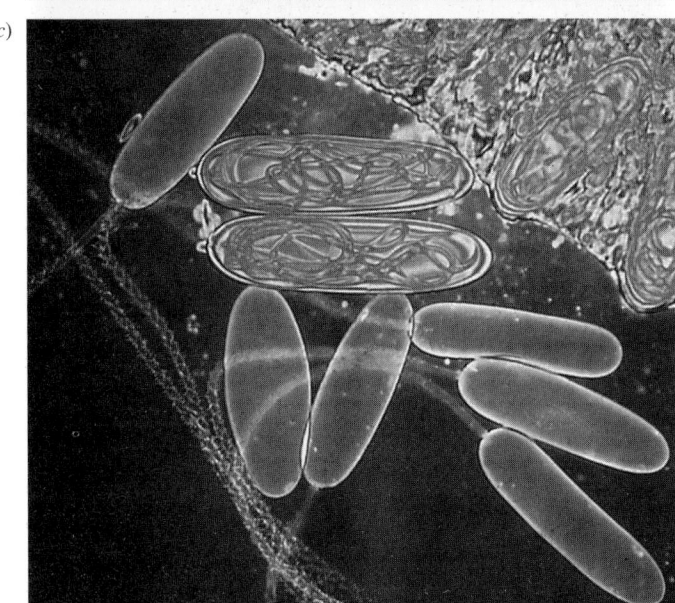

(c)

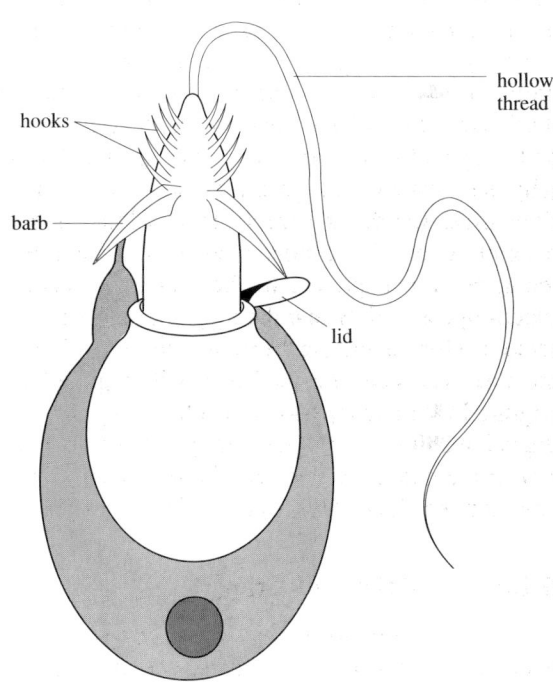

hooks

barb

hollow
thread

lid

after discharge

Fig 8.6 (a) Hydra *capturing a water flea (*Daphnia*).
(b) *Nematoblast before and after discharge.* (c) *Light
micrograph of a group of nematocysts of the sea anemone*
Rhodactis rhodostoma. *All but two of the nematocysts have
discharged their stinging threads.* (d) *Scanning electron
micrograph of* Trichodina *trapped on the tentacles of a
hydra.*

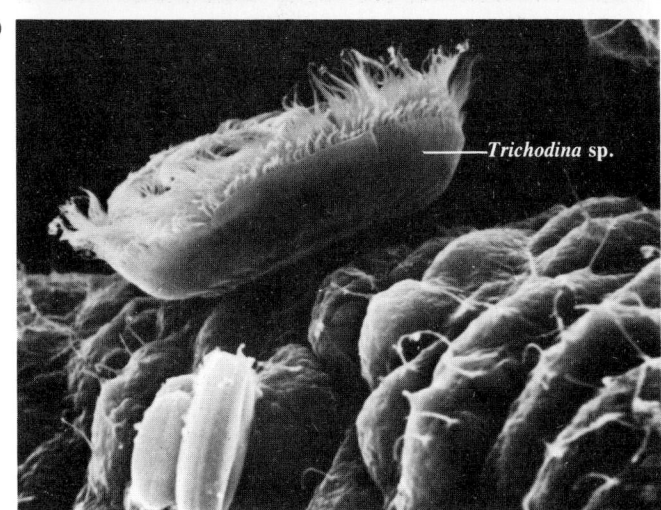

(d)

Trichodina sp.

(a)

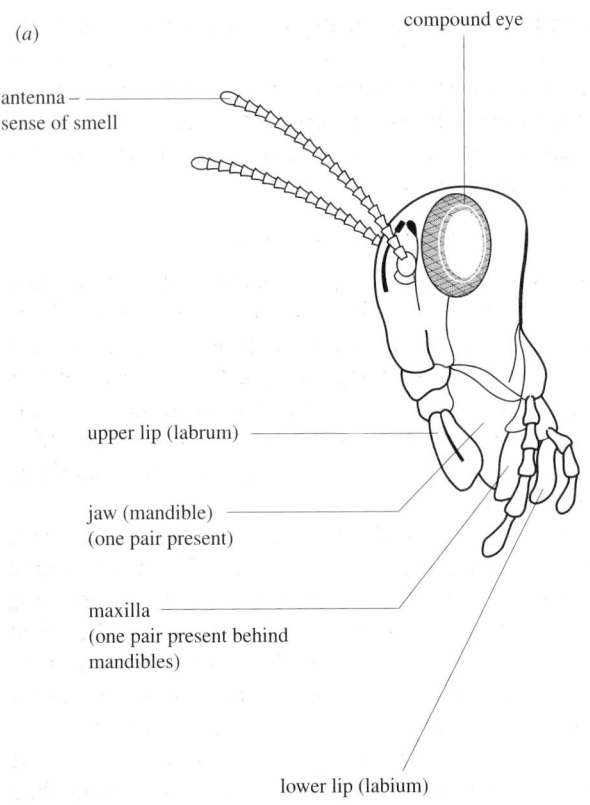

antenna –
sense of smell

compound eye

upper lip (labrum)

jaw (mandible)
(one pair present)

maxilla
(one pair present behind
mandibles)

lower lip (labium)

front views

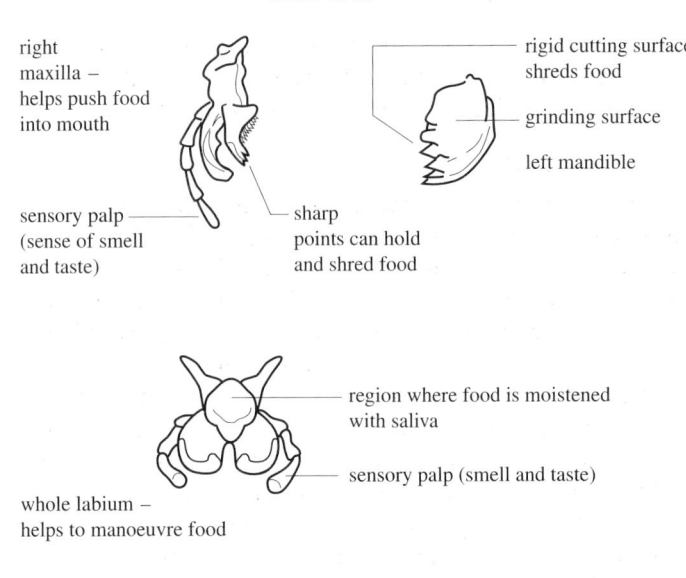

right
maxilla –
helps push food
into mouth

sensory palp
(sense of smell
and taste)

sharp
points can hold
and shred food

rigid cutting surface
shreds food

grinding surface

left mandible

region where food is moistened
with saliva

sensory palp (smell and taste)

whole labium –
helps to manoeuvre food

Fig 8.7 (a) *Mouthparts of a locust.* (b) *Front view of head of locust showing mouthparts.*

populations are now constantly monitored. This, and studies of their migratory behaviour, means that swift responses can now be made to minimise damage. Places most at risk can be identified and sprayed with insecticide before the arrival of the locusts. Swarms can be tracked and destroyed with the aid of aeroplanes and land vehicles.

(b)

Fig 8.8 *Swarming locusts.*

8.2.5 Fluid feeding

Some insects feed on fluids using specialised mouthparts for **sucking**, for example butterflies, or **piercing and sucking**, for example aphids and mosquitoes.

Sucking

Butterflies, such as the cabbage white butterfly (fig 2.60), possess a feeding device called a **proboscis**. This is formed from the two **maxillae** (which, as noted above, have a completely different structure and function in the locust). Part of each maxilla is greatly elongated and C-shaped in cross section (fig 8.9). The two C-shapes fit together precisely to form the walls of a long tube, the proboscis. Mandibles (jaws) are absent, unlike the locust, and sensory palps are less well developed than in the locust. At rest, the proboscis is coiled up under the head. When feeding, a reflex causes contraction of muscles inside each half of the proboscis which uncoil and straighten the proboscis.

Butterflies feed on nectar from flowers. The proboscis is extended into the corolla (petals) of a flower and its tip placed directly on the nectar, which is a dilute solution of sugar. Muscles in the pharynx (fig 8.9) then begin to contract, causing the nectar to be sucked into the mouth of the insect. It is frequently the case that the depth of the corolla tube of the flower corresponds to the length of the butterfly's proboscis, so that each species of butterfly tends to visit one or a few species of flower only. The butterfly often acts as a vital agent of pollination, so these species often depend on each other for their survival, an example of mutualism.

Piercing and sucking

Aphids (greenfly) feed on plant juices from leaves and stems. Like the butterfly, the aphid has specialised elongated mouthparts that form a proboscis, but these have to be modified for piercing the plant tissue as well as sucking. They have to penetrate the sieve tubes of the phloem, which are the long tubes which conduct high concentrations of the sugar sucrose and other nutrients through the plant.

In the aphid, the maxillae fit together to form a sharp piercing tube called the **stylet** (fig 8.10). This is enclosed in a sheath formed by an elongated labium (lower lip) and mandibles. The stylet can be pushed through the plant tissues and into the sieve tube. The aphid's work is now done because the contents of the sieve tube are under pressure and are forced up the stylet tube into its gut.

Aphids have been used by scientists to analyse the contents of sieve tubes. After anaesthetising the feeding aphid, its body can be cut off and the stylet continues to exude juice from the sieve tubes. Aphids are a serious pest in agriculture and horticulture. They attack most crops, important examples being cereals, beans, potatoes, fruit trees and bushes, and cotton. They are a common pest of greenhouses. Both biological and chemical controls are used. Ladybirds, for example, are an important predator. However, spraying with insecticides can kill ladybirds and other insect predators, as well as aphids, and populations of aphids have sometimes benefited from the use of insecticides. As well as being important crop pests in their own right, aphids can act as vectors in spreading virus disease from one plant to another.

8.3 The alimentary canal in humans

Digestion and absorption occurs in the alimentary canal, or more plainly the gut, which runs from the mouth to the anus. As the gut wall is continuous with the outside surface of the body, the food in the gut is considered to be 'outside' the body. Food can only be absorbed into the body after it has been **ingested** and broken down physically by the teeth and muscles of the gut wall (**mechanical digestion**), and chemically by its enzymes into molecules of a suitably small size to be absorbed through the gut wall (**chemical digestion**). From here the nutrients enter the blood or lymph and are delivered to the cells of the body tissues where they undergo **assimilation**. Undigested food is **egested** through the anus. A reminder of the stages of nutrition might be useful at this stage (section 8.1.1).

(a)

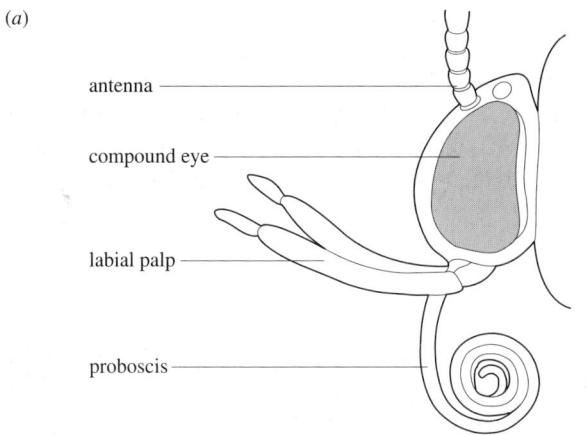

antenna

compound eye

labial palp

proboscis

(b)

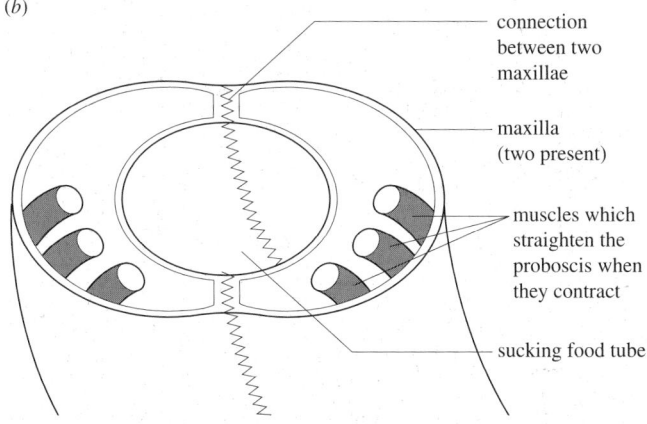

connection between two maxillae

maxilla (two present)

muscles which straighten the proboscis when they contract

sucking food tube

Fig 8.9 (a) *Mouthparts of a butterfly.* (b) *Detail of the proboscis, shown cut transversely.*

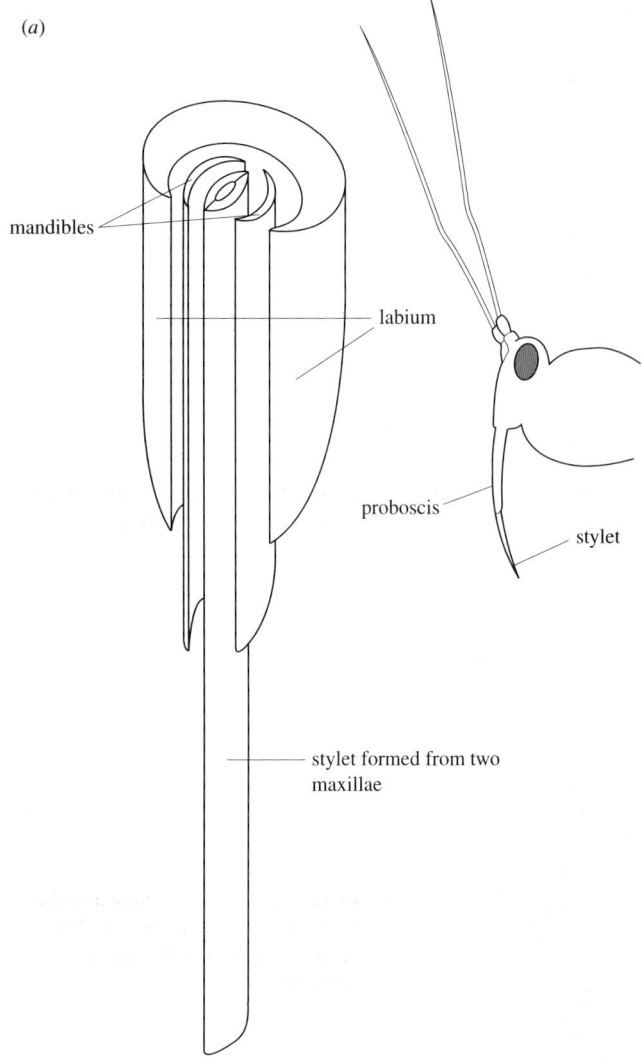

(a)

mandibles

labium

proboscis

stylet

stylet formed from two
maxillae

(b)

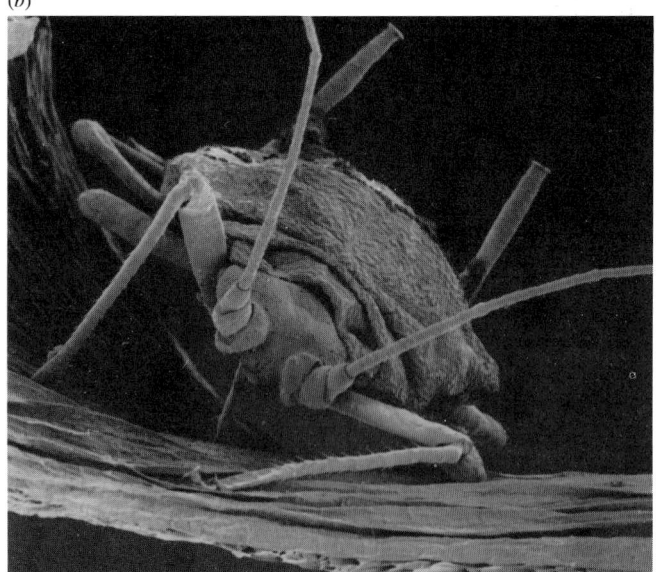

Fig 8.10 (a) *Aphid mouthparts (based on figs 28.15a and 28.16a, p152, Introduction to Biology, 5th ed., D.G. Mackean, John Murray (1973)). (b) Scanning electron micrograph of aphid showing stylet piercing a leaf.*

The gut is specialised into different regions, each designed to carry out a different role in the overall processes of digestion and absorption. These regions and a summary of their functions are shown in fig 8.11.

8.3.1 Generalised structure of the human gut

Although each different region of the gut possesses its own special characteristics, all have a basic common structure as shown in fig 8.12. This consists of four distinct layers: the mucosa, submucosa, muscularis externa and serosa.

Mucosa

This is the innermost layer of the gut and has three layers, the **epithelium**, **lamina propria** and **muscularis mucosa**. It is the major absorbing and secreting layer.

The **epithelium** secretes large quantities of mucus which lubricates the food, helping its passage through the gut. It also prevents digestion of the gut wall by its own enzymes. Some of the epithelial cells have microvilli on their free surfaces. These contain enzymes embedded in their cell surface membranes. The microvilli form a border which is just visible as a fuzzy line in the light microscope and is known as a **'brush border'**. The epithelial cells rest on a basement membrane beneath which is the **lamina propria**. This contains a supporting layer of connective tissue, through which runs blood and lymph vessels. In most regions the lamina propria also contains glands which are formed by infoldings of the epithelium. Outside the lamina propria is a thin layer of smooth muscle, the **muscularis mucosa**. This helps to produce folds of the mucosa and submucosa in certain regions of the gut.

Submucosa

This is a layer of connective tissue containing nerves, blood and lymph vessels, collagen and elastic fibres. In the duodenum it contains some mucus-secreting glands which deposit their contents onto the surface via ducts.

Muscularis externa

This layer is composed of an inner circular and an outer longitudinal layer of smooth muscle. Smooth muscle is involuntary muscle, meaning that it is not under voluntary control from the brain. Coordinated movements of the two layers provide the wave-like peristaltic movements of the gut wall which force food along. Their movements also mix the food (section 8.3.5).

Between the circular and the longitudinal muscle layers is **Auerbach's plexus**. A plexus is a mass of nerve tissue. Auerbach's plexus consists of nerves from the autonomic (involuntary) nervous system which control peristalsis. Impulses travelling along sympathetic nerves cause the gut muscles to relax and the sphincters to close, whilst impulses travelling via the parasympathetic nerves stimulate the gut wall to contract and sphincters to open.

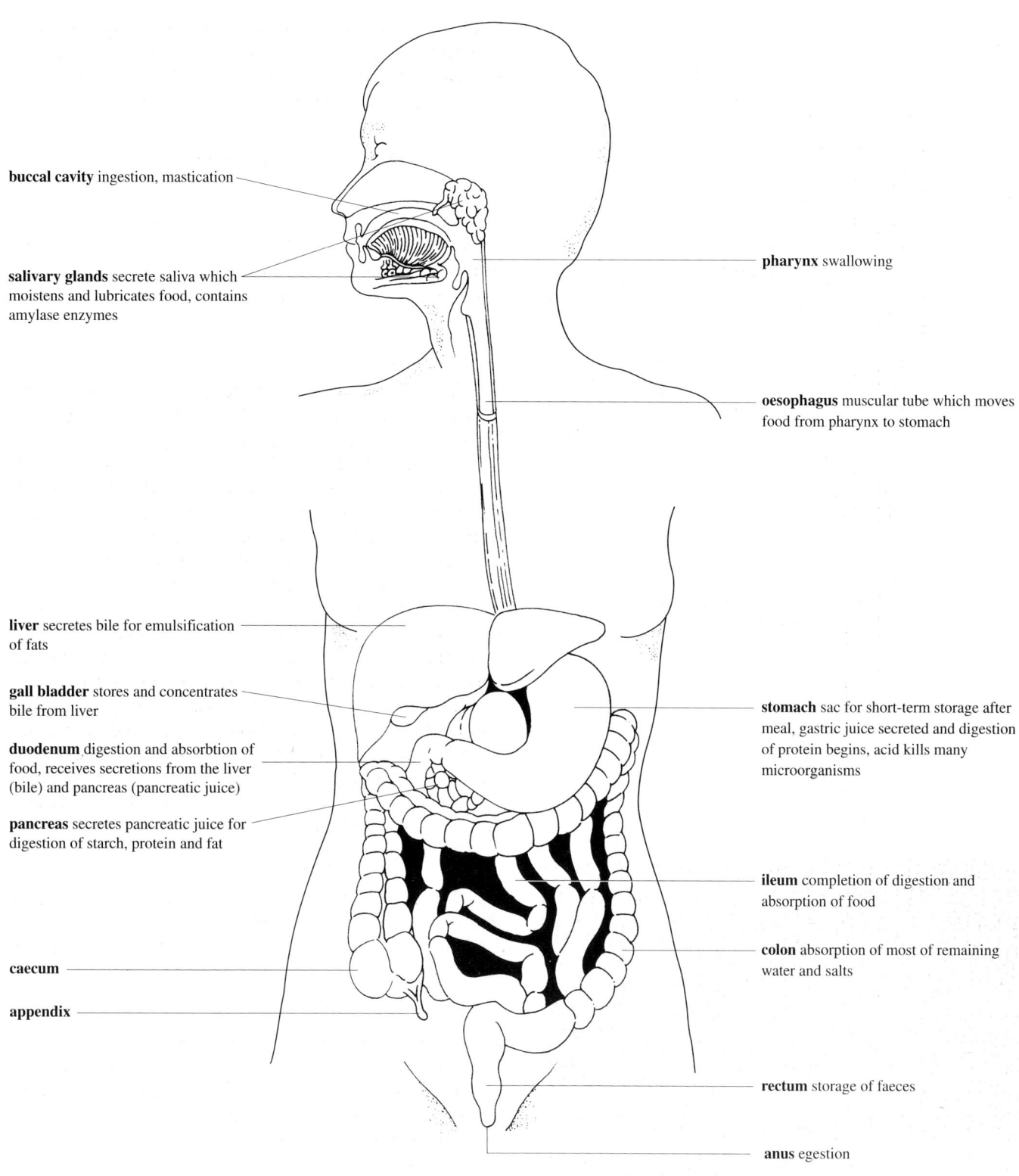

buccal cavity ingestion, mastication

salivary glands secrete saliva which moistens and lubricates food, contains amylase enzymes

pharynx swallowing

oesophagus muscular tube which moves food from pharynx to stomach

liver secretes bile for emulsification of fats

gall bladder stores and concentrates bile from liver

duodenum digestion and absorbtion of food, receives secretions from the liver (bile) and pancreas (pancreatic juice)

pancreas secretes pancreatic juice for digestion of starch, protein and fat

stomach sac for short-term storage after meal, gastric juice secreted and digestion of protein begins, acid kills many microorganisms

ileum completion of digestion and absorption of food

colon absorption of most of remaining water and salts

caecum

appendix

rectum storage of faeces

anus egestion

Fig 8.11 *General layout of the organs of the human digestive system and their functions.*

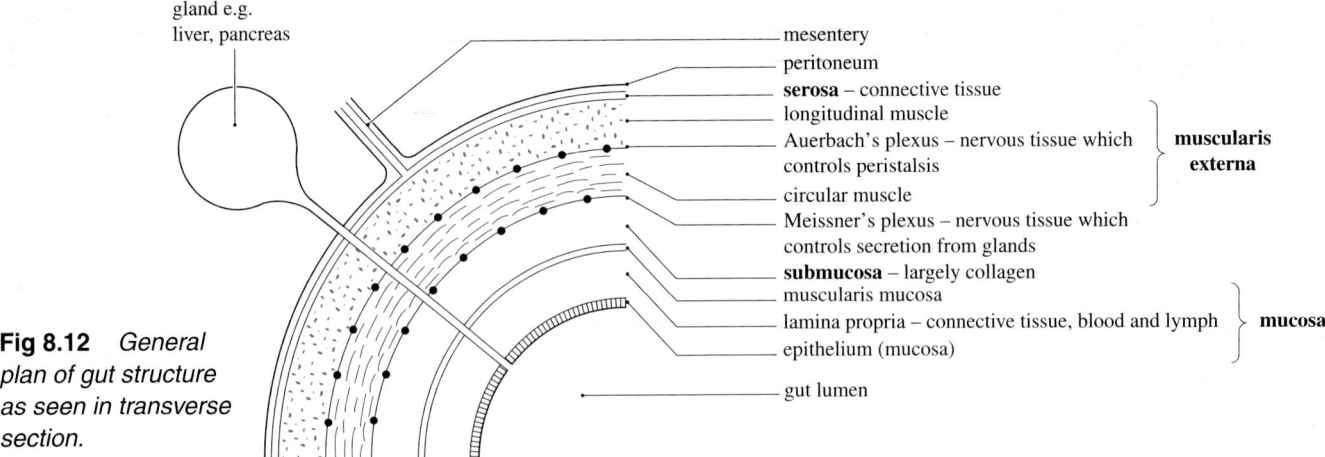

Fig 8.12 *General plan of gut structure as seen in transverse section.*

Labels (top to bottom, right side):
- mesentery
- peritoneum
- **serosa** – connective tissue
- longitudinal muscle
- Auerbach's plexus – nervous tissue which controls peristalsis
- circular muscle
- Meissner's plexus – nervous tissue which controls secretion from glands
- **submucosa** – largely collagen
- muscularis mucosa
- lamina propria – connective tissue, blood and lymph
- epithelium (mucosa)
- gut lumen

muscularis externa

mucosa

gland e.g. liver, pancreas

Between the circular muscle and submucosa is another nerve plexus, **Meissner's plexus**. This controls secretion from glands in the gut wall.

At a number of points along the gut the circular muscle thickens into structures called **sphincters**. When these relax or contract they control the movement of food from one part of the alimentary canal to another. They are found at the junctions of the oesophagus and stomach (cardiac sphincter), stomach and duodenum (pyloric sphincter), ileum and caecum, and at the anus.

Serosa

This is the outermost coat of the gut wall. It is composed of loose fibrous connective tissue.

The whole of the outer surface of the gut is covered by a **peritoneum**. This tissue also lines the abdominal cavity, where most of the gut is located, and forms the **mesenteries** which suspend and support the stomach and intestines from the body wall. Mesenteries consist of double layers of peritoneum containing nerves, blood vessels and lymph vessels that pass to and from the gut. The peritoneum cells are moist and help to reduce friction when the gut wall slides over the portions of itself or other organs.

8.3.2   Human teeth

Types of teeth

In humans there are two jaws, the fixed upper jaw and the movable lower jaw. Both jaws bear teeth which are used to chew or **masticate** food into smaller pieces. This is mechanical digestion and increases the surface area of the food for efficient enzyme attack. The teeth are very hard structures and ideally suited to their task. Humans have two successive sets of teeth. The **deciduous** or milk teeth appear first, and are progressively replaced by the **permanent teeth**. Human teeth have different shapes and sizes and possess uneven biting surfaces. Humans possess up to 32 permanent teeth, consisting of eight incisors (i), four canines (c), eight premolars (pm) and up to 12 molars (m). The arrangement of the teeth can be conveniently expressed in the form of a **dental formula**. Human permanent dentition is:

$$2 \left[\text{i } \frac{2}{2} \text{ c } \frac{1}{1} \text{ pm } \frac{2}{2} \text{ m } \frac{3}{3} \right]$$

where the letters indicate the type of tooth, the top number represents the number of each type of tooth in the upper jaw on one side of the head and the bottom number represents the number of teeth in the lower part of the jaw on the same side (fig 8.13).

The number, size and shape of the teeth is related to diet. The basic structure and function of each type of tooth is as follows.

- *Incisors* are situated at the front of the buccal cavity. They have flat, sharp edges which are used for cutting and biting food (fig 8.13).
- *Canines* are pointed teeth. They are poorly developed in humans, but highly developed in carnivores where they are designed for piercing and killing prey, and tearing flesh.
- *Premolars* possess one or two roots and two cusps (projections on the surface of a tooth). They are specialised for crushing and grinding food, although in humans they may also be used to tear food.
- *Molars* have more than one root; upper molars have three roots, lower molars two. Each has four or five cusps. They are used to crush and grind food. They are not present in the deciduous dentition of humans.

Generalised structure of a tooth

The visible part of the tooth, termed the **crown**, is covered with **enamel** (fig 8.14), the hardest substance in the body. It is relatively resistant to decay. The neck of the tooth is surrounded by the **gum**, whilst the root is embedded in the jawbone. Beneath the enamel is **dentine** which forms the bulk of the tooth. Though tough, it is not as hard as enamel or as resistant to decay. It contains numerous small canals (canaliculi) containing cytoplasmic extensions of **odontoblasts**, the dentine-producing cells. The **pulp cavity** contains odontoblasts, sensory endings of nerves, and blood

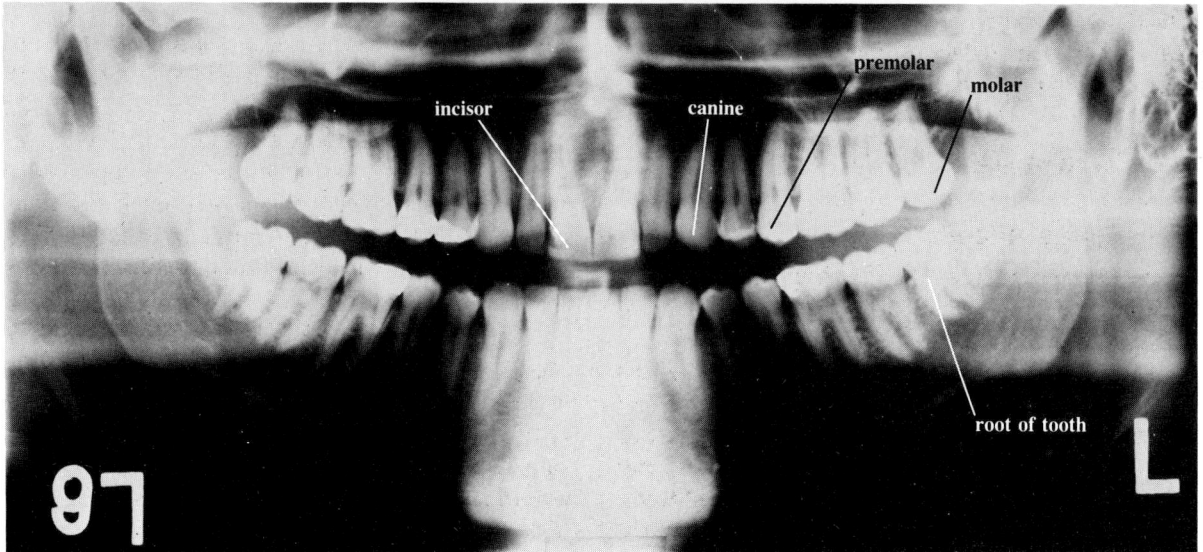

Fig 8.13 *(a) X-ray of side of human head to show permanent dentition on one side.
(b) X-ray of head from the front to show a complete permanent dentition.* Dental formula $2\left[\text{i } \dfrac{2}{2} \text{ c } \dfrac{1}{1} \text{ pm } \dfrac{2}{2} \text{ m } \dfrac{3}{3} \right]$

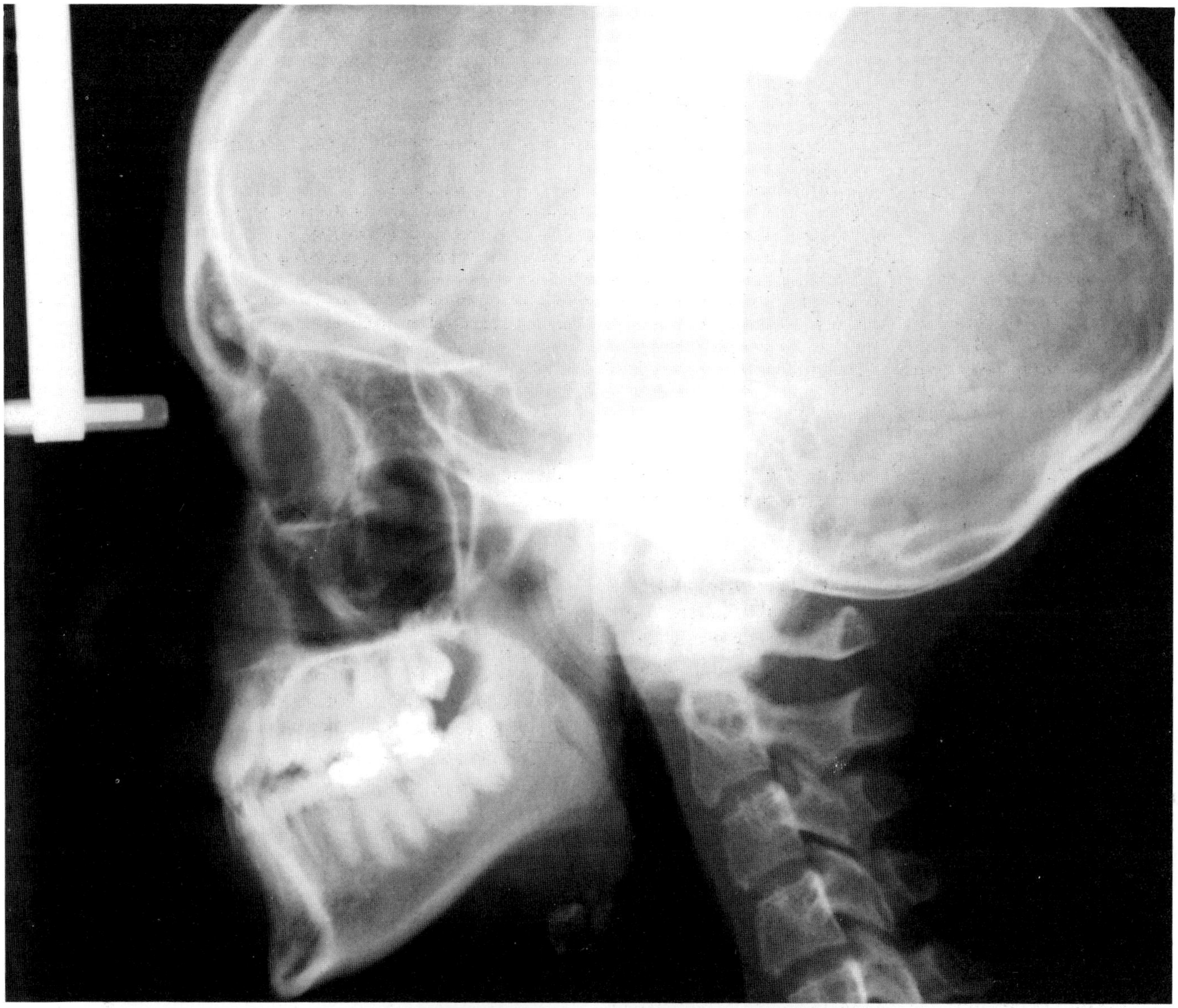

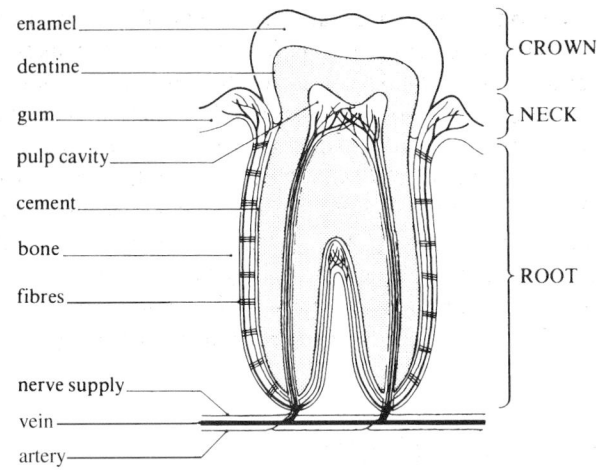

Fig 8.14 *Vertical section of a premolar tooth.*

Labels: enamel, dentine, gum, pulp cavity, cement, bone, fibres, nerve supply, vein, artery. CROWN, NECK, ROOT.

vessels which deliver nutrients to the living tissues of the tooth and remove their waste products.

The root of the tooth is covered with **cement**, a substance similar to bone. Numerous **fibres**, connected to the cement at one end and the jawbone at the other, anchor the tooth firmly in place. However, it is still able to move slightly and this reduces the chances of it being sheared off during chewing.

Dental disease

Two major dental diseases exist, periodontal disease and dental caries. Both are caused by **plaque**, which is a mixture of bacteria and salivary materials. If allowed to accumulate, the bacteria cause inflammation of the gums (**periodontal disease**). Plaque also combines with certain chemicals in the saliva which make it harden and calcify to form deposits of calculus which cannot be removed by brushing. Some of the bacteria in plaque convert sugar into acid which starts the process of **dental caries** (fig 8.15).

Periodontal disease. This is a disease of the gums caused by microorganisms that are normally present in the mouth in dental plaque, especially in the areas between the gums and the teeth. Neglect of oral hygiene creates favourable conditions for the spread of this disease. At first periodontal disease causes inflammation of the gums. If this condition, which is generally painless, is allowed to continue, the inflammation may spread to the root of the tooth and destroy the fibres which anchor it in place. Eventually the tooth becomes loose and may have to be extracted.

Dental caries. The microorganisms in dental plaque convert sugar in the mouth to acid. Initially the enamel is slowly and painlessly dissolved by the acid. However, when the dentine and pulp of the tooth are attacked, this is accompanied by severe pain or 'toothache', and the possible loss of teeth. Several factors contribute to the spread of dental caries. They include prolonged exposure to sugary foodstuffs, disturbance of saliva

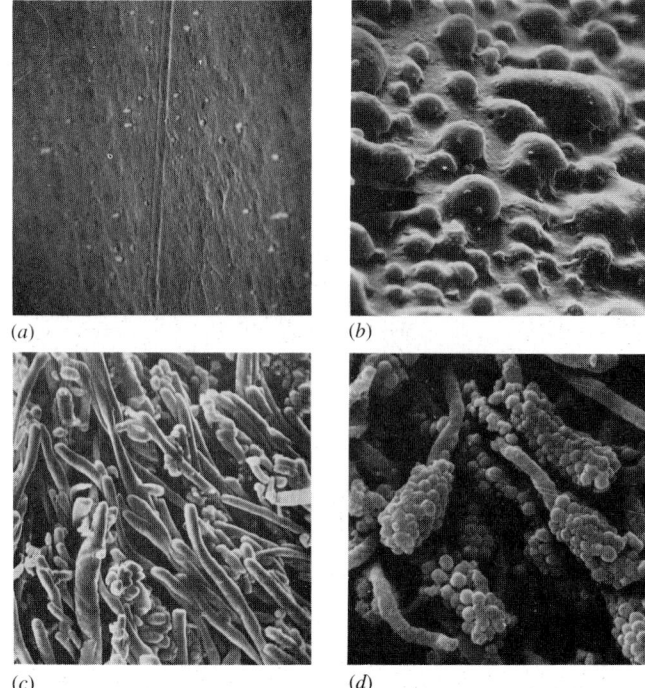

Fig 8.15 *Development of dental plaque. (a) Spherical bacteria called cocci deposit as 'pioneer' species and then multiply to form a film. (b) Organisms embedded in a matrix of secretions of bacterial and salivary origin. (c) The complexity of the community increases and rod- and filament-shaped populations appear. (d) In the 'climax' community many unusual associations between different populations can be seen, including 'corn cob' arrangements.*

composition, lack of oral hygiene and low levels of fluoride in drinking water. Prevention of dental caries may be helped by adding fluoride to drinking water, fluoridation of some foods such as milk, children taking fluoride tablets, brushing teeth with fluoridated toothpaste, good oral hygiene and regular visits to the dentist and oral hygienist, and care with the composition of the diet.

8.3.3 Buccal cavity

The buccal cavity is the chamber just inside the mouth in which food is chewed. During chewing the muscular tongue moves food around the mouth and mixes and moistens it with saliva. The tongue possesses **taste buds** (fig 8.16)) that contain receptors sensitive to sweet, salty, sour and bitter substances. A simple (inborn) or conditioned (learned) reflex results in stimulation of the salivary glands to secrete saliva. The eye and the olfactory (smell) receptors in the nose are also important receptors in triggering reflexes that bring about salivation (see section 8.4.1).

About $1.5\,dm^3$ of saliva are produced by humans each day by the **salivary glands**. Saliva is a watery secretion containing the enzymes salivary **amylase** and **lysozyme**. It also contains **mucus** and various **mineral salts**, including chloride ions which speed up the activity of the enzymes. The mucus moistens and lubricates food and makes it easier to swallow. Salivary amylase begins the digestion of starch, first to shorter polysaccharides, and then to the disaccharide maltose. Lysozyme helps to kill bacteria, which are potentially harmful, by catalysing the breakdown of their cell walls (section 5.10.6). Eventually the semi-solid, partially digested food particles are stuck together and moulded into a **bolus** (or pellet) by the tongue, which then pushes it towards the pharynx. From here, as a result of a reflex action, it is swallowed into the oesophagus via the pharynx.

8.3.4 Oesophagus

This is a narrow muscular tube lined by stratified squamous epithelium (see section 6.3.2) containing mucus glands (fig. 8.17). In humans it is about 25 cm long and quickly conveys food and fluids by peristalsis from the pharynx to the stomach.

8.3.5 Peristalsis

Food is pushed through the gut by the muscles of the muscularis externa, the outer longitudinal and inner circular layers of muscle in the gut wall (fig 8.12). Behind the bolus (pellet of food) the circular muscles contract, squeezing and constricting the gut. In front of the food, the longitudinal muscles contract, shortening this section of the gut and pulling it past the advancing bolus (fig 8.18).

Other types of movement are possible in the stomach and small intestine which ensure stirring and mixing of food.

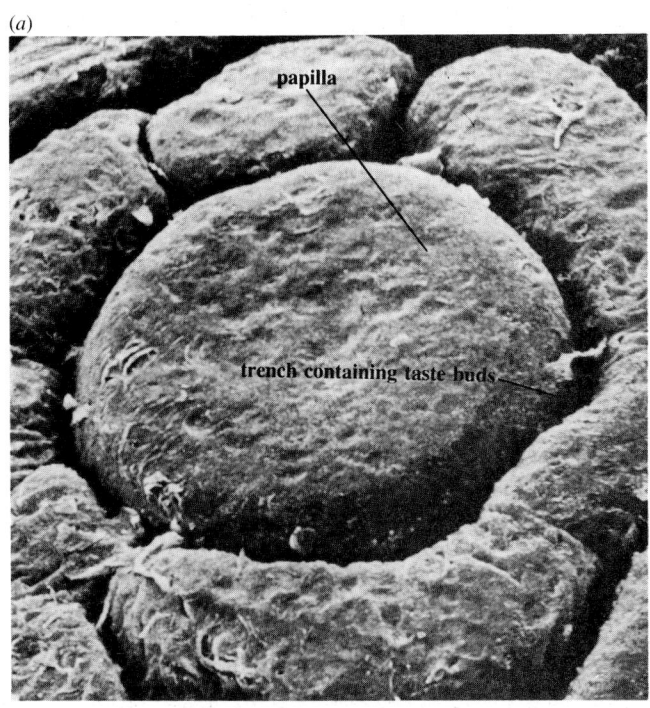

(a)

Fig 8.16 (a) *Scanning electron micrograph of the tongue surface of a three-week-old puppy. The taste buds are in the trenches surrounding the surface papillae.* (b) *VS taste buds in the tongue.*

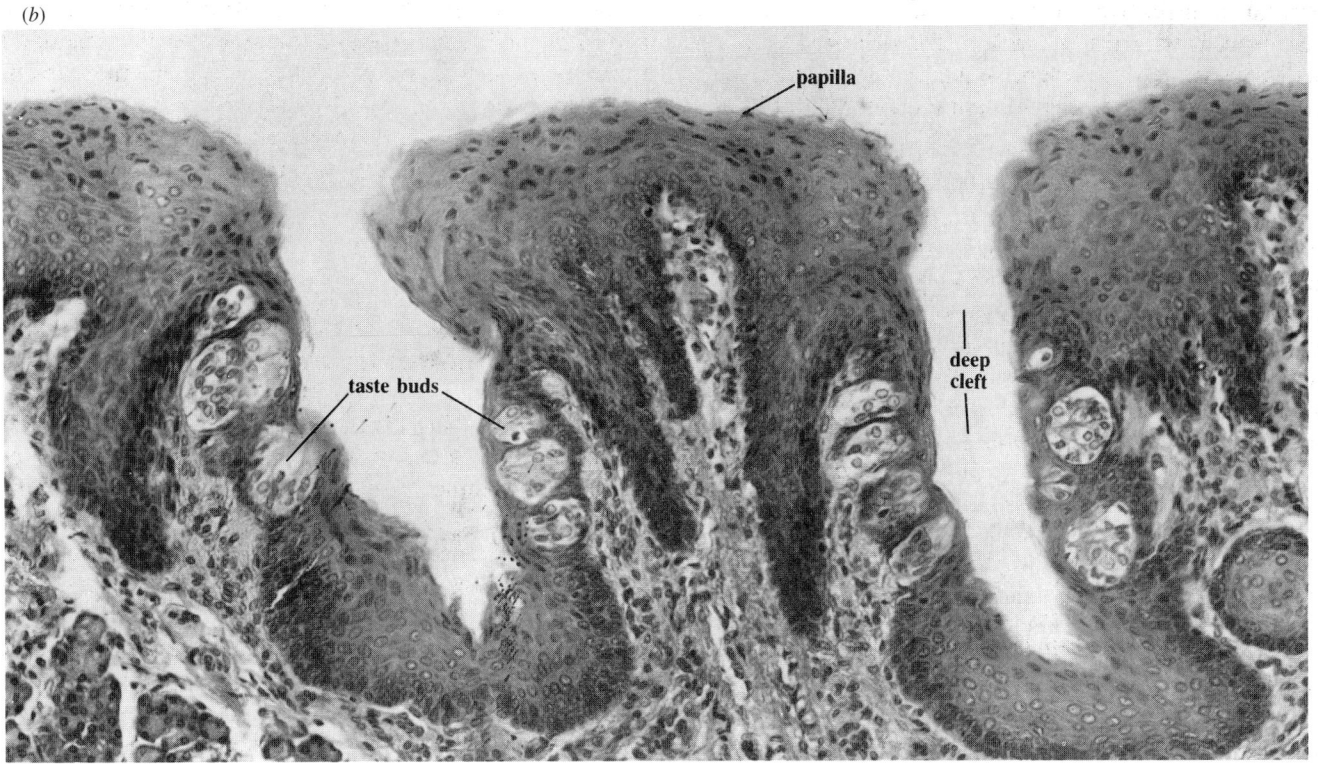

(b)

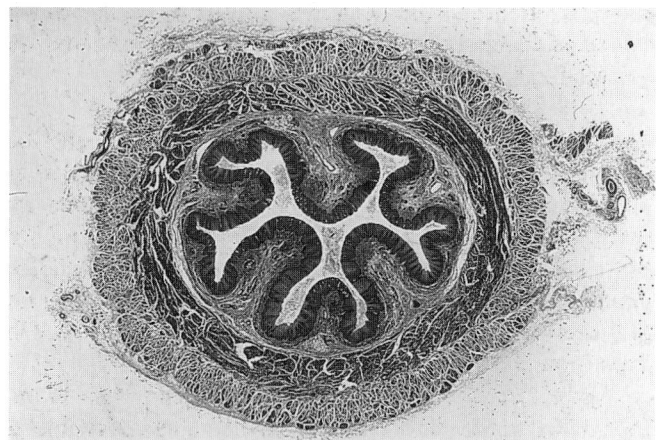

Fig 8.17 *TS human oesophagus.*

Strictly speaking these are not described as peristaltic movements. For example, the gut may be constricted in several parts at once (segmental movements) and sometimes sections of the intestine suddenly and rapidly shorten, throwing food from one end to the other and thus thoroughly mixing it.

8.3.6 Stomach

The stomach in humans is situated below the diaphragm and on the left side of the abdominal cavity (fig 8.11). It is a muscular bag which can stretch to take in food. When unstretched the stomach wall lies in folds, but when fully distended it can hold nearly $5\,dm^3$ of food and the folds disappear. It has a number of functions.

- It stores food temporarily after meals, releasing food slowly into the rest of the gut.
- It continues mechanical digestion by its churning action. This is made more efficient by the fact that unlike the other regions of the gut it possesses three layers of smooth muscle instead of two, namely the outer longitudinal, middle circular and inner oblique layers.
- The thick mucosa contains mucus-secreting epithelial cells. The mucus provides a barrier between the stomach mucosa and gastric juice (see below) and prevents the stomach self-digesting.
- The main part of the stomach is dotted with numerous gastric pits (figs 8.19 and 8.20). These lead into long, tubular gastric glands formed by infoldings of the epithelium. The glands are lined with cells which secrete the gastric juice. There are two specialised types of cell, the **parietal cells** and the **chief cells**.

    Chief cells (also known as zymogen cells) secrete the inactive enzymes **pepsinogen** and **prorennin**. (Inactive enzymes are known as zymogens).

    Parietal cells (also known as oxyntic cells) secrete a dilute solution of hydrochloric acid which itself has a number of functions. It makes the stomach contents pH 1–2·5, ideal for the optimum activity of the stomach

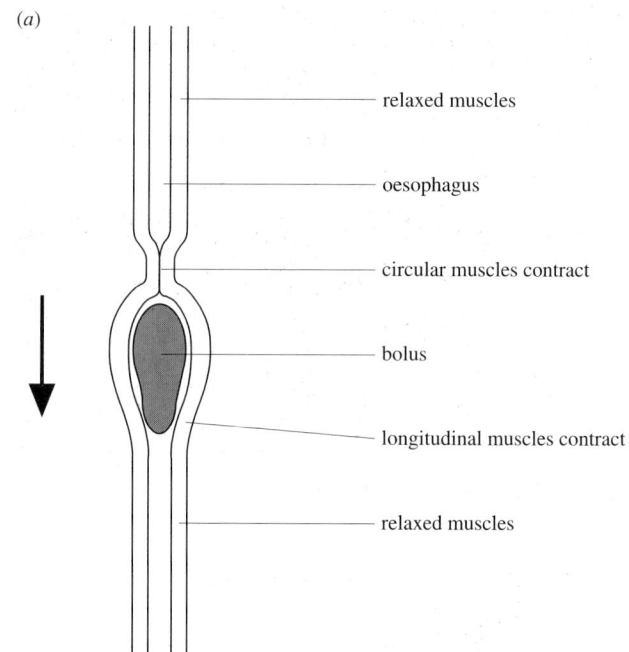

relaxed muscles

oesophagus

circular muscles contract

bolus

longitudinal muscles contract

relaxed muscles

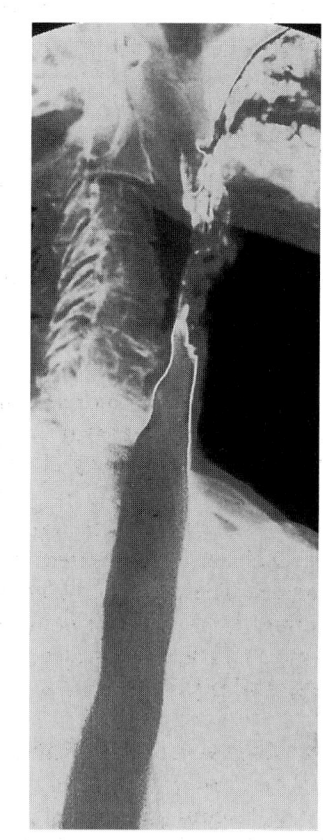

Fig 8.18 (a) *Diagram of peristalsis in the oesophagus.* (b) *X-ray of peristalsis in the human oesophagus. The patient has just swallowed a barium meal, which is opaque to X-rays. The muscles in the oesophagus above the meal are constricted, forcing the meal down towards the stomach.*

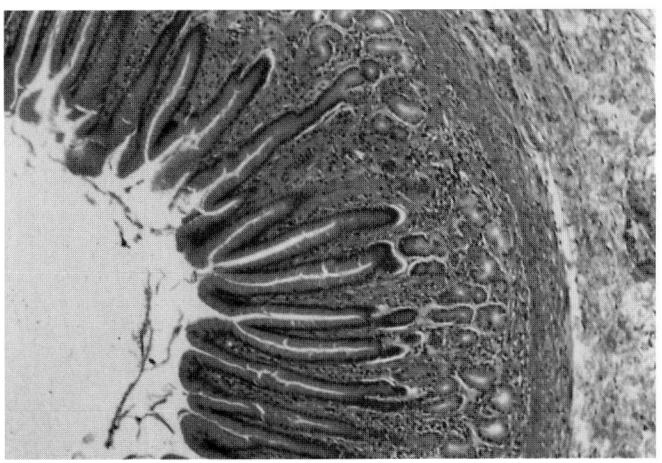

Fig 8.19 *TS gastric pits of a mammal.*

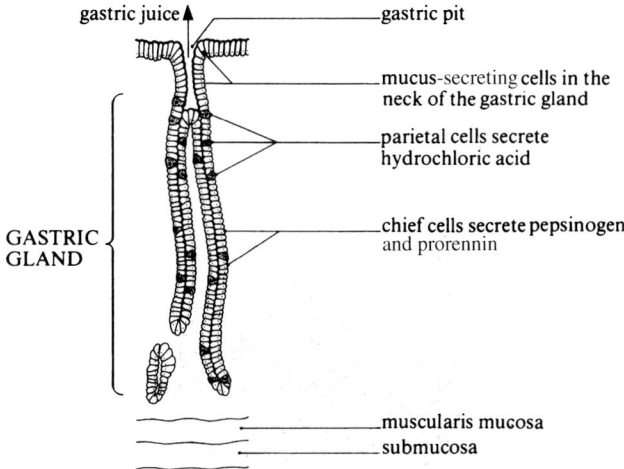

Fig 8.20 *VS stomach wall showing gastric gland. Cells which secrete the hormone gastrin are also present in the gland.*

enzymes. The acid kills many bacteria, thus acting as a defence mechanism. It denatures many proteins: their tertiary structure is altered, making them unfold and so easier to digest. This is particularly important for fibrous proteins, some of which are very common, such as collagen which is found extensively in animal connective tissues. The acid also loosens fibrous and cellular components of tissue. It converts pepsinogen and prorennin to their active forms pepsin and rennin and begins the hydrolysis of sucrose to glucose and fructose.

- Pepsin hydrolyses protein into smaller polypeptides. Rennin coagulates casein, the soluble protein of milk, into the insoluble calcium salt of casein in the presence of calcium ions. This calcium salt is then digested by pepsin.

> **8.3** Why is it necessary for pepsin to be secreted in an inactive state?

- The stomach also contains endocrine cells which secrete the hormone gastrin. This is discussed in section 8.4.

The cardiac sphincter, at the junction between the oesophagus and the stomach, and the pyloric sphincter, at the junction between the stomach and the duodenum, prevent the uncontrolled exit of food from the stomach. Both act as valves and retain food in the stomach for periods of up to four hours. Relaxation of the pyloric sphincter releases small quantities of the food into the duodenum at regular intervals.

The muscles of the stomach wall thoroughly mix up the food with gastric juice and eventually convert it into a semi-liquid mass called **chyme**. Gradually the stomach squirts the chyme into the duodenum through the relaxed, ring-shaped pyloric sphincter.

8.3.7 Structure of the small intestine

The first part of the small intestine is the **duodenum**. It is short, about 25 cm long, and the pancreatic and bile ducts open into it. The duodenum leads on to the **ileum** which is about 3 m long in a living body (it relaxes and gets much longer after death) (figs 8.11 and 8.21). The submucosa and mucosa together are folded (fig 8.21*a*). In addition, the mucosa possesses numerous finger-like projections called **villi**, whose walls are richly supplied with blood capillaries and lymph vessels and contain smooth muscle (fig 8.21*d* and *e*). They are able to contract and relax continuously, thus bringing themselves into close contact with the food in the small intestine. The individual cells on the surface of the villi possess tiny microvilli on their free surfaces (figs 8.21*f*, 6.16 and section 5.10.8). Between them these features greatly increase the surface area of the small intestine (table 8.2).

> **8.4** (*a*) List the features of the small intestine which increase its surface area.
>
> (*b*) Why is this an advantage?

At the base of the villi the epithelium folds inwards in places to form narrow tubes called **crypts of Lieberkühn** (fig 8.21*d*). It is here that new epithelial cells are made to replace those which are constantly being shed from the villi (the average life of these cells is about five days). The cells in the crypts also secrete **intestinal juice**, a slightly alkaline fluid which contains water and mucus and helps to increase the volume of fluid in the gut. **Paneth cells** at the base of the crypts secrete lysozyme, the antibacterial enzyme already mentioned in saliva.

Throughout the small intestine, special epithelial cells called **goblet cells** secrete mucus, whose function has been described in section 8.3.1 (mucosa). The duodenum also secretes an alkaline fluid which helps to neutralise the acid

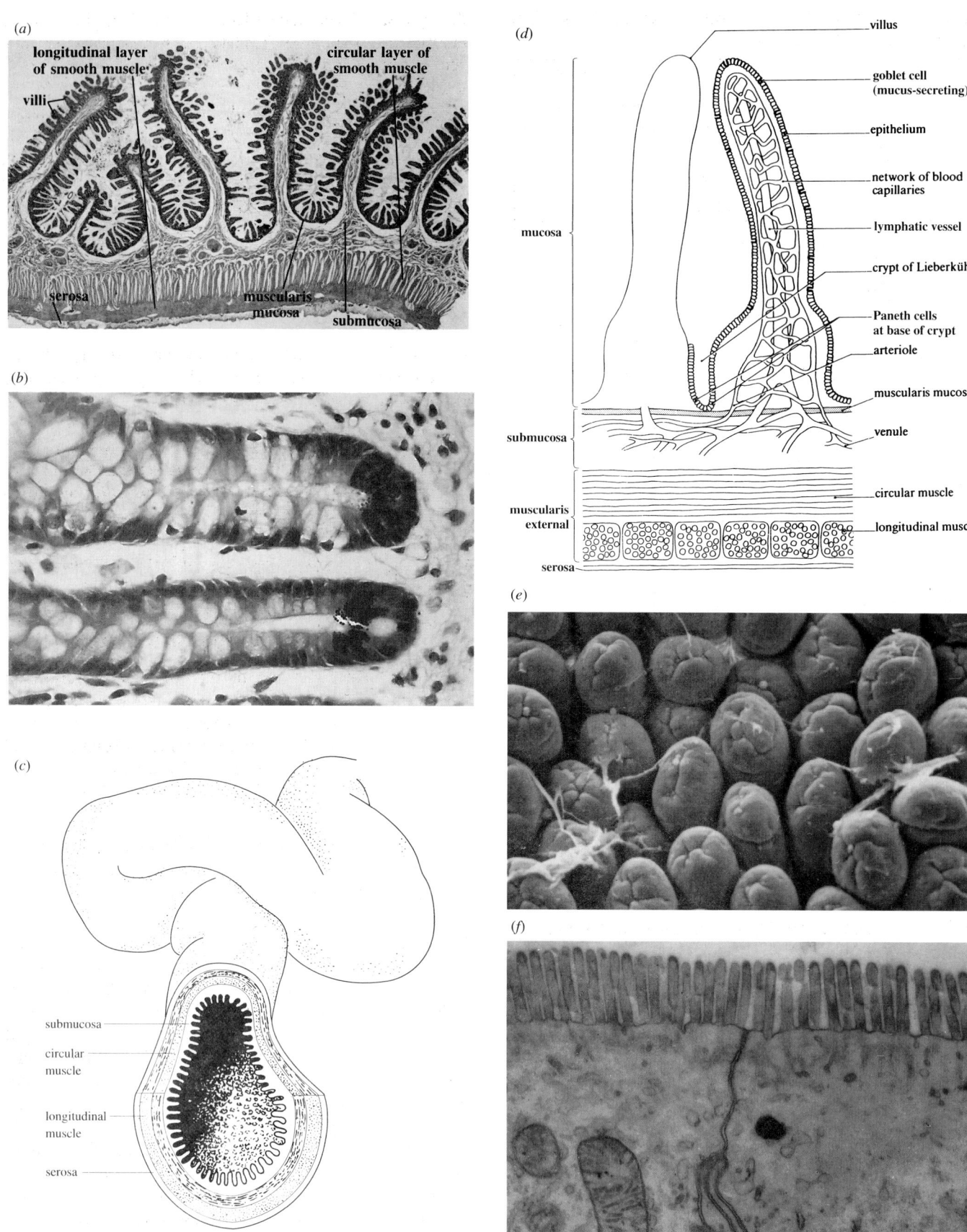

Fig 8.21 (a) *Vertical section through ileum.* (b) *Crypts of Lieberkühn in the ileum.* (c) *Artist's impression of a cross-section of the small intestine.* (d) *Diagram of TS ileum showing a villus.* (e) *Scanning electron micrograph showing villi on surface of small intestine (×200).* (f) *Electron micrograph of epithelial cells showing microvilli (×18 000)*

Table 8.2 Structural features which increase the surface area of the small intestine.

Structure	Increase in surface area relative to simple cylinder
simple cylinder	×1
visible with naked eye folds of submucosa and mucosa	×3
visible with light microscope villi villi	×30
two epithelial cells with microvilli 1 villus 0.5–1 mm high 10–40 per mm^2 give a velvety appearance visible with electron microscope	×600

of the stomach and provide an optimum pH of 7–8 for the enzymes of the small intestine.

> **8.5** What would happen to the activity of the intestinal enzymes if the pH in the small intestine remained at 2?

8.3.8 Digestion by enzymes in the small intestine

The general pattern of carbohydrate, protein and lipid digestion is shown in fig 8.22. All the enzymes involved in digestion in the small intestine, apart from those made by the pancreas, are bound to the cell surface membranes of the microvilli of the epithelium (fig 8.21f) or located within the epithelial cells. It is at these sites that the final hydrolysis of disaccharides, dipeptides and some tripeptides occurs (fig 8.23). The end-products are monosaccharides and amino acids respectively. A full list of the enzymes involved can be found in table 8.3.

In addition to its own set of enzymes, the small intestine receives alkaline pancreatic juice and bile from the pancreas and liver respectively. **Bile** is produced by liver cells and stored in the gall bladder. It contains a mixture of salts (bile salts) which, in the small intestine, act as natural

detergents, reducing the surface tension of fat globules and emulsifying them into droplets, so increasing their total surface area. (This process is called emulsification.) These small droplets are then acted upon more efficiently by the enzyme lipase. Further information about the composition of bile is given in chapter 18.

The pancreas is a large gland located next to the stomach (fig 8.11). Within the pancreas are groups of cells which produce a variety of digestive enzymes that are poured into the duodenum via the pancreatic duct (fig 5.29). They include:

- **amylase** to convert amylose to maltose;
- **lipase** to convert lipids (fats and oils) to fatty acids and glycerol;
- **trypsinogen** which, when converted to **trypsin** by **enterokinase** from the microvilli, digests proteins into smaller polypeptides and more trypsinogen into trypsin;
- **chymotrypsinogen** which is converted to chymotrypsin that digests proteins to amino acids;
- **carboxypeptidases** that converts peptides to amino acids.

A summary of the enzymes secreted by the human gut and their action is given in table 8.3.

8.3.9 Absorption of food in the ileum

Absorption of the end-products of digestion occurs through the villi of the ileum. The structure of the villus is ideally suited for this function as can be seen in figs 8.21d, e, and f. **Monosaccharides**, **dipeptides** and **amino acids** are absorbed either by diffusion or active transport into the blood capillaries (fig 8.23 and fig 5.22).

> **8.6** Suggest one advantage of using active transport in the absorption of monosaccharides, dipeptides and amino acids.

From the villi the blood capillaries join to form the hepatic portal vein which delivers the absorbed food to the liver.

Fatty acids and **glycerol** diffuse into the columnar epithelial cells of the villi. Here they are reconverted into lipids. Proteins present in the epithelial cells coat the lipid molecules to form lipoprotein droplets called **chylomicrons**. These pass out of the epithelial cells by exocytosis and into lymphatic vessels in the villi (fig 8.21d). They make the lymph in the lymphatic vessels appear white, so the vessels are sometimes called lacteal vessels (lacteal meaning milky). The chylomicrons are carried by lymph in the lymphatic system to veins near the heart where they enter the liquid part of the blood, the plasma. An enzyme in the blood plasma then hydrolyses the lipids back to fatty acids and glycerol in which form they are taken up by cells. They may be used in respiration or stored as fat in the liver, muscles, mesenteries or below the skin.

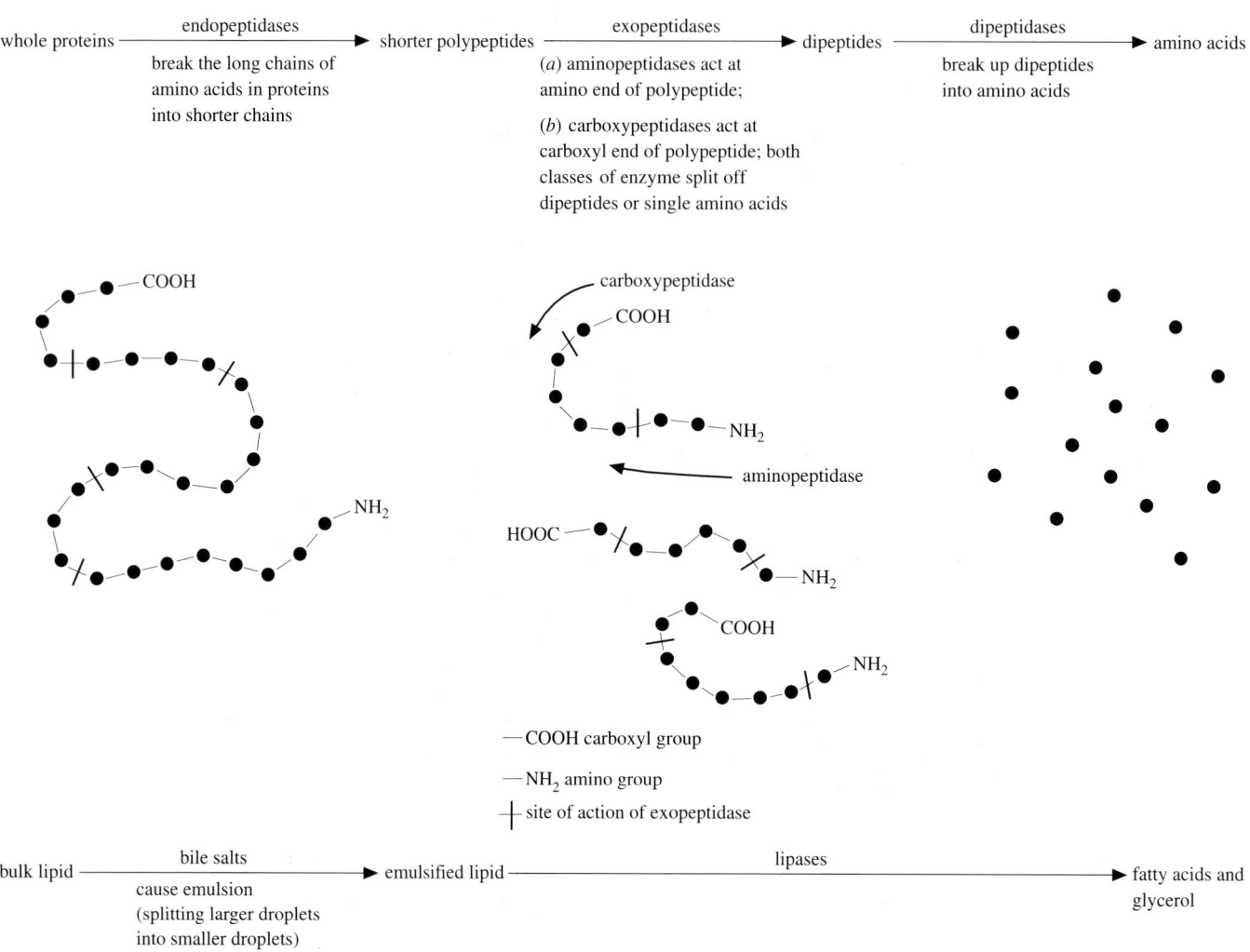

polysaccharides ——— amylases ——→ disaccharides ——————— disaccharases ——————————→ monosaccharides

whole proteins ——— endopeptidases ——→ shorter polypeptides ——— exopeptidases ——→ dipeptides ——— dipeptidases ——→ amino acids
break the long chains of amino acids in proteins into shorter chains

(*a*) aminopeptidases act at amino end of polypeptide;

(*b*) carboxypeptidases act at carboxyl end of polypeptide; both classes of enzyme split off dipeptides or single amino acids

break up dipeptides into amino acids

carboxypeptidase
aminopeptidase

—COOH carboxyl group

—NH$_2$ amino group

—|— site of action of exopeptidase

bulk lipid ——— bile salts ——→ emulsified lipid ——————— lipases ——————————→ fatty acids and glycerol
cause emulsion (splitting larger droplets into smaller droplets)

Fig 8.22 *General pattern of enzyme digestion in the human gut.*

Inorganic salts, **vitamins** and **water** are also absorbed in the small intestine.

The sphincter muscle between the ileum and the caecum opens and closes from time to time to allow small amounts of material from the ileum to enter the large intestine.

8.3.10 Large intestine

No digestion takes place in the large intestine or **colon**. Most of the fluids (about 90%) and salts in the gut are absorbed in the small intestine. The colon and caecum remove about 90% of any remaining liquid. Some metabolic waste and inorganic substances, notably calcium and iron, in excess in the body are excreted in the large intestine as salts. Epithelial cells secrete mucus which lubricates the solidifying undigested food remains known as **faeces**. Many symbiotic bacteria present in the large intestine synthesise amino acids and some vitamins,

especially vitamin K, which are absorbed into the bloodstream.

In humans the appendix is a blind-ended pouch leading from the caecum and possesses no known function. It is, however, of great significance in herbivores (section 8.6.2). The bulk of the faeces consists of dead bacteria, cellulose and other plant fibres, dead epithelial cells, mucus, cholesterol, bile pigment derivatives and water. Faeces can remain in the colon for 36 h before being passed on to the rectum where they are stored briefly before egestion through the anus. Two sphincters surround the anus, an internal one of smooth (involuntary) muscle and under the control of the autonomic (involuntary) nervous system, and an outer one of striated (voluntary) muscle controlled by the voluntary nervous system.

Table 8.4 summarises the differences in structure between the major regions of the alimentary canal in humans.

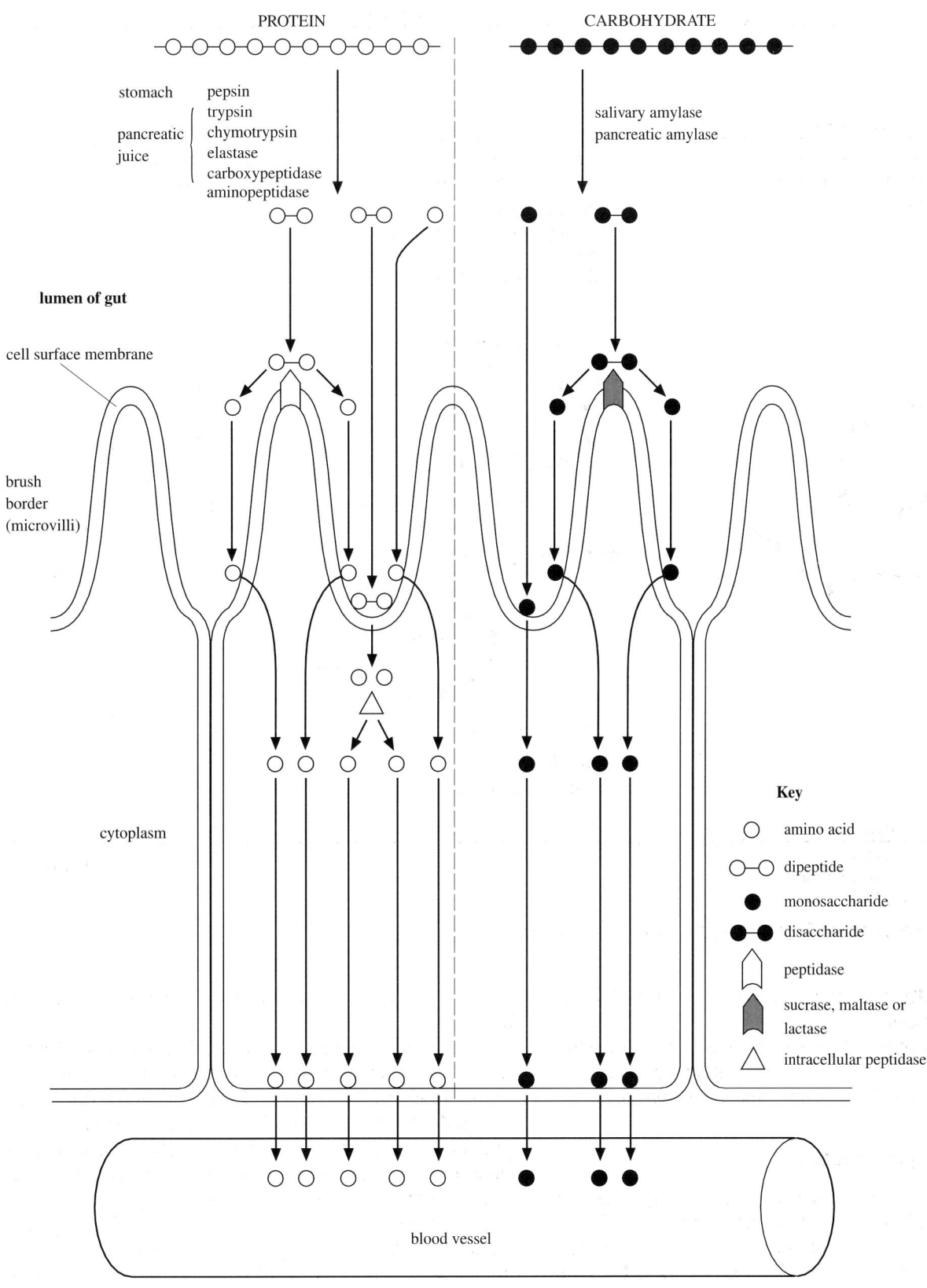

Fig 8.23 *Diagram of an epithelial cell in the ileum with microvilli. The left half shows the final phase of protein digestion, with the absorption of amino acids. The right half shows the corresponding processes for carbohydrates.*

Table 8.3 Summary of digestive secretions and their action.

Secretion	Source	Enzymes	Site of action	Optimum pH	Substrate	Products
saliva	salivary glands	salivary amylase	buccal cavity	6.5–7.5	amylose in starch	maltose
gastric juice	stomach mucosa (gastric glands)	rennin** (in young)	stomach	2.00	casein	insoluble salt of casein
		pepsin**	stomach	2.00	proteins	peptides
		hydrochloric acid (not an enzyme)	stomach	–	pepsinogen prorennin	pepsin rennin
membrane-bound enzymes in microvilli of small intestine	small intestine mucosa	amylase	microvilli of epithelium of small intestine	8.5	amylose	maltose
		maltase		8.5	maltose	glucose
		lactase		8.5	lactose	glucose + galactose
		sucrase		8.5	sucrose	glucose + fructose
		exopeptidases* (aminopeptidase		8.5	peptides and	aminoacids
		dipeptidase)		8.5	dipeptides	amino acids
		enterokinase	small intestine	8.5	trypsinogen	trypsin
pancreatic juice	pancreatic glands	amylase	small intestine	7.00	amylose	maltose
		endopeptidases* (trypsin**	small intestine	7.00	proteins chymotrypsinogen	peptides chymotrypsin
		elastase	small intestine	7.00	proteins	peptides
		chymotrypsin**)	small intestine	7.00	proteins	amino acids
		exopeptidase* (carboxypeptidase)	small intestine	7.00	peptides	amino acids
		lipase	small intestine	7.00	lipids	fatty acids + glycerol
bile	liver	bile salts (not enzymes)	small intestine	7.6–8.6	lipids	lipid droplets

*Exopeptidases split off terminal amino acids from proteins (polypeptides)
Endopeptidases break bonds between amino acids within proteins thus producing smaller peptides
**Rennin and pepsin are secreted in the inactive forms prorennin and pepsinogen respectively
Trypsin is secreted in the inactive form trypsinogen, and chymotrypsin as the inactive chymotrypsinogen

Collectively these enzymes break up polypeptides into their constituent amino acids so that they can be absorbed by the villi of the ileum

Table 8.4 Comparison of structures of the major regions of the gut.

Layer	Oesophagus	Stomach	Small intestine	Large intestine
	specialisation – a few mucus glands located in the lamina propria and submucosa	specialisation – gastric glands located in lamina propria, four cell types: (i) mucus (ii) parietal (iii) chief (iv) endocrine	specialisation – (i) intestinal glands in crypts of Lieberkühn (ii) Paneth cells (iii) endocrine cells	specialisation – intestinal glands in lamina propria
mucosa (a) epithelium	stratified, squamous (see fig 6.19)	simple columnar (fig 6.16)	simple columnar, absorptive and mucus cells (fig 6.16)	simple columnar, absorptive and mucus cells (fig 6.16)
(b) lamina propria	some mucus glands	many gastric glands	intestinal glands and prominent lymphatic vessels to transport lipids	tubular glands
(c) muscularis mucosa	present	present	present	present
submucosa	some deep mucus glands	present	glands in duodenum	intestinal glands
muscularis externa (inner circular, outer longitudinal muscle)	transitional from striated (voluntary) muscle in upper region to smooth (involuntary) muscle in lower region	extra innermost layer of oblique muscle; circular muscle forms cardiac and pyloric sphincters	present	present
serosa	present	present	present	incomplete

8.4 Nervous and hormonal control of digestive secretions

Secretion of digestive enzymes and other substances, such as hydrochloric acid, is an energy-consuming process. It would be extremely wasteful of both energy and materials if the body carried on producing them in the absence of food. Instead, the bulk of digestive juice is produced only when there is digestive work to be done. The overall control of digestive activity is coordinated and regulated, and this control involves both the nervous system and the endocrine system (the system of hormone-producing glands). This control is discussed in the following sections.

8.4.1 Saliva

Secretion of saliva into the buccal cavity from the salivary glands is controlled by two types of reflex action. First, a simple unconditional (inborn) reflex occurs when food is present in the buccal cavity. Contact with the taste buds of the tongue (fig 8.16) stimulates receptors sensitive to sweet, salty, sour and bitter tastes. Sensory neurones carry nerve impulses from these receptors to the brain. From there, nerve impulses travel along motor neurones to the salivary glands, the effectors, which are stimulated to secrete saliva. Reflexes which pass through the brain are known as cranial reflexes. Secondly, there are the conditioned reflexes of seeing, smelling or thinking of food. If you relax and think of lemon juice dripping onto your tongue it will probably make you start to produce saliva. A **conditioned reflex** is one which has been learned through experience. A well-known example is the experiment carried out by I.P. Pavlov, in which a bell was rung every time he fed some dogs. Eventually the dogs would salivate at the sound of the bell, even when there was no food present. They were said to have been **conditioned**. The reflex is cranial and operates in the same way as the simple reflex described above. The eye, the ear and the olfactory (smell) receptors in the nose are the important receptors.

8.4.2 Gastric juice

Secretion of gastric juice occurs in three phases. The first is the **nervous phase**. The presence of food in the buccal cavity and its swallowing trigger reflex nerve impulses which pass along the vagus nerve from the brain to the stomach. The sight, smell, taste and even the thought of food can trigger the same reflex. The gastric glands of the stomach are stimulated to secrete gastric juice. This takes place before the food has reached the stomach and therefore prepares it to receive food. The nervous phase of gastric secretion lasts for approximately one hour.

The second phase is the **gastric phase** which takes place in the stomach. It involves both nervous and hormonal control. Stretching of the stomach by the food it contains stimulates stretch receptors in the wall of the stomach. These send nerve impulses to Meissner's plexus (see fig 8.11) in the submucosa, which in turn sends nerve impulses to the gastric glands, stimulating the flow of gastric juice. Stretching of the stomach and the presence of food also stimulates special endocrine cells in the mucosa to secrete the hormone **gastrin**. This reaches the gastric glands by way of the bloodstream and stimulates them to produce gastric juice rich in hydrochloric acid for about four hours.

The third phase is the **intestinal phase** which takes place in the small intestine. When acidified chyme enters and makes contact with the walls of the duodenum, it triggers both nervous and hormonal responses. Receptors in the small intestine are stimulated by the presence of food, but the reflexes, which pass through the brain, *inhibit* secretion of gastric juice and slow the release of chyme from the stomach. This prevents too much food being released into the small intestine at once. In addition, the mucosa of the duodenum produces two hormones, **cholecystokinin (CCK)** and **secretin**. (CCK may also be known as pancreozymin, but use only one of these names! CCK is easier and more widely used.) The two hormones are taken in the bloodstream to the stomach, pancreas and the liver. In the stomach secretin inhibits secretion of gastric juice and CCK inhibits stomach emptying.

8.4.3 Pancreatic juice and bile

Secretin and CCK are produced in the duodenum when acidified chyme enters it from the stomach (see above). Secretin is produced in response to the acid, whereas partially digested fats and protein stimulate CCK production. Both hormones are important regulators of the production of pancreatic juice and bile. Secretin is, in effect, an anti-acid hormone. It stimulates the production of hydrogencarbonate ions in the pancreas and the liver, making the pancreatic juice and the bile more alkaline as a result. This helps to neutralise the acid from the stomach. CCK stimulates synthesis of digestive enzymes by the pancreas and the contraction of the gall bladder to release bile into the duodenum (see fig 8.11 for the location of the pancreas, liver and gall bladder). Bile is made in the liver, but stored and concentrated in the gall bladder. It has a pH of 7.6–8.6.

The secretion of bile and pancreatic juice is also stimulated by nervous reflexes. During the nervous and gastric phases of gastric digestion (see section 8.4.2) the vagus nerve also stimulates the liver to secrete bile and the pancreas to secrete enzymes.

Table 8.5 summarises the endocrine control of the various secretions of the alimentary canal and its associated organs.

8.5 The fate of the absorbed food materials – a summary

Monosaccharides and amino acids are both absorbed into blood vessels in the villi and passed to the liver in the hepatic portal vein. Most of the glucose is stored here or in muscle as glycogen and fats, though some leaves the liver in the hepatic vein to be distributed round the body where it is needed for oxidation during respiration or for use in other functions. Between meals, if the body requires more energy, glycogen in the liver can be reconverted to glucose and transported by the blood to those tissues in need.

Amino acids are used for the synthesis of proteins. The functions of proteins are summarised in table 3.9. They are used particularly for growth and repair, being some of the main constituents of protoplasm. Enzymes and some hormones are proteins. Surplus amino acids cannot be stored and are deaminated in the liver. Their amino (NH_2) groups are removed and converted to urea which is taken in the blood to the kidneys and excreted in the urine. The remainder of the amino acid molecule is converted to glycogen and stored.

Absorbed fats bypass the liver by entering the lymphatic system and being released into veins near the heart. Fats represent the major energy store of the body. Normally, however, glucose is in adequate supply and the fats are not required for energy production. In this case they are stored in adipose tissue below the skin, around the heart and kidneys and in the mesenteries. Some fat is incorporated into cell membranes as phospholipids.

Further details of most of these processes will be found elsewhere in this book.

8.6 Herbivores

8.6.1 Teeth

The dentition of herbivores is closely related to their feeding habits and diet. The sheep is a suitable example. A sheep eats grass. Its dental formula is:

$$2 \left[i\, \frac{0}{3} \quad c\, \frac{0}{1} \quad pm\, \frac{3}{2} \quad m\, \frac{3}{3} \right]$$

Upper incisors and canines are absent. In their place is a horny pad against which the chisel-shaped lower incisors and canines bite when the sheep is cropping grass. Between the front and cheek teeth is a large gap, the **diastema**, which provides space for the tongue to manipulate the cropped grass in such a way that grass being chewed is kept apart from that which is freshly gathered.

The cheek teeth possess broad grinding surfaces. The surface area of the upper teeth is further increased by being folded into a W-shape and that of the lower teeth by being folded into an M-shape. The ridges of the teeth are composed of hard enamel whilst the troughs are of dentine. The jaw joint is very loose and allows forward, backward and sideways movement. During chewing the lower jaw moves from side to side, with the W-shaped ridges of the upper cheek teeth fitting closely into the grooves of the M-shaped lower teeth as they grind the grass. The masseter muscle, which provides the power for grinding, is large and the temporal muscle, which is used for biting, is small (fig 8.24). (In contrast, the temporal muscle is large in carnivores, where a powerful bite is needed, and the masseter muscle is small.)

8.6.2 Cellulose digestion in ruminants

A **ruminant** is an animal which has a complicated digestive system in which the 'stomach' typically has several chambers. Among the ruminant animals are deer, giraffe, antelope, cattle, sheep and goats. The first chamber of the stomach is called the **rumen** (fig 8.25). This acts as a fermentation chamber where food, mixed with saliva, undergoes fermentation by mutualistic (symbiotic) microorganisms such as bacteria, protozoans and fungi. Many of these produce cellulases which digest cellulose. Their presence is absolutely essential to the ruminant which is unable to manufacture cellulase itself. The end-products of fermentation are carboxylic acids

Table 8.5 Summary of hormonal control of the secretions of the gut and its associated organs.

Hormone	Site of production	Main stimulus for secretion	Target organ	Response
gastrin	stomach mucosa	stretching of stomach by food	stomach	increased secretion of HCl
cholecystokinin (CCK)	mucosa of duodenum	fatty food and protein in the duodenum	pancreas	increased secretion of pancreatic juice rich in enzymes
			gall bladder	contraction of gall bladder to release bile
secretin	mucosa of duodenum	acid chyme in the duodenum	pancreas	increased flow of hydrogen-carbonate in pancreatic juice
			liver	synthesis of bile rich in hydrogen-carbonate
			stomach	inhibits secretion of gastric juice

(particularly ethanoic, propanoic and butanoic acids), carbon dioxide and methane. The acids are absorbed by the host, which uses them as a major source of energy in respiration. In return the microorganisms obtain their energy requirements through the chemical reactions of fermentation, and have an ideal temperature in which to live.

The partially digested food, the 'cud', is passed to the second chamber, the **reticulum**, where it is formed into pellets. It is then regurgitated and thoroughly rechewed. This is called rumination or 'chewing the cud'. The food is then reswallowed and undergoes further fermentation. Eventually the partially digested food is passed through the first three chambers of the gut to reach the **abomasum** which corresponds to the stomach in humans (fig 8.25). From here onwards food undergoes digestion by the usual mammalian digestive enzymes.

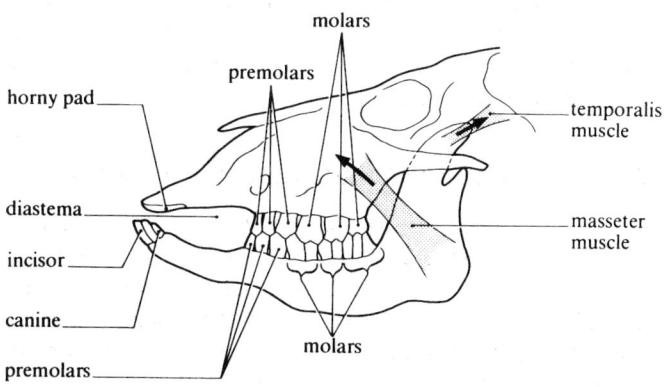

Fig 8.24 *Jaws, dentition and related muscles of the sheep.*

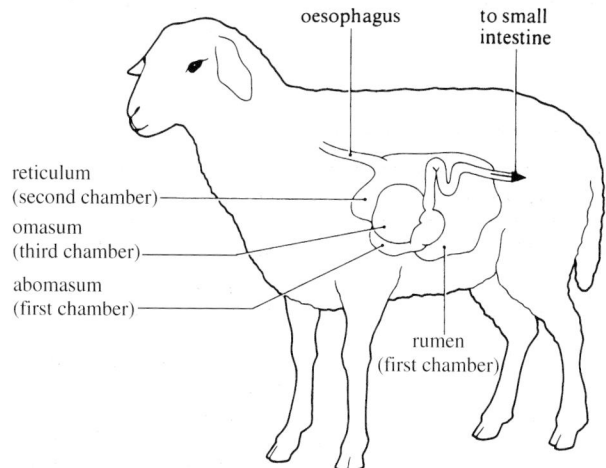

Fig 8.25 *Complex arrangement of chambers preceding the small intestine in a ruminant.*

8.7 Nutrition in humans

Good nutrition has sometimes been described as the key to health. It follows that the opposite, namely malnutrition, can cause ill-health, or disease. **Malnutrition** is, literally, bad nutrition. We tend to associate it with undernutrition, or eating too little, but in its broad sense malnutrition can equally refer to overeating (overnutrition).

Undernutrition not only kills directly by starvation, but indirectly by lowering the resistance of the body to disease. This type of malnutrition is mainly associated with developing countries. In contrast, overnutrition is a leading cause of premature death in developed countries. It can be responsible for, or contribute to, diseases such as coronary heart disease and strokes. Both good nutrition and malnutrition will be examined in this section.

8.7.1 Nutrition, nutrients, food and diet

Nutrition is the acquiring of energy and raw materials needed to maintain life. The two basic nutritional requirements are energy and building materials. These are supplied in the form of chemicals known as **nutrients**. They may be organic, such as carbohydrates, lipids, proteins and vitamins, or inorganic, such as mineral salts. We eat **food** that largely contains these nutrients. **Diet** is the quantity and nature of the food we eat, that is which nutrients and how much of each.

8.7.2 Balanced diet

A **balanced diet** is one which contains the correct proportions and quantity of the various nutrients, water and dietary fibre required to maintain health. Broadly speaking, carbohydrates and fats are needed for energy, proteins for growth and repair processes, and vitamins and minerals for 'protection' of good health and prevention of deficiency diseases.

The ideal diet will vary greatly in different individuals, depending on factors such as their sex, age, activity, body size and the temperature of their external environment (less food is eaten per individual in warm climates).

8.7.3 Water

Water has a wide variety of functions in living cells. It is not therefore regarded simply as a nutrient. Water makes up 65–70% of the total body weight. The importance of water is clear from the fact that a human deprived of water will live for only a few days, whereas it is possible to survive for more than 60 days without food.

8.7.4 Dietary fibre

Dietary fibre is a complex mixture of indigestible compounds derived mainly from plant cell walls. It consists mainly of polysaccharides, particularly cellulose fibres. Its bulk stimulates the movement of food through the gut. There is evidence that fibre helps to reduce blood cholesterol levels, and the risk of bowel cancer and gall stones.

8.7.5 Energy

About 80–85% of the energy content of the average adult diet is provided by carbohydrates and lipids, 15–20% by proteins (up to 5% may be provided by alcohol). Carbohydrates and lipids normally provide the energy actually used. It is needed for three main reasons. These are:

- to maintain the **basal metabolic rate (BMR)**, that is the activities of the body at rest. This includes the energy for growth when it occurs;
- physical exercise (muscle contraction);
- generation of heat to maintain the body at 37 °C.

BMR accounts for the largest proportion of the energy used.

8.7 Why does a mouse require a larger number of joules per unit weight than a human?

8.8 It has been calculated that 1 g glucose combines with 774 cm^3 oxygen releasing 15.8 kJ heat, and 1 g long-chain fatty acid combines with 2012 cm^3 oxygen releasing 39.4 kJ heat. Why does 1 g of fatty acid release more than twice as much heat as 1 g glucose?

Energy units

Energy units used are joules. In the past calories were used.

4.18 joules = 1 calorie
1000 calories = 1 kilocalorie (kcal) = 1 Cal
1000 joules = 1 kJ (kilojoule) = 1 Joule
1000 kJ = 1 MJ (megajoule)

8.7.6 Carbohydrates

Carbohydrates include sugars and starch (a polysaccharide). Carbohydrates are a major energy source, but sugars are also building blocks for more complex molecules such as nucleic acids, nucleotides (e.g. ATP, NAD) and glycogen.

8.7.7 Lipids (fats and oils)

Lipids include fats, which are solid at room temperature, and oils, which are liquid at room temperature. Like carbohydrates, lipids are a major energy source. Fatty tissues form a convenient long-term energy store in the body. Fats in the diet may also be a source of fat-soluble vitamins (A, D, E and K).

The following are some key facts about lipids.

- The lipids found in foods are mainly triglycerides made from glycerol and three fatty acids.
- There is a large variety of fatty acids in food, but all are either saturated or unsaturated.
- **Saturated** fatty acids have no double bonds (they are saturated with hydrogen). Fats are rich in saturated fatty acids. They have been linked with cardiovascular disease (chapter 15).
- **Unsaturated** fatty acids have one or more double bonds. Oils are rich in unsaturated fatty acids.
- Unsaturated fatty acids may be **monounsaturated** (one double bond) or **polyunsaturated** (more than one double bond).
- Unsaturated fatty acids can be converted to saturated fatty acids by adding hydrogen, a process known as **hydrogenation**. In this way oils can be hardened to make margarines.
- Most natural fatty acids exist in the 'cis' form where the molecules are fairly straight. When unsaturated fatty acids are partially hydrogenated some of the remaining unsaturated fatty acids are converted to the 'trans' form in which the molecules are kinked. These have the same effect on our bodies as saturated fatty acids.

A balanced diet will contain both saturated and unsaturated fatty acids, but because of the link between saturated fatty acids and cardiovascular disease (chapter 15) it has been recommended that most people need to reduce their saturated fatty acid intake.

Essential fatty acids (EFAs)

An **essential fatty acid** is one which must be included in the diet because it cannot be made in the body. Without it, ill-health would result. Only two are strictly essential, namely linoleic acid and alpha linolenic acid. (Note spelling carefully.) They are both polyunsaturated fatty acids (PUFAs) and exist in the cis form. Linoleic acid has two double bonds and linolenic acid has three. They have a number of important functions.

- EFAs are used in the manufacture of phospholipids which form part of the structure of membranes.
- They are involved in the transport, breakdown and excretion of cholesterol. Cholesterol is an essential component of membranes and needed for the manufacture of steroids, including the sex hormones, and vitamin D. However, an excess of cholesterol can be harmful to health because it can be a cause of atherosclerosis (fatty deposits in the arteries) which can lead to cardiovascular disease. Thus precise regulation of its metabolism is essential. Linoleic acid and some other PUFAs help to reduce cholesterol levels in the blood, whereas saturated fatty acids tend to raise them. The best dietary advice is to reduce saturated fatty acid intake.

- Linolenic acid may inhibit the blood clotting associated with atherosclerosis and reduces risk of heart attack in people who have already had one heart attack.
- EFAs are needed to make certain other fatty acids which are physiologically important, such as prostaglandins which are a group of fatty acids that have a wide range of effects on the body. For example, they influence the action of certain hormones, can stimulate inflammatory responses and regulate blood flow to some organs. They are involved in the birth process and have been used in the morning-after pill as an anti-progesterone drug to prevent implantation of a fertilised egg in the uterus.
- Linolenic acid is one of the fatty acids needed for normal development and functioning of the retina and brain.

Deficiency of EFAs is rare since large reserves usually exist in the body fat and daily intake is usually more than adequate.

8.7.8   Proteins

Proteins are used mainly for growth and repair. They have many functions (section 3.5). They can also be used as a source of energy if the diet is deficient in carbohydrate and fat.

Proteins are made of amino acids. There are 20 different amino acids commonly used to make protein, and like fatty acids they can be divided into two types, essential and non-essential.

An **essential amino acid** is one which must be included in the diet because either it cannot be made in the body at all, or it is made too slowly to meet needs. Ill-health would result from insufficient intake. Eight of the 20 amino acids are essential for adult humans, and ten for infants. Non-essential amino acids can be made from essential amino acids in the body. Proteins which are rich in essential amino acids are called first class or high quality proteins. They are most commonly animal proteins, as found in milk and its products, meat, fish and eggs, but soya protein is a useful source of first class protein for vegetarians. Other proteins are referred to as second class or low quality proteins.

8.7.9   Vitamins

Vitamins are organic compounds required in small quantities for good health. They cannot be made within the body, so must be present in the diet.

If a given vitamin is lacking, a characteristic set of symptoms will develop known as a **deficiency disease**. Table 8.6 shows some of the sources and functions of the main vitamins and the deficiency diseases caused by a lack of them. Vitamins A, D, E and K are fat-soluble and the rest are water-soluble.

Vitamin A (retinol)

The proper chemical name of vitamin A is **retinol**. It is found in food of animal origin. The orange pigment carotene, familiar in carrots, and similar pigments called carotenes, are found widely in plants and can be converted to vitamin A during digestion. The structure of carotenes and vitamin A is particularly well adapted for light absorption, both in plants in the form of carotenes and in animals where vitamin A is converted to the light-absorbing molecule **retinal**. The three groups of animals which possess eyes (molluscs, arthropods and vertebrates) all use retinal as the light-absorbing part of their photoreceptor molecules. Light brings about a relatively large change in the structure of retinal, sufficient to trigger the generation of a nerve impulse.

Vitamin A is also needed for healthy skin and other epithelial (surface) tissues and is required by young children for growth.

Deficiency disease.   A deficiency of vitamin A affects the rods (which react to light intensity) in the eye much more than the cones (which react to colour) and leads at first to a condition known as **'night blindness'**. This is poor adaptation to conditions of low light intensity when vision is mainly dependent on the rods. Night blindness is caused by a deficiency of retinal in the rods. Eventually the rods themselves become damaged. At the same time the conjunctiva and the cornea become drier and uncomfortable. This can lead to a condition known as **xerophthalmia** (*xero*, dry; *ophthalmia*, eye) with ulcers occurring on the cornea leading to blindness (**keratomalacia**).

Young children are particularly susceptible to vitamin A deficiency because it also reduces growth. Prolonged deficiency can lead to death. The condition is still common in some developing countries and is the most common cause of blindness in children. About 3 million children under the age of 10 years are blind as a result. A person with a healthy diet could be expected to have up to two years' supply in the liver, where it is stored. Average daily consumption in Britain is about twice that needed.

Excess vitamin A.   Rare cases have been reported of vitamin A liver poisoning resulting from intake of excess amounts, often from prolonged consumption of large amounts of vitamin pills. Bone damage, hair loss, double vision, vomiting and other problems may also occur. High intakes (in excess of 3300 µg per day) during pregnancy may cause birth defects. In the UK, pregnant women are generally advised not to take vitamin supplements containing vitamin A unless advised to do so at antenatal classes or by a doctor.

Regular intakes should not exceed 6000 µg per day for adolescents, 7500 µg per day for adult women and 9000 µg per day for adult men.

Table 8.6 Sources and functions of the main vitamins required in the human diet and deficiency diseases caused by a lack of them.

Name of vitamin and its designated letter	Principal sources	Function	Deficiency diseases and symptoms
Fat-soluble vitamins			
A (Retinol)	Fish-liver oil, liver, milk and derivatives, carrots, spinach, watercress	Controls normal epithelial structure and growth. Used to make retinal, which is essential for the formation of the visual pigment rhodopsin. Aids 'night vision'	Skin becomes dry, cornea bcomes dry and mucous membranes degenerate. Poor 'night vision'. Serious deficiency results in complete night blindness (xerophthalmia). Permanent blindness (keratomalacia) may occur if the vitamin is not present in the diet.
D (Calciferol)	Fish-liver oil, egg yolk, dairy products, margarine, made by the action of sunlight on a cholesterol-like compound in the skin	Controls calcium absorption from the gut, and concerned with calcium metabolism. Important in bone and tooth formation. Aids absorption of phosphorus.	**Rickets** – this is the failure of growing bones to calcify. Bow legs are a common feature in young children and knock knees in older ones. Deformation of the pelvic bones in adolescent girls can occur which may lead to complications when they give birth. **Osteomalacia** – an adult condition where the bones are painful and spontaneous fractures may occur.
E (Tocopherol)	Wheat germ, brown flour, liver, green vegetables	In rats, it affects muscles and the reproductive system and prevents breakdown of red blood cells. Function in humans is still unknown.	Can cause sterility in rats. Muscular dystrophy. **Anaemia** – increased breakdown of red blood cells.
K (Phylloquinone)	Spinach, cabbage, brussels sprouts, synthesised by bacteria in the intestine	Essential for final stage of prothrombin synthesis in the liver. Therefore it is a necessary factor for the blood-clotting mechanism.	Mild deficiency leads to a prolonged blood-clotting time. Serious deficiency means blood fails to clot at all.
Water-soluble vitamins			
B_1 (Thiamin)	Wheat or rice germ, yeast extract, wholemeal flour, liver, kidney, heart	Acts as a coenzyme for decarboxylation in respiration, especially in Krebs cycle.	**Beriberi** – nervous system affected. Muscles become weak and painful. Paralysis can occur. Heart failure. Oedema (tissues swollen with fluid). Children's growth is reduced. Keto acids, e.g. pyruvic acid, accumulate in the blood.
B_2 (Riboflavin)	Yeast extract, liver, eggs, milk, cheese	Forms part of the prosthetic group of flavoproteins which are used in electron transport.	Tongue sores. Sores at the corners of the mouth.
B_6 (Pyridoxine)	Eggs, liver, kidney, whole grains, vegetables, fish	Converted to a coenzyme for amino acid and fatty acid metabolism	Depression and irritability. Anaemia. Diarrhoea. Dermatitis.
B_5 (Pantothenic acid)	In most foods	Forms part of coenzyme A molecule which is involved in activation of carboxylic acids in cell metabolism.	Poor nerve/muscle coordination. Fatigue. Muscle cramp.
B_3 (Nicotinic acid (niacin) or pp)	Meat, wholemeal bread, yeast extract, liver	Essential component of the coenzymes NAD, NADP which are hydrogen acceptors for a range of dehydrogenase enzymes. Also a part of coenzyme A.	**Pellagra** – skin lesions, rashes. Diarrhoea.
B_{12} (Cyanocobalamin)	Meat, milk, eggs, fish, cheese	RNA nucleoprotein synthesis. Prevents pernicious anaemia.	Pernicious anaemia.
Folic acid (M or Bc)	Liver, white fish, green vegetables	Formation of red blood corpuscles. Synthesis of nucleoproteins.	**Anaemia** – particularly in women during pregnancy.

Table 8.6 *(cont.)*

Name of vitamin and its designated letter	Principal sources	Function	Deficiency diseases and symptoms
H (Biotin)	Yeast, liver, kidney, egg white, synthesis by intestinal bacteria	Used as a coenzyme for a number of carboxylation reactions. Involved in protein synthesis and transamination.	Dermatitis. Muscle pains.
C (Ascorbic acid)	Citrus fruits, green vegetables, potatoes, tomatoes, other fruits e.g. blackcurrants	Concerned with the metabolism of connective tissue and the production of strong skin. Essential for collagen fibre synthesis.	**Scurvy** – skin of gums becomes weak and bleeds. Wounds fail to heal. Connective tissue fibres fail to form. Anaemia. Heart failure.

Vitamin D (calciferol)

For most people enough vitamin D can be made by the action of sunlight on the skin. The light-absorbing molecule found in the skin is made from cholesterol. The active part of the light is ultraviolet (UV) light. There is almost no UV radiation of the suitable wavelength of 280–310 nm in Britain from the end of October to the end of March. Normally, stores of vitamin D build up in the liver in the summer months and provide the body's requirements during the rest of the year.

Most naturally occurring foods are low in vitamin D. Oily fish, such as mackerel, sardines and herring, fish-liver oils and egg yolk are exceptions. These days vitamin D is added as a supplement to some foods, such as margarine (to which it must be added by law) and breakfast cereals.

Vitamin D is converted through reactions first in the liver and then in the kidney (and placenta in pregnant women) to an active form which promotes calcium and phosphate absorption from the intestine. The manufacture of active vitamin D is closely linked with calcium levels in the blood and increases rapidly if calcium levels drop. The active form of vitamin D also affects deposition of calcium and phosphate in bone (bone deposition) and the removal of these from bone (bone reabsorption). In an adult, bone deposition and reabsorption are normally kept in balance so that total bone mass remains constant. A constant re-modelling of bones goes on which allows them to adjust in strength and shape to stresses.

In pregnancy and lactation there is extra demand for calcium for the growth of the baby. Vitamin D content of breast milk is relatively low so, where exposure to sunlight is low, supplements may be recommended.

Deficiency disease. A deficiency of vitamin D is particularly damaging in childhood because the skeleton is growing rapidly. For this reason a dietary supply is recommended for children up to the age of 4 years. The deficiency disease is called **rickets**, and is caused by too little calcium and phosphate being added to the bones. This makes the bones too weak and soft to support the weight of the body, causing bowing of the legs and bending of the spine.

In adults vitamin D deficiency leads to a condition known as **osteomalacia** (*osteon*, bone; *malakia*, softness). Here the bones are weakened and soften, becoming less mineralised with calcium and phosphate. Those most at risk are people who receive little exposure to sunlight. In Britain the two groups most at risk are the elderly and the Asian community. Many elderly people lack mobility and spend much of their time indoors. For cultural reasons the Asian diet may be relatively low in calcium as well as vitamin D. The traditional clothing of Asian women leaves little skin exposed to sunlight and darker skins also filter out UV light more effectively than pale skins. Asian children are also particularly at risk. Incidence of rickets in Britain has risen among some poor inner city communities, particularly among Asian communities.

Excess vitamin D. Excess intake of vitamin D can lead to excess calcium uptake. If the excess cannot all be excreted in the urine it may become deposited in the kidneys where it can cause damage. It is more dangerous for infants than for adults.

8.7.10   Minerals

Minerals are inorganic and needed for a wide range of functions. Those needed in the human diet are shown in table 8.7. Seven minerals are needed in only trace amounts for good health, and these are known as **trace elements**. They include manganese, copper, zinc and iodine. Only tiny quantities of trace elements are required in the daily diet. Examples of the roles of minerals are given in table 8.7.

8.7.11   Milk

The only food that most mammals receive during the first weeks of their lives is milk. It provides an almost complete diet during this stage of their development, containing carbohydrate, protein, fat, minerals (especially calcium, magnesium, phosphorus and potassium) and a variety of vitamins. The one major element that milk lacks is iron, a constituent of haemoglobin in blood. However,

Table 8.7 The essential mineral ions needed in a balanced diet and their functions.

Major minerals in order of total amount in body	Examples of functions
Calcium	synthesis of bones and teeth
Phosphorus /phosphate	75% is combined with calcium in bones and teeth
	synthesis of nucleic acids (DNA and RNA)
	synthesis of ATP
	synthesis of phospholipids in membranes
Sulphur	mainly present as part of the amino acids cysteine and methionine
Potassium	needed with sodium to maintain electrical potential across cell membranes
	conduction of nerve impulses
Sodium	important constituent of fluid outside cells (tissue fluid)
	helps maintain water balance
	conduction of nerve impulses
	needed with potassium to maintain electrical potential across cell membranes
Chlorine	as sodium (not as important for nerve impulses)
	also a constituent of hydrochloric acid in the stomach
Magnesium	synthesis of bones and teeth
Iron	constituent of the haem group in haemoglobin and myoglobin

Trace elements in order of total amount in body	
Fluorine	associated with structure of bones and teeth, increasing resistance to decay
Zinc	constituent of bone and some enzymes
Copper	constituent of cytochrome oxidase, an electron acceptor in respiration
Iodine	synthesis of the hormone thyroxine
Manganese	constituent of some enzymes involved in respiration and the development of bone
Chromium	involved in the use of glucose
Cobalt	part of vitamin B_{12}

this problem is overcome by the embryo gaining iron from its mother and storing it in its body before birth. It stores enough to allow development until it begins to ingest solid food.

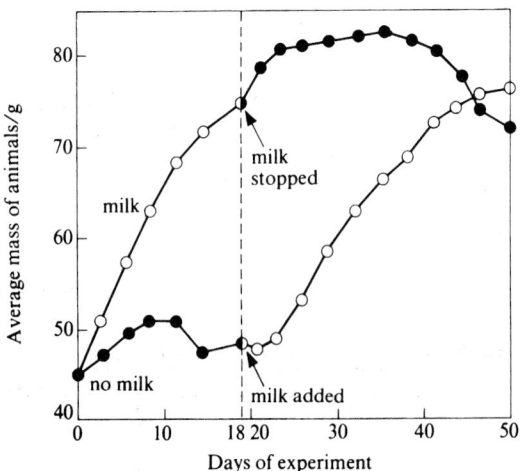

Fig 8.26 *Gowland Hopkins' experiment on feeding milk to rats.*

8.9 Early this century, Frederick Gowland Hopkins in Cambridge performed a famous experiment where he took two sets of eight young rats and fed both on a diet of pure casein (a milk protein), starch, sucrose, lard, inorganic salts and water. The first set also received 3 cm³ of milk per day for the first 18 days. On day 18, the extra milk was denied the first set, but given to the second set of rats instead. The result of the experiment is shown in fig 8.26.

(a) What hypothesis can you deduce from the graph?

(b) Support your answer with comments.

(c) Why is a diet of milk only inadequate for an adult?

8.8 Recommended intakes of nutrients and reference values

The first set of recommendations for human nutritional requirements was made by the League of Nations in 1937. So during the Second World War the government in Britain was able to plan a food policy on a scientific basis. The government later set up a Committee on Medical Aspects of Food Policy (COMA).

In 1979 COMA published tables which summarised the **Recommended Daily Amounts** (**RDAs**) of food energy and nutrients for particular groups of the population. They took account of age, sex, level of activity, and whether a woman is pregnant or lactating (producing milk) and represented the needs of most people within each group, *including those with relatively high needs.*

8.8.1 Dietary Reference Values (DRVs)

In 1987 COMA began reviewing the RDAs, and published another report in 1991. This time they considered 40 nutrients in detail, compared with the previous 10. They also argued that the term RDA was often being misinterpreted as a recommended ideal or a minimum requirement which everyone should be trying to achieve for a healthy life.

> **8.10** Explain why it is a misinterpretation of the term RDA to assume that it is an ideal which everyone should try to achieve.

The term Recommended Daily Amount (RDA) was therefore changed to **Reference Nutrient Intake** (**RNI**) and two further terms were introduced. The two new terms are **Estimated Average Requirement** (**EAR**) and **Lower Reference Nutrient Intake** (**LRNI**). The three terms now used are known collectively as **Dietary Reference Values** (**DRVs**). In tables, DRVs are expressed as amounts per day (tables 8.8 and 8.9). The terms are defined below. Fig 8.27 shows how DRVs relate to the population as a whole. It is assumed that the requirements for energy or any given

nutrient within a population is represented by a normal distribution curve (a bell-shaped curve whose mean value occurs with the highest frequency).

- **EAR Estimated Average Requirement**
  This value is given for energy (table 8.8), protein, vitamins and minerals. It represents the estimated

Table 8.8 Estimated Average Requirements (EARs) for energy in the UK (per day).

Age range	Males		Females	
	MJ	kcal	MJ	kcal
0–3 months (formula fed)	2.28	545	2.16	515
4–6 months	2.89	690	2.69	645
7–9 months	3.44	825	3.20	765
10–12 months	3.85	920	3.61	865
1–3 years	5.15	1230	4.86	1165
4–6 years	7.16	1715	6.46	1545
7–10 years	8.24	1970	7.28	1740
11–14 years	9.27	2220	7.92	1845
15–18 years	11.51	2755	8.83	2110
19–50 years	10.60	2550	8.10	1940
51–59 years	10.60	2550	8.00	1900
60–64 years	9.93	2380	7.99	1900
65–74 years	9.71	2330	7.96	1900
75+ years	8.77	2100	7.61	1810
Pregnant			+0.80[a]	+200[a]
Lactating:				
1 month			+1.90	+450
2 months			+2.20	+530
3 months			+2.40	+570
4–6 months			+2.00	+480
>6 months			+1.00	+240

[a] last three months only.
From *Manual of Nutrition*, Reference Book 342 (HMSO) 10th ed. (1995) table 24, p.68.

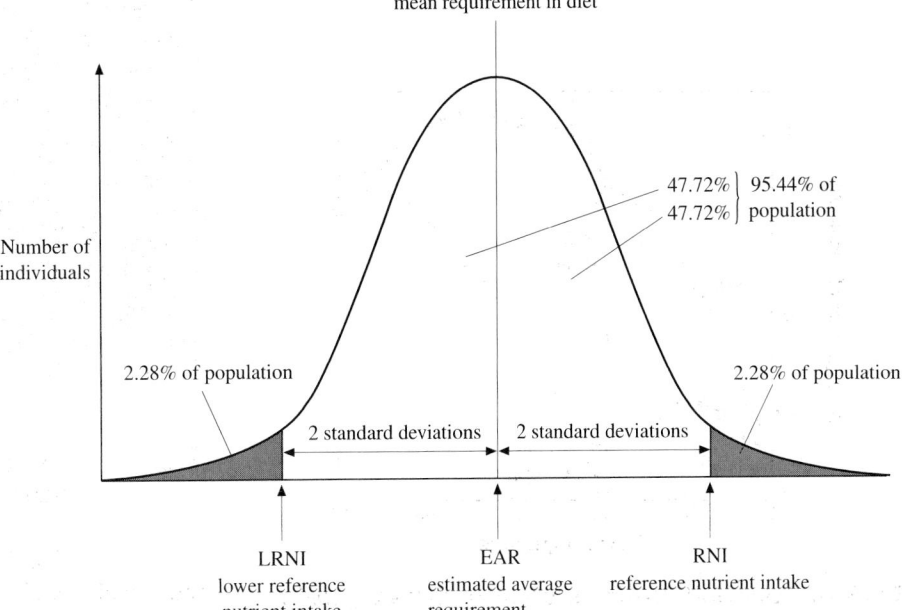

Fig 8.27 *The relationship between LRNI, EAR and RNI in a population.*

Table 8.9 Reference Nutrient Intakes (RNIs) for selected nutrients for the UK (per day).

Age range	Protein (g)	Calcium (mg)	Iron (mg)	Zinc (mg)	Vitamin A (µg)	Thiamin (mg)	Vitamin B_6[a] (mg[a])	Folic acid (µg)	Vitamin C (mg)	Vitamin D (µg)
0–3 months (formula fed)	12.5	525	1.7	4.0	350	0.2	0.2	50	25	8.5
4–6 months	12.7	525	4.3	4.0	350	0.2	0.2	50	25	8.5
7–9 months	13.7	525	7.8	5.0	350	0.2	0.3	50	25	7
10–12 months	14.9	525	7.8	5.0	350	0.3	0.4	50	25	7
1–3 years	14.5	350	6.9	5.0	400	0.5	0.7	70	30	7
4–6 years	19.7	450	6.1	6.5	500	0.7	0.9	100	30	–
7–10 years	28.3	550	8.7	7.0	500	0.7	1.0	150	30	–
Males										
11–14 years	42.1	1000	11.3	9.0	600	0.9	1.2	200	35	–
15–18 years	55.2	1000	11.3	9.5	700	1.1	1.5	200	40	–
19–50 years	55.5	700	8.7	9.5	700	1.0	1.4	200	40	–
50+ years	53.3	700	8.7	9.5	700	0.9	1.4	200	40	*
Females										
11–14 years	41.2	800	14.8[b]	9.0	600	0.7	1.0	200	35	–
15–18 years	45.0	800	14.8[b]	7.0	600	0.8	1.2	200	40	–
19–50 years	45.0	700	14.8[b]	7.0	600	0.8	1.2	200	40	–
50+ years	46.5	700	8.7	7.0	600	0.8	1.2	200	40	*
Pregnant	+6.0	c	c	c	+100	+0.1[d]	c	+100	+10	10
Lactating:										
0–4 months	+11.0	+550	c	+6.0	+350	+0.2	c	+60	+30	10
4 months	+8.0	+550	c	+2.5	+350	+0.2	c	+60	+30	10

[a] Based on protein providing 14.7% of the EAR for energy.
[b] These RNIs will not meet the needs of approximately 10% of women with the highest menstrual losses, who may need iron supplements.
[c] No increment.
[d] Last three months only.
* After age 65 the RNI is 10 µg per day for men and women.

From *Manual of Nutrition*, table 25, p.69 (see table 8.8).

average requirement of that nutrient per day. About half the population will usually need more than the EAR and half will need less.

- **RNI   Reference Nutrient Intake**
  This value is given for protein, vitamins and minerals (table 8.9). It replaces the old term RDA, and represents the amount of nutrient that is enough, or more than enough, for about 97% of people in a group. If average intake of a group is at RNI, then the risk of deficiency in the group is very small. In other words, intake at or above this amount will almost certainly be adequate for good health.
- **LRNI   Lower Reference Nutrient Intake**
  This value is given for protein, vitamins and minerals. It represents the amount of nutrient that is enough for

the few people in a group who have low needs. In other words, intakes below this amount will almost certainly be inadequate, with harmful consequences for health.

Energy is excluded from RNIs and LRNIs because appetite is usually closely related to the energy required, and because consuming more energy than required can lead to obesity. EARs for energy are shown in table 8.8.

Fat and carbohydrate

The 1979 COMA report did not include RDAs for fat and carbohydrate because the contribution of these two nutrients was included in the RDA for energy. However, in view of the health concern over the relative amounts of fat and carbohydrate in the diet, and the relative proportions of saturated and unsaturated fats, the 1991 report included recommendations which would help to guide those who plan diets. Table 8.10 shows the energy intake of the average British diet at the time the report was published, and the DRVs. DRVs are not expressed as RNI, LRNI or EAR because, apart from the essential fatty acids, carbohydrates and fats have not been shown to be essential nutrients. Instead, another DRV has been used, namely **recommended percentage of daily energy intake** (average for the whole population).

> **8.11** Compare the average intakes in 1990 with the DRVs (table 8.10). What are the main ways in which it is recommended that diet should change?
>
> **8.12** Suggest two problems that might be encountered in trying to keep an accurate record of an individual's diet.

Note that DRVs are *not recommendations for intakes by individuals or particular groups*. They are reference values which can be used in a variety of ways. However, there is still insufficient data to be able to calculate DRVs with great confidence.

8.8.2 Uses of DRVs

DRVs can be used for a variety of purposes and different DRVs are appropriate in different circumstances.

- **Planning diets**
  When health professionals such as dieticians plan diets for groups, individuals or institutions, or when the government makes national recommendations, it is safest to use the RNIs as the recommended values.

> **8.13** Explain why this is so.

- **Assessing the diet of individuals**
  One of the least suitable uses of DRVs is in *assessing* the diet of an individual. Assessing diet means judging whether the existing diet is suitable; it is *not* the same as planning a diet. DRVs can be used only as a rough guide to the adequacy of a person's diet.

> **8.14** Explain why this is the case based on the discussion of DRVs so far.

Table 8.10 Fat, fatty acids and carbohydrates in the diet of British adults – intake in 1990 and DRVs.

Nutrient	Average intake in 1990 (g/day)	Approximate % of daily energy intake	DRV (recommended % of daily energy intake) (1991)
Total fat (glycerol + fatty acids)	87.8	40%	33%
Fatty acids:			
cis-polyunsaturated	13.3	6%	6%
cis-monounsaturated	26.7	12%	12%
saturated	36.5	16%	10% (achieved by only about 5% of adults)
trans-unsaturated	4.8	2%	2%
Total fatty acids	81.3	36%	30%
Total carbohydrate	232	40%	47%
Sugars (excluding those in cell walls and milk)	60	10%	10%
Starch (+ cell wall and milk sugars)	170	30%	37%
Dietary fibre	11.6	11.6 g/day	18 g/ day
Energy	8.6 MJ per day (2061 kcal per day)		
Total energy (actual averages)			
Fat and carbohydrate (excluding dietary fibre)		80%	
Protein		15%	
Alcohol*		5%	
	Total	100%	

* Alcohol contains energy. If the diet contains no alcohol, all the recommendations in the table would be slightly higher.
Data on g/day from Gregory, J., Foster, K., Tyler, H. & Wiseman, M., *The Dietary and Nutritional Survey of British Adults*, HMSO, (1990). Data on sugars and starch have been changed by the author to be comparable with DRVs.

- **Assessing the diets of particular groups**

  The larger the group, the more likely that errors and variations among individuals will be averaged out, and therefore the more accurate will be estimates of mean nutrient intakes of that group. Estimates can then be made of the risks of deficiency within the group.

- **Food labelling**

  RDAs have been used on food labels. Thus the consumer might be informed that 100 g of the food contains one-quarter (or 25%) of the recommended daily amount of protein. This is more useful to the average consumer than being informed that the food contains 15 g of protein per 100 g.

> **8.15** State one disadvantage of providing RDAs on food labels.

COMA suggested that a system of labelling based on EARs would be more useful than using RDAs. Since EAR is an indication of the average amount of food required rather than the upper limit, this would reduce attempts to reach inappropriately high consumption levels.

- **General use**

  DRVs can also be of more general use. They have relevance to agricultural policy. They may also be used by economists and sociologists in tackling some of the wider issues in society, such as poverty.

> **8.16** How might DRVs be of use to a sociologist investigating poverty?

8.8.3 Effect of age, sex and activity on DRVs

Nutritional requirements vary with age, sex, and activity. DRVs have been set for the two sexes and for different age groups as shown in tables 8.8 and 8.9. They are based on average body weights for the particular group, and apply to healthy people.

Energy (table 8.8)

Energy is needed to maintain the basal metabolic rate (BMR), that is the activities of the body at rest. BMR accounts for a large proportion of the energy used and can be estimated accurately. BMR for a 65 kg man is about 7.56 MJ per day. For a 55 kg woman it is about 5.98 MJ per day.

Any movement requires extra energy because it involves muscular activity, and muscle contraction requires energy. The more physically active a person, the more energy they consume. It is useful to express the amount of energy needed for a given activity as a multiple of BMR. This is known as the **physical activity ratio** (**PAR**). For example the PAR for walking is 4, meaning that walking requires four times as much energy as BMR.

Physical activity varies with both occupation and leisure. Occupations are traditionally described as follows. PARs are averaged over the whole working day.

- sedentary, meaning non-active or sitting: PAR is 1.7.
- moderately active: PAR is 2.2 in women and 2.7 in men.
- very active: PAR is 2.3+ in women and 3.0+ in men.

These days leisure activities are at least as important as occupation in determining energy requirements and should, therefore, be taken into account. It has been suggested that the following categories are used: sedentary (PAR 2), moderately active (PAR 3) and very active (PAR 4).

Men have proportionately more muscle and less fat than women. They also weigh more on average (growing, maintaining and moving a heavier body requires more energy). The average energy expenditure of men is therefore higher (table 8.8).

For women during the first six months of pregnancy, reductions in physical activity and metabolic rate compensate for the extra energy needed for growth of the fetus and deposition of fat ready for lactation (producing milk for breastfeeding). It is only in the final three months that extra energy is needed (table 8.8). This is needed for growth of the baby and to build up a store of about 2 kg of fat in the mother in preparation for lactation. Breastfeeding requires extra energy because all the baby's energy comes from the milk and the baby continues to grow rapidly after birth.

Protein

RNIs which take into account age and sex are shown in table 8.9. RNIs for infants and children are higher than for adults on a body weight for weight basis, because protein is needed for growth and maintenance. RNIs are the same, on a weight for weight basis, for all adults (age 19+).

In practice, actual average intakes of protein by adults in the UK are higher than the RNIs. Men consume on average 84 g of protein per day, and women 64 g.

The higher average muscle:fat ratio and average body weight of males compared with females means that males require extra protein from the age of 11 (table 8.9).

There is no need to consume extra protein if there is increased activity because it is not usually used as a source of energy. However, if extra body mass occurs as a result of muscle development, a corresponding increase in protein intake may be justified.

Extra protein is required during pregnancy (table 8.9) to allow for growth of the fetus and extra tissue in the mother, such as uterus, placenta, blood and breasts. Breast milk contains the protein needed for growth of the baby so, during lactation, the mother continues to require extra protein.

Minerals

During pregnancy and lactation, particular attention should be paid to making sure that the mother's diet contains sufficient iron, calcium, vitamin C, vitamin D and folic acid (table 8.9). These are needed for making the baby's haemoglobin, bones, teeth and muscle. A good mixed diet will normally satisfy these requirements. Extra folic acid is sometimes given to pregnant women to reduce the risk of spina bifida in the baby.

8.9 Malnutrition

Malnutrition in its broad sense means bad nutrition, and can be applied to both undernutrition and overnutrition (overeating). In the following sections four examples of malnutrition will be examined. Two of these are typical of developed countries, namely anorexia nervosa and obesity. Two are typical of developing countries, namely starvation or general undernutrition, and protein deficiency. Two examples of vitamin deficiency diseases, caused by lack of vitamin A and vitamin D, are discussed in section 8.7.9.

8.9.1 Anorexia nervosa

Anorexia nervosa is sometimes referred to as 'slimmer's disease'. It has become more common in the last 30 years and is associated mainly with affluent western societies, perhaps because such societies tend to stress that 'thin is beautiful'. The term anorexia nervosa means literally 'loss of appetite through nervous causes', but, strictly speaking, the condition is not caused by a loss of appetite because the typical victim will be extremely hungry. Despite this there is a constant fear of putting on weight and this overcomes the desire to eat.

Anorexia is associated mainly with young women (only 10% of cases are men), often at the beginning of adolescence. It most commonly starts as a result of dieting. Gradually the dieting becomes more and more exaggerated and the woman eats less and less until the fear of putting on weight becomes an obsession. At this stage, psychologically, the woman may still be thinking of herself as overweight even if she is becoming severely underweight and beginning to show signs of starvation.

Physically the body returns to a pre-adolescent state, for example menstruation may cease. Also soft, downy hair may grow around the edges of the face and over the shoulders, as in marasmus (section 8.9.4). Starvation may lead to emaciation, which is an extremely thin body, and other symptons typical of marasmus may appear. The body is usually deprived particularly of carbohydrate and fat, which are the foods that diets focus on. The body may therefore start to use protein as a source of energy. Muscles contain a high proportion of the body's protein, so muscles and other body tissues start to waste away. Other side effects include increased incidence of constipation, low blood pressure, tooth decay (dental caries) and susceptibility to infection. Vitamin and mineral deficiencies may occur. Severe cases may be fatal.

A full discussion of the psychology of the condition and its treatment is outside the scope of this book. However, it is very important for anorexics to recognise that they have a problem and to want to seek help. Self-help groups exist and counselling by experts is available. Voluntary organisations exist which can advise on the best approach. Sometimes a period in hospital is necessary.

8.9.2 Obesity

Obesity is the most common nutritional disorder in Britain today and is just as great a problem in most European countries and in North America. A survey of British adults in 1991 showed that 13% of men and 15% of women were obese. A person is described as obese if they weigh at least 20% more than the average for someone of their height and overall frame size (fig. 8.28). It can be measured more scientifically by measuring the amount of fat in the body compared with total body weight. For young men fat is about 12% of normal body weight and for young women about 26%. A figure of more than 20% for men and 30% for women could be considered as indicating obesity.

Obesity is caused when energy input as a result of eating is greater than energy used. Extra fat, carbohydrate, protein or alcohol can be converted into body fat. This does not necessarily mean that the person eats a lot. Surveys have shown that many obese people eat no more than thin people. Other factors such as little physical exercise may be important. There are exceptions. One man who weighed 365 kg (57 stone) used to eat 15 chickens at a time. The amount of excess food needed to produce obesity may be relatively small. Over time regular small excesses accumulate and cause obesity. Apart from quantity of food, the nature of the food may also be a factor. High energy foods such as carbohydrates and fats are more likely to cause problems.

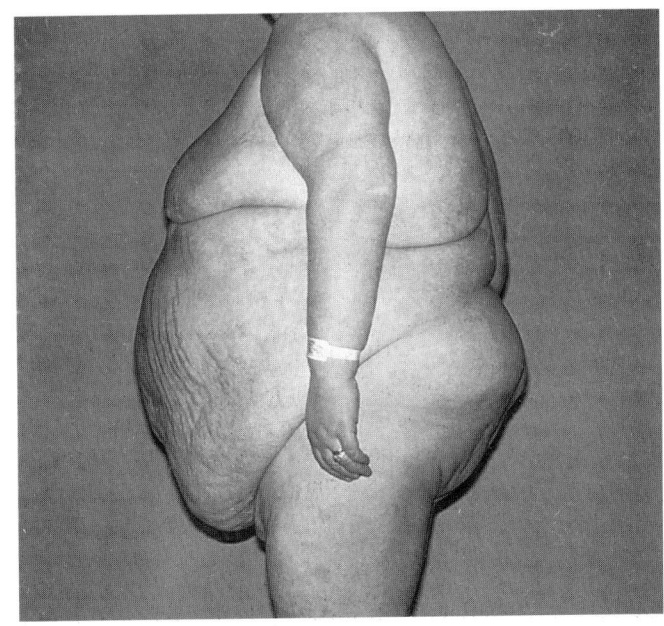

Fig 8.28 *Obese person.*

Obesity often runs in families and there is probably some genetic predisposition in some sufferers. Occasionally it is due to a physiological disorder, particularly involving the hypothalamus or underactivity of the thyroid gland.

Cardiovascular disease is more common in obese people because blood cholesterol levels are typically high and high blood pressure is more common. There is a greater tendency for atherosclerosis in the coronary arteries, with more heart attacks in middle life as a result. There is also an increased incidence of varicose veins.

The extra load on the skeleton commonly causes mechanical difficulties. Flat feet, osteoarthritis of joints, slipped disc and back problems are more common. Hernias are also more common. Movement becomes restricted and difficult and is often slow and awkward. Accidents may happen as a result. Diabetes and some cancers (e.g. gall bladder) are more common in obese people.

Obesity can create emotional problems. Children may become figures of fun and subject to teasing and bullying. Adults are constantly reminded of the association between attractiveness and a slim body by advertising.

Not surprisingly, life expectancy is reduced as a result of obesity. Insurance companies have calculated that a man of 45 who is 10 kg overweight reduces his life expectancy by 25%. The risks are slightly less for women.

To combat obesity, the energy content of the diet must be reduced to the point where energy output is greater than energy input. This should continue until normal weight is restored. This involves counselling the person so that they understand the nature of the problem and can start a low energy diet. A programme of physical exercise may also be recommended.

8.9.3 Starvation and general undereating

The body must maintain a supply of energy for survival. During starvation energy reserves gradually get used up until death results. The first reserve to be used is the carbohydrate glycogen which is stored in the liver and muscles. This supplies energy only for about half a day in the absence of food. Fat stores are then used. In an average person fat can supply enough energy for about 50 days. Fat is broken down in the liver to release fatty acids which are then used instead of glucose in cell respiration. However, ketones made from the fatty acids also tend to build up in the blood, causing a condition called **ketosis** and making the blood acidic. One ketone produced is acetone. It is made in small quantities but can be smelt on the breath and is a sign of ketosis.

For about the first week of fasting, muscle protein is also used as a source of energy. It is converted to glucose, a process called gluconeogenesis. Use of protein then more or less ceases until the fat begins to run out. The renewed use of protein represents the final phase of starvation before death (fig 8.29). Body tissues such as muscle begin to waste away and the person becomes emaciated. Death usually occurs when about half the body's proteins have been used. Complete starvation leads to death in 40 to 60 days.

Children who are undernourished over an extended period of time have stunted growth, and are usually thin. They may develop marasmus (section 8.9.4). It is only relatively recently that the problem of undernourishment has been largely overcome in developed countries, but there are still many problems remaining in providing sufficient food in developing countries.

8.9.4 Protein deficiency, kwashiorkor and marasmus

Protein deficiency can arise in two basic ways. Firstly it may occur when the diet contains sufficient energy, but not enough protein. This occurs in some parts of Africa where the staple food (the food that makes up the bulk of the diet) is corn meal (maize), yam or cassava, all of which are starchy and therefore energy-rich, but deficient in protein in some way. Corn meal lacks one of the essential amino acids, tryptophan, without which proteins cannot be made. Protein deficiency is not common in wheat-growing areas.

A second cause of protein deficiency is lack of sufficient energy in the diet. In this situation the body's own protein is used as a source of energy, as explained for starvation.

Kwashiorkor

In both types of protein-deficiency, a disease called **kwashiorkor** can develop. This term was first adopted in 1935 from the Ghanaian word meaning 'the disease of the child removed from the breast by the birth of the next one'. Switching the child from a milk diet to a starchy diet results in protein deficiency.

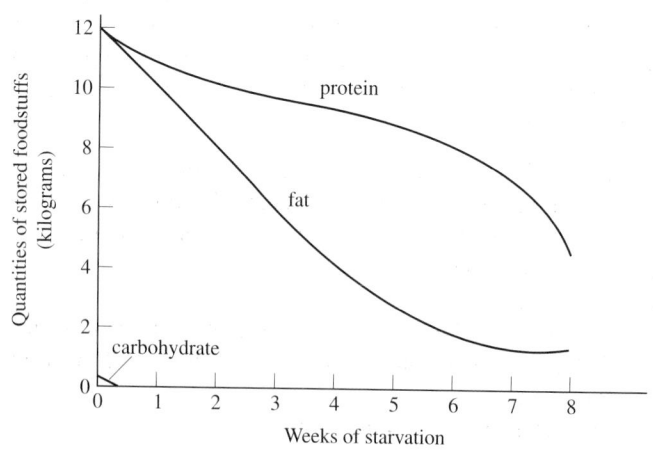

Fig 8.29 *Effect of starvation on the food stores of the body. (From* Textbook of Medical Physiology, *9th ed., A.C. Guyton & J.E. Hall (1996), W.B. Saunders & Co.)*

The characteristic appearance of a child suffering from kwashiorkor can be seen in fig 8.30a. Signs and symptoms are:

- the hair changes, becoming thin, straight, sparse and easily removed. It loses pigment and may become white or red.
- the lower cheeks develop large swellings, giving a characteristic 'moon-faced' appearance.
- swollen abdomen due to accumulation of gases and distention of the small intestine caused by abnormal growth of bacteria.
- oedema. This is swelling of the body tissues with fluid, particularly noticeable in the feet and lower legs (later the hands). It is caused by a reduction in blood plasma protein. Water potential of the blood therefore increases and water moves from the blood into the tissue fluid, causing swelling.
- thin muscles, underweight and reduced growth, particularly height. Mental development is also slower.
- skin lesions which cause a 'flaky paint' or 'crazy paving' appearance of the skin. The skin becomes rough. Wound healing is delayed. Jaundice may occur.
- little interest in surroundings and irritability. Babies avoid eye contact, even with their mothers. They may cry continuously and often do not respond to pain or comfort.
- fatty liver. Biochemical changes cause accumulation of fat in the liver which can cause permanent damage.
- vitamin deficiency diseases may be associated with the condition, particularly those due to lack of vitamins A and D.
- reduced resistance to infection.

Kwashiorkor is often fatal.

Marasmus

Another common condition caused by undernutrition is **marasmus**. Originally this was thought to be due to a lack of energy in the diet, but it may not be as clear cut as this, as discussed below. The appearance of a child suffering from some symptoms of marasmus is shown in fig 8.30b and can be compared with the child suffering from kwashiorkor. Signs and symptoms are:

- wizened and shrunken features, giving the face the appearance of an old man's face, with sunken eyes.
- thin muscles, thin arms and legs, and low body fat.
- hair is not affected.
- no oedema.
- very underweight. One definition of marasmus states that the child should be more than 60% underweight for its age.
- reduced resistance to infection.
- vitamin deficiency as with kwashiorkor.

As we have learned more about malnutrition caused by undereating, the distinctions between the causes of marasmus and kwashiorkor have become less and less clear. Different children in the same family have developed the two different conditions while feeding on the same diet, and sometimes a child develops marasmus after kwashiorkor. The child in fig 8.30b shows the thin limbs associated with marasmus and also the swollen abdomen associated with kwashiorkor. There is a tendency to refer to both conditions now simply as malnutrition, or **protein–energy malnutrition (PEM)**. This always involves stunted growth and reduced resistance to infectious diseases.

(a)

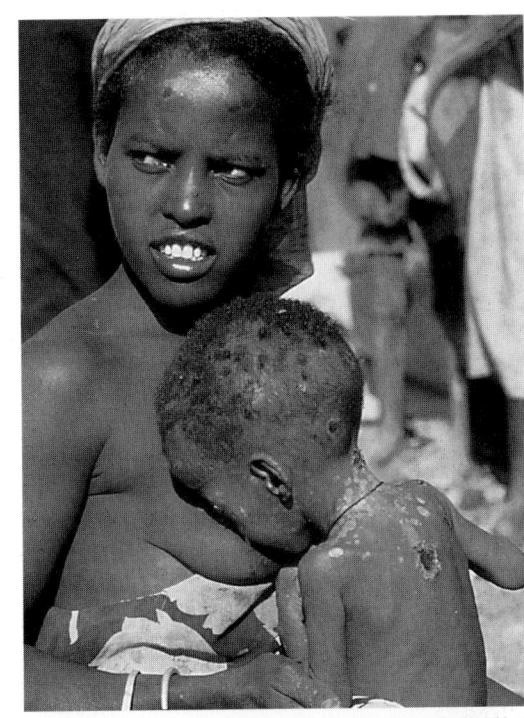

(b)

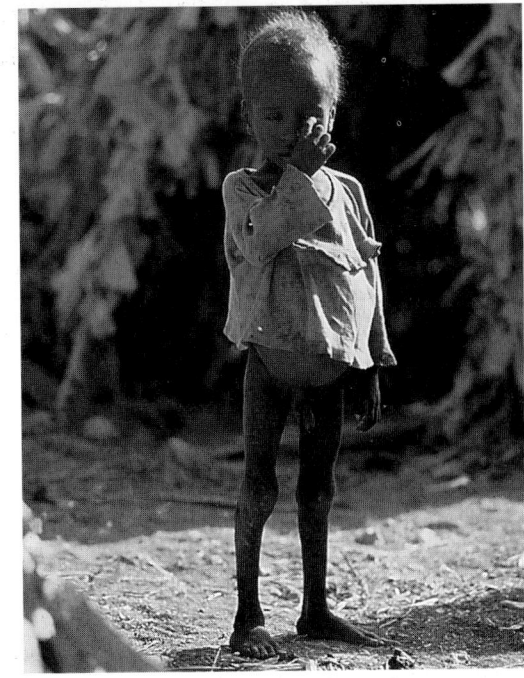

Fig 8.30 (a) *Child showing thin hair and skin lesions associated with kwashiorkor.* (b) *Child showing symptoms of marasmus and kwashiorkor.*

Chapter Nine

Energy utilisation

At the beginning of chapter 7 we considered what energy is and why living organisms need energy. From the examples given, we can see that energy exists in various forms, such as chemical, electrical, mechanical, light and heat energy. You should be able to give examples of the uses of these different forms of energy in living organisms. (If you can't, look back at section 7.1.)

Energy is an important theme in biology. All systems, from cells to ecosystems, require energy so that they can work. Just as a cell would soon die if its energy supply were cut off (cyanide can do this effectively to aerobic cells, as you will see later), so an ecosystem would soon collapse without a constant input of energy from the Sun.

> **9.1** Explain why animals are dependent on light energy.

Acquiring the energy needed by an individual is one of the two functions of nutrition, the other being to acquire the materials needed to build and repair cells. However the energy in the food has to be made available to cells in a usable form. This is the role of respiration which is the theme of this chapter. The relationship between autotrophic nutrition, heterotrophic nutrition and respiration is shown in fig 7.1. Another way of showing the energy transfer between the environment and cells is given in fig 9.1.

9.1 What is respiration?

Respiration is the process by which chemical energy in organic molecules is released by oxidation. This energy is then made available to living cells in the form of ATP. The biochemical process which occurs within cells is called **cell respiration**. If it requires oxygen, it is described as **aerobic respiration**; if the process takes place in the absence of oxygen, it is described as **anaerobic respiration**.

The organic molecules most commonly used as substrates in cell respiration are carbohydrates, for example glucose, or fats. They are broken down gradually by a series of enzyme-controlled reactions. Each releases a small

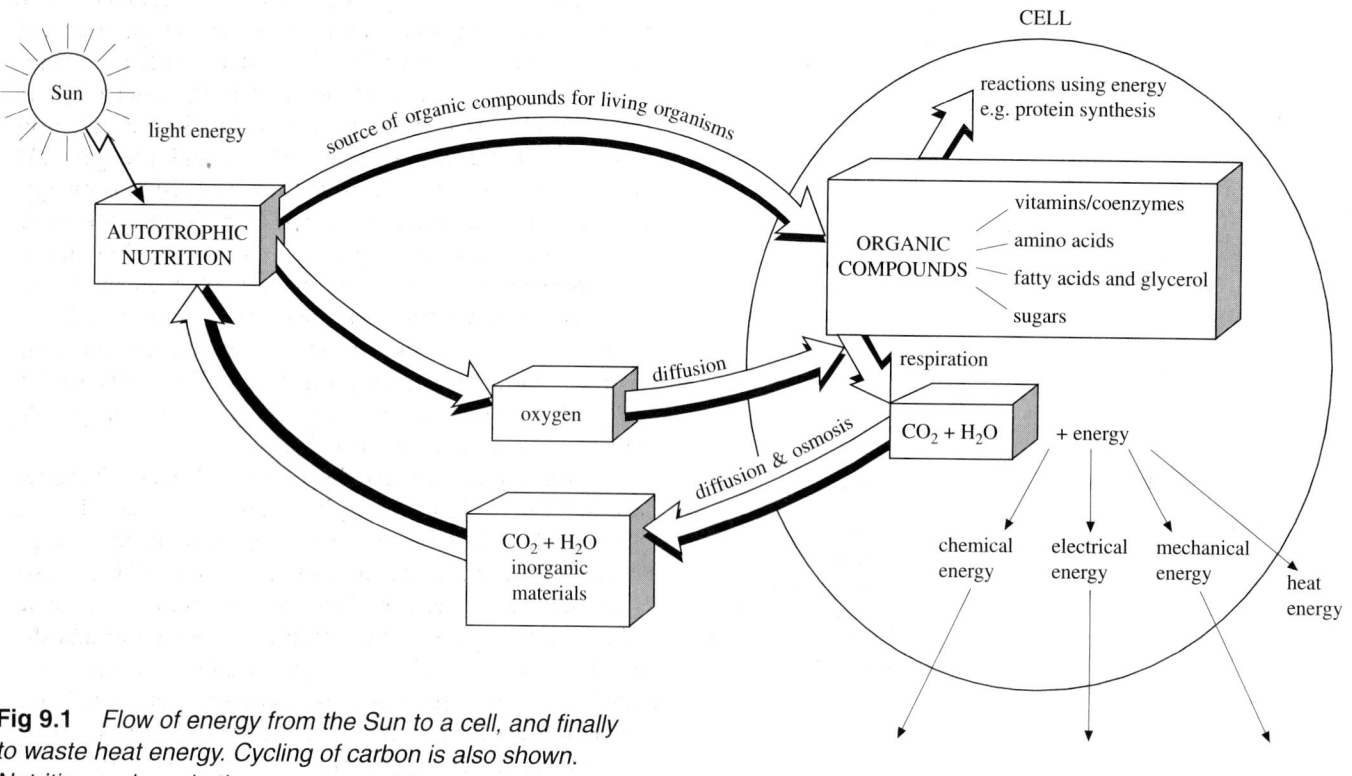

Fig 9.1 *Flow of energy from the Sun to a cell, and finally to waste heat energy. Cycling of carbon is also shown. Nutrition and respiration are responsible.*

amount of energy, some of which is transferred to molecules of a chemical called **adenosine triphosphate** (**ATP**). The rest of the energy is lost as heat. ATP is the energy carrier of cells. The energy in the ATP can then be used when required in reactions in the cell which require energy.

Cell respiration should not be confused with gaseous exchange, which is the process of acquiring oxygen from, and getting rid of carbon dioxide into, the environment. Gaseous exchange may involve organs or structures with specialised surfaces for the efficient exchange of gases, such as lungs and gills (section 9.4).

9.2 ATP

9.2.1 Structure of ATP

Two ways of representing the structure of ATP are shown in fig 9.2.

ATP is adenosine triphosphate, ADP is adenosine diphosphate and AMP is adenosine monophosphate.

AMP is a nucleotide. This is best shown in fig 9.2*a*. A **nucleotide** is made up of a sugar, base and phosphate (section 5.6.1). In AMP the sugar is ribose and the base is adenine. ATP has two extra phosphate groups, making a total of three.

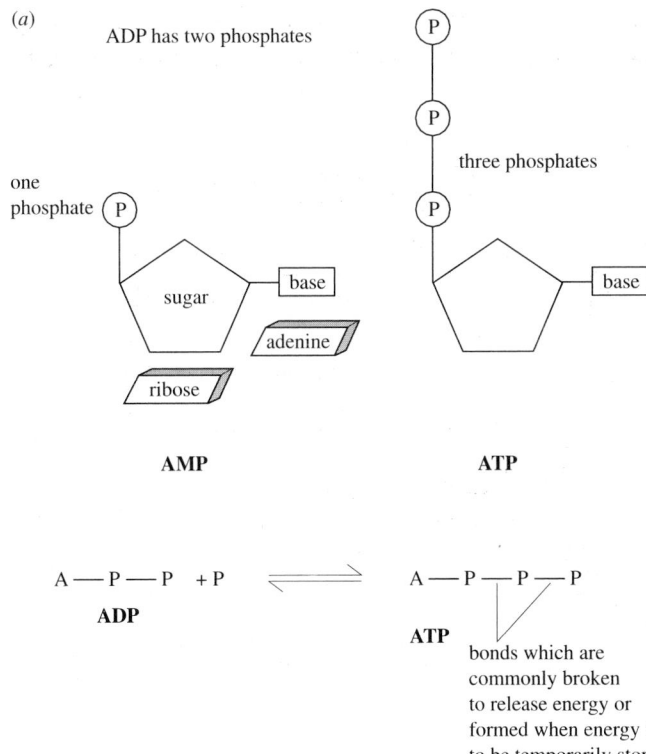

Fig 9.2 *Two ways of representing the structure of ATP.*

9.2.2 Significance of ATP

ATP can be converted to ADP and inorganic phosphate (P_i). This reaction releases energy.

$$ATP + H_2O \xrightarrow{\text{hydrolysis}} ADP + P_i + energy$$
$$(30.6\,kJ \text{ per mole of ATP})$$

The reaction requires water and is described as a **hydrolysis** reaction. This is a common type of biochemical reaction and was encountered many times in chapter 3. The third phosphate group is split from the ATP, and this phosphate remains in the cell in inorganic form. The reaction releases 30.6 kJ for every mole of ATP that is hydrolysed. (A mole is a convenient known quantity of a substance.)

ADP and phosphate can be converted back to ATP, but this requires 30.6 kJ of energy per mole of ATP.

$$30.6\,kJ + ADP + P_i \xrightarrow{\text{condensation}} ATP + H_2O$$

This reaction releases water and is known as **condensation**. Adding phosphate to ADP is known as **phosphorylation**. Putting the two reactions together:

$$ATP + H_2O \underset{\text{condensation}}{\overset{\text{hydrolysis}}{\rightleftharpoons}} ADP + P_i + 30.6\,kJ \text{ per mole of ATP}$$

The enzyme which catalyses this reaction is known as **ATPase**.

All cells require energy, as already explained, and all cell in every kind of organism use ATP as their source of energy when performing their work. ATP is therefore known as the '**universal energy carrier**' or the '**energy currency**' of cells. A useful analogy is the battery. Think of all the uses to which you can put a battery. How could you get light energy, mechanical energy, sound energy, electrical energy, from it? The convenience of a battery is that the same source of energy, the battery, can be used in a wide range of ways to perform work – it is merely 'plugged in' to the right piece of apparatus. ATP does the same in cells. It can be used to make muscles contract, make nerves function, drive active transport and synthesise proteins, and is used in all the other work the cell has to do by being 'plugged in' to the correct piece of cell machinery.

The analogy can be extended further because batteries have to be made in the first place and some, like ATP, are rechargeable. When batteries are made in a factory, energy has to be used in their manufacture. Likewise ATP is made using energy, in this case from the oxidation of organic molecules during respiration. (Since the energy to add the phosphate to the ADP (phosphorylation) comes from oxidation, the process is known as oxidative phosphorylation. In photosynthesis ATP is made using energy from light – photophosphorylation, section 7.6.2). In the manufacture of ATP, the equivalent of the factory is the mitochondrion, a specialised site where the chemical assembly lines for efficiently producing most of the ATP in aerobic respiration are located. Finally there is the recharging of the battery once its energy has been used. Once ATP has been converted to ADP and P_i and released this energy, the ADP and P_i can be rapidly converted back to ATP by re-entering the process of respiration and receiving more energy from the oxidation of more organic molecules.

The actual amount of ATP in the cell at any one time is surprisingly small. ATP should therefore be thought of, not as a store of energy, but as a carrier of energy. Long-term storage of energy takes place in molecules like fats and glycogen. The cell is very sensitive to the amount of ATP present. As soon as the rate at which it is being used goes up, the rate of respiration goes up as well to keep up the supply.

The role played by ATP as the link between cell respiration and the cell's energy requirements is summarised in fig 9.3. This diagram looks simple but it summarises a very important principle.

We can say that the overall function of respiration is to make ATP.

> **9.2** Copy fig 9.3 and add an extra part to the left to show how the Sun's energy enters glucose.

Summary

- To make ATP from ADP and inorganic phosphate requires 30.6 kJ of energy per mole.
- ATP is found in all living cells and is therefore known as the universal energy carrier. No other carriers are used. This makes things simpler – it reduces the amount of cell machinery needed and is more efficient and economical.
- ATP is mobile and can carry energy to energy-consuming processes anywhere in the cell.
- ATP can release energy quickly. Only one chemical reaction, hydrolysis, is required.
- The rate at which ATP can be re-formed from ADP and inorganic phosphate (the rate of respiration) can be varied quickly according to demand.

- ATP is made during respiration using chemical energy from the oxidation of organic molecules such as glucose, and during photosynthesis using light energy from the Sun. Making ATP from ADP and inorganic phosphate is a phosphorylation reaction. When the energy to carry out the phosphorylation comes from oxidation it is called oxidative phosphorylation (this happens in respiration) and when the energy comes from light it is called photophosphorylation (this happens in photosynthesis).

9.3   Cell respiration

9.3.1   Respiratory substrates

Respiration involves oxidation of an organic compound, the respiratory substrate. Carbohydrates, fats and proteins may all be used.

Carbohydrates. When these are available they are usually used first by most cells. Polysaccharides such as starch (in plants) and glycogen (in animals and fungi) are hydrolysed to monosaccharides before they enter the respiratory pathway.

Lipids (fats or oils). Lipids are used mainly when carbohydrate reserves have been exhausted. They are first converted to glycerol and fatty acids. Fatty acids are energy-rich and some cells such as skeletal muscle cells, in particular, gain some of their energy in this way during normal activity.

Proteins. Since proteins have other essential functions, they are only used when all carbohydrate and lipid reserves have been used up, as during prolonged starvation (section 8.9.3). Proteins are first hydrolysed to amino acids and then deaminated (their amino groups are removed). The remaining acid can enter the Krebs cycle (section 9.3.5) or be converted first to a fatty acid for oxidation (section 9.3.5).

9.3.2   Some key reactions

Two types of reaction are fundamental in cell respiration, namely oxidation and decarboxylation.

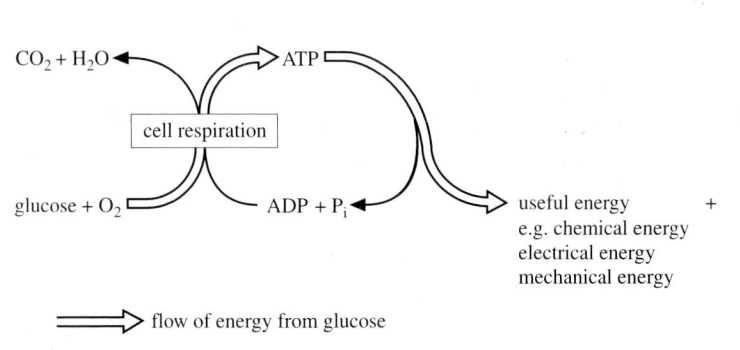

Fig 9.3 *Flow of energy from glucose through ATP to useful work. Once in ATP the energy can be used to do work in the cell, before being lost as heat. ATP is constantly being made in respiration and used in cell reactions. It continuously recycles in cells.*

Oxidation

This may occur in three ways during cell respiration.

(1) Adding oxygen.

$$A + O_2 \longrightarrow AO_2$$

(2) Removal of hydrogen (dehydrogenation). During aerobic respiration glucose is oxidised by a series of **dehydrogenations**. At each dehydrogenation, hydrogen is removed and used to reduce a coenzyme, known as a hydrogen carrier:

$$AH_2 + B \xrightarrow{\text{dehydrogenase}} A + BH_2$$

AH_2	$+ B$	A	$+ BH_2$
reduced respiratory substrate	coenzyme (hydrogen carrier)	oxidised respiratory substrate	reduced coenzyme

Most of these oxidations occur in the mitochondrion, where the usual hydrogen carrier is NAD (nicotinamide adenine dinucleotide):

$$NAD + 2H \longrightarrow NADH_2$$

or, more accurately,

$$NAD^+ + 2H \longrightarrow NADH + H^+$$

NADH (reduced NAD) is later reoxidised, releasing energy, as explained later (section 9.3.5). Enzymes that catalyse dehydrogenation reactions are called **dehydrogenases**. Gradually all the hydrogen is removed from glucose and added to hydrogen carriers. This hydrogen will then be oxidised to water, using oxygen and releasing the energy needed to make ATP. You may have witnessed the energy which can be released from the oxidation (burning) of hydrogen, when a lighted taper is introduced into a test tube of hydrogen. A small explosion, heard as a pop, occurs. In the cell the same amount of energy is released but in a series of small steps known as the respiratory chain.

(3) Removal of electrons.

$$\text{For example} \quad Fe^{2+} \longrightarrow Fe^{3+} + e^-$$

Electrons can be transferred from one compound to another, like hydrogen in the reactions described in (2) above. The compounds involved are called electron carriers. This occurs in mitochondria (section 9.3.5).

Decarboxylation

This is the removal of carbon from a compound by using the carbon to make carbon dioxide. Glucose contains six carbon atoms, as well as hydrogen and oxygen. Since only the hydrogen is needed (see (2) above) carbon is removed by decarboxylation and the carbon dioxide released as a waste product in aerobic respiration.

9.3.3 An overview of cell respiration

Before studying the details of cell respiration it is useful to have an overview of the process. Fig 9.4 outlines the stages of aerobic and anaerobic respiration. Note that there is one aerobic pathway and two anaerobic pathways. Note also that the first stage in all these pathways is **glycolysis**.

9.3.4 Glycolysis

Glycolysis is the oxidation of glucose to pyruvate. One glucose molecule (six carbon atoms, or 6C) is broken down into two molecules of pyruvate (3C) as shown in fig 9.5. It occurs in the cytoplasm of cells, not in the mitochondria, and does not require the presence of oxygen. The process may be divided into three stages:

- **phosphorylation of the sugar** – this 'activates' the sugar, making it more reactive. The process *uses* some ATP. Bearing in mind that the whole point of respiration is to *make* ATP, this may seem unfortunate, but it can be regarded as an investment which allows ATP-producing reactions to occur later.
- **lysis** – the phosphorylated 6C sugar is split into two 3C sugar phosphates. This is the origin of the term glycolysis, which means 'sugar splitting'. The sugar phosphates are isomers of each other. One is converted to the other before continuing, giving two identical 3C sugar phosphates.
- **oxidation by dehydrogenation** – each 3C sugar phosphate is converted to pyruvate. This involves a dehydrogenation, making a reduced NAD molecule, and production of two ATP molecules. The process happens twice, once for each 3C sugar phosphate molecule, so two reduced NAD and four ATP molecules are made (fig 9.5).

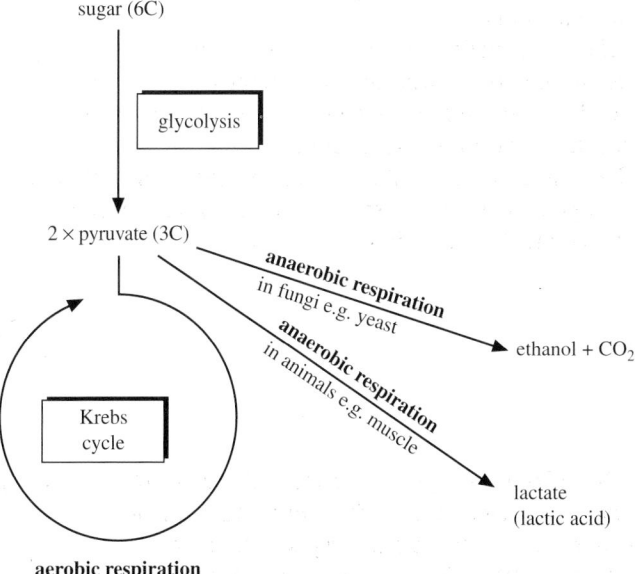

Fig 9.4 *Summary of respiration.*

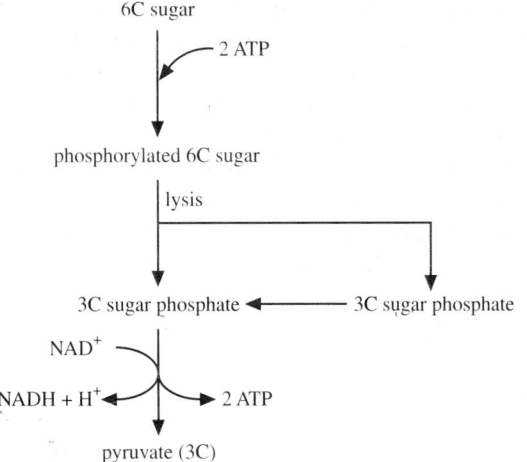

Fig 9.5 *Glycolysis in outline. Only the three key stages are shown.*

Overall two ATP molecules are used for phosphorylation reactions in the first stage, whilst four ATP molecules are produced in the third stage. Therefore there is a net gain of two ATP molecules. Four hydrogen atoms are also released and added to NAD. Their fate will be discussed later. The overall reaction is:

$$\text{glucose} + 2\text{NAD}^+ \longrightarrow \text{2pyruvate} + 2\text{ATP} + 2\text{NADH} + 2\text{H}^+$$

The input and output of materials during glycolysis is shown in table 9.1.

In the respiration of lipids, the glycerol is easily converted to a 3C sugar phosphate which can join glycolysis. This conversion uses one ATP, but yields three ATPs.

The fate of pyruvate depends on the availability of oxygen in the cell. If it is present, pyruvate will enter a mitochondrion and be completely oxidised into carbon dioxide and water (**aerobic respiration**). If oxygen is unavailable, pyruvate will be converted into ethanol or lactate (**anaerobic respiration**) (fig 9.4).

9.3.5   Aerobic respiration

In aerobic respiration, the pyruvate from glycolysis is completely oxidised to carbon dioxide and water using oxygen. In the first stage, pyruvate is broken down to carbon dioxide and hydrogen. This takes place in the matrix of mitochondria and involves the Krebs cycle. In the second stage, the hydrogen is oxidised by oxygen to water in a series of reactions called the respiratory chain. This takes place on the cristae (inner membranes) of the mitochondria.

The first stages of aerobic respiration are summarised in fig 9.6.

Transition stage between glycolysis and Krebs cycle

Each pyruvate molecule enters the matrix of a mitochondrion where it is converted to an acetyl group ($\text{CH}_3\text{COO}-$). These are carried by coenzyme A as

Table 9.1 Budget for glycolysis. ADP, P_i and H_2O are ignored.

Total input	Total output
1 molecule of glucose (6C)	2 molecules of pyruvate ($2 \times 3C$)
2 ATP	4 ATP
$2 \times \text{NAD}^+$	$2 \times (\text{NADH} + \text{H}^+)$

Overall 'profit': $2\text{ATP} + 2(\text{NADH} + \text{H}^+)$

acetylcoenzyme A (acetylcoA). Acetyl groups have two carbon atoms (2C), so the conversion of pyruvate (3C) to acetyl (2C) involves loss of carbon. This is lost as carbon dioxide in a decarboxylation reaction. A dehydrogenation also occurs, so that reduced NAD is made from NAD.

Krebs cycle

The details of this cycle were worked out by Sir Hans Krebs in the 1930s. (It is also known as the TCA cycle (tricarboxylic acid cycle) and the citric acid cycle because of the acids it contains. The acids exist as salts in the cell, so their names end with -ate. Thus citric acid is referred to as citrate).

The Krebs cycle takes place in the matrix of the mitochondrion. A summary is shown in fig 9.6. Acetyl groups (2C) enter the cycle by combining with a 4C compound, oxaloacetate, to form a 6C compound, citrate. As the acetyl groups pass round the cycle, the two carbon atoms are lost in carbon dioxide in two decarboxylation reactions, and the hydrogen is added to hydrogen carriers in four dehydrogenation reactions, resulting in a total of three reduced NAD and one reduced FAD molecules. One molecule of ATP is also made directly for every turn of the

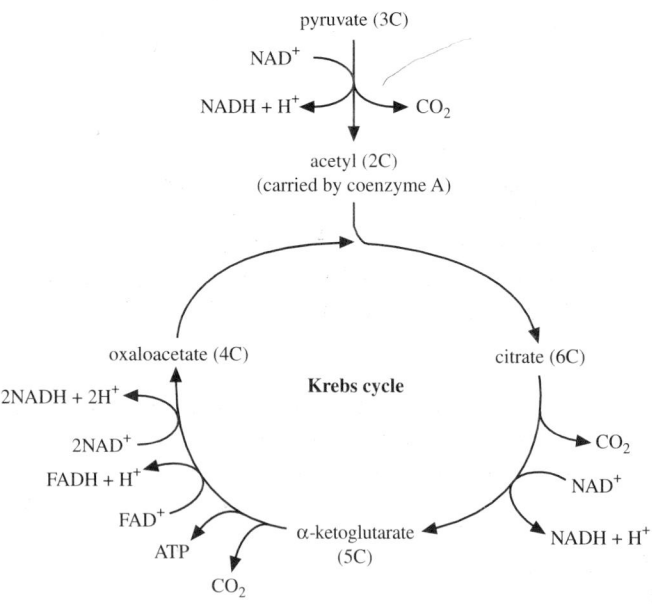

Fig 9.6 *Simplified diagram of the Krebs cycle. The link reaction between glycolysis and the Krebs cycle (pyruvate to acetylcoenzyme A) is also shown. This diagram joins to fig 9.5.*

cycle. (Remember that two acetyl groups were made from one glucose molecule, so two turns of the cycle occur per glucose molecule used.) Oxaloacetate is regenerated at the end of the cycle, ready to accept another acetyl group.

The overall budget for aerobic respiration so far is summarised in table 9.2.

The overall equation is:

$$C_6H_{12}O_6 + 6H_2O \longrightarrow 6CO_2 + 4ATP + 12H_2$$

The hydrogen is on the hydrogen carriers NAD and FAD. All the hydrogen from the original glucose is now on hydrogen carriers. All the carbon is lost in carbon dioxide. (You may be puzzled to note from the equation that six molecules of water have also been used. Water is needed as a source of oxygen in decarboxylation reactions – some of the oxygen in the carbon dioxide comes from this water. This is a detail which you can ignore.)

The respiratory chain and oxidative phosphorylation

The hydrogens (carried as 10 reduced NAD and two reduced FAD molecules) now move to the inner membrane of the mitochondrion. This has folds called **cristae** which increase its surface area (fig 9.12). Hydrogen is a fuel. As already explained, it can be oxidised to water using oxygen, thus releasing energy:

$$2H_2 + O_2 \longrightarrow 2H_2O + energy$$

Some of the energy is used to make ATP from ADP and inorganic phosphate, in the process of oxidative phosphorylation which was mentioned in section 9.2.2. The energy is not released all in one reaction, but in a series of smaller steps, some of which release enough energy to make ATP. This series of reactions is known as the **respiratory chain**. The respiratory chain is a series of hydrogen and electron carriers ending with oxygen. Hydrogen or electrons are passed from one carrier to the next, moving downhill in energy terms, until they reach oxygen, which is reduced to water as a result. At each transfer some energy is released and in some of the transfers this is coupled to the formation of ATP (fig 9.7 – follow the arrowheads carefully in this figure). The caption

to the figure explains the process in more detail. The final stage involves cytochrome oxidase which contains copper. This stage can be specifically inhibited by cyanide (or carbon monoxide). Cyanide combines with the copper and prevents oxygen combining with it.

Fig 9.7 shows that for each reduced NAD that enters the respiratory chain, 3ATP can be made as the hydrogen or electrons flow to oxygen. However, for each reduced FAD, only 2ATP are made because reduced FAD enters the chain at a lower energy level.

The overall budget for the respiratory chain is shown in table 9.3.

The overall equation for the respiratory chain is:

$$12H_2 + 6O_2 \longrightarrow 12H_2O + 34ATP$$

Combining the two equations, we have:

$$(1)\ C_6H_{12}O_6 + 6H_2O \xrightarrow[\text{Krebs cycle}]{\text{glycolysis}} 6CO_2 + 12H_2 + 4ATP$$

$$(2)\ 12H_2 + 6O_2 \xrightarrow{\text{respiratory chain}} 12H_2O + 34ATP$$

Add (1) and (2):

$$C_6H_{12}O_6 + 6O_2 \longrightarrow 6CO_2 + 6H_2O + 38ATP$$

Thus 38 molecules of ATP are produced for every glucose molecule oxidised in aerobic respiration.

> **9.3** What is the *precise* role of oxygen in respiration?

A summary of aerobic respiration is provided in fig 9.8.

Oxidation of fatty acids

When lipids are used as the respiratory substrate, each fatty acid molecule which is released from lipid is oxidised by a process which involves 2C acetyl fragments being split off from the acid so that the long fatty acid molecule is shortened 2C atoms at a time. Each acetyl group is carried by coenzyme A, forming acetylcoenzyme A. This can enter

Table 9.2 Overall budget for aerobic respiration of one glucose molecule. Remember that two turns of the Krebs cycle take place per glucose molecule.

	CO_2	ATP	$NADH + H^+$	$FADH + H^+$
Glycolysis	–	2	2	–
Pyruvate $\rightarrow$ Acetyl coA	2	–	2	–
Krebs cycle	4	2	6	2
TOTAL	$6CO_2$	4ATP	$10(NADH + H^+)^*$	$2(FADH + H^+)^*$

*enter respiratory chain in cristae of mitochondria.

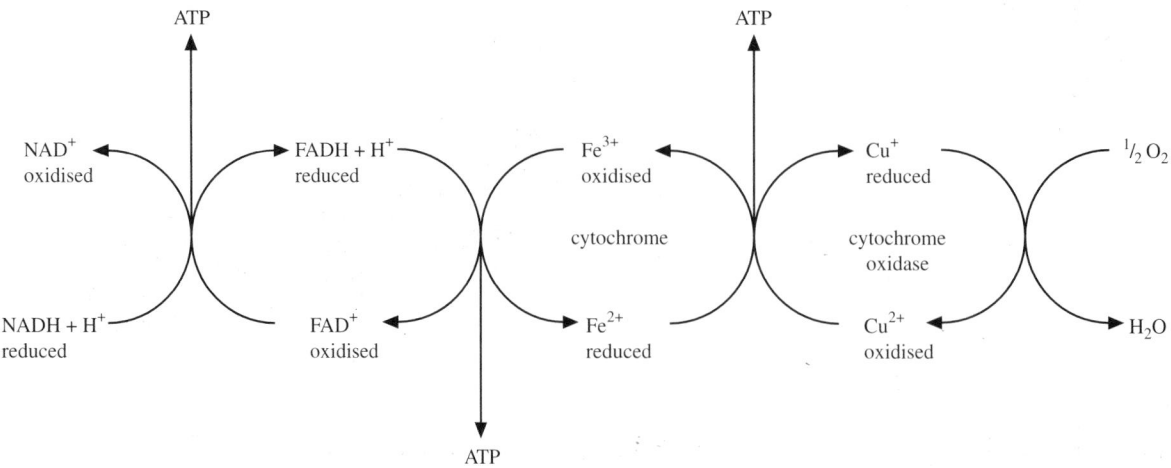

ATP

NAD$^+$ oxidised	FADH + H$^+$ reduced	Fe^{3+} oxidised

cytochrome

cytochrome oxidase

NADH + H$^+$ reduced	FAD$^+$ oxidised	Fe^{2+} reduced

Cu$^+$ reduced $\frac{1}{2}$O$_2$

Cu^{2+} oxidised   H$_2$O

ATP

Fig 9.7 *Simplified diagram of the respiratory chain. Hydrogen passes from reduced NAD to FAD. Hydrogen then splits into hydrogen ion (H$^+$) and electrons. Electrons flow from reduced FAD to iron (Fe), copper (Cu), and oxygen, where they are re-united with the hydrogen ions to form water. (Addition of an electron is reduction, loss of an electron is oxidation (section 9.3.2).) The iron is part of a haem group in a protein molecule called a cytochrome. Like haemoglobin, which is also an iron-containing protein, cytochrome is coloured (pink). Copper is part of a group of proteins known collectively as cytochrome oxidase. Cytochromes carry electrons rather than hydrogen.*

Table 9.3 Budget for the respiratory chain. Each reduced NAD molecule results in production of three ATP and the release of hydrogen which combines with oxygen to form water, H$_2$O. Therefore, 10 reduced NAD molecules result in the production of 30ATP, 10H$_2$O and use of 10 oxygen atoms, or five molecules of oxygen. Each reduced FAD molecule results in the production of two ATP.

Entering	Produced	Used
12H$_2$ in the form of 10NADH + H$^+$ and	30ATP + 10H$_2$O	5O$_2$
2FADH + H$^+$	4ATP + 2H$_2$O	O$_2$
TOTAL	34ATP + 12H$_2$O	6O$_2$

12H$_2$O are made, but 6H$_2$O are used earlier in respiration (see equation at end of section 9.3.5). Therefore there is an overall production of 6H$_2$O.

Krebs cycle as usual. A great deal of energy is released from each fatty acid molecule thus oxidised, for instance 147ATP per molecule of stearic acid. Not surprisingly, therefore, fatty acids are important energy sources, contributing, for example, at least half the normal energy requirements of heart muscle, resting skeletal muscle, liver and kidneys.

9.3.6   Anaerobic respiration

Anaerobic respiration is often referred to as fermentation. A variety of microorganisms use anaerobic respiration as their major source of ATP. Some bacteria are actually killed by normal atmospheric levels of oxygen and have to live where there is no oxygen. They are termed **obligate anaerobes** (for example *Clostridium tetani* which causes tetanus).

Other organisms, such as yeasts and gut parasites (such as tapeworms), can exist whether oxygen is available or not. These can survive on anaerobic respiration when they have to, although respire aerobically when possible, and are called **facultative anaerobes**. Also some cells that are temporarily short of oxygen (such as muscle cells) are able to respire anaerobically.

Like aerobic respiration, the first part of anaerobic respiration is glycolysis. This makes pyruvate from glucose and produces a 'profit' of two ATP and two reduced NAD molecules (table 9.1). In aerobic respiration the hydrogen on the reduced NAD is oxidised to water with release of energy, but this is not possible in anaerobic respiration because oxygen is absent. Instead, the hydrogen is added back to the pyruvate, and its potential for releasing energy is therefore wasted. We shall look at how this happens in animals and fungi. The details are shown below.

Anaerobic respiration in fungi, e.g. yeast

pyruvate ⟶ ethanal + CO$_2$
                 enzyme: pyruvate decarboxylase
ethanal + NADH + H$^+$ ⟶ ethanol + NAD$^+$
                 enzyme: alcohol dehydrogenase
Overall: pyruvate ⟶ ethanol + CO$_2$

No more ATP is made. Ethanol is the alcohol found in alcoholic drinks. This process is known as **alcoholic fermentation** and its occurrence in yeast is made use of in the manufacture of beer, wine and other alcoholic drinks. Production of carbon dioxide by yeast is used in bread making, to make dough rise. Ethanol is a waste product that

Fig 9.8 *Summary of aerobic respiration.*

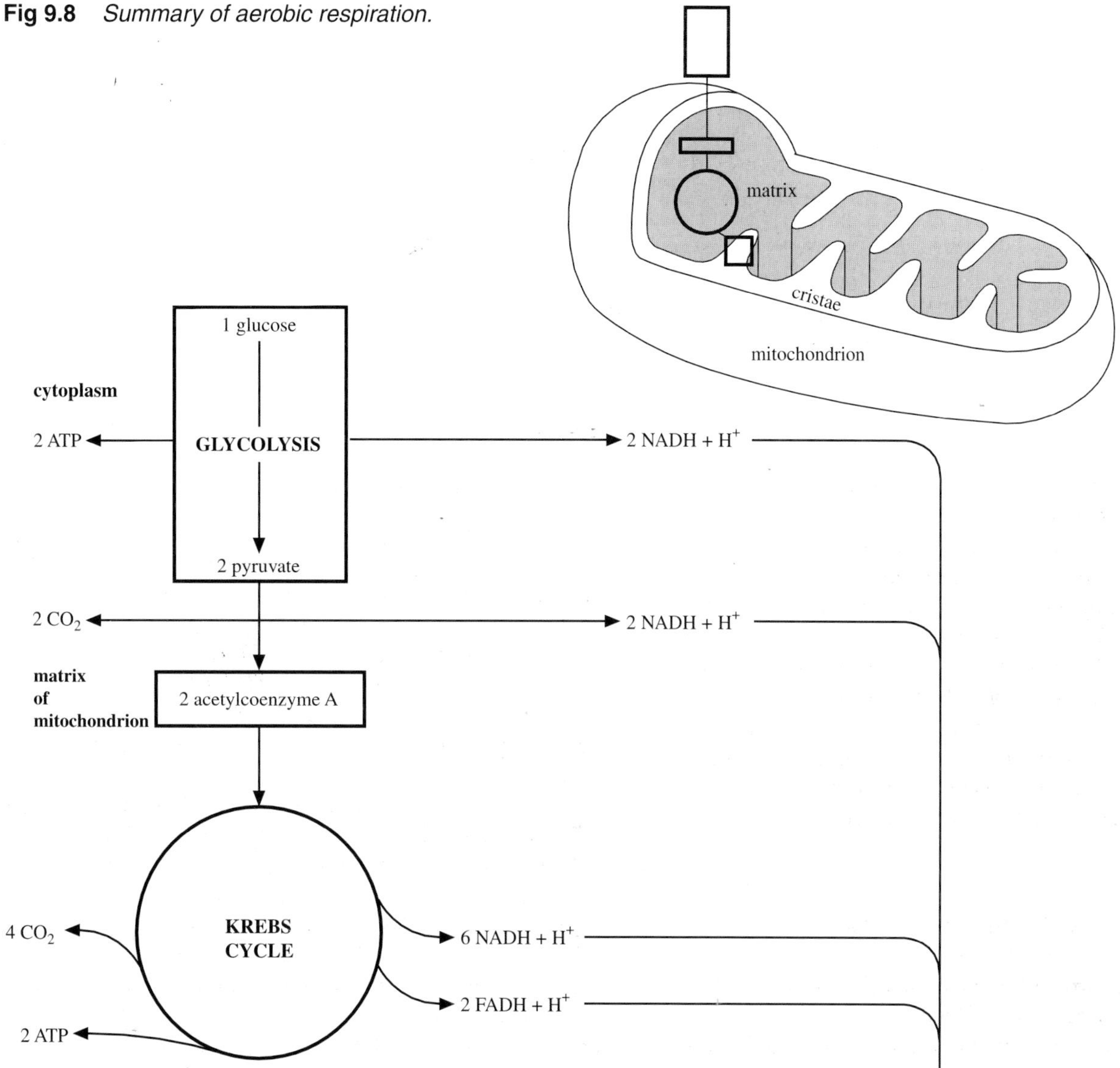

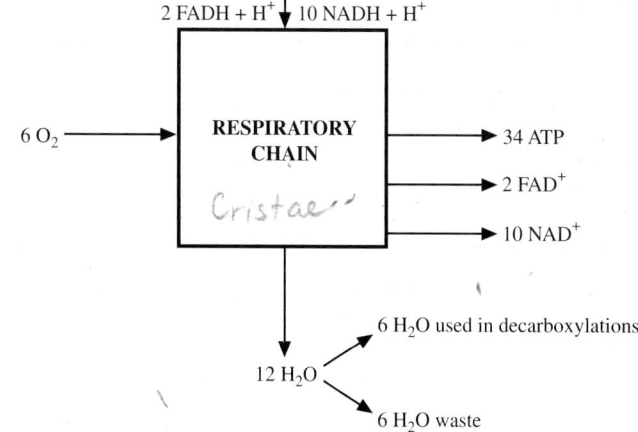

1 glucose

cytoplasm

GLYCOLYSIS → 2 ATP

2 NADH + H$^+$

2 pyruvate

2 CO$_2$ ← 2 NADH + H$^+$

matrix of mitochondrion

2 acetylcoenzyme A

KREBS CYCLE

4 CO$_2$

6 NADH + H$^+$

2 FADH + H$^+$

2 ATP

matrix

cristae

mitochondrion

2 FADH + H$^+$ 10 NADH + H$^+$

6 O$_2$ → **RESPIRATORY CHAIN** → 34 ATP

Cristae

→ 2 FAD$^+$

→ 10 NAD$^+$

12 H$_2$O

6 H$_2$O used in decarboxylations

6 H$_2$O waste

still contains a lot of energy (for example, it is used to make gasohol, a fuel that is used for cars in Brazil). The energy in ethanol is unavailable in the absence of oxygen.

Overall two molecules of ATP are produced per glucose molecule.

Anaerobic respiration in animals, e.g. muscle tissue

pyruvate + NADH + H$^+$ → lactate + NAD$^+$

enzyme: lactate dehydrogenase

Note that no carbon dioxide is produced, unlike in fungi. Also, alcohol is not made. Instead, the product is lactate (lactic acid) whose build-up in muscles contributes to the sensation of fatigue and can contribute to cramp. The build-up of an oxygen debt during vigorous exercise is discussed in section 9.3.8.

As with anaerobic respiration in fungi, overall only two molecules of ATP are produced per glucose molecule and the waste product, lactate, still contains a lot of energy.

A summary of anaerobic respiration is given in fig 9.9.

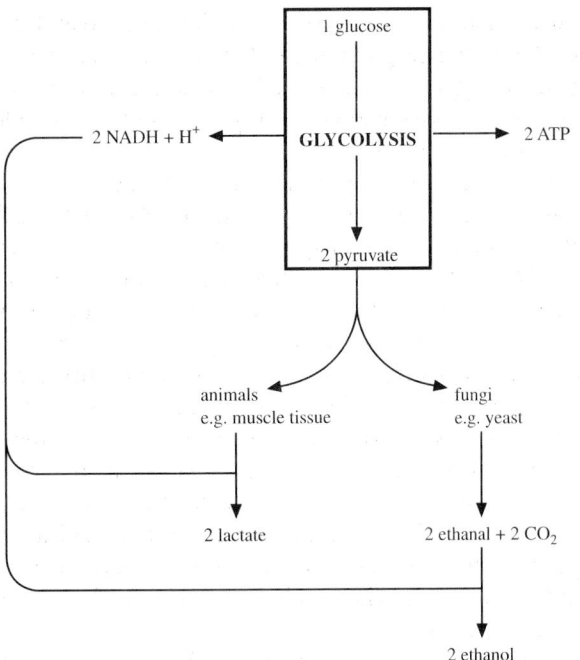

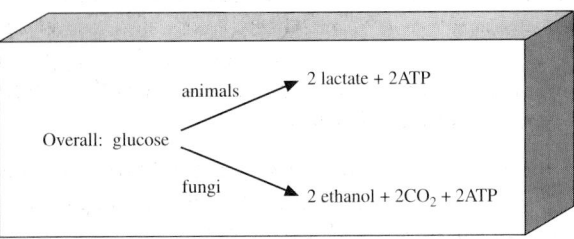

Fig 9.9 *Summary of anaerobic respiration.*

9.3.7 Efficiency of aerobic and anaerobic respiration

Aerobic respiration

During aerobic respiration 38 molecules of ATP are produced for every molecule of glucose that is oxidised.

$$C_6H_{12}O_6 + 6O_2 \longrightarrow 6CO_2 + 6H_2O + 38ATP$$

The energy released by the complete oxidation of glucose is 2880 kJ per mole.

The energy contained in one mole of ATP is 30.6 kJ.

Therefore the energy contained in 38 moles of ATP is $30.6 \times 38 = 1162.8$ kJ.

Therefore the efficiency of transfer of energy in aerobic respiration is = 1162.8/2880 = 40.4%.

Anaerobic respiration

(1) Yeast (alcoholic fermentation). During alcoholic fermentation, two molecules of ATP are produced for every molecule of glucose used.

$$glucose \longrightarrow 2 \text{ ethanol} + 2CO_2 + 2ATP$$

The total energy released by conversion of glucose to ethanol is 210 kJ per mole.

The energy contained in two molecules of ATP is $2 \times 30.6 = 61.2$ kJ.

Therefore the efficiency of transfer of energy during alcoholic fermentation is 61.2/210 = 29.1%.

(2) Muscle (lactate fermentation). During lactate fermentation, two molecules of ATP are produced for every molecule of glucose used.

$$glucose \longrightarrow 2 \text{ lactate} + 2ATP$$

The total energy released by conversion of glucose to lactate is 150 kJ per mole.

Therefore the efficiency of transfer of energy during lactate fermentation is 61.2/150 = 40.8%.

Study of the above figures indicates that the efficiency of each system is relatively high when compared with petrol engines (25–30%) and steam engines (8–12%).

The amount of energy captured as ATP during aerobic respiration is 19 times as much as for anaerobic respiration (38ATP compared with 2ATP). From this point of view aerobic respiration is much more efficient than anaerobic respiration. This is because a great deal of energy remains locked within lactate and ethanol. The energy in ethanol is permanently unavailable to yeast, which clearly indicates that alcoholic fermentation is an inefficient energy-producing process. However, much of the energy locked in lactate may be liberated at a later stage if oxygen is made available. In the presence of oxygen, lactate is converted to pyruvate in the liver. Pyruvate then enters the Krebs cycle and is fully oxidised to carbon dioxide and water, releasing many more ATP molecules in the process. Alternatively the pyruvate can be converted back to glucose by the reverse of glycolysis, using energy from ATP.

9.3.8 Oxygen debt and the immediate effects of exercise

There is only a small store of ATP in cells. Normally the body can replace the ATP as fast as it is used, but if a sudden change is made from rest to exercise, it takes a little while to adjust. The body has evolved mechanisms by which it can supply energy to the muscles at the required rate until the rate of aerobic respiration has increased sufficiently. One of these mechanisms is anaerobic respiration. It is important to realise that it is a supplement to aerobic respiration (an extra) rather than an alternative.

Fig 9.10 shows a graph of oxygen uptake during and immediately after a period of exercise. To satisfy the energy demands of the exercise aerobically, 3 dm³ of oxygen per minute must be supplied (see graph). In the example shown, this is not achieved until six minutes after exercise began. The **oxygen deficit** (the amount of oxygen that was

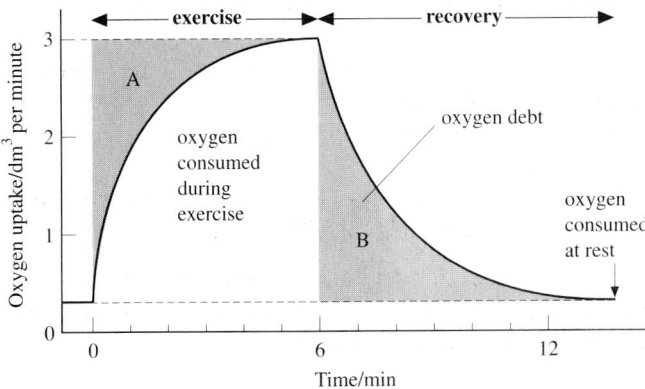

Fig 9.10 *Oxygen uptake during exercise and recovery. This shows the principle of oxygen debt.*

needed, but not supplied from outside the body by breathing), is shown in region A in the graph. During that first six minutes various mechanisms would be used to maintain the supply of energy as described below.

> **9.4** The rate of uptake of oxygen increases immediately exercise starts. How is the supply of oxygen from outside the body to the cells increased during exercise?

Oxygen reserves

The body has reserve oxygen capacity. This includes extracting more oxygen than usual from the lungs, the body fluids and haemoglobin. Also in the muscles, oxygen is stored in a molecule known as **myoglobin**. This is very similar to haemoglobin (fig. 3.36) and, like haemoglobin, can combine reversibly with oxygen. However, it does not release its oxygen until oxygen levels become very low and haemoglobin has already released most of its oxygen. It is therefore only used at times of high demand.

Creatine phosphate system

The amount of ATP in muscles is sufficient only for about three seconds of maximal muscle contraction. Creatine phosphate is another chemical like ATP which contains a phosphate group that can be removed to release energy. It releases enough energy to make ATP from ADP and P_i. Muscle cells have 2–4 times as much creatine phosphate as ATP, so energy can very rapidly be switched to ATP from creatine phosphate when needed. ATP and creatine phosphate together can provide maximum muscle power for about 8–10 seconds.

Anaerobic respiration – the glycogen–lactic acid system

Although anaerobic respiration only produces two molecules of ATP per glucose molecule compared with 38ATP for aerobic respiration, anaerobic respiration can operate much faster than aerobic respiration. In fact, its rate of ATP production is about 2.5 times faster than that of aerobic respiration (five molecules of ATP produced for

every two produced by aerobic respiration in a given time period). Anaerobic respiration can therefore supply energy rapidly. It uses glycogen stored in the muscle as a source of glucose. It can provide enough energy for about 90 seconds of maximum muscle activity.

All these systems are improved by regular exercise.

Overall we can see that the creatine phosphate and anaerobic systems supply energy rapidly, but only for short periods of time. The aerobic system supplies energy for an unlimited time, providing the supply of raw materials is adequate. Sports or activities which rely on short explosive bursts of activity, such as a 100 m race or weightlifting, use mainly the creatine phosphate system. Additional energy from anaerobic respiration could be used in a 200 m race. Most of the energy in a 400 m race would come from anaerobic respiration, and sports like tennis, squash and soccer would rely almost entirely on anaerobic respiration during active phases of the game. Endurance sports such as marathon running, jogging and cross-country skiing are almost entirely aerobic.

After exercise, the graph in fig 9.10 does not return immediately to the resting requirement of $0.25 \, dm^3$ of oxygen per minute. Instead, the body continues to breathe in and use extra oxygen. The amount of this oxygen is shown in region B of the graph and is known as the **oxygen debt**. It is used for the following.

- It replaces the oxygen reserves in the body, including restoring normal levels of oxygen in the lungs, tissue fluids, haemoglobin and myoglobin.
- It restores creatine phosphate – after exercise the creatine combines with the phosphate again, using energy from aerobic respiration.
- Replacement of oxygen reserves and creatine phosphate takes place rapidly, which explains the steep downward part of the curve in the first few minutes of recovery (fig 9.10). The slow part of the recovery is the removal of lactic acid resulting from anaerobic respiration. This first diffuses into the blood where it is carried away from the muscles, mainly to the liver. Here it is reconverted to pyruvate and reduced NAD. Some of the pyruvate enters the normal aerobic pathway through the Krebs cycle to be oxidised, yielding ATP. This ATP can be used to convert the rest of the pyruvate back to glucose by the reverse of glycolysis (up to 75% of the pyruvate). The heart can also convert lactic acid back to pyruvate and reduced NAD as an extra energy source during heavy exercise.

> **9.5** Why does the lactic acid level in the blood continue to rise *after* exercise when anaerobic respiration has ceased?

9.3.9 Fermentation in industry

Fermentation processes are commercial or experimental processes in which microorganisms are cultured in containers, called **fermenters** or **bioreactors**. They are an important part of modern industry and are discussed in chapter 12.

Experiment 9.1: To investigate the oxidation of a Krebs cycle intermediate

The most efficient way of releasing energy from a substrate and storing this for future use is by a series of smaller reactions, each one reversible and enzyme-controlled. One of the intermediate reactions involved is the oxidation, by removal of hydrogen, of succinate to fumarate.

There are substances which accept such hydrogen atoms and, doing so, change colour. One example is 2,6 dichlorophenolindophenol (DCPIP). It is blue in its oxidised form but loses its colour when reduced.

If the coloured form of DCPIP is decolourised by a tissue extract, one explanation could be that it has accepted hydrogen atoms from succinate. If the rate of decolourisation increased when succinate was added this would tend to confirm the hypothesis that DCPIP was a hydrogen acceptor of atoms from succinate.

As most living processes are governed by enzymes, these must be present before the oxidation will occur. The enzyme succinate dehydrogenase reduces succinate and further experiments could reveal the presence of the enzyme. In this experiment mitochondria are isolated from germinating mung bean seedlings and a suspension of these used as a source of enzyme. It is essential to carry out the extraction as quickly as possible. Once cells are disrupted, further metabolism is short-lived.

The experiment is divided into two parts. The first part consists of the extraction of the enzyme required and the second uses the extracted enzyme to oxidise succinic acid. DCPIP is used to indicate that a reaction has or has not occurred.

Ideally all the apparatus concerned with the first part of this experiment (the preparation of the enzyme extract) should be placed in a refrigerator for at least one hour before it is required for the experiment.

Materials

4 centrifuge tubes (capacity 15 cm^3)
2 glass rods
2 × 10 cm^3 graduated pipettes
2 × 1000 cm^3 beakers (polythene preferably)
ice
salt
mung beans
test-tubes and rack
1 cm^3 graduated pipette
stopclock
Solutions (see notes)
buffer/sucrose solution
buffer/sucrose + succinate (succinic acid) solution
0.1% DCPIP (solution made up in buffer/sucrose solution)
distilled water

Method

(1) Germinate some mung beans by placing the dry beans on damp cotton wool in the dark for 3–4 days (24 beans are needed for the whole experiment per student or group).
(2) Prepare an ice bath by placing ice in a 1000 cm^3 polythene beaker and adding a little salt to lower the temperature further.
(3) Place the flask containing buffer/sucrose solution and two centrifuge tubes in the ice bucket.
(4) Take 12 mung beans and remove their testas and radicles.
(5) Place six beans in each centrifuge tube.
(6) Add 1 cm^3 of buffer/sucrose solution which does not contain succinate to each tube.
(7) Crush the beans thoroughly using a cold glass rod, keeping the tubes in the ice bucket.
(8) Add a further 10 cm^3 of buffer/sucrose solution to each centrifuge tube.
(9) Place the centrifuge tubes on opposite sides of the centrifuge head and spin the tubes at maximum speed for 3 min.
(10) Place the centrifuge tubes back in the ice bucket.
(11) Pipette 15 cm^3 of distilled water into a test-tube and mark the position of the meniscus.
(12) Pour off the distilled water and carefully fill the tube to the mark with supernatant from the centrifuge tubes.
(13) The next step must be carried out very quickly: add 0.5 cm^3 of DCPIP solution to the reaction tube and mix the contents by placing a thumb over the end of the tube and inverting the tube.
(14) Start the stopclock as the solutions are mixing.
(15) Note the colour of the solution after 20 min.
(16) Repeat the entire experiment using the buffer/sucrose solution containing succinate.

The experiment can be monitored colorimetrically. This is done as follows.
(1) Using a red filter, switch on the colorimeter and allow it to warm up for 5 min.
(2) Add 0.5 cm^3 of DCPIP solution to 15 cm^3 of supernatant as before.
(3) Mix the solutions and start the stopclock.
(4) Place the tube in the colorimeter and adjust the needle to 0% transmission.
(5) Take readings after 1, 2, 5, 10 and 20 min.
(6) Repeat the experiment using buffer/sucrose containing succinate.
(7) Plot a graph of percentage transmission (vertical axis) against time.
(8) Draw your own conclusions from the results that you obtain.

Notes on how to make solutions

Buffer/sucrose solution (100 cm³)

disodium hydrogen phosphate (Na_2HPO_4)	0.76 g
potassium dihydrogen phosphate (KH_2PO_4)	0.18 g
sucrose	13.60 g
magnesium sulphate	0.10 g

Buffer/sucrose + succinic acid (100 cm³)

As for buffer/sucrose, plus

succinate	1.36 g
sodium hydrogencarbonate	1.68 g

The best method for making up these solutions is to make up enough buffer/sucrose solution for both halves of the experiment (solutions are made up in distilled water). Divide the solution into two and add succinate and sodium hydrogencarbonate (in the correct concentration) to one half.

There will be effervescence when succinate and sodium hydrogencarbonate are added to the buffer/sucrose solution. The solution should be shaken well to get rid of as much carbon dioxide as possible as this could affect the experiment.

DCPIP solution

Use 0.1 g of dichlorophenolindophenol in 10 cm³ of buffer/sucrose solution (without succinate for both experiments). The solid does not dissolve very well and so after thorough mixing the suspension should be filtered.

9.3.10   Mitochondria

Mitochondria are present in all eukaryotic cells and are the major sites of aerobic respiration within cells. They were first seen as granules in muscle cells in 1850.

The number of mitochondria per cell varies considerably and depends on the type of organism and nature of the cell. Cells with high energy requirements possess large numbers of mitochondria (for example, liver cells contain upwards of 1000 mitochondria) whilst less active cells possess far fewer. Mitochondrial shape and size are also tremendously variable. They may be spiral, spherical, elongated, cup-shaped and even branched, and are usually larger in active cells than in less active ones. Their length ranges from 1.5–10 μm, and width from 0.25–1.00 μm, but their diameter does not exceed 1 μm.

> **9.6** Why should the diameter of mitochondria remain fairly constant when the length is so variable?

Mitochondria are able to change shape, and some are able to move to areas in the cell where a lot of activity is taking place. This provides the cell with a large concentration of mitochondria in areas where ATP need is

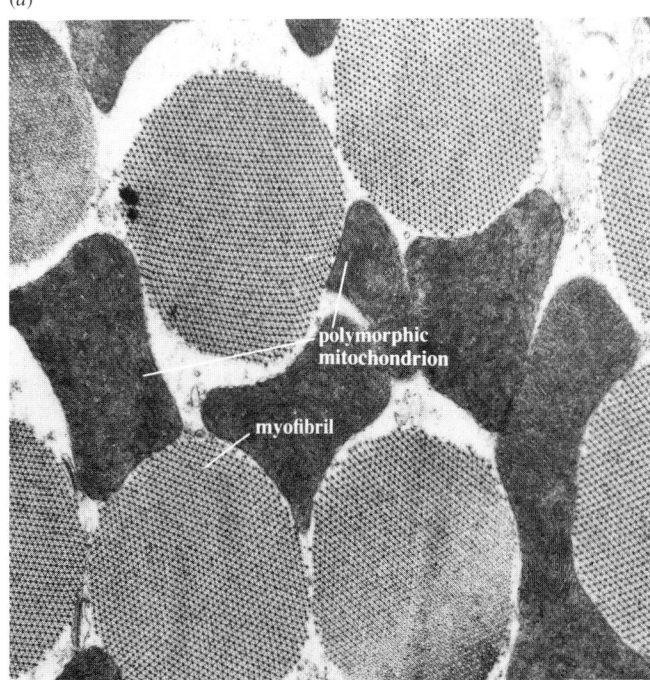

(a)

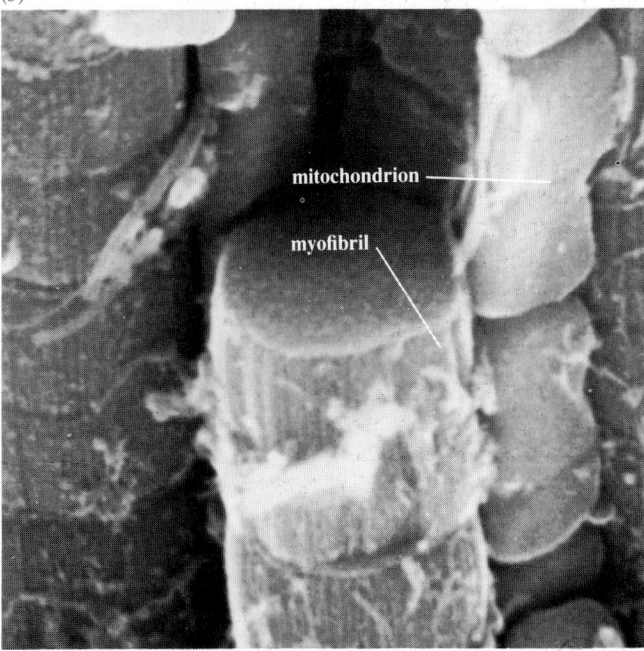

(b)

Fig 9.11 (a) *Transmission electron micrograph, and (b) scanning electron micrograph of the flight muscle of a house fly. Each muscle fibril (myofibril) is surrounded by polymorphic mitochondria (mitochondria with variable shape). Myofibrils are the part of the muscle that contracts, a process that requires a lot of energy.*

greater. Other mitochondria have a more fixed position (as in insect flight muscle, fig 9.11).

Structure of mitochondria

Mitochondria can be extracted from cells by cell homogenisation and ultracentrifugation techniques as described in chapter 5 (section 5.7). Once isolated they may be examined with an electron microscope using various techniques such as sectioning or negative staining.

Each mitochondrion is bounded by two membranes (an envelope), the outer one being separated from the inner by a narrow space, the intermembranal space. The inner membrane is folded inwards into a number of shelf-like **cristae** (fig 9.12). The cristae increase its surface area, providing space for the components of the respiratory chain which are located in the membrane. Active transport mechanisms are responsible for the movement of ADP and ATP across it. Negative staining techniques which stain the space around structures rather than the structures themselves (fig 9.12e) show the presence of **elementary particles** on the matrix side of the inner membrane. Each particle consists of a head piece, stalk and base (fig 9.12c and d). Whilst the photograph (fig 9.12f) suggests that the particles stick out from the membrane into the matrix, it is

known that this is an artefact produced by the method of preparation, and that the particles are tucked into the membrane. The head piece is associated with ATP synthesis and is the coupling enzyme, **ATPase**, which links ('couples') the making of ATP to the respiratory chain. At the base of the particle, and extending through the inner membrane, are the components of the respiratory chain itself. The mitochondrial matrix contains most of the enzymes of the Krebs cycle. Fatty acid oxidation also takes place here. In addition, mitochondrial DNA, RNA and 70S ribosomes are present.

9.7 Name four chemical substances which are involved in respiration which would enter the mitochondrion from the cytoplasm and four which would leave.

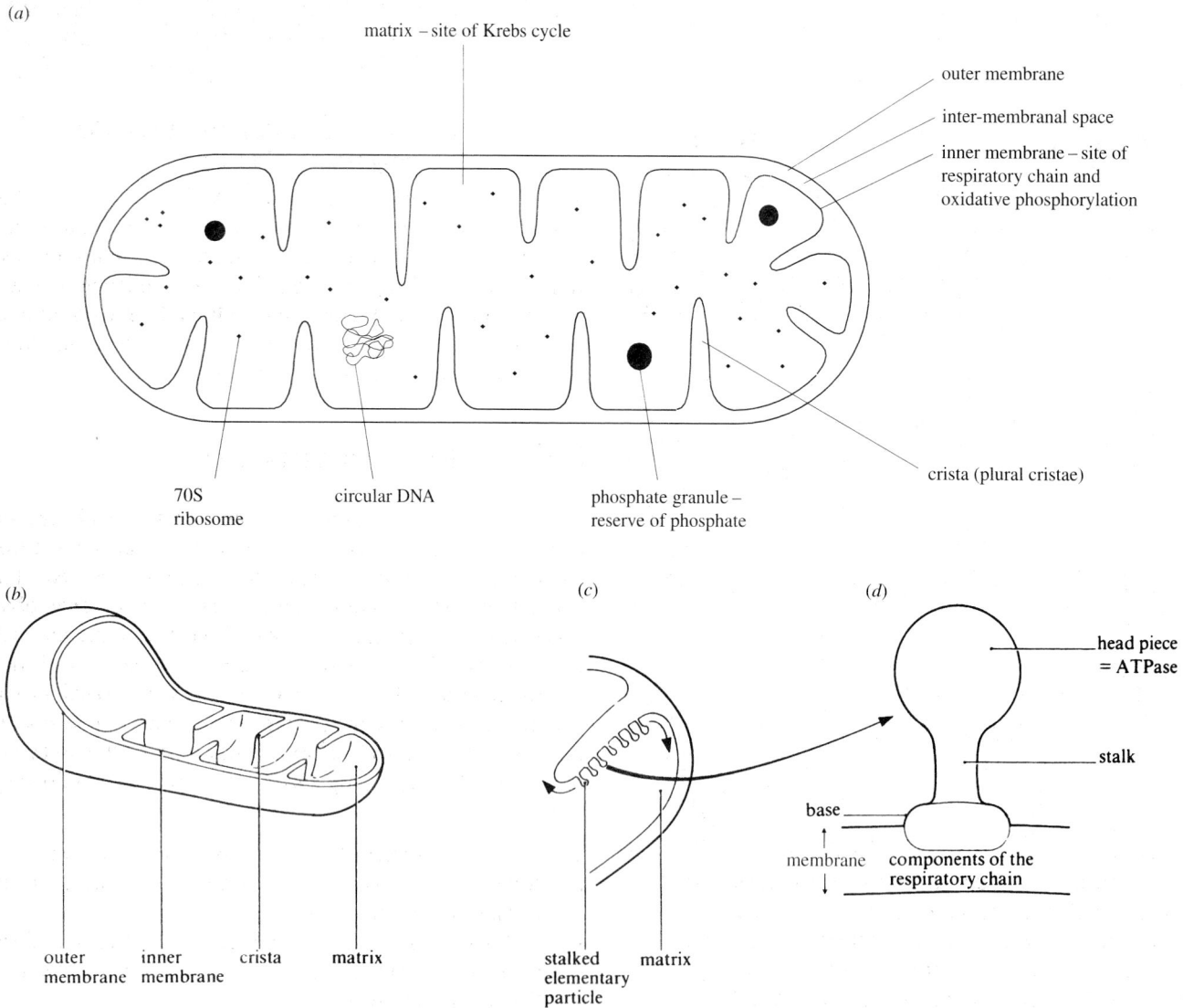

Fig 9.12 *Structure of mitochondrion. (a) Diagram of mitochondrion. (b) Three-dimensional structure. (c) Diagram of crista showing inner membrane particles. (d) Structure of inner membrane particle.*

(e)

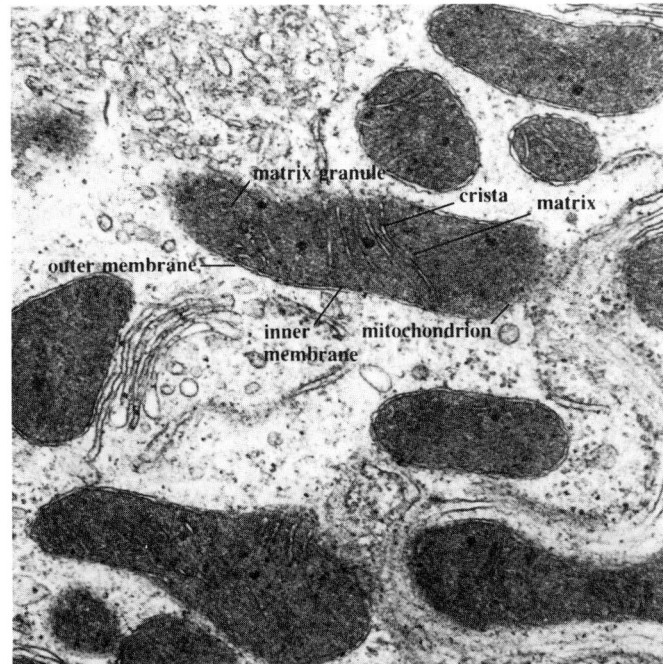

(g)

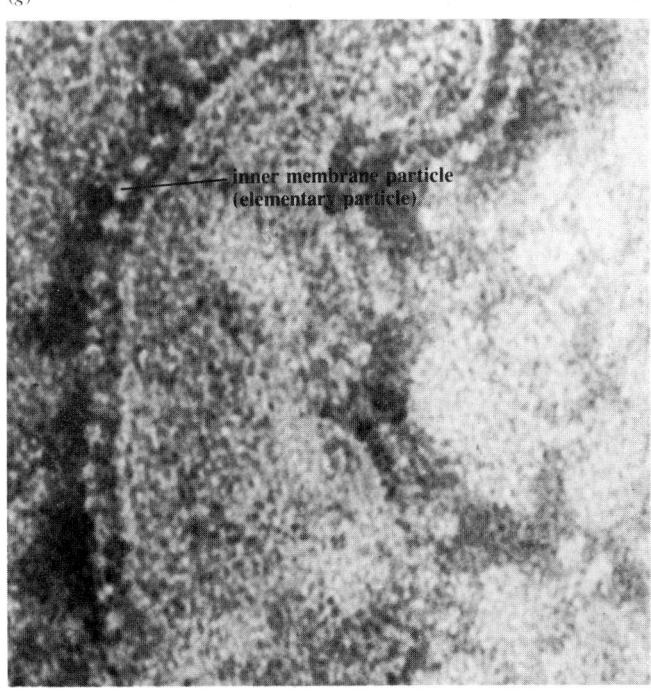

(f)

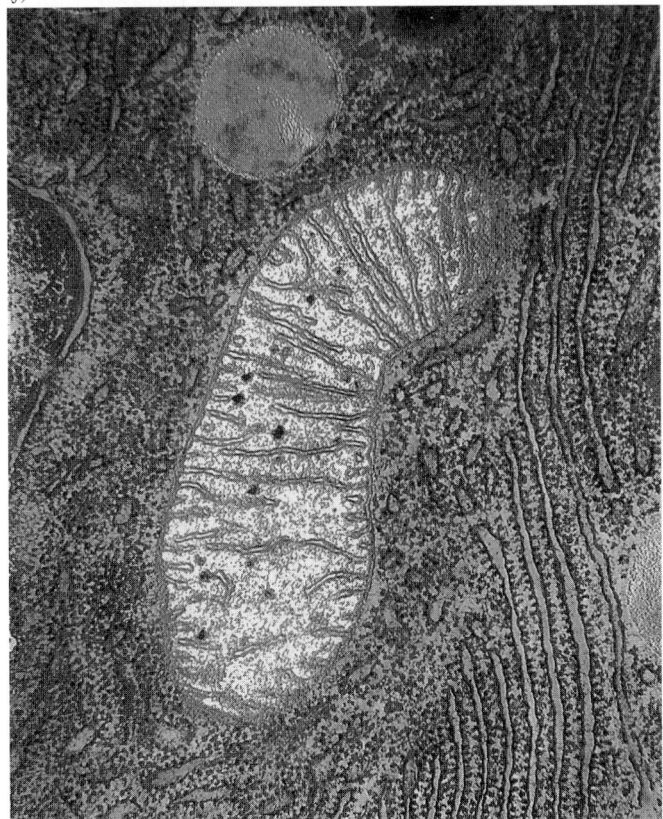

Fig. 9.12 (cont.) (e) *Low power electron micrograph of mitochondria.* (f) *High power electron micrograph of mitochondrion.* (g) *Transmission electron micrograph of negatively stained inner membrane particles from osmotically disrupted mitochondria of the house-fly.*

Evolution of mitochondria – the endosymbiont theory

Mitochondria contain circular DNA (fig 9.13) and 70S ribosomes like bacteria (prokaryotes). This and other evidence suggests that mitochondria, like chloroplasts, were once free-living bacteria. They are believed to have invaded an ancestral eukaryote cell and entered into a successful mutualistic (symbiotic) union with it. (See section 2.6.1 for further information.)

9.4 Gaseous exchange

Gaseous exchange refers to the exchange of respiratory gases between the cells of the organism and the environment. Aerobic organisms require oxygen for respiration whilst both aerobic and most anaerobic organisms must get rid of carbon dioxide, a waste product of respiration. The area where gaseous exchange with the environment actually takes place is called the **respiratory surface**. Gaseous exchange takes place in all organisms by the physical process of **diffusion**. In order for this to occur effectively the respiratory surface must have the following properties.

- It must be **permeable**, so that gases can pass through.
- It must be **thin**, because diffusion is only efficient over distances of 1 mm or less.
- It should possess a **large surface area** so that sufficient amounts of gases are able to be exchanged according to the organism's need.
- It should possess a **good blood supply** (and sometimes a good ventilation mechanism) in those organisms (larger animals) which use blood as a transport

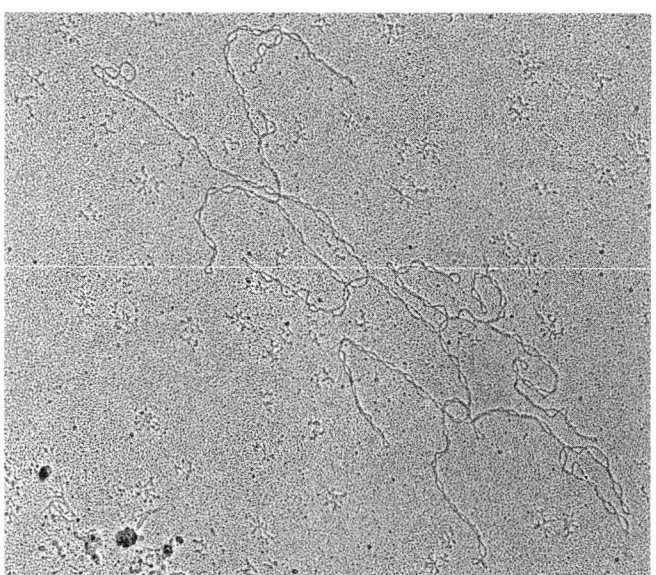

Fig 9.13 *Electron micrograph of mitochondrial DNA from the brewer's yeast* Saccharomyces carlsbergensis. *The molecule is a 'supercoiled' circle of DNA with a circumference of 26 μm. It is made up of some 75 000 nucleotides. It codes for some, but not all, of the mitochondrial proteins. Nuclear DNA contains the remaining genes needed to control mitochondria.*

medium. This helps to maintain a steep diffusion gradient, that is a large difference in concentration, across the respiratory surface.

Fick's law provides a way of considering how the maximum rate of diffusion of respiratory gases is achieved in the examples we shall study. From the law we can predict that the diffusion rate of a respiratory gas through a respiratory surface is proportional to:

surface area* × difference in concentration**/thickness*

* of the respiratory surface
** of the gas either side of the membrane

A similar relationship with membranes has already been noted in section 5.9.8.

Organisms acquire their oxygen either direct from the atmosphere or from oxygen dissolved in water. There are marked differences in the oxygen content of air and water. A given volume of air contains far more oxygen (21% by volume) than an equal volume of water (0.8% by volume). Therefore it follows that an aquatic organism such as a fish must pass a correspondingly much greater volume of water over its gaseous exchange surface than an air-breathing vertebrate passes air in order to obtain sufficient oxygen for its metabolic needs. This requires a different ventilation mechanism. Water is also more than 700 times denser than air and 100 times more viscous. It therefore requires more energy to pass water over the respiratory surface. Oxygen diffuses about 1 000 times slower through water than

through air, which means that it is harder to maintain a steep concentration gradient across the respiratory surface. It is not surprising then that fish are unable to achieve the higher metabolic rates of animals with lungs.

9.4.1 A unicellular organism, e.g. *Amoeba*

Amoeba is a single-celled organism which belongs to a group commonly known as protozoans in the kingdom Protoctista. Its shape varies as it moves. It measures less than 1 mm in diameter and possesses a large surface area to volume ratio, typical of unicellular organisms. The respiratory surface is the cell surface membrane. Diffusion of gases therefore occurs over the whole surface of the animal, and is fast enough to satisfy its metabolic needs. Oxygen enters the cell and carbon dioxide leaves, each down its own diffusion gradient. Diffusion across membranes is described in section 5.9.8.

9.4.2 The need for special respiratory structures and pigments

As animals increase in size, so their surface area to volume ratio decreases. This makes simple diffusion over the body surface inadequate to supply oxygen to any cells of the organism that are not in direct contact with the surrounding medium. Also the increased metabolic activity of many of these larger animals increases their rate of oxygen consumption.

In order to cope with the increased demand, certain regions of the body have developed into specialised respiratory surfaces. Different organisms possess different types of gaseous exchange surface. Each has evolved to work efficiently in a particular environment. They can be classified as shown in fig 9.14. Generally they have a large surface area and are often associated with a transport system, the blood vascular system. The possession of a transport system provides a link between the respiratory surface and all the other tissues of the organism, and enables oxygen and carbon dioxide to be continuously exchanged between the respiratory surface and cells. The presence of a respiratory pigment in the blood further increases the efficiency of the blood's oxygen-carrying capacity (see below). In addition there may be special ventilation movements which assist in ensuring a rapid exchange of gases between the animal and the surrounding environment by maintaining steep diffusion gradients.

Respiratory pigments

Respiratory pigments are coloured molecules which act as oxygen carriers by binding reversibly to oxygen. All known respiratory pigments contain a coloured non-protein portion, such as haem in haemoglobin, linked to a protein molecule. Haemoglobin is red. At high oxygen concentrations, the pigment combines with oxygen, whereas at low oxygen concentrations the oxygen is quickly released. Blood that contains any form of

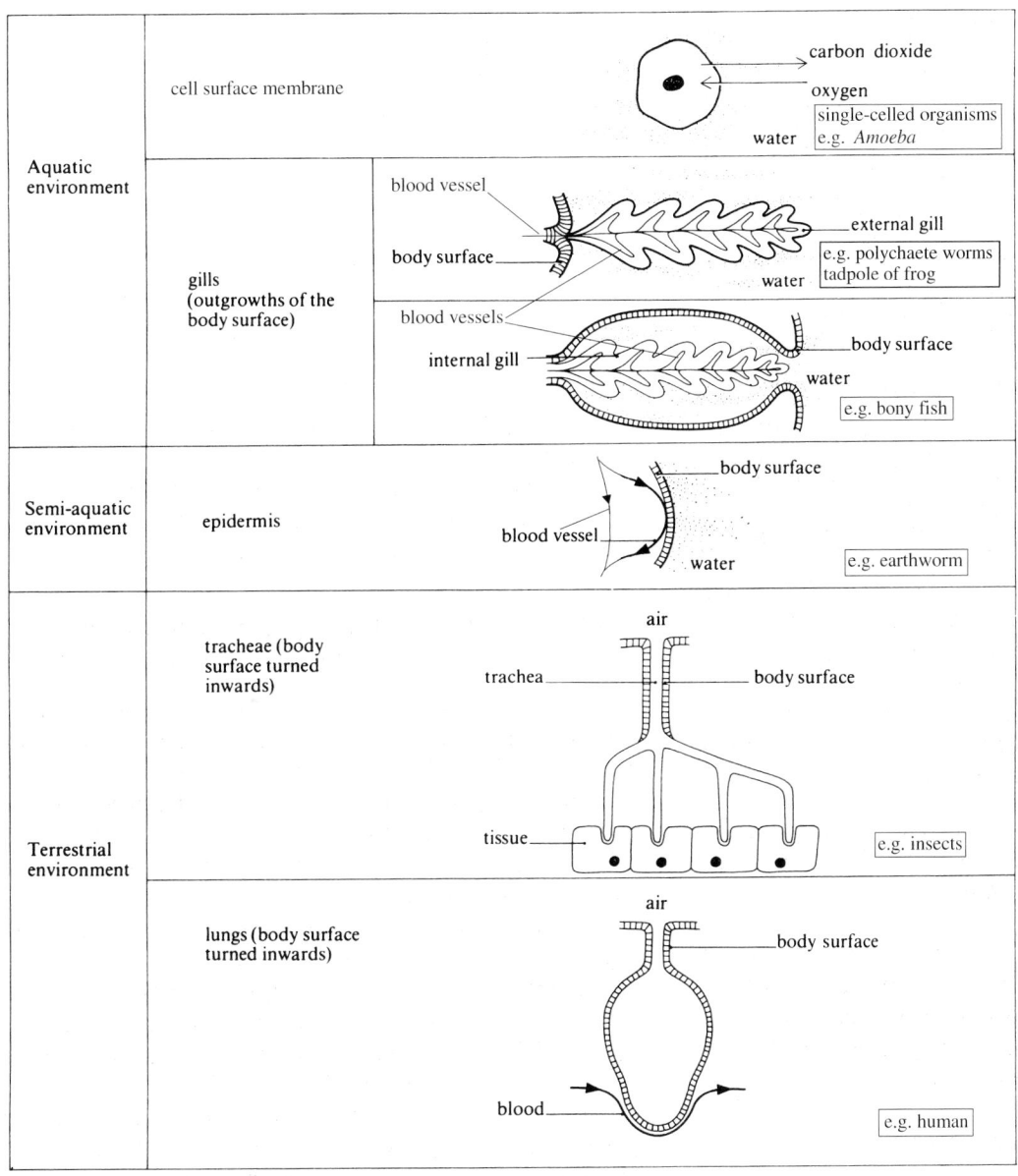

Fig 9.14 *Some types of respiratory surface in animals.*

respiratory pigment is a more efficient oxygen carrier than blood without one. This is because the pigment permits far greater amounts of oxygen to be taken up and transported. In mammals and other vertebrates the pigment is haemoglobin which is enclosed in red blood cells.

A more detailed account of the transport of oxygen by haemoglobin can be found in chapter 14.

9.4.3 Segmented worms, e.g. earthworm

The earthworm belongs to a group of animals known as segmented worms. There are no special organs designed for gaseous exchange in the earthworm. Gas exchange takes place by diffusion over the whole body surface. Special organs are unnecessary as the cylindrical shape of the worms gives a high surface area to volume ratio, and their relative inactivity means that there is only a low rate of oxygen consumption.

Segmented worms do, however, possess a blood vascular system, unlike some simpler animals and unicellular organisms. This contains the respiratory pigment haemoglobin in solution. Pumping activity by the major blood vessels circulates blood and dissolved gases round the body and maintains steep diffusion gradients.

The earthworm lives on land and keeps its thin skin (cuticle) moist by glandular secretions from the epidermis. Looped blood capillaries are present in the epidermis immediately below the cuticle (fig 9.14). The distance between body surface and blood vessels is small enough to enable rapid diffusion of oxygen into the blood. Earthworms have little protection against desiccation (drying out) and therefore they tend to stay in moist conditions.

9.4.4 Insects, e.g. locust

In insects gaseous exchange occurs by means of a system of tubes called the **tracheal system**. This system allows oxygen to diffuse from the outside air directly to the tissues, without the need for transportation by blood. This is much faster than diffusion of dissolved oxygen through the tissues and allows higher metabolic rates.

Pairs of holes called **spiracles**, found on the second and third thoracic segments, and first eight abdominal segments, lead into air-filled sacs. Extending from these are branched tubes called **tracheae** (singular **trachea**) (fig 9.15). Each trachea secretes a thin layer of strong, supporting chitinous material around its outer surface. This is usually further strengthened by spiral or circular patterns of thickening which maintain an open pipeline even when the lumen of the trachea is subjected to reduced pressure (compare the cartilage hoops in the trachea and bronchi of humans). In each body segment the tracheae branch into numerous smaller tubes called tracheoles which spread among the insect tissues, and in the more active ones, such as flight muscle, end within cells. The degree of branching may be adjusted according to the metabolic needs of individual tissues.

Tracheoles lack a chitinous lining. At rest they are filled with watery fluid (fig 9.16) and the rate at which oxygen diffuses through them, and carbon dioxide in the reverse direction, satisfies the insect's requirements. However, during exercise, increased metabolic activity by the muscles leads to accumulation of products such as lactic acid, so making the tissue's solute potential more negative. When this occurs the water in the tracheoles leaves by osmosis into the tissues, causing more air and therefore more

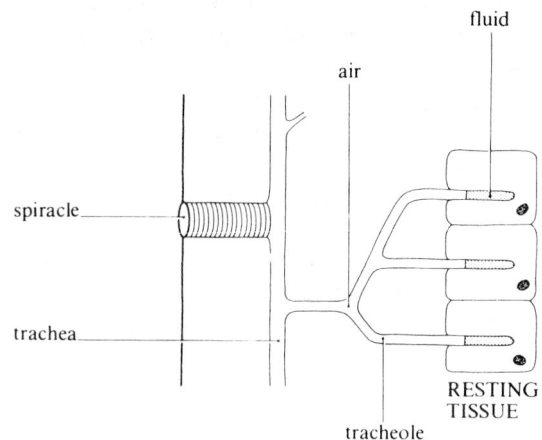

Fluids of a higher water potential surround the the tracheole; fluids diffuse into the tracheole

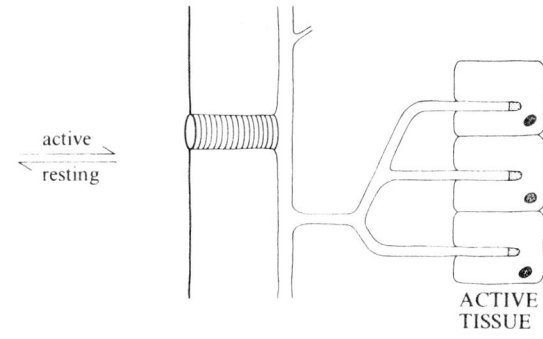

Increased lactate (lactic acid) lowers the water potential of the surrounding fluid; fluid withdrawn from the tracheoles; air moves in to replace it

Fig 9.16 *The functioning of tracheoles – conditions in resting and active insect tissues.*

oxygen to enter the tracheoles and come into close contact with the tissues just at the time when it is required.

The overall flow of air in and out of the insect is regulated by a valve mechanism at the spiracles. Each spiracle is controlled by a system of valves operated by tiny muscles. It also has hairs around its edges which prevent foreign bodies entering and reduce loss of water vapour. The size of the aperture is adjusted according to the level of carbon dioxide in the body.

Increased activity leads to increased carbon dioxide production. This is detected by chemoreceptors and the spiracles are opened accordingly. Ventilation (breathing) movements by the body may also be triggered by the same stimulus, notably in larger insects such as the locust. Muscles contract and flatten the insect body, decreasing the volume of the tracheal system, thus forcing air out (expiration). Inspiration (intake of air) is achieved passively when the elastic nature of the body segments returns them to their original shape.

There is evidence to suggest that the thoracic and abdominal spiracles open and close alternately, and that

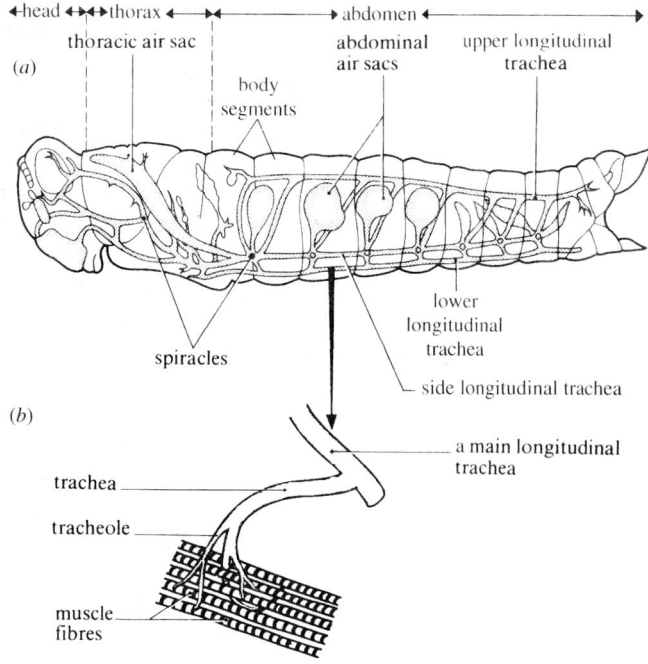

Fig 9.15 (a) *Tracheal system of locust.* (b) *Structure of insect trachea.*

this, in conjunction with ventilation movements, provides a one-way flow of air through the animal, with air entering in through the thorax and out via the abdomen.

Even though the tracheal system is a highly effective means of gaseous exchange, in most insects it relies entirely on diffusion of oxygen through the body. Since this can only occur efficiently across small distances, it imposes severe limitations on the size that insects can attain. Diffusion is only effective over distances of up to 1 cm; therefore, even though some stick insects may be up to 30 cm in length, no insects can be more than 2 cm broad!

9.4.5 Bony fish, e.g. herring

Fish possess **gill slits** in the wall of the pharyngeal region of the gut (the region between the buccal cavity and oesophagus). These connect with the outside environment, water. The tissue between the slits forms supports known as branchial arches or **gill arches**. In bony fish there are four pairs of gill arches separating five pairs of gill slits (fig 9.17a). Each gill is made up of two rows of **gill filaments** arranged in the shape of a V (fig 9.17b). The filaments possess **lamellae** (fig 9.17c), thin plates which have a rich supply of blood capillaries. These plates greatly increase the surface area of the respiratory surface. The barrier between blood and water is only several cells thick so diffusion between the two is rapid.

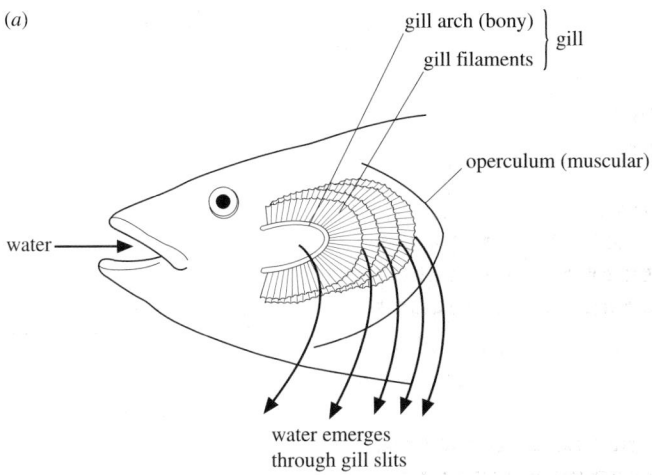

(a)

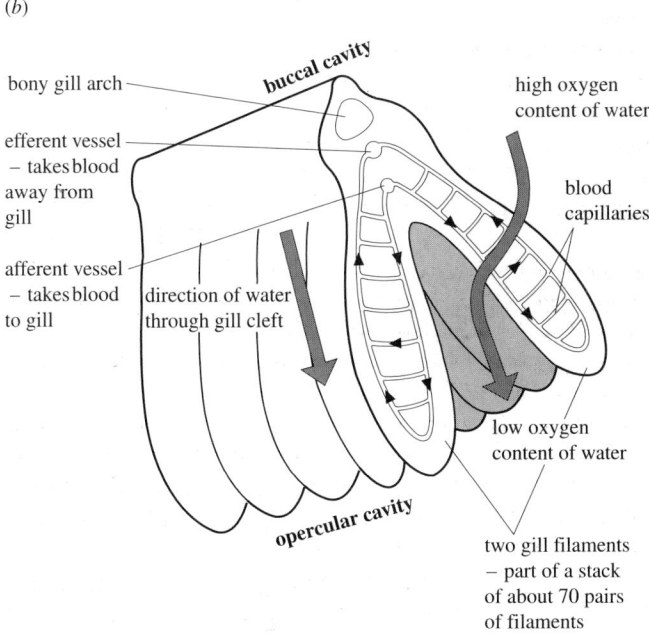

(b)

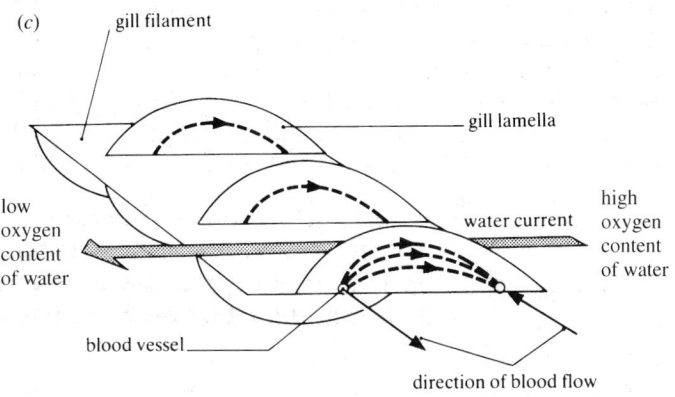

(c)

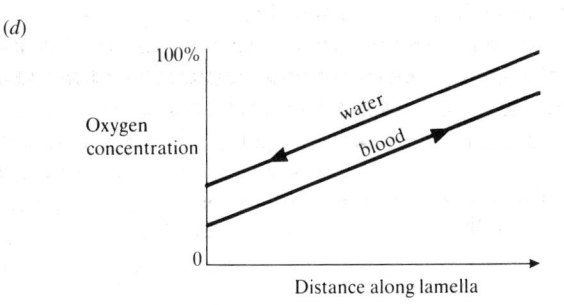

(d)

Fig 9.17 (a) *External view of the gills of a bony fish. The operculum is shown as transparent for convenience.*
(b) *Part of a stack of gill filaments.* (c) *Detail of part of one gill filament showing the lamellae which increase the surface area.* (d) *Variation in the oxygen concentration of blood and water as they pass across a gill lamella.*

A moveable gill cover, the **operculum**, which is reinforced with thin layers of bone, encloses and protects the gills. There is a space between the inside surface of the operculum and the gills called the **opercular cavity** (fig 9.18). This plays a part in the fish's ventilation mechanism. The operculum can shut tight against the side of the fish or open, controlling movement of water in and out of the opercular cavity like a valve.

During inspiration the buccal cavity expands, and this decreases the pressure within, causing water to be drawn in through the mouth. At the same time, the outside water pressure presses the posterior (rear) end of the operculum shut, preventing entry of water from this region. However, also active at this time are muscles in the operculum which contract, causing the opercular cavity to be enlarged. The pressure in the opercular cavity is less than that in the buccal cavity and hence water is drawn from the buccal cavity over the gills into the opercular cavity. Therefore gaseous exchange is able to continue even when the fish is taking in a fresh supply of water.

When expiration takes place the mouth closes, as does the entrance to the oesophagus, and the floor of the buccal cavity is raised. This forces water over the gills, through the gill slits, and into the opercular cavity where the increased pressure forces open the posterior end of the operculum. Water therefore leaves to the outside environment. The coordinated activity of the buccal cavity and the opercular muscles ensures that a continuous flow of water passes over

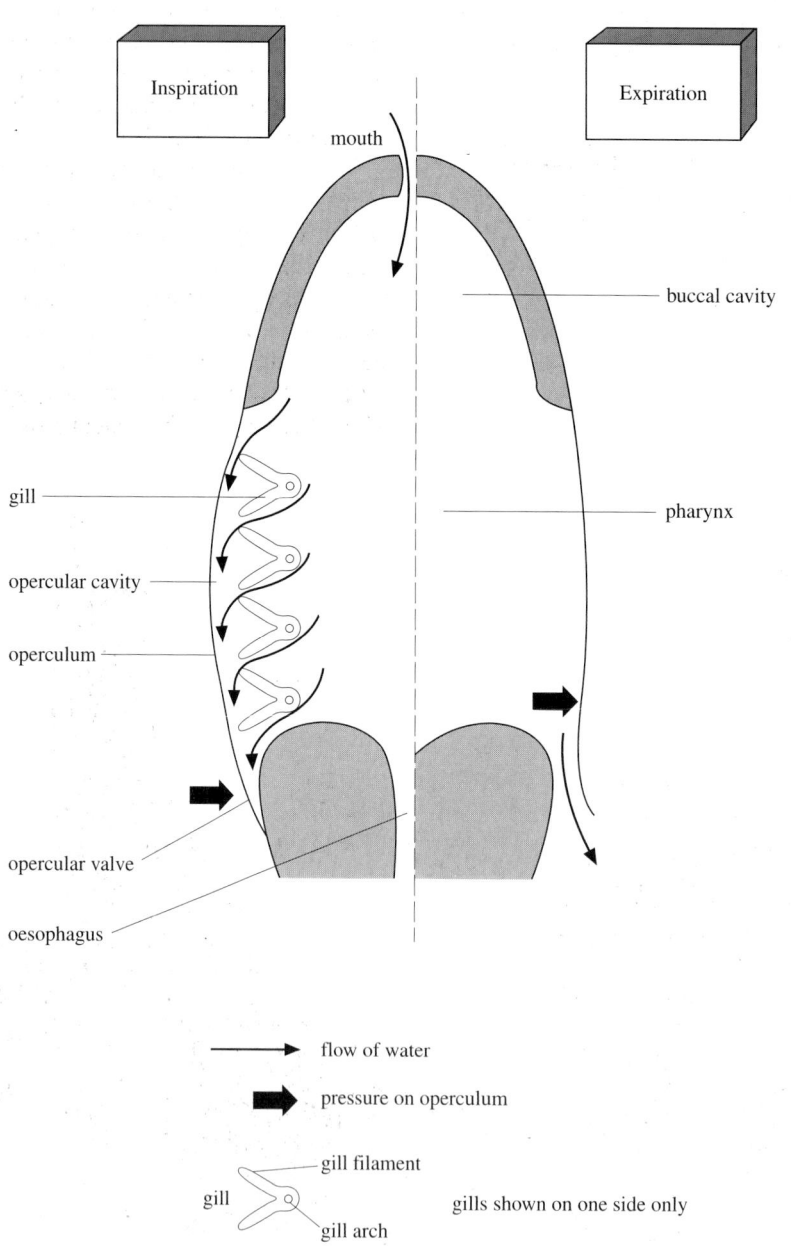

Fig 9.18   *Ventilation mechanism of a bony fish.*

the gills for most of the time, thus maintaining a high concentration of oxygen in water near the gills and low concentration of carbon dioxide.

Neighbouring gill filaments overlap at their tips, providing resistance to water flow. This slows down the passage of water over the gill lamellae, thus increasing the time available for gaseous exchange to take place. The blood in the lamellae flows in the opposite direction to that of the water (fig 9.17c). This is called a **countercurrent system** (fig 9.17d), and is a more efficient arrangement than a parallel current system in which the two fluids would travel in the same direction. A countercurrent system ensures that blood will constantly meet water with a relatively higher concentration of dissolved oxygen in it, and that a concentration gradient will be maintained between blood and water throughout the entire length of the filament and across each lamella. In this way bony fish are able to extract 80% of the oxygen in water.

9.8 Try to explain why blood flowing in the same direction as the water current (a parallel current system) would be a relatively inefficient mechanism for exchange of gases.

9.5 Gaseous exchange in a mammal

9.5.1 Structure of the respiratory system

The respiratory surface of a mammal consists of many air sacs called **alveoli** inside a pair of **lungs**. The lungs are situated next to the heart in the thoracic cavity and are connected to the atmosphere by tubes (fig 9.19). Air passes into the lungs through these tubes. Twelve pairs of bony **ribs** surround and protect the lungs and heart. **Intercostal muscles** are attached to the ribs, and a large **diaphragm** separates the thorax from the abdomen. These are involved in the ventilation mechanism, as described in section 9.5.4.

Air enters the body through two nostrils, each of which possesses a border of large hairs which trap particles in the air and filter them out of the system. While passing through the nasal passages the air is warmed and moistened and its odour detected. Air passes from the nasal passages, through the pharynx and into the trachea. This is a tube which lies in front of the oesophagus and extends into the thoracic cavity. The wall of the tube is strengthened and held open by horizontally arranged C-shaped bands of cartilage. The open section of the C is next to the oesophagus (fig 9.19). The cartilage prevents collapse of the tube during inspiration (breathing in). The cartilage can be seen in a section of the trachea (fig 9.20).

At its lower end the trachea splits into two **bronchi**. Within the lungs each bronchus subdivides many times into

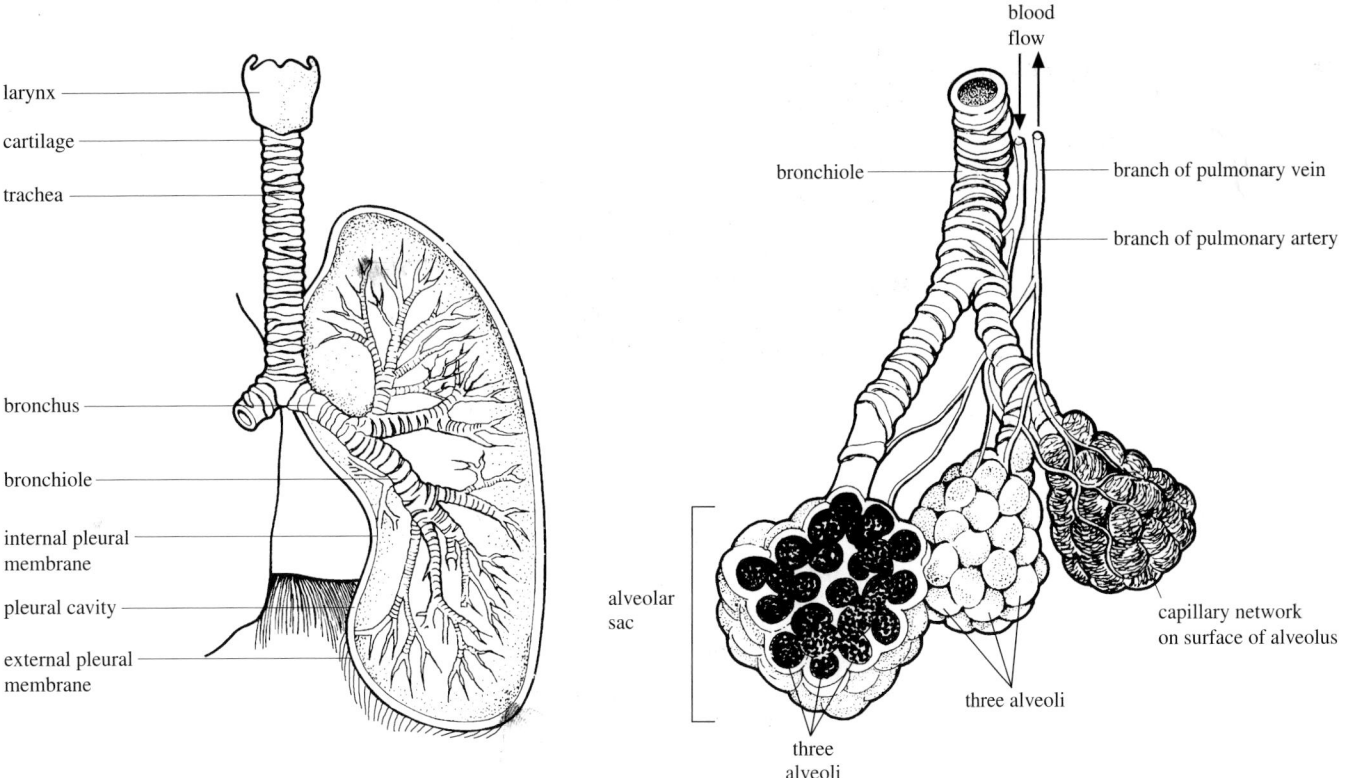

Fig 9.19 *Human trachea and lungs.*

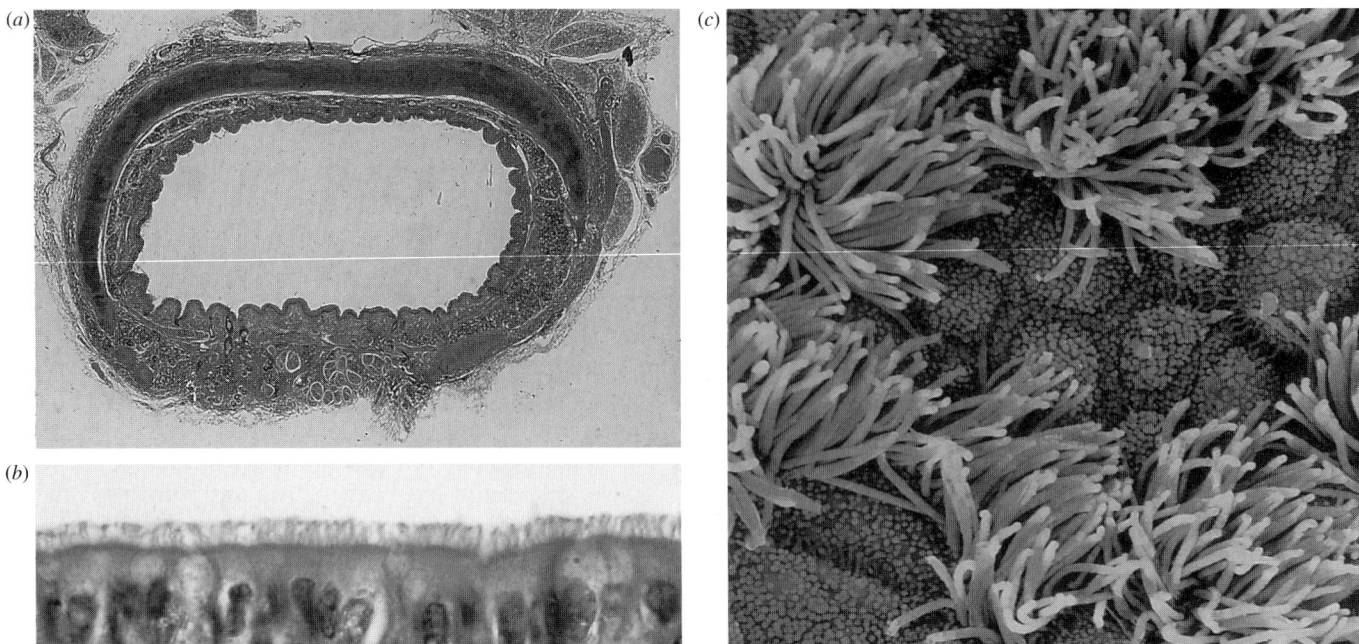

Fig 9.20 (a) *TS trachea seen at low power with a light microscope.* (b) *High power, showing ciliated epithelium and goblet cells.* (c) *Scanning electron micrograph of the surface of ciliated epithelium.*

much smaller tubes called **bronchioles**. These in turn branch into finer and finer tubes, ending with the **alveolar ducts** which lead into sacs called **alveolar sacs**. Into each alveolar sac opens a group of alveoli. A summary of these structures and their main features is provided in fig 9.21.

The walls of most of the respiratory passage are lined with ciliated epithelial cells and goblet cells, which secrete mucus (see figs 9.20 and 6.17). Mucus traps any particles, such as dust and bacteria, that have managed to pass through the hairs of the nostrils. The beating of the cilia then carries the trapped particles to the back of the buccal cavity where the mucus is swallowed. Note that it is not the cilia which trap the particles – don't confuse them with the hairs in the nose. Mucus also moistens the incoming air.

Structure of the alveolus

The alveoli form the gas exchange surface (fig 9.22). There are over 700 million alveoli present in the human lungs, representing a total surface area of 70–90 m². The wall of each alveolus is only 0.0001 mm thick (0.1 μm). On its outside is a dense network of blood capillaries, all of which originate from the pulmonary artery and rejoin to form the pulmonary vein (fig 9.23 and 9.24). Lining each alveolus is moist squamous epithelium. This consists of very thin, flattened cells (fig 6.14), reducing the distance over which

diffusion must occur (fig 9.24). Collagen and elastic fibres are also present. The latter allow the alveoli to expand and recoil easily during breathing.

Special cells in the alveolus wall secrete a detergent-like chemical on to the inside lining of the alveolus. This is called a **surfactant**. It lowers the surface tension of the fluid layer lining the alveolus, and thereby reduces the amount of effort needed to breathe in and inflate the lungs. Surfactant also speeds up the transport of oxygen and carbon dioxide between the air and the liquid lining the alveolus and helps to kill any bacteria which reach the alveoli. Surfactant is constantly being secreted and reabsorbed in a healthy lung. It is first made in the lungs of a fetus when about 23 weeks old. This is the main reason why the fetus is considered to be incapable of independent existence before 24 weeks, and therefore determines the legal age limit for abortion in the UK. Babies born prematurely are at risk of being deficient in surfactant. This causes a condition known as respiratory distress syndrome in which breathing is very difficult, and is one of the main causes of premature death. Without surfactant the surface tension of the fluid in the alveoli is about 10 times higher than normal and the alveoli collapse after each expiration. It also requires much greater effort to expand them again when breathing in than when surfactant is present.

Fig 9.21 *Summary of the histology of the respiratory pathway.*

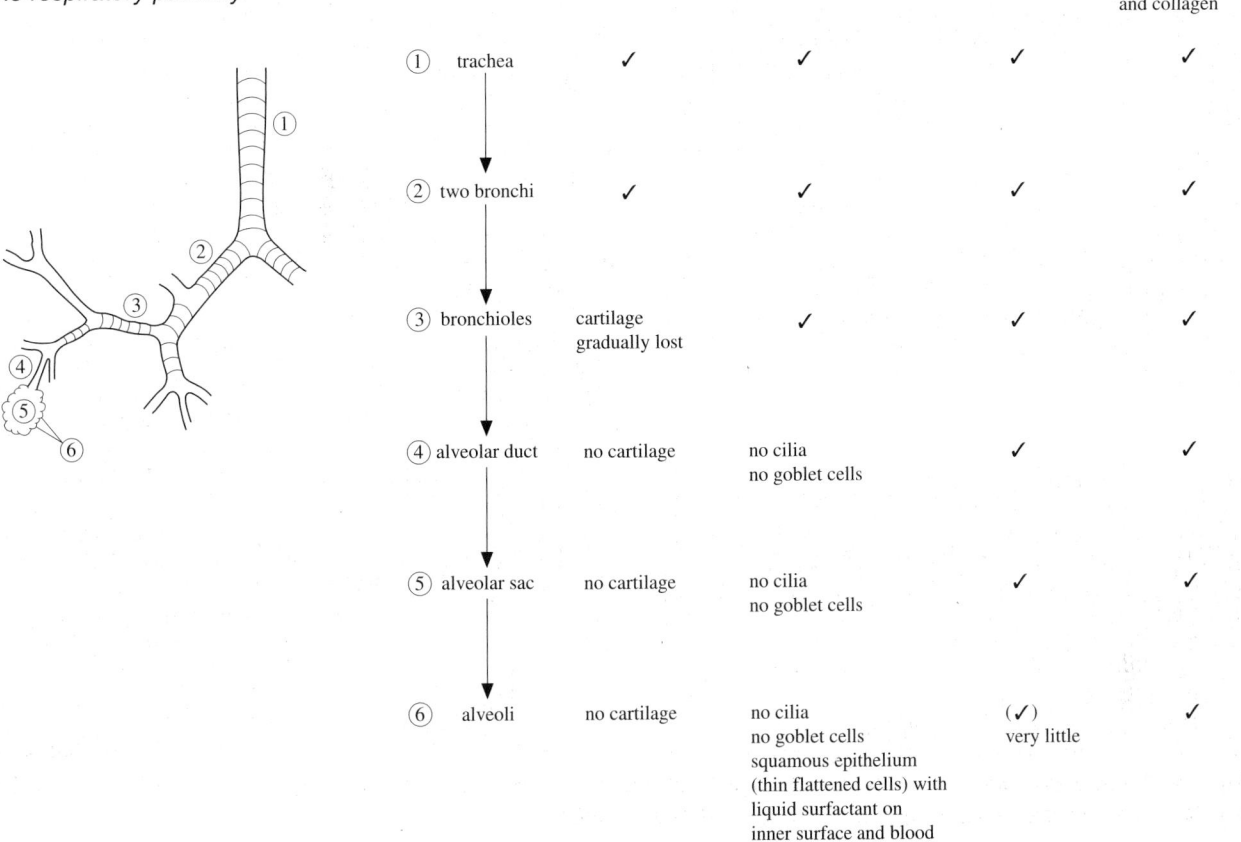

	Cartilage	Ciliated epithelium with goblet cells	Smooth muscle	Connective tissue with elastic fibres and collagen
① trachea	✓	✓	✓	✓
② two bronchi	✓	✓	✓	✓
③ bronchioles	cartilage gradually lost	✓	✓	✓
④ alveolar duct	no cartilage	no cilia no goblet cells	✓	✓
⑤ alveolar sac	no cartilage	no cilia no goblet cells	✓	✓
⑥ alveoli	no cartilage	no cilia no goblet cells squamous epithelium (thin flattened cells) with liquid surfactant on inner surface and blood capillaries on outer surface	(✓) very little	✓

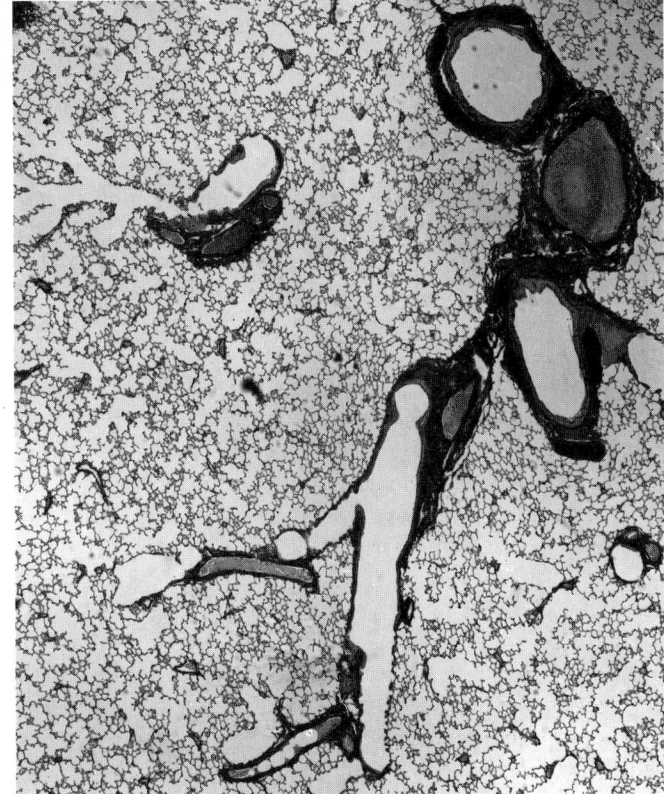

Fig 9.22 (a) *Human lung tissue as seen with a light microscope at low power.*

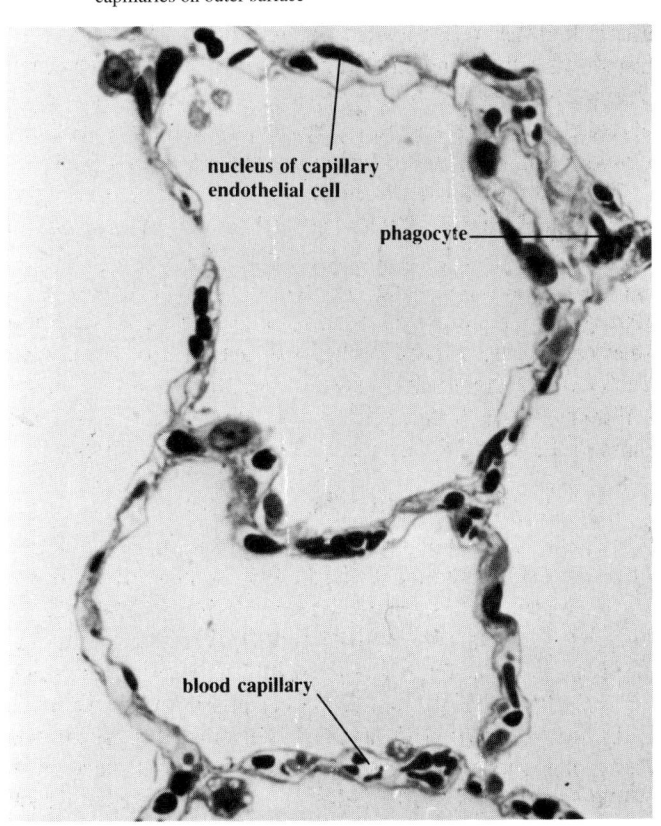

(b) *High power view of alveoli.*

nucleus of capillary endothelial cell

phagocyte

blood capillary

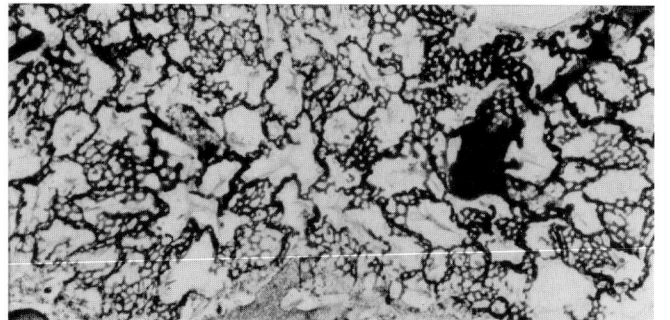

Fig 9.23 *Human lung injected to show blood vessels.*

Gaseous exchange at the alveolus

Oxygen diffuses across the thin barrier represented by the epithelium of the alveolus and the endothelium of the capillary (fig 9.24*b*). It passes first into the blood plasma and then combines with haemoglobin in the red blood cells to form oxyhaemoglobin. Carbon dioxide diffuses in the reverse direction from the blood to the alveoli.

Diffusion is efficient because:

- alveoli have a large surface area,
- the gases have a short distance to travel,
- a steep diffusion gradient is maintained by ventilation, a good blood supply and the presence of an oxygen-carrying compound, haemoglobin,
- surfactant is present.

9.9   How many times must a molecule of oxygen diffuse across a cell surface membrane in passing from the inside of an alveolus to haemoglobin?

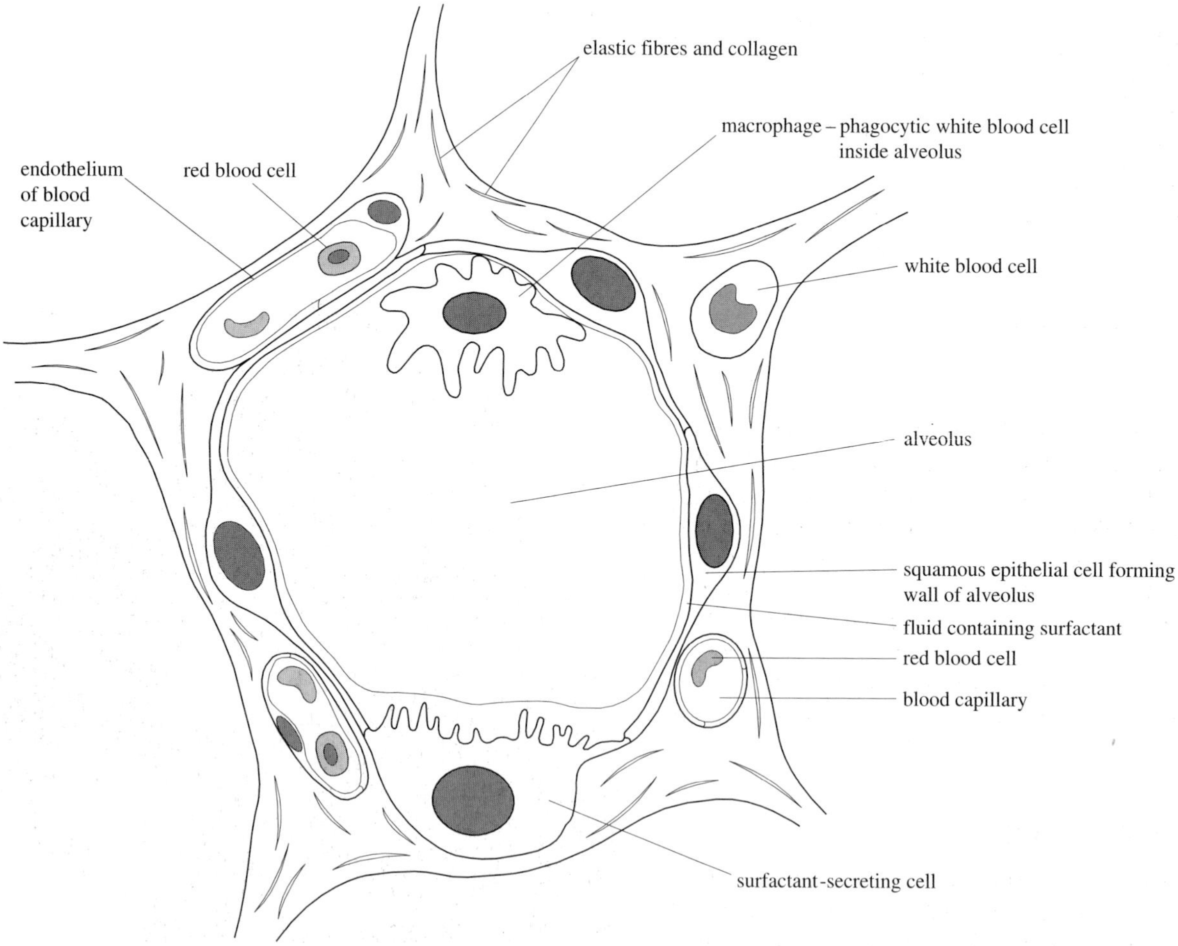

---

elastic fibres and collagen

macrophage – phagocytic white blood cell inside alveolus

white blood cell

endothelium of blood capillary

red blood cell

alveolus

squamous epithelial cell forming wall of alveolus

fluid containing surfactant

red blood cell

blood capillary

surfactant-secreting cell

Fig 9.24   (a) *Cross-section through an alveolus. Five neighbouring alveoli are also partly shown, together with the structures between the alveoli.*

Fig 9.24 (b) *Relationship between an alveolus and a capillary.*

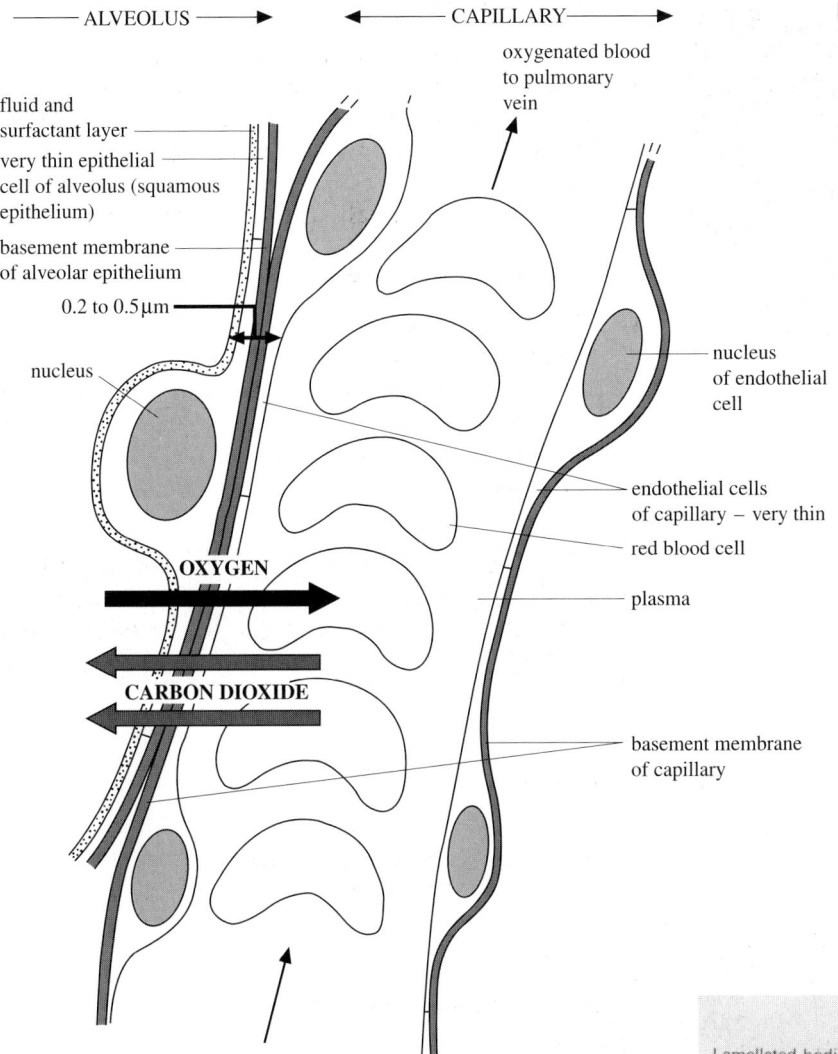

ALVEOLUS ⟶ ⟵ CAPILLARY ⟶

oxygenated blood to pulmonary vein

fluid and surfactant layer

very thin epithelial cell of alveolus (squamous epithelium)

basement membrane of alveolar epithelium

0.2 to 0.5 μm

nucleus

OXYGEN

CARBON DIOXIDE

nucleus of endothelial cell

endothelial cells of capillary – very thin

red blood cell

plasma

basement membrane of capillary

deoxygenated blood from pulmonary artery

The diameter of the blood capillaries is smaller than the diameter of the red blood cells passing through them. This means that the red blood cells have to be squeezed through the capillaries by blood pressure. During this process they bend into an umbrella shape (fig 9.25), exposing more of their surface area to the surface of the alveolus and allowing greater uptake of oxygen. Progress of the cells is also relatively slow, thus increasing the time available for gaseous exchange to take place. When blood leaves the alveolus it possesses the same concentration of oxygen and carbon dioxide as the air in the alveoli.

9.5.3 Pleural cavity

Each lung is surrounded by a pleural cavity. This is a space lined by two tough, flexible, transparent pleural membranes (pleura). These protect the lungs, stop them leaking air into the thoracic cavity and reduce friction between the lungs and the wall of the thorax. The inner membrane is in contact with the lungs, whilst the outer membrane lines the walls of the thorax and diaphragm. The

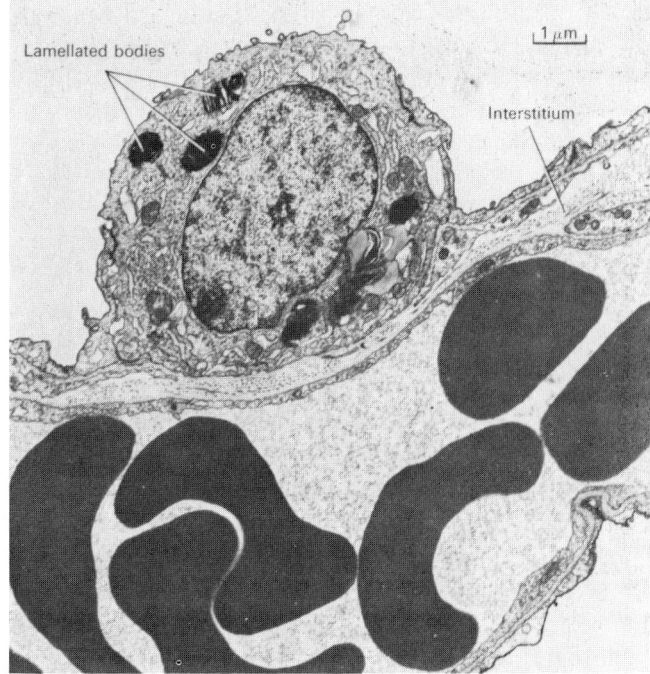

Lamellated bodies

1 μm

Interstitium

Fig 9.25 *Electron micrograph of a section through a capillary on the surface of an alveolus (dog lung). Red blood cells can be seen as dark objects in the lower part of the photograph*

287

pleural cavity contains pleural fluid which is secreted by the membranes. This lubricates the pleura, thus reducing friction as the membranes rub against each other during breathing movements. The cavity is air-tight and its pressure stays at 3–4 mmHg lower than that in the lungs. This negative pressure is maintained during inspiration and helps the alveoli to inflate and the lungs to fill any extra available space provided by the expanding thorax.

9.5.4 The mechanism of ventilation (breathing)

Air is passed in and out of the lungs by movements of the intercostal and diaphragm muscles which alter the volume of the thoracic cavity. There are two sets of intercostal muscles between each pair of ribs. The external intercostals are outside the internal intercostals. The muscle fibres run diagonally but in opposite directions in the two sets of muscles (fig 9.26). The diaphragm consists of circular and radial muscle fibres arranged around the edge of a circular inelastic sheet of white fibres (collagen).

Inspiration (breathing in)

This is an active process.

- The external intercostal muscles contract and the internal intercostals relax.
- This pulls the rib cage up and out. (You can easily feel this by placing a hand on your chest as you breathe in.)
- At the same time, the diaphragm muscles contract.
- This flattens the diaphragm.
- Both actions increase the volume of the thorax.
- As a result the pressure in the thorax, and hence the lungs, is reduced to less than atmospheric pressure.
- Air therefore enters the lungs, inflating the alveoli, until the air pressure in the lungs is equal to that of the atmosphere (fig 9.27).

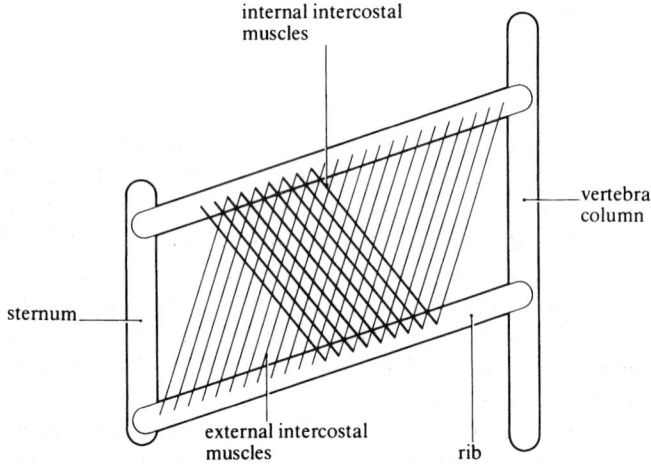

Fig 9.26 *Diagrammatic representation of the position of the intercostal muscles.*

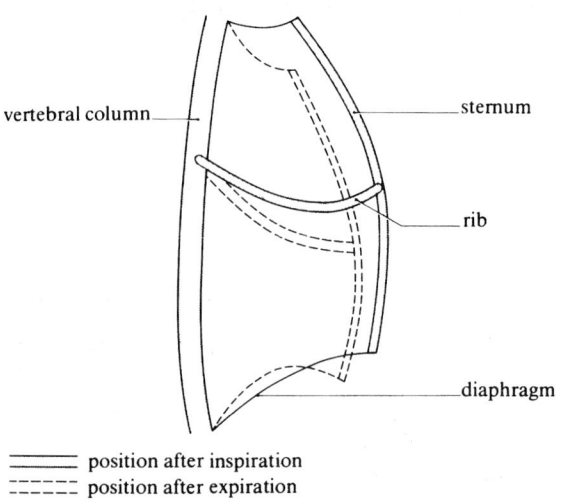

_____ position after inspiration
- - - - - - position after expiration

Fig 9.27 *Side view of thorax to show movements during breathing (only one rib shown).*

Expiration (breathing out)

This is largely a passive process under resting conditions, and is brought about by the elastic recoil of the lung tissue, respiratory muscles (see below) and the weight of the rib cage. The respiratory muscles act as follows.

- The external intercostal muscles relax and the internal intercostals contract. The rib cage drops, mainly due to its own weight.
- At the same time, the diaphragm relaxes. The dropping rib cage forces the diaphragm into a domed shape, pushing it up into the thoracic cavity.
- These events reduce the volume of the thorax and raise its pressure above that of the atmosphere.
- Consequently air is forced out of the lungs.

Under conditions of exercise, forced breathing occurs. When this happens additional muscles are brought into action and expiration becomes a much more active, energy-consuming process. The internal intercostals contract more strongly and move the ribs vigorously downwards. The abdominal muscles also contract strongly, causing more active upward movement of the diaphragm. This also happens when sneezing or coughing.

9.5.5 Control of ventilation

Normally we are not conscious of our breathing because it is controlled involuntarily. We can take over some voluntary control, and this will be discussed after considering involuntary control.

Involuntary control of breathing is carried out by a **breathing centre** located in the medulla of the brain (the medulla is part of the hindbrain) (fig 9.28). The ventral (lower) portion of the breathing centre acts to increase the rate and depth of inspiration and is called the **inspiratory centre**. The dorsal (top) and lateral (side) portions inhibit

Fig 9.28 *Nervous control of breathing.*

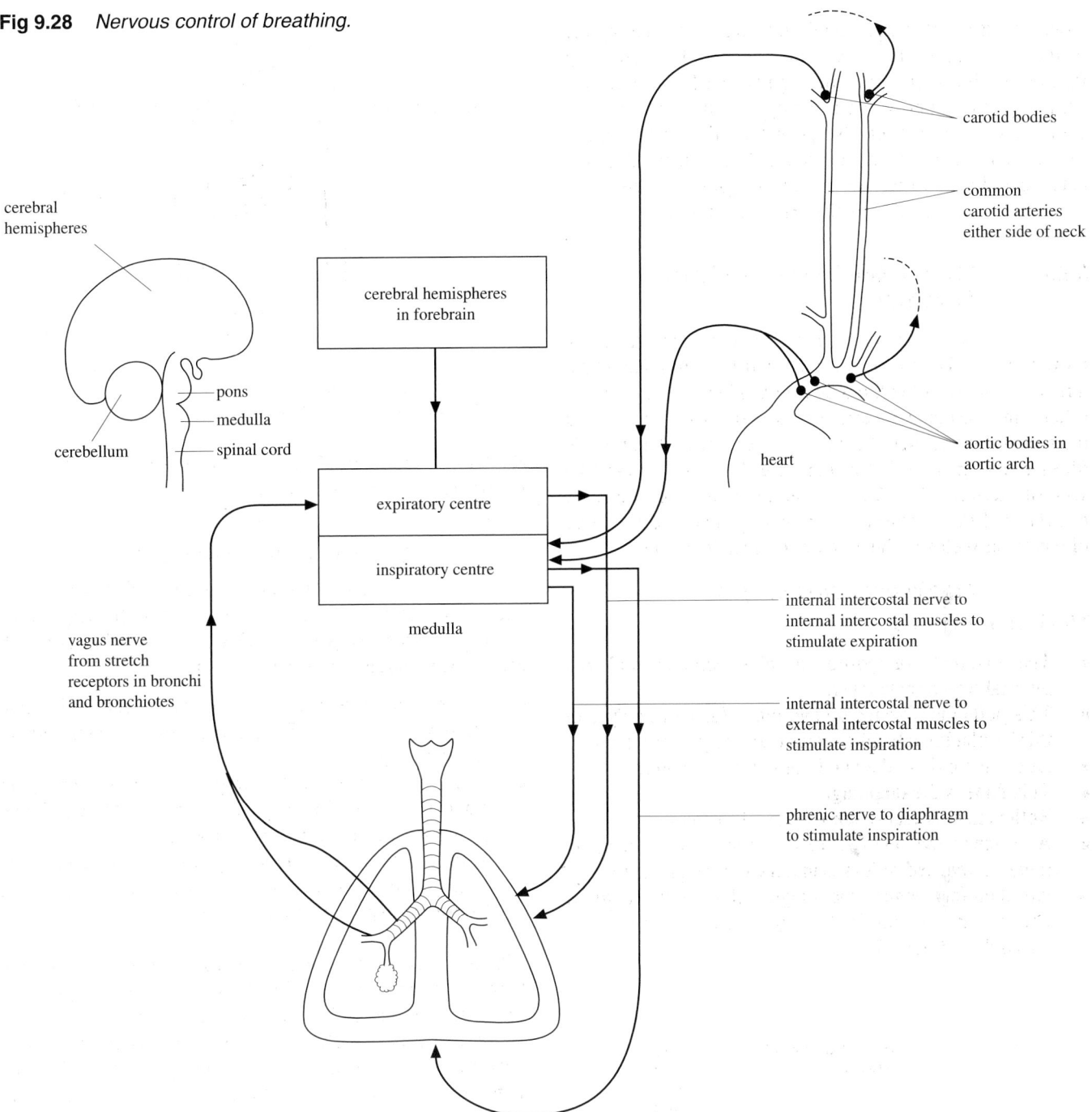

inspiration and stimulate expiration. These regions form the **expiratory centre**. The breathing centre communicates with the intercostal muscles by way of the **intercostal nerves** and with the diaphragm by way of the **phrenic nerves**. The bronchial tree (the mass of bronchioles and the bronchi) is connected to the brain by the **vagus nerve** (fig 9.28). Rhythmic nerve impulses to the diaphragm and intercostal muscles bring about ventilation movements.

Inspiration inflates the lungs and, as they inflate, stretch receptors (also known as proprioceptors) located in the bronchial tree are stimulated to send more and more nerve impulses via the vagus nerve to the expiratory centre. This temporarily inhibits the inspiratory centre and inspiration.

The external intercostal muscles therefore relax, elastic recoil of the lung tissues occurs and expiration takes place. After this has occurred, the bronchial tree is no longer stretched and the stretch receptors no longer stimulated. Therefore the expiratory centre becomes inactive and inspiration can begin again. The whole cycle is repeated rhythmically throughout the life of the organism. Forcible expiration can be achieved by contraction of the internal intercostal muscles.

A basic rhythm of breathing is maintained by the medulla even if all nervous input is cut. However, under normal circumstances various stimuli modify this basic rhythm. The main stimulus that controls breathing is the concentration of carbon dioxide in the blood, rather than the oxygen concentration. When carbon dioxide levels increase (as, for example, during exercise) **chemoreceptors** in the **carotid** and **aortic bodies** of the blood system (fig 9.28) are stimulated and they send nerve impulses to the inspiratory centre. The medulla itself also contains such chemoreceptors. The inspiratory centre then sends out impulses via the external intercostal and phrenic nerves to the external intercostal muscles and diaphragm causing them to increase the rate at which they contract. This increases the rate of inspiration. Carbon dioxide quickly becomes harmful if allowed to build up in the body. It dissolves to form an acid which can start to denature enzymes and other proteins. The body has therefore evolved extremely rapid responses to any increase. An increase of 0.25% in concentration of carbon dioxide in the air can double the ventilation rate. It takes a reduction in oxygen concentration in the air from 20% to 5% to produce a doubling in ventilation rate. Oxygen concentration also has an effect on the breathing rate. However, under normal circumstances there is an abundance of oxygen available, and its influence is relatively minor. Chemoreceptors sensitive to oxygen concentration are located in the medulla and aortic and carotid bodies, as with the carbon dioxide receptors.

Within limits, the rate and depth of breathing are also under **voluntary control** as shown by the ability to hold the breath. Voluntary control is also used during forced breathing, speech, singing, sneezing and coughing. When such control is being exerted, impulses originating in the cerebral hemispheres pass to the breathing centre which then carries out the appropriate action.

The control of inspiration by stretch receptors and chemoreceptors is an example of negative feedback. Negative feedback can be overridden by voluntary activity of the cerebral hemispheres.

9.5.6 Lung volumes and capacities

The average young adult female has a lung capacity of approximately $4\,dm^3$ and the average young adult male $5\,dm^3$. Some definitions and typical figures for a young adult male are given below (see also fig 9.29). Figures for females are about 80% of those for males, reflecting differences in overall body mass.

- **Tidal volume** is the volume of gas exchanged during one breath in and out. It is about $450\,cm^3$ during quiet breathing. After maximal exercise it rises to about $3\,dm^3$.
- If after normal inspiration the male continues to inhale, he can take in an extra $1500\,cm^3$ of air. This is called the **inspiratory reserve volume**.
- If after a normal expiration the male continues to exhale, he can force out an extra $1500\,cm^3$ of air. This is termed the **expiratory reserve volume**.
- **Vital capacity** is the maximum volume of air that can be exchanged during one breath in and out (forced inspiration and expiration). This is about $5.7\,dm^3$ for the male and $4.25\,dm^3$ for the female.
- Even after forced expiration $1500\,cm^3$ of air remain in the lungs. This cannot be expelled and is called the **residual volume**.

During inspiration about $300\,cm^3$ of the tidal volume reaches the alveoli, whilst the remaining $150\,cm^3$ remains in the respiratory tubes, where gaseous exchange does not occur. When expiration follows, this air is expelled from the body as unchanged room air and is termed **dead space air**. The air that reaches the alveoli mixes with the $1500\,cm^3$ of air already present in the alveoli. Its volume is small compared to that of the alveolar air and complete renewal of air in the lungs is therefore necessarily a slow process. The slow exchange between fresh air and alveolar air affects the composition of gases in the alveoli to such a small extent that they remain relatively constant at 13.8% oxygen, 5.5% carbon dioxide and 80.7% nitrogen. Comparison of the composition of gases of inspired, expired and alveolar air is interesting (table 9.4). It is clear that one-fifth of the oxygen inspired is retained for use by the body, and 100 times the amount of carbon dioxide inspired is expelled. The air that comes into close contact with the blood is alveolar air. It contains less oxygen than inspired air, but more carbon dioxide.

Fig 9.29 *Lung volumes and lung capacities as shown by a spirometer. It is normal, as in this case, to publish graphs upside down compared with an actual trace from a spirometer. When using a spirometer the graph goes down while breathing in (air being removed from the lid and lid dropping) and up while breathing out (lid filling and rising).*

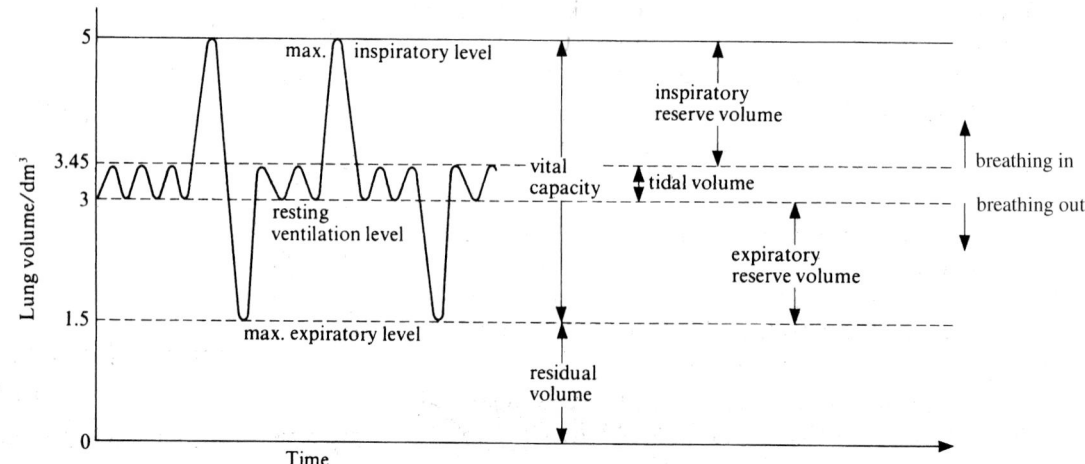

Table 9.4 Percentage composition by volume of gases in inspired, alveolar and expired air.

Gas	Inspired air	Alveolar air	Expired air
Oxygen	20.95	13.8	16.4
Carbon dioxide	0.04	5.5	4.0
Nitrogen	79.01	80.7	79.6

9.5.7 Using a spirometer to measure respiratory activity

An instrument commonly used in schools, laboratories and hospitals for measuring the volume of air which enters and leaves the lungs is the spirometer. Essentially it consists of an air-filled lid (like a box with no bottom) with a capacity of six dm^3 or more, which fits inside a box of water. The lid has an entry tube and an exit tube which come together at a mouthpiece which is placed in the subject's mouth during use. A valve ensures that the air breathed out enters the lid through one tube and leaves through the other. On its return the carbon dioxide can be removed by soda-lime in a canister. (A gradually increasing concentration of carbon dioxide in the spirometer being re-breathed would be dangerous.) Medical grade oxygen may also be used to fill the lid. The air in the subject's lungs and the air in the spirometer is therefore a sealed system.

The lid is counterbalanced so that when gas is passed in or out, it rises or falls accordingly. When the subject breathes out, the lid fills and is raised; when he or she breathes in, the lid drops. A pen attached to the lid writes on a piece of graph paper attached to a slowly rotating drum (**kymograph**), recording the up and down movements of the lid (fig 9.29).

Detailed instructions for the operation of the spirometer are supplied by the manufacturer and will not be dealt with here. However, it is important to be able to analyse the tracings recorded by the spirometer, and to understand what information can be derived from them.

From spirometer tracings the metabolic rate, respiratory quotient, tidal volume, rate of breathing and consumption of oxygen can be measured.

The breathing rate (or ventilation rate) is calculated as the number of breaths taken per minute. Pulmonary ventilation (PV) is expressed in terms of the breathing rate multiplied by the tidal volume:

PV = breathing rate × tidal volume

For example, if breathing rate is 15 breaths per minute and tidal volume is $400\,cm^3$, then PV = $15 \times 400\,cm^3$ = $6000\,cm^3$ per minute (that is $6\,dm^3$ of air will be exchanged between subject and outside environment each minute).

> **9.10** The volume of air exchanged in the alveoli is in fact less than that of the pulmonary ventilation. Suggest why this is the case.

Some further typical figures are as follows:

breathing rate at rest: 15 breaths per minute
breathing rate after maximal exercise: 40–50 breaths per minute
PV at rest: $6.75\,dm^3$ per minute
PV after maximal exercise (tidal volume $3\,dm^3$ per minute × breathing rate 45 per minute) = $135\,dm^3$ per minute
oxygen consumption at rest: 0.25–$0.4\,dm^3$ per minute
oxygen consumption after maximal exercise: $3.6\,dm^3$ per minute (up to $5.1\,dm^3$ per minute for a marathon runner)

Measuring the metabolic rate of an organism

As respiration is directly involved with most metabolic activities within the body, its measurement gives a relatively accurate indication of metabolic activity. The metabolic rate can be calculated by measuring the rate of oxygen consumption. As the oxygen in the spirometer is used, the lid gradually gets lower, assuming carbon dioxide is being absorbed and not returned to the spirometer. The rate of oxygen consumption is measured as the overall drop in the lid over a given time period (see question 9.16, section 9.5.9).

> **9.11** Consider fig 9.30. It can be seen that the smaller the mammal the higher its metabolic rate. Why is this so?
> **9.12** How can you compare the metabolic rates of mammals of different size?

9.5.8 The basal metabolic rate (BMR)

The BMR of an organism is the minimum rate of energy conversion required just to stay alive during complete rest or sleep. Before the BMR of human subjects is measured they undergo a standardised rest period of 12–18 h physical and mental relaxation. No meal is eaten

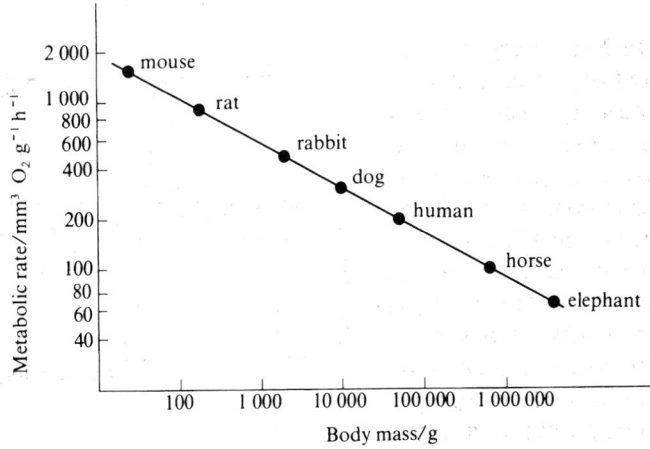

Fig 9.30 *Metabolic rate of animals, calculated per gram body mass, plotted on logarithmic coordinates.*

291

during this time. This ensures that the alimentary canal is empty before measurements are taken. The BMR varies with age, sex, size and state of health of the individual and is clearly correlated with body surface area to volume ratio.

9.5.9 Respiratory quotient (RQ)

Consider the equation:

$$C_6H_{12}O_6 + 6O_2 \longrightarrow 6CO_2 + 6H_2O + energy$$

From this it is quite clear that in a given time the volume of carbon dioxide produced during respiration of carbohydrate is equal to the volume of oxygen consumed (remember, one mole of any gas occupies the same volume under the same conditions of temperature and pressure). The ratio of $CO_2:O_2$ is called the **respiratory quotient**, and for respiration using carbohydrate its value is 1, that is

RQ = volume of CO_2 evolved/volume of O_2 absorbed
(from direct observations)

Or

RQ = moles or molecules of CO_2 evolved/moles or molecules of O_2 evolved (from equations)

Therefore, from the above equation,

RQ = CO_2/O_2 = 6/6 = 1.

> **9.13** The equation for respiration of the fat tripalmitin is:
> $$2C_{51}H_{98}O_6 + 145O_2 \rightarrow 102CO_2 + 98H_2O$$
> What is the RQ for tripalmitin?
>
> **9.14** What is the RQ when glucose is respired anaerobically to ethanol and carbon dioxide?

Determination of respiratory quotients can yield valuable information about the nature of the substrate being used for respiration and the type of metabolism that is taking place (table 9.5).

Table 9.5 Respiratory quotients of a variety of substrates.

RQ	Substrate	
>1.0	carbohydrates plus some anaerobic respiration	
1.0	carbohydrates	
0.9	protein	
0.7	fat, such as tripalmitin	
0.5	fat associated with carbohydrate synthesis	carbon dioxide released during respiration is being put to other uses and therefore not released from the body
0.3	carbohydrate with associated organic acid synthesis	

> **9.15** Why is the usual RQ for humans between 0.7 and 1.0?
>
> **9.16** From the spirometer trace given in fig 9.31 calculate
> (a) breathing rate;
> (b) tidal volume;
> (c) pulmonary ventilation;
> (d) oxygen consumption.

Experiment 9.2: Use of a respirometer to measure oxygen uptake in small terrestrial nonvertebrates such as woodlice

The oxygen uptake by the nonvertebrates in this experiment is measured using a manometer. Fig 9.32 shows the apparatus which is used. It is called a **respirometer** (don't confuse this with a spirometer).

In respiration, oxygen is taken up and carbon dioxide is given off. So to ensure that the manometer is recording oxygen consumption alone, soda-lime is incorporated in the apparatus in order to absorb the carbon dioxide evolved. The apparatus can be used to investigate the effect of temperature on oxygen uptake. A water bath is used in order to keep the temperature of the atmosphere surrounding the organisms constant whilst readings are being taken.

Materials

manometer	clamps and stands
manometer fluid	water bath
1 cm³ syringe	thermometer
2 boiling tubes	stopclock
2 pieces of zinc gauze	graph paper
(to fit the diameter of a	small nonvertebrates such
boiling tube)	as woodlice or blowfly
glass beads (or any	larvae
equivalent non-	soda-lime
absorbent material of	
equal volume to the	
nonvertebrates)	

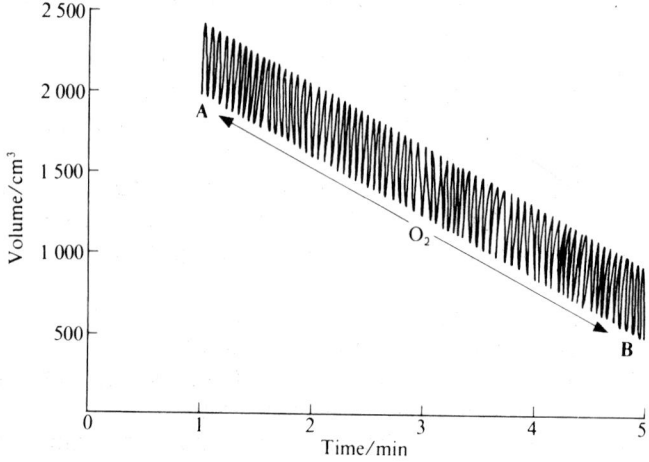

Fig 9.31 *Spirometer tracing of subject at rest.*

Fig 9.32 *Apparatus used in the investigation of oxygen uptake in small terrestrial nonvertebrates.*

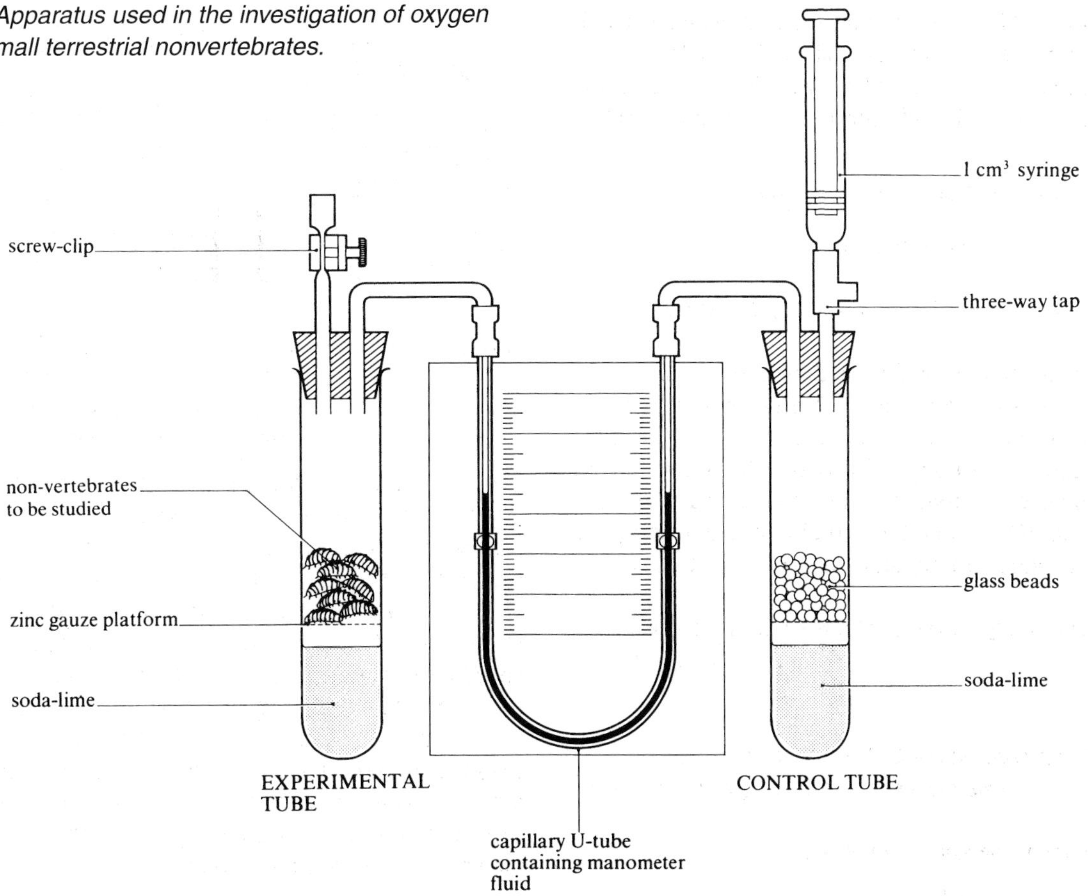

Method

(1) Half fill a manometer with fluid and connect a $1\,cm^3$ syringe to the three-way tap attached to one arm of the manometer.

(2) Place equal volumes of soda-lime in the bottom of each of two boiling tubes and then place a zinc-gauge platform 1 cm above the soda-lime.

(3) Place some nonvertebrates in one boiling tube (experimental) and an equal volume of glass beads in the other tube (control). The animals must not come into contact with the soda-lime and so the platform must be an absolute barrier between the animals and the soda-lime.

(4) Connect the manometer to the two boiling tubes as shown in fig 9.32, and adjust the three-way tap and screw-clip so that the apparatus is open to the atmosphere.

(5) Clamp the apparatus so that the boiling tubes are in a water bath at 20 °C and leave the apparatus at this temperature with the taps open for at least 15 min.

(6) Close the tap and screw-clip, note the position of the manometer fluid and start the stopclock.

(7) At regular intervals, read off the position of the manometer fluid against the scale.

(8) At the end of the experiment open the tap and screw-clip again.

(9) Plot a graph of the change in fluid level against time.

(10) Calculate the rate of oxygen uptake.

(11) Repeat the experiment several times over a range of temperatures, such as 20, 25, 30, 35 and 40 °C.

(12) Plot a graph of rate of oxygen consumption against temperature.

Notes

(1) The fluid that is used in the manometer can be dyed water, oil or mercury. The less dense the fluid, the greater the displacement in the manometer.

(2) In order to measure the change in the manometer fluid levels, a scale must be attached to the manometer. This can be done by attaching the manometer U-tube to a piece of hardboard on which a scale or graph paper has been glued. Alternatively an adhesive metric scale can be attached to the arm of the manometer itself. The scale is available from Philip Harris Ltd.

(3) Before any readings are taken in the experiment, the apparatus must be checked to ensure that it is air-tight. This can be done by pushing air into the apparatus using the syringe, causing the manometer fluid to be displaced. The tap should then be used to close off the apparatus to the atmosphere and, if the apparatus is air-tight, the difference in levels of fluid should not decrease.

9.6 Gaseous exchange in flowering plants

Plants require less energy per unit mass than animals as they possess lower metabolic rates. They do not therefore need to maintain the high rates of gaseous exchange of the more complex animals, and rely on diffusion through spaces between the cells (intercellular air spaces). No special ventilation mechanisms exist. Flowering plants exchange gases by diffusion through pores called **stomata** in their leaves and on their green stems, or if the stems are woody, through cracks in the bark or slits called **lenticels**. Leaves are thin and have a large surface area, as seen in chapter 7 (fig 7.5), and so they are the main sites of gaseous exchange. Inside the leaf of a dicotyledon, there is a spongy mesophyll with large air spaces which allow efficient diffusion. There are also specially large air spaces around the stomata (fig 7.5). Since the system relies on diffusion, water can diffuse out of the plant just as easily. This can be a handicap, as is obvious when plants wilt. Even a small amount of water stress may reduce plant growth (and therefore yield if it is a crop plant). Plants have protective mechanisms whereby they can close their stomata if water is in short supply. This depends on the action of plant hormones, particularly abscisic acid.

Once inside the plant, movement of oxygen is determined by the diffusion gradients that exist in the intercellular air spaces. In this way oxygen travels towards the cells and dissolves in the surface moisture of their walls. From here it passes by diffusion into the cells themselves. Carbon dioxide leaves the plant by the same pathway but in the reverse direction.

The whole situation becomes more complex in photosynthesising plants. Here oxygen is also produced by the chloroplasts as a waste product of photosynthesis. The oxygen may be used up immediately in respiration by mitochondria contained in the same cell, and waste carbon dioxide from respiration may be used by the chloroplasts for photosynthesis.

> **9.17** (*a*) Construct a table showing the major differences between photosynthesis and aerobic respiration.
> (*b*) Make a list of similarities (including biochemical similarities), between photosynthesis and aerobic respiration.

9.7 Respiratory disease and ill health

9.7.1 Short-term effects of smoking on ventilation and gaseous exchange

Smoking has some relatively short-term effects on breathing and gaseous exchange, as well as long-term effects discussed in the following sections (9.7.2–9.7.5):

- nicotine causes constriction of the finer bronchioles, increasing resistance to the flow of air.
- nicotine paralyses the cilia which remove dirt and bacteria; the accumulation of extra material in the air passages can restrict air flow.
- smoke acts as an irritant; this causes secretion of excess mucus from goblet cells and excess fluid into the airways, making it more difficult for air to pass through them.

9.7.2 Asthma

Asthma is a form of difficult or heavy breathing which is caused by spasms of smooth (involuntary) muscle in the walls of the bronchioles. The contractions of the muscle cause the bronchioles to narrow or even close. The person has more difficulty breathing out than breathing in because the pressure from the lungs during breathing out squeezes the tubes even more. During an attack, a characteristic whistling or wheezing sound is caused by breathing, particularly during breathing out. A second problem with asthma is the secretion of excess mucus which is thick and difficult to cough away. This collects in the bronchioles and makes breathing even more difficult. In the long term the mucus can trap bacteria and their growth may cause an infection leading to bronchitis. This will make the asthma even worse. A third factor causing breathing difficulty is swelling of the lining of the respiratory pathway.

The cause of asthma is an over-reaction to one of a variety of possible stimuli. These stimuli normally have no or little effect on the air passages of people who do not suffer from the condition. Commonly, there is an allergic response to substances like pollen, household dust (which contains many possible causes such as mites and the spores of moulds), a particular food, or feathers from a pillow. Emotional disturbance may also provoke an attack. Other triggers include cold air, exercise and smoking. The worrying increase in asthma among children in urban environments is thought to be related to increases in atmospheric pollution from traffic. Certain particles, as well as gases, emitted from exhaust pipes may be responsible, and legal limits on such emissions are gradually becoming stricter in industrialised countries. Asthma, though, is a complex problem and more research is needed to establish who are most at risk and why. Anti-inflammatory drugs are prescribed to help control the problem.

9.7.3 Emphysema

Emphysema is caused by the gradual breakdown of the thin walls of the alveoli. Gradually the air spaces become larger (fig 9.33) and the total surface area for gaseous exchange decreases. The most obvious sign is therefore increasing breathlessness. In advanced cases, patients find it difficult even to walk across a room, and in extreme cases may be confined to a chair unable even to

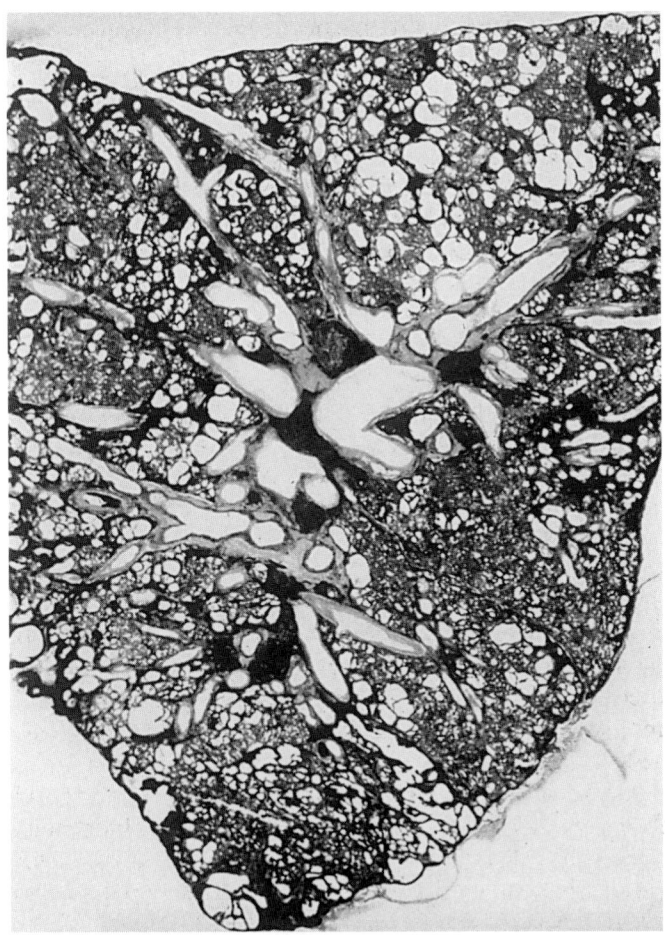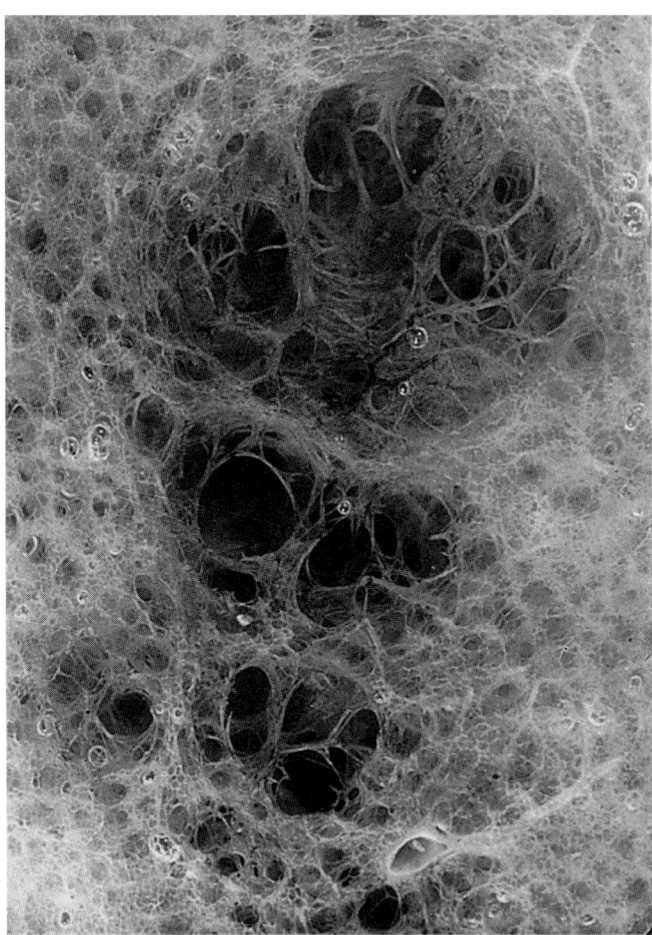

Fig 9.33 (a) *Section of lung from a patient who suffered from emphysema. Note that there are fewer alveoli than usual and the air spaces are larger (compare fig 9.22).* (b) *Close-up view of lung tissue from emphysema lung.*

raise an arm without a noticeable increase in breathing stress. The lungs also lose elasticity, so that it becomes more difficult to exhale air. A lot of air remains in the lung during expiration. This is easily demonstrated by measuring 'forced expiratory volume' (FEV), the amount of air that can be forcibly exhaled in a given time (usually one second) after a maximum inspiration. FEV also declines in asthma sufferers. Breathing out becomes a more conscious activity – the patient is forced to think about it and work to achieve it. Inflammation and narrowing of the finer bronchioles also occurs.

The root cause of emphysema is long-term irritation of the lungs, most commonly by cigarette smoke, air pollution or industrial dust. The damage is caused by both chemical and physical factors. Chemicals in cigarette smoke, for example, disturb the normal balance between breakdown and replacement of elastic tissue. They inhibit enzymes which prevent the breakdown of elastic tissue in the walls of the alveoli and also inhibit repair processes. White blood cells in the lungs secrete protein-digesting enzymes in response to the increasing stress and these also break down the walls of the alveoli. Heavy coughing associated with bronchitis (see below) may also physically damage the walls of the alveoli.

Emphysema is very common in Britain. About 1 person in 100 suffers from it and it is 10 times more common in men than women. Death is typically preceded by years of increasing disability.

9.7.4 Bronchitis

Bronchitis is inflammation of the lining of the air passages and may be chronic or acute. A **chronic** disease is one with a gradual onset and of long duration. An **acute** condition flares up quickly and dies down in a relatively short space of time. **Acute bronchitis** usually lasts a few days only and is a side-effect of an infection like a cold.

Chronic bronchitis is a much more serious and common problem. Britain has the highest death rate in the world from this disease (one person in 2000 every year, about 30 000 people per year). About 1 million others are affected, three times as many men as women. Death rate is six times higher among smokers. It is often associated with emphysema, especially in its late stages. Like emphysema, it is most commonly caused by smoking and to a lesser extent by air pollution. The same sensation of breathlessness occurs, due to reduced gaseous exchange.

The tars in cigarette smoke are the chemicals which are mainly responsible for the inflammation. One symptom of the disease is secretion of excess mucus from the goblet cells in response to the irritation. Smoking destroys or paralyses the cilia which normally sweep away the mucus. The main sign is therefore a cough in which the excess mucus is coughed up as a thick and greenish-yellow sputum. Coughing and breathlessness increase as the disease progresses and the more damaged the system becomes, the more likely infections such as pneumonia are to occur.

9.7.5 Lung cancer

Lung cancer is the most common form of cancer in men in the UK (breast cancer is the most common for women). It is the third most common cause of death in the UK after coronary heart disease and strokes (fig 9.34).

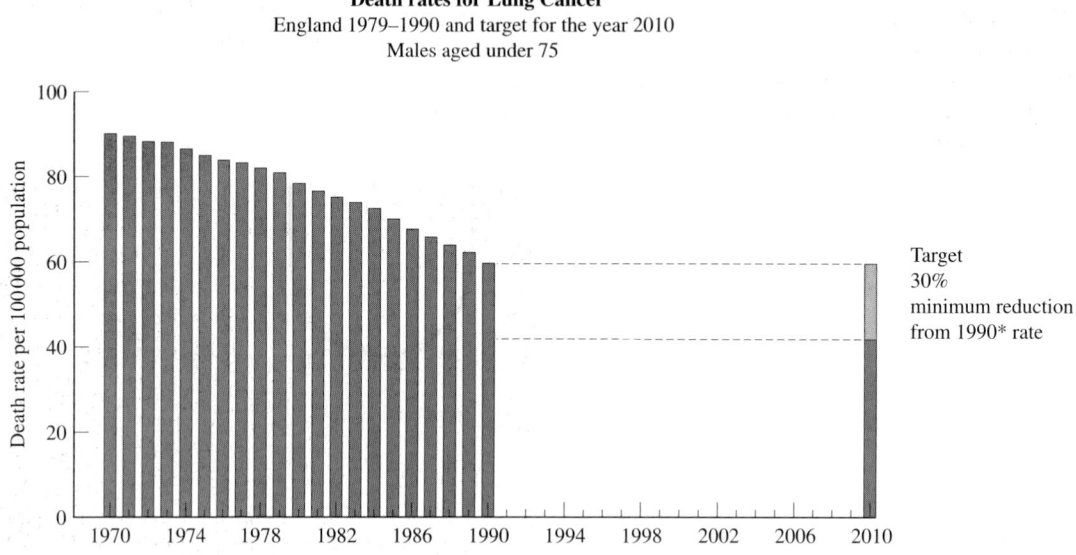

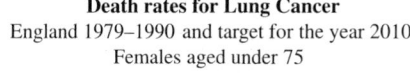

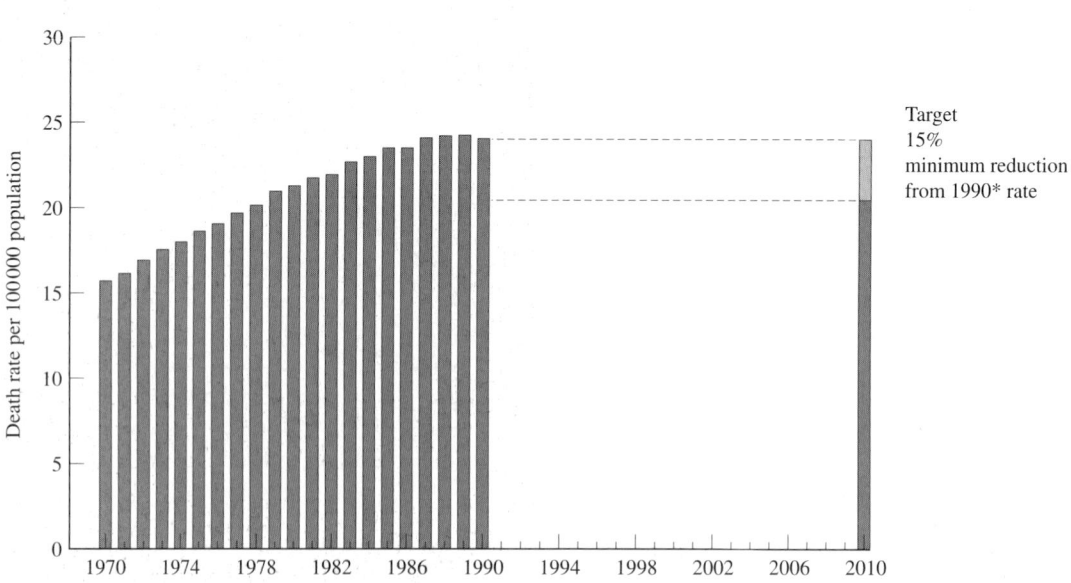

Fig 9.34 *Death rates from lung cancer.*

296

It accounted for about 1 in 18 deaths (5–6%) in Britain during the 1980s. Cancer is caused by cells dividing repeatedly out of control. They cease to respond to the normal signals around them and form unspecialised masses of cells called **tumours** (fig 9.35). Sometimes these cells break away from the original site and invade other tissues of the body to start secondary tumours. Lung cancer usually starts in the epithelium of the bronchioles, so-called bronchial carcinoma. It then usually spreads throughout the lungs. It is caused almost exclusively by smoking (99.7% of those who die from lung cancer are smokers). The tars in the smoke are responsible. They contain chemicals which cause cancer ('carcinogens'). The irritation causes thickening of the epithelium by extra cell division and it may be this that triggers the cancer. As a result of campaigns against smoking, there has been a decline in deaths from lung cancer (fig 9.34).

9.7.6 Effects of ageing on the respiratory system

There is a decline in the efficiency of the respiratory system with ageing. There is a gradual loss of elastic tissue and the chest wall becomes less capable of expansion. These changes show up as a reduction in vital capacity (the maximum volume of air that can be expired after a maximum inspiration). This may decrease by as much as 35% by the age of 70. All other aspects of function decline in performance, notably the action of cilia and the protective activity of white blood cells. This leaves the system more prone to diseases like pneumonia, bronchitis and emphysema.

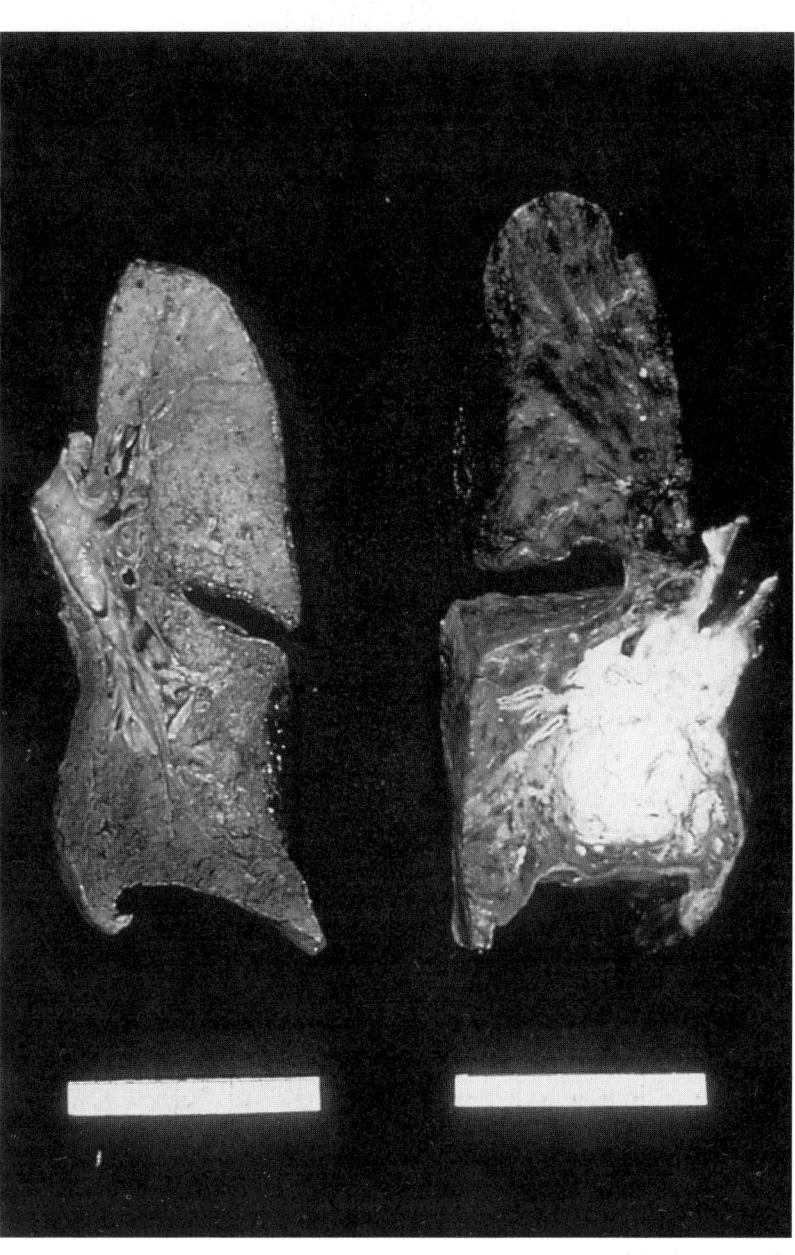

Fig 9.35 *The effect of lung cancer. The lung on the left shows the normal healthy condition. The one on the right shows a large white cancerous growth in the lower part.*

Chapter Ten

Organisms and the environment

Ecology is the study of the relationships of living organisms with each other and their non-living or physical surroundings. Ecological studies give us the scientific foundations for our understanding of agriculture, forestry and fisheries. Ecology also gives us the basis for predicting, preventing and remedying pollution. It helps us to understand the likely consequences of massive environmental intervention, as in the construction of dams or diversion of rivers, and provides the rationale underpinning biological conservation.

The relationship of ecology to other branches of biology is summarised in fig 10.1, which shows that living organisms can be studied at different levels of organisation. Ecology spans the right-hand portion of the diagram, which includes individual organisms, populations and communities. Ecologists regard these as the living part (**biotic component**) of a system called the **ecosystem**. This also includes a non-living part (the **abiotic component**) which contains matter and energy. Populations, communities and ecosystems are terms which have precise meanings in ecology. They are defined in fig 10.1. The different ecosystems together form the **biosphere**, or **ecosphere**, which includes all living organisms and the physical environments with which they interact. Thus, the oceans, land surface and lower parts of the atmosphere all form part of the biosphere.

10.1 Approaches to ecology

The holistic approach (one in which a whole picture is built up that is more important than its parts) is the distinctive characteristic of ecological science. Ecologists must simultaneously consider all of the factors interacting in a particular place. The sheer scope of this task presents problems, and in practice most ecologists adopt one of several main approaches when undertaking a new investigation. These approaches are described below.

- *Ecosystem approach* This approach uses studies which focus on the **exchange of energy and matter** between living and non-living components of the system. The functional relationships between organisms (such as feeding) and between organisms and their environment are emphasised, rather than species composition and identification of rarities.
- *Community approach* Community ecology (synecology) is mainly concerned with the biotic components of ecosystems. One important aspect of community studies is the concept of **succession** and **climax communities** (section 10.6.1).
- *Population approach* Modern population studies (autecology) are concerned with the characteristic mathematical forms of the growth, maintenance and

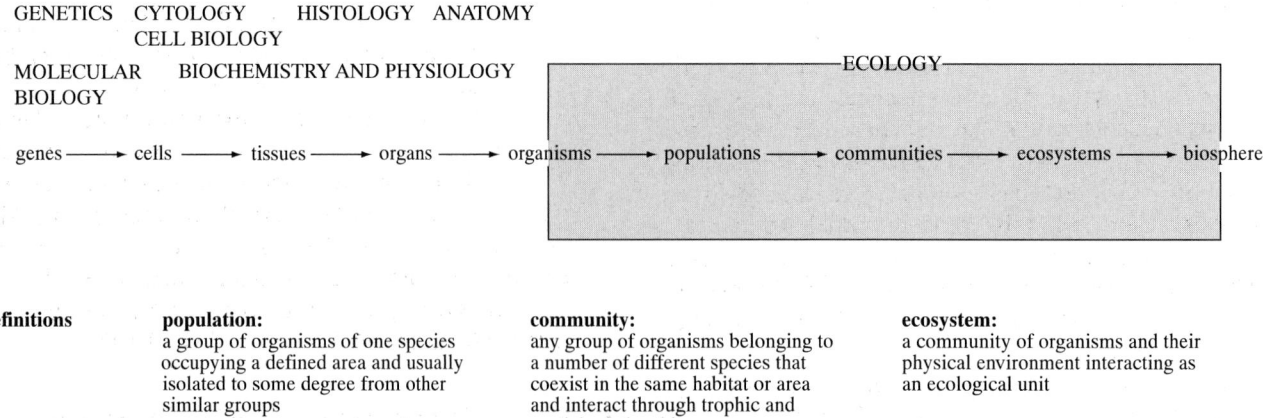

Fig 10.1 *Levels of organisation from genes to ecosystems. The whole planet, the Earth, operates as an ecosystem. The oceans, forests, grasslands etc. are smaller ecosystems which are linked, by energy flow and exchange of materials, to form the overall planetary ecosystem.*

decline of species populations. They provide the scientific basis for understanding 'outbreaks' of pests and disease in agriculture and medicine, and help us to predict the critical numbers of individuals needed for continued survival of a species. Traditional autecology focuses on the environmental relationships of a particular species. It examines how characteristics such as an organism's morphology, behaviour, food preferences and so on are linked with its habitat, distribution and evolutionary history.

- *Habitat approach* **Habitat** is a spatial concept. It describes the typical environment of a particular organism, population, community or ecosystem (section 10.5). Particular locations within the same overall habitat may have their own special conditions and are sometimes referred to as **microhabitats**, such as the bark of a rotting log in an oakwood. The habitat approach is also convenient for studying those characteristics of the physical environment which are intimately linked with plants and animals, such as soils, moisture and light.

- *Evolutionary or historical approach* By studying how ecosystems, communities, populations and habitats have changed over time we can gain insights into why these changes occurred. This gives us a good basis for predicting the likely nature of future change. **Evolutionary ecology** views the changes since life evolved. It examines how events, such as the formation of a mountain barrier, have influenced the form and distribution of species and taxa. It answers questions such as 'why are kangaroos only found in Australia?' and 'why are tropical rain forests so species diverse?' It helps us to understand the triggers for extinction and speciation and at a detailed level to understand why species have a particular size or form, and reproductive strategy. **Palaeoecology** applies our modern knowledge of ecosystems to the study of fossil organisms. It attempts to reconstruct past ecosystems and, in particular, to see how ecosystems and communities functioned before humans became a major influence. **Historical ecology** is concerned with change since the developing technology and culture of humans made human activity a major influence on ecological systems. Understanding the human impact is a vital aspect of conservation management. Distinguishing human-induced and natural biosphere change is an important part of this process which may have economic significance. For example, is acidification a natural ecosystem process or is it wholly due to industrial pollutants and thus avoidable if we modify human behaviour?

These approaches to ecology interact and overlap. However, they provide a useful framework for study. In this chapter it is not possible to consider all in equal depth. We will focus on ecosystems, communities and populations.

10.2 Ecosystems

10.2.1 Definitions and key concepts

Ecosystems are made up of **biotic** and **abiotic** components. The organisms which comprise the biotic component are collectively known as the **community**.

Key points about ecosystems

- **There is a close association between living (biotic) and non-living (abiotic) components.** Both affect each other and are equally important for the ecosystem.

- **Ecosystems can be studied at any level of organisation.** For example you can apply ecosystem principles to a:

puddle ⟶ pond ⟶ lake ⟶ sea ⟶ ocean ⟶ planet

You can also study ecosystems over different time periods. A puddle is best studied over hours or days, whereas the ecological relationships in a lake ecosystem may only become fully apparent over many years.

- **All organisms and all features of the physical environment are necessary for the system to be maintained and flourish.** The tendency for a system to maintain a stable state, a balance between the contributions of all its parts, is known as **homeostasis** (self-regulation). Changes move the system away from equilibrium. Small changes will normally be countered by **feedback** processes within the system and the original equilibrium will be restored. Large changes can alter the state of the system in a major way and move it well away from its original equilibrium point. This happens when the feedback mechanisms cannot respond rapidly enough to maintain the original equilibrium. A new equilibrium will be reached but the original ecosystem may be radically changed or altered.

Changes are not necessarily detrimental; for example the development of scrubland or forest from initial bare ground during ecological succession (section 10.6.1). However, there are many examples where human manipulation of ecosystems has produced unexpected and unwished-for side effects, such as problems with insect pests in simplified agricultural ecosystems. Also, changes may not be immediately obvious. For example, we have only recently understood the link between waste products of fuel combustion and acid damage to lakes and forests (section 10.8.1).

10.2.2 Overall structure of ecosystems

The general structure of an ecosystem can be seen in fig 10.2 which shows, in a simplified way, the overall structure of a terrestrial and an aquatic ecosystem.

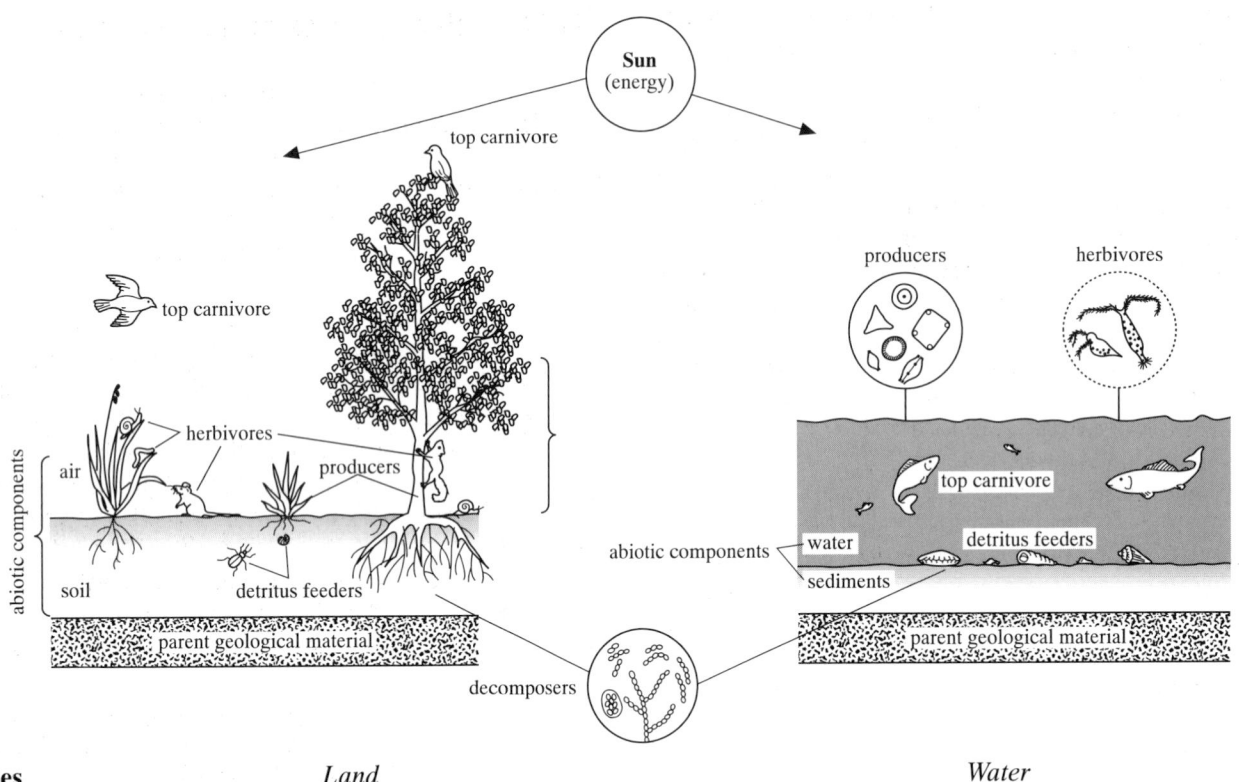

Notes

	Land	Water
producers	trees, herbs, grasses	phytoplankton
primary consumers	small animals e.g. field mouse, squirrel, caterpillar	zooplankton
secondary consumers (top carnivores)	bird of prey	large fish
detritivores	soil non-vertebrates	bottom-living non-vertebrates
decomposers	bacteria and fungi	bacteria and fungi

Fig 10.2 *A simple schematic comparison of terrestrial and aquatic ecosystems (see also section 10.3.2). (Modified from E. P. Odum (1975)* Ecology, *2nd ed., Holt, Rinehart & Wilson.)*

The most striking point is the similarity in ecosystem structure found in these two very different environments. The biotic component of all ecosystems can usefully be subdivided into autotrophic and heterotrophic organisms. Heterotrophs are dependent on autotrophs for their existence. This point is fundamental to our understanding of **food chains** and **food webs** and the movement of energy and nutrients in ecosystems (sections 10.3 and 10.4).

The non-living or abiotic component of an ecosystem includes soil, water and climate. Soil and water contain a mixture of inorganic and organic nutrients. Soil derives most of its physical and chemical properties from its geological parent material. Similarly water quality and salinity are influenced by bedrock and basal sediments and by the soils and rocks of the surrounding area. Climate includes such environmental variables as light, temperature, humidity and rain or snow, which are important influences on the types of living organisms that can flourish in an ecosystem.

The essence of ecosystem studies, however, lies in understanding how connections between the different organisms and their abiotic environment work. **Energy flow** and **biogeochemical cycling** are the important functional links between the different ecosystem components.

10.2.3 Energy flow and biogeochemical cycling

Energy may be defined as the capacity to do work and living organisms can be likened to machines in that they require energy to keep working and stay alive. The energy that powers most ecosystems is ultimately derived from the Sun.* Solar energy is captured by photoautotrophs

---

* Recently deep sea exploration has found areas near hot vents linked to underwater volcanoes which are unexpectedly rich in life. Organisms include previously unknown species. Sunlight cannot reach the ocean depths and life in the deep waters is often sparse, being dependent on organic debris from surface illuminated waters as a food source. In these hot vents, however, it appears that autotrophic bacteria are the primary food suppliers for some unique tube worms and clams. These bacteria feed on hydrogen sulphide released from the hot vents and are therefore chemoautotrophs.

in photosynthesis. Autotrophs in turn form the food source or potential chemical energy supply for all other organisms in the ecosystem.

The chemicals found in living organisms are derived originally from the abiotic components of ecosystems, such as soil, water and air, to which they eventually return by way of the decomposition of the waste products or dead bodies of organisms. Bacteria and fungi bring about decomposition, obtaining energy from the waste products and dead organisms in the process. Thus a constant cycling of the chemical materials needed by living organisms occurs within an ecosystem. Since both living and non-living parts of the ecosystem are involved in these chemical cycles they are called **biogeochemical cycles**.

The energy to drive these cycles is also supplied by the Sun because it drives the Earth's weather systems and regulates Earth surface climates. Temperature, wind speed and direction, evaporation and rainfall, all ultimately depend on the input of solar energy. Rates of erosion and weathering, the breakdown of rocks to fine particles, in turn reflect climatic conditions. Thus the supply of abiotic nutrient elements is also ultimately dependent on solar energy.

While the chemicals in ecosystems are constantly recycled and used again, some of the energy transferred within the ecosystem is changed into forms which cannot be used again by the system, mainly heat energy. To maintain the ecosystem, frequent and regular inputs of solar energy are needed. Thus we make an important distinction between chemical elements which are *recycled* and energy which is said to *flow* through ecosystems. This is illustrated in fig 10.3.

10.3 Ecosystems and energy flow

The study of energy flow through ecosystems is called energetics. The SI unit of energy is the joule, though the traditional unit, the calorie, is still often used. Both units are defined in table 10.1, which also includes references to the energy content of representative foods and organisms, and to daily food requirements of representative organisms.

> **10.1** Why are the figures for energy content in table 10.1 quoted for dry mass rather than fresh (wet) mass?
>
> **10.2** Account for the large difference in daily energy requirements of humans and small birds or mammals on a weight for weight basis.

Table 10.1 Units of energy and energy content of some living organisms and biological molecules.

Energy units

calorie (cal) or gram calorie	–	the amount of heat (or energy) needed to raise the temperature of one gram of water through 1 °C (14.5 °C to 15.5 °C)
kilocalorie (kcal or Cal)	–	1000 cal
joule (J)	–	10^7 ergs: 1 erg is the amount of work done when 1 newton moves through 1 metre (1 newton (N) is a unit of force) Alternatively 981 ergs is the work done in raising a gram weight against the force of gravity to a height of 1 cm
kilojoule (kJ)		1000 J

[1 J = 0.239 cal   1 cal = 4.186 J]

Energy content (*averages or approximations*)

	joules per gram dry mass (energy value)
carbohydrate	16.7
protein	20.9
lipid	38.5
terrestrial plants	18.8
algae	20.5
non-vertebrates	12.6
(excl. insects)	22.6
vertebrates	23.4

(differences between these groups of organisms are due partly to different mineral contents)

Daily food requirements	*kJ per kg live body mass*
humans	167 (about 12 500 kJ day^{-1} for a 70 kg adult)
small bird or mammal	4186
insect	2093

Based on data from table 3.1, Odum, E.P. (1971) *Fundamentals of Ecology*, 3rd. ed. Saunders.

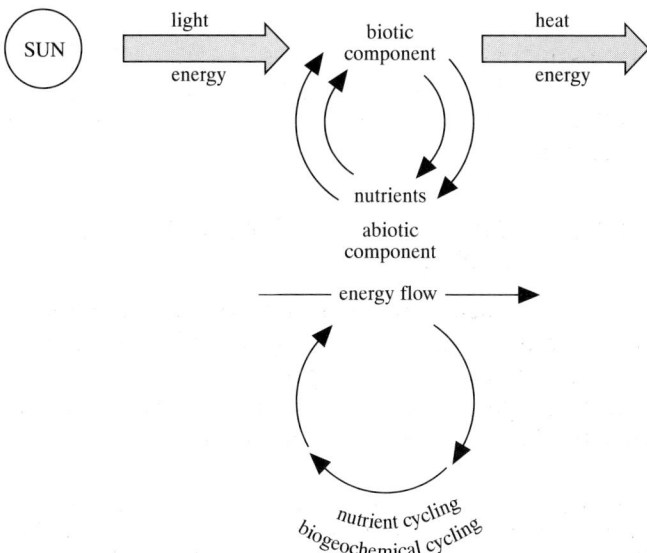

Fig 10.3 *Schematic summary of an ecosystem showing energy flow and nutrient or biogeochemical cycling.*

10.3.1 The Sun as a source of energy

As we have seen the Sun is usually the ultimate source of energy in ecosystems. Of the Sun's energy which reaches the Earth, about 40% is reflected immediately from the clouds, dust in the atmosphere and the Earth's surface without having any heating effect. A further 15% is absorbed and converted to heat energy in the atmosphere, particularly by ozone in the stratosphere, and by water vapour. The ozone layer absorbs almost all short-wave ultraviolet radiation which is important because such radiation is hazardous to exposed living material. The remaining 45% of incoming energy penetrates to the Earth's surface. This represents an average of about $5 \times 10^6 \, kJ \, m^{-2} \, yr^{-1}$, though the actual amount for a given locality varies with latitude and local features such as aspect and climate. Just under half the radiation striking the Earth's surface is in the **photosynthetically active range (PAR)**, the visible wavelengths. However, even under optimum conditions only a very small proportion, about 5% of incoming radiation (or 10% PAR) is converted in photosynthesis into **gross primary productivity (GPP)**. A more typical figure for good conditions is 1% of total radiation (2% PAR) while the biosphere average is about 0.2% of total incident radiation. **Net primary productivity (NPP)** (the net gain of organic material in photosynthesis after allowing for losses due to respiration) varies between 50 and 80% of gross primary productivity (see section 10.3.5).

As a global average the energy fixed by Earth's green plants is only 0.1% of that received by the Earth. Terrestrial systems, which cover the 30% of the Earth which is not covered by oceans, fix half the total sunlight captured. Cultivated crops achieve higher rates of GPP and NPP during their short growing periods, but so far it has proved impossible to achieve higher rates of photosynthetic fixation on a sustained basis under normal field conditions.

10.3.2 Energy transfers: food chains and trophic levels

The energy-containing organic molecules produced by autotrophic organisms are the source of food (materials and energy) for heterotrophic organisms. These animals may in turn be eaten by other animals, and in this way energy is transferred through a series of organisms, each feeding on the preceding organism and providing raw materials and energy for the next organism. Such a sequence is called a **food chain**, or the **grazing link** in the ecosystem. Each stage of the food chain is known as a **trophic level** (*trophos*, food). The first trophic level is occupied by the autotrophic organisms, called **producers**. The organisms of the second trophic level are usually called **primary consumers** while those of the third level are called **secondary consumers**, and so on.

There are usually four or five trophic levels, and seldom more than six. This is partly because at every feeding stage some energy is wasted from the chain of animals feeding on each other. This point is also evident from figs 10.4 and 10.10 and relates to the discussion in section 10.3.5. Recent work has, however, suggested that factors other than energy loss may also be important in limiting the length of food chains. The availability of sufficient food of the preferred types and territorial space may also restrict the numbers of end-of-chain organisms and thus the length of food chains.

It is estimated that in some ecosystems as much as 80% of primary production is not eaten by primary consumers. Instead, on death, plant material is consumed in various ways by detrital feeders and decomposer organisms. Food chains in which most primary production is decomposed or consumed as detritus are termed **detrital food chains**. Tropical moist forests are a noteworthy example of ecosystems where the detrital link is more important than the grazing link.

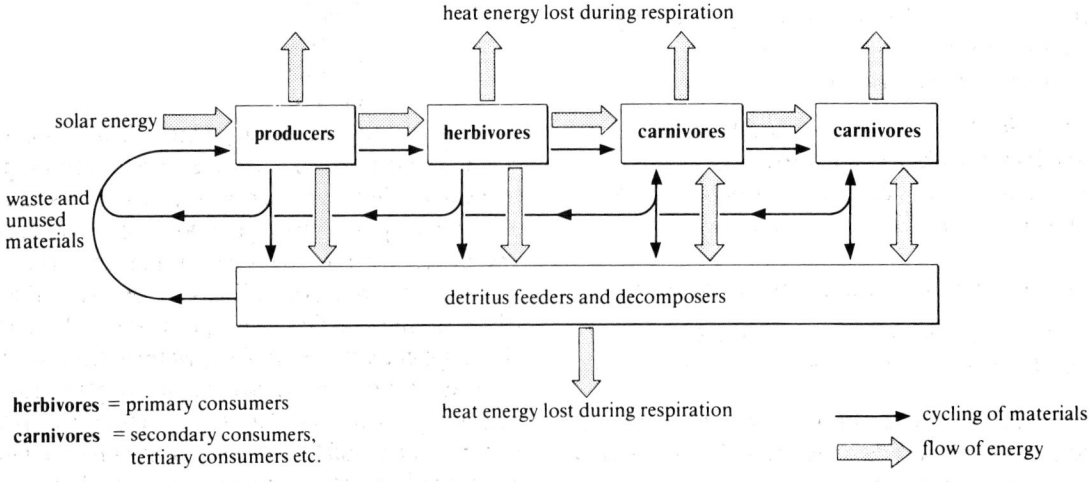

Fig 10.4 *Flow of energy and cycling of materials through a typical food chain. Note that a two-way exchange is possible between carnivores and detritus feeders/decomposers. The latter feed on dead carnivores; carnivores may eat living detritus feeders/decomposers.*

Producers

The producers are autotrophic organisms, and are typically green plants and algae. Some bacteria, such as blue-green bacteria, also photosynthesise and are thus also producers. Microscopic algae and blue-green bacteria are the main producers in aquatic ecosystems and are known as **phytoplankton**. These contrast with terrestrial ecosystems in which larger plants dominate, such as the grasses characteristic of savannah, steppe and many agricultural ecosystems and the conifer and broadleaf trees of forest ecosystems.

Primary consumers

Primary consumers feed on producers. They are therefore also called **herbivores**. Some primary consumers do not eat the producer but live as plant parasites, such as aphids, some fungi and even other plants (e.g. broomrape, *Orobanche*, an unusual plant with no chlorophyll). More common are plants such as mistletoe, which parasitises its host tree for nutrients but has its own chlorophyll system and thus is also a producer.

On land, herbivores typically include insects, reptiles, birds and mammals. In aquatic ecosystems (freshwater and marine) herbivores are typically small crustaceans, such as water fleas, crab larvae and barnacles, and molluscs which include bivalves such as mussels and clams. Most are filter-feeders and extract the producers from the water as described in section 8.2.1. Together with protozoans, many of them form the **zooplankton**, the small or microscopic drifting animals which feed on the phytoplankton. Life in the oceans and lakes is almost totally dependent on planktonic organisms which are found at the beginning of virtually all food chains.

Secondary and tertiary and other top consumers

Secondary consumers feed on herbivores and are thereby flesh eaters or carnivores. Tertiary and other higher order consumers that feed on the secondary (or tertiary as appropriate) consumers are also carnivores.

Secondary and tertiary consumers may be:

- **predators**, which hunt, capture and kill their prey;
- **carrion feeders**, which feed on corpses;
- **parasites** which do not eat their prey but feed off the host organism while it continues to live.

Two examples of predator food chains are given below.

plant (such as leaves) → slug → frog → grass snake → stoat
rosebush sap → aphid → ladybird → spider → insectivorous bird → hawk

Typically carnivores become larger and fewer in number at each successive trophic level. Parasite food chains are very different; the parasites get smaller at successive trophic levels and typically increase in number.

10.3 Give example food chains for any major habitat you have investigated, e.g. marine, freshwater, woodland, grassland, etc.

Decomposers and detrivores (detrital food chains)

When organisms die their bodies form a source of energy and raw materials (nutrients) for other organisms. Similarly waste materials passed from the bodies of living organisms are also a source of energy and nutrients. These materials are not wasted by ecosystems. They form the food for many other organisms referred to as **decomposers** and **detritivores**.

Decomposers are microorganisms, mainly fungi and bacteria, which live as saprotrophs on **dead organic matter (DOM)**. They secrete digestive enzymes onto dead or waste material and absorb the products of digestion. **Detritivores** feed on small fragments of decomposing or dead material termed detritus. Many small animals in both terrestrial and aquatic ecosystems are detrital feeders. Examples include ragworms in estuarine environments, sludgeworms in fresh waters and on land earthworms, woodlice and very small animals such as mites and springtails. Methods for isolating and examining some of these organisms are given in section 11.2.

Detritivores may be fed upon by carnivores which may then be consumed by other carnivores, thus building up a food chain based on detritus. These are termed **detrital food chains** to distinguish them from the **grazing food chains** we have already described where living primary producers form the base of the food chain. Two typical detritus food chains of woodlands are:

leaf litter → earthworms → blackbird → sparrowhawk
Lumbricus spp. *Turdus nerula* *Accipiter nisus*

dead animal → blowflies and blowfly maggots (larvae) *Calliphora vomitoria* → common frog → grass snake
Rana temporaria *Natrix natrix*

Rates of decomposition vary with substrate and climate. The organic matter of animal urine, faeces and corpses may be consumed within a matter of weeks, whereas fallen trees and branches may take many years to decompose. Essential to the breakdown of wood (and other plant material) is the action of fungi which produce cellulase, softening the wood and allowing small animals to penetrate and ingest material. Decomposition is most rapid in warm and moist environments, such as tropical rainforest, but takes place slowly in cool and/or dry conditions. The virtual absence of litter from the rainforest floor and the low content of humus in rainforest soils by comparison with the conspicuous litter layer and significant humus content of soils in temperate oakwoods or beechwoods reflect this point. This has important implications for human use of these systems (see section 10.9.5).

10.3.3 Food webs

In food chains each organism is shown as feeding on only one other type of organism. However, the feeding relationships within an ecosystem are usually far more complex than this. Most organisms feed on more than one other organism. Some feed in both grazing and detrital food chains. This is particularly true of carnivores at the higher trophic levels. Many carnivores have highly varied diets and operate as secondary, tertiary, quaternary and higher consumers. Some animals, including humans, feed on organisms at all trophic levels; plants, animals and fungi. These organisms are called **omnivores**.

Grazing and detrital food chains interlink in a complex manner. An earthworm, for example, may feed as both a herbivore (fine rootlets) and a detritivore. Waste products and dead bodies from every trophic level form the raw materials for detrital food chains. This mesh of interlinking food chains that characterises the real world is called a **food web**. Fig 10.5 illustrates woodland and freshwater food webs. Only some of the many possible interrelationships can be shown on such diagrams and it is usual to include only one or two carnivores at the highest level. Such diagrams illustrate the feeding relationships among organisms in an ecosystem and provide a basis for more quantitative studies of energy flow and exchange of material through the biotic component of ecosystems.

10.3.4 Ecological pyramids

The first pyramid diagrams were prepared by Charles Elton in the 1920s. His pyramids were based on field observations of the numbers of animals in different size classes. He did not include primary producers, nor distinguish detritivores and decomposers in his model. However, Elton observed that predators were typically larger than their prey and realised that this relationship was quite specialised for particular sizes of predator and prey. In the 1940s, the American ecologist Raymond Lindeman suggested that Elton's idea could be adapted to a trophic model, that is one based directly on the feeding levels of organisms irrespective of their sizes. However, while it is a straight-forward matter to assign animals to different size classes, it is much more difficult to identify their trophic level. We can do this only in the most general terms.

> **10.4** Using the information from fig 10.5a and section 10.3.2 on consumer organisms, identify and write out food chains for a hawk at trophic levels 3, 4, 5 and 6.

Feeding relationships and the efficiency of energy transfer through the biotic component of ecosystems have traditionally been summarised in pyramid diagrams. These give an apparently simple and fundamental basis for comparing:

- different ecosystems;
- seasonal variation within a particular ecosystem;
- change in an ecosystem.

Three types of pyramid have been used. These are:

- pyramids of numbers, based on counting the numbers of organisms at each trophic level;
- pyramids of biomass, which note the weight (usually dry weight) of organisms at each trophic level;
- pyramids of energy, which monitor the energy content of the organisms at each trophic level.

Energy pyramids are considered the most important since they deal directly with the fundamentals of food chains, the flow of energy.

Pyramids of numbers

In a numbers pyramid based on trophic levels, the organisms of a given area are first counted and then grouped into their trophic levels (as best one can). When this is done, a progressive decrease in the number of organisms at each successive level is often found. For diagrammatic purposes the number of organisms in a given trophic level can be represented as a rectangle whose length (or area) is proportional to the number of organisms in a given area (or volume if aquatic). An idealised numbers pyramid is shown in fig 10.6a.

Although the data needed to construct pyramids of numbers may be relatively easy to collect by straightforward sampling techniques, there are a number of complications associated with their use. Three important problems are as follows.

- Producers vary greatly in size, but a single grass plant or alga, for example, is given the same status as a single tree. This explains why a true pyramid shape is often not obtained (see fig 10.6b). Parasitic food chains may also give inverted pyramids.
- The range of numbers is so great that it is often difficult to draw the pyramids to scale. Although logarithmic scales may be used, their interpretation needs care.
- The trophic level of an organism may be difficult to ascertain.

> **10.5** What changes would you expect to occur to the pyramid of numbers shown in fig 10.6b during the midwinter season?

Pyramids of biomass

Some of the disadvantages of using pyramids of numbers can be overcome by using a **pyramid of biomass** in which the total mass of the organisms (**biomass**) is estimated for each trophic level. Such estimates involve weighing representative individuals, as well as recording numbers, and so are more laborious and expensive in terms of time

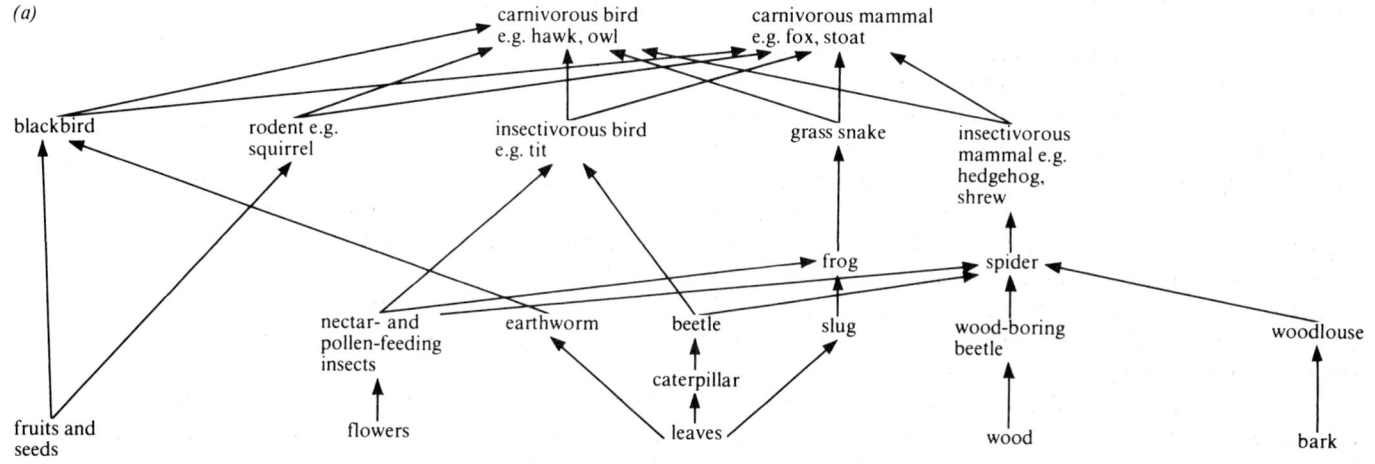

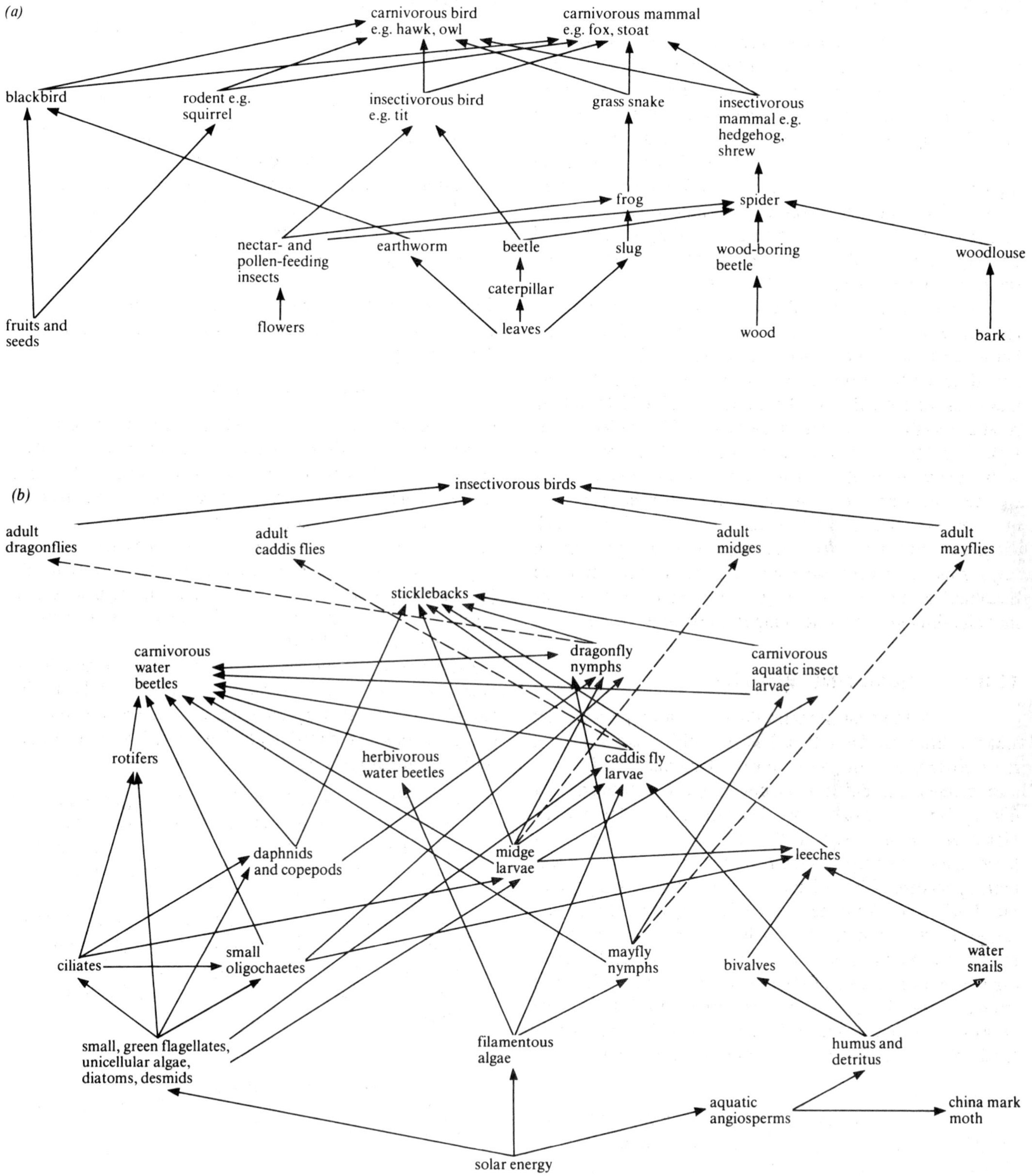

(a)

(b)

Fig 10.5 *(a) Feeding relationships in a woodland, forming a food web. (b) Food web of a freshwater habitat (based on Popham (1955) Some aspects of life in fresh water, Heinemann).*

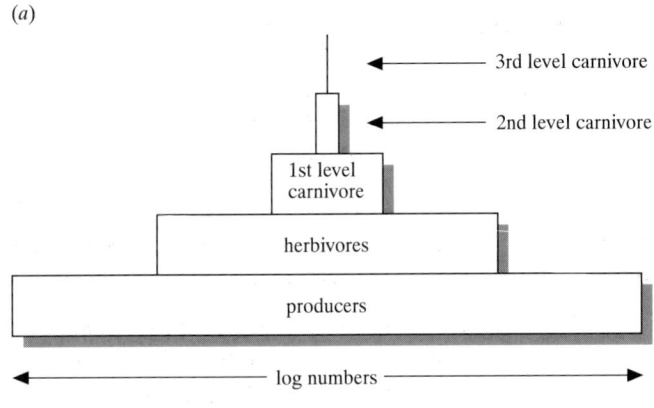

(a)

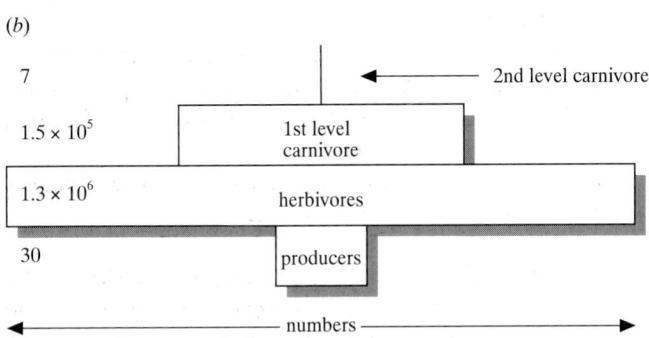

(b)

7
1.5×10^5
1.3×10^6
30

Fig 10.6 *(a) Schematic diagram of a typical pyramid of numbers. The width of the boxes indicates the relative numbers of organisms at each trophic level. The most convenient horizontal scale is logarithmic. The highest carnivores are sometimes referred to as 'top carnivores'. (b) Inverted pyramid of numbers in Wytham oak wood, Oxford. The horizontal scale is logarithmic. The numbers at the left-hand side refer to the numbers of the organisms at each trophic level per hectare. Only oaks were counted as producers. (Data from Varley, 1970.)*

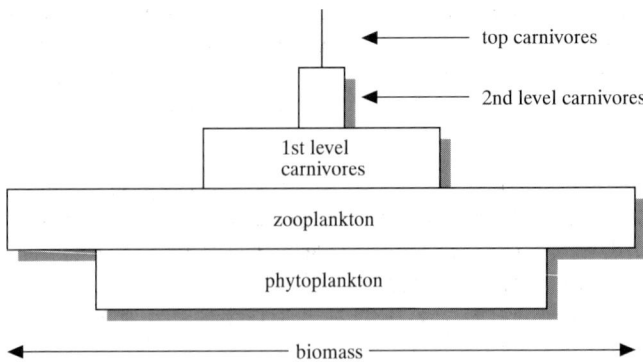

Fig 10.7 *A biomass pyramid from an aquatic ecosystem. The width of the boxes indicates the relative amounts of biomass present at each trophic level. The pyramid is inverted, as frequently happens in food chains which start with phytoplankton. These organisms are very small and have a much more rapid turnover than their zooplankton predators.*

- If the rate of consumption (loss through being used as food) more or less equals the rate of production, the standing crop does not necessarily give any indication of productivity, that is the amounts of material and energy passing from one trophic level to the next in a given time period such as one year. For example, a fertile, intensely grazed pasture may have a smaller standing crop of grass, but a higher productivity, than a less fertile and ungrazed pasture.

- If the producers are small, such as algae, they have a high turnover rate, that is a high rate of growth and reproduction balanced by a high rate of consumption or death. Thus, although the standing crop may be small compared with large producers such as trees, the productivity may be the same. Put another way, a group of phytoplankton with the same productivity as a tree would have a much smaller biomass than a tree, even though it could support the same amount of animal life. In general, the larger, longer-lived plants and animals have lower 'turnover rates' than the smaller, shorter-lived plants or algae and animals, and accumulate materials and energy over a longer time period. One possible consequence of this is shown in fig 10.7 where the first two levels of the pyramid of biomass are inverted. The zooplankton are shown to have a higher biomass than the phytoplankton on which they feed. This is characteristic of ocean and lake planktonic communities at certain times of year; phytoplankton biomass exceeds zooplankton biomass during the spring 'bloom', but at other times the reverse is often true. Such apparent anomalies are avoided by using pyramids of energy as described below.

These differences may also highlight useful information. For example, persistence of an algal bloom and a broad-based biomass pyramid in an aquatic ecosystem may indicate the onset of eutrophication (section 10.8.2).

and equipment. Ideally, dry masses should be compared. These can either be estimated from wet masses or can be determined by destructive methods (experiment 11.2). The rectangles used in constructing the pyramid then represent the masses of organisms at each trophic level per unit area or volume. Fig 10.7 shows a pyramid of biomass from an aquatic ecosystem. Note that the biomass of the producers (phytoplankton) is smaller than the primary consumers (zooplankton), but the pyramid becomes a typical shape above this level. The biomass at the time of sampling, in other words at a given moment in time, is known as the **standing biomass** or **standing crop biomass**. It is important to realise that this figure gives no indication of the *rate* of production (**productivity**) or consumption of biomass. This can be misleading in two ways.

Similarly, the frequent inversion of marine pyramids suggests that for these systems harvesting plant or algal material rather than animal biomass is not the sensible strategy it appears to be for many terrestrial ecosystems.

10.6 Fig 10.8 shows the standing crop biomass of producers and primary consumers in a lake throughout the year, as well as certain environmental variables.
(a) In what months could an inverted pyramid of biomass be obtained?
(b) What factors account for (i) the spring rise in phytoplankton production, (ii) the rapid decline in phytoplankton in the summer, (iii) the increase in phytoplankton in the autumn, (iv) the decrease in phytoplankton during the winter?

Pyramids of energy

The most fundamental and ideal way of representing relationships between organisms in different trophic levels is by means of a pyramid of energy. This has a number of advantages.

- It takes into account the *rate* of production, in contrast to pyramids of numbers and biomass which depict the standing states of organisms at a particular moment in time. Each bar of a pyramid of energy represents the amount of energy per unit area or volume that flows through that trophic level in a given time period. In fig 10.9 a pyramid of energy for an aquatic ecosystem is shown.

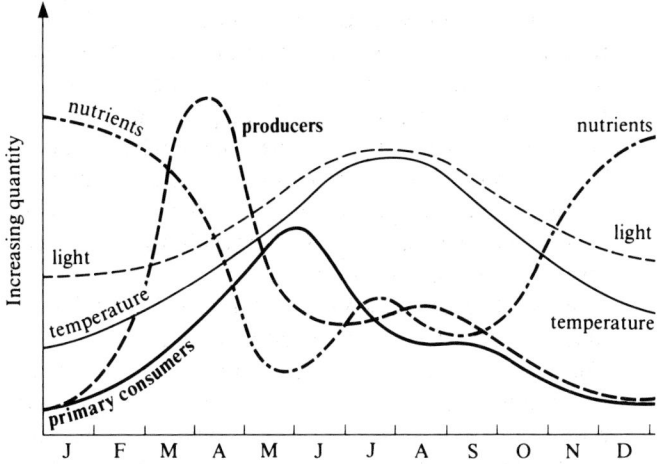

Fig 10.8 *Changes in standing crop biomass of producers and primary consumers and in certain environmental variables in a lake during one year. (From M.A. Tribe, M.R. Erant and R.K. Snook (1974)* Ecological principles, Basic Biology Course 4, *CUP.)*

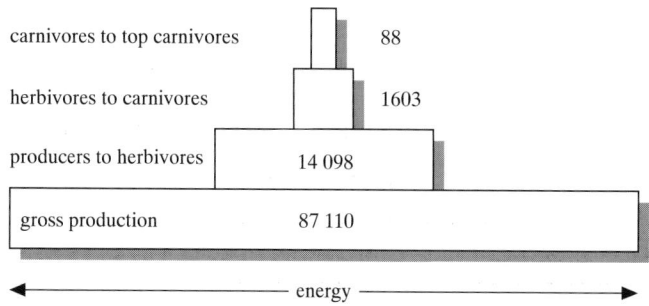

Fig 10.9 *An energy pyramid for Silver Springs, Florida. The figures represent energy flow in kJ m^{-2} yr^{-1}. (From E.P. Odum (1971)* Fundamentals of ecology, *3rd edition, W.B. Saunders.)*

- Weight for weight, two species do not necessarily have the same energy content, as table 10.1 indicates. Comparisons based on biomass may therefore be misleading.
- Apart from allowing different ecosystems to be compared, the relative importance of populations within one ecosystem can be compared and inverted pyramids are not obtained.
- Input of solar energy can be added as an extra rectangle at the base of the pyramid of energy.

Although pyramids of energy are sometimes considered the most useful of the three types of ecological pyramid, they are the most difficult to obtain data for because they require even more measurements than pyramids of biomass. One extra piece of information needed is the energy values for given masses of organisms. This requires combustion of representative samples. In practice, pyramids of biomass can sometimes be converted to pyramids of energy with reasonable accuracy, based on previous experiments.

Problems with ecological pyramids

- The most fundamental problem is that of identifying an organism's trophic level. As discussed above, many organisms feed at several trophic levels.
- Some ecologists also consider that assigning all plant material to the producer level may be inappropriate. Many plants have organs such as tubers or produce fruits and seeds which do not contain chlorophyll. These structures are plant products rather than primary producing photosynthetic organs. Many herbivores cannot digest chlorophyll; others are highly selective in their diet, eating only seeds or fruits or nectar. Many ecologists think that the trophic level model described by ecological pyramids should be adapted to take account of these important differences.
- Another difficulty is that DOM is often omitted from pyramid diagrams. Yet, as we have already noted, as much as 80% of all energy fixed by producers may not be eaten by consumers but by detritivores or is used by decomposers.

10.3.5 Efficiency of energy transfer: production ecology

The study of productivity is known as **production ecology**, and involves the study of energy flow through ecosystems. Energy enters the biotic component of the ecosystem through the producers, and the rate at which this energy is stored by them in the form of organic substances which can be used as food materials is known as **primary productivity**. This is an important parameter to measure as it determines the total energy flow through the biotic component of the ecosystem, and hence the amount (biomass) of life which the ecosystem can support.

> **10.7** In considering the primary productivity of an ecosystem, which groups of organisms other than plants make a contribution?

As mentioned in section 10.3.1, the amount of the Sun's radiation intercepted by the Earth's surface varies with latitude and with details of location such as aspect and altitude. The amount intercepted by plants also varies with light quality and the organisation and amount of vegetation cover. In Britain, incident radiation on plants averages about $1 \times 10^6 \text{ kJ m}^{-2} \text{ yr}^{-1}$. Of this, as much as 95–99% is immediately lost from the plant by reflection, radiation or heat of evaporation. The remaining 1–5% of incoming radiation is absorbed by the chlorophyll and used in the production of organic molecules. The rate at which this chemical energy is stored by plants is known as **gross primary productivity (GPP)**. Between 20–25% of the GPP is used by the plant in simultaneous respiration and photorespiration, leaving a net gain known as the **net primary productivity (NPP)** which is stored in the plant.

It is this energy which is potentially available to the next trophic level.

When herbivores and carnivores consume other organisms, food (materials and energy) is thereby transferred from one trophic level to the next. Not all of the energy and materials available in the food is used by the consumer organisms for production. Some energy is lost as heat in respiration. Other losses occur in the organic waste products of metabolism and are **excreted**. Some food materials remain undigested and are lost immediately in the process of **egestion**.

food consumed = growth + respiration + egesta + excreta

These waste products are used as food sources by decomposers and detritivores.

Some of these terms can be measured easily in domestic animals or in laboratory studies of wild animals. Growth is measured as increase in biomass, or better as increase in energy value of the body, with time. Faeces and excreta can be collected, weighed and subtracted from the mass of food consumed to determine food retained and used for growth and respiration.

The energy remaining in heterotrophs after losses through egestion, excretion and respiration is available for production, that is growth, repair and reproduction. Production by heterotrophs is called **secondary production** (whatever the trophic level).

Fig 10.10 shows clearly that energy is lost at every stage in the food chain and the length of the food chain is obviously limited by the extent of these losses. The proportion of energy lost in the first transfer of energy from solar energy received to net primary production is high. Subsequent transfers are much more efficient. The average efficiency of transfer from plants to herbivores is about 10% and from animal to animal is about 20%. In general, herbivores make less efficient use of their food than do

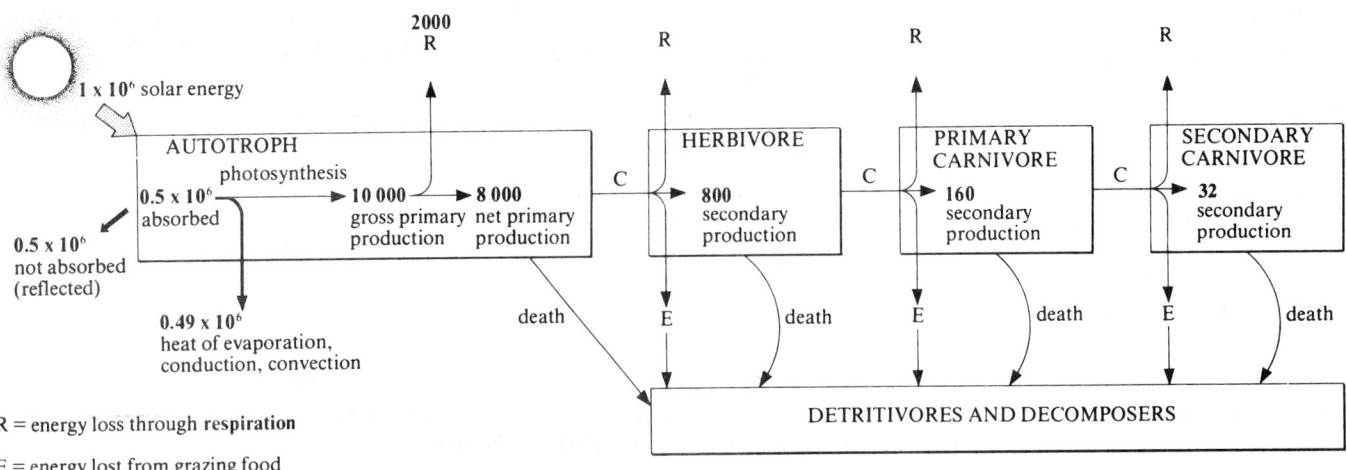

R = energy loss through **respiration**

E = energy lost from grazing food chain to detritivores and decomposers through **excretion** (e.g. urine) and **egestion** (e.g. faeces)

C = **consumption** by organisms at the higher trophic level

all energy values given in kilojoules (kJ)

Fig 10.10 *Energy flow through a grazing chain, such as a grazed pasture. Figures represent kJ m^{-2} yr^{-1}.*

carnivores because plants contain a high proportion of cellulose and sometimes wood which are relatively indigestible and therefore unavailable as energy sources for most herbivores.

Energy lost in respiration cannot be transferred to other living organisms. However, the energy lost from a food chain in the form of excreta and egesta is not lost to the ecosystem because it is transferred to detritivores and decomposers. Similarly, any dead organisms, fallen leaves, twigs and branches and so on will start detritus and decomposer food chains. Detrital pathways are often complex and are less well understood than the conventionally described grazing pathways. Nevertheless they are just as important and, in terms of energy flow, frequently more important than grazing pathways.

The proportion of net primary production flowing directly into detritus and decomposer food chains varies from one system to another. In a forest ecosystem most of the primary production enters the detrital rather than the grazing pathway, with the result that the litter and humus on the forest floor is the centre of much of the consumer activity, even though the organisms involved are mostly inconspicuous. However, in an ocean ecosystem or an intensively grazed pasture more than half the net primary production may enter the grazing food chain. Most intensive agricultural systems ignore the potential value of detritus-based food production.

The figures quoted in this section have been on an annual basis. If the ecosystem is stable, that is not changing such as during succession (section 10.6.1), the total biomass at the end of the year will be the same as at the beginning. All the energy that went into primary production will then have passed through the various trophic levels and none retained as net production. Quite often, however, an ecosystem will be in a process of change. A young forest, for example, would retain some of the energy input in the form of increased biomass at the end of the year. A year is a useful period over which to express productivity because it takes into account seasonal variations where these exist. For example, primary productivity is usually greater in the part of the year when new plant or algal growth commences and secondary production increases later.

One of the reasons for studying energy flow through ecosystems is that it has important implications for the way in which humans obtain their own food and energy requirements. It opens the way to analysing agricultural systems for their efficiency, and suggests where improvements can be made. Since energy is lost at each trophic level, it is clear that, for omnivores like humans, eating plants is a more efficient way of extracting energy from a system (table 10.2). However, in suggesting improved methods for providing food, other factors must be considered. For example, animal protein is generally a better source of the essential amino acids, though some pulse crops, such as soyabean, are richer sources than most plants. Also animal protein is more easily digested, since the tough plant cell walls must first be broken down before the plant protein is released. Finally, there are many ecosystems where animals can concentrate food from large areas where it would be difficult to grow or harvest plant crops. Examples are grazing on poor quality pasture land, such as by sheep in Britain, reindeer in Scotland and Scandinavia and eland in East Africa, or taking fish from aquatic ecosystems.

Table 10.2 Outputs of agricultural food chains in UK.

Food chain	Example	Energy yield of food to humans ($kJ \times 10^3\ ha^{-1}$)	Protein yield of food to humans ($kg\ ha^{-1}\ yr^{-1}$)
(a) Cultivated plant crop ⟶ humans	Monocultures of wheat and barley	7800–11 000	42
(b) Cultivated plant crop ⟶ livestock ⟶ humans	Barley-fed beef and bacon pigs	745–1423	10–15
(c) Intensive grassland ⟶ livestock ⟶ humans	Intensive beef herd on carefully managed pasture		
	Meat	339	4
	Milk	3813	46
(d) Grassland and crops ⟶ livestock ⟶ humans	Mixed dairy farm		
	Milk	1356	17

Data from Duckham, A.N. & Mansfield, G.B. (1970) *Farming systems of the world*, Chatto and Windus.

10.4 Biogeochemical cycles – the cycling of matter

Biogeochemical cycling is the other major feature of ecosystems (along with energy flow). For many elements in an ecosystem, a cycle can be drawn which summarises the movement of the element through the living components of the ecosystem. During the cycle the element may be combined within complex organic molecules. These are later broken down in decomposition to simpler organic and inorganic forms which can be used again to make the living material of living organisms. As well as this actively **cycling pool** of an element, all cycles have a larger **reservoir pool** which is usually abiotic. Exchanges between the reservoir and active cycling pools are typically limited and often slow processes, for example the chemical weathering of phosphate rock, and fixation by lightning of nitrogen into nitrates during thunderstorms.

An understanding of biogeochemical cycling and maintenance of effective cycling is important. Human activity generally speeds movement of material through the cycles and may fundamentally upset the balance of cycles. This may lead to build-up of material at one point in the cycle, in other words, **pollution** (section 10.8).

The biogeochemical cycles for nitrogen and carbon are summarised in figs 10.11 and 10.12. Hydrogen, which has vital importance in photosynthesis, cycles in the water or hydrological cycle as shown in fig 10.13.

10.4.1 The nitrogen cycle

Nitrogen in the atmosphere (N_2) is very inert, and it takes a lot of energy to split the bonds in the nitrogen molecule so that it can form other compounds, such as nitrites and nitrates. However, nitrogen is an essential component of biological molecules such as proteins and DNA. The only organisms capable of splitting the nitrogen molecule are a few bacteria. They use it to form nitrites or nitrates, a process known as **nitrogen fixation** (fig 10.11). This is the major way in which nitrogen enters the biotic component of an ecosystem.

Nitrogen fixation

Nitrogen fixation is an energy-consuming process because the two nitrogen atoms of the nitrogen molecule must first be separated. Nitrogen-fixers achieve this using an enzyme, nitrogenase, and energy from ATP. Non-enzymic separation requires the much greater energy of industrial processes or of ionising events in the atmosphere, such as lightning and cosmic radiation.

Nitrogen is so important for soil fertility, and the demand for food production so great, that colossal amounts of ammonia are produced industrially each year to be used mainly for nitrogenous fertilisers such as ammonium nitrate (NH_4NO_3) and urea ($CO(NH_2)_2$).

The amounts of nitrogen fixed commercially are now approximately equivalent to the amounts fixed naturally.

We are still relatively ignorant of the likely effects of this gradual accumulation of fixed nitrogen on the biosphere. There is no new counterbalancing removal mechanism taking industrially fixed nitrogen back to the atmospheric reservoir pool.

A relatively small amount of fixed nitrogen (5–10%) is formed by ionising events in the atmosphere. The resulting nitrogen oxides dissolve in rain, forming nitrates.

The legumes, such as clover, soyabean, lucerne and pea, are probably the greatest natural source of fixed nitrogen. Their roots possess characteristic swellings called **nodules** which are caused by colonies of nitrogen-fixing bacilli (genus *Rhizobium*) living within the cells. The relationship is mutualistic because the plant gains fixed nitrogen in the form of ammonia from the bacteria and, in return, the bacteria gain energy and certain nutrients, such as carbohydrates, from the plants. In a given area legumes can contribute as much as 100 times more fixed nitrogen than free-living bacteria. It is not surprising, therefore, that they are frequently used to add nitrogen to the soil, especially since they have the added benefit of making good fodder crops.

> **10.8** Farmers often say that legumes are 'hard on the soil', meaning that they place a large demand on soil minerals. Why should this be so?

All nitrogen-fixers incorporate nitrogen into ammonia, but this is immediately used to make organic compounds, mainly proteins.

Decay and nitrification

Most plants depend on a supply of nitrate from the soil for their nitrate source. Animals in turn depend directly or indirectly on plants for their nitrogen supply. Fig 10.11 shows how nitrates are recycled from proteins in dead organisms by saprotrophic bacteria and fungi. The sequence from proteins to nitrate is a series of oxidations, requiring oxygen and involving aerobic bacteria. Proteins are decomposed via amino acids to ammonia when an organism dies. Animal wastes and excreta are similarly decomposed. Chemosynthetic bacteria (*Nitrosomonas* and *Nitrobacter*) then oxidise ammonia to nitrate, a process called **nitrification**.

> **10.9** In which of the nutritional categories would you place bacteria and fungi which are decomposers?

Denitrification

Nitrification can be reversed by denitrifying bacteria (**denitrification**) whose activities can therefore reduce soil fertility. They only do this under anaerobic conditions, when nitrate is used instead of oxygen as an oxidising agent (electron acceptor) for the oxidation of organic compounds.

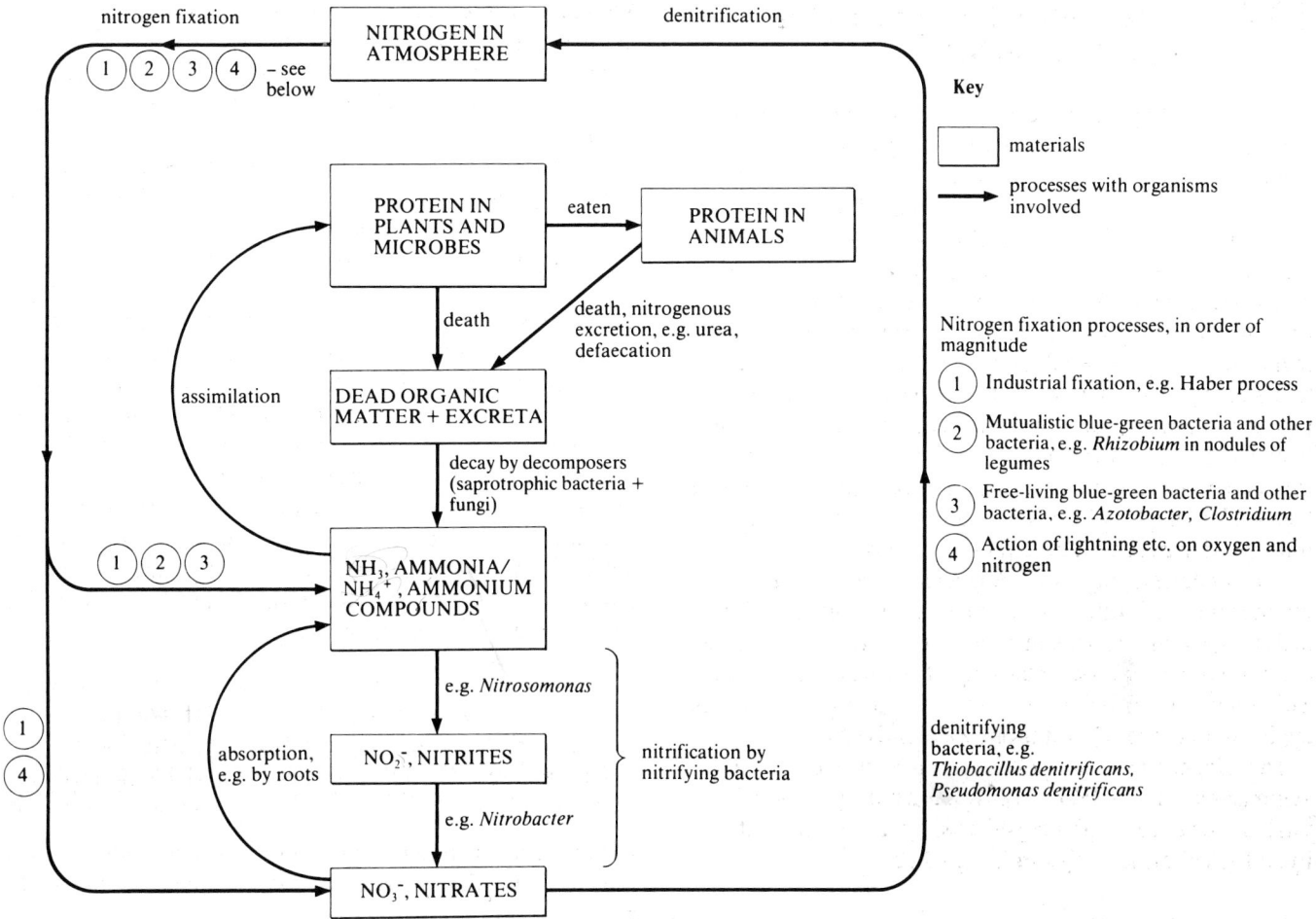

Fig 10.11 *Nitrogen cycle. 79% by volume of the atmosphere is nitrogen. This is the main nitrogen reservoir.*

Nitrate itself is reduced. The bacteria are therefore **facultative aerobes**.

> **10.10** What natural areas or situations might favour denitrification?
>
> **10.11** Why should good drainage and ploughing increase soil fertility?

10.4.2 The carbon cycle

The main carbon store is the estimated 75 million billion tonnes in the Earth's rocks. A further 5000 billion tonnes are found in fossil fuel reserves: coal, oil, gas and peat, and about 150 billion tonnes are held in the uppermost ocean bed sediments. These carbon sources are not normally available to living organisms; they represent the main carbon reservoirs. Of more importance to living organisms are the exchange or cycling pools of carbon shown in fig 10.12.

The main carbon source for living organisms is carbon dioxide present in the atmosphere or dissolved in surface waters. In photosynthesis green plants, algae and blue-green bacteria convert carbon dioxide to simple carbohydrates, the building blocks for all other organic molecules. This conversion of carbon dioxide in photosynthesis, and the counterbalancing release of carbon dioxide in respiration, is an important mechanism helping to maintain the balance of the natural carbon cycle. However, not all carbon dioxide fixed is returned to the atmosphere by respiration. In anaerobic environments, such as waterlogged soils, or at the bottom of still waters with poor illumination, decomposition is very slow and organic matter accumulates. These accumulating peat deposits and organic sediments may in the very long term generate new 'fossil' fuel deposits.

In oceans, the main removal mechanisms taking carbon dioxide from the atmosphere are photosynthesis, mostly by phytoplankton, and dissolving in surface waters. Much of this carbon dioxide is quickly released back into the atmosphere, either directly from the water or by respiration. However, as in terrestrial ecosystems, some carbon dioxide is locked away for a longer time, such as when cool surface

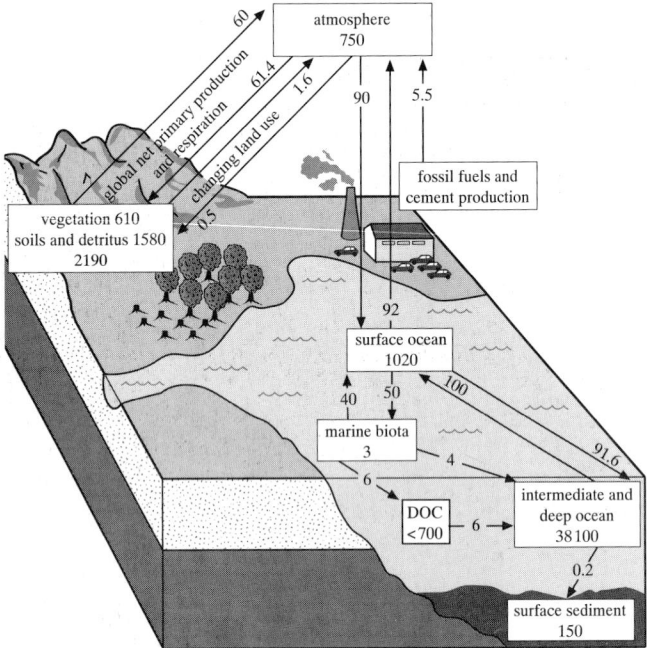

Fig 10.12 *Global carbon reservoirs and flows at the present day. Units are* 10^9 *tonnes of carbon for reservoir sizes and* 10^9 *tonnes of carbon per year for flows. (Climate change 1994, Radiative forcing of climate change (1995) IPCC/CUP.)*

waters sink below warmer currents, or when marine organisms form carbonate shells that later form carbonate rocks such as limestone.

In practice rates of carbon exchange between the active cycling pools can vary from year to year depending on climate. The balance is also affected by human activities, notably by changing land-use as in deforestation or reforestation and in human use of fossil fuels and in cement manufacture. Records show that human activity has led to a marked build-up of carbon dioxide in the atmosphere since the industrial revolution (section 10.8.1).

The effect of human activities in increasing the rate of release of carbon dioxide from long-term stores, such as fossil fuels and carbonates used in cement manufacture, and how this might affect the Earth's climate and ecosystems is the subject of much current research and debate (section 10.8.1). The general feeling is that we may be risking major environmental change by adding carbon dioxide to the atmosphere at the present rates. Efforts are now being made by governments to reduce carbon dioxide emissions by combustion in industry, and to reduce the rate of use of fossil fuels by finding alternative sources of energy, such as solar or wind power.

10.4.3 The hydrological cycle

Water is an essential component of all living organisms. It is important as a solvent and as a medium for chemical reactions. The oceans are the main reservoir for the hydrological cycle, containing 97% of all water on Earth (fig 10.13). Evaporation from the oceans and subsequent condensation and precipitation is the source of all fresh water for terrestrial and freshwater organisms. Fresh water may rapidly evaporate into the atmosphere or quickly return to the oceans via surface run-off and river flow. Some precipitation, especially in areas of vegetation, may soak into the underlying soils and enter longer-term storage as ground water. Fresh water may also be stored as ice for long periods in icecaps and glaciers of polar and mountain areas.

The hydrological cycle plays a major part in regulating the Earth's surface temperature and its distribution. Evaporating liquids take in heat and condensing gases give out heat. Similarly, heat is absorbed when ice melts and released when water freezes. These energy exchanges are important in the development of large-scale weather systems which are a key mechanism for transporting heat energy from equatorial to polar regions. Without this heat transfer, the poles would become progressively colder and the tropics increasingly hotter. As major stores of water, the oceans and icecaps are also important regulators of heat energy and thus of surface temperatures.

Water vapour in the atmosphere is an important greenhouse gas, like carbon dioxide (section 10.8.1). Thus water vapour also has an important influence on surface temperatures of the Earth. Understanding how interactions between the carbon and water cycles operate and, in turn, influence surface temperatures of the Earth, is an important challenge for current research. This knowledge would help us to predict and minimise the likely impact of human activity on the greenhouse effect.

10.5 Factors influencing environments and habitats

The environment in which an organism lives will be determined by a range of physical or abiotic factors such as light, heat and moisture (table 10.3). However, the real details of an individual's environment may be much more precise than this. For example, for a beetle living on a fallen tree trunk it is the details of temperature and moisture *on* the log which matter. However, an organism's habitat is not solely a matter of *physical conditions*. Its environment may be modified, or even mainly determined, by *other living organisms* (biotic factors). No matter how good the abiotic conditions, an organism may not thrive if this is also

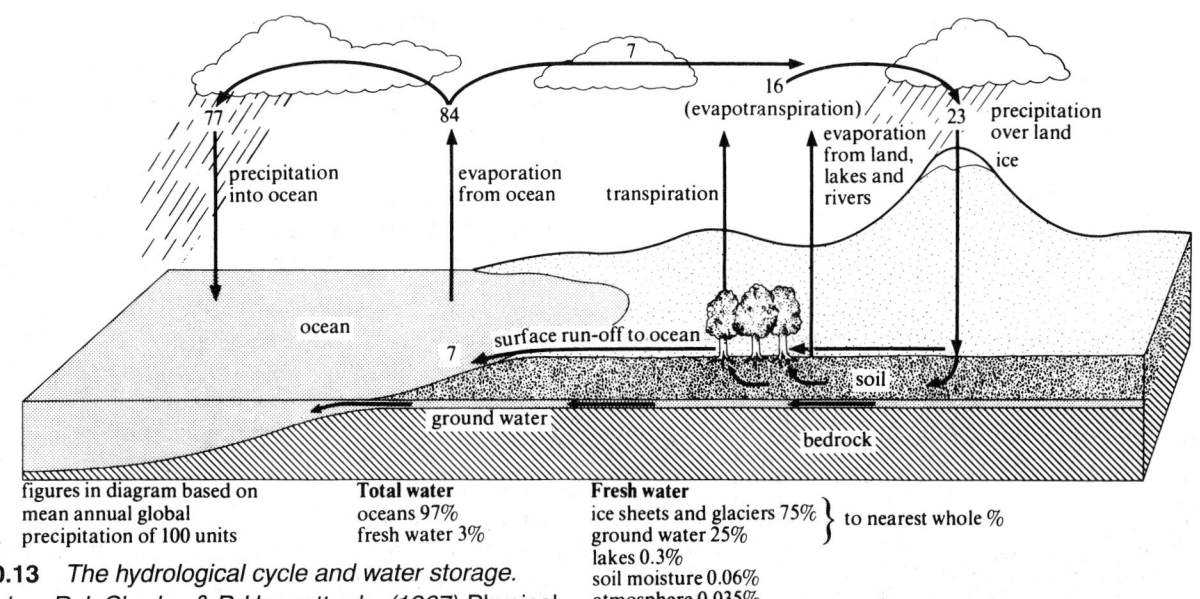

Fig 10.13 *The hydrological cycle and water storage. (Based on R.J. Chorley & P. Haggett eds. (1967)* Physical and information models in geography, *Methuen.)*

figures in diagram based on mean annual global precipitation of 100 units

Total water
oceans 97%
fresh water 3%

Fresh water
ice sheets and glaciers 75% } to nearest whole %
ground water 25%
lakes 0.3%
soil moisture 0.06%
atmosphere 0.035%
rivers 0.03%

Table 10.3 Factors influencing the distribution of organisms.

Abiotic factors		*Biotic factors*		*Combined factors*	
Factor	*Main examples*	*Factor*	*Main examples*	*Factor*	*Main examples*
light	quantity	competition		soil type	texture
	quality	predation			organic content
	duration	mutualism			soil air
					soil water
heat	temperature	human	pesticides	fire	
	extremes	activity	fire		
	seasonality		domestication of plants and animals		
water	salinity, nutrients		land use change e.g. in agriculture		
	rain, snow, hail, dew		and dam construction		
	humidity				
	water currents and				
	pressure				
atmosphere	gaseous content: e.g.		deforestation		
	carbon dioxide,		pollution e.g. linked with use		
	oxygen		of fossil fuels		
	air currents and air				
	pressure				
	weather systems				
topography	altitude		contaminated land		
	aspect				
	gradient				
		(You can probably think of many other examples.)			

the perfect location for its main competitors and predators or lacks its preferred food or nesting materials and so on. An organism's habitat is thus determined by both abiotic and biotic factors.

A related, useful and important concept is the **ecological niche** which combines the ideas of spatial habitat with the functional relationships of the organism. An organism's niche thus describes both its location and 'job' (e.g. pollinator, decomposer, predator and so forth) within a particular community or ecosystem. To understand more completely why an organism not only exists but flourishes in a particular place, you must study its absolute physical and biotic constraints, which will determine its **potential niche** (where it could occur), and its preferences and behaviour, which will determine the more restricted range of its **realised niche** (where it does occur).

If two species occupy the same niche they will generally compete with one another until one is displaced (see also section 10.7.5). Similar habitats have similar ecological niches and in different parts of the world may contain morphologically similar but taxonomically different animal and plant species. Open grassland and scrub, for example, will typically provide a niche for fast running herbivores, but these may be horses, antelope, bison, kangaroos, and so on.

A summary of the main abiotic and biotic factors influencing the distribution of organisms is given in table 10.3. Note that some factors such as soil type do not neatly fit these categories and are listed as **combined factors**.

10.5.1 The abiotic factors

Light

As the source of energy for photosynthesis light is essential for life, but it also influences living organisms in many other ways. The intensity, quality (wavelength or colour), and duration (photoperiod) of light can all have different effects.

Light intensity is affected by the angle of incidence of the Sun's rays to the surface of the Earth. This varies with latitude, season, time of day and aspect of slope. Photoperiod or daylength is a more or less constant 12 hours at the equator but at higher latitudes it varies seasonally. Plants and animals of higher latitudes typically show photoperiodic responses that synchronise their activities with the seasons, such as flowering and germination of plants (chapter 16), migration, hibernation and reproduction of animals (chapter 17). Light quality is important to plants. Only light at certain wavelengths can be used by chlorophyll. In aquatic systems some seaweeds, such as red algae, have different light intercepting pigments and can thus survive in locations where green algae would find light quality limiting.

The need for light by plants has an important effect on the structure of communities. Aquatic plants are confined to surface layers of water, and in terrestrial ecosystems competition for light favours certain strategies such as gaining height through growing tall or climbing, and increasing leaf surface area. In woodland this results in stratification (fig 10.15).

> **10.12** Identify the various ways in which light affects the activity of organisms.

Temperature

The main source of heat is the Sun's radiation. Geothermal sources are important only in a minority of habitats, such as the growth of bacteria in hot springs. A given organism will survive only within a certain temperature range for which it is metabolically and structurally adapted. If the temperature of a living cell falls far below freezing, the cell is usually physically damaged and killed by the formation of ice crystals. At the other extreme, if temperatures are too high, proteins become denatured. Between the extremes enzyme-controlled reactions, and hence metabolic activity, double in rate with every 10°C rise. Most organisms are able to exert some degree of control over their temperature by a variety of responses and adaptations so that extremes and sudden changes of environmental temperature can be 'smoothed out' (chapter 19). Aquatic environments undergo less extreme temperature changes, and therefore provide more stable habitats than terrestrial environments owing to the high heat capacity of water.

As with light intensity, temperature is broadly dependent on latitude, season, time of day and aspect of slope. However, local variations are common, particularly in microhabitats which have their own microclimates. Vegetation often has some microclimatic effect on temperature, as in forests, or on a smaller scale within individual clumps of plants or the shelter of leaves and buds of individual plants.

Moisture and salinity

Water is essential for life and is one of the major limiting factors in terrestrial ecosystems. It is precipitated from the atmosphere as rain, snow, sleet, hail or dew. There is a continuous cycling of water, the **hydrological cycle**, which governs water availability over land surfaces. Terrestrial plants mainly absorb water from the soil. Rapid drainage, low rainfall and high evaporation, or a combination of these factors, can result in dry soils, whereas the opposite extremes can lead to permanent waterlogging.

Plants can be classified according to their ability to tolerate water shortage as xerophytes (high tolerance), mesophytes (medium tolerance) and hydrophytes (low tolerance/water-adapted). Some of the xeromorphic adaptations are summarised in table 10.4 (see chapters 14 and 20 for a fuller discussion). Similarly, terrestrial animals show adaptations for gaining and conserving water, particularly in dry habitats (see chapter 20 and table 10.4).

Aquatic organisms also have problems with water regulation (chapter 20). Salinity of water is important, as can be seen in the differences between freshwater and marine species. Relatively few plants and animals can withstand large fluctuations in salinity, such as are found in estuaries or salt marshes. One example is the snail *Hydrobia ulvae* which can survive a range of salinities from 50–1600 mmol dm^{-3} of sodium chloride. Salinity may also be important in terrestrial habitats; if evaporation exceeds precipitation, soils may become saline. This is a serious problem in some irrigated areas.

Atmosphere

The atmosphere is a major part of the ecosphere. Like the oceans, it is constantly circulating. This is a mass flow phenomenon. The energy which drives these circulations comes from the Sun.

On a large scale, atmospheric circulation is important in the distribution of water vapour because this can be picked

Table 10.4 Adaptations of plants and animals to dry conditions.

	Examples
Reducing water loss	
Leaves reduced to needles or spines	Cactaceae, Euphorbiaceae (spurges), conifers
Sunken stomata	*Pinus, Ammophila*
Leaf rolls into cylinder	*Ammophila*
Thick waxy cuticle	Leaves of most xerophytes; insects
Swollen stem with large volume to surface area ratio	Cactaceae and Euphorbiaceae
Hairy leaves	Many alpine plants
Leaf-shedding in drought	*Fouquieria splendens* (ocotillo or candle plant)
Stomata open at night, close during day	Crassulaceae (stonecrops)
Efficient carbon dioxide fixation at night with partial opening of stomata	C_4 plants, e.g. *Zea mais*
Uric acid as nitrogenous waste	Insects, birds and some reptiles
Long loop of Henlé in kidneys	Desert mammals, e.g. camel, desert rat
Tissues tolerant of high temperatures, reducing sweating or transpiration	Many desert plants, camel
Burrowing behaviour	Many small desert mammals, e.g. desert rat
Spiracles covered with flaps	Many insects
Increasing water uptake	
Extensive shallow root system and deep roots	Some Cactaceae, e.g. *Opuntia*, and Euphorbiaceae
Long roots	Many alpine plants, e.g. *Leontopodium alpinum* (edelweiss)
Burrow for water	Termites
Water storage	
In mucilaginous cells and cell walls	Cactaceae and Euphorbiaceae
In specialised bladder	Desert frog
As fat (water is a product of oxidation)	Desert rat
Physiological tolerance of water loss	
Apparent dehydration can occur without death	Some epiphytic ferns and clubmosses, many bryophytes and lichens, *Carex physiodes* (sedge)
Loss of high proportion of body mass with rapid recovery when water is available	*Lumbricus terrestris* (70% loss of body mass), camel (30% loss)
Evasion	
Pass unfavourable season as seed	Californian poppy
Pass unfavourable season as bulbs or tubers	Some lilies
Seed dispersal, with some reaching more favourable conditions	
Escape behaviour	Soil organisms, e.g. mites, earthworm
Aestivation in mucus-containing sheath	Earthworm, lungfish

up locally (by evaporation), carried in moving air masses and deposited in a distant location (by precipitation). Similarly pollutant gases, such as sulphur dioxide, released into the atmosphere at industrial locations may be deposited in solution in rainfall many miles from the source (section 10.8.1). The pattern of atmospheric circulation will thus affect the distribution of pollutants and their eventual precipitation in rainfall.

Wind can interact with other environmental variables to affect growth of vegetation, particularly trees in exposed places, where they may become stunted and distorted on their windward sides. Wind is also important in increasing evaporation and transpiration under conditions of low humidity.

Dispersal of spores, seeds and so on, through the atmosphere, aided by wind, increases the spread of non-motile organisms like plants, fungi and some bacteria. Winds may also influence the dispersal or migration of flying animals.

Topography

The influence of topography is intimately connected with the other abiotic factors since it can strongly influence local climate and soil development. The main topographic factor is altitude. Higher altitudes are associated with lower average temperatures and a greater diurnal temperature range, higher precipitation (including snow), increased wind speeds, more intense radiation, lower atmospheric pressures, all of which have an influence on plant and animal life. As a result, vertical **zonations** are common, as shown in fig 10.14 (see also section 10.6.4).

Mountain chains can act as climatic barriers. As air rises over mountains it cools and precipitation tends to occur. Thus a rain 'shadow' occurs on the leeward side of the mountains where air is drier and precipitation is less. This affects the ecosystems. Mountains also act as barriers to dispersal and migration and may play important roles as isolating mechanisms in the process of speciation, as described in chapter 26.

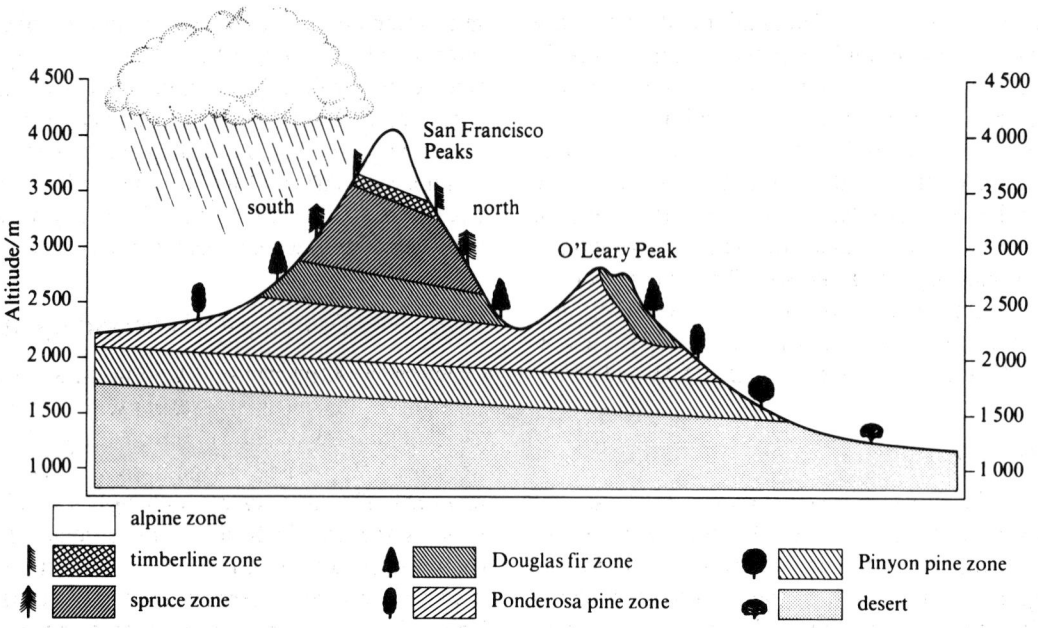

Fig 10.14 *Zonation of vegetation on San Francisco Peaks, Arizona, as viewed from the south east. (From Merriam (1890). Redrawn and modified from W.D. Billings (1972)* Plants, man and the ecosystem, *2nd ed. Macmillan.)*

Another important topographic factor is **aspect**. In the northern hemisphere south-facing slopes receive more sunlight, and therefore higher light intensities and temperatures, than valley bottoms and north-facing slopes (the reverse being true in the southern hemisphere). This has striking effects on the natural vegetation and on land use by humans.

Steepness of slope (**gradient**) is a third topographic factor. Steep slopes generally suffer from faster drainage and run-off, and the soils are therefore thinner and drier, with more xeromorphic vegetation. At slope angles in excess of 35° soil and vegetation are typically unable to develop, and screes of loose material form.

10.5.2 Soils

Soil is a complex mixture of organic and inorganic materials. It is the medium for plant growth. Understanding the characteristics of soil, in particular knowing how to maintain good quality soil and how to improve difficult soils, is of importance for successful agriculture. It thus has considerable economic significance.

Soils have four main constituents. These are:

- the mineral matter;
- the organic matter;
- the soil air;
- the soil water. (This may be better described as the '**soil solution**' since it is not pure water but contains dissolved ions.)

The soil mineral matter

Soils are composed of mineral fragments of widely varying size: gravel and stones, and fine earth. In practice the fine earth is commonly further subdivided into clays, silts and sands. The relative proportions of the main particle size groups determine soil texture.

Soil texture importantly influences drainage, nutrient retention and the soil temperature regime. It is thus important agriculturally. Medium- and fine-textured soils, such as clays, clay loams and silt loams, are generally more suitable for plant growth because they have the most satisfactory nutrient and water retention. Sandy soils are faster draining and lose nutrients through leaching, but may be advantageous in obtaining early crops as the surface dries more rapidly than that of a clay soil in early spring, resulting in a warmer soil. Stone content of the soil (particles >2 mm) may also have importance agriculturally since it will affect wear and tear on agricultural implements, and will modify the drainage characteristics of fine earth. Generally, as the stone content of a soil increases, its water-holding capacity decreases.

The soil organic matter

The organic matter content of a soil, although only a small percentage by volume, is very important. It is a major source of the key soil nutrients phosphorus, nitrogen and sulphur; it increases the water-holding capacity of the soil; it encourages the formation of aggregates in the soil and thus is particularly useful in clay rich soils; and it is a source of energy and materials for microorganisms. Soil organic matter comprises two main constituents, namely DOM and living organisms.

Humus is organic material formed from the partial decomposition of DOM. Much of the soil humus is present not as individual molecules but as complexes with inorganic molecules, especially the clay minerals. These clay–humus complexes are fundamental to almost every physical, chemical and biological process that occurs in soils. For example they influence water and nutrient retention and affect crumb structure and aeration.

Earthworms are particularly important soil organisms. They feed on DOM and at the same time ingest large amounts of mineral particles. Because they migrate between the upper and lower layers of the soil, earthworms are important mixing agents in the soil. They also open up channels for air and water and so help to improve soil texture and related properties. Earthworms thrive best in neutral to acid soils and are rarely found where the pH is less than 4.5.

The soil air

The soil air occupies the pore spaces within the soils. It is readily displaced by the soil water. In a waterlogged soil there is no soil air. The soil air differs from air in the outside atmosphere in several important ways. It contains more carbon dioxide and water vapour but has less oxygen.

The soil water

The soil water or the **soil solution** contains dissolved chemicals that have been produced by weathering and by mineralisation in the process of decomposition. There is a continuous movement of solutes (dissolved chemicals) from the mineral and organic components of the soil into the soil solution and from the soil solution into plants.

10.5.3 Biotic factors

The biotic factors which affect the survival and distribution of an organism include:

- intraspecific factors – those which occur between members of the same species, such as competition for food and territory (section 10.7.4).
- interspecific factors – those which occur between members of different species, such as predator–prey interactions, host–parasite interactions, competitive exclusion and resource partitioning (section 10.7.5).
- other detailed mutualistic relationships such as species-specific pollinators and fruit dispersal agents.

However, as shown in table 10.3, humans have become the predominant biotic influence on the distribution and success of other species as discussed in sections 10.8 and 10.9.

10.6 Community ecology

A **community** is a group of interacting organisms or species populations living together in a particular place. It represents the living (biotic) part of an ecosystem and could be seen as a dynamic unit with a web of energy flow and an exchange or cycling of matter as described in sections 10.3 and 10.4. Community ecology focuses on the interactions between the community members. This means understanding competition, predator–prey relationships (including herbivory) and mutualism (section 10.7.5).

Community structure is often very diverse. A woodland community, for example, will generate many different niches and microhabitats, and supply many different food sources, as a result of its vertical structure (fig 10.15) and spatial variation beneath and between the mature tree canopies.

10.6.1 Primary and secondary succession

All biotic communities are continually changing. They change in response to external factors, such as changing climates, or as a result of internal factors caused by the organisms themselves, such as accumulation of DOM. The time scales of change are highly variable. So long as the abiotic factors remain relatively constant, the biotic community will develop through time from an initial bare rock or open water start point to a **climax community**. The climax community is considered to be the most complex, diverse and productive community a given area can *sustain*. It may vary seasonally or fluctuate in a minor way, but it is essentially stable unless some catastrophic intervention occurs. A volcanic eruption or human-induced fire or deforestation would be a typical catastrophic event. The climax community would be destroyed but DOM and chance survivors would remain. These would start a new sequence of changes until a fairly stable community was once again established.

The change from bare rock or open water is rapid, especially in the initial stages, and follows a series of recognisable and hence predictable stages. This process is called **succession**. Individual successions are known as **seres** and the developmental phases are called **seral stages**. A succession developing on newly emerged land or water is termed a **primary succession**. A succession developing following a fire or similar major disruption to an established community is called a **secondary succession**.

Opportunities for primary succession are relatively uncommon. Examples would be land or lakes emerging during glacier retreat, or a new island created by volcanic activity as occurred when Surtsey appeared off Iceland in 1963. Secondary successions are much more common. Scrub invasion on the lowland heaths and chalk downlands of southern England are widespread examples of secondary succession (fig 10.16). Here the disruption to the natural succession was caused by forest clearance by humans, and has subsequently been reinforced by centuries of grazing activity by sheep and cattle. A community where human intervention has led to the long-term establishment of a community very different from the original climax is termed a **plagioclimax**. The succession is said to have been **deflected**. If pressures such as grazing and burning management which caused the succession to be deflected are removed then, inevitably, a renewed succession will occur. This is an important consideration for the conservation management of these communities.

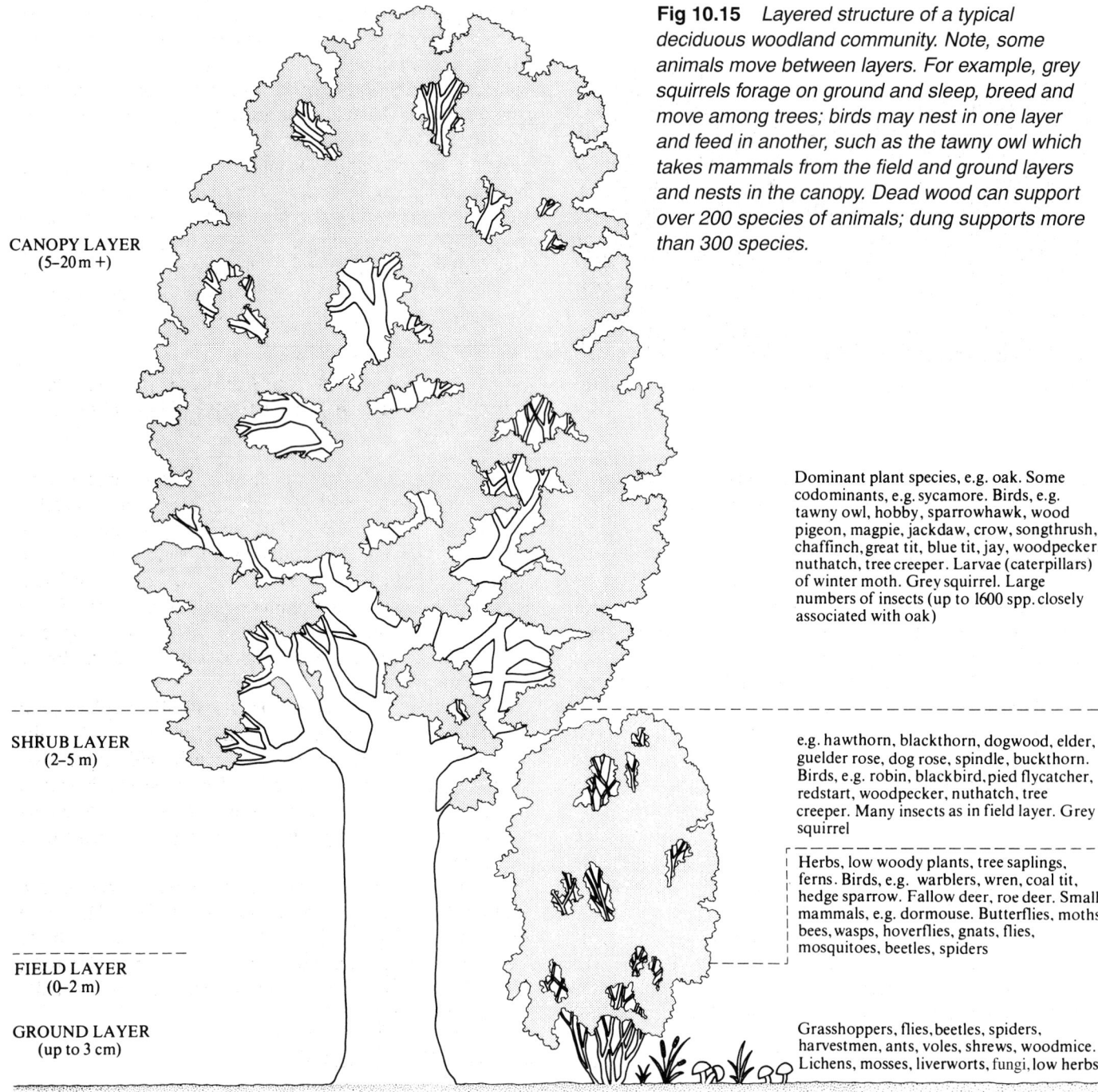

CANOPY LAYER
(5–20 m +)

SHRUB LAYER
(2–5 m)

FIELD LAYER
(0–2 m)

GROUND LAYER
(up to 3 cm)

LITTER

TOPSOIL
(lowest organic layer)

SUBSOIL
(weathered bedrock)

Fig 10.15 *Layered structure of a typical deciduous woodland community. Note, some animals move between layers. For example, grey squirrels forage on ground and sleep, breed and move among trees; birds may nest in one layer and feed in another, such as the tawny owl which takes mammals from the field and ground layers and nests in the canopy. Dead wood can support over 200 species of animals; dung supports more than 300 species.*

Dominant plant species, e.g. oak. Some codominants, e.g. sycamore. Birds, e.g. tawny owl, hobby, sparrowhawk, wood pigeon, magpie, jackdaw, crow, songthrush, chaffinch, great tit, blue tit, jay, woodpecker, nuthatch, tree creeper. Larvae (caterpillars) of winter moth. Grey squirrel. Large numbers of insects (up to 1600 spp. closely associated with oak)

e.g. hawthorn, blackthorn, dogwood, elder, guelder rose, dog rose, spindle, buckthorn. Birds, e.g. robin, blackbird, pied flycatcher, redstart, woodpecker, nuthatch, tree creeper. Many insects as in field layer. Grey squirrel

Herbs, low woody plants, tree saplings, ferns. Birds, e.g. warblers, wren, coal tit, hedge sparrow. Fallow deer, roe deer. Small mammals, e.g. dormouse. Butterflies, moths, bees, wasps, hoverflies, gnats, flies, mosquitoes, beetles, spiders

Grasshoppers, flies, beetles, spiders, harvestmen, ants, voles, shrews, woodmice. Lichens, mosses, liverworts, fungi, low herbs

Dead and decaying material. Decomposers (bacteria and fungi). Earthworms, moth larvae, fly larvae, dung and carrion beetles, centipedes, millipedes, woodlice, springtails, mites, nematode worms. Moles

Burrows of rabbits, badgers, foxes

10.6.2 The process of succession

The concept of succession is most easily illustrated for a bare rock surface. The initial rock surface presents a hostile environment for most living organisms.

Early colonisers will need to be autotrophs which can tolerate these hostile conditions. They will also need good dispersal mechanisms to ensure arrival at the site. Typical organisms are lichens, algae and blue-green bacteria.

Fig 10.16 *Scrub invasion of lowland heath in south-east England.*

Lichens, for example, colonise rock surfaces. They exude chemicals which help to break down the rock surface, at the same time supplying themselves with essential inorganic materials. When they die, these primary colonisers provide DOM which may accumulate in the small depressions and cracks in the rock. This debris is a good food source for decomposers and marks the beginning of soil formation and accumulation of readily available nutrients for plant growth. A series of increasingly demanding plant species can then colonise the area. First arrivals and early colonisers will be those with good seed dispersal mechanisms and a wide range of tolerance. We call these species **opportunists** or **generalists**. Each organism in turn contributes to the developing biomass (living and dead) of the community. This paves the way for later arrivals which will typically be more competitive longer-living species. These characteristically show a narrower range of tolerance to environmental conditions.

During a succession more and more of the available nutrients become locked up in the biomass of the community, with a consequent decrease in nutrients in the abiotic component of the ecosystem. The amount of detritus produced also increases and detritus feeders take over from grazers as the main primary consumers. Appropriate changes in food webs occur and detritus becomes the main source of nutrients. These and other trends that can be expected to occur in successions are summarised in table 10.5.

Succession is a good example of organisms modifying their environment and thereby creating opportunities for other organisms. Of course, as the plant community develops so new niches for herbivores, secondary consumers, detrital feeders and decomposers emerge until a complex biotic community and ecosystem develops. A schematic summary of this process is shown in fig 10.17.

10.13 What factors are likely to affect the number and diversity of species reaching an area?

In the latter stages of succession, biotic interactions become more important in forming the detailed community structure. The variety of living organisms tends to increase, so inevitably their interactions become more complex (section 10.7.5). The tropical rainforest communities, which are among the longest established climax communities, are renowned for their species richness and the extreme complexity of their biotic interactions.

The outline given above is an idealised picture of succession for a terrestrial community. In real life the situation may be less clear cut. Much will depend on available spores and seed supplies. This is especially true in secondary succession where colonisers will also reflect surviving seed stores and vegetative organs in cleared or abandoned land.

The climax community is often described as having one **dominant** or several **co-dominant** species. The term dominance is rather subjective but normally refers to those species with the greatest collective biomass or productivity, although physical size of individuals is also usually considered important.

Table 10.5 Summary of changes in an ecosystem during a typical secondary succession.

	Stage of ecosystem development	
Characteristic	*Immature (early)*	*Mature (late)*
Gross production/community respiration (P/R ratio)	high (>1)	approaches 1
Food chains	linear, mainly grazing	web-like, mainly detritus-feeding
Total organic matter (or biomass)	small	large
Species diversity	low	high*
Structure of community	simple	complex (stratification, many microhabitats)
Niche specialisation	broad	narrow
Size of organism	small	large
Strategies adopted by species	opportunist	specialist

* Most plant and some animal examples of succession show a peak of species diversity before climax.

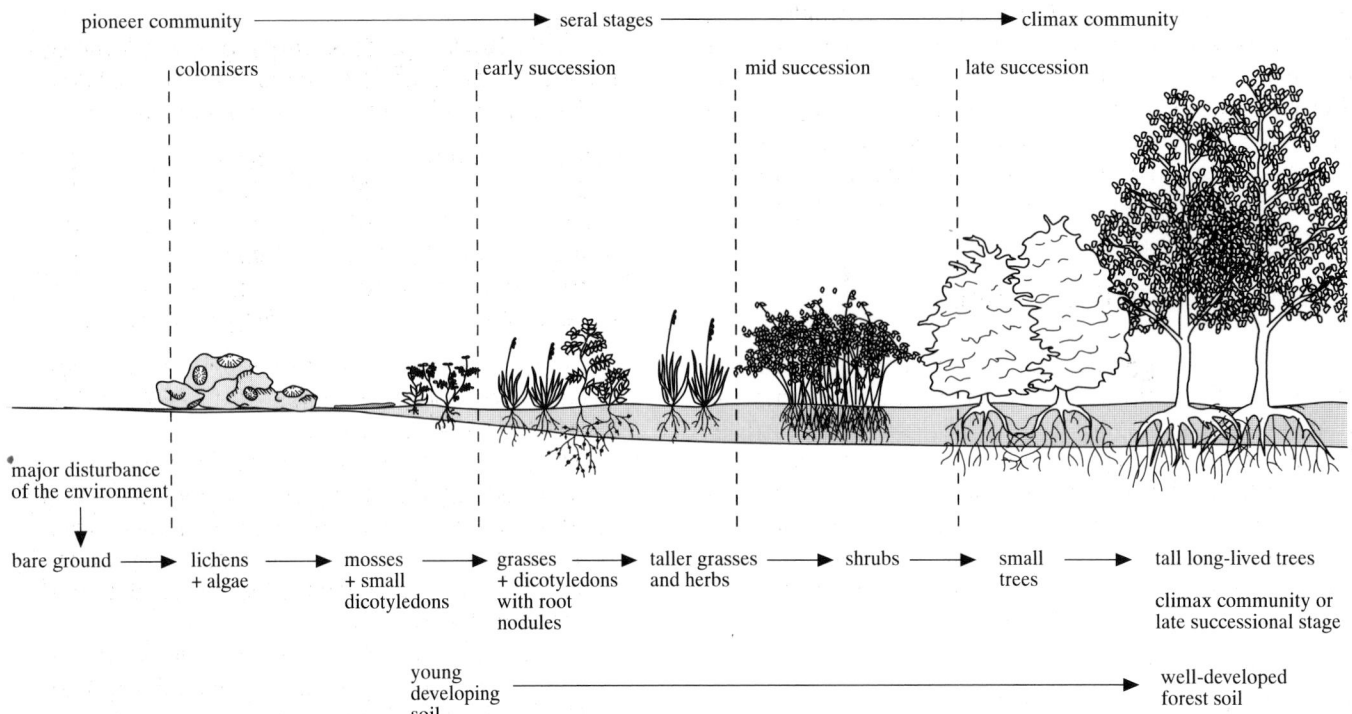

pioneer community ⟶ seral stages ⟶ climax community

colonisers   early succession   mid succession   late succession

major disturbance
of the environment

bare ground ⟶ lichens ⟶ mosses ⟶ grasses ⟶ taller grasses ⟶ shrubs ⟶ small ⟶ tall long-lived trees
                + algae   + small   + dicotyledons and herbs   trees
                           dicotyledons with root   climax community or
                                         nodules   late successional stage

young   well-developed
developing   forest soil
soil

Fig 10.17 *Schematic summary of a sere showing characteristic vegetational change during succession.*

The time scales of succession are very difficult to specify. Initial changes may be rapid but subsequent rates of change are often slow. For example on the skeletal soils of moraines left by retreating glaciers a well-developed soil and plant community has been observed to occur in 30–70 years. Whether this represents the final climax stage is much more difficult to judge. Indeed some ecologists argue that since climate is always changing, biotic communities too must always be changing in sympathy with the new climatic conditions. The optimum stable climax community must therefore also be changeable. In other words as human observers of this process we are much better informed about the early stages of succession than about changes that may occur after 200 or 300 years, the lifespan of some trees which in many terrestrial environments are the major determinants of climax community structure.

10.6.3 Applying succession principles to land restoration

In practical terms, the speed with which successional change takes place can be very important. Mining wastes, motorway verges and railway embankments are just three examples where colonisation by vegetation is an important means of stabilisation. In the case of mine waste, land reclamation and landscape improvement are also important objectives. Some wastes are quickly colonised. China clay waste has been observed to establish woody vegetation in very short time periods, such as 10–20 years. It also quickly establishes a self-sustaining nitrogen cycle essential to the maintenance of tree cover. This latter point is important. It means that very little, if any, human help is needed to revegetate these areas. Commonly an initial seeding will include a mix of grasses and nitrogen-fixing legumes, to enable a vegetation cover to establish quickly, but little subsequent treatment is needed.

Other wastes such as colliery spoil are more difficult to colonise. These wastes are often very acidic and may also be contaminated with heavy metals. Relying on natural succession would take a very long time since few organisms can tolerate these conditions. We can help succession in these circumstances in several ways. Lime can be added to reduce acidity and top soil (very expensive) or some organic material may be added. This material will improve water retention by the waste. It will also bind toxic heavy metals and help to buffer extremes of pH. The organic material also provides a food source for earthworms. Earthworm activity will increase the aeration and mixing of the soil. Organic amendments are often readily and cheaply available as the waste products of other industries, for example sewage sludge, finely shredded domestic waste and farmyard manure.

10.6.4 Zonation

Within a community at any one time species may be spatially distributed according to variations of the physical environment. This is called **zonation**. A good example is the zonation of seaweeds and marine animals that occurs on rocky shores from low-tide to high-tide level and into the splash zone. Physical conditions vary through these zones, notably length of exposure to air between successive tides, and each zone is occupied by species adapted for its particular conditions. Zonation on a seashore is described and illustrated in section 11.4. Another good example of zonation is the vertical zonation that occurs on mountains with increasing altitude (shown in fig 10.14). Superficially zonations may resemble succession, but it is important to recognise the basic difference, namely that with zonation the species vary in space (spatially), whereas with succession the species vary in time (temporally).

10.7 Population ecology

A **population** may be defined as a group of organisms of one species occupying a particular place and usually isolated to some extent from other similar groups by geography or topography. The roe deer of a particular woodland, the frogs of a particular valley or trout of a particular lake are all examples of ecological populations. Population studies are not just about numbers of a given species living in a given area at a given moment in time. More importantly we want to know

- how populations grow;
- how populations are maintained;
- and how and why populations decline.

The study of how and why population size changes over time is called **population dynamics**. Typically, it examines the characteristics of a group of organisms, such as their density, natality (birth rate), mortality (death rate), survivorship, age structure, migration and form of growth of the population. Population interactions such as competition, predation and parasitism not only regulate growth of a given population but influence the structure of communities.

10.7.1 Birth rate (natality) and death rate (mortality)

Population size may increase as a result of **immigration** from neighbouring populations, or by reproduction of individuals within the population. For mammals, rate of reproduction is expressed as **birth rate** or **natality**, the number of young produced per female per unit time (usually per year).

Population size may decrease as a result of **emigration** or death (**mortality**). In population biology, mortality strictly means *rate* of death and may be expressed in terms of per cent, or numbers per thousand, dying per year.

10.7.2 Survivorship curves

The percentage of individuals that die before reaching reproductive age (**pre-reproductive mortality**) is one of the chief factors affecting population size, and for a given species is much more variable than birth rate. Many populations remain more or less the same size year after year. In these cases, an average of only two offspring from each male–female pair must survive to reproductive age.

10.14 The data below give the average number of fertilised eggs produced in their lifetime by females of different organisms (fecundity).

oyster	100×10^6	mouse	50
cod	9×10^6	dogfish	20
plaice	35×10^4	penguin	8
salmon	10×10^4	elephant	5
stickleback	5×10^2	Victorian	
winter moth	200	Englishwoman	10

(a) If each population remains stable in numbers, how many fertilised eggs from each female must, on average, survive?

(b) For each species write down the number of fertilised eggs which must die before becoming adult if the population remains stable. Then express this number as a percentage of the total number produced (this gives the pre-reproductive mortality).

(c) Try to suggest why the fecundities of the stickleback and dogfish are so much lower than for the other fish in the table.

Source of question: Open University, S100, Unit 20, *Species and Populations*, p. 26.

If we start with a population of newborn individuals and the numbers of survivors is plotted against time, a **survivorship curve** is obtained. On the vertical axis, actual numbers of survivors may be plotted, or percentage survival:

$$\frac{\text{number of survivors}}{\text{number in original population}} \times 100\%$$

Different species have characteristic survivorship curves. Some representative examples are shown in fig 10.18.

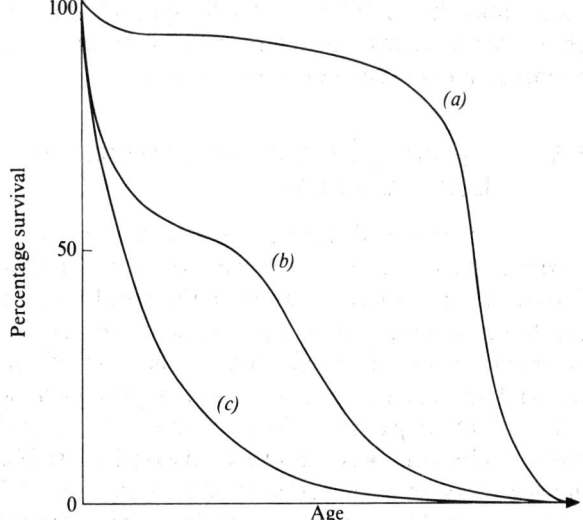

Fig 10.18 *Three types of survivorship curve. Curves (a), (b) and (c) are explained in the text.*

Most animals and plants exhibit a phenomenon called senescence or ageing, manifested as a declining vigour with increasing age beyond maturity. Once senescence begins, there is increasing likelihood of death occurring within a given time period. The immediate cause of death can vary, but the underlying cause is a reduced resistance to external factors such as disease.

Curve (a) in fig 10.18 shows an almost ideal curve for a population in which senescence is the major factor affecting mortality. A curve like (a) would also be obtained for an annual crop plant such as wheat, where all the plants in a given field survive well early in life and then senesce simultaneously.

Curve (b) is for a population with a high mortality rate early in life, such as might occur for mountain sheep or for humans in a country in which starvation and disease are prevalent. Curve (c) shows the kind of smooth curve that would be obtained if there was a constant mortality rate throughout life (50% per unit time). Such a curve is obtained if chance is the major factor influencing mortality and the organisms die out before senescence becomes evident. Some animal populations show survivorship curves which approximate closely to this model curve, for example *Hydra*, where there is no special risk attached to being young. Most nonvertebrates and plants show a curve similar to (c), but with high juvenile mortality superimposed so that the initial part of the curve descends even more steeply.

10.15 Which population, (a) or (b), would need the higher reproductive rate to maintain a stable population? Explain your choice.

By plotting survivorship curves of species it is possible to determine the mortality rates of individuals of different ages and hence to determine at which ages they are most vulnerable. By identifying the factors causing death at these ages, an understanding can be gained of how population size is regulated.

10.16 The following figures apply to sockeye salmon in a Canadian river system. Each female salmon lays 3200 eggs in a gravelly shallow in the river in autumn. 640 fry (young fish derived from these eggs) enter a lake near the shallow in the following spring. 64 smolts (older fish survivors from the fry) leave the lake one year later and migrate to the sea. Two adult fish (survivors of these smolts) return to the spawning grounds $2\frac{1}{2}$ years later; they spawn and then die. Calculate the percentage mortalities for sockeye salmon for each of the following periods:

(a) from laying eggs to movement of fry into the lake six months later;
(b) from entering the lake as fry to leaving the lake as smolts 12 months later;
(c) from leaving the lake as smolts to returning to the spawning grounds as adult salmon 30 months later.

Draw a survivorship curve for the sockeye salmon in this river system (plot percentage survival against age). What is the pre-reproductive mortality for these salmon?

Source of question: Open University, S100, Unit 20, *Species and Populations*, p. 71.

10.7.3 Population growth and growth curves

Populations grow and decline in characteristic ways. The size of population increase will be determined by the **reproductive potential** of the organisms concerned and by **environmental resistance**. The maximum reproductive potential is the rate of reproduction given unlimited environmental resources. It will vary according to the age structure of a population and will be influenced by male:female ratios.

Environmental resistance means the sum total of limiting factors, both biotic and abiotic, which act together to prevent the maximum reproductive potential from being realised. It includes external factors such as predation, food supply, heat, light and space, and internal regulatory mechanisms such as intraspecific competition and behavioural adaptations. Strong feedback links exist between all these factors, for example intraspecific competition arises in response to some resource (such as space) which is in limiting supply.

The balance between biotic potential and environmental resistance defines the **carrying capacity** for a particular organism with a given set of environmental resources.

Growth curves

Two basic forms of growth curve can be identified, the J-shaped growth curve and the S-shaped or sigmoidal growth curve.

The **S-shaped** or **sigmoidal growth curve** describes a situation in which, in a new environment, the population density of an organism increases slowly initially, as it adapts to new conditions and establishes itself, then increases rapidly, approaching an exponential growth rate. It then shows a declining rate of increase until a zero population growth rate is achieved where rate of reproduction (natality) equals rate of death (mortality) (fig 10.19a). The slowing rate of population growth results from increasing competition for essential resources, such as food or nesting materials. The decline in growth rate continues until eventually feedback in terms of increased mortality and reproduction failures (fewer matings, stress-induced abortion) reduces population growth rate to zero.

This type of population growth is said to be **density-dependent** since, for a given set of resources, growth rate depends on the numbers present in the population. The point of stabilisation or zero growth rate is the maximum **carrying capacity** of the given environment for the organism concerned.

(a)

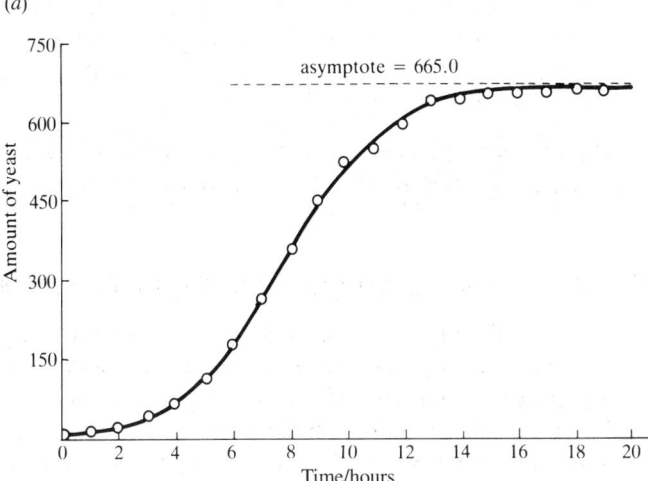

(b)

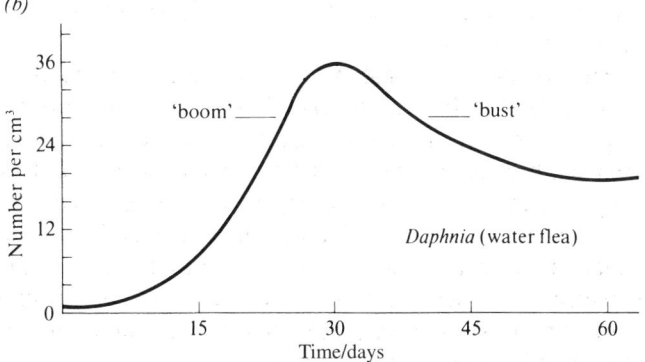

Fig 10.19 *Types of population growth curve. (a) The sigmoidal growth curve (S-shaped curve). The growth of yeast in a culture. A simple case of the sigmoid growth form in which environmental resistance (in this case detrimental factors produced by the organisms themselves) is linearly proportional to density. (b) The diagram shows the curve of water fleas grown in culture. These curves are sometimes called 'boom and bust' curves.*

Many populations of microorganisms, plants and animals, under both laboratory and field conditions broadly follow this basic sigmoidal pattern. A useful example is when a fresh culture medium is inoculated with bacteria (fig 12.8). Phytoplankton in lakes and oceans may show sigmoidal growth in spring, as do insects such as flour beetles or mites introduced into a new habitat with abundant food and no predators.

The **J-shaped growth curve** describes a situation in which, after the initial establishment phase (lag phase), population growth continues in an exponential form until stopped *abruptly*, as environmental resistance becomes *suddenly* effective (fig 10.19b). Growth is said to be **density-independent** since regulation of growth rate is not tied to the population density until the final crash. The crash may be triggered by factors such as seasonality or the end of a breeding phase, either of the organism itself or of an important prey species. It may be associated with a particular stage in the life cycle, such as seed production, or it may be induced by human intervention as when an insecticide is used to control an insect pest population. Following the crash, such populations typically show a fluctuating recovery pattern giving the 'boom and bust' cycles characteristic of some insect species and associated with algal blooms.

10.7.4 Factors within species which affect population size

Once a population has finished its initial growth phase there usually continues to be fluctuations in population size over time. Important influences are likely to be variations in climatic conditions (such as temperature), food supply and predation. Sometimes fluctuations are regular and may be called **cycles**.

Population size may change as a result of changes in birth rate or death rate, or possibly both. Factors which bring about these changes often become more effective as population density increases. Hence they may be described as density-dependent factors. Food shortage and increased predation are two factors which sometimes operate in this way. They have direct effects on mortality for obvious reasons. Two regulatory mechanisms which affect birth rate are **territorial behaviour** and the physical effects of **overcrowding**.

Territorial behaviour

Territorial behaviour or **territoriality** occurs in a wide range of animals, including certain fish, reptiles, birds, mammals and social insects. It has been particularly well studied in bird populations. Either the male bird, or both the male and the female, of a pair may establish a breeding territory which they will defend against intruders of the same species. The song of the bird and often a visual display, such as that of the robin's red breast, are means of asserting territorial claims, and intruders usually retreat, sometimes after a brief 'ritual fight' in which neither

Fig 10.20 *Display of territoriality.*

competitor is seriously damaged. There is little or no overlap between neighbouring territories of the same species and, in areas where the territory includes the food of the species, it will contain sufficient food to support the birds and their young (fig 10.20). As population sizes grow, territories usually become smaller and able to support fewer new birds. In extreme cases, some birds may be unable to establish territories and therefore fail to breed. Regulation is therefore due to spatial interactions.

Overcrowding

Another factor which may affect birth rate is overcrowding. Laboratory experiments with rats show that when a certain high population density is reached, birth rate is greatly reduced even if there is no food shortage. Various hormonal changes occur which affect reproductive behaviour in a number of ways; for example failure to copulate, infertility, number of abortions and eating of young by the parents all increase, and parental care decreases. The young abandon the nest at an earlier age, with consequent reduction in chances of survival. There is also an increase in aggressive behaviour. Changes like these have been demonstrated for a number of mammals and could operate under natural circumstances outside the laboratory. Natural populations of voles, for example, show a similar kind of regulation.

Another density-dependent factor that may affect the population size of a species is dispersal. For example, at high aphid densities not only does the rate of reproduction of the aphids decrease but a higher proportion develop wings and leave the plant on which they are feeding.

Some factors regulating population sizes such as climate have been regarded as density-independent, but it is inevitable that they interact with other factors that are density-dependent. Thus, although the terms are useful, it is better to avoid stressing the difference between density-dependent and density-independent factors because complex interactions may occur.

10.7.5 Factors between species which affect population size

It is seldom possible to confine studies of population dynamics to single species. A number of well-recognised types of interaction may occur between populations of different species. These are termed **interspecific interactions**. Populations from different trophic levels may also interact, as, for example, in the cases of predator–prey relationships and host–parasite relationships. Other relationships exist, some of which are subtle and complex, including some mutualistic relationships where both partners benefit. At a given trophic level there may be **interspecific competition**, that is competition between members of different species for available resources such as food and space. This can result in resource partitioning.

Predator–prey relationships

A commonly used and simple model of predator–prey relationships is one that has been well illustrated by laboratory experiments with two mites, one predatory (*Typhlodromus*) and one herbivorous (*Eotetranychus*). Fig 10.21 shows the cyclic fluctuations that occur in their numbers, the cycles for the two species being slightly out of phase with each other.

The explanation for these cycles is that an increase in numbers of the prey supports a subsequent increase in numbers of the predator. The predators then cause a crash in numbers of the prey, followed by an inevitable decline in numbers of predators. The cycles are completed when the decline in predators allows an increase in numbers of the prey. Each cycle occurs over a number of generations.

Although it may not be the only factor, there is no doubt that predation plays an important part in regulating natural populations. Some indication of the importance of predator–prey relationships in this respect, and the long-term advantage it has for the prey, can be gained from the

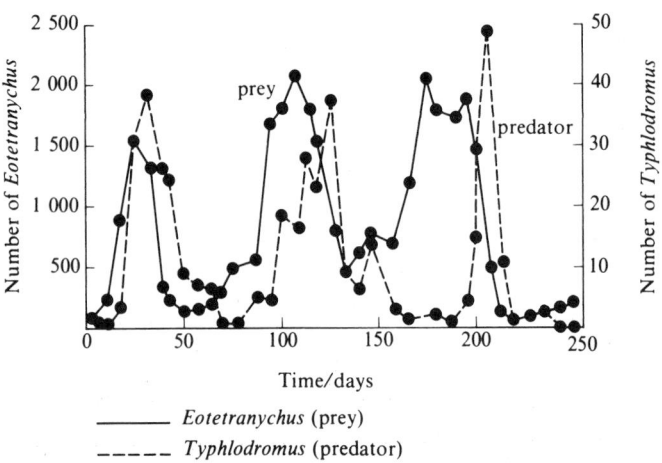

Fig 10.21 *Oscillations in the populations of the predatory mite* Typhlodromus *and its prey, the plant mite* Eotetranychus, *in a laboratory habitat. (From M.K. Sands (1978)* Problems in ecology, *Mills & Boon Limited.)*

fate of a population of deer on the Kaibab Plateau in Arizona. In 1906 the area was declared a wildlife refuge, and in order to protect the deer from their predators, a culling programme of the deers' main predators, such as pumas, wolves and coyotes, was planned for the next 30 years. Until 1906 the deer population had remained stable at about 4000, but subsequently a 'population explosion' occurred, as shown in fig 10.22, with the result that the carrying capacity of the rangeland, thought to be about 30 000 deer, was exceeded. The population grew rapidly to an estimated 100 000 by 1924, following a J-shaped growth curve instead of its normal sigmoidal curve. The deer population then crashed due to starvation and disease. Meanwhile the rangeland had been seriously damaged by overgrazing and did not recover to its 1906 level. As a result the carrying capacity of the area dropped to 10 000 deer.

Host–parasite relationships

In some of the cases studied host and parasite populations show similar out-of-phase cycles to those described above, notably when insects parasitise other insects.

Interspecific competition

Competition may occur between populations within an ecosystem for any of the available resources, such as food, space, light or shelter. If two species occur at the same trophic level then they are likely to compete with each other for food if they eat the same prey. Specialisation by one or both species over a period of time may lead to resource partitioning, so that they come to occupy separate niches within the trophic level and minimise the extent of competition (see below). Alternatively, if the competitors occupy the same niche, or strongly overlapping niches, an equilibrium situation may be reached in which neither succeeds as well as it would in the absence of the competitor, or one of the competitors declines in numbers

to the point of extinction. The latter phenomenon is known as **competitive exclusion**.

Interspecific competition is difficult to study in wild populations but some classic work on laboratory populations was done by the Russian biologist Gause in 1934 who worked on competition between several species of *Paramecium*. Some of his results are shown in fig 10.23.

> **10.17** With reference to fig 10.23,
> (a) what type of population growth curve is shown by the two species when grown in isolation?
> (b) what resources might the two species be competing for in the mixed culture?
> (c) what factors give *P. aurelia* a competitive advantage over *P. caudatum*?

When the two species are cultured together *P. aurelia* has a competitive advantage over *P. caudatum* for gaining food and after five days the numbers of *P. caudatum* start to decrease until, after about 20 days, the species has become 'extinct', that is it has been competitively excluded. *P. aurelia* takes longer to reach the stationary phase of growth than when grown in isolation, so is also affected adversely by the competition, even though it is more successful than its competitor. This helps to explain the selection pressure for competitors to adapt to separate niches. Under natural circumstances, the less successful competitor rarely becomes extinct, but merely becomes rare.

The **competitive exclusion principle** (or **Gausian exclusion principle**) has since been confirmed in further animal experiments. Competitive exclusions have also been shown to occur in plant populations, such as in mixed cultures of duckweed (*Lemna*) species.

The study of natural populations is made more complex by the larger number of interacting populations and by the fact that the environmental variables such as temperature, moisture and food supply cannot be controlled.

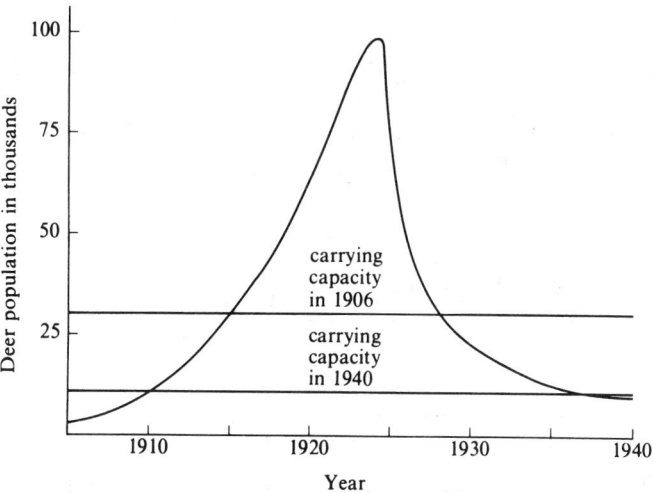

Fig 10.22 *Deer population on the Kaibab Plateau following eradication of predators.*

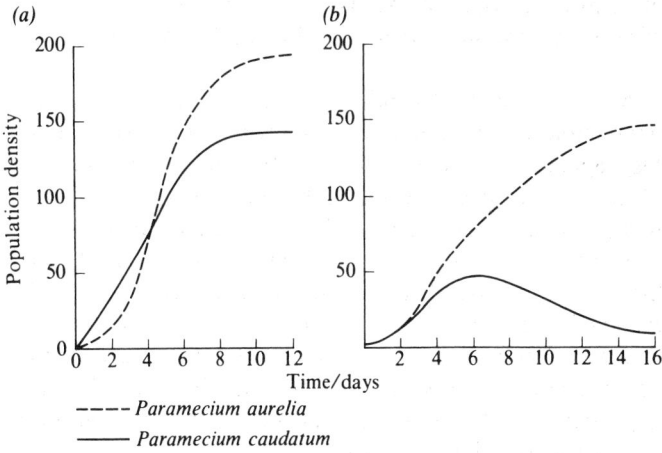

Fig 10.23 *Population growth of two species of* Paramecium, *(a) cultured separately, (b) cultured together.*

One form of competition which has attracted a lot of interest involves complex organic molecules that are produced by plants and animals which affect the growth of other living organisms. They include antibiotics and growth inhibitors, such as penicillin which is produced by the fungus *Penicillium* and has antibiotic properties against Gram positive bacteria (section 2.2.2). Chemical competition among microorganisms is very intense and the relationships between them very complex.

Resource partitioning

The more specialised an organism becomes for a particular niche, the less chance there is of direct competition. So, in long-established communities which are species-rich, **resource partitioning** (specialisation by different species to make use of different resources) leads to less competition and a more stable community structure.

Resource partitioning may take several forms, for example:

● specialisation of morphology and behaviour for different foods, such as the beaks of birds which may be modified for picking up insects, drilling holes, cracking nuts, tearing flesh and so on;

● vertical separation (stratification, see fig 10.15), such as canopy dwellers and forest floor dwellers;

● horizontal separation, such as the occupation of different microhabitats.

However, despite a tendency for each species to evolve its own particular niche, some direct competition between species for available resources will still occur.

10.8   Human impacts on ecosystems

Until the last ten thousand years or so, living systems evolved in response to changes in the abiotic environment, unaffected by human activity. Since the development of agriculture and technology, an increasing human impact on the environment has occurred. In the last two centuries especially, widespread industrialisation has led to potentially damaging environmental pollution.

Pollution may be defined as the release into the environment of substances or energy in such quantities and for such duration that they cause harm to people or other organisms or their environment. Pollution can affect all aspects of environment, human-made and natural, abiotic and biotic, and may be readily transferred between components of the life support system.

10.8.1   Air pollution

Until fairly recently air pollutants were generally considered a local problem associated with urban and industrial centres. Now it has become apparent that pollutants may be transported long distances in the air, causing adverse effects in environments far removed from the source of emission. Air pollution and its control is thus a global issue demanding international cooperation. Important atmospheric pollutants include gases such as chlorofluorocarbons (CFCs), sulphur dioxide (SO_2), hydrocarbons (HCs) and the oxides of nitrogen (NO_x). Increasing levels of natural gases, such as carbon dioxide, in the atmosphere as a result of human activity can also be considered as a form of pollution.

Gases occurring naturally in the atmosphere may be affected seriously by pollution, such as the depletion of ozone (O_3) high in the atmosphere. Paradoxically in some locations ozone is occurring with increasing frequency as a ground-level air pollutant. These raised levels damage many crop plants and, in association with hydrocarbons and NO_x pollutants, are an important constituent of photochemical smog and may generate a direct human health hazard. Dust, noise, waste heat, radioactivity and electromagnetic pulses may also pollute the atmosphere.

Carbon dioxide and the greenhouse effect

The main exchange pathways in the carbon cycle were summarised in fig 10.12. Much of the carbon is locked away in complex inorganic forms, such as carbonates in rocks, and in complex organic forms in fossil fuels and biomass. The release of some of this stored carbon into the atmosphere, as carbon dioxide, has increased in recent times with the burning of large amounts of fossil fuels and with large-scale deforestation (section 10.8.3).

10.18 How does deforestation increase atmospheric carbon dioxide?

Carbon dioxide is normally present in the lower atmosphere, the troposphere, in very small amounts, about 300 ppm or 0.03% by volume. Its importance lies in its contribution to the planetary greenhouse effect. Carbon dioxide is transparent to incoming short-wave radiation from the Sun, but absorbs strongly the long-wave radiation which the Earth re-radiates into Space. It therefore 'traps' outgoing radiation, warming the lower atmosphere which in turn radiates energy back to the surface of the Earth. Ultimately, of course, any given 'package' of incoming energy will be dissipated and lost to Space, but the atmosphere–surface exchanges induced by the presence of carbon dioxide (and other near-surface greenhouse gases) are sufficient to raise planetary surface temperatures some 32 °C above those that would otherwise occur.

It is important to realise that without this basic greenhouse effect, which has varied little for millions of years, living systems as we know them would not exist. The contemporary concern lies with the clear evidence that carbon dioxide levels (and those of other greenhouse gases, notably carbon monoxide, methane and chloro-fluorocarbons (CFCs)), are rising at a rate unprecedented in recent Earth history and their increased presence may lead to an increasingly warmer surface environment (fig 10.24), namely an **enhanced greenhouse effect**. This may in turn lead to increased evaporation and a greater atmospheric water vapour content. Since water vapour also acts as a powerful long-wave absorber, this may further increase surface temperatures. A resulting rise in surface

temperatures would cause changes in the distribution pattern and intensity of the major planetary weather systems which would profoundly affect human activities and the distribution of organisms.

In 1988 an Intergovernmental Panel on Climate Change (IPCC) was established to coordinate scientific information and research on the likely causes and consequences of increased levels of carbon dioxide and other greenhouse gases and to identify effective remedies. The Earth Summit in 1992 attempted to secure international agreement on targets for CO_2 emissions for all countries. We cannot be certain whether enhanced greenhouse warming will happen though some scientists consider that is has already begun. Nevertheless international governmental action to control pollutant greenhouse gases is a welcome trend.

Ozone depletion

The atmosphere provides a thermal blanket and radiation shield to the Earth. In the upper atmosphere, 15–50 km above the Earth, oxygen and ozone absorb much of the incoming short-wave radiation which is mostly very harmful to living organisms, in particular in damaging their genetic material. Although ultraviolet radiation of certain wavelengths has a beneficial effect in the production of vitamin D (section 8.7.9), overexposure to strong sunlight is known to increase the risk of skin cancer. Furthermore radiation absorption by ozone high in the atmosphere warms these higher levels and creates a deep temperature inversion layer (where the highest temperatures are at greatest altitude). This effectively limits the movement of air in the atmosphere by convection. Any change or weakening of this inversion layer would profoundly alter global weather patterns and hence Earth surface climates.

Ozone is produced high in the atmosphere by the action of sunlight on oxygen molecules. Chlorofluorocarbons are a group of chemicals, including carbon tetrachloride and chloroform, which are commonly used as solvents, aerosol propellants and refrigerator coolants. They are not readily broken down in the atmosphere and may contribute to increased 'greenhouse' warming. Eventually they diffuse into the stratosphere. High in the atmosphere they are broken down by sunlight, releasing chlorine and fluorine. These react with ozone and break it down into oxygen faster than it can be reformed from oxygen into ozone. CFC pollution thus shifts the oxygen–ozone equilibrium.

In 1987 a seasonal, but complete, depletion of the ozone layer occurred above Antarctica for the first time and, in the 1990s, ozone thinning over the Arctic has been regularly observed. Scientists are not certain why this is happening. A possible explanation may be that increased cooling of the stratosphere is taking place due to the enhanced greenhouse effect which is trapping more radiated heat near Earth's surface. This may in turn mean the Arctic stratosphere is more frequently cold enough to enable formation of stratospheric ice clouds. Rapid ozone depletion then takes place. A worrying outcome may be that in spite of worldwide efforts to reduce emissions of CFCs the

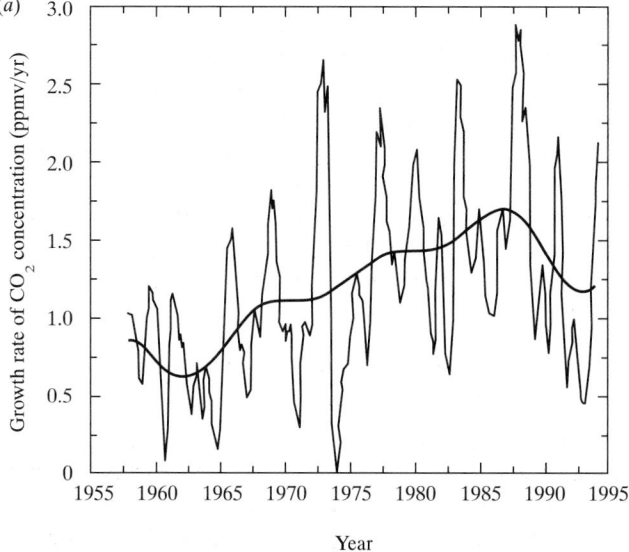

(*a*) 3.0

(*b*) Industrial carbon emissions and global reservoir changes since the mid-nineteenth century.

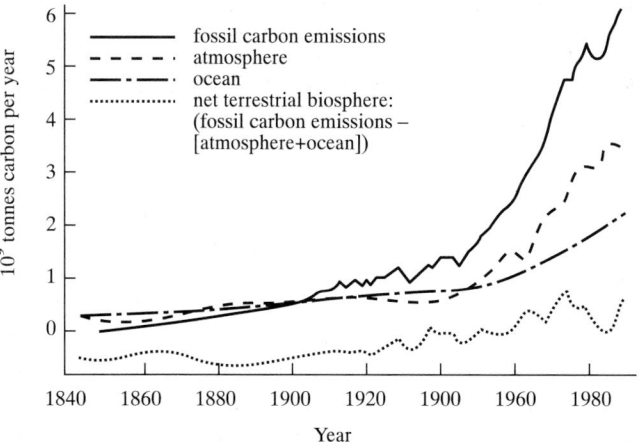

Fig 10.24 *(a) Growth rate of carbon dioxide concentration since 1958 (from the Mauna Loa record). The smooth curve shows the same data filtered to suppress any variations on a time scale less than 10 years. Currently atmospheric carbon dioxide concentration is about 355 ppmv.*
(b) Industrial carbon emissions and global reservoir changes since the mid-nineteenth century. The calculation implies that the terrestrial biosphere was a net source of carbon before 1940 (negative values) and has been a net sink since about 1960. (From Climate Change *(1994) IPCC Scientific Assessment, WMO/UNEP, CUP.)*

stratospheric ozone layer may not, as previously predicted, recover quickly in the next century. Recovery may also depend on controlling the enhanced greenhouse effect.

Acid rain

Acid rain is neither a simple nor a single phenomenon. The acid gases sulphur dioxide (SO_2) and oxides of nitrogen (NO_x) are produced by burning fossil fuels. Incomplete combustion of these fuels also releases hydrocarbons. These may have effects as dry gases or they may be washed out of the atmosphere to produce acid precipitation in rain and snow (fig 10.25). The most industrialised areas of the world, such as the eastern USA, western Europe, north-east China and Japan, have all experienced rainfall with a pH well below 4.0.

Acid rainfall (pH <5) often causes major changes in ecosystems and damage to buildings. This often happens in countries bordering those which are major sources of pollutants. Norway and Sweden, for example, receive acid rain as a result of air pollutants emitted in the UK and industrial centres of Europe which are transported by prevailing high-level winds. Acid rainfall in central Sweden and southern Norway has affected salmon and trout fisheries (fig 10.26) and damaged forests. Tree injury associated with acid pollution is now widespread in Europe (fig 10.27) and evidence for damage to beech and yew has been recorded in Britain.

Acid rain leaches magnesium and calcium from soils and from damaged leaves. Eventually aluminium, manganese and heavy metals such as iron and cadmium come into solution and may reach toxic concentrations, causing damage to tree roots and the breakdown of mycorrhizas. This decreases the capacity of the tree to take up water and nutrients. Disease induced by mineral deficiencies becomes common, a situation made worse by dry conditions.

Cures, such as adding lime to lakes (Sweden) and forests (W. Germany) can only be viewed as temporary stop-gaps. The remedy lies in reducing the release of pollutant gases.

Attention has been focused on reducing sulphur dioxide emissions since these have significant and clearly identifiable industrial sources, most notably coal-fired electricity generators. Furthermore the desulphurisation technology is available and effective, though costly. In the long term, however, it may be equally important to reduce hydrocarbon and nitrogen oxide emissions.

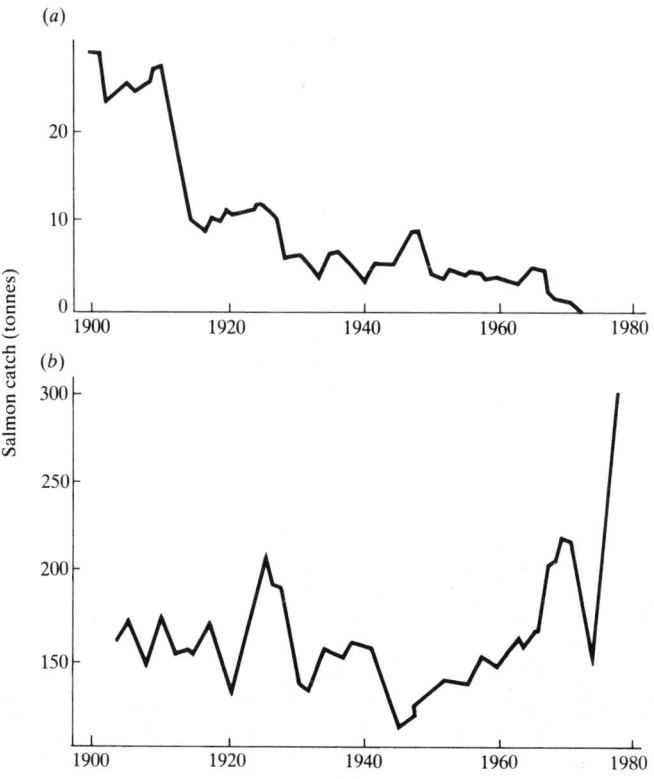

Fig 10.26 *Trends in the salmon catch from Norwegian rivers; (a) southern rivers, the area most affected by acid rain, (b) 68 other rivers in Norway. (From F. Pearce (1986)* Unravelling a century of acid pollution, New Scientist 11, *1527, p.33.)*

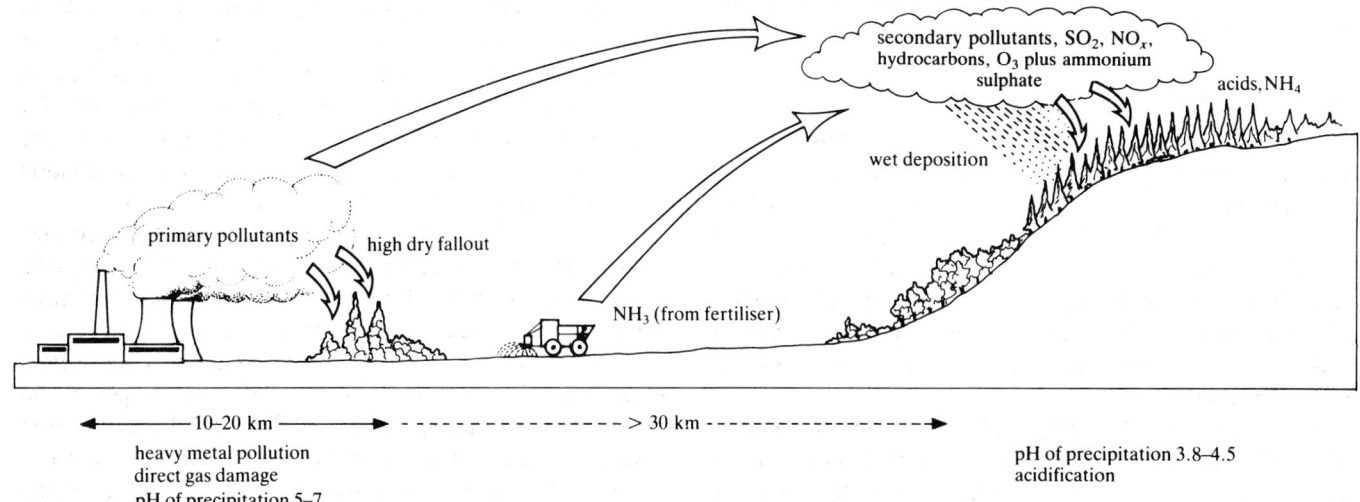

Fig 10.25 *The complexity of 'acid rain', a schematic representation of how air pollutants interact in complex ways to produce different effects in different areas. (From C. Rose (1985)* Acid rain falls on British woodland, New Scientist, *108, 1482, 52–7.)*

328

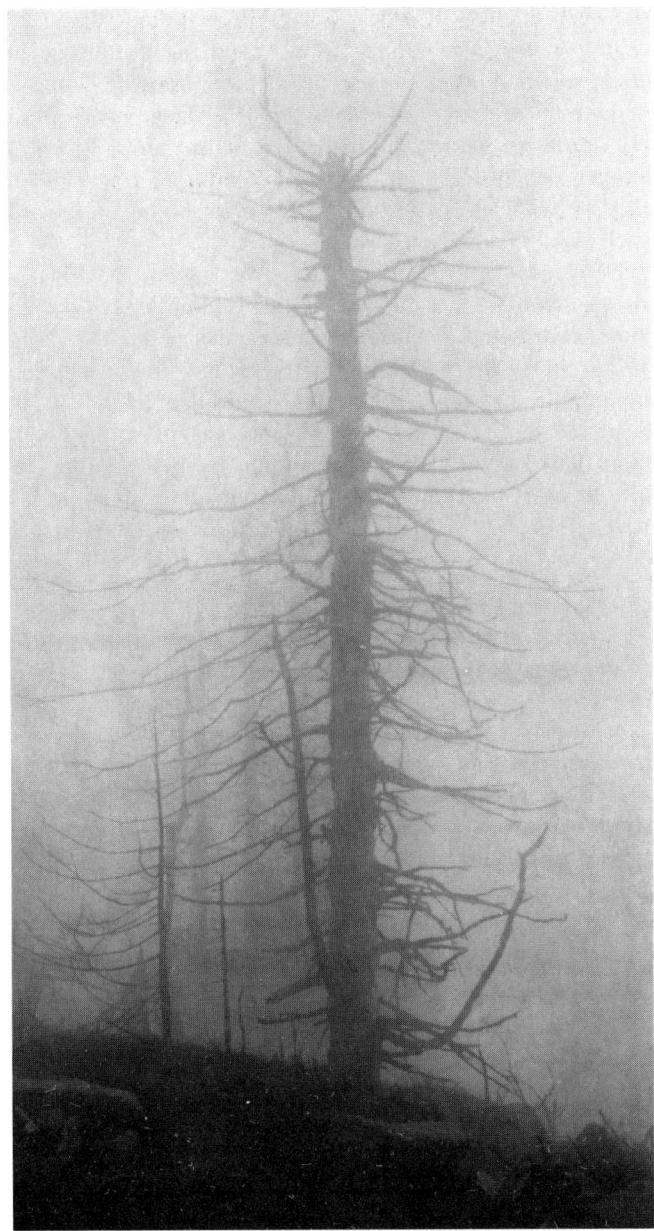

Fig 10.27 *Acid dieback in a German forest.*

10.8.2 Water pollution

Until recently water pollution has been a relatively local problem of the developed world. **Eutrophication** is the most common problem, where inland waters and rivers are polluted with nitrogen and phosphorus run-off from fertilisers used in intensive agriculture and discharge of phosphate-rich sewage effluents. Such problems are increasingly occurring on a worldwide basis and now affect marine as well as freshwater ecosystems.

Sewage from coastal settlements discharges, sometimes untreated, into coastal waters where it generates a direct health hazard for recreational bathers as well as marine organisms. Land drainage from urban areas, industrial and waste disposal sites is often contaminated with heavy metals or hydrocarbons. Biological concentration of heavy metals in marine food chains may give lethal doses, as occurred following the industrial discharge of mercury into coastal waters at Minimata in Japan. Here, concentrations in fish led to the deaths of many humans and other animal predators. At sub-lethal levels heavy metals and contaminants such as pesticide and oil derivatives may lower resistance to disease.

During the last decade measures to control and eventually stop toxic waste dumping and incineration at sea have been introduced by countries bordering the North Sea in an attempt to reduce pollution and damage to this ecosystem.

Another major problem is caused by excessive soil erosion on the land surface. This increases the silt load of rivers and coastal waters which may beneficially enrich fisheries. However, it can also be destructive. For example, it is leading to coral reef destruction in the Australian Great Barrier Reef as a result of deforestation on the mainland.

Other important forms of water pollution include thermal pollution and oil pollution.

Eutrophication

Eutrophication means nutrient enrichment. Over a long time period, typically several thousand years, lake ecosystems classically show a natural progression from an **oligotrophic** (few nutrients) to a **eutrophic** or even **dystrophic** (rich in nutrients) state (table 10.6). In the twentieth century, however, rapid eutrophication has occurred in many lakes, in semi-enclosed seas such as the Baltic, Mediterranean and Black Sea, and in river systems worldwide. This is due to human activity.

The main factors that cause eutrophication are heavy use of nitrogen fertilisers on agricultural land and the increased discharge of phosphates from sewage works. The phosphate problem reflects not only a larger human population but also the modern tendency for more people to live in urban areas and the development of mains sewage systems.

Eutrophication generates acute economic as well as ecological problems. Good quality water resources are important for many industrial processes, vital for human and livestock drinking water supplies, essential for commercial and recreational fisheries and necessary for the maintenance of recreational amenities and navigation routes on major waterways (table 10.7).

Nitrates and particularly phosphates are the nutrients most commonly limiting primary productivity in aquatic ecosystems. Additional nitrate and phosphate, therefore, favours an increase in rapidly growing competitive planktonic species. As it takes longer for consumer organisms to increase in number in response to environmental change, this means that not all the increased primary production is eaten by the consumer organisms. Instead the excess material enters the decomposition pathway. Breakdown to simple inorganic nutrients is an oxygen-demanding process. Dissolved oxygen levels may be reduced below those necessary for the successful growth

Table 10.6 The general characteristics of oligotrophic and eutrophic lakes.

	Oligotrophic	Eutrophic
Depth	deeper	shallower
Summer oxygen in hypolimnion	present	absent
Algae and blue-green bacteria	high species diversity, with low density and productivity, often dominated by green algae	low species diversity with high density and productivity, often dominated by blue-green bacteria
Blooms	rare	frequent
Plant nutrient flux	low	high
Animal production	low	high
Fish	salmonids (e.g. trout, char) and coregonids (whitefish) often dominant	coarse fish (e.g. perch, roach, carp) often dominant

(Source: C.F. Mason (1981) *Biology of freshwater pollution*, Longman.)
Note
In the classic mode of natural lake eutrophication a newly formed deep lake (a classic situation would be following retreat of an ice sheet) contains few nutrients since there has been no opportunity for weathering and sediment removal from the surrounding catchment. Primary and secondary productivity are hence low, the waters are clear, and oxygen status is good throughout.

With time, as weathering proceeds, nutrient status increases, primary and secondary productivity rise, organic and inorganic sediments accumulate and the lake becomes shallower. The more productive waters are less clear and the hypolimnion (see fig 10.29) may become seasonally oxygen-depleted.

A **dystrophic** lake is one which receives large quantities of organic matter from terrestrial plants giving the water a brown colouration. Such lakes typically have peat-filled margins and may develop into peat bogs.

Table 10.7 The main effects of eutrophication on the receiving ecosystem and the problems for human societies associated with these effects.

Effects
(1) Species diversity decreases and the dominant biota change
(2) Plant, algal and animal biomass increase
(3) Turbidity increases
(4) Rate of sedimentation increases, shortening the life span of the lake
(5) Anoxic conditions may develop

Problems
(1) Treatment of drinking water may be difficult and the supply may have an unacceptable taste or odour
(2) The water may be injurious to health
(3) The amenity value of the water may decrease
(4) Increased vegetation may impede water flow and navigation
(5) Commercially important species (such as salmonids and coregonids) may disappear

(Source: C.F. Mason (1981) *Biology of freshwater pollution*, Longman.)

and reproduction of other species. In extreme cases, the death of fish and other species and their subsequent decomposition can impose a further oxygen demand, making the situation increasingly worse. This may not just be a problem for the immediately affected area. Zones of oxygen depletion on an otherwise unaffected river system may be sufficient to disrupt breeding in migratory species such as salmon and eels.

Deoxygenation of a river caused by organic wastes is a slow process so that the point of maximum deoxygenation may occur some distance downstream of a discharge (fig 10.28). In the River Thames in 1967, at low flow in autumn, minimum oxygen conditions prevailed for 40 km downstream of London Bridge, whereas in spring, with high flow, only 12 km had minimum oxygen. During the last 30 years major efforts have been made to clean up the River Thames. Oxygen depletion on this scale no longer occurs and fish are found throughout the course of the river.

> **10.19** List the factors that will determine the degree of deoxygenation.

In lake ecosystems the problem of eutrophic oxygen depletion may be made worse by seasonal water **stratification**, when the water forms layers with different temperatures. In temperate regions thermal stratification typically establishes in early summer (fig 10.29). This occurs for two main reasons.

- The Sun heats the surface water. Warmer water is less dense so it remains in the top layer of the lake (**epilimnion**). Heat transfer to deeper layers can only take place by conduction which is a slow process in water.
- Rivers and streams draining into the lake are shallow by comparison. Their water will have become warmed throughout its depth. This warmer water, being also lighter and less dense, mixes only with the surface waters of the lake further raising its temperature by comparison with the deeper water (the **hypolimnion**).

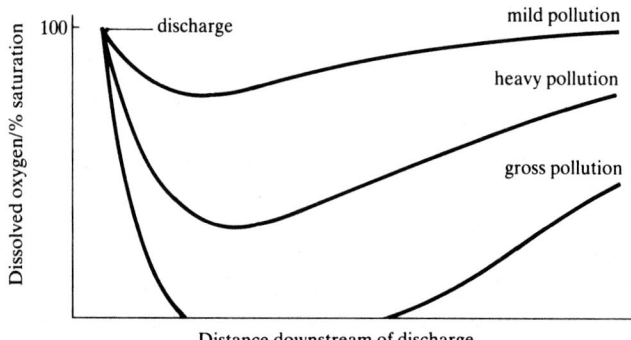

Fig 10.28 *A typical 'oxygen sag' curve; the effect of organic discharge on the oxygen content of river water. (From C.F. Mason (1981)* Biology of fresh water pollution, *Longman.)*

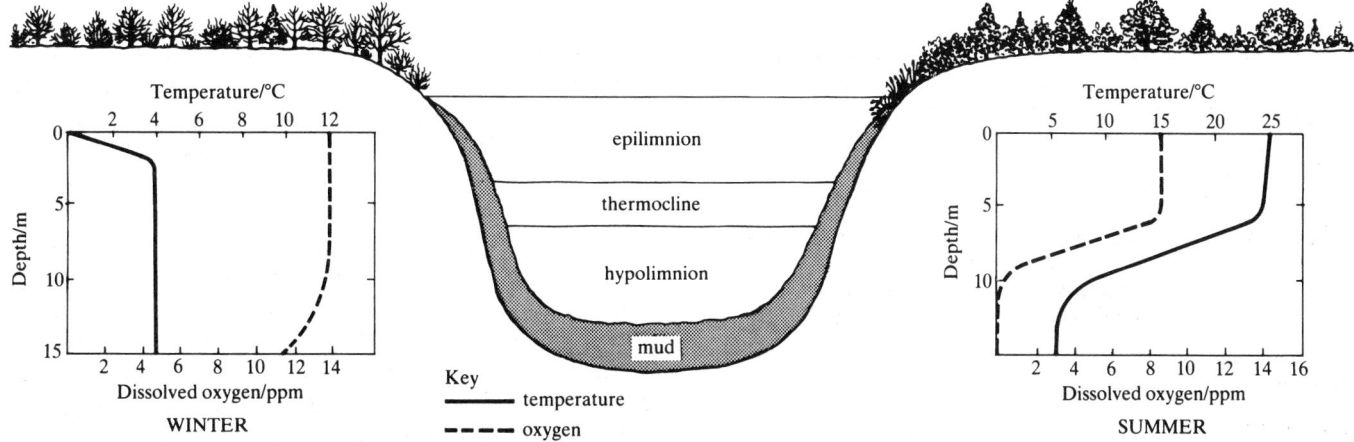

Fig 10.29 *Thermal stratification in a mid-latitude lake (Linsley ponds, Conn. USA). In summer, a warm oxygen-rich circulating layer of water, the epilimnion, is separated from cold oxygen-poor hypolimnion waters by a broad zone of rapid temperature change called the thermocline. A similar gradient in oxygen also occurs across the thermocline. (Modified from E.P. Odum (1971)* Fundamentals of ecology, *Saunders.)*

This has important consequences for lake ecosystems. In particular it affects the supply of oxygen to the deep waters.

Oxygen supplies in lake waters come from three main sources. These are:

- photosynthesis which requires light and is therefore most rapid in the surface waters;
- diffusion from the atmosphere;
- oxygen in stream and river waters draining into the lake.

These sources all primarily enrich the surface waters. Oxygen in the deeper water will depend on effective diffusion from above or extreme turbulence linked with storm events. Storminess and good mixing of the water is more characteristic of the winter season. So once the thermal stratification pattern has become established life in the deep waters will be dependent on the oxygen supplies locked away in spring.

In a healthy lake ecosystem most primary producers are eaten. Very few die and form food materials for detritivores and decomposers. However, if increased phytoplankton production occurs in the surface waters, encouraged by the warmth and increased nutrient status of the epilimnion or by eutrophication, then the excess primary producers not consumed by herbivores will fall into the hypolimnion when they die. Here their decomposition makes an additional oxygen demand on a restricted oxygen resource. Providing sufficient oxygen is present to meet this extra demand, as well as the needs of existing fauna, no major problem will arise. However, if there is insufficient oxygen, sudden and catastrophic fish kills may result in late summer when oxygen supplies approach exhaustion.

Monitoring eutrophication

Changes associated with eutrophication can be monitored biologically and chemically. This gives the opportunity for remedial action before catastrophic ecosystem damage occurs. Changes in phytoplankton species present may help to indicate eutrophication, for example blue-green bacterial blooms are common. Eutrophic waters characteristically show high abundance and low species diversity of phytoplankton.

A useful chemical indicator of eutrophication is the **biochemical oxygen demand (BOD)** (Experiment 11.9), which measures the rate of oxygen depletion by organisms. It is assumed this primarily reflects microorganism activity in decomposing organic matter present in waters. (As discussed, organic matter typically increases as waters become nutrient-enriched.) However, oxygen consumption by algae will inevitably also be included in the test. In practice this is normally not important, but in some cases it may account for up to 50% of the total BOD. BOD is thus an approximate rather than precise guide to water quality. It is most useful when used in conjunction with other water quality indicators.

> **10.20** What are the advantages and disadvantages of biological rather than chemical monitoring of eutrophication?

Thermal pollution

Thermal pollution can be a problem in rivers and coastal areas. It most typically arises from the use of water as a coolant in industrial processes, such as in electricity generating plants. Water discharging from electricity stations may be warmer than that taken in. Warm water has a lower dissolved oxygen content than cold water. At the same time the increased warmth raises the metabolic rate of organisms in the water and thus increases their oxygen demand. With small temperature differences no major biotic change occurs. However, where the difference in temperature is large, significant changes may result. For example migratory species such as salmon and trout may be prevented from returning to spawning sites or from moving downstream to the open sea by intervening stretches of warmer water with reduced oxygen content.

In a river or estuary contaminated with sewage or other organic effluents, addition of warm water may actually *improve* conditions. The coolant water will have become well oxygenated during use and may contain more oxygen than the water it is joining. This may promote increased microbial activity within the polluted water and lead to more rapid restoration of good water quality.

Oil pollution

Oil pollution is a major hazard for marine and coastal environments. The main sources of marine oil pollution are:

- damage to oil tanker ships through collision with other ships, explosion, or wrecking;
- seepage from offshore installations;
- flushing of tanker holds.

Each year about 10 million tonnes of crude oil is spilt into the Earth's oceans from incidents of this type.

Crude oil kills seaweeds, molluscs and crustaceans when washed onto rocky shores. Marine mammals may also be affected by oil spills, for example when their fur is oiled. However, usually the worst casualties of major oil spills are fish-eating birds because oil penetrates and mats the plumage making flight impossible; heat insulation is lost and birds may die of hypothermia; buoyancy is also reduced causing birds to drown; attempts to preen leads to ingestion of oil and gut irritation. Phytoplankton, however, do not appear to be greatly affected by the oil, though shading may temporarily restrict light penetration and reduce photosynthesis.

The long-term damage to ecosystems caused by major oil spills is minimal. Recovery is more rapid and complete when oil is left to disperse naturally. Bacterial decomposition aided by break-up of the slick by wind and wave action can mean complete recovery in 3 or 4 years in warm or temperate climates. In colder environments, such as the Alaskan coast affected by the *Exxon Valdez* spill in 1989, effects are more persistent since bacterial activity is slower. Use of **dispersants** may accelerate break up of oil slicks, but the agents used often cause lasting damage because detergents are toxic and are not readily biodegradable.

Studies have shown, however, that the less spectacular but persistent spills and leakages, linked for example with coastal refineries and oil terminals, have a more damaging effect on marine and coastal ecosystems than the well-publicised major incidents.

Techniques for treating and preventing oil pollution have improved. These include:

- use of floating booms to prevent slicks from reaching sensitive shore lines;
- burning heavy oil residues (where feasible);
- collection of oil and pumping back into special collection ships;
- spraying onto oil slicks naturally occurring bacteria such as *Pseudomonas* that can digest oil (see chapter 25);
- use of new specially designed oil spill cleaners that are less toxic and more biodegradable than those used previously;
- careful routing of supertankers to avoid hazardous waters and ecologically sensitive areas;
- introduction of double-skinned tanker hulls;
- introduction of new ballast systems.

10.8.3   Degradation of terrestrial ecosystems

Since prehistoric times, humans have manipulated ecosystems in their search for food, shelter, fuel and other resources and by the impact of discarded waste materials. The first hunter–gatherer communities had minimal impact but, as human societies became increasingly settled, numerous and technically advanced, their impact on Earth's ecosystems increased dramatically. For example, deforestation in Britain, which began in Neolithic times, expanded rapidly to the point where at the start of the twentieth century only 3% of the land surface remained wooded. Deforestation on a global scale is now an issue of great concern.

The destruction of woodlands and forests is usually in response to the need for more land for growing crops and rearing livestock, and results in the creation of completely new, managed ecosystems. Mismanagement of these ecosystems has created other problems, such as soil erosion, desertification and adverse effects associated with the widespread use of new synthetic organic compounds as pesticides.

Global deforestation

Forests are the natural climax vegetation of many parts of the world covering, until recent years, a third of the land surface. Today temperate forests are not significantly decreasing in area though in the past large scale deforestation has occurred. In fact major replanting and conservation initiatives are underway in many countries. Tropical forests on the other hand are declining at a rate that will decrease their 1950 extent (15% of global land surface) to 300 million hectares (7% of global land surface) by the year 2000 AD. It has been estimated that twelve million hectares of forest, an area the size of England, are disappearing annually and a further ten million hectares are being degraded by removal of good timber species, inappropriate management and inattention to conservation needs.

Where human population densities are low, tropical forest clearance for agriculture using traditional shifting cultivation methods does little lasting damage. A small area is felled and the timber burnt leaving a clearing for cultivation. Ash from the burn provides nutrients for the crops and the burn destroys pests. Crops planted in the ash enriched soil are initially very productive, though, as the nutrient supply from the ash becomes exhausted, crop productivity declines. At the same time rainforest understorey species will begin to invade the clearing. After 3 or 4 years the plot is abandoned as it is easier and more rewarding to clear and fire a new area than to try to maintain and cultivate the existing plot. The original plot will then quite quickly regenerate to mature forest, typically taking 30 to 40 years to establish a mature rainforest canopy.

Re-establishment of mature vegetation is important. In tropical moist forests the main biomass store and the main nutrient store is in the above-ground vegetation. Tropical forest soils often lack any significant nutrient store. The main nutrient supply for the vegetation comes from recycled nutrients. Litter is rapidly decomposed and its nutrients are recycled within five or six weeks or less. The trees have a thick surface root mat and the fine rootlets absorb 99.9% of all inorganic nutrients percolating down through them. Many trees are legumes and have root nodules with nitrogen-fixing bacteria; others commonly have mycorrhizas which, in their feeding process, transfer nutrients from decomposing litter direct to the tree roots. Maintaining an unbroken cycle is important to maintaining fertility. This is quite easy in shifting cultivation, where the small-scale clearances resemble the natural gaps which occur from time to time in the forest canopy. It is very difficult to maintain fertility when large-scale clearance takes place.

Small gap size clearances and long fallow periods between felling produce a sustainable forest agriculture. If the vegetation is felled again before reaching maturity, then the ash produced will be less abundant and the nutrient supply for new crops will be reduced. The clearing will be less productive and will be abandoned more quickly, increasing demands on the surrounding forested areas.

As human population size increases, larger areas of land may be cultivated to supply food. In addition, fuel wood gathering will lead to further deforestation. Changing land use may make the situation much worse, such as clearance of large areas for the growth of cash crops or for ranching. In some forests commercial logging for tropical hardwoods such as teak and mahogany is another major cause of deforestation.

Loss of forests is serious for many reasons.

- There is a loss of traditionally harvested products such as timber, poles, twine, fuel-wood, honey, fruit, game animals and herbs, that at one time supplied local people with their needs.

- The demand for softwood timber (for building), pulp wood (for making paper) and tropical hardwood (for furniture) is rising globally. Long-term supplies are threatened.

- Forests are often on uplands and on watersheds. Here they catch large amounts of rain. An intact forest canopy softens the impact of intense tropical rainfall in many ways. It releases large amounts of water back to the atmosphere in evaporation and transpiration and channels water gently through the vegetation to the soil. Infiltration to the soil is high and there is a long delay before water percolates through to the streams and rivers. If the forest canopy is removed, the tropical soil surface bakes hard in the intense heat. Rainfall cannot easily penetrate the surface and is rapidly lost from the area in surface run-off. Regeneration is difficult and, at the same time a flood hazard is created in the plains below. For example, in Bangladesh in the summer of 1988, flooding occurred on an unprecedented scale affecting most of the country, largely due to the deforestation in the mountains to the north in India and Nepal.

- More rapid run-off of rainwater results in soil erosion. This can remove the topsoil and leave ground unsuitable for growing crops. It can also lead to silting of reservoirs which reduces their useful life, whilst harbours and estuaries must be continually dredged to keep them open.

- Deforestation increases global carbon dioxide (see section 10.8.1) which may have long-term effects on the global climate.

- Forests have species-rich and diverse wildlife communities. Their destruction will lead to innumerable extinctions of little-known forms of life with the consequent loss of genetic variety and potential resources. Tropical forests have already given us anti-cancer and anti-malaria drugs and scientists are actively investigating tropical moist forest plants for drugs to control HIV and many other diseases.

Fig 10.30 *Villager planting maniok in a clearing in Madagascar rainforest produced by slash and burn.*

Soil erosion and desertification

Deforestation is not the only cause of soil erosion. Mismanagement of farmland and grassland may lead to a rapid loss of soil. Soil formation is a slow process. Hilly areas with steep slopes which are regularly cultivated and also have high rainfall are especially susceptible to soil erosion. Parts of south-east Asia have long-established systems of terracing that have proved very effective in holding soil. These are in areas where forests have been cleared. Principal soil conservation measures are terrace cultivation, contour ploughing and making ridges to stop run-off of rain. Annually, five million hectares of farmed land are coming out of crop production, worldwide, because of erosion losses. Grasslands that are overgrazed by livestock frequently lose the plant cover that holds the topsoil. Plants are eaten to their roots and die, with the result that water running freely across the land surface causes sheet erosion, carrying off the topsoil. Channelled rainwater forms gullies which cut deep into the land surface. About seven million hectares of grazing land are lost this way each year and much of this will become desert.

Deserts may form naturally, for example when rains persistently fail in semi-arid areas, but their creation can be accelerated by human activity in a process called **desertification**. This is a general term for the degradation of dry land areas so that formerly productive land becomes useless. It usually results from:

- overgrazing by livestock,
- overcultivation,
- deforestation (as mentioned above),
- poor irrigation practices.

Overgrazing reduces the sparse vegetation cover, and trampling by livestock may break up the soil. Erosion of top soil by wind or during flash floods commonly results. Overcultivation can lead to the removal of nutrients and humus from the soil, leading again to sparse vegetation cover and the increased risk of erosion.

In irrigated areas, waterlogging and salinisation are the main problems. **Waterlogging** occurs when the water table lies close to the soil surface. Excess water use during irrigation may increase and extend the problem. This is a particular problem when the cultivated crops are intolerant of waterlogging, such as wheat and cotton. **Salinisation** is the increase in the concentration of soluble salts in the soil. This occurs when high rates of evaporation draw water and salts to the surface of the soil by capillary action. It also happens when saline irrigation water is used on soils which are not very permeable, and when deep ground water sources, which are naturally more salty than most other 'fresh' water, are used for irrigation. Few crops can tolerate a salt concentration of above 0.5–1.0%, so salinisation can be economically very important.

Restoration of desertified land is a complex problem. It may require the exclusion of people and their livestock from the area to allow surface vegetation to recover. Other practices may be used to reduce soil removal by flooding, such as the planting of trees, terracing on slopes or fencing to prevent soil loss. Installation of good drainage and efficient leaching systems can reduce the problems of waterlogging or salinisation. However, this can be administratively, socially, economically and politically difficult. Unless the socio-economic factors that trigger the use of dry lands are resolved, it is unlikely that local projects to alleviate the problems of land degradation will make a significant impact on desertification.

10.8.4 Pesticides and the environment

Pesticides are chemical substances used by humans to control pests. The term pesticide is an all-embracing word for **herbicides** (which kill plants), **insecticides** (which kill insects), **fungicides** (which act on fungi), and so on. Most pesticides are poisons and aim to kill the target species, but the term also includes chemosterilants (chemicals causing sterility) and growth inhibitors.

In Britain pesticide use is mainly associated with agriculture and horticulture, though pesticides are also widely used in food storage and to protect wood, wool and other natural products. In many countries pesticides are used in forestry and they are also used extensively to control human and animal disease vectors (as in malaria, chapter 15).

Ecological characteristics of pesticides

The important ecological characteristics of pesticides are toxicity, persistence and specificity.

Toxicity. For a particular species toxicity is commonly defined by the **lethal dose 50** (LD_{50}). This is the single dose which kills half an experimental laboratory population. In the field, when the organism is subjected to additional environmental stresses, a higher proportion may die. Nevertheless, by definition, some survive. (In short the aim in agriculture is to reduce crop injury to an acceptable level, this point being largely a question of economics). Unfortunately the survivors form the basis of a resistant pest population and, in organisms such as insects with a rapid life cycle, resistance and pest resurgence are common problems.

Persistence. This is the length of time that the pesticide remains in the environment, including within organisms, without being broken down. An example of a persistent insecticide is the organochlorine DDT which was commonly used between the 1940s and 1960s. Though persistence is generally an undesirable quality (particularly on food crops) in some instances, for example in the control of animal parasites and soil-borne diseases, some degree of persistence is an important practical and economic requirement. However, long-term persistence can be very damaging. For example, in the mid-1960s DDT was detected in the livers of penguins in the Antarctic, a habitat far from areas where DDT might have been used.

Toxicity and persistence are linked in that a lethal but non-persistent chemical may in the long run do less damage than a sublethal persistent chemical. This is because the latter has more opportunity for incorporation into food chains where it may be metabolised to a more toxic form or more typically accumulate to toxic concentrations in predators at the top of the chain (see question 10.21).

Pesticide poisoning has had devastating effects on some top carnivores, most notably birds. The peregrine falcon, for example, disappeared completely from the eastern USA as a result of DDT poisoning. Birds are especially vulnerable because DDT induces hormonal changes that affect calcium metabolism and result in the production of thinner egg shells with a consequently high loss of eggs through breakage.

DDT is now banned in most developed countries such as Britain and the USA. However, it is relatively cheap to produce and is still considered a good option for certain tasks, such as malaria control. When considering whether to use pesticides it is often a case of choosing the lesser of two evils. For example, DDT has completely eradicated malaria in many parts of the world.

Specificity. Pesticides vary in their specificity, that is the range of organisms they affect. DDT is an example of a broad-spectrum pesticide, because it seriously affects many different kinds of animals. Narrow-spectrum pesticides only affect a restricted range of organisms, for example pirimicarb only kills aphids and flies but does not affect beetles and most other insects. Likewise dalapon kills monocotyledonous plants but does not affect dicotyledons, whereas phenoxyacetic acid weedkillers eliminate dicotyledons but do not affect monocotyledons.

Use of broad-spectrum pesticides can lead to **pest resurgence**, that is when numbers of the pest after treatment increase to *more than before* the treatment. This is because the pesticide not only kills the pest, but also the predators of the pest.

A good example of this was seen in a study of the use of DDT to control cabbage white butterfly, *Pieris rapae*, on brussels sprouts. Initial pesticide application gave good control but subsequently numbers of butterfly larvae *exceeded* those in an unsprayed control area (fig 10.31). This effect was even more pronounced following repeat applications of DDT to 'control' the new infestation. Examination of the crop ecosystem showed that pesticide concentrations on the leaves were rapidly reduced due to subsequent growth of existing and new leaves. However, levels in the soil remained high, especially if crop residues were ploughed in. Thus eggs deposited by adults entering the crop from surrounding areas after spraying were little affected by the pesticide, but the main larval predators, the soil-dwelling ground beetle *Harpalus rufipes* and the harvestman *Phalangium opilio*, showed reduced numbers and survivors fed less frequently. Larval predation was thus significantly reduced and larval numbers exceeded pre-spraying levels. Further applications of DDT merely made this situation worse (fig 10.31). Predatory species are often more badly affected by pesticide use than the pest species. This is because they occur in lower numbers than their prey and therefore the population is more vulnerable and recovers more slowly.

(a)   1964 (after one application of DDT, 6 July 1964)

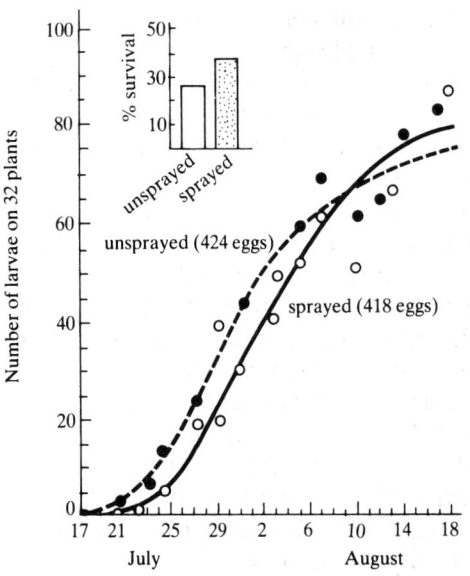

(b)   1965 (after three applications of DDT, 6 July, 20 August 1964 and 28 June 1965)

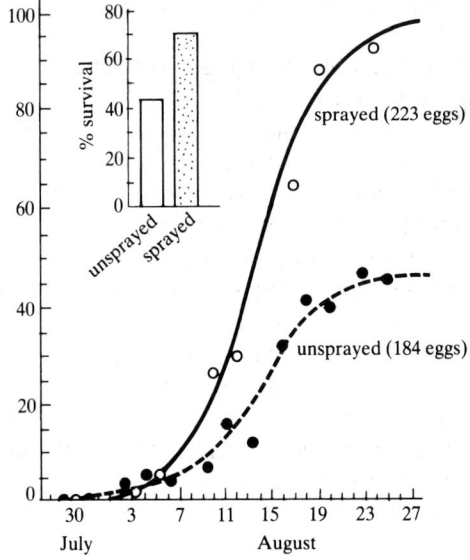

Fig 10.31   *An illustration of the differential effects of DDT on crop and soil fauna.* Pieris *lives on crops; spraying with DDT to control it is effective for only a very short period in the first year (a). As the soil-living predators of* Pieris *are affected by residuals in the soil,* Pieris *increases markedly after repeat spraying (b). (From J.D. Dempster (1968) The control of* Pieris rapae *with DDT, J. Appl. Ecol. 5, 451–62.)*

10.21 Fig 10.32 shows the amount of DDT at different levels in a food chain, the data for which were collected in the USA.

(a) If the concentration of DDT in the water surrounding the algae was 0.02 ppm, what was the final concentration factor for DDT in passing **from water** into (i) producers, (ii) small fish, (iii) large fish, (iv) the top carnivore.

(b) What conclusions can you draw from your answers to (a)?

(c) At which trophic level (i) is DDT likely to have the most marked effect, (ii) would DDT be most easily detected, (iii) are insect pests of crops found (a typical target of DDT)?

(d) Suggest ways in which penguins in the Antarctic might have come to contain DDT.

(e) Clear Lake, California, is a large lake used for recreational activities such as fishing. Disturbance of the natural ecosystem by eutrophication (nutrient enrichment, see section 10.8.2) led to increased populations of midges during the 1940s and these were treated by spraying with DDD, a close relative of DDT, in 1949, 1954 and 1957. The first and second applications killed about 99% of the midges but they recovered quickly and the third application had little effect on the population.

Analysis of small fish from the lake showed levels of 1–200 ppm of DDD in the flesh eaten by humans, and 40–2500 ppm in fatty tissues. A population of 1000 western grebes that bred at the lake died out and levels of 1600 ppm of DDT were found in their fatty tissues.

(i) Suggest a reason why the DDD did not succeed in eradicating the midges and why they recovered so quickly after the third application.

(ii) It has been observed that many animals die from DDT poisoning in times of food shortage. Suggest a reason for this based on the data given so far.

(f) In Great Britain, the winters of 1946–7 and 1962–3 were particularly severe. The death toll of birds was high in both winters, but much higher in 1962–3. Suggest a possible reason for this in the light of the data given about DDT.

Long-term consequences of pesticide exposure, even at low doses, and possible synergistic links with other contaminants or disease vectors are little known due to the relative newness of most pesticides. There is mounting concern that the 'harmless' traces of pesticide metabolites left as residues on food, though not directly toxic and certainly not lethal, may, nevertheless, lower disease resistance or be biologically accumulated to significant levels. Pesticide residues in the North Sea are thought by many scientists to be linked with the rapid spread of viral disease in the common seal population during summer 1988.

The general effect of pesticide use is to reduce species diversity. It also tends to increase productivity at lower levels of ecosystems and lessen productivity at higher levels. The effects on decomposer organisms are poorly understood and the implications of all these for nutrient cycling and soil fertility need further study. Fig 10.33 summarises the main ways in which pesticides affect ecosystems. You should consider the implications of these changes.

Problems such as those outlined, especially resistance, resurgence and health risk to the human population, have led to more extensive consideration of alternative control techniques. The main alternatives, **biological control** and **integrated control** (more carefully targeted use of pesticides linked with biological control), are now briefly considered.

Biological control of pests

Biological control of pests has traditionally meant regulation by natural enemies: predators, parasites and pathogens. As such it represents a form of population management preventing unchecked exponential growth of pest species (section 10.7.3, growth curves). Some scientists take a wider view and include other techniques, such as genetic manipulation. **Cultural control** methods such as crop rotation, tillage, mixed cropping, removal of crop residues and adjustment of harvest or sowing times to favour crop or natural enemies rather than pest may also be considered biological control.

Classic biological control has been most successfully applied to introduced species which may lack natural controls, either biological or physical in a new environment. The control of cottony cushion scale, *Icerya purchasi*, on newly established citrus plantations in California in the late-nineteenth century is the first truly successful example of scientifically planned biological control. This pest was introduced with nursery stock from its native Australia. Field searches in Australia identified two natural enemies, a parasitic fly *Cryptochetum iceryae* and a predatory ladybeetle, *Rodolia cardinalis*, commonly known as Vedalia. These were taken to California and, after careful study and successful controlled release in canvas tents, were released into the wild. Both parasite and predator spread rapidly and effective and persistent control was achieved within months.

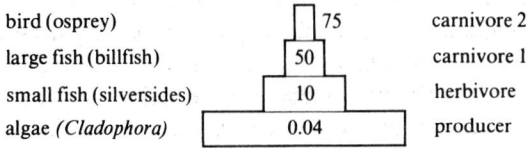

Fig 10.32 *Biomass and amounts of DDT at different trophic levels in a food chain. Figures represent amounts of DDT in parts per million (ppm).*

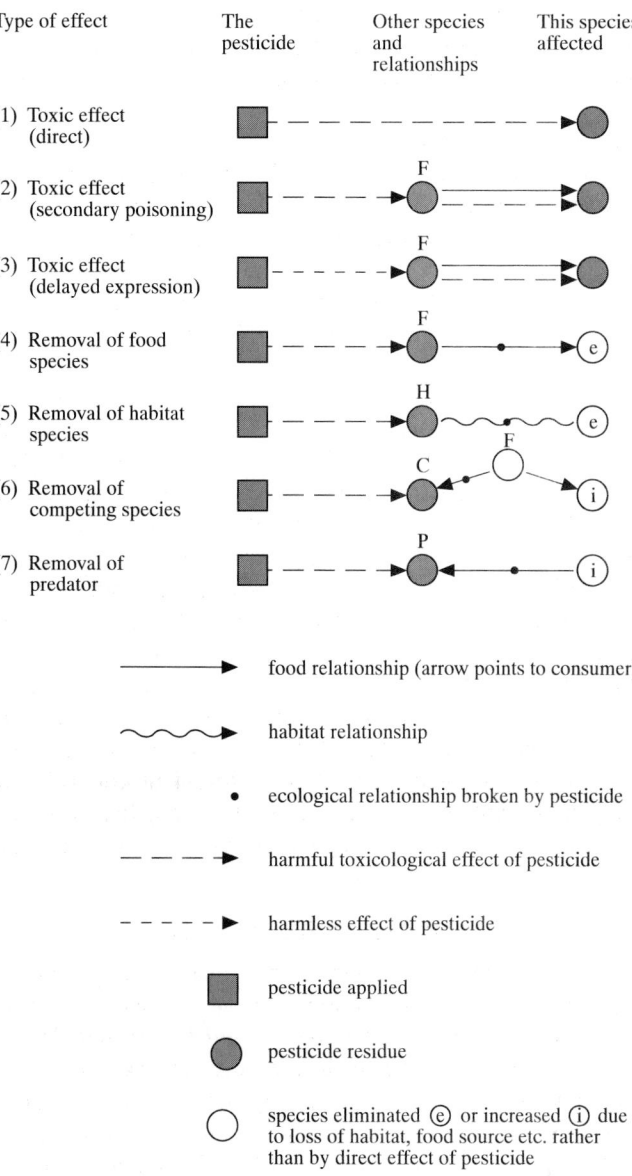

Type of effect	The pesticide	Other species and relationships	This species affected
(1) Toxic effect (direct)			
(2) Toxic effect (secondary poisoning)		F	
(3) Toxic effect (delayed expression)		F	
(4) Removal of food species		F	e
(5) Removal of habitat species		H	e
(6) Removal of competing species		C / F	i
(7) Removal of predator		P	i

⟶ food relationship (arrow points to consumer)

∿⟶ habitat relationship

• ecological relationship broken by pesticide

– – –▶ harmful toxicological effect of pesticide

- - - -▶ harmless effect of pesticide

■ pesticide applied

● pesticide residue

○ species eliminated ⓔ or increased ⓘ due to loss of habitat, food source etc. rather than by direct effect of pesticide

Fig 10.33 *The main ways in which pesticides affect ecosystems. C, competing species; F, food species; H, habitat species; P, predator species. (Modified from N.W. Moore (1967) A synopsis of the pesticide problem, Advances in Ecological Research, J.B. Cragg (ed.) pp. 75–126, Blackwell.)*

Success is not always so immediate. Careful matching of climatic conditions and monitoring of interactions with native species is essential. In attempts to control the walnut aphid, *Chromaphis juglandicola*, in California a parasitic wasp, *Trioxys pallidus*, was introduced from Cannes in France. It was moderately successful in coastal areas but in the hot interior, the main walnut-growing area, the wasp died out after one season. Ten years later after extensive searching in similar hot and dry environments a new strain of *Trioxys* was introduced from Iran. It successfully overwintered and within a year over 50 000 square miles were cleared of the pest and parasitisation exceeded 90%.

Biological control is widely used in commercial glasshouses which are enclosed environments. Soil sterilisation in winter kills all beneficial predatory controls. New plants introduced the following spring typically bring in some pests. With no natural enemies present, populations grow rapidly unless pesticides are used or natural enemy control is quickly re-established. Release of predators, once pest populations have reached a large enough number to provide sufficient food for the predators, can be very effective in keeping pest numbers to a low level where damage to the crop is minimum.

All biological control requires careful analysis of the ecosystem into which it is being introduced. In particular, where predatory control is planned it is essential to identify all the likely prey organisms. Unwished-for consequences may otherwise result. For example the mongoose which was introduced to Jamaica to control the black rat showed a preference for the existing natural enemies of the rat. It also severely reduced some bird populations and caused the extinction of several reptiles.

Integrated control of pests

Integrated control is pest population management which combines and integrates biological and chemical controls in a sensitive way. Pesticides are used as necessary in a manner least disruptive to complementary biological control. It aims to keep pest populations below the level of economic injury, or even prevent their development, while causing minimum harm and disruption to a crop (agroecosystem) or 'natural' ecosystem and especially the beneficial natural enemies of the crop or host species.

One example of this is to use more-selective chemicals, such as the aphicide pirimicarb. Its use has enabled development of an integrated control programme for peach–potato aphid, *Myzus persicae*, and for red spider mite, *Tetranychus* sp., on glasshouse chrysanthemums in Britain. Both were formerly controlled by organophosphate insecticides which are relatively unselective and to which the aphid was developing resistance.

For economic reasons (research and development costs versus the smaller market for selective chemicals) another approach that is used is the better targeted use of broad-spectrum chemicals. Targeting may be improved spatially and by better timing of pesticide applications. The development of pheromones (chapter 17) has greatly aided spatial targeting. Sex attractants can be used to lure insects to some other control measure, such as a pesticide or chemosterilant. Alternatively, a pheromone might be used to aggregate a population in an area to be treated with a pesticide. In this way much less pesticide is used, with minimal effects on non-target species and the wider environment. Another promising use of pheromones alone is to inhibit behavioural responses such as mating by saturating the atmosphere with the appropriate pheromone (very low concentrations will do this). Insects become habituated to the constant stimulus and the appropriate reaction is suppressed.

Frequency of pesticide application can be reduced by careful timing to cause maximum damage to the pest (such as at mating) while minimising effects on associated species. This requires close study of the life histories of all the species concerned and a clear understanding of the ecosystems involved.

10.9   Conservation

Conservation is about maintaining the biosphere. It means taking action to avoid species decline and extinction and permanent detrimental change to the environment. To achieve conservation we need to understand how the biosphere functions or, more immediately, how organisms and environment interact. In other words we must apply our knowledge of ecology and the related environmental sciences.

Successful conservation, however, is not just a matter of science. It also requires public and governmental support. For this reason conservationists often stress the utilitarian benefits of successful conservation.

Extinction

Extinction, as the fossil record shows, has always been part of the story of life on Earth. Since the emergence of humans, however, many new causes of extinction have arisen which are directly attributable to human use of biosphere resources. Extinction due to overhunting probably began this trend, whereas pollution of land, air and water (section 10.8), the widespread use of pesticides, habitat fragmentation and loss, and agricultural intensification are among the prime causes of species rarity and extinction during the last 400 years. As fig 10.34 shows there is considerable evidence that rates of extinction have accelerated since the agricultural and industrial revolutions.

Research shows that extinction rates for birds and mammals are presently between 10 and 100 times greater than the 'natural' background rate. Many more species are rare and their long-term survival is also in doubt. Rare species are typically **genetically eroded**, which means that their gene pool is reduced and with it their capacity to adapt to change in their environment. Chance adversity or environmental change can easily bring about the extinction of a rare species.

Biodiversity

The most obvious definition of **biodiversity** is the variety of species on Earth. Biodiversity can, however, be viewed at much smaller and larger scales. We may wish to conserve as much genetic diversity as possible within each species as insurance against future environmental change or

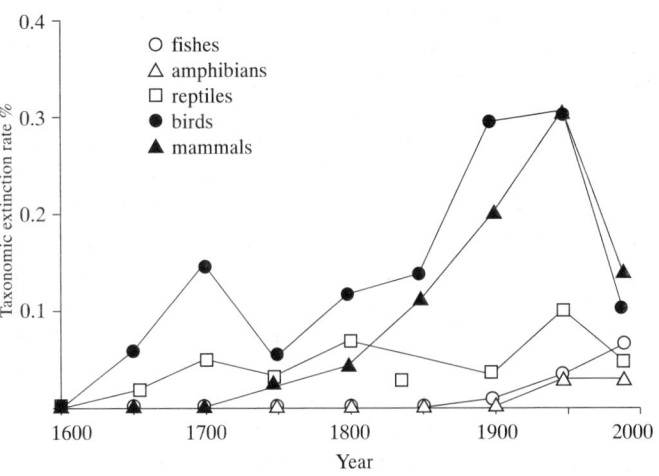

Fig 10.34 *Trends in extinction rates for vertebrates since 1600 for which a date is known. (From Begon* et al. *(1996) Ecology: individuals, populations and communities, 3rd ed, Blackwell.)*

new human uses of these resources. We may, therefore, wish to focus attention on genetically distinct sub-populations or subspecies such as heavy metal tolerant strains of common grasses. We may be interested in phylogenetic distinctiveness to ensure that organisms with no close living relatives are conserved, to aid our understanding of evolution or perhaps because of their unique properties. Alternatively our focus may be on conservation of biotic communities and ecosystems. If we maintain full representation of all Earth's ecosystems, this should help to ensure the survival of species.

10.9.1   Why conserve?

To many people, the need to conserve wildlife and avoid environmental degradation is undeniable. Others, though, have questioned the value of conservation. In particular the justification for financial investment in species and countryside conservation has been challenged. Policy decisions are overwhelmingly matters of economics. Yet standard economics has failed to assign more than nominal value to ecological resources.

Developing a new ecological or 'green' economics is an important contemporary challenge. This may be relatively straightforward for species with obvious resource value such as crop plants or plants with known medicinal use. It is much more difficult for species with only indirect or potential value, for example as a tourist attraction or as part of a landscape in a National Park or as an essential but unattractive decomposer organism.

Most justifications for nature conservation centre on the human benefits that will accrue from maintaining a full range of biodiversity and avoiding environmental degradation. These can broadly be summarised as aesthetic, utilitarian, and ecological or scientific reasons for conservation. To these we must add one further category, ethical reasons for conservation.

Ethical reasons. Cultural tradition, religious beliefs, political persuasion and other similar concepts all shape our attitudes to nature. Some people argue very strongly that nature does not exist simply for humans to transform and modify as they please for their own purposes. They assert that all living species have a right to coexist with us on Earth, and we have no right to cause the extinction or to diminish the quality of life of any organism. Sometimes linked with this idea is the concept of **custodianship** which challenges us to pass on to future generations all the diversity of life and quality of environment that we, ourselves, inherited. Implicit in custodianship, however, is the notion of beneficial human inheritance, whereas the ethical argument accepts no justification of human benefit or need for guardianship.

Aesthetic reasons. Humans derive pleasure from natural environments and the presence of other living organisms. This can be hard to measure objectively but is undeniably true, as shown by the numerous local, national and international organisations that exist worldwide to promote wildlife and countryside conservation. Our appreciation of nature permeates art, design, literature and music and influences our recreational pursuits. Some people consider that contact with nature is essential for human well-being.

Utilitarian reasons. Wildlife contributes to our immediate needs in many fundamental ways. Obvious examples are agriculture and forestry and fisheries. As well as direct crop benefits, we make use of pollinating insects and beneficial predators in pest control. Many plant species have important medical uses; animal studies have enabled us to understand and treat human diseases more effectively. Numerous industrial processes depend on plant and animal materials and, increasingly, microorganisms are being used industrially, for example to concentrate valuable metals from low-grade metal ores.

Ecological or scientific reasons. It is not just the direct benefits of species and their genetic resources that are important to humans. Our well-being also depends on the maintenance of a fully functional biosphere. In particular maintenance of balanced biogeochemical cycles is vital to the avoidance of pollution, as discussed for acidification and eutrophication in sections 10.8.1 and 10.8.2, and to the regulation of Earth's climatic systems as discussed in section 10.8.1. As you will have read in the discussion of deforestation and desertification (section 10.8.3), loss of vegetation cover can have profound effects on soil erosion, lead to siltation of rivers and coasts and may even result in changes in rainfall and climate patterns.

10.9.2   Conservation of genetic diversity

Rare and endangered species

Human pressures on the biosphere have caused the extinction of many species. The woolly mammoth, dodo, great auk and Bengal tiger are all examples of species made extinct by humans. It is estimated that, at present, one species is lost every day.

If we are to prevent the continued rapid extinction of species due to human activity we must:

- identify the species at greatest risk;
- investigate why they have become vulnerable;
- attempt to remedy the problem.

The IUCN publishes detailed lists of species at risk of extinction in a series known as the **Red Data Books**. Four categories of risk are identified.

Rare	Species with small populations either restricted geographically with localised habitats or with widely scattered individuals. These species are at risk of becoming more rare, but they are not in immediate danger of extinction.
Vulnerable	These are species under threat of or actually declining in number, or species which have been seriously depleted in the past and have not yet recovered.
Endangered	Species with low population numbers that are in considerable danger of becoming extinct.
Extinct	Species which cannot be found in areas they recently inhabited nor in other likely habitats.

The Red Data Books for vertebrates list all known species in these four categories. This is impossible for plants since it is estimated that over 10% of all known plants, up to 60 000 species, are either rare or in danger of genetic erosion or extinction in the next 30 to 40 years.

We can help to prevent extinctions by:

- protecting and restoring habitats;
- establishing game parks, national parks, nature reserves and similar protected areas;
- controlling and reducing the impacts of modern intensive agriculture;
- reducing the use of bio-poisons such as pesticides;
- restricting trade in endangered species;
- providing refuges and assisted breeding programmes for endangered species, for example in zoos and botanic gardens;
- establishing sperm banks and seed stores to maintain the full range of genetic diversity of species.

The giant panda, *Ailuropoda melanoleuca*, symbol of the Worldwide Fund for Nature (WWF), is an example of an endangered species whose extinction has so far been prevented by a combination of habitat restoration measures and a captive breeding programme.

Giant pandas are found in eastern Tibet and southwest China. At one time the species was very much endangered since its habitat, of bamboo forest, was being encroached upon increasingly by the human population. Giant pandas feed almost exclusively on arrow bamboo, a plant that goes through cycles of abundance and scarcity. In Sichuan province in 1983 large areas of forest suddenly died back and at least 59 pandas died of starvation. Without human help this endangered species might have become extinct altogether.

By the early 1990s sufficient studies had been made of this species to begin to understand its physiology and ecology in the wild. It is now easy to see how ill-equipped giant pandas are to cope with change. Pandas live solitary lives and only come together for breeding. Adults spend 95% of their waking hours feeding on bamboo, which is a poor diet, but they will rarely eat anything else in preference. Breeding captive pandas has been successful at Wolong in Sichuan province. Use has been made of the latest techniques in reproduction technology, such as artificial insemination and sperm banking. Since interest in its survival has developed and forest reserves for it have been made, the giant panda population has increased to nearly one thousand.

Genetic resources for human use

Only 30 of the 250 000 known higher plant species currently account for 95% of human nutrition (fig 10.35). In developed countries it is common for just a few varieties of these species to be used. For example, half of all the wheat grown in the Canadian wheatlands is of one variety, 'Neepawa'. The danger of this is that if major physical or biotic environmental change occurs, the species or varieties in use will not continue to thrive. Problems of pest attack are an obvious hazard of monocultural practice. This was clearly shown by the catastrophic spread of potato blight and resulting crop failure that led to widespread famine in Ireland in the 1840s.

The solution to problems on this large scale is to find a wild relative that is naturally resistant to the pest, or better adapted to the new climatic situation. The desired genes from the new stock can then be transferred into the crop cultivar by a careful programme of crossbreeding. Similarly, disease resistance in stock animals can be improved by incorporating genes from wild relatives.

Such options clearly will not continue to be possible if human activity eliminates wild relatives of important crop and animal species. Conservation in seed stores, sperm banks, field gene banks and cryopreservation have obvious importance for domesticated plant and animal species. Maintaining genetic diversity in non-domesticated species is also important for humans, since some wild species have become important sources of drugs used in medicine. Aspirin was originally derived from the leaves of a species of willow, *Salix alba*, whilst the rosy periwinkle,

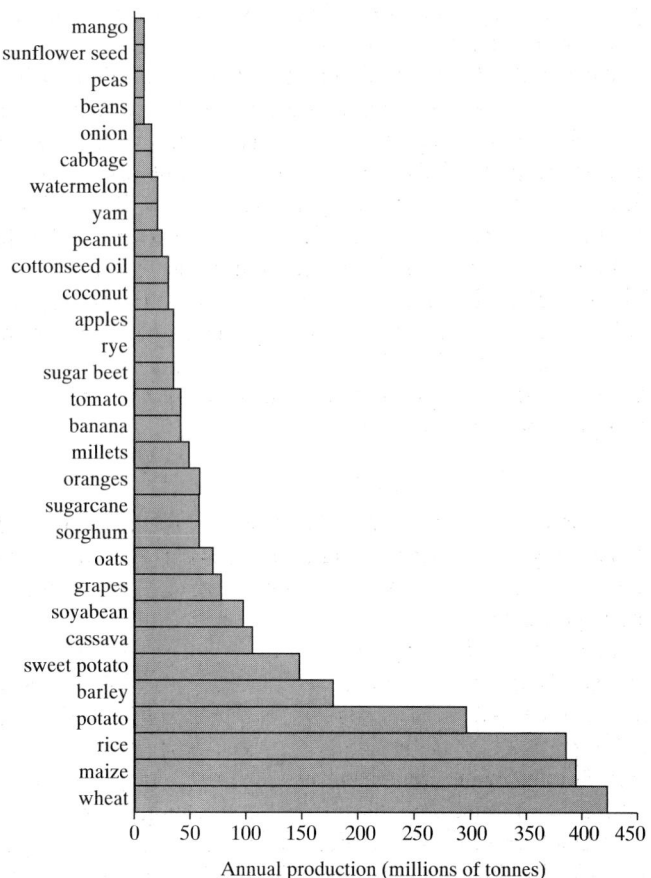

Fig 10.35 *Annual production of the major crop plants. (From O. Sattaur (1989)* The shrinking gene pool, New Scientist, *29.7.89, 37–41.)*

Catharanthus roseus, has yielded potent anti-cancer drugs for the treatment of Hodgkin's disease and some types of lymphatic cancer. Recently a variant of this plant was found in the West Indies that had the capacity to produce ten times the yield of this valuable anti-cancer drug.

In 1982 the world value of plant-based prescription drugs was estimated at $40 billion. These drugs came from just 41 species out of 5000 plants tested. Given a world total of 250 000 known plant species, it seems quite probable that many useful plant-based drugs have yet to be discovered. Realising that potential obviously depends on conserving the maximum plant genetic diversity possible.

Botanic gardens

Plants are best conserved **in situ**, that is where they occur naturally. In situ conservation can achieve maintenance of a large number of individuals for minimum management effort and cost. Species protected in their natural habitat can continue to evolve alongside their pollinators, symbionts, competitors and predators. This will ensure that they retain their 'fitness' and adaptiveness.

However, where habitats are particularly fragmented and vulnerable to exploitation in situ conservation may not be feasible. This is true for many tropical species where rates of habitat loss are very high. Ex situ conservation in botanic gardens and special tree collections, called arboreta, is a possible solution to this problem.

Worldwide there are about 1500 botanic gardens. Most are located in North America, Europe and the former Soviet Republics, whereas plant diversity is greatest in the tropics and subtropics. This poses obvious problems, such as differing day length and temperature regimes, if the aim is not merely to preserve examples of living specimens but to ensure reproduction and long-term survival of the species. These difficulties may be overcome by combining the cultivation expertise of botanic gardens with the more innovative methods of germ plasm conservation based on establishment of seed banks, field gene banks and cryopreservation (see below).

Seed banks

Seed banks are a convenient and space-saving method of conserving germ plasm. Originally focused on food crops and their wild relatives, they now include stores of many endangered wild species.

The seeds of many species can remain dormant for thousands of years if kept at low humidity (5–10%) and low temperature (−20 °C). Seeds that can be stored in this way are termed **orthodox** and include major crop plants such as cereals, soyabean, cotton and many vegetable species. One difficulty is ensuring that the seed remains viable. At Wakefield House, the major seed store for the Royal Botanic Gardens at Kew in Britain, all seed is X-rayed before storage to check an embryo is present. Subsamples are regularly tested for germination and if viability falls below acceptable levels, about 85%, new seed for storage is generated by growing the stored seed and harvesting the seed. This can prove a challenging and costly exercise. Even when successful, the enforced inbreeding may lead to a loss of vigour in the stored seed.

Some seeds, called **recalcitrant**, are damaged by drying and cannot be conserved for long periods in a seed bank. About 20% of all species, and 70% of tropical species, have recalcitrant seeds, including several commercially important species such as cocoa, rubber and tea. Other plants like potatoes, that mainly reproduce vegetatively, also require an alternative long-term conservation strategy to seed stores. For these species deep frozen germ plasm, rather than whole seed storage, and field gene banks are possible alternatives.

Cryopreservation

Cryopreservation involves storage of cells from embryos and shoot tips in liquid nitrogen at −196 °C. This stops all metabolic processes, which means that the material can be preserved indefinitely assuming no mechanical failure of the storage system occurs. The main biological drawback of this approach is that germ plasm is evolutionarily frozen. It is no longer subject to adaptation processes and may therefore prove biologically 'unfit' after prolonged storage so that it loses its value for reintroduction of species to the wild or for breeding into modern crop cultivars.

Field gene banks

Field gene banks are permanent living plant collections, not just of trees, as in arboreta, but also of savannah grasses, varieties of wheat, rice, cotton and others. A small plot or strip of each variety of a particular species is grown. For example the International Cocoa Genebank in Trinidad, which specialises in cocoa types from Latin America, grows 16 trees of each of 2500 types of *Theobroma cacao* that it holds. These plots give useful information on plant requirements, especially for germination and seed production, which is also vital companion information for seed banks. The main drawbacks are the space required and the inevitable susceptibility to pests and natural disasters such as fire and flood.

In 1989 a Botanic Gardens Conservation Strategy was drawn up by a group of major international agencies concerned with conservation. This aims to ensure integration of local, national and global conservation schemes and to standardise procedures for ex situ conservation, including the exchange and duplication of material and data between major collections. The Strategy also advises botanic gardens how they can stop illegal trade in endangered species.

Zoos

Zoos were originally established as collections of animals for curiosity's sake. Conservation, involving captive breeding, is a relatively recent aim. The aim of captive breeding programmes is to preserve the genetic stocks of threatened species so that they can be reintroduced into the wild when conditions permit. Therefore a complementary programme remedying conditions in the natural habitat that caused the species to become endangered is also needed.

Most zoos have only a few individuals of each species. To avoid inbreeding and weakening of stock, cooperation with other zoos is essential. The International Species Inventory System (ISIS) based at Minnesota Zoo in the USA coordinates advice on which individuals to exchange for breeding.

Transporting would-be suitors around the world is expensive and has no guarantee of successful breeding as was most famously demonstrated by giant pandas at London Zoo. Artificial insemination is one solution to this problem. In captive wild animals, sperm can be collected from anaesthetised males using a probe which electrically stimulates the genitals. This approach can also be used for sperm collection from animals living in the wild, so that the gene pool of captive breeding lines can be increased without further depleting wild stocks.

In practice many captive breeding programmes have proved so successful that, in zoos, overpopulation problems have resulted, especially where return to the wild has not been possible. Overpopulation occurs because life in captivity poses fewer threats, whereas mortality in the wild is high. Lions, for example, rarely live more than 7 years in the wild but, in zoos, a 20-year lifespan is common.

Reducing birth rates is rarely an appropriate solution. An ageing, less viable population results, and continuity of important learning patterns achieved by copying adult role models, such as mothering, is broken.

Reintroductions pose many problems and have achieved limited success so far, often because the problems that originally threatened the species still remain. The story of the Hawaiian goose illustrates this point well. In 1949 the wild population was reduced to 12 birds. Captive breeding programmes have since ensured its survival and to date over 3000 birds have been released back into the wild. Yet a viable wild population has not been re-established since the introduced predators, that caused the original problem, still remain.

Nevertheless reintroduction is an essential aim. Captive breeding without rapid reintroduction into the wild will inevitably lead to changed characteristics in the captive population, such as docility. Equally, learned behaviour such as finding food, establishing territories, wariness of enemies, especially humans, would be lost, reducing the prospects for long-term survival and successful reproduction of captive bred animals in the wild. As in the case of plants, successful animal conservation requires close collaboration between ex situ and in situ conservation efforts.

10.22 How can sperm banks contribute to the conservation of a species such as the African rhinoceros, populations of which are becoming increasingly isolated and unable to meet each other?

10.9.3 A case study in species conservation: the African elephant

The main herds of non-domesticated elephants are found in Africa (*Loxodonta africana africana* (bush elephant) and *L. africana cyclotis* (forest elephant)). They have no serious natural predators, yet their numbers are in decline, dropping from 1.2 million in 1981 to 623 000 in 1989. Humans are the main threat to the elephants' survival. They compete with the elephants for land for forestry, agriculture and settlement, destroying their habitat. They kill elephants which threaten crops or property and, above all, kill elephants for their ivory.

It is not just the absolute decline in elephant numbers that is causing concern. Changing population structure caused by illegal poaching is also a problem. Poachers select the animals with the largest tusks. Males, which have a typical tusk weight of 9.3 kg compared with 4.7 kg for cows and mature calves, have been preferentially eliminated. As a result, by 1987 cows and calves were the main source of poached ivory in parts of East Africa. One tonne of ivory represented 113 dead elephants compared with 54 in 1979 and the mainly female harvest was estimated to cause the deaths of an additional 55 calves orphaned too young to survive. Surveys in Ambroseli National Park in Kenya in 1988 showed that just 22% of the population was male; data from Mikimu Reserve in Tanzania showed only 0.4% of the population was male. These data suggest that the long-term prospects of elephant populations seem very poor. Some researchers have predicted their extinction by the year 2010 unless effective conservation action is taken.

Elephants are an important **keystone species** (one on which many others depend) in the ecology of the African savannah. A medium-density herd will generate a wide diversity of habitats and promote a varied community of associated grazing and browsing game animals (table 10.8). In Kenya the revenue from tourism related to game viewing is ten times greater than the estimated income from sales of poached ivory and benefits many more people. Ensuring the elephants' survival has clear utilitarian benefits, as well as other conservation benefits.

Since 1989 the African elephant has been protected by a total ban on ivory sales under international legislation known as CITES (Convention on International Trade in Endangered Species). Not all African states support this ban. Southern African countries of Zimbabwe, Botswana, Malawi, Zambia and South Africa objected, since they already have successful sustainable management

Table 10.8 Schematic summary of the relationship between changing elephant population density and associated plant and animal communities.

Density of elephant population	low	medium	high
Plants	mainly woody plants low species diversity	mixed trees and grasses high species diversity and good abundance of each species	mainly open grassland a few species dominant
Animals	browsers, e.g. giraffe, impala, Grant's gazelle	mixed browsers and grazers	grazers, e.g. zebra, wildebeest, Thompson's gazelle, buffalo
Level of protection	outside Game/ National Park	Park boundary area	central Park area

programmes. Elephant populations in these countries have a good age and sex structure and are stable, or in some cases rising and requiring culling to maintain rangeland. Sustainably managed herds generate income from sale of ivory, meat and hide, and at the same time encourage tourism. Elephants are regarded as a valuable resource, generating jobs and income which is used for development projects. Local support for maintenance of elephant herds is therefore strong and poaching is considered antisocial.

However, some people consider that a total ban on ivory sales is the only way to prevent extinction. They argue that we must educate people worldwide so that they no longer want carved ivory products and compare the ivory trade with the fur trade: it is no longer acceptable to wear fur coats made from the skins of exotic and rare species. Public disapproval has killed demand for fur products and helped to save many endangered species.

The debate continues: while ivory remains available from sustainably managed herds it is difficult to enforce a ban elsewhere. The pro-ivory lobby point out that the black rhino has continued to decline in spite of maximum protection under CITES. The anti-ivory group argue that illegally obtained ivory is marketable only because the legal trade continues. They claim that as herds elsewhere diminish, illegal poaching of sustainably managed herds will inevitably take place.

10.9.4 Planning for the future

Knowledge from ecological studies of how we are changing our environment is forcing us to look critically at how we use the Earth's resources. We need to reduce pollution and conserve resources while achieving a good standard of living for all people. The Earth Summit held at Rio de Janeiro in 1992 was an important milestone in raising political and public awareness of environmental concerns and the need to promote **sustainable development**. This has been defined as 'meeting the needs of the present without compromising the ability of future generations to meet their own needs'.

The Earth Summit identified 27 principles for environmental and social development into the twenty-first century. Together these initiatives are known as **Agenda 21**. What is important is how the general public, business community, industry and politicians, respond to Agenda 21. One target set in Rio acknowledged the importance of local community participation. Local communities in each participating country were charged with consulting the people they represent to formulate a **Local Agenda 21** by 1996.

10.23 Has your local authority identified a Local Agenda 21?

What local conservation measures are proposed?

You may expect to find new schemes for collection, separation and recycling of waste from households and local businesses.

How are local environment action groups contributing to Local Agenda 21.

What is happening in your school or college?

Is your home a 'green' household?

Some resources, such as food crops, are easily renewed in short time scales. Regular, typically annual, harvests are produced. We call these **renewable resources**. Providing we do not catastrophically damage our environment, as in desertification, these resources are potentially always available. Other resources, notably mineral resources and fossil fuels, were formed thousands or millions of years ago. They cannot be replenished on human time-scales. These resources are called **non-renewable**. For example, it is estimated that in 70 years almost all the known oil deposits that are recoverable with current technology will be used up unless we reduce our rates of consumption. Similarly, natural gas reserves will be exhausted in 150 years unless we change our pattern of use.

10.9.5 Sustainable use of plant and animal resources

The discussions of deforestation (section 10.8.3) and African elephants (section 10.9.3) show how valuable resources can be diminished or destroyed by over-exploitation due to ignorance or greed. In contrast, management based on ecological knowledge brings continued benefits, though short-term profits may be less. The attempt to regulate sea fishing using an agreed international quota system is one example of this. Long-lived species and ecosystems such as elephants and forests also require sensitive management if future stocks are to be maintained. Productive and sustainable management of woodland ecosystems is a long-established concern of human populations.

Overfishing

A state of chronic overfishing now exists in the world's oceans. Fig 10.36 shows landings of sea fish since 1950. Today nine of the world's 17 major fishing grounds show a steep decline in size of catch and four are fished out. In 1992 the cod fisheries off Newfoundland in Canada were closed indefinitely. In the North Sea mackerel have declined by more than 50% since the 1960s, while the herring industry which was closed between 1977 and 1982 has never recovered its former abundance. The world's largest fishery, anchovies off the coasts of Peru and Chile, has collapsed completely.

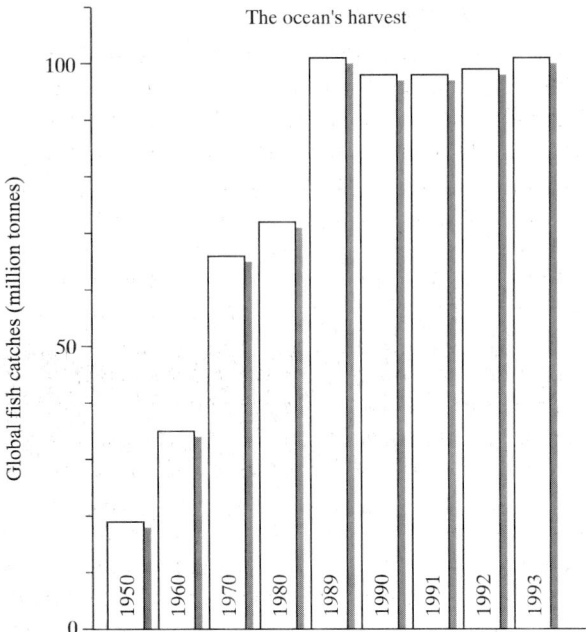

The ocean's harvest

Fig 10.36 *Global fish catches 1950–93. (From F. Pearce New Scientist, 2016, 10th February 1996 p. 4.)*

Overfishing is the root cause of these problems. Signs of overfishing were clearly evident in the 1960s, yet during the subsequent decades the recorded global marine fish catch rose by nearly 50%. These increased landings reflected the development of large 'factory' fishing fleets (that is ships equipped not only to freeze but to completely process the catch at sea) and the targeting of one fish species after another. In other words, as one fishery or fish species became exhausted another species would be substituted.

Heavy fishing produces a population of mainly young small individuals because fish are caught as soon as they reach a catchable size. These young fish would make rapid growth if left longer in the sea and would soon reach a more valuable size, giving heavier landings of better quality fish per unit fishing effort, and yielding a better profit margin. However, individual fishermen are tempted to achieve weight quotas and maintain income by catching more rather than fewer fish. If this reaches the point where fish are caught before spawning, so that the reproductive capacity of the stock is seriously impaired, then a catastrophic reduction in numbers occurs and local extinction may result.

Fisheries quotas are intended to safeguard fish stocks. However, although scientists use quite sophisticated population ecology models on which to base their recommendations, there are many problems with the quota system. These include:

- acquiring reliable data with which to model the fish populations;
- allowing for climate change;
- persuading governments to accept scientific recommendations;
- policing international agreements;

- accommodating the needs of traditional local fishing communities as well as major commercial fleets.

Tropical rainforests

Some ecosystems are very difficult to manage in a way that provides sustainable resources. In parts of Amazonia agricultural success following rainforest clearance has been very transient. Even schemes with substantial external financial support and agricultural expertise have been abandoned after 10 or 15 years. Weed invasion, pest and disease problems and, above all, declining soil fertility make projects no longer economically viable. Mature rainforest rarely re-establishes on these sites. In the intervening period soil nutrients are lost and soil structure is impaired; no forest seed store remains and, even when dispersal brings seeds of mature rainforest species, germination is poor in the exposed conditions. (Rainforest species require the high humidity found beneath a mature canopy for successful germination.) At best, a secondary forest of lower productivity than the original rainforest is established, in which only very low intensity shifting cultivation can be practised. Intensive agriculture is clearly not a sustainable use of these areas. It wastes resources since the secondary forest is less productive than the original. At the same time many mature forest species are permanently lost. Sustainable use of tropical moist forests which also allows economic and social development of the region concerned is a major contemporary challenge for the world community.

Traditional woodland management systems in Britain

For centuries Britain's woodlands were an important source of fuel and timber resources. Management practices evolved to ensure their continued regeneration and productivity. The broadleaved woodland remnants we seek to conserve today reflect this management history, and are in most cases very different from the original forest cover of Britain. These woodlands include many species in semi-natural communities that will die out if we do not continue to manage them in a traditional manner.

There are very few woodlands that are primary forest remnants and even these have been modified by human activities. Most broadleaved woodlands are secondary, having developed from formerly cleared sites. 'Ancient woodlands' are those that date from before 1600 AD and have the highest conservation value. They often contain great species diversity, particularly of slow-growing, long-lived organisms such as lichens, and they bear the marks of human management back to very early times.

Most woodlands were managed in one of two traditional systems as wood pastures or coppice. **Wood pastures** were common on poorer soils and livestock grazing, as well as timber produce, was important in these woodlands. Grazing pressure restricted regeneration, a problem overcome by **pollarding**, the cutting of the main stem above the browse line (c. 2 m) to encourage new growth of lateral branches which could be periodically harvested. Over centuries the more palatable species, such as hazel, have been lost and browse-tolerant species, such as holly and hawthorn, have become dominant in the understorey. The future of many of these woodlands depends on regeneration by the control of grazing pressure.

On richer soils the **coppice system** predominated. Understorey species, such as ash and hazel, were cut close to ground level on a 5–20 year cycle depending on the rate of regrowth and the products required. The larger coppice poles were used to provide materials for house building, furniture and fencing; lighter materials were used for basket weaving, sheep bundles or wattle (to hold wall plaster) or were used in thatching. Woods provided much fuel and very little was wasted. Occasional **standard** trees were allowed to grow to near full maturity. These were felled on a longer time scale and sawn into planks or fashioned into beams. This management pattern of coppice with standards resulted in periodic expanses of flowers on the woodland floor. Such woods have a species-rich ground flora, with many rare and historically interesting plants.

Conserving ancient woodland helps to retain the rich plant and animal communities of the primary forests, many members of which are now rare.

Fig 10.37 *Wood pasture in the New Forest.*

Hedgerows

Many people consider that hedgerows have high value to wildlife conservation. Hedges were used in Saxon times to divide and mark out land plots and to contain livestock. Over the centuries hedgerows have increased their species richness. On average, one new species of woody shrub is added to every 27 m length of hedgerow every hundred years. Ancient hedgerows have therefore the greatest diversity of wildlife and some are the only places in an arable area where plants typical of ancient woodland are found.

Between 1950 and 1980 many thousands of kilometres of hedgerow were lost in lowland Britain to make fields larger for arable farming and to make ploughing and harvesting by large machines easier. This also removed what farmers perceived as a reservoir of weeds, pests and diseases. Hedgerows, however, undoubtedly conserve many species of animals which act as predators of many plant pests. They reduce wind speeds, providing important areas of livestock shelter in their lee and helping to reduce soil erosion. Hedgerows also provide a refuge and home for song birds, game birds and other woodland species and give shelter to beneficial pollinating insects. They can also act as 'corridors' between isolated broadleaved woodlands in agricultural areas. Small mammal species, such as the dormouse, which do not readily colonise new areas may benefit from the habitat continuity that hedgerows can provide. Plants with only localised dispersal mechanisms may also benefit from these hedgerow 'corridors'.

In some parts of Britain farmers can now get grants to re-establish hedgerows. However, a newly planted hedge, although quickly providing the benefits of shelter, will be much less diverse in species than the long-established hedgerows removed during the 1960s.

10.9.6 Waste management and recycling

Human societies generate large amounts of waste. Many wastes contain valuable materials that can be reclaimed and re-used, reducing the need to exploit new supplies of a resource. Reclamation and recycling of scrap metals rather than mining new materials is an obvious example. The energy requirements and pollution associated with recycling are often much less than those caused by mining and ore processing methods. For example, in Europe the steel industry re-uses scrap metal, so achieving energy savings up to 50%; aluminium recycling achieves 95% in energy savings. Also, many businesses are reducing packaging on products in an attempt to save energy costs in production and reduce waste and pollution.

Recycling also beneficially reduces the total volume of waste requiring disposal. In Britain most household and municipal waste is sent to landfill sites. These are rapidly becoming filled, especially in the densely populated south-east. In 1996, as part of its response to Agenda 21, the UK government introduced a new landfill tax designed to encourage business and consumers to dispose of less waste and to recover more of the waste which is produced using recycling and waste-to-energy incineration schemes (where the energy generated is used for other purposes).

At present in Britain between 1% and 8% of municipal waste is recycled, whereas the government target for recycled household materials is 25% by the year 2000.

The difficulties of recycling include:

- the need for effective separation of wastes. For example, one piece of Pyrex in a consignment of glass can render the recycled product worthless.
- the fluctuating price received for materials saved for recycling. For example, the price for waste paper in 1996 was only $\frac{1}{3}$ the price paid in 1995.
- the need for easily accessible recycling points for householders. Most waste collection authorities rely on the 'bring system', where the householder takes recyclables to a collection point which restricts those who can participate. More recently authorities have experimented with kerbside collection schemes for different wastes in an attempt to increase householder participation rates.

Much municipal waste is biodegradable. During this process methane, a highly flammable and important greenhouse gas, is produced. Using carefully designed recovery systems the methane can be collected and used for generating electricity. A landfill site at Mucking in Essex which serves several London boroughs generates 3.8 MW of electricity, sufficient to run the plant and supply a small community of 30 000 people. At the same time the potential fire hazard associated with uncontrolled methane release is reduced, and the carbon dioxide released as waste is a far less active greenhouse gas than the original methane.

In the future waste-to-energy incineration plants are likely to become the main method of waste disposal. Such energy production from waste beneficially reduces demands on fossil fuel reserves as well as reducing demand for landfill.

Sewage processing uses decay microorganisms, normally present in the soil and fresh water, to break down human wastes. If these organic rich wastes were discharged to the receiving waters without pre-treatment their inevitable subsequent decomposition would lead to rapid and extreme deoxygenation in the receiving water. Sewage works employ the natural decomposition processes of the microorganisms and produce, as byproducts, nutrient-rich dried sludge and methane. Providing it has not become contaminated with heavy metals (such as by lead from petroleum wastes) the sludge may be used on the land as fertiliser. Sewage sludge is also often used in reclamation schemes since it improves 'soil' structure as well as providing vital missing nutrients (section 10.5.2). The methane (biogas) that is also produced during decomposition can be burnt to provide the heating and electricity for the sewage processing works and, in some cases, small local communities or businesses.

New sources of energy

In Britain most of our energy is provided from the burning of fossil fuels which are non-renewable. About 10% of our electrical energy is generated from nuclear power, which apart from its inherent dangers and the problems of nuclear waste disposal and decommissioning of obsolete nuclear plants, is also dependent on a non-renewable resource, uranium. An awareness of the rate of depletion of fossil fuels and pollution caused by their use, coupled with unease about nuclear power, has prompted many people to think creatively about alternative sources of energy.

Globally, biomass energy (wood, charcoal, crop residues, dung and other organic materials) is the most important fuel energy source aside from fossil fuel. This source supplies 14% of the world's energy needs and is the main source of energy in the developing world, supplying 35% of needs. Biotechnology can also be used to produce alternative sources of energy based on naturally produced organic materials. For example, Brazil has large industrial plants for converting sugar, from cane, into ethanol (gasohol) which can be used to fuel cars. In North America cereals such as maize, wheat and barley are fermented to produce a variety of products including fuel alcohol. Sugar beet widely grown in northern Europe could similarly be processed for fuel alcohol. Fuel alcohol is potentially a cleaner source of energy than fossil fuels since it is sulphur-free and does not require a lead additive.

New and renewable sources of energy come in many forms. Solar, wind, hydro, tides and waves, biomass technologies, geothermal sources and others present an almost limitless potential if we can find suitable ways to harness them.

Hydro power is the most widely used form of renewable energy. It currently produces energy equivalent to 500 000 MW worldwide, supplying about 23% of the world's electricity. Most remaining potential hydro resources are concentrated in developing countries. Massive schemes, such as the Itaipu dam in Brazil, produce cheap electricity but distribution systems are often poor, limiting the benefits of the schemes. High environmental and social costs typically include:

- displacement of people as environmental refugees;
- flooding of valuable farmland and forests;
- increased incidence of water-borne diseases such as bilharzia;
- disrupted river flow;
- increased soil erosion.

Silting and acidification problems often limit the productive life of these schemes, sometimes to as little as 30 years.

Most renewable energy resources, however, have a less damaging environmental impact than fossil fuels and nuclear power, though many are not suitable for large-scale centralised power generation. The resources themselves, such as waves, wind and sunshine, are too dispersed to make it easy to generate large amounts of power. They are also often unreliable, for example because of cloudiness or lack of wind, so for essential energy supplies a back-up capacity is needed.

Renewable energy resources can, however, play a useful part in an integrated power generation system for greater energy needs. For example, wind-generated electricity already makes a small contribution to Britain's energy needs and is widely used in other countries. In California, the use of solar energy for space and water heating has become a regular feature of modern house design. It has been also proposed that solar energy should provide the estimated 10 MW of power needed to supply the Olympic Games in Sydney, Australia in the year 2000. Tidal power has been successfully harnessed at La Rance, France. However, though several designs have been proposed for using wave power to generate electricity none, as yet, has proved commercially successful.

Renewable energy sources are ideally suited to supplying small-scale dispersed power needs, such as in remote island communities, mountain regions and semi-arid areas. They are particularly useful in developing countries where sunshine is plentiful, providing energy for local industries, schools, health clinics, water pumping stations and many other small-scale projects.

10.9.7   Conservation agencies in Britain

There are many individuals, groups and organisations concerned with conservation. Some operate locally, others have national or even international agendas. All contribute in different ways to changing the way we think about and act towards the environment.

Non-governmental organisations (NGOs)

In Britain membership of environmental organisations such as the National Trust (NT), the Royal Society for the Protection of Birds (RSPB) and the various Wildlife Trusts has doubled since 1980. Every county and major urban area in Britain has a Wildlife Trust which owns and manages small nature reserves. These Trusts, which are largely staffed by volunteers, provide protection for locally important conservation sites and involve many of their members in wildlife recording and fund-raising. The 48 County Wildlife Trusts collectively own or manage over 2000 nature reserves. They are linked with the more recently formed 50 Urban Wildlife Groups in a Wildlife Trusts Partnership under the umbrella of the Royal Society for Nature Conservation (RSNC). Their junior club 'WATCH' has promoted many nationwide educational schemes typically linked with industrial sponsors. Recent examples include an ozone monitoring project sponsored by Volvo and a three-year Riverwatch project sponsored by National Power. The RSPB owns 126 generally quite large reserves. Though primarily aimed at conservation of birds, these sites also importantly conserve a wide variety of other wildlife as well. The RSPB junior membership is the Young Ornithologist's Club.

Other conservation charities, such as the NT, are not solely concerned with wildlife and landscape conservation. Nevertheless the NT owns 340 **Sites of Special Scientific Interest** (**SSSI**) and is an important coastal and countryside land owner. Groups, such as the Wildfowl Trust (ducks, geese and swans), the Rare Breeds Trust (conserving domesticated animal varieties) and the Woodland Trust, are more specific in their concerns. Organisations such as Friends of the Earth (FoE) and the Councils for the Protection of Rural England, Scotland and Wales (CPRE, CPRS, CPRW) are concerned with political lobbying and direct action at a wider level. Greenpeace is an important international agency renowned for its controversial, sometimes confrontational but often very effective, direct action. The Flora and Fauna Preservation Society is an international voluntary agency based in Britain which specialises in work promoting species conservation and protection. Much more widely known and also based in Britain is WWF, the Worldwide Fund for Nature. WWF raises large sums of money in support of species and habitat conservation and is particularly active on the international scene. It also sponsors a wide range of environmental education activities.

Statutory Conservation Organisations

Although the voluntary movement is important in Britain, there are also many statutory (government and state-funded) organisations concerned with conservation and the environment. The main nature and countryside conservation agencies were established immediately following the Second World War. These were the Nature Conservancy and the National Parks Commission. Both organisations have subsequently experienced several reorganisations in an attempt to clarify their role and widen their achievements. The Nature Conservancy (since 1973 the Nature Conservancy Council (NCC)) was responsible for establishing National Nature Reserves (NNRs) intended to conserve the best examples of Britain's wildlife and habitats. Over 200 had been designated in mainland Britain by 1990. The Conservancy also identified SSSIs. Today these form an important countrywide series of about 6000 protected locations.

The National Parks Commission was charged with setting up Britain's National Parks. It had limited success since it had no land-owning powers. The Commission's role was to persuade, cajole and advise local authorities and county councils to act. Ten parks were designated in the 1950s in England and Wales, mainly in upland and coastal locations. The Norfolk and Suffolk Broads finally achieved National Park status in 1988.

In 1968 the Countryside Commission (CC) replaced the National Parks Commission. The Countryside Commission deals with the wider countryside as well as the National Parks. It is responsible for designating Areas of Outstanding Natural Beauty (AONBs), the definition of Heritage Coasts and the establishment of long-distance footpaths. It advises local and regional planning authorities on countryside matters, taking a particular interest in urban fringe areas. It has encouraged the setting up of Country Parks, whose recreational and educational emphasis has relieved pressure on the more-sensitive and scientifically important sites managed by the former NCC (see below).

Since 1987 government funds have also been available for **Environmentally Sensitive Areas** (ESAs) giving support to farmers to maintain traditional agricultural practices in countryside that might otherwise be spoilt by modern farming methods. The South Downs, which were rejected as a National Park in the 1950s, is included in this scheme. Since 1990, to reduce the levels of overproduction of food in Europe, farmers have been required to 'set-aside' land from agricultural production. Properly managed, this scheme offers another new opportunity for diversifying the countryside and promoting wildlife conservation.

Other significant statutory organisations are the Forestry Commission, which was established in 1919, and the National Rivers Authority (NRA), which was set up in 1989 and, since April 1996 has been linked with the former Pollution Inspectorate in the new Environment Agency. The Forestry Commission is the statutory body responsible for timber production. It is required to take account of conservation interests on its estates and co-operates with both statutory and voluntary nature conservation organisations. Although much criticised in the past for extensive use of regimented plantings of non-native conifers, the Forestry Commission today takes account of scenic, wildlife and recreational issues. Native hardwoods are now also used on its estates which have been important in re-establishing woodland habitats in Britain. The National Rivers Authority (now the Environment Agency) has responsibility, in England and Wales, for water quality and conservation where this is related to matters of water abstraction, flood control, water quality and similar issues.

In 1990 the British government passed major new environmental legislation. This brought pollution control, environmental assessment and wildlife and countryside conservation into one legislative framework. It included major reorganisation of the Britain's nature conservation agencies to form separate, national organisations for England, Scotland and Wales. In England, English Nature replaced the NCC but remained separate from the Countryside Commission. In Wales and Scotland, however, the national branches of the NCC were amalgamated with the Welsh and Scottish Countryside Commissions to give single unified wildlife and countryside conservation agencies. These are the Countryside Council for Wales and Scottish National Heritage. A new umbrella agency, the Joint Nature Conservation Committee (JNCC) which includes representatives from all these national groups, was formed to deal with issues such as management of major estuaries like the Severn and Solway Firth which require co-operation between the national bodies.

European Environmental initiatives are increasingly influencing nature conservation in Britain. An important current development is the European Habitats Directive. The aim of this directive is to promote the maintenance of biodiversity. Each member state in the European Union has to identify Sites of Community Interest. A final list of key European nature conservation sites will then be agreed in consultation with the European Union. Termed Special Areas for Conservation (SACs), these sites will be strongly protected under European law. The year 2004 is the target date for full establishment of this scheme which will be known as **Natura 2000**.

Chapter Eleven

Quantitative ecology

The principles of ecology, as outlined in the previous chapter, are based on qualitative and quantitative data obtained from studies carried out on animals, plants, microorganisms and the abiotic environment. This chapter deals with both qualitative and quantitative aspects of ecological investigation, and presents a general introduction to some of the methods and techniques of obtaining, presenting and analysing data relating to the abiotic and biotic environments.

Before attempting any ecological investigation it is essential to identify the exact aims and objectives of the study and the degree of accuracy required. These, in turn will clarify the methods and techniques to be employed and will ensure that the data collected are relevant to the study and are adequate to form a basis for valid conclusions. In many cases, this simplifies the methods and techniques and reduces the time, money, resources and effort needed for the study. However, it must be stressed that investigations frequently have to be modified in the light of problems encountered during the investigation.

11.1 Methods of measuring environmental factors

The main environmental factors which must be studied in order to complement biotic analyses are soil factors, water, topography and climatic factors, such as humidity, temperature, light and wind. Many of the methods used to measure environmental factors are included below in experiments. Other methods of quantitative study are described in outline only.

11.1.1 Soil factors

Soils vary considerably in structure and chemical composition. In order to obtain a basic idea of the structure or profile of the soil, a pit is dug so that a clean-cut vertical section of the soil can be seen. The various thicknesses of clearly differentiated bands (horizons), shown in terms of colour and texture, can be measured directly, and samples removed from these horizons and used for the various analyses described below.

Alternatively a soil auger, which is an elongated cork-screw implement, is screwed into the ground to the desired depth and then removed (fig 11.1). Soil trapped in the threads of the screw at various levels is removed into

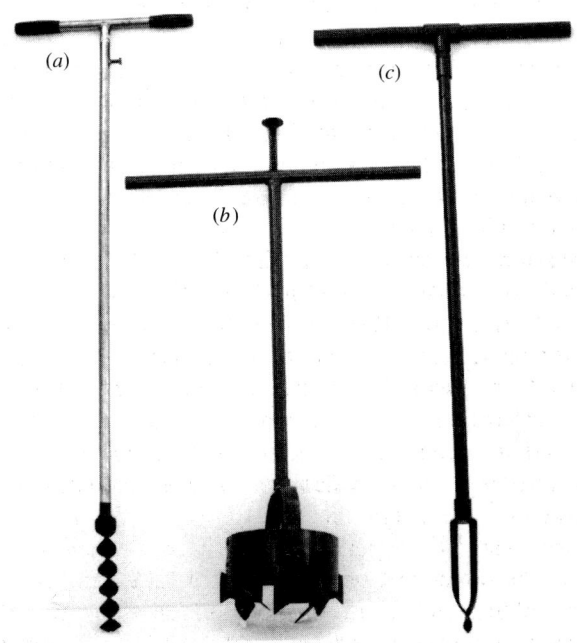

Fig 11.1 (a) Simple screw auger, (b) post-hole auger and (c) 'Dutch' auger.

separate bags for subsequent analysis. When using this method of obtaining a soil sample, it is important to keep a record of the level each part of the sample occupied in the ground. This information should be recorded on the relevant bag.

Notes

(a) Soil samples should not be stored in polythene bags for long periods before analysis because they tend to 'sweat'. The humidity and temperature changes will affect microorganisms present and will therefore affect the pH of the sample and the form in which nutrient elements are held in the soil.

(b) Screw auger sampling is most useful as an indicator of soil profile and hence soil type. Though sufficient material can be taken this way for pH testing and field estimation of soil texture, samples from a soil pit, or taken with a Dutch or post-hole borer (fig 11.1), are preferable to screw auger samples for accurate tests of water content, organic matter content, soil organisms and so on. It is particularly difficult to take reliable uncontaminated samples in sufficient bulk from coarse-textured soils using a screw auger.

Experiment 11.1: To investigate the water content of a soil sample

Materials

about 80 g soil
aluminium foil pie dish
balance accurate to 0.1 g
thermostatically controlled oven
thermometer reading up to 150 °C
desiccator
tongs

Method

(1) Weigh the aluminium foil dish while still empty. Record the mass (*a*).
(2) Add a broken-up soil sample to the dish and weigh. Record the mass (*b*).
(3) Place the dish with the soil sample in the oven at 110 °C for 24 hours.
(4) Remove the sample from the oven and cool in a desiccator.
(5) Weigh the sample when cool and record the mass.
(6) Return the sample to the oven at 110 °C for a further 24 hours.
(7) Repeat stages (4) and (5) until consistent weighings are recorded (constant mass). Record the mass (*c*).
(8) Calculate the percentage water content as follows:

$$\frac{b-c}{b-a} \times 100\%$$

(9) Retain the soil sample in the desiccator for experiment 11.2.

Notes

The value obtained in the experiment is the percentage total water present. This amount will depend upon recent rainfall. Alternative estimates of water content include field capacity and available water. The **field capacity** is the amount of water retained in the soil after excess water has drained off under the influence of gravity. To obtain this value the soil in the field should be flooded until surface water persists for several minutes, 48 hours before the sample is removed for investigation. The **available water** is the water which is available to be taken up by plants, and may be estimated by drying the weighed sample to constant mass at room temperature. The difference between wet mass and dry mass is the amount of available water present.

Experiment 11.2: To investigate the organic (humus) content of a soil sample

Materials

dried soil sample from experiment 11.1 in desiccator
crucible and lid

tripod, bunsen burner, heat proof mat, fireclay triangle
desiccator
tongs

Method

(1) Heat the crucible and lid strongly in the bunsen flame to remove all traces of moisture. Place in the desiccator to cool. Weigh and record the mass (*a*).
(2) Add the dried soil sample (kept from the previous experiment) from the desiccator and weigh. Record the mass (*b*).
(3) Heat the soil sample in the crucible, covered with the lid, to red-heat for 1 h to burn off all the organic matter. Allow to cool for 10 min and remove to the desiccator.
(4) Weigh the crucible and sample when cool.
(5) Repeat (3) and (4) until constant mass is recorded. Record the mass (*c*).
(6) Calculate the percentage organic content as follows:

$$\frac{b-c}{b-a} \times 100\%$$

(7) Repeat the experiment on soil samples taken from different areas to demonstrate variations in organic content.

Note

The percentage organic content obtained in this experiment is relative to dried soil and not to fresh (wet) soil. The organic content of a soil may be quoted as a percentage of fresh (wet) soil using the data obtained in experiment 11.1.

> **11.1** 60 g of a fresh sample of soil produced the following data on analysis. After repeatedly heating at 110 °C and cooling in a desiccator, consistent readings of dry mass of 45 g were obtained. The dry soil was heated repeatedly to red-heat in a crucible, cooled in a desiccator and weighed. The mass was now found to be 30 g. Calculate the water content and organic content of the fresh soil sample.

Experiment 11.3: To investigate the air content of a soil sample

Materials

tin can of volume about 200 cm³
500 cm³ beaker
water
100 cm³ measuring cylinder
chinagraph pencil
drill
metal seeker

Method

(1) Place the empty can, open end uppermost, into the 500 cm^3 beaker and fill the beaker with water above the level of the can. Mark the water level in the beaker.

(2) Carefully remove the can containing the water and measure this volume of water in a measuring cylinder. Record the volume (*a*). The water level in the beaker will fall by an amount corresponding to the volume of water in the can.

(3) Perforate the base of the can using a drill, making about eight small holes.

(4) Push the open end of the can into soil from which the surface vegetation has been removed until soil begins to come through the perforations. Gently dig out the can, turn it over and remove soil from the surface until it is level with the top of can.

(5) Place the can of soil, with open end uppermost, gently back into the beaker of water and loosen soil in the can with seeker to allow air to escape.

(6) The water level in the beaker will be lower than the original level because water will be used to replace the air which was present in the soil.

(7) Add water to the beaker from a full 100 cm^3 measuring cylinder until the original level is restored. Record volume of water added (*b*).

(8) The percentage air content of the soil sample can be determined as follows:

$$\frac{b}{a} \times 100\%.$$

(9) Repeat the experiment on soil samples from different areas.

Experiment 11.4: To investigate the approximate relative proportions of solid particles (soil texture) in a soil sample

Materials

500 cm^3 measuring cylinder
100 cm^3 soil sample
300 cm^3 water

Method

(1) Add the soil sample to the measuring cylinder and cover with water.

(2) Shake the contents vigorously.

(3) Allow the mixture to settle out, according to density and surface area of particles, for 48 hours.

(4) Measure the volume of the various fractions of soil sample.

Results

A gradation of soil components is seen. Organic matter floats at the surface of the water, some clay particles remain in suspension, larger clay particles settle out as a layer on top of sand and stones which are layered according to their sizes.

Experiment 11.5: To investigate the pH of a soil sample

Materials

long test-tube (145 mm) and bung
test-tube rack
barium sulphate
BDH universal indicator solution and colour chart
soil sample
spatula
distilled water
10 cm^3 pipette

Method

(1) Add about 1 cm of soil to the test-tube and 1 cm of barium sulphate, which ensures flocculation of clay particles that remain in suspension.

(2) Add 10 cm^3 of distilled water and 5 cm^3 of BDH universal indicator solution. Seal the test-tube with the bung. Shake vigorously and allow contents to settle for 5 min.

(3) Compare the colour of liquid in the test-tube with the colours on the BDH reference colour chart and read off the corresponding pH.

(4) Repeat the experiment on soil samples from different areas.

Note

pH is one of the most useful measurements which can be made on a soil. Although a simple measurement, it is a product of many interacting factors and is likely to be a good guide to nutrient status and to types of plants (and therefore animals) that flourish. Acid soils tend to be less nutrient-rich (poorer cation-holding capacity).

11.1.2 Water factors

Water, like soil, is an important medium for life. This section outlines some of the basic practical methods used in monitoring the physical and chemical water properties that are of vital importance to living organisms.

Experiment 11.6: To investigate the pH of a water sample

Materials

universal indicator test paper or pH meter
water sample

Method

Either

(1) Dip a piece of universal indicator test paper into the water sample and compare the colour produced with the colour chart. Read off the pH value.

or

(2) Rinse the probe of the pH meter with distilled water, dip it into the water sample and read off the pH value. (This method is more precise, but the meter must be accurately calibrated using prepared solutions of known pH before the experiment begins.) Rinse the probe with distilled water before returning it to buffer solution for storage.

Experiment 11.7: To investigate the chloride content of a water sample (giving a rough estimate of salinity)

Materials

water sample
$10\,cm^3$ pipette
burette
distilled water in a wash bottle
3 conical flasks
white tile
potassium chromate indicator
$50\,cm^3$ silver nitrate solution ($2.73\,g\ 100\,cm^{-3}$)

Method

(1) Place $10\,cm^3$ of the water sample into a conical flask and add two drops of potassium chromate indicator solution.

(2) Titrate silver nitrate solution from the burette, shaking the conical flask constantly.

(3) The end-point of the titration is given by a reddening of the silver chloride precipitate.

(4) Repeat the titration on a further two $10\,cm^3$ water samples. Calculate the mean volume of silver nitrate used.

(5) The volume of silver nitrate solutions used is approximately equal to the chloride content of the water sample (in $g\,dm^{-3}$).

Experiment 11.8: To investigate the dissolved oxygen content of a water sample

The technique described here is the Winkler method which gives an accurate measure of oxygen content but requires many reagents. A simpler but less accurate method is described in Nuffield Advanced Science, *Biological Science*.

Miniaturised 'field kit' versions of the Winkler method are now available from several suppliers (e.g. Hanna dissolved oxygen test kit).

Materials

$10\,cm^3$ of alkaline iodide solution ($3.3\,g$ NaOH, $2.0\,g$ KI in $10\,cm^3$ distilled water) (CARE)
$10\,cm^3$ of manganese chloride solution ($4.0\,g$ $MnCl_2$ in $10\,cm^3$ distilled water)
$5\,cm^3$ of concentrated hydrochloric acid (CARE)
starch solution (as indicator)
distilled water in a wash bottle
0.01 M sodium thiosulphate solution (see point (8) in method)
$3 \times 5\,cm^3$ graduated pipettes
burette
white tile
3 conical flasks
$250\,cm^3$ water sample in glass bottle with ground glass stopper

Method

(1) Collect the water sample carefully without splashing and stopper the sample bottle under water to prevent entry of air bubbles.

(2) Add $2\,cm^3$ of manganese chloride solution and $2\,cm^3$ of alkaline iodide solution to the sample using pipettes whose tips are placed at the bottom of the sample bottle. The heavier salt solutions will displace an equal volume of water from the top of the sample bottle. Replace the stopper carefully (the bottle should be completely filled by the sample). Shake well to mix reagents throughout the water sample. A complex precipitate of manganic-oxide-hydroxide will form in direct proportion to the amount of oxygen present in the sample. The sample may now be set aside (e.g. transported back to a laboratory before continuing the analysis).

(3) Add $2\,cm^3$ of concentrated hydrochloric acid and stopper the bottle so that no air bubbles are trapped. Shake the bottle thoroughly to dissolve the precipitate. This leaves a solution of iodine in an excess of potassium iodide. The iodine formed is directly proportional to the oxygen originally present in the water sample. The dissolved oxygen is now fixed and exposure to air will not affect the result.

(4) Remove a $50\,cm^3$ sample of this solution and place it in a conical flask. Titrate with 0.01 M sodium thiosulphate solution from the burette as follows:
(*a*) add thiosulphate solution whilst shaking the flask until the yellow colour becomes pale;
(*b*) add three drops of starch solution and continue to titrate and shake until the blue-black colouration of the starch disappears.
Record the volume of thiosulphate used.

(5) Repeat stage (4) with two further $50\,cm^3$ samples of water and obtain the mean volume used (*x*).

(6) Using these solutions, $1\,cm^3$ of 0.01 M thiosulphate solution corresponds to $0.056\,cm^3$ of oxygen at standard temperature and pressure (STP).

(7) Calculate the concentration of oxygen per dm^3 of water using the following formula:

$$\text{oxygen in } cm^3 dm^{-3} = 0.056 \times x \times 1000/50 \text{ at STP}$$

where x = volume of thiosulphate solution required for the titration of $50\,cm^3$ of samples.

(8) In comparative studies for water pollution work and estimating BOD, dissolved oxygen levels are commonly expressed in $mg\,dm^{-3}$. Calculation of the final result is simpler if a working solution of $0.0125\,M$ sodium thiosulphate is used. Then $1\,cm^3$ sodium thiosulphate solution is equivalent to $0.1\,mg$ oxygen.

(a) Prepare a stock solution of $0.1\,M$ sodium thiosulphate. To do this, dissolve $24.82\,g$ $Na_2S_2O_3.5H_2O$ (sodium thiosulphate) in distilled water. Add a pellet of NaOH (sodium hydroxide) and dilute to $1\,dm^3$. Store in a brown bottle. This solution may be kept for two or three weeks.

(b) Prepare, as needed, a working solution of $0.0125\,M$ sodium thiosulphate. To do this take $125\,cm^3$ of the stock solution and dilute to $1\,dm^3$ ($\times 8$ dilution).

(c) Carry out the method following the procedure outlined above but using $0.0125\,M$ sodium thiosulphate in step (4):

$$\text{mg } O_2 \text{ in } 1\,dm^3 \text{ sample} = x \times 0.1 \times 1000/50$$
$$\text{or } x \times 2$$

where x = mean volume of $0.0125\,M$ thiosulphate solution required for the titration of $50\,cm^3$ of sample.

(9) It may be useful to compare the actual oxygen content with the potential maximum value, the **saturation level**. This will be especially relevant if you are sampling a stream or river at different seasons of the year, in other words under different temperature conditions. The amount of oxygen that can be held in solution is temperature-dependent. Thus to estimate the percentage saturation one further measurement, the temperature of the water sample at collection, is needed. This can be easily achieved using a simple mercury thermometer. By reference to table 11.1 the percentage oxygen saturation value for the water can easily be calculated:

$$\frac{\text{mg } O_2 \, dm^{-3} \text{ present in sample tested}}{\text{mg } O_2 \, dm^{-3} \text{ held at saturation}} \times 100\%.$$

Notes

(1) It is quite common to use $25\,cm^3$ water samples, thus saving on reagent, with appropriate adjustment

of the final calculation ($mg\,O_2\,dm^{-3} = x \times 4$).

(2) It is essential to dissolve all the precipitate present, since this contains all the oxygen from the water. It may sometimes be necessary to add extra acid to achieve this.

(3) It is important to add enough manganese chloride and alkaline iodide solution to ensure all oxygen is trapped in the precipitate. In practice any convenient size of glass-stoppered bottle can be used, providing these two reagents are added in equal amounts and in the approximate ratio of $1\,cm^3$ manganese

Table 11.1 The solubility of oxygen in water.

Temperature/ °C	Saturation value for O_2/ $mg\,dm^{-3}$	Adjustment for saline waters/ $mg\,dm^{-3}$
0	14.63	0.0925
1	14.23	0.0890
2	13.84	0.0857
3	13.46	0.0827
4	13.11	0.0798
5	12.77	0.0771
6	12.45	0.0745
7	12.13	0.0720
8	11.84	0.0697
9	11.55	0.0675
10	11.28	0.0653
11	11.02	0.0633
12	10.77	0.0614
13	10.53	0.0595
14	10.29	0.0577
15	10.07	0.0559
16	9.86	0.0543
17	9.65	0.0527
18	9.46	0.0511
19	9.27	0.0496
20	9.08	0.0481
21	8.91	0.0467
22	8.74	0.0453
23	8.57	0.0440
24	8.42	0.0427
25	8.26	0.0415
26	8.12	0.0404
27	7.97	0.0393
28	7.84	0.0382
29	7.70	0.0372
30	7.57	0.0362

Notes: The solubility of oxygen in water varies with temperature, atmospheric pressure and the concentration of dissolved salts. In saline waters saturation values will be lower and suitable adjustment must be made. The data show the necessary adjustment in $mg\,dm^{-3}$ for each 1 part per thousand (ppt) change in salinity.
Data are based on work by Montgomery, Thorn and Cockburn at the Water Pollution Research Laboratory. It has been reproduced from Klein, L., (1966) *River Pollution*, Vol. 3, Butterworth.

chloride and $1\,cm^3$ alkaline iodide to $100\,cm^3$ of water sample.

(4) When collecting samples in the field the bottles should be rinsed at least three times with the water to be tested before collecting the test sample. The bottle should be pointing upstream so that water flows in easily without splashing. Bottles should be thoroughly cleaned before use, if possible including acid rinsing.

(5) Waterproof gloves (e.g. washing-up gloves) should always be worn when taking samples from rivers, streams and ponds which may be polluted. In shallow rivers and streams, samples should be taken mid-stream; deeper water samples may be taken from bridges or using a boat, as suitable. Appropriate safety procedures should always be followed.

Experiment 11.9 To investigate the biochemical oxygen demand (BOD) of a water sample

A dissolved oxygen test measures the current oxygen status of a stream or river. This is a useful starting point. However, dissolved oxygen content can vary considerably from day to day due to a range of other environmental factors such as sunlight and windiness. Of more fundamental significance is the rate at which oxygen is being used by organisms present in the water. If water contains large amounts of organic wastes, then the rate of microorganism activity (effectively decomposition) may be high and the water may rapidly become depleted of oxygen. This will have important consequences for continued microorganism activity and the lives of other aerobic organisms.

Materials

$500\,cm^3 - 1\,dm^3$ water sample and

either
reagents and glassware as described for the Winkler method in experiment 11.8 above
or
an appropriately calibrated oxygen electrode

Method

Pre-checks

(1) If necessary adjust the sample pH to a range of 6.5–8.5 (to optimise microorganism activity).

(2) If the oxygen content of the sample is known to be very low (e.g. you have already measured the dissolved oxygen) the sample should be oxygenated for 5–10 min. This is important since the test measures the rate of oxygen consumption and microorganism activity. The results will be misleading if there is an insufficient initial oxygen supply.

(3) If high organic contamination is suspected, prepare sample dilutions (see note at end of method) before

incubating. Remember to check that the BOD of the dilution water itself is negligible. To do this incubate dilution water in the same way as samples. If necessary (that is if there is a significant decrease in dissolved oxygen) adjust results for oxygen loss in dilution water controls as well as for dilution factor itself.

Test procedure

(1) Place portions of the sample (dilute if necessary) into three glass-stoppered bottles of $125\,cm^3$ or $250\,cm^3$ capacity. Pour carefully to avoid trapping air bubbles. Ensure bottles are completely full.

(2) Immediately determine the oxygen content of one bottle (express as $mg\,dm^{-3}$).

(3) Incubate the remaining two bottles *in the dark* (no photosynthesis) at a standard temperature (20 °C) or the temperature of the original sample for 1–5 days. The standard procedure is to incubate in darkness at 20 °C for five days.

(4) Determine the oxygen content of the incubated bottles ($mg\,dm^{-3}$).

(5) Subtract the mean value for the incubated samples from the original sample. This gives the sample BOD in $mg\,dm^{-3}$, unless the sample was diluted before incubation. In this case use the following formula:

$$BOD = (x - y)(a + 1)\,mg\,dm^{-3}$$

where x is the initial dissolved oxygen in $mg\,dm^{-3}$, y is the mean final dissolved oxygen in $mg\,dm^{-3}$, and a is the volume(s) of dilution water to 1 volume of sample.

Note

River water does not usually require dilution. A badly polluted stream or pond might require up to four parts dilution water to one part sample. Such contaminated water is a health risk and requires great care in handling and is best avoided for student class work. Tap water was formerly commonly used for dilution but high chlorination now often makes this unsuitable. Synthetic dilution water is preferable (distilled or deionised water with appropriate chemicals added). Advice on the preparation of synthetic dilution waters is given in H.L. Golterman, R.S. Clymo & M.A.M. Ohnstad (1978) *Methods for physical and chemical analysis of fresh waters*, IBP Handbook No. 8, Blackwell Scientific Publications, 2nd edition.

Any samples absorbing more than $6\,mg\,dm^{-3}$ oxygen or having a final dissolved oxygen content less than 40% saturation should be diluted.

In some cases a considerable part of the BOD may be due to oxidation of ammonia. If wished this nitrification can be inhibited by adding $1\,cm^3$ of $0.5\,g\,dm^{-3}$ solution of allylthiourea to each sample. For a fuller discussion see Golterman *et al.* as cited above.

Water current

The simplest method of measuring water current is to record the time taken for a floating object to cover a known distance. In order to eliminate the effects of wind, it is preferable to use an object which is mainly submerged. Alternatively an L-shaped tube 50 cm high, 10 cm long and 2 cm in diameter can be placed in a stream with the short end facing upstream. By measuring the height to which water rises in the long limb, the velocity of the current can be measured using the formula:

$$v = \sqrt{(2hg)}$$

where v is the speed of the current (cm s^{-1}), g is the acceleration due to gravity (981 cm s^{-2}) and h is the height of the column (cm).

11.1.3 Climatic factors

Some simple approaches to the measurement of key atmospheric and climatic characteristics are outlined below.

Humidity

The relative humidity of air is a measure of the moisture content of air relative to air fully saturated with water vapour. It varies with temperature, since air expands on heating and can hold more water vapour. Relative humidity is measured by a **whirling hygrometer**, which is a wet and a dry bulb thermometer mounted on a wooden frame resembling a football rattle (fig 11.2). It is whirled around until both thermometers give constant temperature readings. These temperatures are then examined in hygrometer tables, or on a specially calibrated slide rule supplied with the whirling hygrometer kit, and the corresponding relative humidity read off. Dew-point values (the temperature at which the same air sample would become saturated) can also be estimated from these data.

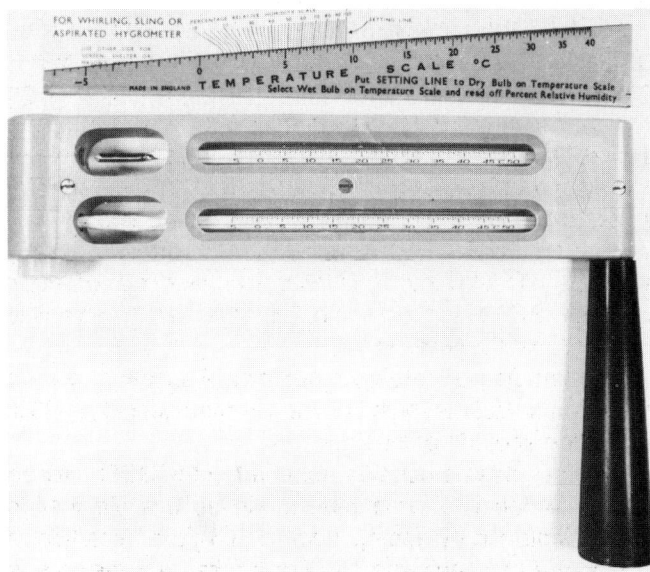

Fig 11.2 *Whirling hygrometer.*

Temperature

Air, water and soil temperatures can be measured using a mercury thermometer, but measurements of temperature at a point in time provide little real information of ecological significance. It is the range of temperatures over a period of time which has more significance in ecological studies. Hence sophisticated time-based recordings of temperature are normally used, or the maximum and minimum temperatures recorded using a maximum–minimum thermometer.

Temperatures in microhabitats and inaccessible habitats, such as the centre of a tree, are measured using a thermistor (fig 11.3). This is an electrical device which can be miniaturised to fit into the tip of a ballpoint pen and whose resistance varies with temperature. By measuring the resistance of the thermistor, and comparing this with previous temperature-calibrated resistances, the environmental temperature can be obtained.

The temperature extremes of microhabitats (microclimates) are also useful in ecological studies since they can often explain the disappearance of a particular species from an area, such as frost-sensitive plants.

Light

Light varies in intensity, duration and quality (wavelength). Measurements of all three aspects are required to provide the information relevant to ecological study, and specialised techniques are required to record them. For practical purposes some indication of intensity related to particular areas is generally required, so that the incident light in

Fig 11.3 *A thermistor in use.*

different areas can be compared. For this purpose an ordinary photographic exposure meter is adequate. Light intensities over a given period of time can be recorded using Ozalid papers which have a cumulative sensitivity to light.

Wind speed and direction

The wind speed in a habitat at a given point in time is not as ecologically significant as the degree of exposure to wind experienced by the habitat. In this respect wind frequency, intensity and direction are all important. However, for most practical purposes a simple wind-gauge, indicating the direction of the wind, and a simple anemometer (fig 11.4), indicating wind speed, are adequate for comparing features of wind in different habitats.

11.2   Biotic analysis

In analysing the organisms living in a given habitat (the biotic component of the ecosystem) the community structure must be determined in terms of species present in the habitat and numbers within each population. It is obviously impractical to attempt to find and count all the members of a given species, and so sampling techniques have to be devised which will give indications of species present and their numbers. Generally speaking, the more accurate the results required the more time-consuming the method, so it is necessary to be clear about objectives. Also, if possible, non-destructive techniques should be used.

In all cases reliable methods of sampling (recording

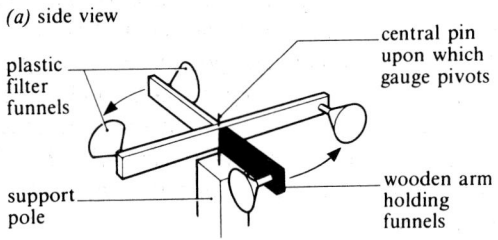

(a) side view

plastic filter funnels

central pin upon which gauge pivots

support pole

wooden arm holding funnels

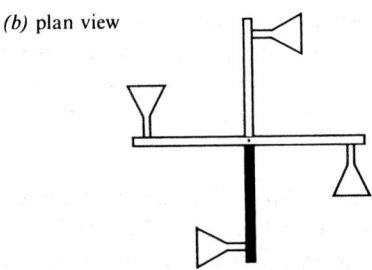

(b) plan view

Fig 11.4 *Simple anemometer which may be used to determine wind speed in terms of the rate of turning of the wooden arm painted black.*

and/or collecting) organisms are required, and it is safe to say that 'no stone should be left unturned' (providing it is replaced!) since organisms will occupy almost all available microhabitats. For example, at first sight a square metre of grass, soil, sand, rocky shore or stream bed may not appear to support many species, but closer examination, involving hand-sorting the soil, grass and weeds, turning over stones and examining roots, stems, flowers and fruits of plants and holdfasts of seaweeds, will reveal many more species.

In recording data, as many species as possible (plant and animal) should be identified in the field, using keys if necessary. Only if the species are obviously common locally and not known to be rarities should they be collected. Over-collection can have serious effects on local communities. In the case of collected animals, attempts should be made to keep them alive and to release them in a similar microhabitat to that in which they were collected. It is necessary to identify the organisms as accurately as possible, that is to the level of species. This cannot always be done, but it should be possible to identify them at least as far as class, order or family. Identification of specimens depends upon familiarity with keys. The principles of classification, key construction and details of how to use a key are described in appendix 3 in Book 2.

A list of all the species in the habitat gives some indication of the diversity of structure of the community, the **species richness** or **diversity**. (There are various numerical ways of expressing species richness using mathematical formulae. The numerical value is called the **diversity index** but details of this will not be considered here.)

These data provide information enabling possible food chains and food webs to be constructed, but are inadequate in providing information related to quantitative aspects of the community. The extent of the diversity is only fully revealed when the numbers of organisms within each species, that is the population sizes, are determined. This information enables a more detailed picture of the community to be constructed, such as a pyramid of numbers (section 10.3.4).

Obtaining the qualitative and quantitative data of a habitat depends on specific methods of collecting, sampling and estimating organisms within the habitat, and the method chosen is related to the mode of life, behaviour and size of the organism.

11.2.1   Methods of collecting organisms

There are several points to consider when collecting organisms and these are summarised below.

(1) Always observe sensible safety precautions for yourself and others. These will vary with the nature of your investigation and the environment being studied. Always check your safety arrangements with an experienced field worker **before starting** any ecological project work.

(2) Observe the Countryside Code at all times.

(3) Respect the environments, communities and ecosystems in which you are working. Be sure you cause no damage nor permanent change.

(4) Always obtain permission from the landowner before beginning an ecological study in an area.

(5) Consult the local Wildlife Trust, university, college or the statutory countryside conservation organisations such as English Nature about where and what you are to study and what you may collect.

(6) Never remove organisms from their habitat or destroy them unnecessarily.

(7) Leave the habitat as undisturbed as possible, for example replace stones, turf, logs and so on to their original positions.

(8) Where it is necessary to remove organisms from the habitat for identification, take as few as possible and, if practicable, return them to the habitat.

(9) Keep specimens separate when removing them to the laboratory for identification, to prevent contamination or being eaten by predators, for example do not put ragworm and crabs in the same collecting vessel. Useful collecting equipment includes jam jars, Kilner jars, polythene bottles, specimen tubes and polythene bags.

(10) Always record as much information as possible concerning the topography of the habitat and climate at the time of collection as the information may have a bearing on what is collected:

(a) nature of rock or substratum (grass, mud, soil etc.);

(b) nature of aspect (for example flat, south-facing, angle of slope etc.);

(c) drainage;

(d) soil, mud or sand profile;

(e) temperature of substrate, water and air;

(f) substrate or water pH;

(g) cloud cover and rainfall;

(h) relative humidity of air;

(i) light intensity (such as shaded or open, possibly a meter reading);

(j) wind speed and direction (such as still, gentle breeze, gale, south-west);

(k) time of day and date.

An example of how some of these features may be recorded is shown in table 11.2.

There are a variety of methods of collecting specimens. A summary of methods and their applications is shown in table 11.3 and in figs 11.5–11.10. Specimens should be collected from traps at regular intervals, identified, counted and, where possible, released. In the case of pitfall traps it should be realised that if natural predators and prey are collected it is probable that the prey will not be present when the trap is emptied. Where this is believed to be happening, 70% alcohol should be placed in the trap to kill

Table 11.2 Field booking sheet for recording edaphic, physiographic and climatic features.

Area .... Grid reference .... Date ....

(1) **Underlying rock**
(2) **Substratum/soil**
  (a) surface feature...
  (b) depth of horizon A ....
  (c)   ,,   ,,   ,,   B ....
  (d)   ,,   ,,   ,,   C ....
  (e) pH ....
  (f) temperature ....

(3) **Topography**
  (a) aspect, direction......... angle ....
  (b) height above sea level ....
  (c) relief ....
  (d) drainage ....
  (e) land use ....
  (f) high or low water, time......... height ....

(4) **Climate**
  (a) air temperature, range ....
  (b) rainfall...
  (c) cloud cover/sunlight......................................
  (d) relative humidity ....
  (e) wind direction...
  (f) wind speed ....
  (g) light intensity (horizontal), N....., S....., E....., W ....
  (h) time of day...

the organisms as they fall in. Imagination and ingenuity are required in collecting specimens.

Generally, sites where specimens are collected are not randomly chosen and consequently the results obtained from the collections must be interpreted in the light of biased selection of collecting site. Whilst this may not affect the species of organism collected, so that community structure will be accurately represented, it is likely to give biased indications of numbers present. For example, the use of baits and lures to attract organisms to sticky traps, pitfall traps and mammal traps will influence the results, and conclusions based on quantitative data will reflect this bias. Therefore in discussion of results it is necessary to state clearly that bias exists.

11.2.2   Methods of sampling an area

In order to standardise the sites where abiotic and biotic aspects of ecosystems are investigated, transects and/or quadrats are commonly used and collecting and sampling is often confined to the area of the transect or quadrat.

Line transect.   This may be used to sample a uniform area but is particularly useful where it is suspected that there is a transition in habitats and populations through an area (fig 11.10). For example, a tape or string running along the ground in a straight line between two poles indicates the position of the transect and sampling is rigorously confined to species actually touching the line.

Table 11.3 A summary of various methods used to collect organisms.

Collecting method	Structure and function	Organisms collected
beating tray	A fabric sheet of known area is attached to a collapsible frame and held under a branch which is beaten with a stick or shaken. Organisms fall onto the sheet and are removed using a pooter (see later notes).	non-flying insects, larval stages, spiders
kite net	A muslin net is attached to a handle and swept through the air. Organisms become trapped in the net. All netting techniques must be standardised to ensure uniformity of sampling, e.g. eight, figure-of-eight sweeps per examination of the net.	flying insects
sweep net	A nylon net is attached to a steel handle and swept through grass, bushes, ponds or streams.	insects, crustaceans
plankton net	A bolting silk net is attached to a metal hoop and rope harness and towed through the water. A small jar is attached to the rear of the net to collect specimens.	plankton
sticky trap	Black treacle and sugar are boiled together and smeared onto a sheet of thick polythene which is then attached to a piece of chipboard with drawing pins. This can be hung in various situations and at various heights. Jam and beer can be added to the sticky substances to act as attractants.	flying insects
pitfall trap	A jam jar or tin is buried in the soil with the rim level with ground level. This is best placed where the ground falls away from rim level to prevent water entering the jar. A piece of slate supported on three stones acts as a lid preventing rainwater from entering. The trap can be baited with either sweet foods such as jam or decaying meat. Traps should be regularly cleared (fig 11.5).	walking/crawling insects, myriapods, spiders, crustaceans
light trap	A mercury vapour light trap attracts flying organisms which hit baffles and fall down into the base and become trapped in cardboard egg boxes or crumpled-up paper. Cotton wool soaked in chloroform is added before examining the contents to anaesthetise or kill the organisms (fig 11.6).	night-flying insects, particularly moths and caddis flies
mammal trap	A Longworth mammal trap (fig 11.7) is left in a runway and filled with bedding material. Bait, e.g. grain or dried fruit, can be left outside and inside the trap. The trap can be left unset for some time until organisms become accustomed to it and then set. Animals are captured alive so the trap must be visited regularly. Some animals may remain 'trap shy' and never enter it, whereas others become 'trap happy' and visit it regularly. These two patterns can present problems when using the technique to estimate population sizes.	shrews, voles and mice
kick sampling	This is used for collecting in running fresh water. An open sweep or plankton net is held vertically downstream of the area being sampled by turning over stones and scraping off organisms which are then swept into the net. Alternatively the area being sampled is agitated by kicking and stamping so that organisms are displaced vertically and swept into the net by the current.	aquatic insects and crustaceans
pooter	This is used to collect small insects from beating trees or directly off vegetation for closer examination and/or counting (fig 11.11).	aphids, small insects and spiders
hand-sorting	Samples of soil or vegetation, e.g. grass, leaf litter, pond and seaweed, are placed at one end of a tray and small amounts of material are systematically examined between the fingers, specimens are removed to a collecting jar and sorted material passed to the other end of the tray. The sample is then examined as it is moved back to the original end of the tray.	mites, enchytraeid worms, insect larvae and small insects
extractions	$5\,cm^3$ of 4% formaldehyde are added to $50\,cm^3$ of water and used to water a square metre of lawn or grassland. Earthworms are driven out from their burrows and collected and immediately washed in water to remove the formaldehyde.	earthworms
flotation	Add a known mass of soil to a beaker of saturated salt solution, stir vigorously for several minutes and allow soil to settle. Organisms float to surface in dense salt solution. Pour off surface layer of fluid into a petri dish and examine under binocular microscope. Remove all specimens into another petri dish containing 70% alcohol to kill and fix the specimens. Mount each specimen separately in glycerine on a microscope slide, cover with a cover-slip and identify under binocular microscope or low power of compound microscope.	mites, insects, eggs, cocoon, larval and pupal stages
Tullgren funnel (dry extraction)	Many soil and leaf litter-dwelling organisms move away from a source of heat and towards moister conditions. A soil or leaf litter sample is placed in the sieve about 25 cm below a 25 W bulb in a metal reflector (fig 11.8). Every two hours the bulb is moved 5 cm nearer to the sample until the bulb is 5 cm from the soil sample. The apparatus is left for a total of 24 h. All small arthropods move downwards and drop through the metal gauze into the alcohol beneath.	small arthropods e.g. millipedes, centipedes, mites, springtails and collembola
Baermann funnel (wet extraction)	A soil sample is placed in a muslin bag, submerged in a funnel containing water and suspended 25 cm from a 60 W bulb in a metal reflector (fig 11.9). The apparatus is left for 24 h. The water and the gentle heating encourage organisms to leave the sample, move out into the water and sink to the base of the funnel. They are removed at intervals by opening the clip in the apparatus and allowing them to fall into the alcohol.	small arthropods, enchytraeid worms and nematodes

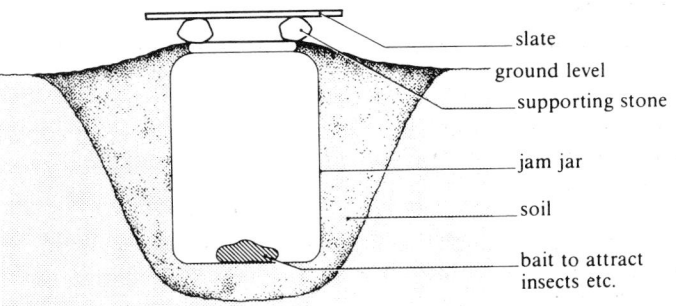

Fig 11.5 *Simple pitfall trap made by sinking a jam jar into the soil.*

Fig 11.6 *Mercury vapour lamp in use attracting insects.*

Labels for Fig 11.5:
- slate
- ground level
- supporting stone
- jam jar
- soil
- bait to attract insects etc.

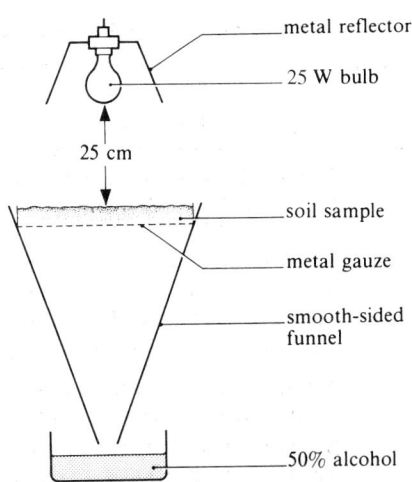

Fig 11.8 *Tullgren funnel.*

Labels for Fig 11.8:
- metal reflector
- 25 W bulb
- 25 cm
- soil sample
- metal gauze
- smooth-sided funnel
- 50% alcohol

Fig 11.7 *(below) Longworth mammal trap.*

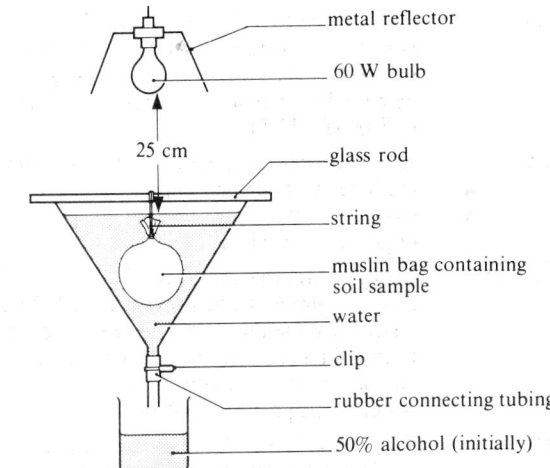

Fig. 11.9 *Baermann funnel.*

Labels for Fig 11.9:
- metal reflector
- 60 W bulb
- 25 cm
- glass rod
- string
- muslin bag containing soil sample
- water
- clip
- rubber connecting tubing
- 50% alcohol (initially)

Fig 11.10   *The position of a line transect a cross a rocky shore.*

Belt transect.   A belt transect is simply a strip of chosen width through the habitat, made by setting up two line transects, say 0.5 m or 1 m apart, between which species are recorded. An easier method of obtaining both qualitative and quantitative data from a belt transect is to use a quadrat frame in conjunction with a line transect.

Height variations recorded along line or belt transects produce a profile of the transect, sometimes known as a **profile transect**, which can be used when presenting data (fig 11.21).

A decision over which type of transect to use depends on the qualitative and quantitative nature of the investigation, the degree of accuracy required, the nature of the organisms present, the size of the area to be investigated and the time available. Over a short distance a line transect might be used and a continuous record kept of each plant species lying immediately beneath it. Alternatively, over a longer distance the species present every metre, or other suitable distance along the transect, may be recorded.

Quadrat.   A quadrat frame is typically a metal or wooden frame, preferably collapsible to facilitate carrying, which forms a square of known area, such as 0.25 m^2 or 1 m^2 (fig 11.12). The size of quadrat used will depend on the organisms being studied. A 0.25 m^2 (flexible*) quadrat would be suitable for a study of lichens on trees, but a 10 m^2 or 20 m^2 quadrat** would be needed for an investigation of a woodland.

The quadrat is placed to one side of a line transect and sampling carried out. It is then moved along the line transect to different positions. Both the species present within the frame and the numbers or abundance (section 11.2.3) of these may be recorded, depending upon the nature of the investigation. In all cases the method of recording the species must be consistent, for example all species partially or completely visible within the quadrat are listed. The structure of the quadrat frame can be modified according to the demands of the investigation. For example, it can be divided by string or wire into convenient sections to assist in counting or estimating numbers or abundance of the species (fig 11.12). This is particularly useful when studying a habitat supporting several species of plants.

* A small flexible quadrat can be made by marking out the quadrat dimensions, in waterproof ink, onto a clear plastic sheet.

** Instant portable quadrats, of any size, can be made using tent pegs or canes to fix the corner posts and strong nylon string, looped at appropriate intervals (10 m or 20 m) to mark the quadrat sides. The string should be mounted on a dispenser board for tangle-free assembly and dismantling. If needed, matching lengths of dividing strings can be mounted on separate dispenser boards or, for smaller quadrat sizes, they can be wound separately onto the quadrat dispenser (fig 11.13).

Fig 11.11 *Pooter in use collecting small non-vertebrates.*

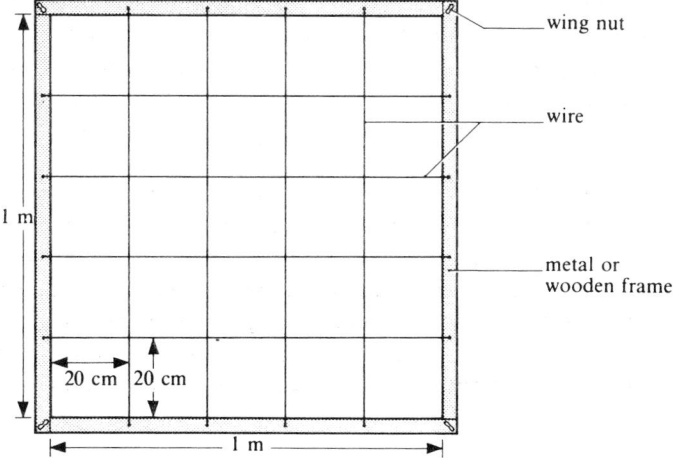

Fig 11.12 *Quadrat frame (1 m^2) with wire sub-quadrats (each 400 cm^2) forming a graduated quadrat.*

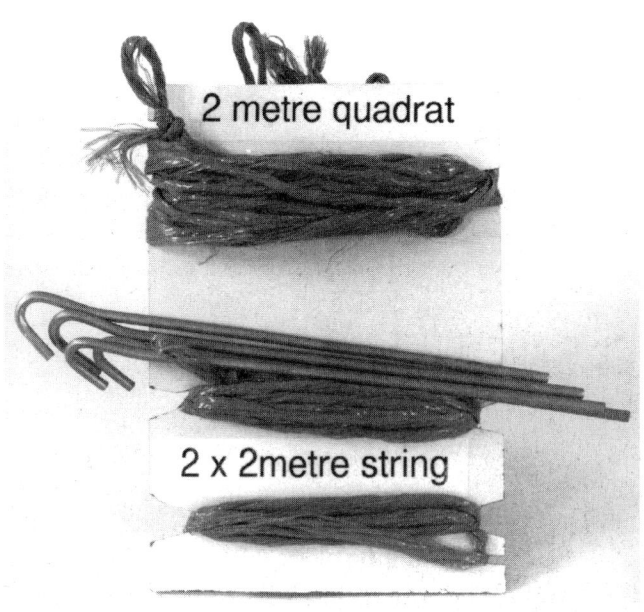

Fig 11.13 *Quadrat dispenser.*

A quadrat may be used without a transect when studying an apparently uniform habitat. In this case the quadrat is used randomly. One fairly random and traditionally used sampling technique is to fling a robust quadrat over the shoulder and record the species within it wherever it falls. This is repeated several times so that a representative sample of the area is covered. This obviously needs care and the resultant sample may still be biased, for example according to the investigator's throwing skills. An alternative, and sounder, approach is to choose a sampling point using a table of random numbers or random numbers generated on an suitable pocket calculator. Each pair of random numbers can be used to identify a random coordinate, the **sampling point**, on an imaginary grid laid over the area. The sides of the grid may be marked by measuring tapes. Alternatively random number pairs may be used to plot a random walk using one number to determine the distance walked and the second to indicate the direction of the walk.

Investigations have shown that in a uniform habitat there comes a point beyond which analysing the species within a quadrat becomes unnecessary, as it does not increase the number of different species recorded. This relationship is shown in fig 11.14. As a rule of thumb, once five quadrats have failed to show any new species it may be assumed that no further species will be found. However, when an assumption such as this is made it must be stated in the ecological report as it may affect the reliability of the results.

Pin frame (point quadrat). This is a frame bearing a number of holes through which a 'pin', such as a knitting needle can be passed (fig 11.15). It is particularly useful with transect studies of overgrown habitats where

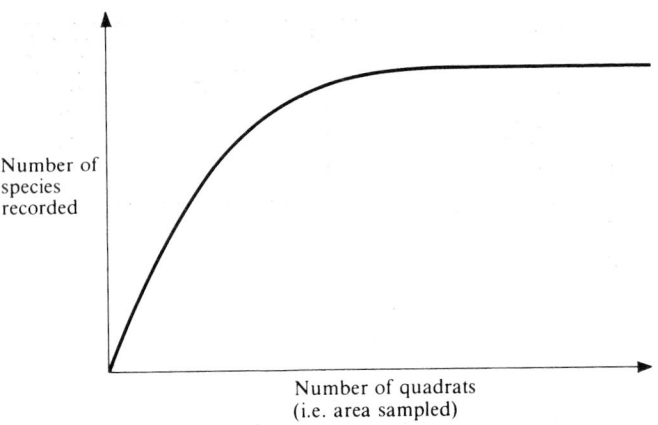

Fig 11.14 *Graph showing the relationship between the number of species recorded in an area and the number of quadrats studied. (In quantitative studies there is no point in sampling more quadrats beyond a certain point as it is unrewarding and uneconomical of time.)*

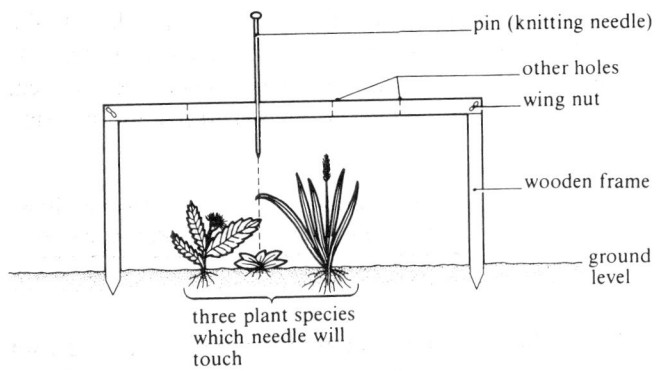

Fig 11.15 *Pin frame or point quadrat.*

several plant species may overlap. All species touched by the pin as it descends to the ground are recorded for each of the holes.

Permanent quadrat. In long-term ecological investigations involving the study of community change (succession) or seasonal changes, a permanent quadrat or transect is used. Metal pegs and nylon rope are used to mark out an area of ground. Periodic samples of abiotic and biotic factors can be taken and the results presented in such a way as to reveal trends and changes and possible factors accounting for, or associated with, these changes.

11.2.3 Methods of estimating population size

In all studies in quantitative ecology it is essential to be able to estimate, with a reasonable degree of accuracy, the number of organisms within a given area of ground or volume of water or air. In most cases this is equivalent to estimating the population size, and the methods employed are determined by the size and mode of life of organisms involved and the size of the area under investigation. The numbers of plants and sessile or slow-moving animals in a small area may be counted directly, or their percentage cover or abundance estimated, whereas indirect methods may be required for fast-moving organisms in large open areas. In habitats where organisms are difficult to observe, because of their behaviour and mode of life, it is necessary to estimate numbers of organisms using either the removal method or the capture–recapture method. Methods of estimating populations may be either objective or subjective.

Objective methods

The use of quadrats, direct observation and photography are known as direct counting methods, whereas the removal and capture–recapture techniques are indirect counting methods.

Quadrat method. If the number of organisms within a number of quadrats, representing a known fraction of the total area, are determined, an estimate of the total numbers in the whole area can be obtained by simple multiplication. This method provides a means of calculating three aspects of species distribution.

(1) **Species density.** This is the number of individuals of a given species in a given area. It is obtained by counting the number of organisms in randomly thrown quadrats. The method has the advantages of being accurate, enabling different areas and different species to be compared, and providing an absolute measure of abundance. The disadvantages are that it is time-consuming and requires individuals to be defined, for example is a grass tussock counted as one plant or does each plant of the tussock need to be counted?

(2) **Species frequency.** This is a measure of the probability (chance) of finding a given species with any one throw of a quadrat in a given area. For example, if the species occurs once in every ten quadrats it has a frequency of 10%. This measure is obtained by recording the presence or absence of the species in a randomly thrown quadrat. (The number present is irrelevant.) In this method the size of the quadrat must be stated since it will influence the results, and also whether the frequency refers to 'shoot' or 'rooted' frequency. (For 'shoot' frequency the species is recorded as present even if foliage only overlaps into the quadrat from outside. For 'rooted' frequency the species is only recorded as present if it is actually rooted in the quadrat.) This method has the advantage of being quick and easy and useful in certain large-scale ecosystems such as woodland. The disadvantages are that quadrat size, plant size and spatial distribution (that is random, uniform or clumped) (see appendix section A2.8, Book 2) all affect the species frequency.

11.2 What is the species frequency of the species recorded in 86 quadrats out of 200 studied?

(3) **Species cover.** This is a measure of the proportion of ground occupied by the species and gives an estimate of the area covered by the species as a percentage of the total area. It is obtained either by observing the species covering the ground at a number of random points, by the subjective estimate of percentage of quadrat coverage or by the use of a pin frame (fig 11.15). This is a useful method for estimating plant species, especially grasses, where individuals are hard to count and are not as important as cover. However it has the disadvantages of being slow and tedious.

11.3 If a pin frame containing ten pins was used ten times and 36 units were recorded for plant X, what is the percentage cover of X?

Direct observation. Direct counting is not only applicable to sessile or slow-moving animals but also to many larger mobile organisms such as deer, wild ponies and lions, and wood pigeons and bats as they leave their roost.

Photography. It is possible to obtain population sizes of larger mammals and sea birds which congregate in open spaces by direct counting from aerial photographs.

Removal method. The removal method is very suitable for estimating numbers of small organisms, particularly insects, within a known area of grassland or volume of water. Using a net in some form of standard sweep, the number of animals captured is recorded and the animals kept. This procedure is repeated a further three times and the gradually reducing numbers recorded. A graph is plotted of number of animals captured per sample against the previous cumulative number of animals captured. By extrapolating the line of the graph to the point at which no further animals would be captured (that is number in sample = 0) the total population may be estimated, as shown in fig 11.16.

Capture–recapture method. This method involves capturing the organism, marking it in some way without causing it any damage, and replacing it so that it can resume a normal role in the population. For example, fish are netted and their operculum tagged with aluminium discs; birds are netted and rings attached to their legs; small mammals may be tagged by dyes, or by clipping the fur in a distinctive pattern; and arthropods are marked with paint. In all cases some form of coding may be adopted so that individual organisms are identified. Having trapped,

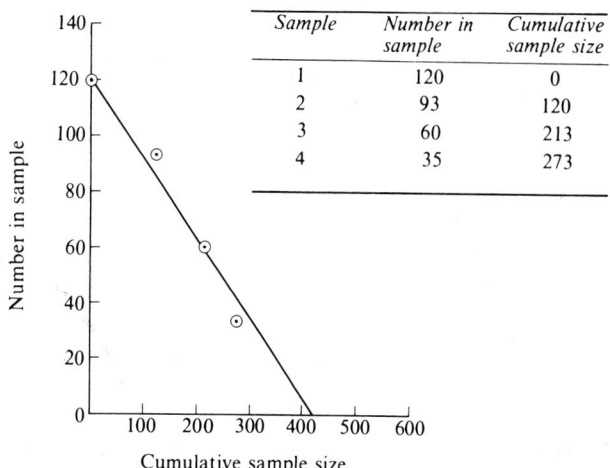

Sample	Number in sample	Cumulative sample size
1	120	0
2	93	120
3	60	213
4	35	273

Fig 11.16 *Graph of number in sample against cumulative sample size. Extrapolation of the line to the point when the number in the sample equals zero gives an estimate of the number in the population.*

counted and marked a representative sample of the population, the individuals are released in the same area. At a later stage the population is trapped again and counted, and the population size estimated using the expression below:

$$\text{Estimated total population} = \frac{\text{number of organisms in initial sample} \times \text{number of organisms in second sample}}{\text{number of marked organisms recaptured}}$$

This estimate of population size is called the **Lincoln index**. It relies on a number of assumptions which are summarised below.

(1) Organisms mix randomly within the population. (This does not always apply since some organisms live in colonies, troops or shoals.)
(2) Sufficient time must elapse between capture and recapture to allow random mixing. The less mobile the species the longer the time lapse must be.
(3) It is only applicable to populations whose movement is restricted geographically.
(4) Organisms disperse evenly within the geographical area of the population.
(5) Changes in population size as a result of immigration, emigration, births and deaths are negligible.
(6) Marking does not hinder the movement of the organisms or make them conspicuous to predators.

11.4 In an attempt to estimate the number of trout in a small lake, 625 trout were netted, marked and released. One week later 873 trout were netted and of these 129 had been marked. What was the estimated size of the population?

Where plants and small animals, such as barnacles, are concerned, direct counting becomes very tedious and, depending upon the degree of accuracy required from the study, may be replaced by estimating percentage cover or abundance within a quadrat frame. In the early stages of estimation it is advisable to use a graduated quadrat frame (fig 11.12) to increase the accuracy of estimation. Various schemes may be adopted for representing percentage cover or abundance, some being totally subjective, others partially, or completely, objective.

Subjective methods

These involve some form of frequency assessment, frequency scale or estimate of abundance in terms of cover. For example, an arbitrary scale devised by Crisp and Southward for limpets on a rocky shore uses the following letters, frequencies and percentages.

A	abundant	>50%
C	common	10–50%
F	frequent	1–10%
O	occasional	<1%
R	rare	present – only a few found in 30 min searching

These assessments and scales are arbitrary and the frequencies can be adjusted to varying percentage values, for example in a particular study, abundant may represent >90%. The value of using the five categories above is that they can be applied to methods of presenting data, such as in constructing kite diagrams, as described in appendix section A2.7.3 in Book 2. The major disadvantage of this method is that it is subjective and tends to rate small species with poor cover lower than conspicuous species, flowering species and species occurring in clumps.

Table 11.4 Five-point scale for water pollution studies using presence and absence indicator species.

Level of pollution	Oxygen concentration	Indicator organisms
(A) clean water or very low pollution levels	high	stonefly nymph mayfly nymph
(B) low pollution levels		caddis fly larva freshwater shrimp
(C) high pollution levels		water louse bloodworm
(D) very high pollution levels	low	sludgeworm rat tailed maggot
(E) extreme pollution levels	no oxygen	no apparent life

This point scheme is used in the Philip Harris and Griffin water pollution study packs. The Philip Harris scheme includes colour photographs of key indicator species. The Griffin package has an excellent series of black and white drawings of a wider range of indicator organisms as well as procedures for calculating the Trent Biotic Index and other simple pollution indicator tests.

11.2.4 Biotic indices

In some situations organisms make good indicators of environmental quality. Examples are the use of lichens as air pollution indicators and the use of non-vertebrates to monitor river pollution. Diatoms and plants can also be used as biological indicators of water quality.

Assessment of water quality using non-vertebrates is now in widespread use. Techniques rely on the assessment of non-vertebrates found in the stream sediment and the presence and absence of key taxa or families. Several different schemes have been proposed from the simple five-point scale shown in table 11.4 to the Biological Monitoring Working Party (BMWP) scores which are now routinely used in the water industry in Britain. The example which follows shows how to estimate the Trent Biotic Index (TBI), the first scheme used in the water industry and essentially the basis for subsequent methods.

Method for estimating the Trent Biotic Index (TBI)

Principles. The approach is based on a two-way classification which looks at the number of non-vertebrate taxa present from certain defined groups in relation to the presence of six key indicator organisms. Each group denotes the limit of identification which can be reached for a given set of organisms without needing to use lengthy identification techniques. Thus molluscs and crustacea are identified to species level whereas mayflies are distinguished to genus level only (see table 11.5). The mayfly *Baetis rhodani* is an important exception which is separately identified in the scheme since it is more pollution tolerant than other mayfly species. It is grouped with the caddis fly larvae in terms of pollution tolerance.

An example of the two-way approach used in the Trent Biotic Index is shown in table 11.5. The combination of the total number of groups present and the highest (most pollution sensitive) indicator organism present gives a score ranging from 0, very polluted, to 10, very clean with many groups present and several species of stoneflies. In the example highlighted several species of caddis fly larvae (Trichoptera) are the highest indicator species present. Overall, representatives of 7 groups were found and thus a TBI of 6 is recorded. If only one species of caddis fly larvae was present then the TBI would be 5.

Materials.
waterproof footwear (waders or wellingtons)
waterproof gloves
white sample tray
stiff brush
handlens ($\times 10$)
sweep net (see table 11.3)
identification key

Method. Kick sample the river bed to disturb bottom-living non-vertebrates. Use the sweep net downstream of the disturbed area to capture the organisms.

Table 11.5 The Trent Biotic Index.

Summary table
The maximum value is 10. Biotic indices are effectively marks out of ten with zero representing virtually lifeless heavily polluted waters.

	Indicator species		0–1	2–5	6–10	11–15	16+
					Trent Biotic Index		
Clean	Plecoptera nymph present (stoneflies)	More than one species	–	7	8	9	10
		One species only	–	6	7	8	9
	Ephemeroptera nymph present (mayflies)	More than one species*	–	6	7	8	9
		One species only*	–	5	6	7	8
	Trichoptera larvae present (caddisflies)	More than one species**	–	5	6	7	8
		One species only**	4	4	5	6	7
	Gammarus present (freshwater shrimps)	All above species absent	3	4	5	6	7
	Asellus present (water louse, water skaters)	All above species absent	2	3	4	5	6
	Tubificid worms and/or red chironomid larvae present	All above species absent	1	2	3	4	–
	All above types absent	Some organisms such as *Eristalis tenax* not requiring dissolved oxygen may be present	0	1	2	–	–

Organisms in order of tendency to disappear as degree of pollution increases

Heavily polluted

* Baetis rhodani excluded
** Baetis rhodani (Ephemeroptera) is counted in this section for the purpose of classification.

Groups used in calculating the TBI
The term 'group', for the purposes of calculating the TBI, means any one of the organisms included in the following list.

Each known species of Platyhelminthes (flatworms).	*Baetis rhodani* (mayfly).
Annelida (worms) excluding genus *Nais*.	Each family of Trichoptera (caddisfly).
Genus *Nais* (worms).	Each species of Neuroptera (alderfly).
Each known species of Hirudinae (leeches).	Family Chironomidae (midge larvae) except *Chironomus thummi*.
Each known species of Mollusca (snails).	*Chironomus thummi* (blood worms).
Each known species of Crustacea (*Asellus*, shrimps).	Family Simulidae (blackfly larvae).
Each known species of Plecoptera (stonefly).	Each known species of other fly larvae.
Each known genus of Ephemeroptera (mayfly) excluding *Baetis rhodani*.	Each known species of Coleoptera (beetles and beetle larvae).
	Each known species of Hydracarina (watermites).

Procedure (see also text)
(1) Sort each sample, separating the animals according to group (see above groups list). Count the total number of groups present.
(2) Note which indicator species are present, starting from the top of the list.
(3) To find the Trent Biotic Index, take the highest indicator species, e.g. caddis fly, *Trichoptera*, and work along the line. Note from the top the group number and read off the Trent Biotic Index.

e.g.	Highest indicator animal	Trichoptera
	Number of indicator species	more than one
	Total numbers of groups	7
	Trent Biotic Index	6

(Source: The Griffin Pollution test kit: handbook for users.)

Empty the contents into the white tray for identification. Record all the groups and key indicator organisms present. Return organisms to the river when identification is complete. Use table 11.5 to establish the Trent Biotic Index.

It is important to standardise the kick time if you are comparing rivers or different locations on the same river. The recommended kick sample time is 3 minutes. You should also investigate beneath stones and boulders and use the brush to disturb and remove organisms from these locations. A one-minute search is standard.

The TBI has been criticised since it takes no account of the relative abundance of organisms. This can lead to misclassification of sites. For example, it can often happen that a single stonefly is swept downstream to a polluted location following heavy rain. It may have poor survival prospects but if you are sampling soon after the rain event your results will be distorted by its chance presence.

The TBI has also been criticised for its taxonomic inconsistency. In other words it requires identification of some organisms to species level, such as *B. rhodani*, whereas others are not distinguished beyond genus or family level.

Alternative approaches have been devised to overcome these criticisms. The Biological Monitoring Working Party was set up to identify a rigorous universally applicable scheme for Britain. Its recommended method is now widely used. Similar schemes are used in other countries. Estimating BMWP scores requires much more taxonomic knowledge than the simpler Trent Biotic Index. Full discussion of the BMWP method is beyond the scope of this text.

11.3 Ecological research projects and investigations

Ecological projects are broadly concerned with studying either the organisms in an area (**community ecology** or **synecology**) or a single species (**autecology**). In both cases it is necessary to spend time reading about and discussing the project, so as to clarify the aims, nature and extent of the project. All investigations should include problems which have to be solved or hypotheses to be tested.

The aims of the project should be stated clearly and should include both general and specific aims. For example:

(1) to develop and encourage an attitude of curiosity and enquiry;
(2) to develop the ability to plan an investigation, construct hypotheses and design experiments;
(3) to develop the ability to formulate questions and collect relevant qualitative and quantitative data to answer these;
(4) to develop practical and observational skills including the use of apparatus and biological keys;
(5) to develop the ability to record data accurately;

(6) to develop the ability to apply existing knowledge to the interpretation of data;
(7) to develop a critical attitude to data, assessment of their validity and conclusions based on them;
(8) to develop the ability to communicate biological information by means of tables, graphs and the spoken and written word;
(9) to develop an appreciation of organisms and the importance of conservation;
(10) to develop an understanding of the interrelationships between organisms, between organisms and their environment, and the dynamic aspects of ecology. This can be extended to include very specific aims, such as those described for autecological investigations (section 11.5).

11.3.1 Writing up the project or investigations

Irrespective of the quality of both the investigation and the data obtained, the project or investigation is of little use to other scientists until it is presented as a report and this should take the following form.

(1) **Introduction:** including the idea, the problems, hypotheses and aims (what you set out to do and why).
(2) **Method:** the strategy of the project (what you did (was done), where and how it was done, including all practical details of apparatus and techniques employed both in the field and in the laboratory).
(3) **Results and observations:** tabulated data, graphs, histograms, profiles, presence–absence graphs, kite diagrams and any other relevant and realistic way of representing data and relationships clearly and concisely.
(4) **Discussion of results:** this involves an analysis of the results, preferably quantitative if possible, tentative conclusions based on data presented and references to already published material.
(5) **Discussion of significance of conclusions:** criticisms of the techniques employed, sources of error and suggestions for further study.
(6) **List of references consulted.**

11.4 A synecological investigation

A synecological investigation involves studying the abiotic and biotic elements associated with a natural community (biotic element of ecosystem) found in a particular defined geographical area (or ecosystem) such as an oak woodland or a rocky shore, which may contain several plant and animal species and possibly several habitats. In such an investigation it is necessary to carry out the following exercises:

(1) map the area and habitat(s) in plan view and, if necessary, in profile;

(2) identify the species and estimate the number of each species present;

(3) measure (possibly collect and analyse) the abiotic factors within the habitat(s).

The overall aim of such an investigation is to determine the qualitative and quantitative relationships between the plant and animal populations within the area being studied and the possible interactions between these and soil, topographic and climatic factors. Given this information, it is possible to explain the nature and extent of the factors governing the number and distribution of organisms in terms of a food web and, depending upon the sophistication of the investigation, pyramids of numbers, standing crop biomass and energy.

11.4.1 Mapping an area

Plan view

The following simple method is designed primarily for mapping a small area, such as a grassland 10 m × 10 m or a small pond, but can be used on a large scale, for example to map the whole rocky shore of a bay.

(1) Select the approximate area to study and stretch a measuring tape along one side of the area. This marks the base line AY (fig 11.17).

(2) From the base line measure the perpendicular distance to certain natural landmarks within the area or marker poles showing the limit of the study area. Record these measurements.

(3) Transfer the measurement of AY and the various perpendicular distances to a sheet of squared paper using a suitable scale.

(4) Using the base line and measured distances to perpendicular landmarks drawn in (3) above as a guide, complete the map freehand.

(5) If the area is relatively small divide the actual base line AY into an equal number of sections and from these lay out perpendicular string line transects. Repeat the procedure using the extreme left transect AF as a new

base line to produce a string grid, as shown in fig 11.18. Draw these grid lines on the map and label them using A, B, C etc. along one edge and 1, 2, 3 etc. along the other edge.

(6) Mark the positions of obvious structural and vegetational zones.

(7) Using a quadrat frame, pin frame or sweep net, depending on the area, systematically sample the area from, say, left to right and record the species present and their numbers or abundance.

(8) If the area is extremely large and a qualitative and quantitative study is required, belt transects spaced out at set intervals across the area, and set at right-angles to any suspected zonation, can be used in conjunction with random quadrats to sample the area at particular points called **stations**. If the area has no obvious zonation then a number of random quadrat samples should be used (and their positions noted) rather than a transect approach. Direct measurement of the abiotic features of the environment should be made as frequently as possible or samples removed for subsequent analysis.

Plotting a height profile

In some areas, distribution of organisms may be influenced by a factor related to height, such as on a rocky shore. Here the length of time each part of the shore is exposed due to the vertical motion of tides is height dependent. In such cases it is necessary to produce a height profile showing how the height along the transect varies, as from high to low water marks in the rocky shore example used below. At each point (station) along the transect where the community is sampled, the height should be obtained accurately by the use of a surveying theodolite and measuring points. Over short distances a simple home-made levelling device attached to a reference pole, and a graduated pole can achieve relatively accurate results as described below (fig 11.19).

(1) Attach the levelling device at a convenient height (h_1), such as 1.5 m, on the measuring pole.

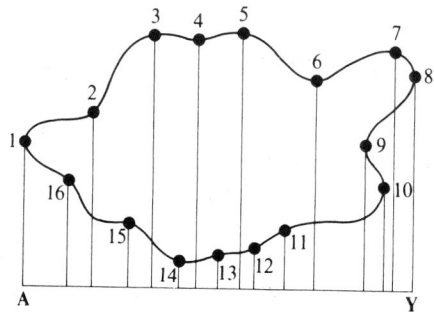

Fig 11.17 *A suggested method of mapping the significant aspects of an area, such as a small, irregularly shaped pond.*

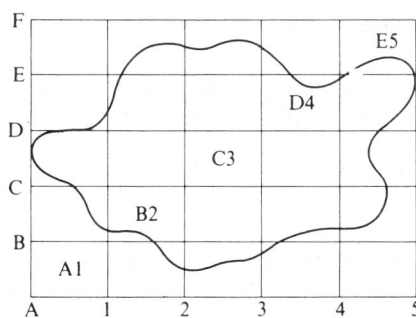

Fig 11.18 *Map of the area under investigation showing the various sub-sections, for example A1–E5, obtained by the use of a string grid. These provide reference areas for subsequent study.*

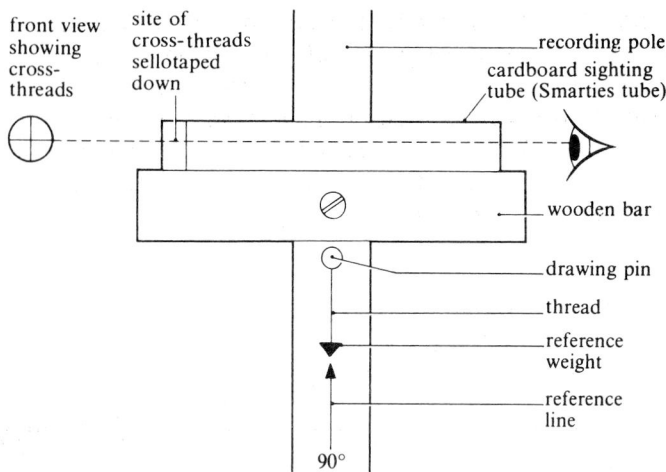

Fig 11.19 *A simple home-made levelling device attached to a reference pole. The position of the pole is adjusted until the sighting bar is shown to be horizontal by the thread indicating 90° on the reference point on the pole. Holding the pole steady, the observer looks along the sighting tube and indicates to the person holding the graduated pole the corresponding level position on their pole, as shown by the cross-wire sights. This height is recorded.*

(2) Set out a line transect from high water mark to the water's edge.

(3) Set up the reference pole at a specific point, such as high water mark, on the transect and the marker pole at a known distance (x) further down the shore. Mark these positions on the transect and label them A and B. Keep to one side of the transect line whilst taking readings to avoid trampling on the specimens to be studied.

(4) When the wooden sighting bar is horizontal, look along the sighting tube identifying the point where the centre of the cross-threads 'hits' the marker pole. The exact position of this point is then located by the person holding the marker pole and the height (h_2) recorded. The height difference between the stations is equal to $h_2 - h_1$.

(5) Move the reference pole to station B and the marker pole a known distance (x_1) to station C. Repeat stages

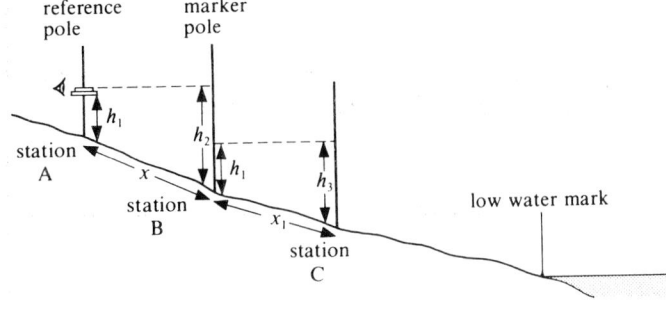

Fig 11.20 *Methods of obtaining heights and horizontal distances of stations above low water mark.*

(3) and (4) and record the new height (h_3) (fig 11.20).

(6) Continue to obtain readings h_4, h_5 and so on, distances x_2, x_3 and so on and stations D, E and so on, to the water's edge at low water. Record all distances as shown in table 11.6, and calculate the heights and horizontal distances of the stations above the low water mark.

(7) Transfer these data to a scale representation of the shore profile and mark on the positions of the stations (fig 11.21).

11.4.2 Identifying and estimating the number of each species present

Line and belt transects, frame quadrats and pin frames are used to sample systematically the area as described in section 11.2.2. Specimens are identified using a key and the number of organisms are either counted directly or estimated as described in section 11.2.3.

11.4.3 Recording and representing data

Data should be recorded directly they are obtained using some form of field booking sheet. In the case of synecological investigations of marine habitats the information shown on the booking sheets illustrated in tables 11.7 and 11.8 has proved successful. These sheets are best attached to a clipboard, completed in pencil and kept in a large polythene bag to protect them from rain. Once all the data have been collected they must be represented in some suitably efficient diagrammatic form that will highlight relationships between organisms and/or the nature of the environment. Methods of representing data are given in appendix section A2.7 in Book 2 and include presence–absence graphs, kite diagrams, and histograms. Trophic pyramids are described in section 10.3.4. Some examples of the use of all four methods of representation are included in figs 11.22–11.24.

Table 11.6 Horizontal and vertical distances recorded at stations A–K on a rocky shore. Northumberland 1968.

Station	Horizontal distance/m (x, x_1 etc.)	Height between stations/m ((h_2-h_1) etc.)	Height above low water/m ((h_2-h_1) etc.)
A	0		9.6
B	20	1.5	8.1
C	40	1.7	6.4
D	60	1.8	4.6
E	80	0.8	3.8
F	100	0.6	3.2
G	120	0.7	2.5
H	140	0.9	1.6
I	160	0.8	0.8
J	180	0.4	0.4
K	200	0.4	0

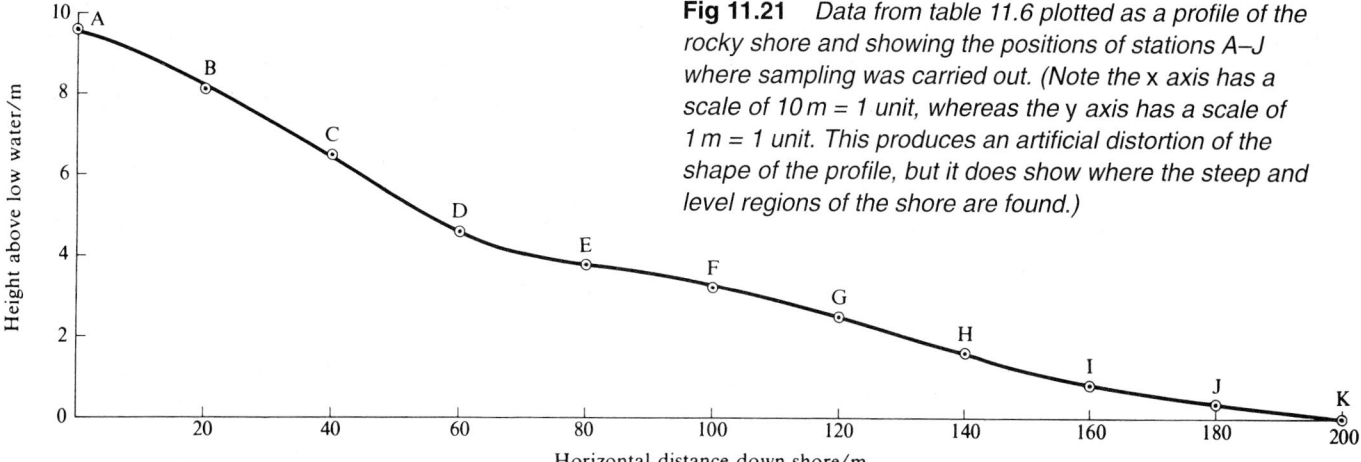

Fig 11.21 *Data from table 11.6 plotted as a profile of the rocky shore and showing the positions of stations A–J where sampling was carried out. (Note the x axis has a scale of 10 m = 1 unit, whereas the y axis has a scale of 1 m = 1 unit. This produces an artificial distortion of the shape of the profile, but it does show where the steep and level regions of the shore are found.)*

Table 11.7 Suggested format of field booking sheet.

Field Booking Sheet – Marine Ecology

(1) Name of site and grid reference . . . .
(2) Nature of profile (rocky, sandy, muddy, dune) . . . .
(3) Sketch map of area showing area(s) of study/position(s) of transects.

(4) Special features (exposure, aspect, etc.) . . . .
(5) Date . . . .
(6) Weather, conditions . . . .
(7) Tide data:
    predicted high water . . . .
        "   low water . . . .
    observed high water . . . .
        "   low water . . . .
    predicted tidal range . . . .
(8) Notes and key to recorded data (abundance scales – % cover, reference height of level, e.g. h_1 etc.)

Table 11.8 Data required on a booking sheet for investigating the synecology of marine habitats.

Station name	Horizontal distance from origin/m	Level reading (h_2)/m etc.	Change in height (h_2-h_1 etc.)/m	Height above low water/m	Time exposed	Time covered	ANIMALS (species and abundance)	PLANTS (species and abundance)	NOTES

Table 11.9 The distribution of four common species of the periwinkle, *Littorina* on a rocky shore on the Dale peninsula, Pembrokeshire. April 1976. These data are represented graphically by the kite-diagrams shown in fig 11.22.

Height above low water/m	L. neritoides		L. saxatalis		L. littorea		L. littoralis	
	number	scale	number	scale	number	scale	number	scale
9–10	63	10	–	–	–	–	–	–
8–9	54	10	–	–	–	–	–	–
7–8	7	4	3	2	–	–	–	–
6–7	–	–	8	4	1	1	–	–
5–6	–	–	17	8	3	2	2	2
4–5	–	–	6	4	13	6	9	4
3–4	–	–	1	1	6	4	16	8
2–3	–	–	–	–	2	2	5	4
1–2	–	–	–	–	1	1	1	1
0–1	–	–	–	–	–	–	–	–

Abundance scale: ≥20 = 10; 19–15 = 8; 14–10 = 6, 9–5 = 4; 4–2 = 2; 1 = 1.

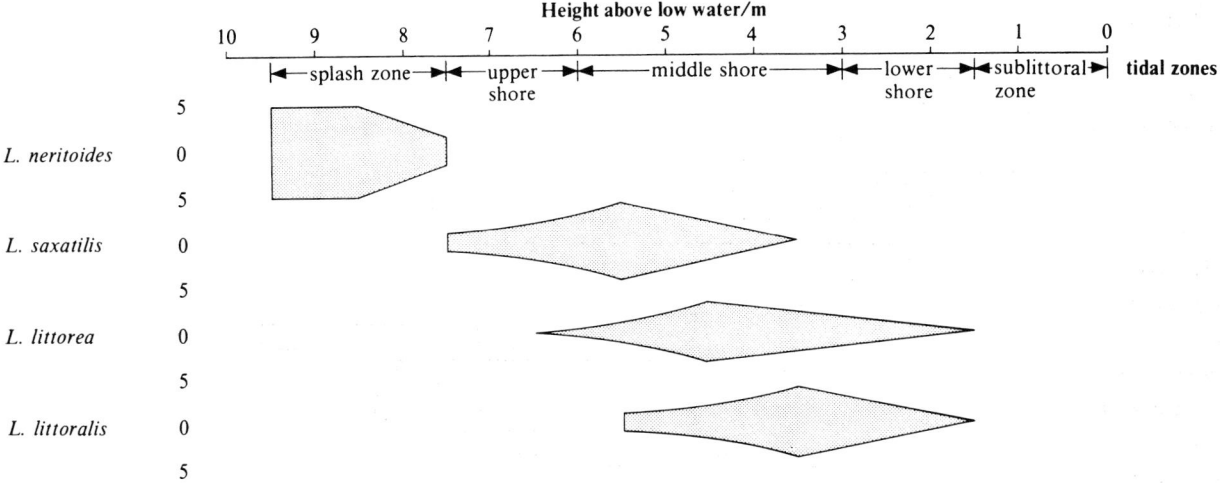

Fig 11.22 *Kite-diagrams showing the frequency and distribution of four common species of periwinkle,* Littorina, *on a rocky shore on the Dale peninsula, Pembrokeshire, April 1976. See table 11.8 for data.*

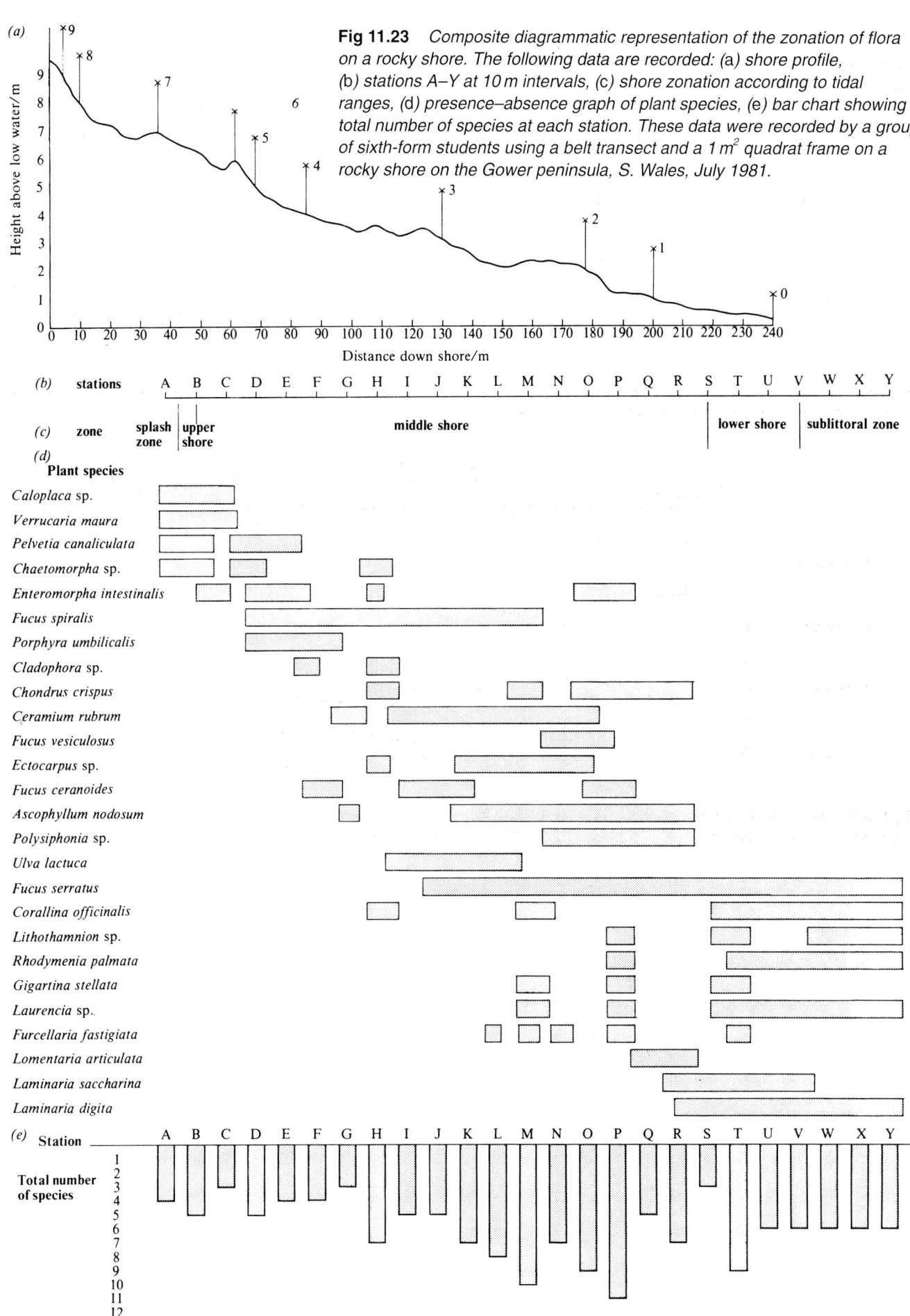

(a)

Height above low water/m

Fig 11.23 *Composite diagrammatic representation of the zonation of flora on a rocky shore. The following data are recorded: (a) shore profile, (b) stations A–Y at 10 m intervals, (c) shore zonation according to tidal ranges, (d) presence–absence graph of plant species, (e) bar chart showing total number of species at each station. These data were recorded by a group of sixth-form students using a belt transect and a 1 m² quadrat frame on a rocky shore on the Gower peninsula, S. Wales, July 1981.*

Distance down shore/m

(b)   stations   A B C D E F G H I J K L M N O P Q R S T U V W X Y

(c)   zone   splash zone | upper shore | middle shore | lower shore | sublittoral zone

(d)
Plant species

Caloplaca sp.
Verrucaria maura
Pelvetia canaliculata
Chaetomorpha sp.
Enteromorpha intestinalis
Fucus spiralis
Porphyra umbilicalis
Cladophora sp.
Chondrus crispus
Ceramium rubrum
Fucus vesiculosus
Ectocarpus sp.
Fucus ceranoides
Ascophyllum nodosum
Polysiphonia sp.
Ulva lactuca
Fucus serratus
Corallina officinalis
Lithothamnion sp.
Rhodymenia palmata
Gigartina stellata
Laurencia sp.
Furcellaria fastigiata
Lomentaria articulata
Laminaria saccharina
Laminaria digita

(e) Station   A B C D E F G H I J K L M N O P Q R S T U V W X Y

Total number of species

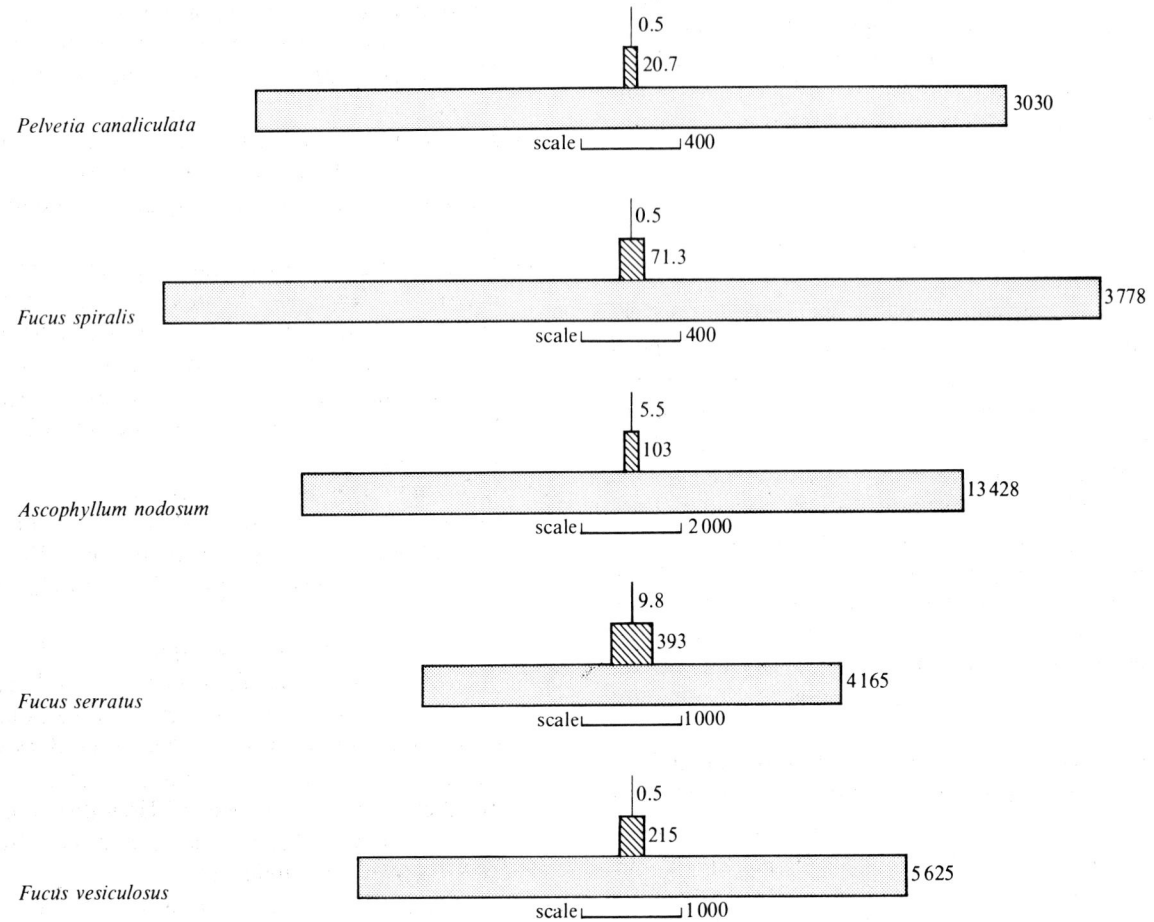

Fig 11.24 *Trophic pyramids of standing crop biomass for five rocky shore communities based on particular algal primary producers. The numerical values represent estimates of standing crop biomass in* g m^{-2}. *The stippled areas represent producers, the cross-hatched areas represent primary consumers (herbivores and detritus feeders) and the solid areas represent secondary consumers (carnivores). It must not be assumed, however, that each trophic level is supported entirely by the level beneath. Northumberland coast, March 1969. (After D.A.S. Smith (1970)* School Science Review, *ASE.)*

11.4.4 Collecting and analysing abiotic factors

The amount of time spent on this stage of a synecological investigation will depend upon the nature of the area being studied. It is more applicable to areas where soil factors predominate, such as woodland, grassland and salt marsh, than to a rocky shore. The abiotic factors to be studied and the methods of study are described in section 11.1.

11.5 An autecological investigation

An autecological investigation involves studying all the ecological factors related to a single plant or animal species throughout its life cycle. The aim of the investigation is to describe as precisely as possible the ecological niche of the species. The species selected for study should be one which is both common and locally available. Initially the investigation should concern itself with undertaking extensive background reading on the species selected. During the reading, notes should be made on all aspects of the biology of the species and also on opportunities for practical work. This may involve either repeating investigations carried out by others or developing new investigations to be undertaken as part of the current study.

A straightforward approach to an autecological study is to prepare a comprehensive list of the questions which must be answered in order to reveal all there is to know about the species under investigation. The study should be undertaken as rigorously as possible and treated as a research project. Therefore it must involve some measure of original investigation including observation, measurement and experimentation. It must not simply be a report based on knowledge gleaned from reading books, journals and magazines. The species under investigation should be studied over a period of at least one full year.

A guide to the sorts of questions to be asked in the investigations of an **animal** is given below.

(1) **Classification.** What is the name of the species? What other groups of organisms does it resemble most closely? What are the similarities and differences between related species? What is its full taxonomic description?

(2) **Habitat.** Where is it found? What are the characteristic abiotic features of the area? How do these factors change over the course of a year?

(3) **Structure.** What is its adult structure? What are its characteristic external features? What are its dimensions and mass?

(4) **Movement.** How does it move from place to place? Which parts of the organism are involved in the movement and what are the functions of these parts? How are these parts adapted to the environment?

(5) **Nutrition.** What are the food sources of the organism? When does the organism feed? How much food is eaten? How is the food captured and ingested? What special features assist ingestion? Are there any unusual features of digestion and absorption.

(6) **Respiration.** Where is the gaseous exchange surface? How does gaseous exchange occur? How much oxygen is required by the organism?

(7) **Excretion.** What are the waste products of metabolism? How are these removed from the organism? What special organs of excretion are present?

(8) **Reproduction.** Are the sexes separate? What visible external differences are there between the sexes? Does any form of courtship occur? Does the organism defend a territory? How does mating occur? When does mating occur? How often does mating occur? How many gametes are produced? Where does fertilisation occur?

(9) **Life cycle.** How long does development take? What degree of parental care is shown? Are there larval stages? When do adults become sexually mature? What is the typical lifespan of an individual of the species?

(10) **Behaviour.** How does the organism receive stimuli? To which stimuli does the organism mainly respond? How are the major sense organs adapted to the mode of life of the organism? To what extent does learning occur? How does the organism react to other members of the same species? How does the species react to unfavourable weather conditions? How does the organism communicate?

(11) **Ecology.** How many organisms occur in the population? What other organisms live in the same habitat? How are the various species distributed within the habitat? How is the species related to other species in the same habitat in terms of position in food chains and food webs? Is the organism a host, parasite or symbiont? What is the ecological niche of the species?

Similarly the sorts of questions to be asked in the investigation of a **flowering plant** are given below.

(1) **Classification.** What is the name of the species? What subspecies, varieties and ecotypes of the species exist? What are the similarities and differences between closely related species? What is its full taxonomic description?

(2) **Habitat.**
(a) *Edaphic factors* – What is the parent rock type? What type of soil profile is shown? How thick are the various horizons? What is the percentage water content (field capacity) of the soil? What is the percentage organic content of the soil? What is the mineral composition of the soil? What is the pH of the soil?

What is the height and seasonal variation of the water table in relation to the life history and distribution of the species?

(*b*) *Climatic factors* – What are the extremes and mean temperatures in the habitats? What is the annual rainfall in the habitats? What is the mean relative humidity of the air in the habitats? What is the direction of the prevailing wind? How much light is received by the plant?

(*c*) *Topographical factors* – To which direction is the species normally exposed? Does the species appear to prefer exposed or sheltered sites? Does the species appear to prefer sloping or flat habitats? Does altitude appear to affect the distribution of the species?

(3) **Structure.** How extensive is the root system? What form does the root system take? How does the stem branch? How many leaves are carried on each branch? What shapes are the leaves? What variations in length and breadth exist between the leaves? How tall does the plant grow?

(4) **Physiology.** What pigments are present in the leaves and petals? Which surface of the leaf has the highest transpiration rate? What effect has darkness on transpiration rate? Do diurnal changes in water content of leaves occur?

(5) **Reproduction.**

(*a*) *Flower* – How many flowers are produced per plant? How many and of what shape and size are the sepals, petals, anthers, carpels or pistil? What variation in petal colour exists? What pigments are present in the leaves? When does flowering begin? How long is the flowering period? How does pollination occur? What adaptations to insect or wind pollination are shown?

(*b*) *Fruits and seeds* – How are the fruits formed? What is the structure of the fruit? How many seeds are produced per flower? How are the fruits and seeds dispersed? How far are fruits and seeds dispersed?

(*c*) *Perennation* – How does vegetative propagation occur? What are the organs of perennation? At what rate does the species colonise an area?

(6) **Life cycle.** What type of seed is produced? What conditions are required for germination? When do the seeds germinate? What percentage of seeds germinate? Which form of germination occurs? At what rate does the shoot system develop? What is the extent of growth in terms of space and time? (Why do some of the seedlings not become mature?)

(7) **Ecology.** Does the species grow as solitary plants or in patches? What size are the patches? Which species grow in the same habitat? What degree of competition exists between the species being studied and other species? Is the species a parasite, host or symbiont? How is the species related to animals in terms of position in the food web? Does the species offer protection or shelter to animals? If so, which animals and how is this provided? What is the ecological niche of the species?

Fungi, algae, mosses, liverworts or conifers may be used in autecological studies and questions above may be modified as appropriate to the species under investigation.

Chapter Twelve

Microbiology and biotechnology

What is microbiology?

Microbiology is the study of microorganisms, those organisms which are so small that they can only be seen clearly, if at all, with the use of a microscope. They include bacteria, viruses, fungi and protoctists such as protozoa and microscopic algae. The classification and some of the chief characteristics of these organisms have been described in chapter 2.

Microorganisms show great diversity and have enormous potential for exploitation by humans. They grow and multiply rapidly given suitable conditions, and use and make a huge range of chemicals. It is this versatility which makes them so useful. They can even be genetically engineered to make further useful products, such as human insulin. Our exploitation of microorganisms is probably only in its infancy, but already it makes an important contribution to our industrial production. One word has come to symbolise the use of microorganisms and other biological systems, namely biotechnology.

What is biotechnology?

Biotechnology has been defined as the application of organisms, biological systems or biological processes to manufacturing and servicing industries. It does not refer simply to microorganisms, although microorganisms play an important role. In fact, use of any biological process in a manufacturing process could be regarded as biotechnology. This would include, for example, genetic engineering and cloning of plants in agriculture, horticulture and forestry. Examples of biotechnology are shown in fig 12.1.

Biotechnology provides both **products** and **services**. Examples of products are alcohol in the brewing industry and newer products such as human insulin from genetically engineered bacteria. Examples of services are treatment of sewage or detection of pollution using a biosensor. Here the process rather than an end-product is important.

Biotechnology could be defined more broadly as the use of other living organisms for the benefit of humans. It would then include the breeding and improvement of domesticated animals such as cattle or pigs, and crops such as wheat and potatoes. New techniques of genetic engineering are particularly relevant here because they give us a way of introducing new desirable factors into living organisms much more precisely and quickly than the breeding programmes of the past.

In this chapter we shall examine some of the principles of large-scale manufacture in biotechnology and look at some examples of biotechnology. The new technologies will continue to change our society just as the old ones have done. Inevitably they will raise new social and ethical issues, and some of these are discussed at the end of chapter 25 on applied genetics.

12.1 Requirements for growth

Scientists first began trying to grow bacteria and fungi under controlled conditions in the mid-nineteenth century. The two great pioneers working on bacteria were Louis Pasteur, working in Paris, and Robert Koch, working in Berlin. These and other scientists realised the importance of being able to grow pure cultures of the organisms they were trying to study. This meant somehow developing techniques by which different microorganisms could be isolated from each other. In addition, suitable nutrients and environmental conditions for growing the microorganisms had to be developed. Some microorganisms, particularly those that cause disease and therefore live parasitically, have complex requirements; others have relatively simple requirements.

12.1.1 Essential nutrients

Raw materials are needed for growth, maintenance, and multiplication. In addition, a source of energy is needed. When microorganisms are grown, nutrients are supplied in a suitable medium known as the **nutrient medium**. The following are typical components of nutrient media.

- **A source of carbon** – Most bacteria and all fungi and protozoans are heterotrophic, meaning that they need an *organic* source of carbon (see section 2.5.4 and table 2.3). This is often provided in the form of glucose or the salt of an organic acid such as sodium ethanoate (acetate). However, as a group, bacteria in particular can use a vast range of organic compounds as a source of carbon, including fatty acids, alcohols, proteins, hydrocarbons and methane. Some soil bacteria and fungi, and some bacteria that live in the guts of herbivores such as ruminants, can digest cellulose and use it as a carbon source. All disease-causing bacteria are heterotrophic.

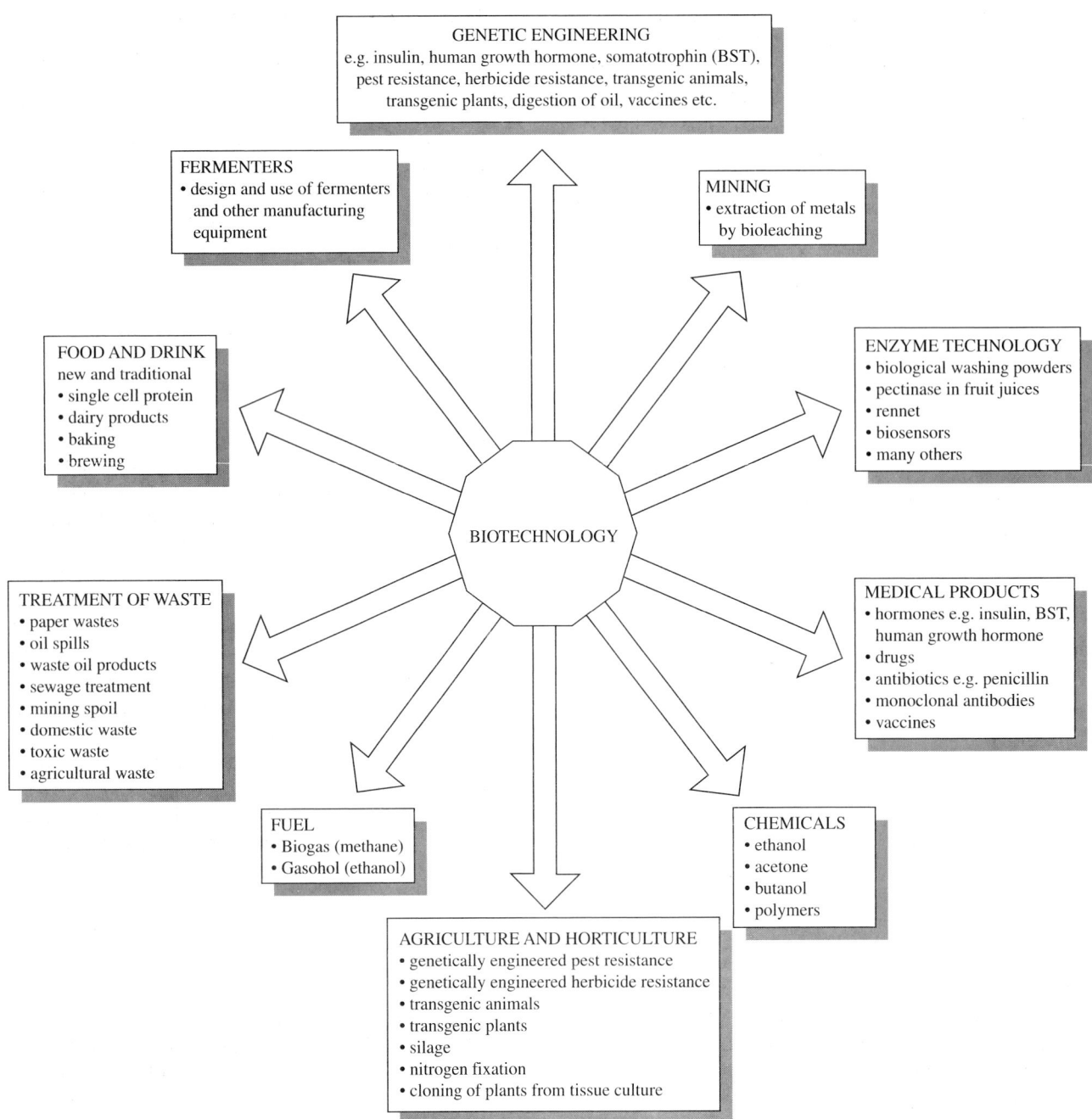

Fig 12.1 *Some of the applications of biotechnology. Categories are not rigid and may overlap. Genetic engineering is an important technique in biotechnology. It can be involved in any of the categories shown in order to 'improve' microorganisms, plants and animals. It will become increasingly important in the twenty-first century.*

All the algae and some bacteria, such as the blue-green bacteria, are autotrophic, meaning that their source of carbon is carbon dioxide. The algae are photosynthetic, but some of the bacteria are photosynthetic and some are chemosynthetic (table 2.3).

- **A source of nitrogen** – This may be organic, for example amino acids, peptides and proteins, or inorganic, for example ammonium salts and nitrates. Amino acids are often supplied in the form of partially digested proteins called peptones.

- **Growth factors** or **vitamins** are sometimes needed. Growth factors are the equivalent of the vitamins needed by animals, and many *are* vitamins. They are organic compounds which are essential for growth and are needed in very small amounts. They include some of the B vitamins (thiamine or B_1, riboflavine or B_2, niacin or B_3, and B_6) as well as folic acid and para-amino benzoic acid. Trace amounts only are needed for healthy growth. Other organic compounds may also be important, such as purines and pyrimidines.

Microorganisms vary in their ability to make their own growth factors from simpler substances. If their needs are complex, the medium used to grow them in a laboratory is often derived from natural substances in which they normally grow, such as blood, soil, meat extract or yeast extract.

- **Mineral salts** – Those most commonly needed are the positive ions calcium, potassium, sodium, iron and magnesium, and the negative ions chloride, phosphate (a possible source of phosphorus) and sulphate (a possible source of sulphur). As mentioned above, nitrogen may be supplied as ammonium or nitrate. The needs of algae are similar to those of plants (see tables 7.7 and 7.8).

12.1 Give one example of the role of each of the following: (i) iron and phosphate in heterotrophic bacteria, (ii) nitrate and magnesium in autotrophic bacteria. (Use table 7.7 for help if you need it.)

- **A source of energy** – The need for energy by living cells is discussed at the beginning of chapters 7 and 9. The energy may be supplied as chemical energy or light energy. If it uses chemical energy, the organism is described as chemotrophic; if it uses light energy, it is described as phototrophic or photosynthetic (table 2.3). Photosynthetic microorganisms include some bacteria, such as the blue-green bacteria, and algae. When chemical energy is needed it is usually supplied as a sugar such as glucose.
- **Water** – Although this is not strictly a nutrient, it is required by all living cells. In general bacteria need more moisture than yeasts, and yeasts need more than moulds.

An example of a relatively simple culture medium is given in table 12.1.

12.2 What is each of the ingredients in the medium in table 12.1 needed for?

12.1.2 Environmental variables

As well as nutrients, environmental variables have to be carefully controlled. All microorganisms will grow best at a particular temperature and pH, and they may be sensitive to factors such as oxygen concentration and light intensity. **Optimum conditions** are the conditions which give the shortest generation time. Each species of microorganism will be adapted for a particular environment.

Temperature

Microorganisms differ widely in their temperature requirements, so temperature has an important effect on which microorganisms grow in a particular environment. The effect of temperature is best understood by considering its effects on enzymes. All cells contain enzymes, and the rate at which enzymes work, and therefore the rate of cell reactions and growth, is affected by temperature. A given microorganism will have an optimum temperature at which it grows best and a temperature range outside of which it will not grow. The upper limit is usually the point at which certain vital enzymes begin to denature. The optimum temperature ranges from 0 °C to 5 °C for some ocean-dwelling bacteria at or near the poles, to 70 °C or higher for bacteria living in hot springs or rotting vegetation such as compost heaps or silage where temperatures can be relatively high. There are bacteria which live in or close to volcanic vents in the ocean floor which thrive in temperatures of 118 °C.

Microorganisms can be placed in four categories according to their temperature requirements. The temperatures quoted below are only a general guide because there is a continuous range of types.

- **thermophiles** – optimum temperature for growth is above 45 °C, e.g. some species of *Lactobacillus* (found in milk).
- **mesophiles** – optimum temperature for growth is 25–45 °C. For bacteria living in mammals the optimum temperature is about 37 °C with a maximum of 42–43 °C, e.g. *Escherichia coli* (*E. coli*), a bacterium which is common in the human gut. Yeast (a fungus) is also mesophilic.
- **psychrophiles** – optimum temperature for growth is below 15 °C and they cannot grow above 20 °C. These can be a problem in refrigerated food.
- **psychrotrophs** – optimum temperature above 15 °C but can grow at much lower temperatures (5 °C or lower), e.g. some *Candida* yeasts, some moulds. These organisms are important in the spoilage of refrigerated dairy products.

pH

As with temperature, each species has its own minimum, maximum and optimum pH at which it will grow. For most bacteria the optimum is around pH 7 (neutral). Microorganisms that thrive in acid conditions, such as the

Table 12.1 A relatively simple medium used for growth of *Escherichia coli*, a bacterium which is common in the human gut.

		Concentration/ g dm^{-3}
K$_2$HPO$_4$	dipotassium hydrogen phosphate	7.0
KH$_2$PO$_4$	potassium dihydrogen phosphate	2.0
(NH$_4$)$_2$SO$_4$	ammonium sulphate	1.0
MgSO$_4$	magnesium sulphate	0.1
CaCl$_2$	calcium chloride	0.02
glucose		10.0
distilled water to 1 dm^3		

bacteria that produce vinegar, are described as **acidophiles**, while those that thrive in alkaline conditions are described as **alkalophiles**. Most yeasts are capable of growing in acid conditions, with an optimum pH of 4.5–5.0 being typical. Moulds prefer slightly acid conditions.

Oxygen concentration

Oxygen is needed for aerobic respiration. Microorganisms differ in their oxygen requirements as follows.

- **Obligate aerobes** – Microorganisms that can only live if oxygen is present, e.g. *Mycobacterium tuberculosis*, the bacterium that causes tuberculosis, moulds, e.g. *Penicillium*, algae and most protozoans. Most bacteria and fungi are obligate aerobes.
- **Facultative aerobes** – These use oxygen if it is present but can survive anaerobically in its absence, e.g. *E. coli* and many other bacteria, yeasts and some protozoans.
- **Obligate anaerobes** – Microorganisms which survive only in anaerobic conditions such as mud or the rumen, e.g. *Clostridium tetani* which lives in soil and is the cause of tetanus, and *Clostridium botulinum* which can be found in damaged tins of food rich in protein such as meat, and causes botulism, an often fatal form of food poisoning.
- **Microaerophiles** – These microorganisms grow best at concentrations of oxygen much lower than air, e.g. *Lactobacillus* in milk.

> **12.3** If bacteria of types (i) to (iv) below were mixed with nutrient agar in four separate test tubes, show by means of dots the distribution you would expect to find: (i) aerobic, (ii) anaerobic, (iii) facultative aerobic, (iv) microaerophilic.

Ionic and osmotic balance

When a cell is in a solution which is more concentrated than its contents, it usually loses water by osmosis. However, halophiles are organisms which are specialised for living in high salt concentrations, for example in the Salt Lakes of America, the Dead Sea in Israel and in salt marshes. An example of a halophile is *Halobacterium*. In contrast, if protozoans did not have a contractile vacuole which collects excess water and removes it, they would swell and burst in dilute media because they do not have a cell wall (section 2.3.1). The correct balance of ions is also important.

12.2   Culture media

A **medium** (plural *media*) is a solid or liquid preparation containing nutrients for the culture (growth) of microorganisms, animal cells or plant tissue cultures. A **culture** is a collection of microbial cells growing on or in a medium.

12.2.1   Solid and liquid media

Microorganisms may be cultured in a **solid** medium or a **liquid** medium (a **broth**).

Solid media

Solid media are particularly suitable for bacteria and fungi and are prepared by mixing the liquid nutrient solution with a gelling agent, usually **agar**, at a concentration of about 1–2%, thus producing **nutrient agar**. Agar is an extract from red algae. At a concentration of 1–2% agar melts at 95–100 °C and sets at about 44 °C. It can be sterilised by heating first (section 12.2.4) and then cooling. Microorganisms can either be added to the surface of the agar after setting or, if they are not damaged by temperatures of around 44 °C, can be added just before setting so that they can be distributed throughout the medium. Agar has the advantage that it is transparent and, being a complex polysaccharide, is not easily broken down by microorganisms. Examples of the uses of solid and liquid media are given in the following sections. Plant tissue cultures are sometimes grown on solid media (chapter 22).

Liquid media

Liquid media are often useful for measuring population growth (section 12.5). They may be placed in a test tube, stoppered by a plug of cotton wool or a metal cap, or in a glass, screw-capped bottle such as a universal bottle (McCartney bottle, fig 12.3) which holds about 25 cm^3, enough for one agar plate. The medium must be sterilised before it can be used for growth of a cell culture. Adding a small quantity of cells to the medium is called **inoculation**. After inoculation, the medium is left in a thermostatically controlled incubator at the optimum growth temperature. Cells grown are evenly spread throughout the medium.

If large volumes of medium are used, they should be

agitated to ensure mixing and to prevent the cells from settling out. Mechanical shakers or a magnetic stirrer can be used. Large volumes should also have sterile air passed through them in order to maintain the oxygen concentration throughout the medium. Commercial filters or use of glasswool or non-absorbent cottonwool can be used to filter the air and sterilise it. Air is introduced through a sparger, a device with many small holes to give fine bubbles. It is fitted to the end of a tube leading to the bottom of the culture vessel. Liquid cultures may be grown as batch cultures or continuous cultures (section 12.10).

12.2.2 Enrichment and selective media

An **enrichment medium** is a medium in which substances are added to meet the requirements of certain microorganisms in preference to others. As a result, certain microorganisms grow better than others. Starting with a mixed culture, often taken from the 'wild', one or a few types eventually come to dominate. Using a suitable medium, it is therefore possible to selectively grow the microorganism wanted. Conditions such as temperature, pH, carbon source and energy source are modified until those are found that favour the chosen organism as much as possible. For example, the Salmonella bacteria that cause typhoid (*Salmonella typhi*) can be selected for and later positively identified by growing a sample of food or faeces in a medium containing a selenium compound (selenium is an element with similar properties to sulphur). Normal gut bacteria such as *E. coli* which might be present in a faecal sample are inhibited by the selenium. Enrichment culture is one of the most powerful tools available to the microbiologist for isolating microorganisms.

A **selective medium** is one in which one or more substances are added which inhibit the growth of all but one or a few organisms. Examples include the addition of penicillin to a culture to select for those organisms resistant to it, or the selection of hybridised cells during the production of monoclonal antibodies (section 12.11.2).

> **12.4** How would you set about trying to isolate from the soil an organism which could use atmospheric nitrogen as its only source of nitrogen (a nitrogen-fixing organism)?

12.2.3 Indicator media

These are media which contain an indicator which enables colonies of one organism to be visibly distinguished from those of another. For example, certain bacteria can break down ('ferment') the sugar lactose to an acid. In a medium known as MacConkey's agar, which contains the pH indicator neutral red and bile salts, colonies of lactose fermenters will appear red and non-lactose fermenters colourless or pale pink. This is useful, for example, in detecting whether water is contaminated by sewage. Such water contains gut bacteria such as *E. coli* which ferment lactose. Similarly, if *Salmonella* were present in a sample of gut bacteria it would form colourless colonies in MacConkey's agar.

12.2.4 Preparing media

Dried media can be bought commercially, already containing agar. They are normally soaked for 15 minutes in water and then autoclaved in bottles or flasks for 15 minutes at 121 °C to sterilise. The medium mixes and dissolves during autoclaving. Inside an autoclave, water is boiled under pressure. The autoclave has a lid with a safety valve to let out the steam when the required pressure has been reached. The higher the pressure, the higher the boiling point of the water. It is used to sterilise solutions and equipment such as glassware. In order to kill all bacteria and their resistant spores, a pressure of 103 kPa (15 pounds per square inch) for 15 or 20 minutes is normally recommended. At this pressure, the temperature inside the autoclave will reach 121 °C.

12.3 Aseptic technique

Aseptic technique is using sterilised equipment and solutions and preventing their contamination while in use. Bacteria and fungal spores are abundant in most environments, including laboratories. The microbiologist uses a range of special techniques and apparatus which are designed to prevent contamination of nutrient media. Although a 'nuisance', these quickly become part of the daily routine of being a microbiologist. You will only be able to take basic precautions in school or college laboratories. Special laboratories are needed for routine microbiological work. These will have easily cleaned surfaces and special enclosed benches which receive filtered sterile air (fig 12.2).

Fig 12.2 *A modern microbiology laboratory with a laminar flow bench in use.*

12.3.1 Pouring plates

This is one of the most basic and useful of microbiological techniques. A **plate** is a petri dish containing nutrient agar. Petri dishes are specially designed shallow circular dishes made of glass or plastic. They are used for growth of bacteria, fungi or tissues on a solid nutrient medium. They are typically about 9 cm in diameter. Glass dishes can be re-used after autoclaving. Plastic dishes are disposable and are usually autoclaved to destroy the culture. They melt in the process. They are bought in sealed packs which have been sterilised, usually by radiation with gamma rays. The lid prevents contamination, but gas molecules can diffuse between the inside of the dish and the environment through microscopic irregularities where the base meets the lid. Oxygen can therefore reach the culture and carbon dioxide can escape.

The procedure for pouring molten nutrient agar into a petri dish ('pouring a plate') is shown in fig 12.3. It is assumed that the agar has been prepared in small bottles (McCartney bottles).

12.4 Methods of inoculation

The introduction of a small number of microorganisms into a nutrient medium is called **inoculation**. Aseptic technique must be used to avoid contamination. The procedure differs for solid and liquid media.

12.4.1 Inoculating a solid medium

Streak plate or dilution plate

The technique is illustrated in fig 12.4. It is suitable for isolating pure colonies of bacteria from a mixture of bacteria. An inoculating loop is used, which must first be 'flamed', as shown in fig 12.4a, to sterilise it. The wire loop is then used to lift a thin film of liquid suspension, or a small amount of solid material, containing the microorganisms being investigated from the previous culture or source of the microorganisms. The loop is gently stroked across the surface of the medium in a series of sets of streaks. The plate is partly rotated between each set of streaks so that each set spreads out the bacteria from the previous set of streaks, diluting them until they are separated into single bacteria (fig 12.4). (Don't expect to see anything along the final streaks until after incubation!) The streaks can be made very rapidly once the technique has been practised.

Bacteria from natural habitats like soil, milk and water can be isolated in this way. In the case of a solid medium like soil, it may be easier to suspend a sample in water, or to grow a sample in liquid medium first. Pasteurised milk is a safe source for routine work. Safety regulations and guidelines should always be consulted before carrying out experiments with bacteria or fungi to minimise the risk of harmful organisms being cultivated.

Spread plate

This technique is illustrated in fig 12.5. It is suitable for inoculating solid media with cells from a liquid suspension. It is used when determining the number of living cells (the 'viable count') in a sample after serial dilutions (see section 12.6.1). It can also be used to produce a continuous 'lawn' of microorganisms over the surface of the agar by using a heavy inoculation. This is convenient for testing the activity of inhibitors, such as antibiotics or disinfectants, which can be added to wells cut in the agar or to filter paper discs added to the surface of the agar. The inhibitor can diffuse through the agar, causing a zone of inhibition around the wells or filter paper which is visible after incubation. The diameter of the zone can be used as a measure of the degree of inhibition.

Pour plate

This is an alternative to the spread plate method for inoculating with cells from a liquid suspension and for counting living cells. Larger numbers can be counted, up to 1000 colonies per plate, because the cells grow throughout the medium, not just on its surface. Smaller colonies result (fig 12.6).

A known, small volume (up to $0.5\,cm^3$) of cell suspension is added to a suitable volume (about $15\text{–}20\,cm^3$) of sterilised molten nutrient agar in a small bottle which has been cooled to about 45 to 50 °C in a water bath. The lid of the bottle should be removed and the mouth of the bottle flamed as shown in figs 12.3a and b before adding the cell suspension. Mix the cell suspension thoroughly with the nutrient agar in the bottle by rotating (not shaking) the bottle back and forth between the palms of the hands as shown in fig 12.6a. Then pour the mixture into a sterile petri dish as shown in fig 12.3c. Label the base of the dish and incubate. The final appearance of the plate is shown in fig 12.6b.

(a)

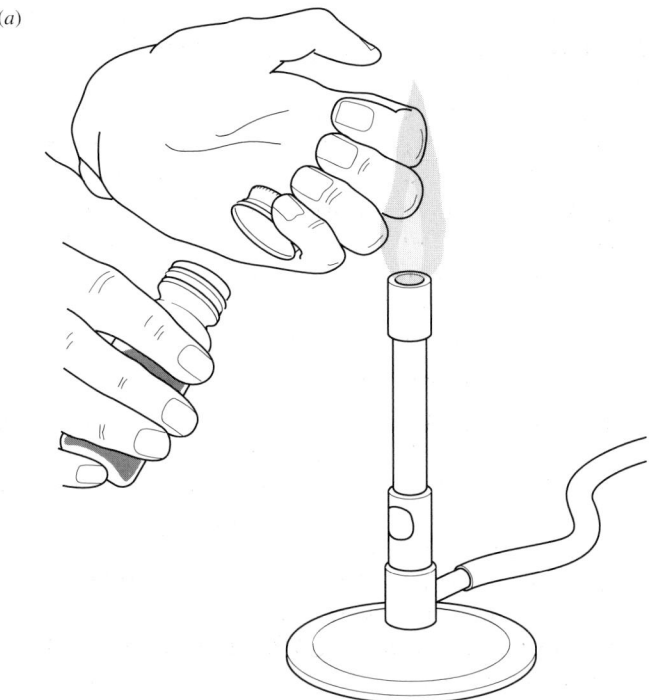

Allow liquid nutrient agar to cool to about 50 °C (just cool enough for comfortable handling) after removal from autoclave. Unscrew cap of bottle with little finger as shown. It can be held by the little finger during the procedure to avoid placing it on the bench where it could become contaminated.

(b)

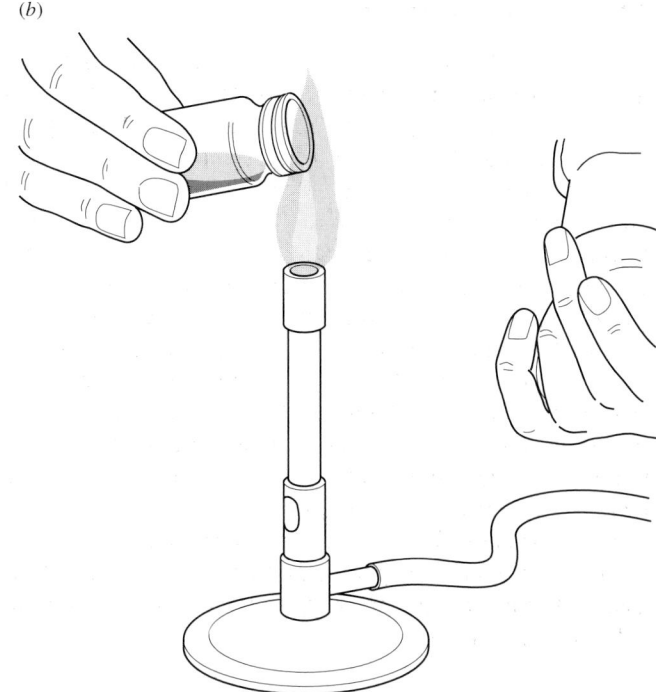

'Flame' mouth of bottle for a few seconds. This is done to produce an upward flow of air from the bottle so that any organisms in the area will not fall into the bottle. (It is not done to kill microorganisms – the bottle would have to be heated for too long to achieve this effect.)

(c)

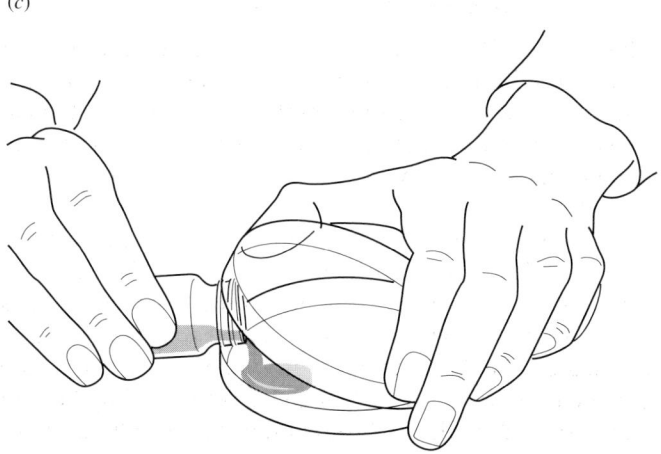

Pour the molten agar (about 15–20cm³) slowly into the base of the sterile petri dish, lifting the lid only as much as necessary. Do not spill agar on the edges of the dish (if so, start again). Replace the lid and allow the agar to set.

Fig 12.3 *Procedure for pouring a plate.*

(d)

plates are dried with base resting on lid as shown

drying several plates

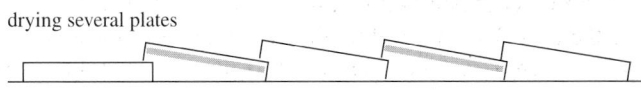

If the plate is to be used for 'streaking' or 'spreading' the surface of the agar and lid can be dried once the agar is set. They are best dried upside down in an incubator at about 37 °C, and arranged as shown to minimise the risk of contamination (slight in these circumstances).

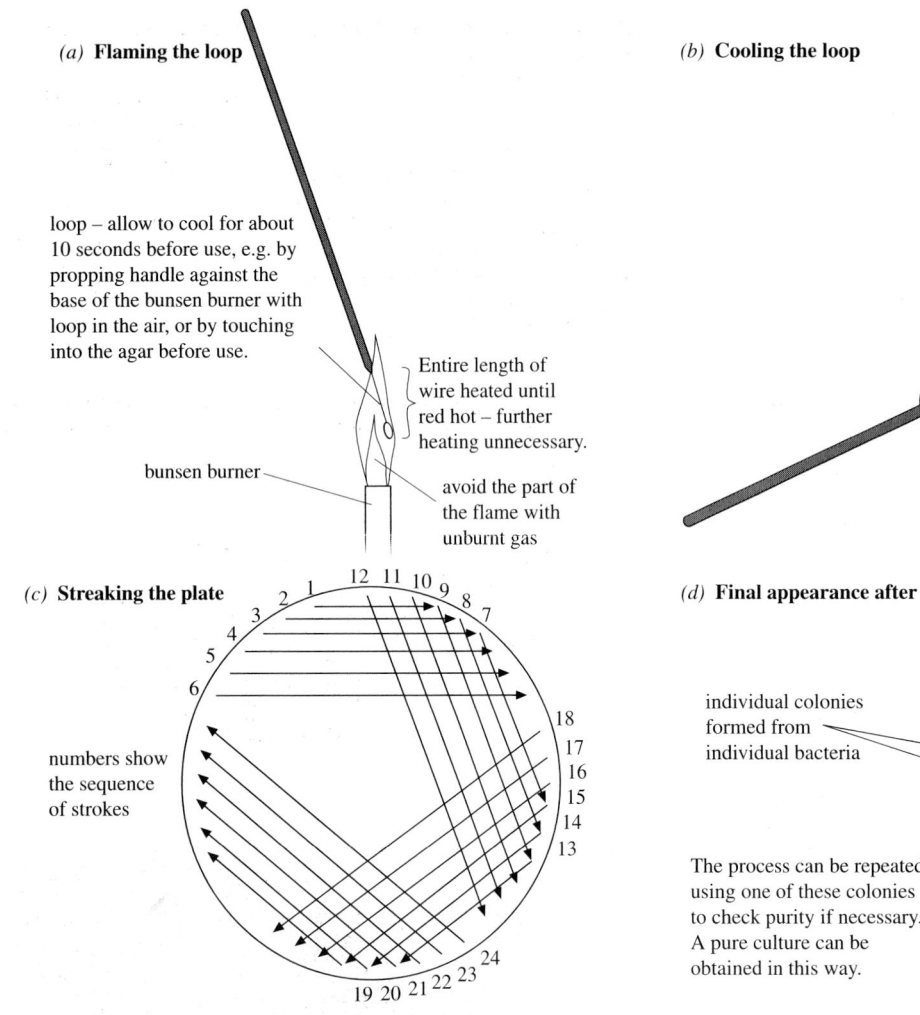

(a) **Flaming the loop**

loop – allow to cool for about 10 seconds before use, e.g. by propping handle against the base of the bunsen burner with loop in the air, or by touching into the agar before use.

Entire length of wire heated until red hot – further heating unnecessary.

bunsen burner

avoid the part of the flame with unburnt gas

(b) **Cooling the loop**

(c) **Streaking the plate**

numbers show the sequence of strokes

Collect a loopful of the sample if liquid. Touch the sample with the loop if solid. Raise the lid of the petri dish only as far as necessary and lightly spread the sample as shown, without damaging the surface of the agar. Keep the loop flat and hold the handle at the balance point near the centre. Each line represents one stroke with the wire loop. Flame the loop and cool between each set of six lines. Flame again at the end. Label the base of the plate*. Incubate upside down to prevent any condensation falling onto the cultures.

(d) **Final appearance after incubation**

individual colonies formed from individual bacteria

The process can be repeated using one of these colonies to check purity if necessary. A pure culture can be obtained in this way.

* Labelling the plate
• date
• initials
• contents
If you use mirror-writing you will be able to read it through the lid

Fig 12.4 *Streak or dilution culture.*

(a) Stand the spreader in a small beaker of alcohol.

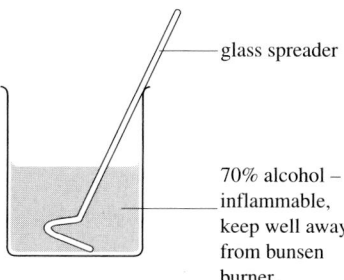

glass spreader

70% alcohol – inflammable, keep well away from bunsen burner.

(c) Remove the spreader from the alcohol and allow excess alcohol to drain from it.

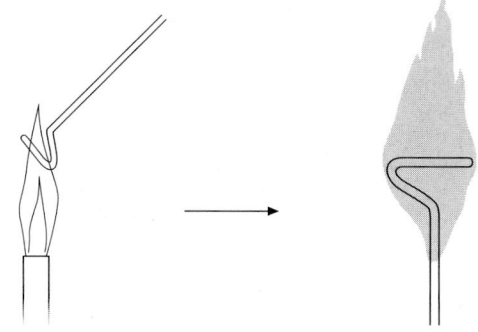

Ignite the alcohol by passing the spreader through a bunsen flame. Do not leave in the bunsen flame or it may crack. (Alcohol burns at a much lower temperature than that of the bunsen flame.) After the flame has disappeared, allow to cool for about 10 seconds. Store in the beaker after use.

(e) **Final appearance after incubation**

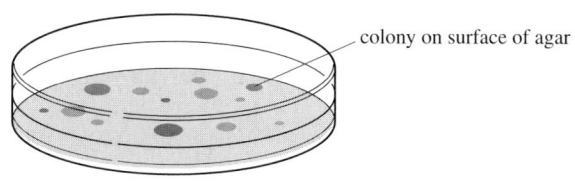

colony on surface of agar

Count the number of colonies. This corresponds to the number of bacteria originally inoculated.

Fig 12.5 *Spread culture (above).*

(b) Transfer a known, small volume (up to 0.5 cm³) of cell suspension to the surface of the nutrient agar in a petri dish. A teat on the end of the pipette helps to control delivery.

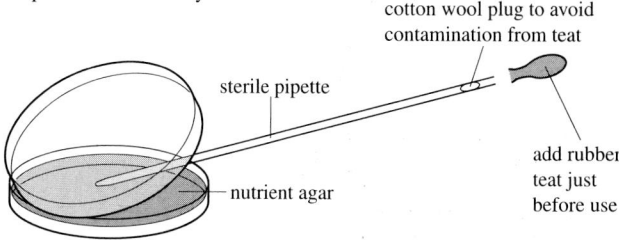

cotton wool plug to avoid contamination from teat

sterile pipette

nutrient agar

add rubber teat just before use

(d) Push the liquid over the surface of the agar using the spreader. Rotate the plate at the same time to ensure an even coverage. Label the base of the plate and incubate.

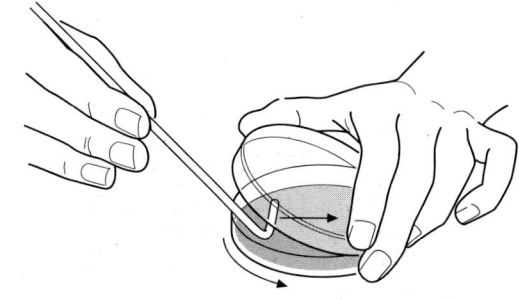

(a)

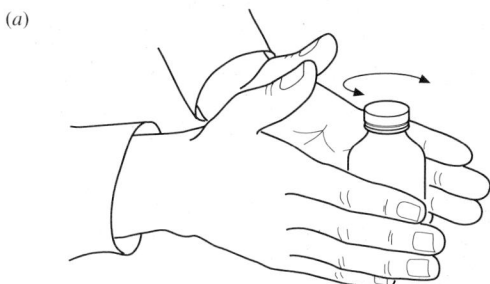

(b)

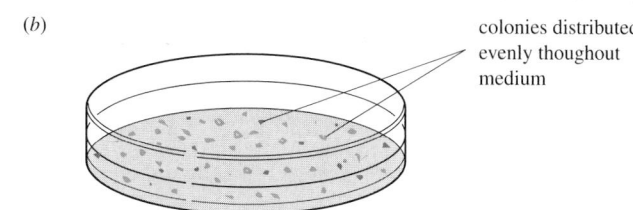

colonies distributed evenly thoughout medium

Fig 12.6 *Pour plate.*

Stab culture

This is used for anaerobic organisms or those that thrive in conditions of low oxygen concentration, namely microaerophiles. A nutrient agar medium in a test tube is normally used. The greater depth of agar, and the small surface area in the tube compared with a dish, means less oxygen can diffuse into the agar. Inoculation is done with a straight wire (no loop). A sample (liquid or solid) is collected at the tip of the wire which is then stabbed vertically through the medium (fig 12.7). The culture grows out from the stab line.

12.4.2   Inoculating a liquid medium

If the cells to be inoculated are in a liquid, for example water, milk or a broth, a sterile wire loop is used to transfer a sample to the medium, which is often in a test tube. The wire loop is simply agitated gently inside the medium. Remember to flame the necks of bottles if caps or cotton wool plugs are removed.

If the cells to be inoculated are in or on a solid medium, such as soil or nutrient agar, a wire loop may also be used for transfer to the liquid medium. It can be rubbed on the inside surface of the vessel containing the liquid medium to ensure successful transfer.

In both cases the tube containing the liquid medium can be tapped afterwards to help mix the culture.

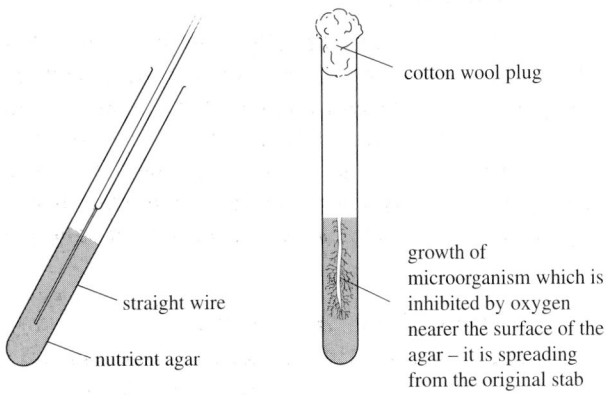

Fig 12.7 *Stab culture.*

12.5   Bacterial growth

12.5.1   Population growth

When bacteria reach a certain size they divide by a form of asexual reproduction called **binary fission** in which the cell divides into two identical daughter cells (fig 2.11). Further details of this process are given in section 2.5.3. In this chapter we shall look at growth of the whole population in more detail.

If a single bacterium is placed in a nutrient medium in optimum growth conditions, it, and its descendants, should divide every 30 minutes, as shown in table 12.2.

> **12.5** If you have not already answered question 2.1 in chapter 2, use the data from table 12.2 to draw graphs of number of bacteria (graph A) and $\log_{10}$ number of bacteria (graph B) on the vertical axes against time (horizontal axis). What do you notice about the shapes of the graphs?

The kind of growth shown in table 12.2 is known as **logarithmic** or **exponential growth**. This can be explained by looking at line C in table 12.2 where the number of bacteria is expressed as a power of 2. The power can be called the logarithm (log) or exponent. The logs or exponents form a linearly increasing series 0, 1, 2, 3, etc., corresponding with the number of divisions.

The numbers in line A of table 12.2 can be converted to logs to the base 2 as shown in line D. (Compare line C with line D.) However, it is conventional to use logs to the base 10, as in line B. Thus 1 is 10^0, 2 is $10^{0.3}$, 4 is $10^{0.6}$, etc.

The curve for graph A in question 12.5 is known as a **logarithmic** or **exponential curve**. Such growth curves can be converted to straight lines by plotting the logs of growth against time. Under ideal conditions, then, bacterial growth is exponential. The time taken for the number of bacteria to double is constant during exponential growth. This is

Table 12.2 Growth of a model population of bacteria.

		0	0.5	1	1.5	2	2.5	3	3.5	4	4.5	5
	Time /h											
	*	0	1	2	3	4	5	6	7	8	9	10
A	**	1	2	4	8	16	32	64	128	256	512	1024
B	***	0.0	0.3	0.6	0.9	1.2	1.5	1.8	2.1	2.4	2.7	3.0
C	****	2^0	2^1	2^2	2^3	2^4	2^5	2^6	2^7	2^8	2^9	2^{10}
D	*****	0	1	2	3	4	5	6	7	8	9	10

* Number of divisions
** Number of bacteria
*** Log$_{10}$ number of bacteria

**** Number of bacteria expressed as power of 2
***** Log$_2$ number of bacteria

known as the **doubling time** or the **generation time** and can be calculated from the graph.

The ideal model of bacterial growth can be compared with the growth of a real population in a closed vessel (with no external changes such as renewal of nutrients). Fig 12.8 shows such growth. Note that two curves are shown, one for the total number of bacteria, including all those that have died. In practice, this is an easier number to determine (section 12.6.2). A more useful graph to study, though, is the number of living bacteria, known as the **viable count** (section 12.6.1). This curve has four distinct phases. The first is the **lag phase** in which the bacteria are adapting to their new environment and growth has not yet achieved its maximum rate. The bacteria may, for example, be synthesising new enzymes to digest the particular range of nutrients available in the new medium.

The next phase is the **log phase** when growth is proceeding at its maximum rate, closely approaching an ideal logarithmic increase in numbers when the growth curve would be a straight line. During this phase the doubling time is constant and at its shortest. Eventually growth of the colony begins to slow down, doubling time starts to increase, and it starts to enter the **stationary phase** where growth rate of the population is zero and there is much greater competition for resources. Rate of production of new cells is slower and may cease altogether. Any increase in the number of cells is offset by the death of other cells, so that the number of living cells remains constant. This phase is a result of several factors, including exhaustion of essential nutrients, accumulation of toxic waste products, such as alcohol, and possibly, if the bacteria are aerobic, shortage of oxygen. Changes in pH sometimes occur which also slow down growth.

During the final phase, the **phase of decline**, the death rate increases and becomes greater than the rate of multiplication. Eventually the cells stop multiplying altogether. Methods of counting bacteria are described in the next section.

12.6 What would be the shape of the graph obtained if a sample of bacteria was taken from the culture at the beginning of the stationary phase, inoculated into fresh medium and the bacterial population growth measured?

12.7 A culture of bacteria was set up in a nutrient solution and kept at 30 °C. From time 0, and at the times indicated in table 12.3, a count was made of the number of bacterial cells in the culture.

Using the data in table 12.3, draw graphs to show what happened. Explain, using your graphs, what you think was affecting the changes in cell numbers.

12.8 What is the shortest doubling time (generation time) of the bacteria in question 12.7?

Similar principles to these can be applied to the growth of any population and have even been applied to human populations. Any population can, in theory, achieve exponential growth if the doubling time remains constant. However, limiting factors always come into operation sooner or later and a study of these factors is the basis of population ecology (section 10.7).

12.5.2 Diauxic growth

Diauxic means literally that the growth has two phases. It occurs when a bacterium is in a medium containing two different and alternative nutrients. It will often use one in preference to the other until the preferred one is exhausted. It will then switch to the alternative. However, growth usually slows noticeably while the change is being achieved. An example is *E. coli*, the common gut

Table 12.3 Culture of bacteria at 30 °C.

| Time/h | Number of cells in millions | |
	living	living and dead
0	9	10
1	10	11
2	11	12
5	18	20
10	400	450
12	550	620
15	550	700
20	550	850
30	550	950
35	225	950
45	30	950

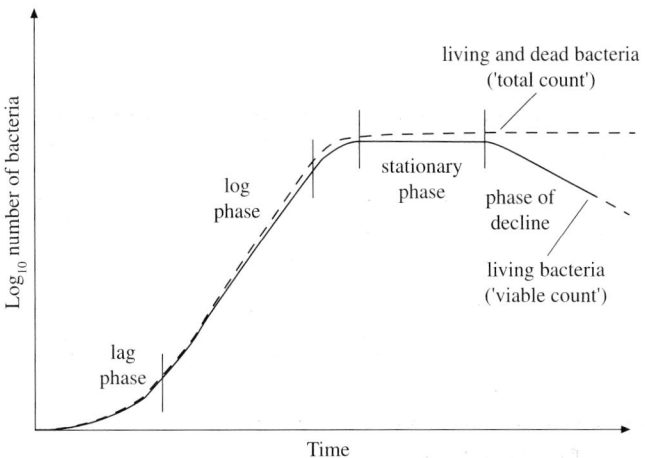

Fig 12.8 *Typical growth of a bacterial population.*

bacterium. This can use glucose or lactose as an energy and carbon source. If both are present, the glucose is used first and then growth slows while enzymes are made which can digest the lactose.

12.5.3 Production of primary and secondary metabolic products

Primary metabolites are products of metabolism needed for growth and are vital for survival.

Secondary metabolites are products of metabolism which are not needed for growth and are not vital for survival. However, they do serve useful functions and are often protective or inhibitory to other competing microorganisms. Some are toxic to animals; they may therefore be a form of chemical warfare. They are often not produced during the most active periods of growth. Once growth slows, spare materials become available for their manufacture. Some important antibiotics are secondary metabolites.

12.6 Measuring population growth of bacteria and fungi

The typical growth curve of a population of bacteria was examined in the previous section. A similar growth curve could be expected for yeast, a unicellular fungus, or the growth of any population.

When measuring the growth of a population of bacteria or yeast, we can do it directly by counting the number of cells, or indirectly by measuring some indication of the number of cells, such as the cloudiness of a solution, or production of a gas. It is usual to inoculate a small sample of the microorganism into a sterilised nutrient medium and to place the culture in an incubator at the optimum temperature for growth. Other conditions should be as close as possible to optimum (section 12.1). Growth can be measured from the time of inoculation.

It is good practice in all scientific investigations to set up replicates and controls where possible and appropriate. Some of the techniques for measuring population growth require practice and are not very precise even in the hands of experts. It is therefore wise, if possible, to set up at least two samples (one replicate) for each treatment. Controls with no microorganisms added to the nutrient medium can test whether your technique is genuinely aseptic. All the techniques described improve with experience and it is advisable to practice them first if they are to be used for project work.

Two types of cell count are possible, namely viable counts and total counts. The **viable count** is the total of *living* cells only. The **total count** is the total number of cells, *living* and *dead*, and is often easier to measure.

12.6.1 Viable counts

It may be important to know the number of living cells. For example, the effectiveness of pasteurising milk in killing certain bacteria could be measured by making viable counts before and after pasteurisation. In an industrial process it is only the living cells which will be contributing to the process, so here again it is important to know the number of living cells in the culture. Viable counts are made using spread plates or pour plates, though viable yeast cells can also be counted using an adaptation of haemocytometry.

Spread plates

This method has already been described in section 12.4.1 (fig 12.5). A known, small volume of sample is added to the nutrient agar in a petri dish. One problem with the technique is that traces of the sample are bound to remain on the spreader and in the pipette, so the final count will be a slight underestimate. However, this is usually not important.

The method relies on the principle that each bacterium will grow into a single colony after a suitable time period, such as two days. The number of bacteria in the original added sample is therefore equal to the number of colonies after incubation. Only those colonies with about 100 000 or more individuals are visible to the naked eye. Typically a colony contains several million bacteria.

Providing the sample does not have too few or too many bacteria, the number of colonies can be counted easily although, for safety reasons, lids of petri dishes should not be removed during counting. It is usual to prepare a dilution series, so that the ideal number of colonies is obtained from one of the series. A dilution series is a series of samples of different known dilutions (fig 12.9). Once a suitable dilution has been found, further replicates can be carried out at this dilution to improve accuracy and reliability. In experiment 12.3 in section 12.9.2 the number of bacteria in milk samples is estimated using this method. Some limitations of the method are discussed at the end of this section.

Pour plates

This method has already been described in section 12.4.1 (fig 12.6). The method is similar in principle to spread plating, but the sample is mixed with the nutrient agar before it sets so the colonies are spread throughout the medium instead of growing only on the surface.

Yeast

Viable counting of yeast cells can be made using a haemocytometer and methylene blue. This technique is described in more detail in the next section.

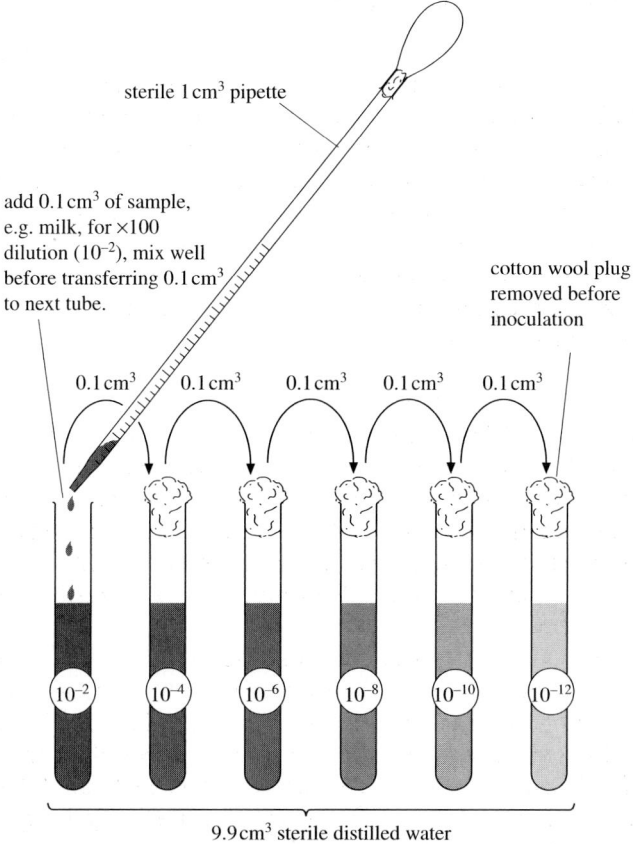

sterile 1 cm³ pipette

add 0.1 cm³ of sample, e.g. milk, for ×100 dilution (10^{-2}), mix well before transferring 0.1 cm³ to next tube.

cotton wool plug removed before inoculation

0.1 cm³   0.1 cm³   0.1 cm³   0.1 cm³   0.1 cm³

10^{-2} 10^{-4} 10^{-6} 10^{-8} 10^{-10} 10^{-12}

9.9 cm³ sterile distilled water

Fig 12.9 *Making a serial dilution.*

Problems associated with viable counting

There are a number of problems associated with viable counting.

- Some bacteria form chains or groups of cells, for example streptococci and staphylococci (fig 2.10). Each group of cells will give rise to only one colony. The results of viable counts are therefore sometimes expressed as numbers of colony-forming units (cfu) rather than number of bacteria.
- If more than one type of bacterium is present, as for example in a soil, milk or water sample, conditions will not favour all types equally. Some will therefore grow more rapidly than others, giving variable numbers of visible colonies.

12.6.2   Total counts

Haemocytometer

The number of bacteria or yeast cells in a liquid culture, such as a broth culture, can be counted directly using a microscope. The technique is easier for yeast because the cells are much larger. With bacteria, an oil immersion lens is required (see section 5.11.2).

A special counting slide called a **haemocytometer slide** is most commonly used (fig 12.10). The technique is known

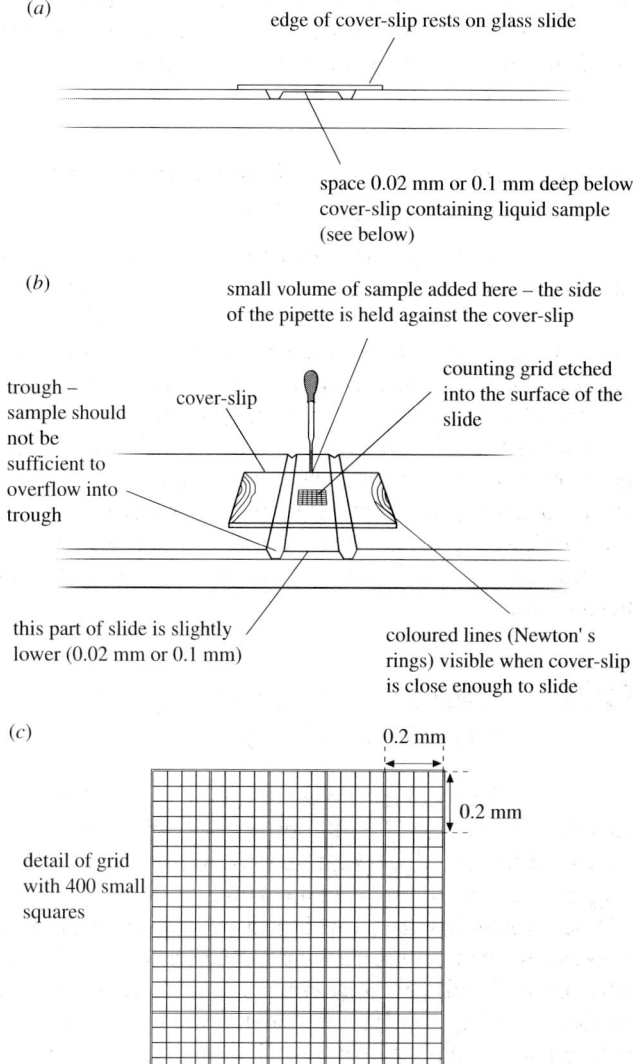

(a) edge of cover-slip rests on glass slide

space 0.02 mm or 0.1 mm deep below cover-slip containing liquid sample (see below)

(b) small volume of sample added here – the side of the pipette is held against the cover-slip

trough – sample should not be sufficient to overflow into trough

cover-slip

counting grid etched into the surface of the slide

this part of slide is slightly lower (0.02 mm or 0.1 mm)

coloured lines (Newton's rings) visible when cover-slip is close enough to slide

(c) 0.2 mm   0.2 mm

detail of grid with 400 small squares

Fig 12.10 *Haemocytometry.*

as **haemocytometry**. To ensure close enough contact between slide and cover-slip, the cover-slip should be pressed down firmly either side of the counting chamber (but don't break the cover-slip!). It should be moved slightly until coloured lines appear as indicated in fig 12.10. The liquid sample in the pipette is drawn under the cover-slip by capillary action. The slide should be left for 2 to 30 minutes to allow cells to settle, making counting easier. The microscope is focused on the grid and the number of cells in the entire grid, or a representative sample, can be counted. At least 600 cells should be counted. Where cells lie on a boundary, they can be judged as in the square on two sides (e.g. upper and right boundaries) and out of the square on the other two sides, rather than trying to count half cells. Each small square is a known area and the depth of liquid below the cover-slip is constant (usually either 0.02 mm or 0.1 mm). The volume of each square can therefore be calculated, and the number of cells in a given volume can be estimated. The sample should be diluted if there are more than about 30 cells in some of the squares. Remember to allow for any dilution in the calculations.

In the grid shown in fig 12.10 the small squares are each $0.05\,\text{mm} \times 0.05\,\text{mm} = 0.0025\,\text{mm}^2$, a total area for the grid of $1\,\text{mm}^2$. If the gap between the cover-slip and the grid is $0.02\,\text{mm}$, the total volume above the grid is therefore $1 \times 0.02\,\text{mm} = 0.02\,\text{mm}^3$. The number of cells in a given volume of sample can therefore be counted. Remember $1000\,\text{mm}^3 = 1\,\text{cm}^3$ and $1000\,\text{cm}^3 = 1\,\text{dm}^3$ (1 litre).

With yeast, methylene blue stain can be used. This stains only dead cells blue. Living cells actively transport the dye back out of the cell. This would enable a viable count to be determined by counting only colourless or very pale blue cells.

Measuring turbidity

This technique is simple in principle. The more cells there are in a suspension, the greater will be its **turbidity** or 'cloudiness'. The degree of turbidity is measured, a technique known as **turbidimetry**.

The simplest way of doing this is to have a set of standard tubes (Brown's tubes). These can be purchased and contain suspensions of different concentrations of barium sulphate, ranging from transparent (tube 1) to opaque (tube 10). A sample of the suspension of microorganisms under investigation is placed into an identical tube and the turbidity of the suspension is matched with one of the standard tubes. A table is supplied with the tubes showing how the turbidity of the microorganisms can be converted to concentrations of cells for a range of different microorganisms.

Alternatively turbidity can be measured as the change in percentage transmission of light (or **optical density**) of the suspension using a colorimeter or a spectrophotometer. The cell mass is directly proportional to the optical density. A red light (red filter) is most useful because it is not interfered with by the yellowish colour of many culture media.

Measuring turbidity is likely to be subject to errors if cells grow in clumps like some bacteria (see viable counting). Also, the most accurate estimates are obtained from population densities that are not too high or too low. Dilution of the sample may be necessary for an ideal density of cells (10^6–10^{10} cells per cm^3).

12.6.3 Non-counting methods

Various other methods for measuring the growth of microorganisms can be devised. For example, with fungi, the growth in diameter of the mycelium can be measured over time. This would be suitable, for example, if the effect of temperature on fungal growth were being investigated, or the effect of an inhibitory substance in the medium. If a fungus is growing in a liquid medium, samples of the culture could be filtered or centrifuged at suitable intervals and the fresh or dry mass of the mycelium measured.

12.7 Staining bacteria – the Gram stain

Although direct microscopic examination of living bacteria is possible using a phase contrast microscope, it is more common to kill and stain bacteria before examination.

One stain which is important in the identification of bacteria is the Gram stain. It was first developed by a Danish physician, Christian Gram, in 1884. Before staining, all bacteria are colourless. Afterwards Gram positive bacteria are stained violet and Gram negative bacteria are stained red. The difference between the two types of bacteria is described in section 2.5.1 (cell wall).

Details of the procedure are given in experiment 12.2, section 12.9.

12.8 Growing viruses

The culture, or growth, of viruses is made more difficult than the culture of bacteria or fungi by the fact that viruses will only grow and multiply inside living cells. This can be done by infecting whole organisms such as plants or animals, but, where possible, cell or tissue cultures are now used (fig 12.11). An early technique was to grow certain viruses in chick embryos while the embryo was still growing inside the egg. A similar procedure was used to grow viruses for mumps and influenza vaccines in the amniotic fluid surrounding the chick embryo.

Fig 12.11 *Cell cultures for growing viruses in petri dishes, incubated in a sterile hot room.*

Cell cultures are a suspension of cells in a liquid medium and tissue cultures are small pieces of plant or animal organ grown in liquid or on a solid medium. In plant tissue culture, meristems are usually used, that is regions such as the root and shoot tips where cells are actively dividing. The material can be taken from a suitably infected plant or inoculated with the appropriate virus when in culture. Animal tissue culture is usually set up by growing individual cells to form a single layer of cells over the surface of a glass container (a **monolayer culture**). The polio virus was originally grown in such cultures derived from monkey kidney. Human cells from the lung, amnion or human cancers have also been used in tissue culture work.

12.9 Experimental work

The following practical work is designed to cover some of the basic microbiological techniques associated with bacteriology, using milk as a relatively safe source of bacteria. Milk is a useful food source for bacteria as well as mammals, and certain bacteria are characteristically associated with it.

12.9.1 Bacterial content of milk

Bacteria inevitably enter milk during milking and handling, even under the most hygienic conditions. Milking is normally followed immediately by cooling to retard bacterial growth. The untreated (raw) milk is pasteurised, a heat process intended to kill pathogenic bacteria, though many non-pathogenic bacteria survive. Bacteria present are:

15–30 °C *Streptococcus lactis* (Gram +) dominates, together with many other streptococci (Gram +) and coryneform (club-shaped) bacteria (for example *Microbacterium*, *Brevibacterium*) which resemble *Lactobacillus* but may have swollen ends to the rods.

Streptococcus lactis grows well at 10 °C but growth ceases at >40 °C.

30–40 °C *Lactobacillus* (Gram +) and gut-living bacilli (Gram –) dominate, such as *E. coli*.

Streptococcus lactis and *Lactobacillus* are lactic acid bacteria. They produce lactic acid during fermentation (anaerobic respiration) of lactose (milk sugar) and the accumulating acid causes souring of milk. Colonies of *S. lactis* and *Lactobacillus* are relatively small (maximum diameter of a few millimetres on a culture) and never coloured, appearing chalky white. *S. lactis* forms smooth-textured colonies with entire edges. If finely divided calcium carbonate is included in the nutrient agar, streptococci show clear zones around each colony where lactic acid dissolves the calcium carbonate. Streptococci are responsible for the normal souring of milk. They are spherical and form chains (fig 12.12). Lactobacilli are rods

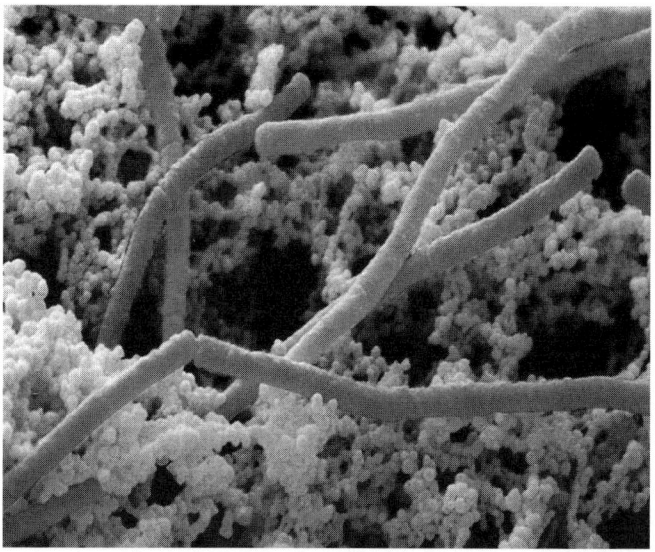

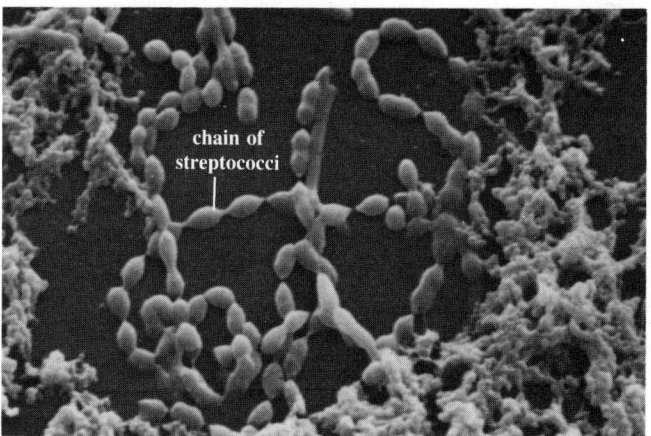

Fig 12.12 *(a) Scanning electron micrograph of* Lactobacillus bulgaricus, *a rod-shaped Gram positive bacterium which causes souring of milk. (b) Light micrograph of chains of streptococci, recovered from milk by filtration.*

which tend to stick together in long chains (fig 12.12). Colonies may have a rough surface texture with irregular edges.

A number of other bacteria may be found in milk, including the gut-living rod *Alcaligenes* (Gram –) found singly or in chains. It may be recognised on MacConkey's agar by a yellowish (alkaline) zone around each colony.

12.9.2 Bacteriology experiments

The following three experiments are exercises in the use of microbiological techniques, all including aseptic technique. The first experiment is to culture milk bacteria and involves pouring agar plates and producing a streak culture. The second experiment is to use Gram-staining bacteria from experiment 12.1 for examination with a light microscope. The third involves the counting of bacterial colonies using the technique of serial dilution.

Experiment 12.1: To investigate the bacterial content of fresh and stale milk

The aims of the experiment are to determine the effect of leaving milk unrefrigerated for 24 hours and why milk becomes stale. Milk is almost a complete food for humans and the experiments show that it is also a good culture medium for certain bacteria.

Materials

4 sterile nutrient agar plates
inoculating loop
bunsen burner
indelible marker or wax pencil
fresh pasteurised milk
stale milk (milk left at room temperature for 24 h)
incubator set at 35 °C

Method

(1) Place the inoculating loop in the bunsen burner flame until the loop is red hot (fig 12.4).
(2) Allow the loop to cool and then dip it into a sample of fresh, well shaken milk.
(3) Lift the lid of a sterile agar plate slightly with the other hand and lightly spread the contents of the inoculating loop over the surface of the agar as described in fig 12.4.
(4) Close the lid of the plate and return the loop to the bunsen burner flame until red hot.
(5) Label the base of the plate with an indelible marker (or wax pencil).
(6) Repeat with a second plate and another sample of fresh milk.
(7) Flame the loop again and, having allowed it to cool, dip it into a sample of stale milk.
(8) Spread the contents of the loop over the surface of a third plate and then close the lid.
(9) Label the base of the plate with an indelible marker.
(10) Repeat with a fourth plate and a second sample of stale milk.
(11) Place the four plates in an incubator at 35 °C for about three days. They should be placed upside down to prevent condensation falling onto the cultures. After incubation, the two halves of each plate should be taped together for safety reasons.
(12) Record the appearance of the colonies and compare with the description in section 12.9.1.

Notes

(1) Students may pour their own plates, if McCartney tubes of sterile molten nutrient agar are supplied.
(2) The particular streaking technique used progressively reduces the number of bacteria in each streak. It is suitable in situations where large numbers of bacteria are present, as in milk, and is normally used to isolate pure colonies of bacteria from mixed cultures.

(3) The plates can be placed in a refrigerator after incubation until required. This prevents further bacterial growth.
(4) When the plates are no longer required they should be placed in a disposable autoclave bag and autoclaved for 15 min before final disposal.
(5) Other experiments using milk could be performed. The experiment above is the simplest. The effect of refrigeration could be studied. Also, if samples of raw (unpasteurised) milk could be obtained (for instance direct from a dairy farm) the effect of the process of pasteurisation on the bacterial content of milk could be studied. Pasteurisation of milk can be accomplished by placing raw milk in a sterile test-tube plugged with cotton wool and heating at 63 °C for 35 min in a water bath. A third variation would be to incubate some plates at 10 °C instead of 35 °C. This lower temperature favours growth of *Streptococcus lactis* compared with *Lactobacillus*.

Experiment 12.2: To stain bacteria for examination with a light microscope

Although direct microscopic examination of living bacteria is possible using a phase contrast microscope, it is more common to kill and stain bacteria before examination.

One stain which is important in the identification of bacteria is the Gram stain. Before staining, all bacteria are colourless. Afterwards **Gram positive** bacteria are stained violet and **Gram negative** bacteria are red. The difference between the two types of bacteria is described in section 2.5.1 (cell wall).

Materials

basic stain = crystal violet (0.5% aqueous)
mordant = Lugol's iodine
decolouriser = acetone–alcohol (50:50 acetone: absolute alcohol)
counterstain = safranin (1% aqueous)
wire loop
bunsen burner
glass slides scrupulously clean (wipe with alcohol)
forceps
staining rack set up over sink or dish
distilled water in wash bottle
blotting paper
immersion oil and microscope with oil immersion lens

Method

(Stages 1 to 6 should take about 5 min.) (Based on *Bacteriology*, J. Humphries, John Murray, 1974.)

(1) **Prepare a smear** of bacteria on the slide as follows. Flame a wire loop and cool. Place a loopful or two of tap water on the centre of a clean slide. Touch the wire loop lightly on a selected bacterial colony from the experiment above, opening the lid of the plate a

minimal amount for safety reasons. Transfer the bacteria to the slide and gently mix with the water. Spread the bacteria over the slide, using the loop, to cover an area about $3 \times 1\,cm$. Flame the loop again. It is important to achieve the correct thickness of the smear. It should appear only faintly opalescent and is more usually too thick than too thin. It should also be of even thickness. Allow the smear to become perfectly dry in air (a few minutes).

(2) **Fix the bacteria.** Holding the slide with forceps, pass it horizontally just over a yellow bunsen flame three times. It is important that it is not overheated and should feel comfortable against the skin after each passage over the flame. Fixing kills the bacteria by coagulating the cytoplasm and also makes them stick to the slide.

(3) **Stain the bacteria.** Staining is likely to soil the bench so should be done on a rack over a sink or dish. A rack can be made by arranging two glass or metal rods across the sink or dish 5 cm apart and absolutely horizontal. If supported on plasticine they are easily adjusted. Flood the slide with crystal violet stain. Leave for 30 s. This makes all bacteria violet.

(4) Wash off with Lugol's iodine; flood with Lugol's iodine and leave for 30 s. Wash off the iodine with distilled water from a wash bottle. The iodine fixes the stain more permanently into the cells.

(5) Flood the slide with acetone–alcohol until no more colour is seen to come off (about 3 s); *immediately* wash with water to prevent excessive decolourisation. Repeat if necessary (only experience will show how much washing is needed). This decolourises Gram negative bacteria. Gram positive bacteria stay violet.

(6) Flood the slide with safranin and leave for 1 min. Wash off the stain with water. Gently dry the slide between sheets of clean blotting paper and allow to dry finally in air. Safranin is described as a counterstain. It is used after the crystal violet to stain any Gram negative bacteria red.

(7) Apply a drop of immersion oil and examine under the oil immersion lens (section 5.11.2).

Results

Are your observations in agreement with the description given in section 12.9.1 of the bacterial content of milk?

Experiment 12.3: To compare the numbers of bacteria present in fresh and stale milk

If a single bacterium is placed on nutrient agar it will grow to form a colony which is easily seen with the naked eye, unlike the original bacterium. This can be made use of when counting bacteria.

After sterilising the apparatus, the first part of the experiment involves the technique of serial dilution. The numbers of bacteria in milk are vast, so counting can be made more manageable by diluting by a known factor and taking a small sample of known volume. A series of dilutions is prepared. In the second part of the experiment samples of each dilution are cultured and the one giving the most suitable number of colonies (a reasonably large number but with no overlap of colonies) when grown on agar is used to calculate the number of bacteria in a given volume of milk.

Materials

6 sterile nutrient agar plates
8 1 cm^3 graduated pipettes
10 cm^3 graduated pipette
6 test-tubes and test-tube rack
cotton wool
oven at 160 °C
indelible marker
bunsen burner
100 cm^3 distilled water
fresh milk
stale milk
70% alcohol
aluminium foil
glass spreader

Sterilisation of apparatus

(1) Place cotton wool plugs in each of six test-tubes and cover plugs loosely with aluminium foil.
(2) Place a small piece of cotton wool in the top of each of eight 1 cm^3 graduated pipettes and the 10 cm^3 graduated pipette and wrap each pipette separately in aluminium foil.
(3) Place the test-tubes and pipettes in a hot air oven at 160 °C for 60 min (bottles of media and water should not be sterilised in an oven).
(4) Allow all apparatus to cool before use.

Serial dilution of milk and inoculation of agar plates

(1) Label the six sterile plugged test-tubes F1, F2, F3, S1, S2 and S3, and remove the aluminium foil covers from the plugs.
(2) Label the base of each of six sterile nutrient agar plates F1, F2, F3, S1, S2 and S3.
(3) Transfer 9.9 cm^3 of sterile distilled water to each of the six test-tubes using the following technique.
   (*a*) Remove the cotton wool plug from the flask containing sterile distilled water using the little finger and fourth finger of one hand.
   (*b*) Whilst holding the plug, draw up 9.9 cm^3 of water using the sterile 10 cm^3 graduated pipette held in the other hand.
   (*c*) Replace the plug.
   (*d*) Remove the plug from the first test-tube using the same method as in (*a*).
   (*e*) Transfer 9.9 cm^3 of water to the test-tube.
   (*f*) Replace the plug.
   (*g*) Repeat for the five remaining test-tubes.

(4) Shake the sample of fresh milk and transfer 0.1 cm^3 of this milk using a sterile 1 cm^3 pipette to tube F1, removing and replacing the plug as before. This gives a ×100 dilution.

(5) Shake the tube gently to ensure thorough mixing.

(6) Using a fresh pipette, transfer 0.1 cm^3 from tube F1 to the sterile plate labelled F1, lifting the lid by a minimal amount.

(7) Dip the glass spreader in 70% alcohol, allow excess alcohol to drip off and then hold the spreader vertically in a bunsen burner flame.

(8) Cool the spreader and spread the sample milk over the surface of the plate.

(9) Re-sterilise the spreader.

(10) Using the same pipette as in point (6), transfer 0.1 cm^3 from tube F1 to tube F2, removing and replacing the bungs as before.

(11) Shake the tube F2 to ensure thorough mixing. This gives a ×10 000 dilution.

(12) Repeat from (10)–(11), using F3 for F2. This gives a ×1 000 000 dilution. Repeat (6)–(9) using F3 for F1.

(13) Repeat the serial dilution technique using the sample of stale milk and prepare plates S1, S2 and S3.

(15) Incubate the six plates upside down at 35 °C for about three days.

(16) The lids of the plates should then be taped down to avoid the risk of pathogens being spread.

(17) Examine the plates for bacterial growth. Count the numbers of individual colonies where practical. Record results in the form of a table and use them to calculate the number of bacteria in 1 cm^3 of undiluted milk.

Notes

See notes (3) and (4) at the end of experiment 12.1.

12.9.3　Practical work with fungi

The methods for handling fungi are in many cases the same as those for bacteria, being standard microbiological techniques. Many saprotrophic fungi, like bacteria, can be cultured on nutrient agar and, if pure cultures are required, the sterile techniques described in sections 12.3 and 12.4 should be used. Common fungi suitable for culture in this way are *Mucor*, *Rhizopus* and *Penicillium*. A suitable culture medium is a 2% malt agar prepared in petri dishes. Selected fungi can be isolated from mixed cultures grown by chance contamination of substrates such as bread, fruit and other moist foods. Spores can be transferred and added to the culture medium by a sterile mounted needle. Cultures can be conveniently examined with low power stereoscopic microscopes.

12.10　Large scale production

You have read about, and may have attempted, some of the practical aspects of working with microorganisms in the previous sections. Moving from a laboratory scale to an industrial scale presents new problems for biotechnologists. The problems may involve any area of science, including engineering, chemistry and biology. Economic, social and sometimes ethical issues also start to be important factors in decision-making. In this section we shall consider some of the practical aspects of large-scale production before looking at specific examples and related issues in later sections.

Microorganisms are particularly suitable for industrial processes for the following reasons:

- they have simple nutritional requirements;
- growth conditions can be controlled very precisely in fermenters (large vessels in which the microorganisms are grown);
- they have fast growth rates;
- reactions can be carried out at lower temperatures than conventional industrial procedures – energy costs are therefore lower;
- they produce higher yields and have higher specificity than conventional processes;
- a wide range of chemicals can be used and produced;
- some complex chemicals, such as hormones and antibiotics, can be manufactured which are difficult to produce by other methods, and specific isomers (such as L-amino acids) can be produced;
- the genetics of microorganisms are relatively simple and techniques for genetic manipulation are continually advancing.

However, there are specialist techniques, such as aseptic techniques and complex methods of separation, which can make the process more technically demanding.

12.10.1　An overview

Fig 12.13 is a flow diagram showing some of the key stages which are typically involved in setting up a biotechnological process.

12.10.2　Screening

We know that microorganisms show great diversity in the chemical reactions they carry out and the products they can form. However, only a tiny fraction of their potential has been exploited. There is a constant search for potentially useful microorganisms, particularly by commercial companies such as drugs companies. Microorganisms are cultured from all over the world, and from many different environments, in the hope of discovering new commercially useful products or more efficient means of producing existing products. Very often

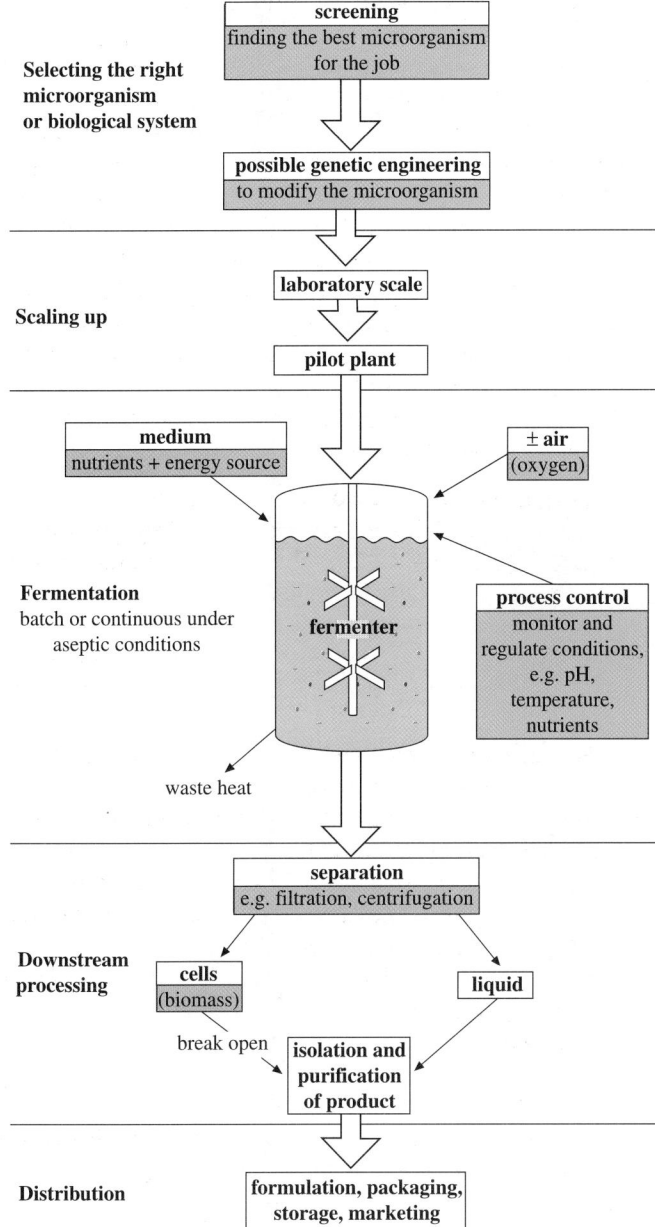

Fig 12.13 *Overview of a biotechnological process.*

Antibiotics are used to treat bacterial or fungal diseases of humans and domesticated animals. Some also inhibit growth of cancer. They appear to be products of secondary metabolism (section 12.5.3). With systematic screening there is always the hope of finding a new 'wonder-drug' or a microorganism which will improve on the performance of one currently in use.

12.10.3 Scaling up

Any new biotechnological manufacturing process must first be tried out on a laboratory scale. After initial investigations using ordinary laboratory apparatus it is usual to make a 'pilot plant'. This involves use of a relatively small fermenter, anything from 2 to 200 dm³ (fig 12.14). The **fermenter** is the tank or vessel in which the process will be carried out. Optimum nutrient and physical conditions for maximum yields must be determined.

New factors come into play when the process has to be scaled up from pilot production to full-scale, involving thousands of dm³ (fig 12.15). Sometimes a successful transition is not possible. Some of the important factors are as follows.

- A major problem is maintaining aseptic conditions. It is easy to contaminate both inputs and outputs to the main fermenter. Engineering techniques have improved with experience and a good example of success with aseptic technique was the manufacture of Pruteen (section 12.12.3).
- Physical factors, such as mixing and aerating the media and getting rid of waste heat, create the biggest problems in moving from one scale to another. Chemical engineers are needed to solve these problems. Some of these problems are discussed below.
- To supply enough oxygen in large-scale cultures, air must be forced through the medium because the simple agitation used at the laboratory scale is inadequate. Small bubbles are more effective than large bubbles, so a **sparger** is used (a tube with small holes). The mixture may also be stirred. **Baffles** in the vessel walls increase turbulence and improve the efficiency with which bubbles dissolve in the medium since they take longer to reach the top of the fermenter.
- Anti-foaming agents are required to reduce the foaming caused by stirring and aeration.
- Heat is produced by the activity of microorganisms and large-scale production. Cooling water must be circulated around the fermenter.
- It is more difficult to keep conditions constant, such as supply of nutrients, pH and oxygen concentration, throughout the medium on a large scale. Sophisticated monitoring devices and control processes are needed. Overcoming these difficulties, for example by stirring the medium, may have other undesirable consequences such as affecting the distribution of organisms in the culture. In the manufacture of Pruteen, for example, the

this work is purely empirical, meaning that chance plays a large part in any discovery. Testing microorganisms in this way is known as **screening**. A good example is the constant screening that takes place for new antibiotics. The first antibiotic was discovered in 1928 by Alexander Fleming and named penicillin after the fungus that produces it, *Penicillium*. Natural antibiotics are chemicals which are made by microorganisms and which kill or inhibit the growth of other microorganisms. Since 1928 more than 5000 different antibiotics have been isolated from microorganisms, including a range of different penicillins with slightly different structures and activities. Most of the antibiotics discovered are unsuitable for medical use, mainly because they are too toxic. However, *Streptomyces* species have been a particularly rich source of different antibiotics, including streptomycin.

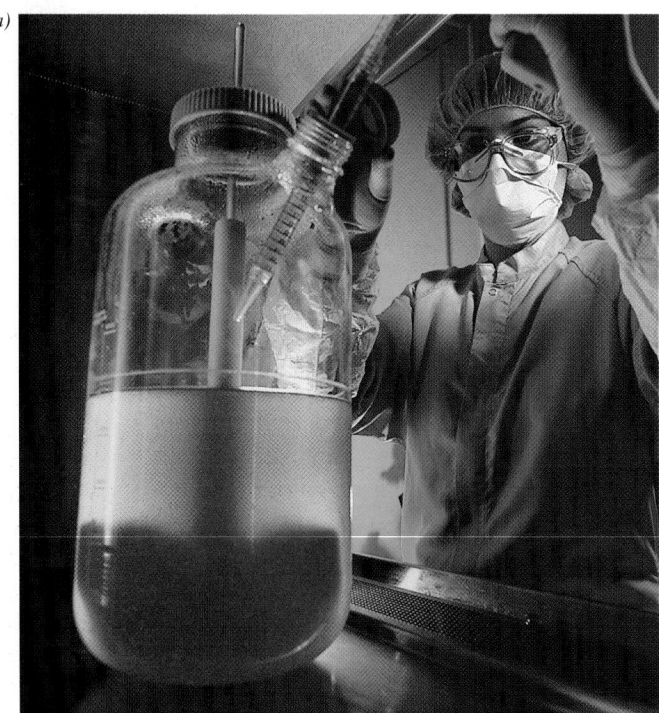

Fig 12.15 *A large-scale fermenter (2000 dm³) used in commercial production of monoclonal antibodies.*

- Microorganisms may change their metabolism according to conditions, and precise control of conditions is much more difficult on a large scale. Any small changes in the product may have harmful effects on people or animals using it.

- The more complex the equipment and procedures, the more opportunity there is for faults or accidents to occur. These may have economically disastrous consequences and have to be considered when deciding whether the operation is economically worthwhile.

- Large quantities of water must be supplied, sterilised and disposed of.

- Because of the large quantities involved, raw materials should be readily available, stable, and easy to handle and store. Chemical changes and microbial contamination of stored material must be minimal. They must be economic because cost is a major concern.

- Sometimes the strains of microorganisms selected for use in fermentation processes can easily revert by mutation to lower yielding strains which grow more rapidly. This is more likely as the scale of manufacture increases.

- Handling powders in bulk can be a health hazard to workers.

- Materials used in construction of the fermenter must be corrosion-resistant, to prevent traces of metal contamination. They should also be non-toxic to microorganisms and must be able to resist repeated sterilisation with high pressure steam.

- Extra hazards are posed by large-scale fermentation, especially of genetically modified organisms. These are due to the scale of the operation and the opportunity for a greater degree of exposure to an organism and its biologically active products compared to laboratory scale work.

Fig 12.14 *(a) Start-up flask of mammalian cell culture used for the commercial production of monoclonal antibodies. The hybridoma cells formed in the flask are later multiplied in fermenters to produce the antibodies. (b) Pilot-scale commercial fermentation unit in a biotechnology laboratory.*

yields originally obtained were significantly lower than predicted from the laboratory and pilot plant scales. It was discovered that because the methanol, which was the only carbon and energy source, was being added at one point only, the circulating bacteria were going through successive 'feast and famine' periods as they rotated once every several minutes. Yields were raised to those predicted by adding the methanol at various points around the fermenter.

12.10.4 Fermenter design and use

Fermenters, also known as **bioreactors**, are chambers in which microorganisms are cultured in a liquid or solid medium. The processes which take place in fermenters are referred to as **fermentations**. The term fermentation originally applied only to anaerobic processes but is now used more broadly to include all the processes, whether aerobic or anaerobic. Fig 12.16 shows a typical fermenter. It is a complex diagram so you will need to spend some time studying the different parts. Bear in mind the list of scale-up problems identified in the previous section. The contents of most fermenters are stirred during operation, but this is not always the case, as with the now discontinued production of the single cell protein Pruteen by ICI, where air introduced at high velocity at the bottom of the vessel was used to achieve mixing. The **product** is either the cells themselves (biomass) or some useful cell product. *All* operations must be carried out under sterile conditions to avoid contamination of the culture. In addition, it must be possible to keep all inlets and outlets of the fermenter sterile. The fermenter and the medium used are sterilised before use, either together or separately. Stock cultures of the organism to be used in the fermentation are kept in an inactive form (for example stored frozen). A sample is re-activated, grown up to sufficient bulk using aseptic techniques (**scale-up**), and then added to the fermenter, a process known as **inoculation**. Once inside the fermenter, the organism grows and multiplies, using the nutrient medium.

The fermenter is usually made of high grade stainless steel so that it does not corrode and leak toxic metal salts into the medium. All equipment, materials and air used must be sterile. Equipment is sterilised by steam under pressure. All surfaces must be accessible to the steam and as smooth and polished as possible to avoid cracks or rough surfaces where microorganisms can collect. The medium may be sterilised before inoculation by passing steam through the cooling coils. Air is sterilised by filtration.

For safety reasons air leaving the fermenter may also need to be sterilised, for example to prevent escape of genetically engineered microorganisms.

12.10.5 Batch, fed-batch and continuous culture

Two basic types of fermentation are possible, **batch fermentation** (or **closed system**) and **continuous culture** (or **open system**). In the more common batch fermentation the conditions are set up and not changed from outside once the fermentation starts; for example, no more nutrients are added. This is why the process is described as a closed system. The process is stopped once sufficient product has been formed. The contents of the fermenter are then removed, the product isolated, the microorganism discarded and the fermenter is cleaned and set up for a fresh batch.

Continuous culture involves continuous long-term operation over many weeks, during which nutrient medium is added as fast as it is used, and the overflow is harvested. Although this is closer to the situation in natural environments, such as the gut, continuous culture has found only limited application. However, it is used for the production of single cell protein where a large biomass of cells is required. ICI, for example, used to produce the single cell bacterial protein (SCP) Pruteen from the bacterium *Methylophilus methylotrophus* (section 12.12.3). The fermenter was run continuously for as long as 100 days and could produce 150 tonnes per day.

Although continuous culture is still not commonly used, increasing use is being made of **'fed-batch' culture**. This is a compromise between the two systems. With fed-batch culture more control of the process is involved than with batch culture. The period of growth is extended by adding nutrients at low concentrations during the fermentation, and not adding all the nutrients at the beginning. One advantage of this is that the rate of growth can be regulated to keep pace with the rate at which oxygen can be supplied. The process is commonly used to produce yeast cells for the baking industry. If the yeast has too much sugar it starts to respire anaerobically and produce alcohol at the expense of biomass. The process is also used in the production of penicillin (section 12.11.1).

The advantages and disadvantages of batch and continuous culture are summarised in table 12.4.

12.10.6 Downstream processing

Downstream processing is the name given to the stage after fermentation when the desired product is recovered and purified. Usually the contents of the fermenter are first separated into a liquid component and a solid component which contains the cells. This is usually done by filtration or centrifugation. The liquid may contain the desired product in solution or it may be the cells or some product inside the cells that is needed.

A whole range of biochemical separation and purification techniques is available, such as drying, chromatography, solvent extraction and distillation. As an indication of the importance of downstream processing, it involves over 90% of the 200 staff employed by Eli Lilly in their human insulin plant. The techniques used in downstream processing during the production of penicillin and mycoprotein are considered later in sections 12.11.1 and 12.12.3 respectively.

12.11 Medical products

One of the most economically successful ways of using the technology of large-scale fermentation is to manufacture medical products. Such products are effective in relatively small amounts and command relatively high prices. There is the additional advantage of an obvious

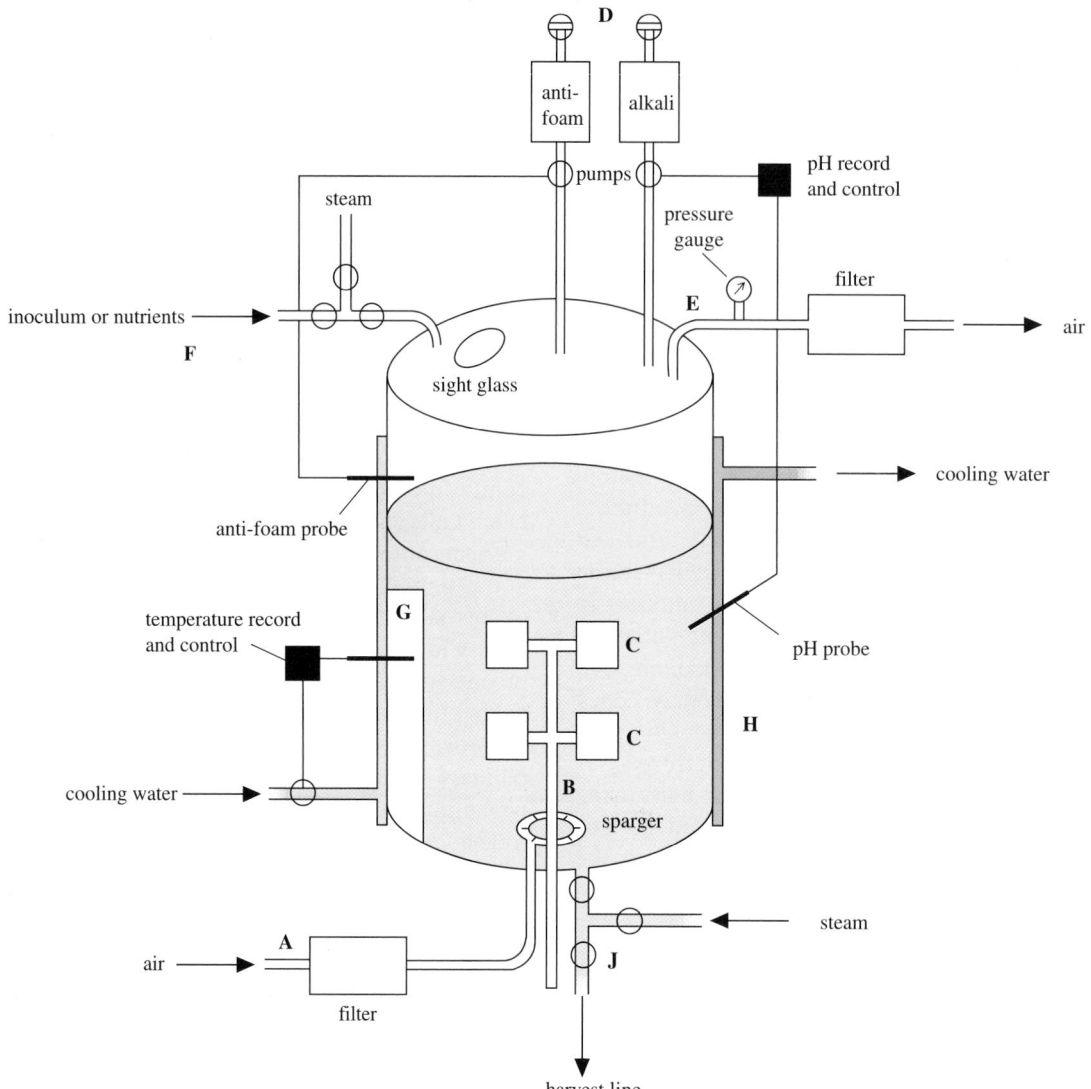

Fig 12.16 *A typical fermenter. Size of vessel is very variable, ranging from 1 dm³ (experimental) to 500 000 dm³ (commercial production). Shape and material used in construction are also variable, although cylindrical stainless steel vessels are common.*

Key:

A Air inlet – most fermentations are aerobic, requiring large volumes of sterile air. The sparger is a specially designed part that releases air bubbles to help the mixing process, provide oxygen for aerobic respiration and aid release of volatile waste products.

B Stirrer shaft – present in most fermenters. Agitation increases the rate at which oxygen dissolves; maintains diffusion gradients of oxygen and nutrients into cells and products out of cells; prevents clumping of cells or mycelia of fungi; promotes heat exchange between medium and cooling surfaces. Shaft bearings must be strong and sterile.

C Stirrer paddles – usually flat and vertical.

D Alkali and anti-foam inlets - these are connected to pH and anti-foam probes which monitor the contents of the fermenter. Aeration and agitation generate foam, particularly from proteins, and prevent escape of contents through the exhaust. When foam touches the anti-foam probe, it completes an electrical circuit which activates a pump connected to a supply of anti-foaming agent. Other probes are connected by electrical circuits to other 'effectors'. Alkali is added if (as is usual) acidity increases during fermentation, so that pH is kept constant.

E Exhaust – contents of fermenter are under pressure, so a pressure gauge and safety valve are attached.

F Top of fermenter has a part where medium and inoculum (microorganism) can be added, and which gives access for cleaning.

G Baffle – vertical fin on inside wall, helps to increase agitation and reduce swirling of contents as culture is rotated. This improves efficiency of oxygen transfer.

H Cooling jacket – reduces temperature because the culture generates heat during growth.

J Harvest – samples may be taken here during fermentation so that the process can be monitored.

Table 12.4 Advantages and disadvantages of batch and continuous culture.

	Advantages	*Disadvantages*
Batch culture	Suitable for production of secondary metabolites whose production is not associated with growth, e.g. antibiotics. Can use strains which are too unstable for continuous culture. Easier to set up and run than continuous culture. Fermenters are less specialised and may be used for a greater variety of processes, depending on demand.	Turnaround time between batches can be prolonged, wasting possible production time. Environment changes in the fermenter as the fermentation progresses. Nutrients get used up and products build up. Heat output, acid or alkali production, oxygen consumption increase in rate as growth progresses. Therefore, conditions gradually become unfavourable and growth rate gradually declines. See graph fig 12.8.
Continuous culture	Gives more control. Aim is to keep environmental conditions constant. Nutrients are replaced as fast as they are used and products are removed as fast as they are made. Productivity is greater because there is no turnaround time (continuous process). Therefore more cost effective in some situations. Optimum (maximum or exponential) growth rate is maintained once achieved. Smaller fermenters are needed because higher yields are obtained. More suitable for production of biomass. Also used for production of ethanol whose synthesis is proportional to rate of growth. Demand for labour is more regular.	Greater risk of contamination, although good engineering design can solve this problem. Control is more complex. When used for brewing gives greater yields but has given flavour problems.

social benefit. Some of the most successful products are considered in the following sections.

12.11.1 Penicillin production

Production of the antibiotic penicillin is a good example of the use of fed-batch culture for the production of a secondary metabolite.

> **12.9** What is meant by (*a*) antibiotic, (*b*) fed-batch culture, (*c*) secondary metabolite?

Since its discovery in 1928 (see section 12.10.2) penicillin has probably saved millions of lives. It was first used on a large scale during the Second World War where it was mainly used to cure troops suffering from the sexually transmitted disease gonorrhoea. Its use against more life-threatening diseases, such as pneumonia, followed when sufficient supplies were available. The death rate from pneumonia was about 30% before its use. Penicillin acts by inhibiting cell wall synthesis in some bacteria, particularly Gram positive bacteria (section 2.5.1, cell wall). Only growing cells are killed. Some bacteria contain plasmids which make them resistant to penicillin (section 2.5.1, plasmids). There are now several hundred penicillins, all with the same basic structure but with different side chains

on the molecule. Some are synthetic, some semi-synthetic and some are natural. They have different specifications, in other words they vary in their effectiveness against different bacteria. This provides the incentive for looking for alternative forms of the antibiotic.

The original screening process for a suitable strain of the fungus *Penicillium*, from which penicillin is obtained, was carried out at the beginning of the Second World War in the USA, although Fleming discovered penicillin in England (in *Penicillium notatum*). The search was started by a scientist from Oxford University, Sir Howard Florey, who was helped by the greater resources of the Americans. Cultures and soil samples from all round the world were tested, but the highest yields were obtained from a strain of *Penicillium chrysogenum* found growing on a mouldy melon purchased locally. Since then yields have increased about 2000-fold due to selection of high-yielding mutant strains and better culturing, extraction and purification techniques.

The composition of the medium used in the fermentation is critical. The preferred carbon source now is glucose. Glucose promotes growth but tends to inhibit production of the enzymes needed for penicillin synthesis. It is usual, therefore, to stimulate rapid growth of the fungus for the first 30 to 40 hours, and then to add glucose at low concentrations, either in regular doses, or as a continuous feed (hence it is a fed-batch culture). Nitrogen is supplied in the form of a cheap protein such as soyabean flour or fishmeal. Other nutrients added are phosphate, calcium carbonate and phenylacetic acid which increases yields because it is used to help make the penicillin molecule. Since penicillin is a secondary metabolite, its production starts after the initial rapid growth phase. The primary metabolites of the first phase of growth include carbon dioxide and ethanol from respiration.

The culture is started from spores of the fungus. About 3–5 tonnes of mycelium is eventually used to inoculate a $50\,000\,dm^3$ fermenter. Fermenters up to $200\,000\,dm^3$ have been built for penicillin production because the demand is so huge. About half a tonne of glucose is used per day. Production is very sensitive to temperature, which can rise by as much as $2\,°C$ per hour, so temperature is very carefully controlled. pH is also carefully controlled between 6.5 and 7.0. The process is allowed to run for up to 15 days.

Downstream processing involves removal of the mycelium by filtration. The penicillin remains behind in solution in the liquid part of the medium. It is extracted by a series of solvents. With each extraction some of the impurities are removed, so the penicillin gets more and more pure until it is left dissolved in water in a pure state. The water is then removed by vacuum evaporation and the penicillin crystallises as a sodium or potassium salt (penicillin itself is a weak acid).

12.11.2 Monoclonal antibodies

Humans have an immune system which is able to respond to the invasion of certain foreign molecules by making antibodies (chapter 14). Molecules which stimulate the formation of antibodies are called **antigens**. They are usually proteins or glycoproteins. Each antigen stimulates the production of a specific antibody which matches it exactly and is able to combine with it and bring about its destruction. Thus if, for example, the body is invaded by a particular type of bacterium, the antigens in the cell surface membranes of the bacterial cells will be recognised as foreign by the immune system, and antibodies specific to those antigens will be made. Antibodies are made by special lymphocytes (a type of white blood cell) called B cells.

In the 1970s César Milstein and Georges Köhler working in Cambridge, were looking for a way to make pure antibodies of one type only. Up to that time antibodies were prepared from the blood of animals that had been deliberately exposed to the relevant antigen. However, the final product was still impure and contained hundreds of different antibodies. Milstein and Köhler solved the problem by developing a technique for producing monoclonal antibodies, work for which they were awarded the Nobel prize in 1984. **Monoclonal** means belonging to one clone. Each type of antibody is made by one type of B cell which clones itself, in other words multiplies to make many identical copies of itself, in response to a particular antigen. In theory, if a particular type of B cell could be isolated and cultured, large quantities of a single pure antibody could be collected. Since antibodies produced in this way are all from one clone, they are described as monoclonal. However, B cells survive only a few days in a culture medium. Milstein and Köhler solved this problem by fusing B cells with cancer cells, which are immortal, to form **hybridoma cells**. The hybridoma cells continue to multiply and can be cloned so that large quantities of antibody can be produced.

Production of monoclonal antibodies

The relevant antigen is injected into an experimental animal, usually a mouse. After allowing time for an immune response to take place, lymphocytes are removed from the spleen of the animal and mixed with a special type of cancer cell in a suitable culture medium. Fusion of some of the lymphocytes with the cancer cells is stimulated by adding polyethylene glycol to the medium. Conditions are arranged so that only hybridised cells will survive. It is then possible to select the ones making the relevant antibodies from all the others, and to culture these separately. The cells continue to multiply indefinitely and are a constant source of pure antibody.

Uses of monoclonal antibodies

Monoclonal antibodies are specific for a particular antigen. They can be used to 'find' or identify that antigen and possibly to destroy it. A large number of applications have been found and are being developed. So far, they are used mainly for diagnostic purposes.

Pregnancy testing. Nearly one-third of the 150 diagnostic monoclonal antibodies currently in use are for pregnancy testing. As soon as the embryo reaches the uterus (within four days of conception) it begins to grow into the wall of the uterus, a process called **implantation**. It is vital that the embryo sends a signal to the woman's ovaries at this stage so that they can respond appropriately. If the signal is received, the ovaries continue to produce the hormones that maintain the lining of the uterus, and the woman will not have a period and lose the embryo. The signal to the ovaries is a hormone produced by finger-like extensions of the chorion, a layer of cells which grows out from the embryo into the uterus wall. The name of the hormone is human chorionic gonadotrophin (HCG for short – chapter 21). It circulates in the mother's blood to reach the ovaries. By the time her period should normally have started (about 14 days after conception) HCG has built up to a high enough level to be detectable in the urine. It is a glycoprotein, so monoclonal antibodies can be produced against it by the method described above. Modern pregnancy tests work by detecting HCG in a sample of the woman's urine using these monoclonal antibodies. The procedure is described in fig 12.17. The kit can be bought in chemists for testing at home and gives a result in five minutes. Even earlier detection of pregnancy is possible if a doctor tests the blood.

Fig 12.17 *Use of home pregnancy kit.*

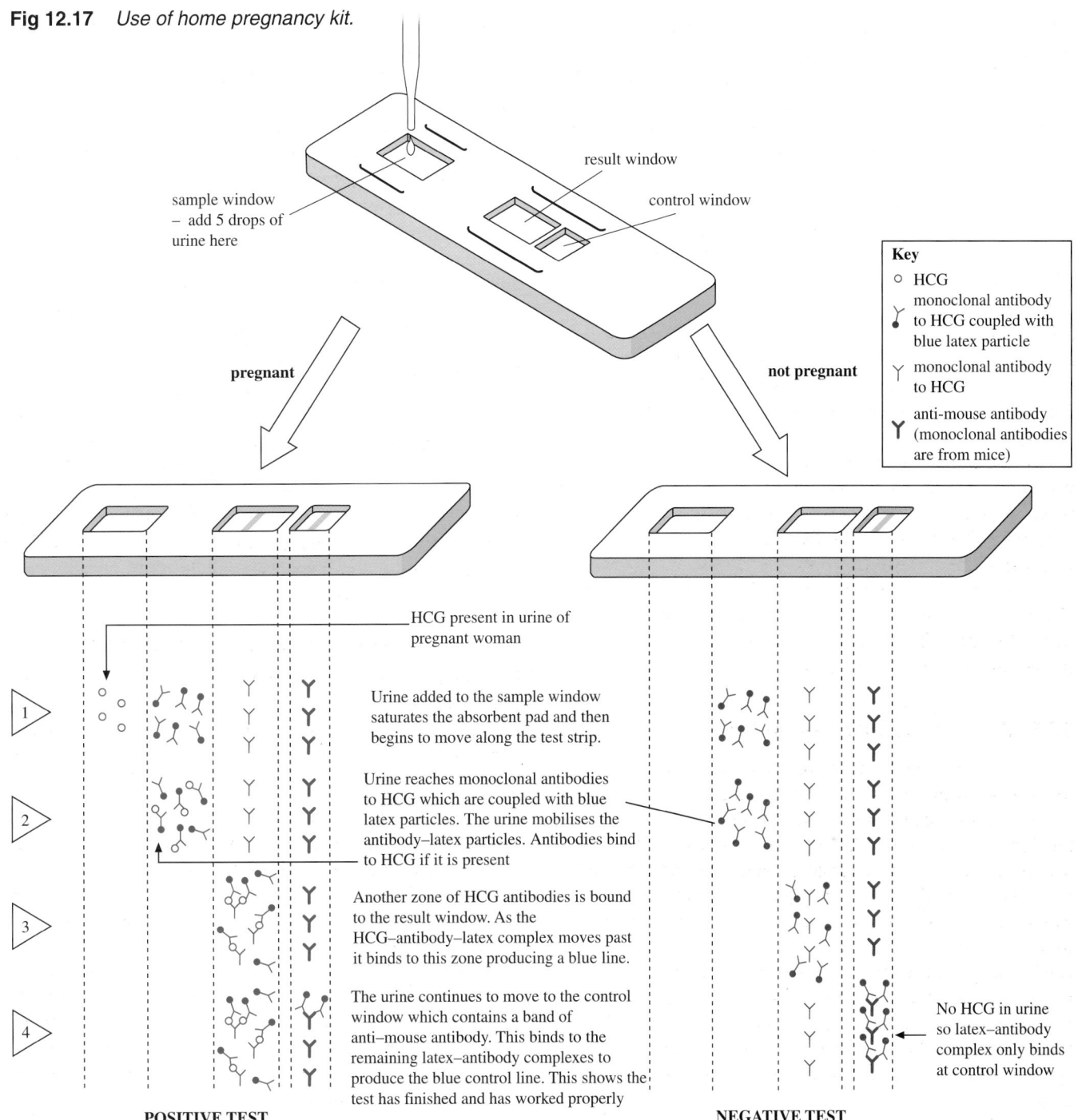

result window

control window

sample window
– add 5 drops of
urine here

Key
○ HCG

Y monoclonal antibody
to HCG coupled with
blue latex particle

Y monoclonal antibody
to HCG

Y anti-mouse antibody
(monoclonal antibodies
are from mice)

pregnant

not pregnant

HCG present in urine of
pregnant woman

1 Urine added to the sample window
saturates the absorbent pad and then
begins to move along the test strip.

2 Urine reaches monoclonal antibodies
to HCG which are coupled with blue
latex particles. The urine mobilises the
antibody–latex particles. Antibodies bind
to HCG if it is present

3 Another zone of HCG antibodies is bound
to the result window. As the
HCG–antibody–latex complex moves past
it binds to this zone producing a blue line.

4 The urine continues to move to the control
window which contains a band of
anti–mouse antibody. This binds to the
remaining latex–antibody complexes to
produce the blue control line. This shows the
test has finished and has worked properly

No HCG in urine
so latex–antibody
complex only binds
at control window

POSITIVE TEST

NEGATIVE TEST

12.10 Suggest three advantages of
being able to conduct a pregnancy test at home.

Diagnosis of disease. One of the most
common sexually transmitted diseases (STD) is *Chlamydia*.
It is a small Gram negative bacterium which is unusual in
that it grows inside cells. Symptoms of infection are very
mild and are sometimes hard to distinguish from
gonorrhoea, another common STD. Both diseases can
cause pelvic inflammatory disease in women if they spread
through the uterus and into the Fallopian tubes. This causes
pain and discomfort and may cause infertility. *Chlamydia*
was particularly difficult to diagnose until monoclonal
antibodies became available. Use of monoclonals has made
tests for both diseases much more rapid and reliable.
Results can be obtained within 15–20 minutes rather than
involving laborious procedures in hospitals which take
several days.

Another use of monoclonal antibodies is in a diagnostic
kit for streptococcal throat infections, which is available for
use by local doctors, enabling immediate diagnosis and
treatment. This might previously have had to wait several
days for tests to be completed in a hospital laboratory.

Monoclonal antibodies have also been developed that can distinguish between the closely related herpes virus 1, which causes cold sores on the lips, and herpes virus 2, which causes genital infections. About 10–20% of these genital infections, however, are caused by herpes virus 1. Since the recommended treatment differs for the two viruses, it is important to distinguish between them. Again, the test takes only about 15–20 minutes.

One exciting aspect of diagnosis with monoclonal antibodies is the research being carried out to try to detect cancers much earlier than is now possible. Leukaemias and lymphomas are both cancers of white blood cells (lymphocytes) which are sometimes difficult to distinguish between. Early precise diagnosis with monoclonals which recognise the different antigens on these cells is now becoming possible. The importance of this is that early treatment of cancer greatly increases the chances of survival.

Work is also proceeding on early diagnosis of the most common cancers such as lung, breast, colon and rectal cancers. At present, samples of body fluids such as blood and fluids from around the lungs are tested most frequently. However, techniques for identifying directly tumours inside the body are also being developed. One method is to add a radioactive isotope, such as iodine-131, to a monoclonal antibody which is specific for an antigen associated with a cancer cell. The antibody will seek out these antigens in the body and accumulate at cells possessing them. The location of these cells can then be detected from outside the body using special equipment sensitive to the radiation from the isotope. Eventually such targetting may be used in treating the cancer because the radiation could be used to kill the cancer cells (see below).

Treatment of disease – magic bullets. It is hoped that eventually monoclonal antibodies will be able to be used in the *treatment* of disease, not just in its diagnosis. The way they seek out and attach themselves to specific targets such as cancer cells has led to their being called 'magic bullets'. If a radioactive isotope or a toxic drug is attached to the antibody, the hope is that this would destroy the target cell. One problem is that the antigens most characteristic of cancer cells are also found on some normal cells, so these would also be killed. Another is that the antibody attaches to the *surface* of the cancer cell but does not enter it to deliver the toxin. However, some progress is being made on this work.

Preventing rejection of transplants. The main problem with transplants is that the body's immune system recognises the new organ as foreign and attacks it. One way around this problem is to try to suppress the immune system of the patient. A monoclonal antibody has been developed which is very effective at preventing rejection of transplanted kidneys. It reacts with an antigen found on all T cells. T cells are a type of lymphocyte which normally attack virus-infected cells and cancer-causing cells. However, they are also involved in the rejection of transplanted organs (chapter 14). A monoclonal antibody is more effective than the usual drugs which are used to suppress the immune system. It also only suppresses the T cells rather than the whole immune system which the drugs affect, leaving the patient with more protection against disease.

Tissue typing for transplants. To reduce the risk of rejection, before carrying out a transplant, a donor who is as compatible as possible must be found. This means that the donor's antigens must be as close a match as possible to those of the recipient. The more unlike the antigens are, the greater the chance of rejection. Monoclonal antibodies can be used to find out the types of antigens present in the donor and increase the accuracy of matching.

12.11.3 Insulin and human growth hormone

Both these products can now be produced from genetically engineered bacteria. Although genetic engineering can be regarded as a branch of biotechnology, it is dealt with in chapter 25 with other applications of genetics. Insulin and human growth hormone are discussed in chapter 25.

12.12 Food and drink

Some of the oldest biotechnologies are concerned with the making of foods and drinks. The making of bread, cheese, yogurt, vinegar and alcoholic drinks, such as beer and wine, date back thousands of years to prehistoric times. There are many references to wine in the Old Testament of the Bible, the Romans drank beer and wine, and as long ago as 4000 BC the ancient Egyptians are known to have made beer and used wild yeasts to raise dough in the making of bread. By some definitions, the breeding of animals and plants for food can also be regarded as biotechnology, and agriculture dates back more than 10 000 years.

In this section we shall not only be looking at modern approaches to some of these old technologies but also at some of the newer methods for producing food.

12.12.1 Yeast fermentation – bread, beer and wine

Yeast is a unicellular fungus. Wild yeasts are common and it is not difficult to imagine how the raising of dough and the fermentation of sugars to produce alcohol could have been discovered, even though the actual cause of the process could not have been understood. It was Louis Pasteur, in the nineteenth century, who first showed that fermentation was due to the activity of microorganisms.

Bread

Bread is made from flour obtained by grinding cereal grain, usually wheat. The flour is mainly starch (the white part of the grain), which is part of the food store normally used at germination of the grain. Enzymes present in the grain partially digest the starch to sugars like maltose and glucose. Amylases from fungi, which digest starch, can be added to increase the sugar content. Yeast uses sugars as a source of energy in respiration. Both aerobic and anaerobic respiration result in production of carbon dioxide gas. When making bread, bubbles of the gas are trapped inside the warm dough causing it to rise. This stage is called **proving**. Strains of the yeast *Saccharomyces cerevisiae* are selected for their high production of carbon dioxide. Alcohol is also a product of anaerobic respiration but this evaporates during the baking process that follows proving.

Beer

The oldest fermentation industry is that of brewing. Beer is brewed from barley grain which has been partially germinated to convert its starch store to sugars such as maltose, a process known as **malting**. Gibberellins are used to speed up this process and to control it more precisely (chapter 16). Also, more enzymes, such as amylase, are sometimes added to increase the amount of sugar produced. This in turn leads to more alcohol being produced. Nitrogen is also present from the digestion of proteins.

The grain is then killed by slow roasting to about 80 °C, although 'malts' for lager production are roasted at lower temperatures. The exact conditions affect flavour and colour. The grain is then crushed between rollers and added to hot water to extract the sugars. The liquid obtained is called **wort**. Hops are added for their bitter flavour and antimicrobial properties. The mash is boiled to concentrate it and the hops are removed before cooling the mash to a suitable temperature for fermentation. It is added to a large batch fermenter where it is inoculated with brewer's yeast, usually from a previous batch (fig 12.18). Two commonly used species are *Saccharomyces cerevisiae* and *Saccharomyces carlsbergensis*. The latter is used to make lager. Fermentation is anaerobic. During this process sugar is converted to alcohol and carbon dioxide as in baking. After 2–5 days, the alcohol reaches a final concentration of 3.5–8% (mostly 3.5–5%). Traditionally, lager yeasts grow at the bottom of the fermenter and are called **bottom fermenters**, whereas beer yeasts float at the top and are called **top fermenters**. However, newer types of beer yeast are bottom fermenters, enabling the same type of fermenter to be used for both processes. After fermentation the beer is separated from the yeast.

Wine

The source of sugar for the fermentation, which lasts several days, is grapes. Different grape varieties and different yeasts are responsible for the different flavours of wines. Red wines get their colour from the skin of the grapes used. White wines are made from grapes which have usually had their skins removed. Commercially selected strains of yeast are now used in preference to wild yeasts because they are more reliable. Fermentation starts when

Fig 12.18 *Reading the temperature of a brew of beer in a brewery.*

the grapes are crushed to form the 'must'. A second fermentation by lactic acid bacteria may take place during which malic acid is converted to lactic acid and carbon dioxide. This reduces the acidity of the wine.

12.12.2 Lactic acid fermentation – dairy products

A range of products, known as dairy products, can be made by the fermentation of milk. Milk contains lactic acid bacteria which break down lactose, the sugar found in milk, to lactic acid during anaerobic respiration. These bacteria may be killed during pasteurisation, so it is usual to add them back again if fermentation is to be carried out. Different products are obtained depending on the conditions under which fermentation takes place, the additives used and the exact composition and source of the milk. Final textures and flavours are very variable, as can be seen from the range of products which include all the cheeses, butter, yogurt, sour cream and fromage frais (fig 12.19).

Yogurt

Unlike cheese, which is made from part of the milk (see below), yogurt is made by fermenting the whole milk. Originally it was thinner and more acidic, but in western countries it has been modified to suit national tastes. Since it is already acidic (pH 3.7–4.3), fruits can be added for flavour.

A variety of milks may be used, either alone or mixed, including whole, semi-skimmed, skimmed, evaporated and dried milks. Each combination will give a particular type of yogurt. Low-fat varieties have become increasingly popular. A flow diagram of the manufacturing process is shown in fig 12.20.

Fig 12.19 *Range of dairy products.*

All milk in the UK is heat treated (pasteurised), usually at 72 °C for 15 seconds. This is needed to destroy any pathogenic (disease-causing) microorganisms. These are not commonly present, but milk is an ideal medium for the growth of microorganisms and contamination by harmful bacteria such as *Salmonella*, or fungi, is always a possibility. In addition, some bacteria which are not harmful nevertheless affect the quality of milk if allowed to grow in it. Extra heat treatment is required for yogurt manufacture for the reasons shown in fig 12.20. In order to replace the lactic acid bacteria killed by the heat, a 'starter culture' is added. This is a culture of selected bacteria which gives a controlled and predictable fermentation. The starter normally contains *Lactobacillus bulgaricus*, which produces lactic acid and ethanal, a characteristic yogurt flavour, and *Streptococcus thermophilus* which adds a characteristic creamy flavour. These bacteria can be seen in roughly equal proportions if Gram staining of a sample of yogurt is carried out (section 12.9.2). Both types are Gram positive and will therefore appear purple. If you would like to try counting the bacteria, you should find something like 10^8 per gram of each of the two types mentioned.

Cheese

To make cheese the milk must first be separated into curds and whey. This is done by inoculating the milk in carefully controlled, hygienic conditions with a starter culture containing the required microorganisms. As fermentation proceeds, lactic acid builds up and starts to sour the milk, causing the soluble milk protein casein to coagulate (solidify). This is what happens when milk 'curdles'. Coagulation is increased and controlled more precisely by adding rennet which contains the enzyme rennin. Traditionally this is obtained from calves' stomachs, but increasingly similar proteinase enzymes are being obtained from certain fungi or from genetically engineered bacteria. The advantage of these newer sources is that they can be used to make vegetarian and kosher cheeses. The solid part of the milk, mainly protein and fat, is known as **curds** and the liquid is **whey**. The curds are separated and pressed into

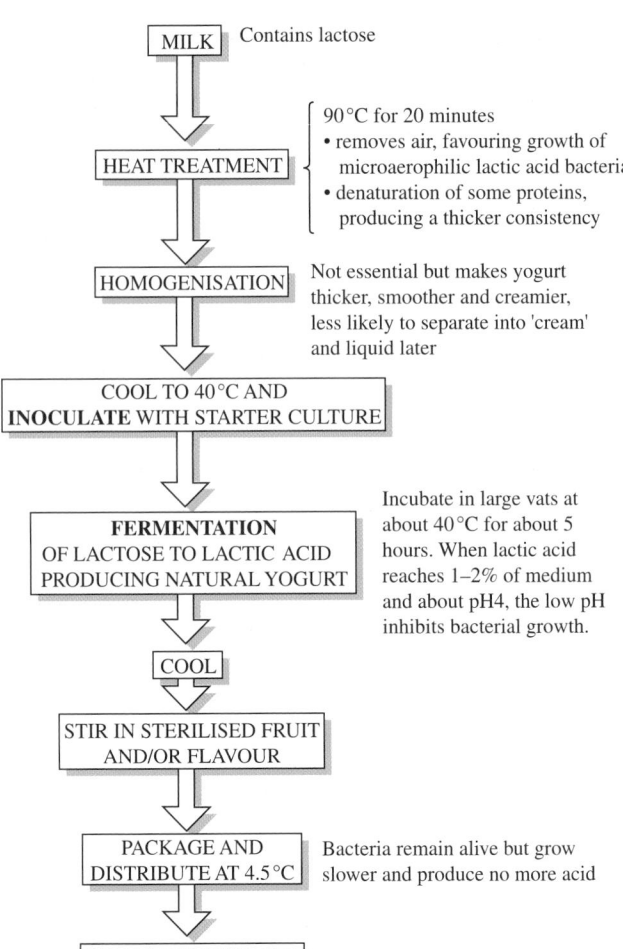

Fig 12.20 *Flow diagram of yogurt manufacture.*

the desired shape and drained. The whey can be used as a food source for yeasts which in turn can be processed and added to cattle feed. The product is rich in protein and certain vitamins.

Maturing or ripening of the cheese then adds its characteristic flavour and texture. This is done by adding further microorganisms, either bacteria (e.g. Cheddar), or mould fungi (e.g. Roquefort and other blue cheeses) or a combination of the two (e.g. Camembert). All these processes are done under controlled conditions which vary for different cheeses. Some cheeses, such as cottage cheese and cream cheese, are unripened.

Butter

Butter is made from the cream of fresh milk and must by law contain at least 80% fat. The cream is first pasteurised and later it is churned.

12.12.3 Single cell protein (SCP)

A relatively new food source is 'single cell protein' (SCP). Its production began in the late 1960s. The term refers to protein obtained from the large-scale growth of microorganisms such as bacteria, yeasts and other fungi, and algae. The protein may be used for human consumption or animal feed. It may also be a useful source of minerals, vitamins, fat and carbohydrate. In theory this should release proteins, such as soyabean meal and grain, which are currently used in animal feeds, for human consumption. However, there are agricultural surpluses in the western world which mean that this has not happened, as we shall see. Although there is a global shortage of protein, the shortage is in developing countries which cannot afford this technology.

There are several advantages in using microorganisms as a food source.

- They occupy less room than conventional crops and animals.
- They grow much more rapidly.
- They can grow on a wide range of cheap or waste products of agriculture and industry, e.g. petroleum products, methane, methanol, ethanol, sugar, molasses, cheese, whey, and waste from pulp and paper mills. They may therefore have the secondary advantage that they can help to recycle materials and clean up waste.
- There are fewer ethical issues associated with their exploitation and no animal rights issues.
- They are more easily modified by genetic engineering.
- They have a relatively high protein content.
- They are independent of climate and do not occupy large areas of land.

One of the first major SCP products was Pruteen, whose production was an excellent example of good engineering design in a continuous fermentation process. Pruteen was marketed as an animal feed additive. Early hopes for SCP were dampened by changes in the economic and political aspects of its production. Problems were as follows.

- A rise in oil prices in the late 1970s greatly increased the cost of production since the process, including production of methanol, is very energy-demanding.
- In the developed countries such as the USA and Europe where SCP was to be made, agricultural surpluses became common, particularly of rival high-protein products like grain, soya bean and dairy products.
- Developing countries, where protein is scarce, could not afford the investment necessary to set up SCP production themselves, and did not have the necessary expertise.
- There was an increase in production and reduction in price of competitive animal feed additives like soya bean, fishmeal, and gluten from maize. The latter is a byproduct of biotechnological fuel production.

Pruteen was made by ICI. After its failure as a commercial product, the production plant was dismantled, but ICI made use of the expertise gained by collaborating with Rank, Hovis, McDougall to produce a protein from a fungus called *Fusarium*. This mycoprotein (*myco-* refers to fungus) is unusual in being used for human consumption. It is marketed as Quorn, and its manufacture is described later in this section.

Pruteen

In 1980 ICI built a huge fermenter at Billingham on the north bank of the Tees in north-east England. It cost £40 million, had a capacity of 1500 cubic metres (1.5 million dm^3) and was 60 m tall. It had a potential to produce 70 000 tonnes of SCP per year. The organism used was a bacterium, *Methylophilus methylotrophus*, and its organic carbon and energy source was the cheap and readily available methanol. The process was aerobic. A summary of the process shows the raw materials required and the products made:

$$\text{organic carbon (methanol)} + \text{nitrogen} + \text{mineral salts} + \text{oxygen} \longrightarrow \text{SCP (biomass)} + CO_2 + H_2O + \text{heat energy}$$

The waste carbon dioxide was bottled and sold.

Screening for a suitable bacterium involved looking for one with a rapid growth rate capable of growing on a relatively cheap source of carbon and energy, heat-tolerant due to the heat released during the process, non-pathogenic to any other organisms and with a high percentage of protein in its dry mass. The bacterium chosen, *M. methylotrophus*, was found locally and has a generation time (doubling time) of 2–5 hours. Nitrogen was added as ammonium salts, and additional minerals that were needed included phosphorus, calcium and potassium. Methanol was obtained from natural gas on the same industrial site at Billingham. It produces no harmful by-products. Temperature was carefully monitored and kept within the range 30–40 °C, and pH was kept at 6.7. The fermenter could be run continuously for several months.

Pruteen manufacture is a classic example of continuous batch culture and the basic principles of manufacture are as described in section 12.10.5. The fermenter was tall and narrow, making aeration and cooling easier. It had a unique air-lift system to aerate the medium. Compressed air was introduced at the bottom of the fermenter and the rising bubbles mixed the contents (rather than using paddles). 6000 tonnes were produced per month. 2 tonnes of methanol produced 1 tonne of dried Pruteen, which is 72% protein and 8% moisture. It was rich in essential amino acids, had a high vitamin content and was twice as nutritious as soyabean meal. It was used as an animal feed.

Being a continuous culture, bacteria were harvested continuously once they had reached their maximum growth rate (exponential growth). Some of the contents of the fermenter were removed, treated with a chemical which caused the bacteria to clump together and then centrifuged. The separated cells were then spray-dried and the useful components of the liquid recycled to the fermenter. After drying, the bacterial cells were ground up to improve digestibility and the pH and mineral balance adjusted before packaging.

Mycoprotein

Fungi are another possible source of SCP. Yeast is used for both animal and human consumption (see yeast extract below) in processes similar to those for bacteria. Moulds are also used. These have the typical fungal body described in section 2.5.2 which consists of a mass of fine thread-like hyphae called a mycelium. A good example of the use of moulds is the manufacture of mycoprotein (Quorn). In 1985 Rank, Hovis, McDougall jointly formed a company with ICI, called Marlow Foods, to produce and market mycoprotein under the trade name of Quorn. The fungus used is *Fusarium graminearum*. It was originally isolated in the early 1960s from soil in a field near Marlow in Buckinghamshire, hence the name of the company. Product development was started in 1964. It was passed as safe for human consumption and launched in 1986, the first commercial product being a savoury pie sold by J. Sainsbury. Although originally used as an ingredient of manufactured foods such as pies and curries, Quorn pieces became available for home cooking in 1990 and minced Quorn in 1992. It is given a mild savoury flavour and has been a commercial success.

The doubling time of the fungus in culture is 5.5 hours, which is slower than bacteria, and it uses glucose as a carbon and energy source. This comes from any convenient cheap source of starch such as corn, wheat, rice, potato or molasses. It produces 0.5 kg dry biomass per kilogram of sugar used. Fungi have the advantage that they can be grown at a pH which is acidic enough to inhibit the growth of bacteria, thus reducing the risk of contamination. *Fusarium* is grown at 30 °C in continuous culture. Ammonium salts are the nitrogen source and mineral salts are also added to maintain growth, as with bacteria. Sterilisation of all materials used, and aeration and cooling of the medium are required as described for previous processes. Agitation of the medium is achieved by a special aeration mechanism because the hyphae would tend to become tangled up with stirrers and not be evenly distributed inside the fermenter. This mechanism is called an air-lift fermenter because the culture is circulated continuously, once every 2 minutes, by the air through a vertically elongated loop about 40 m high. The fermenter contains about 40 000 dm³. As it is a continuous process, the product is harvested and fresh medium added continuously to keep the volume constant.

Eukaryotic cells contain a higher proportion of nucleic acid than prokaryotic cells, so the mycoprotein product contains a significant amount of nucleic acid (5–15% dry mass). This is mostly RNA and must be reduced because consumption of more than 2 g a day in the human diet can lead to gout and kidney stones. It is removed by heating the culture to 64 °C for 20–30 minutes in a separate steam-heated vessel. This inactivates fungal proteases (so the protein is not digested) but allows natural RNAase enzymes to break down the RNA. RNA is reduced to about 1%, well below the recommended limit of 2% set by the World Health Organisation.

An advantage of using fungi is that the mycelium is easier to separate from the medium than are bacterial cells. Filtration is sufficient and centrifugation is not needed. Filtering and drying leaves a thin flexible sheet of Quorn. At this stage it looks and tastes a little like raw pastry. Vegetable flavours and a little egg white are added. It is then sliced, diced or shredded for use. The fungus is already fibrous (one reason why it was chosen), so it is easy to give it the texture of meat.

For human consumption, factors other than just economics are important. Very strict safety guidelines must be adhered to, and the nutritional value of the food has to be acceptable. Long-term studies (10 or more years) with 11 species of animals, including rats, pigs and cows, for up to four generations have shown no long-term harmful effects. Human trials were also carried out before its release on the mass market. The final product has several health advantages over meat. Its composition compared with some typical animal protein sources is shown in table 12.5. It is cholesterol-free and high in fibre, unlike meat. It is low in fat and 'calories' (energy) with a good polyunsaturated:saturated fatty acid ratio (see section 8.7). It is also a good source of vitamin B_{12} and zinc, which are often lacking in the diets of vegetarians.

There are also psychological barriers to overcome in adopting new foods. Presentation, including packaging and advertising, is important (fig 12.21). Odour, colour, taste and texture must all be carefully planned. It was decided to market Quorn originally as a meat substitute. It can easily be woven into fibres which successfully mimic the texture of meat, and it can be flavoured to taste like chicken or, less commonly, beef.

Fig 12.21 *Food containing Quorn.*

Table 12.5 Typical composition of Quorn mycoprotein compared with traditional animal protein sources.

Component per 100 g	Myco-protein (cooked)	Raw lean beef	Cooked stewing steak	Roast chicken, meat only	Cheddar cheese	Fresh cod	Grilled beef sausage
Protein	12.3	20.3	30.9	24.8	26.0	17.4	13.0
Fat	3.2	4.6	11.0	5.4	34.4	0.7	17.3
Dietary fibre	4.8	0	0	0	0	0	0
Cholesterol	0	59	82	76	70	50	40
Energy (kJ)	355	514	932	621	1708	318	1104
Ratio PUFAs to SFAs*	2.5	0.1	0.1	0.5	0.2	2.2	0.1

* PUFA = polyunsaturated fatty acids – these are beneficial to health (section 8.7.7)
SFAs = saturated fatty acids

12.11 In advertising, the source of Quorn is usually referred to as a 'natural, tiny plant' or as a 'tiny relative of the mushroom'. Suggest why this is so.

Yeast extract

The left-over yeast from brewing can be used in a number of ways. One example is the manufacture of whisky which, like beer, depends on fermentation of sugars from germinating barley. Whisky, however, is distilled from the fermented malt. This requires boiling and kills the yeast. Yeast produced during brewing can be used as a replacement.

Yeast cells are rich in B vitamins, particularly niacin (B_6), riboflavin (B_2), thiamin (B_1), folic acid and B_{12}. They can be dried and made into vitamin-rich tablets or converted into products like Marmite. This involves heating the yeast in large vats to 50 °C and adding salt to encourage the process of autolysis (section 5.10.6). **Autolysis** is self-digestion and is carried out by enzymes in dying cells. The products are filtered and centrifuged to remove cell walls and then concentrated into a thick paste. Vegetable extract is added to Marmite.

An alternative to autolysis is **hydrolysis** with hydrochloric acid. This is later neutralised with sodium hydroxide. The product is also used in a whole variety of foods as a meaty, salty flavouring, for example in crisps, hamburgers, soups, sauces and gravy powders.

SCP from photosynthetic organisms

Both photosynthetic bacteria, such as blue-green bacteria, and algae are used to make SCP. *Spirulina* is an example of a blue-green bacterium that is used. It was made into cakes by the Aztecs and is the main food of flamingoes in the lakes of the Rift Valley in East Africa. *Spirulina* has been grown on a small scale in Mexico and Hawaii for sale in health food shops. It has a very high protein content and a high growth rate. It can be skimmed off from pond or lake surfaces. *Chlorella* is a unicellular alga which is commonly used. In Japan and Taiwan dried *Chlorella* is sold as health food.

The nutritional and environmental requirements of photosynthetic organisms used in SCP production have been discussed in sections 12.1.1 and 12.1.2. The fact that they all need light and most need carbon dioxide as a carbon source are the obvious differences compared with fungi and non-photosynthetic bacteria. They are generally cultured in non-sterile conditions in warm, mineral-rich open ponds and are usually in a mixed culture (one that contains different species).

Growing algae on sewage serves the dual purpose of purifying the sewage and producing SCP for animal feed. This has been done in Israel.

12.13   Agriculture

This section deals with some of the ways in which production of food using biotechnology can be extended to agriculture.

12.13.1   Genetic engineering

Some of the most important applications of genetic engineering are in agriculture. As already discussed, genetic engineering can be regarded as an aspect of biotechnology. Examples of its use in agriculture which are considered in this book are production of somatotrophin (BST), pesticide and herbicide resistance, and transgenic plants and animals. These are all discussed in chapter 25 which deals with the practical applications of genetics.

12.13.2　Silage

The making of silage is a traditional anaerobic fermentation process carried out on farms. It preserves the nutritive value of grass for winter feed for farm animals, particularly dairy cattle. Grass has a natural population of lactic acid bacteria such as *Lactobacillus* on its surface. After harvest it is finely chopped and can be loaded into a large 'bin' called a silo or silage clamp or, more recently, it is sometimes stacked in a large bale wrapped in black plastic. The bacteria use the natural sugars in grass, such as glucose, fructose and sucrose, as an energy source in anaerobic respiration (traditional fermentation) and convert them to lactic acid. Other fermentation products are also formed which add flavour, but lactic acid is the main product. It reduces the pH to about 4, which is low enough to inhibit the activity of decomposing bacteria which would otherwise completely rot the grass and lower its nutritive value. Temperatures in fermenting grass can become quite high, so the bacteria must be heat resistant. Contamination with *Listeria* bacteria must be avoided because this can lead to blood poisoning or stillbirth of farm animals. Providing fermentation is active and the pH is less than 5.5 this should not be a problem.

Improved reliability and quality of silage production is now possible by adding commercially prepared inoculants of fast-growing lactic acid bacteria. These are applied as powders or sprays to the newly harvested grass. ICI produce three products in fermenters at Billingham, named Ecosyl, Ecohay and Ecobale. Increased productivity of the animals is reported to occur, partly because the conversion to lactic acid is more efficient and partly because the silage tastes better and therefore the cattle eat more.

12.13.3　Nitrogen fixation

Crops of the legume family (Papilionaceae), which includes peas, beans, clover and alfalfa, have been used for centuries in crop rotation schemes because their roots add nitrogen to the soil. In the nineteenth century it was discovered that the characteristic swellings on the roots of these plants, root nodules, contain bacteria which can 'fix' nitrogen from the air and convert it to nitrate. This process is described in more detail in section 10.4.1. The bacteria are various strains of *Rhizobium* (fig 12.22). Individual strains are adapted to infect different legume species. The bacteria normally infect the roots as they grow in the natural habitat where *Rhizobium* occurs naturally. However, for situations where seed is to be grown in places where the bacteria may not exist, for example if the seed is for export, a technique has been developed for 'inoculating' the seed with the bacterium. Cultures of the required *Rhizobium* strain are grown in fermenters and afterwards added to a suitable medium, commonly sterile peat. This can be added to the soil as the seeds are planted, for example by being added to the seed drill. Inoculated seed is not needed where the crop has been grown regularly because *Rhizobium* can survive in

Fig 12.22　*The effect of* Rhizobium *inoculant on pea seedlings. The pea seedling on the left has its roots growing under sterile conditions in a flask. The plant has been fed with a mineral salts medium lacking any source of nitrogen. Consequently, it shows poor growth and yellow leaves. The roots of the similar pea seedling on the right were inoculated with* Rhizobium, *which converts nitrogen gas in the atmosphere into forms which the plant can use. Consequently this plant is healthy and shows no sign of nitrogen deficiency.*

the soil for many years using simple organic compounds and ammonium or nitrate as a nitrogen source. The bacterium only fixes nitrogen when in plant roots.

Examples of seeds that have been exported are clover to Australia, soya beans to N. America and alfalfa to Europe. Using such crops in rotation reduces the need for industrially produced nitrogen fertiliser. The advantages of this are discussed in section 10.8.2.

12.14　Fuel from biomass – new energy sources

Biomass is a traditional fuel in the form of products like coal, gas, oil, wood, peat, and dried animal dung. Some of these products are becoming scarcer and more expensive. Many new methods are being explored for using living organisms and biological processes as sources of fuel. **Artificial photosynthesis**, producing hydrogen gas as a fuel from water, is a long-term possibility. Another basic approach is to change the energy trapped in biomass into another form which can be used as fuel. Among the raw materials being investigated are **waste materials** such as animal manures, sewage sludge, domestic wastes, food wastes, paper wastes, spoilt crops, sugarcane tops and molasses. Various **crops** (such as maize, sugarcane, sugar beet) and water plants (such as kelps and water hyacinth) might also be used. Two processes currently dominate, namely production of biogas (methane) by bacteria, and production of ethanol by yeast. Both processes are anaerobic.

12.14.1 Biogas

Overall equation:

$$C_6H_{12}O_6 \longrightarrow 3CH_4 + 3CO_2$$

glucose   methane   carbon dioxide

energy value: $16\,kJ\,g^{-1}$ $56\,kJ\,g^{-1}$

Biogas is about 54–70% methane. Most of the rest is carbon dioxide, with traces of nitrogen, hydrogen and other gases. (Natural gas is about 80% methane.) A mixture of microorganisms is used in the fermentation, including a group of bacteria called **methanogens**, e.g. *Methanobacterium*, which can produce methane from carbon dioxide and hydrogen. These are **archaebacteria**, an ancient group of organisms closely related to the true bacteria. A wide range of waste materials or plant products can be used as a substrate for fermentation (see above). In the USA the water hyacinth, a vigorous plant which can block canals and waterways, has been used. The process is ideal for small-scale use and therefore for local fuel use. This is now common in India and China for example (fig 12.23).

The manure from one cow in one year can be converted to an amount of methane which is equivalent to over 227 litres (dm^3) of petrol. For example, 0.5 kg of cow manure could generate enough gas to cook a family's meals for a day. In China, over 18 million family-scale digesters have been built. The gas is typically used for cooking, lighting, tractor or car fuel and for running electricity generators.

On a larger scale, the gas can be produced as a by-product of landfill, sewage or waste from factories such as sugar factories and distilleries. It can be used to drive electricity generators in sewage works and waste treatment plants. In Britain, rubbish could be a major source of methane, with up to $20\,dm^3$ of gas being obtained per kilogram of rubbish. At the moment the gas is collected from landfill sites by sinking pipes into the compacted rubbish and sucking out the gas.

Bearing in mind the growing shortage of landfill sites and the nuisance they cause, it may be worth developing processes for *fermenting* products like paper and cardboard, even if the fuel produced is no cheaper than conventional fuels. The economics are usually more favourable in developing countries which lack their own fossil fuel reserves and have dwindling supplies of timber. Raw sewage and dried animal dung can also be used in a fermenter. The fuel value of fermented dung is six times greater than that of dried dung.

Fig 12.23 *Biogas digester in India. Animal manure is put into the digester, where it decomposes and gives off methane gas.*

12.14.2 Ethanol

Overall equation:

$$C_6H_{12}O_6 \longrightarrow 2C_2H_5OH + 2CO_2$$

glucose   ethanol

energy value: $16\,kJ\,g^{-1}$ $30\,kJ\,g^{-1}$

Ethanol has been produced successfully for use as a fuel in Brazil since 1975. Sugarcane is the starting material. It is crushed by rollers after harvest to extract the juice. Sucrose is extracted from the juice as a commercial product, but this leaves a syrup called **molasses** which contains glucose and fructose. The molasses can be used as material for fermentation by the yeast *Saccharomyces cerevisiae*. Ethanol is distilled to separate it from the other fermentation products. The dry fibrous material left behind when the sugarcane is crushed can be used as fuel in the distillery.

Some Brazilian cars are adapted to run on pure alcohol, although the ethanol is mixed with a little petrol to stop people drinking it. Over 11 000 million dm^3 were produced in 1985. The process started to save Brazil money when oil prices rose in 1983, and since then oil consumption has been cut by 20%. Some cars in Brazil and in the USA can run on mixtures of alcohol and petrol called **gasohol** (fig 12.24). In the USA the starting biomass is starch from maize. Over 2280 million dm^3 per year were being produced in the mid 1980s.

Although the Brazilian scheme seems to have been a success, not all is straightforward. Debate continues about the most economic use for molasses and whether other crops might be a better source of carbohydrate. For example, molasses could be used instead of oil as a raw material in the plastics industry.

Fig 12.24 *An ethanol-powered car filling up with Alcool (gasohol) in Brazil.*

12.15 Microbiological mining

Useful metals such as copper, iron, uranium, gold, lead, nickel and cobalt are found naturally as minerals, otherwise known as ores. Where these ores are sufficiently concentrated they can be mined and the metals extracted. It is only recently that the important role and potential of microorganisms in the extraction process has been realised. Copper will be used as an example to illustrate the principles involved.

Copper was one of the first metals used by humans. Bronze, which is an alloy of copper and tin, was first made over 5000 years ago, leading to the 'Bronze Age' when bronze was valued for its strength and cutting power as well as its decorative value. Copper naturally occurs mainly as copper sulphides. For example, more than 50% of the world's supply comes from copper pyrites, $CuFeS_2$, which contains iron as well as sulphur. Extraction of copper from the ore is difficult. It has long been known, though, that copper can be recovered from water which has drained through rocks containing the copper ores. This process of metal **leaching** is now known to be due to the action of bacteria. The bacteria convert insoluble metal compounds to soluble metal compounds such as copper sulphate, from which copper can be more easily extracted.

The bacterium chiefly responsible for the leaching of metal sulphides was identified in 1947 as *Thiobacillus ferrooxidans*. Other important bacteria are *T. thiooxidans* and *Leptospirillum ferrooxidans*. These bacteria thrive in acid conditions and can often work at high temperatures. They obtain their energy by oxidising inorganic substances. *T. ferrooxidans*, for example, obtains energy by oxidising Fe^{2+} in ores to Fe^{3+} and reduced forms of sulphur, like the sulphides in ores, to sulphuric acid. *T. ferrooxidans* is autotrophic, so can be classified as chemoautotrophic or chemosynthetic (table 2.3).

Bacterial leaching is now used throughout the world as an additional technique for extracting metals from ores, mainly for copper and uranium (fig 12.25). Suitable

Fig 12.25 *An open pit mine in Rio Tinto, Spain, which produces 2.3 million tonnes per year of gold, silver and copper.*

combinations of bacteria are used, each making its own unique contribution. More than 10% of the copper extracted in the USA in 1983, worth over 300 million dollars, was recovered using this method. Advantages of bacterial leaching include the following.

- Lower grade ores can be exploited commercially. The expense of extracting by conventional methods meant that only ores particularly rich in the metal could be used, so there was much loss of potential product in the mining areas.

- Deep mining can be avoided by washing out the metal using bacterial leaching. The rock is fractured first by explosive charges and the leaching solution is then pumped in. The leaching solution containing the soluble metal compounds is recovered by pumping from wells sunk into the rock. This saves the cost, danger and environmental damage of deep mining which brings large quantities of rock to the surface, creating waste tips.

- Traditional methods of extracting the copper from the ore use high temperatures. They consume fossil fuels and therefore contribute to pollution such as acid rain as well as being expensive. (Bacterial leaching might also be used in future to clean fossil fuels by leaching out sulphur compounds.)

- Uncontrolled leaching from the waste of mines has led to pollution of surrounding waters with heavy metals. This can be avoided by controlled leaching with recovery of the metal. It is estimated that more than 33 thousand million kilograms of copper are located in mine dumps in the western USA alone. A good location for a dump is a valley so that it can be sprayed with water from a river. The water, containing soluble leached metal, can then be collected at a dam downstream and pumped through a metal recovery plant. Cleaned water can be recycled to the dump if desired.

- Improvements are being attempted by genetically engineering the bacteria, particularly *T. ferrooxidans*.

12.16   Enzyme technology

This section will be concerned with the use in biotechnology of enzymes which have been separated from cells.

Enzymes are the biological catalysts which make possible the organised chemical activity of cells. Although we have made use of them for thousands of years, we did not begin to understand how they work until the late nineteenth century. We now know that they are complex protein molecules with specific three-dimensional shapes and that their structure is coded for by DNA. The number of possible overall shapes is infinite.

To the industrialist, enzymes have two major attractions. Firstly, because of their variety, they have the potential to catalyse a vast range of industrially important chemical reactions. Secondly, they are much more efficient and specific than the inorganic catalysts commonly used. As a result, they may achieve at normal temperatures and pressures what might otherwise require extremely high temperatures and pressures. For example, one of the world's largest industrial processes is the Haber process in which ammonia (NH_3) is produced from nitrogen and hydrogen gases at a temperature of $500\,°C$ and at high pressures. Nitrogen-fixing bacteria, however, can make ammonia from atmospheric nitrogen and hydrogen at room temperature and normal atmospheric pressure using enzymes, with ATP as an energy source. If the technology could be devised to do this with enzymes, great energy savings would be made. Another advantage is that, because of their specificity, enzymes also give purer products, which is important in the pharmaceutical, food and agricultural industries.

There are disadvantages however, mainly relating to the instability of proteins once they are removed from the cell environment. They are easily denatured by temperature and pH change, and by the organic solvents which often have to be used in industrial processes. They may also be inhibited by products of the reaction. Two other problems are that they are expensive to produce and that they must be taken from 'safe' (for example, non-pathogenic) organisms if they are to be used to make products for use in animals, including humans. Less than 200 enzymes are used out of the roughly 2500 which have been isolated and described so far (which in turn is only about 10% of those found in nature). Most come from only 11 species of fungi, four species of yeasts and eight species of bacteria.

In the future there are exciting opportunities opening up for re-designing enzymes. One possibility is to deliberately change individual amino acids by changing the genes that code for the enzymes. As we learn more about the rules governing the way that proteins fold into their specific three-dimensional shapes, we may even start to be able to make completely new *designer enzymes*. This is known as **protein engineering**. Also, the more we learn about the ways in which enzymes work, the more likely it will be that we can design non-protein or part-protein catalysts which are far more stable than normal enzymes. This is probably the direction most industrialists would favour. Of more immediate benefit is the search for natural enzymes which offer improved alternatives to the processes currently used. All this requires the investment of large sums of money in research and development.

Pharmaceutical companies, cheese-makers, brewers and distillers, wine producers, detergent manufacturers, textiles manufacturers, fruit juice producers and many others now use enzymes in manufacturing processes. Worldwide sales of enzymes now exceed 1 billion dollars per year. Table 12.6 gives some idea of the range of uses of enzymes.

12.16.1   Source of enzymes

Microorganisms are preferred to plants and animals as a source of enzymes because:

- they have high growth rates;
- they can be grown economically in bulk in fermenters under controlled conditions;
- they carry out a wide range of chemical reactions;
- they can be genetically engineered relatively easily, and mutant varieties can relatively easily be produced, to improve performance;
- they have simple nutritional requirements;
- they can be grown on cheap, often waste, substrates;
- production rate can be altered to suit demand;
- they produce a lot of extracellular enzymes; because these leave the cell, they are easier to recover and purify.

12.16.2   Why isolate enzymes?

Since the enzymes used come mainly from microorganisms, it might be argued that it would be simpler to use whole cells in fermenters rather than isolate the enzymes first. Where more than one chemical reaction is

Table 12.6 Some common industrial uses of enzymes.

Application	Enzymes used	Uses
Biological detergents	Primarily proteases, produced in an extracellular form by bacteria	Used for pre-soak or main wash, break down protein stains on clothes; also used in dishwashers to remove food residues
	Amylases	Remove starch stains from clothes; also used in dishwashers to remove resistant starch residues
	Cellulase	Softens and brightens colour of cotton fabrics
Brewing industry	**Enzymes produced from barley** during mashing stage of beer production	Digest starch to sugars and proteins to amino acids and peptides for use by yeast in growth and alcohol production
	Enzymes from microorganisms	
	Amylases	Digest polysaccharides in the malt
	Proteases	Digest proteins in the malt; remove cloudiness during cold storage
	β-glucanase	Digests polysaccharides in beer and prevents cloudiness
Baby foods	Trypsin	To predigest baby foods
Dairy industry	Rennet (rennin) from stomachs of young calves	Used to coagulate protein in manufacture of cheese
Leather industry	Proteases	Removal of hair from hides; also makes leather more pliable
Paper industry	Amylases	Degrade starch to smaller molecules which have lower viscosity and are used for sizing (filling in spaces between cellulose fibres to make a smoother product) and coating paper
Photographic industry	Proteases	Dissolve gelatin off scrap film allowing recovery of silver present

Modified from Table 5.2 *Biotechnology*, 2nd ed., John E. Smith, New Studies In Biology (1988), Edward Arnold, and *Enzymes, their nature and role*, Wiseman & Gould, Hutchinson Educational.

required to make a product, and therefore more than one enzyme, this is what is normally done. However, using purified enzymes rather than whole microorganisms can be an advantage for several reasons.

- Building and running fermenters in which to grow microorganisms is expensive.
- Fermentations must be carried out in aseptic conditions.
- Aeration and mixing of whole cells is energy-consuming.
- Products in fermenters are in an impure form.
- Wastes from fermenters have to be disposed of and may cause pollution.

Manufacturing processes carried out with purified enzymes involve the use of specially designed 'reactors'. The design of these is outside the scope of this book, but they are much simpler than fermenters.

12.16.3 Producing isolated enzymes

When the source of the enzyme is a microorganism, the microorganism is first grown in bulk in a fermenter as discussed earlier in this chapter. Glucose is usually avoided as a nutrient because it inhibits the production of many useful enzymes. Batch fermentations are used, except for the production of glucose isomerase from *Bacillus coagulans*, which is a continuous fermentation. Many enzymes are secreted from the cells as extracellular enzymes. These can be purified more easily than those which remain inside the cells. In the latter case, the cells are separated from the liquid contents of the fermenter and then broken open by various means to release their contents. Purification is then carried out as far as is necessary. Some enzymes do not need to be completely pure.

The enzymes may be used as they are, for example in fruit juice production, meat tenderisation and in washing powders, or may be immobilised before use (section 12.16.7).

12.16.4 Fruit juice production

During the manufacture of fruit juices the fruit must first be crushed. Like any other part of the plant, fruits are made up of cells with cell walls. These contain cellulose and other complex polysaccharides called hemicelluloses. Cell walls are very tough and difficult to break open. In order to improve yields and the quality of the product, cellulases and hemicellulases are added during the crushing stage to digest the cellulose and hemicelluloses in the walls, making them more 'soluble' and ensuring more complete disintegration of the tissues. The enzymes are selected to work at low pH because fruit juice is acidic. Their pH optimum is about 4–5.

Plant cells are held together by other complex polysaccharides called pectins. These are the sticky compounds which cause jam to set. They tend to be converted into water-soluble pectins during the storage and processing of fruits, and are therefore present in fruit juices in solution even if the 'bits', the unbroken cells and cell wall debris, are removed. At low temperatures, the pectins start to come out of solution and form a colloidal suspension (a suspension of tiny particles which do not settle). This gives the drink a cloudy appearance. This is an unattractive feature to some consumers, particularly in the USA and Britain, although it should, perhaps, be regarded more as a sign of high fruit content. If enzymes called pectinases are added to the juice they partially digest the pectins to smaller polysaccharides and sugars which remain in solution even at low temperatures. The pectinases therefore clarify the drink (fig 12.26). The drink is then described as 'chill-proofed'. The source of the pectinases is bacteria.

The same principle is applied to beers and wine, although the haze in beer is due to protein and tannins rather than polysaccharides. Proteases such as pepsin and papain are added to beer to break down the proteins and reduce the haze when it is chilled.

12.16.5 Meat tenderisation

Meat is mainly muscle protein. Muscles are bundles of protein fibres wrapped in blocks by connective tissue. Connective tissue also contains structural proteins, particularly collagen and elastin. Collagen forms 'white fibres', which are tough and non-elastic; elastin forms 'yellow fibres' which are elastic in nature. The meat can be made easier to chew, in other words more tender, by predigesting some of these connective tissue proteins and some of the muscle fibres. The fibres become shorter and more easily separated and the meat therefore breaks down more easily.

Enzymes that break down proteins are called proteases and the one most commonly used for meat tenderisation is **papain**. It comes from the sap of the papaya plant. Meat tenderisers containing this enzyme can be purchased for home use. The meat should be left 'marinading' in the juice

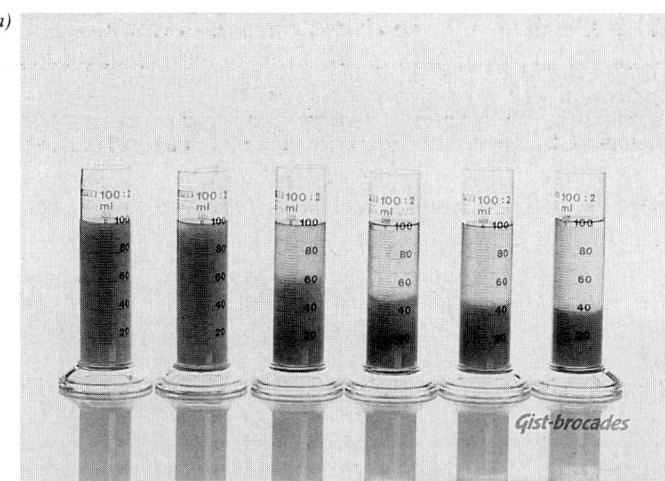

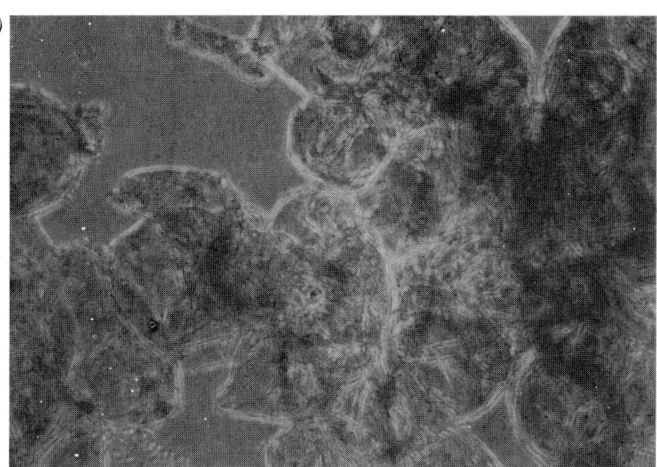

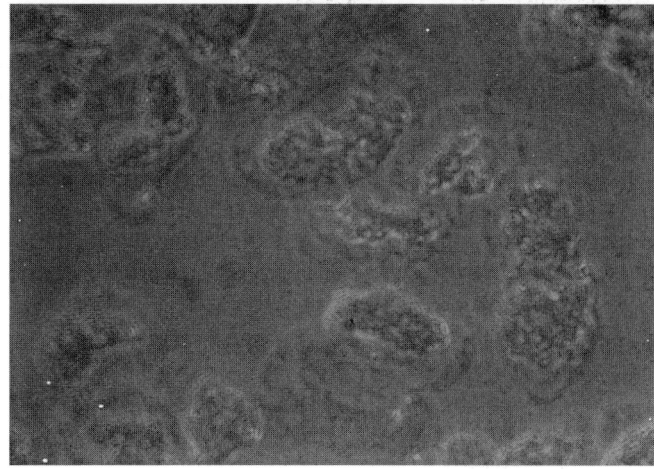

Fig 12.26 (a) A series of flasks showing the effect of increasing pectinase dosage on apple juice. The two cloudy flasks on the left have no enzyme. The others, from left to right, contain 0.5, 1.0, 1.5 and 2.0 grams per 100 dm³.
(b) Apple pulp before (middle) and after (bottom) the action of pectinase. You can see that the pectinases (Rapidase) are removing the pectin coating of the apple cells, making them more fragile and less viscous.

for some time before cooking, to allow the enzyme to work, because it is denatured once cooking starts. In some countries, though not in the UK, papain can be injected into the blood of animals just before or after slaughter to make the meat more tender.

A similar tenderising process occurs naturally in meat after death. Lysosomes in the dying cells break down and release their digestive enzymes which begin the process of digestion. This is known as autolysis (section 5.10.6). It is the main reason why it is usual to hang meat in cold storage for several days before use.

12.16.6 Biological washing powders

The first commercially successful biological washing powders were introduced in the mid 1960s. They contained proteases (protein-digesting enzymes) which are particularly useful for removing stains of biological origin, such as blood, grass and egg, formed from protein and other materials. These are dislodged by digestion of the protein. Lower temperature washes are possible, saving energy, although the enzymes used have been selected to function over a wide range of temperatures (10–90 °C, optimum about 55 °C), having been obtained originally from thermophilic (heat-loving) bacteria. In washing powders, proteases must also function in alkaline conditions (pH 9–10) and in the presence of the high levels of phosphate found in some detergents. They are particularly useful for pre-wash and soak use and for low temperature washes. In western Europe 25% of domestic energy consumption is from washing machines, a high proportion compared with the rest of the world.

Soon after the introduction of biological washing powders, health problems began to occur, particularly among the workers in the factories making the detergents. Some people developed allergies to the powders, and lung irritation and respiratory disorders were experienced after breathing in fine detergent dust from the air. This led to the withdrawal in the early 1970s of the powders from sale in the USA, although they remained in use in Europe. The product was re-formulated to overcome these problems (fig 12.27), an inert wax being added to the powder to make it safer on contact and less likely to be airborne. Liquids were also developed. They have now been re-introduced in the USA and by the mid 1990s made up 15% of the market there compared with 85% in western Europe.

New enzymes have been added to biological washing powders to improve effectiveness. Cellulase digests the loose cellulose microfibrils from damaged cotton fibres, making cotton fabrics brighter, softer and smoother. Enzymes are also added that digest carbohydrates, for example amylases that digest starches. One problem is that proteases can digest some other enzymes since enzymes are proteins! This has made finding suitable enzymes more difficult. Even more recently a suitable lipase has been found in a fungus which is active at normal temperatures.

Fig 12.27 *SEM of biological washing powder, showing encapsulation of granules. Some granules are partially opened to show the enzymes inside.*

The relevant gene has been transferred by genetic engineering into another fungus which is more suitable for growing in a fermenter. Lipases digest lipids, in other words fat, oil and grease stains.

An organism which is commonly used as a source of enzymes for washing powders is the bacterium *Bacillus*. Several species are used. The enzymes produced are extracellular, making it relatively easy to collect and purify them.

12.16.7 Immobilised enzymes

Advantages of immobilised enzymes

As already discussed in the introduction to this section, commercial use of enzymes is limited by a number of factors. Two important ones are the instability of enzymes and their high cost. The cost can be greatly reduced by **immobilising** the enzyme. This means binding it to, or trapping it in, a solid support which can be recovered easily from the reaction mixture during downstream processing. The enzyme can then be re-used which greatly reduces the cost of the process.

Another advantage of immobilisation is that it sometimes makes the enzyme more stable, possibly by restricting its ability to change shape and denature as a result of changes in pH, temperature, and solvents. For example, glucose isomerase is stable for almost a year at 65 °C when immobilised, whereas it denatures within a few hours at 45 °C when in solution.

Immobilising the enzyme can also mean that continuous (open) production can be achieved more easily by passing the reactants over the enzyme and collecting the product at the end.

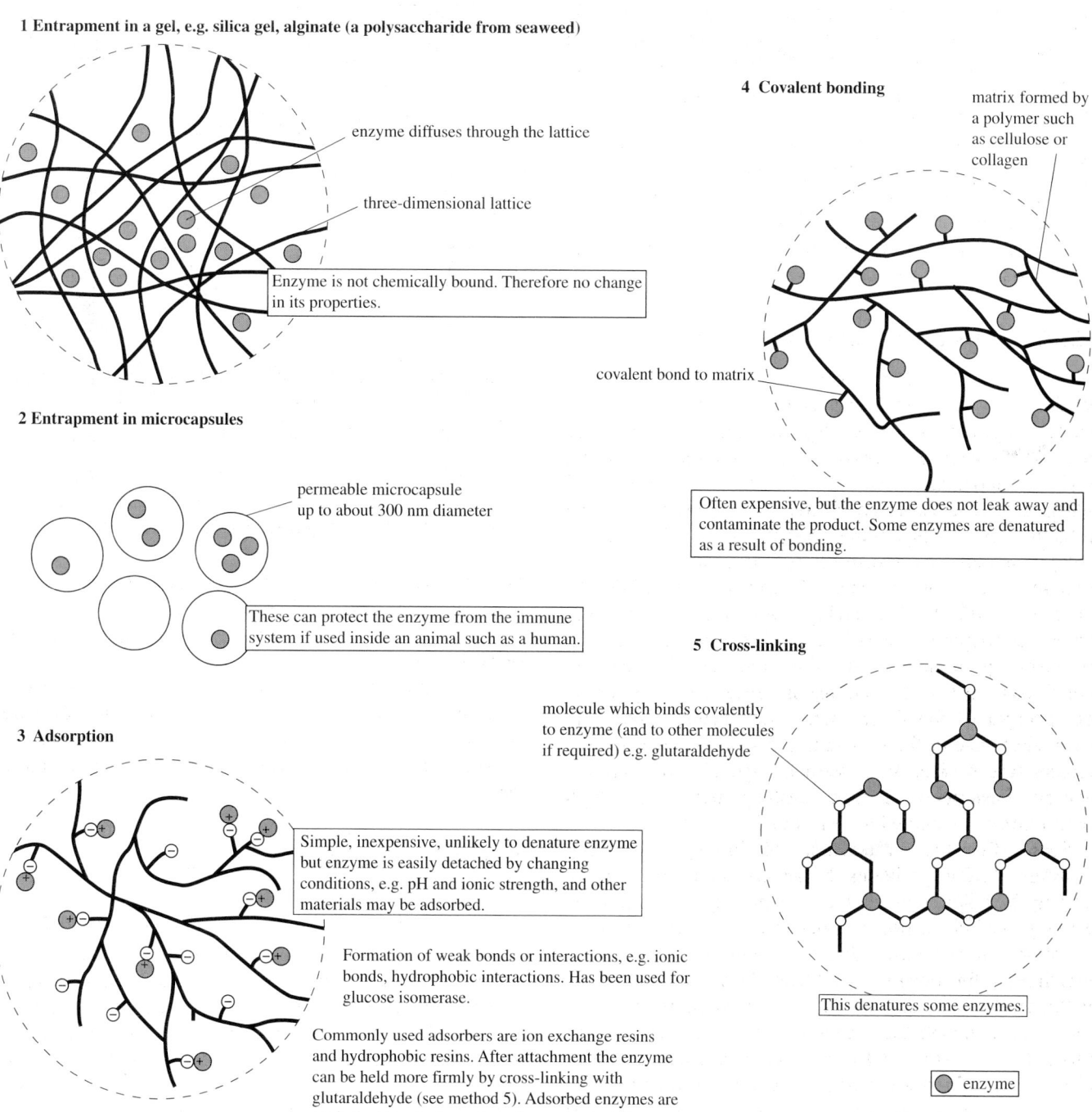

1 Entrapment in a gel, e.g. silica gel, alginate (a polysaccharide from seaweed)

enzyme diffuses through the lattice

three-dimensional lattice

Enzyme is not chemically bound. Therefore no change in its properties.

2 Entrapment in microcapsules

permeable microcapsule up to about 300 nm diameter

These can protect the enzyme from the immune system if used inside an animal such as a human.

3 Adsorption

Simple, inexpensive, unlikely to denature enzyme but enzyme is easily detached by changing conditions, e.g. pH and ionic strength, and other materials may be adsorbed.

Formation of weak bonds or interactions, e.g. ionic bonds, hydrophobic interactions. Has been used for glucose isomerase.

Commonly used adsorbers are ion exchange resins and hydrophobic resins. After attachment the enzyme can be held more firmly by cross-linking with glutaraldehyde (see method 5). Adsorbed enzymes are equivalent to membrane-bound enzymes in cells.

4 Covalent bonding

matrix formed by a polymer such as cellulose or collagen

covalent bond to matrix

Often expensive, but the enzyme does not leak away and contaminate the product. Some enzymes are denatured as a result of bonding.

5 Cross-linking

molecule which binds covalently to enzyme (and to other molecules if required) e.g. glutaraldehyde

This denatures some enzymes.

○ enzyme

Fig 12.28 *Methods for immobilising enzymes.*

Methods for immobilising enzymes

There are various ways of immobilising enzymes, as shown in fig 12.28. They involve either trapping the enzyme (**entrapment**) or attaching it to a fixed structure or matrix. Entrapment has the advantage that the enzyme remains in its natural state. However, it is difficult for large molecules to reach the enzyme.

Entrapment in beads of alginate is easily demonstrated in a class experiment and is a commonly used method in industry. A solution containing the enzyme and sodium alginate is dripped into a solution of calcium chloride. The droplets start to gel immediately they contact the calcium chloride and perfectly spherical beads of gel, with the enzyme entrapped inside, are formed. The gel can be further stabilised with polyacrylamide for long-term use. It can also be prepared in the form of sheets if supported by a woven cloth.

Applications of immobilised enzymes

The best example of a successful process involving immobilised enzymes is the production of high fructose corn syrup. This is widely used as a sweetener in the USA and Japan, for example in fruit drinks, because it is cheaper than sucrose. It is made from starch obtained from corn cobs (maize), a relatively cheap source of carbohydrate. Millions of tonnes are converted to a product known as **high fructose corn syrup** (**HFCS**) each year, a process requiring three enzymes. A starch slurry is obtained by milling (grinding) the corn and two amylases convert the starch to a glucose syrup. This can be decolourised and concentrated and used in a range of foods and drinks, or it can be finally converted to a roughly equal mixture of glucose and fructose by the enzyme glucose isomerase. This is done by passing it through a column in which the enzyme is immobilised by adsorption on a cellulose ion exchanger (method 3, fig 12.28). The activity of the enzyme gradually decreases with time, so it is usual to have several columns working at the same time. Fructose is sweeter than glucose, though both contain the same number of calories per unit mass. This means that by using high fructose corn syrup the same level of sweetness can be obtained in foods with fewer calories. About 4 million tonnes per year are produced in the USA.

The first immobilised enzyme to be used on an industrial scale was aminoacylase in Japan in 1969. It is used in the production of amino acids for animal feed supplements, for which there is a large market worldwide. Each amino acid molecule can exist in two forms which are mirror images of each other, like right and left hands. The two forms are known as optical isomers and are referred to as right and left-handed forms, or D- and L-forms (according to the direction in which they rotate the plane of polarised light). All naturally occurring amino acids are L-amino acids. Chemical synthesis of amino acids is easier than extracting amino acids from cells, but those made 'artificially' are an equal mix of L- and D-isomers. The solution to this problem is to use the specificity of enzymes to select one form only. A diagrammatic summary of the process is shown in fig 12.29.

The enzyme is immobilised by ionic binding to a column of matrix material (method 3, fig 12.28). After continuous and automated operation at 50 °C for 30 days, activity of the enzyme has dropped by 40%, at which point fresh enzyme can be added. A saving of 40% is made by immobilising the enzyme rather than using it in solution.

Another use of immobilised enzymes is in the manufacture of semisynthetic penicillins from natural penicillins. The immobilised enzyme chemically modifies one of the side groups on the basic penicillin structure which increases the antibiotic activity of the penicillins.

12.17 Biosensors

A **biosensor** is an electronic monitoring device which uses a biological material, such as a cell, an enzyme or an antibody, to detect or measure a chemical compound. Enzymes and antibodies are particularly useful

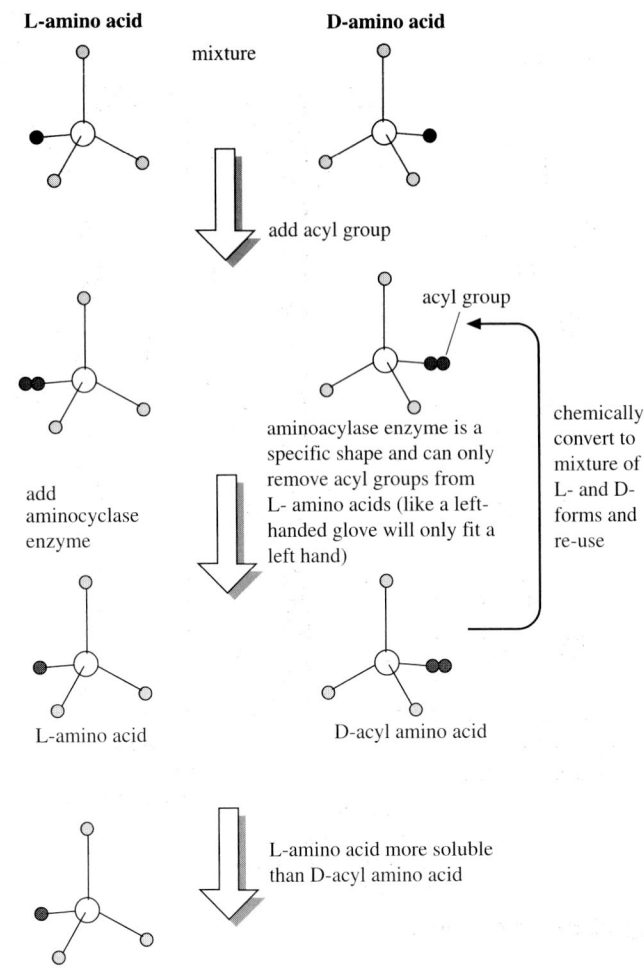

Fig 12.29 *Summary of the process for making L-amino acids for animal feed.*

because they are so specific and can pick out (detect) particular molecules in a complex mixture.

The reaction between the biological material and the substrate brings about a change which is converted into an electrical signal by an appropriate **transducer** (fig 12.30). This is designed to detect and respond to the change, much as an animal sense organ does. (For example, the rods and cones in the retina at the back of the eye are transducers. They respond to light by producing a nerve impulse, which is an electrical event.) The electrical signal in the biosensor is amplified to give some form of read-out, such as a digital display or print-out. Many types of change may occur, such as release of heat, light, a change in pH or mass, a flow of electrons or production of a new chemical.

12.17.1 Advantages and problems with biosensors

The main advantages are:

- they are specific – complex mixtures can be analysed for a particular chemical without the need for purification;

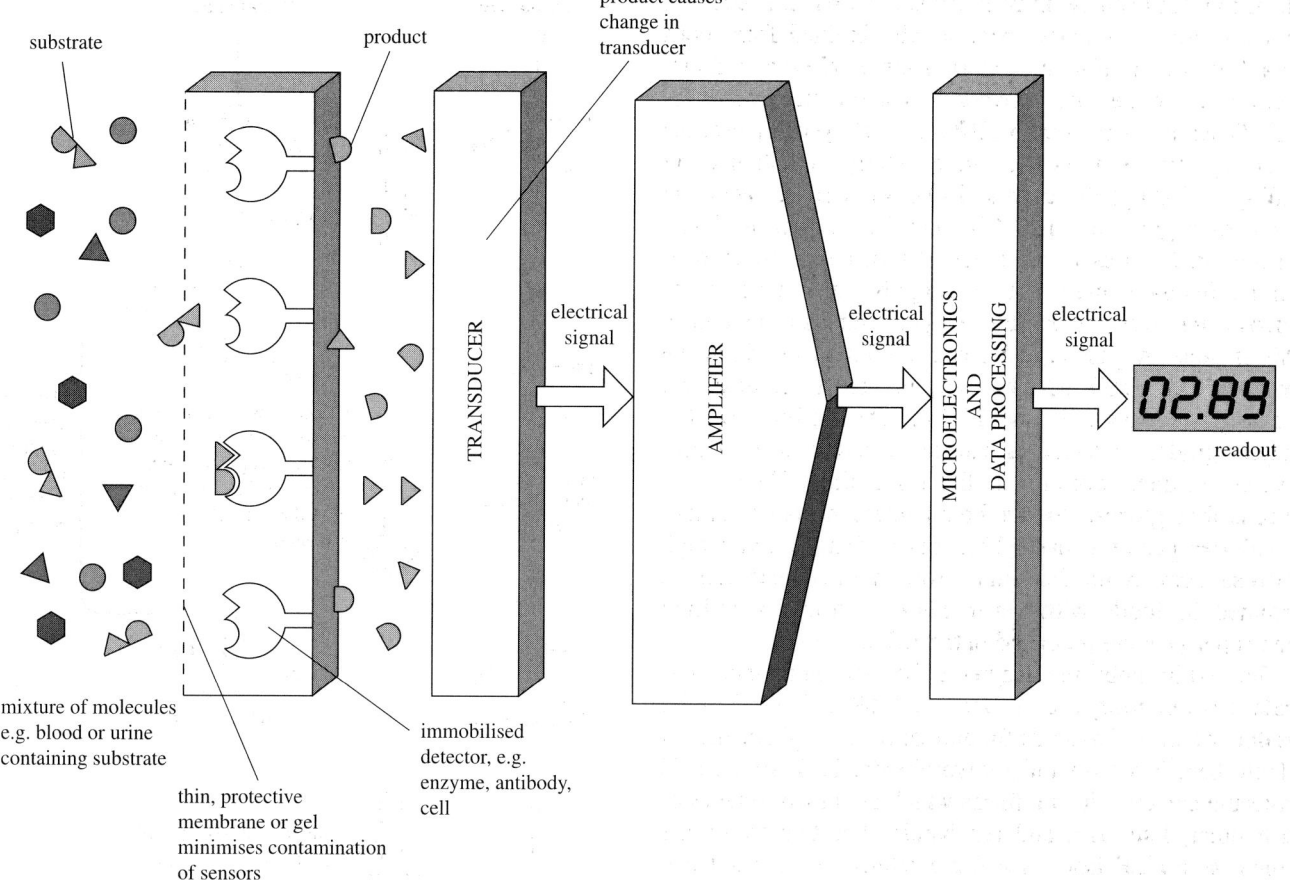

substrate — **product** — **product causes change in transducer** — **electrical signal** — **electrical signal** — **electrical signal** — **02.89** **readout**

TRANSDUCER — AMPLIFIER — MICROELECTRONICS AND DATA PROCESSING

mixture of molecules e.g. blood or urine containing substrate

thin, protective membrane or gel minimises contamination of sensors

immobilised detector, e.g. enzyme, antibody, cell

Fig 12.30 *A biosensor.*

- they are very sensitive, so only very small samples are needed and very low concentrations can be detected;
- they are rapid in response;
- they are safe to use;
- they are accurate;
- they can be made very small;
- they can be mass produced.

The main problems are:

- they are not very robust and need careful handling;
- they are not very stable;
- they are not sterilisable.

12.17.2   Monitoring blood glucose

An example of a commonly used biosensor is the one developed for detecting glucose in the blood of diabetics (fig 12.31). This contains the enzyme **glucose oxidase** in an immobilised form. The enzyme oxidises glucose in the blood to release electrons. These are collected and converted into an electrical current. The current generated is proportional to the *amount* of glucose present. It is extremely sensitive and can measure the glucose concentration in a single drop of blood and display the result within 20 seconds.

It is hoped that eventually it will be possible to implant such devices in blood vessels in the skin of diabetics, allowing them to monitor more accurately their insulin requirements. If this is linked to a minipump so that insulin is automatically released when needed, the diabetic will have, in effect, an automatic pancreas. This fine control would reduce the common secondary effects of diabetes, such as eye and kidney damage, suffered by some diabetics as a result of the relatively crude peaks and troughs of insulin concentration obtained with occasional injections.

12.17.3   Medical applications

The largest application of biosensors at present is in medicine. Enzymes are being used increasingly for routine automatic analysis of body fluids for metabolites, drugs and hormones. They are particularly useful for clinical diagnosis. Using biosensors reduces the risk of errors in diagnosis and also reduces costs once the biosensors are mass produced. Less time and less expertise is needed. It allows GPs to do tests in their surgeries without involving hospital laboratories. This saves money and avoids the need for patients to make return visits to receive a diagnosis. Treatment can also be started quicker. Another advantage is that there is less chance of a sample being mishandled, lost or contaminated. This would also be particularly useful in testing for use of drugs in sport. Kits

Fig 12.31 *A patient takes a blood sugar measurement using an Exactech biosensor. The patient places a drop of blood from a pin prick onto the lighter of the two panels at the end of the disposable strip (seen projecting from the left). An electronic readout then gives the blood sugar measurement, allowing the user to calculate the correct*

are already in use by police and doctors for detecting small amounts of drugs in humans.

Home diagnosis kits may become possible since many people would like to have this facility. However, care would be needed to make counselling available if tests for serious conditions became possible.

Biosensors are already in use which enable critical metabolites to be monitored during surgery. Such monitoring of metabolite levels in the body could become more general with the use of miniature implants, so that corrective action could be taken if any changes took place. Biosensors which are more sensitive and smaller could be developed by using '**biochips**'. Just as large computers have been reduced in size by the introduction of silicon microchips, so further size reduction of biosensors may be possible by using semiconducting organic molecules in place of silicon. Electrical signals could pass along these molecules and electrical circuits could be just one molecule wide. Biochips would be small enough to implant in the human body. Devices such as artificial sense organs and heart pacemakers might then become possible.

12.17.4 Other uses

The second largest use of biosensors is in the control of industrial processes. Living cells (yeasts or bacteria) have been used in conjunction with electrodes to measure L-amino acids, alcohol, phenols, methane, various sugars, ethanoic acid (vinegar) and antibiotics. They allow monitoring of conditions inside fermenters, which is particularly useful for continuous cultures.

An oxygen-detecting system which is about 100 times more sensitive has been developed which uses bacteria which become luminous when exposed to traces of oxygen. The light emitted is detected by a photoelectric cell. Optical biosensors are generating a lot of interest. One reason is that remote sensing may be possible in hazardous environments by using fibre optics.

Many enzyme reactions produce heat. Thermal biosensors can detect temperature changes as small as 0.0001 °C. They can be used to detect the presence of lactic acid.

Future applications are expected in the fields of agriculture, veterinary science, defence (detection of nerve gases, toxins and explosives), and the environment (mainly detection of pollution). Annual growth in the use of biosensors is 30% or over in all these cases. The markets, though, are still relatively small, worth less than £50 million in 1992. This is due partly to the disadvantages noted above.

Answers and discussion

Chapter 2

2.1

Time (in units of 20 min)	0	1	2	3	4	5	6	7	8	9	10
A Number of bacteria	1	2	4	8	16	32	64	128	256	512	1024
B $\log_{10}$ number of bacteria	0.0	0.3	0.6	0.9	1.2	1.5	1.8	2.1	2.4	2.7	3.0
C Number of bacteria expressed as power of 2	2^0	2^1	2^2	2^3	2^4	2^5	2^6	2^7	2^8	2^9	2^{10}

Graph A increases in steepness as time progresses. Graph B (a logarithmic plot) is a straight line (increases linearly with time). See fig 2.1(ans).

2.2 Consult tables 2.6 and 2.7, chapter 2.

2.3 The sporangiophores bear the sporangia above the main mycelium so that the spores are more likely to catch air currents and be dispersed.

2.4 Amphibians, like liverworts and mosses, are only partially adapted to life on land, having bodies which easily lose water, and they still rely on water for sexual reproduction. Both groups of organisms are thought by some scientists to represent intermediate stages in the evolution towards more advanced forms which are better adapted to life on land.

2.5 The sporophyte has become adapted for life on land although the gametophyte is still dependent on water for swimming gametes.

The sporophyte generation has true vascular tissue and true roots, stem and leaves with which to exploit the land environment more successfully.

The sporophyte is the dominant generation, the life of the gametophyte being short.

The mature sporophyte is no longer dependent on the gametophyte.

2.6 Sexual reproduction is dependent on water since it involves free-swimming sperm.

The gametophyte thallus is susceptible to desiccation.

The plants are often relatively intolerant of high light intensities.

2.7 The *Dryopteris* spore can develop wherever it falls, providing conditions are moist and fertile. Pollen grains must reach the female parts of the sporophyte.

2.8 The megaspore is large because it must contain sufficient food reserves to support the female gametophyte and subsequent development of the embryo sporophyte until the latter becomes self-supporting. Microspores, by being small, can be produced economically in large numbers and are light enough to be carried by air currents, thus increasing the chances of the male gametes that they contain reaching the female parts of the plants.

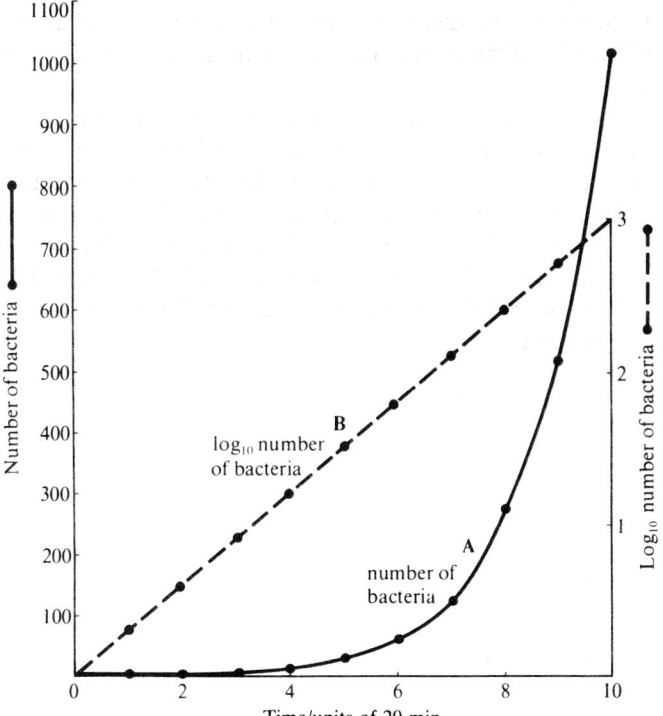

Fig 2.1(ans) *Growth of a model population of bacteria as plotted on arithmetic and logarithmic scales.*

Chapter 3

3.1 The molecular formula shows the number of each type of atom. The structural formula shows the arrangement of the atoms relative to each other. Note that angles of bonds can also be shown; see figs 3.3 and 3.5, for example.

3.2 (*a*) C_8H_{18}, octane

(*b*) C_6H_6, benzene

3.3

3.4 pentose $C_5H_{10}O_5$ hexose $C_6H_{12}O_6$

3.5 (*a*) Valency of C = 4, O = 2, H = 1.

(*b*) Molecular formula is $C_3H_6O_3$ in both cases; the compounds are therefore trioses.

(c) Each contains two hydroxyl groups. This could have been predicted, since it has already been explained that in monosaccharides all the carbon atoms except one have a hydroxyl group attached.

3.6 The principal sources of variation are as follows.

(a) Both pentoses and hexoses can be used to make polysaccharides, although normally only one type of monosaccharide is used in each type of polysaccharide.

(b) Two types of linkage, 1,4 and 1,6, are common between sugar units. Thus branching can occur.

(c) Lengths of chains and branches, and extent of branching can vary enormously.

(d) α- and β-forms of monosaccharides are important. (Compare starch and cellulose.)

(e) Sugars may be ketoses or aldoses.

(f) The high chemical reactivity of sugars (aldehyde, ketone and hydroxyl groups) means that they are very reactive molecules.

3.7 One that occurs when two compounds are joined by the elimination of a water molecule.

3.8 Body temperatures of poikilothermic animals become lower in cold environments. Lipids rich in unsaturated fatty acids (which have low melting points) generally remain liquid at temperatures lower (usually 5°C or lower) than those rich in saturated fatty acids. This may be necessary if the lipid is to maintain its function, such as a constituent of membranes.

3.9 Triolein because it contains three *unsaturated* oleic acid molecules. Tristearin is a fat, triolein an oil.

3.10 (a) Cell respiration (internal or tissue respiration). Fat undergoes oxidation.

(b) Only the hydrogen part of carbohydrate and fat molecules yields water on oxidation ($2H_2 + O_2 \longrightarrow 2H_2O$) and fats contain relatively more hydrogen than carbohydrates on a weight basis (nearly twice as much).

3.11

*peptide bond.

3.12 (a) AAA AAB ABA ABB
BAA BAB BBA BBB

(b) $2^3 = 8$

(c) $2^{100} = 1.27 \times 10^{30}$

(d) $20^{100} = 1.27 \times 10^{130}$ This is much larger than the number of atoms in the Universe (estimated at about 10^{100})! Thus, there is effectively an infinite potential for variation among protein structures.

(e) 20^n where n is the number of amino acids in the molecule.

3.13 The outstanding feature is that the ratio of adenine to thymine is always about 1.0, and so is the ratio of guanine to cytosine. In other words, the number of adenine molecules equals the number of thymine molecules and guanine = cytosine. Note also that the number of purine residues (adenine + guanine) therefore equals the number of pyrimidine residues (thymine + cytosine). Also revealed is the fact that the DNAs of different organisms have different base compositions, in other words the ratio of A:G or T:C is variable.

3.14 Adenine must pair with thymine and guanine with cytosine to account for the observed base ratios.

3.15 Compare the volume of the unknown sample needed to reduce the dye with the volume of 0.1% ascorbic acid solution needed in the standard described.

Percentage ascorbic acid in unknown sample =

$$\frac{\text{volume 0.1\% ascorbic acid used in standard}}{\text{volume of unknown sample used}} \times \frac{0.1}{100}$$

3.16 (a) Carry out Benedict's test on all three solutions. The sucrose solution would not give a brick-red precipitate on boiling. The glucose and glucose/sucrose solutions could be distinguished by pre-treating both as for hydrolysis (see non-reducing sugar test) and repeating Benedict's test. The glucose/sucrose mix will now show a greater amount of reducing sugar. (In practice, different dilutions of the solutions may have to be tried for convincing results. 0.05% glucose solution, 0.5% sucrose solution and a mixture of equal volumes of 0.1% glucose solution and 1.0% sucrose solution are suitable.)

(b) (i) Paper chromatography or thin-layer chromatography.

(ii) Effect on plane-polarised light using a polarimeter (both sucrose and glucose are dextro-rotatory, but sucrose produces a greater degree of rotation than glucose).

(iii) Sucrose is converted to reducing sugars (glucose + fructose) by the enzyme sucrase (invertase). The reaction may either be followed using a polarimeter or by Benedict's test.

3.17 Dissolve 10 g glucose in distilled water and make up to 100 cm³. (Do not add 10 g glucose to 100 cm³ distilled water because the final volume would be greater than 100 cm³.)

3.18 Add 10 cm³ of 10% glucose to 50 cm³ of 2% sucrose solution and make up to 100 cm³ with distilled water.

Chapter 4

4.1 (a) Initially the reactions A and B are fast and a lot of product is formed. Later, product formation levels off and there is no further increase. This may be because (i) all substrate has been converted to product, (ii) the enzyme has become inactivated, or (iii) the equilibrium point of a reversible reaction has been reached, and substrate and product are present in balanced concentrations.

(b) When the temperature is raised, (i) initial reaction rate is increased, and (ii) the enzyme becomes less stable and is inactivated more rapidly.

(c) Sensitivity to heat is an indication of the protein nature of the enzymes.

(d) At lower temperatures (as in curve C) rate of formation of product remains constant over 1 h.

4.2 (a) 5.50

(b) (i) pepsin, (ii) salivary amylase

(c) The active site of the enzyme is being destroyed. The ionisable groups of the enzyme, especially those of the active site, are being modified. Hence the substrate no longer fits easily into the active site and catalytic activity is diminished.

(d) A change in pH results in a change in the activity of most enzymes. Each enzyme would have its rate of reaction modified to a different extent as each possesses its own particular pH activity curve. All cells rely on a delicate balance between their enzyme systems, and so any changes in enzyme activity could cause the death of the cell or multicellular organism.

(e) See fig 4.2 (ans).

Optimum pH for enzyme activity is 6.00.

From pH 4–6, ionisable groups of the active site are modified such that the active site becomes more efficient at receiving and complexing with its substrate. The reverse is true when the pH changes from 6–8.

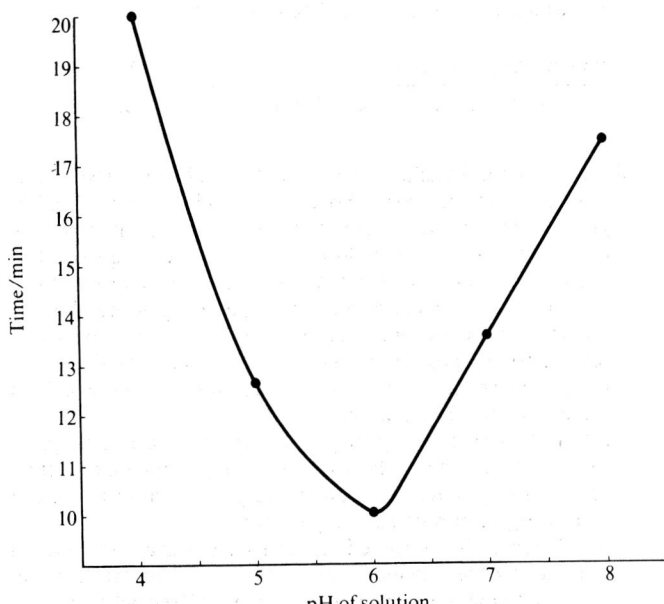

Fig 4.2(ans) *Activity of catalase on hydrogen peroxide at varying pH.*

4.3 Increasing the substrate concentration increases the probability of substrate molecules fitting into the active sites rather than inhibitor molecules.

4.4 Increased substrate concentration has no effect on the overall rate as there is no competition for the active site.

4.5 (*a*) The two sites are located on different parts of the enzyme, an active site for binding with the substrate and an allosteric site for binding with X.

(*b*) (i) X could act as an allosteric inhibitor of e_1 and therefore only permit production of S along the A–S pathway. This situation could remain until the surplus of X had been used up.

(ii) X could act as an allosteric inhibitor of e_5, again enhancing the production of S at the expense of X.

(*c*) Feedback inhibition.

4.6 (1) All are proteins and synthesised within living organisms.

(2) They catalyse chemical reactions by lowering the activation energy required to start the reaction.

(3) Only small amounts of enzyme are needed to catalyse reactions.

(4) At the end of a reaction the enzymes are unchanged.

(5) Each enzyme is specific and possesses an active site where enzyme and substrate combine temporarily to form an enzyme/substrate complex before products are released.

(6) Enzymes work best at an optimum pH and optimum temperature.

(7) Being proteins, enzymes are denatured by extremes of pH and temperature.

Chapter 5

5.1 Endoplasmic reticulum, ribosomes, microtubules, microvilli (visible as a 'brush border' in the light microscope).

In addition, small structures that are difficult to identify with certainty using a light microscope can be easily identified with the electron microscope, such as lysosomes and mitochondria.

5.2 (*a*) Cell wall with middle lamella and plasmodesmata, chloroplasts, large central vacuole (animal cells do possess small vacuoles, such as food vacuoles, contractile vacuoles)

(*b*) Centrioles, microvilli. (Pinocytotic vesicles are more commonly seen in animal cells.)

5.3 A: polar head of phospholipid (hydrophilic)
B: non-polar hydrocarbon tails of phospholipid (hydrophobic)
C: phospholipid
D: phospholipid layer

5.4 (*a*) A, (*b*) B, (*c*) A, (*d*) B, (*e*) –1000 kPa.

5.5 (*a*) A Na^+/K^+ pump operates whereby pumping out of Na^+ is linked to pumping in of K^+. Without K^+, no pumping out of Na^+ can occur, so Na^+ accumulates within the cells by diffusion and K^+ leaves the cells by diffusion.

(*b*) ATP is a source of energy for active transport of Na^+ ions.

Chapter 7

7.1 Photoautotrophic organisms use light energy from the Sun as an energy source for synthesising organic compounds from inorganic materials, with carbon dioxide as a source of carbon. Chemoheterotrophic organisms use organic compounds which are synthesised from pre-existing organic sources of carbon, using energy from chemical reactions.

7.2 **Overall form and position**
Large surface area to volume ratio for maximum interception of light and efficient gaseous exchange.
Blade often held at right-angles to incident light, particularly in dicotyledons.

Stomata
Pores in the leaf allow gaseous exchange. Carbon dioxide needed for photosynthesis, with oxygen a waste product.
In dicotyledons, stomata are located mainly in the shady lower epidermis, thus minimising loss of water vapour in transpiration.

Guard cells
Regulate opening of stomata (ensure stomata open only in light when photosynthesis occurs).

Mesophyll
Contains special organelles for photosynthesis, the chloroplasts, containing chlorophyll.
In dicotyledons, palisade mesophylls cells, with more chloroplasts, are located near the upper surface of the leaf for maximum interception of light. Length of the cells increases the chance for light absorption.
Chloroplasts are located near the periphery of the cell for maximum absorption of light and easier gas exchange with intercellular spaces.
Chloroplasts may be phototataxic (that is move within the cell towards light).

In dicotyledons, spongy mesophyll has large intercellular spaces for efficient gaseous exchange.

Vascular system
Supplies water, a reagent in photosynthesis; also mineral salts. Removes the products of photosynthesis.
Supporting skeleton provided together with collenchyma and sclerenchyma.

7.3 Chlorophyll *a* absorption in red light is about twice that of chlorophyll *b* and the absorption peak is at a slightly longer wavelength (lower energy). Absorption in the blue is lower and shifted to a slightly shorter wavelength (higher energy). Note that only very slight differences in chemical structure cause these differences.

7.4 If an isotope has a shorter half-life (for example 11C, 20.5 min) it rapidly decays to the point at which it is undetectable, thus severely restricting its usefulness in biological experiments, which often take hours or days to complete.

7.5 Photosynthesis in *Chlorella* and higher plants is biochemically similar so that *Chlorella* was used for the following reasons:
(1) *Chlorella* culture is virtually a chloroplast culture since a large volume of every cell is occupied by a single chloroplast;
(2) greater uniformity of growth can be achieved;
(3) the cells are very rapidly exposed to radioactive carbon dioxide and also quickly killed, so handling techniques are easier.

7.6 For maximum illumination of algae.

7.7

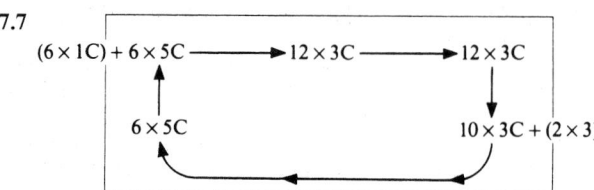

This emphasises the cyclic flow of carbon; the complexity of Calvin's cycle is due mainly to the difficulty of converting $10 \times 3C$ into $6 \times 5C$.

7.8 Availability of carbon dioxide, water, light and chlorophyll.

7.9 (*a*) In region A light intensity is the limiting factor.
(*b*) B: some factor other than light intensity is becoming the limiting factor. In region B, both light intensity and the other factor(s) are limiting. C: light intensity is no longer a limiting factor.
(*c*) D: the 'saturation point' for light intensity under these conditions, that is the point beyond which an increase in light intensity will cause no further increase in the rate of photosynthesis.
(*d*) E: the maximum rate of photosynthesis attainable under the conditions of the experiment.

7.10 X, Y and Z are the points at which light ceases to be the major limiting factor in the four experiments. Up to these points there is a linear relationship between light intensity and rate of photosynthesis.

7.11 Enzymes would start to become denatured.

7.12 Some likely situations would be (*a*) in a shaded community such as a wood; dawn and twilight in a warm climate; (*b*) a bright winter's day.

7.13 Mesophyll chloroplasts for light reactions, bundle sheath chloroplasts for dark reactions.

7.14 Oxygen would compete with carbon dioxide for the active site of RuBP carboxylase.

7.15 **Carbon dioxide pump.** By acting as a carbon dioxide pump, the malate shunt increases carbon dioxide concentration in the bundle sheath cells, thus increasing the efficiency with which RuBP carboxylase works.
Hydrogen pump. Malate carries hydrogen from $NADPH_2$ in the mesophyll to NADP in the bundle sheath cells, where $NADPH_2$ is regenerated. The advantage is that $NADPH_2$ is generated by the efficient light reaction in the mesophyll chloroplasts and can be used as reducing power in the Calvin cycle of bundle sheath chloroplasts, whose own synthesis of $NADPH_2$ is limited.

7.16 (*a*) Lowering oxygen concentrations stimulates C_3 photosynthesis because it reduces competition between oxygen and carbon dioxide for the active site of RuBP carboxylase.
(*b*) Lowering oxygen concentration does not affect C_4 photosynthesis because PEP carboxylase does not accept oxygen.

7.17 The dark blue colour of the dye should disappear as it is reduced, leaving the green of the chloroplasts.

7.18 The DCPIP should have remained blue in tubes (2) and (3), which were controls. Tube (2) shows that light alone cannot induce the colour change, and that chloroplasts must be present for the Hill reaction to occur. Tube (3) shows that light must be present as well as chloroplasts for the Hill reaction to occur.

7.19 The two organelles closest in size to the chloroplasts are nuclei (slightly larger) and mitochondria (slightly smaller). More rigorous differential centrifugation or density gradient centrifugation would be necessary to isolate pure chloroplasts.

7.20 Indirect evidence suggests that nuclei and mitochondria were not involved in reducing DCPIP because light was needed, and these organelles lack chlorophyll or any other conspicuous pigment.

7.21 To reduce enzyme activity. During homogenisation destructive enzymes may be released from other parts of the cell, such as from lysosomes or vacuoles.

7.22 Cell reactions operate efficiently only at certain pHs; any significant change in pH, caused for example by release of acids from other parts of the cell, might have affected chloroplast activity.

7.23 (*a*) water (*b*) DCPIP

7.24 Non-cyclic photophosphorylation only: (i) oxygen was evolved (ii) electrons were accepted by DCPIP, therefore they could not recycle into PSI.

7.25 (*a*) The chloroplasts lack chloroplast envelopes (bounding membranes) and stroma. Only the internal membrane system remains.
(*b*) The medium lacking sucrose was hypotonic to the chloroplasts. Without the protection of the cell walls, broken during homogenisation, chloroplasts absorb water by osmosis, swell and burst. The stroma dissolves, leaving only membranes.
(*c*) The change was desirable because bursting the chloroplasts allows more efficient access of DCPIP to the membranes where the Hill reaction is located.

7.26 The discovery of the Hill reaction was a landmark for several reasons:
(1) it showed that oxygen evolution could occur without reduction of carbon dioxide, providing evidence for separate light and dark reactions and the splitting of water;
(2) it showed that chloroplasts could carry out a light-driven reduction of an electron acceptor;
(3) it gave biochemical evidence that the light reaction of photosynthesis was entirely located in the chloroplast.

7.27 The plant continues to use sugars in the dark, for example for respiration. Photosynthesis ceases in the dark, so as sugars are depleted starch reserves are converted to sugars, including sucrose which travels from the leaves to other parts of the plant.

7.28 It should be placed in an identical flask but with water replacing potassium hydroxide solution. Unsoaked cotton wool should secure the leaf stalk. (The stalk itself could be surface-treated with lime water to check whether possible injury here could affect photosynthesis.)

7.29 Rates of carbon dioxide uptake, oxygen production and carbohydrate production could be used. Rate of increase in the dry mass of leaves may also be measured. This is particularly suitable for crop plants over a growing season when relatively large samples may be taken. An experiment for measuring carbon dioxide uptake is described in experiment 7.5.

7.30 (*a*) The rate of gas production is directly proportional to *LI* up to a *LI* of *x* units. At this point light saturation began to occur and this was complete at *y* units (*x* and *y* values depend on experimental conditions). Thereafter some factor other than light was limiting the rate of gas production.
(*b*) The laboratory was darkened to avoid extra light which could have stimulated extra photosynthesis. Temperature was kept constant because this also affects the rate of photosynthesis.

7.31 (a) Temperature may vary as the lamp heats the water (this should be avoided by the water bath).

(b) The carbon dioxide concentration of the water may vary during the experiment, especially if potassium hydrogen-carbonate was added earlier.

(c) Any stray light which is admitted to the laboratory will affect photosynthesis.

7.32 As the bubble of oxygen rises through the water, some of the dissolved nitrogen will come out of solution and enter the bubble, and some of the oxygen will dissolve. This exchange is due to the different partial pressures (concentrations) of oxygen and nitrogen in the bubble and the water, there being a tendency for them to come to equilibrium with time. Traces of water vapour and carbon dioxide will also be present in the collected gas. Once the gas has been collected, it will tend to come into equilibrium with atmospheric air by diffusion of gases through the water.

7.33 The amount of oxygen produced by photosynthesis in the experiment must all be collected. If the water is not saturated with air, some of the oxygen released in photosynthesis will dissolve in the water and reduce the amount recorded.

7.34 Specimen results are given in the following table.

Time/h	Colour of indicator			
	tube A	tube B	tube C	tube D
0	red	red	red	red
18	yellow	purple	red	red

The control tubes, C and D, were necessary to prove that any changes that took place in tubes A and B were due to the presence of leaves. In tube A conditions became more acidic as a result of carbon dioxide being produced during respiration. Photosynthesis did not take place in the absence of light. In tube B conditions became less acidic, indicating a net uptake of carbon dioxide. The carbon dioxide produced by respiration was used in photosynthesis, together with that already in the air inside the leaf and dissolved in the indicator solution. The rate of photosynthesis was greater than the rate of respiration.

7.35 The carbon dioxide compensation point. At this point rate of photosynthesis equals rate of respiration.

Chapter 8

8.1 (1) Decompose organic matter and therefore help recycling of elements from dead to living organisms.

(2) Render food unfit for human consumption (such as make bread mouldy).

(3) In the Far East *Mucor* has been used to produce alcohol. A mixture of *Mucor* and yeast was added to rice. *Mucor* converted the rice to sugars which the yeast then converted to alcohol.

8.2 See section 2.10.3 and table 8.1.

8.3 Active pepsin would digest cells that produce it, there being no mucus barrier within the gastric glands.

8.4 (a) The folds of the wall of the small intestine, villi and microvilli.

(b) It increases tremendously the surface area for secretion and absorption and makes it very efficient at these processes.

8.5 Rate of enzyme activity would decrease or stop as the enzymes would be denatured by the low pH.

8.6 It ensures that even if the soluble food molecules are in concentrations lower than those already in the blood, they will still pass into the blood.

8.7 Because of the continual heat loss from the relatively larger body surface of the mouse.

8.8 Fats are much richer in hydrogen than carbohydrates. As most of the energy that is released in the body arises by the oxidation of hydrogen to water, so fats liberate more heat than carbohydrates.

8.9 (a) Certain 'factors' (now known as vitamins) are needed in small amounts in the diet, which are essential for healthy growth and development.

(b) The growth 'factors' must be contained in the 3 cm^3 rations of milk provided for the rats, which confirms that only minute amounts are required. When the milk was stopped, growth was quickly curtailed. Rats without milk did grow initially, therefore they must have had a small store of vitamins in their body initially.

(c) It is deficient in iron, vitamin B and roughage.

8.10 The RDA quoted for a particular group is not the *average* requirement for that group, but a level which would cover the needs of almost everyone in that group. Many people regard it as a minimum desirable intake. For most people, though, the RDA is much more than they need. Its misuse could result in an average person over-eating.

8.11 The contribution of fat to energy intake should decrease, from 40% to 33%. This should be achieved by cutting down intake of saturated fatty acids from 16% to 10% of energy intake. There should be an equivalent rise in carbohydrate in the form of starch, and cell wall sugars from dietary fibre. (Milk contains saturated fats.)

8.12 There are many possible answers, e.g. the individual may make an error in estimating amount of intake; day-to-day and long-term variations in diet occur; food composition tables are not perfectly accurate and are based on assumptions such as the amount of fat in any meat consumed.

8.13 The risk of deficiency would be very small for any individual. Most individuals, though, would be eating more than they need.

8.14 It is difficult to measure accurately the existing intake of an individual. An individual's intake may vary over time.

If an individual's consumption is between the LRNI and the RNI one can only state that the nearer the RNI, the less likelihood of a deficiency. Unless there are physical signs or symptoms of deficiency it is impossible to state whether the diet is inadequate.

8.15 The consumer might believe that this is the average requirement and that he or she should try to consume the full RDA, whereas most people do not need this amount.

8.16 Purchasing food takes up a high proportion of the income of lower income groups. Such groups might be more at risk from nutrient deficiencies and assessment and planning of diet would be particularly important in such a situation.

Chapter 9

9.1 Light energy is needed for photosynthesis. Photosynthetic organisms (mainly plants and algae) are at the beginning of almost all food chains. Animals are therefore dependent on plants, either directly or indirectly, for their energy and materials.

9.2 See fig 9.2 (ans).

9.3 Oxygen is the final hydrogen acceptor in the respiratory chain.

9.4 Oxygen supply is increased by increased rate and depth of breathing, and an increase in the power and rate of heart beat.

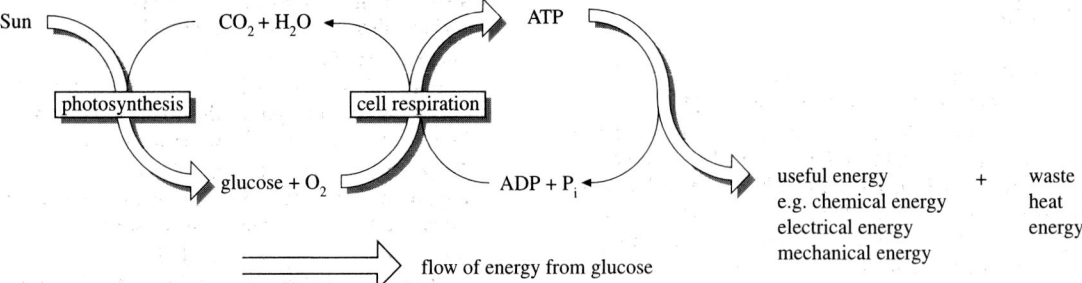

Fig 9.2(ans)

9.5 Lactic acid is being removed from the muscle by the blood, to be taken to the liver.

9.6 For rapid diffusion of molecules between cytoplasm and mitochondrion.

9.7

Entering	*Leaving*
pyruvate	
oxygen	carbon dioxide
reduced hydrogen carrier,	oxidised hydrogen carrier,
e.g. reduced NAD	e.g. NAD
ADP	ATP
phosphate	water

9.8 When blood and water first meet, the concentration gradient of oxygen between them will be great. However, as blood and water flow along together the gradient will decrease until blood shows a percentage saturation for oxygen equal to that of the water. This would be well below the blood's maximum possible saturation point and therefore inefficient (fig 9.8 (ans)).

9.9 Five – into epithelial cell lining alveolus, out of this cell, into endothelial cell of blood capillary, out of this cell, and into red cell.

9.10 Because not all the air exchanged reaches the alveoli. Some is in the bronchioles, bronchi and trachea ('dead space air').

9.11 Smaller mammals have a large surface area to volume ratio from which heat can be lost and therefore must use up more oxygen in order to maintain a constant body temperature.

9.12 By relating oxygen consumed per gram of body weight in unit time.

9.13 $RQ = \dfrac{CO_2}{O_2} = \dfrac{102}{145} = 0.70$. An RQ of 0.7 is typical of fats (lipids).

9.14 $RQ = \dfrac{CO_2}{O_2} = \dfrac{2}{0} = \infty$ (infinity).

This is typical of anaerobic respiration. If anaerobic and aerobic respiration are occurring at the same time, very high RQ values are obtained.

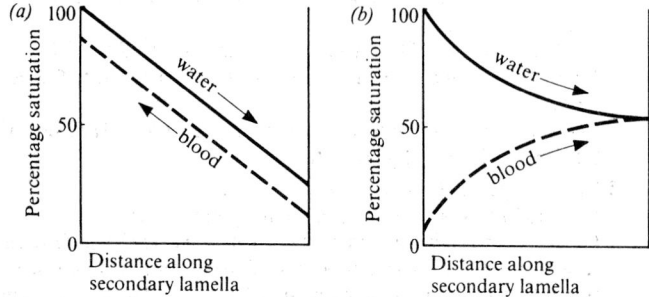

Fig 9.8(ans) (a) *Counterflow of water and blood.* (b) *Parallel flow of water and blood.*

9.15 Because humans generally respire a mixture of carbohydrate and fat.

9.16 (a) Breathing rate is about 17 breaths min^{-1}.
(b) Tidal volume is 450 cm^3 (average).
(c) Pulmonary ventilation is 17×450 cm^3 = 7.65 dm^3 min^{-1}.
(d) Oxygen uptake is given by the slope of the line AB. Therefore oxygen consumption is 1500 cm^3 in 4 min = 375 cm^3 min^{-1}.

9.17 (a)

Aerobic respiration	*Photosynthesis*
This is a catabolic process and results in the breakdown of carbohydrate molecules into simple inorganic compounds	An anabolic process which results in the synthesis of carbohydrate molecules from simple inorganic compounds.
Energy is incorporated into ATP for immediate use.	Energy is accumulated and stored in carbohydrate. Some ATP is formed.
Oxygen is used up.	Oxygen is released.
Carbon dioxide and water are released.	Carbon dioxide and water are used up.
The process results in a decrease in dry mass.	Results in an increase in dry mass.
In eukaryotes the process occurs in mitochondria.	In eukaryotes the process occurs in chloroplasts.
Takes place continuously throughout the lifetime of all cells, and is independent of chlorophyll and light.	Occurs only in cells possessing chlorophyll and only in the presence of light.

(b) *List of similarities between photosynthesis and aerobic respiration*
Both are energy-converting processes.
Both require mechanisms for exchange of carbon dioxide and oxygen.
Both require special organelles in eukaryotes, that is mitochondria for respiration and chloroplasts for photosynthesis; mitochondria and chloroplasts resemble prokaryotic organisms in possessing circular DNA and a prokaryote-type protein-synthesising system.
The light reactions of photosynthesis resemble cell respiration in the following ways:
(i) phosphorylation occurs (that is synthesis of ATP from ADP and P);
(ii) this is coupled to flow of electrons along a chain of electron carriers;
(iii) the electron carriers must be organised on membranes for coupling to take place; these are cristae in mitochondria and thylakoids in chloroplasts.

Chapter 10

10.1 Dry mass is used because the water content of food samples or organisms may vary and water contributes no energy.

10.2 Small birds or mammals have a much higher surface area to volume ratio than humans and therefore lose body heat relatively more rapidly. Since small mammals and birds are endothermic ('warm-blooded') like humans they must consume relatively more energy to maintain body heat. (Birds also have a higher metabolic rate and body temperature than mammals.)

10.3 Example for grassland:

grass $\longrightarrow$ sheep $\longrightarrow$ human.
Festuca ovina,
sheep's fescue

10.4 seed – blackbird – hawk; trophic level 3, T3
leaf litter – earthworm – blackbird – hawk, T4
leaf – caterpillar – beetle – insectivorous bird – hawk, T5
rose bush (sap) – aphid – ladybird – spider – insectivorous bird – hawk, T6

10.5 Since the main primary producers are trees, their numbers would not be changed during the winter season. However herbivores dependent on the leaves, flowers and fruits for their food sources would be greatly reduced in number since in a mid-latitude deciduous woodland their food source would not be available in winter. It is likely that in winter the pyramid of numbers for this woodland would no longer be inverted; certainly any inversion between trophic levels 1 and 2 would be greatly reduced. In winter detritus pathways are more important than grazing food chains.

10.6 (*a*) May, June and July
(*b*) (i) Increase in light intensity and duration, and increase in temperature coupled with the availability of nutrients. Photosynthesis and growth are therefore favoured.
(ii) Grazing by primary consumers, such as zooplankton, and decrease in production due to depletion of nutrients. (The latter is due to the dead remains of producers sinking through the lake to colder, non-circulating water.)
(iii) Decline in numbers of zooplankton. Increase in nutrients (circulation of nutrients improves in the autumn as the surface layers of water cool and mix more freely with the colder, deeper layers). Temperature and light are still favourable.
(iv) Light and temperature unfavourable for photosynthesis and growth.

10.7 Blue-green bacteria and some other bacteria are also photosynthetic (they are prokaryotes, not plants). Chemosynthetic bacteria are also autotrophic (section 7.2) and therefore make a contribution to primary productivity. The total contribution of all these organisms is small compared with autotrophic eukaryotes (photosynthetic protoctista and plants).

10.8 Mutualistic bacteria in the root nodules of legumes fix nitrogen which leads to increased growth and thus to increased demand for other minerals, notably potassium and phosphorus. (However, ploughing-in of legumes is sometimes done, thus keeping the minerals in the soil.)

10.9 Chemoheterotrophic. They can be classified further as saprotrophic.

10.10 Anywhere there is insufficient oxygen for decomposition of all accumulating organic matter, such as bogs, aquatic sediments like mud deposits, arctic tundra, deeper zones of soil and waterlogged soils.

10.11 Both increase aeration and hence oxygen content of soil. This stimulates decomposition and nitrification. It also inhibits denitrification, oxygen being used instead of nitrate.

10.12 *Photosynthesis* (see chapter 7 and section 10.3)
On average 1–5% of the radiation incident on plants is used in photosynthesis

Source of energy for rest of food chain
Light is also needed for chlorophyll synthesis
Transpiration (see chapter 13)
About 75% of the radiation incident on plants is wasted in causing water to evaporate thereby causing transpiration
Important implications for water conservation
Photoperiodism (see chapters 16 and 17)
Important for synchrony of plant and animal behaviour (particularly reproduction) with seasons
Movement (see chapters 16 and 18)
Phototropism and photonasty in plants: important for reaching light
Phototaxic movements of animals and unicellular plants; important for locating suitable habitat
Vision in animals (see chapter 17)
One of the major senses
Other roles
Synthesis of vitamin D in humans
Prolonged exposure to ultra-violet damaging, particularly to animals, therefore pigmentation, avoidance behaviour, etc.

10.13 Geographical barriers, such as oceans; ecological barriers, such as unfavourable habitats separating areas of favourable habitats; distance over which dispersal must operate; air and water currents: size and nature of invasion areas

10.14 (*a*) Two eggs from each female must, on average, survive.
(*b*)

	Number of fertilised eggs that must die for stable population	Pre-reproductive mortality
oyster	$(100 \times 10^6) - 2$	>99.9%
codfish	$(9 \times 10^6) - 2$	>99.9%
plaice	$(35 \times 10^4) - 2$	>99.9%
salmon	$(10 \times 10^4) - 2$	>99.9%
stickleback	498	498/500= 99.6%
winter moth	198	99.0%
mouse	48	96.0%
dogfish	18	90.0%
penguin	6	75.0%
elephant	3	60.0%
Victorian Englishwoman	8	80.0%

(*c*) The stickleback and dogfish give birth to live young, that is they are viviparous. Therefore fewer eggs need to be produced owing to the greater degree of parental involvement in the development of offspring. Also, the female parent could not physically support any greater numbers of offspring.

10.15 Population (*b*), since a high percentage of individuals would die before reproductive age is reached. Population (*a*) would have to combine its high survival rate with low reproductive rate to maintain a stable population size.

10.16 (*a*) Out of 3200 eggs, 640 survive, so 2560 die – a mortality of 80%.
(*b*) Out of 640 fry, 64 survive, so 576 die – a mortality of 90%.
(*c*) Out of 64 smolts, 2 survive, so 62 die – a mortality of about 97%.
The total pre-reproductive mortality for salmon is 3198 out of 3200 = 99.97% (see fig 10.16 (ans)).

10.17 (*a*) A sigmoid (S-shaped) growth curve.
(*b*) Food and space. Food is more likely in this case.
(*c*) Faster reproductive rate. More efficient feeding. Greater resistance to toxic waste products, either of *Paramecium* or of bacteria growing in the same culture (*P. aurelia* has been shown to be more resistant than *P. caudatum*). Production of a poison or growth inhibitor (allelopathy). Predation.

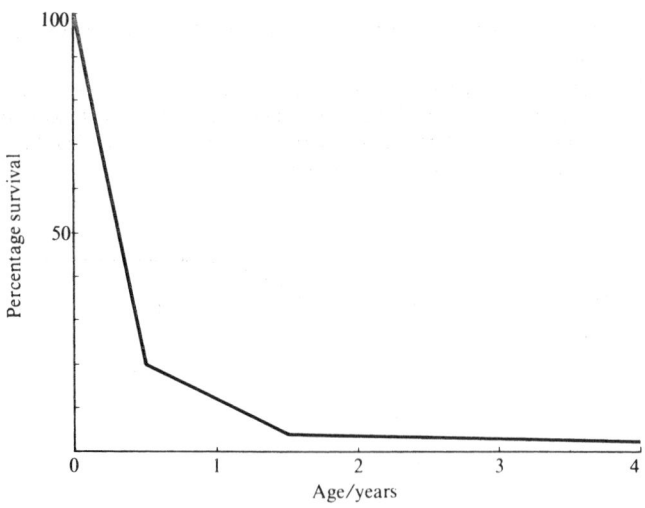

Fig 10.16(ans) *Graph showing pre-reproductive mortality for salmon.*

10.18 (*a*) Deforestation reduces the total world volume of photosynthetic material and thus reduces consumption of atmospheric carbon dioxide in photosynthesis.

(*b*) Removal of the tree canopy exposes the forest floor to sunlight and warmer temperatures. In forests or woodlands with significant litter and soil humus contents this exposure will favour accelerated rates of decomposition and carbon dioxide release.

10.19 BOD of discharge
BOD of receiving water
Nature of organic material
Total organic load of the river
Temperature
Extent of aeration from atmosphere (varies with wind etc.)
Dissolved oxygen in stream
Numbers and type of bacteria in effluent and stream
Ammonia content of effluent

10.20 Organisms live in their environment all the time. Their presence (or absence) therefore reflects the suitability of that environment for their living requirements at all times. A short-lived but severe pollution incident occurring at night would be reflected by the absence of sensitive organisms long after visible and chemical evidence of the pollution incident had disappeared. Biological indicators can therefore be a more sensitive and representative reflection of environmental conditions. 24 hour continuous chemical monitoring can be done but is not usually a viable routine practice for most water courses. This is especially true of small rivers and streams and remote areas. It also requires much time-consuming and, in the long term, expensive laboratory analysis. The main drawbacks of biological methods are that they require reasonable expertise at identification and will also be affected by seasonal factors.

10.21 (*a*) (i) $\times$ 2 (ii) $\times$ 500 (iii) $\times$ 2500 (iv) $\times$ 3750

(*b*) DDT is subject to progressive concentration as it passes along the food chain. This suggests that it is a persistent chemical, not easily broken down, and that it is stored rather than metabolised in living organisms. (In fact, it remains active for 10–15 years in soil.)

(*c*) (i) and (ii) 4th trophic level (top carnivore) (iii) 2nd trophic level (herbivore)

(*d*) DDT has spread all over the world as a result of two factors. First, it is carried at very low concentrations in water. If it is washed off agricultural land and into rivers some of it reaches the sea and becomes concentrated in marine food chains. Penguins feed on fish and are part of these food chains.

Secondly, DDT can be carried in the atmosphere, both because it is volatile and because it is sprayed as a dust which can be carried by wind systems over large distances.

(*e*) (i) A small proportion of the original midges were resistant to DDD and these were not killed by the spraying procedure. Between sprays their numbers increased and after successive sprays they continued to breed and eventually constituted the greater part of the population. In other words the population had undergone intensive selection pressure (see chapter 26).

(ii) The data given suggest that DDD (and therefore DDT) is stored predominantly in fatty tissues. (This is because DDD and DDT are soluble in fat rather than water.) During times of food shortage, fat is mobilised and used so that the DDD or DDT accumulated over a long period is released into the bloodstream in relatively high concentrations.

(*f*) It has been suggested that the high death toll of birds in the winter of 1962–3 compared with 1946–7 was due to the additional effects of DDT mobilisation from fatty tissues. In 1946–7 the use of DDT was limited: in the late 1950s and early 1960s its use was widespread.

10.23 A population with a common gene pool will slowly evolve over time. If the population is very small its members may become inbred and lose vigour. In the recent past the black rhino has been hunted, for its horn, to near extinction. Each local population is now a tiny fraction of the original population and physically isolated. Such animals will be increasingly inbred. Outbreeding strengthens genetic diversity and, where populations are very small, this may be important for the health of the animals. Semen may be collected from anaesthetised wild or captive males and used to inseminate anaesthetised captive females at oestrus (the time of ovulation). Such artificial insemination technology makes it less necessary to move the animals themselves yet allows the spread of genes. It also makes possible the storage of genetic material (by cryopreservation – deep-frozen semen) in the event of a lack of males, in a local population, where females are still found.

Chapter 11

11.1 Fresh mass of soil $= 60\,g$
dry mass of soil $= 45\,g$
therefore mass of water $= 60\,g - 45\,g = 15\,g$

therefore percentage water content of fresh soil $= \dfrac{15}{60} \times 100 = 25\%$

Dry mass of soil $= 45\,g$
dry mass of soil after combustion $= 30\,g$
therefore mass of organic material $= 15\,g$

therefore percentage organic content of fresh soil $= \dfrac{15}{60} \times 100 = 25\%$

11.2 43%.

11.3 36%.

11.4 4230.

Chapter 12

12.1 (i) iron   – found in cytochromes which are electron carriers in respiration

     phosphate   – synthesis of nucleic acids, ATP, phospholipids in membranes

(ii) nitrate   – source of nitrogen for synthesis of proteins, nucleic acids and many other organic molecules

     magnesium   – part of structure of chlorophyll (bacteriochlorophyll) and cofactor for many enzymes, eg AT Pase

12.2 K_2HPO_4 and KH_2PO_4 – source of K and P. (These also act as buffers, tending to resist changes in pH caused by products of bacterial growth.)

$(NH_4)_2SO_4$ – source of N and S.

$MgSO_4$ – source of Mg and S.

$CaCl_2$ – source of Ca and Cl.

Glucose – source of C and energy.

12.3 See fig 12.3(ans).

12.4 Prepare a medium which is free from any nitrogen-containing compounds but which contains all other nutrients needed for growth. Inoculate with soil, place in contact with nitrogen and incubate under sterile conditions. The only organisms which will be able to grow and multiply will be nitrogen fixers.

12.5 Graph A increases in steepness as time progresses. Graph B (a logarithmic plot) is a straight line (increases linearly with time). See fig 2.1(ans).

12.6 The graph would be a typical growth curve for a bacterial population (see fig 12.8) except that there would be no lag phase because the bacteria are already adapted for that medium.

12.7 See fig 12.7(ans). Factors responsible for the changes are discussed in section 12.1. The difference in the growth curve of living bacteria compared with living and dead bacteria is due to the following:

(*a*) a few cells die during lag and log phases;

(*b*) during the stationary phase the combined total of living plus dead cells continues to increase slowly for some time since some cells are still reproducing;

(*c*) during the phase of decline the combined total of living plus dead cells remains constant, though many are dying.

12.8 Doubling time is between 2.5 and 3 hours.

12.9 (*a*) See section 12.10.2.

(*b*) See section 12.10.5.

(*c*) See section 12.5.3.

12.10 Any of the following: confidentiality – the user is the first to know if she is pregnant; a rapid result is obtained; can be used from the first day a period is due because it is very sensitive;

simple, giving confidence that the test has been performed correctly.

12.11 Fungi may have a bad image. Eating fungi may seem unappealing or even dangerous to some consumers. Emphasis on 'natural' and 'plants' is reassuring. Reference to familiar food like mushrooms is also reassuring.

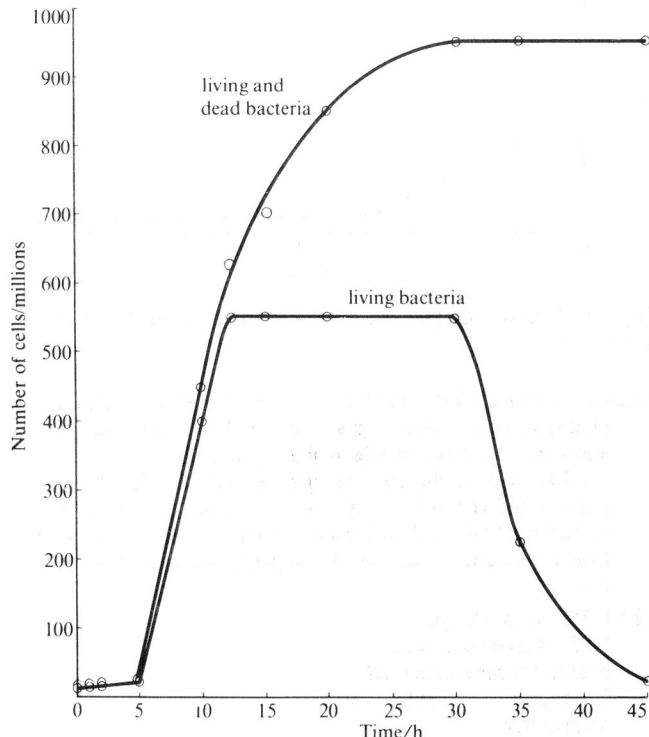

Fig 12.7(ans)   *Growth of a bacterial population.*

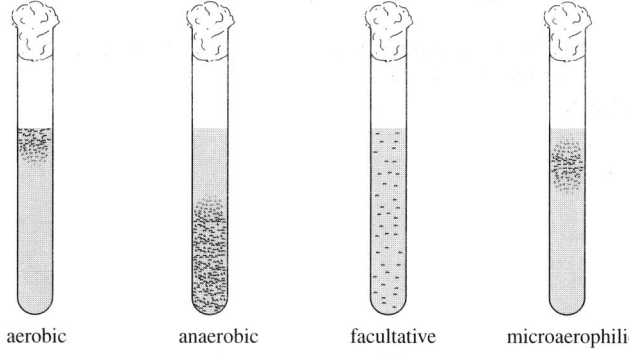

Fig 12.3(ans)   *Distribution of different bacteria.*

Index

References to figures are <u>underlined</u>; to tables are <u>*underlined italics*</u>

426